Maximilian J. Hommel

Selected National, European and International Provisions
from Public and Private Law

Europa Law Publishing, Groningen 2010

Selected National, European and International Provisions from Public and Private Law

The Maastricht Collection

Edited by Philipp Kiiver & Nicole Kornet

Second edition

Europa Law Publishing is a publishing company specializing in European Union law, international trade law, public international law, environmental law and comparative national law.
For further information please contact Europa Law Publishing via email: info@europalawpublishing.com or visit our website at: www.europalawpublishing.com.

All rights reserved. No part of this publication may be reproduced or transmitted, in any form or by any means, or stored in any retrieval system of any nature, without the written permission of the publisher. Application for permission for use of copyright material shall be made to the publishers. Full acknowledgement of author, publisher and source must be given.

Voor zover het maken van kopieën uit deze uitgave is toegestaan op grond van artikel 16h t/m 16m Auteurswet 1912 *juncto* het Besluit van 27 november 2002, Stb. 575, dient men de daarvoor wettelijk verschuldigde vergoedingen te voldoen aan de Stichting Reprorecht (Postbus 3060, 2130 KB Hoofddorp).
Voor het overnemen van (een) gedeelte(n) uit deze uitgave in bloemlezingen, readers en andere compilatiewerken (artikel 16 Auteurswet 1912) dient men zich tot de uitgever te wenden.

© Europa Law Publishing, P. Kiiver, N. Kornet, 2010

Typeset in Scala and Scala Sans, Graphic design by G2K Designers, Groningen/Amsterdam

NUR 828; ISBN 978-90-8952-093-7

Preface to the second edition

The Faculty of Law of Maastricht University attaches great importance to the study of European and comparative law. Its curriculum includes several internationally oriented Master programmes, and the European Law School as a Bachelor programme in which law is taught in a European and comparative perspective in English from the very first day. This volume, *The Maastricht Collection*, is based on the Maastricht Law Faculty's expertise in teaching European, international and comparative law.

The Maastricht Collection comprises a selection of legal instruments and provisions which have proven to be particularly relevant and useful to students and practitioners of European and comparative law. It includes statutory law, including codes, from France, Germany, the Netherlands and the United Kingdom; international treaties; and legal instruments of the European Union. In addition, selected sources from the United States are provided. The main content is divided into chapters corresponding to different areas of law, such as constitutional law, criminal law and contract law.

This second edition constitutes not only an update but also an expansion with respect to the first edition. New chapters on international human rights law, civil procedure, European private law, international business law and international tax law have been added. The private law chapter has been revised and expanded to include domestic company law provisions. More sources have been added to the constitutional law chapter, and the national constitutions are now all rendered in full.

The provisions in this volume are reproduced in the original English or in the authentic English version, where applicable, or they are freshly translated under critical editorship. Many existing translations of written law, including officious translations available on government websites, are not faithful enough to the original. They often seek to turn old-fashioned or ambiguous original texts into modern and elegant English. Or, instead of translating, they seek to *explain* how certain terms or formulations are interpreted in practice. *The Maastricht Collection* remains true to the content, style and syntax of the original, allowing the reader to appreciate not only the substance but also the authentic form of legal sources.

Formatting styles, such as the use of §§ ('Paragraphen') rather than 'Articles' in most German statutes, and 'Sections' in UK legislation, or the absence of paragraph numbering in French legislation, are preserved. In the interest of consistency of style, the headings of individual Articles are always suppressed. Enactment formulas are always omitted; preambles are retained unless indicated otherwise. For easy reference within translated texts, key legal terms and proper names are added in the original language as in-text citations between square brackets.

We are very grateful to all the staff members of the Maastricht Law Faculty who have contributed to the work on this volume: Dr. Bram Akkermans, Prof. Chris Backes, Prof. Fons Coomans, Merel Dekker, Prof. Sjef van Erp, Dr. Nicola Gundt, Prof. René de Groot, Sascha Hardt, Heike Hauröder, Prof. Aalt Willem Heringa, Dr. Sander Jansen, Prof. Anselm Kamperman Sanders, Prof. André Klip, Maartje Krabbe, Gisela Kristoferitsch, Prof. Raymond Luja, Prof. Gerrit van Maanen, Dr. Mieke Olaerts, Eveline Ramaekers, Dr. Stephan Rammeloo, Prof. Remco van Rhee, Dr. David Roef, Gereon Rotering, Dr. Kees Saarloos, Dr. René Seerden, Prof. Taru Spronken, Dr. Ilse Van den Driessche, Dr. Jakob van der Velde, Prof. Luc Verhey, Dr. Remme Verkerk, Yvonne Walhof, Dr. Stefan Weishaar, Daniëlle Wenders, Rob van de Westelaken, Irene Wieczorek and Prof. Jan Willems. It is the synergy between the experts in the various areas of law that made *The Maastricht Collection* possible. Special thanks to the Public Law department for their financial support.

Maastricht, August 2010

Dr. Philipp Kiiver LL.M., Associate Professor of European and Comparative Constitutional Law, Maastricht University

Dr. Nicole Kornet LL.M., Assistant Professor of Commercial Law, Maastricht University

		Preface to the second edition	v
		Contents	vii
PART	I	**Constitutional Law**	
		France: Constitution	3
		France: Declaration of 1789	21
		France: Electoral Code	23
		Germany: Basic Law	27
		Germany: Federal Elections Act	61
		The Netherlands: Charter for the Kingdom	63
		The Netherlands: Constitution	71
		The Netherlands: Elections Act	85
		United Kingdom: Bill of Rights 1689	89
		United Kingdom: Parliament Acts 1911/1949	91
		United Kingdom: Human Rights Act 1998	93
		United Kingdom: Scotland Act 1998	99
PART	II	**Administrative Law**	
		France: Code of Administrative Justice	103
		France: Reasons for Administrative Decisions Act	109
		Germany: Administrative Procedure	111
		Germany: Administrative Court Procedure	127
		The Netherlands: General Administrative Law Act	133
		United Kingdom: Civil Procedure Rules 1998	153
PART	III	**Criminal Justice**	
		France: Criminal Code	159
		Germany: Criminal Code	165
		The Netherlands: Criminal Code	171
		United Kingdom: Criminal Attempts Act 1981	177
		EU: European Arrest Warrant 2002/584/JHA	179
		EU: Framework Decision on Combating Terrorism 2002/475/JHA	189
		EU: Framework Decision on Freezing Orders 2003/577/JHA	193
PART	IV	**Human Rights Law**	
		European Convention on Human Rights	201
		ECHR: Protocols	209
		ECHR: Rules of Court	213
		Convention on the Rights of the Child	225
		CRC: Protocols	235

PART	V	**Private Law**	
		France: Civil Code	245
		France: Miscellaneous Private Law Codes	271
		Germany: Civil Code	275
		Germany: Miscellaneous Private Law Statutes and Codes	303
		The Netherlands: Civil Code	309
		United Kingdom: Sale of Goods Act 1979	347
		United Kingdom: Miscellaneous Private Law Statutes	363
PART	VI	**Civil Procedure**	
		France: Code of Civil Procedure	379
		Germany: Code of Civil Procedure	383
		The Netherlands: Code of Civil Procedure	391
		United Kingdom: Civil Procedure Rules 1998	393
		EU: Evidence Directive 1206/2001	403
		EU: European Enforcement Order 805/2004	409
		EU: Order for Payment Regulation 1896/2006	415
		EU: Small Claims Regulation 861/2007	421
		EU: Service Regulation 1393/2007	427
		EU: ADR Directive 2008/52/EC	433
PART	VII	**Private International Law**	
		Germany: Implementation Act of the Civil Code	437
		The Netherlands: Private International Law Act Relating to Divorce	441
		The Netherlands: Private International Law Act Relating to Parentage	443
		The Netherlands: Private International Law Act Relating to Corporations	447
		The Netherlands: Pro Forma Foreign Companies Act	449
		The Netherlands: Private International Law Act Relating to Property Law	451
		EU: Brussels I Regulation	453
		EU: Brussels II Regulation	467
		EU: Rome II Regulation	483
		EU: Rome I Regulation	491
		Rome Convention	501
		Convention on Law Applicable to Names	505
		Convention on Recognition of Decisions Concerning the Marriage Bond	507
		Convention on Recognition of Divorces and Legal Separations	511

CONTENTS

PART	VIII	**European Company Law**	
		Directive 2009/101 on Coordination of Safeguards	517
		Directive 77/91 on Coordination of Safeguards	523
		Directive 78/855 on Mergers	537
		Directive 78/660 on Annual Accounts	545
		Directive 83/349 on Consolidated Accounts	569
		Directive 2005/56 on Cross-Border Mergers	587
		Directive 89/666 on Disclosure Requirements	595
		Directive 2009/102 on Single-Member Companies	599
		Directive 2004/25 on Takeover Bids	603
		Directive 2007/36 on Certain Rights of Shareholders	613
		Directive 2004/109 on Transparency Requirements	621
		Directive 2003/6 on Market Abuse	639
		Regulation 2137/85 on European Economic Interest Grouping	649
		Regulation 2157/2001 on Statute for a European Company (SE)	659
		Directive 2001/86 on SE Employee Involvement	675
		Proposal Regulation on Statute for European Private Company	683
		Directive 2009/38 European Works Council	697
		Directive 98/59 on Collective Redundancies	709
PART	IX	**European Private Law**	
		Directive 85/374 on Product Liability	715
		Directive 85/577 on Doorstep Selling	719
		Directive 86/653 on Commercial Agency	721
		Directive 87/102 on Consumer Credit	727
		Directive 93/7 on Return of Cultural Objects	733
		Directive 93/13 on Unfair Terms in Consumer Contracts	737
		Directive 97/7 on Distance Contracts	743
		Directive 1999/44 on Consumer Sales and Associated Guarantees	749
		Directive 2000/31 on Electronic Commerce	755
		Directive 2000/35 on Combating Late Payment	769
		Directive 2002/47 on Financial Collateral Arrangements	773
		Directive 2005/29 on Unfair Commercial Practices	781
		Directive 2008/122 on Timeshare	793
		Regulation 1346/2000 on Insolvency Proceedings	805
PART	X	**International Business Law**	
		Convention on the International Sale of Goods	821
		Convention on Carriage of Goods by Road (CMR)	835
		Hague Visby Rules	845

		Convention on Carriage of Goods by Sea (Rotterdam Rules)	849
		New York Convention	871
		UNCITRAL Model Law on International Commercial Arbitration	875
		UNIDROIT Principles of International Commercial Contracts	885
PART	XI	**International Tax Law**	
		OECD Model Tax Convention	905
PART	XII	**United States Law**	
		United States: Constitution and Amendments	917
		United States: Uniform Commercial Code	927

PART I

Constitutional Law

CONST

Constitution (of the Fifth Republic) [Constitution (de la Ve République)] of 4 October 1958 as last amended by constitutional statute 2008-724 of 23 July 2008.[1]

Preamble

The French people solemnly proclaim their attachment to human rights and the principles of national sovereignty as they are defined by the Declaration of 1789, confirmed and complemented by the Preamble to the Constitution of 1946, as well as to the rights and obligations as defined in the Charter on the Environment of 2004. By virtue of these principles and that of the self-determination of peoples, the Republic offers to the overseas territories that express the will to adhere to them, new institutions founded on the common ideal of liberty, equality and fraternity and conceived with a view to their democratic development.

Article 1. France is an indivisible, secular, democratic and social Republic. It ensures the equality of all citizens before the law, without distinction of origin, race or religion. It respects all beliefs. Its organization is decentralized.

Statute promotes equal access of women and men to elected offices and electoral functions as well as to professional and social positions.

Title I. On sovereignty

Article 2. The language of the Republic is French.
The national emblem is the tricolour flag of blue, white, red.
The national anthem is the Marseillaise.
The motto of the Republic is Liberty, Equality, Fraternity.
Its principle is: government of the people, by the people and for the people.

Article 3. National sovereignty belongs to the people, who exercise it through their representatives and by means of referendum.
No part of the population nor any individual may arrogate the exercise thereof.
Suffrage may be direct or indirect in accordance with the condition of the Constitution. It is always universal, equal and secret.
All French nationals of the age of majority and of both sexes, who enjoy their civil and political rights, have the right to vote, under the conditions provided by statute.

Article 4. Political parties and groups contribute to the expression of suffrage. They establish themselves and carry out their activity freely. They must respect the principles of national sovereignty and of democracy.
They contribute to the giving effect to the principle enshrined in the second paragraph of Article 1 under the conditions provided by statute.
Statute guarantees pluralist expressions of opinions and the fair participation of political parties and groups in the democratic life of the Nation.

Title II. The President of the Republic

Article 5. The President of the Republic sees that the Constitution is respected. He ensures, by his arbitration, the proper functioning of the public authorities as well as the continuity of the State.
He is the guarantor of national independence, territorial integrity and observance of treaties.

Article 6. The President of the Republic is elected for five years by direct universal suffrage.
No-one may serve more than two consecutive terms.
The details of the implementation of this Article are determined by an organic statute.

---

[1] Translation by Ph. Kiiver, S. Hardt & G. Kristoferitsch. The entry into force of the amended wording of Articles 11, 13, 25 (last paragraph), 34-1, 39, 44, 56, 61-1, 65, 69, 71-1 and 73 as rendered here were, when it was adopted in July 2008, made subject to the entry into force of organic statutes necessary for the amendments' application.

Part I. Constitutional Law

Article 7. The President of the Republic is elected by the absolute majority of votes cast. If this is not obtained in the fist round of elections, a second round is held on the fourteenth day thereafter. Only the two candidates may run who, after the withdrawal of candidates with more votes where applicable, find themselves having obtained the largest number of votes in the first round.
The elections are opened by a call of the Government.
The election of a new President takes place at least twenty days and, at most, thirty-five days before the expiry of the powers of the incumbent President.
In case of a vacancy of the Presidency of the Republic for whatever reason, or in case the President is prevented from exercising his functions as declared by the Constitutional Council [Conseil Constitutionnel] by absolute majority of its members upon request by the Government, the functions of the President of the Republic, with the exception of those provided by Articles 11 and 12 below, are provisionally exercised by the president of the Senate and, if he in turn is prevented from exercising his functions, by he Government.
In case of a vacancy or when the prevention from the exercise of functions is declared definitive by the Constitutional Council, a vote for an election of a new President takes place, except in cases of force majeure established by the Constitutional Council, at least twenty days and at most thirty-five days after the opening of the vacancy or the declaration of the definitive character of the prevention.
If within seven days prior to the deadline for the filing of candidacies, one of the persons who has publicly announced his decision to be a candidate less than thirty days before that date, dies or finds himself prevented from running, the Constitutional Council may decide to postpone the elections.
If before the first round one of the candidates dies or finds himself prevented from running, the Constitutional Council declares the postponement of the elections.
In the case of death or prevention of one of the two candidates with the largest number of votes in the first round before any withdrawals, the Constitutional Council declares that the election procedure must start entirely anew; the same applies in the case of death or prevention of one of the two remaining candidates for the second round.
In all cases, the Constitutional Council is seized under the conditions prescribed by the second paragraph of Article 61 below or under those provided for the running as a candidate by the organic statute stipulated by Article 6 above.
The Constitutional Council may extend the periods provided by the third and fifth paragraph as long as the vote does not take place any later than thirty-five days after the date of the decision of the Constitutional Council. If the application of the provisions of the present paragraph has as an effect that elections are postponed to a date after the expiry of the powers of the incumbent President, he remains in office until the proclamation of his successor.
Neither Articles 49 and 50 nor Article 89 of the Constitution may be applied during a vacancy of the Presidency of the Republic or during the period between the declaration of the definitive character of the prevention of the President of the Republic from exercising his functions and the election of his successor.

Article 8. The President of the Republic appoints the Prime Minister. He terminates the functions of the Prime Minister when the latter tenders the resignation of the Government.
On the proposal of the Prime Minister, he appoints the other members of the Government and terminates their functions.

Article 9. The President of the Republic presides over the Council of Ministers.

Article 10. The President of the Republic promulgates statutes within fifteen days following the transmission to the Government of the statute finally adopted.
He may, before the expiry of this period, ask Parliament to deliberate anew on the statute or certain provisions of it. Such new deliberation may not be refused.

Article 11. The President of the Republic, on proposal of the Government during sessions or on joint proposal of the two chambers, which are published in the Official Journal [Journal Officiel], may submit to a referendum any government bill [projet de loi] regarding the organization of public authorities, reforms relating to the economic, social or environmental policy of the nation and the public services which contribute to it, or proposing the authorization of the ratification of a treaty which, while not being contrary to the Constitution, would have an effect on the functioning of the institutions.
Where a referendum is organized on the proposal of the Government, it makes a declaration before each chamber, which is followed by a debate.
A referendum regarding a subject mentioned in the first paragraph may be organized on the initiative of one-fifth of the members of Parliament, supported by one-tenth of the voters registered in the electoral lists. Such initiative

takes the form of a private member's bill and may not have as its subject the repeal of a statutory provision promulgated less than one year earlier.

The conditions of its submission and those under which the Constitutional Council controls the compliance with the provisions of the preceding paragraph are established by an organic statute.

If the private member's bill has not been considered by the two chambers within a period determined by organic statute, the President of the Republic submits it to referendum.

Where the private member's bill has not been adopted by the French people, no new proposal for referendum regarding the same subject may be submitted before the expiry of a period of two years following the date of the vote.

Where a referendum has resulted in the adoption of a government bill or private member's bill, the President of the Republic promulgates the statute within fifteen days following the proclamation of the results of the referendum.

Article 12. The President of the Republic may, after consultations with the Prime Minister and the presidents of the chambers, declare the dissolution of the National Assembly.

General elections take place at least twenty days and at the latest forty days after the dissolution.

The National Assembly reconvenes by operation of law on the second Thursday following its election. If this convention takes place outside the period envisaged for an ordinary session, a session is opened by operation of law for a period of fifteen days.

No new dissolution may take place during the year following these elections.

Article 13. The President of the Republic signs ordinances [ordonnances] and decrees [décrets] debated in the Council of Ministers.

He appoints civil servants and military personnel of the State.

The members of the Council of State [conseillers d'État], the grand chancellor of the Legion of Honour, the ambassadors and special envoys, the magistrates of the Court of Auditors [Cour des Comptes], the prefects, the representatives of the State in overseas entities governed by Article 74 and in New Caledonia, generals, the rectors of the academies and the directors of the central administration are appointed in the Council of Ministers.

An organic statute determines the other posts to be filled in the Council of Ministers as well as the conditions under which the power of the President of the Republic to make appointments may be delegated by him to be exercised in his name.

An organic statute determines the posts or functions, other than those mentioned in the third paragraph, for which, by reason of their importance to the guarantee of rights and freedoms or the economic and social life of the Nation, the power of appointment of the President of the Republic is exercised on public advice by the competent permanent committee of each chamber. The President of the Republic may not proceed with an appointment where the added negative votes in each committee represent at least three-fifths of votes cast in the two committees. Statute determines the competent permanent committees for the posts or functions concerned.

Article 14. The President of the Republic accredits ambassadors and special envoys to foreign states; foreign ambassadors and special envoys are accredited before him.

Article 15. The President of the Republic is the commander-in-chief of the armies. He presides over the supreme councils and committees of National Defence.

Article 16. Where the institutions of the Republic, the independence of the Nation, the integrity of its territory or the execution of its international commitments is jeopardized in a serious and immediate manner and the regular functioning of the constitutional public authorities is interrupted, the President of the Republic takes measures as the circumstances demand, after official consultation with the Prime Minister, the presidents of the chambers as well as the Constitutional Council.

He informs the Nation in an address.

These measures must be inspired by the will to ensure the constitutional public authorities, in the shortest of periods, of the means to accomplish their mission. The Constitutional Council is consulted regarding their subject.

The Parliament convenes by operation of law.

The National Assembly may not be dissolved during the exercise of exceptional powers.

After thirty days of exercise of exceptional powers, the Constitutional Council may be seized by the president of the National Assembly, the president of the Senate, sixty deputies or sixty senators, with a view to examining whether the conditions provided in the first paragraph remain met. It decides within the shortest of periods by a public advice. It commences such examination by operation of law and decides under the same conditions after a period of sixty days of exercise of exceptional powers and at any further moment after that period.

PART I. CONSTITUTIONAL LAW

Article 17. The President of the Republic has the right to grant pardons in individual cases.

Article 18. The President of the Republic communicates with the two chambers of the Parliament by addresses which he orders to be read out and which are not followed by any debate.
He may speak before Parliament assembled for that purpose in Congress. His statement may, in his absence, be followed by a debate which may not be the object of any vote.
Outside sessions, the parliamentary chambers convene especially for that purpose.

Article 19. The acts of the President of the Republic other than those stipulated in Articles 8 (first paragraph), 11, 12, 16, 18, 54, 56 and 61 are countersigned by the Prime Minister and, where appropriate, the competent ministers.

Title III. The Government

Article 20. The Government determines and conducts the policy of the Nation.
It has at its disposal the administration and the armed forces.
It is responsible before the Parliament under the conditions and following the procedures stipulated in Articles 49 and 50.

Article 21. The Prime Minister directs the actions of the Government. He is responsible for the National Defence.
He ensures the execution of statutes. Save for the provisions of Article 13, he exercises the power of regulation [pouvoir réglementaire] and appoints civilian and military personnel.
He may delegate some of his powers to the ministers.
He substitutes, where appropriate, the President of the Republic in the presidency over the councils and committees stipulated in Article 15.
He may, by way of exception, substitute him in the presidency over a Council of Ministers by virtue of an express delegation and for a fixed agenda.

Article 22. The acts of the Prime Minister are countersigned, where appropriate, by the ministers who are charged with the execution thereof.

Article 23. The functions of a member of the Government are incompatible with the exercise of any parliamentary mandate, any function of professional representation at national level and any public employment or any professional activity.
An organic statute determines the conditions under which a replacement of the holders of such mandates, functions or employments is provided for.
The replacement of members of the Parliament takes place in accordance with the provisions of Article 25.

Title IV. The Parliament

Article 24. The Parliament adopts statutes [loi]. It controls the action of the government. It evaluates public policies.
It comprises the National Assembly [Assemblée Nationale] and the Senate [Sénat].
The deputies of the National Assembly, whose number may not exceed five hundred seventy-seven, are elected by direct suffrage.
The Senate, the number of whose members may not exceed three hundred forty-eight, is elected by indirect suffrage. It ensures the representation of the territorial entities of the Republic.
The French established outside France are represented in the National Assembly and in the Senate.

Article 25. An organic statute determines the length of the powers of each chamber, the number of its members, their remuneration, the conditions of eligibility, the regime regarding disqualification and incompatibilities.
It equally determines the conditions under which the persons are elected who are called upon to ensure, in case of a vacancy of a seat, the replacement of deputies or senators until new general or partial elections of the chamber to which they belonged or their temporary replacement in case of the acceptance by them of governmental functions.
An independent commission, the composition and rules of organization and functioning of which are determined by statute, pronounces itself in a public advice on government proposals for texts and private member's bills for

statutes delimiting the districts for the election of deputies or modifying the distribution of seats of deputies or senators.

Article 26. No member of Parliament may be prosecuted, investigated, arrested, detained or tried based on the opinions or votes expressed by him in the exercise of his functions.
No member of Parliament may be subject to an arrest or any other measure of a criminal or correctional nature depriving him of or restricting his liberty, except with the authorization of the Bureau of the chamber to which he belongs. Such authorization is not required in case of a crime or misdemeanour in flagrante or in case of a final conviction.
The detention, the measures depriving of or restricting liberty or the prosecution of a member of Parliament are suspended for the period of the session if the chamber to which he belongs so demands.
The affected chamber convenes by operation of law for supplementary meetings in order to allow, where appropriate, the application of the preceding paragraph.

Article 27. Any binding mandate is void. The right to vote of the members of Parliament is personal. An organic statute may authorize, by way of exception, the delegation of a vote. In such case, no-one may receive the delegation of more than one mandate.

Article 28. The Parliament convenes by operation of law in an ordinary session [session ordinaire] which starts on the first working day of October and ends on the last working day of June.
The number of meeting days [jours de séance] which each chamber may hold during an ordinary session may not exceed one hundred and twenty. The meeting weeks are determined by each chamber.
The Prime Minister, after consultations with the president of the chamber concerned, or the majority of the members of each chamber may decide on holding additional meeting days.
The meeting days and hours are determined by the rules of procedure [règlement] of each chamber.

Article 29. The Parliament convenes in an extraordinary session upon the demand of the Prime Minister or of the majority of the members composing the National Assembly, under a fixed agenda.
Where the extraordinary session is held upon the demand of the members of the National Assembly, a decree of closure intervenes as soon as the Parliament has exhausted the agenda for which it has been convened and, at the latest, twelve days from its convention.
Only the Prime Minister may demand a new session before the expiry of the month that follows the decree of closure.

Article 30. Outside the cases where the Parliament convenes by operation of law, the extraordinary sessions are opened and closed by decree from the President of the Republic.

Article 31. The members of the Government have access to the two chambers. They are heard when they so demand.
They may be assisted by Government agents [commissaires].

Article 32. The president of the National Assembly is elected for the legislative term. The president of the Senate is elected after each partial elections.

Article 33. The meetings of the two chambers are public. The complete minutes of the debates are published in the Official Journal [Journal officiel].
Each chamber may meet in closed committee upon the demand of the Prime Minister or of a tenth of its members.

Title V. The relations between Parliament and the Government

Article 34. Statute determines the rules regarding:
• the civil rights and fundamental guarantees granted to citizens for the exercise of the civil liberties; the freedom, pluralism and independence of the media; the duties imposed on the person and property of citizens by the National Defence;
• the nationality, the status and capacity of persons, the matrimonial regime, inheritance and gifts;
• the determination of crimes and misdemeanours as well as the penalties applicable to them; criminal procedure; amnesty; the establishment of new court systems and the status of magistrates;

Part I. Constitutional Law

• the basis, rate and method of collection of taxes and charges of any nature; the regime for the issuing of currency.
Statute equally determines the rules regarding:
• the electoral system for the parliamentary chambers and local assemblies and the representative bodies for the French established outside France as well as the conditions for the exercise of elected offices and electoral functions for members of the deliberative assemblies of the territorial entities;
• the establishment of categories of public bodies;
• the fundamental guarantees granted to civil servants and members of the armed forces of the State;
• the nationalization of enterprises and the transfer of property of enterprises from the public to the private sector.
Statute determines the fundamental principles:
• of the general organization of the National Defence;
• of the self-administration of territorial entities, their competences and their revenue;
• of education;
• of the preservation of the environment;
• of the property system, real rights and civil and commercial obligations;
• of labour law, trade union law and social security law.
Financial statutes [lois de finances] determine the revenue and the expenditure of the State subject to the conditions and with the reservations provided for by an organic statute.
Social security financing statutes determine the general conditions of their financial equilibrium and, taking into account anticipated revenue, set expenditure objectives subject to the conditions and with the reservations provided for by an organic statute.
Programming statutes [lois des programmation] determine the objectives of the action of the State.
The multiannual directions for public finances are defined by programming statutes. They are in line with the objective of a balance of accounts of the public administration.
The provisions of the present Article may be specified and completed by an organic statute.

Article 34-1. The chambers may pass resolutions under the conditions set by an organic statute [loi organique]. Bills for resolutions of which the Government considers that their adoption or rejection would become a matter of its responsibility or that they contain injunctions against it are inadmissible and may not be included in the agenda.

Article 35. A declaration of war is authorized by Parliament.
The Government informs Parliament of its decision to have the Armed Forces intervene abroad, at the latest three days after the start of the intervention. It specifies the objectives pursued. This information may lead to a debate which is not followed by any vote.
Where the length of the intervention exceeds four months, the Government submits its extension to Parliament for authorization. It may ask the National Assembly to decide in final instance.
If Parliament is not in session after four months have expired, it decides at the opening of the following session.

Article 36. A state of siege is decreed in the Council of Ministers.
Its extension beyond twelve days may only be authorized by Parliament.

Article 37. Matters other than those falling under the scope of statute [loi] are of regulatory nature [réglementaire]. Texts of statutory form enacted with regard to these matters may be modified by decree issued after an opinion by the Council of State [Conseil d'État]. Of these texts, those enacted after the entry into force of the present Constitution may not be modified by decree except if the Constitutional Council [Conseil Constitutionnel] has declared that they are of a regulatory nature pursuant to the foregoing paragraph.

Article 37-1. Statute and regulation may contain, for a limited purpose and time, provisions of an experimental nature.

Article 38. The Government may, in order to implement its programme, request Parliament to authorize, for a limited period of time, the taking of measures by ordinances [ordonnances] which normally fall under the scope of statute.
Ordinances are issued in the Council of Ministers after an opinion by the Council of State. They enter into force upon their publication but become ineffective if the government bill for their ratification is not submitted to Parliament before the date set by the enabling statute. They may only be ratified in an explicit manner.
Upon the expiry of the period of time referred to in the first paragraph of the present Article, ordinances may not be modified except by statute in matters within the scope of statute.

Article 39. The right of initiative for statutes rests both with the Prime Minister and the members of Parliament. Government bills [projets de loi] are discussed in the Council of Ministers after an opinion by the Council of State and submitted to the bureau of one of the two chambers. Government bills for financial statutes and social security financing statutes are submitted to the National Assembly first. Without prejudice to the first paragraph of Article 44, government bills having as their primary object the organization of the territorial entities are submitted to the Senate first.

The presentation of government bills [projets de loi] submitted to the National Assembly or the Senate meets the conditions set by an organic statute [loi organique].

Government bills may not be included in the agenda if the conference of the presidents of the first chamber seized declares that the rules set by the organic statute have been disregarded. In case of disagreement between the conference of presidents and the Government, the president of the chamber concerned or the Prime Minister may refer the matter to the Constitutional Council which decides within eight days.

Under the conditions stipulated by statute, the president of a chamber may submit to the Council of State [Conseil d'État] a private member's bill submitted by one of the members of that chamber, before its examination in a committee, for its opinion, unless that member objects.

Article 40. Private member's bills [propositions] and amendments formulated by members of Parliament are not admissible if their adoption would have as a consequence either a diminution of public revenue or the creation or aggravation of public expenditure.

Article 41. If it appears, during the legislative process, that a private member's bill or amendment is not a matter of statute or is contrary to a delegation granted by virtue of Article 38, the Government or the president of the chamber seized may oppose it as inadmissible.

In case of disagreement between the Government and the president of the chamber concerned, the Constitutional Council, at the request of either party, rules within a period of eight days.

Article 42. Debate on government bills [projets] and private member's bills [propositions de loi] in the meeting takes place on the basis of the text adopted by the committee seized by application of Article 43 or, by default, the text referred to the chamber.

However, the debate in the meeting on government bills for constitutional amendment statutes [projets de révision constitutionnelle], financial statutes [projets de loi de finances] and social security financing statutes [projets de loi de financement de la sécurité sociale] takes place, in the first reading in front of the first chamber seized, on the basis of the text presented by the Government and, in the other readings, the text transmitted by the other chamber.

The debate in the meeting, in the first reading, of a government bill or a private member's bill may only take place before the first chamber seized after the expiry of a period of six weeks after its submission. It may only take place before the second chamber seized after the expiry of a period of four weeks from the moment of its transmission.

The previous paragraph does not apply if the accelerated procedure has been initiated under the conditions stipulated in Article 45. Nor does it apply to government bills for financial statutes, social security financing statutes and to government bills relating to a state of crisis [états de crise].

Article 43. Government and private member's bills are sent for examination to one of the permanent committees, the number of which is limited to eight in each chamber.

Upon the demand of the Government or the chamber seized, government or private member's bills are sent for examination to a committee set up especially for that purpose.

Article 44. Members of Parliament and the Government have the right of amendment. This right is exercised in the meeting or in a committee under the conditions prescribed in the rules of procedure of the chambers, within the framework determined by an organic statute.

After the opening of the debate, the Government may object to the consideration of any amendment which has not previously been submitted to a committee.

If the Government so demands, the chamber seized decides by a single vote on the whole or part of the debated text, containing only the amendments proposed or accepted by the Government.

Article 45. Every government or private member's bill is considered successively in the two chambers of Parliament with a view to the adoption of an identical text. Without prejudice to the application of Articles 40 and 41, any amendment that has a link, even an indirect one, with the text submitted or transmitted is admissible in the first reading.

Where, as a result of a disagreement between the two chambers, a government or private member's bill could not be adopted after two readings by each chamber or, if the Government has decided to apply the accelerated procedure without the conference of presidents being jointly opposed, after one reading by each of them, the Prime Minister or, for a private member's bill, the presidents of the two chambers acting jointly, have the right to convene a joint committee, composed of an equal number of members of each chamber, charged with the task to propose a text on the provisions still under debate.

The text drafted by the joint committee may be submitted by the Government to the two chambers for adoption. No amendment is admissible except with the consent of the Government.

If the joint committee does not succeed in agreeing on a common text or if this text is not adopted under the conditions provided for by the foregoing paragraph, the Government may, after a new reading by the National Assembly and by the Senate, request the National Assembly to adopt a definitive decision. In that case, the National Assembly may reconsider either the text drafted by the joint committee or the last text adopted by itself, modified, where appropriate, by one or more amendments adopted by the Senate.

Article 46. Statutes which the Constitution defines as organic statutes [lois organiques] are adopted and amended under the following conditions.

The government or private member's bill may not be subjected to deliberation and to a vote of the chambers in the first reading until the expiry of the period fixed in the third paragraph of Article 42. However, if the accelerated procedure has been applied under the conditions stipulated in Article 45, the government or private member's bill may not be subjected to deliberation in the first chamber seized until the expiry of a period of fifteen days after its submission.

The procedure of Article 45 applies. However, failing agreement between the two chambers, the text may be adopted by the National Assembly in final reading only by an absolute majority of its members.

Organic statutes relating to the Senate must be adopted in the same terms by the two chambers.

Organic statutes may not be promulgated until the Constitutional Council has declared their conformity with the Constitution.

Article 47. Parliament adopts government bills for financial statutes under the conditions provided by an organic statute.

If the National Assembly has not reached a decision in the first reading within a period of forty days after the submission of a government bill, the Government seizes the Senate which must reach a decision within a period of fifteen days. Thereafter the procedure of Article 45 is applied.

If Parliament has not reached a decision within a period of seventy days, the provisions of the government bill may be enacted by ordinance.

If a financial statute setting revenues and expenditure for a financial year has not been submitted in time for promulgation before the beginning of that financial year, the Government requests from Parliament, as a matter of urgency, the authorization to collect taxes and make available by decree the funds needed for measures already adopted. The time limits set by the present Article are suspended when Parliament is not in session.

Article 47-1. Parliament adopts government bills for social security financing statutes under the conditions provided by an organic statute. If the National Assembly has not reached a decision in the first reading within a period of twenty days after the submission of a government bill, the Government seizes the Senate which must reach a decision within a period of fifteen days. Thereafter the procedure of Article 45 is applied. If Parliament has not reached a decision within a period of fifty days, the provisions of the government bill may be put into effect by ordinance.

The time limits set by the present Article are suspended when Parliament is not in session and, with respect to each chamber, during the weeks during which it has decided not to meet in conformity with the second paragraph of Article 28.

Article 47-2. The Court of Auditors [Cour des Comptes] assists the Parliament with the control of the action of the Government. It assists the Parliament and the Government with the control of the execution of financial statutes and the implementation of social security financing statutes as well as with the assessment of public policies. With its public reports, it contributes to the informing of the citizens.

The accounts of the public administration are regular and sincere. They provide a picture that faithfully shows the results of their management, their assets and their financial situation.

Article 48. Without prejudice to the application of the last three paragraphs of Article 28, the agenda is fixed by each chamber.
Two weeks of meetings out of four are reserved with priority, in the order that the Government has fixed, for the examination of texts and for debates which it requests to be included in the agenda.
Furthermore, the examination of government bills for financial statutes, social security financing statutes and, subject to the provisions of the following paragraph, texts transmitted by the other chamber at least six weeks earlier, government bills relating to a state of crisis and requests for authorization envisaged by Article 35, is, upon request of the Government, included in the agenda with priority.
One week of meetings out of four is reserved, with priority and in the order fixed by each assembly, for the control of the action of the Government and for the assessment of public policies.
One day of meeting per month is reserved for an agenda determined by each chamber upon the initiative of opposition groups of the chamber concerned, as well as of minority groups.
At least one meeting per week, including during extraordinary sessions provided for in Article 29, is reserved, with priority, for questions of members of Parliament and answers by the Government.

Article 49. The Prime Minister, after deliberation by the Council of Ministers, ties the responsibility of the Government before the National Assembly to the Government's programme or possibly a general policy statement.
The National Assembly invokes the responsibility of the Government by a vote on a motion of censure. Such a motion is only admissible if it is signed by at least one tenth of the members of the National Assembly. The vote may not take place until forty-eight hours have elapsed after the tabling. Solely votes in favour of the motion of censure are counted, which may only be adopted by a majority of the members composing the Assembly. Except in the case stipulated by the paragraph hereunder, a deputy may not be a signatory to more than three motions of censure during one ordinary session and to more than one during one extraordinary session.
The Prime Minister may, after deliberation by the Council of Ministers, make a matter of the responsibility of the Government before the National Assembly the adoption of a government bill for a financial statute or a social security financing statute. In that event, the government bill is considered adopted unless a motion of censure, tabled within the twenty-four hours that follow, is adopted under the conditions provided for by the foregoing paragraph. The Prime Minister may furthermore resort to this procedure for one other government bill or one private member's bill per session.
The Prime Minister has the option to request from the Senate the approval of a general policy statement.

Article 50. When the National Assembly adopts a motion of censure or when it disapproves the programme or a general policy statement of the Government, the Prime Minister must tender the resignation of the Government to the President of the Republic.

Article 50-1. Before one of the chambers the Government may, on its own initiative or at the request of a parliamentary group in the sense of Article 51-1, make a statement on a specified subject that is followed by a debate and that may, if it so decides, be the object of a vote without making it a matter of its responsibility.

Article 51. The closure of an ordinary session or of extraordinary sessions is postponed by operation of law in order to allow, where applicable, the application of Article 49. For that same purpose, supplementary meetings are held by operation of law.

Article 51-1. The rules of procedure of each chamber determine the rights of parliamentary groups constituted within it. It recognizes the rights specific to opposition groups of the chamber concerned as well as to minority groups.

Article 51-2. For the exercise of the controlling and evaluation tasks defined in the first paragraph of Article 24, commissions of inquiry may be created within each chamber in order to gather information under the conditions stipulated by statute.
Statute determines their rules of organization and functioning. The conditions of their establishment are determined by the rules of procedure of each chamber.

Title VI. On international treaties and agreements

Article 52. The President of the Republic negotiates and ratifies treaties [traités].

Part I. Constitutional Law

He is informed of any negotiation for the conclusion of an international agreement [accord international] not subject to ratification.

Article 53. Peace treaties, treaties on trade, treaties or agreements relating to international organization, those which affect the finances of the State, those which modify provisions of statutory nature, those which relate to the status of persons, those which entail the cession, exchange or acquisition of territory, may only be ratified or approved by statute.
They do not take effect until they have been ratified or approved.
No cession, no exchange, no acquisition of territory is valid without the consent of the population concerned.

Article 53-1. The Republic may conclude, with European States bound by commitments identical to its own in matters of asylum and the protection of human rights and fundamental freedoms, agreements determining their respective competences for the consideration of requests for asylum submitted to them.
However, even if, pursuant to these agreements, a request does not fall under its competences, the authorities of the Republic always have the right to grant asylum to any foreigner persecuted for his action in pursuit of freedom or who seeks protection by France for another reason.

Article 53-2. The Republic may recognize the jurisdiction of the International Criminal Court under the conditions provided by the treaty signed on 18 July 1998.

Article 54. If the Constitutional Council, seized by the President of the Republic, by the Prime Minister, by the president of one of the chambers or by sixty deputies or sixty senators, has declared that an international commitment contains a clause contrary to the Constitution, the authorization to ratify or approve the international commitment in question may only be given after amendment of the Constitution.

Article 55. Treaties or agreements duly ratified or approved have, upon their publication, authority superior to that of statutes, subject, with respect to each agreement or treaty, to their application by the other party.

Title VII. The Constitutional Council

Article 56. The Constitutional Council [Conseil Constitutionnel] comprises nine members whose mandate lasts nine years and is not renewable. One third of the Constitutional Council is renewed every three years. Three of the members are appointed by the President of the Republic, three by the president of the National Assembly, three by the president of the Senate. The procedure stipulated in the last paragraph of Article 13 is applicable to these appointments. The appointments made by the president of each chamber are submitted for an opinion only to the competent permanent committee of the relevant chamber.
In addition to the nine members provided for above, former Presidents of the Republic are by operation of law members of the Constitutional Council for life.
The president is appointed by the President of the Republic. He has the decisive vote in case of a tie.

Article 57. The office of a member of the Constitutional Council is incompatible with that of a minister or a member of Parliament. Other incompatibilities are established by an organic statute.

Article 58. The Constitutional Council ensures the proper conduct of the election of the President of the Republic. It examines complaints and proclaims the result of the election.

Article 59. The Constitutional Council rules, in case of a challenge, on the proper conduct of the election of deputies and senators.

Article 60. The Constitutional Council ensures the proper conduct of referendums as provided for by Articles 11 and 89 and by Title XV. It proclaims the results thereof.

Article 61. Organic statutes, prior to their promulgation, private member's bills mentioned in Article 11 before they have been submitted to referendum, and the rules of procedure of the parliamentary chambers, before coming into force, must be submitted to the Constitutional Council which rules on their conformity with the Constitution.

For the same purpose, statutes may be referred to the Constitutional Council, before their promulgation, by the President of the Republic, the Prime Minister, the president of the National Assembly, the president of the Senate or sixty deputies or sixty senators.
In the cases provided for by the two foregoing paragraphs, the Constitutional Council must rule within a period of one month. However, at the request of the Government, in cases of urgency, this period is reduced to eight days. In the same cases, referral to the Constitutional Council suspends the time period for promulgation.

Article 61-1. When, in the course of proceedings before a court, it is submitted that a statutory provision jeopardizes the rights and freedoms which the Constitution guarantees, the Constitutional Council may be seized on that question by reference from the Council of State or the Court of Cassation which decide within a determined period.
An organic statute determines the conditions for the application of the present Article.

Article 62. A provision declared unconstitutional on the basis of Article 61 may neither be promulgated nor implemented.
A provision declared unconstitutional on the basis of Article 61-1 is repealed from the moment of the publication of the decision of the Constitutional Council or a later date established in that decision. The Constitutional Council determines the conditions and limits within which the effects that the provision has created may be called into question.
The decisions of the Constitutional Council are not open to any appeal. They are binding on public authority and on all administrative and judicial authorities.

Article 63. An organic statute determines the organization and functioning of the Constitutional Council, the procedure followed before it and, in particular, the time limits for submitting complaints to it.

Title VIII. On the judicial authority

Article 64. The President of the Republic is the guarantor of the independence of the judicial authority.
He is assisted by the High Council of the Judiciary [Conseil Supérieur de la Magistrature].
An organic statute contains the rules governing magistrates.
Judges [magistrats du siège] are irremovable.

Article 65. The High Council of the Judiciary comprises a section competent with regard to judges [magistrats du siège] and one competent with regard to public prosecutors [magistrats du parquet].
The section competent with regard to judges is presided over by the first president of the Court of Cassation [Cour de cassation]. It comprises furthermore five judges and one public prosecutor, one member of the Council of State nominated by the Council of State [Conseil d'État], one advocate [avocat] as well as six distinguished persons who are not members of either Parliament or the judiciary or the administration. The President of the Republic, the president of the National Assembly and the president of the Senate each appoint two distinguished persons. The procedure stipulated in the last paragraph of Article 13 is applicable to the appointment of distinguished persons. The appointments made by the president of each chamber of Parliament are submitted for an opinion only to the competent permanent committee of the relevant chamber.
The section competent with regard to public prosecutors is presided over by the procurator-general at the Court of Cassation. It comprises furthermore five public prosecutors and one judge, as well as the member of the Council of State, the advocate and the six distinguished persons mentioned in the second paragraph.
The section of the High Council of the Judiciary competent with regard to judges submits proposals for the appointments of judges at the Court of Cassation, for those of the first president of a court of appeals [cour d'appel] and for those of the president of a district court [tribunal de grande instance]. The other judges are appointed upon its assent.
The section of the High Council of the Judiciary competent with regard to public prosecutors gives its opinion on appointments that affect public prosecutors.
The section of the High Council of the Judiciary competent with regard to judges rules as a disciplinary council for judges. It then comprises besides the members envisaged in the second paragraph the judge who is a member of the section competent with regard to public prosecutors.
The section of the High Council of the Judiciary competent with regard to public prosecutors gives its opinion on those disciplinary sanctions that affect them. It then comprises besides the members envisaged in the third paragraph, the public prosecutor who is a member of the section competent with regard to judges.

PART I. CONSTITUTIONAL LAW

The High Council of the Judiciary meets in plenary composition in order to answer requests for an opinion made by the President of the Republic in application of Article 64. It gives, in the same composition, its opinion on questions regarding the ethics of magistrates as well as on any question regarding the functioning of the justice system on which it is seized by the minister of justice. The plenary composition comprises three of the five judges mentioned in the second paragraph, three of the five public prosecutors mentioned in the third paragraph as well as the member of the Council of State, the advocate and the six distinguished persons mentioned in the second paragraph. It is presided over by the first president of the Court of Cassation who may be substituted by the procurator-general at that Court.

Except in disciplinary matters the minister of justice may participate in the meetings of the sections of the High Council of the Judiciary.

The High Council of the Judiciary may be seized by a person undergoing a trial under the conditions determined by organic statute.

An organic statute determines the conditions for the application of the present Article.

Article 66. No-one may be detained arbitrarily.
The judicial authority, guardian of individual liberty, ensures the observance of this principle under the conditions provided by statute.

Article 66-1. No-one may be sentenced to the death penalty.

Title IX. The High Court

Article 67. The President of the Republic is not liable for any acts committed in this capacity, subject to the provisions of the Articles 53-2 and 68.

He may not, during his mandate and before no French court or administrative authority, be required to testify, nor be the object of a court action, investigatory action, instruction or prosecution. Any period of prescription or foreclosure is suspended.

All actions and proceedings thus barred may be resumed or brought against him upon expiry of a period of one month after the end of his office.

Article 68. The President of the Republic may only be removed from office in case of a breach of his duties manifestly incompatible with the exercise of his mandate. The removal is proclaimed by Parliament sitting as the High Court [Haute Cour].

The proposal to convene the High Court adopted by one of the chambers of Parliament is immediately transmitted to the other, which reaches its decision within fifteen days.

The High Court is chaired by the president of the National Assembly. It rules within a period of one month, by secret ballot, on the removal from office. Its decision is of immediate effect.

The decisions taken in the application of the present Article are taken by two thirds of the members composing the chamber concerned or the High Court. Any delegation of votes is prohibited. Only the votes in favour of the proposal to convene the High Court or of the removal from office are counted.

An organic statute determines the conditions for the application of the present Article.

Title X. On the criminal liability of members of the government

Article 68-1. The members of the government are liable for acts committed in the exercise of their office and qualified as crimes [crime] or misdemeanours [délit] at the time they were committed.

They are tried by the Court of Justice of the Republic [Cour de justice de la République].

The Court of Justice of the Republic is bound by such definition of crimes and misdemeanours as well as by such determination of penalties as follows from statute.

Article 68-2. The Court of Justice of the Republic consists of fifteen judges: twelve parliamentarians elected from among their ranks and in equal number by the National Assembly and by the Senate after each general or partial election of these chambers, and three judges at the Court of Cassation, one of whom presides over the Court of Justice of the Republic.

Any person who claims to be a victim of a crime or misdemeanour committed by a member of the government in the exercise of his office may file a complaint with a petitions committee.

This committee orders either the closure of the procedure or its transmission to the procurator-general at the Court of Cassation for the seizing of the Court of Justice of the Republic.
The procurator-general at the Court of Cassation may also upon his own motion seize the Court of Justice of the Republic upon the assent of the petitions committee.
An organic statute determines the conditions for the application of the present Article.

Article 68-3. The provisions of the present Title are applicable to acts committed before its entry into force.

Title XI. The Economic, Social and Environmental Council

Article 69. The Economic, Social and Environmental Council [Conseil économique, social et environnemental], seized by the Government, gives its opinion on government bills, draft ordinances or draft decrees as well as on private member's bills which are submitted to it.
A member of the Economic, Social and Environmental Council may be appointed by it to present to the parliamentary chambers the opinion of the Council on the government or private member's bills which have been submitted to it.
The Economic, Social and Environmental Council may be seized by way of petition under the conditions determined by organic statute. After examination of the petition, it notifies the Government and Parliament of the follow-up actions that it proposes to take.

Article 70. The Economic, Social and Environmental Council may be consulted by the Government and Parliament on any problem of an economic, social or environmental nature. The Government may equally consult it on government bills for programming statutes defining the multiannual directions for public finances. Any plan or any government bill for a programming statute of an economic, social or environmental nature is submitted to it for its opinion.

Article 71. The composition of the Economic and Social and Environmental Council, the number of whose members may not exceed two hundred and thirty-three, and its rules of procedure are determined by an organic statute.

Title XI bis. The Defender of Rights

Article 71-1. The Defender of Rights guards the respect of rights and liberties by the administrations of the State, the territorial entities, public bodies, as well as by any body charged with a public service task, or with respect to which an organic statute confers competences on him.
He may be seized, under the conditions stipulated by an organic statute, by any person who considers himself harmed by the functioning of a public service or a body envisaged in the first paragraph. He may consider a matter on his own initiative.
An organic statute specifies the competences and the terms of intervention of the Defender of Rights. It determines the conditions under which he may be assisted by a collegiate body in the exercise of some of his competences.
The Defender of Rights is appointed by the President of the Republic for a non-renewable term of six years after application of the procedure stipulated in the last paragraph of Article 13. His functions are incompatible with those of a member of Government and of a member of Parliament. Other incompatibilities are determined by organic statute.
The Defender of Rights gives account of his activity to the President of the Republic and to Parliament.

Title XII. The territorial entities

Article 72. The territorial entities [collectivités territoriales] of the Republic are the municipalities [communes], the departments [départements], the regions [régions], the special-status entities and the overseas entities governed by Article 74. Any other territorial entity is created by statute, where appropriate in place of one or more entities referred to in the present paragraph.
Territorial entities are charged with taking decisions on the entirety of competences that can best be exercised at their level.

Under the conditions provided by statute, the entities administer themselves freely through elected councils and possess regulatory powers [réglementaire] for the exercise of their competences.

Under the conditions provided by organic statute, provided that the essential conditions for the exercise of a public liberty or a constitutionally guaranteed right is not affected, territorial entities or associations thereof may, where such is provided by statute or regulation, as the case may be, derogate on an experimental basis for limited purpose and duration from statutory or regulatory provisions governing the exercise of their competences.

No territorial entity may exercise tutelage over another. However, where the exercise of a competence requires the co-operation of several territorial entities, statute may authorize one of them or one of their associations to organize the modalities of their joint action.

In the territorial entities of the Republic, the representative of the State, representing each of the members of the Government, is responsible for the national interests, administrative supervision and the observance of statutes.

Article 72-1. Statute determines the conditions under which voters in each territorial entity may, by exercising the right of petition, request that a question relevant to its competence be included in the agenda of the deliberative assembly of that entity.

Under the conditions determined by organic statute, government bills for deliberation or acts relevant to the competence of a territorial entity may, on its initiative, by means of referendum, be submitted to the decision of the voters of that entity.

When it is envisaged that a territorial entity be created or provided with a special status or its organization be modified, it may be decided by statute to consult the voters registered in the concerned entities. The modification of the borders of territorial entities may equally give rise to a consultation of the voters under the conditions provided by statute.

Article 72-2. Territorial entities enjoy resources of which they may dispose freely under the conditions determined by statute.

They may receive all or a part of the revenue from taxes of any nature. Statute may authorize them to specify the basis and rate thereof within the limits it determines.

Fiscal revenue and other own resources of the territorial entities represent, for each category of entities, a decisive share of the entirety of their resources. Organic statute determines the conditions under which this rule is given effect.

Any transfer of competences between the State and the territorial entities is accompanied by an allocation of resources equivalent to what had been dedicated to the exercise of those competences. Any creation or extension of competences having as a consequence an increase in expenditures of territorial entities is accompanied by resources determined by statute.

Statute provides for equalization mechanisms designed to promote equality between territorial entities.

Article 72-3. The Republic recognizes, within the French people, the overseas populations in a common ideal of liberty, equality and fraternity.

Guadeloupe, Guiana, Martinique, Réunion, Mayotte, Saint-Barthélemy, Saint-Martin, Saint-Pierre-and-Miquelon, the Islands of Wallis and Futuna and French Polynesia are governed by Article 73 for departments and overseas regions and for territorial entities created by application of the last paragraph of Article 73, and by Article 74 for the other entities.

The status of New Caledonia is governed by Title XIII.

Statute determines the legislative regime and the special organization of the French Southern and Antarctic Territories and of Clipperton.

Article 72-4. No change, regarding the whole or a part of one of the entities mentioned in the second paragraph of Article 72-3, of one towards the other of the regimes provided for by Articles 73 and 74, takes place unless the consent of the voters of the entity or the part of the entity concerned has been obtained beforehand under the conditions provided by the following paragraph. This change of regime is decided on by organic statute.

The President of the Republic, on a proposal of the Government during sessions or on joint proposal of the two chambers, which are published in the Official Journal [Journal officiel], may decide to consult the voters of a territorial entity situated overseas on a question relating to its organization, to its competences or to its legislative regime. Where this consultation concerns a change stipulated in the foregoing paragraph and is organized on proposal of the Government, it makes a statement before each chamber, which is followed by a debate.

Article 73. In the overseas departments and regions, statutes and regulations are applicable by operation of law. They may be the object of adaptations in view of the particular characteristics and constraints of these entities.

These adaptations may be decided by the entities on matters where they exercise their competences and if they were enabled to do so, as the case may be, by statute or by regulation.

By derogation from the first paragraph and in order to take account of their specificities, entities governed by the present Article may be enabled, as the case may be by statute or by regulation, to themselves determine the rules applicable on their territory in a limited number of matters that can fall under the scope of statute or regulation.

These rules may not concern nationality, civil rights, guarantees of civil liberties, the status and capacity of persons, the organization of justice system, criminal law, criminal procedure, foreign policy, defence, public security and order, currency, credit and exchange, as well as electoral law. This enumeration may be specified and completed by organic statute.

The provisions stipulated in the two preceding paragraphs are not applicable to the department and to the region of Réunion.

The enabling provided for in the second and third paragraph is decided, upon request of the entity concerned, subject to the conditions and with the reservations provided by an organic statute. They may not be carried out where the essential conditions for the exercise of a public liberty or a constitutionally guaranteed right is at issue.

The creation by statute of an entity substituting an overseas department and region or the establishment of a single deliberative assembly for those two entities may not take place unless the consent of the voters registered in the territory of these entities has been obtained according to the procedure provided in the second paragraph of Article 72-4.

Article 74. The overseas entities governed by the present Article have a status that takes account of their particular interests within the Republic.

This status is defined by organic statute, adopted after an opinion of the deliberative assembly, which determines:
- the conditions under which statutes and regulations are applicable there;
- the competences of this entity; subject to those already exercised by it, the transfer of competences by the State may not concern the matters enumerated in the fourth paragraph of Article 73, specified and complemented, as the case may be, by organic statute;
- the rules on the organization and functioning of the institutions of the entity and the electoral regime of its deliberative assembly;
- the conditions under which its institutions are consulted on government bills and private member's bills and drafts of ordinances or decrees containing provisions that are specific to the entity as well as to the ratification or approval of international commitments concluded in matters relevant to its competence.

The organic statute may equally determine, for those entities that are provided with autonomy, the conditions under which:
- the Council of State exercises specific judicial review over certain categories of acts of the deliberative assembly effected on the basis of competences that it exercises within the scope of statute;
- the deliberative assembly may amend a statute promulgated after the entry into force of the status of the entity, where the Constitutional Council, seized in particular by the authorities of that entity, has established that the statute has intervened in the scope of competence of that entity;
- measures justified by local needs may be taken by the entity in favour of its population, in matters of access to employment, the right of establishment for the exercise of a professional activity or the protection of land property;
- the entity may participate, under the control of the State, in the exercise of the competences it retains, respecting the guarantees granted to the entire national territory for the exercise of public liberties.

The other modalities of the organization specific to the entities subject to the present Article are determined and amended by statute after consultation of their deliberative assembly.

Article 74-1. In the overseas entities envisaged by Article 74 and in New Caledonia, the Government may, by ordinance, in the matters that remain in the competence of the State, extend, with the necessary adaptations, the provisions of statutory nature in force in Metropolitan France or adapt the provisions of statutory nature in force to the specific organization of the entity concerned, provided that the statute did not explicitly exclude, for the provisions in question, recourse to this procedure.

The ordinances are issued in the Council of Ministers after an opinion of the deliberative assembly concerned and the Council of State. They enter into force upon their publication. They become ineffective in the absence of ratification by Parliament within a period of eighteen months after that publication.

Article 75. The citizens of the Republic who do not have ordinary civil status, only envisaged in Article 34, retain their personal status as long as they have not renounced it.

PART I. CONSTITUTIONAL LAW

Article 75-1. Regional languages belong to the heritage of France.

Title XIII. Transitional provisions regarding New Caledonia

Article 76. The population of New Caledonia is called upon to pronounce itself before the 31 December 1998 on the provisions of the agreement signed at Nouméa on 5 May 1998 and published on 27 May 1998 in the Official Journal of the French Republic.
Admitted to participate in the vote are the persons who fulfil the conditions determined in Article 2 of statute no. 88-1028 of 9 November 1988.
The measures necessary for the organization of the vote are taken by decree in consultation with the Council of State [Conseil d'Etat] after having been discussed in the council of ministers.

Article 77. After adoption of the agreement by the vote provided in Article 76, an organic statute, passed after an opinion of the deliberative assembly of New Caledonia, determines, in order to ensure the development of New Caledonia respecting the directions defined by that agreement and in accordance with the terms necessary in order to give it effect:
- the competences of the State that will be transferred definitively to the institutions of New Caledonia, the time scale and the modalities of the transfer, as well as the allocation of the expenditures resulting therefrom;
- the rules of the organization and functioning of the institutions of New Caledonia and in particular the conditions under which certain categories of acts of the deliberative assembly of New Caledonia may be submitted for review to the Constitutional Council [Conseil Constitutionnel] before publication;
- the rules relating to citizenship, to the electoral regime, to employment and to the customary civil status;
- the conditions and time limits within which the population concerned in New Caledonia will be led to pronounce themselves on the attainment of full sovereignty.
The other measures necessary for giving effect of the agreement mentioned in Article 76 are defined by statute.
For the definition of the electoral body called upon to elect the members of the deliberative assemblies of New Caledonia and its provinces, the list to which the agreement mentioned in Article 76 and in Article 188 and 189 of the organic statute no. 99-209 of 19 March 1999 relating to New Caledonia refer is the list drawn up in the course of the vote provided for in Article 76 and including the persons not admitted to participate in it.

Articles 78 to 86. (Repealed).

Title XIV. On the French-speaking World and on Association Agreements

Article 87. The Republic takes part in the development of solidarity and cooperation between the States and peoples which have the French language in common.

Title XV. On the European Union

Article 88-1. The Republic participates in the European Union, constituted by States that have freely chosen to exercise certain of their powers conjointly by virtue of the Treaty on European Union and the Treaty on the Functioning of the European Union as they result from the Treaty signed at Lisbon on 13 December 2007.

Article 88-2. Statute determines the rules regarding the European arrest warrant by application of the acts taken by the institutions of the European Union.

Article 88-3. Subject to reciprocity and in accordance with the terms laid down by the Treaty on European Union signed on 7 February 1992, the right to vote and to stand in municipal elections may be granted only to citizens of the Union residing in France. These citizens may neither exercise the office of mayor or deputy mayor, nor participate in the designation of senatorial electors and in the election of senators. An organic statute adopted in identical terms by both chambers determines the conditions under which the present Article is applied.

Article 88-4. The Government submits to the National Assembly and to the Senate, when they have been transmitted to the Council of the European Union, drafts of or proposals for acts of the European Communities and of the European Union.

In accordance with the terms set by the rules of procedure of each chamber, European resolutions may be adopted, also outside sessions where appropriate, on the drafts and proposals mentioned in the first paragraph, as well as on any document emanating from an institution of the European Union.
Within each parliamentary chamber a committee responsible for European affairs is established.

Article 88-5. Any government bill authorizing the ratification of a Treaty regarding the accession of a State to the European Union and to the European Communities is submitted to referendum by the President of the Republic. However, by a vote on a motion adopted in identical terms by each assembly by a majority of three fifths, Parliament may authorize the adoption of the government bill in accordance with the procedure stipulated in the third paragraph of Article 89.

[Note: This Article does not apply to accessions made following an intergovernmental conference whose convocation was decided by the European Council before 1 July 2004.]

Article 88-6. The National Assembly or the Senate may adopt a reasoned opinion on the compliance of a draft European legislative act with the principle of subsidiarity. The opinion is addressed by the president of the chamber concerned to the presidents of the European Parliament, of the Council and of the European Commission. The Government is informed of this.
Each chamber may bring an action before the Court of Justice of the European Union against a European legislative act for a violation of the principle of subsidiarity. The action is transmitted to the Court of Justice of the European Union by the Government.
To that end, resolutions may be adopted, also outside sessions where appropriate, in accordance with the terms on initiative and debate set by the rules of procedure of each chamber. Upon request of sixty deputies or of sixty senators, the action is brought by operation of law.

Article 88-7. By adoption of a motion passed in identical terms by the National Assembly and the Senate, Parliament may oppose an amendment of the rules for the adoption of acts of the European Union in the cases envisaged, under the simplified treaty revision procedure or judicial cooperation in civil matters, by the Treaty on European Union and the Treaty on the Functioning of the European Union as they result from the Treaty signed at Lisbon on 13 December 2007.

Title XVI. On amendments

Article 89. The right of initiative for a revision of the Constitution lies concurrently with the President of the Republic, upon a proposal by the Prime Minister, and with the members of Parliament.
A government or private member's bill for a revision must be examined under the conditions of the fixed periods determined in the third paragraph of Article 42 and adopted by both chambers in identical terms. The revision is final after having been approved by referendum.
However, a government bill for a revision is not submitted to referendum where the President of the Republic decides to submit it to Parliament convened in Congress [Congrès]; in that case, the government bill for revision is not approved unless it is adopted by a majority of three fifths of the votes cast. The bureau of the Congress is that of the National Assembly.
No procedure of revision may be initiated or continued where the integrity of the territory is jeopardized.
The republican form of Government may not be the object of a revision.

Title XVII. (Repealed).

Declaration of the Rights of Man and the Citizen [Déclaration des Droits de l'homme et du Citoyen] of 26 August 1789.[2]

The Representatives of the French People, organized in a National Assembly, considering that ignorance, neglect or contempt of the rights of man are the only causes of the public misfortunes and of Governments' corruption, have decided to expose, in a solemn Declaration, the natural, inalienable and sacred rights of man, so that this Declaration, constantly present to all members of the social body, continually reminds them of their rights and their duties; so that the acts of the legislative power and those of the executive power may be compared at any time with the aim of every political institution, and that they would be more respected; so that the grievances of citizens, founded henceforth on simple and incontestable principles, result in the preservation of the Constitution and in the happiness of all.

Therefore the National Assembly recognizes and proclaims, in the presence and under the auspices of the Supreme Being, the following rights of man and of the citizen:

First Article. Men are born and remain free and equal in rights. Social distinctions may be based only on the common good.

Article II. The aim of every political association is the conservation of the natural and imprescriptible rights of man. These rights are liberty, property, safety and resistance to oppression.

Article III. The principle of all Sovereignty resides essentially in the Nation. No body, no individual may exercise any authority that does not expressly emanate from it.

Article IV. Liberty consists of being able to do everything that does not harm anybody else: thus the exercise of the natural rights of every man has no boundaries except those that ensure to other Members of the Society the enjoyment of those same rights. Those boundaries may be defined only by Law.

Article V. The Law does not have the right to forbid any action except those that are harmful to society. Nothing which is not forbidden by the Law may be barred, and no-one may be forced to do what it does not dictate.

Article VI. The Law is the expression of the general will. All Citizens have the right to contribute personally, or through their Representatives, to its formation. It must be the same for everybody, whether it protects or punishes. All citizens, being equal before it, are equally eligible to all public dignities, positions and employments, according to their capacities, without any distinction other than those of their virtues and their talents.

Article VII. No man may be accused, arrested or detained except in the cases determined by Law and in the forms that it has prescribed. Those who solicit, send, execute or let execute arbitrary orders must be punished; however every Citizen summoned or arrested pursuant to the Law must obey immediately: he makes himself guilty with his resistance.

Article VIII. The Law must establish only strictly and evidently necessary penalties, and no-one may be punished except pursuant to a Law established and promulgated prior to the crime, and lawfully applied.

Article IX. Every man being presumed innocent until he has been declared guilty, if it is deemed indispensable to arrest him, any harshness which is not necessary for the securing of his person must be severely repressed by Law.

Article X. No-one may be disquieted because of his opinions, even religious, provided that their manifestation does not disturb the public order established by Law.

Article XI. The free communication of thoughts and of opinions is one of the most precious rights of Man; every Citizen may therefore speak, write, print freely, save answering for the abuse of this freedom in the cases determined by the Law.

---

[2] Translation by I. Wieczorek.

Article XII. The guarantee of the rights of Man and the Citizen requires a public force: such force is therefore established for the advantage of all and not for the specific utility of those who have been entrusted with it.

Article XIII. For the maintenance of the public force, and for the expenses of the administration, a common contribution is indispensable. It must be equally distributed among the citizens according to their means.

Article XIV. All Citizens have the right to ascertain, personally or through their Representatives, the necessity of the public contribution, to freely consent to it, to monitor its use and to determine its proportion, base, collection and duration.

Article XV. Society has the right to call every public Agent to account for the administration.

Article XVI. Any society in which the guarantee of Rights is not ensured and the separation of Powers is not determined, has no Constitution.

Article XVII. Property being an inviolable and sacred right, no-one may be deprived of it, except when public necessity, lawfully assessed, evidently requires it, and under the condition of a just and prior indemnity.

Electoral Code [Code Electoral], as last amended in its relevant parts by organic statute no. 2009-38 of 13 January 2009. Selected provisions: Book I, Title II: Chapters I and II as well as Articles L 162 and L 163 of Chapter V; Book II: Title I, Title II, Articles L 283 to L 285 of Title III, and Chapter I of Title IV.[3]

Statutory part

Book I. The election of deputies, members of the departmental councils and members of the municipal councils

[Title I is omitted.]

Title II. Special provisions regarding the election of deputies

Chapter I. Composition of the National Assembly and the length of the mandate of the deputies

Article LO 119. The number of deputies is five hundred seventy seven.

Article LO 120. The National Assembly is re-elected in full.

Article LO 121. The powers of the National Assembly expire on the third Tuesday of June in the fifth year following its election.

Article LO 122. Save for a case of dissolution, general elections take place within sixty days prior to the expiry of the powers of the National Assembly.

Chapter II. Election procedure

Article L 123. The deputies are elected in single-vote majority voting with two rounds.

Article L 124. The vote takes place in electoral districts.

Article L 125. The electoral districts are determined in conformity with Table 1 annexed to the present Code. A revision of the borders of the electoral districts takes place, according to demographic developments, after the second general census of the population following the last redistricting.

Article L 126. No-one is elected in the first round of the vote if he has not received:
1. the absolute majority of votes cast;
2. a number of votes equal to one quarter of the number of registered voters.
In the second round, a relative majority suffices.
In case of a tie, the oldest of the candidates is elected.

[Chapters III and IV are omitted.]

Chapter V. Declarations of candidacies

[Articles L 154 to L 161 are omitted.]

Article L 162. The declarations of candidacies for the second round of the vote must be filed before 18.00 hours on the Tuesday that follows the first round.
However if, because of a case of force majeure, the counting of the votes could not be completed in the period prescribed in Article L 175, declarations are accepted until 18.00 hours on Wednesday.
Save for the provisions of Article L 163, no-one may be candidate in the second round if he did not run in the first round and if he did not receive a number of votes at least equal to 12.5 % of the number of registered voters.

---

[3] Translation by Ph. Kiiver.

In case a single candidate fulfils these conditions, the candidate who has received, after him, the largest number of votes in the first round may proceed to the second.

In case no candidate fulfils these conditions, the two candidates who have received the largest number of votes in the first round may proceed to the second.

A candidate may not present in the second round of the vote any alternate other than the one he designated in his declaration of candidacy for the first round.

The provisions of the second and third paragraph of Article L 157 and those of Article L 159 are applicable to declarations of candidacies for the second round of the vote. In that case, the administrative tribunal decides within a period of twenty-four hours.

Article L 163. Where a candidate dies after the expiry of the period prescribed for filing declarations of candidacies, his alternate becomes candidate and may designate a new alternate.

Where an alternate dies during the same period, the candidate may designate a new alternate.

[The remainder of Book I is omitted.]

Book II. The election of senators of the departments

Title I. Composition of the Senate and the length of the mandate of the senators

Article LO 274. The number of Senators elected within the departments is 326.

Article LO 275. Senators are elected for six years.

Article LO 276. The Senate is re-elected by half. For this purpose, the senators are divided into two classes, 1 and 2, of approximately equal importance, in accordance with Table 5 annexed to the present Code.
[Note: Until the partial elections of 2010, Article LO 276 provides: The Senate is re-elected by thirds. For this purpose, the senators are divided into three classes, A, B and C, of approximately equal importance, in accordance with Table 5 annexed to the present Code.]

Article LO 277. In each class, the mandate of the senators begins at the opening of the ordinary session which follows their election, at which date the mandate of the senators previously in office expires.

Article LO 278. The election of senators takes place within sixty days prior to the date of the beginning of their mandate.

Title II. Composition of the electoral college

Article L 279. The seats of the senators representing the departments are distributed in accordance with Table 6 annexed to the present Code.

Article L 280. The senators are elected in each department by an electoral college composed of:
1. deputies;
2. members of the regional council [conseillers régionaux] from the departmental section corresponding to the department and the members of the Assembly of Corsica [Assemblée de Corse] designated under the conditions envisaged by Title III bis of the present Book;
3. members of the departmental council [conseillers généraux];
4. delegates of the municipal councils or the substitutes of these delegates.

Article L 281. The deputies, the members of the regional council, the members of the Assembly of Corsica and the members of the departmental council who have been appointed by the census commissions are registered in the list of senatorial electors and take part in the vote even if their election is contested. In case they are prevented by a major hindrance, they may exercise, upon written request, their right to vote by proxy. The mandatary must be a member of the senatorial electoral college and may not dispose of more than one proxy.

Article L 282. In the case where a member of the departmental council is a deputy, a member of the regional council or a member of the Assembly of Corsica, a replacement is designated for him, upon his proposal, by the president of the departmental council.

In the case where a member of the regional council or a member of the Assembly of Corsica is a deputy, a replacement is designated for him, upon his proposal, by the president of the regional council or the one of the Assembly of Corsica.

Title III. Designation of delegates of municipal councils

Article L 283. The decree calling up the senatorial electors determines the day on which the delegates of the municipal councils and their substitutes must be designated. An interval of at least six weeks must separate these elections and the ones of the senators.

Article L 284. In municipalities of less than 9,000 inhabitants, the municipal councils elect from among their members:
- one delegate for municipal councils of nine and eleven members;
- three delegates for municipal councils of fifteen members;
- five delegates for municipal councils of nineteen members;
- seven delegates for municipal councils of twenty-three members;
- fifteen delegates for municipal councils of twenty-seven and twenty-nine members.

In case the municipal council is formed by application of Articles L 2113-6 and L 2113-7 of the General Code of Territorial Entities [code général des collectivités territoriales] regarding mergers of municipalities, the number of delegates is equal to the number to which the former municipalities would have been entitled before the merger.

Article L 285. In municipalities of 9,000 inhabitants and more, all members of the municipal council are delegates ex officio.

Furthermore, in municipalities of more than 30,000 inhabitants, the municipal councils elect additional delegates, namely 1 for every 1,000 inhabitants in excess of 30,000.

[The remainder of Title III as well as Title IIIbis are omitted.]

Title IV. Election of senators

Chapter I. Election procedure

Article L 294. In departments where three senators or less are elected, the election takes place by majority voting with two rounds.
No-one is elected senator in the first round of the vote if he has not obtained:
1. the absolute majority of votes cast;
2. a number of votes equal to one quarter of registered voters.
In the second round of the vote, a relative majority suffices. In case of a tie, the oldest of the candidates is elected.

Article L 295. In departments where four senators or more are elected, the election takes place by proportional representation following the rule of largest averages, without spreading votes over multiple lists [panachage] and without preference votes.
On each list, seats are attributed to candidates in the order of nomination.

[The remainder of the Code is omitted.]

Basic Law for the Federal Republic of Germany [Grundgesetz für die Bundesrepublik Deutschland] of 23 May 1949 as last amended by federal statute of 21 July 2010 (*BGBl.* I p. 944).[4]

Preamble
Conscious of its responsibility before God and man, inspired by the will to serve world peace as an equal partner in a united Europe, the German people, by virtue of its constituent power, has adopted for itself this Basic Law. Germans in the States of Baden-Württemberg, Bavaria, Berlin, Brandenburg, Bremen, Hamburg, Hesse, Mecklenburg-Western Pomerania, Lower Saxony, North Rhine-Westphalia, Rhineland-Palatinate, Saar, Saxony, Saxony-Anhalt, Schleswig-Holstein and Thuringia have achieved the unity and freedom of Germany in free self-determination. This Basic Law thus applies to the entire German people.

I. The fundamental rights

Article 1. (1) Human dignity is inviolable. To respect and protect it is the duty of all state authority.
(2) The German people therefore acknowledges inviolable and inalienable human rights as the basis of every community of people, of peace and of justice in the world.
(3) The following fundamental rights bind the legislature, the executive and the judiciary as directly applicable law.

Article 2. (1) Everyone has the right to the free development of his personality, as far as he does not infringe on the rights of others and does not violate the constitutional order or the law of morality.
(2) Everyone has the right to life and physical integrity. The freedom of the person is inviolable. These rights may be interfered with only pursuant to a statute.

Article 3. (1) All people are equal before the law.
(2) Men and women have equal rights. The state promotes the actual implementation of equal rights for women and men and takes measures to remove existing disadvantages.
(3) No-one may be disadvantaged or preferred because of his sex, his descent, his race, his language, his homeland and origin, his faith, his religious or political views. No-one may be disadvantaged because of his disability.

Article 4. (1) The freedom of faith, of conscience, and the freedom to manifest one's religious and world-view conviction, are inviolable.
(2) The undisturbed exercise of religion is ensured.
(3) No-one may be forced against his conscience into armed military service. Details are regulated by a federal statute.

Article 5. (1) Everyone has the right to freely express and disseminate his opinion in speech, writing and picture and to inform himself without interference from generally accessible sources. The freedom of the press and the freedom of reporting through radio and film are ensured. Censorship does not take place.
(2) These rights find their limits in the regulations of general statutes, in statutory provisions for the protection of the youth and in the right to personal honour.
(3) Art and science, research and teaching are free. The freedom of teaching does not release from the loyalty to the constitution.

Article 6. (1) Marriage and family are placed under the special protection of the state order.
(2) The care and upbringing of children are the natural right of the parents and are an obligation that is primarily theirs. The community of the state watches over their performance.
(3) Children may be separated from the family pursuant to a statute against the will of their custodians only when the custodians fail or when the children are in danger of becoming victims of neglect for other reasons.
(4) Every mother is entitled to the protection and care of the community.
(5) Legislation is to provide children born outside wedlock with conditions for their physical and mental development and their position in society equal to those of children born within wedlock.

---

[4] Translation by Ph. Kiiver, G. Kristoferitsch & G. Rotering.

Part I. Constitutional Law

Article 7. (1) The entire school system is placed under the supervision of the state.
(2) Custodians have the right to decide over the participation of their child in religion classes.
(3) Religion classes are a regular course at public schools with the exception of non-denominational schools. Without prejudice to the state right of supervision, religious classes are taught in accordance with the principles of the religious communities. No teacher may be obliged against his will to teach religion classes.
(4) The right to establish private schools is ensured. Private schools as a substitute for public schools require the approval of the state and are subject to State legislation. Approval is to be granted when private schools are not inferior to state schools in their teaching aims and facilities as well as the scientific training of their teaching staff, and when a segregation of pupils according to the economic standing of the parents is not promoted. Approval is to be denied when the economic and legal position of the teaching staff is insufficiently secured.
(5) A private primary-cum-secondary school is only to be allowed if the curriculum administration recognizes a special educational interest or, upon custodians' request, if it is to be established as a community school, a denominational school or as a school based on a particular world view and a public primary-cum-secondary school of that kind is lacking in the municipality.
(6) Nursery schools remain abolished.

Article 8. (1) All Germans have the right to assemble peacefully and unarmed without notification or permission.
(2) Regarding gatherings outdoors, this right may be limited by or pursuant to a statute.

Article 9. (1) All Germans have the right to form clubs and societies.
(2) Associations whose purposes or activities run counter to criminal law or which are aimed against the constitutional order or the idea of understanding between nations are prohibited.
(3) The right to form associations for the promotion of working and economic conditions is ensured for everyone and for all professions. Agreements that limit or seek to hinder this right are void, measures taken with a view thereto are illegal. Measures in the sense of Articles 12a, 35 (2) and (3), Article 87a (4) and Article 91 may not be directed against industrial dispute action that is taken for the protection and promotion of working and economic conditions by associations in the meaning of the first sentence.

Article 10. (1) The privacy of correspondence as well as the privacy of mail and telecommunications are inviolable.
(2) Limitations may be ordered only pursuant to a statute. If the limitation serves the protection of the liberal-democratic fundamental order or of the integrity or security of the Federation or a State, then statute may provide that it not be notified to those affected and that recourse to the courts be replaced by review by organs and auxiliary organs appointed by the parliament.

Article 11. (1) All Germans enjoy freedom of movement on the entire territory of the Federation.
(2) This right may be limited only by or pursuant to a statute and only for those cases where sufficient means to support life are lacking and where this would result in a special burden on the community or where it is necessary for the aversion of a danger to the integrity or the liberal democratic fundamental order of the Federation or a State, for the countering of an epidemic threat, natural disasters or very serious accidents, for the protection of the youth from neglect or for the prevention of criminal acts.

Article 12. (1) All Germans have the right to freely choose their profession, place of work and of their training. The exercise of a profession may be regulated by or pursuant to a statute.
(2) No-one may be forced to perform a particular work, except within the framework of a regular general public service obligation that is the same for everyone.
(3) Forced labour is permissible only in the context of a court-ordered deprivation of freedom.

Article 12a. (1) Men from the age of eighteen onwards can be obliged to serve in the armed forces, the Federal Border Guard [Bundesgrenzschutz] or in a civil defence organization.
(2) He who refuses armed military service on conscientious grounds may be obliged to serve in an alternative service. The length of the alternative service may not exceed the length of the military service. Details are regulated by a statute which may not compromise the freedom of conscientious decision and which must also provide for an alternative service option which is not connected with the units of the armed forces and the Federal Border Guard.
(3) Persons liable to conscription who have not been drafted in accordance with paragraphs 1 or 2 may in a state of defence, by or pursuant to a statute, be committed to an employment for civilian services for defence purposes including the protection of the civilian population; commitment to public employment is only permissible for the

exercise of police tasks or such sovereign tasks of public administration that can be fulfilled only within a public employment. Employments in the meaning of the first sentence may be established with the armed forces, in the context of their supply, as well as in the public administration; commitment to employment in the context of the supply of the civilian population is permissible only to secure its basic needs or to maintain its safety.
(4) If in a state of defence the demand for civilian services in the civilian medical and health system as well as in the stationary military hospital system cannot be met on a voluntary basis, women from the age of eighteen until the age of fifty-five may be drafted to such services by or pursuant to a statute. They may in no event be drafted to armed service.
(5) For the time period before the state of defence, obligations under paragraph 3 may only be established within the guidelines of Article 80a (1). For the preparation to services according to paragraph 3 for which special knowledge or skills are required, by or pursuant to a statute the participation in training courses may be made mandatory. In that respect, the first sentence does not apply.
(6) If in a state of defence the demand for workers in the contexts stipulated in paragraph 3, second sentence, cannot be met on a voluntary basis, the freedom of Germans to give up a profession or a place of work may be limited, in order to meet this demand, by or pursuant to a statute. Prior to the beginning of a state of defence, paragraph 5, first sentence, applies mutatis mutandis.

Article 13. (1) The home is inviolable.
(2) Searches may be ordered only by a judge or, in case of an imminent threat, also by other organs provided for by statutes, and may be conducted only in the form stipulated there.
(3) When certain facts support the suspicion that someone has committed a certain very serious crime defined individually by statute, then, for the prosecution of this act, on the basis of a court order, technical means for the acoustic surveillance of homes in which the suspect is presumably staying may be used, if the investigation of the case by other means would be disproportionately burdensome or futile. The measure is to be of a limited duration. The order is to be given by a body staffed with three judges. In case of an imminent threat, it may also be given by a single judge.
(4) To avert acute threats to public safety, especially a threat to the public or to life, technical means for the surveillance of homes may be used only on the basis of a court order. In case of an imminent threat, the measure may also be ordered by another instance stipulated by statute; a court decision must afterwards be obtained without delay.
(5) If technical means are exclusively meant for the protection of persons operating in a home, the measure may be ordered by an instance stipulated by statute. Any other use of the information thus obtained is permissible only for the purpose of criminal prosecution or the aversion of dangers and only if the lawfulness of the measure has been established by a court; in case of an imminent threat, a court decision must afterwards be obtained without delay.
(6) The Federal Government informs the Bundestag annually about the use that has been made of technical means under paragraph 3, under paragraph 4 within the competence of the Federation, and under paragraph 5 in as far as it requires judicial review. A body elected by the Bundestag exercises parliamentary control on the basis of this report. The States ensure an equivalent parliamentary control.
(7) Interferences and limitations may otherwise be effected only for the aversion of a threat to the public or to the life of individual persons, pursuant to a statute also for the prevention of acute threats to public safety and order, especially to address a shortage of housing space, to combat epidemic threats or to protect endangered adolescents.

Article 14. (1) Property and the right of inheritance are ensured. The content and limits thereof are defined by statutes.
(2) Property entails obligations. Its use should also serve the public good.
(3) An expropriation is only permissible for the public good. It may be effected only by or pursuant to a statute which regulates the kind and extent of compensation. The compensation is to be established by justly weighing the interests of the community and of those involved. Recourse to the ordinary courts is open in case of a dispute regarding the amount of the compensation.

Article 15. Land, natural resources and means of production may, for the purpose of socialization, by a statute which regulates the kind and extent of compensation, be transferred into public ownership or into other forms of collective concern. As regards the compensation, Article 14 (3), third and fourth sentence, applies mutatis mutandis.

Article 16. (1) German citizenship may not be withdrawn. A loss of citizenship may occur only pursuant to a statute and, if against the will of the person affected, only when the person affected does not become stateless as a result.

PART I. CONSTITUTIONAL LAW

(2) No German may be extradited to a foreign state. By statute a different regime may be established concerning extraditions to a member state of the European Union or an international tribunal, as long as principles of the rule of law are secured.

Article 16a. (1) Those politically persecuted enjoy the right to asylum.
(2) He who arrives from a member state of the European Communities or from another third country where the application of the Convention relating to the status of refugees and the Convention for the protection of human rights and fundamental freedoms is ensured, cannot rely on paragraph 1. The states outside the European Communities to which the conditions of the first sentence apply are designated by a statute which requires the consent of the Bundesrat. In cases stipulated by the first sentence, measures for the termination of a stay may be taken irrespectively of any court actions filed against them.
(3) By a statute which requires the consent of the Bundesrat, states may be designated where, based on the state of the law, the application of the law and the general political circumstances, it appears certain that neither political persecution nor inhuman or degrading punishment or treatment takes place. It is presumed that an alien from such a state is not being persecuted as long as he does not provide facts which support the conclusion that he is being politically persecuted contrary to this presumption.
(4) The execution of measures for the termination of a stay are, in the cases of paragraph 3 and in other cases that are manifestly ill-founded or are presumed manifestly ill-founded, suspended by a court only when serious doubts exist as to the lawfulness of the measure; the scope of review may be limited and belated submissions be disregarded. Details are to be regulated by statute.
(5) Paragraphs 1 to 4 do not bar any international treaties of member states of the European Communities among themselves and with third countries which, while respecting the obligations under the Convention relating to the status of refugees and the Convention for the protection of human rights and fundamental freedoms, the application of which must be ensured in the contracting states, provide for rules on jurisdiction for the review of applications for asylum, including the mutual recognition of decisions regarding asylum.

Article 17. Everyone has the right, individually or together with others in a group, to address in writing the competent authorities and parliament with petitions or complaints.

Article 17a. (1) Statutes regarding military and alternative service may provide that for members of the armed forces and the alternative service, for the duration of the military or alternative service, the fundamental right to freely express and disseminate one's opinion in speech, writing and picture (Article 5 (1), first sentence, first clause), the fundamental right of freedom of assembly (Article 8) and the right of petition (Article 17) in as far as it grants the right to submit petitions or complaints together with others in a group, be limited.
(2) Statutes which serve the purpose of defence, including the protection of the civilian population, may provide that the fundamental rights of free movement (Article 11) and the inviolability of the home (Article 13) be limited.

Article 18. He who abuses the freedom of expression, in particular the freedom of the press (Article 5 (1)), the freedom of teaching (Article 5 (3)), the freedom of assembly (Article 8), the freedom of association (Article 9), the privacy of the correspondence, the mail and telecommunications (Article 10), property (Article 14) or the right to asylum (Article 16a) in order to fight against the liberal democratic fundamental order, forfeits these fundamental rights. The forfeiture and its scope are established by the Federal Constitutional Court [Bundesverfassungsgericht].

Article 19. (1) In as far as a fundamental right may be limited by or pursuant to a statute in accordance with this Basic Law, such statute must be of a general nature and may not merely apply to an individual case. In addition, the statute must state the fundamental right and the Article concerned.
(2) In no event may a fundamental right be compromised in its essence.
(3) The fundamental rights also cover domestic legal persons, in as far as they are applicable in the light of their nature.
(4) If someone's rights are violated by public authority, he has recourse to the courts. In as far as no other jurisdiction applies, recourse may be had to the ordinary courts. Article 10 (2), second sentence, remains unaffected by this.

II. The Federation and the States

Article 20. (1) The Federal Republic of Germany is a democratic and social federal state.

(2) All state authority derives from the people. It is exercised by the people through elections and votes and through specific organs of the legislature, of executive power and the judiciary.
(3) The legislature is bound by the constitutional order, the executive power and the judiciary by law and justice.
(4) All Germans have the right to resist any person seeking to abolish this order, if no other remedy is available.

Article 20a. The state protects, also under its responsibility for future generations, the natural foundations of life and the animals, within the framework of the constitutional order through legislation and within the guidelines of law and justice through executive power and the judiciary.

Article 21. (1) Political parties contribute to the political will-formation of the people. Their establishment is free. Their internal order must correspond to democratic principles. They must render account about the origin and use of their means as well as about their assets in public.
(2) Political parties which, based on their aims or the conduct of their followers, are committed to jeopardizing or eliminating the liberal democratic fundamental order or to threatening the integrity of the Federal Republic of Germany, are unconstitutional. The Federal Constitutional Court [Bundesverfassungsgericht] rules on the question of unconstitutionality.
(3) Details are regulated by federal statutes.

Article 22. (1) The capital of the Federal Republic of Germany is Berlin. The representation of the state as a whole in the capital is a matter for the Federation. Details are regulated by statute.
(2) The federal flag is black-red-gold.

Article 23. (1) With a view to achieving a united Europe, the Federal Republic of Germany participates in the development of the European Union which is committed to democratic, rule-of-law, social, and federal principles and to the principle of subsidiarity, and which guarantees a level of protection of fundamental rights essentially comparable to that afforded by this Basic Law. To this end the Federation may, by a statute with the consent of the Bundesrat, transfer sovereign powers. For the establishment of the European Union, as well as for changes to its treaty foundations and comparable regulations that amend or supplement this Basic Law in its content, or that make such amendments or supplements possible, Article 79 (2) and (3) applies.
(1a) The Bundestag and the Bundesrat have the right to bring an action before the Court of Justice of the European Union if a legislative act of the European Union infringes upon the principle of subsidiarity. The Bundestag is obliged to do so on application by a quarter of its members. A statute which requires the consent of the Bundesrat may, with respect to the exercise of the rights accorded to the Bundestag and the Bundesrat in the treaty framework of the European Union, make deviations from the first sentence of Article 42 (2), first sentence, and Article 52 (3), first sentence.
(2) The Bundestag and, through the Bundesrat, the States, participate in matters concerning the European Union. The Federal Government must inform the Bundestag and the Bundesrat comprehensively and at the earliest possible time.
(3) The Federal Government provides the Bundestag with an opportunity to state its opinion prior to its participation in legislative acts of the European Union. The Federal Government takes into account the statements of opinion of the Bundestag during negotiations. Details are regulated by a statute.
(4) The Bundesrat is to be included in the will-formation of the Federation in as far as it would have had to participate in an equivalent domestic measure or in as far as the States would have been competent domestically.
(5) In as far as, in an area of exclusive competence of the Federation, interests of the States are affected, or in as far as the Federation has otherwise legislative competence, the Federal Government takes into account the statements of opinion of the Bundesrat. If primarily legislative competences of the States, the organization of their authorities or their administrative procedures are affected, the opinion of the Bundesrat must to that extent be given greatest consideration during the will-formation of the Federation; the responsibility of the Federation for the state as a whole must in that context be upheld. In matters that may result in an increase in spending or a decrease in revenue for the Federation, the consent of the Federal Government is required.
(6) If primarily exclusive legislative competences of the States in the areas of schooling, culture or broadcasting are affected, the exercise of the rights that the Federal Republic of Germany has as a member state of the European Union is transferred from the Federation to a representative of the States appointed by the Bundesrat. The exercise of these rights is carried out with the participation of and in coordination with the Federal Government; the responsibility of the Federation for the state as a whole must in that context be upheld.
(7) Details regarding paragraphs 4 to 6 are regulated by a statute that requires the consent of the Bundesrat.

Part I. Constitutional Law

Article 24. (1) The Federation may, by statute, transfer sovereign powers to international organizations.
(1a) In as far as the States are competent for the exercise of state power and the fulfilment of state tasks, they may, with the consent of the Federal Government, transfer sovereign powers to cross-border neighbourhood institutions.
(2) The Federation may, for the preservation of peace, enter into a system of mutual collective security; it will in that context agree to limitations of its sovereign powers which bring about and secure a peaceful and permanent order in Europe and between the nations of the world.
(3) For the settlement of international disputes, the Federation will accede to agreements regarding general, comprehensive and mandatory international arbitration.

Article 25. The general rules of international law are an integral part of federal law. They take precedence over statutes and directly create rights and obligations for the inhabitants of the territory of the Federation.

Article 26. (1) Acts that are capable of and are committed with the intent to disturb the peaceful coexistence of nations, in particular prepare the conduct of a war of aggression, are unconstitutional. They are to be made punishable offences.
(2) Weapons designed for warfare may be produced, transported and brought into circulation only with the consent of the Federal Government. Details are regulated by a federal statute.

Article 27. All German merchant vessels form a uniform merchant fleet.

Article 28. (1) The constitutional order in the States must comply with the principles of a republican, democratic and social state based on the rule of law in the meaning of this Basic Law. In the States, rural counties [Kreise] and municipalities [Gemeinden], the people must have a representative body that is formed in general, direct, free, equal and secret-ballot elections. At elections within rural counties and municipalities, persons with the citizenship of a member state of the European Community, within the guidelines of the law of the European Community, also have the right to vote and may be elected. In municipalities, a municipal assembly may take the place of an elected body.
(2) Municipalities must have the secured right to regulate all affairs of the local community, within the framework of statutes, on their own responsibility. Also associations of municipalities [Gemeindeverbände] have, within the framework of their statutory function, within the guidelines of statutes, the right to self-government. The securing of self-government also includes the foundations of financial autonomy; part of these foundations is a source of revenue related to economic strength to which municipalities with the right to set tax rates are entitled.
(3) The Federation ensures that the constitutional order of the States complies with fundamental rights and the provisions of paragraphs 1 and 2.

Article 29. (1) The territory of the Federation may be restructured so as to ensure that the States, in the light of their size and capacity, are able to effectively fulfil the tasks vested in them. Account is to be taken of regional attachment, historical and cultural connections, economic opportunity, as well as the requirements of regional planning and zoning.
(2) Measures for the restructuring of the territory of the Federation are effected by a federal statute which requires approval in a referendum [Volksentscheid]. The affected States are to be heard.
(3) The referendum takes place in those States from the territory or from parts of the territory of which a new or a redrawn State is to be formed (affected States). The object of the referendum is the question whether the affected States should continue to exist as before or whether the new or redrawn State should be formed. A referendum in favour of a new or redrawn State is established when majorities vote in favour of the change both within its future territory and within the territories or parts of territories of an affected State whose State affiliation is to be changed. It is not established when a majority within the territory of one of the affected States rejects the change; such rejection is however ineffective if in a part of a territory whose affiliation with the affected State is to be changed, a two-thirds majority votes in favour of the change, except when within the territory of the affected State as a whole a two-thirds majority rejects the change.
(4) If within a contiguous, separated residential and economic area whose parts lie in several States and which has at least one million inhabitants, one-tenth of the population entitled to vote for the Bundestag there demands by popular initiative [Volksbegehren] that for this area a single State affiliation be created, then within two years a federal statute is either to determine whether the State affiliation will be changed in accordance with paragraph 2 or that a consultative referendum [Volksbefragung] will be held in the affected States.
(5) The consultative referendum is aimed at establishing whether a change of State affiliation to be proposed by the statute finds approval. The statute may subject different, yet not more than two proposals to the consultative referendum. If a majority votes in favour of a proposed change of State affiliation, then within two years a federal

statute is to determine whether the State affiliation will be changed in accordance with paragraph 2. If a proposal subjected to a consultative referendum receives an approval corresponding with the provisions of paragraph 3, third and fourth sentence, then within two years after the consultative referendum a federal statute regarding the creation of the proposed State is to be adopted, which does no longer require approval by referendum.
(6) A majority in a referendum and in a consultative referendum is the majority of the votes cast, if that includes at least one quarter of the population entitled to vote for the Bundestag. As for the rest, details regarding the referendum, the popular initiative and the consultative referendum are regulated by a federal statute; this statute may also provide that popular initiatives may not be repeated within a time period of five years.
(7) Further changes to the territorial shape of the States may be effected by inter-State agreements [Staatsverträge] between the affected States or by a federal statute with the consent of the Bundesrat, if the territory whose State affiliation is to be changed has no more than 50,000 inhabitants. Details are regulated by a federal statute which requires the consent of the Bundesrat and the approval of the majority of the members of the Bundestag. It must provide for a hearing of the affected municipalities and rural counties.
(8) The States may regulate a restructuring of their territory or parts of their territory, in deviation from the provisions of paragraphs 2 to 7, by inter-State agreement. The affected municipalities and rural counties are to be heard. The inter-State agreement requires approval by referendum in each participating State. If the inter-State agreement concerns parts of the territories of States, the approval may be confined to referendums in these parts of the territories; the fifth sentence, second clause, does not apply. In a referendum the majority of votes cast decides if it includes at least one quarter of the population entitled to vote for the Bundestag; details are regulated by a statute. The inter-State agreement requires the consent of the Bundestag.

Article 30. The exercise of state power and the fulfilment of state tasks is a matter for the States, in as far as this Basic Law does not stipulate or permit otherwise.

Article 31. Federal law prevails over State law.

Article 32. (1) The conduct of relations with foreign states is a matter for the Federation.
(2) Before the conclusion of a treaty which affects the special circumstances of a State, that State is to be heard.
(3) In as far as the States have legislative competence, they may conclude treaties with foreign states with the consent of the Federal Government.

Article 33. (1) Every German has the same citizenship rights and obligations in all States.
(2) Every German has, in view of his aptitude, ability and professional performance, equal access to every public office.
(3) The enjoyment of civil and political rights, the admission to public offices as well as the rights acquired in public service are independent of religious conviction. No-one may be subject to disadvantage due to his adherence or non-adherence to a conviction or world view.
(4) The exercise of sovereign powers as a permanent task is, as a rule, to be transferred to members of the public service who are in a public-law relation of service and loyalty.
(5) The law on the public service is to be regulated and developed further, taking into account the traditional principles of the professional civil service.

Article 34. If someone violates his official duties with respect to a third person in the exercise of a public office entrusted to him, then liability lies in principle with the state or with the entity in the service of which he is. In case of intent or gross negligence, individual liability for indemnity is reserved. For the right to damages and indemnity, recourse to the ordinary courts may not be excluded.

Article 35. (1) All authorities of the Federation and the States provide to each other legal and inter-administrative assistance.
(2) In order to maintain or restore public safety or order, a State may in cases of special significance request forces and facilities of the Federal Border Guard to support its police, if the police could, without such support, not fulfil a task at all or only with great difficulty. For relief in case of a natural disaster or a very serious accident, a State may request police forces of other States, forces and facilities of other administrations as well as the Federal Border Guard and the armed forces.
(3) If the natural disaster or the accident threatens the territory of more than one State, the Federal Government may, in as far as that is necessary for effective relief, give the State governments the order to make police forces available to other States, and use units of the Federal Border Guard and the armed forces to support the police

forces. Measures of the Federal Government under the first sentence must at any time be lifted upon request of the Bundesrat, otherwise without delay after the removal of the threat.

Article 36. (1) In the supreme federal authorities, civil servants from all States must be employed in appropriate proportions. Persons employed in the other federal authorities should, as a rule, be drawn from the State in which they serve.
(2) Statutes regarding the military must also take into account the division of the Federation into States and their special regional attachments.

Article 37. (1) If a State does not fulfil its federal duties according to the Basic Law or another federal statute, the Federal Government may, with the consent of the Bundesrat, take the necessary measures to compel that State to fulfil its duties by way of federal enforcement [Bundeszwang].
(2) For the execution of federal enforcement, the Federal Government or its representative has the right to give instructions to all States and their authorities.

III. The Bundestag

Article 38. (1) The members of the German Bundestag are elected in general, direct, free, equal and secret-ballot elections. They are the representatives of the whole people, not bound by orders or instructions, and responsible only to their conscience.
(2) He who has attained the age of eighteen years has the right to vote; he who has reached the age at which majority begins, has the right to be elected.
(3) Details are regulated by a federal statute.

Article 39. (1) The Bundestag is elected, subject to the following provisions, for four years. Its term ends with the convention of a new Bundestag. New elections take place at the earliest forty-six, at the latest forty-eight months after the beginning of a term. In the case of a dissolution of the Bundestag, new elections take place within sixty days.
(2) The Bundestag convenes, at the latest, on the thirtieth day after elections.
(3) The Bundestag determines the end and the beginning of its sessions. The president of the Bundestag may convene it earlier. He is obliged to do so if one-third of the members, the Federal President or the Federal Chancellor so demand.

Article 40. (1) The Bundestag elects its president, his deputy and the secretaries. It adopts its rules of procedure.
(2) The president exercises proprietary and police powers in the Bundestag building. Without his permission, no search or seizure may take place on the premises of the Bundestag.

Article 41. (1) Review of elections is a matter for the Bundestag. It also decides whether a member of the Bundestag has lost his membership.
(2) Complaints against the decision of the Bundestag are admissible before the Federal Constitutional Court.
(3) Details are regulated by a federal statute.

Article 42. (1) The Bundestag deliberates in public. Upon the request of one-tenth of its members or upon request of the Federal Government, the public may be excluded by a two-thirds majority. The decision on the request takes place in a non-public session.
(2) A decision of the Bundestag requires a majority of the votes cast, in as far as this Basic Law does not provide otherwise. For the elections to be carried out by the Bundestag, the rules of procedure may allow for exceptions.
(3) Truthful reports about the public sessions of the Bundestag and its committees do not give rise to any liability.

Article 43. (1) The Bundestag and its committees may demand the presence of any member of the Federal Government.
(2) The members of the Bundesrat and the Federal Government as well as their representatives have access to all sessions of the Bundestag and its committees. They have the right to be heard at all times.

Article 44. (1) The Bundestag has the right and, upon request of one quarter of its members the obligation, to establish an investigative committee [Untersuchungsausschuss] which gathers the necessary evidence in public deliberation. The public may be excluded.

(2) The rules regarding criminal procedure are applicable mutatis mutandis to the gathering of evidence. The privacy of the correspondence, mail and telecommunications remains unaffected.
(3) Courts and administrative authorities are obliged to provide legal and inter-administrative assistance.
(4) The decisions of investigative committees are outside the scope of judicial assessment. In the consideration and qualification of the facts subject to the investigation, the courts are free.

Article 45. The Bundestag establishes a committee for the affairs of the European Union. It may authorize it to exercise the rights of the Bundestag under Article 23 with respect to the Federal Government. It may also authorize it to exercise the rights that have been accorded to the Bundestag in the treaty framework of the European Union.

Article 45a. (1) The Bundestag establishes a committee for foreign affairs and a committee for defence.
(2) The committee for defence also has the rights of an investigative committee. Upon the request of one quarter of its members it has the obligation to make a matter the subject of an investigation.
(3) Article 44 (1) does not apply to the area of defence.

Article 45b. For the protection of fundamental rights and as an auxiliary organ of the Bundestag in the exercise of parliamentary control, a commissioner for the armed forces [Wehrbeauftragter] is appointed. Details are regulated by a federal statute.

Article 45c. (1) The Bundestag establishes a petitions committee which has as its task the consideration of petitions and complaints addressed to the Bundestag under Article 17.
(2) The competences of the committee for the consideration of complaints are regulated by a federal statute.

Article 45d. (1) The Bundestag establishes a body to control the intelligence activities of the Federation.
(2) Details are regulated by a federal statute.

Article 46. (1) A member of the Bundestag may at no time be prosecuted by judicial or disciplinary means or be in any other way held liable outside the Bundestag because of his voting or because of a statement which he made in the Bundestag or in one of its committees. This does not apply to defamatory insults.
(2) A member of the Bundestag may be held liable or arrested because of a punishable act only with the permission of the Bundestag, unless he is arrested as he committed the act or on the following day.
(3) Permission of the Bundestag is furthermore required for any other limitation of the personal freedom of a member of the Bundestag or for the commencement of a procedure against a member of the Bundestag under Article 18.
(4) Any criminal procedure and any procedure under Article 18 against a member of the Bundestag, any detention and any other limitation of his personal freedom must be suspended upon demand of the Bundestag.

Article 47. The members of the Bundestag have the right to refuse to testify regarding persons who have confided information to them in their capacity as members of the Bundestag or to whom they have in that capacity confided information, as well as regarding the information itself. In as far as this right to refuse to testify applies, the seizure of written documents is not permissible.

Article 48. (1) He who runs as a candidate for a seat in the Bundestag has a right to the leave necessary for the preparation of his election.
(2) No-one may be hindered from assuming and exercising the office of a member of the Bundestag. A dismissal or discharge from employment on this ground is not permissible.
(3) The members of the Bundestag have the right to an appropriate allowance that secures their independence. They have the right to the free use of all state-run means of transport. Details are regulated by a federal statute.

Article 49. (Repealed).

IV. The Bundesrat

Article 50. Through the Bundesrat, the States participate in the legislation and administration of the Federation and in matters concerning the European Union.

Part I. Constitutional Law

Article 51. (1) The Bundesrat consists of members of the State governments, which appoint and recall them. They may be represented by other members of their governments.
(2) Each State has at least three votes; States with more than two million inhabitants have four, States with more than six million inhabitants five, States with more than seven million inhabitants six votes.
(3) Each State may send as many members as it has votes. The votes of each State may be cast only as a unit and only by members present or their alternates.

Article 52. (1) The Bundesrat elects its president for one year.
(2) The president convenes the Bundesrat. He must convene it if the representatives of at least two States or the Federal Government so demand.
(3) The Bundesrat takes its decisions with at least a majority of its votes. It adopts its rules of procedure. It deliberates in public. The public may be excluded.
(3a) For matters concerning the European Union, the Bundesrat may establish a European affairs chamber whose decisions are considered decisions of the Bundesrat; the number of votes of the States to be cast as a unit is determined by Article 51 (2).
(4) In the committees of the Bundesrat, other members or representatives of the governments of the States may be members.

Article 53. The members of the Federal Government have the right and, upon demand, the duty to participate in the deliberations of the Bundesrat and its committees. They have the right to be heard at all times. The Bundesrat is to be kept informed by the Federal Government about the conduct of affairs.

IVa. The Joint Committee

Article 53a. (1) Two-thirds of the members of the Joint Committee [Gemeinsamer Ausschuss] comprise members of the Bundestag and one-third members of the Bundesrat. The members of the Bundestag are appointed by the Bundestag according to the relative strength of the political party groups; they may not be members of the Federal Government. Each State is represented by a member of the Bundesrat appointed by it; these members are not bound by any instructions. The establishment of the Joint Committee and its procedures are regulated by rules of procedure which are to be adopted by the Bundestag and which require the consent of the Bundesrat.
(2) The Federal Government must inform the Joint Committee about its planning for the state of defence. The rights of the Bundestag and its committees under Article 43 (1) are not affected.

V. The Federal President

Article 54. (1) The Federal President is elected without debate by the Federal Convention [Bundesversammlung]. Any German may be elected who is entitled to vote for the Bundestag and who has attained the age of forty.
(2) The term of office of the Federal President is five years. A subsequent re-election is permissible only once.
(3) The Federal Convention consists of the members of the Bundestag and an equal number of members who are elected by the parliaments of the States on the basis of proportional representation.
(4) The Federal Convention convenes, at the latest, thirty days before the expiry of the term of office of the Federal President, and in case of an early termination thirty days after that moment at the latest. It is convened by the president of the Bundestag.
(5) After the expiry of a term, the period under paragraph 4, first sentence, begins with the first convention of the Bundestag.
(6) He who has received the votes of a majority of the members of the Federal Convention is elected. If after two ballots such majority is not obtained by any candidate, then he who receives the most votes in a further ballot is elected.
(7) Details are regulated by a federal statute.

Article 55. (1) The Federal President may not be a member of the Federal Government or of a legislative body of the Federation or of a State.
(2) The Federal President may not exercise any other remunerated office, he may pursue no trade or profession and may not be a member of either the board or the supervisory board of a profit-oriented company.

Article 56. The Federal President, when assuming office, takes the following oath before the assembled members of the Bundestag and the Bundesrat:
"I swear that I shall dedicate my strength to the well-being of the German people, promote its welfare, protect it from harm, uphold and defend the Basic Law and the legislation of the Federation, fulfil my duties conscientiously, and do justice to all. So help me God."
The oath may also be taken without the religious assertion.

Article 57. The powers of the Federal President, in case he is prevented from exercising his functions or in case of an early termination of his term, are exercised by the president of the Bundesrat.

Article 58. Instructions and orders of the Federal President require for their validity the countersignature by the Federal Chancellor or the competent federal minister. This does not apply to the appointment and dismissal of the Federal Chancellor, the dissolution of the Bundestag under Article 63 and the request under Article 69 (3).

Article 59. (1) The Federal President represents the Federation under international law. He concludes, in the name of the Federation, treaties with foreign states. He accredits and receives envoys.
(2) Treaties which regulate the political relations of the Federation, or which refer to objects of federal legislation, require the consent or participation of the organs competent for such federal legislation in the form of a federal statute. For administrative agreements, the regulations regarding the federal administration apply mutatis mutandis.

Article 59a. (Repealed).

Article 60. (1) The Federal President appoints and dismisses federal judges, federal civil servants, officers and non-commissioned officers, as far as statutory regulations do not provide otherwise.
(2) He exercises, in individual cases, the right of pardon for the Federation.
(3) He may transfer these competences to other authorities.
(4) Paragraphs 2 to 4 of Article 46 apply to the Federal President mutatis mutandis.

Article 61. (1) The Bundestag or the Bundesrat may impeach the Federal President for an intentional violation of the Basic Law or another federal statute before the Federal Constitutional Court. The motion to impeach must be tabled by at least a quarter of the members of the Bundestag or a quarter of the votes of the Bundesrat. The decision to impeach requires a majority of two-thirds of the members of the Bundestag or two-thirds of the votes of the Bundesrat. The prosecution is conducted by a representative of the impeaching organ.
(2) If the Federal Constitutional Court establishes that the Federal President is guilty of having committed an intentional violation of the Basic Law or another federal statute, it may declare that he is removed from office. By interim order after impeachment it may rule that he is prevented from exercising his functions.

VI. The Federal Government

Article 62. The Federal Government consists of the Federal Chancellor [Bundeskanzler] and the federal ministers.

Article 63. (1) The Federal Chancellor is elected, on the proposal of the Federal President, by the Bundestag without debate.
(2) He who receives the votes of a majority of the members of the Bundestag is elected. The person elected is to be appointed by the Federal President.
(3) If the nominee is not elected, the Bundestag may within fourteen days after the ballot, by the votes of more than half of its members, elect a Federal Chancellor.
(4) If no election is successful within this period, a new ballot takes place without delay, in which he who receives the most votes is elected. If the person elected receives the votes of a majority of the members of the Bundestag, the Federal President must appoint him within seven days after the election. If the person elected does not receive such a majority, then within seven days the Federal President must either appoint him or dissolve the Bundestag.

Article 64. (1) The federal ministers are appointed and dismissed by the Federal President on the proposal of the Federal Chancellor.
(2) The Federal Chancellor and the federal ministers, when assuming office, take the oath as stipulated in Article 56 before the Bundestag.

Article 65. The Federal Chancellor determines the guidelines of policy and bears responsibility for that. Within these guidelines, each federal minister directs his portfolio autonomously and on his own responsibility. The Federal Government rules in case of disagreements between federal ministers. The Federal Chancellor directs its affairs according to rules of procedure as adopted by the Federal Government and approved by the Federal President.

Article 65a. (1) The federal minister of defence has the command over the armed forces.
(2) (Repealed).

Article 66. The Federal Chancellor and the federal ministers may not exercise any other remunerated office, they may pursue no trade or profession and may not be a member of either the board or, without consent of the Bundestag, the supervisory board of a profit-oriented company.

Article 67. (1) The Bundestag may express its lack of confidence in the Federal Chancellor only by electing a successor by the vote of a majority of its members and by requesting the Federal President to dismiss the Federal Chancellor. The Federal President must comply with the request and appoint the person elected.
(2) Forty-eight hours must pass between the motion and the election.

Article 68. (1) If a motion of the Federal Chancellor for a vote of confidence is not supported by the majority of the members of the Bundestag, the Federal President may, on the proposal of the Federal Chancellor, dissolve the Bundestag within twenty-one days. The right of dissolution lapses as soon as the Bundestag elects another Federal Chancellor by the vote of a majority of its members.
(2) Forty-eight hours must pass between the motion and the vote.

Article 69. (1) The Federal Chancellor appoints a federal minister as his deputy.
(2) The office of the Federal Chancellor ends in any event with the convention of a new Bundestag, the office of a federal minister ends also with any other termination of the office of the Federal Chancellor.
(3) On the request of the Federal President, the Federal Chancellor is obliged, and on the request of the Federal Chancellor or the Federal President a federal minister is obliged to continue the affairs until the appointment of a successor.

VII. The legislation of the Federation

Article 70. (1) The States have the right to legislate in as far as this Basic Law does not confer legislative power on the Federation.
(2) The delimitation of competences between the Federation and the States is guided by the provisions of this Basic Law regarding exclusive and concurrent legislation.

Article 71. In the area of exclusive legislative power of the Federation, the States have power to legislate only when and in as far as they are expressly authorized to do so by a federal statute.

Article 72. (1) In the area of concurrent legislative power, the States have power to legislate so long as and to the extent that the Federation has not exercised its legislative power through a statute.
(2) The Federation has legislative power in the areas of Article 74 (1) no. 4, 7, 11, 13, 15, 19a, 20, 22, 25 and 26 when and to the extent that the bringing about of equivalent living standards throughout the territory of the Federation or the upholding of legal or economic unity in the interest of the state as a whole require a federal statutory regulation.
(3) If the Federation has made use of its legislative competence, the States may by statute adopt regulations that deviate therefrom regarding:
1. hunting (except the law on hunting permits);
2. nature conservation and landscape management (except the general principles of nature conservation, the law on the protection of species or maritime nature conservation);
3. the distribution of land;
4. regional planning;
5. water resources (except regulations on substances and facilities);
6. admissions to higher education and higher education diplomas.

Federal statutes in these areas enter into force at the earliest six months after their publication, in as far as nothing is provided otherwise with the consent of the Bundesrat. In the areas of the first sentence, in the relation between federal law and State law the later statute prevails.
(4) A federal statute may determine that a federal statutory regulation a need for which in the sense of paragraph 2 no longer exists, may be replaced by State law.

Article 73. (1) The Federation has exclusive legislative power regarding:
1. foreign relations as well as defence including the protection of the civilian population;
2. citizenship in the Federation;
3. free movement, the passport regime, population registers and identity documents, immigration, emigration and extradition;
4. currency, the money and coinage regime, measures and weights as well as the determination of the time;
5. the unity of the customs and trade area, trade and navigation agreements, the free movement of goods and the movement of goods and capital with foreign states including customs and border protection;
5a. the protection of German cultural assets from transfers abroad;
6. air traffic;
6a. rail traffic which falls entirely or predominantly under the ownership of the Federation (the railways of the Federation), the construction, maintenance and operation of tracks of the railways of the Federation as well as the levying of charges for the use of these tracks;
7. post and telecommunications;
8. legal relations of persons in the service of the Federation and of directly federal entities of public law;
9. intellectual property, copyright and publishing law;
9a. the protection from the dangers of international terrorism by the Federal Criminal Investigations Police Office [Bundeskriminalpolizeiamt] in cases where a danger transcending State borders is at hand, where the jurisdiction of a State police authority is not apparent or where a supreme State authority requests a takeover of jurisdiction;
10. the cooperation between the Federation and the States
a. regarding criminal police investigation,
b. for the protection of the liberal democratic fundamental order, the integrity and security of the Federation or a State (domestic intelligence [Verfassungsschutz]) and
c. for the protection against attempts within the territory of the Federation which jeopardize, through the use of force or preparatory acts with such aim, the external interests of the Federal Republic of Germany,
as well as the establishment of a Federal Criminal Investigations Police Office and the international fight against crime;
11. statistics for federal purposes;
12. the law on weapons and explosives;
13. care for those disabled in war and surviving dependants of war dead, and support for former prisoners of war;
14. the production and use of nuclear energy for peaceful purposes, the establishment and operation of facilities serving these purposes, the protection against dangers arising from the release of nuclear energy or from ionizing radiation, and the disposal of radioactive material.
(2) Statutes under paragraph 1 no. 9a require the consent of the Bundesrat.

Article 74. (1) Concurrent legislative power extends to the following areas:
1. private law, criminal law, the court system, judicial procedure (except the law on the execution of detentions pending criminal investigation), the advocacy, the notary and legal advice system;
2. the civil status registry;
3. the law on associations;
4. the law on the sojourn and establishment of aliens;
5. (repealed);
6. the affairs of refugees and expellees;
7. public welfare (except the law on homes);
8. (repealed);
9. war damages and reparations;
10. war graves and the graves of other victims of war and victims of tyranny;
11. commercial law (mining, industry, energy, crafts, trade, commerce, banking and stock exchange, private insurance) except the law on the closing times for shops, on bars and restaurants, on gambling halls, on acting performance by persons, fairs, exhibitions and markets;
12. labour law including the organization of enterprises, work safety and job agency services, as well as social security including unemployment insurance;

PART I. CONSTITUTIONAL LAW

13. the regulation of education allowances and the promotion of scientific research;
14. the law on expropriation in as far as it is relevant in the areas of Articles 73 and 74;
15. the transfer of land, natural resources and means of production into public ownership or other forms of collective concern;
16. the prevention of abuses of economically powerful positions;
17. the promotion of agricultural and forestry production (except the law on rearrangements of terrain), the securing of food supply, the import and export of agricultural and forestry products, high-seas and coastal fisheries and coastal protection;
18. the transfer of urban real estate, land law (except the law on contributions for land development) and the law on housing allowances, the law on old debt relief, the law on homebuilding premiums, the law on homebuilding for miners and miner settlement law;
19. measures against human and animal diseases that are dangerous to the public or communicable, the admission to medical and other healing professions and the healing services, as well as the law on the pharmacy system, medicines, medical products, cures, narcotics and poisons;
19a. the securing of the economic viability of hospitals and the regulation of hospital charges;
20. the law on food including the animals used for the production thereof, the law on recreational consumables, on commodities for use and on feed, as well as the safety in the trade in agricultural and forestry seeds and seedlings, the protection of plants against diseases and pests as well as animal protection;
21. high-seas and coastal shipping as well as naval signaling, inland navigation, meteorological services, shipping routes and inland waterways serving general traffic;
22. road traffic, motor transport, the construction and maintenance of country roads for long-distance traffic, as well as the levying and distribution of fees or charges for the use of public roads by vehicle;
23. railways, which are not railways of the Federation, with the exception of mountain railways;
24. waste management, air pollution control and noise abatement (except protection from behaviour-related noise);
25. state liability;
26. the medically assisted creation of human life, the analysis and artificial modification of genetic information as well as regulations concerning transplantation of organs, tissues and cells;
27. the rights and obligations deriving from the status of civil servants of States, municipalities and other public-law entities as well as judges in the States except careers, salary and support;
28. hunting;
29. nature conservation and landscape management;
30. the distribution of land;
31. regional planning;
32. water resources;
33. admissions to higher education and higher education diplomas.
(2) Statutes under paragraph 1 no. 25 and 27 require the consent of the Bundesrat.

Articles 74a and 75. (Repealed).

Article 76. (1) Bills are introduced in the Bundestag by the Federal Government, from the floor of the Bundestag, or by the Bundesrat.
(2) Bills of the Federal Government must first be transmitted to the Bundesrat. The Bundesrat is entitled to give a reaction to such bills within six weeks. If it demands for important reasons, especially with regard to the size of a bill, an extension of the period, then the period is nine weeks. The Federal Government may transmit a bill, which it has by way of exception, when transmitting it to the Bundesrat, qualified as particularly urgent, to the Bundestag after three weeks or, if the Bundesrat has made a demand pursuant to the third sentence, after six weeks, even when it has not yet received the reaction of the Bundesrat; it must in that case transmit the reaction of the Bundesrat to the Bundestag without delay. In the case of bills for an amendment of this Basic Law and for the transfer of sovereign powers pursuant to Article 23 or Article 24, the period for a reaction is nine weeks; the fourth sentence does not apply.
(3) Bills of the Bundesrat must be transmitted to the Bundestag by the Federal Government within six weeks. The Federal Government, when transmitting them, is to give a statement of its opinion. If it demands for important reasons, especially with regard to the size of a bill, an extension of the period, the period is nine weeks. If the Bundesrat has by way of exception qualified a bill as particularly urgent, the period is three weeks or, if the Federal Government has made a demand pursuant to the third sentence, six weeks. In the case of bills for an amendment of this Basic Law and for the transfer of sovereign powers pursuant to Article 23 or Article 24, the period is nine weeks; the fourth sentence does not apply. The Bundestag must deliberate and decide on the bills within a reasonable time.

Article 77. (1) Federal statutes are adopted by the Bundestag. They must, after their adoption, be transmitted to the Bundesrat by the president of the Bundestag without delay.
(2) The Bundesrat may, within three weeks after receiving an adopted bill, demand that a committee for the joint consideration of bills, composed of members of the Bundestag and of the Bundesrat, be convened. The composition and procedure of this committee is regulated by rules of procedure which are adopted by the Bundestag and which require the consent of the Bundesrat. The members of the Bundesrat sent to this committee are not bound by instructions. If a statute requires the consent of the Bundesrat, then also the Bundestag and the Federal Government may demand a convention. If the committee proposes an amendment to the adopted bill, the Bundestag must decide again.
(2a) In as far as a statute requires the consent of the Bundesrat, the Bundesrat, if a demand under paragraph 2, first sentence, is not made or the conciliation procedure is concluded without any proposals for an amendment to the adopted bill, must decide on its consent within a reasonable time.
(3) In as far as a statute does not require the consent of the Bundesrat, the Bundesrat, once the procedure under paragraph 2 is completed, may within two weeks object to a statute adopted by the Bundestag. The period for objection starts, in the case under paragraph 2, last sentence, with the receipt of the new decision adopted by the Bundestag, and in all other cases with the receipt of the statement of the chairman of the committee stipulated under paragraph 2 that the procedure before the committee has been concluded.
(4) If the objection is adopted by the majority of the votes of the Bundesrat, it may be rejected by a decision of the majority of the members of the Bundestag. If the Bundesrat has adopted the objection by a majority of at least two-thirds of its votes, then its rejection by the Bundestag requires a two-thirds majority, including at least a majority of the members of the Bundestag.

Article 78. A statute adopted by the Bundestag is successfully completed if the Bundesrat consents to it, or does not make a demand pursuant to Article 77 (2), or does not enter an objection within the period stipulated in Article 77 (3) or withdraws such objection, or if the objection is overridden by the Bundestag.

Article 79. (1) The Basic Law may be amended only by a statute which expressly amends or supplements its text. In the case of international treaties which have as their object a peace settlement, the preparation of a peace settlement or the phasing out of an occupation regime, or which are intended to serve the defence of the Federal Republic, a clarification that the provisions of the Basic Law do not preclude the conclusion and entry into force of such treaties requires only a supplement to the text of the Basic Law which is confined to such clarification.
(2) Any such statute requires the approval by two-thirds of the members of the Bundestag and two-thirds of the votes of the Bundesrat.
(3) Any amendment to this Basic Law affecting the division of the Federation into States, the participation of the States in principle in the legislative process, or the principles laid down in Articles 1 and 20, is inadmissible.

Article 80. (1) By statute, the Federal Government, a federal minister or the State governments may be authorized to adopt ordinances [Rechtsverordnungen]. In that case, the content, purpose and scope of the given authorization must be determined in the statute. The legal basis must be stated in the ordinance. If by statute it is provided that an authorization may be delegated further, then such authorization of a delegation requires an ordinance.
(2) The consent of the Bundesrat is required, save for federal statutory regulations providing otherwise, for ordinances of the Federal Government or a federal minister regarding the principles and charges for the use of the facilities of the post and telecommunications system, regarding the principles of the levying of charges for the use of the facilities of the railways of the Federation, regarding the construction and operation of railways, as well as ordinances based on federal statutes which require the consent of the Bundesrat or which are executed by the States on behalf of the Federation or as their own affairs.
(3) The Bundesrat may transmit to the Federal Government proposals for the adoption of ordinances which require its consent.
(4) In as far as State governments are authorized to adopt ordinances by federal statute or pursuant to federal statutes, the States are also competent to regulate by statute.

Article 80a. (1) If this Basic Law or a federal statute regarding defence including the protection of the civilian population provides that regulations may be applied only within the guidelines of this Article, then such application except in a state of defence is only permissible when the Bundestag has declared the beginning of a state of tension [Spannungsfall] or when it has approved such application explicitly. The declaration of a state of tension and the special approval in the cases of Article 12a (5), first sentence, and (6), second sentence, require a majority of two-thirds of votes cast.
(2) Measures pursuant to regulations under paragraph 1 must be lifted when the Bundestag so demands.

PART I. CONSTITUTIONAL LAW

(3) By deviation from paragraph 1, the application of such regulations is permissible also on the basis and within the guidelines of a decision that is taken by an international body in the framework of an alliance treaty with the consent of the Federal Government. Measures under this paragraph must be lifted when the Bundestag by the majority of its members so demands.

Article 81. (1) If in the case of Article 68 the Bundestag is not dissolved, the Federal President may, upon request of the Federal Government with the consent of the Bundesrat, declare a legislative emergency [Gesetzgebungsnotstand] for a bill if the Bundestag rejects it although the Federal Government has qualified it as urgent. The same applies when a bill has been rejected although the Federal Chancellor had linked it to a motion under Article 68.
(2) If the Bundestag rejects the bill after the declaration of a legislative emergency again or if it adopts it in a version qualified as unacceptable by the Federal Government, then the statute is deemed adopted if the Bundesrat consents to it. The same applies when the bill has not been adopted by the Bundestag within four weeks after the new introduction.
(3) During the term of office of a Federal Chancellor, also any other bill rejected by the Bundestag may be adopted within a period of six months following the first declaration of a legislative emergency under paragraphs 1 and 2. After the period has lapsed, during the term of office of that same Federal Chancellor another declaration of a legislative emergency is not permissible.
(4) The Basic Law may be neither amended nor wholly or partly suspended or rendered inapplicable by a statute that has been adopted under paragraph 2.

Article 82. (1) Statutes completed in accordance with the provisions of this Basic Law are, after counter-signature, certified by the Federal President and published in the Federal Law Gazette [Bundesgesetzblatt]. Ordinances are certified by the organ which adopts them and are, save for other statutory regulations, published in the Federal Law Gazette.
(2) All statutes and all ordinances are to determine the day of entry into force. If such a provision is lacking, they enter into force on the fourteenth day after the end of the day when the Federal Law Gazette has been published.

VIII. The execution of federal statutes and the federal administration

Article 83. The States execute federal statutes as their own affairs in as far as this Basic Law does not otherwise provide or permit.

Article 84. (1) Where the States execute federal statutes as their own affairs, they regulate the establishment of authorities and the administrative procedure. Where federal statutes provide otherwise, the States may make adopt regulations in deviation therefrom. Where a State has adopted a deviating regulation pursuant to the second sentence, subsequent federal regulations regarding the establishment of authorities and the administrative procedure relating to this enter into force in that State at the earliest six months after their publication, in as far as nothing is provided otherwise with the consent of the Bundesrat. Article 72 (3) third sentence applies mutatis mutandis. In exceptional cases the Federation may, because of a special need for uniform federal regulation, regulate the administrative procedure without a possibility of deviation for the States. Such statutes require the consent of the Bundesrat. A federal statute may not delegate tasks to municipalities and associations of municipalities.
(2) The Federal Government may, with the consent of the Bundesrat, issue general administrative regulations.
(3) The Federal Government exercises supervision to ensure that the States execute federal statutes in accordance with applicable law. The Federal Government may, for this purpose, send agents to the highest State authorities, with their consent or, if such consent is refused, with the consent of the Bundesrat, also to subordinate authorities.
(4) Should shortcomings which the Federal Government has established in the execution of federal statutes in the States not be corrected, the Bundesrat decides, at the request of the Federal Government or the State concerned, whether the State has violated the law. The decision of the Bundesrat may be challenged before the Federal Constitutional Court.
(5) The Federal Government may, by federal statute which requires the consent of the Bundesrat, be granted authorization, for the execution of federal statutes, to issue individual instructions in particular cases. They are, unless the Federal Government considers the matter urgent, to be addressed to the highest States authorities.

Article 85. (1) Where the States execute federal statutes on behalf of the Federation, the establishment of the authorities remains the concern of the States, unless federal statutes with the consent of the Bundesrat provide otherwise. A federal statute may not delegate tasks to municipalities and associations of municipalities.
(2) The Federal Government may, with the consent of the Bundesrat, issue general administrative regulations. It may regulate the uniform training of civil servants and employees. The heads of intermediate authorities are to be appointed with its approval.
(3) The State authorities are subordinate to the instructions of the competent highest federal authorities. The instructions are, unless the Federal Government considers the matter urgent, to be addressed to the highest State authorities. Execution of the instructions is to be ensured by the highest State authorities.
(4) Federal supervision extends to the lawfulness and expediency of execution. The Federal Government may, for this purpose, require reporting and submission of files and send agents to all authorities.

Article 86. Where the Federation executes statutes by direct federal administration or by directly federal entities or institutions of public law, the Federal Government issues, to the extent that a statute does not provide details, the general administrative regulations. It regulates, unless statute provides otherwise, the establishment of the authorities.

Article 87. (1) The Foreign Service [Auswärtiger Dienst], the Federal Revenue Administration [Bundesfinanzverwaltung] and, pursuant to Article 89, the administration of the federal waterways and navigation are managed by direct federal administration with a dedicated administrative substructure. By federal statute federal border guard authorities [Bundesgrenzschutzbehörden], and central offices for police information and communications, for the criminal police and for the collection of documents for the purposes of domestic intelligence [Verfassungsschutz] and of protection against endeavours on federal territory which, through the use of force or preparatory acts thereto endanger the foreign interests of the Federal Republic of Germany, may be established.
(2) Social insurance institutions whose competence extends beyond the territory of one State are managed as directly federal entities of public law. Social insurance institutions whose competence extends beyond the territory of one State but not more than three States are managed in deviation from the first sentence as directly State entities of public law if the supervising State is determined by the States involved.
(3) In addition, for matters on which the Federation is competent to legislate, independent higher federal authorities as well as new directly federal entities and institutions of public law may be established by federal statute. Where new tasks arise for the Federation in matters on which it has the power to legislate, then in cases of urgent need federal authorities at the intermediate and lower levels may be established with the consent of the Bundesrat and of the majority of the members of the Bundestag.

Article 87a. (1) The Federation establishes armed forces for the purpose of defence. Their numerical strength and the general outline of their organization must follow from the budget.
(2) Except for defence, the armed forces may only be deployed to the extent explicitly permitted by this Basic Law.
(3) The armed forces have, in a state of defence and in a state of tension [Spannungsfall], the competence to protect civilian objects and to perform tasks of traffic control to the extent that this is required for the accomplishment of their defence mission. Furthermore, during a state of defence or a state of tension the armed forces may also be assigned to protect civilian objects so as to support police measures; in such case the armed forces cooperate with the competent authorities.
(4) In order to avert an imminent danger to the existence or liberal democratic fundamental order of the Federation or of a State, the Federal Government may, if the conditions of Article 91 (2) are fulfilled and the police forces as well as the Federal Border Guard [Bundesgrenzschutz] are not sufficient, deploy the armed forces to support the police and the Federal Border Guard in protecting civilian objects and in fighting organized and militarily armed insurgents. The deployment of the armed forces is to be discontinued if the Bundestag or the Bundesrat so demands.

Article 87b. (1) The Federal Armed Forces Administration [Bundeswehrverwaltung] is managed by direct federal administration with a dedicated administrative substructure. It performs tasks of personnel management and tasks to cover the immediate material requirements of the armed forces. Tasks related to the maintenance of injured persons or construction work may only be delegated to the Federal Armed Forces Administration by federal statute which requires the consent of the Bundesrat. The consent of the Bundesrat is furthermore required for statutes to the extent that they authorize the Federal Armed Forces Administration to interfere with the rights of third parties; this does not apply to statutes in the area of personnel management.

(2) In addition, federal statutes concerning defence, including recruitment for military service and the protection of the civilian population may, with the consent of the Bundesrat, provide that they be executed, wholly or in part, by direct federal administration with a dedicated administrative substructure or by the States on behalf of the Federation. Where such statutes are executed by the States on behalf of the Federation, they may, with the consent of the Bundesrat, provide that the powers appertaining to the Federation and the competent supreme federal authorities pursuant to Article 85 are delegated wholly or in part to higher federal authorities; in such case it may be provided that these authorities do not require the consent of the Bundesrat in issuing general administrative regulations pursuant to Article 85 (2) first sentence.

Article 87c. Statutes that are enacted pursuant to Article 73 (1) no. 14, may, with the consent of the Bundesrat, provide that they be executed by the States on behalf of the Federation.

Article 87d. (1) The air traffic administration is managed by federal administration. Tasks related to air traffic control may also be executed by foreign air traffic organizations that are authorized pursuant to European Community law. Details are regulated by a federal statute.
(2) A federal statute requiring the consent of the Bundesrat may delegate tasks relating to air traffic administration to the States as commissioned administration [Auftragsverwaltung].

Article 87e. (1) The railway transport administration for railways of the Federation is managed by direct federal administration. By federal statute tasks relating to the railway transport administration may be delegated to the States as their own affairs.
(2) The Federation discharges tasks relating to the railway transport administration extending beyond the area of the railways of the Federation that are delegated to it by federal statute.
(3) Railways of the Federation are managed as commercial enterprises established under private law. These are owned by the Federation, to the extent that the activities of the commercial enterprise comprise the construction, maintenance and the operation of railroads. The transfer of federal shares in these commercial enterprises under to the second sentence is effected pursuant to a statute; the majority of the shares remains with the Federation. Details are regulated by a federal statute.
(4) The Federation ensures that account be taken of the benefit of the general public, especially the transportation needs, in developing and maintaining the federal railroad network of the railways of the Federation as well as in their transportation services on that railroad network, to the extent that they do not concern local passenger rail services. Details are regulated by a federal statute.
(5) Statutes enacted pursuant to paragraphs 1 to 4 require the consent of the Bundesrat. The consent of the Bundesrat is furthermore required for statutes which regulate the dissolution, merger and splitting-up of railway enterprises of the Federation, the transfer of railway tracks of the railways of the Federation to third parties as well as the abandonment of railroad tracks of railways of the Federation or which affect local passenger rail services.

Article 87f. (1) Within the guidelines of a federal statute requiring the consent of the Bundesrat, the Federation ensures area-wide adequate and sufficient services in the area of post and telecommunications.
(2) Services within the meaning of paragraph 1 are provided as private commercial activities by the enterprises that emerged from the special asset German Federal Post Office [Deutsche Bundespost] and by other private providers. Sovereign tasks in the area of post and telecommunications are performed by direct federal administration.
(3) Without prejudice to paragraph 2 second sentence, the Federation, in the form of a directly federal institution of public law, performs particular tasks with respect to the enterprises that emerged from the special asset German Federal Post Office within the guidelines of a federal statute.

Article 88. The Federation establishes a currency bank and bank of issue as the Federal Bank [Bundesbank]. Its tasks and powers may, within the framework of the European Union, be transferred to the European Central Bank, which is independent and committed to the primary goal of securing price stability.

Article 89. (1) The Federation is the owner of the former Reich waterways.
(2) The Federation manages the federal waterways through its own authorities. It performs the state tasks of inland navigation extending beyond the area of a single State and the tasks of maritime navigation which are assigned to it by statute. It may assign the management of federal waterways, to the extent that they lie within the territory of one State, upon request to that State as commissioned administration. If a waterway touches the territory of several States, the Federation may commission the State which is designated by the States concerned.

(3) In the administration, development and new construction of waterways, the requirements of land and water management are to be observed in agreement with the States.

Article 90. (1) The Federation is the owner of the former Reich motorways [Reichsautobahnen] and Reich roads.
(2) The States or the self-governing entities competent under State law manage the federal motorways [Bundesautobahnen] and other federal roads for long-distance traffic on behalf of the Federation.
(3) Upon the request by a State, the Federation may place federal motorways and other federal roads for long-distance traffic, to the extent that they lie within the territory of that State, under direct federal administration.

Article 91. (1) In order to avert an imminent danger to the existence or the liberal democratic fundamental order of the Federation or of a State, a State may request the services of the police forces of other States as well as forces and institutions of other administrations and of the Federal Border Guard [Bundesgrenzschutz].
(2) If the State where such danger is imminent is not itself prepared or able to combat the danger, the Federal Government may place the police in that State and police forces of other States under its own authority and deploy units of the Federal Border Guard. The order is to be lifted after the removal of the danger and, otherwise, at any time upon the demand of the Bundesrat. Where the danger extends to the territory of more than one State, the Federal Government may, to the extent that this is necessary for the effective combating, issue instructions to the State governments; the first and second sentence remain unaffected.

VIIIa. Joint tasks

Article 91a. (1) The Federation participates in the fulfilment of the tasks of the States in the following areas, if these tasks are important for the whole and the participation of the Federation is necessary for the improvement of living standards (joint tasks):
1. improvement of regional economic structure,
2. improvement of agricultural structure and coastal protection.
(2) By federal statute with the consent of the Bundesrat, joint tasks as well as the details of coordination are determined.
(3) The Federation bears in the cases of paragraph 1 no. 1 half of the costs in each State. In the cases of paragraph 1 no. 2, the Federation bears at least half; the contribution must be fixed uniformly for all States. Details are regulated by statute. The making available of funds remains a matter for the adoption of the budgets of the Federation and the States.

Article 91b. (1) The Federation and the States may, on the basis of agreements in cases of importance that transcends regions, cooperate in the promotion of:
1. establishments and projects of scientific research outside the universities;
2. projects of science and research at universities;
3. research facilities at universities including large machines.
Agreements under the first sentence, no. 2, require the consent of all States.
(2) The Federation and the States may cooperate on the basis of agreements for the assessment of the effectiveness of the educational system in international comparison and on reports and recommendations in that matter.
(3) The allocation of the financial burden is regulated in the agreement.

Article 91c. (1) The Federation and the States may cooperate in the planning, establishment and operation of the information systems needed for the fulfilment of their tasks.
(2) The Federation and the States may on the basis of agreements establish the standards and security requirements necessary for the communication between their information systems. Agreements concerning the principles of the cooperation pursuant to the first sentence may provide for individual tasks, circumscribed with regard to their content and extent, that details enter into force for the Federation and the States with the consent of a qualified majority to be determined by the agreement. They require the consent of the Bundestag and the parliaments of the participating States; the right to terminate these agreements may not be excluded. The agreements also regulate the bearing of burdens.
(3) The States may furthermore agree on the joint operation of information systems and the establishment of dedicated institutions.
(4) The Federation establishes a connecting network in order to connect the information systems of the Federation and of the States. The details regarding the establishment and the operation of the connecting network are regulated by federal statute which requires the consent of the Bundesrat.

PART I. CONSTITUTIONAL LAW

Article 91d. The Federation and the States may, in order to determine and promote the performance of their administrations, conduct comparative studies and publish the results.

Article 91e. (1) In the execution of federal statutes in the area of basic social security for jobseekers, the Federation and the States or the municipalities and associations of municipalities competent under State law cooperate, as a rule, in joint institutions.
(2) The Federation may allow that a limited number of municipalities and associations of municipalities, on their request and with the consent of the supreme State authority, excercises the tasks under paragraph 1 alone. The necessary expenditure including administrative costs are borne by the Federation, to the extent that in an execution of statutes pursuant to paragraph 1 the tasks are to be exercised by the Federation.
(3) Details are regulated by a federal statute which requires the consent of the Bundesrat.

IX. The judiciary

Article 92. Judicial power is vested in the judges; it is exercised by the Federal Constitutional Court, by the federal courts provided for in this Basic Law, and by the courts of the States.

Article 93. (1) The Federal Constitutional Court [Bundesverfassungsgericht] rules:
1. on the interpretation of this Basic Law in the event of disputes concerning the extent of the rights and duties of a supreme federal body or of other parties vested with rights of their own by this Basic Law or by the rules of procedure of a supreme federal body;
2. in the event of disagreements or doubts regarding the formal or substantive compatibility of federal law or State law with this Basic Law, or the compatibility of State law with other federal law, on application of the Federal Government, a State government or one-quarter of the members of the Bundestag;
2a. in the event of disagreements whether a statute complies with the conditions under Article 72 (2) on application of the Bundesrat, a State government or the parliament of a State;
3. in the event of disagreements regarding the rights and duties of the Federation and the States, especially as regards the execution of federal law by the States and the performance of federal supervision;
4. in other public-law disputes between the Federation and the States, between different States, or within one State, in as far as another recourse is not available;
4a. on constitutional complaints, which may be filed by any person with the allegation that one of his fundamental rights or one of his rights contained in Article 20 (4), 33, 38, 101, 103 and 104 has been violated by public authority;
4b. on constitutional complaints of municipalities or associations of municipalities based on a violation of the right to self-government pursuant to Article 28 by a statute, or by State legislation yet only in as far as no complaint may be filed with the State constitutional court;
5. in the other cases provided by this Basic Law.
(2) The Federal Constitutional Court furthermore rules on the application of the Bundesrat, a State government or the parliament of a State whether in the case of Article 72 (4) the need for a federal statutory regulation under Article 72 (2) no longer exists or whether in the cases of Article 125a (2), first sentence, federal law could no longer be adopted. The finding that the need has ceased to exist or that federal law could no longer be adopted replaces a federal statute under Article 72 (4) or Article 125a (2), second sentence. An application under the first sentence is admissible only when a bill under Article 72 (4) or Article 125a (2), second sentence, has been rejected in the Bundestag or is not deliberated and decided upon within one year or when such bill has been rejected in the Bundesrat.
(3) The Federal Constitutional Court furthermore becomes active in the other cases assigned by federal statute.

Article 94. (1) The Federal Constitutional Court is composed of federal judges and other members. Half of the members of the Federal Constitutional Court are elected by the Bundestag and half by the Bundesrat. They may not be members of the Bundestag, the Bundesrat, the Federal Government or equivalent bodies of a State.
(2) A federal statute regulates its organization and its procedures and determines in which cases its decisions have statutory force. It may make the prior exhaustion of judicial remedies a precondition for constitutional complaints and stipulate a special admissibility procedure.

Article 95. (1) For the areas of general, administrative, tax, labour and social-security jurisdiction, the Federation establishes as supreme courts the Federal Supreme Court [Bundesgerichtshof], the Federal Administrative Court, the Federal Tax Court, the Federal Labour Court and the Federal Social-Security Court.

(2) The appointment of judges at these courts is decided by the federal minister competent for the respective subject-matter together with a judicial nomination committee [Richterwahlausschuss] which is composed of the ministers from the States competent for the respective subject-matter and an equal number of members who are elected by the Bundestag.
(3) For the upholding of the unity of jurisprudence, a Joint Chamber of the courts stipulated in paragraph 1 must be established. Details are regulated by a federal statute.

Article 96. (1) The Federation may establish a federal court for intellectual property law.
(2) The Federation may establish courts of military criminal justice for the armed forces as federal courts. They may exercise criminal law jurisdiction only in a state of defence as well as over members of the armed forces who are deployed abroad or are serving on board of warships. Details are regulated by a federal statute. These courts fall within the competence of the Federal minister of justice. Their salaried judges must possess the qualifications to be a judge.
(3) The supreme court for the courts stipulated in paragraphs 1 and 2 is the Federal Supreme Court.
(4) The Federation may, for persons in a public-law service relation to it, establish federal courts to decide in disciplinary and complaint procedures.
(5) For criminal procedures in the following areas, a federal statute with the consent of the Bundesrat may provide that State courts are to exercise the jurisdiction of the Federation:
1. genocide;
2. crimes against humanity under international criminal law;
3. war crimes;
4. other acts that are capable of and are committed with the intent to disturb the peaceful coexistence of nations (Article 26 (1));
5. protection of the state.

Article 97. (1) Judges are independent and are subject only to the law.
(2) Judges who are salaried and appointed permanently may be dismissed or suspended in their function permanently or temporarily or be transferred to another post or made to retire before the expiry of their term against their will only by virtue of a judicial decision and only for reasons and in the form provided by statutes. Legislation may determine age limits upon the reaching of which judges appointed for life retire. In the context of changes to the organization of courts or their districts, judges may be transferred to another court or removed from office, yet only while preserving their full salary.

Article 98. (1) The legal position of federal judges is to be regulated by a special federal statute.
(2) If a federal judge violates, in the exercise of his office or outside, the principles of the Basic Law or the constitutional order of a State, then the Federal Constitutional Court may order by a two-thirds majority upon request of the Bundestag that the judge be transferred to a different post or be made to retire. In case of an intentional violation, dismissal may be ordered.
(3) The legal position of judges in the States is to be regulated by special State statutes, in as far as Article 74 (1) no. 27 does not provide otherwise.
(4) The States may provide that the State minister of justice decides together with a judicial nomination committee over the appointment of judges in the States.
(5) The States may, as regards State judges, provide for a regulation corresponding to paragraph 2. State constitutional law in force remains unaffected. The Federal Constitutional Court may decide over the prosecution of a judge.

Article 99. By State statute, the Federal Constitutional Court may be assigned the jurisdiction to decide in constitutional disputes within one State, and the supreme courts stipulated in Article 95 (1) may be assigned last-instance jurisdiction to decide in cases where the application of State law is of the issue.

Article 100. (1) If a court concludes that a statute on the validity of which its decision depends is unconstitutional, then the proceedings are to be stayed, and, where a violation of the constitution of a State is of the issue, a decision is to be obtained from the State court which is competent for constitutional disputes, or, when a violation of this Basic Law is of the issue, a decision from the Federal Constitutional Court is to be obtained. The same applies where a violation of this Basic Law by State law or an incompatibility between State statute and a federal statute is of the issue.

(2) If in a judicial dispute it is doubtful whether a rule of international law is part of federal law and whether it directly creates rights and obligations for individuals (Article 25), then the court must obtain a decision from the Federal Constitutional Court.
(3) If the constitutional court of a State wishes to deviate from a decision of the Federal Constitutional Court or the constitutional court of another State in the interpretation of the Basic Law, then the constitutional court must obtain a decision from the Federal Constitutional Court.

Article 101. (1) Extraordinary tribunals are inadmissible. No-one may be deprived of his right to a lawful judge.
(2) Courts for special subject-areas may be established only by statute.

Article 102. The death penalty is abolished.

Article 103. (1) Before a court, everyone has the right to a hearing in accordance with the law.
(2) An act may be punished only when the liability to punishment was determined by statute before the act was committed.
(3) No-one may be punished several times on the basis of general criminal statutes for the same act.

Article 104. (1) The freedom of a person may be limited only pursuant to a formal statute and only in accordance with the form prescribed therein. Detained persons may not be abused either psychologically or physically.
(2) The permissibility and continuation of a deprivation of freedom is decided only by a judge. In all cases of a deprivation of freedom that are not based on a court order, a judicial decision must be obtained without delay. The police may, based on their own powers, detain no-one any longer than until the end of the day following the arrest. Details must be regulated statutorily.
(3) Everyone provisionally detained based on the suspicion of a criminal act must, at the latest on the day following the arrest, be brought before a judge who must inform him of the reasons for the arrest, question him, and give him an opportunity to object. The judge must without delay either issue a written arrest warrant stating the reasons, or order a release.
(4) A relative [Angehöriger] of the detainee or a person of his trust must be notified without delay of any judicial decision regarding the order or continuation of a deprivation of freedom.

X. The finances system

Article 104a. (1) The Federation and the States bear the costs resulting from the exercise of their tasks separately to the extent that this Basic Law does not provide otherwise.
(2) Where the States act on behalf of the Federation, the Federation bears the costs resulting therefrom.
(3) Federal statutes that confer pecuniary benefits and are executed by the States may provide that the pecuniary benefits are borne wholly or in part by the Federation. Where the statute provides that the Federation bears half of the costs or more, it is executed on behalf of the Federation.
(4) Federal statutes that establish obligations for the States to provide pecuniary benefits, benefits in kind with pecuniary value, or comparable services with respect to third parties and that are executed by the States as their own affairs or pursuant to paragraph 3, second sentence, on behalf of the Federation, require the consent of the Bundesrat, if the costs resulting therefrom are to be borne by the States.
(5) The Federation and the States bear the administrative costs arising for their administrative authorities and are liable to each other for ensuring a proper administration. Details are regulated by a federal statute which requires the consent of the Bundesrat.
(6) The Federation and the States bear the burdens of a violation of supranational or international-law obligations of Germany according to the domestic distribution of responsibilities and tasks. In cases of financial corrections of the European Union affecting several States, the Federation and the States bear these burdens at a ratio of 15 to 85. In such case the collectivity of the States bears 35 percent of the total burdens in mutual solidarity pursuant to a general key; 50 percent are borne by the States that caused the burdens, proportionate to the amount of the funds received. Details are regulated by a federal statute which requires the consent of the Bundesrat.

Article 104b. (1) The Federation may, to the extent that this Basic Law confers legislative competences upon it, grant financial aids to the States for particularly significant investments of the States and municipalities (associations of municipalities) that are required to
1. avert a disturbance of the macro-economic equilibrium or to
2. equalize diverging economic strengths in the federal territory or to

3. stimulate economic growth.
In deviation from the first sentence, the Federation may, in cases of natural disasters or exceptional emergencies that are beyond the state's control and substantially compromise the state financial situation, grant financial aids even without legislative competences.
(2) Details, particularly the kinds of investments to be supported, are regulated by federal statute which requires the consent of the Bundesrat, or pursuant to the Federal Budget Act [Bundeshaushaltsgesetz] by administrative agreement. The funds are to be granted for a limited time period and to be reviewed at regular intervals with respect to their use. The financial aids are to be administered with annual sums decreasing over time.
(3) The Bundestag, the Federal Government and the Bundesrat are, upon request, to be informed about the execution of the measures and the improvements achieved.

Article 105. (1) The Federation has exclusive legislative power regarding customs duties and fiscal monopolies.
(2) The Federation has concurrent legislative power regarding other taxes where it is entitled, wholly or in part, to the revenue generated by these taxes, or where the conditions of Article 72 (2) are met.
(2a) The States have competence to legislate regarding local consumption and expenditure taxes for as long as and to the extent that they are not equivalent to taxes regulated by federal statute. They have competence to determine the tax rate of the real estate acquisition tax.
(3) Federal statutes regarding taxes whose revenue flows wholly or in part to the States or the municipalities (associations of municipalities) require the consent of the Bundesrat.

Article 106. (1) The Federation is entitled to the yield of fiscal monopolies and to the revenue from the following taxes:
1. customs duties;
2. consumption taxes, to the extent that they are not due to the States pursuant to paragraph 2 or jointly to the Federation and the States pursuant to paragraph 3 or to the municipalities pursuant to paragraph 6;
3. the road freight transportation tax, the motor vehicle tax and other traffic taxes related to motorized transportation;
4. capital transactions taxes, the insurance tax and the exchange tax;
5. one-time levies on property and compensation levies raised for the implementation of the equalization of burdens;
6. the supplementary levy on the income tax and corporation tax;
7. levies within the framework of the European Communities.
(2) The States are entitled to the revenue from the following taxes:
1. the property tax;
2. the inheritance tax;
3. the traffic taxes to the extent that they are not due to the Federation pursuant to paragraph 1 or jointly to the Federation and the States pursuant to paragraph 3;
4. the beer tax;
5. the levies of casinos.
(3) The revenue from the income tax, the corporation tax and the turnover tax is due to the Federation and the States jointly (joint taxes) to the extent that pursuant to paragraph 5 the revenue from the income tax and pursuant to paragraph 5a the revenue from the turnover tax is not allocated with the municipalities. The revenue from the income tax and the corporation tax is shared equally between the Federation and the States. The respective shares of the Federation and the States in the revenue from the turnover tax are determined by a federal statute that requires the consent of the Bundesrat. This determination is to be based on the following principles:
1. Within the framework of current revenues, the Federation and the States have an equal claim to recover their necessary expenditures. The extent of these expenditures is to be determined with regard to multi-annual financial planning.
2. The coverage requirements of the Federation and the States are to be coordinated in such way that a fair balance is achieved, an excessive burden on the taxpayers is avoided, and uniformity of living standards throughout the federal territory is maintained.
In addition, in the determination of the respective shares of the Federation and the States in the revenue from the turnover tax, losses in tax revenue incurred by the States from 1 January 1996 because of the consideration of children in income tax law are also to be taken into account. Details are regulated by the federal statute enacted pursuant to the third sentence.
(4) The respective shares of the Federation and the States in the turnover tax is to be determined anew when the ratio between revenue and expenditure of the Federation and the States develops in a substantially different manner; losses of revenue that are additionally taken into account under paragraph 3, fifth sentence, in determining

the respective shares in the turnover tax remain disregarded in that context. Where additional tasks are assigned to or revenue is withdrawn from the States by federal statute, then the additional burden may be compensated by federal grants pursuant to a federal statute which requires the consent of the Bundesrat, if it is limited to a short time period. In the statute, the principles for calculating these grants and for their distribution among the States are to be established.
(5) The municipalities receive a share in the revenue of the income tax that is to be passed on by the States to their municipalities on the basis of the income tax payments of their inhabitants. Details are regulated by a federal statute which requires the consent of the Bundesrat. It may provide that municipalities may establish rate factors [Hebesatz] for the municipalities' share.
(5a) The municipalities receive a share in the revenue of the turnover tax from 1 January 1998. It is passed on by the States on the basis of a geographical and economic key. Details are regulated by a federal statute requiring the consent of the Bundesrat.
(6) The revenue from the real property tax and the trade tax is due to the municipalities; revenue from local consumption and expenditure taxes is due to the municipalities or, in accordance with State legislation, to the associations of municipalities. Municipalities are to be granted the right to establish rate factors for the real property tax and the trade tax within the framework of the statutes. Where there are no municipalities in a State, revenue from the real property tax and the trade tax as well as revenue from local consumption and expenditure taxes is due to the State. The Federation and the States may, by virtue of an apportionment, share in the revenue from the trade tax. Details regarding the apportionment are regulated by a federal statute which requires the consent of the Bundesrat. In accordance with State legislation, the real property tax and the trade tax as well as the municipalities' share of the revenue from the income tax and turnover tax may be taken as a calculation basis for determining apportionments.
(7) From the State' share of the total revenue from joint taxes, a percentage to be determined by State legislation flows to the municipalities and associations of municipalities collectively. For the rest, State legislation determines whether and to what extent revenues from State taxes are due to municipalities (associations of municipalities).
(8) Where the Federation arranges for special facilities in individual States or municipalities (associations of municipalities) which directly result in an increase of expenditure or a loss of revenue (special burdens) for these States or municipalities (associations of municipalities), the Federation grants the necessary compensation where and to the extent that States or municipalities (associations of municipalities) cannot reasonably be expected to bear the special burdens. Compensations from third parties and financial benefits arising for the States or municipalities (associations of municipalities) from the facilities are to be taken into account in granting the compensation.
(9) Revenues and expenditures of municipalities (associations of municipalities) are considered to be States revenues and expenditures for the purposes of this Article.

Article 106a. The States are entitled, from 1 January 1996, to a sum from the tax revenue of the Federation for local public transport. Details are regulated by a federal statute which requires the consent of the Bundesrat. The sum pursuant to the first sentence is not taken into account in the assessment of financial strength pursuant to Article 107 (2).

Article 106b. The States are entitled from 1 July 2009 to a sum from the tax revenue of the Federation in consequence of the transfer of the motor vehicle tax to the Federation. Details are regulated by a federal statute which requires the consent of the Bundesrat.

Article 107. (1) The revenue from State taxes and the States' share of revenue from the income tax and the corporation tax belongs to the individual States to the extent that the taxes are collected by tax authorities within their territories (local revenue). A federal statute which requires the consent of the Bundesrat is to make more detailed provisions for the corporation tax and the wage tax regarding the delimitation as well as the manner and scope of the disaggregation of the local revenue. The statute may also make provision for the delimitation and disaggregation of local revenue from other taxes. The States' share of revenue from the turnover tax belongs to the individual States in accordance with their population numbers; for a part, but not for more than a quarter of that States' share, a federal statute which requires the consent of the Bundesrat may provide for supplementary shares for those States whose revenue per capita from State taxes, from the income tax and the corporation tax and pursuant to Article 106b is below the average of the States; for the real estate acquisition tax, the tax capacity is to be taken into account.
(2) It is to be ensured by statute that the diverging financial strengths of the States is appropriately equalized; at this the financial strength and financial requirements of municipalities (associations of municipalities) are to be taken into account. The conditions governing equalization claims of States entitled to equalization payments as

well equalization duties of States obliged to provide equalization payments as well as the criteria for determining the amounts of equalization payments are to be specified in the statute. It may also provide that the Federation provides grants from its own funds to financially weak States in order to complement the coverage of their general financial requirements (supplementary grants).

Article 108. (1) Customs duties, fiscal monopolies, consumption taxes regulated by federal legislation including the import turnover tax, as well as the motor vehicle tax and other traffic taxes related to motorized transportation from 1 July 2009 onwards and charges within the framework of the European Communities are administered by federal tax authorities. The organization of these authorities is regulated by a federal statute. Where intermediate authorities are established, their heads are appointed in consultation with the State governments.
(2) The remaining taxes are administered by State tax authorities. The organization of these authorities and the uniform training of their civil servants may be regulated by a federal statute which requires the consent of the Bundesrat. Where intermediate authorities are established, their heads are appointed in agreement with the Federal Government.
(3) Where State tax authorities administer taxes which flow wholly or in part to the Federation, they act on behalf of the Federation. Article 85 (3) and (4) applies with the proviso that the Federal Government is substituted by the Minister of Finance.
(4) A federal statute which requires the consent of the Bundesrat may provide for a collaboration in the administration of taxes between federal and State tax authorities as well as in the case of taxes under Paragraph 1 for administration by State tax authorities or in the case of other taxes for their administration by federal tax authorities if and to the extent that the execution of tax laws will thereby be substantially facilitated or improved. For the taxes flowing exclusively to the municipalities (associations of municipalities), the administration that State tax authorities are entitled to may be delegated by the States to the municipalities (associations of municipalities) wholly or in part.
(5) The procedures to be applied by federal tax authorities are regulated by a federal statute. The procedures to be applied by State tax authorities, or, as provided by the second sentence of paragraph 4, by municipalities (associations of municipalities) may be regulated by a federal statute which requires the consent of the Bundesrat.
(6) Financial jurisdiction is uniformly regulated by a federal statute.
(7) The Federal Government may issue general administrative rules, which require the consent of the Bundesrat to the extent that the administration is incumbent upon State tax authorities or municipalities (associations of municipalities).

Article 109. (1) The Federation and the States are autonomous and independent from one another in their budget management.
(2) The Federation and the States jointly fulfil the responsibilities of the Federal Republic of Germany arising from legal acts of the European Community on the basis of Article 104 of the Treaty establishing the European Community for compliance with budgetary discipline and, within this framework, take due account of the requirements of the macro-economic equilibrium.
(3) The budgets of the Federation and the States are in principle to be balanced without revenue from credits. The Federation and the States may provide regulations regarding the consideration that is symmetrical for the upturn and downturn of the effects of an economic development that is deviating from the normal situation as well as an exception for natural disasters or exceptional emergencies that are beyond the state's control and that substantially compromise the state financial situation. For the exception, a corresponding redemption regulation is to be provided. Further details for the budget of the Federation are regulated by Article 115 with the proviso that the first sentence is complied with if the revenue from credits does not exceed 0.35 percent in proportion to the nominal gross domestic product. Details for the budgets of the States are regulated by them within the framework of their constitutional competences with the proviso that the first sentence is only complied with if no revenue from credits is admitted.
(4) By federal statute which requires the consent of the Bundesrat, common principles applying to the budgetary law, to budget management in line with cyclical economic requirements and to multi-annual financial planning may be established for the Federation and the States.
(5) Sanctions imposed by the European Community in relation to the provisions of Article 104 of the Treaty establishing the European Community for compliance with budgetary discipline are borne by the Federation and the States in a ratio of 65 to 35. The collectivity of the States bears 35 percent of the burdens allocated with the States in mutual solidarity and in proportion to their population; 65 percent of the burdens allocated with to the States is borne by the States in accordance with their share of causation. Details are regulated by a federal statute which requires the consent of the Bundesrat.

Part I. Constitutional Law

Article 109a. In order to avoid budgetary emergencies, a federal statute which requires the consent of the Bundesrat regulates
1. the continuous supervision of the budget management of the Federation and the States by a common panel (stability council [Stabilitätsrat]),
2. the requirements and the procedures for determining an imminent budgetary emergency,
3. the principles for establishing and executing restructuring programmes to avoid budgetary emergencies.
The decisions of the stability council and the underlying documentation of the deliberations are to be published.

Article 110. (1) All revenues and expenditures of the Federation are to be included in the budget; for federal enterprises and special assets only allocations or withdrawals need to be included. The budget is to be balanced for revenues and expenditures.
(2) The budget is established for one or more fiscal years divided by years, in a budget statute before the beginning of the first fiscal year. Parts of the budget may apply to different periods of time, divided by fiscal years.
(3) Bills pursuant to the first sentence of paragraph 2 as well as bills to amend the budget statute and the budget are to be submitted to the Bundesrat simultaneously with their transmission to the Bundestag; the Bundesrat is entitled to give a reaction on the bills within six weeks or, in the case of amendment bills, within three weeks.
(4) The budget statute may only contain provisions relating to revenues and expenditures of the Federation and to the period for which the budget statute is enacted. The budget statute may prescribe that its provisions expire only upon publication of the next budget statute or, in the event of an authorization pursuant to Article 115, at a later date.

Article 111. (1) If, by the end of a fiscal year, the budget for the following year has not been established by a statute, the Federal Government is authorized, until its entry into force, to make all expenditures that are necessary
a. to maintain statutory institutions and to carry out statutory measures,
b. to fulfil the legal obligations of the Federation,
c. to continue constructions, acquisitions and other services, or to continue to grant benefits for these purposes, to the extent that amounts have already been approved in the budget of a previous year.
(2) To the extent that revenues not based upon specific statutes from taxes, charges or other sources or the operational capital reserves do not cover the expenditures referred to in paragraph 1, the Federal Government may mobilize the funds necessary for sustaining operational management up to a maximum of one quarter of the total amount of the previous budget by way of a credit.

Article 112. Expenditures in excess of or outside the budgetary planning require the consent of the Minister of Finance. It may only be granted in the case of an unforeseen and irrefutable necessity. Details may be regulated by a federal statute.

Article 113. (1) Statutes which increase the expenditures of the budget proposed by the Federal Government or which comprise or will bring about in the future new expenditures require the consent of the Federal Government. The same applies to statutes that comprise or will bring about in the future decreases in revenue. The Federal Government may demand that the Bundestag suspend its decision-making on these statutes. In such case the Federal Government is to transmit a statement to the Bundestag within six weeks.
(2) The Federal Government may, within four weeks after the Bundestag has adopted this statute, demand that it make a decision again.
(3) Where the statute has become effective pursuant to Article 78, the Federal Government may withhold its consent only within six weeks and only after having initiated the procedure provided for in the third and fourth sentence of paragraph 1 or in paragraph 2. Upon the expiry of that period, consent is deemed to have been given.

Article 114. (1) The Minister of Finance is to render annually to the Bundestag and to the Bundesrat an account of all revenues and expenditures as well as of assets and debts during the following fiscal year, for the relief of the Federal Government.
(2) The Federal Court of Audit [Bundesrechnungshof] whose members enjoy judicial independence audits the account as well as the economic efficiency and regularity of the budget and operational management. It is to report annually directly to the Bundestag and to the Bundesrat in addition to the Federal Government. In all other respects, the competences of the Federal Court of Audit are regulated by federal statute.

Article 115. (1) The raising of credit and the assumption of co-signing of obligations, of guaranties or of other commitments which may lead to expenditures in future fiscal years require authorization to a quantified or quantifiable amount by a federal statute.

(2) Revenues and expenditures are in principle to be balanced without revenues from credits. This principle is complied with if the revenues from credits do not exceed 0.35 percent in proportion to the nominal gross domestic product. In addition, for an economic development that is deviating from the normal situation, the effects on the budget are to be considered symmetrically for the upturn and the downturn. Deviations in the effective raising of credit from the credit maximum permissible pursuant to the first through third sentences are registered on a control account; burdens that exceed the threshold of 1.5 percent in proportion to the nominal gross domestic product are to be reduced in line with the economic development. Details, especially the correction of revenues and expenditures for financial transactions and the procedure for calculating the maximum limit of the annual net borrowing taking into account the economic developments on the basis of a procedure for economic development correction as well as the control and the offsetting of deviations in the effective raising of credit from the maximum limit, are regulated by a federal statute. In the case of natural disasters or exceptional emergencies that are beyond the state's control and that substantially compromise the state financial situation, these maximum credit limits may be exceeded on the basis of a decision of the majority of the members of the Bundestag. The decision is to be connected with a redemption plan. The redemption of the credits raised pursuant to the sixth sentence is to take place within an adequate timeframe.

Xa. State of defence

Article 115a. (1) The finding that the territory of the Federation is being attacked by force of arms or that there is an imminent threat of such an attack (state of defence) is pronounced by the Bundestag with the consent of the Bundesrat. The finding is pronounced on request of the Federal Government and requires a majority of two-thirds of votes cast, including at least the majority of the members of the Bundestag.
(2) If the situation imperatively requires immediate action and insurmountable impediments prevent the timely convention of the Bundestag or if it does not have capacity to take decisions, then the Joint Committee pronounces the finding with a majority of two-thirds of votes cast, including a majority if its members.
(3) The finding is published by the Federal President in accordance with Article 82 in the Federal Law Gazette. If this cannot be done in time, the publication takes place in another manner; it must later be effected in the Federal Law Gazette as soon as the circumstances permit.
(4) If the territory of the Federation is being attacked by force of arms and the competent federal organs are incapable of immediately pronouncing a finding under paragraph 1, first sentence, such finding is deemed pronounced and published as from the time when the attack started. The Federal President specifies that time as soon as the circumstances permit.
(5) If the finding of a state of defence has been published and the territory of the Federation is being attacked by force of arms, the Federal President may, with the consent of the Bundestag, make declarations under international law regarding the existence of a state of defence. Under the conditions of paragraph 2, the position of the Bundestag is assumed by the Joint Committee.

Article 115b. With the publication of the state of defence, the command over the armed forces passes to the Federal Chancellor.

Article 115c. (1) The Federation has the right of concurrent legislation for the state of defence also in the matters that fall within the legislative power of the States. These statutes require the consent of the Bundesrat.
(2) To the extent that the circumstances during the state of defence so require, for the state of defence a statute may
1. in case of expropriations in deviation from Article 14 (3) second sentence, regulate the compensation provisionally,
2. regarding deprivations of freedom, provide for a time limit deviating from Article 104 (2) third sentence and (3) first sentence, at most however one of four days, for the case that a judge could not act within the time limit applied in normal times.
(3) To the extent that it is necessary for the aversion of a present or immediately threatening attack, for the state of defence by federal statute with the consent of the Bundesrat the administration and the finances system of the Federation and the States may be regulated in deviation from the sections VIII, VIIIa and X, in which case the viability of the States, municipalities and associations of municipalities, especially in a financial perspective, is to be respected.
(4) Federal statutes in the sense of Paragraph 1 and 2 no. 1 may for the purpose of the preparation of their execution already be applied before the beginning of the state of defence.

Article 115d. (1) Regarding legislation of the Federation in a state of defence, the provisions of Paragraphs 2 and 3 apply in deviation from Article 76 (2), Article 77 (1) second sentence and (2) to (4), Article 78 and Article 82 (1).
(2) Bills of the Federal Government which it has qualified as urgent are to be transmitted to the Bundesrat at the same time as their submission to the Bundestag. The Bundestag and the Bundesrat immediately deliberate on these bills jointly. In as far as the consent of the Bundesrat is required for a statute, the majority of its votes are required for the adoption of the statute. Details are regulated by rules of procedure which are adopted by the Bundestag and which require the consent of the Bundesrat.
(3) For the publication of statutes, Article 115a (3) second sentence applies mutatis mutandis.

Article 115e. (1) If the Joint Committee declares in a state of defence with a majority of two thirds of the votes cast, at least with the majority of its members, that an insurmountable impediments prevent the timely convention of the Bundestag or that it does not have capacity to take decisions, the Joint Committee has the position of Bundestag and Bundesrat and exercises their rights unitarily.
(2) By statute of the Joint Committee the Basic Law may neither be amended nor wholly or partly suspended or rendered inapplicable. The Joint Committee is not entitled to adopt statutes under Article 23 (1) second sentence, Article 24 (1) or Article 29.

Article 115f. (1) The Federal Government may, in a state of defence, in as far as the circumstances so require,
1. use the Federal Border Guard throughout the entire territory of the Federation;
2. give orders, besides to the federal administration, also to the State governments and, if it considers it to be urgent, to the State authorities and transfer this power to members of the State governments to be determined by it.
(2) The Bundestag, the Bundesrat and the Joint Committee are to be informed of the measures taken under Paragraph 1 immediately.

Article 115g. The constitutional position and the fulfilment of the constitutional tasks of the Federal Constitutional Court and its judges may not be jeopardized. The statute regarding the Federal Constitutional Court may be amended by a statute of the Joint Committee only to the extent that this is also in the opinion of the Federal Constitutional Court required in order to maintain the capacity of the Court to function. Until the adoption of such a statute the Federal Constitutional Court may take the measures necessary for maintaining the capacity of the Court to function. The Federal Constitutional Court takes decisions under the second and third sentence by majority of the judges present.

Article 115h. (1) Electoral terms of the Bundestag or the parliaments of the States expiring during a state of defence end six months after the termination of the state of defence. The term of the Federal President expiring during a state of defence as well as the exercise of his powers in case of early termination of his term by the president of the Bundesrat end nine months after the termination of the state of defence. The term of a member of the Federal Constitutional Court expiring during a state of defence ends six months after the termination of the state of defence.
(2) Where a new election of a Federal Chancellor by the Joint Committee becomes necessary, it elects a new Federal Chancellor by a majority of its members; the Federal President submits a proposal to the Joint Committee. The Joint Committee may express its lack of confidence in the Federal Chancellor only by electing a successor by the vote of two-thirds of its members.
(3) For the duration of the state of defence, a dissolution of the Bundestag is excluded.

Article 115i. (1) If the competent federal organs are incapable of taking the measures necessary for the aversion of the danger and the situation imperatively requires an immediate autonomous action in certain parts of the territory of the Federation, the State governments or authorities or representatives appointed by them are authorized to take measures in the sense of Article 115f (1) in matters within their competence.
(2) Measures under Paragraph 1 may at any time be repealed by the Federal Government, in relation to State authorities and subordinated federal authorities also by the prime ministers of the States.

Article 115k. (1) For the duration of their applicability, statutes under Articles 115c, 115e and 115g and ordinances that are adopted pursuant such statutes render conflicting law inapplicable. This does not apply to earlier law that has been adopted pursuant to Articles 115c, 115e and 115g.
(2) Statutes that the Joint Committee has adopted and ordinances that were adopted pursuant to such statutes expire at the latest six months after the termination of the state of defence.

(3) Statutes that contain rules deviating from Articles 91a, 91b, 104a, 106 and 107 apply at the latest until the end of the second fiscal year following the termination of the state of defence. They may, after the termination of the state of defence, be amended by federal statute with the consent of the Bundesrat, in order to lead over to the regime under sections VIIIa and X.

Article 115l. (1) The Bundestag may at any time with the consent of the Bundesrat repeal statutes of the Joint Committee. The Bundesrat may demand that the Bundestag decide on this matter. Other measures taken for the aversion of the danger by the Joint Committee or the Federal Government are to be lifted when the Bundestag and the Bundesrat so decide.
(2) The Bundestag may at any time with the consent of the Bundesrat, by a decision which is to be published by the Federal President, declare the state of defence terminated. The Bundesrat may demand that the Bundestag decide on this matter. The state of defence is to be declared terminated immediately when the conditions for its declaration are no longer present.
(3) The conclusion of peace is decided by federal statute.

XI. Transitional and final provisions

Article 116. (1) German within the meaning of this Basic Law is, subject to other statutory provisions, he who has the German citizenship or who, as a refugee or expellee of German ethnicity or as his spouse or descendant found admittance to the territory of the German Reich as it existed on 31 December 1937.
(2) Former German citizens, who, between 30 January 1933 and 8 May 1945, had their citizenship revoked for political, racial or religious reasons, and their descendants, are, on application, to be renaturalized. They are considered as not denaturalized if they, after 8 May 1945, took up residence in Germany and have not expressed a contrary intention.

Article 117. (1) Law contrary to Article 3 (2) remains in force until its adaptation to that provision of the Basic Law, but not for longer than until 31 March 1953.
(2) Statutes which limit the right to freedom of movement due to the current shortage of living space remain in force until their repeal by federal statute.

Article 118. The reorganization in the territories comprising the States of Baden, Württemberg-Baden and Württemberg-Hohenzollern may be effected, in derogation from the provisions of Article 29, by agreement between the States concerned. If no agreement is reached, the reorganization will be regulated by federal statute which must provide for a consultative referendum.

Article 118a. The reorganization in the territory comprising the States of Berlin and Brandenburg may be effected, in derogation from the provisions of Article 29, by agreement, with the participation of their eligible voters, between the States concerned..

Article 119. In matters relating to refugees and expellees, in particular as regards their distribution among the States, the federal government, until the adoption of a settlement by federal statute, may, with the consent of the Bundesrat, issue ordinances having the force of statute. For special cases, the federal government may be authorized to issue individual instructions. These instructions are, unless in case of an imminent danger, to be addressed to the highest States authorities.

Article 120. (1) The Federation bears the expenses for occupation costs and other internal and external burdens resulting from the war, in accordance with the more detailed federal statutes. To the extent that these burdens resulting from the war have been regulated by federal statutes by 1 October 1969, the Federation and the States bear such expenses in the proportion established by such federal statutes. To the extent that expenditures for burdens resulting from the war which neither have been nor are regulated by federal statutes have been assumed by 1 October 1965 by the States, municipalities (associations of municipalities) or other agencies performing functions of the States or municipalities, the Federation is not obliged to assume expenditures of this nature even after that date. The Federation bears the supplementary contributions towards the expenses of social security, including unemployment insurance and unemployment assistance. The distribution of burdens resulting from the war between the Federation and the States regulated by this paragraph does not affect the statutory regulation of compensation claims for effects of the war.
(2) Revenues pass to the Federation at the same time as it takes over the expenditures.

Part I. Constitutional Law

Article 120a. (1) The statutes concerning the implementation of the equalization of burdens may, with the consent of the Bundesrat, stipulate that in the field of equalization payments they will be executed partly by the Federation and partly by the States on behalf of the Federation and that the powers appertaining to the federal government and the competent highest federal authorities pursuant to Article 85 are delegated to the Federal Equalization of Burdens Office [Bundesausgleichsamt]. The Federal Equalization of Burdens Office does not require the consent of the Bundesrat in the exercise of these competences; its instructions are, except in cases of urgency, to be directed to the highest States authorities (State equalization of burdens offices).
(2) Article 87 (3), second sentence, remains unaffected.

Article 121. A majority of the members of the Bundestag and the Federal Convention within the meaning of this Basic Law is the majority of their statutory number.

Article 122. (1) From the convention of the Bundestag onwards, statutes are exclusively enacted by the legislative bodies recognized by this Basic Law.
(2) Legislative bodies and entities participating in the legislative process in an advisory capacity whose competence expires pursuant to paragraph 1 are dissolved from that moment.

Article 123. (1) Law predating the convention of the Bundestag remains in force to the extent that it does not conflict with the Basic Law.
(2) Treaties concluded by the German Reich, which pursuant to this Basic Law concern matters falling within the competence of State legislation, if under general principles of law they are and continue to be valid, remain in force, subject to all rights and objections of the parties, until new treaties are concluded by the authorities competent pursuant to this Basic Law or until their termination is otherwise effected by virtue of provisions contained in them.

Article 124. Law concerning matters falling within the exclusive legislative competence of the Federation becomes federal law within its scope of application.

Article 125. Law concerning matters falling within concurrent legislative powers of the Federation becomes federal law within its scope of application,
1. insofar as it applies uniformly within one or more occupation zones,
2. insofar as it is law by which after 8 May 1945 former Reich law has been amended.

Article 125a. (1) Law which has been enacted as federal law, but due to the amendment of Article 74 (1), the insertion of Article 84 (1) seventh sentence, Article 85 (1) second sentence or Article 105 (2a) second sentence or due to the repeal of Articles 74a, 75 or 98 (3) second sentence could no longer be enacted as federal law remains in force as federal law. It may be replaced by State law.
(2) Law which has been enacted pursuant to Article 72 (2) in the version applicable until 15 November 1994, but which due to the amendment of Article 72 (2) could no longer be enacted as federal law, remains in force as federal law. By federal statute it may be stipulated that it may be replaced by State law.
(3) Law which has been enacted as State law but due to the amendment of Article 73 could no longer be enacted as State law remains in force as State law. It may be replaced by federal law.

Article 125b. (1) Law which has been enacted pursuant to Article 75 in the version applicable until 1 September 2006 and which also after this date could be enacted as federal law, remains in force. Competences and obligations of the States to legislate remain in place in that respect. With respect to the areas mentioned in Article 72 (3) first sentence, the States may adopt regulations in deviation from this law; in the areas of Article 72 (3) first sentence, nos. 2, 5 and 6 however only when and to the extent that the Federation has exercised its legislative powers after 1 September 2006, in the cases of numbers 2 and 5 from 1 January 2010 at the latest, in the case of number 6 from 1 August 2008 at the latest.
(2) The States may adopt regulations in deviation from federal legal provisions that have been enacted pursuant to Article 84 (1) in the version applicable until 1 September 2006, they may adopt regulations in deviation from regulations regarding administrative procedure until 31 December 2008 however only if after 1 September 2006 regulations regarding administrative procedure have been amended in the relevant federal statute.

Article 125c. (1) Law which has been enacted pursuant to Article 91a (2) in conjunction with paragraph 1 no. 1 in the version applicable until 1 September 2006 remains in force until 31 December 2006.

(2) The legal provisions in the areas of municipal traffic financing and promotion of social housing created pursuant to Article 104a (4) in the version applicable until 1 September 2006 remain in force until 31 December 2006. The legal provisions created for special programmes pursuant to § 6 (1) of the Municipal Traffic Financing Act [Gemeindeverkehrsfinanzierungsgesetz] in the area of municipal traffic financing as well as the other legal provisions created pursuant to Article 104a (4) in the version applicable until 1 September 2006 remain in force until 31 December 2019, unless a prior date is or will be set for expiry.

Article 126. Disagreements about the continuance of law as federal law are resolved by the Federal Constitutional Court.

Article 127. The federal government may, with the consent of the governments of the States concerned, within one year after the promulgation of this Basic Law, enact law of the Bizone administration [Vereinigtes Wirtschaftsgebiet], to the extent that it remains in force as federal law under Article 124 or 125, in the States of Baden, Greater Berlin, Rhineland-Palatinate and Württemberg-Hohenzollern..

Article 128. To the extent that law remaining in force provides for powers to issue instructions within the meaning of Article 84 (5), they remain in force until statutory regulation provides otherwise.

Article 129. (1) To the extent that legal provisions that remain in force as federal law contain an authorization to enact ordinances or general administrative regulations or to issue administrative acts, it passes to the authorities henceforth competent in the subject matter. In cases of doubt, the federal government decides in agreement with the Bundesrat; the decision is to be published.
(2) To the extent that legal provisions that remain in force as State law contain such an authorization, it is exercised by the authorities competent under State law.
(3) To the extent that legal provisions within the meaning of paragraphs 1 and 2 authorize their amendment or supplementation or the enactment of legal provisions in the place of statutes, such authorization is expired.
(4) The provisions of paragraphs 1 and 2 apply mutatis mutandis where legal provisions refer to provisions no longer in force or to institutions no longer existent.

Article 130. (1) Administrative bodies and other institutions serving the public administration or the administration of justice that are not based on State law or agreements between States as well as the administration of the South West German Railways and the administrative board for postal and telecommunications services for the French occupation zone are subordinate to the federal government. The latter regulates with the consent of the Bundesrat their transfer, dissolution or liquidation.
(2) The supreme disciplinary superior of the members of these administrations and institutions is the competent federal minister.
(3) Institutions and entities under public law not directly subordinate to a State and not based on agreements between the States are under the supervision of the competent supreme federal authority.

Article 131. The legal relationships of persons including refugees and expellees who on 8 May 1945 were employed in the public service, who have left it for reasons related to other than to civil servant or labour agreement law and who have not yet been employed or not in a position corresponding to their former one, are to be regulated by federal statute. The same applies mutatis mutandis to persons including refugees and expellees who on 8 May 1945 were entitled to support and who for reasons related to other than to civil servant or labour agreement law no longer receive support or equivalent support. Until the entry into force of the federal statute, no legal entitlements may be claimed save for other regulations under State law.

Article 132. (1) Civil servants and judges who, on the moment of the entry into force of this Basic Law, are appointed for life, may within six months after the first convention of the Bundestag be retired, suspended or transferred to an office with a lower salary if they lack the personal or professional aptitude required for their office. This provision applies mutatis mutandis to employees with a non-terminable employment. In the case of employees whose employment can be terminated, periods of notice exceeding those set by labour agreement may be terminated within the same time period.
(2) This provision does not apply to members of the public service who are not affected by the provisions regarding the "Liberation from National Socialism and Militarism" or who are recognized victims of National Socialism, unless an important personal ground obtains.
(3) Those affected may have recourse to the courts pursuant to Article 19 (4).
(4) Details are regulated by an ordinance of the federal government which requires the consent of the Bundesrat.

PART I. CONSTITUTIONAL LAW

Article 133. The Federation succeeds to the rights and obligations of the Bizone administration [Vereinigtes Wirtschaftsgebiet].

Article 134. (1) The assets of the Reich in principle become federal assets.
(2) To the extent that they were, pursuant to their originally intended use, to be used principally for administrative tasks which pursuant to this Basic Law are not administrative tasks of the Federation, they are to be transferred free of charge to the authorities now competent and, to the extent that they, pursuant to their current and not merely temporary use, serve for administrative tasks that pursuant to this Basic Law are now to be performed by the States, they are to be transferred to the States. The Federation may also transfer other assets to the States.
(3) Assets that were placed at the disposal of the Reich free of charge by States and municipalities (associations of municipalities) become assets of the States and municipalities (associations of municipalities) again, to the extent that the Federation does not require them for its own administrative tasks.
(4) Details are regulated by a federal statute which requires the consent of the Bundesrat.

Article 135. (1) If after 8 May 1945 and before the entry into force of this Basic Law the affiliation of a territory to a State has changed, then the State to which the territory now belongs is entitled to the assets of the State to which it previously belonged that are located in that territory.
(2) The assets of no longer existing States and other entities and institutions under public law, to the extent that, pursuant to their originally intended use, they were to be used principally for administrative tasks or, pursuant to their current and not merely temporary use, serve principally administrative tasks, pass to the State or entity or institution under public law that now performs these tasks.
(3) Land property of no longer existing States including appurtenances pass to the State within which it is located to the extent that it is not already included among the assets within the meaning of paragraph 1.
(4) To the extent that an overriding interest of the Federation or the particular interest of a territory so requires, arrangements deviating from the provisions of paragraphs 1 to 3 of this Article may be adopted by federal statute.
(5) In all other respects, the succession and disposition of assets, to the extent that it has not been resolved by 1 January 1952 by agreement between the States or entities or institutions under public law concerned, is regulated by a federal statute which requires the consent of the Bundesrat.
(6) Holdings of the former State of Prussia in private-law enterprises pass to the Federation. Details are regulated by a federal statute which may also deviate from this provision.
(7) To the extent that assets which would fall to a State or entity or institution under public law pursuant to paragraphs 1 to 3 had been used by the beneficiary by a State statute, pursuant to a State statute or in any other manner at the entry into force of this Basic Law, the transfer of assets is considered to have taken place before the use.

Article 135a. (1) By federal legislation reserved pursuant to Article 134 (4) and Article 135 (5) it may be provided that the following do not have to be fulfilled or do not have to be fulfilled in full:
1. liabilities of the Reich as well as liabilities of the former State of Prussia and other no longer existing entities and institutions under public law,
2. liabilities of the Federation or other entities or institutions under public law which are related to the passing of assets pursuant to Article 89, 90, 134 and 135 and liabilities of these legal bodies that are based on measures taken by the legal bodies designated under subparagraph 1,
3. liabilities of the States and municipalities (associations of municipalities) which have arisen from measures which these legal bodies have taken before 1 August 1945 in order to implement orders of the occupying powers or to remedy a state of emergency resulting from the war within the framework of the administrative tasks incumbent upon or delegated by the Reich.
(2) Paragraph 1 applies mutatis mutandis to liabilities of the German Democratic Republic or its legal bodies as well as to liabilities of the Federation or other entities or institutions under public law which are related to the passing of assets of the German Democratic Republic to the Federation, States and municipalities, and to liabilities arising from measures of the German Democratic Republic or its legal bodies.

Article 136. (1) The Bundesrat convenes for the first time on the day of the first convention of the Bundestag.
(2) Until the election of the first Federal President, his competences are exercised by the president of the Bundesrat. He does not have the right to dissolve the Bundestag.

Article 137. (1) The right of civil servants, employees in the public service, professional soldiers, temporary volunteer soldiers and judges to run in elections in the Federation, in the States and the municipalities may be restricted by statute.

(2) The electoral law to be adopted by the Parliamentary Council [Parlamentarischer Rat] applies to the election of the first Bundestag, the first Federal Convention and the first Federal President of the Federal Republic.
(3) The competence of the Federal Constitutional Court pursuant to Article 42 (2) is, until its establishment, exercised by the German High Court for the Bizone [Deutsches Obergericht für das Vereinigte Wirtschaftsgebiet] which decides in accordance with its own rules of procedure.

Article 138. Changes to the constitutions of the profession of notary public as it now exists in the States of Baden, Bavaria, Württemberg-Baden and Württemberg-Hohenzollern require the consent of the governments of these States.

Article 139. The legal provisions enacted for the "Liberation of the German People from National Socialism and Militarism" [Befreiung des deutschen Volkes vom Nationalsozialismus und Militarismus] are not affected by the provisions of this Basic Law.

Article 140. The provisions of Articles 136, 137, 138, 139 and 141 of the German Constitution of 11 August 1919 are part of this Basic Law.

Article 141. Article 7 (3) first sentence does not apply in any State where State law providing otherwise was in force on 1 January 1949.

Article 142. Notwithstanding the provision of Article 31, provisions of State constitutions remain in force to the extent that they guarantee fundamental rights in conformity with Articles 1 to 18 of this Basic Law.

Article 142a. (Repealed).

Article 143. (1) Law in the territory specified in Article 3 of the Unification Treaty [Einigungsvertrag] may deviate from the provisions of this Basic Law at the latest until 31 December 1992, to the extent and so long as, due to the differing circumstances, a complete adaptation to the order of the Basic Law cannot be achieved yet. Deviations may not violate Article 19 (2) and must be compatible with the principles stipulated in Article 79 (3).
(2) Deviations from Titles II, VIII, VIIIa, IX, X and XI are permissible at the latest until 31 December 1995.
(3) Notwithstanding paragraphs 1 and 2, Article 41 of the Unification Treaty and provisions for its implementation remain in force to the extent that they provide that interference with property in the territory specified in Article 3 of that Treaty cannot be reversed.

Article 143a. (1) The Federation has exclusive legislative competence in all matters arising from the transformation of the federal railways administered by the Federation into commercial enterprises. Article 87e (5) applies mutatis mutandis. Civil servants of the federal railways may be assigned by statute, without prejudice to their legal status or the responsibility of the employer, to provide services for railways of the Federation organized under private law.
(2) The Federation executes statutes enacted pursuant to paragraph 1.
(3) The performance of the tasks relating to local public railway transport of the former federal railways is the responsibility of the Federation until 31 December 1995. The same applies to the corresponding tasks of the Rail Transport Administration [Eisenbahnverkehrsverwaltung]. Details are regulated by a federal statute that requires the consent of the Bundesrat.

Article 143b. (1) The special assets of the German Federal Post Office [Deutsche Bundespost] is transformed into private-law enterprises pursuant to a federal statute. The Federation has exclusive legislative competence in all matters arising herefrom.
(2) The exclusive rights of the Federation existing before the transformation may be conferred by a federal statute for a transitional period on the enterprises that succeed the postal service of the German Federal Post Office [Deutsche Bundespost Postdienst] and the telecommunications service of the German Federal Post Office [Deutsche Bundespost Telekom]. The majority interest in the enterprise that succeeds the postal service of the German Federal Post Office may be surrendered by the Federation at the earliest five years after the entry into force of the statute. To do so requires a federal statute with the consent of the Bundesrat.
(3) The federal civil servants employed by the German Federal Post Office are employed by the private enterprises without prejudice to their legal status and the responsibility of their employer. The enterprises exercise employer's authority. Details are regulated by a federal statute.

Article 143c. (1) The States are entitled from 1 January 2007 until 31 December 2019 to receive amounts out of the federal budget annually for the discontinuation of the Federation's share in financing due to the abolition of the joint tasks of upgrading and constructing universities including university hospitals and educational guidance and due to the abolition of financial aid for the improvement of the traffic situation of the municipalities and for social housing subsidies. Until 31 December 2013, these amounts are calculated on the basis of the average financing shares of the Federation in the 2000 to 2008 frame of reference.
(2) The amounts are, until 31 December 2013, distributed among the States as follows:
1. as annual fixed amounts whose height is calculated on the basis of the average share of each State over the time period of 2000 to 2003;
2. for a specific purpose of the responsibilities under the previous mixed financing.
(3) The Federation and the States review until the end of 2013 to what extent the financing means the States have been assigned under paragraph 1 are still suitable and necessary for the performance of the States' tasks. From 1 January 2014 onwards, the purpose-bound appropriation designated in paragraph 2 (2) of the financing means assigned pursuant to paragraph 1 will lapse; the investment-related appropriation of the median volume remains valid. The agreements from the Second Solidarity Agreement [Solidarpakt II] remain unaffected.
(4) Details are regulated by a federal statute that requires the consent of the Bundesrat.

Article 143d. (1) Articles 109 and 115 in the version applicable until 31 July 2009 are to be applied for the last time to the 2010 fiscal year. Articles 109 and 115 in the version applicable as from 1 August 2009 are to be applied for the first time to the 2011 fiscal year; credit authorizations existing on 31 December 2010 for special assets [Sondervermögen] already established remain unaffected. The States may, in the period from 1 January 2011 to 31 December 2019, deviate from the target of Article 109 (3) in accordance with the applicable provisions of State law. The States' budgets are to be shaped in such way that in the 2020 fiscal year the target under Article 109 (3) fifth sentence is met. The Federation may, in the time period from 1 January 2011 to 31 December 2015 deviate from the target of Article 115 (2) second sentence. The reduction of the existing deficit shall begin in the 2011 fiscal year. The annual budgets are to be shaped in such way that in the 2016 fiscal year the target under Article 115 (2) second sentence is met; details are regulated by a federal statute.
(2) As an aid for compliance with the target under Article 109 (3) from 1 January 2020 onwards, the States of Berlin, Bremen, Saarland, Saxony-Anhalt and Schleswig-Holstein may be granted a total of 800 million euros in consolidation aids per year out of the federal budget for the time period of 2011 to 2019. Thereof, 300 million euros are allotted to Bremen, 260 million euros to Saarland, and 80 million euros each to Berlin, Saxony-Anhalt and Schleswig-Holstein. The aids are provided on the basis of an administrative agreement pursuant to a federal statute with the consent of the Bundesrat. The granting of aids presupposes a complete clearing of the financing deficits by the end of 2020. Details, in particular the annual stages of reduction of the financing deficit, the supervision of the reduction of the financing deficits by the Stability Council [Stabilitätsrat] as well as consequences in case of non-compliance with the stages of reduction are regulated by a federal statute with the consent of the Bundesrat and an administrative agreement. A simultaneous granting of consolidation aids and stabilization aids due to an extreme budgetary emergency is excluded.
(3) The financing burden resulting from the granting of consolidation aids is distributed in equal parts between the Federation and the States, in the case of the latter from their share of the turnover tax. Details are regulated by a federal statute with the consent of the Bundesrat.

Article 144. (1) This Basic Law requires ratification by the representative assemblies in two thirds of the States in which it is to apply initially.
(2) To the extent that the application of this Basic Law is subject to restrictions in one of the States listed in Article 23 or in a part of these States, that State or that part of the State has the right to send representatives to the Bundestag pursuant to Article 38 and to the Bundesrat pursuant to Article 50.

Article 145. (1) The Parliamentary Council [Parlamentarischer Rat], with the participation of the representatives of Greater Berlin, declares the adoption of this Basic Law in public session, promulgates and publishes it.
(2) This Basic Law enters into force at the end of the day on which it is published.
(3) It is to be published in the Federal Law Gazette [Bundesgesetzblatt].

Article 146. This Basic Law, which since the completion of the unity and freedom of Germany applies to the entire German people, shall cease to apply on the day on which a constitution enters into force which has been freely adopted by the German people.

Germany: Federal Elections Act

Federal Elections Act [Bundeswahlgesetz] as last amended by federal statute of 17 March 2008 (*BGBl.* I p. 394). Selected provisions: Chapter 1 (§§ 1 to 7).[5]

I. Electoral system

§ 1. (1) The German Bundestag is composed, subject to the deviations resulting from this Act, of 598 members. They are elected in general, direct, free, equal and secret-ballot elections by the Germans entitled to vote, according to the principle of proportional representation combined with person-based voting.
(2) 299 of the members of the Bundestag are elected upon electoral district candidacies within electoral districts and the other members upon State candidacies (State lists).

§ 2. (1) The electoral territory is the territory of the Federal Republic of Germany.
(2) The division of the electoral territory into electoral districts is based on the Annex to this Act.
(3) Each electoral district is, for the purposes of polling, divided into polling districts.

§ 3. (1) During the division of electoral districts, the following principles must be observed:
1. The State borders must be respected.
2. The number of electoral districts in the individual States must correspond as far as possible to their share of the population. It is established with the same calculation method which is applied to the distribution of seats to the State lists in accordance with § 6 (2), second to seventh sentence.
3. The population size of an electoral district should not deviate from the average population size of electoral districts by more than 15 per cent, above or below; if the deviation is more than 25 per cent, a re-districting must take place.
4. An electoral district is to form a contiguous area.
5. The borders of municipalities, rural counties and autonomous cities are to be respected if possible.
During the calculation of population numbers, aliens (§ 2 (1) Sojourn Act [Aufenthaltsgesetz]) are not taken into account.
(2) The Federal President appoints a permanent electoral district commission. It consists of the president of the Federal Statistics Office [Statistisches Bundesamt], one judge at the Federal Administrative Court [Bundesverwaltungsgericht] and five other members.
(3) The electoral district commission has the task to report on changes of population numbers in the electoral territory and to submit whether and which changes in the division of electoral districts it considers necessary in that light. It may submit in its report proposals for changes also for other reasons. Regarding its proposals for changes in the division of electoral districts it must respect the principles stipulated in paragraph 1; if following the calculation under paragraph 1 no. 2, several possible affiliations with electoral districts may result, it draws up proposals in that matter.
(4) The report of the electoral district commission must be submitted to the Federal Ministry of Internal Affairs within fifteen months following the beginning of the term of the German Bundestag. The Federal Ministry of Internal Affairs transmits it without delay to the German Bundestag and publishes it in the Federal Gazette [Bundesanzeiger]. Upon request of the Federal Ministry of Internal Affairs, the electoral district committee must submit a supplementary report; for this case, the second sentence applies mutatis mutandis.
(5) If State borders are being redrawn in accordance with statutory provisions regarding the procedure on further changes to the territorial shape of the States under Article 29 (7) of the Basic Law, then the borders of the affected electoral districts also change accordingly. If in the receiving State two or more electoral districts are affected or if an exclave of a State is being created, then the electoral district affiliation of the new part of the State is determined by the electoral district affiliation of the municipality, municipal district or autonomous area to which it has been attached. Changes to State borders which are carried out after the end of the thirty-second month following the beginning of the term have an effect on the division of electoral districts only in the following term.

§ 4. Each voter has two votes, a first vote for the election of a member of the Bundestag from the electoral district, and a second vote for the election of a State list.

---

[5] Translation by Ph. Kiiver. Editor's note: by judgment of 3 July 2008 (2 BvC 1/07 / 2 BvC 7/07), the Federal Constitutional Court declared § 7 (3) second sentence in conjunction with § 6 (4) and (5) unconstitutional, leaving the provisions in force and allowing the lawmaker until 30 June 2011 to change the electoral regime.

§ 5. In each electoral district, one member of the Bundestag is elected. The candidate who receives the most votes is elected. In case of a tie, a lot to be drawn by the district returning officer decides.

§ 6. (1) For the distribution of seats to be filled from State lists, the second votes cast for each State list are added. The second votes of those voters who have cast their first vote for a candidate who was successful in his electoral district and who has been put forward in accordance with § 20 (3) or by a political party for which in the respective State no State list was admitted, are not taken into account. The number of successful electoral district candidates who are stipulated in the second sentence or who are put forward by a political party not to be taken into account under paragraph 6 is subtracted from the total number of members of the Bundestag (§ 1 (1)).
(2) The seats remaining pursuant to paragraph 1, third sentence, are distributed as follows among the State lists on the basis of the second votes to be taken into account under paragraph 1, first and second sentence. Each State list receives as many seats as result from the division of the sum of its second votes received in the electoral territory by a distribution divisor. Decimals under 0.5 are rounded off to the whole number below, those above 0.5 are rounded off to the whole number above. Decimals which are equal to 0.5 are rounded off upwards or downwards so that the whole number of seats to be distributed is maintained; if several possible assignments of seats result from this, a lot to be drawn by the federal returning officer decides. The distribution divisor is to be established so that, in total, as many seats are assigned to State lists as there are seats to be distributed. For that purpose, first the total number of second votes of all State lists to be taken into account is divided by the total number of the seats remaining pursuant to paragraph 1, third sentence. If more seats are assigned to the State lists than there are seats to be distributed, then the distribution divisor is to be increased so that in the calculation the number of seats to be distributed is obtained; if too few seats are assigned to the State lists, the distribution divisor is to be lowered accordingly.
(3) If following the distribution of seats according to paragraph 2 a State list, which has received more than half of the total number of second votes of all State lists to be taken into account, has not received more than half of the seats to be distributed, it is assigned at first, in deviation from paragraph 2, second to seventh sentence, one additional seat. Seats to be distributed after that are assigned according to paragraph 2, second to seventh sentence.
(4) The number of seats won by the political party in the electoral districts of the State is subtracted from the number of members of the Bundestag for each State list thus calculated. The remaining seats are filled from the State list in the order determined therein. Candidates who have been elected in an electoral district are not taken into account on the State list. If a State list receives more seats than it nominates candidates, these seats remain vacant.
(5) Seats won in the electoral districts remain with a political party even when they exceed the number calculated under paragraphs 2 and 3. In such case, the total number of seats (§ 1 (1)) increases with the difference; a new calculation under paragraphs 2 and 3 does not take place.
(6) During the distribution of seats among State lists, only political parties are taken into account which have received at least 5 per cent of valid second votes cast in the electoral territory or which have won a seat in at least three electoral districts. The first sentence does not apply to lists submitted by political parties of national minorities.

§ 7. (1) State lists of the same political party are considered combined in as far as it is not declared that one of more participating State lists are excluded from the combination of lists.
(2) Combined lists are considered, during the distribution of seats, as one list in relation to the other lists.
(3) Seats assigned to a combination of lists are distributed among the participating State lists in accordance with § 6 (2). § 6 (4) and (5) applies mutatis mutandis.

[The remaining Chapters are omitted.]

Charter for the Kingdom of the Netherlands [Statuut voor het Koninkrijk der Nederlanden] of 28 October 1954 as last amended by Kingdom Statute of 7 September 1998 (*Stb.* 597).[6]

Preamble
The Netherlands, the Netherlands Antilles and Aruba,
noting that the Netherlands, Surinam and the Netherlands Antilles in 1954 have declared by free will to accept a new legal order in the Kingdom of the Netherlands, in which they conduct their own interests autonomously and pursue their common interests on a basis of equality and accord each other assistance, and have resolved in mutual consultation to adopt the Charter for the Kingdom;
noting that the connection with Surinam under the Charter has come to an end as per 25 November 1975 by virtue of an amendment of the Charter by Kingdom Statute of 22 November 1975, Stb. 617, PbNA 233;
considering that Aruba has declared by free will to accept this legal order as a country;
have resolved in mutual consultation to adopt the Charter for the Kingdom as follows.

§ 1. General provisions

Article 1. The crown of the Kingdom is held by inheritance by Her Majesty Queen Juliana, Princess of Orange-Nassau, and, by succession, by her lawful successors.

Article 2. (1) The King heads the government of the Kingdom and of each of the countries. He is inviolable, the ministers are responsible.
(2) The King is represented in the Netherlands Antilles and Aruba by the Governor [Gouverneur]. The competences, duties and responsibility of the Governor as representative of the government of the Kingdom are regulated by Kingdom Statute [rijkswet] or, where applicable, by Kingdom Ordinance [algemene maatregel van rijksbestuur].
(3) Kingdom Statute regulates that which relates to the appointment and the dismissal of the Governor. The appointment and the dismissal are effected by the King as head of the Kingdom.

Article 3. (1) Notwithstanding what is provided elsewhere in the Charter, matters for the Kingdom are:
a. the maintenance of the independence and the defence of the Kingdom;
b. foreign relations;
c. Dutch citizenship;
d. the regulation of chivalric orders as well as the flag and the coat of arms of the Kingdom;
e. the regulation of the nationality of vessels and the laying down of conditions regarding the safety and navigation of seagoing vessels which fly the flag of the Kingdom, except sailing vessels;
f. oversight over the general rules regarding the admission and expulsion of Dutch citizens;
g. the laying down of general conditions for the admission and expulsion of aliens;
h. extradition.
(2) Other matters may in mutual consultation be declared to be matters for the Kingdom. In that context, Article 55 applies mutatis mutandis.

Article 4. (1) Royal authority is exercised in matters for the Kingdom by the King as head of the Kingdom.
(2) Legislative authority is exercised in matters for the Kingdom by the legislator of the Kingdom. In cases of bills for Kingdom Statutes, consideration takes place with due regard to Articles 15 to 21.

Article 5. (1) The monarchy and the succession to the throne, the organs of the Kingdom referred to in the Charter, the exercise of royal and legislative authority in matters for the Kingdom are regulated, in as far as that is not provided for by the Charter, by the Constitution [Grondwet] for the Kingdom.
(2) The Constitution respects the provisions of the Charter.
(3) To a proposal for an amendment of the Constitution containing provisions regarding matters for the Kingdom, as well as to bills stating that there is reason to consider such a proposal, Articles 15 to 20 apply.

---

[6] Translation by Ph. Kiiver.

PART I. CONSTITUTIONAL LAW

§ 2. The conduct of matters for the Kingdom

Article 6. (1) The matters for the Kingdom are conducted in cooperation between the Netherlands, the Netherlands Antilles and Aruba in accordance with the following provisions.
(2) During the conduct of these matters, organs of the countries are involved where possible.

Article 7. The council of ministers of the Kingdom is composed of the ministers appointed by the King and the Minister Plenipotentiary [Gevolmachtigde Minister] appointed by the government of the Netherlands Antilles and of Aruba, respectively.

Article 8. (1) The Ministers Plenipotentiary act on behalf of the governments of their country, which appoint and dismiss them. They must be Dutch citizens.
(2) The government of the country involved determines who replaces the Minister Plenipotentiary in case of his being hindered or absent. That which is provided in this Charter regarding the Minister Plenipotentiary applies mutatis mutandis with respect to his substitute.

Article 9. (1) The Minister Plenipotentiary, before assuming his office, takes an oath or makes a promise of allegiance to the King and the Charter before the Governor. The formula for the oath or promise is established by Kingdom Ordinance.
(2) When in the Netherlands, the Minister Plenipotentiary takes the oath or makes the promise before the King.

Article 10. (1) The Minister Plenipotentiary participates in the deliberations in the meetings of the council of ministers and of the permanent bodies and special commissions of the council regarding matters for the Kingdom which affect the country in question.
(2) The governments of the Netherlands Antilles and Aruba each have the right – if a certain subject-matter calls for such action – to also let a minister with an advisory vote participate next to the Minister Plenipotentiary in the deliberations stipulated in the preceding paragraph.

Article 11. (1) Proposals for an amendment of the Constitution containing provisions regarding matters for the Kingdom affect the Netherlands Antilles and Aruba.
(2) As regards defence, it is assumed that the defence of the territory of the Netherlands Antilles or of Aruba, respectively, as well as agreements or understandings regarding an area that belongs to their sphere of interests, affect the Netherlands Antilles and Aruba, respectively.
(3) As regards foreign affairs, it is assumed that foreign affairs where the interests of the Netherlands Antilles or of Aruba, respectively, are involved, or where the conduct thereof can have serious consequences for these interests, affect the Netherlands Antilles and Aruba, respectively.
(4) The determination of the contribution to the costs referred to in Article 35 affects the Netherlands Antilles and Aruba, respectively.
(5) Proposals for naturalization are only considered to affect the Netherlands Antilles and Aruba, respectively, if persons are concerned who reside in the country in question.
(6) The government of the Netherlands Antilles and of Aruba, respectively, may state which matters for the Kingdom other than those stipulated in the first to fourth paragraph affect its country.

Article 12. (1) If the Minister Plenipotentiary of the Netherlands Antilles or of Aruba, respectively, indicating his reasons based on which he expects serious detriment to his country, has declared that his country should not be bound by a proposed instrument containing generally binding regulations, such instrument may not be adopted in a way that it applies in the country in question, unless this would be incompatible with the ties of the country within the Kingdom.
(2) If the Minister Plenipotentiary of the Netherlands Antilles or of Aruba, respectively, has serious objections to the initial opinion of the council of ministers regarding the requirement of binding nature as stipulated in the first paragraph, or regarding any other matter in the consideration of which he has participated, then upon his request deliberations are continued, if necessary with due regard to a time limit to be determined by the council of ministers.
(3) The deliberations referred to above are conducted between the prime-minister, two ministers, the Minister Plenipotentiary and a minister or special plenipotentiary to be nominated by the government involved.
(4) If both Ministers Plenipotentiary wish to participate in continued deliberations, then these deliberations are conducted between the prime-minister, two ministers and both Ministers Plenipotentiary. The second paragraph of Article 10 applies mutatis mutandis.

(5) The council of ministers decides in accordance with the result of the continued deliberations. If the opportunity for continued deliberations has not been seized within the specified time limit, then the council of ministers takes its decision.

Article 13. (1) There is a Council of State of the Kingdom [Raad van State van het Koninkrijk].
(2) If the government of the Netherlands Antilles or of Aruba, respectively, makes known such wish, the King appoints a member to the Council of State for the Netherlands Antilles or Aruba, respectively, whose appointment is effected in agreement with the government of the country involved. His dismissal is effected after consultation with that government.
(3) The member of the Council of State for the Netherlands Antilles or Aruba, respectively, participates in the activities of the Council of State in case the Council or a division of the Council is heard regarding bills for Kingdom Statutes and Kingdom Ordinances which shall apply in the Netherlands Antilles or Aruba, respectively, or regarding other matters which, in accordance with Article 11, affect the Netherlands Antilles or Aruba, respectively.
(4) By Kingdom Ordinance, regulations may be adopted with respect to the mentioned members of the Council of State that deviate from the provisions of the Council of State Act [Wet op de Raad van State].

Article 14. (1) Regulations regarding matters for the Kingdom – in as far as the relevant matter is not regulated in the Constitution and save for international regulations and that which is provided in the third paragraph – are established by Kingdom Statute [rijkswet] or, in cases where that is applicable, by Kingdom Ordinance [algemene maatregel van rijksbestuur]. The Kingdom Statute or the Kingdom Ordinance may charge other organs with, or leave to other organs, the establishment of more detailed regulations. The charging of or leaving to the countries is effected with respect to the legislator or the government of the countries.
(2) If the regulation is not reserved for Kingdom Statute, it may be effected by Kingdom Ordinance.
(3) Regulations regarding matters for the Kingdom which apply neither in the Netherlands Antilles nor Aruba are established by statute [wet] or ordinance [algemene maatregel van bestuur].
(4) The naturalization of persons resident in the Netherlands Antilles or Aruba is effected by or pursuant to Kingdom Statute.

Article 15. (1) The King transmits a bill for a Kingdom Statute, simultaneously with its introduction in the States-General, to the representative bodies of the Netherlands Antilles and Aruba.
(2) In case of a proposal for a bill for a Kingdom Statute emanating from the States-General, the transmission of the bill by the Second Chamber [Tweede Kamer] is effected immediately after it has been introduced in the Chamber.
(3) The Minister Plenipotentiary of the Netherlands Antilles or Aruba, respectively, has the right to propose to the Second Chamber to make a proposal for a bill for a Kingdom Statute.

Article 16. The representative body of the country where the regulation shall apply has the right to scrutinize it before the public consideration of the bill in the Second Chamber and, if necessary within a time period determined for that purpose, to issue a written report on it.

Article 17. (1) The Minister Plenipotentiary of the country where the regulation shall apply is offered the opportunity to attend the oral consideration of the bill for a Kingdom Statute in the Chambers of the States-General and to provide such information to the Chambers as he considers appropriate.
(2) The representative body of the country where the regulation shall apply may decide, for the consideration of a specific matter in the States-General, to delegate one or more special delegates who also have the right to attend the oral consideration and to provide information in that context.
(3) The Ministers Plenipotentiary and the special delegates are not liable to judicial prosecution for that which they have said in the meeting of the Chambers of the States-General or which they have submitted to them in writing.
(4) The Ministers Plenipotentiary and the special delegates have the right, during the consideration in the Second Chamber, to propose amendments to the bill.

Article 18. (1) The Minister Plenipotentiary of the country where the regulation shall apply is given the opportunity, before the final vote on a bill for a Kingdom Statute in the Chambers of the States-General, to give a statement regarding that bill. If the Minister Plenipotentiary declares his opposition to the bill, he may also request the Chamber to postpone the vote until the following meeting. If the Second Chamber, after the Minister Plenipotentiary has declared his opposition to the bill, adopts it with a majority smaller than three-fifths of the

number of votes cast, the consideration is suspended and further deliberations regarding the bill take place in the council of ministers.
(2) If special delegates are attending the meeting of the Chambers, the right stipulated in the first paragraph also applies to the delegate nominated by the representative body for that purpose.

Article 19. Articles 17 and 18 apply mutatis mutandis to the consideration in the joint session of the States-General.

Article 20. By Kingdom Statute, further regulations may be established regarding that which is provided in Articles 15 to 19.

Article 21. If, after concluded deliberations with the Ministers Plenipotentiary of the Netherlands Antilles and Aruba, in case of war or in other special cases where action must be taken swiftly, it is impossible in the opinion of the King to wait for the result of the scrutiny stipulated in Article 16, the provision of that Article may be deviated from.

Article 22. (1) The government of the Kingdom ensures the publication of Kingdom Statutes and Kingdom Ordinances. It is effected where the regulation shall apply in the official journal. The governments of the countries provide the necessary assistance in that context.
(2) They enter into force on the moment to be stipulated by or pursuant to these regulations.
(3) The enactment formula of Kingdom Statutes and of Kingdom Ordinances states that the provisions of the Charter for the Kingdom have been respected.

Article 23. (1) The jurisdiction of the Supreme Court of the Netherlands [Hoge Raad der Nederlanden] as regards disputes in the Netherlands Antilles or Aruba, respectively, is regulated by Kingdom Statute.
(2) If the government of the country involved so requests, by that Kingdom Statute the possibility is opened for a member, an extraordinary member or an advisory member to be added to the Court.

Article 24. (1) Agreements with foreign states and with international organizations which affect the Netherlands Antilles or Aruba, respectively, are submitted, simultaneously with the submission to the States-General, to the representative body of the Netherlands Antilles or Aruba, respectively.
(2) In case the agreement is submitted to the States-General for tacit approval, the Minister Plenipotentiary may, within the period set for the Chambers of the States-General for that purpose, express the wish that the agreement be submitted to explicit approval by the States-General.
(3) The preceding paragraphs apply mutatis mutandis with respect to the termination of international agreements, the first paragraph applies with the provision that the intention of termination is notified to the representative body of the Netherlands Antilles or Aruba, respectively.

Article 25. (1) The King does not commit the Netherlands Antilles or Aruba, respectively, to international economic and financial agreements if the government of the country, indicating the reasons based on which it expects serious detriment from the commitment to the country, has declared that the country should not be committed.
(2) The King does not terminate international economic and financial agreements as regards the Netherlands Antilles or Aruba, respectively, if the government of the country, indicating the reasons based on which it expects serious detriment from the termination to the country, has declared that for the country a termination should not take place. Termination may nevertheless be effected if it is incompatible with the provisions of the agreement that the country be excluded from the termination.

Article 26. If the government of the Netherlands Antilles or of Aruba, respectively, expresses the wish that an international economic or financial agreement should be concluded which is to apply exclusively to the country involved, the government of the Kingdom shall cooperate with a view to such an agreement unless this would be incompatible with the ties of the country within the Kingdom.

Article 27. The Netherlands Antilles and Aruba, respectively, are involved in the preparation of agreements with foreign states which affect them in accordance with Article 11. They are also involved in the execution of agreements which affect them thus and which are binding upon them.

Article 28. On the basis of international agreements concluded by the Kingdom, the Netherlands Antilles and Aruba, respectively, may, if such wish exists, join international organizations as members.

Article 29. (1) The acquisition or guarantee of a credit outside the Kingdom in the name of or at the expense of one of the countries takes place in agreement with the government of the Kingdom.
(2) The council of ministers agrees with the acquisition or guarantee of such credit unless this would be contrary to the interests of the Kingdom.

Article 30. (1) The Netherlands Antilles and Aruba provide the armed forces that are present in their territory with help and assistance which they require in the fulfilment of their task.
(2) By country statute, rules are established to ensure that the armed forces of the Kingdom in the Netherlands Antilles and in Aruba, respectively, can fufil their task.

Article 31. (1) Persons who are resident in the Netherlands Antilles and Aruba may be obliged to serve in the armed forces or in civilian service only by country statute.
(2) It is reserved to the Regulation of State [Staatsregeling] to determine that servicemen serving in the armed forces may be deployed abroad without their consent only pursuant to country statute.

Article 32. In the armed forces for the defence of Netherlands Antilles and of Aruba, respectively, as far as possible persons shall be included who are resident in these countries.

Article 33. (1) For the purposes of defence, the confiscation of property and use of goods, the limitation of property and usage rights, the requisition of services and quartering is effected only under observance of general rules to be laid down by Kingdom Statute which also contain provisions regarding compensation.
(2) In that Kingdom Statute, further regulation is assigned where possible to country institutions.

Article 34. (1) The King may, for the maintenance of external or internal security, in case of war or threat of war or where a threat to or disruption of internal order and peace can lead to a substantial infringement on the interests of the Kingdom, declare each part of the territory in state of war or in state of siege.
(2) By or pursuant to Kingdom Statute the manner is determined in which such declaration is effected and the consequences are regulated.
(3) In this regulation is may be provided that and in which manner competences of bodies of civilian authority regarding public order and policing pass wholly or partly to other bodies of civilian authority or to military authority and that the civilian authorities in that latter case are subordinate to military authorities. Regarding the passing of competences, consultation with the government of the affected country takes place where possible. In that regulation it may be deviated from provisions regarding the freedom of the press, the right of association and assembly as well as the inviolability of the home and the respect for correspondence.
(4) For the territory declared in state of siege, in case of war in a manner determined by Kingdom Statute, military penal law and military penal jurisdiction may be wholly or partly declared applicable to everyone.

Article 35. (1) The Netherlands Antilles and Aruba share, in accordance with their economic strength, the costs connected to the maintenance of the independence and defence of the Kingdom as well as the costs connected to the maintenance of other affairs of the Kingdom to the extent that this benefits the Netherlands Antilles or Aruba respectively.
(2) The share for the Netherlands Antilles and for Aruba, respectively, stipulated in the first paragraph, is determined by the council of ministers for one fiscal year or for several consecutive fiscal years. Article 12 applies mutatis mutandis, with the exception that decisions are taken by unanimity.
(3) Where the determination stipulated in the second paragraph does not take place in time, pending that, for the duration of at most one fiscal year, the share determined in accordance with that paragraph for the previous fiscal year applies.
(4) The preceding paragraphs do not apply to measures for which special arrangements have been established.

§ 3. Mutual assistance, consultation and cooperation

Article 36. The Netherlands, the Netherlands Antilles and Aruba provide to each other aid and assistance.

PART I. CONSTITUTIONAL LAW

Article 36a. (1) The Netherlands, the Netherlands Antilles and Aruba take part in a fund for the maintenance of proper standards of administration in the island territories of Bonaire, Saba and Saint Eustatius of the Netherlands Antilles.
(2) This fund is established by Kingdom Statute.

Article 37. (1) The Netherlands, the Netherlands Antilles and Aruba shall conduct as much consultation as possible regarding all matters where the interests of the countries or of two of them are effected. For that purpose, special representatives may be appointed and common institutions may be established.
(2) As matters in the meaning of this Article are considered, among other things:
a. the promotion of cultural and social ties between the countries;
b. the promotion of effective economic, financial and monetary relations between the countries;
c. questions regarding the coinage and monetary system, banking and foreign-currency policy;
d. the promotion of economic resilience through mutual aid and assistance by the countries;
e. the exercise of professions and businesses by Dutch citizens in the countries;
f. matters regarding aviation, including the policy on unregulated air transportation;
g. matters regarding shipping;
h. cooperation in the field of telegraphy, telephony and radio communications.

Article 38. (1) The Netherlands, the Netherlands Antilles and Aruba may establish regulations between each other.
(2) In mutual consultation it may be provided that such regulations and the change thereof are established by Kingdom Statute or Kingdom Ordinance.
(3) Regarding matters of private law and criminal law of an inter-regional or international nature, regulations may be established by Kingdom Statute if agreement over such regulations exists between the governments of the countries involved.
(4) The matter of the relocation of the seat of legal persons is regulated by Kingdom Statute. On this regulation, agreement between the governments of the countries is required.

Article 39. (1) Private and commercial law, civil procedure, criminal law, criminal procedure, copyright law, industrial property, the office of the notary, as well as provisions regarding measures and weights are regulated as far as possible in an equivalent manner in the Netherlands, the Netherlands Antilles and Aruba.
(2) A proposal for a far-reaching change in the existing legislation on this matter is not introduced in the representative body – or taken into consideration by the representative body – before the governments in the other countries have been given the opportunity to express their views in that matter.

Article 40. Judgments given by the judge in the Netherlands, the Netherlands Antilles or Aruba, and orders issued by him, as well as engrossments of authentic acts issued there, may be executed in the entire Kingdom with due regard to the legal provisions of the country where the execution takes place.

§ 4. The constitutional system of the countries

Article 41. (1) The Netherlands, the Netherlands Antilles and Aruba conduct their own affairs autonomously.
(2) The matters for the Kingdom are among the subjects of concern for the countries.

Article 42. (1) In the Kingdom, the constitutional system of the Netherlands is regulated in the Constitution [Grondwet], the one of the Netherlands Antilles and the one of Aruba in the Regulation of State [Staatsregeling] of the Netherlands Antilles and of Aruba.
(2) The Regulations of State of the Netherlands Antilles and of Aruba are established by country statute [landsverordening]. Each proposal for an amendment of the Regulation of State indicates clearly the proposed amendment. The representative body may not adopt the bill for such a country statute unless by two-thirds of votes cast.

Article 43. (1) Each of the countries ensures the realization of the fundamental human rights and freedoms, legal certainty and proper administration.
(2) The guarantee of these rights, freedoms, legal certainty and proper administration is a matter for the Kingdom.

Article 44. (1) A country statute for an amendment of the Regulation of State regarding:
a. the Articles relating to the fundamental human rights and freedoms;

b. the provisions relating to the competences of the Governor;
c. the Articles relating to the competences of the representative bodies of the countries;
d. the Articles relating to the judiciary,
is transmitted to the government of the Kingdom. It does not enter into force until after the government of the Kingdom has expressed its consent herein.
(2) The provision of the first paragraph also applies to a country statute for an amendment of the Regulation of State of the Netherlands Antilles as regards the distribution of seats in the representative body of the Netherlands Antilles among the different island territories, as well as the regulation of the island territories.
(3) A bill for a country statute regarding the preceding provisions is not presented to the representative body, nor taken into consideration by that body by way of a private member's initiative, until the opinion of the government of the Kingdom is obtained.

Article 45. Amendments to the Constitution [Grondwet] regarding:
a. the Articles relating to the fundamental human rights and freedoms;
b. the provisions relating to the competences of the government;
c. the Articles relating to the competences of the representative body;
d. the Articles relating to the judiciary,
are – notwithstanding the provisions of Article 5 – considered to affect the Netherlands Antilles and Aruba in the meaning of Article 10.

Article 46. (1) The representative bodies are elected by the residents of the country involved who are Dutch citizens, who have reached an age to be determined by the countries, which may not be higher than 25 years. Each voter only casts one vote. The elections are free and secret. If a necessity thereto appears, the countries may establish restrictions. Every Dutch citizen may run in elections, with the provision that the countries may establish a requirement of residence and an age limit.
(2) The countries may confer the right to elect representative bodies to Dutch citizens who are not residents of the country involved, as well as the right to elect representative bodies and the right to run in elections to residents of the country involved who are not Dutch citizens, in any case provided that in that context at least the requirements for residents who are also Dutch citizens are observed.

Article 47. (1) The ministers and the members of the representative body in the countries, before assuming their office, take an oath or make a promise of allegiance to the King and the Charter.
(2) The ministers and the members of the representative body in the Netherlands Antilles and in Aruba take the oath or make the promise before the representative of the King.

Article 48. The countries respect the provisions of the Charter in their legislation and administration.

Article 49. By Kingdom Statute, regulations may be established regarding the binding effect of legislative measures which are incompatible with the Charter, an international regulation, a Kingdom Statute or a Kingdom Ordinance.

Article 50. (1) Legislative and administrative measures in the Netherlands Antilles and Aruba which are incompatible with the Charter, an international regulation, a Kingdom Statute or a Kingdom Ordinance, or with interests the promotion or safeguarding of which is a matter for the Kingdom, may be suspended or annulled by the King as the head of the Kingdom by way of reasoned decree. The proposal for an annulment is issued by the council of ministers.
(2) For the Netherlands, this matter is regulated, where necessary, in the Constitution.

Article 51. (1) If an organ in the Netherlands Antilles or Aruba does not, or does insufficiently perform what it must perform pursuant to the Charter, an international regulation, a Kingdom Statute or a Kingdom Ordinance, then a Kingdom Ordinance, while stating the legal grounds and reasons on which it is based, may determine in which manner this shall be performed.
(2) For the Netherlands, this matter is regulated, where necessary, in the Constitution.

Article 52. Country statute may confer competences with respect to country affairs, with the approval of the King, to the King as head of the Kingdom and to the Governor as an organ of the Kingdom.

PART I. CONSTITUTIONAL LAW

Article 53. If the Netherlands Antilles or Aruba express such wish, the independent supervision of the spending of funds in accordance with the budget of the Netherlands Antilles and the island territories, or of Aruba, respectively, is exercised by the General Chamber of Audit [Algemene Rekenkamer]. In that case, regulations are established after consultation with the Chamber of Audit by Kingdom Statute regarding the cooperation between the Chamber of Audit and the country involved. Thereafter, the government of the country may, upon a proposal from the representative body, appoint someone who is given the opportunity to participate in the deliberations on all matters of the country involved.

§ 5. Transitional and final provisions

Article 54. (Repealed).

Article 55. (1) Amendments to this Charter are effected by Kingdom Statute.
(2) A proposal for an amendment adopted by the States-General is not approved by the King until it has been accepted by the Netherlands Antilles and Aruba. Such acceptance is effected by country statute. Such country statute is not adopted until it has been approved by the Parliaments [Staten] in two readings. If the bill is adopted in the first reading by two-thirds of the votes cast, the adoption is effective immediately. The second reading takes place within one month after the bill has been adopted in first reading.
(3) If and in as far as a proposal for an amendment of the Charter deviates from the Constitution [Grondwet], the proposal is considered in such manner as the Constitution prescribes for proposals for an amendment of the Constitution, with the exception that both Chambers may adopt the proposed amendment in second reading by an absolute majority of votes cast.

Article 56. Authorities, binding statutes, decrees and decisions existing on the moment of the entry into force of the Charter remain in place until they are replaced by others under observance of this Charter. To the extent that the Charter itself regulates any matter differently, the regulation by the Charter applies.

Article 57. Statutes and ordinances which apply in the Netherlands Antilles acquire the status of Kingdom Statute or Kingdom Ordinance, respectively, with the exception that, to the extent that they may pursuant to the Charter be amended by country statute, they acquire the status of country statute.

Article 58. (1) Aruba may declare by country statute that it wishes to terminate the legal order laid down by the Charter regarding Aruba.
(2) The proposal for such country statute is accompanied, when tabled, by an outline of a future constitution including at least provisions regarding fundamental rights, government, representative body, legislation and administration, judiciary and amendment of the constitution.
(3) Parliament may only adopt the proposal by a majority of two thirds of the votes of the sitting members.

Article 59. (1) Within six months after the Parliament of Aruba has adopted the proposal stipulated in Article 58 a referendum regulated by country statute is held whereby those entitled to vote may voice their opinion on the adopted proposal.
(2) The adopted proposal is adopted as country statute only if in the referendum a majority of those entitled to vote has voted in favour of the proposal.

Article 60. (1) After the adoption of the country statute in accordance with Articles 58 and 59 and the approval of the future constitution by the Parliament of Aruba by a majority of two thirds of the votes of the sitting members, by royal decree the moment of the termination of the legal order laid down by the Charter regarding Aruba is established in accordance with the wishes of the government of Aruba.
(2) That moment lies at the latest one month after the date of the adoption of the constitution. That adoption takes place at the latest one year after the date of the referendum stipulated in Article 59.

Article 61. The Charter enters into force on the moment of its ceremonial declaration, after it has been affirmed by the King.
Before the affirmation takes place, the Charter requires, for the Netherlands, approval in a manner provided by the Constitution; for Surinam and the Netherlands Antilles by a decision of the representative body.
This decision is taken by two thirds of votes cast. If such majority is not obtained, the Parliament is dissolved and it is decided by the new Parliament by an absolute majority of votes cast.

Constitution for the Kingdom of the Netherlands [Grondwet voor het Koninkrijk der Nederlanden] of 24 August 1815 as last amended by statute of 16 March 2006 (*Stb.* 170).[7]

Chapter 1. Fundamental rights

Article 1. All persons in the Netherlands are treated equally in equal circumstances. Discrimination on the grounds of religion, belief, political opinion, race, sex or any other ground is not permissible.

Article 2. (1) Statute regulates who is a Dutch citizen.
(2) Statute regulates the admission and expulsion of aliens.
(3) Extradition may only be effected pursuant to a treaty. Further regulations regarding extradition are provided by statute.
(4) Everyone has the right to leave the country, save for cases provided by statute.

Article 3. All Dutch citizens are eligible for appointment in the public service on an equal footing.

Article 4. Every Dutch citizen has the equal right to elect the members of general representative bodies as well as to be elected member of these bodies, save for limitations and exceptions provided by statute.

Article 5. Everyone has the right to submit petitions in writing to the competent authorities.

Article 6. (1) Everyone has the right to freely express his religion or belief, individually or in community with others, save for everybody's responsibility according to law.
(2) Statute may, regarding the exercise of this right outside of buildings and closed locations, provide for regulations for the protection of health, in the interest of traffic and for the combat against and prevention of disorder.

Article 7. (1) No-one requires prior permission in order to publish thoughts or feelings via the press, save for everybody's responsibility according to law.
(2) Statute provides for regulations regarding radio and television. There is no supervision in advance of the content of a radio or television broadcast.
(3) For the publication of thoughts or feelings via means other than the ones stipulated in the preceding paragraphs, no-one requires prior permission regarding the content thereof, save for everybody's responsibility according to law. Statute may regulate the rendering of displays accessible to persons younger than sixteen years of age for the protection of good morals.
(4) The preceding paragraphs do not apply to commercial advertisement.

Article 8. The right of association is recognized. By statute this right may be limited in the interest of the public order.

Article 9. (1) The right of assembly and demonstration is recognized, save for everybody's responsibility according to law.
(2) Statute may provide for regulations for the protection of health, in the interest of traffic and for the combat against and prevention of disorder.

Article 10. (1) Everyone has, save for limitations to be provided by or pursuant to statute, the right to respect for his private life.
(2) Statute provides for regulations for the protection of private life in the context of the recording and transmission of personal data.
(3) Statute provides for regulations regarding the entitlements of persons to insight into the data recorded on them and into the use made thereof, as well as to a correction of such data.

---

[7] Translation by Ph. Kiiver.

PART I. CONSTITUTIONAL LAW

Article 11. Everyone has, save for limitations to be provided by or pursuant to statute, the right to inviolability of his body.

Article 12. (1) The entry into a home without consent of the occupant is permissible only in cases provided by or pursuant to statute, by those who are designated to that end by or pursuant to statute.
(2) An entry in accordance with the preceding paragraph requires prior identification and notification of the purpose of the entry, save for exceptions provided by statute.
(3) A written report on the entry is delivered to the occupant as soon as possible. If the entry has been effected in the interest of national security or of criminal prosecution, the delivery of the report may be postponed in accordance with regulations to be provided by statute. In cases to be provided by statute, the delivery may be omitted if the interest of national security is permanently incompatible with such delivery.

Article 13. (1) The privacy of the correspondence is inviolable except, in cases provided by statute, by order of a judge.
(2) The privacy of telephone and telegraph communications is inviolable except, in cases provided by statute, by or with the authorization of those designated to that end by statute.

Article 14. (1) Expropriation may be effected only in the general interest and for a previously guaranteed compensation, all of which in accordance with regulations to be provided by or pursuant to statute.
(2) Compensation need not be guaranteed beforehand if in a case of emergency immediate expropriation is called for.
(3) In cases provided by or pursuant to statute there is a right to compensation or partial compensation if, in the general interest, by competent authorities property is being destroyed or made unusable or the exercise of ownership rights is being limited.

Article 15. (1) Save for cases provided by or pursuant to statute, no-one may be deprived of his freedom.
(2) He who is deprived of his freedom on a basis other than upon court order may request his release to a judge. In that case he is heard by the judge within a period to be provided by statute. The judge orders immediate release if he considers the deprivation of freedom unlawful.
(3) The trial of him who is deprived of his freedom with a view thereto, takes place within reasonable time.
(4) He who is lawfully deprived of his freedom may be limited in the exercise of his fundamental rights in as far as such exercise is not compatible with the deprivation of freedom.

Article 16. No act is punishable except by virtue of a prior statutory criminal provision.

Article 17. No-one may against his will be barred from access to the judge that statute accords him.

Article 18. (1) Everyone may be aided in court and in administrative appeal.
(2) Statute provides for regulations regarding the provision of legal aid to persons of limited means.

Article 19. (1) The promotion of sufficient employment is a subject of concern for the state authority.
(2) Statute provides for regulations regarding the legal position of those who are engaged in an employment and regarding their protection therein, as well as regarding co-determination.
(3) The right of every Dutch citizen to a free choice of his occupation is recognized, save for limitations provided by or pursuant to statute.

Article 20. (1) The securing of means of subsistence of the population and the promotion of welfare is a subject of concern for the state authority.
(2) Statute provides for regulations regarding entitlements to social security.
(3) Dutch citizens in this country who cannot provide for their own subsistence have a right to state assistance to be regulated by statute.

Article 21. Concern of the state authority is directed at the habitability of the land and the protection and improvement of the environment.

Article 22. (1) State authority takes measures to promote public health.
(2) The promotion of sufficient living space is a subject of concern for the state authority.
(3) It creates conditions for social and cultural development and for leisure activity.

Article 23. (1) Education is a subject of permanent concern for the government.
(2) Teaching is free, save for state supervision and, as regards forms of education designated by statute, the monitoring of the competence and morality of those who teach, all of which is to be regulated by statute.
(3) Public education is regulated by statute with due respect to the religion or belief of everyone.
(4) In each municipality, sufficient public primary education is offered by the state in a sufficient number of public schools. In accordance with regulations to be provided by statute, deviations from this provision may be permitted as long as an opportunity to receive such education is provided, whether or not in a public school.
(5) The requirements of the appropriateness to be applied to education to be financed wholly or partly from the public purse are regulated by statute with due respect for, as far as special education [bijzonder onderwijs] is concerned, the freedom of underlying direction.
(6) These requirements are regulated for primary education in such manner that the appropriateness of special education financed wholly from the public purse and of public education is equally ensured. In the context of such regulation, in particular the freedom of special education regarding the choice of means of teaching and employment of teachers is respected.
(7) Special primary education which complies with the conditions to be provided by statute is financed from the public purse under the same criteria as public education. Statute provides the conditions under which contributions from the public purse are granted to special secondary and higher secondary education.
(8) The government reports annually to the States-General on the state of the education system.

Chapter 2. Government

§1. The King

Article 24. The crown is vested by hereditary succession in the lawful successors of King William I, Prince of Orange-Nassau.

Article 25. The crown passes, in the case of the death of the King, by virtue of hereditary succession to his lawful descendants, in which case the oldest child takes precedence, with further passage of the crown taking place according to the same rule. When there are no descendants of his own, the crown passes in an equal manner to the lawful descendants first of his parent, then of his grandparent, in the line of hereditary succession as long as they are blood relatives not more than thrice removed from the deceased King.

Article 26. The child which a woman carries at the moment of the death of the King is deemed already born for the purposes of hereditary succession. If it is stillborn, it is deemed never to have existed.

Article 27. Abdication leads to hereditary succession in accordance with the rules provided in the preceding Articles. Children born after the abdication, and their descendants, are excluded from hereditary succession.

Article 28. (1) The King who enters into a marriage without approval granted by statute thereby abdicates.
(2) If someone who can inherit the crown from the King enters into such marriage, then he is, together with the children born within that marriage, and their descendants, excluded from hereditary succession.
(3) The States-General deliberate and decide on a bill to grant approval in joint session.

Article 29. (1) If exceptional circumstances so require, one or more persons may be excluded from hereditary succession by statute.
(2) The bill for that purpose is submitted by or on behalf of the King. The States-General deliberate and decide on the matter in joint session. They may adopt the bill only with at least two-thirds of the number of votes cast.

Article 30. (1) If there is a prospect that there shall be no successor, he may be appointed by statute. The bill for that purpose is submitted by or on behalf of the King. After the submission of the bill, the Chambers are dissolved. The new Chambers deliberate and decide on the matter in joint session. They may adopt the bill only with at least two-thirds of the number of votes cast.
(2) If at the death of the King or at abdication there is no successor, the Chambers are dissolved. The new Chambers convene within four months after the death or abdication in joint session in order to decide on the appointment of a King. They may appoint a successor only with at least two-thirds of the number of votes cast.

PART I. CONSTITUTIONAL LAW

Article 31. (1) An appointed King may be succeeded by hereditary succession only by his lawful descendants.
(2) The provisions regarding hereditary succession and the first paragraph of this Article apply mutatis mutandis to an appointed successor as long as he is not yet King.

Article 32. After the King has assumed the exercise of royal authority, he is as soon as possible sworn in and inaugurated in the capital city of Amsterdam in a public joint session of the States-General. He swears or promises allegiance to the Constitution and loyal exercise of his office. Statute provides further regulations.

Article 33. The King exercises royal authority only after he has attained the age of eighteen years.

Article 34. Statute regulates parental authority and guardianship over the King who is a minor and the supervision thereof. The States-General deliberate and decide on the matter in joint session.

Article 35. (1) If the council of ministers concludes that the King is incapable of exercising royal authority, it reports this, submitting the advice of the Council of State requested on the matter, to the States-General, which convene on the matter in a joint session.
(2) If the States-General share this conclusion, they declare that the King is incapable of exercising royal authority. Such declaration is published by order of the chairman of the session and enters into force immediately.
(3) As soon as the King is capable again of exercising royal authority, this is declared by statute. The States-General deliberate and decide on the matter in joint session. Immediately after the publication of this statute, the King resumes the exercise of royal authority.
(4) Statute regulates, where necessary, the supervision over the person of the King if he is declared incapable of exercising royal authority. The States-General deliberate and decide on the matter in joint session.

Article 36. The King may temporarily suspend the exercise of royal authority and resume such exercise by virtue of a statute, the bill for which is submitted by or on behalf of himself. The States-General deliberate and decide on the matter in joint session.

Article 37. (1) Royal authority is exercised by a regent:
a. as long as the King has not attained the age of eighteen years;
b. if a child not yet born can be called to take over the crown;
c. if the King has been declared incapable of exercising royal authority;
d. if the King has temporarily suspended the exercise of royal authority;
e. as long as after the death of the King or his abdication there is no successor.
(2) The regent is appointed by statute. The States-General deliberate and decide on the matter in joint session.
(3) In the cases stipulated in the first paragraph under c. and d., the descendant of the King who is his presumed successor is regent by operation of law, if he has attained the age of eighteen years.
(4) The regent swears or promises allegiance to the Constitution and loyal exercise of his office in a joint session of the States-General. Statute provides further regulations regarding regency and may provide for succession and replacement therein. The States-General deliberate and decide on the matter in joint session.
(5) Articles 35 and 36 apply to the regent mutatis mutandis.

Article 38. As long as the exercise of royal authority is not secured, it is exercised by the Council of State [Raad van State].

Article 39. Statute regulates who is a member of the royal house.

Article 40. (1) The King annually receives allowances charged to the Kingdom in accordance with rules to be provided by statute. That statute determines which other members of the royal house receive allowances charged to the Kingdom and regulates these allowances.
(2) The allowances charged to the Kingdom received by them, as well as assets which serve the exercise of their function, are exempt from personal taxation. Furthermore, what the King or his presumed successor receives from a member of the royal house by virtue of inheritance or gift, is exempt from inheritance, transfer and gift taxation. Further exemption from taxation may be granted by statute.
(3) The Chambers of the States-General may adopt bills for statutes stipulated in the preceding paragraphs only with at least two-thirds of the number of votes cast.

Article 41. The King organizes, with due respect for the public interest, his household.

§ 2. King and ministers

Article 42. (1) The government comprises the King and the ministers.
(2) The King is inviolable; the ministers are responsible.

Article 43. The Prime-Minister [minister-president] and the other ministers are appointed and dismissed by royal decree.

Article 44. (1) Ministries are established by royal decree. They are placed under the direction of a minister.
(2) Furthermore, ministers may be appointed who are not charged with directing a ministry.

Article 45. (1) The ministers together form the council of ministers [ministerraad].
(2) The Prime-Minister is chairman of the council of ministers.
(3) The council of ministers deliberates and decides on general government policy and promotes the unity of that policy.

Article 46. (1) Secretaries of state may be appointed by royal decree.
(2) A secretary of state [staatssecretaris] assumes, in the cases where the minister finds it necessary and with due regard to his instructions, his position as minister. The secretary of state is in that context responsible, notwithstanding the responsibility of the minister.

Article 47. All statutes and royal decrees are signed by the King and by one or more ministers or secretaries of state.

Article 48. The royal decree whereby a Prime-Minister is appointed, is signed also by him. The royal decrees whereby the other ministers and the secretaries of state are appointed or dismissed are signed also by the Prime-Minister.

Article 49. In a manner provided by statute, the ministers and secretaries of state, when assuming office, take an oath or make a declaration and promise before the King of their integrity, and swear or promise allegiance to the Constitution and loyal exercise of their office.

Chapter 3. States-General

§1. Organization and composition

Article 50. The States-General [Staten-Generaal] represent the entire Dutch people.

Article 51. (1) The States-General consist of the Second Chamber [Tweede Kamer] and the First Chamber [Eerste Kamer].
(2) The Second Chamber consists of one hundred and fifty members.
(3) The First Chamber consists of seventy-five members.
(4) In a joint session, the two Chambers are considered as one.

Article 52. (1) The term of session of both Chambers is four years.
(2) If for the provincial assemblies [provinciale staten] a term other than four years is established by statute, the term of session of the First Chamber is changed accordingly.

Article 53. (1) The members of both Chambers are elected on the basis of proportional representation within the limits to be provided by statute.
(2) Elections take place by secret ballot.

Article 54. (1) The members of the Second Chamber are elected directly by Dutch citizens who have attained the age of eighteen years, save for exceptions to be provided by statute with regard to Dutch citizens who are not residents.
(2) The following are excluded from the right to vote:

a. he who has been convicted to a prison sentence of at least one year for a criminal act so designated by statute in a final court judgment and who has at the same time been disqualified from the right to vote;
b. he who by virtue of a final court judgment has been declared incapable of carrying out legal acts because of a mental disorder.

Article 55. The members of the First Chamber are elected by the members of the provincial assemblies [provinciale staten]. The elections take place, save for the event of a dissolution of the Chamber, within three months following the elections of the members of the provincial assemblies.

Article 56. In order to be able to become a member of the States-General, it is required that one be a Dutch citizen, have attained the age of eighteen years, and not be disqualified from the right to vote.

Article 57. (1) No-one may be a member of both Chambers.
(2) A member of the Second Chamber may not at the same time be a minister, secretary of state, member of the Council of State, member of the General Chamber of Audit, National Ombudsman or substitute ombudsman, or a member of or procurator-general or advocate-general at the Supreme Court.
(3) Nevertheless a minister or secretary of state, who has tendered his resignation, may combine this office with a membership of the States-General, until a decision has been taken regarding that resignation.
(4) Statute may provide with regard to other public offices that they may not be exercised at the same time as the membership of the States-General or of one of the Chambers.

Article 57a. Statute regulates the temporary replacement of a member of the States-General because of pregnancy and delivery as well as because of illness.

Article 58. Each Chamber examines the letters patent of its newly appointed members and decides, with due regard to the regulations to be provided by statute, on disputes that arise with respect to the letters patent or the election itself.

Article 59. Everything else regarding the right to vote and the elections is regulated by statute.

Article 60. In a manner provided by statute, the members of the Chambers, when assuming their office, take an oath or make a declaration and promise in the assembly of their integrity, and swear or promise allegiance to the Constitution and loyal exercise of their office.

Article 61. (1) Each of the Chambers appoints a president from among the members.
(2) Each of the Chambers appoints a secretary. He and the other administrative staff of the Chambers may not at the same time be members of the States-General.

Article 62. The president of the First Chamber has the chairmanship over the joint session.

Article 63. Financial consideration for members and former members of the States-General and their surviving dependants are regulated by statute. The Chambers may adopt a bill on this matter only with at least two-thirds of the number of votes cast.

Article 64. (1) Each of the Chambers may be dissolved by royal decree.
(2) Each decree on such dissolution also contains an order for new elections to the dissolved Chamber and for the convention of the newly elected Chamber within three months.
(3) The dissolution takes effect on the day when the newly elected Chamber convenes.
(4) Statute determines the duration of the term of session of a Second Chamber operating after dissolution; the period may not be longer than five years. The term of session of a First Chamber operating after dissolution ends on the moment when the term of the dissolved Chamber would have ended.

§ 2. Procedures

Article 65. Annually, on the third Tuesday of September or at an earlier moment to be determined by statute, an explanation is given by or on behalf of the King in a joint session of the States-General regarding the policies to be pursued by the government.

Article 66. (1) The meetings of the States-General are public.
(2) The doors are closed when a tenth part of the number of members present so demand or when the president deems it necessary.
(3) The Chamber or the Chambers in joint session, respectively, then decide whether they should deliberate and decide with closed doors.

Article 67. (1) The Chambers may, each separately and in joint session, deliberate and decide only if more than half of the number of members in office is present at the meeting.
(2) Decisions are taken by a majority of votes.
(3) The members vote without any instructions.
(4) Matters are voted on orally and by individual calls when one member so demands.

Article 68. The ministers and the secretaries of state provide the Chambers, separately and in joint session, orally or in writing the information demanded by one or more members, where such provision is not in conflict with the interest of the state.

Article 69. (1) The ministers and the secretaries of state have access to the meetings and may participate in deliberations.
(2) They may be invited by the Chambers, separately and in joint session, to be present at the meeting.
(3) They may be assisted at the meeting by persons designated by them for that purpose.

Article 70. Both Chambers, both separately and in joint session, have the right of inquiry (enquête) to be regulated by statute.

Article 71. The members of the States-General, the ministers, the secretaries of state and other persons who participate in deliberations may not be prosecuted or held liable for what they have said in the meetings of the States-General or in committees thereof, of for what they have submitted to them in writing.

Article 72. The Chambers, both separately and in joint session, adopt rules of procedure.

Chapter 4. Council of State, General Chamber of Audit, National Ombudsman and permanent advisory bodies

Article 73. (1) The Council of State [Raad van State] or a division of the Council is heard on bills and drafts for ordinances [algemene maatregelen van bestuur] as well as proposals for the ratification of treaties by the States-General. In cases to be provided by statute, such hearing may be omitted.
(2) The Council or a division of the Council is charged with the investigation in administrative disputes that are decided by royal decree, and proposes a decision.
(3) Statute may charge the Council or a division of the Council with deciding in administrative disputes.

Article 74. (1) The King is the president of the Council of State. The presumed successor of the King is a member of the Council by operation of law after having attained the age of eighteen years. By or pursuant to statute, other members of the royal house may be granted membership of the Council.
(2) The members of the Council are appointed for life by royal decree.
(3) They are dismissed upon their own request and because they have attained an age to be provided by statute.
(4) In cases provided by statute they may be suspended or dismissed by the Council.
(5) Statute regulates the further details of their legal position.

Article 75. (1) Statute regulates the organization, composition and competence of the Council of State.
(2) By statute, also other tasks may be assigned to the Council or a division of the Council.

Article 76. The General Chamber of Audit [Algemene Rekenkamer] is charged with investigating the revenue and expenditure of the Kingdom.

Article 77. (1) The members of the General Chamber of Audit are appointed by royal decree for life from a proposal of three persons drawn up by the Second Chamber of the States-General.
(2) They are dismissed upon their own request and because they have attained an age to be provided by statute.

(3) In cases provided by statute they may be suspended or dismissed by the Supreme Court [Hoge Raad].
(4) Statute regulates the further details of their legal position.

Article 78. (1) Statute regulates the organization, composition and competence of the General Chamber of Audit.
(2) By statute, also other tasks may be assigned to the General Chamber of Audit.

Article 78a. (1) The National Ombudsman, upon request or on his own motion, conducts investigations into the conduct of administrative authorities of the Kingdom and of other administrative authorities designated by or pursuant to statute.
(2) The National Ombudsman and a substitute ombudsman are appointed for a term to be provided by statute by the Second Chamber of the States-General. They are dismissed upon their own request and because they have attained an age to be provided by statute. In cases provided by statute they may be suspended or dismissed by the Second Chamber of the States-General. Statute regulates the further details of their legal position.
(3) Statutes regulates the competence and procedures of the National Ombudsman.
(4) By or pursuant to statute, also other tasks may be assigned to the National Ombudsman.

Article 79. (1) Permanent advisory bodies in matters of legislation and administration of the Kingdom are established by or pursuant to statute.
(2) Statute regulates the organization, composition and competence of such bodies.
(3) By or pursuant to statute, also tasks other than advisory ones may be assigned to such bodies.

Article 80. (1) The opinions of the bodies stipulated in this chapter are published in accordance with procedures to be provided by statute.
(2) Opinions given on the matter of bills which are introduced by or on behalf of the King are, save for exceptions to be provided by statute, transmitted to the States-General.

Chapter 5. Legislation and administration

§ 1. Statutes and other regulations

Article 81. Statutes [wetten] are adopted jointly by the government and the States-General.

Article 82. (1) Bills may be introduced by or on behalf of the King and by the Second Chamber of the States-General.
(2) Bills for which deliberation in the States-General in joint session is prescribed may be introduced by or on behalf of the King and, as far as the relevant Articles of Chapter 2 allow, by the joint session.
(3) Bills to be introduced by the Second Chamber or the joint session, respectively, are tabled by one or more of the members.

Article 83. Bills introduced by or on behalf of the King are transmitted to the Second Chamber or, if deliberation in the States-General in joint session is prescribed, to that assembly.

Article 84. (1) As long as a bill introduced by or on behalf of the King has not yet been adopted by the Second Chamber or the joint session, respectively, it may be amended by it, on the proposal of one or more members, and by the government.
(2) As long as the Second Chamber or the joint session, respectively, has not yet adopted a bill to be introduced by itself, it may be amended by it on the proposal of one or more members and by the member or members who have tabled the bill.

Article 85. As soon as the Second Chamber has adopted a bill or has decided to introduce a bill, it transmits it to the First Chamber, which considers it as transmitted to it by the Second Chamber. The Second Chamber may instruct one or more of its members to defend a bill introduced by it in the First Chamber.

Article 86. (1) As long as a bill has not yet been adopted by the States-General, it may be withdrawn by or on behalf of the initiator.
(2) As long as the Second Chamber or the joint session, respectively, has not yet adopted a bill to be introduced by it, it may be withdrawn by the member or members who have tabled it.

Article 87. (1) A bill becomes a statute as soon as it has been adopted by the States-General and confirmed by the King.
(2) The King and the States-General inform each other of their decision regarding any bill.

Article 88. Statute regulates the publication and entry into force of statutes. They do not enter into force before they have been published.

Article 89. (1) Ordinances [algemene maatregelen van bestuur] are adopted by royal decree.
(2) Regulations to be enforced by sanctions are provided there only pursuant to statute. Statute regulates the sanctions to be imposed.
(3) Statute regulates the publication and entry into force of ordinances. They do not enter into force before they have been published.
(4) The second and third paragraph apply mutatis mutandis to other generally binding regulations adopted by the Kingdom.

§ 2. Further provisions

Article 90. The government promotes the development of the international legal order.

Article 91. (1) The Kingdom is not bound by treaties and they are not terminated without prior approval of the States-General. Statute provides the cases where no such approval is required.
(2) Statute provides the manner in which approval is given and may provide for tacit approval.
(3) If a treaty contains provisions which deviate from the Constitution or necessitate such deviation, the Chambers may give approval only with at least two-thirds of the number of votes cast.

Article 92. Subject, where necessary, to the provisions of Article 91 (3), legislative, executive and judicial powers may be conferred upon international organizations by or pursuant to a treaty.

Article 93. Provisions of treaties and of decisions of international organizations, which by virtue of their content can be binding upon everyone, become binding after they have been published.

Article 94. Statutory regulations in force within the Kingdom are not applicable if such application is incompatible with provisions of treaties and decisions of international organizations that are binding on everyone.

Article 95. Statute provides regulations regarding the publication of treaties and decisions of international organizations.

Article 96. (1) The Kingdom is not declared to be in a state of war unless after prior consent of the States-General.
(2) Such consent is not required when consultation with the States-General has proven to be impossible as a result of a state of war existing in fact.
(3) The States-General deliberate and decide on the matter in a joint session.
(4) The provisions of the first and the third paragraph apply mutatis mutandis to a declaration that a war has ended.

Article 97. (1) For the purposes of defence and for the protection of the interests of the Kingdom, as well as for the upholding and promotion of the international legal order, there are armed forces.
(2) The government has the supreme command over the armed forces.

Article 98. (1) The armed forces consist of volunteers and may also comprise conscripts.
(2) Statute regulates compulsory military service and the power to defer drafting into actual service.

Article 99. Statute regulates exemption from military service because of serious conscientious objections.

Article 99a. In accordance with regulations to be provided by statute, obligations may be imposed for the purposes of civil defence.

Article 100. (1) The government provides the States-General with information in advance regarding the deployment or the making available of the armed forces for the upholding and promotion of the international legal

order. That includes information in advance regarding the deployment or the making available of the armed forces for humanitarian assistance in case of an armed conflict.
(2) The first paragraph does not apply if pressing reasons prevent the provision of information in advance. In that case, information is provided as soon as possible.

Articles 101 and 102. (Repealed).

Article 103. (1) Statute regulates in which cases, for the maintenance of external and internal security, a state of emergency to be designated as such by statute may be declared by royal decree; statute regulates the consequences.
(2) In that context, deviations are permissible from the constitutional provisions regarding the competences of the governments of the provinces, municipalities and water boards, from the fundamental rights regulated in Article 6, in as far as the exercise of the right stipulated in that Article outside buildings and closed locations is concerned, 7, 8, 9, 12 (2) and (3) and 13, as well as from Article 113 (1) and (3).
(3) Immediately after the declaration of a state of emergency and then, as long as it has not been lifted by royal decree, each time they consider it necessary, the States-General decide on the continuation thereof; they deliberate and decide on the matter in joint session.

Article 104. Taxes of the Kingdom are raised by virtue of a statute. Other charges of the Kingdom are regulated by statute.

Article 105. (1) The budget of the revenue and expenditure of the Kingdom is established by statute.
(2) Annually, bills for general budget statutes are introduced by or on behalf of the King on the moment provided in Article 65.
(3) Account for the revenue and expenditure of the Kingdom is given to the States-General in accordance with the provisions of statute. The accounts approved by the General Chamber of Audit are submitted to the States-General.
(4) Statute provides regulations regarding the administration of the finances of the Kingdom.

Article 106. Statute regulates the monetary system.

Article 107. (1) Statute regulates private law, criminal law and civil and criminal procedure in general codes, save for the power to regulate certain subject-matters in separate statutes.
(2) Statute provides general rules of administrative law.

Article 108. (Repealed).

Article 109. Statute regulates the legal position of civil servants. It also provides regulations regarding their protection at work and regarding co-determination.

Article 110. The state respects openness in the exercise of its tasks in accordance with regulations to be provided by statute.

Article 111. Chivalric orders are established by statute.

Chapter 6. Judiciary

Article 112. (1) The judiciary is charged with adjudicating in disputes over rights and claims of private law.
(2) Statute may assign the adjudication in disputes which did not arise from private law relations either to the judiciary or to courts which do not form part of the judiciary. Statute regulates the procedures and the consequences of decisions.

Article 113. (1) The judiciary is furthermore charged with adjudicating on criminal acts.
(2) Disciplinary jurisdiction established by the state is regulated by statute.
(3) A sentence of deprivation of freedom may be imposed only by the judiciary.
(4) For adjudication outside the Netherlands and for military criminal law, statute may provide deviating regulations.

Article 114. The death penalty may not be imposed.

Article 115. With regard to disputes stipulated in Article 112 (2), administrative appeal may be allowed.

Article 116. (1) Statute designates the courts that form part of the judiciary.
(2) Statute regulates the organization, composition and competence of the judiciary.
(3) Statute may provide that persons not belonging to the judiciary participate in the jurisprudence thereof.
(4) Statute regulates the supervision by members of the judiciary charged with jurisprudence to be exercised over the exercise of the office of such members and of persons stipulated in the preceding paragraph.

Article 117. (1) The members of the judiciary charged with jurisprudence and the procurator-general at the Supreme Court are appointed by royal decree for life.
(2) They are dismissed upon their own request and because they have attained an age to be provided by statute.
(3) In cases provided by statute they may be suspended or dismissed by a court forming part of the judiciary designated by statute.
(4) Statute regulates the further details of their legal position.

Article 118. (1) The members of the Supreme Court [Hoge Raad] of the Netherlands are appointed from a proposal of three persons drawn up by the Second Chamber of the States-General.
(2) The Supreme Court is charged, in the cases and within the boundaries provided by statute, with cassation of judicial decisions because of a violation of the law.
(3) By statute, also other tasks may be assigned to the Supreme Court.

Article 119. The members of the States-General, the ministers and the secretaries of state are prosecuted for crimes committed in office, also after their leaving office, before the Supreme Court. The order to prosecute is given by royal decree or by a decision of the Second Chamber.

Article 120. The judge does not enter into a review of the constitutionality of statutes and treaties.

Article 121. Save for cases provided by statute, trials are conducted in public and judgments contain the reasons on which they are based. The judgment is handed down in public.

Article 122. (1) Pardon is granted by royal decree after the advice of a court designated by statute and with due regard to regulations to be provided by or pursuant to statute.
(2) Amnesty is granted by or pursuant to statute.

Chapter 7. Provinces, municipalities, water boards and other public entities

Article 123. (1) By statute, provinces [provincies] and municipalities [gemeenten] may be dissolved and new ones may be established.
(2) Statute regulates the change of provincial and municipal borders.

Article 124. (1) For provinces and municipalities, the power of regulation and administration regarding their local affairs [huishouding] is left to their governments.
(2) Regulation and administration may be demanded of the governments of provinces and municipalities by or pursuant to statute.

Article 125. (1) The head of the province and the municipality is the provincial assembly [provinciale staten] and the municipal council [gemeenteraad], respectively. Their meetings are public, save for exceptions to be regulated by statute.
(2) The government [bestuur] of the province also includes the provincial executive [gedeputeerde staten] and the King's Commissioner, the government of the municipality also includes the board of burgomaster and aldermen and the burgomaster.
(3) The King's Commissioner and the burgomaster are chairmen of the meetings of the provincial assembly and the municipal council, respectively.

Part I. Constitutional Law

Article 126. Statute may provide that the King's Commissioner is furthermore charged with the execution of an official instruction given by the government.

Article 127. The provincial assembly and the municipal council adopt, save for exceptions provided by statute or by them pursuant to statute, the provincial and the municipal ordinances [verordeningen], respectively.

Article 128. Save for the cases stipulated in Article 123, the conferral of powers within the meaning of Article 124 (1) to organs other than the ones stipulated in Article 125 may be effected only by the provincial assembly and the municipal council, respectively.

Article 129. (1) The members of the provincial assembly and of the municipal council are elected directly by Dutch citizens who are at the same time residents of the province or municipality, respectively, who fulfil the conditions that apply to elections of the Second Chamber of the States-General. For membership the same conditions apply.
(2) The members are elected on the basis of proportional representation within the limits to be provided by statute.
(3) Articles 53 (2) and 59 apply. Article 57a applies mutatis mutandis.
(4) The term of session of the provincial assembly and the municipal council is four years, save for exceptions to be provided by statute.
(5) Statute provides which offices may not be exercised simultaneously with membership. Statute may provide that disqualifications derive from family relation or marriage and that the commission of acts designated by statute may lead to a loss of membership.
(6) Members vote without instructions.

Article 130. Statute may confer the right to elect the members of the municipal council and the right to be a member of the municipal council to residents who are not Dutch citizens, as long as they at least fulfil the conditions that apply to residents who are also Dutch citizens.

Article 131. The King's Commissioner and the burgomaster are appointed by royal decree.

Article 132. (1) Statute regulates the organization of provinces and municipalities as well as the composition and competence of their governments.
(2) Statute regulates supervision of these governments.
(3) Decisions of these governments may be subjected to supervision in advance only in cases to be provided by or pursuant to statute.
(4) Annulment of decisions of these governments may only be effected by royal decree because of a violation of the law or the general interest.
(5) Statute regulates provisions in case of a non-performance with regard to regulation and administration demanded by virtue of Article 124 (2). By statute, provisions in deviation from Articles 125 and 127 may be effected in case the government of a province or a municipality grossly neglects its tasks.
(6) Statute provides which taxes may be raised by the governments of provinces and municipalities and regulates their financial relation with the Kingdom.

Article 133. (1) The dissolution and establishment of water boards [waterschappen], the regulation of their tasks and organization, as well as the composition of their governing bodies is effected, in accordance with regulations to be provided by statute, by provincial ordinance, in as far as nothing is provided otherwise by or pursuant to statute.
(2) Statute regulates the regulatory and other competences of the governing bodies of water boards, as well as the public character of their meetings.
(3) Statute regulates the provincial and further supervision of these governing bodies. Annulment of decisions of these governing bodies may be effected only because of a violation of the law or the general interest.

Article 134. (1) By or pursuant to statute, public entities for professions and enterprises and other public entities may be established and dissolved.
(2) Statute regulates the tasks and the organization of these public entities, the composition and competence of their governing bodies, as well as the public character of their meetings. By or pursuant to statute, regulatory competence may be conferred upon their governing bodies.
(3) Statute regulates the supervision of these governing bodies. Annulment of decisions of these governing bodies may be effected only because of a violation of the law or the general interest.

Article 135. Statute provides regulations for provisions in cases where two or more public entities are involved. In that context, the establishment of a new public entity may be provided for, in which case Article 134 (2) and (3) applies.

Article 136. Disputes between public entities are resolved by royal decree, unless they fall under the jurisdiction of the judiciary or such resolution is assigned by statute to others.

Chapter 8. Revision of the Constitution

Article 137. (1) A statute declares that an amendment of the Constitution as it proposes shall be considered.
(2) The Second Chamber may, whether or not upon such proposal introduced by or on behalf of the King, split a bill for such a statute.
(3) After the publication of the statute stipulated in the first paragraph, the Second Chamber is dissolved.
(4) After the new Second Chamber has convened, both Chambers consider in second reading the proposal for an amendment stipulated in the first paragraph. They may adopt it only with at least two-thirds of the number of votes cast.
(5) The Second Chamber may, whether or not upon such proposal introduced by or on behalf of the King, split a proposal for an amendment with at least two-thirds of the number of votes cast.

Article 138. (1) Before the proposals for an amendment of the Constitution adopted in second reading are confirmed by the King, by statute:
a. the adopted proposals and the provisions of the Constitution left unchanged may be adjusted to one another as far as necessary;
b. the division and position of chapters, sections and Articles as well as the titles may be modified.
(2) The Chambers may adopt a bill containing provisions stipulated in the first paragraph, sub a., only with at least two-thirds of the number of votes cast.

Article 139. The amendments of the Constitution, adopted by the States-General and confirmed by the King, enter into force immediately after they have been published.

Article 140. Existing statutes and other regulations and decisions which are incompatible with an amendment of the Constitution remain in force until a provision on that matter is effected in accordance with the Constitution.

Article 141. The text of the revised Constitution is published by royal decree, in which context chapters, sections and Articles may be renumbered and references be changed accordingly.

Article 142. The Constitution may by statute be brought into line with the Charter for the Kingdom of the Netherlands [Statuut voor het Koninkrijk der Nederlanden]. Articles 139, 140 and 141 apply mutatis mutandis.

[The supplementary provisions are omitted.]

Elections Act [Kieswet] of 28 September 1989 as amended. Selected provisions: Articles P1, P5 to P7, P9, P10, P15, P19, U1, U2(1), U3, U7 to U10 and U15.[8]

[Part I is omitted.]

Part II. The elections of the members of the Second Chamber of the States-General, of provincial assemblies and of the municipal councils

[Chapters B to O are omitted.]

Chapter P. The establishment of the election results by the central polling office

§ 1. General provision

Article P 1. Immediately after the copies of the records of all main polling offices have been received, the central polling office starts carrying out the activities for the establishment of the results of the elections. If elections of the municipal council or the provincial assembly of a province which forms a single polling district is concerned, the central elections office starts these activities immediately after the activities stipulated in Articles O 1 and O 2 have been concluded.

§ 2. The distribution of seats

[Articles P2 to P4 are omitted.]

Article P 5. (1) The central polling office divides the sum of the number of votes of all lists by the number of seats to be distributed.
(2) The quotient thus obtained is called electoral divisor.

Article P 6. A list is assigned a seat so many times as the electoral divisor is accommodated in the number of votes of that list.

Article P 7. (1) The remaining seats, which are called rest seats, are, if the number of seats to be distributed is nineteen or more, consecutively assigned to those lists which after assignment of a seat have the largest average number of votes per assigned seat. If averages are equal, the lot decides where necessary.
(2) If the election of the members of the Second Chamber is concerned, lists the number of votes of which is lower than the electoral divisor are not entitled to such assignment.

[Article P 8 is omitted.]

Article P 9. If a list which has received an absolute majority of votes cast is assigned a number of seats that is smaller than the absolute majority of seats to be distributed, that list is assigned one additional seat and, at the same time, one seat is forfeited that had been assigned to the list which had received a seat for the smallest average or the smallest remainder. If two or more lists had received a seat for the same smallest average or the smallest remainder, the lot decides.

Article P 10. If in the application of the preceding provisions a list would have to be assigned more seats than there are candidates, the remaining seat or seats pass by continued application of these provisions to one or more of the other lists on which candidates appear to whom no seat has been assigned.

[Articles P 11 to P 14 are omitted.]

---

[8] Translation by Ph. Kiiver.

PART I. CONSTITUTIONAL LAW

§ 3. The assignment of the seats to the candidates

Article P 15. (1) In the order of the number of votes cast for them, those candidates are elected who, on the common lists on which they appear, have received a number of votes that is larger than 25% of the electoral divisor, as long as that group of lists, that number of identical lists that do not belong to a group of lists or that separate list has received sufficient seats. If numbers are equal, the lot decides where necessary.
(2) If the number of seats to be distributed in the elections is lower than nineteen, then, in the application of the first paragraph, not 25% of the electoral divisor but half of the electoral divisor shall be applied.

[Articles P 16 to P 18a are omitted.]

Article P 19. (1) The central polling office ranks, with respect to each list or number of identical lists, the candidates appearing thereon in such manner that the candidates to whom a seat is assigned by application of Article P 15 come on top, in the order in which the seats have been assigned.
(2) Subsequently, in the order of the numbers cast for them, candidates appearing on the list or number of identical lists are ranked who have, on the common lists on which they appear, received a number of votes that is larger than 25% of the electoral divisor or larger than half of the electoral divisor, respectively, but who have not been declared elected by application of Article P 15 (1) or (2), respectively. If numbers are equal, the order of the list decides.
(3) Finally, in the order of the list, the other candidates appearing on the list or number of identical lists are ranked.
(4) Article P 18 remains inapplicable at the ranking.
(5) Save for elections of the members of municipal councils with nine or eleven members, the ranking shall be omitted as far as lists or numbers of identical lists are concerned on which no candidates have been declared elected and which do not form part of a combination of lists or group of lists to which one or more seats have been assigned.

[The remainder of Chapter P is omitted.]

Part III. The election of the members of the First Chamber of the States-General

[Chapters Q to T are omitted.]

Chapter U. The establishment of the election results by the central polling office

§ 1. General provisions

Article U 1. Immediately after the records have been received, the central polling office starts carrying out the activities for the establishment of the results of the elections.

Article U 2. (1) Each vote counts, depending on the province where it has been cast, as a number of votes that is equal to the number that is obtained by dividing the population number of the province by one hundred times the number of members of which the provincial assembly is composed. The quotient is thereafter rounded towards a full number upwards if a fraction is greater than 1/2 and downwards if a fraction is less than 1/2. This number is called the vote value.
[The remainder of Article U2 is omitted.]

§ 2. The distribution of seats

Article U 3. With respect to each province, the central polling office multiplies the numbers of votes cast for each candidate and the numbers of votes of the lists by the vote value that applies to that province. For the establishment of the result of the election, the products thus obtained count as the number of votes cast for each candidate or the number of votes of the lists, respectively.

[Articles U 4 to U 6 are omitted.]

Article U 7. (1) The central polling office divides the sum of the number of votes of all lists by the number of seats to be distributed.
(2) The quotient thus obtained is called electoral divisor.

Article U 8. A list is assigned a seat so many times as the electoral divisor is accommodated in the number of votes of that list.

Article U 9. The remaining seats, which are called rest seats, are consecutively assigned to those lists which after assignment of a seat have the largest average number of votes per assigned seat. If averages are equal, the lot decides where necessary.

Article U 10. If in the application of the preceding provisions a list would have to be assigned more seats than there are candidates, the remaining seat or seats pass by continued application of these provisions to one or more of the other lists on which candidates appear to whom no seat has been assigned.

[Articles U 11 to U 14 are omitted.]

§ 3. The assignment of the seats to the candidates

Article U 15. (1) Those candidates from the list are elected who are designated as such by application, mutatis mutandis, of Articles P 15 to P 18a.
(2) The ranking of candidates is carried out in accordance with the provisions of Article P 19.
(3) In deviation from Articles P 15 (1) and P 19 (2), candidates who have, on the common lists on which they appear, received a number of votes that is larger than half of the electoral divisor, are elected or are ranked, respectively, in the order of the number of votes cast for them.

[The remainder of the Act is omitted.]

Bill of Rights 1689 [An Act declareing the Rights and Liberties of the Subject and Setleing the Succession of the Crowne], as amended. Selected provisions: first part.

Whereas the Lords Spirituall and Temporall and Comons assembled at Westminster lawfully fully and freely representing all the Estates of the People of this Realme did upon the thirteenth day of February in the yeare of our Lord one thousand six hundred eighty eight present unto their Majesties then called and known by the Names and Stile of William and Mary Prince and Princesse of Orange being present in their proper Persons a certaine Declaration in Writeing made by the said Lords and Comons in the Words following viz

Whereas the late King James the Second by the Assistance of diverse evill Councellors Judges and Ministers imployed by him did endeavour to subvert and extirpate the Protestant Religion and the Lawes and Liberties of this Kingdome.
By Assumeing and Exerciseing a Power of Dispensing with and Suspending of Lawes and the Execution of Lawes without Consent of Parlyament.
By Committing and Prosecuting diverse Worthy Prelates for humbly Petitioning to be excused from Concurring to the said Assumed Power.
By issueing and causeing to be executed a Commission under the Great Seale for Erecting a Court called The Court of Commissioners for Ecclesiasticall Causes.
By Levying Money for and to the Use of the Crowne by pretence of Prerogative for other time and in other manner then the same was granted by Parlyament.
By raising and keeping a Standing Army within this Kingdome in time of Peace without Consent of Parlyament and Quartering Soldiers contrary to Law.
By causing severall good Subjects being Protestants to be disarmed at the same time when Papists were both Armed and Imployed contrary to Law.
By Violating the Freedome of Election of Members to serve in Parlyament.
By Prosecutions in the Court of Kings Bench for Matters and Causes cognizable onely in Parlyament and by diverse other Arbitrary and Illegall Courses.
And whereas of late yeares Partiall Corrupt and Unqualified Persons have beene returned and served on Juryes in Tryalls and particularly diverse Jurors in Tryalls for High Treason which were not Freeholders,
And excessive Baile hath beene required of Persons committed in Criminall Cases to elude the Benefitt of the Lawes made for the Liberty of the Subjects.
And excessive Fines have beene imposed.
And illegall and cruell Punishments inflicted.
And severall Grants and Promises made of Fines and Forfeitures before any Conviction or Judgement against the Persons upon whome the same were to be levyed. All which are utterly directly contrary to the knowne Lawes and Statutes and Freedome of this Realme.

And whereas the said late King James the Second haveing Abdicated the Government and the Throne being thereby Vacant His Hignesse the Prince of Orange (whome it hath pleased Almighty God to make the glorious Instrument of Delivering this Kingdome from Popery and Arbitrary Power) did (by the Advice of the Lords Spirituall and Temporall and diverse principall Persons of the Commons) cause Letters to be written to the Lords Spirituall and Temporall being Protestants and other Letters to the severall Countyes Cityes Universities Burroughs and Cinque Ports for the Choosing of such Persons to represent them as were of right to be sent to Parlyament to meete and sitt at Westminster upon the two and twentyeth day of January in this Yeare one thousand six hundred eighty and eight in order to such an Establishment as that their Religion Lawes and Liberties might not againe be in danger of being Subverted, Upon which Letters Elections haveing beene accordingly made.

And thereupon the said Lords Spirituall and Temporall and Commons pursuant to their respective Letters and Elections being now assembled in a full and free Representative of this Nation takeing into their most serious Consideration the best meanes for attaining the Ends aforesaid Doe in the first place (as their Auncestors in like Case have usually done) for the Vindicating and Asserting their auntient Rights and Liberties, Declare

That the pretended Power of Suspending of Laws or the Execution of Laws by Regall Authority without Consent of Parlyament is illegall.
That the pretended Power of Dispensing with Laws or the Execution of Laws by Regall Authoritie as it hath beene assumed and exercised of late is illegall.

That the Commission for erecting the late Court of Commissioners for Ecclesiasticall Causes and all other Commissions and Courts of like nature are Illegall and Pernicious.

That levying Money for or to the Use of the Crowne by pretence of Prerogative without Grant of Parlyament for longer time or in other manner then the same is or shall be granted is Illegall.

That it is the Right of the Subjects to petition the King and all Commitments and Prosecutions for such Petitioning are Illegall.

That the raising or keeping a standing Army within the Kingdome in time of Peace unlesse it be with Consent of Parlyament is against Law.

That the Subjects which are Protestants may have Arms for their Defence suitable to their Conditions and as allowed by Law.

That Election of Members of Parlyament ought to be free.

That the Freedome of Speech and Debates or Proceedings in Parlyament ought not to be impeached or questioned in any Court or Place out of Parlyament.

That excessive Baile ought not to be required nor excessive Fines imposed nor cruell and unusuall Punishments inflicted.

That Jurors ought to be duely impannelled and returned.

That all Grants and Promises of Fines and Forfeitures of particular persons before Conviction are illegall and void.

And that for Redresse of all Grievances and for the amending strengthening and preserveing of the Lawes Parlyaments ought to be held frequently.

And they doe Claime Demand and Insist upon all and singular the Premises as their undoubted Rights and Liberties and that noe Declarations Judgements Doeings or Proceedings to the Prejudice of the People in any of the said Premisses ought in any wise to be drawne hereafter into Consequence or Example. To which Demand of their Rights they are particularly encouraged by the Declaration of this Highnesse the Prince of Orange as being the onely meanes for obtaining a full Redresse and Remedy therein. Haveing therefore an intire Confidence That his said Highnesse the Prince of Orange will perfect the Deliverance soe farr advanced by him and will still preserve them from the Violation of their Rights which they have here asserted and from all other Attempts upon their Religion Rights and Liberties. The said Lords Spirituall and Temporall and Commons assembled at Westminster doe Resolve That William and Mary Prince and Princesse of Orange be and be declared King and Queene of England France and Ireland and the Dominions thereunto belonging to hold the Crowne and Royall Dignity of the said Kingdomes and Dominions to them the said Prince and Princesse dureing their Lives and the Life of the Survivour of them And that the sole and full Exercise of the Regall Power be onely in and executed by the said Prince of Orange in the Names of the said Prince and Princesse dureing their joynt Lives And after their Deceases the said Crowne and Royall Dignitie of the said Kingdoms and Dominions to be to the Heires of the Body of the said Princesse And for default of such Issue to the Princesse Anne of Denmarke and the Heires of her Body And for default of such Issue to the Heires of the Body of the said Prince of Orange. And the Lords Spirituall and Temporall and Commons doe pray the said Prince and Princesse to accept the same accordingly.

And that the Oathes hereafter mentioned be taken by all Persons of whome the Oathes of Allegiance and Supremacy might be required by Law instead of them And that the said Oathes of Allegiance and Supremacy be abrogated.

I A B doe sincerely promise and sweare That I will be faithfull and beare true Allegiance to their Majestyes King William and Queene Mary Soe helpe me God.

I A B doe sweare That I doe from my Heart Abhorr, Detest and Abjure as Impious and Hereticall this damnable Doctrine and Position That Princes Excommunicated or Deprived by the Pope or any Authority of the See of Rome may be deposed or murdered by their Subjects or any other whatsoever. And I doe declare That noe Forreigne Prince Person Prelate, State or Potentate hath or ought to have any Jurisdiction Power Superiority Preeminence or Authoritie Ecclesiasticall or Spirituall within this Realme Soe helpe me God.

Upon which their said Majestyes did accept the Crowne and Royall Dignitie of the Kingdoms of England France and Ireland and the Dominions thereunto belonging according to the Resolution and Desire of the said Lords and Commons contained in the said Declaration. And thereupon their Majestyes were pleased That the said Lords Spirituall and Temporall and Commons being the two Houses of Parlyament should continue to sitt and with their Majesties Royall Concurrence make effectuall Provision for the Setlement of the Religion Lawes and Liberties of this Kingdome soe that the same for the future might not be in danger againe of being subverted, To which the said Lords Spirituall and Temporall and Commons did agree and proceede to act accordingly.

[The remainder is omitted.]

Parliament Act 1911 [An Act to make provision with respect to the powers of the House of Lords in relation to those of the House of Commons, and to limit the duration of Parliament] as amended by, inter alia, the **Parliament Act 1949** [An Act to amend the Parliament Act 1911].

Whereas it is expedient that provision should be made for regulating the relations between the two Houses of Parliament:

And whereas it is intended to substitute for the House of Lords as it at present exists a Second Chamber constituted on a popular instead of hereditary basis, but such substitution cannot be immediately brought into operation:

And whereas provision will require hereafter to be made by Parliament in a measure effecting such substitution for limiting and defining the powers of the new Second Chamber, but it is expedient to make such provision as in this Act appears for restricting the existing powers of the House of Lords:

Section 1. (1) If a Money Bill, having been passed by the House of Commons, and sent up to the House of Lords at least one month before the end of the session, is not passed by the House of Lords without amendment within one month after it is so sent up to that House, the Bill shall, unless the House of Commons direct to the contrary, be presented to His Majesty and become an Act of Parliament on the Royal Assent being signified, notwithstanding that the House of Lords have not consented to the Bill.

(2) A Money Bill means a Public Bill which in the opinion of the Speaker of the House of Commons contains only provisions dealing with all or any of the following subjects, namely, the imposition, repeal, remission, alteration, or regulation of taxation; the imposition for the payment of debt or other financial purposes of charges on the Consolidated Fund, the National Loans Fund or on money provided by Parliament, or the variation or repeal of any such charges; supply; the appropriation, receipt, custody, issue or audit of accounts of public money; the raising or guarantee of any loan or the repayment thereof; or subordinate matters incidental to those subjects or any of them. In this subsection the expressions "taxation," "public money," and "loan" respectively do not include any taxation, money, or loan raised by local authorities or bodies for local purposes.

(3) There shall be endorsed on every Money Bill when it is sent up to the House of Lords and when it is presented to His Majesty for assent the certificate of the Speaker of the House of Commons signed by him that it is a Money Bill. Before giving his certificate the Speaker shall consult, if practicable, two members to be appointed from the Chairmen's Panel at the beginning of each Session by the Committee of Selection.

Section 2. (1) If any Public Bill (other than a Money Bill or a Bill containing any provision to extend the maximum duration of Parliament beyond five years) is passed by the House of Commons in two successive sessions (whether of the same Parliament or not), and, having been sent up to the House of Lords at least one month before the end of the session, is rejected by the House of Lords in each of those sessions, that Bill shall, on its rejection for the second time by the House of Lords, unless the House of Commons direct to the contrary, be presented to His Majesty and become an Act of Parliament on the Royal Assent being signified thereto, notwithstanding that the House of Lords have not consented to the Bill: Provided that this provision shall not take effect unless one year has elapsed between the date of the second reading in the first of those sessions of the Bill in the House of Commons and the date on which it passes the House of Commons in the second of these sessions.

(2) When a Bill is presented to His Majesty for assent in pursuance of the provisions of this section, there shall be endorsed on the Bill the certificate of the Speaker of the House of Commons signed by him that the provisions of this section have been duly complied with.

(3) A Bill shall be deemed to be rejected by the House of Lords if it is not passed by the House of Lords either without amendment or with such amendments only as may be agreed to by both Houses.

(4) A Bill shall be deemed to be the same Bill as a former Bill sent up to the House of Lords in the preceding session if, when it is sent up to the House of Lords, it is identical with the former Bill or contains only such alterations as are certified by the Speaker of the House of Commons to be necessary owing to the time which has elapsed since the date of the former Bill, or to represent any amendments which have been made by the House of Lords in the former Bill in the preceding session, and any amendments which are certified by the Speaker to have been made by the House of Lords in the second session and agreed to by the House of Commons shall be inserted in the Bill as presented for Royal Assent in pursuance of this section:

Provided that the House of Commons may, if they think fit, on the passage of such a Bill through the House in the second session, suggest any further amendments without inserting the amendments in the Bill, and any such suggested amendments shall be considered by the House of Lords, and, if agreed to by that House, shall be treated as amendments made by the House of Lords and agreed to by the House of Commons; but the exercise of this

Part I. Constitutional Law

power by the House of Commons shall not affect the operation of this section in the event of the Bill being rejected by the House of Lords.

Section 3. Any certificate of the Speaker of the House of Commons given under this Act shall be conclusive for all purposes, and shall not be questioned in any court of law.

Section 4. (1) In every Bill presented to His Majesty under the preceding provisions of this Act, the words of enactment shall be as follows, that is to say:
"Be it enacted by the King's most Excellent Majesty, by and with the advice and consent of the Commons in this present Parliament assembled, in accordance with the provisions of the Parliament Acts 1911 and 1949 and by authority of the same, as follows."
(2) Any alteration of a Bill necessary to give effect to this section shall not be deemed to be an amendment of the Bill.

Section 5. In this Act the expression "Public Bill" does not include any Bill for confirming a Provisional Order.

Section 6. Nothing in this Act shall diminish or qualify the existing rights and privileges of the House of Commons.

Section 7. Five years shall be substituted for seven years as the time fixed for the maximum duration of Parliament under the Septennial Act 1715.

Section 8. This Act may be cited as the Parliament Act 1911.

Parliament Act 1949 [An Act to amend the Parliament Act 1911].

Section 1. The Parliament Act, 1911, shall have effect, and shall be deemed to have had effect from the beginning of the session in which the Bill for this Act originated (save as regards that Bill itself), as if –
(a) there had been substituted in subsections (1) and (4) of section two thereof, for the words "in three successive sessions", "for the third time", "in the third of those sessions", "in the third session", and "in the second or third session" respectively, the words " in two successive sessions", "for the second time", "in the second of those sessions", "in the second session", and "in the second session" respectively; and
(b) there had been substituted in subsection (1) of the said section two, for the words "two years have elapsed" the words "one year has elapsed":
Provided that, if a Bill has been rejected for the second time by the House of Lords before the signification of the Royal Assent to the Bill for this Act, whether such rejection was in the same session as that in which the Royal Assent to the Bill for this Act was signified or in an earlier session, the requirement of the said section two that a Bill is to be presented to His Majesty on its rejection for the second time by the House of Lords shall have effect in relation to the Bill rejected as a requirement that it is to be presented to His Majesty as soon as the Royal Assent to the Bill for this Act has been signified, and, notwithstanding that such rejection was in an earlier session, the Royal Assent to the Bill rejected may be signified in the session in which the Royal Assent to the Bill for this Act was signified.

Section 2. (1) This Act may be cited as the Parliament Act 1949.
(2) This Act and the Parliament Act 1911, shall be construed as one and may be cited together as the Parliament Acts 1911 and 1949.

Human Rights Act 1998 [An Act to give further effect to rights and freedoms guaranteed under the European Convention on Human Rights; to make provision with respect to holders of certain judicial offices who become judges of the European Court of Human Rights; and for connected purposes] as amended. Selected provisions: Sections 1 – 10 and Schedule 2.

Section 1. (1) In this Act "the Convention rights" means the rights and fundamental freedoms set out in –
(a) Articles 2 to 12 and 14 of the Convention,
(b) Articles 1 to 3 of the First Protocol, and
(c) Articles 1 and 2 of the Sixth Protocol,
as read with Articles 16 to 18 of the Convention.
(2) Those Articles are to have effect for the purposes of this Act subject to any designated derogation or reservation (as to which see sections 14 and 15).
(3) The Articles are set out in Schedule 1.
(4) The Lord Chancellor may by order make such amendments to this Act as he considers appropriate to reflect the effect, in relation to the United Kingdom, of a protocol.
(5) In subsection (4) "protocol" means a protocol to the Convention –
(a) which the United Kingdom has ratified; or
(b) which the United Kingdom has signed with a view to ratification.
(6) No amendment may be made by an order under subsection (4) so as to come into force before the protocol concerned is in force in relation to the United Kingdom.

Section 2. (1) A court or tribunal determining a question which has arisen in connection with a Convention right must take into account any –
(a) judgment, decision, declaration or advisory opinion of the European Court of Human Rights,
(b) opinion of the Commission given in a report adopted under Article 31 of the Convention,
(c) decision of the Commission in connection with Article 26 or 27 (2) of the Convention, or
(d) decision of the Committee of Ministers taken under Article 46 of the Convention,
whenever made or given, so far as, in the opinion of the court or tribunal, it is relevant to the proceedings in which that question has arisen.
(2) Evidence of any judgment, decision, declaration or opinion of which account may have to be taken under this section is to be given in proceedings before any court or tribunal in such manner as may be provided by rules.
(3) In this section "rules" means rules of court or, in the case of proceedings before a tribunal, rules made for the purposes of this section –
(a) by the Lord Chancellor or the Secretary of State, in relation to any proceedings outside Scotland;
(b) by the Secretary of State, in relation to proceedings in Scotland; or
(c) by a Northern Ireland department, in relation to proceedings before a tribunal in Northern Ireland –
(i) which deals with transferred matters; and
(ii) for which no rules made under paragraph (a) are in force.

Section 3. (1) So far as it is possible to do so, primary legislation and subordinate legislation must be read and given effect in a way which is compatible with the Convention rights.
(2) This section –
(a) applies to primary legislation and subordinate legislation whenever enacted;
(b) does not affect the validity, continuing operation or enforcement of any incompatible primary legislation; and
(c) does not affect the validity, continuing operation or enforcement of any incompatible subordinate legislation if (disregarding any possibility of revocation) primary legislation prevents removal of the incompatibility.

Section 4. (1) Subsection (2) applies in any proceedings in which a court determines whether a provision of primary legislation is compatible with a Convention right.
(2) If the court is satisfied that the provision is incompatible with a Convention right, it may make a declaration of that incompatibility.
(3) Subsection (4) applies in any proceedings in which a court determines whether a provision of subordinate legislation, made in the exercise of a power conferred by primary legislation, is compatible with a Convention right.
(4) If the court is satisfied –
(a) that the provision is incompatible with a Convention right, and

(b) that (disregarding any possibility of revocation) the primary legislation concerned prevents removal of the incompatibility,
it may make a declaration of that incompatibility.
(5) In this section "court" means –
(a) the House of Lords;
(b) the Judicial Committee of the Privy Council;
(c) the Courts-Martial Appeal Court;
(d) in Scotland, the High Court of Justiciary sitting otherwise than as a trial court or the Court of Session;
(e) in England and Wales or Northern Ireland, the High Court or the Court of Appeal.
(6) A declaration under this section ("a declaration of incompatibility") –
(a) does not affect the validity, continuing operation or enforcement of the provision in respect of which it is given; and
(b) is not binding on the parties to the proceedings in which it is made.

Section 5. (1) Where a court is considering whether to make a declaration of incompatibility, the Crown is entitled to notice in accordance with rules of court.
(2) In any case to which subsection (1) applies –
(a) a Minister of the Crown (or a person nominated by him),
(b) a member of the Scottish Executive,
(c) a Northern Ireland Minister,
(d) a Northern Ireland department,
is entitled, on giving notice in accordance with rules of court, to be joined as a party to the proceedings.
(3) Notice under subsection (2) may be given at any time during the proceedings.
(4) A person who has been made a party to criminal proceedings (other than in Scotland) as the result of a notice under subsection (2) may, with leave, appeal to the House of Lords against any declaration of incompatibility made in the proceedings.
(5) In subsection (4) –
"criminal proceedings" includes all proceedings before the Courts-Martial Appeal Court; and
"leave" means leave granted by the court making the declaration of incompatibility or by the House of Lords.

Section 6. (1) It is unlawful for a public authority to act in a way which is incompatible with a Convention right.
(2) Subsection (1) does not apply to an act if –
(a) as the result of one or more provisions of primary legislation, the authority could not have acted differently; or
(b) in the case of one or more provisions of, or made under, primary legislation which cannot be read or given effect in a way which is compatible with the Convention rights, the authority was acting so as to give effect to or enforce those provisions.
(3) In this section "public authority" includes –
(a) a court or tribunal, and
(b) any person certain of whose functions are functions of a public nature,
but does not include either House of Parliament or a person exercising functions in connection with proceedings in Parliament.
(4) In subsection (3) "Parliament" does not include the House of Lords in its judicial capacity.
(5) In relation to a particular act, a person is not a public authority by virtue only of subsection (3)(b) if the nature of the act is private.
(6) "An act" includes a failure to act but does not include a failure to –
(a) introduce in, or lay before, Parliament a proposal for legislation; or
(b) make any primary legislation or remedial order.

Section 7. (1) A person who claims that a public authority has acted (or proposes to act) in a way which is made unlawful by section 6 (1) may –
(a) bring proceedings against the authority under this Act in the appropriate court or tribunal, or
(b) rely on the Convention right or rights concerned in any legal proceedings,
but only if he is (or would be) a victim of the unlawful act.
(2) In subsection (1)(a) "appropriate court or tribunal" means such court or tribunal as may be determined in accordance with rules; and proceedings against an authority include a counterclaim or similar proceeding.
(3) If the proceedings are brought on an application for judicial review, the applicant is to be taken to have a sufficient interest in relation to the unlawful act only if he is, or would be, a victim of that act.

(4) If the proceedings are made by way of a petition for judicial review in Scotland, the applicant shall be taken to have title and interest to sue in relation to the unlawful act only if he is, or would be, a victim of that act.
(5) Proceedings under subsection (1)(a) must be brought before the end of –
(a) the period of one year beginning with the date on which the act complained of took place; or
(b) such longer period as the court or tribunal considers equitable having regard to all the circumstances,
but that is subject to any rule imposing a stricter time limit in relation to the procedure in question.
(6) In subsection (1)(b) "legal proceedings" includes –
(a) proceedings brought by or at the instigation of a public authority; and
(b) an appeal against the decision of a court or tribunal.
(7) For the purposes of this section, a person is a victim of an unlawful act only if he would be a victim for the purposes of Article 34 of the Convention if proceedings were brought in the European Court of Human Rights in respect of that act.
(8) Nothing in this Act creates a criminal offence.
(9) In this section "rules" means –
(a) in relation to proceedings before a court or tribunal outside Scotland, rules made by the Lord Chancellor or the Secretary of State for the purposes of this section or rules of court,
(b) in relation to proceedings before a court or tribunal in Scotland, rules made by the Secretary of State for those purposes,
(c) in relation to proceedings before a tribunal in Northern Ireland –
(i) which deals with transferred matters; and
(ii) for which no rules made under paragraph (a) are in force,
rules made by a Northern Ireland department for those purposes,
and includes provision made by order under section 1 of the Courts and Legal Services Act 1990.
(10) In making rules, regard must be had to section 9.
(11) The Minister who has power to make rules in relation to a particular tribunal may, to the extent he considers it necessary to ensure that the tribunal can provide an appropriate remedy in relation to an act (or proposed act) of a public authority which is (or would be) unlawful as a result of section 6 (1), by order add to –
(a) the relief or remedies which the tribunal may grant; or
(b) the grounds on which it may grant any of them.
(12) An order made under subsection (11) may contain such incidental, supplemental, consequential or transitional provision as the Minister making it considers appropriate.
(13) "The Minister" includes the Northern Ireland department concerned.

Section 8. (1) In relation to any act (or proposed act) of a public authority which the court finds is (or would be) unlawful, it may grant such relief or remedy, or make such order, within its powers as it considers just and appropriate.
(2) But damages may be awarded only by a court which has power to award damages, or to order the payment of compensation, in civil proceedings.
(3) No award of damages is to be made unless, taking account of all the circumstances of the case, including –
(a) any other relief or remedy granted, or order made, in relation to the act in question (by that or any other court), and
(b) the consequences of any decision (of that or any other court) in respect of that act,
the court is satisfied that the award is necessary to afford just satisfaction to the person in whose favour it is made.
(4) In determining –
(a) whether to award damages, or
(b) the amount of an award,
the court must take into account the principles applied by the European Court of Human Rights in relation to the award of compensation under Article 41 of the Convention.
(5) A public authority against which damages are awarded is to be treated –
(a) in Scotland, for the purposes of section 3 of the Law Reform (Miscellaneous Provisions) (Scotland) Act 1940 as if the award were made in an action of damages in which the authority has been found liable in respect of loss or damage to the person to whom the award is made;
(b) for the purposes of the Civil Liability (Contribution) Act 1978 as liable in respect of damage suffered by the person to whom the award is made.
(6) In this section –
"court" includes a tribunal;
"damages" means damages for an unlawful act of a public authority; and
"unlawful" means unlawful under section 6 (1).

Part I. Constitutional Law

Section 9. (1) Proceedings under section 7(1)(a) in respect of a judicial act may be brought only –
(a) by exercising a right of appeal;
(b) on an application (in Scotland a petition) for judicial review; or
(c) in such other forum as may be prescribed by rules.
(2) That does not affect any rule of law which prevents a court from being the subject of judicial review.
(3) In proceedings under this Act in respect of a judicial act done in good faith, damages may not be awarded otherwise than to compensate a person to the extent required by Article 5(5) of the Convention.
(4) An award of damages permitted by subsection (3) is to be made against the Crown; but no award may be made unless the appropriate person, if not a party to the proceedings, is joined.
(5) In this section –
"appropriate person" means the Minister responsible for the court concerned, or a person or government department nominated by him;
"court" includes a tribunal;
"judge" includes a member of a tribunal, a justice of the peace and a clerk or other officer entitled to exercise the jurisdiction of a court;
"judicial act" means a judicial act of a court and includes an act done on the instructions, or on behalf, of a judge; and
"rules" has the same meaning as in section 7 (9).

Section 10. (1) This section applies if –
(a) a provision of legislation has been declared under section 4 to be incompatible with a Convention right and, if an appeal lies –
(i) all persons who may appeal have stated in writing that they do not intend to do so;
(ii) the time for bringing an appeal has expired and no appeal has been brought within that time; or
(iii) an appeal brought within that time has been determined or abandoned; or
(b) it appears to a Minister of the Crown or Her Majesty in Council that, having regard to a finding of the European Court of Human Rights made after the coming into force of this section in proceedings against the United Kingdom, a provision of legislation is incompatible with an obligation of the United Kingdom arising from the Convention.
(2) If a Minister of the Crown considers that there are compelling reasons for proceeding under this section, he may by order make such amendments to the legislation as he considers necessary to remove the incompatibility.
(3) If, in the case of subordinate legislation, a Minister of the Crown considers –
(a) that it is necessary to amend the primary legislation under which the subordinate legislation in question was made, in order to enable the incompatibility to be removed, and
(b) that there are compelling reasons for proceeding under this section,
he may by order make such amendments to the primary legislation as he considers necessary.
(4) This section also applies where the provision in question is in subordinate legislation and has been quashed, or declared invalid, by reason of incompatibility with a Convention right and the Minister proposes to proceed under paragraph 2(b) of Schedule 2.
(5) If the legislation is an Order in Council, the power conferred by subsection (2) or (3) is exercisable by Her Majesty in Council.
(6) In this section "legislation" does not include a Measure of the Church Assembly or of the General Synod of the Church of England.
(7) Schedule 2 makes further provision about remedial orders.

[The remainder of the Act proper and Schedule 1 are omitted.]

Schedule 2 (Remedial Orders)

Paragraph 1. (1) A remedial order may –
(a) contain such incidental, supplemental, consequential or transitional provision as the person making it considers appropriate;
(b) be made so as to have effect from a date earlier than that on which it is made;
(c) make provision for the delegation of specific functions;
(d) make different provision for different cases.
(2) The power conferred by sub-paragraph (1) (a) includes –

(a) power to amend primary legislation (including primary legislation other than that which contains the incompatible provision); and
(b) power to amend or revoke subordinate legislation (including subordinate legislation other than that which contains the incompatible provision).
(3) A remedial order may be made so as to have the same extent as the legislation which it affects.
(4) No person is to be guilty of an offence solely as a result of the retrospective effect of a remedial order.

Paragraph 2. No remedial order may be made unless –
(a) a draft of the order has been approved by a resolution of each House of Parliament made after the end of the period of 60 days beginning with the day on which the draft was laid; or
(b) it is declared in the order that it appears to the person making it that, because of the urgency of the matter, it is necessary to make the order without a draft being so approved.

Paragraph 3. (1) No draft may be laid under paragraph 2(a) unless –
(a) the person proposing to make the order has laid before Parliament a document which contains a draft of the proposed order and the required information; and
(b) the period of 60 days, beginning with the day on which the document required by this sub-paragraph was laid, has ended.
(2) If representations have been made during that period, the draft laid under paragraph 2(a) must be accompanied by a statement containing –
(a) a summary of the representations; and
(b) if, as a result of the representations, the proposed order has been changed, details of the changes.

Paragraph 4. (1) If a remedial order ("the original order") is made without being approved in draft, the person making it must lay it before Parliament, accompanied by the required information, after it is made.
(2) If representations have been made during the period of 60 days beginning with the day on which the original order was made, the person making it must (after the end of that period) lay before Parliament a statement containing –
(a) a summary of the representations; and
(b) if, as a result of the representations, he considers it appropriate to make changes to the original order, details of the changes.
(3) If sub-paragraph (2) (b) applies, the person making the statement must –
(a) make a further remedial order replacing the original order; and
(b) lay the replacement order before Parliament.
(4) If, at the end of the period of 120 days beginning with the day on which the original order was made, a resolution has not been passed by each House approving the original or replacement order, the order ceases to have effect (but without that affecting anything previously done under either order or the power to make a fresh remedial order).

Paragraph 5. In this Schedule –
"representations" means representations about a remedial order (or proposed remedial order) made to the person making (or proposing to make) it and includes any relevant Parliamentary report or resolution; and
"required information" means –
(a) an explanation of the incompatibility which the order (or proposed order) seeks to remove, including particulars of the relevant declaration, finding or order; and
(b) a statement of the reasons for proceeding under section 10 and for making an order in those terms.

Paragraph 6. In calculating any period for the purposes of this Schedule, no account is to be taken of any time during which –
(a) Parliament is dissolved or prorogued; or
(b) both Houses are adjourned for more than four days.

Paragraph 7. (1) This paragraph applies in relation to –
(a) any remedial order made, and any draft of such an order proposed to be made, –
(i) by the Scottish Ministers; or
(ii) within devolved competence (within the meaning of the Scotland Act 1998) by Her Majesty in Council; and
(b) any document or statement to be laid in connection with such an order (or proposed order).

(2) This Schedule has effect in relation to any such order (or proposed order), document or statement subject to the following modifications.
(3) Any reference to Parliament, each House of Parliament or both Houses of Parliament shall be construed as a reference to the Scottish Parliament.
(4) Paragraph 6 does not apply and instead, in calculating any period for the purposes of this Schedule, no account is to be taken of any time during which the Scottish Parliament is dissolved or is in recess for more than four days.

[The remaining Schedules are omitted.]

Scotland Act 1998

Scotland Act 1998 [An Act to provide for the establishment of a Scottish Parliament and Administration and other changes in the government of Scotland; to provide for changes in the constitution and functions of certain public authorities; to provide for the variation of the basic rate of income tax in relation to income of Scottish taxpayers in accordance with a resolution of the Scottish Parliament; to amend the law about parliamentary constituencies in Scotland; and for connected purposes] as amended. Selected provisions: Sections 1, 28 and 29.

Part I. The Scottish Parliament

Section 1. (1) There shall be a Scottish Parliament.
(2) One member of the Parliament shall be returned for each constituency (under the simple majority system) at an election held in the constituency.
(3) Members of the Parliament for each region shall be returned at a general election under the additional member system of proportional representation provided for in this Part and vacancies among such members shall be filled in accordance with this Part.
(4) The validity of any proceedings of the Parliament is not affected by any vacancy in its membership.
(5) Schedule 1 (which makes provision for the constituencies and regions for the purposes of this Act and the number of regional members) shall have effect.

[Sections 2 – 27 are omitted.]

Section 28. (1) Subject to section 29, the Parliament may make laws, to be known as Acts of the Scottish Parliament.
(2) Proposed Acts of the Scottish Parliament shall be known as Bills; and a Bill shall become an Act of the Scottish Parliament when it has been passed by the Parliament and has received Royal Assent.
(3) A Bill receives Royal Assent at the beginning of the day on which Letters Patent under the Scottish Seal signed with Her Majesty's own hand signifying Her Assent are recorded in the Register of the Great Seal.
(4) The date of Royal Assent shall be written on the Act of the Scottish Parliament by the Clerk, and shall form part of the Act.
(5) The validity of an Act of the Scottish Parliament is not affected by any invalidity in the proceedings of the Parliament leading to its enactment.
(6) Every Act of the Scottish Parliament shall be judicially noticed.
(7) This section does not affect the power of the Parliament of the United Kingdom to make laws for Scotland.

Section 29. (1) An Act of the Scottish Parliament is not law so far as any provision of the Act is outside the legislative competence of the Parliament.
(2) A provision is outside that competence so far as any of the following paragraphs apply –
(a) it would form part of the law of a country or territory other than Scotland, or confer or remove functions exercisable otherwise than in or as regards Scotland,
(b) it relates to reserved matters,
(c) it is in breach of the restrictions in Schedule 4,
(d) it is incompatible with any of the Convention rights or with Community law,
(e) it would remove the Lord Advocate from his position as head of the systems of criminal prosecution and investigation of deaths in Scotland.
(3) For the purposes of this section, the question whether a provision of an Act of the Scottish Parliament relates to a reserved matter is to be determined, subject to subsection (4), by reference to the purpose of the provision, having regard (among other things) to its effect in all the circumstances.
(4) A provision which –
(a) would otherwise not relate to reserved matters, but
(b) makes modifications of Scots private law, or Scots criminal law, as it applies to reserved matters,
is to be treated as relating to reserved matters unless the purpose of the provision is to make the law in question apply consistently to reserved matters and otherwise.

[The remainder of the Act is omitted.]

PART II

Administrative Law

ADMIN

Code of Administrative Justice [Code de justice administrative]. Selected provisions: Statutory part, Preliminary Title; Book I: Title 1, Article L 121-1 of Chapter 1 of Title 2, Section 2 of Chapter 2 of Title 2; Book II: Title 1, Chapters 1 and 2 of Title 2; Book III: Title 1, Chapter 1, Articles L 311-1 – L 311-5, Titles 2 and 3; Book VII: Titles 2 and 3; Book VIII.[9]

Statutory Part

Preliminary Title

Article L 1. The present code applies to the Council of State [Conseil d'Etat], to the administrative appeal courts [cours administratives d'appel] and to the administrative tribunals [tribunaux administratifs].

Article L 2. Judgments are delivered in the name of the French people.

Article L 3. Judgments are delivered in a collegial composition, unless otherwise provided by statute.

Article L 4. Save for specific statutory provisions, appeals do not have suspensive effect unless otherwise prescribed by the court [juridiction].

Article L 5. The proceedings are adversarial [contradictoire]. The requirements of adversarial proceedings are adapted to those of urgency.

Article L 6. The oral proceedings take place in a public hearing.

Article L 7. A member of the court, charged with the functions of commissioner of the government, reveals publicly, and in complete independence, his opinion concerning the questions which the appeals present for adjudication and concerning the solutions that they call for.

Article L 8. The deliberation of the judges is secret.

Article L 9. Judgments are substantiated with reasons.

Article L 10. Judgments are public. They mention the name of the judges who have delivered them.

Article L 11. The judgments are executory.

Book I. The Council of State

Title 1. Attributions

Chapter 1. Contentious attributions

Article L 111-1. The Council of State [Conseil d'Etat] is the supreme administrative court. It rules sovereignly on appeals in cassation directed against decisions delivered in last instance by the several administrative courts as well as on those on which it is seized in the capacity of judge of first instance or appeals judge.

Chapter 2. Attributions in administrative and statutory matters

Article L 112-1. The Council of State participates in the drafting of statutes and ordinances. It is seized by the Prime-Minister on proposals drafted by the Government.
The Council of State issues an opinion on private member's bills, submitted to the bureau of a parliamentary chamber and not yet examined in a committee, on which it is seized by the president of that chamber.

---

[9] Translation by E. Ramaekers.

PART II. ADMINISTRATIVE LAW

The Council of State gives its opinion on proposals for decrees and on every other proposed text for which its involvement is prescribed by constitutional, statutory or regulatory provisions or which are submitted to it by the Government.
Seized on a proposed text, the Council of State gives its opinion and proposes modifications which it deems necessary.
Furthermore, it prepares and draws up texts that are requested of it.

Article L 112-2. The Council of State may be consulted by the Prime-Minister or the ministers concerning difficulties that arise in administrative matters.

Article L 112-3. The Council of State may, on its own initiative, draw the attention of the public authorities to reforms of a statutory, regulatory or administrative nature which it deems in conformity with the general interest.

Article L 112-4. The vice-president of the Council of State may, at the request of the Prime-Minister or of a minister, designate a member of the Council of State for an investigative mission.
The vice-president may, at the request of ministers, designate a member of the Council of State to assist their administration in the elaboration of a specified proposed text.

Article L 112-5. The Council of State is charged with a permanent investigative task with regard to the administrative courts.

Article L 112-6. As stated in Article 100 of organic statute no. 99-209 of 19 March 1999 relating to New Caledonia, "government bills for statutes for the country are submitted, for advice, to the Council of State before their adoption by the government deliberating in council.
Private member's bills for statutes for the country are submitted, for advice, to the Council of State by the president of the congress before their first reading. The vote of the congress takes place after the Council of State has given its opinion.
The opinion is considered given within a period of one month.
The opinions mentioned in the present Article are transmitted to the president of the government, to the president of the congress, to the high commissioner and to the Constitutional Council."

Chapter 3. The opinion on a question of law

Article L 113-1. Before ruling on an appeal raising a new question of law, presenting a serious difficulty and arising in numerous disputes, the administrative tribunal [tribunal administratif] or the administrative appeal court [cour administrative d'appel] may, by a decision which is not susceptible to any appeal, transfer the file of the case to the Council of State, which examines the question raised within a period of three months. Any decision on the merits is postponed until an opinion of the Council of State or, by lack thereof, until the expiry of this time period.

Title 2. Organization and functioning

Chapter 1. General provisions

Article L 121-1. The presidency of the Council of State is assumed by the vice-president.
The general assembly of the Council of State may be chaired by the Prime-Minister and, in his absence, by the keeper of the seals, the minister of justice.

[The remainder of Chapter 1 is omitted.]

Chapter 2. The Council of State in the exercise of its contentious attributions

Section 2. The forming of judgments

Article L 122-1. The decisions of the Council of State ruling on contentious proceedings are rendered by the chamber for contentious proceedings, by the division for contentious proceedings or by the formation of joint subdivisions. They may equally be rendered by each subdivision sitting in a composition for the rendering of judgments.

The president of the division for contentious proceedings and the presidents of the subdivisions may, by ordinance, regulate matters the nature of which does not justify the composition of a collegial body.

[The remainder of Chapter 2 is omitted; Title 3 is omitted.]

Book II. The administrative tribunals and the administrative appeal courts

Title 1. Attributions

Chapter 1. Contentious attributions

Article L 211-1. The administrative tribunals [tribunaux administratifs] are, in first instance and without prejudice to the competences attributed to the Council of State, judges of general jurisdiction in administrative disputes.

Article L 211-2. The administrative appeal courts [cours administratives d'appel] hear cases adjudicated in first instance by the administrative tribunals, without prejudice to the competences attributed to the Council of State in its capacity of appeals judge and to those defined in Articles L 552-1 and L 552-2.

Article L 211-3. The administrative appeal courts equally hear appeals brought against the judgments rendered by the committees for contentious proceedings on the compensation of French persons expropriated of property situated in a territory previously placed under the sovereignty, the protectorate or the tutelage of France.

Article L 211-4. The administrative tribunals may exercise a mission of arbitration.

Chapter 2. Administrative attributions

Article L 212-1. Apart from their judicial attributions, the administrative tribunals and the administrative appeal courts exercise advisory functions.

Article L 212-2. The administrative tribunals rule on the exercise by the tax-payers of actions belonging to certain territorial entities and to their public institutions, under the conditions established by the General Code of Territorial Entities [code général des collectivités territoriales].

Title 2. Organization and functioning

Chapter 1. Organization of the administrative tribunals and the administrative appeal courts

Section 1. Common provisions

Article L 221-1. The administrative tribunals and the administrative appeal courts consist of a president and several members of the body of administrative tribunals and administrative appeal courts. They may equally contain other members assigned to that body under the conditions defined by the statutes and regulations in force.

Section 2. Organization of the administrative tribunals

Article L 221-2. The administrative tribunals may, in case of a vacancy or an inability to attend, deliberate while completed, for lack of a member belonging to another administrative tribunal, by the addition of an advocate registered with the bar at the seat by following the order of the list.

Section 3. Organization of the administrative appeal courts

Article L 221-3. Each administrative appeal court contains chambers.

Chapter 2. Functioning of the administrative tribunals and the administrative appeal courts

Section 1. Common provisions

Article L 222-1. The judgments of the administrative tribunals and the judgments of the administrative appeal courts are rendered in collegial formation, save for exceptions pertaining to the object of the litigation or the nature of the questions to be adjudicated.
The judges deliberate in odd numbers.

Article L 222-2. Where the participation of a magistrate of the administrative tribunal in a committee is provided for, the appointment may be granted to a magistrate of an administrative appeal court.
If the provision states that the appointment is granted by the president of the administrative tribunal or upon his proposal, the latter may ask the president of the competent administrative appeal court to appoint or propose a magistrate of the court.
In all cases where the participation of a magistrate of an administrative tribunal or an administrative appeal court in a committee is provided for, the appointment may be granted to an honorary magistrate.

Section 2. Functioning of the administrative tribunals

Article L 222-2-1. The president of the administrative tribunal may appoint an honorary administrative magistrate chosen from among the registered magistrates, for a renewable term of three years, from a list drawn up by the vice-president of the Council of State, to rule in disputes regarding decisions on escorts back to the border.

Section 3. Functioning of the administrative appeal courts

Article L 222-3. Each administrative appeal court is presided over by a member of the Council of State in ordinary service.

Article L 222-4. The assignment to the position of president of an administrative appeal court is pronounced by decree on the proposal of the vice-president of the Council of State deliberating with the presidents of the divisions.

[Chapters 3 – 7 are omitted.]

Book III. Competence

Title 1. Competence in first instance

Chapter 1. Competence by virtue of the subject matter

Article L 311-1. The administrative tribunals are, in first instance, judges of general jurisdiction in administrative disputes, save for the competences that the object of the dispute or the interest of a proper administration of justice require to be attributed to the Council of State.

Article L 311-2. The Council of State is competent to hear, in first and final instance, objections to changes of names pronounced by virtue of Article 61 of the Civil Code [code civil].

Article L 311-3. The Council of State is competent in first and final instance to hear objections made against:
1. The election of representatives to the European Parliament, in accordance with Article 25 of statute no. 77-729 of 7 July 1977 relating to the election of representatives to the European Parliament;
2. The elections for regional councils and for the Assembly of Corsica in accordance with Articles L 361 and L 381 of the Electoral Code [code electoral];
[The remainder of the Article is omitted.]

Article L 311-4. The Council of State hears, in first and final instance, appeals in full jurisdiction which are attributed to it by virtue of:

1. Paragraph IV of Article L 612-16 of the Monetary and Financial Code [code monétaire et financier] as against the decisions of sanction taken by the Authority for prudential control;
2. Article L 313-13 of the Construction and Housing Code [code de la construction et de l'habitation] as against the decisions of sanction taken by the minister charged with housing;
[The remainder of the Article is omitted.]

Article L 311-5. The Council of State is competent in first and final instance to hear appeals brought against the decisions of the administrative tribunals envisaged in Article L 212-2.

[Articles L 311-6 – L 311-12 are omitted.]

Title 2. Competence in appeal

Chapter 1. Competence by virtue of the subject matter

Article L 321-1. The administrative appeal courts [cours administratives d'appel] hear cases adjudicated in first instance by the administrative tribunals [tribunaux administratifs], save for the competences which the interest of a proper administration of justice requires to be attributed to the Council of State [Conseil d'Etat] and those defined in Articles L 552-1 and L 552-2.

Article L 321-2. In all cases where statute does not provide otherwise, the Council of State hears appeals brought against decisions rendered in first instance by the other administrative courts.

Title 3. The Council of State as judge in cassation

Article L 331-1. The Council of State is solely competent to adjudicate appeals in cassation brought against the decisions rendered in final instance by all administrative courts.

[Book V is omitted.]

Book VII. The judgment

Title 2. Abstention and recusation

Article L 721-1. The recusation of a member of the court is pronounced, at the request of a party, if there is a serious reason to question his impartiality.

Title 3. The procedure of the hearing

Article L 731-1. By derogation from the provisions of Article L 6, the president of the chamber sitting in the composition to render judgments may, on exceptional grounds, decide that the hearing will take place or will be continued without the presence of the public, if the maintenance of the public order or the respect for the privacy of the persons or the secrets protected by statute so require.
The provisions of the preceding paragraph are applicable to Mayotte, to Saint-Pierre and Miquelon, to New Caledonia, to French Polynesia and to the islands of Wallis and Futuna.

[Titles 4 – 8 are omitted.]

Book VIII. The means of appeal

Title 1. The appeal

Article L 811-1. In the case where a judgment rendered in first instance is susceptible to appeal, it is brought before the instance of appeal competent in view of the provisions of Book III.

Title 2. The appeal in cassation

Chapter 1. General provisions

Article L 821-1. The judgments rendered by the administrative appeal courts [cours administratives d'appel] and, generally, all the decisions rendered in final instance by the administrative courts may be referred to the Council of State [Conseil d'Etat] by way of appeal in cassation.

Article L 821-2. If it pronounces the annulment of a decision of an administrative court ruling in final instance, the Council of State may either refer the case back to the same court which rules in a different composition except in case of impossibility relating to the nature of the court, or refer the case to another court of the same nature, or adjudicate the case on the merits if the interest of a proper administration of justice justifies it.
Where the case forms the object of a second appeal in cassation, the Council of State rules definitively in this case.

Chapter 2. Procedure of admission

Article L 822-1. The appeal in cassation before the Council of State is subject to a preliminary admission procedure. Admission is refused by jurisdiction order if the appeal is inadmissible or is not based on any serious footing.

[Book IX is omitted.]

Statute No. 79-587 of 11 July 1979 regarding the substantiation of reasons for administrative acts and the improvement of the relations between the authorities and the general public [Loi relative à la motivation des actes administratifs et à l'amélioration des relations entre l'administration et le public], as last amended by Statute No. 86-76 of 17 January 1986. Selected provisions: Articles 1 – 7.[10]

Article 1. Natural or legal persons have the right to be informed without delay of the reasons for individual unfavourable administrative decisions that concern them.
To that effect, decisions must be substantiated [motivées] that:
- restrict the exercise of public liberties or, in a general manner, constitute a policing measure;
- impose a sanction;
- make the grant of an authorisation subject to restrictive conditions or impose burdens;
- withdraw or repeal a decision creating rights;
- oppose a prescription, a foreclosure or a deprivation;
- refuse a benefit the attribution of which constitutes a right for the persons who fulfil the legal conditions to obtain it;
- refuse authorisation, except where the communication of the reasons could be of such a nature as to prejudice one of the secrets or interests protected by the provisions of the second to the fifth paragraph of Article 6 of statute [Loi] no. 78-753 of 17 July 1978 containing certain measures of improvement of the relations between the authorities and the general public.

Article 2. Individual administrative decisions that derogate from the general rules laid down by statute or regulation must equally be substantiated.

Article 3. The substantiation required by the present statute must be written and contain a statement of the considerations of law and of fact that constitute the foundation of the decision.

Article 4. Where absolute urgency has prevented that a decision is substantiated, the lack of substantiation does not entail the illegality of that decision. Nevertheless, upon request by the interested party, formulated within the period for appeal, the authority that has taken the decision will, within a period of one month, have to communicate the reasons to him.
The provisions of the present statute do not derogate from the statutory texts prohibiting the disclosure or the publication of facts covered by secrecy.

Article 5. An implicit decision taken in the case where an explicit decision should have been substantiated is not illegal due to the sole fact that it is not accompanied by such substantiation. Nevertheless, upon request by the interested party, formulated within the period for appeal, the reasons for every implicit decision of rejection will have to be communicated to him within the month following that request. In that case, the period for appeal against that decision is suspended until the expiry of two months following the day on which the reasons have been communicated to him.

Article 6. The organizations of social security and the institutions stipulated in Article L 351-2 of the Labour Code [code du travail] must make known the reasons for their individual decisions by which they refuse a benefit the attribution of which constitutes a right for the persons who fulfil the legal conditions to obtain it.
The obligation to substantiate extends to decisions by which the organizations and institutions in the meaning of the preceding paragraph refuse the attribution of aid or of subsidies within the framework of their public-health and social activity.

Article 7. Decrees of the Council of State [Conseil d'Etat] specify, to the extent necessary, the categories of decisions that must be substantiated by application of the present statute.

[The remainder of the Act is omitted.]

---

[10] Translation by E. Ramaekers.

Germany: Administrative Procedure

Administrative Procedure Act [Verwaltungsverfahrensgesetz] of 25 May 1976, as last amended by statute of 14 August 2009 (*BGBl.* I p. 2827). Selected provisions: Part I, Chapters 1, 2 and §8a of Chapter 3, and Parts II and III.[11]

Part I. Scope of application, local competence, electronic communication, inter-administrative assistance

Chapter 1. Scope of application

§ 1. (1) This Act applies to the administrative activity under public law of the authorities
1. of the Federation, the directly federal entities, institutions and foundations under public law,
2. of the States, the municipalities and associations of municipalities, the other legal persons under public law subject to supervision by the State where they execute federal law on behalf of the Federation,
as far as legal rules of the Federation do not contain identical as to their content or conflicting provisions.
(2) This Act also applies to the administrative activity under public law of the authorities indicated in sub-paragraph 1 no. 2 where the States execute federal law, which concerns subjects of the exclusive or concurrent legislation of the Federation, as their own affairs, as far as legal rules of the Federation do not contain identical as to their content or conflicting provisions. To the execution of federal statutes enacted after the entry into force of this Act, this applies only as far as the federal statutes, with the consent of the Bundesrat, declare this Act applicable.
(3) To the execution of federal law by the States this Act does not apply as far as the administrative activity of the authorities is regulated by an administrative procedure act under State law.
(4) An authority in the meaning of this Act is every office which performs tasks of public administration.

§2. (1) This Act does not apply to the activity of the churches, the religious associations and world-view communities as well as their organizations and institutions.
(2) This Act does further not apply to
1. procedures of the federal or State tax authorities under the Tax Code [Abgabenordnung],
2. criminal prosecution, the prosecution and sanctioning of administrative offences, legal aid for foreign countries in criminal and civil cases and, irrespective of § 80 (4), to measures under the law on the service of judges,
3. procedures before the German Patent and Brand Office [Deutsches Patent- und Markenamt] and the arbitration boards established with it,
4. procedures under the Social Security Code [Sozialgesetzbuch],
5. the law on the equalization of burdens,
6. the law on compensation.
(3) To the activity
1. of the court administrations and the authorities of the judicial administration, including the entities under public law subject to their supervision, this Act only applies as far as the activity is subject to review in proceedings before the courts of the administrative jurisdiction;
2. of the authorities in performance, aptitude or similar tests of persons only the §§ 3a to 13, 20 to 27, 29 to 38, 40 to 52, 79, 80 and 96 apply;
3. of the representations of the Federation abroad, this Act does not apply.

§ 3. (1) Locally competent is
1. in matters which relate to immovable property or a right or legal relationship attached to a certain location, the authority in whose district the property or the location is situated;
2. in matters which relate to the operation of an undertaking or one of its business premises, to the practicing of a profession or to another permanent occupation, the authority in whose district the undertaking or the premises are, or are to be, operated or the profession or the occupation is, or is to be, practiced;
3. in other matters,
a. concern a natural person, the authority in whose district the natural person has or last had its habitual sojourn,
b. concern a legal person or an association, the authority in whose district the legal person or the association has or last had its seat;

---

[11] Translation by S. Hardt & Ph. Kiiver.

Part II. Administrative Law

4. in matters for which the competence does not flow from the nos. 1 to 3, the authority in whose district the cause for the official action arises.
(2) If several authorities are competent in accordance with sub-paragraph 1, then the authority which has first been concerned with the matter decides, unless the common supervisory authority which is competent for the subject matter determines that another locally competent authority has to decide. In cases in which a matter relates to several business premises of a business or undertaking, it may specify one of the authorities competent under sub-paragraph 1 no. 2 as the commonly competent authority if, with due regard to the interests of those involved, this is appropriate for a comprehensive decision. This supervisory authority further decides on the local competence if several authorities consider themselves competent or not competent or if competence is doubtful for other reasons. If a common supervisory authority is lacking, then the supervisory authorities which are competent for the subject matter take the decision together.
(3) If the circumstances that form the basis for the competence change in the course of the administrative procedure, then the authority which has been competent so far may continue the administrative procedure, if, with due regard to the interests of those involved, this serves the easy and effective completion of the procedure and if the authority which is now competent agrees.
(4) In case of an imminent danger, every authority is locally competent for urgency measures in whose district the cause for the official action arises. The authority which is locally competent under sub-paragraph 1 nos. 1 to 3 must be informed immediately.

§3a. (1) The transmission of electronic documents is permissible as far as the recipient opens an access for this purpose.
(2) A written form prescribed by legal rule may, as far as a legal rule does not provide otherwise, be replaced by the electronic form. In this case, the electronic document must be provided with a qualified electronic signature under the Signature Act [Signaturgesetz]. Signing with a pseudonym which does not allow for the identification of the person holding the signature key is not permissible.
(3) If an electronic document transmitted to the authority is not suitable for being processed by it, then it immediately informs the addressor thereof, stating the technical requirements that are applicable to it. If a recipient asserts that he is unable to process the electronic document transmitted by the authority, then it has to transmit it to him again in a suitable electronic format or as a written document.

§ 4. (1) Every authority renders supplementary assistance (inter-administrative assistance) [Amtshilfe] to other authorities upon request.
(2) There is no inter-administrative assistance where
1. authorities render assistance to each other within an existing hierarchical relationship;
2. the assistance consists of acts which the seized authority is responsible for as its own task.

§ 5. (1) An authority may in particular request inter-administrative assistance if it
1. cannot perform the official action itself for legal reasons;
2. cannot perform the official action itself for factual reasons, especially because it lacks the staff or facilities required for the performance of the official action;
3. depends, for the performance of its tasks, on the knowledge of facts which are unknown to it and which it is unable to investigate itself;
4. requires, for the performance of its tasks, documents or other evidence which is in the possession of the seized authority;
5. could perform the official action only with a significantly greater effort compared to the seized authority.
(2) The seized authority may not render assistance if
1. it is not able to do so for legal reasons;
2. by the rendering of assistance significant disadvantages would arise for the well-being of the Federation or of a State.
The seized authority is in particular not obliged to provide documents or files as well as to provide information if the processes must be kept secret according to statute or by virtue of their nature.
(3) The seized authority does not need to render assistance if
1. another authority can provide the assistance significantly more easily or with a significantly smaller effort;
2. it could only render the assistance with a disproportionately great effort;
3. it would, taking into account the tasks of the requesting authority, seriously jeopardize the performance of its own tasks by the assistance.

(4) The seized authority may not refuse the assistance because it considers the request inexpedient for reasons other than those mentioned in sub-paragraph 4 or because it considers the measure to be realized with the assistance inexpedient.
(5) If the seized authority considers itself not to be obliged to render assistance, then it informs the requesting authority of its opinion. If the latter insists on the inter-administrative assistance, then the common supervisory authority competent for the subject matter or, where such a common supervisory authority does not exist, the supervisory authority competent for the seized authority for the subject matter decides on the obligation to render inter-administrative assistance.

§ 6. If, for the inter-administrative assistance, several authorities come into consideration, then, if possible, an authority of the lowest administrative level of the administrative branch to which the requesting authority belongs shall be seized.

§ 7. (1) The admissibility of the measure which is to be realized by the inter-administrative assistance is determined by the law applicable to the requesting authority, the execution of the inter-administrative assistance by the law applicable to the seized authority.
(2) The requesting authority is responsible to the seized authority for the lawfulness of the measure to be taken. The seized authority is responsible for the execution of the inter-administrative assistance.

§ 8. (1) The requesting authority does not have to pay any administrative fee to the seized authority for the inter-administrative assistance. It must reimburse the seized authority upon demand for expenses if they exceed 35 euro in an individual case. If authorities of the same legal body [Rechtsträger] render inter-administrative assistance to each other, then the expenses are not reimbursed.
(2) If the seized authority performs an official action subject to costs in order to carry out the inter-administrative assistance, then it is entitled to the costs (administrative fees, utilization fees and expenses) owed by a third person in that context.

Chapter 3. European administrative cooperation

§ 8a. (1) Every authority accords the authorities of other member states of the European Union assistance upon request, to the extent that this is required pursuant to legal acts of the European Community.
(2) Authorities of other member states of the European Union may be requested to provide assistance to the extent that this is allowed pursuant to legal acts of the European Community. Assistance is to be requested to the extent that this is required pursuant to legal acts of the European Community.
(3) §§ 5, 7 and 8 (2) are to be applied mutatis mutandis to the extent that this does not contravene legal acts of the European Community.

[§§ 8b to 8e are omitted.]

Part II. General provisions regarding the administrative procedure

Chapter 1. Procedural principles

§ 9. For the purpose of this Act, the administrative procedure is the externally effective activity of the authorities which aims at the examination of the conditions, the preparation and the issuing of an administrative act or at the conclusion of a contract under public law; it includes the issuing of the administrative act and the conclusion of the contract under public law.

§ 10. The administrative procedure is not bound to specific forms as far as no specific legal rules exist as to the form of the procedure. It must be carried out easily, expediently and quickly.

§ 11. Capable of participating in the procedure are
1. natural and legal persons,
2. associations, as far as they can be the carrier of a right,
3. authorities.

PART II. ADMINISTRATIVE LAW

§ 12. (1) Capable of carrying out procedural acts are
1. natural persons that have capacity to act [geschäftsfähig] under private law,
2. natural persons that are restricted in their capacity to act under private law, as far as they are recognized for the subject matter of the procedure as having capacity to act by rules of private law or as able to act by rules of public law,
3. legal persons and associations (§11 no. 2) through their legal representatives or through special agents,
4. authorities through their directors, their representatives or assignees.
(2) If a reserve for consent under § 1903 of the Civil Code [Bürgerliches Gesetzbuch] concerns the subject matter of the procedure, then a person under custody who has capacity to act is only capable to carry out procedural acts as far as he may act without consent of the custodian under the rules of private law or is recognized as able to act by rules of public law.
(3) The §§ 53 and 55 of the Code of Civil Procedure [Zivilprozessordnung] apply mutatis mutandis.

§ 13. (1) Participants are
1. applicant and respondent,
2. those to whom the authority intends to address or has addressed the administrative act,
3. those with whom the authority intends to conclude or has concluded a contract under public law,
4. those who have been involved in the procedure by the authority under sub-paragraph 2.
(2) The authority may upon its own motion or upon application involve those as participants whose legal interests can be affected by the outcome of the procedure. If the outcome of the procedure creates an effect in law for a third party, then this third party must upon application be involved as a participant; as far as he is known to the authority, it has to inform him of the initiation of the procedure.
(3) He who must be heard without the conditions of sub-paragraph 1 being fulfilled does not thereby become a participant.

§ 14. (1) A participant may be represented by an agent [Bevollmächtigter]. The agency [Vollmacht] entitles to all procedural acts relating to the administrative procedure as far as not otherwise follows from its content. The agent has to provide written evidence for his agency on demand. A revocation of the agency only becomes effective as regards the authority when it reaches it.
(2) The agency is revoked neither by the death of the principal nor by a change in his capacity to act or in his legal representation; however, the agent must, where he acts on behalf of the legal successor in the administrative procedure, provide the agency from the legal successor in writing on demand.
(3) If an agent is appointed for the procedure, then the authority shall address him. It may address the participant himself as far as he is obliged to cooperate. If the authority addresses the participant, then the agent shall be informed. Rules regarding the delivery to agents remain unaffected.
(4) A participant may attend hearings and consultations with a counsel [Beistand]. What is put forward by the counsel is deemed to be put forward by the participant as far as he does not contradict immediately.
(5) Agents and counsels must be rejected where they take care of the legal matters of others in a businesslike manner without being authorized to do so.
(6) Agents and counsels may be barred from making submissions if they are inapt for this purpose; from oral submissions they may only be barred if they are incapable of making appropriate submissions. Persons who are authorized to represent in administrative court proceedings pursuant to § 67 (2) first and second sentence no. 3 to 7 of the Administrative Court Procedure Act [Verwaltungsgerichtsordnung] may not be barred.
(7) The bar under sub-paragraphs 5 and 6 must also be communicated to the participant whose agent or counsel is being barred. Procedural acts of the barred agent or counsel which he carries out after the bar are ineffective.

§ 15. A participant without a place of residence or habitual sojourn, seat or headquarters within the country must on demand, within a reasonable time, specify to the authority an agent authorized to receive [Empfangsbevollmächtigter] within the country. If he fails to do so, then a written document addressed to him is deemed received on the seventh day after its posting and an electronically transmitted document is deemed received on the third day after its sending. This does not apply if it is established that the document has not reached the addressee or has reached him on a later moment. The legal consequences of the failure must be brought to the knowledge of the participant.

§ 16. (1) If there is no representative, then the court of guardianship [Vormundschaftsgericht] must appoint a suitable representative upon request by the authority
1. for a participant whose identity is unknown;
2. for an absent participant whose sojourn is unknown or who is unable to take care of his matters;

3. for a participant without sojourn within the country if he has failed to comply, within the fixed time, with the demand by the authority to appoint a representative;
4. for a participant who is unable to become active in the administrative procedure himself as a result of a mental illness or a physical, mental or psychological disability;
5. in case of ownerless goods to which the procedure relates, for the safeguarding of the rights and obligations that arise in relation to the good.
(2) For the appointment of the representative in the cases of sub-paragraph 1 no. 4 the court of guardianship is competent in whose district the participant has his habitual sojourn; otherwise the court of guardianship is competent in whose district the requesting authority has its seat.
(3) The representative is entitled toward the legal body [Rechtsträger] of the authority which has requested his appointment to an appropriate remuneration and to reimbursement of his cash outlays. The authority may claim compensation for its expenses from the represented party. It fixes the remuneration and quantifies the outlays and expenses.
(4) Otherwise, in the cases of sub-paragraph 1 no. 4 the rules on guardianship [Pflege], in the remaining cases the rules on care for legal interests [Pflegschaft] apply mutatis mutandis to the appointment and to the office of the representative.

§ 17. (1) In case of applications and submissions in an administrative procedure which have been signed by more than 50 persons on signature lists or have been submitted in the form of multiple copies of identical texts (uniform submissions), the signatory is deemed representative of the other signatories for the procedure who is indicated there by his name, his profession and his address as representative as far as he has not been appointed by them as an agent. Only a natural person can be a representative.
(2) The authority has the right not to take into consideration uniform submissions which do not contain the specifications under sub-paragraph 1 clause 1 clearly visible on every page containing a signature or which do not fulfil the requirement of sub-paragraph 1 clause 2. If the authority intends to proceed like this, it must notify this by way of publication according to local custom. The authority has furthermore the right not to take into consideration uniform submissions in as far as signatories have not stated their name or their address, or have done so in an illegible manner.
(3) The authority of representation expires as soon as the representative or the represented gives written notice of this to the authority; the representative may give such notice only with regard to all those represented. Where the represented gives such notice, he shall state at the same time whether he maintains his submission and whether he has appointed an agent.
(4) Where the authority of the representative comes to an end, the authority may request those no longer represented to appoint a common representative within a reasonable time. If more than 50 persons must be requested, then the authority may publish the request according to local custom. Where the request is not complied with in the time period set, the authority may appoint a common representative upon its own motion.

§ 18. (1) Where more than 50 persons are participating in an administrative procedure with the same interest without being represented, the authority may request them to appoint a common representative within a reasonable time if otherwise the due carrying out of the administrative procedure would be compromised. If they do not comply with the request within the time period set, then the authority may appoint a common representative upon its own motion. Only a natural person can be a representative.
(2) The authority of representation expires as soon as the representative or the represented gives written notice of this to the authority; the representative may give such notice only with regard to all those represented. Where the represented gives such notice, he shall state at the same time whether he maintains his submission and whether he has appointed an agent.

§ 19. (1) The representative has to take care of the interests of those represented conscientiously. He may carry out all procedural acts relating to the administrative procedure. He is not bound by instructions.
(2) § 14 (5) to (7) applies mutatis mutandis.
(3) The representative appointed by the authority is entitled toward its legal entity [Rechtsträger] to an appropriate remuneration and to reimbursement of his cash outlays. The authority may claim compensation for its expenses from those represented in equal shares. It fixes the remuneration and quantifies the outlays and expenses.

§ 20. (1) In an administrative procedure a person may not act for an authority
1. who is a participant himself,
2. who is a relative [Angehöriger] of a participant,
3. who represents a participant in general or in this administrative procedure pursuant to law or an agency,

4. who is a relative of a person who represents a participant in this procedure,
5. who is employed by a participant for remuneration or is active for him as a member of the board, of the supervisory board or of a similar organ; this does not apply to him whose employing public entity [Anstellungskörperschaft] is a participant;
6. who has outside his official capacity delivered an expert opinion or has otherwise become active in the subject matter.
Equal to the participant is he who can attain an immediate advantage or disadvantage by the activity or by the decision. This does not apply where the advantage or disadvantage is only based on the fact that someone belongs to a profession or population group whose common interests are affected by the subject matter.
(2) Sub-paragraph 1 does not apply to elections for honorary [ehrenamtlich] posts and to the dismissal of persons working in an honorary capacity.
(3) He who is excluded under sub-paragraph 1 may take urgent measures in case of an imminent danger.
(4) Where a member of a committee (§ 88) considers himself excluded or where it is doubtful if the conditions of sub-paragraph 1 are met, the chairman of the committee has to be notified of this. The committee decides on the exclusion. The person concerned may not participate in this decision. The excluded member may not be present at the further deliberation and decision-making.

(5) Relatives in the sense of sub-paragraph 1 no. 2 and 4 are:
1. the fiancé,
2. the spouse,
3. relatives and in-laws in direct line,
4. siblings,
5. children of the siblings,
6. spouses of the siblings and siblings of the spouses,
7. siblings of the parents,
8. persons connected to each other like parents and children by virtue of a foster relationship with a common household instituted for a longer period of time (foster children and foster parents).
The persons indicated in clause 1 are also relatives if
1. in the cases of the nos. 2, 3 and 6 the marriage forming the basis of the relation no longer exists;
2. in the cases of the nos. 3 to 7 the relatedness or in-law relatedness has lapsed by adoption as a child;
3. in the case of no. 8 the common household no longer exists as far as the persons continue to be connected to each other like parents and child.

§ 21. (1) If a reason exists which is suitable to justify distrust against an unprejudiced exercise of office, or if the existence of such a reason is alleged by a participant, then he who is to become active in an administrative procedure for an authority has to notify the director of the authority or his assignee and to abstain from involvement upon his order. Where the concern of prejudice relates to the director of the authority, the supervisory authority issues this order as far as the director of the authority does not abstain from involvement himself.
(2) To members of a committee (§ 88), § 20 (4) applies mutatis mutandis.

§ 22. The authority decides according to its best judgment whether and when it carries out an administrative procedure. This does not apply where, by virtue of legal rules, the authority
1. must become active upon its own motion or upon application;
2. may only become active upon application and no application exists.

§ 23. (1) The official language is German.
(2) Where applications are made or submissions, evidence, certificates or other documents are presented to an authority in a foreign language, the authority shall immediately demand the presentation of a translation. In justified cases the presentation of a certified translation or a translation produced by a publicly appointed or sworn interpreter or translator may be demanded. If the demanded translation is not presented immediately, then the authority may obtain a translation itself at the expense of the participant. Where the authority has involved interpreters or translators, they receive a remuneration under application mutatis mutandis of the Judiciary Remuneration and Compensation Act [Justizvergütungs- und -entschädigungsgesetz].
(3) If by notification, application or submission of a declaration of will a period of time is to be initiated during which the authority must become active in a certain manner, and if these are received in a foreign language, then the period of time will only start on the moment that a translation is available to the authority.
(4) If by notification, application or a declaration of will which are received in a foreign language a period of time toward the authority is to be observed in favour of the participant, a claim under public law is to be asserted or a

performance is to be requested, then the notification, the application or the declaration of will are deemed submitted on the moment of receipt by the authority if, on demand of the authority, a translation is presented within a reasonable time to be fixed by it. Otherwise the moment of receipt of the translation is decisive, as far as not otherwise follows from international agreements. Notice of this legal consequence has to be given with the fixing of the time period.

§ 24. (1) The authority investigates the facts of the case upon its own motion. It decides on the manner and the scope of the investigations; it is not bound by the submissions and the motions to hear evidence from the participants.
(2) The authority has to take into consideration all circumstances significant for the individual case, also those in favour of the participants.
(3) The authority may not refuse the receipt of declarations or applications which fall within its area of competence because of the fact that it considers the declaration or the application inadmissible or unfounded on the substance.

§ 25. (1) The authority shall encourage the submission of declarations, the filing of applications or the correction of declarations or applications where it is evident that they have only by mistake or out of unawareness been omitted or submitted or filed incorrectly. It provides, as far as necessary, information about the rights to which participants are entitled in the administrative procedure and about the duties incumbent on them.
(2) The authority deliberates, to the extent necessary, already before the filing of an application with the future applicant which proofs and documents are to be provided by him and in which manner the procedure can be expedited. To the extent that it serves the expedition of procedure, it shall inform the applicant immediately after the receipt of the application on the estimated length of the procedure and the completeness of the documents in the application.

§ 26. (1) The authority avails itself of the evidence which it deems necessary according to its best judgment for the investigation of the facts of the case. In particular it may
1. obtain information of any sort,
2. hear participants, question witnesses and experts or obtain the written or electronic statement of participants, experts and witnesses,
3. consult documents and files,
4. conduct inspections [Augenschein].
(2) The participants shall co-operate in the investigation of the facts of the case. They shall in particular disclose the facts and evidence known to them. A further-reaching obligation to co-operate in the investigation of the facts of the case, in particular an obligation to appear in person or to make a statement, only exists as far as it is especially provided for by a legal rule.
(3) For witnesses and experts an obligation to make a statement or to give an expert opinion exists as far as it is provided for by a legal rule. If the authority has involved witnesses and experts, they receive on application a compensation or remuneration under application mutatis mutandis of the Judiciary Remuneration and Compensation Act [Justizvergütungs- und -entschädigungsgesetz].

§ 27. (1) The authority may only demand and receive a statutory affirmation [Versicherung an Eides statt] in the investigation of the facts of the case if the receipt of the affirmation about the subject concerned and in the procedure concerned is provided for by statute or ordinance [Rechtsverordnung] and if the authority has been declared competent by a legal rule. A statutory affirmation shall only be demanded where other means for the exploration of the truth are not available, have led to no result or require a disproportional effort. Of persons not having capacity take an oath in the meaning of § 393 of the Code of Civil Procedure [Zivilprozessordnung], a statutory affirmation may not be demanded.
(2) If the statutory affirmation is recorded by the authority in writing, then only the director of the authority, his general substitute and members of the public service who are qualified to hold a judgeship or who fulfil the conditions of § 110 clause 1 of the German Judges Act [Deutsches Richtergesetz] are authorized to take the record. The director of the authority or his general substitute may authorize in writing, in general or for the individual case, other members of the public service for this purpose.
(3) The affirmation consists of the fact that the affirmant confirms the truthfulness of his statement regarding the subject concerned and declares: "I affirm in lieu of an oath that I have told the whole truth to the best of my knowledge and have not concealed anything." Agents and counsels are entitled to participate in the recording of the statutory affirmation.

(4) Before the recording of the statutory affirmation, the affirmant must be informed about the meaning of the statutory affirmation and the consequences under criminal law of an incorrect or incomplete statutory affirmation. The information has to be noted in the record.
(5) The record must further contain the names of all persons present as well as the location and the day of recording. The record must be read to the one who issues the statutory affirmation for approval or must on demand be presented to him for review. The given approval must be noted and signed by the affirmant. The record must then be signed by the one who has received the statutory affirmation as well as by the secretary.

§ 28. (1) Before an administrative act is issued that interferes with the rights of a participant, he must be given the opportunity to speak out on the facts relevant for the decision.
(2) The hearing may be abstained from where it is not necessary under the circumstances of the individual case, in particular where
1. an immediate decision appears necessary because of imminent danger or in the public interest;
2. by the hearing the observance of a time limit significant to the decision would be jeopardized;
3. the statements of fact made by a participant in an application or declaration are not to be deviated from to his detriment;
4. the authority intends to issue a general order [Allgemeinverfügung] or a larger number of similar administrative acts or administrative acts by means of automatic facilities;
5. measures are to be taken in administrative enforcement [Verwaltungsvollstreckung].
(3) A hearing does not take place where it is in conflict with a pressing public interest.

§ 29. (1) The authority must grant the participants access to the files concerning the procedure as far as the knowledge thereof is necessary for the assertion or defence of their legal interests. Until the completion of the administrative procedure, clause 1 does not apply to draft decisions as well as to works for their immediate preparation. As far as a representation takes place under §§ 17 and 18, only the representatives are entitled to access to the files.
(2) The authority is not obliged to grant access to the files as far as thereby the proper performance of the tasks of the authority would be jeopardized, the making known of the content of the files would cause disadvantages for the well-being of the Federation or of a State, or as far as the processes must be kept secret by virtue of statute or by virtue of their nature, especially because of the legitimate interests of the participants or of third persons.
(3) Access to the files takes place at the authority which keeps the files. In individual cases, access may also take place at another authority or at a diplomatic or salaried consular representation of the Federal Republic of Germany abroad; further exceptions may be permitted by the authority which keeps the files.

§ 30. The participants have the right that their secrets, in particular the secrets belonging to the personal sphere of life as well as business and commercial secrets, not be disclosed by the authority without authorization.

Chapter 2. Periods of time, fixed moments in time, restoration

§ 31. (1) To the calculation of periods of time [Fristen] and the fixing of moments in time [Termine] the §§ 187 to 193 of the Civil Code [Bürgerliches Gesetzbuch] apply mutatis mutandis as far as not otherwise is provided by the sub-paragraphs 2 to 5.
(2) A period of time fixed by an authority starts on the day which follows the notification of the period of time, except where otherwise is communicated to the person concerned.
(3) Where the end of a period of time falls on a Sunday, a public holiday or a Saturday, the period of time ends at the end of the next-following working day. This does not apply if, with reference to this rule, a specific day has been communicated to the person concerned as the end of the period of time.
(4) Where an authority has to render a performance for a certain period of time only, then this period ends at the end of its last day even if this day falls on a Sunday, a public holiday or a Saturday.
(5) The moment in time fixed by an authority must be observed even if it falls on a Sunday, a public holiday or a Saturday.
(6) Where a period of time is specified in hours, then Sundays, public holidays and Saturdays are counted as well.
(7) Periods of time which are fixed by an authority may be extended. Where such periods of time have already expired, they may be extended retroactively, especially if it would be inequitable [unbillig] to leave the legal consequences, which have occurred due to the expiry of the period of time, in existence. The authority may combine the extension of the period of time with a supplementary provision under § 36.

§ 32. (1) Where someone has been prevented without fault [Verschulden] from observing a period of time, he must be granted restoration in his previous state upon application. The fault of a representative must be imputed to the represented.
(2) The application must be made within two weeks after the disappearance of the impediment. The facts for the justification of the application must be substantiated with the submission of the application or in the procedure on the application. Within the period of time for application, the act missed must be made up for. Where this has happened, restoration may also be granted without application.
(3) After one year since the end of the missed period of time, restoration may no longer be applied for or the act missed no longer be made up for, except where this has been impossible before the expiry of the one-year period due to force majeure [höhere Gewalt].
(4) The authority which has to decide on the act missed decides on the application for restoration.
(5) Restoration is inadmissible where it follows from a legal rule that it is excluded.

Chapter 3. Official authentication

§ 33. (1) Every authority is authorized to authenticate copies of documents which it has issued itself. Furthermore the authorities in the meaning of § 1 (1) no. 1 specified by the Federal Government by ordinance [Rechtsverordnung] and the authorities competent under State law are authorized to authenticate copies where the original has been issued by an authority or where the copy is needed for submission with an authority, as far as the issuing of authenticated copies from official registers and archives is not exclusively reserved for other authorities by legal rule; the ordinance does not require the consent of the Bundesrat.
(2) Copies may not be authenticated where circumstances justify the assumption that the original content of the written document, the copy of which is to be authenticated, has been altered, in particular where this written document contains gaps, deletions, insertions, changes, illegible words, numbers or characters, traces of the erasure of words, numbers and characters or where the coherence of a document consisting of several pages is broken.
(3) A copy is authenticated by a statement of authentication which must be added under the copy. The statement must contain
1. the exact indication of the written document the copy of which is authenticated,
2. the ascertainment that the authenticated copy matches the presented document,
3. the notice that the authenticated copy is only issued for presentation with the specified authority if the original has not been issued by an authority,
4. the location and the day of the authentication, the signature of the civil servant competent for the authentication and the official seal.
(4) The sub-paragraphs 1 to 3 apply mutatis mutandis to the authentication of
1. photocopies, heliographies and similar duplicates produced by use of technical means,
2. negatives of written documents produced by way of photography which are kept with an authority,
3. print-outs of electronic documents,
4. electronic documents
a. which have been produced to depict a written document,
b. which have received another technical format than the original document which has been provided with a qualified electronic signature.
(5) The statement of authentication must, in addition to the specifications under sub-paragraph 3 clause 2, for the authentication
1. of the print-out of an electronic document provided with a qualified electronic signature, contain the ascertainment
a. whom the signature check identifies as holder of the signature,
b. which time the signature check identifies for the placement of the signature and
c. which certificate with which data formed the basis of the signature;
2. of an electronic document, contain the name of the civil servant competent for the authentication and the indication of the authority which carries out the authentication; the signature of the civil servant competent for the authentication and the official seal under sub-paragraph 3 clause 2 no. 4 are replaced by a permanently verifiable qualified electronic signature.
Where an electronic document is authenticated under clause 1 no. 2 which has received another technical format than the original document which has been provided with a qualified electronic signature, the statement of authentication must additionally contain the ascertainments under clause 1 no. 1 for the original document.

(6) The documents produced under sub-paragraph 4 are, as far as they are authenticated, equal to authenticated copies.

§ 34. (1) The authorities in the meaning of § 1 (1) no. 1 specified by ordinance [Rechtsverordnung] by the Federal Government and the authorities competent under State law are authorized to authenticate signatures if the signed written document is needed for submission with an authority or another office to which the written document must be submitted by virtue of a legal rule. This does not apply to
1. signatures without a corresponding text,
2. signatures which require public authentication (§ 129 of the Civil Code [Bürgerliches Gesetzbuch])
(2) A signature shall only be authenticated if it is given or approved in the presence of the authenticating civil servant.
(3) The statement of authentication must be added directly next to the signature which is to be authenticated. It must contain
1. the affirmation that the signature is authentic,
2. the precise indication of the person whose signature is being authenticated as well as a notice whether the civil servant competent for the authentication has established certainty about this person and if the signature has been given or approved in his presence,
3. the notice that the authentication is only intended for presentation to the specified authority or office,
4. the location and the day of the authentication, die signature of the civil servant competent for the authentication and the official seal.
(4) The sub-paragraphs 1 to 3 apply mutatis mutandis to the authentication of paraphs.
(5) The ordinances under sub-paragraphs 1 and 4 do not require the consent of the Bundesrat.

Part III. Administrative Act

Chapter 1. Formation of the administrative act

§ 35. An administrative act [Verwaltungsakt] is every order, decision or other sovereign measure which an authority issues for the regulation of an individual case in the area of public law and which is aimed at direct external legal effect. A general order [Allgemeinverfügung] is an administrative act which is aimed at a group of people defined or definable on the basis of general characteristics or which concerns the public-law character of a good or its use by the general public.

§ 36. (1) An administrative act to which there is an entitlement may only be furnished with a supplementary provision where it is permitted by a legal rule or where it is to ensure that the statutory conditions of the administrative act are fulfilled.
(2) Notwithstanding sub-paragraph 1 an administrative act may, according to best judgment, be issued with
1. a provision under which a benefit or burden begins, ends or applies for a certain period of time (limitation in time);
2. a provision under which the creation or the lapse of a benefit or a burden depends on the uncertain occurrence of a future event (conditionality);
3. a reserve of revocation
or be combined with
4. a provision by which an action, toleration or omission is imposed on the beneficiary (obligation);
5. a reserve of subsequent incorporation, alteration or supplementation of an obligation.
(3) A supplementary provision may not be contrary to the purpose of the administrative act.

§ 37. (1) An administrative act must be sufficiently precise as regards its content.
(2) An administrative act may be issued in writing, electronically, orally or in another manner. An oral administrative act must be confirmed in writing or electronically where there is a legitimate interest therein and the person concerned demands it immediately. An electronic administrative act must be confirmed in writing under the same conditions; § 3a (2) does not apply in this respect.
(3) A written or electronic administrative act must indicate the issuing authority and contain the signature or the name of the director of the authority, his substitute or his assignee. Where the electronic form is applied to an administrative act for which the written form is prescribed by a legal rule, also the qualified certificate which forms the basis of the signature or a corresponding attributive certificate must indicate the issuing authority.

(4) For an administrative act, the permanent verifiability of the signature required under § 3a (2) may be prescribed by a legal rule.
(5) In a written administrative act which is issued by means of automatic facilities, signature and name may be omitted in deviation from sub-paragraph 3. For the indication of contents, key codes may be used if he to whom the administrative act is addressed or who is affected by it is able to clearly apprehend the content of the administrative act on the basis of the explanations given with it.

§ 38. (1) A promise given by the competent authority to issue or omit a certain administrative act later (assurance) requires the written form for its validity. Where prior to the issuing of the assured administrative act a hearing of participants or the co-operation of another authority or of a committee in required on the basis of a legal rule, the assurance may only be given after the hearing of the participants or after the co-operation of this authority or of the committee.
(2) To the invalidity of the assurance, notwithstanding sub-paragraph 1 clause 1, § 44, to the remedying of defects in the hearing of participants and the co-operation of other authorities or committees § 45 (1) nos. 3 to 5 and (2), to the withdrawal § 48, to the revocation, notwithstanding sub-paragraph 3, § 49 apply mutatis mutandis.
(3) Where after the issuing of the assurance the factual or legal situation changes in such a way that the authority, if aware of the subsequent change, would not have issued or would not have been allowed for legal reasons to issue the assurance, the authority is no longer bound by the assurance.

§ 39. (1) A written or electronic administrative act as well as an administrative act confirmed in writing or electronically must be provided with a substantiation of reasons [Begründung]. In the substantiation, the essential factual and legal reasons must be communicated which have led the authority to its decision. The substantiation of discretionary decisions shall also indicate the considerations which the authority based itself on in exercising its discretion.
(2) No substantiation of reasons is required
1. as far as the authority grants an application or follows a declaration and the administrative act does not affect the rights of others;
2. as far as the opinion of the authority about the factual or legal situation is already known or easily apprehensible to the person to whom the administrative act is addressed or who is affected by it;
3. where the authority issues a larger number of similar administrative acts or administrative acts by means of automatic facilities and substantiation is not necessary under the circumstances of the individual case;
4. where this follows from a legal rule;
5. where a general order is announced publicly.

§ 40. Where the authority is authorized to act in its discretion [Ermessen], it must exercise its discretion according to the purpose of its authorization and must observe the legal limits of the discretion.

§ 41. (1) An administrative act must be notified to the participant to whom it is addressed or who is affected by it. If an agent is appointed, then the notification may be addressed to him.
(2) A written administrative act delivered by mail within the country is deemed notified on the third day after its posting, an administrative act delivered electronically is deemed notified on the third day after its sending. This does not apply where the administrative act has not been received or has been received at a later time; in case of doubt the authority must prove the receipt of the administrative act and the time of receipt.
(3) An administrative act may be notified in public if that is permitted by a legal rule. A general order may also be notified in public where a notification to the participants is undesirable.
(4) The public notification of a written or electronic administrative act is effected by publishing its operative part according to local custom. In the publication according to local custom it must be stated where the administrative act and the substantiation of its reasons can be inspected. The administrative act is deemed notified two weeks after its publication according to local custom. In a general order another day, but at the earliest the day following the publication, may be specified.
(5) Provisions regarding the notification of an administrative act by means of delivery remain unaffected.

§ 42. The authority may correct typing errors, mathematical errors and similar evident mistakes in the administrative act at any time. Correction must be effected in case of a legitimate interest of the participant. The authority is entitled to demand the presentation of the document which is to be corrected.

§ 42a. (1) A permission applied for is considered to have been granted upon expiry of a period of time fixed for the decision (fiction of permission), if this is so determined by a legal rule and the application is sufficiently precise. The provisions regarding the validity of administrative acts and legal remedies apply mutatis mutandis.
(2) The time period under paragraph 1, first sentence, is three months, to the extent that nothing deviating is provided by a legal rule. The period commences with the receipt of the complete set of documents. It may be extended appropriately once, if this is justified due to the difficulty of the matter. The extension of the period is to be substantiated with reasons and to be notified in time.
(3) Upon request he to whom the administrative act under § 41 (1) should have been notified, is to be issued a certification in writing of the entry into force of the fiction of permission.

Chapter 2. Validity of the administrative act

§ 43. (1) An administrative act becomes effective [wirksam] towards him to whom it is addressed or who is affected by it on the moment it is notified to him. The administrative act becomes effective with the content with which it is notified.
(2) An administrative act remains effective as long and as far as it is not withdrawn, revoked, otherwise repealed or has not expired through passage of time or otherwise.
(3) A void [nichtig] administrative act is ineffective.

§ 44. (1) An administrative act is void as far as it suffers from a particularly serious defect and this is evident in a reasonable appraisal of all relevant circumstances.
(2) Without regard to the existence of the conditions of sub-paragraph 1, an administrative act is void
1. which has been issued in writing or electronically but does not identify the issuing authority;
2. which under a legal rule may only be issued by delivery of a certificate but does not satisfy this form;
3. which an authority has issued outside its competence based on § 3 (1) no. 1 without being authorized thereto;
4. which for factual reasons nobody can carry out;
5. which demands the commission of an unlawful act which constitutes a criminal offence or an act subject to a fine;
6. which is against good morals.
(3) An administrative act is not immediately void only for the reason that
1. provisions regarding local competence have not been complied with, except in the case under sub-paragraph 2 no. 3;
2. a person excluded under § 20 (1) clause 1 nos. 2 to 6 has co-operated;
3. a committee assigned to co-operate by legal rule has not taken the decision which is compulsory for the issuing of the administrative act or has not had capacity to take a decision;
4. the co-operation of another authority required under a legal rule has not taken place.
(4) If the voidness only affects a part of the administrative act, then it is void in whole if the void part is so essential that the authority would not have issued the administrative act without the void part.
(5) The authority may at all times establish the voidness upon its own motion; upon application it must be established if the applicant has a legitimate interest therein.

§ 45. (1) A violation of procedural or formal requirements which does not render the administrative act void according to § 44 is negligible if
1. the application necessary for the issuing of the administrative act is subsequently filed;
2. the necessary substantiation of reasons is subsequently given;
3. the necessary hearing of a participant is made up for;
4. the decision of a committee whose co-operation is necessary for the issuing of the administrative act is subsequently taken;
5. the necessary co-operation of an authority is made up for.
(2) Acts under sub-paragraph 1 may be made up for until the completion of the last instance on points of fact in an administrative court procedure.
(3) If an administrative act lacks the necessary substantiation of reasons or if the necessary hearing of a participant has been omitted before the issuing of the administrative act and if thereby the timely challenge of the administrative act has been missed, then the failure to observe the time limit for legal remedies is deemed to be without fault. The event which is decisive for the time limit for restoration in accordance with § 32 (2) occurs on the moment of making up for the omitted procedural act.

§ 46. The repeal of an administrative act which is not void under § 44 may not be demanded only because it has come into being under a violation of provisions on procedure, form or local competence, if it is evident that the violation has not influenced the decision on the substance.

§ 47. (1) A defective administrative act may be reinterpreted as another administrative act if it is aimed at the same objective, could legally have been issued in the followed procedural manner and form by the issuing authority and if the conditions for its issuing are fulfilled.
(2) Sub-paragraph 1 does not apply where the administrative act as which the defective administrative act were to be reinterpreted would contradict the evident intention of the issuing authority or where its legal consequences would be more detrimental to the person concerned than those of the defective administrative act are. A reinterpretation is furthermore inadmissible if the defective administrative act could not be withdrawn.
(3) A decision which may only be issued as a statutorily bound decision may not be reinterpreted as a discretionary decision.
(4) § 28 must be applied mutatis mutandis.

§ 48. (1) An unlawful administrative act may, after it has become unchallengeable, be withdrawn in whole or in part with effect for the future or for the past. An administrative act which has given rise to or confirmed a right or a legally significant advantage (favourable administrative act) may only be withdrawn under the restrictions of the sub-paragraphs 2 to 4.
(2) An unlawful administrative act which grants a one-time or continuous benefit in money or divisible benefit in kind, or is a precondition for it, may not be withdrawn as far as the beneficiary has relied on the continued existence of the administrative act and his reliance, weighed against the public interest in a withdrawal, is worthy of protection. As a rule, the reliance is worthy of protection where the beneficiary has expended the granted benefits or has made a disposition of property which he can no longer, or only under unacceptable disadvantages, revoke. The beneficiary may not invoke reliance where he
1. has effected the administrative act through wilful deceit [arglistige Täuschung], threat or bribery;
2. has effected the administrative act through submissions which were incorrect or incomplete in essential respects;
3. was aware of the unlawfulness of the administrative act or was not aware of it as a result of gross negligence.
In the cases of clause 3 the administrative act is, as a rule, withdrawn with retroactive effect.
(3) Where an unlawful administrative act which does not fall under sub-paragraph 2 is withdrawn, the authority must, upon application, compensate the person concerned for the proprietary disadvantage [Vermögensnachteil] which he incurs as a consequence of having relied on the existence of the administrative act, as far as his reliance, weighed against the public interest, is worthy of protection. Sub-paragraph 2 clause 3 must be applied. The proprietary disadvantage must, however, not be compensated in excess of the amount of the interest which the person concerned has in the existence of the administrative act. The proprietary disadvantage to be compensated is established by the authority. The claim may only be asserted during one year; the period begins as soon as the authority has notified it to the person concerned.
(4) Where the authority is informed of facts which justify the withdrawal of an unlawful administrative act, the withdrawal is only admissible during one year from the moment of information. This does not apply in the case of sub-paragraph 2 clause 3 no. 1.
(5) On the withdrawal decides, after incontestability of the administrative act, the authority competent under § 3; this does also apply where the administrative act to be withdrawn has been issued by another authority.

§ 49. (1) A lawful non-favourable administrative act may, also after it has become incontestable, be revoked in whole or in part with effect for the future, except if an administrative act of identical content would have to be issued again or if revocation is inadmissible for other reasons.
(2) A lawful favourable administrative act may, also after it has become incontestable, be revoked in whole or in part with effect for the future only
1. if revocation is permitted by a legal rule or is reserved in the administrative act;
2. if an obligation is connected with the administrative act and the beneficiary has not fulfilled this obligation or has not fulfilled it within the period of time fixed for him;
3. if the authority would, on the basis of facts that occurred subsequently, have been entitled not to issue the administrative act and if without the revocation the public interest would be jeopardized;
4. if the authority would, on the basis of a changed legal rule, be entitled not to issue the administrative act as far as the beneficiary has not yet made use of the benefit or has not yet received any benefit on the basis of the administrative act and if without the revocation the public interest would be jeopardized;
5. in order to prevent or remove serious disadvantages to public welfare.

§ 48 (4) applies mutatis mutandis.
(3) A lawful administrative act which grants a one-time or continuous benefit in money or a divisible benefit in kind to serve a certain purpose, or is a precondition for it, may, also after it has become incontestable, be revoked in whole or in part also with retroactive effect
1. if the benefit is not used, is not used shortly after its provision, or is no longer used for the purpose stipulated in the administrative act;
2. if an obligation is connected with the administrative act and the beneficiary has not fulfilled this obligation or has not fulfilled it within the period of time fixed to him.
§ 48 (4) applies mutatis mutandis.
(4) The revoked administrative act becomes ineffective with the coming into effect of the revocation if the authority does not specify another time.
(5) On the revocation decides, after incontestability of the administrative act, the authority competent under § 3; this does also apply where the administrative act to be revoked has been issued by another authority.
(6) Where a favourable administrative act is revoked in the cases of sub-paragraph 2 nos. 3 to 5, the authority must, upon application, compensate the person concerned for the proprietary disadvantage which he incurs as a consequence of having relied on the existence of the administrative act as far as his reliance is worthy of protection. § 48 (3) clause 3 to 5 applies mutatis mutandis. In disputes about the compensation, recourse to the ordinary courts is available.

§ 49a. (1) As far as an administrative act has been withdrawn or revoked with retroactive effect or has become ineffective as a result of the occurrence of a dissolving condition, benefits already afforded must be returned. The benefit to be returned must be fixed by means of a written administrative act.
(2) For the amount of the return, with the exception of the payment of interest, the provisions of the Civil Code [Bürgerliches Gesetzbuch] regarding the restitution of an unjustified enrichment are applicable mutatis mutandis. The beneficiary may not invoke the cessation of the enrichment as far as he was aware, or not aware as a result of gross negligence, of the circumstances that led to the withdrawal, the revocation or the ineffectiveness of the administrative act.
(3) From the occurrence of the ineffectiveness of the administrative act onward, interest of five percentage points above the base lending rate must be paid annually on the amount to be returned. The assertion of the interest due may in particular be abstained from if the beneficiary is not responsible for the circumstances that have led to the withdrawal, to the revocation or to the ineffectiveness of the administrative act and if he affords the amount to be returned within the period of time fixed by the authority.
(4) If a benefit is not used for the stipulated purpose shortly after the payment, then interest under sub-paragraph 3 clause 1 may be demanded for the time until use according to purpose is made of it. The same applies mutatis mutandis as far as a benefit is made use of although other means must be employed proportionately or preferentially. § 49 (1) clause 1 no. 1 remains unaffected.

§ 50. § 48 (1) clause 1 and (2) to (4) as well as § 49 (2) to (4) and (6) are not applicable where a favourable administrative act which is challenged by a third party is repealed during the preliminary proceedings or during the administrative court proceedings as far as the complaint or the legal action is thereby satisfied.

§ 51. The authority must upon application by the person concerned decide on the repeal or alteration of an incontestable administrative act if
1. the factual or legal situation which forms the basis of the administrative act has subsequently changed in favour of the person concerned;
2. new evidence is available which would have induced a decision more favourable for the person concerned;
3. reasons for resumption of the procedure according to § 580 of the Code of Civil Procedure [Zivilprozessordnung] are present.
(2) The application is only admissible if the person concerned has been, without serious fault, unable to assert the reason for the resumption in the previous procedure, in particular by a legal remedy.
(3) The application must be made within three months. The period of time begins with the day on which the person concerned has learned of the reason for resumption.
(4) The authority competent under § 3 decides on the application; this does also apply where the administrative act the repeal or alteration of which is desired has been issued by another authority.
(5) The provisions of § 48 (1) clause 1 and of § 49 (1) remain unaffected.

§ 52. If an administrative act is incontestably withdrawn or revoked or if for another reason it is not or no longer effective, then the authority may reclaim the documents or goods awarded on the basis of the administrative act which are intended for the verification of the rights deriving from the administrative act or for their execution. The holder and, as far as he is not the possessor, also the possessor of these documents or goods are obliged to return them. The holder or the possessor may, however, demand that the documents or goods be handed over to him again after having been marked as invalid by the authority; this does not apply to goods for which such marking is not possible or not possible with the necessary clarity or permanence.

Chapter 3. Effects of the administrative act regarding statutes of limitation

§ 53. (1) An administrative act which is issued for the assertion or enforcement of the claim of a public-law legal body [Rechtsträger] impedes the limitation of time of this claim. The impediment ends with the occurrence of the incontestability of the administrative act or six months after its expiry otherwise.

(2) Where an administrative act in the meaning of sub-paragraph 1 has become incontestable, the period of limitation is 30 years. As far as the administrative act has as its content a claim to recurring benefits becoming due in the future, the period of limitation applicable to that claim is maintained.

[The remainder of the Act is omitted.]

Administrative Court Procedure Act [Verwaltungsgerichtsordnung] of 21 January 1960, as last amended by federal statute of 21 August 2009 (*BGBl.* I p. 2870). Selected provisions: Chapters 1 and 6 of Part I.[12]

Part I. Judicial organization [Gerichtsverfassung]

Chapter 1. Courts

§ 1. The administrative jurisdiction is exercised by independent courts that are separate from the administrative authorities.

§ 2. Courts of the administrative jurisdiction are in the States the administrative courts and one Higher Administrative Court [Oberverwaltungsgericht] each, in the Federation the Federal Administrative Court [Bundesverwaltungsgericht] with its seat in Leipzig.

§ 3. (1) By statute are ordered
1. the establishment or dissolution of an administrative court or a Higher Administrative Court,
2. the relocation of the seat of a court,
3. changes in the delimitation of the judicial districts,
4. the allocation of particular subject areas to one administrative court for the districts of several administrative courts,
4a. the allocation of proceedings in which the local jurisdiction flows from § 52 no. 2 clause 1, 2 or 4 to another administrative court or to several administrative courts of the State,
5. the establishment of individual chambers of the administrative court or of individual senates of the Higher Administrative Court in other locations,
6. the referral of pending proceedings to another court in case of measures under the numbers 1, 3, 4 and 4a, if jurisdiction is not to be determined by the provisions applying so far.
(2) Several States may agree upon the establishment of a common court or of common benches of a court or the expansion of court districts beyond State borders, also for particular subject areas.

§ 4. To the courts of the administrative jurisdiction, the provisions of the second title of the Judicial Organization Act [Gerichtsverfassungsgesetz] apply mutatis mutandis. The presidium appoints the members and three alternates of the bench competent for decisions under § 99 (2), each for the period of four years. The members and their alternates must be judges appointed for life.

§ 5. (1) The administrative court consists of the president and of the presiding judges and further judges in necessary numbers.
(2) At the administrative court, chambers are formed.
(3) The chamber of the administrative court decides as a body of three judges and two lay judges, as far as it is not a single judge who decides. In decisions outside the oral proceedings and in court notifications (§ 84) the lay judges do not participate.

§ 6. (1) The chamber shall, as a rule, assign the legal dispute to one of their members as a single judge to decide, if
1. the case does not feature any particular difficulties of a factual or legal nature and
2. the legal issue is of no fundamental importance.
A judge on probation may in the first year after his appointment not be a single judge.
(2) The legal dispute may not be assigned to the single judge if oral proceedings have already taken place before the chamber, unless a provisional, partial or interlocutory judgment has been given in the meantime.
(3) The single judge may, after having heard the parties, refer the legal dispute back to the chamber if it follows from a significant change in the state of proceedings that the legal issue is of fundamental importance or that the case features particular difficulties of a factual or legal nature. A renewed referral to the single judge is inadmissible.
(4) Court orders under sub-paragraphs 1 and 3 may not be challenged. No legal action may be based on a failure to refer.

---

[12] Translation by S. Hardt.

PART II. ADMINISTRATIVE LAW

§§ 7 and 8. (Repealed).

§ 9. (1) The Higher Administrative Court consists of the president and of the presiding judges and further judges in necessary numbers.
(2) At the Higher Administrative Court, senates are formed.
(3) The senates of the Higher Administrative Court decide as bodies of three judges; State legislation may provide that the senates decide as bodies of five judges, two of which may also be lay judges. For the cases of § 48 (1) it may also be provided that the senates decide as bodies of five judges and two lay judges. Clause 1 half-clause 2 and clause 2 do not apply in the cases of § 99 (2).
(4) (Repealed).

§ 10. (1) The Federal Administrative Court consists of the president and of the presiding judges and further judges in necessary numbers.
(2) At the Federal Administrative Court, senates are formed.
(3) The senates of the Federal Administrative Court decide as bodies of five judges, in case of court orders outside the oral proceedings as bodies of three judges.

§ 11. (1) At the Federal Administrative Court, a grand senate is formed.
(2) The grand senate decides where a senate wishes to deviate in a legal question from a decision of another senate or of the grand senate.
(3) A referral to the grand senate is only admissible if the senate whose decision is to be deviated from declares, upon inquiry by the deciding senate, that it maintains its legal opinion. If the senate whose decision is to be deviated from can no longer address the legal question because of a change in the work distribution plan, the senate which would, according to the work distribution plan, now be competent in the case where a deviating decision has been rendered, steps in its place. On the request and the answer the respective senate decides by court order in the composition necessary for judgments.
(4) The deciding senate may refer a question of fundamental importance to the grand senate for decision, if, in its perception, this is necessary for the development of the law or for the safeguarding of the unity of jurisprudence.
(5) The grand senate consists of the president and one judge of each of the revision senates in which the president does not preside. If the referring senate or the senate whose decision is to be deviated from is a senate other than a revision senate, then also a member of that senate is represented in the grand senate. In case of inability of the president to attend, a judge of the senate of which he is a member steps in his place.
(6) The members and the alternates are appointed by the presidium for one business year. This also applies to the member of another senate in the meaning of sub-paragraph 5 clause 2 and to his alternate. The grand senate is presided over by the president, in case of his inability to attend by the member who has seniority. In case of a tie in votes, the vote of the presiding judge is decisive.
(7) The grand senate only decides on the legal question. It may decide without oral proceedings. Its decision is in the case at hand binding upon the deciding senate.

§ 12. (1) The provisions of § 11 are applicable to the Higher Administrative Court mutatis mutandis, as far as it decides in final instance on a question of State law. The appellate senates formed under this Act step in the place of the revision senates.
(2) If a Higher Administrative Court consists of only two appellate senates, then the joint senates step in the place of the grand senate.
(3) By State statute, a deviating composition of the grand senate may be provided for.

§ 13. At each court, a court office is set up. It is staffed with the necessary number of court clerks.

§ 14. All courts and administrative authorities render legal and inter-administrative assistance to the courts of the administrative jurisdiction.

[Chapters 2 – 5 are omitted.]

Chapter 6. Administrative legal recourse and competence

§ 40. (1) The administrative legal recourse is available in all disputes under public law of a non-constitutional nature, as far as the disputes are not explicitly allocated to another court by federal statute. Public law disputes in the field of State law may also be allocated to another court by State statute.
(2) For proprietary claims deriving from sacrifice for the public welfare and from safekeeping under public law as well as for claims to damages deriving from a breach of duties under public law, which are not based on a contract under public law, recourse to the ordinary courts is available; this does not apply to disputes about the existence and the amount of an entitlement to compensation within the scope of Article 14 (1) clause 2 of the Basic Law. The special provisions of the law regarding civil servants as well as the legal recourse in case of compensation of proprietary disadvantages due to a withdrawal of unlawful administrative acts remain unaffected.

§ 41. (Repealed).

§ 42. (1) By legal action, the repeal [Aufhebung] of an administrative act (action to challenge) [Anfechtungsklage] as well as an order for the issue of a refused or omitted administrative act (action to compel) [Verpflichtungsklage] may be requested.
(2) If not otherwise provided statutorily, the legal action is only admissible if the claimant asserts that his rights have been infringed upon by the administrative act or the refusal or omission thereof.

§ 43. (1) By legal action, the declaration of the existence or non-existence of a legal relationship or of the voidness [Nichtigkeit] of an administrative act may be requested if the claimant has a legitimate interest in a speedy declaration (action to declare) [Feststellungsklage].
(2) The declaration may not be requested as far as the claimant is able or could have been able to pursue his rights by an action to modify [Gestaltungsklage] or by an action to perform [Leistungsklage]. This does not apply where a declaration of the invalidity of an voidness act is requested.

§ 44. Several claims may be pursued by the claimant simultaneously in one action if they are directed against the same respondent, are linked to each other, and the same court is competent.

§ 44a. Recourse against procedural acts of the authorities may only be sought together with the recourse admissible against the decision on the merits. This does not apply where procedural acts of the authorities can be executed or are issued against an uninvolved party.

§ 45. The administrative court decides in first instance on all disputes for which the administrative legal recourse is available.

§ 46. The Higher Administrative Court decides on the legal remedy
1. of appeal [Berufung] against judgments of the administrative court,
2. of complaint against other decisions of the administrative court and
3. (repealed).

§ 47. (1) The Higher Administrative Court decides within the scope of its jurisdiction upon request on the validity
1. of executive orders [Satzungen] that have been issued under the provisions of the Building Code [Baugesetzbuch] as well as of ordinances [Rechtsverordnungen] on the basis of § 246 (2) of the Building Code
2. of other legal rules ranking lower than State statute, as far as State law so provides.
(2) Every natural or legal person who asserts that his rights are infringed upon or will be infringed upon in the foreseeable future by the legal rule or its application, as well as every public authority, may submit the request within one year after the publication of the legal rule. It must be directed against the entity, institution or foundation which has issued the legal rule. The Higher Administrative Court may give the State and other legal persons under public law whose competence is affected by the legal rule, the opportunity to comment within a period of time to be determined. § 65 (1) and (4) and § 66 are to be applied mutatis mutandis.
(2a) The request of a natural or legal person which has as its subject matter a development plan or an executive order under § 34 (4) clause 1 no. 2 and 3 or § 35 (6) of the Building Code is inadmissible if the person submitting the request only raises objections which, within the framework of public display (§ 3 (2) of the Building Code) or within the framework of the involvement of the affected public (§13 (2) no. 2 and § 13a (2) no. 1 of the Building Code), it has failed to raise or has raised belatedly but could have raised and if this legal consequence has been pointed out within the framework of involvement.

Part II. Administrative Law

(3) The Higher Administrative Court does not review the compatibility of the legal rule with State law as far as it is provided by statute that the legal rule is only subject to review by the constitutional court of a State.
(4) If a procedure for the review of the validity of the legal rule is pending before a constitutional court, then the Higher Administrative Court may order that proceedings be stayed until the conclusion of the procedure before the constitutional court.
(5) The Higher Administrative Court decides by judgment or, if it considers oral proceedings not necessary, by court order. If the Higher Administrative Court reaches the opinion that the legal rule is invalid, then it declares it ineffective; in that case the decision is generally binding and the formula of the decision must be published by the respondent in the same way the legal rule would have to be notified. For the effect of the decision § 183 applies mutatis mutandis.
(6) Upon request, the court may issue a temporary order if this is urgently required to avert serious disadvantages or for other important reasons.

§ 48. (1) The Higher Administrative Court decides in first instance on all disputes which concern
1. the establishment, the operation, the possession otherwise, the modification, the close-down, the safe sealing and the dismantling of facilities in the meaning of the §§ 7 and 9a (3) of the Atom Act [Atomgesetz],
2. the treatment, processing and other use of nuclear fuels outside the facilities of the sort stipulated in § 7 of the Atom Act (§ 9 of the Atom Act) and the significant deviation or the significant modification in the sense of § 9 (1) clause 2 of the Atom Act as well as the storage of nuclear fuels outside state safekeeping (§ 6 of the Atom Act),
3. the establishment, the operation and the modification of power plants with combustion facilities for solid, liquid or gaseous fuels with a combustion heat capacity of more than three hundred megawatt,
4. planning procedures for the construction and the operation or the modification of overhead high-voltage lines with a nominal voltage of 110 kilovolt or more, buried cables with a nominal voltage of 110 kilovolt or gas supply lines with a diameter of more than 300 millimeters as well as the alteration of the line of each of them,
5. processes for the construction, the operation and the significant modification of stationary facilities for the combustion or thermal decomposition of waste with a yearly throughput (effective output) of more than one hundred thousand tons and of stationary facilities in which wastes in the sense of § 41 of the Circular Flow Economy and Waste Act [Kreislaufwirtschafts- und Abfallgesetz] are stored or landfilled,
6. the creation, the expansion or modification and the operation of commercial airports and of commercial airfields with a restricted protected construction area,
7. planning procedures for the construction or the modification of new lines of tramways, magnet levitation trains and of public railways as well as the construction or modification of railroad shunting yards and container terminals,
8. planning procedures for the construction or the modification of federal long-distance roads,
9. planning procedures for the new construction or extension of federal waterways.
Clause 1 also applies to disputes about approvals that are issued instead of the adoption of a plan as well as to disputes about all approvals and permissions necessary for the project, also as far as they concern ancillary facilities which have a spatial or operational link to it. The States may by statute provide that the Higher Administrative Court decides in first instance on disputes that concern the assignment of property in the cases of clause 1.
(2) The Higher Administrative Court furthermore decides in first instance on legal actions against prohibitions of associations issued by a supreme State authority in accordance with § 3 (2) no. 1 of the Associations Act [Vereinsgesetz] and orders issued in accordance with § 8 (2) clause 1 of the Associations Act.
(3) (Repealed).

§ 49. The Federal Administrative Court decides on the legal remedy
1. of revision [Revision] against judgments of the Higher Administrative Court under § 132,
2. of revision against judgments of the administrative court under §§ 134 and 135,
3. of complaint under § 99 (2) and § 133 (1) of this Act as well as under § 17a (4) clause 4 of the Court Constitution Act [Gerichtsverfassungsgesetz].

§ 50. (1) The Federal Administrative Court decides in first and final instance
1. on disputes under public law of a non-constitutional nature between the Federation and the States and between different States,
2. on legal actions against prohibitions of associations issued by the federal minister of internal affairs under § 3 (2) no. 2 of the Associations Act [Vereinsgesetz] and orders issued under § 8 (2) clause 1 of the Associations Act,
3. on disputes against deportation orders under § 58a of the Sojourn Act [Aufenthaltsgesetz] and their execution,

4. on legal actions the basis of which are processes within the area of operations of the Federal Intelligence Service [Bundesnachrichtendienst],
5. on legal actions against measures and decisions under §44a of the Members of Parliament Act [Abgeordnetengesetz] and the code of conduct for members of the German Bundestag,
6. on all disputes which concern planning procedures and planning approval procedures for projects stipulated in the General Railway Act [Allgemeines Eisenbahngesetz], the Federal Long-Distance Roads Act [Bundesfernstraßengesetz], the Federal Waterways Act [Bundeswasserstraßengesetz] or the Magnet Levitation Train Planning Act [Magnetschwebebahnplanungsgesetz].
(2) (Repealed).
(3) If the Federal Administrative Court under sub-paragraph 1 no. 1 considers a dispute a matter of constitutional law, then it refers the case to the Federal Constitutional Court [Bundesverfassungsgericht] for decision.

§ 51. (1) If according to § 5 (2) of the Associations Act [Vereinsgesetz] the prohibition of the association as a whole instead of the prohibition of a sub-association must be executed, then proceedings on a legal action of that sub-association against the prohibition issued against it must be stayed until the issuing of the decision on a legal action against the prohibition of the association as a whole.
(2) A decision of the Federal Administrative Court binds, in the cases of sub-paragraph 1, the Higher Administrative Courts.
(3) The Federal Administrative Court informs the Higher Administrative Courts about the legal action of an association under § 50 (1) no. 2.

§ 52. As regards local competence, the following applies:
1. In disputes which concern immovable property or a right or legal relationship attached to a certain location, only the administrative court is competent in whose district the property or the location is situated.
2. For actions to challenge against the administrative act of a federal authority or a directly federal entity, institution or foundation under public law, the administrative court is locally competent in whose district the federal authority, entity, institution or foundation has its seat, save for nos. 1 and 4. This also applies to actions to compel in the cases of clause 1. In disputes under the Asylum Procedures Act [Asylverfahrensgesetz], however, the administrative court is locally competent in whose district the alien has to take his sojourn according to the Asylum Procedures Act; if no local competence can be established thereby, then it is to be determined under no. 3. For legal actions against the Federation in subject areas which fall within the competence of the diplomatic and consular representations of the Federal Republic of Germany abroad, the administrative court is locally competent in whose district the Federal Government has its seat.
3. For all other actions to challenge, save for nos. 1 and 4, the administrative court is locally competent in whose district the administrative act has been issued. If it has been issued by an authority whose competence extends to several administrative court districts or by a common authority of several or all States, then the administrative court is competent in whose district the complainant has his seat or residence. If this is lacking within the area of competence of the authority, then the competence is determined under no. 5. For actions to challenge against administrative acts of the central office established by the States for the allocation of university places, however, the administrative court is locally competent in whose district the office has its seat. This also applies to actions to compel in the cases of the clauses 1, 2 and 4.
4. For all legal actions deriving from a present or past service relation as a civil servant, as a judge, in conscription, military service or civilian service and for disputes relating to the formation of such a relation, the administrative court is locally competent in whose district the claimant or the respondent has his business residence or, in case that is lacking, his residence. If the claimant or the respondent has no business residence or no residence within the area of competence of the authority which has issued the original administrative act, then the court is locally competent in whose district that authority has its seat. Clauses 1 and 2 apply mutatis mutandis to legal actions under § 79 of the Act for the regulation of legal relationships of persons falling under Article 131 of the Basic Law.
5. In all other cases the administrative court is locally competent in whose district the respondent has his seat, residence or, in case of a lack of this, his sojourn or where he had his last residence or sojourn.

§ 53. (1) The competent court within the administrative jurisdiction is determined by the next higher court,
1. if in an individual case the court that is in principle competent is legally or factually prevented from exercising jurisdiction,
2. if due to the boundaries of different court districts it is uncertain which court is competent for the legal dispute,
3. if the place of jurisdiction is determined by § 52 and different courts come into consideration,
4. if different courts have effectively declared themselves competent,

Part II. Administrative Law

5. if different courts, of which one is competent for the legal dispute, have effectively declared themselves not to be competent.

(2) If a local competence is not established under § 52, the Federal Administrative Court determines the competent court.

(3) Every person involved in the legal dispute and every court concerned with the legal dispute may appeal to the higher court in the hierarchy of legal recourse or to the Federal Administrative Court. The court appealed to may decide without oral proceedings.

[The remainder of the Act is omitted.]

General Administrative Law Act [Algemene wet bestuursrecht] of 4 June 1994, as last amended by royal decree of 15 January 2007 (*Stb.* 2007, 28). Selected provisions: Chapter 1; Chapter 2, Division 2.1, Article 2:6 of Division 2.2 and Division 2.3; Chapter 3, Division 3.1, 3.2, 3.6 and 3.7; Chapter 4, Title 4.1, 4.2, Division 4.2.1 and Title 4.3; Chapter 6; Chapter 7, Division 7.1 and 7.2; Chapter 8, Title 8.1, Division 8.1.1 and Article 8:10 of Division 8.1.2, Title 8.2, Division 8.2.6; Chapter 10, Title 10.1.[13]

Chapter 1. Introductory provisions

Title 1.1 Definitions and scope

Article 1:1. (1) By 'administrative authority' [bestuursorgaan] are meant:
(a) an organ of a legal entity which has been established under public law, or
(b) another person or body vested with any public authority.
(2) The following organs, persons and bodies are not considered as administrative authorities:
(a) the legislature;
(b) the chambers and the joint assembly of the States-General;
(c) independent authorities established by statute which are charged with adjudication as well as the Council for the Judiciary [Raad voor de rechtspraak] and the College of Deputies [College van afgevaardigden];
(d) the Council of State [Raad van State] and its divisions;
(e) the General Chamber of Audit [Algemene Rekenkamer];
(f) the National Ombudsman and Deputy Ombudsmen in the meaning of Article 9 (1) of the National Ombudsman Act [Wet Nationale ombudsman] and ombudsmen and ombuds-committees in the meaning of Article 9:17 (b);
(g) the chairmen, members, registrars and secretaries of the bodies referred to under b to f, the Procurator-General [procureur-generaal], the Deputy Procurator-General and the Advocates-General of the Supreme Court [Hoge Raad], the directorates of the bodies referred to under c as well as the chairmen of these directorates, as well as committees of members of the bodies referred to under b to f;
(h) the supervisory committee regarding the intelligence and security services stipulated in Article 64 of the Intelligence and Security Services Act 2002 [Wet op de inlichtingen- en veiligheidsdiensten 2002].
(3) An organ, person or body excluded under paragraph 2 is nonetheless considered as an administrative authority in as far as the organ, the person or the body takes administrative decisions or performs acts regarding a civil servant not appointed for life in the meaning of Article 1 of the Civil Servants Act [Ambtenarenwet] himself, his surviving relatives or his legal successors.

Article 1:2. (1) By 'concerned party' [belanghebbende] is meant: the person whose interest is directly affected by an administrative decision.
(2) As regards administrative authorities, the interests entrusted to them are considered their own interests.
(3) As regards legal persons, their interests are considered to include the general and collective interests which they particularly promote by virtue of their objectives and as shown by their factual activities.

Article 1:3. (1) By 'administrative decision' [besluit] is meant: a written decision by an administrative authority containing a legal act under public law.
(2) By 'order' [beschikking] is meant: an administrative decision which is not of a general scope, including the rejection of an application for such order.
(3) By 'application' is meant: the request by a concerned party to take an administrative decision.
(4) By 'policy rule' is meant: a general rule established by administrative decision, not being a generally binding rule, concerning the weighing of interests, the establishment of facts or the interpretation of legal rules in the exercise of a power of an administrative authority.

Article 1:4. (1) By 'administrative judge' is meant: an independent authority established by statute which is charged with administrative adjudication.
(2) A court forming part of the judiciary is considered an administrative judge as far as chapter 8 or the Enforcement of Traffic Regulations under Administrative Law Act [Wet administratiefrechtelijke handhaving verkeersvoorschriften] – with the exception of chapter VIII – applies or applies mutatis mutandis.

---

[13] Translation by S. Hardt and E. Ramaekers.

Part II. Administrative Law

Article 1:5. (1) By 'filing a complaint' [bezwaar] is meant: the making use of the power, existing by virtue of a legal rule, to seek redress against an administrative decision with the administrative authority which has taken the administrative decision.
(2) By 'lodging an administrative appeal' [administratief beroep] is meant: the making use of the power, existing by virtue of a legal rule, to seek redress against an administrative decision with an administrative authority other than the one which has taken the administrative decision.
(3) By 'lodging an appeal' [beroep] is meant: lodging an administrative appeal or an appeal with an administrative judge.

Article 1:6. Chapters 2 to 8 and 10 of this Act do not apply to:
(a) the investigation and prosecution of criminal acts as well as the execution of decisions under criminal law;
(b) the execution of measures depriving persons of their liberty by virtue of the Aliens Act 2000 [Vreemdelingenwet 2000];
(c) the execution of other measures depriving persons of their liberty in an institution which is primarily dedicated to the execution of decisions under criminal law;
(d) administrative decisions and acts for the implementation of the Military Disciplinary Law Act [Wet militair tuchtrecht];
(e) administrative decisions and acts for the implementation of the Review of Termination of Life upon Request and Assisted Suicide Act [Wet toetsing levensbeëindiging op verzoek en hulp bij zelfdoding].

Title 1.2 Implementation of binding decisions of authorities of the European Communities

Article 1:7. (1) Where, pursuant to any legal rule, an opinion must be requested or external consultations must be conducted by an administrative authority regarding an administrative decision before such administrative decision may be taken, that rule does not apply if the sole purpose of the envisaged administrative decision is the implementation of a binding decision of the Council of the European Union, of the European Parliament and the Council jointly or of the Commission of the European Communities.
(2) Paragraph 1 does not apply to the consultation of the Council of State.

Article 1:8. (1) Where, pursuant to any legal rule, a draft administrative decision must be notified by an administrative authority before such administrative decision may be taken, that rule does not apply if the sole purpose of the envisaged administrative decision is the implementation of a binding decision of the Council of the European Union, of the European Parliament and the Council jointly or of the Commission of the European Communities.
(2) Paragraph 1 does not apply to the transmission of a draft of an ordinance [algemene maatregel van bestuur] or ministerial order to the States-General, if:
(a) it is provided by statute that by or on behalf of one of the Chambers of the States-General, or by a number of members thereof, the wish may be expressed that the subject-matter or the entry into force of this ordinance or ministerial order be regulated by statute, or
(b) Article 21.6 (6) of the Environment Management Act [Wet milieubeheer] or Article 33 of the Pollution of Surface Waters Act [Wet verontreiniging oppervlaktewateren] is applicable.

Article 1:9. This title applies mutatis mutandis to bills.

Chapter 2. Relations between citizens and administrative authorities

Division 2.1 General provisions

Article 2:1. (1) Anyone may, for the purpose of representing his interests in relations with administrative authorities, be assisted or be represented by an agent.
(2) The administrative authority may demand a written mandate from an agent.

Article 2:2. (1) The administrative authority may deny assistance or representation by a person against whom there are serious objections.
(2) The concerned party and the person referred to in paragraph 1 are notified in writing of the denial without delay.

(3) Paragraph 1 does not apply with regard to attorneys and procurators.

Article 2:3. (1) The administrative authority forwards documents for the consideration of which obviously another administrative authority is competent to that authority without delay, while at the same time giving notice thereof to the addressor.
(2) The administrative authority returns to the addressor as quickly as possible documents which are not intended for it and which are not forwarded either.

Article 2:4. (1) The administrative authority performs its task without prejudice.
(2) The administrative authority guards that persons belonging to or working for the administrative authority who have a personal interest in an administrative decision do not influence the decision-making.

Article 2:5. (1) Anyone who is involved in the performance of the task of an administrative authority and who in that context gains access to information the confidential nature of which he knows or must reasonably assume and to whom a duty of secrecy regarding such information does not already apply by virtue of his office, profession or any legal rule, is obliged to keep such information secret, except as far as any legal rule obliges him to disclosure or the necessity for disclosure follows from his task.
(2) Paragraph 1 also applies to institutions, and persons belonging to or working for them, involved by an administrative authority in the performance of its task and to institutions, and persons belonging to or working for them, which carry out a task assigned to them by or pursuant to statute.

Division 2.2 The use of language in administrative communication

Article 2:6. (1) Administrative authorities and persons working under their responsibility use the Dutch language, unless otherwise provided for by a legal rule.
(2) In deviation from the first paragraph, another language may be used if such use is more expedient and the interests of third parties are thereby not disproportionately compromised.

[The remainder of Division 2.2 is omitted.]

Division 2.3 Communication by electronic means

Article 2:13. (1) In the communication between citizens and administrative authorities, a message may be sent electronically, provided that the provisions of this division are taken into account.
(2) The first paragraph is not applicable if:
a. this is established by or pursuant to a legal rule, or
b. electronic sending is incompatible with a form requirement.

Article 2:14. (1) An administrative authority may send a message which is addressed to one or more addressees electronically in as far as the addressee has made known that he can be reached to a sufficient extent in this manner.
(2) Unless otherwise is provided by a legal rule, the sending of messages that are not addressed to one or more addressees does not exclusively take place electronically.
(3) If an administrative authority sends a message electronically, this takes place in a sufficiently reliable and confidential manner, given the nature and content of the message and the purpose for which it is used.

Article 2:15. (1) A message may be sent to an administrative authority electronically in as far as the administrative authority has made known that this option is available. The administrative authority may establish further requirements for the use of electronic means.
(2) An administrative authority may refuse information and documents that have been provided electronically to the extent that acceptance thereof would lead to a disproportionate burden for the administrative authority.
(3) An administrative authority may refuse a message sent electronically to the extent that the reliability or confidentiality of this message is insufficiently safeguarded, given the nature and content of the message and the purpose for which it is used.
(4) The administrative authority informs the sender of a refusal on the basis of this Article as soon as possible.

Part II. Administrative Law

Article 2:16. The requirement of signature is met by an electronic signature, if the method which is used for authentication is sufficiently reliable, given the nature and content of the electronic message and the purpose for which it is used. Articles 15a (2) to (6) and 15b of Book 3 of the Civil Code [Burgerlijk Wetboek] apply mutatis mutandis, to the extent that this is not incompatible with the nature of the message. Additional requirements may be established by a legal rule.

Article 2:17. (1) The moment at which a message is sent by an administrative authority is considered to be the moment at which the message reaches a system for data processing over which the administrative authority has no control, or, if the administrative authority and the addressee make use of the same system for data processing, the moment at which the message becomes accessible to the addressee.
(2) The moment at which a message has been electronically received by an administrative authority is considered to be the moment at which the message has reached its system for data processing.

Chapter 3. General provisions regarding administrative decisions

Division 3.1 Introductory provisions

Article 3:1. (1) To administrative decisions containing generally binding rules:
(a) division 3.2 only applies in as far as the nature of the administrative decisions is not incompatible therewith;
(a) divisions 3.6 and 3.7 do not apply.
(2) To acts of administrative authorities other than administrative decisions, divisions 3.2 to 3.4 apply mutatis mutandis in as far as the nature of the acts is not incompatible therewith.

Division 3.2 Duty of care and weighing of interests

Article 3:2. In the preparation of an administrative decision, the administrative authority gathers the necessary knowledge concerning the relevant facts and the interests to be weighed.

Article 3:3. The administrative authority does not use the power to take an administrative decision for any other purpose than that for which this power has been conferred.

Article 3:4. (1) The administrative authority weighs the interests directly affected by the administrative decision in as far as no limitation follows from a legal rule or from the nature of the power to be exercised.
(2) The disadvantageous consequences of an administrative decision for one or more concerned parties may not be disproportionate to the purposes to be served by the administrative decision.

[Divisions 3.3 – 3.5 are omitted.]

Division 3.6 Notification and communication

Article 3:40. An administrative decision does not become effective before it has been notified.

Article 3:41. (1) Notification of administrative decisions which are addressed to one or more concerned parties is effected by sending or delivery to them, including the applicant.
(2) If notification of the administrative decision cannot be effected in the manner provided for in paragraph 1, it is effected in another suitable manner.

Article 3:42. (1) Notification of administrative decisions which are not addressed to one or more concerned parties is effected by means of publication of the administrative decision or of the substantive content thereof in an official government gazette or a daily paper, newspaper or local paper or in another suitable manner.
(2) Except where otherwise is provided by a legal rule, notification is not effected electronically.
(3) If only the substantive content is published, the administrative decision is at the same time deposited for inspection. The publication states where and when the administrative decision is deposited for inspection.

Article 3:43. (1) Simultaneously with, or as quickly as possible after its notification, the administrative decision is communicated to those who have expressed their views during the preparation thereof. It is in any event communicated to an advisor in the meaning of Article 3:5 if the advice is being deviated from.
(2) In communicating an administrative decision it is also stated when and how notification thereof has been effected.

Article 3:44. (1) If in the preparation of the administrative decision division 3.4 has been applied, communication in the meaning of Article 3:43 (1) is effected:
(a) under application mutatis mutandis of Articles 3:11 and 3:12 (1) or (2) and (3) (a), provided that the documents are deposited for inspection until the time limit for appeal has expired, and
(b) by sending a copy of the administrative decision to those who have expressed their views on the draft of the administrative decision.
(2) In deviation from paragraph 1 b, the administrative authority may:
(a) if the extent of the administrative decision gives reason thereto, confine itself to communicating to each of the persons referred to therein the substance of the administrative decision;
(b) if a view has been expressed by more than five persons in the same document, confine itself to sending a copy to the five persons whose names and addresses are given first in that document;
(c) if a view has been expressed by more than five persons in the same document and the extent of the administrative decision gives reason thereto, confine itself to communicating to the five persons whose names and addresses are given first in that document the substance of the administrative decision;
(d) if sending would have to be effected to more than 250 persons, refrain from sending.

Article 3:45. (1) If against an administrative decision a complaint may be filed or an appeal may be lodged, notice is given thereof in the notification and communication of the administrative decision.
(2) Therein it is stated by whom, within which time limit and with which body a complaint may be filed or an appeal may be lodged.

Division 3.7 Stating reasons

Article 3:46. An administrative decision must be based on proper reasons.

Article 3:47. (1) The reasons are stated in the notification of the administrative decision.
(2) In that context it is stated, if possible, by virtue of which legal rule the administrative decision is taken.
(3) If the reasons cannot be stated immediately with the notification of the administrative decision because of urgency, the administrative authority provides them within one week after the notification.
(4) In that case, Articles 3:41 to 3:43 apply mutatis mutandis.

Article 3:48. (1) The statement of reasons may be omitted where it may reasonably be assumed that there is no need for this.
(2) If a concerned party requests within a reasonable time a statement of reasons, then they are provided as quickly as possible.

Article 3:49. For the purpose of stating reasons for an administrative decision or a part thereof, it suffices to refer to an opinion rendered in this regard if the opinion itself contains the reasons and the opinion has been or is being communicated.

Article 3:50. If the administrative authority takes an administrative decision which deviates from an opinion rendered in this regard pursuant to a legal rule, this fact and the reasons for the deviation are stated in the statement of reasons.

Chapter 4. Special provisions regarding administrative decisions

Title 4.1 Orders

Division 4.1.1 The application

Article 4:1. Unless otherwise is provided by a legal rule, an application for the issuing of an order is submitted in writing with the administrative authority which is competent to decide on the application.

Article 4:2. (1) The application shall be signed and contains at least:
(a) the name and the address of the applicant;
(b) the date;
(c) a description of the order which is applied for.
(2) The applicant further provides the information and documents which are necessary for the decision on the application and which he can reasonably be expected to obtain.

Article 4:3. (1) The applicant may refuse to provide information and documents as far as their importance to the decision of the administrative authority does not outweigh the importance of the respect for private life, including the protection of medical and psychological examination results, or the importance of the protection of business and manufacturing information.
(2) Paragraph 1 does not apply to information and documents stipulated by a legal rule for which it is provided that they must be submitted.

Article 4:3a. The administrative authority confirms the receipt of an application submitted electronically.

Article 4:4. The administrative authority which is competent to decide on the application may establish a form for submitting applications and providing information, as far is this is not provided for by a legal rule.

Article 4:5. (1) The administrative authority may decide not to take the application into consideration, if:
(a) the applicant has not complied with any legal rule for the application to be taken into consideration, or
(b) the application has been rejected on the basis of Article 2:15, or
(c) the information and documents submitted are insufficient for the assessment of the application or for the preparation of the order,
provided that the applicant has had the opportunity to supplement the application within a time limit set by the administrative authority.
(2) If the application or one of the pieces of information or documents belonging to it is written in a foreign language and its translation is necessary for the assessment of the application or for the preparation of the order, the administrative authority may decide not to take the application into consideration, provided that the applicant has had the opportunity to supplement the application with a translation within a time limit set by the administrative authority.
(3) If the application or one of the pieces of information or documents belonging to it is extensive or complicated and a summary is necessary for the assessment of the application or for the preparation of the order, the administrative authority may decide not to take the application into consideration, provided that the applicant has had the opportunity to supplement the application with a summary within a time limit set by the administrative authority.
(4) An administrative decision not to take the application into consideration shall be notified to the applicant within four weeks after the application has been supplemented or after the time limit set for this purpose has expired unused.

Article 4:6. (1) If after the issuing of an order rejecting the application in whole or in part a new application is submitted, the applicant is obliged to state newly emerged facts or changed circumstances.
(2) Where no newly emerged facts or changed circumstances are stated, the administrative authority may, without applying Article 4:5, reject the application by referring to its previous rejecting order.

Division 4.1.2 The preparation

Article 4:7. Before an administrative authority rejects an application for the issuing of an order in whole or in part, it gives the applicant the opportunity to state his views if:
(a) the rejection would be based on information about facts and interests which relate to the applicant, and
(b) this information deviates from information which the applicant has provided on the matter himself.
(2) Paragraph 1 does not apply if there is a deviation from the application which can only be of minor importance to the applicant.

Article 4:8. (1) Before an administrative authority issues an order against which a concerned party which has not applied for the order may be expected to have objections, it gives that concerned party the opportunity to state its views if:
(a) the order would be based on information about facts and interests which relate to the concerned party, and
(b) this information has not been provided by the concerned party itself.
(2) Paragraph 1 does not apply if the concerned party has not complied with a legal obligation to provide information.

Article 4:9. In the application of Articles 4:7 and 4:8, the concerned party may choose to state its views either in writing or orally.

Article 4:10. (Repealed).

Article 4:11. The administrative authority may refrain from applying Articles 4:7 and 4:8 in as far as:
(a) urgency precludes this;
(b) the concerned party has already been given the opportunity to state its views and no new facts or circumstances have emerged since then, or
(c) the aim pursued by the order can only be reached if the concerned party is not informed thereof beforehand.

Article 4:12. (1) The administrative authority may furthermore refrain from applying Articles 4:7 and 4:8 in case of an order for establishing a financial obligation or entitlement if:
(a) against this order a complaint may be filed or an administrative appeal may be lodged, and
(b) the disadvantageous consequences can be wholly remedied after a complaint or an administrative appeal.
(2) Paragraph 1 does not apply to an order for:
(a) refusing a subsidy on the basis of Article 4:35 or in accordance with Article 4:5;
(b) fixing a subsidy at a lower amount on the basis of Article 4:46 (2), or
(c) withdrawing or altering to the detriment of the recipient the granting or fixing of a subsidy.

Division 4.1.3 Time limit for decisions

Article 4:13. (1) An order must be issued within the time limit provided for by a legal rule or, in the absence of such a time limit, within a reasonable time after the receipt of the application.
(2) The reasonable time referred to in paragraph 1 has in any event expired where the administrative authority has, within eight weeks after the receipt of the application, neither issued an order, nor given notice in the meaning of Article 4:14 (3).

Article 4:14. (1) If an order cannot be issued within the time limit provided for by a legal rule, the administrative authority gives notice of this fact to the applicant and, at the same time, states a period of time as short as possible within which the order may be expected to be issued.
(2) Paragraph 1 does not apply if after the time limit provided for by a legal rule the administrative authority is no longer competent.
(3) If, in the absence of a time limit provided for by a legal rule, an order cannot be issued within eight weeks, the administrative authority gives notice of this fact to the applicant and states, at the same time, a reasonable period of time within which the order may be expected to be issued.

Article 4:15. The time limit for the issuing of an order is suspended from the day on which the administrative authority, by virtue of Article 4:5, invites the applicant to supplement the application until the day on which the application has been supplemented or the time period set for this purpose has expired unused.

Part II. Administrative Law

Division 4.1.4 (Repealed).

Title 4.2 Subsidies

Division 4.2.1 Introductory provisions

Article 4:21. (1) By 'subsidy' is meant: the entitlement to financial resources provided by an administrative authority for the purpose of certain activities of the applicant, other than as payment for goods or services provided to the administrative authority.
(2) This title does not apply to entitlements or obligations resulting from a legal rule concerning:
(a) taxes,
(b) the levy of a premium or a premium-replacing tax pursuant to the Social Security Financing Act [Wet financiering sociale verzekeringen], or
(c) the levy of an income-dependent contribution or a contribution-replacing tax pursuant to the Nursing Insurance Act [Zorgverzekeringswet].
(3) This title does not apply to the entitlement to financial resources which is provided on the basis of a legal rule which exclusively provides for payment to legal persons established under public law.
(4) This title applies mutatis mutandis to the financing of education and research.

Article 4:22. By 'subsidy ceiling' is meant: the highest amount available for the payment of subsidies during a certain period of time by virtue of a particular legal rule.

Article 4:23. (1) An administrative authority only provides a subsidy on the basis of a legal rule which regulates for which activities a subsidy may be provided.
(2) If such a legal rule is contained in an ordinance not based on statute, this legal rule shall expire four years after it has entered into force, unless before this moment a bill has been introduced in the States-General in which the subsidy is regulated.
(3) Paragraph 1 does not apply:
(a) pending the adoption of a legal rule during one year at most or until within that year a bill introduced in the States-General has been rejected or has been adopted as statute and has entered into force;
(b) if the subsidy is provided directly on the basis of a programme established by the Council of the European Union, the European Parliament and the Council jointly or the Commission of the European Communities;
(c) if the budget states the subsidy recipient and the maximum amount at which the subsidy may be fixed, or
(d) in incidental cases, provided that the subsidy is provided for a maximum of four years.
(4) The administrative authority annually publishes a report on the provision of subsidies in accordance with paragraph 4 a and d.

Article 4:24. If a subsidy is based on a legal rule, a report is published at least once in five years on the effectiveness and the effects of the subsidy in practice, unless otherwise is provided by a legal rule.

[Divisions 4.2.2 – 4.2.8 are omitted.]

Title 4.3 Policy Rules

Article 4:81. (1) An administrative authority may establish policy rules with regard to a power conferred to it or being exercised under its responsibility or delegated by it.
(2) In other cases an administrative authority may only set policy rules in as far as this is provided by a legal rule.

Article 4:82. For the purpose of giving reasons for an administrative decision it suffices to refer to an established practice only in as far as such established practice is laid down in a policy rule.

Article 4:83. When notifying the administrative decision containing a policy rule, the legal rule from which the power follows to which the administrative decision containing a policy rule relates is, if possible, stated at the same time.

Article 4:84. The administrative authority acts in accordance with the policy rule, unless this would have consequences for one or more concerned parties which would, due to special circumstances, be disproportionate in relation to the aims served by the policy rule.

[Chapter 5 is omitted.]

Chapter 6. General provisions regarding complaints and administrative appeals

Division 6.1 Introductory provisions

Article 6:1. Chapters 6 and 7 apply mutatis mutandis if a possibility is provided to file complaints or lodge appeals against acts of administrative authorities other than administrative decisions.

Article 6:2. For the purposes of legal rules regarding complaints and appeals, the following are considered to equal an administrative decision:
(a) the written refusal to take an administrative decision, and
(b) failure to take an administrative decision in due time.

Article 6:3. A decision relating to the procedure for the preparation of an administrative decision is not open to complaints or appeals, unless this decision affects the interests of the concerned party independently of the administrative decision to be prepared.

Division 6.2 Other general provisions

Article 6:4. (1) Filing a complaint is effected by submitting a letter of complaint to the administrative authority which has taken the administrative decision.
(2) Lodging an administrative appeal is effected by submitting a letter of appeal to the administrative appeal authority.
(3) Lodging an appeal with an administrative judge is effected by submitting a letter of appeal to that judge.

Article 6:5. (1) The letter of complaint or appeal shall be signed and contains at least:
(a) the name and address of the submitting person;
(b) the date;
(c) a description of the administrative decision against which the complaint or appeal is directed;
(d) the reasons for the complaint or appeal.
(2) If possible, a copy of the administrative decision to which the dispute relates is submitted together with the letter of appeal.
(3) If the letter of complaint or appeal is written in a foreign language and a translation is necessary for the complaint or appeal to be properly considered, the submitting person must take care that a translation be carried out.

Article 6:6. The complaint or appeal may be declared inadmissible, if:
(a) Article 6:5 or any other requirement imposed by statute for the complaint or appeal to be taken into consideration has not been complied with, or
(b) the letter of complaint or appeal has been wholly or partly rejected on the basis of Article 2:15,
provided that the submitting person has been given the opportunity to remedy the defect within a time limit set for this purpose.

Article 6:7. The time limit for submitting a letter of complaint or appeal is six weeks.

Article 6:8. (1) The period of time begins on the day after that on which the administrative decision has been notified in the prescribed manner.
(2) The period of time for submitting a letter of complaint against an administrative decision against which an administrative appeal could only be lodged by one or more specified concerned parties begins on the day after that on which the period of time for appeals has expired unused.

Part II. Administrative Law

(3) The period of time for submitting a letter of appeal against an administrative decision which is subject to approval begins on the day after that on which the administrative decision containing the approval of that administrative decision has been notified in the prescribed manner.
(4) The period of time for submitting a letter of appeal against an administrative decision which has been prepared in accordance with division 3.4 begins on the day after that on which the administrative decision has been deposited for inspection in accordance with Article 3:44 (1) (a).

Article 6:9. (1) A letter of complaint or appeal has been submitted timely if it has been received before the end of the period of time.
(2) In case of sending by mail, a letter of complaint or appeal has been submitted timely if it has been posted before the end of the period of time, provided that it has not been received any later than one week after the expiry of the period of time.

Article 6:10. (1) As regards a letter of complaint or appeal submitted before the beginning of the period of time, a declaration of inadmissibility for that reason is refrained from if the administrative decision, at the time of submission:
(a) had already come into being, or
(b) had not yet come into being, but the submitting person could reasonably have believed that it had.
(2) The consideration of the complaint or appeal may be suspended until the beginning of the period of time.

Article 6:11. As regards a letter of complaint or appeal submitted after expiry of the period of time, a declaration of inadmissibility for that reason is refrained from if it cannot reasonably be held that the submitting person was in default.

Article 6:12. (1) If the complaint or appeal is directed against a failure to take an administrative decision in due time, it is not bound by a time limit.
(2) The letter of complaint or appeal may be submitted as soon as the administrative authority is in default as regards taking an administrative decision in due time.
(3) The complaint or appeal is declared inadmissible if the letter of complaint or appeal has been submitted unreasonably late.

Article 6:13. No appeal may be lodged with the administrative judge by a concerned party to which it may reasonably be imputed that it did not state any views as stipulated in Article 3:15, has not filed a complaint or has not lodged an administrative appeal.

Article 6:14. (1) The body to which a letter of complaint or appeal has been submitted confirms the receipt thereof in writing.
(2) The body to which the letter of appeal has been submitted gives notice thereof as quickly as possible to the administrative authority which has taken the contested administrative decision.

Article 6:15. (1) If the letter of complaint or appeal is submitted to an administrative authority or administrative judge not competent, it is, after the date of receipt has been noted on it, forwarded as quickly as possible to the competent body, the addressor being informed thereof simultaneously.
(2) Paragraph 1 applies mutatis mutandis if instead of a letter of complaint a letter of appeal has been submitted or vice versa.
(3) The moment of submission to the body not competent is decisive for the question whether the letter of complaint or appeal has been submitted timely, except in case of evidently unreasonable use of procedure.

Article 6:16. The complaint or appeal does not suspend the force of the administrative decision against which it is directed, unless otherwise is provided by or pursuant to a legal rule.

Article 6:17. If someone is being represented, the body competent to decide on the complaint or appeal sends the documents relating to the matter in any event to the agent.

Article 6:18. (1) The fact that a complaint or appeal is pending against an administrative decision does not alter the power, existing independently of the complaint or appeal, to withdraw or alter that administrative decision.
(2) If the administrative authority withdraws or alters a contested administrative decision, it gives notice thereof without delay to the body before which the complaint or appeal is pending.

(3) After withdrawal or alteration, the administrative authority may, as long as the complaint or appeal remains pending, not take any administrative decision the substance or purport of which is identical to the contested administrative decision, unless:
(a) changed circumstances justify this and
(b) the administrative authority would also have had this power independently of the complaint or appeal.
(4) An administrative authority gives notice without delay of an administrative decision as referred to in paragraph 3 to the body before which the complaint or appeal is pending.

Article 6:19. (1) If an administrative authority has taken an administrative decision in the meaning of Article 6:18, the complaint or appeal is deemed also to be directed against the new administrative decision, unless that administrative decision wholly satisfies the complaint or appeal.
(2) The decision on the complaint or appeal against the new administrative decision may, however, be referred to another body before which a complaint or appeal against that new administrative decision is pending or can or could have been filed.
(3) Withdrawal of the contested administrative decision does not bar the annulment of that administrative decision, if the person submitting the letter of complaint or appeal has an interest therein.

Article 6:20. (1) If the complaint or appeal is directed against failure to take an administrative decision in due time, the administrative authority remains under an obligation to take an administrative decision on the application.
(2) The provisions of paragraph 1 do not apply:
(a) during the period that the complaint is pending;
(b) after the decision on the complaint or appeal, if the person who has submitted the application, as a result thereof, no longer has an interest in an administrative decision on the application.
(3) If the administrative authority takes an administrative decision on the application, it gives notice thereof without delay to the body before which the complaint or appeal against failure to decide within due time is pending.
(4) The complaint or appeal is deemed to be directed against the administrative decision on the application, unless that administrative decision wholly satisfies the complaint or appeal.
(5) The decision on the complaint or appeal against the administrative decision on the application may, however, be referred to another body before which a complaint or appeal is pending, can or could have been filed.
(6) The complaint or appeal against failure to decide on the application in due time may still be declared well-founded, if the person submitting the letter of complaint or appeal has an interest therein.

Article 6:21. (1) The complaint or appeal may be withdrawn in writing.
(2) During a hearing, the withdrawal may also be effected orally.

Article 6:22. An administrative decision against which a complaint has been filed or an appeal has been lodged may, despite a violation of a formal requirement, be upheld by the body deciding on the complaint or appeal if it is found that the concerned parties do thereby not incur any disadvantages.

Article 6:23. (1) If an appeal may be lodged against the decision on the complaint or appeal, this is stated in the notification of the decision.
(2) Therein it is stated by whom, within which period of time and with which body an appeal may be lodged.

Article 6:24. This division, with the exception of Article 6:12, applies mutatis mutandis if an appeal to a higher court or an appeal in cassation may be lodged.

Chapter 7. Special provisions regarding complaints and administrative appeals

Division 7.1 Letter of complaint preceding appeal to the administrative judge

Article 7:1. (1) The person who has been given the right to appeal against an administrative decision to an administrative judge must, before lodging an appeal against that administrative decision, file a complaint, unless the administrative decision:
(a) has been taken on a complaint or an administrative appeal,
(b) is subject to approval,

PART II. ADMINISTRATIVE LAW

(c) contains the approval of another administrative decision or the denial of such approval, or
(d) has been prepared in accordance with division 3.4.
(2) Against the decision on the complaint an appeal may be lodged in accordance with the rules that apply to lodging an appeal against the administrative decision against which the complaint has been filed.

Article 7:1a. (1) In the letter of complaint, the submitting person may request the administrative authority to agree to an immediate appeal to the administrative judge, by way of derogation from Article 7:1.
(2) The administrative authority in any event rejects the request, if:
(a) the letter of complaint is directed against failure to take an administrative decision in due time, or
(b) another letter of complaint against the administrative decision has been submitted in which an identical request is missing, unless that other letter of complaint is evidently inadmissible.
(3) The administrative authority may agree to the request if the matter is suitable for this.
(4) The administrative authority decides on the request as quickly as possible. A decision to agree is taken as soon as it may reasonably be assumed that no new letters of complaint will be submitted. Articles 4:7 and 4:8 do not apply.
(5) If the administrative authority agrees with the request, it forwards the letter of complaint, after the date of receipt has been noted on it, without delay to the competent judge.
(6) A letter of complaint received after the agreement is forwarded to the competent judge without delay as well. If this letter of complaint does not contain a request in the meaning of paragraph 1, then by way of derogation from Article 8:41 (1) no registration fee is levied.

Division 7.2 Special provisions regarding complaints

Article 7:2. (1) Before an administrative authority decides on the complaint, it gives concerned parties the opportunity to be heard.
(2) The administrative authority in any event give notice thereof to the person submitting the letter of complaint as well as to the concerned parties who have stated their views during the preparation of the administrative decision.

Article 7:3. The hearing of concerned parties may be refrained from if:
(a) the complaint is evidently inadmissible,
(b) the complaint is evidently ill-founded,
(c) the concerned parties have declared not to be willing to make use of the right to be heard, or
(d) the complaint will be wholly satisfied and the interests of other concerned parties cannot be prejudiced as a result.

Article 7:4. (1) Until ten days before the hearing concerned parties may submit further documents.
(2) The administrative authority deposits the letter of complaint, and all further documents relating to the matter, for inspection by concerned parties for at least one week prior to the hearing.
(3) In the call for the hearing, the attention of concerned parties is drawn to paragraph 1 and it is indicated where and when the documents will be deposited for inspection.
(4) Concerned parties may obtain copies of these documents at no more than cost price.
(5) As far as the concerned parties agree, the application of paragraph 2 may be refrained from.
(6) The administrative authority may, upon request by a concerned party or otherwise, further refrain from applying paragraph 2 as far as secrecy is required for compelling reasons. The application of this provision is notified.
(7) Compelling reasons do in any event not exist as far as pursuant to the Openness of Administration Act [Wet openbaarheid van bestuur] an obligation exists to grant a request for information contained in these documents.
(8) If a compelling reason lies in the fear of damage to the physical or mental health of a concerned party, inspection of the documents concerned may be reserved to an agent who is either an attorney or a physician.

Article 7:5. (1) Unless the hearing is conducted by or also by the administrative authority or by the director or a member thereof, the hearing is conducted by:
(a) a person who has not been involved in the preparation of the contested administrative decision, or
(b) more than one person, of whom the majority, including the person who chairs the hearing, has not been involved in the preparation of the administrative decision.
(2) As far as not otherwise is provided by a legal rule, the administrative authority decides whether the hearing takes place in public.

Article 7:6. (1) Concerned parties are heard in each other's presence.
(2) Upon request or upon the public authority's motion, concerned parties may be heard separately, if it may be assumed that a joint hearing will prejudice proper consideration or that during the hearing facts or circumstances will become known of which secrecy is required for compelling reasons.
(3) Where concerned parties have been heard separately, every one of them is informed of the matters dealt with during the hearing in their absence.
(4) The administrative authority may, upon request by a concerned party or otherwise, refrain from applying paragraph 3 as far as secrecy is required for compelling reasons. Article 7:4 (6) second clause, (7) and (8) applies mutatis mutandis.

Article 7:7. A protocol is made of the hearing.

Article 7:8. Upon request by the concerned party, witnesses and experts whom he has brought with him may be heard.

Article 7:9. Where after the hearing facts or circumstances become known to the administrative authority which may be of considerable importance for the decision to be taken on the complaint, this is communicated to the concerned parties and they are given the opportunity to be heard about this.

Article 7:10. (1) The administrative authority decides within six weeks or - if a committee in the meaning of Article 7:13 has been established - within ten weeks after receipt of the letter of complaint.
(2) The period of time is suspended from the day on which the submitting person is requested to remedy a defect in the meaning of Article 6:6, until the day on which the defect has been remedied or the time limit set for this purpose has expired unused.
(3) The administrative authority may defer the decision for a maximum of four weeks. Written notice is given of the deferral.
(4) Further postponement is possible as far as the person submitting the letter of complaint agrees to this and other concerned parties cannot thereby be prejudiced in their interests or if they agree to this.

Article 7:11. (1) If the complaint is admissible, a reconsideration of the contested administrative decision takes place on the basis thereof.
(2) As far as the reconsideration calls for this, the administrative authority revokes the contested administrative decision and takes, as far as necessary, another administrative decision instead.

Article 7:12. (1) The decision on the complaint must be based on proper reasons which are stated in the notification of the decision. If pursuant to Article 7:3 a hearing has been refrained from, the reason for that is stated at the same time.
(2) The decision is be notified by being sent or delivered to those to whom it is addressed. If an administrative decision is concerned which had not been addressed to one or more concerned parties, then the decision is notified in the same manner as that administrative decision.
(3) As quickly as possible after notification of the decision, notice is given thereof to the concerned parties who have stated their views in the complaint procedure or in the preparation of the contested administrative decision.
(4) Article 6:23 applies mutatis mutandis to the notice in the meaning of paragraph 3, which also states as clearly as possible, with a view to the beginning of the period of time for appeal, when the notification of the decision in accordance with paragraph 2 has taken place.

Article 7:13. (1) This Article applies if an advisory committee has been established for the decision on the complaint:
(a) which consists of a chairman and at least two members,
(b) whose chairman is not part of and does not work under the responsibility of the administrative authority and
(c) which complies with any other requirements as may be imposed by a legal rule.
(2) If a committee will advise on the complaint, the administrative authority communicates this as quickly as possible to the person submitting the letter of complaint.
(3) The hearing is conducted by the committee. The committee may assign the conduct of the hearing to the chairman or to a member who is not part of and who does not work under the responsibility of the administrative authority.
(4) The committee decides on the application of Article 7:4 (6), Article 7:5 (2) and, as far as not otherwise is provided by a legal rule, of Article 7:3.

(5) A representative of the administrative authority is invited to the hearing and is given the opportunity to explain the administrative authority's position.
(6) The advice of the committee is drawn up in writing and contains a protocol of the hearing.
(7) If the decision on the complaint deviates from the advice of the committee, the decision states the reasons for the deviation and the advice is sent together with the decision.

Article 7:14. Article 3:6 (2), division 3.4, Articles 3:41 to 3:45, division 3.7 with the exception of Article 3:49, and chapter 4 do not apply to administrative decisions on the basis of this division.

Article 7:15. (1) No fee is payable for a complaint to be considered.
(2) The costs which the concerned party reasonably had to incur in connection with the consideration of the complaint are reimbursed by the administrative authority only upon request by the concerned party as far as the contested administrative decision is revoked due to unlawfulness which is imputable to the administrative authority. Article 243 (2) of the Code of Civil Procedure [Wetboek van Burgerlijke Rechtsvordering] applies mutatis mutandis.
(3) The request is made before the administrative authority has decided on the complaint. The administrative authority decides on the request simultaneously with the decision on the complaint.
(4) By ordinance, further rules are established regarding the costs which may exclusively be reimbursed and regarding the manner in which the amount of the cost is established.

[Division 7.3 is omitted.]

Chapter 8. Special provisions regarding appeals to the district court

Title 8.1 General provisions

Division 8.1.1 Competence

Article 8:1. (1) A concerned party may appeal to the district court [rechtbank] against an administrative decision.
(2) With an administrative decision is equated any other act by an administrative authority in which a civil servant as such in the meaning of Article 1 of the Civil Servants Act [Ambtenarenwet], or a conscript as such in the meaning of chapter 2 of the Conscription Framework Act [Kaderwet dienstplicht], their surviving relatives or their legal successors are concerned parties.
(3) With an administrative decision are equated:
(a) the written decision containing the denial of an approval of an administrative decision containing a generally binding rule or a policy rule or the withdrawal or the establishment of the entry into force of a generally binding rule or a policy rule, and
(b) the written decision containing the denial of an approval of an administrative decision for the preparation of a legal act under private law.

Article 8:2. No appeal may be lodged against:
(a) an administrative decision containing a generally binding rule or a policy rule,
(b) an administrative decision containing the withdrawal or the establishment of the entry into force of a generally binding rule or a policy rule, and
(c) an administrative decision containing the approval of an administrative decision containing the withdrawal or the establishment of the entry into force of a generally binding rule or a policy rule.

Article 8:3. No appeal may be lodged against an administrative decision for the preparation of a legal act under private law.

Article 8:4. (1) No appeal may be lodged against an administrative decision:
(a) containing the suspension or annulment of an administrative decision of another administrative authority,
(b) based on a power conferred, or obligation imposed, by any legal rule for the case of exceptional circumstances, taken under such circumstances,
(c) taken on the basis of a legal rule for the safeguarding of the military interests of the Kingdom or its allies,

(d) of appointment or employment, unless the appeal is lodged by a civil servant in the meaning of Article 1 of the Civil Servants Act [Ambtenarenwet] as such or a conscript in the meaning of chapter 2 of the Conscription Framework Act [Kaderwet dienstplicht] as such, their surviving relatives or legal successors,
(e) containing an assessment of the knowledge or ability of a candidate or pupil who is examined on the matter or tested in any other way, or containing the establishment of tasks, assessment standards or further rules for such examination or testing,
(f) containing a technical assessment of a vehicle or aircraft, or a measuring device, a part thereof or an auxiliary device therefore,
(g) regarding the numbering of lists of candidates, the validity of combination of candidate lists, the conduct of the voting, the counting of votes and the establishment of results during elections of the members of representative bodies, the declaration of appointment to vacant seats, the admission of new members of a provincial assembly [provinciale staten], a municipal council and the general governing body of a water board [waterschap], as well as the granting of temporary leave due to pregnancy and delivery or illness,
(h) taken on the basis of a legal rule regarding compulsory military service as far as it concerns examination, re-examination, actual service, long leave or discharge, unless the administrative decision relates to the extension of actual service or breadwinner's allowance, or the administrative decision has been taken on the basis of the Armed Forces Reserve Personnel Act 1985 [Wet voor het reservepersoneel der krijgsmacht 1985],
(i) containing an official act of a bailiff [gerechtsdeurwaarder] or notary,
(j) in the meaning of Article 7:1a (4), or
(k) containing a refusal on the basis of Article 2:15.

Article 8:5. (1) No appeal may be lodged against an administrative decision taken on the basis of a legal rule which is included in the annex belonging to this Act.
(2) In case of an amendment of the annex, this annex remains applicable as it was before the coming into effect of the amendment, with respect to the possibility to lodge an appeal against an administrative decision notified before that moment.

Article 8:6. (1) No appeal may be lodged against an administrative decision against which an appeal to another administrative judge may be or could have been lodged.
(2) No appeal may be lodged against an administrative decision against which administrative appeal may be lodged, or could have been lodged by the concerned parties.

Article 8:7. (1) If an appeal is lodged against an administrative decision of an administrative authority of a province, a municipality, a water board or a region in the meaning of Article 21 of the Police Act 1993 [Politiewet 1993] or against an administrative decision of a joint authority or an administrative authority of a public entity which has been established in accordance with the Joint Regulations Act [Wet gemeenschappelijke regelingen], the district court is competent in whose district the administrative authority has its seat.
(2) If an appeal is lodged against an administrative decision of another administrative authority, the district court is competent in whose district the person submitting the letter of appeal has his place of residence in the Netherlands. If the person submitting the letter of appeal does not have a place of residence in the Netherlands, the district court is competent in whose district the administrative authority has its seat.

Article 8:8. (1) If against the same administrative decision appeals are lodged with more than one competent district court, the cases are considered further by the competent district court with which an appeal has been lodged first. If appeals have been lodged simultaneously with more than one competent district court first, the cases are considered further by the competent district court which is mentioned first in the Territorial Division of the Judiciary Act [Wet op de rechterlijke indeling].
(2) The other district court refers, or the other district courts refer, the case or cases pending before them to the district court which will consider the cases further. The documents relating to the case or cases are transmitted to the district court which will consider the cases further.
(3) If against the same administrative decision appeals have been lodged with more than one district court, the administrative authority gives notice thereof to these district courts without delay.
(4) If the administrative authority, pursuant to Article 7:1a (5) or (6), forwards several letters of complaint, it forwards them to the district court which will consider the case in accordance with paragraph 1 clause 2.

Part II. Administrative Law

Article 8:9. The Administrative Jurisprudence Division of the Council of State [Afdeling bestuursrechtspraak van de Raad van State] respectively the Central Council of Appeals [Centrale Raad van Beroep] decide in last instance in disputes between district courts on the application of Article 8:7 in cases which they are competent to take into consideration in higher appeal.

Division 8.1.2 Proceedings before a single judge and a chamber of several judges

Article 8:10. (1) The cases brought before the district court are considered by a single judge.
(2) If a case, in to the opinion of the single judge, is not suitable for consideration by a single judge, he refers it to a chamber of several judges. The single judge may also refer a case to a chamber of several judges in other cases.
(3) If a case, in the opinion of the chamber of several judges, is suitable for consideration by a single judge, it may refer it to a single judge.
(4) Referral may take place at any stage of the proceedings. A referred case is continued from the stage which it has reached.

[The remainder of Division 8.1.2 as well as the Divisions 8.1.3 – 8.1.7 are omitted.]

Title 8.2 Consideration of appeals

[Divisions 8.2.1 – 8.2.5 are omitted.]

Division 8.2.6 Judgment

Article 8:66. (1) Unless judgment is given orally, the district court gives its judgment in writing within six weeks after closure of the investigation.
(2) In special circumstances, the district court may extend this time limit by a maximum of six weeks.
(3) Parties are notified of such extension.

Article 8:67. (1) The district court may give its judgment orally immediately after closure of the investigation in a hearing. Giving judgment may be deferred by a maximum of one week, in which case parties are informed of the date of the judgment.
(2) The oral judgment consists of the decision and the reasons for the decision.
(3) Of the oral judgment a transcript is drawn up by the registrar.
(4) It is signed by the president of the chamber of several judges and by the registrar. In case of inability of the president or the registrar to attend, this is noted in the transcript.
(5) The district court pronounces the decision in the meaning of paragraph 2 in public, in the presence of the registrar. At the same time it is stated by whom, within which time limit and before which administrative judge which legal recourse may be sought.
(6) The statement in the meaning of paragraph 5, clause 2, is noted in the transcript.

Article 8:68. (1) If the district court considers that the investigation has not been complete, it may re-open it. The district court determines in that context in which manner the investigation is to be continued.
(2) The registrar gives, as quickly as possible, notice thereof to parties.

Article 8:69. (1) The district court gives its judgment on the basis of the letter of appeal, the submitted documents, the proceedings during the preliminary investigation and the investigation during the hearing.
(2) The district court supplements the legal bases upon its own motion.
(3) The district court may supplement the facts upon its own motion.

Article 8:70. The judgment provides for:
(a) a declaration of non-competence of the district court,
(b) a declaration of inadmissibility of the appeal,
(c) a declaration of ill-foundedness of the appeal, or
(d) a declaration of the well-foundedness of the appeal.

Article 8:71. As far as a claim may exclusively be brought before the civil judge, this is stated in the judgment. The civil judge is bound by this decision.

Article 8:72. (1) If the district court declares the appeal well-founded, it annuls the contested administrative decision in whole or in part.
(2) The annulment of an administrative decision or of a part of an administrative decision entails the annulment of the legal consequences of that administrative decision or of the annulled part thereof.
(3) The district court may determine that the legal consequences of the annulled administrative decision or the annulled part thereof remain effective in whole or in part.
(4) If the district court declares the appeal well-founded, it may instruct the administrative authority to take a new administrative decision or perform another act with due regard to its judgment, or it may determine that its judgment takes the place of the annulled administrative decision or the annulled part thereof.
(5) The district court may set a time limit for the administrative authority to take a new administrative decision or perform another act, and may also take a provisional measure. In the latter case the district court determines the moment on which the provisional measure will expire.
(6) The district court may determine that a provisional measure will expire at a later moment than the moment at which it has given its judgment.
(7) The district court may determine that, if or as long as the administrative authority does not comply with the judgment, the legal person designated by it is liable to the payment to a party designated by it of a penalty [dwangsom] to be fixed in the judgment. Articles 611a to 611i of the Code of Civil Procedure [Wetboek Burgerlijke Rechtsvordering] apply mutatis mutandis.

Article 8:73. (1) If the district court declares the appeal well-founded, it may, if there are reasons to do so, upon request by a party order the legal person designated by it to pay compensation for the damage suffered by this party.
(2) If the district court is unable to establish, or fully establish, the amount of the compensation in its judgment, it determines in its judgment that the investigation shall be re-opened for the preparation of a further judgment on this matter. The district court determines in that context in which manner the investigation is to be continued.

Article 8:73a. (1) In case of withdrawal of an appeal because the administrative authority has fully or partly satisfied the person submitting the letter of appeal, the district court may, upon request by the submitting person, order by means of a separate judgment the legal person designated by it to pay compensation for the damage suffered by the submitting person in accordance with Article 8:73. The request is submitted simultaneously with the withdrawal of the appeal. If this requirement is not complied with, the request is declared inadmissible.
(2) The district court gives, if necessary, the submitting person the opportunity to explain the request in writing and gives the administrative authority the opportunity to submit a written reply. It sets time limits for these purposes. If the request is submitted orally, the district court may order that the explanation on the request and the reply be submitted orally immediately.
(3) If the explanation or the request and the reply have been submitted orally, the district court closes the investigation. In the other cases, divisions 8.2.4 and 8.2.5 apply mutatis mutandis.

Article 8:74. (1) If the district court declares the appeal well-founded, the judgment further determines that the person submitting the letter of appeal be reimbursed for the registration fee paid by him by the legal person designated by the district court.
(2) In the other cases the judgment may determine that the registration fee paid be reimbursed in whole or in part by the legal person designated by the district court.

Article 8:75. (1) The district court is exclusively authorized to order a party to pay the costs which another party reasonably had to incur in connection with the consideration of the appeal before the district court and of the complaint or administrative appeal. Articles 7:15 (2) to (4) and 7:28 (2), clause 1, (3) and (4) apply. A natural person may only be ordered to pay the costs in case of evidently unreasonable use of procedure. By ordinance further rules are established regarding the costs to which an order in the meaning of the first clause may exclusively relate and regarding the manner in which the amount of the costs are established in the judgment.
(2) In case of an order to reimburse the costs of a party which has been granted legal aid for the appeal to the district court, the complaint or the administrative appeal by virtue of the Legal Aid Act [Wet op de rechtsbijstand], the amount of the costs is paid to the registrar. Article 243 of the Code of Civil Procedure [Wetboek van Burgerlijke Rechtsvordering] applies mutatis mutandis.

(3) If an administrative authority is ordered to pay the costs, the district court designates the legal person which must pay the costs.

Article 8:75a. (1) In case of withdrawal of the appeal because the administrative authority has wholly or partly satisfied the person submitting the letter of appeal, the administrative authority may, upon request by the submitting person, be ordered in a separate judgment in accordance with Article 8:75 to pay the costs. The request is submitted simultaneously with the withdrawal of the appeal. If this requirement is not complied with, the request is declared inadmissible.
(2) Article 8:73a (2) and (3) applies mutatis mutandis.

Article 8:76. As far as a judgment provides for payment of a certain amount of money, it may be executed in accordance with the provisions of the second book of the Code of Civil Procedure [Wetboek van Burgerlijke Rechtsvordering].

Article 8:77. (1) The written judgment states:
(a) the names of the parties and of their representatives or agents,
(b) the reasons for the decision,
(c) the decision,
(d) the name of the judge or the name of the judges who has or have considered the case,
(e) the day on which the decision is pronounced, and
(f) by whom, within which time limit and before which administrative judge which legal recourse may be sought.
(2) If the judgment declares the appeal well-founded, it is stated in the judgment which written or unwritten legal rule or which general principle of law is found to have been violated.
(3) The judgment is signed by the president of the chamber of several judges and by the registrar. In case of inability of the president or the registrar to attend, this is stated in the judgment.

Article 8:78. The district court pronounces the decision in the meaning of Article 8:77 (1) (c) in public, in the presence of the registrar.

Article 8:79. (1) Within two weeks after the date of the judgment, the registrar sends, free of charge, a copy of the judgment or of the transcript of the oral judgment to the parties.
(2) Others than the parties may obtain copies or excerpts of the judgment or of the transcript of the oral judgment. With respect to costs, what is provided by or pursuant to the Payment Amounts in Criminal Cases Act [Wet tarieven in strafzaken] applies mutatis mutandis.

Article 8:80. If the district court determines that its judgment takes the place of the annulled administrative decision, the judgment is furthermore notified in the manner prescribed for that administrative decision by the competent administrative authority.

[Titles 8.3 and 8.4 are omitted.]

[Chapter 9 is omitted.]

Chapter 10. Provisions regarding administrative authorities

Title 10.1 Mandate and delegation

Division 10.1.1 Mandate

Article 10:1. By mandate is meant: the power to take administrative decisions on behalf of the administrative authority.

Article 10:2. An administrative decision taken by the mandatary within the limits of his power is deemed to be an administrative decision of the mandator.

Article 10:3. (1) An administrative authority may grant a mandate, unless otherwise is provided by a legal rule or the nature of the power is incompatible with the granting of a mandate.

(2) A mandate is in any event not granted if it concerns a power:
(a) to adopt a generally binding rule, unless provision has been made for the granting of a mandate when the power was conferred;
(b) to take an administrative decision with regard to which it is provided that it must be taken by qualified majority or the prescribed decision-making procedure of which is otherwise incompatible with the granting of a mandate;
(c) to decide on a letter of appeal;
(d) to annul, or deny the approval of, an administrative decision of another administrative authority.
(3) A mandate to decide on a letter of complaint or on a request in the meaning of Article 7:1a (1) is not granted to the person who has taken, by virtue of a mandate, the administrative decision against which the complaint is directed.

Article 10:4. (1) If the mandatary does not work under the responsibility of the mandator, the granting of the mandate requires the consent of the mandatary and, as the case may be, of the one under whose responsibility he works.
(2) Paragraph 1 does not apply if the power to grant the mandate is provided by a legal rule.

Article 10:5. (1) An administrative authority may grant either a general mandate or a mandate for a specific case.
(2) A general mandate is granted in writing. A mandate for a specific case is in any event granted in writing if the mandatary does not work under the responsibility of the mandator.

Article 10:6. (1) The mandator may, on a case-by-case basis or in general, give the mandatatry instructions regarding the exercise of the mandated power.
(2) The mandatary provides the mandator, upon his request, with information concerning the exercise of the power.

Article 10:7. The mandator remains competent to exercise the mandated power.

Article 10:8. (1) The mandator may withdraw the mandate at any time.
(2) A general mandate is withdrawn in writing.

Article 10:9. (1) The mandator may agree to the granting of a sub-mandate.
(2) The other provisions of this division apply mutatis mutandis to a sub-mandate.

Article 10:10. An administrative decision taken by virtue of a mandate states on behalf of which administrative authority the administrative decision has been taken.

Article 10:11. (1) An administrative authority may determine that administrative decisions taken by it may be signed on its behalf, unless otherwise is provided by a legal rule or the nature of the power is incompatible therewith.
(2) In that case it must appear from the administrative decision that it has been taken by the administrative authority itself.

Article 10:12. This division applies mutatis mutandis if an administrative authority grants powers of attorney to another person, working under its responsibility, to carry out legal acts under private law, or gives authorization for the carrying out of acts which are neither an administrative decision nor a legal act under private law.

Division 10.1.2 Delegation

Article 10:13. By delegation is meant: the transfer by an administrative authority of its power to take administrative decisions to another person who exercises it under his own responsibility.

Article 10:14. Delegation does not occur to subordinates.

Article 10:15. Delegation only occurs if the power thereto is provided by a legal rule.

Article 10:16. (1) The administrative authority may issue only policy rules regarding the exercise of the delegated power.

(2) The person to whom the power has been delegated provides the administrative authority, upon its request, with information regarding the exercise of the power.

Article 10:17. The administrative authority may no longer exercise the delegated power itself.

Article 10:18. The administrative authority may withdraw the administrative decision of delegation at any time.

Article 10:19. An administrative decision which has been taken on the basis of a delegated power cites the administrative decision of delegation and states where it can be found.

Article 10:20. (1) To the transfer by an administrative authority to a third party of the power of another administrative authority to take administrative decisions, this division, with the exception of Article 10:16, applies mutatis mutandis.
(2) By legal rule or by the administrative decision of transfer it may be determined that the administrative authority whose power is transferred may establish policy rules regarding the exercise of this power.
(3) The party to whom the power is transferred provides, at their request, the transferring administrative authority and the originally competent administrative authority with information regarding the exercise of the power.

[Title 10.2 is omitted, the remainder of the Act is omitted.]

Civil Procedure Rules 1998, as amended. Selected provisions: Part 54, Section I.

Section I. Judicial Review

Rule 54.1 (1) This Section of this Part contains rules about judicial review.
(2) In this Section –
(a) a 'claim for judicial review' means a claim to review the lawfulness of –
(i) an enactment; or
(ii) a decision, action or failure to act in relation to the exercise of a public function.
(b) (revoked).
(c) (revoked).
(d) (revoked).
(e) 'the judicial review procedure' means the Part 8 procedure as modified by this Section;
(f) 'interested party' means any person (other than the claimant and defendant) who is directly affected by the claim; and
(g) 'court' means the High Court, unless otherwise stated.

Rule 54.2. The judicial review procedure must be used in a claim for judicial review where the claimant is seeking –
(a) a mandatory order;
(b) a prohibiting order;
(c) a quashing order; or
(d) an injunction under section 30 of the Supreme Court Act 1981 (restraining a person from acting in any office in which he is not entitled to act).

Rule 54.3. (1) The judicial review procedure may be used in a claim for judicial review where the claimant is seeking –
(a) a declaration; or
(b) an injunction.
(2) A claim for judicial review may include a claim for damages, restitution or the recovery of a sum due but may not seek such a remedy alone.

Rule 54.4. The court's permission to proceed is required in a claim for judicial review whether started under this Section or transferred to the Administrative Court.

Rule 54.5. (1) The claim form must be filed –
(a) promptly; and
(b) in any event not later than 3 months after the grounds to make the claim first arose.
(2) The time limit in this rule may not be extended by agreement between the parties.
(3) This rule does not apply when any other enactment specifies a shorter time limit for making the claim for judicial review.

Rule 54.6. (1) In addition to the matters set out in rule 8.2 the claimant must also state –
(a) the name and address of any person he considers to be an interested party;
(b) that he is requesting permission to proceed with a claim for judicial review; and
(c) any remedy (including any interim remedy) he is claiming.
(2) The claim form must be accompanied by the documents required by the relevant practice direction.

Rule 54.7. The claim form must be served on –
(a) the defendant; and
(b) unless the court otherwise directs, any person the claimant considers to be an interested party,
within 7 days after the date of issue.

Rule 54.8. (1) Any person served with the claim form who wishes to take part in the judicial review must file an acknowledgment of service in the relevant practice form in accordance with the following provisions of this rule.
(2) Any acknowledgment of service must be –

Part II. Administrative Law

(a) filed not more than 21 days after service of the claim form; and
(b) served on –
(i) the claimant; and
(ii) subject to any direction under rule 54.7 (b), any other person named in the claim form,
as soon as practicable and, in any event, not later than 7 days after it is filed.
(3) The time limits under this rule may not be extended by agreement between the parties.
(4) The acknowledgment of service –
(a) must –
(i) where the person filing it intends to contest the claim, set out a summary of his grounds for doing so; and
(ii) state the name and address of any person the person filing it considers to be an interested party; and
(b) may include or be accompanied by an application for directions.
(5) Rule 10.3 (2) does not apply.

Rule 54.9. (1) Where a person served with the claim form has failed to file an acknowledgment of service in accordance with rule 54.8, he –
(a) may not take part in a hearing to decide whether permission should be given unless the court allows him to do so; but
(b) provided he complies with rule 54.14 or any other direction of the court regarding the filing and service of –
(i) detailed grounds for contesting the claim or supporting it on additional grounds; and
(ii) any written evidence,
may take part in the hearing of the judicial review.
(2) Where that person takes part in the hearing of the judicial review, the court may take his failure to file an acknowledgment of service into account when deciding what order to make about costs.
(3) Rule 8.4 does not apply.

Rule 54.10. (1) Where permission to proceed is given the court may also give directions.
(2) Directions under paragraph (1) may include a stay of proceedings to which the claim relates.

Rule 54.11. The court will serve –
(a) the order giving or refusing permission; and
(b) any directions,
on –
(i) the claimant;
(ii) the defendant; and
(iii) any other person who filed an acknowledgment of service.

Rule 54.12. (1) This rule applies where the court, without a hearing –
(a) refuses permission to proceed; or
(b) gives permission to proceed –
(i) subject to conditions; or
(ii) on certain grounds only.
(2) The court will serve its reasons for making the decision when it serves the order giving or refusing permission in accordance with rule 54.11.
(3) The claimant may not appeal but may request the decision to be reconsidered at a hearing.
(4) A request under paragraph (3) must be filed within 7 days after service of the reasons under paragraph (2).
(5) The claimant, defendant and any other person who has filed an acknowledgment of service will be given at least 2 days' notice of the hearing date.

Rule 54.13. Neither the defendant nor any other person served with the claim form may apply to set aside an order giving permission to proceed.

Rule 54.14. (1) A defendant and any other person served with the claim form who wishes to contest the claim or support it on additional grounds must file and serve -
(a) detailed grounds for contesting the claim or supporting it on additional grounds; and
(b) any written evidence,
within 35 days after service of the order giving permission.
(2) The following rules do not apply –
(a) rule 8.5 (3) and 8.5 (4); and

(b) rule 8.5 (5) and 8.5(6).

Rule 54.15. The court's permission is required if a claimant seeks to rely on grounds other than those for which he has been given permission to proceed.

Rule 54.16. (1) Rule 8.6 (1) does not apply.
(2) No written evidence may be relied on unless –
(a) it has been served in accordance with any –
(i) rule under this Section; or
(ii) direction of the court; or
(b) the court gives permission.

Rule 54.17. (1) Any person may apply for permission –
(a) to file evidence; or
(b) make representations at the hearing of the judicial review.
(2) An application under paragraph (1) should be made promptly.

Rule 54.18. The court may decide the claim for judicial review without a hearing where all the parties agree.

Rule 54.19. (1) This rule applies where the court makes a quashing order in respect of the decision to which the claim relates.
(2) The court may –
(a) (i) remit the matter to the decision-maker; and
(ii) direct it to reconsider the matter and reach a decision in accordance with the judgment of the court; or
(b) in so far as any enactment permits, substitute its own decision for the decision to which the claim relates.

Rule 54.20. The court may
(a) order a claim to continue as if it had not been started under this Section; and
(b) where it does so, give directions about the future management of the claim.

[Sections II and III are omitted.]

PART III

Criminal Justice

CRIM

Criminal Code [Code Pénal] of 1 March 1994 as consolidated on 11 August 2010. Selected provisions: Articles 121-1 – 122-8, 221-1 – 222-2 and 223-3 and 223-4.[14]

Statutory part

Book I. General provisions

[Title I is omitted.]

Title II. Criminal liability

Chapter I. General Provisions

Article 121-1. Nobody is criminally liable except for his own act.

Article 121-2. Legal persons, with the exception of the state, are criminally liable, according to the distinctions set out in Articles 121-4 to 121-7, for offences committed on their behalf by their organs or representatives.
However, territorial entities and associations thereof are only criminally liable for offences committed in the exercise of activities suitable for being the object of conventions of public service delegation.
The criminal liability of legal persons does not exclude that of natural persons who are perpetrators of or accomplices to the same acts, subject to the reservations of the provisions of the fourth paragraph of Article 121-3.

Article 121-3. There is no crime [crime] or misdemeanour [délit] without there being the intention of committing it.
However, where statute so provides, there is a misdemeanour in the case of deliberately endangering other persons.
There is also a misdemeanour, where statute so provides, in the case of imprudence, negligence or failure to observe a duty of care [obligation de prudence] or of security provided for by statute or regulation [règlement], if it is established that the perpetrator of the acts has failed to apply normal diligence, taking into account, where appropriate, the nature of his tasks or his function, his competences as well as the power and means that were at his disposal.
In the case referred to in the preceding paragraph, natural persons who have not directly caused the damage but who have created or contributed to creating the situation which allowed the damage to occur, or who have failed to take appropriate measures to avoid it, are criminally liable if it is established that they have either breached, in a manifestly deliberate manner, a special duty of care or security provided for by statute or regulation, or that they have made a clear mistake which exposed others to a particularly serious risk of which they could not have been unaware.
There is no contravention [contravention] in the event of force majeure.

Article 121-4. The perpetrator [auteur] of an offence [infraction] is the person who:
1. commits acts prohibited by criminal law;
2. attempts to commit a crime or, in the cases provided for by statute, a misdemeanour.

Article 121-5. An attempt exists where, demonstrated by a beginning of execution, it has been suspended or has failed to have its effect solely through circumstances independent of the will of the perpetrator.

Article 121-6. The accomplice [complice], in the meaning of Article 121-7, shall be punished like the perpetrator of the offence.

Article 121-7. The accomplice of a crime or misdemeanour is the person who intentionally, through aid or assistance, has facilitated its preparation or commission.
The accomplice is equally the person who, through a gift, promise, threat, order, abuse of authority or of power has provoked an offence or has given instructions to commit it.

---

[14] Translation by S. Hardt.

Chapter II. Grounds for absence or mitigation of liability

Article 122-1. A person who was suffering, when the acts were committed, from a mental or neuropsychological disorder which had removed his discernment or the control over his actions, is not criminally liable.
A person who was suffering, when the acts were committed, from a mental or neuropsychological disorder which had altered his discernment or had limited the control over his actions remains punishable; however, the judiciary takes this circumstance into account in determining the penalty and fixing its regime.

Article 122-2. A person is not criminally liable who was acting under the influence of a force or a constraint which he could not resist.

Article 122-3. A person is not criminally liable who credibly shows to have believed, due an error with regard to the law which he was not able to avoid, that he could legitimately perform the act.

Article 122-4. A person is not criminally liable who performs an act prescribed or authorized by statutory or regulatory provisions.
A person is not criminally liable who performs an act ordered by a legitimate authority, except if this act is manifestly illegal.

Article 122-5. A person is not criminally liable who, confronted with an unjustified assault against himself or another person, performs, at the same time, an act required by the necessity of the legitimate defence of himself or others, except where the means of defence used are disproportionate to the seriousness of the attack.
A person is not criminally liable who, in order to interrupt the execution of a crime or of a misdemeanour against a good, performs an act of defence other than wilful homicide [homicide volontaire], where this act is strictly necessary for the objective pursued and where the means used are proportionate to the seriousness of the offence.

Article 122-6. Presumed to have acted in legitimate defence is he who performs the act:
1. to fend off, at night, the entry to an inhabited place by break-in, violence or deceit;
2. to defend himself against the perpetrators of theft or looting carried out with violence.

Article 122-7. A person is not criminally liable who, confronted with a present or imminent danger which threatens himself, others, or a good, performs an act necessary for the protection of the person or the good, except where the means used are disproportionate to the seriousness of the threat.

Article 122-8. Minors capable of discernment are criminally liable for crimes, misdemeanours or contraventions of which they have been found guilty, subject to the conditions laid down by a specific statute which determines measures of protection, assistance, surveillance and education to which they may be subject.
This statute also determines the educational sanctions which may be imposed on minors of ten to eighteen years of age, as well as the penalties to which minors of thirteen to eighteen years of age may be sentenced, taking into account the mitigation of liability which they enjoy by virtue of their age.

[Title III is omitted.]

Book II. Crimes and misdemeanours against persons

[Title I is omitted.]

Title II. Assaults against the human person

Chapter I. Assaults against the life of a person

Section 1. Wilful assaults against life

Article 221-1. The act of wilfully causing the death of another person constitutes murder [meurtre]. It is punished by thirty years of criminal imprisonment.

Article 221-2. Murder which precedes, accompanies or follows another crime is punished by permanent criminal imprisonment.
Murder of which the object is either to prepare or facilitate a misdemeanour, or to assist the escape or to ensure the impunity of the perpetrator or of the accomplice of a misdemeanour is punished by permanent criminal imprisonment.
The first two paragraphs of Article 132-23 regarding the safety period are applicable to the offences set out in the present Article.

Article 221-3. Murder committed with premeditation constitutes an assassination. It is punished by permanent criminal imprisonment.
The two first paragraphs of Article 132-23 regarding the safety period are applicable to the offence set out in the present Article. Nevertheless, where the victim is a minor of fifteen years of age and the assassination is preceded or accompanied by rape, torture or acts of barbarity, the criminal court [cour d'assises] may, by special decision, either prolong the safety period to thirty years or, if it imposes permanent criminal imprisonment, decide that none of the measures referred to in Article 132-23 may be accorded to the convict; in the event of the commutation of the sentence, and unless the decree of pardon provides otherwise, the safety period is equal to the length of the sentence resulting from the measure of pardon.

Article 221-4. Murder is punished by permanent criminal imprisonment where it is committed:
1. against a minor of fifteen years of age;
2. against a legitimate or natural ascendant or against the adoptive father or mother;
3. against a person whose particular vulnerability due to his age, to a disease, to an infirmity, to a physical or mental deficiency or to pregnancy is apparent or known to the perpetrator;
4. against a magistrate, a juror, an attorney, a public officer or high public officer [officier ministériel], a member of the national gendarmerie, a civil servant of the national police, customs authority, penitentiary administration or any other person holding public authority, a professional or voluntary fireman, an accredited guardian of buildings or of groups of buildings or an agent carrying out on behalf of a landlord the task of guarding or watching of inhabited buildings in accordance with Article L. 127-1 of the Construction and Housing Code [code de la construction et de l'habitation], in the exercise or on account of his functions, where the capacity of the victim is apparent or known to the perpetrator;
4bis. against a teacher or any staff member working at schooling institutions, against an employee of an operator of public transport or any other person charged with a public service as well as against a health care professional, in the exercise of his tasks, where the capacity of the victim is apparent or known to the perpetrator;
4ter. against the spouse, the ascendants and the descendants in direct line of the persons referred to under no. 4 and no. 4bis or against any other person habitually living at their domicile, because of the functions carried out by these persons;
5. against a witness, a victim or a civil party to proceedings, either to prevent him to denounce the acts, file a complaint or make a statement before a court, or because of his denunciation, his complaint or his statement;
6. because of the victim's actual or supposed membership or non-membership of a certain ethnic group, nation, race or religion;
7. because of the sexual orientation of the victim;
8. by several persons acting as an organized group;
9. by the spouse or partner [concubin] or partner in a civil union [pacte civil de solidarité] of the victim.
The two first paragraphs of Article 132-23 regarding the safety period are applicable to the offences set out in the present Article. Nevertheless, where the victim is a minor of fifteen years of age and the assassination is preceded or accompanied by rape, torture or acts of barbarity, the criminal court [cour d'assises] may, by special decision, either prolong the safety period to thirty years or, if it imposes permanent criminal imprisonment, decide that none of the measures referred to in Article 132-23 may be accorded to the convict; in the event of the commutation of the sentence, and unless the decree of pardon provides otherwise, the safety period is equal to the length of the sentence resulting from the measure of pardon.

Article 221-5. The act of assaulting the life of another person by the use or administration of substances able to cause death constitutes poisoning [empoisonnement].
Poisoning is punished by thirty years of criminal imprisonment.
It is punished by permanent criminal imprisonment where it is committed in one of the circumstances referred to in Articles 221-2, 221-3 and 221-4.
The two first paragraphs of Article 132-23 regarding the safety period are applicable to the offence set out in the present Article.

Article 221-5-1. The act of making a person offers or promises or of offering him gifts, presents or advantages of any kind so that he commits an assassination or a poisoning is punished, where this crime has neither been committed nor attempted, by ten years of criminal imprisonment and a fine of 150,000 euros.

Article 221-5-2. Legal persons declared criminally liable, under the conditions provided for by Article 121-2, for the offences defined in the present section incur, apart from the fine pursuant to the details provided by Article 131-38, the penalties provided by Article 131-39.
The prohibition referred to under no. 2 of Article 131-39 applies to the activity in the exercise of which or on the occasion of the exercise of which the offence has been committed.

Article 221-5-3. Any person who has attempted to commit the crimes of assassination or poisoning is exempted from punishment if, by having alerted the administrative or judicial authorities, he has allowed for the death of the victim to be prevented and for the other perpetrators or accomplices, where applicable, to be identified.
The custodial sentence incurred by the perpetrator of or the accomplice to a poisoning is reduced to twenty years of criminal imprisonment if, by having alerted the administrative or judicial authorities, he has allowed for the death of the victim to be prevented and for the other perpetrators or accomplices, where applicable, to be identified.

Section 2. Involuntary assaults against life

Article 221-6. The act of causing, subject to the conditions and pursuant to the distinctions provided for by Article 121-3, by inaptness, imprudence, inattentiveness, negligence or failure to observe an obligation of security or care imposed by statute or regulation, the death of another person constitutes involuntary homicide [homicide involontaire] punished by three years of imprisonment and a fine of 45,000 euros.
In case of a manifestly deliberate violation of a specific obligation of security or care imposed by statute or regulation, the penalties incurred are increased to five years of imprisonment and a fine of 75,000 euros.

Article 221-6-1. Where the inaptness, imprudence, inattentiveness, negligence or the failure to observe a statutory or regulatory obligation of security or care provided for by Article 221-6 is committed by the driver of a motor land vehicle, the involuntary homicide is punished by five years of imprisonment and a fine of 75,000 euros.
The penalties are increased to seven years of imprisonment and a fine of 100,000 euros where:
1. the driver has committed a manifestly deliberate violation of a specific obligation of security or care provided for by statute or regulation other than those outlined hereafter;
2. the driver was in a state of manifest drunkenness or was under the influence of an alcoholic state characterized by a concentration of alcohol in the blood or in the exhaled air equal to or higher than the limits fixed by the statutory or regulatory provisions of the Traffic Code [code de la route], or has refused to undergo the examinations provided for by that Code and designed to establish the existence of an alcoholic state;
3. it results from a blood analysis that the driver had used substances or plants classified as narcotics, or has refused to undergo the examinations provided for by the Traffic Code and designed to establish whether he was driving while having used narcotics;
4. the driver did not hold a driver's licence as required by statute or regulation or his licence had been annulled, invalidated, suspended or withdrawn;
5. the driver has committed a transgression of the speed limit by 50 km/h or more;
6. the driver, knowing that he caused or provoked an accident, has not stopped and so has tried to escape the criminal or civil liability he might incur.
The penalties are increased to ten years of imprisonment and to a fine of 150,000 euros where the involuntary homicide has been committed with two or more of the circumstances mentioned in no. 1 onwards of the present Article.

Article 221-7. Legal persons declared criminally liable, subject to the conditions provided for by Article 121-2, for the offence defined in Article 221-6 incur, apart from the fine pursuant to the details provided for by Article 131-38, the penalties mentioned in nos. 2, 3, 8 and 9 of Article 131-39.
The prohibition referred to under no. 2 of Article 131-39 applies to the activity in the exercise of which or on the occasion of the exercise of which the offence has been committed.
In the cases stipulated in the second paragraph of Article 221-6, the penalty referred to under no. 4 of Article 131-39 is also incurred.

Section 3. Complementary penalties applicable to natural persons

Article 221-8. Natural persons guilty of the offences provided for in the present chapter also incur the following complementary penalties:
1. the prohibition, pursuant to the conditions provided for by Article 131-27, either to carry out the professional or social activity in the exercise of which or on the occasion of the exercise of which the offence has been committed, or, for the crimes envisaged in Articles 221-1, 221-2, 221-3, 221-4 and 221-5, to carry out a commercial or industrial profession, to direct, administer, manage or control in whatever capacity, directly or indirectly, in their own name or in someone else's, a commercial or industrial enterprise or a commercial company. These prohibitions may be pronounced cumulatively;
2. the prohibition to hold or to carry, for a maximum period of five years, a weapon subject to authorization;
3. the suspension, for a maximum period of five years, of the driver's licence, with the possibility to limit this suspension to driving outside a professional activity; in the cases provided for by Article 221-6-1, the suspension may not be suspended, even partially, and may not be limited to driving outside a professional activity; in the cases provided for by nos. 1 to 6 and the last paragraph of Article 221-6-1 the period of this suspension is a maximum of ten years;
4. the annulment of the driver's licence with the prohibition to apply for the issuing of a new licence during a maximum period of five years;
4bis. the obligation to participate in an awareness training on the dangers of using narcotic substances, pursuant to the conditions set out in Article 131-35-1;
5. the confiscation of one or more weapons of which the convict is the owner or which he has at his free disposal;
6. the withdrawal of the hunting licence with the prohibition to apply for the issuing of a new licence during a maximum period of five years;
7. in the cases provided for by Article 221-6-1, the prohibition to drive certain motor land vehicles, including those for the driving of which a driver's licence is not required, for a maximum period of five years;
8. in the cases provided for by Article 221-6-1, the obligation to participate, at their own expense, in an awareness training on road safety;
9. in the cases provided for by Article 221-6-1, the immobilization, for a maximum period of one year, of the vehicle of which the convict has made use in committing the offence, if he is its owner;
10. in the case provided for by article 221-6-1, the confiscation of the vehicle of which the convict has made use to commit the offence, if he is the owner.
Any conviction for the misdemeanours provided for by nos. 1 to 6 and the last paragraph of Article 221-6-1 by operation of law entails the annulment of the driver's licence with the prohibition to apply for the issuing of a new licence for a maximum period of ten years. In case of a repeat offence, the period of the prohibition is increased by operation of law to ten years and the court may, by means of a specially reasoned decision, order that the prohibition be definitive.

Article 221-9. Natural persons guilty of the offences set out in section 1 of the present chapter also incur the following complementary penalties:
1. lifting of civic, civil and family rights, under the conditions set out in Article 131-26;
2. prohibition to hold a public office, under the conditions set out in Article 131-27;
3. confiscation as set out in Article 131-21;
4. prohibition of residence, according to the conditions set out in Article 131-31.

Article 221-9-1. Natural persons guilty of the crimes set out in section 1 of the present chapter are also liable to socio-judicial probation under the conditions set out in Articles 131-36-1 to 131-36-13.

Article 221-10. Natural persons guilty of the offences set out in section 2 of the present chapter also incur the complementary penalty of the public display or dissemination of the decision as set out in Article 131-35.

Article 221-11. Banishment from French territory may be ordered under the conditions set out in Article 131-30, either definitively or for a maximum period of ten years, against any alien guilty of one of the offences defined in section 1 of the present chapter.

Chapter II. Assaults against the physical or mental integrity of a person

Section 1. Voluntary assaults against the integrity of a person

Paragraph 1. Torture and acts of barbarity

Article 222-1. The act of subjecting a person to torture or to acts of barbarity is punished by fifteen years of criminal imprisonment.
The two first paragraphs of Article 132-23 regarding the safety period are applicable to the offence set out in the present Article.

Article 222-2. The offence defined in Article 222-1 is punished by permanent criminal imprisonment where it precedes, accompanies or follows a crime other than murder or rape.
The two first paragraphs of Article 132-23 regarding the safety period are applicable to the offence set out in the present Article.

[The remainder of Paragraph 1, the Paragraphs 2 and 3, and the remaining Sections of Chapter II are omitted.]

Chapter III. Endangerment of a person

[Section 1 is omitted.]

Section 2. Abandonment of a person not able to protect himself

Article 223-3. The abandonment in any place of a person who is not able to protect himself due to his age or his physical or mental condition is punished by five years of imprisonment and a fine of 75,000 euros.

Article 223-4. The abandonment which has resulted in a mutilation or a permanent infirmity is punished by fifteen years of criminal imprisonment.
The abandonment which has resulted in death is punished by twenty years of criminal imprisonment.

[The remaining Sections of Chapter III and the remainder of the Criminal Code are omitted.]

Criminal Code [Strafgesetzbuch] of 15 May 1871 as last amended by federal statute of 2 October 2009 (*BGBl.* I p. 3214). Selected provisions: General Part, Division 2 and Special Part, Division 16.[15]

General Part

[Division 1 is omitted.]

Division 2. The act

Title 1. Bases of criminal liability

§ 13. (1) He who fails to avert a result which is part of the constituent elements of a criminal statutory provision is only punishable under this Act if he is legally responsible for the non-occurrence of the result and if the omission is equivalent to the realization of the statutory elements through an action.
(2) The penalty may be mitigated pursuant to § 49 (1).

§ 14. (1) If someone acts
1. as an organ of a legal person authorized to represent it or as a member of such an organ,
2. as a partner [Gesellschafter] in a partnership with legal capacity authorized to represent it or
3. as the legal representative of another,
then a statute according to which particular personal properties, situations or circumstances (particular personal characteristics) form the basis of criminal liability, must also be applied to the representative, if these characteristics are, while not present in him, present in the one represented.
(2) If someone is, by the owner of a business or by someone otherwise so authorized,
1. assigned to manage the business in whole or in part, or
2. expressly assigned to carry out, under his own responsibility, tasks which are incumbent on the owner of the business,
and if he acts on the basis of this assignment, then a statute according to which particular personal characteristics form the basis of criminal liability, must also be applied to the assignee, if these characteristics are, while not present in him, present in the owner of the business. The business within the meaning of clause 1 is equivalent to the undertaking. If someone acts on the basis of a corresponding assignment for an office which performs tasks of public administration, then clause 1 must be applied by analogy.
(3) Sub-paragraphs 1 and 2 must also be applied if the legal act [Rechtshandlung] which was to form the basis of the authorization to represent or of the assignment is invalid.

§ 15. Only intentional [vorsätzlich] action is punishable, unless statute expressly provides for punishment for negligent [fahrlässig] action.

§ 16. (1) He who, in committing the act, is unaware of a circumstance which is part of the statutory elements of the offence, does not act intentionally. Criminal liability for negligent commission remains unaffected.
(2) He who, in committing the act, erroneously assumes circumstances which would satisfy the elements of a more lenient statute, may only be punished for intentional commission under the more lenient statute.

§ 17. If, in committing the act, the perpetrator lacks the discernment of doing something wrong, then he acts without guilt [Schuld] if he was not able to avoid this error. If the perpetrator was able to avoid the error, the penalty may be mitigated pursuant to § 49 (1).

§ 18. If statute attaches a more severe punishment to a particular consequence of the act, then the perpetrator or accessory is only subject to it if, with respect to this consequence, at least negligence can be imputed to him.

§ 19. He who, when committing the act, has not reached the age of fourteen years, lacks capacity to incur guilt [schuldunfähig].

---

[15] Translation by S. Hardt.

§ 20. He who, when committing the act, is unable to discern the wrongfulness of the act or to act according to this discernment due to a pathological psychological disorder, due to a profound disorder of consciousness or due to mental deficiency or to a serious other mental abnormality, acts without guilt.

§ 21. If the ability of the perpetrator to discern the wrongfulness of the act or to act according to this discernment is, in the commission of the act, substantially reduced due to one of the reasons referred to in § 20, the penalty may be mitigated pursuant to § 49 (1).

Title 2. Attempt

§ 22. He who, in accordance with his conception of the act, takes immediate steps to realize the statutory elements of the offence, attempts to commit an offence.

§ 23. (1) The attempt to commit a crime [Verbrechen] is always punishable, the attempt to commit a misdemeanour [Vergehen] is only punishable where statute expressly so provides.
(2) The attempt may be punished more leniently than the completed act (§ 49 (1)).
(3) If the perpetrator, due to a gross lack of understanding, has failed to realize that the attempt, due to the nature of the object on which, or of the means by which, the act was to be committed, could not possibly have led to completion, then the court may refrain from punishment or mitigate the punishment according to its own discretion (§ 49 (2)).

§ 24. (1) He who voluntarily abandons the further execution of the act or averts its completion is not punished for the attempt. If the act is not completed without there being a contribution by the abandoning person, then he is exempted from punishment if he voluntarily and earnestly endeavours to avert the completion.
(2) If several persons participate in the act, he who voluntarily averts the completion is not punished for the attempt. However, his voluntary and earnest endeavour to avert the completion of the act suffices for his exemption from punishment if it is not completed without there being a contribution by him or if it is committed independently of his earlier contribution to the act.

Title 3. Perpetration and complicity

§ 25. (1) He who commits the offence himself or through another is punished as a perpetrator [Täter].
(2) If several persons commit the offence jointly, each is punished as a perpetrator (co-perpetrator) [Mittäter].

§ 26. He who has intentionally induced another to his intentionally committed unlawful act is punished, as an instigator [Anstifter], the same as a perpetrator.

§ 27. (1) He who intentionally has assisted another in his intentionally committed unlawful act is punished as an accomplice [Gehilfe].
(2) The penalty for the accomplice is based on the penalty stipulated for the perpetrator. It must be mitigated pursuant to § 49 (1).

§ 28. (1) If particular personal characteristics (§ 14 (1)), which form the basis of the criminal liability of the perpetrator, are lacking in the accessory [Teilnehmer] (instigator or accomplice), then his penalty must be mitigated pursuant to § 49 (1).
(2) If statute provides that particular personal characteristics aggravate, mitigate or exclude punishment, then this applies only to the participant [Beteiligter] (perpetrator or accessory) in whom they are present.

§ 29. Each participant is punished according to his own guilt without regard to the guilt of the other.

§ 30. (1) He who attempts to induce another to commit a crime, or to instigate thereto, is punished pursuant to the provisions governing the attempt of a crime. However, the penalty must be mitigated pursuant to § 49 (1). § 23 (3) applies mutatis mutandis.
(2) He who declares himself willing, he who accepts the offer of another or he who agrees with another to commit a crime or to instigate thereto, is punished in the same manner.

§ 31. (1) Not punished pursuant to § 30 is he who voluntarily
1. abandons the attempt to induce another to commit a crime and averts a possibly existing danger that the other may commit the act,
2. after he had declared himself willing to commit a crime, abandons his plan or,
3. after he had agreed with, or accepted the offer of, another to commit a crime, averts the act.
(2) If the act is not committed without there being a contribution by the abandoning person, or if it is committed independently of his earlier conduct, then his voluntary and earnest endeavour to avert the act suffices for his exemption from punishment.

Title 4. Necessary defence and emergency

§ 32. (1) He who commits an act which is required as necessary defence [Notwehr] does not act unlawfully.
(2) Necessary defence is the defence which is required in order to fend off an imminent unlawful assault from oneself or from another.

§ 33. If the perpetrator exceeds the boundaries of necessary defence due to confusion, fear or scare, then he is not punished.

§ 34. He who, in an imminent, not otherwise avertable danger to life, limb, freedom, property or another legal interest [Rechtsgut], commits an act in order to fend off the danger from himself or another, does not act unlawfully, if, in weighing the conflicting interests, notably the affected legal interests and the degree of the dangers threatening them, the protected interest significantly outweighs the impaired one. This does, however, only apply as far as the act is an appropriate means to fend off the danger.

§ 35. (1) He who, in an imminent, not otherwise avertable danger to life, limb or freedom, commits an unlawful act in order to fend off the danger from himself, a relative [Angehöriger] or another person close to him, acts without guilt. This does not apply as far as the perpetrator could be expected, according to the circumstances, notably because he has caused the danger himself or because he stood in a special legal relationship, to tolerate the danger; however, the penalty may be mitigated pursuant to § 49 (1) if the perpetrator was not obliged to tolerate the danger with respect to a special legal relationship.
(2) If the perpetrator, in committing the act, erroneously assumes circumstances which would exculpate [entschuldingen] him pursuant to sub-paragraph 1, then he is only punished if he was able to avoid the error. The penalty must be mitigated pursuant to § 49 (1).

Title 5. Exemption from punishment for parliamentary statements and reports

§ 36. Members of the Bundestag, the Federal Convention [Bundesversammlung] or of a legislative organ of a State may at no time be held liable outside the body for their voting or for a statement they have made within the body or within one of its committees. This does not apply to libellous insults [verleumderische Beleidigung].

§ 37. Truthful reports about the public sessions of the bodies referred to in § 36 or their committees remain exempt from all liability.

[The remainder of the General Part is omitted.]

PART III. CRIMINAL JUSTICE

Special Part

[Divisions 1 – 15 are omitted.]

Division 16. Offences against life

§ 211. (1) The murderer [Mörder] is punished with imprisonment for life.
(2) A murderer is he who,
out of lust for killing, for the satisfaction of his sexual drive, out of greed or otherwise for base motives,
heinously [heimtückisch] or cruelly or by means dangerous to the public
or to make possible or conceal another offence,
kills another human being.

§ 212. (1) He who kills a human being without being a murderer is punished, as a manslayer [Totschläger], with no less than five years of imprisonment.
(2) In particularly serious cases, a life sentence must be imposed.

§ 213. If the manslayer, without guilt of his own, has been provoked to rage by a serious abuse inflicted on him or a relative [Angehöriger] or by a serious insult by the killed person and was thereby immediately driven to commit the act or if there is an otherwise less serious case, then the punishment is one to ten years of imprisonment.

§ 214. (Repealed).

§ 215. (Repealed).

§ 216. (1) If someone has been induced to the killing by the express and earnest request of the killed person, imprisonment of six months to five years must be imposed.
(2) The attempt is punishable.

§ 217. (Repealed).

§ 218. (1) He who terminates a pregnancy is punished with a maximum of three years of imprisonment or a fine. Actions the effect of which occurs before the completion of the implantation of the fertilized egg in the uterus are not considered a termination of pregnancy within the meaning of this Act.
(2) In particularly serious cases, the punishment is six months to five years of imprisonment. As a rule, a particularly serious case is present if the perpetrator
1. acts against the will of the pregnant woman or
2. carelessly causes the danger of the death or of serious harm to the health of the pregnant woman.
(3) If the pregnant woman commits the act, the punishment is a maximum of one year of imprisonment or a fine.
(4) The attempt is punishable. The pregnant woman is not punished for the attempt.

§ 218a. (1) The statutory elements of the offence of § 218 are not realized, if
1. the pregnant woman demands the abortion and, by means of an attestation pursuant to § 219 (2) clause 2, has proven to the physician that she has received counselling at least three days prior to the operation,
2. the abortion is performed by a physician and
3. no more than twelve weeks have passed since conception.
(2) The abortion performed by a physician with the consent of the pregnant woman is not unlawful if the termination of the pregnancy, with regard to the present and future living conditions of the pregnant woman, is indicated, according to medical findings, in order to avert a danger to the life or the danger of a significant impairment of the physical or psychological health of the pregnant woman and if the danger cannot be averted in another manner which is reasonable for her.
(3) The conditions of sub-paragraph 2 are also deemed fulfilled in the event of an abortion performed by a physician with the consent of the pregnant woman if, according to medical findings, an unlawful act in accordance with the §§ 176 to 179 of the Criminal Code [Strafgesetzbuch] has been committed against the pregnant woman, weighty reasons support the assumption that the pregnancy results from this act, and no more than twelve weeks have passed since conception.
(4) The pregnant woman is not criminally liable pursuant to § 218 if the abortion has been performed by a physician after counselling (§ 219) and no more than twenty-two weeks have passed since conception. The court

may refrain from imposing a penalty pursuant to § 218 if the pregnant woman has been in particular hardship at the time of the operation.

§ 218b. (1) He who terminates, in the cases of § 218a (2) or (3) a pregnancy without the written statement of a physician, who does not perform the abortion himself, having been presented to him as to whether the conditions of § 218a (2) or (3) are present, is punished with a maximum of one year of imprisonment or a fine, if the act is not made punishable by § 218. He who, as a physician, against better judgment, makes an incorrect statement as to the conditions of § 218a (2) or (3) for presentation pursuant to clause 1, is punished with a maximum of two years of imprisonment or a fine if the act is not made punishable by § 218. The pregnant woman is not criminally liable pursuant to clause 1 or 2.
(2) A physician may not make statements pursuant to § 218a (2) or (3) if the competent office has prohibited him to do so because he has been finally convicted for an unlawful act pursuant to sub-paragraph (1), the §§ 218, 219a or 219b or for another unlawful act which he has committed in connection with an abortion. The competent office may provisionally prohibit a physician to make statements pursuant to § 218a (2) or (3) if main proceedings have been initiated against him due to suspicion of an act referred to in clause 1.

§ 218c. (1) He who terminates a pregnancy
1. without having given the woman the opportunity to explain to him the reasons for her request for a termination of the pregnancy,
2. without having given the pregnant woman medical advice about the significance of the operation, especially about the course, consequences, risks, possible physical and mental effects,
3. in the cases of § 218a (1) and (3), without having previously ascertained, on the basis of a medical examination, the duration of the pregnancy, or
4. despite having counselled the woman in a case of § 218a (1) pursuant to § 219,
is punished with a maximum of one year of imprisonment or a fine if the act is not made punishable by § 218.
(2) The pregnant woman is not criminally liable pursuant to sub-paragraph 1.

§ 219. (1) The counselling serves the protection of the unborn life. It must be guided by the endeavour to encourage the woman to continue the pregnancy and open to her perspectives for a life with the child; it shall help her to take a responsible and conscientious decision. The woman must thereby be aware that the unborn child, at every stage of the pregnancy, has a right to life of its own, also with respect to her, and that therefore, pursuant to the legal order, an abortion can only come into consideration in exceptional cases, if by carrying the child to term a burden would arise for the woman which is so grave and extraordinary that it exceeds the threshold of reasonable sacrifice. The counselling shall contribute, by means of advice and help, to overcoming a situation of conflict which exists in connection with the pregnancy and to remedy a situation of emergency. Further details are regulated in the Pregnancy Conflict Act [Schwangerschaftskonfliktgesetz].
(2) The counselling must take place pursuant to the Pregnancy Conflict Act through a recognized pregnancy conflict counselling institution. After completion of the counselling, the counselling institution must issue to the pregnant woman an attestation, including the date of the last counselling interview and the name of the pregnant woman, in accordance with the Pregnancy Conflict Act. The physician who carries out the abortion is precluded from being a counsellor.

§ 219a. (1) He who publicly, in a gathering or by dissemination of writings (§ 11 (3)), for his proprietary advantage or in a grossly offensive manner offers, announces, advertises
1. his own services for the performance or promotion of an abortion or those of another or
2. means, objects or methods suitable for an abortion, indicating this suitability,
or makes known declarations of such content, is punished with a maximum of two years of imprisonment or a fine.
(2) Sub-paragraph 1 no. 1 does not apply where physicians or counselling institutions recognized pursuant to statute are informed about which physicians, hospitals or institutions are prepared to perform an abortion subject to the conditions of § 218a (1) to (3).
(3) Sub-paragraph 1 no. 2 does not apply where the act is committed with respect to physicians or persons authorized to trade in the means or objects mentioned in sub-paragraph 1 no. 2 or by means of a publication in specialized medical or pharmaceutical journals.

§ 219b. (1) He who, with the intention of promoting unlawful acts pursuant to § 218, brings means or objects into circulation which are suitable for an abortion is punished with a maximum of two years of imprisonment or a fine.
(2) The accessoryship of a woman who prepares the termination of her pregnancy is not punishable pursuant to sub-paragraph 1.

(3) Means or objects to which the act relates may be confiscated.

§219c to §220a. (Repealed).

§ 221. (1) He who
1. places a human being in a helpless situation or
2. abandons him in a helpless situation although he has him in his custody or is otherwise obliged to support him, and thereby exposes him to a danger of death or a serious health damage, is punished with three months to five years of imprisonment.
(2) A prison sentence of one year to ten years must be imposed if the perpetrator
1. commits the act against his child or a person entrusted to him for upbringing or care in leading his life, or
2. by the act causes serious health damage to the victim.
(3) If by the act the perpetrator causes the death of the victim, then the penalty is no less than three years of imprisonment.
(4) In less serious cases of sub-paragraph 2 a prison sentence of six months to five years, in less serious cases of sub-paragraph 3 a prison sentence of one year to ten years must be imposed.

§ 222. He who causes the death of a human being by negligence is punished with a maximum of five years of imprisonment or a fine.

[The remainder of the Code is omitted.]

Criminal Code [Wetboek van Strafrecht]. Selected provisions: Articles 39 – 54a, 255 – 260 and 287 – 309.[16]

Book I. General provisions

[Titles I, II and II A are omitted.]

Title III. Exclusion and increase of criminal liability

Article 39. He who commits an act for which he cannot be held responsible by reason of a defective development or medical disorder of his mental capacities is not criminally liable [strafbaar].

Article 39bis a to Article 39decies. (Repealed).

Article 40. He who commits an act as a result of an irresistible force [overmacht] is not criminally liable.

Article 41. (1) He who commits an act where this is necessary in the defence of his person or the person of another, his or another person's integrity or property, against immediate, unlawful attack, is not criminally liable.
(2) Exceeding the limits of necessary defence, where such excess has been the direct result of a strong emotion brought about by the attack, is not punishable.

Article 42. He who commits an act in carrying out a legal rule is not criminally liable.

Article 43. (1) He who commits an act in carrying out an official order issued by a competent authority is not criminally liable.
(2) An official order issued without authority does not remove criminal liability unless the order was assumed by the subordinate in good faith to have been issued with authority and the compliance lay within the scope of his capacity as subordinate.

Article 43a. The penalty of imprisonment for a determinate period of time or detention for a determinate period of time prescribed for a crime [misdrijf], may, without prejudice to Article 10, be increased by one third, where at the time the crime is committed less than five years had passed since the conviction of the guilty person to a term of imprisonment for a similar crime became final. The term of five years is extended by the time the convicted person was lawfully deprived of his liberty.

Article 43b. 'Similar crimes' are to be taken to include in any case:
(1) The crimes defined in Articles 105, 174, 208 to 210, 213, 214, 216 to 222bis, 225 to 232, 310, 311, 312, 315, 317, 318, 321 to 323a, 326 to 332, 341, 343, 344, 359, 361, 366, 373 (last paragraph), 402, 416, 417, 420bis and 420ter;
(2) The crimes defined in Articles 92, 108, 109, 110, 115, 116, 117 to 117b, 141, 181, 182, 287 to 291, 293 (1), 296, 300 to 303, 381, 382, 395 and 396;
(3) The crimes defined in Articles 111 to 113, 118, 119, 261 to 271, 418 and 419;
(4) The crimes defined in the Opium Act [Opiumwet];
(5) The crimes defined in the Arms and Ammunition Act [Wet wapens en munitie].

Article 43c. In the case of the crimes defined in Articles 208 to 210, 213, and 214, a final conviction pronounced by a court in another member state of the European Union for any crime relating to coinage, government notes or bank notes is to be considered a conviction for a similar offence.

Article 44. Where a public servant in committing a criminal act violates a specific duty of his office or, when committing the criminal act, uses the power, opportunity or means afforded to him by his office, the penalty prescribed for that act may be increased, except in the case of a fine, by one third.

---

[16] Translation by Ph. Kiiver.

PART III. CRIMINAL JUSTICE

Title IIIa. Grounds for a reduction of the sentence

Article 44a. (1) On application by the public prosecutor [officier van justitie], the judge, in accordance with the provisions of paragraph 2, may reduce the sentence that he considered imposing, upon an agreement made pursuant to Article 226h (3) of the Code of Criminal Procedure [Wetboek van Strafvordering]. In reducing the sentence, the judge takes into consideration that the giving of a witness statement provides or may provide a significant contribution to the investigation and prosecution of crimes.
(2) In the application of paragraph 1, the sentence may be reduced as follows:
a. by not more than one half in the case of an unconditional determinate custodial sentence, a sentence for performance [taakstraf] consisting of a labour sentence [werkstraf] or a fine, or
b. commutation of not more than one half of the unconditional part of a custodial sentence, a sentence for performance consisting of a labour sentence or a fine into a conditional part, or
c. substitution of not more than one third of a custodial sentence with a sentence for performance consisting of a labour sentence, or an unconditional fine.
(3) In the application of paragraph 2 (b), Article 14a (1) and (2) remains inapplicable.

Title IV. Attempt and preparation

Article 45. (1) An attempt with a view to a crime [misdrijf] is punishable where the intention of the perpetrator has manifested itself through the initiation of the execution.
(2) In the case of attempt, the maximum principal penalties prescribed for the crime are reduced by one third.
(3) In the case of a crime carrying a sentence of life imprisonment, a term of imprisonment of not more than twenty years is imposed.
(4) The additional penalties for attempt are as for the completed crime.

Article 46. (1) Preparation of a crime which, by statutory definition, carries a term of imprisonment of eight years or more is punishable, where the perpetrator intentionally obtains, manufactures, imports, transits, exports or has at his disposal objects, substances, information carriers, spaces or means of transport intended for the commission of that crime.
(2) In the case of preparation, the maximum principal penalties prescribed for the crime are reduced by one half.
(3) In the case of a crime carrying a sentence of life imprisonment, a term of imprisonment of not more than fifteen years is imposed.
(4) The additional penalties for preparation are as for the completed crime.
(5) Objects are to be taken to include all corporeal objects [zaken] and all patrimonial rights [vermogensrechten].

Article 46a. An attempt to induce another to commit a crime by employing one of the means listed in Article 47 (1), no. 2, is punishable, provided that no sentence is imposed that is heavier than that which may be imposed for an attempt to commit the crime, or, where such attempt is not punishable, for committing the crime itself.

Article 46b. Neither preparation nor attempt to commit exists where the crime has not been completed by reason of circumstances that are dependent on the perpetrator's will.

Title V. Participation in criminal acts

Article 47. (1) The following are punished as perpetrators [daders] of the criminal act:
1. those who commit, let commit or co-commit the act;
2. those who, by means of gifts, promises, abuse of authority, violence, threat or deception or by providing opportunity, means or information intentionally solicit the commission of the act.
(2) With regard to the last category, only those actions intentionally solicited by them and the consequences of such actions are to be taken into consideration.

Article 48. The following are punished as accessories [medeplichtigen] to a crime [misdrijf]:
1. those who intentionally assist during the commission of the crime;
2. those who intentionally provide opportunity, means or information for the commission of the crime.

Article 49. (1) In the case of complicity as an accessory, the maximum of the principal penalties prescribed for the crime are reduced by one third.
(2) In the case of a crime carrying a sentence of life imprisonment, a term of imprisonment of not more than twenty years is imposed.
(3) The additional penalties for complicity as an accessory are as for the crime itself.
(4) Only those actions that were intentionally facilitated or promoted by the accessory and the consequences of such actions are to be taken into consideration in sentencing.

Article 50. In the application of criminal law, such personal circumstances as may exclude, reduce or increase criminal liability are restricted to those which relate directly to the perpetrator or the accessory.

Article 50a. (Repealed).

Article 51. (1) Criminal acts can be committed by natural persons and legal persons.
(2) Where a criminal act is committed by a legal person, criminal proceedings may be initiated and such penalties and measures as are prescribed by law, where applicable, may be imposed:
1. against the legal person, or
2. against those who have ordered the commission of the act, and against those who have in fact supervised the unlawful behaviour, or
3. against the persons mentioned under 1. and 2. jointly.
(3) In the application of the preceding paragraphs, the following are deemed to be equivalent to a legal person: the unincorporated commercial association [vennootschap zonder rechtspersoonlijkheid], the partnership, the ship-owning firm and the special fund [doelvermogen].

Article 52. Complicity as an accessory in misdemeanours [overtredingen] is not punishable.

Article 53. (1) In the case of crimes committed by means of the press, the publisher is not prosecuted in that capacity where his name and place of residence appear on the printed matter and where the perpetrator is known or where his identity was disclosed by the publisher upon the first notice following initiation of the preliminary judicial investigation.
(2) The preceding provision is not applicable where, at the time of publication, the perpetrator was not subject to criminal prosecution or where he was established outside the Kingdom within Europe.

Article 54. (1) In the case of crimes committed by means of the press, the printer is not prosecuted in that capacity where his name and place of residence appear on the printed matter and where the person who ordered the printing is known or where his identity was disclosed by the printer upon the first notice following initiation of the preliminary judicial investigation.
(2) The preceding provision is not applicable where, at the time of the printing, the person who ordered the printing of the matter was not subject to criminal prosecution, or where he was established outside the Kingdom within Europe.

Article 54a. An intermediary who provides a telecommunications service consisting of the onward transmission or storage of data originating from another person, is not prosecuted in that capacity where he complies with an order from the public prosecutor, upon written authorization to be granted by the examining magistrate [rechter-commissaris] on application by the public prosecutor, to take all measures which may be reasonably required of him in order to render the data inaccessible.

[The remaining Titles of Book I are omitted.]

Book II. Crimes

[Titles I – XIV are omitted.]

Title XV. Desertion of persons in distress

Article 255. He who intentionally places or keeps in a helpless condition a person he has, by virtue of law or contract, to support, nurse or care for, is punished by a term of imprisonment of not more than two years or a fine of the fourth category.

Article 256. He who leaves a child under the age of seven as a foundling, or abandons it with the object of ridding himself of it, is punished by a term of imprisonment of not more than four years and six months or a fine of the fourth category.

Article 257. (1) Where serious bodily harm ensues as a result of any of the acts defined in Articles 255 and 256, the guilty person is punished by a term of imprisonment of not more than seven years and six months or a fine of the fifth category.
(2) Where death ensues as a result of any of these acts, he is punished by a term of imprisonment of not more than nine years or a fine of the fifth category.

Article 258. Where the mother or the father is the guilty person of the crime defined in Article 256, the terms of imprisonment prescribed in Articles 256 and 257 may, in his or her case, be increased by one third.

Article 259. Where the mother, under the influence of fear of the discovery of her giving birth to a child, shortly after the delivery leaves her child as a foundling or abandons it with the object of ridding herself of it, the maximum terms of imprisonment mentioned in Articles 256 and 257 are reduced by half and the fine mentioned in Article 257 is reduced to a fine of the fourth category.

Article 260. Upon conviction for any of the crimes defined in Articles 255 to 259, deprivation of the rights listed in Article 28 (1), no. 4, may be imposed.

[Titles XVI – XVIII are omitted.]

Title XIX. Crimes against life

Article 287. He who intentionally takes the life of another is, as guilty of manslaughter [doodslag], punished by a term of imprisonment of not more than fifteen years or a fine of the fifth category.

Article 288. Manslaughter followed, accompanied or preceded by a criminal act and committed with the object of preparing or facilitating the execution of that act or, where one is caught in flagrante delicto, of securing either impunity or the possession of the unlawfully obtained property for himself or for others participating in the act, is punished by life imprisonment or a term of imprisonment of not more than thirty years or a fine of the fifth category.

Article 288a. Manslaughter committed with the object of terrorism is punishable by life imprisonment or a term of imprisonment of not more than thirty years or a fine of the fifth category.

Article 289. He who intentionally and with premeditation takes the life of another person is, as guilty of murder [moord], punished by life imprisonment or a term of imprisonment of not more than thirty years or a fine of the fifth category.

Article 289a. (1) Conspiracy to commit the crime defined in Article 289 with the object of terrorism as well as the crime defined in Article 288a is punishable by a term of imprisonment of not more than ten years or a fine of the fifth category.
(2) Article 96 (2) applies mutatis mutandis.

Article 290. The mother who, under the influence of fear of the discovery of her giving birth to a child, intentionally takes the life of her child at or shortly after the delivery, is, as guilty of manslaughter of an infant [kinderdoodslag], punished by a term of imprisonment of not more than six years or a fine of the fourth category.

Article 291. The mother who, in carrying out a decision taken under the influence of fear of the discovery of her impending delivery, intentionally takes the life of her child at or shortly after the delivery, is, as guilty of murder of an infant [kindermoord], punished by a term of imprisonment of not more than nine years or a fine of the fifth category.

Article 292. The crimes defined in Articles 290 and 291 constitute murder or manslaughter with respect to others participating in the commission thereof.

Article 293. (1) He who intentionally ends the life of another person at that other person's express and earnest request, is punished by a term of imprisonment of not more than twelve years or a fine of the fifth category.
(2) The act specified in the first paragraph is not punishable where it has been committed by a physician who in so doing meets the duty of care requirements specified in Article 2 of the Review of Termination of Life and Assisted Suicide Act [Wet toetsing levensbeëindiging en hulp bij zelfdoding] and who reports it to the municipal coroner pursuant to Article 7 (2) of the Disposal of Bodies of the Dead Act [Wet op de lijkbezorging].

Article 294. (1) He who intentionally incites another to commit suicide, is, where the suicide ensues, punished by a term of imprisonment of not more than three years or a fine of the fourth category.
(2) He who intentionally assists in the suicide of another, or supplies him with the means to commit suicide, is, where the suicide ensues, punished by a term of imprisonment of not more than three years or a fine of the fourth category. Article 293 (2) applies mutatis mutandis.

Article 295. (1) Upon conviction for manslaughter, for murder or for any of the crimes defined in Articles 293 (1) and 296, deprivation of the rights listed in Article 28 (1), nos. 1, 2 and 4 may be imposed.
(2) Where the guilty person of any of the crimes defined in Articles 287 to 289 commits the crime in the practice of his profession, he may be deprived of the right to practice that profession.

Title XIX A. Termination of pregnancy

Article 296. (1) He who subjects a woman to treatment, where he knows or should reasonably suspect that thereby pregnancy may be terminated, is punished by a term of imprisonment of not more than four years and six months or a fine of the fourth category.
(2) Where the death of the woman ensues as a result of the act, a term of imprisonment of not more than six years or a fine of the fourth category is imposed.
(3) Where the act has been committed without the woman's consent, a term of imprisonment of not more than twelve years or a fine of the fifth category is imposed.
(4) Where the act has been committed without the woman's consent and her death also ensues as a result of the act, a term of imprisonment of not more than fifteen years or a fine of the fifth category is imposed.
(5) The act specified in paragraph 1 is not punishable where the treatment was provided by a physician at a hospital or clinic where such treatment may be provided under the Termination of Pregnancy Act [Wet afbreking zwangerschap].

Articles 297 to 299. (Repealed).

Title XX. Physical abuse

Article 300. (1) Physical abuse [mishandeling] is punishable by a term of imprisonment of not more than three years or a fine of the fourth category.
(2) Where serious bodily harm ensues as a result of the act, the guilty person is punished by a term of imprisonment of not more than four years or a fine of the fourth category.
(3) Where death ensues as a result of the act, he is punished by a term of imprisonment of not more than six years or a fine of the fourth category.
(4) Intentionally compromising a person's health is equivalent to physical abuse.
(5) An attempt to commit this crime is not punishable.

Article 301. (1) Physical abuse committed with premeditation is punishable by a term of imprisonment of not more than four years or a fine of the fourth category.
(2) Where serious bodily harm ensues as a result of the act, the guilty person is punished by a term of imprisonment of not more than six years or a fine of the fourth category.
(3) Where death ensues as a result of the act, he is punished by a term of imprisonment of not more than nine years or a fine of the fifth category.

Article 302. (1) He who intentionally inflicts serious bodily harm on another person is, as guilty of serious physical abuse [zware mishandeling], punished by a term of imprisonment of not more than eight years or a fine of the fifth category.
(2) Where death ensues as a result of the act, the guilty person is punished by a term of imprisonment of not more than ten years or a fine of the fifth category.

Article 303. (1) Serious physical abuse committed with premeditation is punishable by a term of imprisonment of not more than twelve years or a fine of the fifth category.
(2) Where death ensues as a result of the act, the guilty person is punished by a term of imprisonment of not more than fifteen years or a fine of the fifth category.

Article 304. The terms of imprisonment prescribed in Articles 300 to 303 may be increased by one third:
(1) where the guilty person commits the crime against his mother, his father with whom he has a relation under family law, his spouse, his partner or his child;
(2) where the crime is committed against a public servant during or in connection with the lawful execution of his duties;
(3) where the crime is committed by administering substances harmful to life or health.

Article 304a. Where a crime punishable under Article 302 or 303 has been committed with the object of terrorism, the determinate period of imprisonment prescribed in that Article is increased by one half and, where a determinate term of imprisonment of not more than fifteen years is prescribed for the crime, life imprisonment or a determinate term of not more than thirty years is imposed.

Article 304b. (1) Conspiracy to commit the crime defined in Article 303, to be committed with the object of terrorism, is punishable by a term of imprisonment of not more than ten years or a fine of the fifth category.
(2) Article 96 (2) applies mutatis mutandis.

Article 305. Upon conviction for any of the crimes defined in Articles 301 and 303, deprivation of the rights listed in Article 28 (1), nos. 1, 2 and 4, may be imposed.

Article 306. Those who intentionally participate in an attack or an affray in which several persons are involved, are punished, without prejudice to the individual responsibility of any one of them for their respective acts:
(1) by a term of imprisonment of not more than two years or a fine of the fourth category, where only serious bodily harm results from the attack or affray;
(2) by a term of imprisonment of not more than three years or a fine of the fourth category, where the death of a person results from the attack or affray.

Title XXI. The causing of imputable death or bodily harm

Article 307. (1) He to whom the death of another person is imputable [schuld] is punished by a term of imprisonment of not more than two years or a fine of the fourth category.
(2) Where the imputability consists of recklessness, he is punished by a term of imprisonment of not more than four years or a fine of the fourth category.

Article 308. (1) He to whom it is imputable that another suffers serious bodily harm or such bodily harm as causes temporary illness or inability to perform the duties of an office or profession, is punished by a term of imprisonment of not more than one year or a fine of the fourth category.
(2) Where the imputability consists of recklessness, he is punished by a term of imprisonment of not more than two years or a fine of the fourth category.

Article 309. Where the crimes defined in this Title are committed in the exercise of any office or profession, the term of imprisonment may be increased by one third, deprivation of the right to practice the profession in which the crime was committed may be imposed, and the judge may order publication of his judgment.

Criminal Attempts Act 1981. Selected Provision: Section 1.

Part I. Attempts etc.

Section 1. (1) If, with intent to commit an offence to which this section applies, a person does an act which is more than merely preparatory to the commission of the offence, he is guilty of attempting to commit the offence.
(1A) Subject to section 8 of the Computer Misuse Act 1990 (relevance of external law), if this subsection applies to an act, what the person doing it had in view shall be treated as an offence to which this section applies.
(1B) Subsection (1A) above applies to an act if –
(a) it is done in England and Wales; and
(b) it would fall within subsection (1) above as more than merely preparatory to the commission of an offence under section 3 of the Computer Misuse Act 1990 but for the fact that the offence, if completed, would not be an offence triable in England and Wales.
(2) A person may be guilty of attempting to commit an offence to which this section applies even though the facts are such that the commission of the offence is impossible.
(3) In any case where –
(a) apart from this subsection a person's intention would not be regarded as having amounted to an intent to commit an offence; but
(b) if the facts of the case had been as he believed them to be, his intention would be so regarded,
then, for the purposes of subsection (1) above, he shall be regarded as having had an intent to commit that offence.
(4) This section applies to any offence which, if it were completed, would be triable in England and Wales as an indictable offence, other than –
(a) conspiracy (at common law or under section 1 of the Criminal Law Act 1977 or any other enactment);
(b) aiding, abetting, counselling, procuring or suborning the commission of an offence;
(c) offences under section 4 (1) (assisting offenders) or 5 (1) (accepting or agreeing to accept consideration for not disclosing information about an arrestable offence) of the Criminal Law Act 1967.

[The remainder of the Act is omitted.]

Council Framework Decision 2002/584/JHA of 13 June 2002 on the European arrest warrant and the surrender procedures between Member States, as amended.

[The Preamble is omitted.]

CHAPTER 1. GENERAL PRINCIPLES

Article 1. 1. The European arrest warrant is a judicial decision issued by a Member State with a view to the arrest and surrender by another Member State of a requested person, for the purposes of conducting a criminal prosecution or executing a custodial sentence or detention order.
2. Member States shall execute any European arrest warrant on the basis of the principle of mutual recognition and in accordance with the provisions of this Framework Decision.
3. This Framework Decision shall not have the effect of modifying the obligation to respect fundamental rights and fundamental legal principles as enshrined in Article 6 of the Treaty on European Union.

Article 2. 1. A European arrest warrant may be issued for acts punishable by the law of the issuing Member State by a custodial sentence or a detention order for a maximum period of at least 12 months or, where a sentence has been passed or a detention order has been made, for sentences of at least four months.
2. The following offences, if they are punishable in the issuing Member State by a custodial sentence or a detention order for a maximum period of at least three years and as they are defined by the law of the issuing Member State, shall, under the terms of this Framework Decision and without verification of the double criminality of the act, give rise to surrender pursuant to a European arrest warrant:
— participation in a criminal organisation,
— terrorism,
— trafficking in human beings,
— sexual exploitation of children and child pornography,
— illicit trafficking in narcotic drugs and psychotropic substances,
— illicit trafficking in weapons, munitions and explosives,
— corruption,
— fraud, including that affecting the financial interests of the European Communities within the meaning of the Convention of 26 July 1995 on the protection of the European Communities' financial interests,
— laundering of the proceeds of crime,
— counterfeiting currency, including of the euro,
— computer-related crime,
— environmental crime, including illicit trafficking in endangered animal species and in endangered plant species and varieties,
— facilitation of unauthorised entry and residence,
— murder, grievous bodily injury,
— illicit trade in human organs and tissue,
— kidnapping, illegal restraint and hostage-taking,
— racism and xenophobia,
— organised or armed robbery,
— illicit trafficking in cultural goods, including antiques and works of art,
— swindling,
— racketeering and extortion,
— counterfeiting and piracy of products,
— forgery of administrative documents and trafficking therein,
— forgery of means of payment,
— illicit trafficking in hormonal substances and other growth promoters,
— illicit trafficking in nuclear or radioactive materials,
— trafficking in stolen vehicles,
— rape,
— arson,
— crimes within the jurisdiction of the International Criminal Court,
— unlawful seizure of aircraft/ships,
— sabotage.

3. The Council may decide at any time, acting unanimously after consultation of the European Parliament under the conditions laid down in Article 39(1) of the Treaty on European Union (TEU), to add other categories of offence to the list contained in paragraph 2. The Council shall examine, in the light of the report submitted by the Commission pursuant to Article 34(3), whether the list should be extended or amended.

4. For offences other than those covered by paragraph 2, surrender may be subject to the condition that the acts for which the European arrest warrant has been issued constitute an offence under the law of the executing Member State, whatever the constituent elements or however it is described.

Article 3. The judicial authority of the Member State of execution (hereinafter 'executing judicial authority') shall refuse to execute the European arrest warrant in the following cases:
1. if the offence on which the arrest warrant is based is covered by amnesty in the executing Member State, where that State had jurisdiction to prosecute the offence under its own criminal law;
2. if the executing judicial authority is informed that the requested person has been finally judged by a Member State in respect of the same acts provided that, where there has been sentence, the sentence has been served or is currently being served or may no longer be executed under the law of the sentencing Member State;
3. if the person who is the subject of the European arrest warrant may not, owing to his age, be held criminally responsible for the acts on which the arrest warrant is based under the law of the executing State.

Article 4. The executing judicial authority may refuse to execute the European arrest warrant:
1. if, in one of the cases referred to in Article 2(4), the act on which the European arrest warrant is based does not constitute an offence under the law of the executing Member State; however, in relation to taxes or duties, customs and exchange, execution of the European arrest warrant shall not be refused on the ground that the law of the executing Member State does not impose the same kind of tax or duty or does not contain the same type of rules as regards taxes, duties and customs and exchange regulations as the law of the issuing Member State;
2. where the person who is the subject of the European arrest warrant is being prosecuted in the executing Member State for the same act as that on which the European arrest warrant is based;
3. where the judicial authorities of the executing Member State have decided either not to prosecute for the offence on which the European arrest warrant is based or to halt proceedings, or where a final judgment has been passed upon the requested person in a Member State, in respect of the same acts, which prevents further proceedings;
4. where the criminal prosecution or punishment of the requested person is statute-barred according to the law of the executing Member State and the acts fall within the jurisdiction of that Member State under its own criminal law;
5. if the executing judicial authority is informed that the requested person has been finally judged by a third State in respect of the same acts provided that, where there has been sentence, the sentence has been served or is currently being served or may no longer be executed under the law of the sentencing country;
6. if the European arrest warrant has been issued for the purposes of execution of a custodial sentence or detention order, where the requested person is staying in, or is a national or a resident of the executing Member State and that State undertakes to execute the sentence or detention order in accordance with its domestic law;
7. where the European arrest warrant relates to offences which:
(a) are regarded by the law of the executing Member State as having been committed in whole or in part in the territory of the executing Member State or in a place treated as such; or
(b) have been committed outside the territory of the issuing Member State and the law of the executing Member State does not allow prosecution for the same offences when committed outside its territory.

Article 4a. 1. The executing judicial authority may also refuse to execute the European arrest warrant issued for the purpose of executing a custodial sentence or a detention order if the person did not appear in person at the trial resulting in the decision, unless the European arrest warrant states that the person, in accordance with further procedural requirements defined in the national law of the issuing Member State:
(a) in due time:
(i) either was summoned in person and thereby informed of the scheduled date and place of the trial which resulted in the decision, or by other means actually received official information of the scheduled date and place of that trial in such a manner that it was unequivocally established that he or she was aware of the scheduled trial; and
(ii) was informed that a decision may be handed down if he or she does not appear for the trial; or
(b) being aware of the scheduled trial, had given a mandate to a legal counsellor, who was either appointed by the person concerned or by the State, to defend him or her at the trial, and was indeed defended by that counsellor at the trial; or

(c) after being served with the decision and being expressly informed about the right to a retrial, or an appeal, in which the person has the right to participate and which allows the merits of the case, including fresh evidence, to be re-examined, and which may lead to the original decision being reversed:
(i) expressly stated that he or she does not contest the decision; or
(ii) did not request a retrial or appeal within the applicable time frame; or
(d) was not personally served with the decision but:
(i) will be personally served with it without delay after the surrender and will be expressly informed of his or her right to a retrial, or an appeal, in which the person has the right to participate and which allows the merits of the case, including fresh evidence, to be re-examined, and which may lead to the original decision being reversed; and
(ii) will be informed of the time frame within which he or she has to request such a retrial or appeal, as mentioned in the relevant European arrest warrant.
2. In case the European arrest warrant is issued for the purpose of executing a custodial sentence or detention order under the conditions of paragraph 1(d) and the person concerned has not previously received any official information about the existence of the criminal proceedings against him or her, he or she may, when being informed about the content of the European arrest warrant, request to receive a copy of the judgment before being surrendered. Immediately after having been informed about the request, the issuing authority shall provide the copy of the judgment via the executing authority to the person sought. The request of the person sought shall neither delay the surrender procedure nor delay the decision to execute the European arrest warrant. The provision of the judgment to the person concerned is for information purposes only; it shall neither be regarded as a formal service of the judgment nor actuate any time limits applicable for requesting a retrial or appeal.
3. In case a person is surrendered under the conditions of paragraph (1)(d) and he or she has requested a retrial or appeal, the detention of that person awaiting such retrial or appeal shall, until these proceedings are finalised, be reviewed in accordance with the law of the issuing Member State, either on a regular basis or upon request of the person concerned. Such a review shall in particular include the possibility of suspension or interruption of the detention. The retrial or appeal shall begin within due time after the surrender.

Article 5. The execution of the European arrest warrant by the executing judicial authority may, by the law of the executing Member State, be subject to the following conditions:
1. (Repealed).
2. if the offence on the basis of which the European arrest warrant has been issued is punishable by custodial life sentence or life-time detention order, the execution of the said arrest warrant may be subject to the condition that the issuing Member State has provisions in its legal system for a review of the penalty or measure imposed, on request or at the latest after 20 years, or for the application of measures of clemency to which the person is entitled to apply for under the law or practice of the issuing Member State, aiming at a non-execution of such penalty or measure;
3. where a person who is the subject of a European arrest warrant for the purposes of prosecution is a national or resident of the executing Member State, surrender may be subject to the condition that the person, after being heard, is returned to the executing Member State in order to serve there the custodial sentence or detention order passed against him in the issuing Member State.

Article 6. 1. The issuing judicial authority shall be the judicial authority of the issuing Member State which is competent to issue a European arrest warrant by virtue of the law of that State.
2. The executing judicial authority shall be the judicial authority of the executing Member State which is competent to execute the European arrest warrant by virtue of the law of that State.
3. Each Member State shall inform the General Secretariat of the Council of the competent judicial authority under its law.

Article 7. 1. Each Member State may designate a central authority or, when its legal system so provides, more than one central authority to assist the competent judicial authorities.
2. A Member State may, if it is necessary as a result of the organisation of its internal judicial system, make its central authority(ies) responsible for the administrative transmission and reception of European arrest warrants as well as for all other official correspondence relating thereto.
Member State wishing to make use of the possibilities referred to in this Article shall communicate to the General Secretariat of the Council information relating to the designated central authority or central authorities. These indications shall be binding upon all the authorities of the issuing Member State.

Article 8. 1. The European arrest warrant shall contain the following information set out in accordance with the form contained in the Annex:

(a) the identity and nationality of the requested person;
(b) the name, address, telephone and fax numbers and e-mail address of the issuing judicial authority;
(c) evidence of an enforceable judgment, an arrest warrant or any other enforceable judicial decision having the same effect, coming within the scope of Articles 1 and 2;
(d) the nature and legal classification of the offence, particularly in respect of Article 2;
(e) a description of the circumstances in which the offence was committed, including the time, place and degree of participation in the offence by the requested person;
(f) the penalty imposed, if there is a final judgment, or the prescribed scale of penalties for the offence under the law of the issuing Member State;
(g) if possible, other consequences of the offence.
2. The European arrest warrant must be translated into the official language or one of the official languages of the executing Member State. Any Member State may, when this Framework Decision is adopted or at a later date, state in a declaration deposited with the General Secretariat of the Council that it will accept a translation in one or more other official languages of the Institutions of the European Communities.

CHAPTER 2. SURRENDER PROCEDURE

Article 9. 1. When the location of the requested person is known, the issuing judicial authority may transmit the European arrest warrant directly to the executing judicial authority.
2. The issuing judicial authority may, in any event, decide to issue an alert for the requested person in the Schengen Information System (SIS).
3. Such an alert shall be effected in accordance with the provisions of Article 95 of the Convention of 19 June 1990 implementing the Schengen Agreement of 14 June 1985 on the gradual abolition of controls at common borders. An alert in the Schengen Information System shall be equivalent to a European arrest warrant accompanied by the information set out in Article 8(1).
For a transitional period, until the SIS is capable of transmitting all the information described in Article 8, the alert shall be equivalent to a European arrest warrant pending the receipt of the original in due and proper form by the executing judicial authority.

Article 10. 1. If the issuing judicial authority does not know the competent executing judicial authority, it shall make the requisite enquiries, including through the contact points of the European Judicial Network, in order to obtain that information from the executing Member State.
2. If the issuing judicial authority so wishes, transmission may be effected via the secure telecommunications system of the European Judicial Network.
3. If it is not possible to call on the services of the SIS, the issuing judicial authority may call on Interpol to transmit a European arrest warrant.
4. The issuing judicial authority may forward the European arrest warrant by any secure means capable of producing written records under conditions allowing the executing Member State to establish its authenticity.
5. All difficulties concerning the transmission or the authenticity of any document needed for the execution of the European arrest warrant shall be dealt with by direct contacts between the judicial authorities involved, or, where appropriate, with the involvement of the central authorities of the Member States.
6. If the authority which receives a European arrest warrant is not competent to act upon it, it shall automatically forward the European arrest warrant to the competent authority in its Member State and shall inform the issuing judicial authority accordingly.

Article 11. 1. When a requested person is arrested, the executing competent judicial authority shall, in accordance with its national law, inform that person of the European arrest warrant and of its contents, and also of the possibility of consenting to surrender to the issuing judicial authority.
2. A requested person who is arrested for the purpose of the execution of a European arrest warrant shall have a right to be assisted by a legal counsel and by an interpreter in accordance with the national law of the executing Member State.

Article 12. When a person is arrested on the basis of a European arrest warrant, the executing judicial authority shall take a decision on whether the requested person should remain in detention, in accordance with the law of the executing Member State. The person may be released provisionally at any time in conformity with the domestic law of the executing Member State, provided that the competent authority of the said Member State takes all the measures it deems necessary to prevent the person absconding.

Article 13. 1. If the arrested person indicates that he or she consents to surrender, that consent and, if appropriate, express renunciation of entitlement to the 'speciality rule', referred to in Article 27(2), shall be given before the executing judicial authority, in accordance with the domestic law of the executing Member State.
2. Each Member State shall adopt the measures necessary to ensure that consent and, where appropriate, renunciation, as referred to in paragraph 1, are established in such a way as to show that the person concerned has expressed them voluntarily and in full awareness of the consequences. To that end, the requested person shall have the right to legal counsel.
3. The consent and, where appropriate, renunciation, as referred to in paragraph 1, shall be formally recorded in accordance with the procedure laid down by the domestic law of the executing Member State.
4. In principle, consent may not be revoked. Each Member State may provide that consent and, if appropriate, renunciation may be revoked, in accordance with the rules applicable under its domestic law. In this case, the period between the date of consent and that of its revocation shall not be taken into consideration in establishing the time limits laid down in Article 17. A Member State which wishes to have recourse to this possibility shall inform the General Secretariat of the Council accordingly when this Framework Decision is adopted and shall specify the procedures whereby revocation of consent shall be possible and any amendment to them.

Article 14. Where the arrested person does not consent to his or her surrender as referred to in Article 13, he or she shall be entitled to be heard by the executing judicial authority, in accordance with the law of the executing Member State.

Article 15. 1. The executing judicial authority shall decide, within the time-limits and under the conditions defined in this Framework Decision, whether the person is to be surrendered.
2. If the executing judicial authority finds the information communicated by the issuing Member State to be insufficient to allow it to decide on surrender, it shall request that the necessary supplementary information, in particular with respect to Articles 3 to 5 and Article 8, be furnished as a matter of urgency and may fix a time limit for the receipt thereof, taking into account the need to observe the time limits set in Article 17.
3. The issuing judicial authority may at any time forward any additional useful information to the executing judicial authority.

Article 16. 1. If two or more Member States have issued European arrest warrants for the same person, the decision on which of the European arrest warrants shall be executed shall be taken by the executing judicial authority with due consideration of all the circumstances and especially the relative seriousness and place of the offences, the respective dates of the European arrest warrants and whether the warrant has been issued for the purposes of prosecution or for execution of a custodial sentence or detention order.
2. The executing judicial authority may seek the advice of Eurojust when making the choice referred to in paragraph 1.
3. In the event of a conflict between a European arrest warrant and a request for extradition presented by a third country, the decision on whether the European arrest warrant or the extradition request takes precedence shall be taken by the competent authority of the executing Member State with due consideration of all the circumstances, in particular those referred to in paragraph 1 and those mentioned in the applicable convention.
4. This Article shall be without prejudice to Member States' obligations under the Statute of the International Criminal Court.

Article 17. 1. A European arrest warrant shall be dealt with and executed as a matter of urgency.
2. In cases where the requested person consents to his surrender, the final decision on the execution of the European arrest warrant should be taken within a period of 10 days after consent has been given.
3. In other cases, the final decision on the execution of the European arrest warrant should be taken within a period of 60 days after the arrest of the requested person.
4. Where in specific cases the European arrest warrant cannot be executed within the time limits laid down in paragraphs 2 or 3, the executing judicial authority shall immediately inform the issuing judicial authority thereof, giving the reasons for the delay. In such case, the time limits may be extended by a further 30 days.
5. As long as the executing judicial authority has not taken a final decision on the European arrest warrant, it shall ensure that the material conditions necessary for effective surrender of the person remain fulfilled.
6. Reasons must be given for any refusal to execute a European arrest warrant.
7. Where in exceptional circumstances a Member State cannot observe the time limits provided for in this Article, it shall inform Eurojust, giving the reasons for the delay. In addition, a Member State which has experienced repeated delays on the part of another Member State in the execution of European arrest warrants shall inform the Council with a view to evaluating the implementation of this Framework Decision at Member State level.

Article 18. 1. Where the European arrest warrant has been issued for the purpose of conducting a criminal prosecution, the executing judicial authority must:
(a) either agree that the requested person should be heard according to Article 19;
(b) or agree to the temporary transfer of the requested person.
2. The conditions and the duration of the temporary transfer shall be determined by mutual agreement between the issuing and executing judicial authorities.
3. In the case of temporary transfer, the person must be able to return to the executing Member State to attend hearings concerning him or her as part of the surrender procedure.

Article 19. 1. The requested person shall be heard by a judicial authority, assisted by another person designated in accordance with the law of the Member State of the requesting court.
2. The requested person shall be heard in accordance with the law of the executing Member State and with the conditions determined by mutual agreement between the issuing and executing judicial authorities.
3. The competent executing judicial authority may assign another judicial authority of its Member State to take part in the hearing of the requested person in order to ensure the proper application of this Article and of the conditions laid down.

Article 20. 1. Where the requested person enjoys a privilege or immunity regarding jurisdiction or execution in the executing Member State, the time limits referred to in Article 17 shall not start running unless, and counting from the day when, the executing judicial authority is informed of the fact that the privilege or immunity has been waived.
The executing Member State shall ensure that the material conditions necessary for effective surrender are fulfilled when the person no longer enjoys such privilege or immunity.
2. Where power to waive the privilege or immunity lies with an authority of the executing Member State, the executing judicial authority shall request it to exercise that power forthwith. Where power to waive the privilege or immunity lies with an authority of another State or international organisation, it shall be for the issuing judicial authority to request it to exercise that power.

Article 21. This Framework Decision shall not prejudice the obligations of the executing Member State where the requested person has been extradited to that Member State from a third State and where that person is protected by provisions of the arrangement under which he or she was extradited concerning speciality. The executing Member State shall take all necessary measures for requesting forthwith the consent of the State from which the requested person was extradited so that he or she can be surrendered to the Member State which issued the European arrest warrant. The time limits referred to in Article 17 shall not start running until the day on which these speciality rules cease to apply. Pending the decision of the State from which the requested person was extradited, the executing Member State will ensure that the material conditions necessary for effective surrender remain fulfilled.

Article 22. The executing judicial authority shall notify the issuing judicial authority immediately of the decision on the action to be taken on the European arrest warrant.

Article 23. 1. The person requested shall be surrendered as soon as possible on a date agreed between the authorities concerned.
2. He or she shall be surrendered no later than 10 days after the final decision on the execution of the European arrest warrant.
3. If the surrender of the requested person within the period laid down in paragraph 2 is prevented by circumstances beyond the control of any of the Member States, the executing and issuing judicial authorities shall immediately contact each other and agree on a new surrender date. In that event, the surrender shall take place within 10 days of the new date thus agreed.
4. The surrender may exceptionally be temporarily postponed for serious humanitarian reasons, for example if there are substantial grounds for believing that it would manifestly endanger the requested person's life or health. The execution of the European arrest warrant shall take place as soon as these grounds have ceased to exist. The executing judicial authority shall immediately inform the issuing judicial authority and agree on a new surrender date. In that event, the surrender shall take place within 10 days of the new date thus agreed.
5. Upon expiry of the time limits referred to in paragraphs 2 to 4, if the person is still being held in custody he shall be released.

Article 24. 1. The executing judicial authority may, after deciding to execute the European arrest warrant, postpone the surrender of the requested person so that he or she may be prosecuted in the executing Member State

or, if he or she has already been sentenced, so that he or she may serve, in its territory, a sentence passed for an act other than that referred to in the European arrest warrant.
2. Instead of postponing the surrender, the executing judicial authority may temporarily surrender the requested person to the issuing Member State under conditions to be determined by mutual agreement between the executing and the issuing judicial authorities. The agreement shall be made in writing and the conditions shall be binding on all the authorities in the issuing Member State.

Article 25. 1. Each Member State shall, except when it avails itself of the possibility of refusal when the transit of a national or a resident is requested for the purpose of the execution of a custodial sentence or detention order, permit the transit through its territory of a requested person who is being surrendered provided that it has been given information on:
(a) the identity and nationality of the person subject to the European arrest warrant;
(b) the existence of a European arrest warrant;
(c) the nature and legal classification of the offence;
(d) the description of the circumstances of the offence, including the date and place.
Where a person who is the subject of a European arrest warrant for the purposes of prosecution is a national or resident of the Member State of transit, transit may be subject to the condition that the person, after being heard, is returned to the transit Member State to serve the custodial sentence or detention order passed against him in the issuing Member State.
2. Each Member State shall designate an authority responsible for receiving transit requests and the necessary documents, as well as any other official correspondence relating to transit requests. Member States shall communicate this designation to the General Secretariat of the Council.
3. The transit request and the information set out in paragraph 1 may be addressed to the authority designated pursuant to paragraph 2 by any means capable of producing a written record. The Member State of transit shall notify its decision by the same procedure.
4. This Framework Decision does not apply in the case of transport by air without a scheduled stopover. However, if an unscheduled landing occurs, the issuing Member State shall provide the authority designated pursuant to paragraph 2 with the information provided for in paragraph 1.
5. Where a transit concerns a person who is to be extradited from a third State to a Member State this Article will apply mutatis mutandis. In particular the expression 'European arrest warrant' shall be deemed to be replaced by 'extradition request'.

CHAPTER 3. EFFECTS OF THE SURRENDER

Article 26. 1. The issuing Member State shall deduct all periods of detention arising from the execution of a European arrest warrant from the total period of detention to be served in the issuing Member State as a result of a custodial sentence or detention order being passed.
2. To that end, all information concerning the duration of the detention of the requested person on the basis of the European arrest warrant shall be transmitted by the executing judicial authority or the central authority designated under Article 7 to the issuing judicial authority at the time of the surrender.

Article 27. 1. Each Member State may notify the General Secretariat of the Council that, in its relations with other Member States that have given the same notification, consent is presumed to have been given for the prosecution, sentencing or detention with a view to the carrying out of a custodial sentence or detention order for an offence committed prior to his or her surrender, other than that for which he or she was surrendered, unless in a particular case the executing judicial authority states otherwise in its decision on surrender.
2. Except in the cases referred to in paragraphs 1 and 3, a person surrendered may not be prosecuted, sentenced or otherwise deprived of his or her liberty for an offence committed prior to his or her surrender other than that for which he or she was surrendered.
3. Paragraph 2 does not apply in the following cases:
(a) when the person having had an opportunity to leave the territory of the Member State to which he or she has been surrendered has not done so within 45 days of his or her final discharge, or has returned to that territory after leaving it;
(b) the offence is not punishable by a custodial sentence or detention order;
(c) the criminal proceedings do not give rise to the application of a measure restricting personal liberty;
(d) when the person could be liable to a penalty or a measure not involving the deprivation of liberty, in particular a financial penalty or a measure in lieu thereof, even if the penalty or measure may give rise to a restriction of his or her personal liberty;

(e) when the person consented to be surrendered, where appropriate at the same time as he or she renounced the speciality rule, in accordance with Article 13;
(f) when the person, after his/her surrender, has expressly renounced entitlement to the speciality rule with regard to specific offences preceding his/her surrender. Renunciation shall be given before the competent judicial authorities of the issuing Member State and shall be recorded in accordance with that State's domestic law. The renunciation shall be drawn up in such a way as to make clear that the person has given it voluntarily and in full awareness of the consequences. To that end, the person shall have the right to legal counsel;
(g) where the executing judicial authority which surrendered the person gives its consent in accordance with paragraph 4.
4. A request for consent shall be submitted to the executing judicial authority, accompanied by the information mentioned in Article 8(1) and a translation as referred to in Article 8(2). Consent shall be given when the offence for which it is requested is itself subject to surrender in accordance with the provisions of this Framework Decision. Consent shall be refused on the grounds referred to in Article 3 and otherwise may be refused only on the grounds referred to in Article 4. The decision shall be taken no later than 30 days after receipt of the request. For the situations mentioned in Article 5 the issuing Member State must give the guarantees provided for therein.

Article 28. 1. Each Member State may notify the General Secretariat of the Council that, in its relations with other Member States which have given the same notification, the consent for the surrender of a person to a Member State other than the executing Member State pursuant to a European arrest warrant issued for an offence committed prior to his or her surrender is presumed to have been given, unless in a particular case the executing judicial authority states otherwise in its decision on surrender.
2. In any case, a person who has been surrendered to the issuing Member State pursuant to a European arrest warrant may, without the consent of the executing Member State, be surrendered to a Member State other than the executing Member State pursuant to a European arrest warrant issued for any offence committed prior to his or her surrender in the following cases:
(a) where the requested person, having had an opportunity to leave the territory of the Member State to which he or she has been surrendered, has not done so within 45 days of his final discharge, or has returned to that territory after leaving it;
(b) where the requested person consents to be surrendered to a Member State other than the executing Member State pursuant to a European arrest warrant. Consent shall be given before the competent judicial authorities of the issuing Member State and shall be recorded in accordance with that State's national law. It shall be drawn up in such a way as to make clear that the person concerned has given it voluntarily and in full awareness of the consequences. To that end, the requested person shall have the right to legal counsel;
(c) where the requested person is not subject to the speciality rule, in accordance with Article 27(3)(a), (e), (f) and (g).
3. The executing judicial authority consents to the surrender to another Member State according to the following rules:
(a) the request for consent shall be submitted in accordance with Article 9, accompanied by the information mentioned in Article 8(1) and a translation as stated in Article 8(2);
(b) consent shall be given when the offence for which it is requested is itself subject to surrender in accordance with the provisions of this Framework Decision;
(c) the decision shall be taken no later than 30 days after receipt of the request;
(d) consent shall be refused on the grounds referred to in Article 3 and otherwise may be refused only on the grounds referred to in Article 4.
For the situations referred to in Article 5, the issuing Member State must give the guarantees provided for therein.
4. Notwithstanding paragraph 1, a person who has been surrendered pursuant to a European arrest warrant shall not be extradited to a third State without the consent of the competent authority of the Member State which surrendered the person. Such consent shall be given in accordance with the Conventions by which that Member State is bound, as well as with its domestic law.

Article 29. 1. At the request of the issuing judicial authority or on its own initiative, the executing judicial authority shall, in accordance with its national law, seize and hand over property which:
(a) may be required as evidence, or
(b) has been acquired by the requested person as a result of the offence.
2. The property referred to in paragraph 1 shall be handed over even if the European arrest warrant cannot be carried out owing to the death or escape of the requested person.

3. If the property referred to in paragraph 1 is liable to seizure or confiscation in the territory of the executing Member State, the latter may, if the property is needed in connection with pending criminal proceedings, temporarily retain it or hand it over to the issuing Member State, on condition that it is returned.
4. Any rights which the executing Member State or third parties may have acquired in the property referred to in paragraph 1 shall be preserved. Where such rights exist, the issuing Member State shall return the property without charge to the executing Member State as soon as the criminal proceedings have been terminated.

Article 30. 1. Expenses incurred in the territory of the executing Member State for the execution of a European arrest warrant shall be borne by that Member State.
2. All other expenses shall be borne by the issuing Member State.

CHAPTER 4. GENERAL AND FINAL PROVISIONS

Article 31. 1. Without prejudice to their application in relations between Member States and third States, this Framework Decision shall, from 1 January 2004, replace the corresponding provisions of the following conventions applicable in the field of extradition in relations between the Member States:
(a) the European Convention on Extradition of 13 December 1957, its additional protocol of 15 October 1975, its second additional protocol of 17 March 1978, and the European Convention on the suppression of terrorism of 27 January 1977 as far as extradition is concerned;
(b) the Agreement between the 12 Member States of the European Communities on the simplification and modernisation of methods of transmitting extradition requests of 26 May 1989;
(c) the Convention of 10 March 1995 on simplified extradition procedure between the Member States of the European Union;
(d) the Convention of 27 September 1996 relating to extradition between the Member States of the European Union;
(e) Title III, Chapter 4 of the Convention of 19 June 1990 implementing the Schengen Agreement of 14 June 1985 on the gradual abolition of checks at common borders.
2. Member States may continue to apply bilateral or multilateral agreements or arrangements in force when this Framework Decision is adopted in so far as such agreements or arrangements allow the objectives of this Framework Decision to be extended or enlarged and help to simplify or facilitate further the procedures for surrender of persons who are the subject of European arrest warrants.
Member States may conclude bilateral or multilateral agreements or arrangements after this Framework Decision has come into force in so far as such agreements or arrangements allow the prescriptions of this Framework Decision to be extended or enlarged and help to simplify or facilitate further the procedures for surrender of persons who are the subject of European arrest warrants, in particular by fixing time limits shorter than those fixed in Article 17, by extending the list of offences laid down in Article 2(2), by further limiting the grounds for refusal set out in Articles 3 and 4, or by lowering the threshold provided for in Article 2(1) or (2).
The agreements and arrangements referred to in the second subparagraph may in no case affect relations with Member States which are not parties to them.
Member States shall, within three months from the entry into force of this Framework Decision, notify the Council and the Commission of the existing agreements and arrangements referred to in the first subparagraph which they wish to continue applying.
Member States shall also notify the Council and the Commission of any new agreement or arrangement as referred to in the second subparagraph, within three months of signing it.
3. Where the conventions or agreements referred to in paragraph 1 apply to the territories of Member States or to territories for whose external relations a Member State is responsible to which this Framework Decision does not apply, these instruments shall continue to govern the relations existing between those territories and the other Members States.

Article 32. 1. Extradition requests received before 1 January 2004 will continue to be governed by existing instruments relating to extradition. Requests received after that date will be governed by the rules adopted by Member States pursuant to this Framework Decision. However, any Member State may, at the time of the adoption of this Framework Decision by the Council, make a statement indicating that as executing Member State it will continue to deal with requests relating to acts committed before a date which it specifies in accordance with the extradition system applicable before 1 January 2004. The date in question may not be later than 7 August 2002. The said statement will be published in the Official Journal of the European Communities. It may be withdrawn at any time.

PART III. CRIMINAL JUSTICE

Article 33. 1. As long as Austria has not modified Article 12(1) of the 'Auslieferungs- und Rechtshilfegesetz' and, at the latest, until 31 December 2008, it may allow its executing judicial authorities to refuse the enforcement of a European arrest warrant if the requested person is an Austrian citizen and if the act for which the European arrest warrant has been issued is not punishable under Austrian law.
2. This Framework Decision shall apply to Gibraltar.

Article 34. 1. Member States shall take the necessary measures to comply with the provisions of this Framework Decision by 31 December 2003.
2. Member States shall transmit to the General Secretariat of the Council and to the Commission the text of the provisions transposing into their national law the obligations imposed on them under this Framework Decision. When doing so, each Member State may indicate that it will apply immediately this Framework Decision in its relations with those Member States which have given the same notification.
The General Secretariat of the Council shall communicate to the Member States and to the Commission the information received pursuant to Article 7(2), Article 8(2), Article 13(4) and Article 25(2). It shall also have the information published in the Official Journal of the European Communities.
3. On the basis of the information communicated by the General Secretariat of the Council, the Commission shall, by 31 December 2004 at the latest, submit a report to the European Parliament and to the Council on the operation of this Framework Decision, accompanied, where necessary, by legislative proposals.
4. The Council shall in the second half of 2003 conduct a review, in particular of the practical application, of the provisions of this Framework Decision by the Member States as well as the functioning of the Schengen Information System.

Article 35. This Framework Decision shall enter into force on the twentieth day following that of its publication in the Official Journal of the European Communities.

[The Annex is omitted.]

Council Framework Decision 2002/475/JHA of 13 June 2002 on combating terrorism (*OJ* L 164, 22.06.2002, pp. 3 – 7) as amended.

[The Preamble is omitted.]

Article 1. 1. Each Member State shall take the necessary measures to ensure that the intentional acts referred to below in points (a) to (i), as defined as offences under national law, which, given their nature or context, may seriously damage a country or an international organisation where committed with the aim of:
— seriously intimidating a population, or
— unduly compelling a Government or international organisation to perform or abstain from performing any act, or
— seriously destabilising or destroying the fundamental political, constitutional, economic or social structures of a country or an international organisation,
shall be deemed to be terrorist offences:
(a) attacks upon a person's life which may cause death;
(b) attacks upon the physical integrity of a person;
(c) kidnapping or hostage taking;
(d) causing extensive destruction to a Government or public facility, a transport system, an infrastructure facility, including an information system, a fixed platform located on the continental shelf, a public place or private property likely to endanger human life or result in major economic loss;
(e) seizure of aircraft, ships or other means of public or goods transport;
(f) manufacture, possession, acquisition, transport, supply or use of weapons, explosives or of nuclear, biological or chemical weapons, as well as research into, and development of, biological and chemical weapons;
(g) release of dangerous substances, or causing fires, floods or explosions the effect of which is to endanger human life;
(h) interfering with or disrupting the supply of water, power or any other fundamental natural resource the effect of which is to endanger human life;
(i) threatening to commit any of the acts listed in (a) to (h).
2. This Framework Decision shall not have the effect of altering the obligation to respect fundamental rights and fundamental legal principles as enshrined in Article 6 of the Treaty on European Union.

Article 2. 1. For the purposes of this Framework Decision, 'terrorist group' shall mean: a structured group of more than two persons, established over a period of time and acting in concert to commit terrorist offences. 'Structured group' shall mean a group that is not randomly formed for the immediate commission of an offence and that does not need to have formally defined roles for its members, continuity of its membership or a developed structure.
2. Each Member State shall take the necessary measures to ensure that the following intentional acts are punishable:
(a) directing a terrorist group;
(b) participating in the activities of a terrorist group, including by supplying information or material resources, or by funding its activities in any way, with knowledge of the fact that such participation will contribute to the criminal activities of the terrorist group.

Article 3. 1. For the purposes of this Framework Decision:
(a) 'public provocation to commit a terrorist offence' shall mean the distribution, or otherwise making available, of a message to the public, with the intent to incite the commission of one of the offences listed in Article 1(1)(a) to (h), where such conduct, whether or not directly advocating terrorist offences, causes a danger that one or more such offences may be committed;
(b) 'recruitment for terrorism' shall mean soliciting another person to commit one of the offences listed in Article 1(1)(a) to (h), or in Article 2(2);
(c) 'training for terrorism' shall mean providing instruction in the making or use of explosives, firearms or other weapons or noxious or hazardous substances, or in other specific methods or techniques, for the purpose of committing one of the offences listed in Article 1(1)(a) to (h), knowing that the skills provided are intended to be used for this purpose.
2. Each Member State shall take the necessary measures to ensure that offences linked to terrorist activities include the following intentional acts:
(a) public provocation to commit a terrorist offence;
(b) recruitment for terrorism;

(c) training for terrorism;
(d) aggravated theft with a view to committing one of the offences listed in Article 1(1);
(e) extortion with a view to the perpetration of one of the offences listed in Article 1(1);
(f) drawing up false administrative documents with a view to committing one of the offences listed in Article 1(1)(a) to (h) and Article 2(2)(b).
3. For an act as set out in paragraph 2 to be punishable, it shall not be necessary that a terrorist offence be actually committed.

Article 4. 1. Each Member State shall take the necessary measures to ensure that aiding or abetting an offence referred to in Article 1(1), Articles 2 or 3 is made punishable.
2. Each Member State shall take the necessary measures to ensure that inciting an offence referred to in Article 1(1), Article 2 or Article 3(2)(d) to (f) is made punishable.
3. Each Member State shall take the necessary measures to ensure that attempting to commit an offence referred to in Article 1(1) and Article 3(2)(d) to (f), with the exception of possession as provided for in Article 1(1)(f) and the offence referred to in Article 1(1)(i), is made punishable.
4. Each Member State may decide to take the necessary measures to ensure that attempting to commit an offence referred to in Article 3(2)(b) and (c) is made punishable.

Article 5. 1. Each Member State shall take the necessary measures to ensure that the offences referred to in Articles 1 to 4 are punishable by effective, proportionate and dissuasive criminal penalties, which may entail extradition.
2. Each Member State shall take the necessary measures to ensure that the terrorist offences referred to in Article 1(1) and offences referred to in Article 4, inasmuch as they relate to terrorist offences, are punishable by custodial sentences heavier than those imposable under national law for such offences in the absence of the special intent required pursuant to Article 1(1), save where the sentences imposable are already the maximum possible sentences under national law.
3. Each Member State shall take the necessary measures to ensure that offences listed in Article 2 are punishable by custodial sentences, with a maximum sentence of not less than fifteen years for the offence referred to in Article 2(2)(a), and for the offences listed in Article 2(2)(b) a maximum sentence of not less than eight years. In so far as the offence referred to in Article 2(2)(a) refers only to the act in Article 1(1)(i), the maximum sentence shall not be less than eight years.

Article 6. Each Member State may take the necessary measures to ensure that the penalties referred to in Article 5 may be reduced if the offender:
(a) renounces terrorist activity, and
(b) provides the administrative or judicial authorities with information which they would not otherwise have been able to obtain, helping them to:
(i) prevent or mitigate the effects of the offence;
(ii) identify or bring to justice the other offenders;
(iii) find evidence; or
(iv) prevent further offences referred to in Articles 1 to 4.

Article 7. 1. Each Member State shall take the necessary measures to ensure that legal persons can be held liable for any of the offences referred to in Articles 1 to 4 committed for their benefit by any person, acting either individually or as part of an organ of the legal person, who has a leading position within the legal person, based on one of the following:
(a) a power of representation of the legal person;
(b) an authority to take decisions on behalf of the legal person;
(c) an authority to exercise control within the legal person.
2. Apart from the cases provided for in paragraph 1, each Member State shall take the necessary measures to ensure that legal persons can be held liable where the lack of supervision or control by a person referred to in paragraph 1 has made possible the commission of any of the offences referred to in Articles 1 to 4 for the benefit of that legal person by a person under its authority.
3. Liability of legal persons under paragraphs 1 and 2 shall not exclude criminal proceedings against natural persons who are perpetrators, instigators or accessories in any of the offences referred to in Articles 1 to 4.

Article 8. Each Member State shall take the necessary measures to ensure that a legal person held liable pursuant to Article 7 is punishable by effective, proportionate and dissuasive penalties, which shall include criminal or non-criminal fines and may include other penalties, such as:
(a) exclusion from entitlement to public benefits or aid;
(b) temporary or permanent disqualification from the practice of commercial activities;
(c) placing under judicial supervision;
(d) a judicial winding-up order;
(e) temporary or permanent closure of establishments which have been used for committing the offence.

Article 9. 1. Each Member State shall take the necessary measures to establish its jurisdiction over the offences referred to in Articles 1 to 4 where:
(a) the offence is committed in whole or in part in its territory. Each Member State may extend its jurisdiction if the offence is committed in the territory of a Member State;
(b) the offence is committed on board a vessel flying its flag or an aircraft registered there;
(c) the offender is one of its nationals or residents;
(d) the offence is committed for the benefit of a legal person established in its territory;
(e) the offence is committed against the institutions or people of the Member State in question or against an institution of the European Union or a body set up in accordance with the Treaty establishing the European Community or the Treaty on European Union and based in that Member State.
2. When an offence falls within the jurisdiction of more than one Member State and when any of the States concerned can validly prosecute on the basis of the same facts, the Member States concerned shall cooperate in order to decide which of them will prosecute the offenders with the aim, if possible, of centralising proceedings in a single Member State. To this end, the Member States may have recourse to any body or mechanism established within the European Union in order to facilitate cooperation between their judicial authorities and the coordination of their action. Sequential account shall be taken of the following factors:
— the Member State shall be that in the territory of which the acts were committed,
— the Member State shall be that of which the perpetrator is a national or resident,
— the Member State shall be the Member State of origin of the victims,
— the Member State shall be that in the territory of which the perpetrator was found.
3. Each Member State shall take the necessary measures also to establish its jurisdiction over the offences referred to in Articles 1 to 4 in cases where it refuses to hand over or extradite a person suspected or convicted of such an offence to another Member State or to a third country.
4. Each Member State shall ensure that its jurisdiction covers cases in which any of the offences referred to in Articles 2 and 4 has been committed in whole or in part within its territory, wherever the terrorist group is based or pursues its criminal activities.
5. This Article shall not exclude the exercise of jurisdiction in criminal matters as laid down by a Member State in accordance with its national legislation.

Article 10. 1. Member States shall ensure that investigations into, or prosecution of, offences covered by this Framework Decision are not dependent on a report or accusation made by a person subjected to the offence, at least if the acts were committed on the territory of the Member State.
2. In addition to the measures laid down in the Council Framework Decision 2001/220/JHA of 15 March 2001 on the standing of victims in criminal proceedings, each Member State shall, if necessary, take all measures possible to ensure appropriate assistance for victims' families.

Article 11. 1. Member States shall take the necessary measures to comply with this Framework Decision by 31 December 2002.
2. By 31 December 2002, Member States shall forward to the General Secretariat of the Council and to the Commission the text of the provisions transposing into their national law the obligations imposed on them under this Framework Decision. On the basis of a report drawn up from that information and a report from the Commission, the Council shall assess, by 31 December 2003, whether Member States have taken the necessary measures to comply with this Framework Decision.
3. The Commission report shall specify, in particular, transposition into the criminal law of the Member States of the obligation referred to in Article 5(2).

Article 12. This Framework Decision shall apply to Gibraltar.

Article 13. This Framework Decision shall enter into force on the day of its publication in the Official Journal.

Council Framework Decision 2003/577/JHA of 22 July 2003 on the execution in the European Union of orders freezing property or evidence (*OJ* L 196, 02.08.2003, pp. 45 – 55).

[The Preamble is omitted.]

Title I. Scope

Article 1. The purpose of the Framework Decision is to establish the rules under which a Member State shall recognise and execute in its territory a freezing order issued by a judicial authority of another Member State in the framework of criminal proceedings. It shall not have the effect of amending the obligation to respect the fundamental rights and fundamental legal principles as enshrined in Article 6 of the Treaty.

Article 2. For the purposes of this Framework Decision:
(a) "issuing State" shall mean the Member State in which a judicial authority, as defined in the national law of the issuing State, has made, validated or in any way confirmed a freezing order in the framework of criminal proceedings;
(b) "executing State" shall mean the Member State in whose territory the property or evidence is located;
(c) "freezing order" property that could be subject to confiscation or evidence;
(d) "property" includes property of any description, whether corporeal or incorporeal, movable or immovable, and legal documents and instruments evidencing title to or interest in such property, which the competent judicial authority in the issuing State considers:
- is the proceeds of an offence referred to in Article 3, or equivalent to either the full value or part of the value of such proceeds, or
- constitutes the instrumentalities or the objects of such an offence;
(e) "evidence" shall mean objects, documents or data which could be produced as evidence in criminal proceedings concerning an offence referred to in Article 3.

Article 3. 1. This Framework Decision applies to freezing orders issued for purposes of:
(a) securing evidence, or
(b) subsequent confiscation of property.
2. The following offences, as they are defined by the law of the issuing State, and if they are punishable in the issuing State by a custodial sentence of a maximum period of at least three years shall not be subject to verification of the double criminality of the act:
- participation in a criminal organisation,
- terrorism,
- trafficking in human beings,
- sexual exploitation of children and child pornography,
- illicit trafficking in narcotic drugs and psychotropic substances,
- illicit trafficking in weapons, munitions and explosives,
- corruption,
- fraud, including that affecting the financial interests of the European Communities within the meaning of the Convention of 26 July 1995 on the Protection of the European Communities' Financial Interests,
- laundering of the proceeds of crime,
- counterfeiting currency, including of the euro,
- computer-related crime,
- environmental crime, including illicit trafficking in endangered animal species and in endangered plant species and varieties,
- facilitation of unauthorised entry and residence,
- murder, grievous bodily injury,
- illicit trade in human organs and tissue,
- kidnapping, illegal restraint and hostage-taking,
- racism and xenophobia,
- organised or armed robbery,
- illicit trafficking in cultural goods, including antiques and works of art,
- swindling,
- racketeering and extortion,
- counterfeiting and piracy of products,

PART III. CRIMINAL JUSTICE

- forgery of administrative documents and trafficking therein,
- forgery of means of payment,
- illicit trafficking in hormonal substances and other growth promoters,
- illicit trafficking in nuclear or radioactive materials,
- trafficking in stolen vehicles,
- rape,
- arson,
- crimes within the jurisdiction of the International Criminal Tribunal,
- unlawful seizure of aircraft/ships,
- sabotage.

3. The Council may decide, at any time, acting unanimously after consultation of the European Parliament under the conditions laid down in Article 39(1) of the Treaty, to add other categories of offence to the list contained in paragraph 2. The Council shall examine, in the light of the report submitted by the Commission pursuant to Article 14 of this Framework Decision, whether the list should be extended or amended.

4. For cases not covered by paragraph 2, the executing State may subject the recognition and enforcement of a freezing order made for purposes referred to in paragraph 1(a) to the condition that the acts for which the order was issued constitute an offence under the laws of that State, whatever the constituent elements or however described under the law of the issuing State.

For cases not covered by paragraph 2, the executing State may subject the recognition and enforcement of a freezing order made for purposes referred to in paragraph 1(b) to the condition that the acts for which the order was issued constitute an offence which, under the laws of that State, allows for such freezing, whatever the constituent elements or however described under the law of the issuing State.

Title II. Procedure for executing freezing orders

Article 4. 1. A freezing order within the meaning of this Framework Decision, together with the certificate provided for in Article 9, shall be transmitted by the judicial authority which issued it directly to the competent judicial authority for execution by any means capable of producing a written record under conditions allowing the executing State to establish authenticity.

2. The United Kingdom and Ireland, respectively, may, before the date referred to in Article 14(1), state in a declaration that the freezing order together with the certificate must be sent via a central authority or authorities specified by it in the declaration. Any such declaration may be modified by a further declaration or withdrawn any time. Any declaration or withdrawal shall be deposited with the General Secretariat of the Council and notified to the Commission. These Member States may at any time by a further declaration limit the scope of such a declaration for the purpose of giving greater effect to paragraph 1. They shall do so when the provisions on mutual assistance of the Convention implementing the Schengen Agreement are put into effect for them.

3. If the competent judicial authority for execution is unknown, the judicial authority in the issuing State shall make all necessary inquiries, including via the contact points of the European Judicial Network(3), in order to obtain the information from the executing State.

4. When the judicial authority in the executing State which receives a freezing order has no jurisdiction to recognise it and take the necessary measures for its execution, it shall, ex officio, transmit the freezing order to the competent judicial authority for execution and shall so inform the judicial authority in the issuing State which issued it.

Article 5. 1. The competent judicial authorities of the executing State shall recognise a freezing order, transmitted in accordance with Article 4, without any further formality being required and shall forthwith take the necessary measures for its immediate execution in the same way as for a freezing order made by an authority of the executing State, unless that authority decides to invoke one of the grounds for non-recognition or non-execution provided for in Article 7 or one of the grounds for postponement provided for in Article 8.

Whenever it is necessary to ensure that the evidence taken is valid and provided that such formalities and procedures are not contrary to the fundamental principles of law in the executing State, the judicial authority of the executing State shall also observe the formalities and procedures expressly indicated by the competent judicial authority of the issuing State in the execution of the freezing order.

A report on the execution of the freezing order shall be made forthwith to the competent authority in the issuing State by any means capable of producing a written record.

2. Any additional coercive measures rendered necessary by the freezing order shall be taken in accordance with the applicable procedural rules of the executing State.

3. The competent judicial authorities of the executing State shall decide and communicate the decision on a freezing order as soon as possible and, whenever practicable, within 24 hours of receipt of the freezing order.

Article 6. 1. The property shall remain frozen in the executing State until that State has responded definitively to any request made under Article 10(1)(a) or (b).
2. However, after consulting the issuing State, the executing State may in accordance with its national law and practices lay down appropriate conditions in the light of the circumstances of the case in order to limit the period for which the property will be frozen. If, in accordance with those conditions, it envisages lifting the measure, it shall inform the issuing State, which shall be given the opportunity to submit its comments.
3. The judicial authorities of the issuing State shall forthwith notify the judicial authorities of the executing State that the freezing order has been lifted. In these circumstances it shall be the responsibility of the executing State to lift the measure as soon as possible.

Article 7. 1. The competent judicial authorities of the executing State may refuse to recognise or execute the freezing order only if:
(a) the certificate provided for in Article 9 is not produced, is incomplete or manifestly does not correspond to the freezing order;
(b) there is an immunity or privilege under the law of the executing State which makes it impossible to execute the freezing order;
(c) it is instantly clear from the information provided in the certificate that rendering judicial assistance pursuant to Article 10 for the offence in respect of which the freezing order has been made, would infringe the ne bis in idem principle;
(d) if, in one of the cases referred to in Article 3(4), the act on which the freezing order is based does not constitute an offence under the law of the executing State; however, in relation to taxes or duties, customs and exchange, execution of the freezing order may not be refused on the ground that the law of the executing State does not impose the same kind of tax or duty or does not contain a tax, duty, customs and exchange regulation of the same kind as the law of the issuing State.
2. In case of paragraph 1(a), the competent judicial authority may:
(a) specify a deadline for its presentation, completion or correction; or
(b) accept an equivalent document; or
(c) exempt the issuing judicial authority from the requirement if it considers that the information provided is sufficient.
3. Any decision to refuse recognition or execution shall be taken and notified forthwith to the competent judicial authorities of the issuing State by any means capable of producing a written record.
4. In case it is in practice impossible to execute the freezing order for the reason that the property or evidence have disappeared, have been destroyed, cannot be found in the location indicated in the certificate or the location of the property or evidence has not been indicated in a sufficiently precise manner, even after consultation with the issuing State, the competent judicial authorities of the issuing State shall likewise be notified forthwith.

Article 8. 1. The competent judicial authority of the executing State may postpone the execution of a freezing order transmitted in accordance with Article 4:
(a) where its execution might damage an ongoing criminal investigation, until such time as it deems reasonable;
(b) where the property or evidence concerned have already been subjected to a freezing order in criminal proceedings, and until that freezing order is lifted;
(c) where, in the case of an order freezing property in criminal proceedings with a view to its subsequent confiscation, that property is already subject to an order made in the course of other proceedings in the executing State and until that order is lifted. However, this point shall only apply where such an order would have priority over subsequent national freezing orders in criminal proceedings under national law.
2. A report on the postponement of the execution of the freezing order, including the grounds for the postponement and, if possible, the expected duration of the postponement, shall be made forthwith to the competent authority in the issuing State by any means capable of producing a written record.
3. As soon as the ground for postponement has ceased to exist, the competent judicial authority of the executing State shall forthwith take the necessary measures for the execution of the freezing order and inform the competent authority in the issuing State thereof by any means capable of producing a written record.
4. The competent judicial authority of the executing State shall inform the competent authority of the issuing State about any other restraint measure to which the property concerned may be subjected.

Part III. Criminal Justice

Article 9. 1. The certificate, the standard form for which is given in the Annex, shall be signed, and its contents certified as accurate, by the competent judicial authority in the issuing State that ordered the measure.
2. The certificate must be translated into the official language or one of the official languages of the executing State.
3. Any Member State may, either when this Framework Decision is adopted or at a later date, state in a declaration deposited with the General Secretariat of the Council that it will accept a translation in one or more other official languages of the institutions of the European Communities.

Article 10. 1. The transmission referred to in Article 4:
(a) shall be accompanied by a request for the evidence to be transferred to the issuing State; or
(b) shall be accompanied by a request for confiscation requiring either enforcement of a confiscation order that has been issued in the issuing State or confiscation in the executing State and subsequent enforcement of any such order; or
(c) shall contain an instruction in the certificate that the property shall remain in the executing State pending a request referred to in (a) or (b). The issuing State shall indicate in the certificate the (estimated) date for submission of this request. Article 6(2) shall apply.
2. Requests referred to in paragraph 1(a) and (b) shall be submitted by the issuing State and processed by the executing State in accordance with the rules applicable to mutual assistance in criminal matters and the rules applicable to international cooperation relating to confiscation.
3. However, by way of derogation from the rules on mutual assistance referred to in paragraph 2, the executing State may not refuse requests referred to under paragraph 1(a) on grounds of absence of double criminality, where the requests concern the offences referred to in Article 3(2) and those offences are punishable in the issuing State by a prison sentence of at least three years.

Article 11. 1. Member States shall put in place the necessary arrangements to ensure that any interested party, including bona fide third parties, have legal remedies without suspensive effect against a freezing order executed pursuant to Article 5, in order to preserve their legitimate interests; the action shall be brought before a court in the issuing State or in the executing State in accordance with the national law of each.
2. The substantive reasons for issuing the freezing order can be challenged only in an action brought before a court in the issuing State.
3. If the action is brought in the executing State, the judicial authority of the issuing State shall be informed thereof and of the grounds of the action, so that it can submit the arguments that it deems necessary. It shall be informed of the outcome of the action.
4. The issuing and executing States shall take the necessary measures to facilitate the exercise of the right to bring an action mentioned in paragraph 1, in particular by providing adequate information to interested parties.
5. The issuing State shall ensure that any time limits for bringing an action mentioned in paragraph 1 are applied in a way that guarantees the possibility of an effective legal remedy for the interested parties.

Article 12. 1. Without prejudice to Article 11(2), where the executing State under its law is responsible for injury caused to one of the parties mentioned in Article 11 by the execution of a freezing order transmitted to it pursuant to Article 4, the issuing State shall reimburse to the executing State any sums paid in damages by virtue of that responsibility to the said party except if, and to the extent that, the injury or any part of it is exclusively due to the conduct of the executing State.
2. Paragraph 1 is without prejudice to the national law of the Member States on claims by natural or legal persons for compensation of damage.

Title III. Final Provisions

Article 13. This Framework Decision shall apply to Gibraltar.

Article 14. 1. Member States shall take the necessary measures to comply with the provisions of this Framework Decision before 2 August 2005.
2. By the same date Member States shall transmit to the General Secretariat of the Council and to the Commission the text of the provisions transposing into their national law the obligations imposed on them under this Framework Decision. On the basis of a report established using this information and a written report by the Commission, the Council shall, before 2 August 2006, assess the extent to which Member States have complied with the provisions of this Framework Decision.

3. The General Secretariat of the Council shall notify Member States and the Commission of the declarations made pursuant to Article 9(3).

Article 15. This Framework Decision shall enter into force on the day of its publication in the Official Journal of the European Union.

PART IV

Human Rights Law

HUMANR

Convention for the Protection of Human Rights and Fundamental Freedoms, Rome, 4 November 1950, as last amended by Protocol 14 (1 June 2010).

Preamble
The governments signatory hereto, being members of the Council of Europe, Considering the Universal Declaration of Human Rights proclaimed by the General Assembly of the United Nations on 10 December 1948; Considering that this Declaration aims at securing the universal and effective recognition and observance of the Rights therein declared;
Considering that the aim of the Council of Europe is the achievement of greater unity between its members and that one of the methods by which that aim is to be pursued is the maintenance and further realisation of human rights and fundamental freedoms;
Reaffirming their profound belief in those fundamental freedoms which are the foundation of justice and peace in the world and are best maintained on the one hand by an effective political democracy and on the other by a common understanding and observance of the human rights upon which they depend;
Being resolved, as the governments of European countries which are likeminded and have a common heritage of political traditions, ideals, freedom and the rule of law, to take the first steps for the collective enforcement of certain of the rights stated in the Universal Declaration,
Have agreed as follows:

Article 1. The High Contracting Parties shall secure to everyone within their jurisdiction the rights and freedoms defined in Section I of this Convention.

Section I. Rights and freedoms

Article 2. (1) Everyone's right to life shall be protected by law. No one shall be deprived of his life intentionally save in the execution of a sentence of a court following his conviction of a crime for which this penalty is provided by law.
(2) Deprivation of life shall not be regarded as inflicted in contravention of this Article when it results from the use of force which is no more than abso-lutely necessary:
(a) in defence of any person from unlawful violence;
(b) in order to effect a lawful arrest or to prevent the escape of a person lawfully detained;
(c) in action lawfully taken for the purpose of quelling a riot or insurrection.

Article 3. No one shall be subjected to torture or to inhuman or degrading treatment or punishment.

Article 4. (1) No one shall be held in slavery or servitude.
(2) No one shall be required to perform forced or compulsory labour.
(3) For the purpose of this Article the term "forced or compulsory labour" shall not include:
(a) any work required to be done in the ordinary course of detention imposed according to the provisions of Article 5 of this Convention or during conditional release from such detention;
(b) any service of a military character or, in case of conscientious objectors in countries where they are recognised, service exacted instead of compulsory military service;
(c) any service exacted in case of an emergency or calamity threatening the life or well-being of the community;
(d) any work or service which forms part of normal civic obligations.

Article 5. (1) Everyone has the right to liberty and security of person. No one shall be deprived of his liberty save in the following cases and in accordance with a procedure prescribed by law:
(a) the lawful detention of a person after conviction by a competent court;
(b) the lawful arrest or detention of a person for non-compliance with the lawful order of a court or in order to secure the fulfilment of any obligation prescribed by law;
(c) the lawful arrest or detention of a person effected for the purpose of bringing him before the competent legal authority on reasonable suspicion of having committed an offence or when it is reasonably considered necessary to prevent his committing an offence or fleeing after having done so;
(d) the detention of a minor by lawful order for the purpose of educational supervision or his lawful detention for the purpose of bringing him before the competent legal authority;

(e) the lawful detention of persons for the prevention of the spreading of infectious diseases, of persons of unsound mind, alcoholics or drug addicts or vagrants;
(f) the lawful arrest or detention of a person to prevent his effecting an unauthorised entry into the country or of a person against whom action is being taken with a view to deportation or extradition.
(2) Everyone who is arrested shall be informed promptly, in a language which he understands, of the reasons for his arrest and of any charge against him.
(3) Everyone arrested or detained in accordance with the provisions of paragraph 1 (c) of this Article shall be brought promptly before a judge or other officer authorised by law to exercise judicial power and shall be entitled to trial within a reasonable time or to release pending trial. Release may be conditioned by guarantees to appear for trial.
(4) Everyone who is deprived of his liberty by arrest or detention shall be entitled to take proceedings by which the lawfulness of his detention shall be decided speedily by a court and his release ordered if the detention is not lawful.
(5) Everyone who has been the victim of arrest or detention in contravention of the provisions of this Article shall have an enforceable right to compensation.

Article 6. (1) In the determination of his civil rights and obligations or of any criminal charge against him, everyone is entitled to a fair and public hearing within a reasonable time by an independent and impartial tribunal established by law. Judgment shall be pronounced publicly but the press and public may be excluded from all or part of the trial in the interests of morals, public order or national security in a democratic society, where the interests of juveniles or the protection of the private life of the parties so require, or to the extent strictly necessary in the opinion of the court in special circumstances where publicity would prejudice the interests of justice.
(2) Everyone charged with a criminal offence shall be presumed innocent until proved guilty according to law.
(3) Everyone charged with a criminal offence has the following minimum rights:
(a) to be informed promptly, in a language which he understands and in detail, of the nature and cause of the accusation against him;
(b) to have adequate time and facilities for the preparation of his defence;
(c) to defend himself in person or through legal assistance of his own choosing or, if he has not sufficient means to pay for legal assistance, to be given it free when the interests of justice so require;
(d) to examine or have examined witnesses against him and to obtain the attendance and examination of witnesses on his behalf under the same conditions as witnesses against him;
(e) to have the free assistance of an interpreter if he cannot understand or speak the language used in court.

Article 7. (1) No one shall be held guilty of any criminal offence on account of any act or omission which did not constitute a criminal offence under national or international law at the time when it was committed. Nor shall a heavier penalty be imposed than the one that was applicable at the time the criminal offence was committed.
(2) This Article shall not prejudice the trial and punishment of any person for any act or omission which, at the time when it was committed, was criminal according to the general principles of law recognised by civilised nations.

Article 8. (1) Everyone has the right to respect for his private and family life, his home and his correspondence.
(2) There shall be no interference by a public authority with the exercise of this right except such as is in accordance with the law and is necessary in a democratic society in the interests of national security, public safety or the economic well-being of the country, for the prevention of disorder or crime, for the protection of health or morals, or for the protection of the rights and freedoms of others.

Article 9. (1) Everyone has the right to freedom of thought, conscience and religion; this right includes freedom to change his religion or belief and freedom, either alone or in community with others and in public or private, to manifest his religion or belief, in worship, teaching, practice and observance.
(2) Freedom to manifest one's religion or beliefs shall be subject only to such limitations as are prescribed by law and are necessary in a democratic society in the interests of public safety, for the protection of public order, health or morals, or for the protection of the rights and freedoms of others.

Article 10. (1) Everyone has the right to freedom of expression. This right shall include freedom to hold opinions and to receive and impart information and ideas without interference by public authority and regardless of frontiers. This Article shall not prevent States from requiring the licensing of broadcasting, television or cinema enterprises.

(2) The exercise of these freedoms, since it carries with it duties and responsibilities, may be subject to such formalities, conditions, restrictions or penalties as are prescribed by law and are necessary in a democratic society, in the interests of national security, territorial integrity or public safety, for the prevention of disorder or crime, for the protection of health or morals, for the protection of the reputation or rights of others, for preventing the disclosure of information received in confidence, or for maintaining the authority and im-partiality of the judiciary.

Article 11. (1) Everyone has the right to freedom of peaceful assembly and to freedom of association with others, including the right to form and to join trade unions for the protection of his interests.
(2) No restrictions shall be placed on the exercise of these rights other than such as are prescribed by law and are necessary in a democratic society in the interests of national security or public safety, for the prevention of disorder or crime, for the protection of health or morals or for the protection of the rights and freedoms of others. This Article shall not prevent the imposition of lawful restrictions on the exercise of these rights by members of the armed forces, of the police or of the administration of the State.

Article 12. Men and women of marriageable age have the right to marry and to found a family, according to the national laws governing the exercise of this right.

Article 13. Everyone whose rights and freedoms as set forth in this Convention are violated shall have an effective remedy before a national authority notwithstanding that the violation has been committed by persons acting in an official capacity.

Article 14. The enjoyment of the rights and freedoms set forth in this Convention shall be secured without discrimination on any ground such as sex, race, colour, language, religion, political or other opinion, national or social origin, association with a national minority, property, birth or other status.

Article 15. (1) In time of war or other public emergency threatening the life of the nation any High Contracting Party may take measures derogating from its obligations under this Convention to the extent strictly required by the exigencies of the situation, provided that such measures are not inconsistent with its other obligations under international law.
(2) No derogation from Article 2, except in respect of deaths resulting from lawful acts of war, or from Articles 3, 4 § 1 and 7 shall be made under this provision.
(3) Any High Contracting Party availing itself of this right of derogation shall keep the Secretary General of the Council of Europe fully informed of the measures which it has taken and the reasons therefor. It shall also inform the Secretary General of the Council of Europe when such measures have ceased to operate and the provisions of the Convention are again being fully executed.

Article 16. Nothing in Articles 10, 11 and 14 shall be regarded as preventing the High Contracting Parties from imposing restrictions on the political activity of aliens.

Article 17. Nothing in this Convention may be interpreted as implying for any State, group or person any right to engage in any activity or perform any act aimed at the destruction of any of the rights and freedoms set forth herein or at their limitation to a greater extent than is provided for in the Convention.

Article 18. The restrictions permitted under this Convention to the said rights and freedoms shall not be applied for any purpose other than those for which they have been prescribed.

Section II. European Court of Human Rights

Article 19. To ensure the observance of the engagements undertaken by the High Contracting Parties in the Convention and the Protocols thereto, there shall be set up a European Court of Human Rights, hereinafter referred to as "the Court". It shall function on a permanent basis.

Article 20. The Court shall consist of a number of judges equal to that of the High Contracting Parties.

Article 21. (1) The judges shall be of high moral character and must either possess the qualifications required for appointment to high judicial office or be jurisconsults of recognised competence.
(2) The judges shall sit on the Court in their individual capacity.

(3) During their term of office the judges shall not engage in any activity which is incompatible with their independence, impartiality or with the demands of a full-time office; all questions arising from the application of this paragraph shall be decided by the Court.

Article 22. The judges shall be elected by the Parliamentary Assembly with respect to each High Contracting Party by a majority of votes cast from a list of three candidates nominated by the High Contracting Party.

Article 23. (1) The judges shall be elected for a period of nine years. They may not be re-elected.
(2) The terms of office of judges shall expire when they reach the age of 70.
(3) The judges shall hold office until replaced. They shall, however, continue to deal with such cases as they already have under consideration.
(4) No judge may be dismissed from office unless the other judges decide by a majority of two-thirds that that judge has ceased to fulfil the required conditions.

Article 24. (1) The Court shall have a Registry, the functions and organisation of which shall be laid down in the rules of the Court.
(2) When sitting in a single-judge formation, the Court shall be assisted by rapporteurs who shall function under the authority of the President of the Court. They shall form part of the Court's Registry.

Article 25. The plenary Court shall
(a) elect its President and one or two Vice-Presidents for a period of three years; they may be re-elected;
(b) set up Chambers, constituted for a fixed period of time;
(c) elect the Presidents of the Chambers of the Court; they may be re-elected;
(d) adopt the rules of the Court;
(e) elect the Registrar and one or more Deputy Registrars;
(f) make any request under Article 26 § 2.

Article 26. (1) To consider cases brought before it, the Court shall sit in a single-judge formation, in Committees of three judges, in Chambers of seven judges and in a Grand Chamber of seventeen judges. The Court's Chambers shall set up Committees for a fixed period of time.
(2) At the request of the plenary Court, the Committee of Ministers may, by a unanimous decision and for a fixed period, reduce to five the number of judges of the Chambers.
(3) When sitting as a single judge, a judge shall not examine any application against the High Contracting Party in respect of which that judge has been elected.
(4) There shall sit as an ex officio member of the Chamber and the Grand Chamber the judge elected in respect of the High Contracting Party concerned. If there is none or if that judge is unable to sit, a person chosen by the President of the Court from a list submitted in advance by that Party shall sit in the capacity of judge.
(5) The Grand Chamber shall also include the President of the Court, the Vice-Presidents, the Presidents of the Chambers and other judges chosen in accordance with the rules of the Court. When a case is referred to the Grand Chamber under Article 43, no judge from the Chamber which rendered the judgment shall sit in the Grand Chamber, with the exception of the President of the Chamber and the judge who sat in respect of the High Contracting Party concerned.

Article 27. (1) A single judge may declare inadmissible or strike out of the Court's list of cases an application submitted under Article 34, where such a decision can be taken without further examin-ation.
(2) The decision shall be final.
(3) If the single judge does not declare an application inadmissible or strike it out, that judge shall forward it to a Committee or to a Chamber for further examination.

Article 28. (1) In respect of an application sub-mitted under Article 34, a Committee may, by a unanimous vote,
(a) declare it inadmissible or strike it out of its list of cases, where such decision can be taken without further examination; or
(b) declare it admissible and render at the same time a judgment on the merits, if the underlying question in the case, concerning the interpretation or the application of the Convention or the Protocols thereto, is already the subject of well-established case-law of the Court.
(2) Decisions and judgments under paragraph 1 shall be final.
(3) If the judge elected in respect of the High Contracting Party concerned is not a member of the Committee, the Committee may at any stage of the proceedings invite that judge to take the place of one of the members of the

Committee, having regard to all relevant factors, including whether that Party has contested the application of the pro-cedure under paragraph 1 (b).

Article 29. (1) If no decision is taken under Article 27 or 28, or no judgment rendered under Article 28, a Chamber shall decide on the admissibility and merits of individual applications submitted under Article 34. The decision on admissibility may be taken separately.
(2) A Chamber shall decide on the admissibility and merits of inter-State applications submitted under Article 33. The decision on admissibility shall be taken separately unless the Court, in exceptional cases, decides otherwise.

Article 30. Where a case pending before a Chamber raises a serious question affecting the interpretation of the Convention or the Protocols thereto, or where the resolution of a question before the Chamber might have a result inconsistent with a judgment previously delivered by the Court, the Chamber may. at any time before it has rendered its judgment, relinquish jurisdiction in favour of the Grand Chamber, unless one of the parties to the case objects.

Article 31. The Grand Chamber shall
(a) determine applications submitted either under Article 33 or Article 34 when a Chamber has relinquished jurisdiction under Article 30 or when the case has been referred to it under Art-icle 43;
(b) decide on issues referred to the Court by the Committee of Ministers in accordance with Article 46 § 4; and
(c) consider requests for advisory opinions submitted under Article 47.

Article 32. (1) The jurisdiction of the Court shall extend to all matters concerning the interpretation and application of the Convention and the Protocols thereto which are referred to it as provided in Articles 33, 34, 46 and 47.
(2) In the event of dispute as to whether the Court has jurisdiction, the Court shall decide.

Article 33. Any High Contracting Party may refer to the Court any alleged breach of the provisions of the Convention and the Protocols thereto by another High Contracting Party.

Article 34. The Court may receive applications from any person, non-governmental organisa-tion or group of individuals claiming to be the victim of a violation by one of the High Contracting Parties of the rights set forth in the Convention or the Protocols thereto. The High Contracting Parties undertake not to hinder in any way the effective exercise of this right.

Article 35. (1) The Court may only deal with the matter after all domestic remedies have been exhausted, according to the generally recognised rules of inter-national law, and within a period of six months from the date on which the final decision was taken.
(2) The Court shall not deal with any application submitted under Article 34 that
(a) is anonymous; or
(b) is substantially the same as a matter that has already been examined by the Court or has already been submitted to another procedure of international investigation or settlement and contains no relevant new infor-mation.
(3) The Court shall declare inadmissible any individual application submitted under Article 34 if it considers that:
(a) the application is incompatible with the provisions of the Convention or the Protocols thereto, manifestly ill-founded, or an abuse of the right of individual application; or
(b) the applicant has not suffered a significant disadvantage, unless respect for human rights as defined in the Convention and the Protocols thereto requires an examination of the application on the merits and provided that no case may be rejected on this ground which has not been duly considered by a domestic tribunal.
(4) The Court shall reject any application which it considers inadmis-sible under this Article. It may do so at any stage of the proceedings.

Article 36. (1) In all cases before a Chamber or the Grand Chamber, a High Contracting Party one of whose nationals is an applicant shall have the right to submit written comments and to take part in hearings.
(2) The President of the Court may, in the interest of the proper administration of justice, invite any High Contracting Party which is not a party to the proceedings or any person concerned who is not the applicant to submit written comments or take part in hearings.
(3) In all cases before a Chamber or the Grand Chamber, the Council of Europe Commissioner for Human Rights may submit written comments and take part in hearings.

Article 37. (1) The Court may at any stage of the proceedings decide to strike an appli-cation out of its list of cases where the circumstances lead to the conclusion that
(a) the applicant does not intend to pursue his application; or
(b) the matter has been resolved; or
(c) for any other reason established by the Court, it is no longer justified to continue the examination of the application.
However, the Court shall continue the examination of the application if respect for human rights as defined in the Convention and the Protocols thereto so requires.
(2) The Court may decide to restore an application to its list of cases if it considers that the circumstances justify such a course.

Article 38. The Court shall examine the case together with the representatives of the parties and, if need be, undertake an investigation, for the effective conduct of which the High Contracting Parties concerned shall furnish all necessary facilities.

Article 39. (1) At any stage of the proceedings, the Court may place itself at the disposal of the parties concerned with a view to securing a friendly settlement of the matter on the basis of respect for human rights as defined in the Convention and the Protocols thereto.
(2) Proceedings conducted under para-graph 1 shall be confidential.
(3) If a friendly settlement is effected, the Court shall strike the case out of its list by means of a decision which shall be confined to a brief statement of the facts and of the solution reached.
(4) This decision shall be transmitted to the Committee of Ministers, which shall supervise the execution of the terms of the friendly settlement as set out in the decision.

Article 40. (1) Hearings shall be in public unless the Court in exceptional circumstances decides otherwise.
(2) Documents deposited with the Registrar shall be accessible to the public unless the President of the Court decides otherwise.

Article 41. If the Court finds that there has been a violation of the Convention or the Protocols thereto, and if the internal law of the High Contracting Party concerned allows only partial reparation to be made, the Court shall, if necessary, afford just satisfaction to the injured party.

Article 42. Judgments of Chambers shall become final in accordance with the provisions of Article 44 § 2.

Article 43. (1) Within a period of three months from the date of the judgment of the Chamber, any party to the case may, in exceptional cases, request that the case be referred to the Grand Chamber.
(2) A panel of five judges of the Grand Chamber shall accept the request if the case raises a serious question affecting the interpretation or application of the Convention or the Protocols thereto, or a serious issue of general importance.
(3) If the panel accepts the request, the Grand Chamber shall decide the case by means of a judgment.

Article 44. (1) The judgment of the Grand Chamber shall be final.
(2) The judgment of a Chamber shall become final
(a) when the parties declare that they will not request that the case be referred to the Grand Chamber; or
(b) three months after the date of the judgment, if reference of the case to the Grand Chamber has not been requested; or
(c) when the panel of the Grand Chamber rejects the request to refer under Article 43.
(3) The final judgment shall be pub-lished.

Article 45. (1) Reasons shall be given for judgments as well as for decisions declaring applications admissible or inadmissible.
(2) If a judgment does not represent, in whole or in part, the unanimous opinion of the judges, any judge shall be entitled to deliver a separate opinion.

Article 46. (1). The High Contracting Parties under-take to abide by the final judgment of the Court in any case to which they are parties.
(2) The final judgment of the Court shall be transmitted to the Committee of Ministers, which shall supervise its execution.

(3) If the Committee of Ministers considers that the supervision of the execution of a final judgment is hindered by a problem of interpretation of the judgment, it may refer the matter to the Court for a ruling on the question of interpretation. A referral decision shall require a majority vote of two thirds of the representatives entitled to sit on the Committee.
(4) If the Committee of Ministers considers that a High Contracting Party refuses to abide by a final judgment in a case to which it is a party, it may, after serving formal notice on that Party and by decision adopted by a majority vote of two-thirds of the representatives entitled to sit on the Committee, refer to the Court the question whether that Party has failed to fulfil its obligation under paragraph 1.
(5) If the Court finds a violation of paragraph 1, it shall refer the case to the Committee of Ministers for consideration of the measures to be taken. If the Court finds no violation of paragraph 1, it shall refer the case to the Committee of Ministers, which shall close its examination of the case.

Article 47. (1) The Court may, at the request of the Committee of Ministers, give advisory opinions on legal questions concerning the interpretation of the Convention and the Protocols thereto.
(2) Such opinions shall not deal with any question relating to the content or scope of the rights or freedoms defined in Section I of the Convention and the Protocols thereto, or with any other question which the Court or the Committee of Ministers might have to consider in consequence of any such proceedings as could be instituted in accordance with the Convention.
(3) Decisions of the Committee of Ministers to request an advisory opinion of the Court shall require a majority vote of the representatives entitled to sit on the Committee.

Article 48. The Court shall decide whether a request for an advisory opinion submitted by the Committee of Ministers is within its competence as defined in Article 47.

Article 49. (1) Reasons shall be given for advisory opinions of the Court.
(2) If the advisory opinion does not represent, in whole or in part, the unanimous opinion of the judges, any judge shall be entitled to deliver a separate opinion.
(3) Advisory opinions of the Court shall be communicated to the Committee of Ministers.

Article 50. The expenditure on the Court shall be borne by the Council of Europe.

Article 51. The judges shall be entitled, during the exercise of their functions, to the privileges and immunities provided for in Article 40 of the Statute of the Council of Europe and in the agreements made thereunder.

Article 52. On receipt of a request from the Secretary General of the Council of Europe any High Contracting Party shall furnish an explanation of the manner in which its internal law ensures the effective implementation of any of the provisions of the Convention.

Article 53. Nothing in this Convention shall be construed as limiting or derogating from any of the human rights and funda-mental freedoms which may be ensured under the laws of any High Contracting Party or under any other agreement to which it is a party.

Article 54. Nothing in this Convention shall prejudice the powers conferred on the Committee of Ministers by the Statute of the Council of Europe.

Article 55. The High Contracting Parties agree that, except by special agreement, they will not avail themselves of treaties, conventions or declarations in force between them for the purpose of submitting, by way of petition, a dispute arising out of the interpretation or application of this Convention to a means of settlement other than those provided for in this Convention.

Article 56. (1) Any State may at the time of its ratification or at any time thereafter declare by notification addressed to the Secretary General of the Council of Europe that the present Convention shall, subject to paragraph 4 of this Article, extend to all or any of the territories for whose international relations it is responsible.
(2) The Convention shall extend to the territory or territories named in the notification as from the thirtieth day after the receipt of this notification by the Secretary General of the Council of Europe.
(3) The provisions of this Convention shall be applied in such territories with due regard, however, to local require-ments.

(4) Any State which has made a declaration in accordance with para-graph 1 of this Article may at any time thereafter declare on behalf of one or more of the territories to which the declaration relates that it accepts the competence of the Court to receive applications from individuals, non-governmental organisations or groups of individuals as provided by Article 34 of the Convention.

Article 57. (1) Any State may, when signing this Convention or when depositing its instrument of ratification, make a reservation in respect of any particular provision of the Convention to the extent that any law then in force in its territory is not in conformity with the provision. Reservations of a general character shall not be permitted under this Article.
(2) Any reservation made under this Article shall contain a brief statement of the law concerned.

Article 58. (1) A High Contracting Party may denounce the present Convention only after the expiry of five years from the date on which it became a party to it and after six months' notice contained in a notification addressed to the Secretary General of the Council of Europe, who shall inform the other High Contracting Parties.
(2) Such a denunciation shall not have the effect of releasing the High
Contracting Party concerned from its obligations under this Convention in respect of any act which, being capable of constituting a violation of such obligations, may have been performed by it before the date at which the denunciation became effective.
(3) Any High Contracting Party which shall cease to be a member of the Council of Europe shall cease to be a party to this Convention under the same conditions.
(4) The Convention may be denounced in accordance with the provisions of the preceding paragraphs in respect of any territory to which it has been declared to extend under the terms of Article 56.

Article 59. (1) This Convention shall be open to the signature of the members of the Council of Europe. It shall be ratified. Ratifications shall be deposited with the Secretary General of the Council of Europe.
(2) The European Union may accede to this Convention.
(3) The present Convention shall come into force after the deposit of ten instruments of ratification.
(4) As regards any signatory ratifying subsequently, the Convention shall come into force at the date of the deposit of its instrument of ratification.
(5) The Secretary General of the Council of Europe shall notify all the members of the Council of Europe of the entry into force of the Convention, the names of the High Contracting Parties who have ratified it, and the deposit of all instruments of ratification which may be effected subsequently.

Protocol (No. 1) to the Convention for the Protection of Human Rights and Fundamental Freedoms. Paris, 20 March 1952.

The governments signatory hereto, being members of the Council of Europe,
Being resolved to take steps to ensure the collective enforcement of certain rights and freedoms other than those already included in Section I of the Convention for the Protection of Human Rights and Fundamental Freedoms signed at Rome on 4 November 1950 (hereinafter referred to as 'the Convention'),
Have agreed as follows:

Article 1. Every natural or legal person is entitled to the peaceful enjoyment of his possessions. No one shall be deprived of his possessions except in the public interest and subject to the conditions provided for by law and by the general principles of international law.
The preceding provisions shall not, however, in any way impair the right of a State to enforce such laws as it deems necessary to control the use of property in accordance with the general interest or to secure the payment of taxes or other contributions or penalties.

Article 2. No person shall be denied the right to education. In the exercise of any functions which it assumes in relation to education and to teaching, the State shall respect the right of parents to ensure such education and teaching in conformity with their own religious and philosophical convictions.

Article 3. The High Contracting Parties undertake to hold free elections at reasonable intervals by secret ballot, under conditions which will ensure the free expression of the opinion of the people in the choice of the legislature.

[Articles 4 – 6 are omitted.]

Protocol No. 4 to the Convention for the Protection of Human Rights and Fundamental Freedoms securing certain rights and freedoms other than those already included in the Convention and in the first Protocol thereto. Strasbourg, 16 September 1963.

[The Preamble is omitted.]

Article 1. No one shall be deprived of his liberty merely on the ground of inability to fulfil a contractual obligation.

Article 2. (1) Everyone lawfully within the territory of a State shall, within that territory,
have the right to liberty of movement and freedom to choose his residence.
(2) Everyone shall be free to leave any country, including his own.
(3) No restrictions shall be placed on the exercise of these rights other than such as are in accordance with law and are necessary in a democratic society in the interests of national security or public safety, for the maintenance of ordre public, for the prevention of crime, for the protection of health or morals, or for the protection of the rights and freedoms of others.
(4) The rights set forth in paragraph 1 may also be subject, in particular areas, to restrictions imposed in accordance with law and justified by the public interest in a democratic society.

Article 3. (1) No one shall be expelled, by means either of an individual or of a collective measure, from the territory of the State of which he is a national.
(2) No one shall be deprived of the right to enter the territory of the state of which he is a national.

Article 4. Collective expulsion of aliens is prohibited.

[Articles 5 – 7 are omitted.]

Protocol No. 6 to the Convention for the Protection of Human Rights and Fundamental Freedoms concerning the abolition of the death penalty. Strasbourg, 28 April 1983.

[The Preamble is omitted.]

Article 1. The death penalty shall be abolished. No-one shall be condemned to such penalty or executed.

Article 2. A State may make provision in its law for the death penalty in respect of acts committed in time of war or of imminent threat of war; such penalty shall be applied only in the instances laid down in the law and in accordance with its provisions. The State shall communicate to the Secretary General of the Council of Europe the relevant provisions of that law.

[Articles 3 – 9 are omitted.]

Protocol No. 7 to the Convention for the Protection of Human Rights and Fundamental Freedoms. Strasbourg, 22 November 1984.

[The Preamble is omitted.]

Article 1. (1) An alien lawfully resident in the territory of a State shall not be expelled therefrom except in pursuance of a decision reached in accordance with law and shall be allowed:
a. to submit reasons against his expulsion,
b. to have his case reviewed, and
c. to be represented for these purposes before the competent authority or a person or persons designated by that authority.
(2) An alien may be expelled before the exercise of his rights under paragraph 1.a, b and c of this Article, when such expulsion is necessary in the interests of public order or is grounded on reasons of national security.

Article 2. (1) Everyone convicted of a criminal offence by a tribunal shall have the right to have his conviction or sentence reviewed by a higher tribunal. The exercise of this right, including the grounds on which it may be exercised, shall be governed by law.
(2) This right may be subject to exceptions in regard to offences of a minor character, as prescribed by law, or in cases in which the person concerned was tried in the first instance by the highest tribunal or was convicted following an appeal against acquittal.

Article 3. When a person has by a final decision been convicted of a criminal offence and when subsequently his conviction has been reversed, or he has been pardoned, on the ground that a new or newly discovered fact shows conclusively that there has been a miscarriage of justice, the
person who has suffered punishment as a result of such conviction shall be compensated according to the law or the practice of the State concerned, unless it is proved that the non-disclosure of the unknown fact in time is wholly or partly attributable to him.

Article 4. (1) No one shall be liable to be tried or punished again in criminal proceedings under the jurisdiction of the same State for an offence for which he has already been finally acquitted or convicted in accordance with the law and penal procedure of that State.
(2) The provisions of the preceding paragraph shall not prevent the reopening of the case in accordance with the law and penal procedure of the State concerned, if there is evidence of new or newly discovered facts, or if there has been a fundamental defect in the previous proceedings, which could affect the outcome of the case.
(3) No derogation from this Article shall be made under Article 15 of the Convention.

Article 5. Spouses shall enjoy equality of rights and responsibilities of a private law character between them, and in their relations with their children, as to marriage, during marriage and in the event of its dissolution. This Article shall not prevent States from taking such measures as are
necessary in the interests of the children.

[Articles 6 – 10 are omitted.]

Protocol No. 12 to the Convention for the Protection of Human Rights and Fundamental Freedoms. Rome, 4 November 2000.

[The Preamble is omitted.]

Article 1. (1) The enjoyment of any right set forth by law shall be secured without discrimination on any ground such as sex, race, colour, language, religion, political or other opinion, national or social origin, association with a national minority, property, birth or other status.
(2) No one shall be discriminated against by any public authority on any ground such as those mentioned in paragraph 1.

[Articles 2 – 6 are omitted.]

Protocol No. 13 to the Convention for the Protection of Human Rights and Fundamental Freedoms Concerning the abolition of the death penalty in all circumstances. Vilnius, 3 May 2002.

[The Preamble is omitted.]

Article 1. The death penalty shall be abolished. No one shall be condemned to such penalty or executed.

[Articles 2 – 8 are omitted.]

European Court of Human Rights: Rules of Court of 1 June 2010. Selected provisions: Rule 1 and Title II.

The European Court of Human Rights,
Having regard to the Convention for the Protection of Human Rights and Fundamental Freedoms and the Protocols thereto,
Makes the present Rules:

Rule 1. For the purposes of these Rules unless the context otherwise requires:
(a) the term "Convention" means the Convention for the Protection of Human Rights and Fundamental Freedoms and the Protocols thereto;
(b) the expression "plenary Court" means the European Court of Human Rights sitting in plenary session;
(c) the expression "Grand Chamber" means the Grand Chamber of seventeen judges constituted in pursuance of Article 26 § 1 of the Convention;
(d) the term "Section" means a Chamber set up by the plenary Court for a fixed period in pursuance of Article 25 (b) of the Convention and the expression "President of the Section" means the judge elected by the plenary Court in pursuance of Article 25 (c) of the Convention as President of such a Section;
(e) the term "Chamber" means any Chamber of seven judges constituted in pursuance of Article 26 § 1 of the Convention and the expression "President of the Chamber" means the judge presiding over such a "Chamber";
(f) the term "Committee" means a Committee of three judges set up in pursuance of Article 26 § 1 of the Convention and the expression "President of the Committee" means the judge presiding over such a "Committee";
(g) the expression "single-judge formation" means a single judge sitting in accordance with Article 26 § 1 of the Convention;
(h) the term "Court" means either the plenary Court, the Grand Chamber, a Section, a Chamber, a Committee, a single judge or the panel of five judges referred to in Article 43 § 2 of the Convention;
(i) the expression "ad hoc judge" means any person chosen in pursuance of Article 26 § 4 of the Convention and in accordance with Rule 29 to sit as a member of the Grand Chamber or as a member of a Chamber;
(j) the terms "judge" and "judges" mean the judges elected by the Parliamentary Assembly of the Council of Europe or ad hoc judges;
(k) the expression "Judge Rapporteur" means a judge appointed to carry out the tasks provided for in Rules 48 and 49;
(l) the term "non-judicial rapporteur" means a member of the Registry charged with assisting the single-judge formations provided for in Article 24 § 2 of the Convention;
(m) the term "delegate" means a judge who has been appointed to a delegation by the Chamber and the expression "head of the delegation" means the delegate appointed by the Chamber to lead its delegation;
(n) the term "delegation" means a body composed of delegates, Registry members and any other person appointed by the Chamber to assist the delegation;
(o) the term "Registrar" denotes the Registrar of the Court or the Registrar of a Section according to the context;
(p) the terms "party" and "parties" mean
– the applicant or respondent Contracting Parties;
– the applicant (the person, non-governmental organisation or group of individuals) that lodged a complaint under Article 34 of the Convention;
(q) the expression "third party" means any Contracting Party or any person concerned or the Council of Europe Commissioner for Human Rights who, as provided for in Article 36 §§ 1, 2 and 3 of the Convention, has exercised the right to submit written comments and take part in a hearing, or has been invited to do so;
(r) the terms "hearing" and "hearings" mean oral proceedings held on the admissibility and/or merits of an application or in connection with a request for revision or an advisory opinion, a request for interpretation by a party or by the Committee of Ministers, or a question whether there has been a failure to fulfil an obligation which may be referred to the Court by virtue of Article 46 § 4 of the Convention;
(s) the expression "Committee of Ministers" means the Committee of Ministers of the Council of Europe;
(t) the terms "former Court" and "Commission" mean respectively the European Court and European Commission of Human Rights set up under former Article 19 of the Convention.

[Title I is omitted.]

PART IV. HUMAN RIGHTS LAW

Title II. Procedure

Chapter I. General rules

Rule 31. The provisions of this Title shall not prevent the Court from derogating from them for the consideration of a particular case after having consulted the parties where appropriate.

Rule 32. The President of the Court may issue practice directions, notably in relation to such matters as appearance at hearings and the filing of pleadings and other documents.

Rule 33. (1) All documents deposited with the Registry by the parties or by any third party in connection with an application, except those deposited within the framework of friendly-settlement negotiations as provided for in Rule 62, shall be accessible to the public in accordance with arrangements determined by the Registrar, unless the President of the Chamber, for the reasons set out in paragraph 2 of this Rule, decides otherwise, either of his or her own motion or at the request of a party or any other person concerned.
(2) Public access to a document or to any part of it may be restricted in the interests of morals, public order or national security in a democratic society, where the interests of juveniles or the protection of the private life of the parties or of any person concerned so require, or to the extent strictly necessary in the opinion of the President of the Chamber in special circumstances where publicity would prejudice the interests of justice.
(3) Any request for confidentiality made under paragraph 1 of this Rule must include reasons and specify whether it is requested that all or part of the documents be inaccessible to the public.
(4) Decisions and judgments given by a Chamber shall be accessible to the public. Decisions and judgments given by a Committee, including decisions covered by the proviso to Rule 53 § 5, shall be accessible to the public. The Court shall periodically make accessible to the public general information about decisions taken by single-judge formations pursuant to Rule 52A § 1 and by Committees in application of Rule 53 § 5.

Rule 34. (1) The official languages of the Court shall be English and French.
(2) In connection with applications lodged under Article 34 of the Convention, and for as long as no Contracting Party has been given notice of such an application in accordance with these Rules, all communications with and oral and written submissions by applicants or their representatives, if not in one of the Court's official languages, shall be in one of the official languages of the Contracting Parties. If a Contracting Party is informed or given notice of an application in accordance with these Rules, the application and any accompanying documents shall be communicated to that State in the language in which they were lodged with the Registry by the applicant.
(3) (a) All communications with and oral and written submissions by applicants or their representatives in respect of a hearing, or after notice of an application has been given to a Contracting Party, shall be in one of the Court's official languages, unless the President of the Chamber grants leave for the continued use of the official language of a Contracting Party.
(b) If such leave is granted, the Registrar shall make the necessary arrangements for the interpretation and translation into English or French of the applicant's oral and written submissions respectively, in full or in part, where the President of the Chamber considers it to be in the interests of the proper conduct of the proceedings.
(c) Exceptionally the President of the Chamber may make the grant of leave subject to the condition that the applicant bear all or part of the costs of making such arrangements.
(d) Unless the President of the Chamber decides otherwise, any decision made under the foregoing provisions of this paragraph shall remain valid in all subsequent proceedings in the case, including those in respect of requests for referral of the case to the Grand Chamber and requests for interpretation or revision of a judgment under Rules 73, 79 and 80 respectively.
(4) (a) All communications with and oral and written submissions by a Contracting Party which is a party to the case shall be in one of the Court's official languages. The President of the Chamber may grant the Contracting Party concerned leave to use one of its official languages for its oral and written submissions.
(b) If such leave is granted, it shall be the responsibility of the requesting Party
(i) to file a translation of its written submissions into one of the official languages of the Court within a time-limit to be fixed by the President of the Chamber. Should that Party not file the translation within that time-limit, the Registrar may make the necessary arrangements for such translation, the expenses to be charged to the requesting Party;
(ii) to bear the expenses of interpreting its oral submissions into English or French. The Registrar shall be responsible for making the necessary arrangements for such interpretation.

(c) The President of the Chamber may direct that a Contracting Party which is a party to the case shall, within a specified time, provide a translation into, or a summary in, English or French of all or certain annexes to its written submissions or of any other relevant document, or of extracts therefrom.
(d) The preceding sub-paragraphs of this paragraph shall also apply, *mutatis mutandis*, to third-party intervention under Rule 44 and to the use of a non-official language by a third party.
(5) The President of the Chamber may invite the respondent Contracting Party to provide a translation of its written submissions in the or an official language of that Party in order to facilitate the applicant's understanding of those submissions.
(6) Any witness, expert or other person appearing before the Court may use his or her own language if he or she does not have sufficient knowledge of either of the two official languages. In that event the Registrar shall make the necessary arrangements for interpreting or translation.

Rule 35. The Contracting Parties shall be represented by Agents, who may have the assistance of advocates or advisers.

Rule 36. (1) Persons, non-governmental organisations or groups of individuals may initially present applications under Article 34 of the Convention themselves or through a representative.
(2) Following notification of the application to the respondent Contracting Party under Rule 54 § 2 (b), the applicant should be represented in accordance with paragraph 4 of this Rule, unless the President of the Chamber decides otherwise.
(3) The applicant must be so represented at any hearing decided on by the Chamber, unless the President of the Chamber exceptionally grants leave to the applicant to present his or her own case, subject, if necessary, to being assisted by an advocate or other approved representative.
(4) (a) The representative acting on behalf of the applicant pursuant to paragraphs 2 and 3 of this Rule shall be an advocate authorised to practise in any of the Contracting Parties and resident in the territory of one of them, or any other person approved by the President of the Chamber.
(b) In exceptional circumstances and at any stage of the procedure, the President of the Chamber may, where he or she considers that the circumstances or the conduct of the advocate or other person appointed under the preceding sub-paragraph so warrant, direct that the latter may no longer represent or assist the applicant and that the applicant should seek alternative representation.
(5) (a) The advocate or other approved representative, or the applicant in person who seeks leave to present his or her own case, must even if leave is granted under the following sub-paragraph have an adequate understanding of one of the Court's official languages.
(b) If he or she does not have sufficient proficiency to express himself or herself in one of the Court's official languages, leave to use one of the official languages of the Contracting Parties may be given by the President of the Chamber under Rule 34 § 3.

Rule 37. (1) Communications or notifications addressed to the Agents or advocates of the parties shall be deemed to have been addressed to the parties.
(2) If, for any communication, notification or summons addressed to persons other than the Agents or advocates of the parties, the Court considers it necessary to have the assistance of the Government of the State on whose territory such communication, notification or summons is to have effect, the President of the Court shall apply directly to that Government in order to obtain the necessary facilities.

Rule 38. (1) No written observations or other documents may be filed after the time-limit set by the President of the Chamber or the Judge Rapporteur, as the case may be, in accordance with these Rules. No written observations or other documents filed outside that time-limit or contrary to any practice direction issued under Rule 32 shall be included in the case file unless the President of the Chamber decides otherwise.
(2) For the purposes of observing the time-limit referred to in paragraph 1 of this Rule, the material date is the certified date of dispatch of the document or, if there is none, the actual date of receipt at the Registry.

Rule 38A. Questions of procedure requiring a decision by the Chamber shall be considered simultaneously with the examination of the case, unless the President of the Chamber decides otherwise.

Rule 39. (1) The Chamber or, where appropriate, its President may, at the request of a party or of any other person concerned, or of its own motion, indicate to the parties any interim measure which it considers should be adopted in the interests of the parties or of the proper conduct of the proceedings before it.
(2) Notice of these measures shall be given to the Committee of Ministers.

(3) The Chamber may request information from the parties on any matter connected with the implementation of any interim measure it has indicated.

Rule 40. In any case of urgency the Registrar, with the authorisation of the President of the Chamber, may, without prejudice to the taking of any other procedural steps and by any available means, inform a Contracting Party concerned in an application of the introduction of the application and of a summary of its objects.

Rule 41. In determining the order in which cases are to be dealt with, the Court shall have regard to the importance and urgency of the issues raised on the basis of criteria fixed by it. The Chamber, or its President, may, however, derogate from these criteria so as to give priority to a particular application.

Rule 42. (1) The Chamber may, either at the request of the parties or of its own motion, order the joinder of two or more applications.
(2) The President of the Chamber may, after consulting the parties, order that the proceedings in applications assigned to the same Chamber be conducted simultaneously, without prejudice to the decision of the Chamber on the joinder of the applications

Rule 43. (1) The Court may at any stage of the proceedings decide to strike an application out of its list of cases in accordance with Article 37 of the Convention.
(2) When an applicant Contracting Party notifies the Registrar of its intention not to proceed with the case, the Chamber may strike the application out of the Court's list under Article 37 of the Convention if the other Contracting Party or Parties concerned in the case agree to such discontinuance.
(3) If a friendly settlement is effected, the application shall be struck out of the Court's list of cases by means of a decision. In accordance with Article 39 § 4 of the Convention, this decision shall be transmitted to the Committee of Ministers, which shall supervise the execution of the terms of the friendly settlement as set out in the decision. In other cases provided for in Article 37 of the Convention, the decision to strike out an application which has been declared admissible shall be given in the form of a judgment. The President of the Chamber shall forward that judgment, once it has become final, to the Committee of Ministers in order to allow the latter to supervise, in accordance with Article 46 § 2 of the Convention, the execution of any undertakings which may have been attached to the discontinuance or solution of the matter.
(4) When an application has been struck out, the costs shall be at the discretion of the Court. If an award of costs is made in a decision striking out an application which has not been declared admissible, the President of the Chamber shall forward the decision to the Committee of Ministers.
(5) The Court may restore an application to its list if it considers that exceptional circumstances justify such a course.

Rule 44. (1) (a) When notice of an application lodged under Article 34 of the Convention is given to the respondent Contracting Party under Rules 53 § 2 or 54 § 2 (b), a copy of the application shall at the same time be transmitted by the Registrar to any other Contracting Party one of whose nationals is an applicant in the case. The Registrar shall similarly notify any such Contracting Party of a decision to hold an oral hearing in the case.
(b) If a Contracting Party wishes to exercise its right under Article 36 § 1 of the Convention to submit written comments or to take part in a hearing, it shall so advise the Registrar in writing not later than twelve weeks after the transmission or notification referred to in the preceding sub-paragraph. Another time-limit may be fixed by the President of the Chamber for exceptional reasons.
(2) If the Commissioner for Human Rights wishes to exercise the right under Article 36 § 3 of the Convention to submit written observations or take part in a hearing, he or she shall so advise the Registrar in writing not later than twelve weeks after transmission of the application to the respondent Contracting Party or notification to it of the decision to hold an oral hearing. Another time-limit may be fixed by the President of the Chamber for exceptional reasons. Should the Commissioner for Human Rights be unable to take part in the proceedings before the Court himself, he or she shall indicate the name of the person or persons from his or her Office whom he or she has appointed to represent him. He or she may be assisted by an advocate.
(3) (a) Once notice of an application has been given to the respondent Contracting Party under Rules 51 § 1 or 54 § 2 (b), the President of the Chamber may, in the interests of the proper administration of justice, as provided in Article 36 § 2 of the Convention, invite, or grant leave to, any Contracting Party which is not a party to the proceedings, or any person concerned who is not the applicant, to submit written comments or, in exceptional cases, to take part in a hearing.
(b) Requests for leave for this purpose must be duly reasoned and submitted in writing in one of the official languages as provided in Rule 34 § 4 not later than twelve weeks after notice of the application has been given to

the respondent Contracting Party. Another time-limit may be fixed by the President of the Chamber for exceptional reasons.
(4) (a) In cases to be considered by the Grand Chamber, the periods of time prescribed in the preceding paragraphs shall run from the notification to the parties of the decision of the Chamber under Rule 72 § 1 to relinquish jurisdiction in favour of the Grand Chamber or of the decision of the panel of the Grand Chamber under Rule 73 § 2 to accept a request by a party for referral of the case to the Grand Chamber.
(b) The time-limits laid down in this Rule may exceptionally be extended by the President of the Chamber if sufficient cause is shown.
(5) Any invitation or grant of leave referred to in paragraph 3 (a) of this Rule shall be subject to any conditions, including time-limits, set by the President of the Chamber. Where such conditions are not complied with, the President may decide not to include the comments in the case file or to limit participation in the hearing to the extent that he or she considers appropriate.
(6) Written comments submitted under this Rule shall be drafted in one of the official languages as provided in Rule 34 § 4. They shall be forwarded by the Registrar to the parties to the case, who shall be entitled, subject to any conditions, including time-limits, set by the President of the Chamber, to file written observations in reply or, where appropriate, to reply at the hearing.

Rule 44A. The parties have a duty to cooperate fully in the conduct of the proceedings and, in particular, to take such action within their power as the Court considers necessary for the proper administration of justice. This duty shall also apply to a Contracting Party not party to the proceedings where such cooperation is necessary.

Rule 44B. Where a party fails to comply with an order of the Court concerning the conduct of the proceedings, the President of the Chamber may take any steps which he or she considers appropriate.

Rule 44C. (1) Where a party fails to adduce evidence or provide information requested by the Court or to divulge relevant information of its own motion or otherwise fails to participate effectively in the proceedings, the Court may draw such inferences as it deems appropriate.
(2) Failure or refusal by a respondent Contracting Party to participate effectively in the proceedings shall not, in itself, be a reason for the Chamber to discontinue the examination of the application.

Rule 44D. If the representative of a party makes abusive, frivolous, vexatious, misleading or prolix submissions, the President of the Chamber may exclude that representative from the proceedings, refuse to accept all or part of the submissions or make any other order which he or she considers it appropriate to make, without prejudice to Article 35 § 3 of the Convention.

Rule 44E. In accordance with Article 37 § 1 (a) of the Convention, if an applicant Contracting Party or an individual applicant fails to pursue the application, the Chamber may strike the application out of the Court's list under Rule 43.

Chapter II. Institution of proceedings

Rule 45. (1) Any application made under Articles 33 or 34 of the Convention shall be submitted in writing and shall be signed by the applicant or by the applicant's representative.
(2) Where an application is made by a non-governmental organisation or by a group of individuals, it shall be signed by those persons competent to represent that organisation or group. The Chamber or Committee concerned shall determine any question as to whether the persons who have signed an application are competent to do so.
(3) Where applicants are represented in accordance with Rule 36, a power of attorney or written authority to act shall be supplied by their representative or representatives.

Rule 46. Any Contracting Party or Parties intending to bring a case before the Court under Article 33 of the Convention shall file with the Registry an application setting out
(a) the name of the Contracting Party against which the application is made;
(b) a statement of the facts;
(c) a statement of the alleged violation(s) of the Convention and the relevant arguments;
(d) a statement on compliance with the admissibility criteria (exhaustion of domestic remedies and the six-month rule) laid down in Article 35 § 1 of the Convention;

Part IV. Human Rights Law

(e) the object of the application and a general indication of any claims for just satisfaction made under Article 41 of the Convention on behalf of the alleged injured party or parties; and
(f) the name and address of the person or persons appointed as Agent; and accompanied by
(g) copies of any relevant documents and in particular the decisions, whether judicial or not, relating to the object of the application.

Rule 47. (1) Any application under Article 34 of the Convention shall be made on the application form provided by the Registry, unless the President of the Section concerned decides otherwise. It shall set out
(a) the name, date of birth, nationality, sex, occupation and address of the applicant;
(b) the name, occupation and address of the representative, if any;
(c) the name of the Contracting Party or Parties against which the application is made;
(d) a succinct statement of the facts;
(e) a succinct statement of the alleged violation(s) of the Convention and the relevant arguments;
(f) a succinct statement on the applicant's compliance with the admissibility criteria (exhaustion of domestic remedies and the six-month rule) laid down in Article 35 § 1 of the Convention; and
(g) the object of the application; and be accompanied by
(h) copies of any relevant documents and in particular the decisions, whether judicial or not, relating to the object of the application.
(2) Applicants shall furthermore
(a) provide information, notably the documents and decisions referred to in paragraph 1 (h) of this Rule, enabling it to be shown that the admissibility criteria (exhaustion of domestic remedies and the six-month rule) laid down in Article 35 § 1 of the Convention have been satisfied; and
(b) indicate whether they have submitted their complaints to any other procedure of international investigation or settlement.
(3) Applicants who do not wish their identity to be disclosed to the public shall so indicate and shall submit a statement of the reasons justifying such a departure from the normal rule of public access to information in proceedings before the Court. The President of the Chamber may authorise anonymity or grant it of his or her own motion.
(4) Failure to comply with the requirements set out in paragraphs 1 and 2 of this Rule may result in the application not being examined by the Court.
(5) The date of introduction of the application for the purposes of Article 35 § 1 of the Convention shall as a general rule be considered to be the date of the first communication from the applicant setting out, even summarily, the subject matter of the application, provided that a duly completed application form has been submitted within the time-limits laid down by the Court. The Court may for good cause nevertheless decide that a different date shall be considered to be the date of introduction.
(6) Applicants shall keep the Court informed of any change of address and of all circumstances relevant to the application.

Chapter III. Judge rapporteurs

Rule 48. (1) Where an application is made under Article 33 of the Convention, the Chamber constituted to consider the case shall designate one or more of its judges as Judge Rapporteur(s), who shall submit a report on admissibility when the written observations of the Contracting Parties concerned have been received.
(2) The Judge Rapporteur(s) shall submit such reports, drafts and other documents as may assist the Chamber and its President in carrying out their functions.

Rule 49. (1) Where the material submitted by the applicant is on its own sufficient to disclose that the application is inadmissible or should be struck out of the list, the application shall be considered by a single-judge formation unless there is some special reason to the contrary.
(2) Where an application is made under Article 34 of the Convention and its examination by a Chamber or a Committee exercising the functions attributed to it under Rule 53 § 2 seems justified, the President of the Section to which the case has been assigned shall designate a judge as Judge Rapporteur, who shall examine the application.
(3) In their examination of applications, Judge Rapporteurs
(a) may request the parties to submit, within a specified time, any factual information, documents or other material which they consider to be relevant;

(b) shall, subject to the President of the Section directing that the case be considered by a Chamber or a Committee, decide whether the application is to be considered by a single-judge formation, by a Committee or by a Chamber;
(c) shall submit such reports, drafts and other documents as may assist the Chamber or the Committee or the respective President in carrying out their functions.

Rule 50. Where a case has been submitted to the Grand Chamber either under Article 30 or under Article 43 of the Convention, the President of the Grand Chamber shall designate as Judge Rapporteur(s) one or, in the case of an inter-State application, one or more of its members.

Chapter IV. Proceedings on Admissibility

Inter-State applications

Rule 51. (1) When an application is made under Article 33 of the Convention, the President of the Court shall immediately give notice of the application to the respondent Contracting Party and shall assign the application to one of the Sections.
(2) In accordance with Rule 26 § 1 (a), the judges elected in respect of the applicant and respondent Contracting Parties shall sit as *ex officio* members of the Chamber constituted to consider the case. Rule 30 shall apply if the application has been brought by several Contracting Parties or if applications with the same object brought by several Contracting Parties are being examined jointly under Rule 42.
(3) On assignment of the case to a Section, the President of the Section shall constitute the Chamber in accordance with Rule 26 § 1 and shall invite the respondent Contracting Party to submit its observations in writing on the admissibility of the application. The observations so obtained shall be communicated by the Registrar to the applicant Contracting Party, which may submit written observations in reply.
(4) Before the ruling on the admissibility of the application is given, the Chamber or its President may decide to invite the Parties to submit further observations in writing.
(5) A hearing on the admissibility shall be held if one or more of the Contracting Parties concerned so requests or if the Chamber so decides of its own motion.
(6) Before fixing the written and, where appropriate, oral procedure, the President of the Chamber shall consult the Parties.

Individual applications

Rule 52. (1) Any application made under Article 34 of the Convention shall be assigned to a Section by the President of the Court, who in so doing shall endeavour to ensure a fair distribution of cases between the Sections.
(2) The Chamber of seven judges provided for in Article 26 § 1 of the Convention shall be constituted by the President of the Section concerned in accordance with Rule 26 § 1.
(3) Pending the constitution of a Chamber in accordance with paragraph 2 of this Rule, the President of the Section shall exercise any powers conferred on the President of the Chamber by these Rules.

Rule 52A. (1) In accordance with Article 27 of the Convention, a single judge may declare inadmissible or strike out of the Court's list of cases an application submitted under Article 34, where such a decision can be taken without further examination. The decision shall be final. The applicant shall be informed of the decision by letter.
(2) In accordance with Article 26 § 3 of the Convention, a single judge may not examine any application against the Contracting Party in respect of which that judge has been elected.
(3) If the single judge does not take a decision of the kind provided for in the first paragraph of the present Rule, that judge shall forward the application to a Committee or to a Chamber for further examination.

Rule 53. (1) In accordance with Article 28 § 1 (a) of the Convention, the Committee may, by a unanimous vote and at any stage of the proceedings, declare an application inadmissible or strike it out of the Court's list of cases where such a decision can be taken without further examination.
(2) If the Committee is satisfied, in the light of the parties' observations received pursuant to Rule 54 § 2 (b), that the case falls to be examined in accordance with the procedure under Article 28 § 1 (b) of the Convention, it shall, by a unanimous vote, adopt a judgment including its decision on admissibility and, as appropriate, on just satisfaction.

(3) If the judge elected in respect of the Contracting Party concerned is not a member of the Committee, the Committee may at any stage of the proceedings before it, by a unanimous vote, invite that judge to take the place of one of its members, having regard to all relevant factors, including whether that Party has contested the application of the procedure under Article 28 § 1 (b) of the Convention.
(4) Decisions and judgments under Article 28 § 1 of the Convention shall be final.
(5) The applicant, as well as the Contracting Parties concerned where these have previously been involved in the application in accordance with the present Rules, shall be informed of the decision of the Committee pursuant to Article 28 § 1 (a) of the Convention by letter, unless the Committee decides otherwise
(6) If no decision or judgment is adopted by the Committee, the application shall be forwarded to the Chamber constituted under Rule 52 § 2 to examine the case.
(7) The provisions of Rules 79 to 81 shall apply, mutatis mutandis, to proceedings before a Committee.

Rule 54. (1) The Chamber may at once declare the application inadmissible or strike it out of the Court's list of cases.
(2) Alternatively, the Chamber or its President may decide to
(a) request the parties to submit any factual information, documents or other material considered by the Chamber or its President to be relevant;
(b) give notice of the application to the respondent Contracting Party and invite that Party to submit written observations on the application and, upon receipt thereof, invite the applicant to submit observations in reply;
(c) invite the parties to submit further observations in writing.
(3) Before taking its decision on the admissibility, the Chamber may decide, either at the request of a party or of its own motion, to hold a hearing if it considers that the discharge of its functions under the Convention so requires. In that event, unless the Chamber shall exceptionally decide otherwise, the parties shall also be invited to address the issues arising in relation to the merits of the application.

Rule 54A. (1) When giving notice of the application to the responding Contracting Party pursuant to Rule 54 § 2 (b), the Chamber may also decide to examine the admissibility and merits at the same time in accordance with Article 29 § 1 of the Convention. The parties shall be invited to include in their observations any submissions concerning just satisfaction and any proposals for a friendly settlement. The conditions laid down in Rules 60 and 62 shall apply, mutatis mutandis. The Court may, however, decide at any stage, if necessary, to take a separate decision on admissibility.
(2) If no friendly settlement or other solution is reached and the Chamber is satisfied, in the light of the parties' arguments, that the case is admissible and ready for a determination on the merits, it shall immediately adopt a judgment including the Chamber's decision on admissibility, save in cases where it decides to take such a decision separately.

Inter-State and individual applications

Rule 55. Any plea of inadmissibility must, in so far as its character and the circumstances permit, be raised by the respondent Contracting Party in its written or oral observations on the admissibility of the application submitted as provided in Rule 51 or 54, as the case may be.

Rule 56. (1). The decision of the Chamber shall state whether it was taken unanimously or by a majority and shall be accompanied or followed by reasons.
(2) The decision of the Chamber shall be communicated by the Registrar to the applicant. It shall also be communicated to the Contracting Party or Parties concerned and to any third party, including the Commissioner for Human Rights, where these have previously been informed of the application in accordance with the present Rules. If a friendly settlement is effected, the decision to strike an application out of the list of cases shall be forwarded to the Committee of Ministers in accordance with Rule 43 § 3.

Rule 57. (1) Unless the Court decides that a decision shall be given in both official languages, all decisions of Chambers shall be given either in English or in French.
(2) Publication of such decisions in the official reports of the Court, as provided for in Rule 78, shall be in both official languages of the Court.

Chapter V. Proceedings after the Admission of an Application

Rule 58. (1) Once the Chamber has decided to admit an application made under Article 33 of the Convention, the President of the Chamber shall, after consulting the Contracting Parties concerned, lay down the time-limits for the filing of written observations on the merits and for the production of any further evidence. The President may however, with the agreement of the Contracting Parties concerned, direct that a written procedure is to be dispensed with.
(2) A hearing on the merits shall be held if one or more of the Contracting Parties concerned so requests or if the Chamber so decides of its own motion. The President of the Chamber shall fix the oral procedure.

Rule 59. (1) Once an application made under Article 34 of the Convention has been declared admissible, the Chamber or its President may invite the parties to submit further evidence and written observations.
(2) Unless decided otherwise, the parties shall be allowed the same time for submission of their observations.
(3) The Chamber may decide, either at the request of a party or of its own motion, to hold a hearing on the merits if it considers that the discharge of its functions under the Convention so requires.
(4) The President of the Chamber shall, where appropriate, fix the written and oral procedure.

Rule 60. (1) An applicant who wishes to obtain an award of just satisfaction under Article 41 of the Convention in the event of the Court finding a violation of his or her Convention rights must make a specific claim to that effect.
(2) The applicant must submit itemised particulars of all claims, together with any relevant supporting documents, within the time-limit fixed for the submission of the applicant's observations on the merits unless the President of the Chamber directs otherwise.
(3) If the applicant fails to comply with the requirements set out in the preceding paragraphs the Chamber may reject the claims in whole or in part.
(4) The applicant's claims shall be transmitted to the respondent Government for comment.

Rule 61. [Deleted].

Rule 62. (1) Once an application has been declared admissible, the Registrar, acting on the instructions of the Chamber or its President, shall enter into contact with the parties with a view to securing a friendly settlement of the matter in accordance with Article 39 § 1 of the Convention. The Chamber shall take any steps that appear appropriate to facilitate such a settlement.
(2) In accordance with Article 39 § 2 of the Convention, the friendly-settlement negotiations shall be confidential and without prejudice to the parties' arguments in the contentious proceedings. No written or oral communication and no offer or concession made in the framework of the attempt to secure a friendly settlement may be referred to or relied on in the contentious proceedings.
(3) If the Chamber is informed by the Registrar that the parties have agreed to a friendly settlement, it shall, after verifying that the settlement has been reached on the basis of respect for human rights as defined in the Convention and the Protocols thereto, strike the case out of the Court's list in accordance with Rule 43 § 3.
(4) Paragraphs 2 and 3 apply, mutatis mutandis, to the procedure under Rule 54A.

Chapter VI. Hearings

Rule 63. (1) Hearings shall be public unless, in accordance with paragraph 2 of this Rule, the Chamber in exceptional circumstances decides otherwise, either of its own motion or at the request of a party or any other person concerned.
(2) The press and the public may be excluded from all or part of a hearing in the interests of morals, public order or national security in a democratic society, where the interests of juveniles or the protection of the private life of the parties so require, or to the extent strictly necessary in the opinion of the Chamber in special circumstances where publicity would prejudice the interests of justice.
(3) Any request for a hearing to be held in camera made under paragraph 1 of this Rule must include reasons and specify whether it concerns all or only part of the hearing.

Rule 64. (1) The President of the Chamber shall organise and direct hearings and shall prescribe the order in which those appearing before the Chamber shall be called upon to speak.
(2) Any judge may put questions to any person appearing before the Chamber.

Part IV. Human Rights Law

Rule 65. Where a party or any other person due to appear fails or declines to do so, the Chamber may, provided that it is satisfied that such a course is consistent with the proper administration of justice, nonetheless proceed with the hearing.

Rules 66 to 69. [Deleted].

Rule 70. (1) If the President of the Chamber so directs, the Registrar shall be responsible for the making of a verbatim record of the hearing. Any such record shall include:
(a) the composition of the Chamber;
(b) a list of those appearing before the Chamber;
(c) the text of the submissions made, questions put and replies given;
(d) the text of any ruling delivered during the hearing.
(2) If all or part of the verbatim record is in a non-official language, the Registrar shall arrange for its translation into one of the official languages.
(3) The representatives of the parties shall receive a copy of the verbatim record in order that they may, subject to the control of the Registrar or the President of the Chamber, make corrections, but in no case may such corrections affect the sense and bearing of what was said. The Registrar shall lay down, in accordance with the instructions of the President of the Chamber, the time-limits granted for this purpose.
(4) The verbatim record, once so corrected, shall be signed by the President of the Chamber and the Registrar and shall then constitute certified matters of record.

Chapter VII. Proceedings before the Grand Chamber

Rule 71. (1) Any provisions governing proceedings before the Chambers shall apply, *mutatis mutandis*, to proceedings before the Grand Chamber.
(2) The powers conferred on a Chamber by Rules 54 § 3 and 59 § 3 in relation to the holding of a hearing may, in proceedings before the Grand Chamber, also be exercised by the President of the Grand Chamber.

Rule 72. (1) In accordance with Article 30 of the Convention, where a case pending before a Chamber raises a serious question affecting the interpretation of the Convention or the Protocols thereto or where the resolution of a question before it might have a result inconsistent with a judgment previously delivered by the Court, the Chamber may, at any time before it has rendered its judgment, relinquish jurisdiction in favour of the Grand Chamber, unless one of the parties to the case has objected in accordance with paragraph 2 of this Rule. Reasons need not be given for the decision to relinquish.
(2) The Registrar shall notify the parties of the Chamber's intention to relinquish jurisdiction. The parties shall have one month from the date of that notification within which to file at the Registry a duly reasoned objection. An objection which does not fulfil these conditions shall be considered invalid by the Chamber.

Rule 73. (1) In accordance with Article 43 of the Convention, any party to a case may exceptionally, within a period of three months from the date of delivery of the judgment of a Chamber, file in writing at the Registry a request that the case be referred to the Grand Chamber. The party shall specify in its request the serious question affecting the interpretation or application of the Convention or the Protocols thereto, or the serious issue of general importance, which in its view warrants consideration by the Grand Chamber.
(2) A panel of five judges of the Grand Chamber constituted in accordance with Rule 24 § 5 shall examine the request solely on the basis of the existing case file. It shall accept the request only if it considers that the case does raise such a question or issue. Reasons need not be given for a refusal of the request.
(3) If the panel accepts the request, the Grand Chamber shall decide the case by means of a judgment.

Chapter VIII. Judgments

Rule 74. (1) A judgment as referred to in Articles 28, 42 and 44 of the Convention shall contain
(a) the names of the President and the other judges constituting the Chamber or the Committee concerned, and the name of the Registrar or the Deputy Registrar;
(b) the dates on which it was adopted and delivered;
(c) a description of the parties;
(d) the names of the Agents, advocates or advisers of the parties;

(e) an account of the procedure followed;
(f) the facts of the case;
(g) a summary of the submissions of the parties;
(h) the reasons in point of law;
(i) the operative provisions;
(j) the decision, if any, in respect of costs;
(k) the number of judges constituting the majority;
(l) where appropriate, a statement as to which text is authentic.
(2) Any judge who has taken part in the consideration of the case by a Chamber or by the Grand Chamber shall be entitled to annex to the judgment either a separate opinion, concurring with or dissenting from that judgment, or a bare statement of dissent.

Rule 75. (1) Where the Chamber or the Committee finds that there has been a violation of the Convention or the Protocols thereto, it shall give in the same judgment a ruling on the application of Article 41 of the Convention if a specific claim has been submitted in accordance with Rule 60 and the question is ready for decision; if the question is not ready for decision, the Chamber or the Committee shall reserve it in whole or in part and shall fix the further procedure.
(2) For the purposes of ruling on the application of Article 41 of the Convention, the Chamber or the Committee shall, as far as possible, be composed of those judges who sat to consider the merits of the case. Where it is not possible to constitute the original Chamber or Committee, the President of the Section shall complete or compose the Chamber by drawing lots.
(3) The Chamber or the Committee may, when affording just satisfaction under Article 41 of the Convention, direct that if settlement is not made within a specified time, interest is to be payable on any sums awarded.
(4) If the Court is informed that an agreement has been reached between the injured party and the Contracting Party liable, it shall verify the equitable nature of the agreement and, where it finds the agreement to be equitable, strike the case out of the list in accordance with Rule 43 § 3.

Rule 76. (1) Unless the Court decides that a judgment shall be given in both official languages, all judgments shall be given either in English or in French.
(2) Publication of such judgments in the official reports of the Court, as provided for in Rule 78, shall be in both official languages of the Court.

Rule 77. (1) Judgments shall be signed by the President of the Chamber or the Committee and the Registrar.
(2) The judgment adopted by a Chamber may be read out at a public hearing by the President of the Chamber or by another judge delegated by him or her. The Agents and representatives of the parties shall be informed in due time of the date of the hearing. Otherwise, and in respect of judgments adopted by Committees, the notification provided for in paragraph 3 of this Rule shall constitute delivery of the judgment.
(3) The judgment shall be transmitted to the Committee of Ministers. The Registrar shall send copies to the parties, to the Secretary General of the Council of Europe, to any third party, including the Commissioner for Human Rights, and to any other person directly concerned. The original copy, duly signed and sealed, shall be placed in the archives of the Court.

Rule 78. In accordance with Article 44 § 3 of the Convention, final judgments of the Court shall be published, under the responsibility of the Registrar, in an appropriate form. The Registrar shall in addition be responsible for the publication of official reports of selected judgments and decisions and of any document which the President of the Court considers it useful to publish.

Rule 79. (1) A party may request the interpretation of a judgment within a period of one year following the delivery of that judgment.
(2) The request shall be filed with the Registry. It shall state precisely the point or points in the operative provisions of the judgment on which interpretation is required.
(3) The original Chamber may decide of its own motion to refuse the request on the ground that there is no reason to warrant considering it. Where it is not possible to constitute the original Chamber, the President of the Court shall complete or compose the Chamber by drawing lots.
(4) If the Chamber does not refuse the request, the Registrar shall communicate it to the other party or parties and shall invite them to submit any written comments within a time-limit laid down by the President of the Chamber. The President of the Chamber shall also fix the date of the hearing should the Chamber decide to hold one. The Chamber shall decide by means of a judgment.

Rule 80. (1) A party may, in the event of the discovery of a fact which might by its nature have a decisive influence and which, when a judgment was delivered, was unknown to the Court and could not reasonably have been known to that party, request the Court, within a period of six months after that party acquired knowledge of the fact, to revise that judgment.
(2) The request shall mention the judgment of which revision is requested and shall contain the information necessary to show that the conditions laid down in paragraph 1 of this Rule have been complied with. It shall be accompanied by a copy of all supporting documents. The request and supporting documents shall be filed with the Registry.
(3) The original Chamber may decide of its own motion to refuse the request on the ground that there is no reason to warrant considering it. Where it is not possible to constitute the original Chamber, the President of the Court shall complete or compose the Chamber by drawing lots.
(4) If the Chamber does not refuse the request, the Registrar shall communicate it to the other party or parties and shall invite them to submit any written comments within a time-limit laid down by the President of the Chamber. The President of the Chamber shall also fix the date of the hearing should the Chamber decide to hold one. The Chamber shall decide by means of a judgment.

Rule 81. Without prejudice to the provisions on revision of judgments and on restoration to the list of applications, the Court may, of its own motion or at the request of a party made within one month of the delivery of a decision or a judgment, rectify clerical errors, errors in calculation or obvious mistakes.

[The remaining Titles are omitted.]

Convention on the Rights of the Child, adopted and opened for signature, ratification and accession by General Assembly resolution 44/25 of 20 November 1989.

Preamble
The States Parties to the present Convention,
Considering that, in accordance with the principles proclaimed in the Charter of the United Nations, recognition of the inherent dignity and of the equal and inalienable rights of all members of the human family is the foundation of freedom, justice and peace in the world,
Bearing in mind that the peoples of the United Nations have, in the Charter, reaffirmed their faith in fundamental human rights and in the dignity and worth of the human person, and have determined to promote social progress and better standards of life in larger freedom,
Recognizing that the United Nations has, in the Universal Declaration of Human Rights and in the International Covenants on Human Rights, proclaimed and agreed that everyone is entitled to all the rights and freedoms set forth therein, without distinction of any kind, such as race, colour, sex, language, religion, political or other opinion, national or social origin, property, birth or other status,
Recalling that, in the Universal Declaration of Human Rights, the United Nations has proclaimed that childhood is entitled to special care and assistance,
Convinced that the family, as the fundamental group of society and the natural environment for the growth and well-being of all its members and particularly children, should be afforded the necessary protection and assistance so that it can fully assume its responsibilities within the community,
Recognizing that the child, for the full and harmonious development of his or her personality, should grow up in a family environment, in an atmosphere of happiness, love and understanding,
Considering that the child should be fully prepared to live an individual life in society, and brought up in the spirit of the ideals proclaimed in the Charter of the United Nations, and in particular in the spirit of peace, dignity, tolerance, freedom, equality and solidarity,
Bearing in mind that the need to extend particular care to the child has been stated in the Geneva Declaration of the Rights of the Child of 1924 and in the Declaration of the Rights of the Child adopted by the General Assembly on 20 November 1959 and recognized in the Universal Declaration of Human Rights, in the International Covenant on Civil and Political Rights (in particular in articles 23 and 24), in the International Covenant on Economic, Social and Cultural Rights (in particular in article 10) and in the statutes and relevant instruments of specialized agencies and international organizations concerned with the welfare of children,
Bearing in mind that, as indicated in the Declaration of the Rights of the Child, "the child, by reason of his physical and mental immaturity, needs special safeguards and care, including appropriate legal protection, before as well as after birth",
Recalling the provisions of the Declaration on Social and Legal Principles relating to the Protection and Welfare of Children, with Special Reference to Foster Placement and Adoption Nationally and Internationally; the United Nations Standard Minimum Rules for the Administration of Juvenile Justice (The Beijing Rules); and the Declaration on the Protection of Women and Children in Emergency and Armed Conflict, Recognizing that, in all countries in the world, there are children living in exceptionally difficult conditions, and that such children need special consideration,
Taking due account of the importance of the traditions and cultural values of each people for the protection and harmonious development of the child, Recognizing the importance of international co-operation for improving the living conditions of children in every country, in particular in the developing countries,
Have agreed as follows:

PART I.

Article 1. For the purposes of the present Convention, a child means every human being below the age of eighteen years unless under the law applicable to the child, majority is attained earlier.

Article 2. 1. States Parties shall respect and ensure the rights set forth in the present Convention to each child within their jurisdiction without discrimination of any kind, irrespective of the child's or his or her parent's or legal guardian's race, colour, sex, language, religion, political or other opinion, national, ethnic or social origin, property, disability, birth or other status.
2. States Parties shall take all appropriate measures to ensure that the child is protected against all forms of discrimination or punishment on the basis of the status, activities, expressed opinions, or beliefs of the child's parents, legal guardians, or family members.

Article 3. 1. In all actions concerning children, whether undertaken by public or private social welfare institutions, courts of law, administrative authorities or legislative bodies, the best interests of the child shall be a primary consideration.
2. States Parties undertake to ensure the child such protection and care as is necessary for his or her well-being, taking into account the rights and duties of his or her parents, legal guardians, or other individuals legally responsible for him or her, and, to this end, shall take all appropriate legislative and administrative measures.
3. States Parties shall ensure that the institutions, services and facilities responsible for the care or protection of children shall conform with the standards established by competent authorities, particularly in the areas of safety, health, in the number and suitability of their staff, as well as competent supervision.

Article 4. States Parties shall undertake all appropriate legislative, administrative, and other measures for the implementation of the rights recognized in the present Convention. With regard to economic, social and cultural rights, States Parties shall undertake such measures to the maximum extent of their available resources and, where needed, within the framework of international co-operation.

Article 5. States Parties shall respect the responsibilities, rights and duties of parents or, where applicable, the members of the extended family or community as provided for by local custom, legal guardians or other persons legally responsible for the child, to provide, in a manner consistent with the evolving capacities of the child, appropriate direction and guidance in the exercise by the child of the rights recognized in the present Convention.

Article 6. 1. States Parties recognize that every child has the inherent right to life.
2. States Parties shall ensure to the maximum extent possible the survival and development of the child.

Article 7. 1. The child shall be registered immediately after birth and shall have the right from birth to a name, the right to acquire a nationality and. as far as possible, the right to know and be cared for by his or her parents.
2. States Parties shall ensure the implementation of these rights in accordance with their national law and their obligations under the relevant international instruments in this field, in particular where the child would otherwise be stateless.

Article 8. 1. States Parties undertake to respect the right of the child to preserve his or her identity, including nationality, name and family relations as recognized by law without unlawful interference.
2. Where a child is illegally deprived of some or all of the elements of his or her identity, States Parties shall provide appropriate assistance and protection, with a view to re-establishing speedily his or her identity.

Article 9. 1. States Parties shall ensure that a child shall not be separated from his or her parents against their will, except when competent authorities subject to judicial review determine, in accordance with applicable law and procedures, that such separation is necessary for the best interests of the child. Such determination may be necessary in a particular case such as one involving abuse or neglect of the child by the parents, or one where the parents are living separately and a decision must be made as to the child's place of residence.
2. In any proceedings pursuant to paragraph 1 of the present article, all interested parties shall be given an opportunity to participate in the proceedings and make their views known.
3. States Parties shall respect the right of the child who is separated from one or both parents to maintain personal relations and direct contact with both parents on a regular basis, except if it is contrary to the child's best interests.
4. Where such separation results from any action initiated by a State Party, such as the detention, imprisonment, exile, deportation or death (including death arising from any cause while the person is in the custody of the State) of one or both parents or of the child, that State Party shall, upon request, provide the parents, the child or, if appropriate, another member of the family with the essential information concerning the whereabouts of the absent member(s) of the family unless the provision of the information would be detrimental to the well-being of the child. States Parties shall further ensure that the submission of such a request shall of itself entail no adverse consequences for the person(s) concerned.

Article 10. 1. In accordance with the obligation of States Parties under article 9, paragraph 1, applications by a child or his or her parents to enter or leave a State Party for the purpose of family reunification shall be dealt with by States Parties in a positive, humane and expeditious manner. States Parties shall further ensure that the submission of such a request shall entail no adverse consequences for the applicants and for the members of their family.

2. A child whose parents reside in different States shall have the right to maintain on a regular basis, save in exceptional circumstances personal relations and direct contacts with both parents. Towards that end and in accordance with the obligation of States Parties under article 9, paragraph 1, States Parties shall respect the right of the child and his or her parents to leave any country, including their own, and to enter their own country. The right to leave any country shall be subject only to such restrictions as are prescribed by law and which are necessary to protect the national security, public order (ordre public), public health or morals or the rights and freedoms of others and are consistent with the other rights recognized in the present Convention.

Article 11. 1. States Parties shall take measures to combat the illicit transfer and non-return of children abroad.
2. To this end, States Parties shall promote the conclusion of bilateral or multilateral agreements or accession to existing agreements.

Article 12. 1. States Parties shall assure to the child who is capable of forming his or her own views the right to express those views freely in all matters affecting the child, the views of the child being given due weight in accordance with the age and maturity of the child.
2. For this purpose, the child shall in particular be provided the opportunity to be heard in any judicial and administrative proceedings affecting the child, either directly, or through a representative or an appropriate body, in a manner consistent with the procedural rules of national law.

Article 13. 1. The child shall have the right to freedom of expression; this right shall include freedom to seek, receive and impart information and ideas of all kinds, regardless of frontiers, either orally, in writing or in print, in the form of art, or through any other media of the child's choice.
2. The exercise of this right may be subject to certain restrictions, but these shall only be such as are provided by law and are necessary:
(a) For respect of the rights or reputations of others; or
(b) For the protection of national security or of public order (ordre public), or of public health or morals.

Article 14. 1. States Parties shall respect the right of the child to freedom of thought, conscience and religion.
2. States Parties shall respect the rights and duties of the parents and, when applicable, legal guardians, to provide direction to the child in the exercise of his or her right in a manner consistent with the evolving capacities of the child.
3. Freedom to manifest one's religion or beliefs may be subject only to such limitations as are prescribed by law and are necessary to protect public safety, order, health or morals, or the fundamental rights and freedoms of others.

Article 15. 1. States Parties recognize the rights of the child to freedom of association and to freedom of peaceful assembly.
2. No restrictions may be placed on the exercise of these rights other than those imposed in conformity with the law and which are necessary in a democratic society in the interests of national security or public safety, public order (ordre public), the protection of public health or morals or the protection of the rights and freedoms of others.

Article 16. 1. No child shall be subjected to arbitrary or unlawful interference with his or her privacy, family, or correspondence, nor to unlawful attacks on his or her honour and reputation.
2. The child has the right to the protection of the law against such interference or attacks.

Article 17. States Parties recognize the important function performed by the mass media and shall ensure that the child has access to information and material from a diversity of national and international sources, especially those aimed at the promotion of his or her social, spiritual and moral well-being and physical and mental health. To this end, States Parties shall:
(a) Encourage the mass media to disseminate information and material of social and cultural benefit to the child and in accordance with the spirit of article 29;
(b) Encourage international co-operation in the production, exchange and dissemination of such information and material from a diversity of cultural, national and international sources;
(c) Encourage the production and dissemination of children's books;
(d) Encourage the mass media to have particular regard to the linguistic needs of the child who belongs to a minority group or who is indigenous;

(e) Encourage the development of appropriate guidelines for the protection of the child from information and material injurious to his or her well-being, bearing in mind the provisions of articles 13 and 18.

Article 18. 1. States Parties shall use their best efforts to ensure recognition of the principle that both parents have common responsibilities for the upbringing and development of the child. Parents or, as the case may be, legal guardians, have the primary responsibility for the upbringing and development of the child. The best interests of the child will be their basic concern.
2. For the purpose of guaranteeing and promoting the rights set forth in the present Convention, States Parties shall render appropriate assistance to parents and legal guardians in the performance of their child-rearing responsibilities and shall ensure the development of institutions, facilities and services for the care of children.
3. States Parties shall take all appropriate measures to ensure that children of working parents have the right to benefit from child-care services and facilities for which they are eligible.

Article 19. 1. States Parties shall take all appropriate legislative, administrative, social and educational measures to protect the child from all forms of physical or mental violence, injury or abuse, neglect or negligent treatment, maltreatment or exploitation, including sexual abuse, while in the care of parent(s), legal guardian(s) or any other person who has the care of the child.
2. Such protective measures should, as appropriate, include effective procedures for the establishment of social programmes to provide necessary support for the child and for those who have the care of the child, as well as for other forms of prevention and for identification, reporting, referral, investigation, treatment and follow-up of instances of child maltreatment described heretofore, and, as appropriate, for judicial involvement.

Article 20. 1. A child temporarily or permanently deprived of his or her family environment, or in whose own best interests cannot be allowed to remain in that environment, shall be entitled to special protection and assistance provided by the State.
2. States Parties shall in accordance with their national laws ensure alternative care for such a child.
3. Such care could include, inter alia, foster placement, kafalah of Islamic law, adoption or if necessary placement in suitable institutions for the care of children. When considering solutions, due regard shall be paid to the desirability of continuity in a child's upbringing and to the child's ethnic, religious, cultural and linguistic background.

Article 21. States Parties that recognize and/or permit the system of adoption shall ensure that the best interests of the child shall be the paramount consideration and they shall:
(a) Ensure that the adoption of a child is authorized only by competent authorities who determine, in accordance with applicable law and procedures and on the basis of all pertinent and reliable information, that the adoption is permissible in view of the child's status concerning parents, relatives and legal guardians and that, if required, the persons concerned have given their informed consent to the adoption on the basis of such counselling as may be necessary;
(b) Recognize that inter-country adoption may be considered as an alternative means of child's care, if the child cannot be placed in a foster or an adoptive family or cannot in any suitable manner be cared for in the child's country of origin;
(c) Ensure that the child concerned by inter-country adoption enjoys safeguards and standards equivalent to those existing in the case of national adoption;
(d) Take all appropriate measures to ensure that, in inter-country adoption, the placement does not result in improper financial gain for those involved in it;
(e) Promote, where appropriate, the objectives of the present article by concluding bilateral or multilateral arrangements or agreements, and endeavour, within this framework, to ensure that the placement of the child in another country is carried out by competent authorities or organs.

Article 22. 1. States Parties shall take appropriate measures to ensure that a child who is seeking refugee status or who is considered a refugee in accordance with applicable international or domestic law and procedures shall, whether unaccompanied or accompanied by his or her parents or by any other person, receive appropriate protection and humanitarian assistance in the enjoyment of applicable rights set forth in the present Convention and in other international human rights or humanitarian instruments to which the said States are Parties.
2. For this purpose, States Parties shall provide, as they consider appropriate, co-operation in any efforts by the United Nations and other competent intergovernmental organizations or non-governmental organizations cooperating with the United Nations to protect and assist such a child and to trace the parents or other members of the family of any refugee child in order to obtain information necessary for reunification with his or her family. In

cases where no parents or other members of the family can be found, the child shall be accorded the same protection as any other child permanently or temporarily deprived of his or her family environment for any reason, as set forth in the present Convention.

Article 23. 1. States Parties recognize that a mentally or physically disabled child should enjoy a full and decent life, in conditions which ensure dignity, promote self-reliance and facilitate the child's active participation in the community.
2. States Parties recognize the right of the disabled child to special care and shall encourage and ensure the extension, subject to available resources, to the eligible child and those responsible for his or her care, of assistance for which application is made and which is appropriate to the child's condition and to the circumstances of the parents or others caring for the child.
3. Recognizing the special needs of a disabled child, assistance extended in accordance with paragraph 2 of the present article shall be provided free of charge, whenever possible, taking into account the financial resources of the parents or others caring for the child, and shall be designed to ensure that the disabled child has effective access to and receives education, training, health care services, rehabilitation services, preparation for employment and recreation opportunities in a manner conducive to the child's achieving the fullest possible social integration and individual development, including his or her cultural and spiritual development.
4. States Parties shall promote, in the spirit of international cooperation, the exchange of appropriate information in the field of preventive health care and of medical, psychological and functional treatment of disabled children, including dissemination of and access to information concerning methods of rehabilitation, education and vocational services, with the aim of enabling States Parties to improve their capabilities and skills and to widen their experience in these areas. In this regard, particular account shall be taken of the needs of developing countries.

Article 24. 1. States Parties recognize the right of the child to the enjoyment of the highest attainable standard of health and to facilities for the treatment of illness and rehabilitation of health. States Parties shall strive to ensure that no child is deprived of his or her right of access to such health care services.
2. States Parties shall pursue full implementation of this right and, in particular, shall take appropriate measures:
(a) To diminish infant and child mortality;
(b) To ensure the provision of necessary medical assistance and health care to all children with emphasis on the development of primary health care;
(c) To combat disease and malnutrition, including within the framework of primary health care, through, inter alia, the application of readily available technology and through the provision of adequate nutritious foods and clean drinking-water, taking into consideration the dangers and risks of environmental pollution;
(d) To ensure appropriate pre-natal and post-natal health care for mothers;
(e) To ensure that all segments of society, in particular parents and children, are informed, have access to education and are supported in the use of basic knowledge of child health and nutrition, the advantages of breastfeeding, hygiene and environmental sanitation and the prevention of accidents;
(f) To develop preventive health care, guidance for parents and family planning education and services.
3. States Parties shall take all effective and appropriate measures with a view to abolishing traditional practices prejudicial to the health of children.
4. States Parties undertake to promote and encourage international co-operation with a view to achieving progressively the full realization of the right recognized in the present article. In this regard, particular account shall be taken of the needs of developing countries.

Article 25. States Parties recognize the right of a child who has been placed by the competent authorities for the purposes of care, protection or treatment of his or her physical or mental health, to a periodic review of the treatment provided to the child and all other circumstances relevant to his or her placement.

Article 26. 1. States Parties shall recognize for every child the right to benefit from social security, including social insurance, and shall take the necessary measures to achieve the full realization of this right in accordance with their national law.
2. The benefits should, where appropriate, be granted, taking into account the resources and the circumstances of the child and persons having responsibility for the maintenance of the child, as well as any other consideration relevant to an application for benefits made by or on behalf of the child.

Article 27. 1. States Parties recognize the right of every child to a standard of living adequate for the child's physical, mental, spiritual, moral and social development.

2. The parent(s) or others responsible for the child have the primary responsibility to secure, within their abilities and financial capacities, the conditions of living necessary for the child's development.
3. States Parties, in accordance with national conditions and within their means, shall take appropriate measures to assist parents and others responsible for the child to implement this right and shall in case of need provide material assistance and support programmes, particularly with regard to nutrition, clothing and housing.
4. States Parties shall take all appropriate measures to secure the recovery of maintenance for the child from the parents or other persons having financial responsibility for the child, both within the State Party and from abroad. In particular, where the person having financial responsibility for the child lives in a State different from that of the child, States Parties shall promote the accession to international agreements or the conclusion of such agreements, as well as the making of other appropriate arrangements.

Article 28. 1. States Parties recognize the right of the child to education, and with a view to achieving this right progressively and on the basis of equal opportunity, they shall, in particular:
(a) Make primary education compulsory and available free to all;
(b) Encourage the development of different forms of secondary education, including general and vocational education, make them available and accessible to every child, and take appropriate measures such as the introduction of free education and offering financial assistance in case of need;
(c) Make higher education accessible to all on the basis of capacity by every appropriate means;
(d) Make educational and vocational information and guidance available and accessible to all children;
(e) Take measures to encourage regular attendance at schools and the reduction of drop-out rates.
2. States Parties shall take all appropriate measures to ensure that school discipline is administered in a manner consistent with the child's human dignity and in conformity with the present Convention.
3. States Parties shall promote and encourage international cooperation in matters relating to education, in particular with a view to contributing to the elimination of ignorance and illiteracy throughout the world and facilitating access to scientific and technical knowledge and modern teaching methods. In this regard, particular account shall be taken of the needs of developing countries.

Article 29. 1. States Parties agree that the education of the child shall be directed to:
(a) The development of the child's personality, talents and mental and physical abilities to their fullest potential;
(b) The development of respect for human rights and fundamental freedoms, and for the principles enshrined in the Charter of the United Nations;
(c) The development of respect for the child's parents, his or her own cultural identity, language and values, for the national values of the country in which the child is living, the country from which he or she may originate, and for civilizations different from his or her own;
(d) The preparation of the child for responsible life in a free society, in the spirit of understanding, peace, tolerance, equality of sexes, and friendship among all peoples, ethnic, national and religious groups and persons of indigenous origin;
(e) The development of respect for the natural environment.
2. No part of the present article or article 28 shall be construed so as to interfere with the liberty of individuals and bodies to establish and direct educational institutions, subject always to the observance of the principle set forth in paragraph 1 of the present article and to the requirements that the education given in such institutions shall conform to such minimum standards as may be laid down by the State.

Article 30. In those States in which ethnic, religious or linguistic minorities or persons of indigenous origin exist, a child belonging to such a minority or who is indigenous shall not be denied the right, in community with other members of his or her group, to enjoy his or her own culture, to profess and practise his or her own religion, or to use his or her own language.

Article 31. 1. States Parties recognize the right of the child to rest and leisure, to engage in play and recreational activities appropriate to the age of the child and to participate freely in cultural life and the arts.
2. States Parties shall respect and promote the right of the child to participate fully in cultural and artistic life and shall encourage the provision of appropriate and equal opportunities for cultural, artistic, recreational and leisure activity.

Article 32. 1. States Parties recognize the right of the child to be protected from economic exploitation and from performing any work that is likely to be hazardous or to interfere with the child's education, or to be harmful to the child's health or physical, mental, spiritual, moral or social development.

2. States Parties shall take legislative, administrative, social and educational measures to ensure the implementation of the present article. To this end, and having regard to the relevant provisions of other international instruments, States Parties shall in particular:
(a) Provide for a minimum age or minimum ages for admission to employment;
(b) Provide for appropriate regulation of the hours and conditions of employment;
(c) Provide for appropriate penalties or other sanctions to ensure the effective enforcement of the present article.

Article 33. States Parties shall take all appropriate measures, including legislative, administrative, social and educational measures, to protect children from the illicit use of narcotic drugs and psychotropic substances as defined in the relevant international treaties, and to prevent the use of children in the illicit production and trafficking of such substances.

Article 34. States Parties undertake to protect the child from all forms of sexual exploitation and sexual abuse. For these purposes, States Parties shall in particular take all appropriate national, bilateral and multilateral measures to prevent:
(a) The inducement or coercion of a child to engage in any unlawful sexual activity;
(b) The exploitative use of children in prostitution or other unlawful sexual practices;
(c) The exploitative use of children in pornographic performances and materials.

Article 35. States Parties shall take all appropriate national, bilateral and multilateral measures to prevent the abduction of, the sale of or traffic in children for any purpose or in any form.

Article 36. States Parties shall protect the child against all other forms of exploitation prejudicial to any aspects of the child's welfare.

Article 37. States Parties shall ensure that:
(a) No child shall be subjected to torture or other cruel, inhuman or degrading treatment or punishment. Neither capital punishment nor life imprisonment without possibility of release shall be imposed for offences committed by persons below eighteen years of age;
(b) No child shall be deprived of his or her liberty unlawfully or arbitrarily. The arrest, detention or imprisonment of a child shall be in conformity with the law and shall be used only as a measure of last resort and for the shortest appropriate period of time;
(c) Every child deprived of liberty shall be treated with humanity and respect for the inherent dignity of the human person, and in a manner which takes into account the needs of persons of his or her age. In particular, every child deprived of liberty shall be separated from adults unless it is considered in the child's best interest not to do so and shall have the right to maintain contact with his or her family through correspondence and visits, save in exceptional circumstances;
(d) Every child deprived of his or her liberty shall have the right to prompt access to legal and other appropriate assistance, as well as the right to challenge the legality of the deprivation of his or her liberty before a court or other competent, independent and impartial authority, and to a prompt decision on any such action.

Article 38. 1. States Parties undertake to respect and to ensure respect for rules of international humanitarian law applicable to them in armed conflicts which are relevant to the child.
2. States Parties shall take all feasible measures to ensure that persons who have not attained the age of fifteen years do not take a direct part in hostilities.
3. States Parties shall refrain from recruiting any person who has not attained the age of fifteen years into their armed forces. In recruiting among those persons who have attained the age of fifteen years but who have not attained the age of eighteen years, States Parties shall endeavour to give priority to those who are oldest.
4. In accordance with their obligations under international humanitarian law to protect the civilian population in armed conflicts, States Parties shall take all feasible measures to ensure protection and care of children who are affected by an armed conflict.

Article 39. States Parties shall take all appropriate measures to promote physical and psychological recovery and social reintegration of a child victim of: any form of neglect, exploitation, or abuse; torture or any other form of cruel, inhuman or degrading treatment or punishment; or armed conflicts. Such recovery and reintegration shall take place in an environment which fosters the health, self-respect and dignity of the child.

Article 40. 1. States Parties recognize the right of every child alleged as, accused of, or recognized as having infringed the penal law to be treated in a manner consistent with the promotion of the child's sense of dignity and worth, which reinforces the child's respect for the human rights and fundamental freedoms of others and which takes into account the child's age and the desirability of promoting the child's reintegration and the child's assuming a constructive role in society.
2. To this end, and having regard to the relevant provisions of international instruments, States Parties shall, in particular, ensure that:
(a) No child shall be alleged as, be accused of, or recognized as having infringed the penal law by reason of acts or omissions that were not prohibited by national or international law at the time they were committed;
(b) Every child alleged as or accused of having infringed the penal law has at least the following guarantees:
(i) To be presumed innocent until proven guilty according to law;
(ii) To be informed promptly and directly of the charges against him or her, and, if appropriate, through his or her parents or legal guardians, and to have legal or other appropriate assistance in the preparation and presentation of his or her defence;
(iii) To have the matter determined without delay by a competent, independent and impartial authority or judicial body in a fair hearing according to law, in the presence of legal or other appropriate assistance and, unless it is considered not to be in the best interest of the child, in particular, taking into account his or her age or situation, his or her parents or legal guardians;
(iv) Not to be compelled to give testimony or to confess guilt; to examine or have examined adverse witnesses and to obtain the participation and examination of witnesses on his or her behalf under conditions of equality;
(v) If considered to have infringed the penal law, to have this decision and any measures imposed in consequence thereof reviewed by a higher competent, independent and impartial authority or judicial body according to law;
(vi) To have the free assistance of an interpreter if the child cannot understand or speak the language used;
(vii) To have his or her privacy fully respected at all stages of the proceedings.
3. States Parties shall seek to promote the establishment of laws, procedures, authorities and institutions specifically applicable to children alleged as, accused of, or recognized as having infringed the penal law, and, in particular:
(a) The establishment of a minimum age below which children shall be presumed not to have the capacity to infringe the penal law;
(b) Whenever appropriate and desirable, measures for dealing with such children without resorting to judicial proceedings, providing that human rights and legal safeguards are fully respected.
4. A variety of dispositions, such as care, guidance and supervision orders; counselling; probation; foster care; education and vocational training programmes and other alternatives to institutional care shall be available to ensure that children are dealt with in a manner appropriate to their well-being and proportionate both to their circumstances and the offence.

Article 41. Nothing in the present Convention shall affect any provisions which are more conducive to the realization of the rights of the child and which may be contained in:
(a) The law of a State party; or
(b) International law in force for that State.

PART II.

Article 42. States Parties undertake to make the principles and provisions of the Convention widely known, by appropriate and active means, to adults and children alike.

Article 43. 1. For the purpose of examining the progress made by States Parties in achieving the realization of the obligations undertaken in the present Convention, there shall be established a Committee on the Rights of the Child, which shall carry out the functions hereinafter provided.
2. The Committee shall consist of eighteen experts of high moral standing and recognized competence in the field covered by this Convention. The members of the Committee shall be elected by States Parties from among their nationals and shall serve in their personal capacity, consideration being given to equitable geographical distribution, as well as to the principal legal systems.
3. The members of the Committee shall be elected by secret ballot from a list of persons nominated by States Parties. Each State Party may nominate one person from among its own nationals.
4. The initial election to the Committee shall be held no later than six months after the date of the entry into force of the present Convention and thereafter every second year. At least four months before the date of each election,

the Secretary-General of the United Nations shall address a letter to States Parties inviting them to submit their nominations within two months. The Secretary-General shall subsequently prepare a list in alphabetical order of all persons thus nominated, indicating States Parties which have nominated them, and shall submit it to the States Parties to the present Convention.
5. The elections shall be held at meetings of States Parties convened by the Secretary-General at United Nations Headquarters. At those meetings, for which two thirds of States Parties shall constitute a quorum, the persons elected to the Committee shall be those who obtain the largest number of votes and an absolute majority of the votes of the representatives of States Parties present and voting.
6. The members of the Committee shall be elected for a term of four years. They shall be eligible for re-election if renominated. The term of five of the members elected at the first election shall expire at the end of two years; immediately after the first election, the names of these five members shall be chosen by lot by the Chairman of the meeting.
7. If a member of the Committee dies or resigns or declares that for any other cause he or she can no longer perform the duties of the Committee, the State Party which nominated the member shall appoint another expert from among its nationals to serve for the remainder of the term, subject to the approval of the Committee.
8. The Committee shall establish its own rules of procedure.
9. The Committee shall elect its officers for a period of two years.
10. The meetings of the Committee shall normally be held at United Nations Headquarters or at any other convenient place as determined by the Committee. The Committee shall normally meet annually. The duration of the meetings of the Committee shall be determined, and reviewed, if necessary, by a meeting of the States Parties to the present Convention, subject to the approval of the General Assembly.
11. The Secretary-General of the United Nations shall provide the necessary staff and facilities for the effective performance of the functions of the Committee under the present Convention.
12. With the approval of the General Assembly, the members of the Committee established under the present Convention shall receive emoluments from United Nations resources on such terms and conditions as the Assembly may decide.

Article 44. 1. States Parties undertake to submit to the Committee, through the Secretary-General of the United Nations, reports on the measures they have adopted which give effect to the rights recognized herein and on the progress made on the enjoyment of those rights
(a) Within two years of the entry into force of the Convention for the State Party concerned;
(b) Thereafter every five years.
2. Reports made under the present article shall indicate factors and difficulties, if any, affecting the degree of fulfilment of the obligations under the present Convention. Reports shall also contain sufficient information to provide the Committee with a comprehensive understanding of the implementation of the Convention in the country concerned.
3. A State Party which has submitted a comprehensive initial report to the Committee need not, in its subsequent reports submitted in accordance with paragraph 1 (b) of the present article, repeat basic information previously provided.
4. The Committee may request from States Parties further information relevant to the implementation of the Convention.
5. The Committee shall submit to the General Assembly, through the Economic and Social Council, every two years, reports on its activities.
6. States Parties shall make their reports widely available to the public in their own countries.

Article 45. In order to foster the effective implementation of the Convention and to encourage international co-operation in the field covered by the Convention:
(a) The specialized agencies, the United Nations Children's Fund, and other United Nations organs shall be entitled to be represented at the consideration of the implementation of such provisions of the present Convention as fall within the scope of their mandate. The Committee may invite the specialized agencies, the United Nations Children's Fund and other competent bodies as it may consider appropriate to provide expert advice on the implementation of the Convention in areas falling within the scope of their respective mandates. The Committee may invite the specialized agencies, the United Nations Children's Fund, and other United Nations organs to submit reports on the implementation of the Convention in areas falling within the scope of their activities;
(b) The Committee shall transmit, as it may consider appropriate, to the specialized agencies, the United Nations Children's Fund and other competent bodies, any reports from States Parties that contain a request, or indicate a need, for technical advice or assistance, along with the Committee's observations and suggestions, if any, on these requests or indications;

(c) The Committee may recommend to the General Assembly to request the Secretary-General to undertake on its behalf studies on specific issues relating to the rights of the child;
(d) The Committee may make suggestions and general recommendations based on information received pursuant to articles 44 and 45 of the present Convention. Such suggestions and general recommendations shall be transmitted to any State Party concerned and reported to the General Assembly, together with comments, if any, from States Parties.

PART III.

Article 46. The present Convention shall be open for signature by all States.

Article 47. The present Convention is subject to ratification. Instruments of ratification shall be deposited with the Secretary-General of the United Nations.

Article 48. The present Convention shall remain open for accession by any State. The instruments of accession shall be deposited with the Secretary-General of the United Nations.

Article 49. 1. The present Convention shall enter into force on the thirtieth day following the date of deposit with the Secretary-General of the United Nations of the twentieth instrument of ratification or accession.
2. For each State ratifying or acceding to the Convention after the deposit of the twentieth instrument of ratification or accession, the Convention shall enter into force on the thirtieth day after the deposit by such State of its instrument of ratification or accession.

Article 50. 1. Any State Party may propose an amendment and file it with the Secretary-General of the United Nations. The Secretary-General shall thereupon communicate the proposed amendment to States Parties, with a request that they indicate whether they favour a conference of States Parties for the purpose of considering and voting upon the proposals. In the event that, within four months from the date of such communication, at least one third of the States Parties favour such a conference, the Secretary-General shall convene the conference under the auspices of the United Nations. Any amendment adopted by a majority of States Parties present and voting at the conference shall be submitted to the General Assembly for approval.
2. An amendment adopted in accordance with paragraph 1 of the present article shall enter into force when it has been approved by the General Assembly of the United Nations and accepted by a two-thirds majority of States Parties.
3. When an amendment enters into force, it shall be binding on those States Parties which have accepted it, other States Parties still being bound by the provisions of the present Convention and any earlier amendments which they have accepted.

Article 51. 1. The Secretary-General of the United Nations shall receive and circulate to all States the text of reservations made by States at the time of ratification or accession.
2. A reservation incompatible with the object and purpose of the present Convention shall not be permitted.
3. Reservations may be withdrawn at any time by notification to that effect addressed to the Secretary-General of the United Nations, who shall then inform all States. Such notification shall take effect on the date on which it is received by the Secretary-General

Article 52. A State Party may denounce the present Convention by written notification to the Secretary-General of the United Nations. Denunciation becomes effective one year after the date of receipt of the notification by the Secretary-General.

Article 53. The Secretary-General of the United Nations is designated as the depositary of the present Convention.

Article 54. The original of the present Convention, of which the Arabic, Chinese, English, French, Russian and Spanish texts are equally authentic, shall be deposited with the Secretary-General of the United Nations. In witness thereof the undersigned plenipotentiaries, being duly authorized thereto by their respective Governments, have signed the present Convention.

Optional Protocol to the Convention on the Rights of the Child on the sale of children, child prostitution and child pornography, adopted and opened for signature, ratification and accession by General Assembly resolution A/RES/54/263 of 25 May 2000.

The States Parties to the present Protocol,
Considering that, in order further to achieve the purposes of the Convention on the Rights of the Child and the implementation of its provisions, especially articles 1, 11, 21, 32, 33, 34, 35 and 36, it would be appropriate to extend the measures that States Parties should undertake in order to guarantee the protection of the child from the sale of children, child prostitution and child pornography,
Considering also that the Convention on the Rights of the Child recognizes the right of the child to be protected from economic exploitation and from performing any work that is likely to be hazardous or to interfere with the child's education, or to be harmful to the child's health or physical, mental, spiritual, moral or social development,
Gravely concerned at the significant and increasing international traffic in children for the purpose of the sale of children, child prostitution and child pornography,
Deeply concerned at the widespread and continuing practice of sex tourism, to which children are especially vulnerable, as it directly promotes the sale of children, child prostitution and child pornography,
Recognizing that a number of particularly vulnerable groups, including girl children, are at greater risk of sexual exploitation and that girl children are disproportionately represented among the sexually exploited,
Concerned about the growing availability of child pornography on the Internet and other evolving technologies, and recalling the International Conference on Combating Child Pornography on the Internet, held in Vienna in 1999, in particular its conclusion calling for the worldwide criminalization of the production, distribution, exportation, transmission, importation, intentional possession and advertising of child pornography, and stressing the importance of closer cooperation and partnership between Governments and the Internet industry,
Believing that the elimination of the sale of children, child prostitution and child pornography will be facilitated by adopting a holistic approach, addressing the contributing factors, including underdevelopment, poverty, economic disparities, inequitable socio-economic structure, dysfunctioning families, lack of education, urban-rural migration, gender discrimination, irresponsible adult sexual behaviour, harmful traditional practices, armed conflicts and trafficking in children,
Believing also that efforts to raise public awareness are needed to reduce consumer demand for the sale of children, child prostitution and child pornography, and believing further in the importance of strengthening global partnership among all actors and of improving law enforcement at the national level,
Noting the provisions of international legal instruments relevant to the protection of children, including the Hague Convention on Protection of Children and Cooperation in Respect of Intercountry Adoption, the Hague Convention on the Civil Aspects of International Child Abduction, the Hague Convention on Jurisdiction, Applicable Law, Recognition, Enforcement and Cooperation in Respect of Parental Responsibility and Measures for the Protection of Children, and International Labour Organization Convention No. 182 on the Prohibition and Immediate Action for the Elimination of the Worst Forms of Child Labour,
Encouraged by the overwhelming support for the Convention on the Rights of the Child, demonstrating the widespread commitment that exists for the promotion and protection of the rights of the child,
Recognizing the importance of the implementation of the provisions of the Programme of Action for the Prevention of the Sale of Children, Child Prostitution and Child Pornography and the Declaration and Agenda for Action adopted at the World Congress against Commercial Sexual Exploitation of Children, held in Stockholm from 27 to 31 August 1996, and the other relevant decisions and recommendations of pertinent international bodies,
Taking due account of the importance of the traditions and cultural values of each people for the protection and harmonious development of the child, Have agreed as follows:

Article 1. States Parties shall prohibit the sale of children, child prostitution and child pornography as provided for by the present Protocol.

Article 2. For the purposes of the present Protocol:
(a) Sale of children means any act or transaction whereby a child is transferred by any person or group of persons to another for remuneration or any other consideration;
(b) Child prostitution means the use of a child in sexual activities for remuneration or any other form of consideration;
(c) Child pornography means any representation, by whatever means, of a child engaged in real or simulated explicit sexual activities or any representation of the sexual parts of a child for primarily sexual purposes.

Article 3. 1. Each State Party shall ensure that, as a minimum, the following acts and activities are fully covered under its criminal or penal law, whether such offences are committed domestically or transnationally or on an individual or organized basis:
(a) In the context of sale of children as defined in article 2:
(i) Offering, delivering or accepting, by whatever means, a child for the purpose of:
a. Sexual exploitation of the child;
b. Transfer of organs of the child for profit;
c. Engagement of the child in forced labour;
(ii) Improperly inducing consent, as an intermediary, for the adoption of a child in violation of applicable international legal instruments on adoption;
(b) Offering, obtaining, procuring or providing a child for child prostitution, as defined in article 2;
(c) Producing, distributing, disseminating, importing, exporting, offering, selling or possessing for the above purposes child pornography as defined in article 2.
2. Subject to the provisions of the national law of a State Party, the same shall apply to an attempt to commit any of the said acts and to complicity or participation in any of the said acts.
3. Each State Party shall make such offences punishable by appropriate penalties that take into account their grave nature.
4. Subject to the provisions of its national law, each State Party shall take measures, where appropriate, to establish the liability of legal persons for offences established in paragraph 1 of the present article. Subject to the legal principles of the State Party, such liability of legal persons may be criminal, civil or administrative.
5. States Parties shall take all appropriate legal and administrative measures to ensure that all persons involved in the adoption of a child act in conformity with applicable international legal instruments.

Article 4. 1. Each State Party shall take such measures as may be necessary to establish its jurisdiction over the offences referred to in article 3, paragraph 1, when the offences are commited in its territory or on board a ship or aircraft registered in that State.
2. Each State Party may take such measures as may be necessary to establish its jurisdiction over the offences referred to in article 3, paragraph 1, in the following cases:
(a) When the alleged offender is a national of that State or a person who has his habitual residence in its territory;
(b) When the victim is a national of that State.
3. Each State Party shall also take such measures as may be necessary to establish its jurisdiction over the aforementioned offences when the alleged offender is present in its territory and it does not extradite him or her to another State Party on the ground that the offence has been committed by one of its nationals.
4. The present Protocol does not exclude any criminal jurisdiction exercised in accordance with internal law.

Article 5. 1. The offences referred to in article 3, paragraph 1, shall be deemed to be included as extraditable offences in any extradition treaty existing between States Parties and shall be included as extraditable offences in every extradition treaty subsequently concluded between them, in accordance with the conditions set forth in such treaties.
2. If a State Party that makes extradition conditional on the existence of a treaty receives a request for extradition from another State Party with which it has no extradition treaty, it may consider the present Protocol to be a legal basis for extradition in respect of such offences. Extradition shall be subject to the conditions provided by the law of the requested State.
3. States Parties that do not make extradition conditional on the existence of a treaty shall recognize such offences as extraditable offences between themselves subject to the conditions provided by the law of the requested State.
4. Such offences shall be treated, for the purpose of extradition between States Parties, as if they had been committed not only in the place in which they occurred but also in the territories of the States required to establish their jurisdiction in accordance with article 4.
5. If an extradition request is made with respect to an offence described in article 3, paragraph 1, and the requested State Party does not or will not extradite on the basis of the nationality of the offender, that State shall take suitable measures to submit the case to its competent authorities for the purpose of prosecution.

Article 6. 1. States Parties shall afford one another the greatest measure of assistance in connection with investigations or criminal or extradition proceedings brought in respect of the offences set forth in article 3, paragraph 1, including assistance in obtaining evidence at their disposal necessary for the proceedings.
2. States Parties shall carry out their obligations under paragraph 1 of the present article in conformity with any treaties or other arrangements on mutual legal assistance that may exist between them. In the absence of such treaties or arrangements, States Parties shall afford one another assistance in accordance with their domestic law.

Article 7. States Parties shall, subject to the provisions of their national law:
(a) Take measures to provide for the seizure and confiscation, as appropriate, of:
(i) Goods, such as materials, assets and other instrumentalities used to commit or facilitate offences under the present protocol;
(ii) Proceeds derived from such offences;
(b) Execute requests from another State Party for seizure or confiscation of goods or proceeds referred to in subparagraph (a);
(c) Take measures aimed at closing, on a temporary or definitive basis, premises used to commit such offences.

Article 8. 1. States Parties shall adopt appropriate measures to protect the rights and interests of child victims of the practices prohibited under the present Protocol at all stages of the criminal justice process, in particular by:
(a) Recognizing the vulnerability of child victims and adapting procedures to recognize their special needs, including their special needs as witnesses;
(b) Informing child victims of their rights, their role and the scope, timing and progress of the proceedings and of the disposition of their cases;
(c) Allowing the views, needs and concerns of child victims to be presented and considered in proceedings where their personal interests are affected, in a manner consistent with the procedural rules of national law;
(d) Providing appropriate support services to child victims throughout the legal process;
(e) Protecting, as appropriate, the privacy and identity of child victims and taking measures in accordance with national law to avoid the inappropriate dissemination of information that could lead to the identification of child victims;
(f) Providing, in appropriate cases, for the safety of child victims, as well as that of their families and witnesses on their behalf, from intimidation and retaliation;
(g) Avoiding unnecessary delay in the disposition of cases and the execution of orders or decrees granting compensation to child victims.
2. States Parties shall ensure that uncertainty as to the actual age of the victim shall not prevent the initiation of criminal investigations, including investigations aimed at establishing the age of the victim.
3. States Parties shall ensure that, in the treatment by the criminal justice system of children who are victims of the offences described in the present Protocol, the best interest of the child shall be a primary consideration.
4. States Parties shall take measures to ensure appropriate training, in particular legal and psychological training, for the persons who work with victims of the offences prohibited under the present Protocol.
5. States Parties shall, in appropriate cases, adopt measures in order to protect the safety and integrity of those persons and/or organizations involved in the prevention and/or protection and rehabilitation of victims of such offences.
6. Nothing in the present article shall be construed to be prejudicial to or inconsistent with the rights of the accused to a fair and impartial trial.

Article 9. 1. States Parties shall adopt or strengthen, implement and disseminate laws, administrative measures, social policies and programmes to prevent the offences referred to in the present Protocol. Particular attention shall be given to protect children who are especially vulnerable to such practices.
2. States Parties shall promote awareness in the public at large, including children, through information by all appropriate means, education and training, about the preventive measures and harmful effects of the offences referred to in the present Protocol. In fulfilling their obligations under this article, States Parties shall encourage the participation of the community and, in particular, children and child victims, in such information and education and training programmes, including at the international level.
3. States Parties shall take all feasible measures with the aim of ensuring all appropriate assistance to victims of such offences, including their full social reintegration and their full physical and psychological recovery.
4. States Parties shall ensure that all child victims of the offences described in the present Protocol have access to adequate procedures to seek, without discrimination, compensation for damages from those legally responsible.
5. States Parties shall take appropriate measures aimed at effectively prohibiting the production and dissemination of material advertising the offences described in the present Protocol.

Article 10. 1. States Parties shall take all necessary steps to strengthen international cooperation by multilateral, regional and bilateral arrangements for the prevention, detection, investigation, prosecution and punishment of those responsible for acts involving the sale of children, child prostitution, child pornography and child sex tourism. States Parties shall also promote international cooperation and coordination between their authorities, national and international non-governmental organizations and international organizations.

2. States Parties shall promote international cooperation to assist child victims in their physical and psychological recovery, social reintegration and repatriation.
3. States Parties shall promote the strengthening of international cooperation in order to address the root causes, such as poverty and underdevelopment, contributing to the vulnerability of children to the sale of children, child prostitution, child pornography and child sex tourism.
4. States Parties in a position to do so shall provide financial, technical or other assistance through existing multilateral, regional, bilateral or other programmes.

Article 11. Nothing in the present Protocol shall affect any provisions that are more conducive to the realization of the rights of the child and that may be contained in:
(a) The law of a State Party;
(b) International law in force for that State.

Article 12. 1. Each State Party shall, within two years following the entry into force of the present Protocol for that State Party, submit a report to the Committee on the Rights of the Child providing comprehensive information on the measures it has taken to implement the provisions of the Protocol.
2. Following the submission of the comprehensive report, each State Party shall include in the reports they submit to the Committee on the Rights of the Child, in accordance with article 44 of the Convention, any further information with respect to the implementation of the present Protocol. Other States Parties to the Protocol shall submit a report every five years.
3. The Committee on the Rights of the Child may request from States Parties further information relevant to the implementation of the present Protocol.

Article 13. 1. The present Protocol is open for signature by any State that is a party to the Convention or has signed it.
2. The present Protocol is subject to ratification and is open to accession by any State that is a party to the Convention or has signed it. Instruments of ratification or accession shall be deposited with the Secretary- General of the United Nations.

Article 14. 1. The present Protocol shall enter into force three months after the deposit of the tenth instrument of ratification or accession.
2. For each State ratifying the present Protocol or acceding to it after its entry into force, the Protocol shall enter into force one month after the date of the deposit of its own instrument of ratification or accession.

Article 15. 1. Any State Party may denounce the present Protocol at any time by written notification to the Secretary- General of the United Nations, who shall thereafter inform the other States Parties to the Convention and all States that have signed the Convention. The denunciation shall take effect one year after the date of receipt of the notification by the Secretary-General.
2. Such a denunciation shall not have the effect of releasing the State Party from its obligations under the present Protocol in regard to any offence that occurs prior to the date on which the denunciation becomes effective. Nor shall such a denunciation prejudice in any way the continued consideration of any matter that is already under consideration by the Committee on the Rights of the Child prior to the date on which the denunciation becomes effective.

Article 16. 1. Any State Party may propose an amendment and file it with the Secretary-General of the United Nations. The Secretary-General shall thereupon communicate the proposed amendment to States Parties with a request that they indicate whether they favour a conference of States Parties for the purpose of considering and voting upon the proposals. In the event that, within four months from the date of such communication, at least one third of the States Parties favour such a conference, the Secretary-General shall convene the conference under the auspices of the United Nations. Any amendment adopted by a majority of States Parties present and voting at the conference shall be submitted to the General Assembly of the United Nations for approval.
2. An amendment adopted in accordance with paragraph 1 of the present article shall enter into force when it has been approved by the General Assembly and accepted by a two-thirds majority of States Parties.
3. When an amendment enters into force, it shall be binding on those States Parties that have accepted it, other States Parties still being bound by the provisions of the present Protocol and any earlier amendments they have accepted.

Article 17. 1. The present Protocol, of which the Arabic, Chinese, English, French, Russian and Spanish texts are equally authentic, shall be deposited in the archives of the United Nations.
2. The Secretary-General of the United Nations shall transmit certified copies of the present Protocol to all States Parties to the Convention and all States that have signed the Convention.

Optional Protocol to the Convention on the Rights of the Child on the involvement of children in armed conflict, adopted and opened for signature, ratification and accession by General Assembly resolution A/RES/54/263 of 25 May 2000.

The States Parties to the present Protocol,
Encouraged by the overwhelming support for the Convention on the Rights of the Child, demonstrating the widespread commitment that exists to strive for the promotion and protection of the rights of the child,
Reaffirming that the rights of children require special protection, and calling for continuous improvement of the situation of children without distinction, as well as for their development and education in conditions of peace and security,
Disturbed by the harmful and widespread impact of armed conflict on children and the long-term consequences it has for durable peace, security and development,
Condemning the targeting of children in situations of armed conflict and direct attacks on objects protected under international law, including places that generally have a significant presence of children, such as schools and hospitals,
Noting the adoption of the Rome Statute of the International Criminal Court, in particular, the inclusion therein as a war crime, of conscripting or enlisting children under the age of 15 years or using them to participate actively in hostilities in both international and non-international armed conflict,
Considering therefore that to strengthen further the implementation of rights recognized in the Convention on the Rights of the Child there is a need to increase the protection of children from involvement in armed conflict,
Noting that article 1 of the Convention on the Rights of the Child specifies that, for the purposes of that Convention, a child means every human being below the age of 18 years unless, under the law applicable to the child, majority is attained earlier,
Convinced that an optional protocol to the Convention that raises the age of possible recruitment of persons into armed forces and their participation in hostilities will contribute effectively to the implementation of the principle that the best interests of the child are to be a primary consideration in all actions concerning children,
Noting that the twenty-sixth International Conference of the Red Cross and Red Crescent in December 1995 recommended, inter alia, that parties to conflict take every feasible step to ensure that children below the age of 18 years do not take part in hostilities,
Welcoming the unanimous adoption, in June 1999, of International Labour Organization Convention No. 182 on the Prohibition and Immediate Action for the Elimination of the Worst Forms of Child Labour, which prohibits, inter alia, forced or compulsory recruitment of children for use in armed conflict,
Condemning with the gravest concern the recruitment, training and use within and across national borders of children in hostilities by armed groups distinct from the armed forces of a State, and recognizing the responsibility of those who recruit, train and use children in this regard,
Recalling the obligation of each party to an armed conflict to abide by the provisions of international humanitarian law,
Stressing that the present Protocol is without prejudice to the purposes and principles contained in the Charter of the United Nations, including Article 51, and relevant norms of humanitarian law,
Bearing in mind that conditions of peace and security based on full respect of the purposes and principles contained in the Charter and observance of applicable human rights instruments are indispensable for the full protection of children, in particular during armed conflict and foreign occupation,
Recognizing the special needs of those children who are particularly vulnerable to recruitment or use in hostilities contrary to the present Protocol owing to their economic or social status or gender,
Mindful of the necessity of taking into consideration the economic, social and political root causes of the involvement of children in armed conflict,
Convinced of the need to strengthen international cooperation in the implementation of the present Protocol, as well as the physical and psychosocial rehabilitation and social reintegration of children who are victims of armed conflict,
Encouraging the participation of the community and, in particular, children and child victims in the dissemination of informational and educational programmes concerning the implementation of the Protocol,

Have agreed as follows:

Article 1. States Parties shall take all feasible measures to ensure that members of their armed forces who have not attained the age of 18 years do not take a direct part in hostilities.

Article 2. States Parties shall ensure that persons who have not attained the age of 18 years are not compulsorily recruited into their armed forces.

Article 3. 1. States Parties shall raise the minimum age for the voluntary recruitment of persons into their national armed forces from that set out in article 38, paragraph 3, of the Convention on the Rights of the Child, taking account of the principles contained in that article and recognizing that under the Convention persons under the age of 18 years are entitled to special protection.
2. Each State Party shall deposit a binding declaration upon ratification of or accession to the present Protocol that sets forth the minimum age at which it will permit voluntary recruitment into its national armed forces and a description of the safeguards it has adopted to ensure that such recruitment is not forced or coerced.
3. States Parties that permit voluntary recruitment into their national armed forces under the age of 18 years shall maintain safeguards to ensure, as a minimum, that:
(a) Such recruitment is genuinely voluntary;
(b) Such recruitment is carried out with the informed consent of the person's parents or legal guardians;
(c) Such persons are fully informed of the duties involved in such military service;
(d) Such persons provide reliable proof of age prior to acceptance into national military service.
4. Each State Party may strengthen its declaration at any time by notification to that effect addressed to the Secretary-General of the United Nations, who shall inform all States Parties. Such notification shall take effect on the date on which it is received by the Secretary-General.
5. The requirement to raise the age in paragraph 1 of the present article does not apply to schools operated by or under the control of the armed forces of the States Parties, in keeping with articles 28 and 29 of the Convention on the Rights of the Child.

Article 4. 1. Armed groups that are distinct from the armed forces of a State should not, under any circumstances, recruit or use in hostilities persons under the age of 18 years.
2. States Parties shall take all feasible measures to prevent such recruitment and use, including the adoption of legal measures necessary to prohibit and criminalize such practices.
3. The application of the present article shall not affect the legal status of any party to an armed conflict.

Article 5. Nothing in the present Protocol shall be construed as precluding provisions in the law of a State Party or in international instruments and international humanitarian law that are more conducive to the realization of the rights of the child.

Article 6. 1. Each State Party shall take all necessary legal, administrative and other measures to ensure the effective implementation and enforcement of the provisions of the present Protocol within its jurisdiction.
2. States Parties undertake to make the principles and provisions of the present Protocol widely known and promoted by appropriate means, to adults and children alike.
3. States Parties shall take all feasible measures to ensure that persons within their jurisdiction recruited or used in hostilities contrary to the present Protocol are demobilized or otherwise released from service. States Parties shall, when necessary, accord to such persons all appropriate assistance for their physical and psychological recovery and their social reintegration.

Article 7. 1. States Parties shall cooperate in the implementation of the present Protocol, including in the prevention of any activity contrary thereto and in the rehabilitation and social reintegration of persons who are victims of acts contrary thereto, including through technical cooperation and financial assistance. Such assistance and cooperation will be undertaken in consultation with the States Parties concerned and the relevant international organizations.
2. States Parties in a position to do so shall provide such assistance through existing multilateral, bilateral or other programmes or, inter alia, through a voluntary fund established in accordance with the rules of the General Assembly.

Article 8. 1. Each State Party shall, within two years following the entry into force of the present Protocol for that State Party, submit a report to the Committee on the Rights of the Child providing comprehensive information on the measures it has taken to implement the provisions of the Protocol, including the measures taken to implement the provisions on participation and recruitment.

2. Following the submission of the comprehensive report, each State Party shall include in the reports it submits to the Committee on the Rights of the Child, in accordance with article 44 of the Convention, any further information with respect to the implementation of the Protocol. Other States Parties to the Protocol shall submit a report every five years.

3. The Committee on the Rights of the Child may request from States Parties further information relevant to the implementation of the present Protocol.

Article 9. 1. The present Protocol is open for signature by any State that is a party to the Convention or has signed it.

2. The present Protocol is subject to ratification and is open to accession by any State. Instruments of ratification or accession shall be deposited with the Secretary-General of the United Nations.

3. The Secretary-General, in his capacity as depositary of the Convention and the Protocol, shall inform all States Parties to the Convention and all States that have signed the Convention of each instrument of declaration pursuant to article 3.

Article 10. 1. The present Protocol shall enter into force three months after the deposit of the tenth instrument of ratification or accession.

2. For each State ratifying the present Protocol or acceding to it after its entry into force, the Protocol shall enter into force one month after the date of the deposit of its own instrument of ratification or accession.

Article 11. 1. Any State Party may denounce the present Protocol at any time by written notification to the Secretary- General of the United Nations, who shall thereafter inform the other States Parties to the Convention and all States that have signed the Convention. The denunciation shall take effect one year after the date of receipt of the notification by the Secretary-General. If, however, on the expiry of that year the denouncing State Party is engaged in armed conflict, the denunciation shall not take effect before the end of the armed conflict.

2. Such a denunciation shall not have the effect of releasing the State Party from its obligations under the present Protocol in regard to any act that occurs prior to the date on which the denunciation becomes effective. Nor shall such a denunciation prejudice in any way the continued consideration of any matter that is already under consideration by the Committee on the Rights of the Child prior to the date on which the denunciation becomes effective.

Article 12. 1. Any State Party may propose an amendment and file it with the Secretary-General of the United Nations. The Secretary-General shall thereupon communicate the proposed amendment to States Parties with a request that they indicate whether they favour a conference of States Parties for the purpose of considering and voting upon the proposals. In the event that, within four months from the date of such communication, at least one third of the States Parties favour such a conference, the Secretary-General shall convene the conference under the auspices of the United Nations. Any amendment adopted by a majority of States Parties present and voting at the conference shall be submitted to the General Assembly of the United Nations for approval.

2. An amendment adopted in accordance with paragraph 1 of the present article shall enter into force when it has been approved by the General Assembly and accepted by a two-thirds majority of States Parties.

3. When an amendment enters into force, it shall be binding on those States Parties that have accepted it, other States Parties still being bound by the provisions of the present Protocol and any earlier amendments they have accepted.

Article 13. 1. The present Protocol, of which the Arabic, Chinese, English, French, Russian and Spanish texts are equally authentic, shall be deposited in the archives of the United Nations.

2. The Secretary-General of the United Nations shall transmit certified copies of the present Protocol to all States Parties to the Convention and all States that have signed the Convention.

PART V

Contract, Tort and Property Law

Civil Code [Code Civil]. Selected provisions from the Preliminary Title, Books I, II, III and IV.[17] Version at 1 October 2010.

Preliminary Title. Of the publication, effects and application of laws in general

[Articles 1 – 2 are omitted.]

Article 3. Laws of public order and security [les lois de police et de sûreté] bind all those residing in the territory. Immovables, even those owned by foreigners, are governed by French law.
Laws concerning the status and capacity of persons govern the French, even while residing in foreign countries.

[Articles 4 – 5 are omitted.]

Article 6. One cannot derogate by private agreements from laws which concern public policy and good morals.

[The remainder of the Preliminary Title is omitted.]

Book I. Of persons

[Titles I – IV are omitted.]

Title VI. Of divorce

[Chapters I – III are omitted.]

Chapter IV. Of divorce and judicial separation

Article 309. Divorce and judicial separation [le divorce et la séparation de corps] are governed by French law:
- where one and the other spouse have the French nationality;
- where both spouses have their domicile on French territory;
- where no foreign law considers itself applicable, whereas French courts have jurisdiction to adjudicate a case of divorce or judicial separation.

Title VII. Of parent and child

Article 310. All children whose parentage has been legally established have the same rights and the same duties in relation to their father and mother. They are taken into the family of each of them.

Chapter I. General provisions

[Articles 310-1 – 310-2 and Section 1 are omitted.]

Section 2. Of the conflict of laws relating to parentage

Article 311-14. Parentage is governed by the personal law of the mother on the day of birth of the child; if the mother is unknown, by the personal law of the child.

Article 311-15. Nevertheless, if the child and his father and mother or either one of them has their habitual residence in France, together or separately, the apparent status produces all the effects according to French law, even if the other elements of parentage would depend on a foreign law.

---

[17] Translation by B. Akkermans and E. Ramaekers.

Article 311-17. Voluntary acknowledgement of paternity or maternity is valid if it has been made in accordance with either the personal law of he who acts, or with the personal law of the child.

Article 311-18. A claim for maintenance is governed, at the choice of the child, either by the law of his habitual residence, or by the law of the habitual residence of the debtor.

[The remainder of Title VII and Titles VIII – IX are omitted.]

Title X. Of minority, of guardianship and of emancipation

Chapter I. Of minority

Article 388. A minor is the individual of one or the other sex who has not yet reached the age of eighteen years.

[The remainder of Chapter I is omitted.]

Chapter II. Of guardianship

Section 1. Of the cases where either statutory administration or guardianship takes place

[Articles 389 – 389-2 are omitted.]

Article 389-3. The legal administrator will represent the minor in all his civil acts, except for the cases in which the law or custom authorizes minors to act themselves.
Where his interests conflict with those of the minor, an ad hoc administrator must be appointed by the court concerned with legal guardianship [Juge des tutelles]. For lack of diligence of the legal administrator, the judge may proceed to this nomination at the request of the public prosecutor, of the minor himself or ex officio. Goods which would have been given or bequeathed to the minor under the condition that they would be administered by a third party are not submitted to the legal administration. This third party administrator will have the powers which will have been conferred on him by the gift or the testament; by lack thereof, he will have those powers of a legal administrator under judicial control.

[The remainder of Book I is omitted.]

Book II. Of things and the different modifications of the right of ownership

Title I. Of the classification of things

Article 516. All things [biens] are movable or immovable.

Chapter 1. Of immovables

Article 517. Things [biens] are immovable, by their nature, by their purpose, or through the object [objet] to which they apply.

Article 518. Land and buildings are immovable by their nature.

[Articles 519 – 525 are omitted.]

Article 526. Immovable are, through the object [objet] to which they apply:
The right of usufruct of immovable objects [choses];
Servitudes or easements [services fanciers];
Actions to revindicate an immovable.

Chapter II. Of movables

Article 527. Things are movable by their nature or by operation of law.

Article 528. Movable are by their nature animals and things [corps] which can be transported from one place to another, whether or not because they move by themselves, or because they can only change places through an external force.

[The remainder of Chapter II is omitted.]

Chapter III. Of things in their relation to those who possess them

Article 537. Private persons have free disposition over the things [biens] that belong to them, within the boundaries established by law.
Things which do not belong to private persons are administered and may not be disposed of other than in the forms and following the rules that apply in particular to them.

Article 539. The things [biens] of persons who have died without any heirs or whose things are abandoned, belong to the State.

[Article 542 is omitted.]

Article 543. One may have in respect to things either a right of ownership, or a simple right of enjoyment, or a servitude.

Title II. Of ownership

Article 544. Ownership is the right to enjoy and dispose of objects [choses] in the most absolute manner, provided they are not used in a way prohibited by statutes or regulations.

Article 545. No one may be compelled to yield his ownership, unless for public purposes and for a fair and previous indemnity.

Article 546. Ownership of an object [chose], whether movable or immovable, gives right to all it produces and to that which is accessory to it, whether naturally or artificially.
This right is called "accession" [droit d'accession].

[Chapter I is omitted.]

Chapter II. On accession of things that unite or incorporate with a thing

Article 552. The ownership of land encompasses the ownership of what is on and below it. The owner may place any plants or constructions that he deems fit on it, except for those exceptions laid down in the title 'on servitudes and land services'. He may place any constructions and conduct any excavations under his land that he deems fit, and draw from those excavations all products that they may provide, except for the amendments resulting from statutes and regulations concerning mines, and of statutes and policing measures [règlements de police].

[The remainder of Title II is omitted.]

Title III. Of usufruct, use and habitation

Chapter I. Of usufruct

Article 578. The right of usufruct is the right to use and enjoy an object [chose] of another in the same way as an owner himself, but on condition that the substance of the object is preserved.

[Articles 579 – 580 are omitted.]

Article 581. It may be created on any kind of movable and immovable things [biens meubles ou immeubles].

Part V. Private Law

Section 1. Of the rights of the usufructuary

Article 582. The usufructuary has the right to enjoy every kind of fruit, whether natural, industrial or civil, which may be produced by the object [objet] in relation to which he has a right of usufruct.

[Articles 583 – 586 are omitted.]

Article 587. Where a right of usufruct is created on objects [choses] which cannot be used without being consumed, such as money, grain, liquors, the usufructuary has a right to use them, but with the obligation to, at the end of the usufruct, return either objects of the same quantity and quality or their value estimated at the date or return.

[The remainder of Section 1 is omitted.]

Section 2. Of obligations of the usufructuary

Article 600. The usufructuary takes the objects [choses] in the way they are, but he may not commence his enjoyment before, in the presence of the owner, drafting an inventory of the movables and an inventory of immovables that are subject to the right of usufruct.

Article 601. He shall guarantee to enjoy as a prudent administrator [bon père de famille], if this is not dispensed with by the instrument creating the usufruct; however, the father and mother who have the legal usufruct of their children's property, a seller or donor, under the condition of the usufruct, are not obliged to give security.

[The remainder of Section 2 is omitted.]

Section 3. Of the ways a usufruct comes to an end

Article 617. A usufruct is destroyed:
By the natural [repealed by implication] death of the usufructuary;
By the expiry of the time for which it was granted;
By the consolidation or vesting in the same person of the two capacities of usufructuary and of owner;
By non-use of the right during thirty years;
By the total loss of the object [chose] on which the usufruct was created.

[Article 618 is omitted.]

Article 619. The right of usufruct which is not granted to private persons lasts no longer than thirty years.

[Articles 620 – 622 are omitted.]

Article 623. Where only a part of an object [chose] subject to the right of usufruct is destroyed, the right of usufruct is preserved on that what remains.

Article 624. Where a right of usufruct is created on a building only, and that building is destroyed by fire or by another accident, or collapses from decay, the usufructuary does not have a right to use and enjoy the land or on the materials.
Where the right of usufruct was created on an area of which the building was a part only, the usufructuary has the right to use and enjoy the land and the materials.

Chapter II. Of use and habitation

Article 625. Rights of use and habitation are created and destroyed in the same manner as the right of usufruct.

[Article 626 is omitted.]

Article 627. The user and he who has a right to reside must enjoy it as prudent administrators [bons pères de famille].

[Articles 628 – 630 are omitted.]

Article 631. The user may not assign nor lease his right to another.

[The remainder of Title III is omitted.]

Title IV. Of servitudes and land services

Article 637. A right of servitude is a burden imposed on a piece of land for the use of that land on behalf of another owner.

[Articles 638 – 639 are omitted.]

Chapter I. Of servitudes that arise from a specific factual situation

Article 640. Lower pieces of land are subjected to those pieces of land that are situated higher, to receive waters that flow naturally from them without the hand of man having contributed thereto.
An owner of a lower piece of land may not raise dams that prevent that flow.
An owner of an upper piece of land may not do anything that worsens the servitude of the lower piece of land.

[Articles 641 – 648 are omitted.]

Chapter II. Of servitudes that arise by operation of law

Article 649. Servitudes created by operation of law [établies par la loi] are for the purpose of public or common use, or for use by private individuals.

Article 650. Those created for public or common use have as their objects towing-paths along public waters [d'eau dominiaux], the construction or repair of roads and of other public or municipal works.
All that relates to that kind of servitudes is determined by statutes or specific regulations.

[Articles 651 – 652 and Sections 1 – 4 are omitted.]

Section 5. Of the right of way

Article 682. An owner whose land is enclosed and who has no way out to the public road, or only one which is insufficient either due to an agricultural, industrial or commercial exploitation of his land, or due to operations of construction or development that are being carried out, is entitled to claim on his neighbor's land a right of way sufficient for complete access to his own land, provided he pays a compensation in proportion to the damage he may cause.

[Articles 683 – 685-1 are omitted.]

Chapter III. Of servitudes created by an act of man

Section 1. Of the different classes of servitudes that may be created in respect to things

Article 686. Owners are permitted to create in respect to their things, or in favour of their things, such servitudes as they deem fit, provided however that the servitudes created are imposed neither on a person, nor in favour of a person, but only on a piece of land and for a piece of land, and provided that those servitudes are not in any way contrary to public policy.
The use and extent of the servitudes so created are regulated by the instrument that creates them; by lack of an instrument, by the following rules.

[Articles 687 – 689 are omitted.]

Part V. Private Law

Section 2: How servitudes are established

Article 690. Continuous and apparent servitudes are acquired on title, or by possession of thirty years.

[Articles 691 – 695 are omitted.]

Article 696. If one creates a servitude, one is obliged to provide all that is necessary to use it. Thus, a servitude to tap water from another's fountain necessarily implies a right of passage.

Section 3. Of the rights of the owner of the piece land on which the servitude runs

Article 697. A person whose land is burdened with a right of servitude has the right to make all works necessary to use and maintain the right.

[Article 698 is omitted.]

Article 699. Even in the case where the owner of the land on which the right of servitude runs is compelled under the instrument of creation to make the works necessary for the use or preservation of a right of servitude at his own expense, he may always exempt himself from that burden by abandoning the servient land to the owner of the land that benefits from the existence of the right of servitude.

[Articles 700 – 702 are omitted.]

Section 4. On how servitudes cease to exist

Article 703. Rights of servitude are destroyed when the things are in such a condition that they can no longer be used.

Article 704. They revive when things are restored in such a manner that they can be continued to be used; unless so much time has already passed to give rise to the presumption that the right of servitude is destroyed, as is stated in Article 707.

Article 705. A right of servitude is destroyed when the ownership of the servient land and the ownership of the dominant land are united in the same hands.

Article 706. A right of servitude is destroyed by non-use for a period of thirty years.

Article 707. The thirty years begin to run, according to the different kinds of servitudes, either from the day a holder of right ceased to enjoy them, with respect to discontinuous servitudes, or from the day when an act contrary to the right of servitude has been performed, with respect to continuous servitudes.

[The remainder of Book II is omitted.]

Book III. Of the various ways in which ownership is acquired

General Provisions

Article 711. Ownership of things [biens] is acquired and transferred through succession, through a donation during life or by testament, and as a result of obligations.

Article 712. Ownership is also acquired through accession or incorporation, and through prescription.

Article 713. Things [biens] that have no master belong to the community on which territory the things are situated. However, the right of ownership is transferred by operation of law to the State when the community waives the exercise of its rights.

Article 714. There are objects [choses] that do not belong to anyone and whose usage is common to all. Public order statutes regulate the manner in which these are to be enjoyed.

[Articles 715 – 717 are omitted.]

Title I. Of succession

[Chapters I – IV are omitted.]

Chapter VII. Of legal regime of co-entitlement [régime légal de l'indivision]

Article 815. Nothing may be restricted to remain in a situation of co-entitlement [indivision] and a division may always be initiated, unless this has been postponed by a judgment or an agreement.

Article 815-1. Persons who are co-entitled [indivisaires] may conclude agreements relating to the exercise of their common rights, in conformity with Articles 1873-1 to 1873-18.

[The remainder of Title I is omitted.]

Title II. Of gifts inter vivos and of wills [Liberalités]

Chapter I. General provisions

[Articles 893 – 900 are omitted.]

Art. 900-1. Non-transferability clauses concerning a thing donated or bequeathed are valid only where they are temporary and justified by a serious and legitimate aim. Even in that case, a donee or legatee may be judicially authorized to dispose of the thing if the aim which justified the clause has disappeared or if it happens that a more important interest so requires.
The provisions of this Article do not prejudice gratuitous transfers granted to legal persons or even to natural persons responsible for forming legal persons.

[The remainder of Chapter I and Chapters II – III are omitted.]

Chapter IV. Of inter vivos gifts

Section 1. Of the form of inter vivos gifts

Article 931. All instruments containing a gift inter vivos shall be passed before a notary in the ordinary form of contracts; and an original shall remain, under penalty of annulment.

[The remainder of Title II is omitted.]

Title III. Of contracts or conventional obligations in general

Chapter I. Preliminary provisions

Article 1101. A contract [contrat] is an agreement [convention] by which one or several persons bind themselves, as against one or several others, to give, to do or not to do something.

Article 1102. A contract is synallagmatic or bilateral where the contracting parties mutually bind themselves as against each other.

Article 1103. It is unilateral where one or several persons are bound as against one or several others, without there being any undertaking on the part of the latter.

Article 1104. It is commutative where each of the parties commits himself to give or to do something which is regarded as the equivalent of what one gives to him, or of what one does for him.
Where the equivalent consists of a chance of gain or loss for each of the parties, depending on an uncertain event, the contract is aleatory.

Article 1105. A contract of benevolence [bienfaisance] is one by which one of the parties procures for the other a purely gratuitous advantage.

Article 1106. An onerous contract is one which obliges each of the parties to give or to do something.

Article 1107. Contracts, whether they have a proper denomination, or whether they do not have one, are subjected to the general rules, which are the subject matter of the present title.

Chapter II. Of the essential requisites for the validity of agreements

Article 1108. Four conditions are essential for the validity of an agreement:
The consent of the party who binds himself;
His capacity to contract;
A certain subject matter [objet] which forms the subject of the undertaking;
A licit cause for the obligation.

[Articles 1108-1 – 1108-2 are omitted.]

Section 1. Of consent

Article 1109. There is no valid consent if the consent has solely been given by error [erreur] or where it has been extorted through duress [violence] or obtained through deceit [dol].

Article 1110. Error is only a cause of nullity of the agreement where it rests on the substance itself of the object which is the object thereof.
It is not a cause of nullity where it rests only on the person with whom one has the intention to contract, unless the considerations relating to this person are the principal cause of the agreement.

Article 1111. Duress exerted against he who has contracted the obligation is a cause for nullity, even though it has been exercised by a third party other than he for whose benefit the agreement has been made.

Article 1112. There is duress where it is of a nature to make an impression on a reasonable person, and where it can instil in him the fear of exposing his person or his wealth to considerable and actual harm.
One takes account, in this matter, of age, sex and the condition of the persons involved.

Article 1113. Duress is a cause for nullity of the contract, not only where it has been exerted against the contracting party, but also where it has been exerted against his or her spouse, against his descendants or his ascendants.

Article 1114. The mere reverential fear towards the father, the mother, or another ascendant, without duress having been exerted, does not suffice to annul the contract.

Article 1115. A contract can no longer be contested for reason of duress, if, since the duress has ceased, that contract has been endorsed either expressly, or tacitly, or by letting the time for restitution determined by law lapse.

Article 1116. Deceit is cause for nullity of the agreement where the manoeuvres used by one of the parties are such that it is evident that, without these manoeuvres, the other party would not have entered into the contract.
It is not to be presumed and must be proven.

Article 1117. The agreement entered into through error, duress or deceit, is not void by operation of law; it only gives rise to an action for invalidity or annulment, in the cases and in the manner explained in Section VII of Chapter V of the present title.

[Articles 1118 – 1122 are omitted.]

Section 2. Of the capacity of contracting parties

Article 1123. Every person can enter into a contract if he has not been declared incapable by law.

Article 1124. Incapable of entering into a contract, to the extent as defined by law, are:
Minors who are not emancipated;
Adults protected in the sense of Article 488 of the present code.

Article 1125. Persons capable of binding themselves cannot put forward the incapacity of those with whom they have entered into a contract.

Article 1125-1. Without judicial authorization, it is prohibited, under penalty of annulment, for whoever exercises a function or holds a position in an establishment which accommodates elderly persons or provides psychiatric care, to designate himself the acquirer of a good or the assignee of a right belonging to a person admitted at the establishment, or to take on lease the accommodation occupied by this person before his admission to the establishment.
For application of the present article, the spouse, the ascendants and descendants of the persons to whom the abovementioned prohibitions apply, shall be deemed intermediaries.

Section 3. Of the object and subject matter of contracts

Article 1126. Every contract has as its subject matter [objet] an object [chose] that a party undertakes to give, or that a party undertakes to do or not to do.

Article 1127. The mere use or the mere possession of an object can be, like the object itself, the subject matter of the contract.

Article 1128. Only objects that may be the subject matter of transactions may be the subject matter of agreements.

Article 1129. The obligation must have as its subject matter an object that is at least determined as regards its kind.
The quantity of the object may be uncertain, provided that it can be determined.

Article 1130. Future objects may be the subject of an obligation.
One cannot however renounce a succession which is not available, nor make a stipulation concerning such a succession, even with the consent of he whose succession it concerns, except under the conditions provided by law.

Section 4. Of cause

Article 1131. An obligation without cause, or based on a false cause, or on an illicit cause, cannot have any effect.

Article 1132. The agreement is no less valid, even though its cause has not been expressed.

Article 1133. The cause is illicit, where it is prohibited by law, where it is contrary to good morals [bonnes moeurs] or to public policy.

PART V. PRIVATE LAW

Chapter III. Of the effect of obligations

Section 1. General provisions

Article 1134. Agreements legally formed constitute law for those who have made them.
They can only be revoked by their mutual consent, or for grounds which the law authorizes.
They must be performed in good faith.

Article 1135. Agreements are not only binding with regard to what has been expressed in them, but also with regard to all the consequences that equity, custom or the law grant to the obligation according to its nature.

Section 2. Of the obligation to give

[Articles 1136 – 1137 are omitted.]

Article 1138. The obligation to deliver an object [chose] is performed by the sole consent of the contracting parties.
It renders its creditor owner and puts the object at his risk at the moment it should have been delivered, even if a transfer has not taken place, unless the debtor is in default of delivery, in which case the object remains at the risk of the latter.

[Articles 1139 – 1140 are omitted.]

Article 1141. If someone has obliged himself to give or deliver a purely movable object [chose] to two persons successively, the person who acquires actual possession is preferred and becomes its owner, even though his right to delivery is of a later date, provided, however, that he is in good faith.

Section 3. Of the obligation to do or not do

Article 1142. Every obligation to do or not do something gives rise to damages and interest in case of non-performance on the part of the debtor.

Article 1143. Nevertheless, the creditor has the right to ask that what has been done in contravention of the undertaking [l'engagement] be undone; and he may have himself authorized to undo it at the expense of the debtor, without prejudice to the damages and interest for which there is a ground.

Article 1144. The creditor may also, in case of non-performance [l'inexécution], be authorized to have the obligation performed himself at the expense of the debtor. The latter may be ordered to make an advance payment for the amount necessary for that performance.

Article 1145. If the obligation is to not do something, he who contravenes it owes damages and interest for the sole reason of the contravention.

Section 4. Of damages resulting from the non-performance of an obligation

Article 1146. The damages and interest are only due where the debtor is in default [en demeure] in fulfilling his obligation, except, however, where the object which the debtor had undertaken to give or to do could only be given or done during a certain time which he let pass.
The notice of default may have the form of a simple letter, if a sufficient interpellation results from it.

Article 1147. The debtor is ordered, if there are grounds, to pay damages and interest either for reason of non-performance of the obligation, or for reason of a delay in performance, every time that he does not prove that the non-performance stems from an external cause which cannot be attributed to him, and where there is no bad faith on his part.

Article 1148. There is no ground for any damages and interest where, as a consequence of *force majeure* or a fortuitous event [cas fortuit], the debtor has been prevented from giving or doing that to which he was obliged, or has done that which was prohibited.

Article 1149. The damages and interest owed to the creditor are, in general, for the loss that he has suffered and for the gain of which he has been deprived, subject to the exceptions and modifications below.

Article 1150. The debtor is only liable for the damages and interest which were foreseen or could have been foreseen at the time of the contract, where it is not through his fault that the obligation has not been performed.

Article 1151. Even in the case where non-performance of the agreement results from the fault of the debtor, the damages and interest may only comprise, as regards the loss incurred by the creditor and the gain of which he has been deprived, that which is an immediate and direct consequence of the non-performance of the agreement.

Article 1152. Where the agreement provides that he who fails to perform it will pay a certain sum under the heading of damages and interest, a higher or lower sum cannot be allocated to the other party. Nevertheless, the judge may, even ex officio, moderate or increase the penalty that was agreed upon, if it is manifestly excessive or derisory. Every stipulation to the contrary shall be deemed unwritten.

[Articles 1153 – 1155 are omitted.]

Section 5. Of the interpretation of agreements

Article 1156. One should search in agreements what has been the common intention of the contracting parties, rather than limit oneself to the literal sense of the terms.

Article 1157. Where a clause is susceptible to two meanings, one must interpret it in the sense in which it can have some effect, rather than in the sense in which it cannot produce any.

Article 1158. Terms that are susceptible to two meanings must be taken in the sense which best suits the subject matter of the contract.

Article 1159. That which is ambiguous must be interpreted in accordance with the custom in the country where the contract is concluded.

Article 1160. Within the contract one must supplement the clauses which are customary, although they have not been expressed therein.

Article 1161. All the clauses of agreements are to be interpreted with reference to one another, by giving each the meaning which results from the act in its entirety.

Article 1162. In case of doubt, the agreement is to be interpreted as against he who has stipulated and in favour of he who has contracted the obligation.

Article 1163. However generous may be the terms in which an agreement is phrased, it only contains the things about which it appears that the parties intended to contract.

Article 1164. Where in a contract one has expressed a case for explanation of the obligation, one is not considered to have wanted to restrict thereby the scope which the undertaking receives by law to cases not expressed.

Section 6. Of the effect of agreements with respect to third parties

Article 1165. Agreements only have effect as between the contracting parties; they do not harm a third party, and they do not profit him except in the case provided by Article 1121.

[Articles 1166 – 1167 are omitted.]

Chapter IV. Of the various kinds of obligations

Section 1. Of conditional obligations

Paragraph 1. Of condition in general and of its various kinds

Article 1168. An obligation is conditional where one makes it dependent upon a future and uncertain event, either by suspending it until the event occurs, or by ending it, whether the event will occur or will not occur.

Article 1169. An incidental condition is one which depends upon coincidence, and which is by no means in the power of the creditor or of the debtor.

Article 1170. A potestative condition is one which makes the execution of the agreement dependent upon an event which is in the power of one or the other of the contracting parties to bring about or prevent.

Article 1171. A mixed condition is one which depends at the same time on the will of one of the contracting parties, and on the will of a third party.

Article 1172. Every condition relating to an impossible thing, or contrary to good morals, or prohibited by law is void, and renders void the agreement which depends on it.

Article 1173. A condition not to do an impossible thing does not render void the obligation contracted under that condition.

Article 1174. Every obligation is void where it has been contracted under a potestative condition on the part of he who binds himself.

Article 1175. Every condition must be fulfilled in the manner which the parties in all likelihood wanted and intended that it should be.

Article 1176. Where an obligation is contracted under the condition that an event will occur within a fixed time period, that condition is deemed to have lapsed where the time period has expired without the event having occurred. If no time period has been fixed, the condition may be fulfilled at any time; and it is only deemed to have lapsed where it has become certain that the event will not occur.

Article 1177. Where an obligation is contracted under the condition that an event will not occur within a fixed time period, that condition is fulfilled where that time period has expired without the event having occurred: it is equally fulfilled, if before the end of the time period it becomes certain that the event will not occur; and if no time period has been determined, it is only fulfilled where it is certain that the event will not occur.

Article 1178. A condition is considered to be fulfilled where it is the debtor, bound by that condition, who has impeded its fulfilment.

Article 1179. A fulfilled condition has retroactive effect to the day on which the undertaking was contracted. If the creditor has died before fulfilment of the condition, his rights pass to his heir.

Article 1180. The creditor can, before the condition is fulfilled, exercise all acts necessary to preserve his right.

[Paragraph 2 is omitted.]

Paragraph 3. Of resolutory conditions

Article 1183. A resolutory condition [condition résolutoire] is one which, where it is fulfilled, brings the obligation to an end, and which returns everything to the same state as if the obligation had not existed. It does not suspend the performance of the obligation; it merely binds the creditor to return what he has received, in the case where the event foreseen by the condition occurs.

Article 1184. A resolutory condition is always implied in synallagmatic contracts, for the case where one of the two parties does not fulfil his obligation.
In that case, the contract is not automatically terminated by law. The party as against whom the undertaking has not been performed, has the choice either to force the other to perform the agreement where it is possible, or to demand its termination with damages and interest.
The termination [résolution] must be applied for in court, and the defendant may be awarded a delay according to the circumstances.

[The remainder of Chapter IV is omitted.]

Chapter V. Of the extinguishment of obligations

Article 1234. Obligations are extinguished:
By payment;
By novation;
By voluntary release;
By set-off;
By merger;
By the loss of the thing;
By nullity or rescission;
By the effect of a resolutory condition, as was explained in the preceding Chapter; and
By prescription, which will be the subject matter of a special title.

[Sections 1 – 6 are omitted.]

Section 7. Of the action for annulment or termination of agreements

Article 1304. In every case where the action for nullity or rescission of an agreement is not limited to a minimum time period by a particular law, that action lasts five years.
That time period only starts running in case of duress from the day on which it has ceased; in case of error or deceit, from the day at which they were discovered.
The time only runs, with regard to acts performed by a minor, from the day of majority or emancipation; and with regard to acts performed by a protected adult, from the day on which he had knowledge thereof, so that he was in a situation to perform them validly again. It only runs as against the heirs of the person under guardianship [de la personne en tutelle ou en curatelle] from the day of decease, if it has not begun to run before.

Article 1305. A mere lesion gives rise to rescission in favour of the non-emancipated minor, with regard to all kinds of agreements.

Article 1306. The minor is not entitled to rescission on the ground of lesion, where it merely results from an incidental and unforeseen event.

Article 1307. The mere declaration of majority, made by the minor, does not form an obstacle to his right to rescission.

Article 1308. A minor who exercises a profession is not entitled to rescission with regard to the obligations that he has undertaken while exercising it.

Article 1309. A minor is not entitled to rescission with regard to the agreements contained in his contract of marriage, where they have been made with the consent and the assistance of those whose consent is required for the validity of his marriage.

Article 1310. He is not entitled to rescission with regard to the obligations resulting from his delicts or quasi-delicts.

Article 1311. He is no longer allowed to repudiate a commitment which he had taken on as a minor, where he has ratified it as an adult, whether that commitment was void in its form, or whether it was only subject to rescission.

Part V. Private Law

Article 1312. Where minors or adults under guardianship are permitted, in those capacities, to obtain rescission as against their undertakings, the reimbursement of that which would, as a consequence of those undertakings, have been paid during minority or guardianship of the adults, may not be claimed, unless it is proven that what has been paid is to their benefit.

Article 1313. Adults will only get rescission for reason of lesion in the cases and under the conditions specifically expressed in the present code.

Article 1314. Where the formalities required with regard to minors or adults under guardianship, either for the transfer of immovables, or for the division of an inheritance, have been fulfilled, they are, in relation to those acts, considered as if they had performed them during adulthood or before the adult became under guardianship.

Chapter VI. Of the proof of obligations and of payment

[Section 1 is omitted.]

Section 2. Of oral evidence

Article 1341. An instrument relating to all things exceeding a sum or a value fixed by decree must be passed before notaries or under private signature, even for voluntary deposits, and no proof is permitted either by witnesses against and beyond the contents of the instruments, or about that which had allegedly been said before, at the time of or after the [passing of the] instruments, even though it concerns a lesser sum or value. All is without prejudice to what is prescribed by laws relating to commerce.

[The remainder of Title III is omitted.]

Title IV. Of undertakings [engagements] formed without an obligation

[Chapter I is omitted.]

Chapter II. Of delicts and quasi-delicts

Article 1382. Any act whatever of a person, which causes damage to another, obliges him by whose fault [faute] the damage was caused to remedy it.

Article 1383. Everyone is liable for the damage which he has caused not only by his act, but also by his negligence or by his carelessness [imprudence].

Article 1384. One is liable not only for the damage caused by one's own act, but also for that which is caused by acts of persons for whom he is responsible, or by objects which are in his care.
Nevertheless, he who holds, under whatever title, whole or part of an immovable or of movable things within which a fire has ignited shall only be liable, vis-à-vis third persons, for the damage caused by that fire, if it is proven that it can be attributed to his fault or to the fault of persons for whom he is responsible.
This provision does not apply to relationships between owners and tenants, who remain governed by Articles 1733 and 1734 of the Civil Code.
The father and mother, while exercising parental authority, are jointly liable for damage caused by their minor children living with them.
Masters and principals, for damage caused by their servants and employees in the functions for which they have been employed;
Teachers and craftsmen, for damage caused by their pupils and apprentices during the time that they are under their supervision.
The abovementioned liability arises, unless the father and mother and the craftsmen prove that they could not have prevented the fact which gave rise to that responsibility.
As regards the teachers, the faults, carelessness or negligence which are alleged against them as having caused the injurious fact, will have to be proven during the proceedings by the claimant in accordance with general law.

Article 1385. The owner of an animal, or he who makes use of one, is liable for the damage caused by the animal while he uses it, whether the animal was in his care, or whether it had strayed or escaped.

Article 1386. The owner of a building is liable for damage caused by its collapse, where it has occurred as a consequence of lack of maintenance or by a defect in its construction.
The rules specific to certain contracts are established under the titles relating to each of them; and the rules specific to commercial transactions are established by the laws relating to commerce.

[The remainder of Title IV and Title V are omitted.]

Title VI. Of sales

Chapter I. Of the nature and the form of sale

Article 1582. Sale is an agreement whereby on party obliges himself to deliver an object [chose], and the other to pay for it.
It may be made by authentic instrument or by an instrument with a private signature.

Article 1583. It is performed between the parties, and ownership is acquired by the buyer as against the seller the moment they have agreed about the object [chose] and the price, even if the object has not yet been delivered or the price not yet been paid.

[The remainder of Chapter I and Chapter II are omitted.]

Chapter III. Of objects that may be sold

[Article 1598 is omitted.]

Article 1599. The sale of an object [chose] of someone else is void: it may give rise to damages where the buyer did not know that the thing belonged to another.

[The remainder of Chapter III is omitted.]

Chapter IV. Of the obligations of the seller

[Sections 1 – 2 are omitted.]

Section 3. Of warranty

Paragraph 2. Of warranty against the defects of the object sold

Article 1641. The seller is held to stand guarantee for latent defects of the object sold which render it unfit for its intended use, or which diminish that use so much that the buyer would not have acquired it, or would only have paid a smaller price for it, if he would have known them.

Article 1642. The seller is not held responsible for apparent defects [vices apparents] and which the buyer could ascertain for himself.

Article 1643. He is held responsible for latent defects [vices cachés], even where he could not have known them, unless, in that case, he has stipulated that he shall not be bound to any guarantee.

Article 1644. In the case of Articles 1641 and 1643, the buyer has the choice to return the object and to have the price repaid to him, or to keep the object and get part of the price back, such as shall be judged by experts.

Article 1645. If the seller knew about the defects of the object, he is held, besides restitution of the price which he has received for it, as against the buyer to pay all the damages and interest.

Article 1646. If the seller did not know the defects of the object, he shall only be held to pay restitution of the price, and to reimburse the buyer for all the costs caused by the sale.

Article 1647. If the object which had defects has perished as a consequence of its bad quality, the loss is for the seller, who will be held as against the buyer to pay restitution of the price and of other indemnities as provided for in the two preceding articles.
However, a loss that occurred due to a fortuitous event shall be for the account of the buyer.

Article 1648. An action resulting from irreparable defects must be initiated by the buyer within a period of two years counting from the discovery of the defect.
In the case foreseen by Article 1642-1, the action must be initiated, upon penalty of foreclosure, in the year which follows the date at which the seller may be discharged from apparent defects [vices] and defects in conformity [défauts de conformité].

[The remainder of Chapter IV and Chapters V – VII are omitted.]

Chapter VIII. On assignment of claims and of other incorporeal rights

[Article 1689 is omitted.]

Article 1690. An assignee [cessionnaire] is vested with regard to third parties only by notice of the assignment to debtor. Nevertheless, the assignee may likewise be vested if he accepts the assignment given by the debtor in an authentic act.

Article 1691. Where, before the debtor has been given notice by the assignor or the assignee, the debtor has paid the assignor, he is lawfully discharged.

Article 1692. The sale or assignment of a claim includes the accessories of the claim, such as the surety, priority right and hypothec.

[The remainder of Title VI and Title VII are omitted.]

Title VIII. On the contract of lease

[Chapter I is omitted.]

Chapter II. Of the lease of objects [louage des choses]

Section 1. General provisions in respect to the lease of houses and agricultural leases

[Articles 1717 – 1742 are omitted.]

Article 1743. If the lessor sells the object [chose] that is leased, the acquirer may not evict the tenant-farmer, share-tenant [colon partiaire] or tenant who has an authentic lease or one the date of which is certain.
He may, however, evict a tenant of non-rural things [biens non ruraux] where he has reserved that right in the contract of lease.

[The remainder of Title VIII and Titles VIIIbis – IX are omitted.]

Title IXbis. On agreements in respect to the exercise of undivided rights [droits indivis]

Chapter 1. On agreements in respect to the exercise of undivided rights in the absence of a right of usufruct

[Article 1873-2 is omitted.]

Article 1873-3. The agreement may be concluded for a determined duration which may not exceed five years. It may be renewed by an express decision of the parties. A division [partage] may be instigated before the agreed term only where there are proper reasons for it.
The agreement may equally be concluded for an indeterminate duration. In that case, a division may be instigated at any time, provided it is not in bad faith or at an inappropriate time.

It may be decided that an agreement for a determined duration will be renewed by tacit extension, for a determined or indeterminate duration. For lack of such an agreement, the co-entitlement [l'indivision] shall be governed by Articles 815 and following at the expiry of the agreement for a determined duration.

[The remainder of Title IXbis and Titles X – XIII are omitted.]

Title XIV. Of trusts [fiducie]

Article 2011. The trust [fiducie] is a transaction through which one or more constituents transfer things [biens], rights or securities, or a collection of things, rights or securities, to one or more fiduciaries [fiduciaires], keeping them segregated from their own patrimony, act so as to further a particular purpose for the benefit of one or more beneficiaries.

Article 2012. The trust is created by law or by contract. It must be express.

Article 2013. A contract of trust is void if it is made with the intention of conferring wealth upon a beneficiary. This nullity is public policy.

Article 2014. A constituant can only be a legal person subject to company taxes, whether as a matter of law or by election [les personnes morales soumises de plein droit ou sur option a l'impôt sur les sociétés]. The rights of a constituant under a trust are neither transmissible by gratuitous title nor by onerous title to persons other than those persons subject by election to company taxes.

Article 2015. A fiduciary must be a lender within the meaning of Article 511-1 of the Monetary and Financial Code, an institution or agency referred to in Article 518-1 of that Code, an investment enterprise referred to in Article 531-4 of that Code, or an insurance company regulated by Article L 310-1 of the Insurance Code.

Article 2016. The constituant or the fiduciary may be the beneficiary or one of the beneficiaries of a contract of trust.

Article 2017. Subject to provision to the contrary in the contract of trust, the constituant may at any time appoint a third party to protect his interests in the context of carrying out the contract. Such third party may exercise any of the powers conferred by law on the constituant.

Article 2018. The contract shall provide, upon penalty of nullity:
(1) the things [biens], rights or securities transferred. If they are future things, rights or securities, they must be identifiable;
(2) the period for which they have been transferred, which must not exceed thirty three years dating from the execution of the contract;
(3) the constituant or constituants;
(4) the fiduciary or fiduciaries;
(5) the beneficiary or beneficiaries, or at least provides for their ascertainment;
(6) the purpose which the fiduciary or fiduciaries have undertaken, and the extent of their powers, both administrative and dispositive.

Article 2019. Upon penalty of nullity, a contract of trust and its variation shall be registered within one month of its date with the tax office of the place where the fiduciary has its seat or, where the fiduciary has no domicile in France, with the tax office for non-residents.
Where it deals with immovable things [immeubles] or immovable property rights [droits réels immobiliers], it is, subject to the same penalty, unless it receives the publicity required by Articles 647 and 657 of the General Tax Code [Code général des impôts].
The transfer of rights resulting from a contract of trust, and, if the beneficiary is not named in the contract, his subsequent designation, upon penalty of nullity, shall give rise to an instrument in writing, to be registered under the same conditions.

Article 2020. A national register of trusts will be constituted in accordance with the requirements of a decree of the Council of State [Conseil d'État].

Part V. Private Law

[Articles 2021 – 2023 are omitted.]

Article 2024. The institution of any safeguard procedure [procédure de sauvegarde], administration [redressement judiciaire], compulsory sale [liquidation judiciaire] for the benefit of the fiduciary has no effect on the trust patrimony.

Article 2025. Without prejudice to the rights of any creditors of the constituants who have a right of recourse against a security, notified before the contract of trust, and except in the case of fraud on the creditors of the constituant, the trust patrimony is subject to execution only for debts arising from the keeping or the management of this patrimony. *[The remainder of this Article is omitted.]*

Article 2026. The fiduciary is personally liable for any wrongs that he commits whilst carrying out his functions.

[Article 2027 is omitted.]

Article 2028. The contract of trust may be revoked by the constituant at any time before it has been accepted by the beneficiary.
After such acceptance, the contract may only be modified or revoked with the consent of the beneficiary or by a decision of the court.

Article 2029. A contract of trust ends if it reaches its expiry date, if its object has been achieved before then, or if the constituant revokes his election for the taxation of companies [impôt sur les sociétés].
It will also end automatically if the contract so provides, or, in default of such provision, if, in the absence of terms providing for the circumstances in which the contract is to continue, all the beneficiaries wish it to come to an end. The same consequence will occur if the fiduciary becomes subject to compulsory sale [liquidation judiciaire] or dissolution, or ceases to exist as a result of an assignment or a merger.

Article 2030. If the contract of trust ends at a time when there are no beneficiaries, the rights, things or securities forming part of the trust patrimony automatically revert to the constituant.

[Titles XV – XIX are omitted.]

Title XX. Of extinctive prescription

Chapter I. General provisions

Article 2219. Extinctive prescription is a way in which rights can be destroyed as a result of their non-use by the holder of the right after a certain period of time.

[Article 2220 is omitted.]

Article 2221. The extinctive prescription is subject to the provisions that are applicable to the right it concerns.

[Articles 2222 – 2223 are omitted.]

Chapter II. Of the prescription period and the start of the prescription period for extinctive prescription

Section 1. Of the common rules on the prescription period and its start

Article 2224. Personal or movable claims are lost through the completion of a prescription period of five years to be calculated from the day that the holder of a right knew or should have known the facts that entitle him to exercise the right.

Section 2. Of some prescription periods and specific starting points

[Articles 2225 – 2226 are omitted.]

Article 2227. The right of ownership cannot be lost through prescription. Taking that into account, real immovable claims prescribe after a period of thirty years to be calculated from the day that the holder of a right knew or should have known the facts that entitle him to exercise the right.

Chapter III. Of the running of the prescription period

Section 1. General provisions

Article 2228. The prescription period is calculated in days, not in hours.

Article 2229. It is completed when the last day of the period has passed.

Article 2230. The suspension of the prescription period brings the running of the prescription period to a temporary halt.

Article 2231. The interruption ends the prescription period that has passed. A new period of the same time as the old one will start to run.

Article 2232. The changing of the starting point of the prescription period as a result of a suspension or interruption may not have the effect of making the prescription period longer than twenty years, to be calculated from the day the right was created. The first paragraph is not applicable in cases mentioned in Articles 2226, 2227, 2233, 2236, first paragraph and Article 2241 until 2244. It does not apply to claims on the state of persons.

[The remainder of Title XX is omitted.]

Title XXI. Of possession and acquisitive prescription

Chapter I. General provisions

Article 2255. Possession is the holding [detention] or the enjoyment of an object [chose] or of a right that we have or hold for ourselves, or by another that has or holds it for us.

Article 2256. One is always presumed to possess for oneself, and in the capacity as owner, where it is not proved that one has started by possessing for another.

Article 2257. Where one has started by possessing for another, one is always presumed to possess in the same capacity, unless there is proof to the contrary.

Chapter II. Of acquisitive prescription

Article 2258. Acquisitive prescription is a way to acquire a thing [bien] or a right through possession without requiring him to show a title for the thing or without opposing him the exception following bad faith.

Article 2259. Articles 2221 and 2222 are applicable to acquisitive prescription, as well as Chapters III and IV of Title XX of this book, except if the provisions in this chapter provide otherwise.

Section 1. Of the requirements for acquisitive prescription

Article 2260. One cannot acquire through prescription things [biens] or rights which are not commercial.

Article 2261. In order to complete the prescription uninterrupted and continuous possession, peaceful, public, unambiguous, and with the title as owner is needed.

Article 2262. Acts which are merely allowed or simply tolerated may not give rise to possession or prescription.

Article 2263. Acts of duress may not give rise to a possession capable of bringing about prescription either. Possession begins to produce effects only from the time the duress has ceased.

Article 2264. A present possessor who proves that he has formerly possessed, is presumed to have possessed during the intervening time, unless there is proof to the contrary.

Article 2265. To complete a prescription, one may join to one's possession that of one's predecessor, in whatever manner one may have succeeded to him, whether by virtue of a universal or specific title, or for value or gratuitously.

Article 2266. Those who possess for another never acquire ownership by prescription, whatever the time elapsed may be.
Thus, a farm tenant, a depositary, a usufructuary, and all those who precariously hold the thing of an owner, may not prescribe it.

[Articles 2267 – 2269 are omitted.]

Article 2270. Prescription cannot have effect against the title, in that regard it is not possible to change, by yourself, the cause and the basis of possession.

Article 2271. Acquisitive prescription is interrupted when the possessor of a thing [bien] is deprived, during more than one year, of the enjoyment of that thing, either by the owner, or even by a third person.

Section 2. Of acquisitive prescription in respect to immovable things

Article 2272. The period required to acquire the ownership in respect to immovables through acquisitive prescription is thirty years. However, he who acquires an immovable in good faith and with a legal title [juste titre] acquires ownership in ten years.

[Article 2273 is omitted.]

Article 2274. Good faith [bonne foi] is always presumed, it is for the person who argues bad faith to prove this.

Article 2275. It is sufficient if good faith exists at the moment of acquisition.

Section 3. Of acquisitive prescription in respect to movable things

Article 2276. As regards movables, possession counts as title.
Nevertheless, the person who has lost an object [chose] or from whom an object has been stolen is, during three years from the day of the loss or theft, able to revindicate the object from the person in whose hands he finds it. This does not exclude the latter's remedy against the person from whom he got the object.

Article 2277. Where the current possessor of an object that is lost or is stolen has bought it at a fair or on a market, or at a public sale, or from a merchant selling similar objects, the original owner may have it returned to him only by reimbursing the possessor for the price that the object has cost him.
A lessor who revindicates, under Article 2332, the movables that have been displaced without his consent and which have been bought in the same conditions, must likewise reimburse the buyer for the price which that the things have cost him.

Chapter III. Of protection of possession

Article 2278. Possession is protected, regardless of the substance of the right, against disturbance which affects or threatens it.
Protection of possession is also granted to a person who holds a thing for another [detenteur] against any other person than the one from whom he derives his rights.

Article 2279. Claims for the protection of possession may be brought under the conditions provided by the Code of Civil Procedure by those who possess or hold for another peacefully.

Book IV. Securities

Article 2284. He who is obliged to something is liable for the performance of that obligation with all his movables and immovables, present and future.

Article 2285. The things [biens] of the debtor are pledge to all the creditors; the value is divided among them according to their contribution, if no rights of preference exist among the creditors.

Article 2286. May claim a right of retention to a thing:
1° The person to whom the object [chose] was handed over until payment of his debt;
2° The person whose outstanding debt results from the contract which binds him to deliver it;
3° The person whose outstanding debt arose at the moment that the object [chose] came in his power [détention].
4° The person who benefits from a right of non-possessory pledge.
A right of retention is lost through voluntary relinquishment.

[Article 2287 is omitted.]

Title I. Of personal security rights

Article 2287-1. The personal security rights dealt with in this title are suretyships [cautionnement], the independent guarantee [garantie autonome] and the letter of intention [lettre d'intention].

[The remainder of Title I is omitted.]

Title II. Of property security rights

Subtitle I. General provisions

Article 2323. Lawful causes of preference are priority rights and hypothecs.

Article 2324. A priority right is a right of a creditor of a claim that arises due to the nature of that claim to have preference over other creditors, even holders of a right of hypothec.

[Articles 2325 – 2328-1 are omitted.]

Subtitle II. Of security rights in respect to movable things

Article 2329. Securities on movables are:
1° Movable priority rights [privileges mobiliers];
2° A right of pledge [gage] on corporeal movables;
3° A right of pledge [nantissement] on incorporeal movables;
4° Retained ownership or ownership transferred for security purposes.

[Chapter I is omitted.]

Chapter II. Of pledge on movable things

Section 1. Of common rules on the right of pledge [gage]

Article 2333. A right of pledge is an agreement by which the pledgor grants a creditor the right to be paid in preference to his other creditors out of a movable thing [bien mobilier] or a set of corporeal things, present or future.
The claims secured may be present or future; in the latter case, they must be determinable.

[Article 2334 – 2336 are omitted.]

Article 2337. A pledge is enforceable against third parties due to the publicity attached to it.
It is likewise so by surrendering possession of the thing [bien] which it concerns into the hands of the creditor or an agreed third party.
Where a pledge has been duly disclosed to the public, the particular successors of the pledgor may not invoke Article 2279.

[Articles 2338 – 2341 are omitted.]

Article 2342. Where a non-possessory pledge attaches to fungible objects [choses fongibles], the pledgor may dispose of them if the agreement so provides, on the condition that they be replaced by the same quantity of equivalent objects.

[Articles 2343 – 2345 are omitted.]

Article 2346. In case of failure to pay the secured debt, a creditor may acquire a court order for the sale of the pledged thing [bien gagé]. That sale shall take place following the rules on enforcement proceedings from which a contract of pledge may not derogate.

Article 2347. A creditor may also acquire a court order that the thing [bien] will remain with him by way of satisfaction.
Where the value of the thing exceeds the amount of the secured debt, the sum which is equal to the difference shall be paid to the debtor or, if there are other pledgee creditors [créanciers gagistes], shall be deposited.

Article 2348. When creating the pledge or afterwards, it may be agreed that in case of failure to perform the secured obligation, the creditor will become owner of the pledged thing [bien gagé].
The value of the thing shall be determined on the day of the transfer by an expert designated by amicable arrangement or judicially, in the absence of an official quotation of the thing on a regulated market within the meaning of the Monetary and Financial Code [code monétaire et financier]. Any clause to the contrary is deemed not written.
Where that value exceeds the amount of the secured debt, the sum equal to the difference shall be paid to the debtor or, if there are other pledgee creditors, shall be deposited.

[The remainder of Chapter II is omitted.]

Chapter III. Of pledge on incorporeal movable things [nantissement]

Article 2355. The pledge [nantissement] on an incorporeal movable thing [bien meubles incorporel] is the connection, in order to secure an obligation, of a movable incorporeal thing or a group of movable incorporeal things, present or future.
It is created by agreement or by court decision.
The pledge created by court decision is regulated by the provisions applicable to the procedure of realization [exécution].
The pledge created by agreement that is created in respect to claims is regulated, in the absence of any particular provisions, by the current chapter.
He who takes incorporeal things is subject, in the absence of any special provisions, by the provisions on the pledge of movable corporeal things.

[The remainder of Chapter III is omitted.]

Chapter IV. Of the right of ownership reserved for security purposes

Article 2367. Ownership of a thing [bien] may be retained as security through a clause of retention of title [clause de réserve de propriéte] that withholds the transferring effect of a contract until payment in full of the obligation which compensates for it.
Ownership so retained is the accessory of the debt the payment of which it secures.

Article 2368. A retention of title shall be agreed upon in writing.

Article 2369. The retention of title of a fungible thing [bien fongible], up to the amount of the debt remaining due, attaches to things of the same nature and quality detained by the debtor or on his behalf.

[Articles 2370 – 2372 are omitted.]

Subtitle III. Of security rights in respect to immovable things

Article 2373. Property security rights in respect to immovables are priority rights, the *antichresis* [le gage immobilier] and rights of hypothec.
The right of ownership in respect to immovable things can also be reserved for security purposes.

[Chapter I is omitted.]

Chapter II. Of the right of *antichresis* [du gage immobilier]

Article 2387. The right of *antichresis* is the connection of an immovable thing in order to secure an obligation. It brings the dispossession of him who creates the right.

[Articles 2388 – 2391 are omitted.]

Article 2392. The rights of a creditor by way of *antichresis* are destroyed in particular:
1° Through the extinguishment of the principal obligation;
2° Through anticipated restoration of the immovable to his owner.

Chapter III. Of the right of hypothec

Section 1. General provisions

Article 2393. A hypothec is a property right on immovables allocated to the discharge of an obligation.
It is, by its nature, indivisible and remains in existence in its entirety on all the immovables concerned, on each one and on each part of those immovables.
It follows them in whatever hands they may pass.

[Articles 2394 – 2396 are omitted.]

Article 2397. Can only be susceptible to a hypothec:
1° Immovable things [biens immobiliers] which may be the subject matter of legal transactions, and their accessories deemed immovable;
2° The usufruct on the same thing and accessories for the time of its duration.
A hypothec covers the improvements which are made to the immovable.

[The remainder of Section 1 and Sections 2 – 3 are omitted.]

Section 4. Hypothecs created by agreement [hypothèques conventionelles]

Article 2413. Rights of hypothec by agreement [hypothèques conventionnelles] can only be consented to by those who have the power to alienate [aliéner] the immovables they burden.

[Articles 2414 – 2415 are omitted.]

Article 2416. A hypothec created by agreement may only be granted by an instrument drawn up by a notary.

[Articles 2417 – 2418 are omitted.]

Article 2419. As a rule, a hypothec may be granted only in respect to existing immovables.

Article 2420. By derogation from the preceding article, a hypothec may be granted with regard to future immovables in the following circumstances and subject to the following conditions:
1° He who does not possess existing and unburdened immovables or who does not possess a sufficient quantity of them to secure the claim may agree that each one which he may subsequently acquire be allocated to the payment of the latter as the acquisitions proceed;
2° He whose existing immovable burdened with a hypothec has perished or suffered deteriorations so that it has become insufficient for the security of the claim may likewise do so, without prejudice to the right of the creditor to enforce at once his reimbursement;
3° He who possesses an existing right which allows him to build for his benefit on another's tenement may burden the buildings whose construction has been started or merely planned with a hypothec; in case of destruction of the latter, the hypothec burdens as of right new buildings erected on the same place.

Article 2421. A hypothec may be granted for security of one or several debts, present or future. Where they are future, they must be determinable.
Their grounds shall be determined in the instrument.

[Article 2422 is omitted.]

Article 2423. A right of hypothec is always created, as regards the capital, up to a fixed sum that the notarial instrument shall specify, on the penalty of annulment. Where appropriate, the parties shall estimate for that purpose the annuities, benefits and undetermined, contingent or conditional rights. Where the debt is subject to an index-linking clause, the guarantee extends to the revalued debt, provided the instrument so specifies.
A hypothec extends, by operation of the law, to interest and other accessories.
Where it is granted for security of one or several future debts and for an undetermined duration, the holder of the right of hypothec may at any time terminate the right subject to him giving a three month notice. Once terminated, the right still exists for security of pre-existing claims.

Article 2424. A hypothec is transferred with the secured debt by operation of law. The mortgagee may subrogate another creditor to the hypothec and retain his debt.
He may also, by a ranking agreement, assign his rank of registration to a creditor of a lower rank, with whom he changes places.

Section 5. Classification of hypothecs

Article 2425. As between creditors, a hypothec, either statutory, or judicial, or conventional, ranks only from the day of the registration made by the creditor at the land registry, in the form and manner prescribed by law.
Where several registrations are required on the same day as regards the same immovable, that which is required by virtue of the instrument of title bearing the least recent date shall be deemed of prior rank, whatever the order resulting from the register provided for in Article 2453 may be.
However, the registrations of separations of patrimony provided for by Article 2283, in the case referred to in Article 2386, second paragraph, as well as those of the statutory hypothecs provided for in Article 2400, 1°, 2° and 3°, shall be deemed of a rank prior to the one of any registration of judicial or conventional hypothecs made on the same day.
Where several registrations are made on the same day as regards the same immovable, either by virtue of instruments of title provided for in the second paragraph but bearing the same date, or for the benefit of requiring parties vested with the prior claim or the hypothecs referred to in the third paragraph, the registrations rank equally whatever the order of the above mentioned register may be.
The registration of a statutory hypothec of the Exchequer [l'hypothèque légale du Trésor] or a conservatory judicial hypothec [hypothèque judiciaire conservatoire] shall be deemed of an earlier rank than that conferred to an agreement for the coverage of new claims where the registration of the aforesaid agreement is subsequent to the registration of that hypothec.
The provisions of the fifth paragraph apply to the registration of the statutory hypothec of administrative organs of an obligatory regime of social protection.
The order of priority between creditors having a prior claim or hypothec and holders of warrants, insofar as the latter are secured on assets deemed immovable, is determined by the dates on which the respective instruments have been published, the publicity of warrants remaining subject to the special statutes which regulate them.

[Chapter IV is omitted.]

Chapter V. Of the effect of priority rights and hypothecs

Article 2458. Unless one takes action to sell the thing [bien] burdened with a hypothec under the terms provided for by the laws which apply to enforcement proceedings, from which a contract of hypothec may not derogate, an unpaid hypothecee may request the court that the immovable remain with him.

Article 2459. It may be agreed in an agreement of hypothec that the creditor shall become owner of the immovable burdened by the hypothec. However, that clause is ineffective in respect to an immovable that is the principal residence of the debtor.

[The remainder of Chapter V is omitted.]

Chapter VI. Of the realization [purge] of priority rights and hypothecs

Article 2475. Where, on the occasion of a sale of an immovable that is burdened with a right of hypothec, all creditors notify to the debtor that the proceeds of the sale is affected completely or partially by their claims or some of these, they exercise their right of preference on the price and they may oppose this right to any acquirer or creditor of the claim to the proceeds of the sale.
By payment, the immovable is relieved from the right to follow that is connected to the right of hypothec.
In absence of an agreement foreseen in the first paragraph, the formalities of realization [purge] apply in conformity with the articles that follow.

[The remainder of Chapter VI is omitted.]

Chapter VII. The destruction of priority rights and hypothecs

Article 2488. Prior charges and hypothecs are destroyed:
1° By extinguishment of the principal obligation except for the case provided for in Article 2422;
2° By the creditor's abandonment of the right of hypothec under the same exception;
3° By the fulfilment of the formalities and conditions prescribed to third parties in possession to redeem the thing that they have acquired;
4° By prescription.
Prescription is acquired to a debtor, as to the things [biens] that are in his hands, by the time prescribed by the statute of limitations in respect of the claims provided by a hypothec or a priority right.
As to the things which are in the hands of a third party in possession, they are acquired by him at the moment regulated for prescription periods of ownership for his benefit: in case where prescription depends upon a title, the prescription period begins to run only from the day when that title has been registered in the land register of the situation of the immovables.
Registrations made by a creditor do not interrupt the running of the prescription period established by law in favour of the debtor or of the third party in possession.
5° By the termination allowed by Article 2423, last paragraph, and as far as provided for by this provision.

[The remainder of the Civil Code is omitted.]

Miscellaneous Private Law Codes[18]

Commercial Code (Code de Commerce). Consolidated version at 7 August 2010, Selected provisions :
Articles L 142-1 ; L142-1 ; L223-18, L223-22, L225-35; L225-56; L225-57; L225-64; L225-66; L225-251; L225-252, L446-II(c), L624-14, L624-16 and L624-18.

Article L 142-1. Businesses may be the subject of a security, without conditions and formalities other than those specified by the present chapter and Chapter III below.
A security on a business does not give the secured creditor the right to have the business allotted to him in payment up to the full amount due.

Article L 142-2. The security subject to the provisions of this chapter may cover the following items only as forming part of a business: style and trademark, leasing rights, clientele and custom, company building, equipment or materials used for the operation of the business, patents, licences, trademarks, industrial drawings and designs, and in general the intellectual property rights attached thereto.
A certificate of addition subsequent to the security, which includes the patent to which it applies shall follow the fate of this patent and, as shall it, be part of the security as constituted.
For lack of an explicit and precise designation in the instrument creating it, the security shall cover only the style and trademark, leasing rights, clientele and custom.
If the security relates to a business and its branches, then these must be designated by the precise indication of their seat.

Article L223-18. A limited liability company is managed by one or more natural persons.
The managers [gérants] may be chosen from outside of the members [associés]. They are appointed by the members, in the articles of association [statuts] or by an ordinary decision, according to the conditions laid down in Article L223-29. Under the same conditions, the reference to the name of a manager in the articles of association can, in the case of the cessation of the functions of this manager for whatever cause, be repealed by way of decision of the shareholders.
In the absence of provisions in the articles of association, they are appointed for the duration of the company.
In his dealings with the shareholders, the powers of the managers are determined by the articles of association, and in case of their silence, according to Article L.221-4.
In his dealings with third parties, the manager is invested with the most extensive powers to act in all circumstances in the name of the company, unless the powers are expressly attributed by the law to the members.
The company is bound in the same way by the acts of the manager which are not covered by the company's purpose, unless it can prove that the third party knew that the act exceeded this purpose or that he could not have been ignorant thereof given the circumstances, excluding that the mere publication of the articles of association suffices to constitute such proof.
Provisions in the articles of association restricting the powers of the managers which result from the present article are inapplicable towards third parties.
In the case of a plurality of managers, they exercise power separately as laid down in the present article.
Opposition formed by one manager against the acts of another manager does not have effect in respect of third parties, unless it can be established that they had knowledge thereof.

Article L223-22. Managers are jointly or severally liable, depending on the case, to the company or to third parties for infringements of the legislative or regulatory provisions applicable to limited liability companies, for violations of the articles of association, and for errors committed in their management.
Should more than one manager have participated in the same facts, the court is to determine the contributory share of each to the compensation of damage.
Besides the proceedings for compensation of loss suffered personally, the member can bring proceedings for civil liability against the managers, either individually or as a group in accordance with the conditions laid down in a decree of the Council of State [Conseil d'État]. The claimants are authorized to pursue compensation for the entirety of the loss suffered by the company to which, if the case arises, damages cam be awarded.

---

[18] Translations by E. Ramaekers/H. Hauröder.

Any clause in the articles of association is deemed not written that have the effect of subordinating the exercise of civil proceedings to prior notice to or authorization of the meeting [assemblée], or which entails in advance a waiver of the exercise of these proceedings.
No decision by the meeting may have the effect of extinguishing civil liability proceedings against the managers for errors committed in the performance of their office.

Article L225-35. The board of directors [conseil d'administration] determines the orientation of the activities of the company and ensures their implementation. Without prejudice to the powers expressly attributed to the shareholders' meetings [assemblée d'actionnaires], and within the limits of the company's purpose, it deals with all matters relevant to the good conduct of the company's business and decides through its deliberations the matters that concern it.
In its dealings with third parties, the company is bound even by acts of its board of directors which are not covered by the company's purpose, unless it can prove that the third party knew that the act exceeded that purpose or that he could not have been ignorant thereof given the circumstances, excluding that the mere publication of the articles of association suffices to constitute such proof.
The board of directors carries out the inspections and verifications which it considers appropriate. The chairman [président] or general manager [directeur général] of the company is required to communicate to each director [adminstrateur] all the documents and information necessary to perform its task.
Securities [cautions], avals and guarantees given by companies other than banking or financial institutions are the subject of an authorization by the board under the conditions laid down in a decree by the Council of State [Conseil d'État]. That decree also lays down the conditions under which the overstepping of that authorization can be raised against third parties.

Article L225-56. I. - The general manager is invested with the most extensive powers to act in the name of the company in all circumstances. He is to exercise these powers within the limits of the company's purpose and those that the law expressly attributes to shareholders' meetings and to the board of directors.
He represents the company in its dealings with third parties. The company is bound even by those acts of the general manager that do not relate to the company's purpose, unless it can prove that the third party knew that the act exceeded that purpose or that he could not have been ignorant thereof given the circumstances, excluding that the mere publication of the articles of association suffices to constitute such proof.
Provisions in the articles of association and decisions of the board of directors limiting the powers of the general manager are inapplicable towards third parties.
II. - In agreement with the general manager, the board of directors shall determine the scope and the duration of the powers conferred upon the assistant general managers [directeurs généraux délégués].
The assistant general managers have the same powers as the general manager with respect to third parties.

Article L225-57. It can be stipulated in the articles of association of any public limited company that it shall be governed by the provisions of this sub-section. In that case, the company remains subject to all rules applicable to public limited companies, with the exception of those contained in Articles L225-17 to L225-56.
The introduction of this stipulation, or its deletion, can be decided during the existence of the company.

Article L225-64. The management board [directoire] is invested with the most extensive powers to act in the name of the company behalf in any circumstances. It exercises them within the limits of the company's purpose and subject to those expressly attributed by the law to the supervisory board and shareholders' meetings.
In dealings with third parties, the company is bound even by acts of the management board that do not relate to the company's purpose, unless it can prove that the third party knew that the act exceeded that purpose or that he could not have been ignorant thereof given the circumstances, excluding that the mere publication of the articles of association suffices to constitute such proof.
Provisions of the articles of association limiting the powers of the management board are inapplicable towards third parties.
The management board considers and takes its decisions in accordance with the conditions laid down by the articles of association.

Article L225-66 The chairman of the management board [président du directoire] or if the case arises the sole general manager [directeur général unique], represents the company in its dealings with third parties.
Nevertheless, the articles of association may empower the supervisory board to attribute the same power of representation to one or more other members of the management board, who will then carry the title of general

manager.
Provisions of the articles of association limiting the powers of representation of the company are inapplicable towards third parties.

Article L225-251. The directors [administrateurs] and general manager [directeur général] are individually or jointly liable, depending on the case, to the company or to third parties either for infringements of legislative or regulatory provisions applicable to public limited companies, for violations of the articles of association, or for faults committed in their management.
If more than one director, or more than one director and the general manager, have participated in the same acts, the Court determines the contributory share of each to the reparation of damage.

Article L225-252. Besides the proceedings for compensation of loss personally, the shareholders may either individually or in an association fulfilling the conditions laid down in Article L.225-120, or as a group in accordance with conditions to be laid down in a decree of the Council of State [Conseil d'Etat], bring proceedings for civil liability against the directors or general manager. The claimants are authorized to pursue compensation for the entirety of the loss suffered by the company to which, if the case arises, damages can be awarded.

Article L 442-6. *[Paragraph I is omitted.]* II. – Clauses or contracts are void when providing a producer, a trader, a manufacturer or a person registered in the index of craftsmen with the possibility:
[Subparagraphs (a) and (b) are omitted.]
(c) to prohibit the fellow contracting party from assigning to third parties claims which he himself has.
[Paragraphs III and IV are omitted.]

Article L 624-14. The seller may retain goods [marchandises] that have not been delivered or dispatched to the debtor or to a third party acting on his behalf.

Article L624-16. Movable things delivered precariously [à titre précaire] to the debtor or those transferred to a patrimony of a fiducie [patrimoine fiduciaire] of which the debtor remains to have the right to use or the right to enjoy in his capacity of constituant, may be claimed if they still exist in kind.
Things [biens] sold under a retention of title clause may equally be claimed if they still exist in kind at the time proceedings are opened. This clause must have been agreed upon by the parties in writing at the latest at the time of delivery. It may be laid down in a document governing a number of commercial operations entered into by the parties.
The recovery claim in kind may be brought under the same conditions with respect to movable things incorporated in another thing where they may be removed without damaging them. A recovery claim in kind may also be made in relation to fungible things where things of the same nature and the same quality are in the possession of the debtor or any person keeping them on his behalf has.
In every instance, the thing may not be recovered if, by decision of the supervisory judge [juge-commissaire], the price is paid immediately. The supervisory judge may also, with the consent of the petitioning creditor, grant a moratorium [délai de règlement]. The payment of the price shall thus be considered equivalent to [the payment] of debts referred to under Article L 622-17(I).

Article L 624-18. The price or a part of the price of the things [biens] as meant in Article L 624-16, which was not paid nor settled in valuables or set off between the debtor and the purchaser at the date of the order opening the proceedings, may be claimed. Insurance payouts subrogated for the property may be claimed under the same conditions.

Part V. Private Law

Construction and Housing Code [Code de la Construction et d l'Habitation]. Version in force from 16 July 2006. Selected provision: Article L 251-3.

Article L 251-3. The construction lease confers upon the lessee an immovable property right [droit réel immobilier].
This right may be burdened with a hypothec, just as the constructions built on the rented land; it can be seized through the prescribed forms for seizure of immovable things [saisie immobilière].
The lessee may assign all or part of his rights or contribute them to a company. The assignees or the company are held to the same obligations as the assignor who remains liable for them until the completion of the whole of the constructions that the lessee has undertaken to build, by application of Article L. 251-1.
The lessee may assign the passive servitudes indispensable to the realization of the constructions provided for by the lease.

Rural Code [Code Rural]. Version in force at 26 August 2010. Selected provision: Article 451-1.

Article 451-1. The right of emphyteusis [bail emphytéotique] of immovable things gives the holder a property right which is susceptible to a hypothec; this right may be assigned and seized in the forms as prescribed for seizure of immovable things [saisie immobilière].
This right must be created for more than eighteen years and may not exceed ninety-nine years; it cannot be tacitly renewed.

Monetary and Financial Code [Code Monétaire et Financier]. Consolidated version of 29 July 2010. Selected provision: Article L 313-23.

Article L 313-23. Any credit which a credit institution grants to a private-law or public-law legal entity, or to a natural person for use in the exercise of his business activities, may give rise to the assignment or pledge [nantissement] by the beneficiary of the credit of any claim which he may have as against a third party, private-law or public-law legal entity, or natural person, if it relates to his business activities, for the benefit of that institution, by simply submitting a list of claims [bordereau].
Claims which are due and payable may be assigned or pledged, even for the future. Claims resulting from an instrument that has already been executed, or which is yet to be executed but the amount and due date of which have not yet been determined, may equally be assigned or pledged.
The invoice must include the following elements:
1. The designation "deed of assignment of receivables" or "deed of pledge of receivables", as applicable;
2. An indication that the document is subject to the provisions of Articles L 313-23 to L 313-34;
3. The name of the credit institution which is the beneficiary;
4. The designation or individualization of the claims assigned or pledged, or of the elements likely to create that designation or that individualization, particularly by indication of the debtor, the place of payment, the amount of the claims or of their valuation and, if applicable, their due date.
However, when the transfer of the claims assigned or pledged is effected via an electronic process which makes it possible to identify them, the invoice may merely indicate, in addition to the elements indicated in 1, 2 and 3 above, the means through which they are transferred, their number and their overall amount.
In the event of a dispute being raised concerning the existence or transfer of one of the claims, the assignee may prove, by any means possible, that the claim which is the object of the dispute is included in the overall amount shown on the invoice.
A document from which one of the above indications is missing does not constitute a valid deed of assignment or pledge of claims within the meaning of Articles L 313-23 to L 313-34.

Civil Code of Germany [Bürgerliches Gesetzbuch (BGB)] of 18 August 1896, in the version promulgated on 2 January 2002 (*BGBl* I p. 42, 2909; 2003 I p. 738), last amended by Article 1 of the law of 24 July 2010 (*BGBl.* I p. 977).[19] Selected provisions from Books 1, 2 and 3.

Book 1. General Part

Division 1. Persons

Title 1. Natural persons, consumers, entrepreneurs

§ 1. The legal personality [Rechtsfähigkeit] of a human being begins on the completion of birth.

§ 2. Majority [Volljährigkeit] begins on the completion of the eighteenth year of age.

§§ 3 – 6. (Repealed.)

[§§ 7 – 9 are omitted.]

§10. (Repealed.)

[§§ 11 – 12 are omitted.]

§ 13. A consumer [Verbraucher] is any natural person who concludes a legal transaction for a purpose that can neither be attributed to his business nor his independent professional activities.

§ 14. (1) An entrepreneur [Unternehmer] is a natural or legal person or a partnership with legal personality who or which, for the conclusion of a legal transaction, acts in exercise of his business or independent professional activity.
(2) A partnership with legal personality is a partnership that has the capacity to acquire rights and to assume liabilities.

§§ 15 – 20. (Repealed.)

[The remainder of Division 1 is omitted.]

Division 2. Objects and animals

§ 90. Objects [Sachen] as it is used in this law can only be corporeal objects [körperliche Gegenstände].

[The remainder of Division 2 is omitted.]

Division 3. Legal transactions [Rechtsgeschäfte]

Title 1. Legal Capacity [Geschäftsfähigkeit]

§ 104. Lacking legal capacity is
1. a person who has not yet completed his seventh year of age,
2. a person who is in a state of mental disturbance caused by disease that excludes the free determination of will [die freie Willensbestimmung ausschließenden Zustand krankhafter Störung der Geistestätigkeit], unless the state by its nature is a temporary one.

§ 105. (1) The declaration of intention [Willenserklärung] of a person lacking legal capacity is void.
(2) A declaration of intention that is made in a state of unconsciousness or temporary mental disturbance is also void.

---

[19] Translation by B. Akkermans, H. Hauröder, N. Kornet and S. Weishaar.

Part V. Private Law

§ 106. A minor who has completed his seventh year of age has, in accordance with the requirements §§107 to 113 limited legal capacity.

§ 107. A minor requires the consent [Einwilligung] of his legal representative for a declaration of intention through which he receives not only a legal benefit.

§ 108 (1) If the minor concludes a contract without the necessary consent of the legal representative, the effectiveness of the contract is subject to the ratification [Genehmigung] of the legal representative.
(2) If the other party requests the representative give a declaration regarding his ratification, the declaration can only be made to the other party; a declaration or refusal of ratification made to the minor before the request is ineffective. The ratification can only be declared before the expiry of two weeks after receipt of the request; if it is not declared, it is held to have been refused.
(3) If the minor has attained full legal capacity, his ratification takes the place of the ratification of the representative.

§ 109. (1) Until the ratification of the contract, the other party is entitled to withdrawal [Widerruf]. The withdrawal may also be made to the minor.
(2) If the other party knew of the minority, he may only withdraw if the minor contrary to the truth claimed the consent of the legal representative; he may not withdraw in this case either if, when the contract was concluded, he knew of the lack of consent.

§ 110. A contract concluded by the minor without the approval [Zustimmung] of the legal representative is held to be effective from the beginning if the minor effects performance under the contract with means that were given to him for this purpose or for free disposal by the legal representative or with his approval by a third party.

§ 111. A unilateral legal transaction undertaken by a minor without the necessary consent of the legal representative is ineffective. If the minor undertakes such a legal transaction with regard to another person with this consent, the legal transaction is ineffective if the minor does not present the consent in writing and the other person rejects the legal transaction for this reason without undue delay. Rejection is excluded if the representative had given the other person notice of the consent

[§§ 112 – 115 are omitted.]

Title 2. Declaration of intention [Willenserklärung]

§ 116. A declaration of intention is not void because the declarant has made a mental reservation that he does not intend the declaration made. The declaration is void if it is to be made to another person and this person knows of the reservation.

§ 117. (1) Where a declaration of intention that is to be made to another person is only made for the sake of appearance, with that person's consent, it is void.
(2) If a sham transaction conceals another legal transaction, the provisions applicable to the concealed transaction apply.

§ 118. A declaration of intention that is not seriously intended, which is made in the expectation that the lack of seriousness will not be mistaken, is void.

§ 119. (1) A person who, when making a declaration of intention, was mistaken about its contents or had no intention of making a declaration with this content at all, may avoid [anfechten] the declaration if it is to be assumed that he would not have made the declaration with knowledge of the factual situation and with a rational appreciation of the circumstances.
(2) Also held to be a mistake about the content of the declaration is a mistake about such characteristics of a person or a thing as are commonly [im Verkehr] regarded as essential is.

§ 120. A declaration of intention that has been incorrectly transmitted by the person or apparatus used for its transmission may be avoided subject to the same condition as a mistakenly given declaration of intention under § 119.

§ 121. (1) Avoidance [Anfechtung] must take place, in the cases set out in §§ 119 and 120, without culpable delay (without undue delay) after the person entitled to avoid has obtained knowledge of the ground for avoidance. Avoidance made to an absent person is held to take place in due time if the declaration of avoidance is dispatched without undue delay.
(2) Avoidance is excluded if ten years have elapsed since the declaration of intention was made.

§ 122. (1) If a declaration of intention is void under § 118, or avoided under §§ 119 and 120, the declarant must, if the declaration was to be made to another person, compensate this person, or failing this any third party, for the damage that the other or the third party suffers as a result of relying on the validity of the declaration; but not in excess of the total amount of the interest which the other or the third party has in the validity of the declaration.
(2) A duty to compensate for damage does not arise if the injured person knew the reason for the nullity or the voidability or did not know it as a result of his negligence [Fahrlässigkeit] (ought to have known it).

§ 123. (1) A person who has been induced to make a declaration of intention by wilful deceit [arglistige Täuschung] or unlawfully by threat [widerrechtlich durch Drohung] may avoid the declaration.
(2) Where a third party carried out this deceit, a declaration that had to be made to another may be avoided only if the latter knew or ought to have known of the deceit. In so far as a person other than the person to whom the declaration was to be made has acquired a right directly under the declaration, the declaration made to him may be avoided if he knew or ought to have known of the deceit.

§ 124. (1) The avoidance of a declaration of intention that is voidable under § 123 may only take place within one year.
(2) The period commences in the case of wilful deceit at the point in time when the person entitled to avoid discovers the deceit, and in case of threat, from the point in time when the predicament ceases. With respect to the course of time, the provisions in §§ 206, 210 and 211 applicable to the limitation period apply mutatis mutandis.
(3) Avoidance is excluded, if ten years have passed since the declaration of intention was made.

§ 125. A legal transaction [Rechtsgeschäft] that lacks the form prescribed by law is void. Lack of the form specified by the legal transaction, in case of doubt, also results in nullity.

§ 126. (1) If written form is prescribed by law, the document must be signed by the creator with his name in his own hand, or by way of his notarially certified mark.
(2) In the case of a contract, the signature of the parties must be made on the same document. Where several identical documents of the contract are drawn up, it suffices if each party signs the document intended for the other party.
(3) Written form may be replaced by electronic form, unless a different consequence follows from the law.
(4) Notarial authentication [Beurkundung] takes the place of the written form.

[§§ 126a – 129 are omitted.]

§130. (1) A declaration of intention that is to be made to another, if made in that person's absence, becomes effective at the point in time at which the declaration reaches him. It does not become effective if a withdrawal [Widerruf] reaches the other person previously or at the same time.
(2) The effectiveness of a declaration of intention is not affected if the declarant dies or becomes legally incapable after it is made.
(3) These provisions apply even if the declaration of intention is to be made to an authority.

[§§ 131 – 132 are omitted.]

§ 133. When interpreting a declaration of intention, the actual intention is to be ascertained rather than adhering to the literal meaning of the expression.

§134. A legal transaction that violates a statutory prohibition is void, unless a different consequence follows from the law.

[§§ 135 – 136 are omitted.]

§137. The power to dispose [Befugnis zur Verfügung] over a transferable right cannot be excluded or limited by a legal transaction. The effectiveness of an obligation not to dispose over such a right is unaffected by this provision.

§ 138. (1) A legal transaction that violates good morals [guten Sitten] is void.
(2) In particular, a legal transaction is void by which a person, by exploiting the predicament, inexperience, lack of sound judgment or considerable weakness of will of another, causes to be promised or granted to himself or a third party, in return for a performance, pecuniary advantages which are clearly disproportionate to the performance.

§ 139. If a part of a legal transaction is void, then the whole legal transaction is void, unless it is to be assumed that it would have been undertaken even without the void part.

§ 140. Where a void legal transaction fulfils the requirements of another legal transaction, then the latter is held to be valid, if it is to be assumed that its validity would be intended if there were knowledge of the nullity.

§ 142. (1) If a voidable legal transaction is avoided, it is to be regarded as having been void from the beginning.
(2) A person who knew or ought to have known of the possibility of avoidance is treated, in case of avoidance, as if he had known or ought to have known of the nullity of the legal transaction.

§ 143. (1) Avoidance occurs by declaration to the opposing party.
(2) The opposing party is, in the case of a contract, the other party to the contract and, in the case of § 123 paragraph (2) sentence 2, the person who has acquired a right directly under the contract.
(3) In the case of a unilateral legal transaction that was to be undertaken in relation to another person, the other person is the opposing party. The same applies to a legal transaction that is required to be undertaken in relation to another person or to an authority, even if the legal transaction has already been undertaken as against the authority.
(4) In the case of any other kind of unilateral legal transaction, any person who has received a legal advantage directly on the basis of the legal transaction is an opposing party. The avoidance may, however, if the declaration of intention was to be made to an authority, be made by declaration to the authority; the authority shall inform the person who was directly affected by the legal transaction of the avoidance.

§ 144. (1) Avoidance is excluded, if the voidable legal transaction is confirmed by the person entitled to avoid.
(2) The confirmation is not required to have the form prescribed for the legal transaction.

Title 3. Contract [Vertrag]

§ 145. A person who offers to another to conclude a contract is bound by the offer [Antrag], unless he has excluded this binding effect.

§ 146. An offer lapses if it is rejected as against the offeror, or if it is not accepted in due time as against this person in accordance with §§ 147 to 149.

§ 147. (1) An offer made to a person who is present may only be accepted immediately. This also applies to an offer made by one person to another using a telephone or another technical apparatus.
(2) An offer made to an absent person may only be accepted up to the point in time when the offeror may expect receipt of the answer under ordinary circumstances.

§ 148. Where the offeror has fixed a period of time for the acceptance of an offer, the acceptance may only occur within this period.

§ 149. Where a declaration of acceptance that reaches the offeror belatedly was sent in such a way that it would have reached him in time if it had been sent by regular delivery, and if the offeror ought to have recognized this, he must notify the acceptor without undue delay after the receipt of the declaration of the delay, unless this has already been done. If he delays in sending the notification, the acceptance is held not to be late.

§ 150. (1) The late acceptance of an offer is held to be a new offer.
(2) An acceptance with additions, limitations or other modifications is held to be a rejection combined with a new offer.

§ 151. A contract is formed by the acceptance of an offer without the offeror needing to be notified of acceptance, if such a declaration is not to be expected according to common practice [Verkehrssitte], or if the offeror has waived it. The point in time at which the offer lapses, is determined in accordance with the intention of the offeror, which is to be inferred from the offer or the circumstances.

§ 152. If a contract is notarially authenticated without both parties being present at the same time, the contract is formed, unless otherwise provided, on the authentication of acceptance effected in accordance with § 128. The provision of § 151 sentence 2 applies.

§ 153. The formation of the contract is not prevented by the offeror dying or becoming legally incapable before acceptance, unless a different intention of the offeror is to be assumed.

§ 154. (1) As long as the parties have not yet agreed on all points of a contract about which an agreement is to be reached according to the declaration of even only one party, the contract is, in case of doubt, not concluded. Agreement on individual points is not legally binding even if a record has been made.
(2) If authentication of the proposed contract has been arranged, the contract is, in case of doubt, not concluded until authentication has taken place.

§ 155. If the parties to a contract which they consider to have been concluded have, in fact, not agreed on a point on which an agreement was required to be reached, whatever is agreed applies in so far as it is to be assumed that the contract would have been concluded even without a provision concerning this point.

[§ 156 is omitted.]

§ 157. Contracts are to be interpreted in accordance with good faith [Treu und Glauben], taking common practice [Verkehrssitte] into consideration.

[Titles 4 and 5 are omitted.]

Title 6. Consent and ratification

§ 182. (1) If the effectiveness of a contract, or of a unilateral legal transaction which is to be undertaken as against another, depends on the approval of a third party, the grant and refusal of approval may be declared either to one party or to the other.
(2) The approval is not required to have the form prescribed for the legal transaction.
(3) If a unilateral legal transaction, the effectiveness of which depends on the approval of a third party, is undertaken with the consent of the third party, then the provisions of § 111 sentences 2 and 3 apply mutatis mutandis.

[§ 183 is omitted.]

§ 184. (1) Subsequent approval (ratification) takes effect retroactively from the point in time when the legal transaction was undertaken, unless otherwise provided.

[§ 185 is omitted.]

Division 4. Periods of time [Fristen, Termine]

[§ 186 is omitted.]

§ 187. (1) If an event [Ereignis] or a certain moment during a day is decisive for the start of a period of time, for the calculation of the period time, the day on which the event or moment occurs is not included.
(2) If the start of a day is decisive for the start of a period of time, this day is included in the calculation of the period of time. The same applies for the day of birth in case of calculation of age.

[The remainder of Division 4 is omitted.]

Part V. Private Law

Division 5. Prescription [Verjährung]

Title 1. Subject matter and duration of prescription

§194. (1) The right of one person to require an act or forbearance of another (claim) [Anspruch] is subject to prescription.
[Paragraph 2 is omitted.]

§ 195. The regular prescription period [regelmäßige Verjährungsfrist] is three years.

§ 196. Claims for the transfer of ownership in respect to a piece of land, as well as in respect to creation, assignment or termination of a right in respect to a piece of land or for the alteration of the content of such a right as well as the claims for the counter-performance of such prescribe after a period of ten years.

§ 197. (1) In so far as is not determined otherwise, the following claims prescribe after a period of 30 years:
1. Claims for the revindication of the right of ownership and other property rights
[The remainder of §197 is omitted]

[§ 198 is omitted.]

§ 199. (1) The regular prescription period starts to run at the end of the year, in which
1. the claim has arisen, and
2. the creditor acquires or, in the absence of gross negligence, should have acquired, knowledge of the circumstances giving rise to the claim and the identity of the debtor.
[Paragraphs 2, 3 and 3a are omitted.]
(4) Other claims, such as claims for compensation for damage, prescribe without regard to the knowledge or grossly negligent knowledge after a period of ten years after they have arisen.
[Paragraph 5 is omitted.]

§ 200. The prescription period that is applicable to claims that are not subject to the regular prescription period, starts at the moment the claim arises, in so far as another commencement of the prescription period is not provided. § 199 paragraph (5) applies mutatis mutandis.

[The remainder of Book 1 is omitted.]

Book 2. Law of Obligation Relationships [Recht der Schuldverhältnisse]

Division 1. Subject matter of obligation relationships

Title 1. Duty of performance

§ 241. (1) By virtue of an obligation relationship the creditor [Gläubiger] is entitled to claim performance from the debtor [Schuldner]. The performance may also consist in a forbearance.
(2) An obligation relationship may also, depending on its contents, oblige each party to take into account the rights, legal interests and other interests of the other party.

[§241a is omitted.]

§ 242. A debtor has a duty to perform according to the requirements of good faith [Treu und Glauben], taking common practice [Verkehrssitte] into consideration.

§ 243. (1) A person who is obliged to provide an object defined only according to its class must provide an object of average kind and quality.
(2) If the debtor has done what is necessary on his part to provide such an object, the obligation relationship is restricted to that object.

[§§ 244 – 248 are omitted.]

§ 249. (1) A person who is obliged to compensate for damage [Schadensersatz] must restore the state of affairs that would have existed if the circumstance obliging him to compensate had not occurred.
(2) Where compensation for damage is to be provided due to injury to a person or damage to a thing, the creditor may instead of restoration [Herstellung] demand the required monetary amount. Where a thing is damaged, the monetary amount required under sentence 1 only includes value-added tax if and to the extent that it is actually incurred.

§ 250. The creditor may fix a appropriate period of time [angemessene Frist] for restoration by the person obliged to compensate through a declaration that he will reject restoration after expiry of this period. After the expiry of the period of time, the creditor may demand compensation in money, if restoration does not occur in due time; the claim to restoration is excluded.

§ 251 (1) To the extent that restoration is not possible or is not sufficient for the indemnification [Entschädigung] of the creditor, the person obliged to compensate must compensate the creditor in money.
(2) The person obliged to compensate may indemnify the creditor in money if restoration is only possible with disproportionate expenditure. Expenditure incurred as a result of the medical treatment of an injured animal is not disproportionate simply because it significantly exceeds its value.

§ 252. The damage to be compensated also encompasses lost profits. Profits that are deemed to be lost are those that in the normal course of events or in the special circumstances, in particular due to the measures and precautions taken, could with probability be expected.

§ 253. (1) For damage that is not pecuniary loss [immaterieller Schaden], indemnification in money may only be demanded in those cases determined by law.
(2) Where compensation for damage is to be made for an injury to body, health, freedom or sexual self-determination, fair indemnification in money may also be demanded for any damage that is not pecuniary loss.

§ 254. (1) If fault on the part of the injured person contributed to the occurrence of the damage, the duty to compensate as well as the extent of compensation to be made will depend on the circumstances, in particular to what extent the damage is caused predominantly by one or the other party.
(2) This also applies if the fault of the injured person is limited to the fact that he failed to draw to the attention of the debtor to the risk of unusually extensive damage, where the debtor neither was nor ought to have been aware of the risk, or he failed to avert or reduce the damage. The provision of § 278 applies mutatis mutandis.

§ 255. A person who must compensate for damage for the loss of a thing or a right is only obliged to compensate in return for the assignment of the claims [Abtretung der Ansprüche] which the person entitled to the compensation holds against third parties on the basis of ownership of the thing or on the basis of the right.

[§§ 256 – 265 are omitted.]

§ 266. The debtor is not entitled to render partial performance.

§ 267. (1) If the debtor does not have to perform in person, a third party may also render performance. The consent of the debtor is not required.
(2) The creditor may reject the performance if the debtor objects.

§ 268. (1) If the creditor carries out compulsory execution [Zwangvollstreckung] against an object belonging to the debtor, anyone who risks losing a right in the object due to execution is entitled to satisfy the creditor. The possessor of a thing is entitled to the same right if he risks losing possession due to the execution.
(2) The satisfaction may also take place by deposit [Hinterlegung] or by set-off [Aufrechnung].
(3) To the extent that the third party satisfies the creditor the claim passes to him. The passing of ownership may not be asserted to the disadvantage of the creditor.

§ 269. (1) If the place of performance is neither specified nor evident from the circumstances, in particular from the nature of the obligation relationship, performance must be made in the place where the creditor had his residence at the time when the obligation relationship arose.

(2) If the obligation arose in the course of business of the debtor, the place of establishment takes the place of the residence if the debtor had his business establishment at another place.
(3) It may not be concluded from the circumstance alone that the debtor has assumed shipping costs that the place to which the shipment is to be made is to be the place of performance.

§ 270. (1) In case of doubt, the debtor must transmit money at his own risk and his own expense to the creditor at the residence of the latter.
(2) If the claim [Forderung] arose in the course of business of the creditor, then, if the creditor has his business establishment in another place, the place of establishment takes the place of the residence.
(3) Where, as the result of a change in the place of residence or business establishment of the creditor occurring after the obligation arises, the costs or risk of transmission increase, the creditor must in the former case bear the additional costs and in the latter case the risk.
(4) The provisions on the place of performance remain unaffected.

§ 271. (1) If the time for performance is neither specified nor evident from the circumstances, the creditor may demand performance immediately, and the debtor may effect it immediately.
(2) If a time has been specified, then in case of doubt it must be assumed that the creditor may not demand performance prior to that time, but the debtor may effect it earlier.

[§ 272 is omitted.]

§ 273. (1) If the debtor has a claim that is due against the creditor under the same legal relationship as that from which his obligation arises, he may, unless another consequence follows from the obligation relationship, refuse the performance owed by him, until the performance owed to him is effected (right of retention) [Zurückbehaltungsrecht].
(2) The person who is obliged to return an object has the same right, if he is entitled to a claim that is due for expenditure on the object or because of damage caused to him by the object, unless he obtained the object by means of an intentionally committed wrongful act [unerlaubte Handlung].
(3) The creditor may avert the exercise of the right of retention by providing security. The provision of security by guarantors is excluded.

§ 274 (1) As against the legal action by the creditor, assertion of the right to of retention only has the effect that the debtor is to be ordered to effect performance in return for receiving the performance owed to him (concurrent performance) [Erfüllung Zug um Zug].
(2) On the basis of such an order the creditor may pursue his claim by way of compulsory execution, without effecting the performance he owes, if the debtor is in delay of acceptance.

§ 275. (1) A claim to performance is excluded in so far as that performance is impossible for the debtor or for any other person.
(2) The debtor may refuse performance to the extent it requires expenditure which, taking into account the content of the obligation relationship and the requirements of good faith, is grossly disproportionate to the interest of the creditor in performance. When determining what efforts may be expected of the debtor, it must also be considered whether he is responsible for the obstacle to performance.
(3) The debtor may further refuse performance if he is to effect the performance in person and, when the obstacle to his performance is weighed against the interest of the creditor in performance, performance cannot be expected of him.
(4) The rights of the creditor are governed by §§ 280, 283 to 285, 311a and 326.

§ 276. (1) The debtor is responsible for intention and negligence, if a stricter or more lenient degree of liability is neither laid down nor to be inferred from the other content of the obligation relationship, in particular from the giving of a guarantee or the assumption of a procurement risk. The provisions of §§ 827 and 828 apply mutatis mutandis.
(2) A person acts negligently if he fails to exercise due and necessary care [im Verkehr erforderliche Sorgfalt].
(3) The debtor may not be released in advance from liability for intention.

§ 277. A person who owes only such standard of care that he has to exercise in his own affairs is not released from liability for gross negligence [grober Fahrlässigkeit].

§ 278. The debtor is responsible for fault on the part of his legal representative, and of persons whom he uses to perform his obligation, to the same extent as for his own fault. The provision of § 276 paragraph (3) does not apply.

§ 279. (Repealed.)

§ 280. (1) If the debtor violates a duty arising from the obligation relationship, the creditor may demand compensation for the damage caused thereby. This does not apply if the debtor is not responsible for the violation of duty.
(2) Compensation for delay in performance may be demanded by the creditor only subject to the additional pre-requisites of § 286.
(3) Compensation instead of performance may be demanded by the creditor only under the additional pre-requisites of §§ 281, 282 or 283.

§ 281. (1) To the extent that the debtor does not effect performance when it is due or does not effect performance as owed, the creditor may, subject to the pre-requisites of § 280 paragraph (1), demand compensation instead of performance, if he has set a reasonable period of time for the debtor for performance or subsequent fulfilment, but without result. If the debtor has effected a partial performance, the creditor may only demand compensation instead of whole performance if he has no interest in the partial performance. If the debtor has not effected performance as owed, the creditor may not demand compensation instead of the whole performance if the violation of duty is immaterial.
(2) The setting of a period of time for performance can be dispensed if the debtor seriously and definitively refuses performance or if there are special circumstances which, on weighing the interests of both parties, justify the immediate assertion of a claim to compensation.
(3) If the nature of the violation of duty is such that setting a period of time is out of the question, a warning notice will take its place.
(4) The claim for performance is excluded as soon as the creditor has demanded compensation instead of performance.
(5) If the creditor demands compensation instead of whole performance, the debtor is entitled to claim the return of his performance under §§ 346 to 348.

§ 282. If the debtor violates a duty under § 241 paragraph (2), the creditor may, subject to the pre-requisites of § 280 paragraph (1), demand compensation instead of performance, if allowing performance by the debtor can no longer reasonably be expected of him.

§ 283. If the debtor is not obliged to perform pursuant to § 275 paragraphs (1) to (3), the creditor may, subject to the pre-requisites of § 280 paragraph (1), demand compensation instead of performance. § 281 paragraph (1) sentences 2 and 3 and paragraph (5) apply mutatis mutandis.

§ 284. In the place of compensation instead of performance, the creditor may demand reimbursement of expenditure which, in reliance on receiving performance, he has made and was fairly [billigerweise] entitled to make, unless its purpose would not have been achieved, even if the debtor had not violated his duty.

§ 285. (1) If the debtor, as a result of the circumstance by reason of which, according to § 275 paragraph (1) to (3), he has no duty of performance, obtains a replacement or a claim to replacement for the object owed, the creditor may demand return of what has been received in replacement or an assignment of the claim to replacement..
(2) If the creditor may demand compensation instead of performance, this will be reduced, if he exercises the right provided for in paragraph (1), by the value of the replacement or the claim to replacement he has obtained.

§ 286. (1) If the debtor fails to perform, following a warning notice from the creditor that is made after performance has become due, he is in delay as a result of the warning notice. Bringing an action for performance as well as the service of default summons in collection proceedings are equivalent to a warning notice.
(2) There is no need for a warning notice if
1. a period of time has been determined for performance according to the calendar,
2. performance must be preceded by an event and a reasonable time for performance has been determined in such a way that it can be calculated, starting from the event, according to the calendar,
3. the debtor seriously and definitively refuses performance,

4. for special reasons, on weighing the interests of both parties, the immediate commencement of the delay is justified.
(3) The debtor of a claim for payment is in delay at the latest if he does not perform within thirty days after the due date and receipt of an invoice or equivalent statement of payment; this only applies to a debtor who is a consumer if these consequences are specifically referred to in the invoice or statement of payment. If the point of time at which the invoice or payment statement is received by the debtor is uncertain, a debtor who is not a consumer is in delay at the latest thirty days after the due date and receipt of the counter-performance.
(4) The debtor is not in delay for as long as performance is not made as the result of a circumstance for which he is not responsible.

§ 287. While he is in delay, the debtor is responsible for all negligence. He is liable for performance even in the case of chance events, unless the damage would also have occurred if performance had been made in due time.

[The remainder of Title 1 and Division 2 are omitted.]

Division 3. Contractual obligation relationships [Schuldverhältnisse aus Verträge]

Title 1. Creation, content and termination

Subtitle 1. Creation

§ 311. (1) In order to create an obligation relationship [Schuldverhältnis] by legal transaction [Rechtsgeschäft] as well as to alter the contents of an obligation relationship, a contract [Vertrag] between the parties is necessary, unless otherwise provided by law.
(2) An obligation relationship with duties under § 241 paragraph (2) also arises by
1. the commencement of contractual negotiations
2. the initiation of a contract where one party, with regard to a potential contractual relationship, grants the other party the possibility of affecting his rights, legal interests and other interests, or entrusts these to him, or
3. similar business contacts.
(3) An obligation relationship with duties under § 241 paragraph (2) may also arise in relation to persons who are not themselves to be contracting parties. Such an obligation arises in particular where the third party, by claiming to have been given a special degree of reliance, substantially influences the contractual negotiations or the conclusion of the contract.

§ 311a. (1) It does not stand in the way of the effectiveness of a contract that according to § 275 paragraphs (1) to (3) the debtor does not need to perform and the obstacle to performance already exists at the conclusion of the contract.
(2) The creditor may, at his option, demand compensation instead of performance or reimbursement of his expenditure to the extent specified in § 284. This does not apply if the debtor did not know of the obstacle to performance at the conclusion of the contract and is also not responsible for his lack of knowledge. § 281 paragraph (1) sentences 2 and 3 and paragraph (5) apply mutatis mutandis.

[§§ 311b – 311c and Subtitle 2 are omitted.]

Subtitle 3. Adaptation and termination of contracts

§ 313. (1) If the circumstances which have become the foundation of the contract have significantly changed after the conclusion of the contract and if the parties would not have concluded the contract or would have concluded it with different contents if they had foreseen this change, adaptation of the contract may be demanded in so far as, taking account of all the circumstances of the individual case, in particular the contractual or statutory distribution of risk, adherence to the unadapted contract cannot be expected of one of the parties [Störung des Geschäftsgrundlage].
(2) It is equivalent to a change of circumstances if material preconceptions that have become the foundation of the contract are found to be incorrect.
(3) If adaptation of the contract is not possible or cannot be expected of one of the parties, the disadvantaged party may withdraw from the contract. For long term obligation relationships a right to cancel [Recht zur Kündigung] takes the place of right of withdrawal [Rücktrittsrecht].

§ 314. (1) Long term obligation relationships can be cancelled by each contracting party for a significant reason without the observance of a notice period. A significant reason arises if the continuation of the contractual relationship until the agreed termination [Beendigung] or until the expiry of a notice period cannot be expected of the cancelling party, taking account of all the circumstances of the individual case and weighing the interests of both parties.
(2) If the significant reason consists of a violation of a duty under the contract, the cancellation is allowed only after the expiry without result of a period specified for relief or after a warning notice without result. §323 paragraph (2) applies mutatis mutandis.
(3) The person so entitled may only cancel within a reasonable period after he has obtained knowledge of the reason for cancellation.
(4) The right to demand compensation for damage is not excluded by the cancellation.

[Subtitle 4 is omitted.]

Title 2. Synallagmatic contracts [Gegenseitiger Verträge]

§ 320. A person who is bound by a synallagmatic contract may refuse the performance incumbent upon him until the effectuation of the counter-performance, unless he is obliged to perform beforehand. If the performance is to be made to several persons, an individual person can be refused the part due to him until the effectuation of the whole counter-performance. The provision of § 273 paragraph (3) is not applicable.
(2) If one party has partially performed, the counter-performance cannot be refused in so far as the refusal in the circumstances, in particular due to the relative triviality the part in arrears, is contrary to good faith.

[§§ 321 – 322 are omitted.]

§ 323. (1) If the debtor, in the case of a synallagmatic contract, does not render the performance which is due, or does not render it in conformity with the contract, the creditor may withdraw from the contract [zurücktreten], if he has determined for the debtor without result, an appropriate period of time for performance or subsequent fulfilment [Nacherfüllung].
(2) The setting of a period of time can be dispensed with if
1. the debtor seriously and definitively refuses performance,
2. the debtor does not render performance by a date determined in the contract or within a determined period and in the contract
3. the creditor has made the continuation of his interest in performance subject to the timeliness of performance, or special circumstances exist which, when upon weighing the interests of both parties, justify immediate withdrawal [Rücktritt].
(3) If in view of the nature of the violation of duty the setting a period of time does not come into consideration, a warning notice takes its place.
(4) The creditor may withdraw already before the occurrence of the due date for performance if it is obvious that the pre-requisites for withdrawal will be met.
(5) If the debtor has effected partial performance, the creditor may only withdraw from the whole contract if he has no interest in partial performance. If the debtor has not effected performance in conformity with the contract, the creditor cannot withdraw from the contract if the violation of duty is trivial.
(6) Withdrawal is excluded if the creditor is solely or very predominantly responsible for the circumstance that would entitle him to withdraw or if the circumstance for which the debtor is not responsible occurs at a time when the creditor is in default of acceptance.

§ 324. If the debtor, in the case of a synallagmatic contract, violates a duty under § 241 paragraph (2), the creditor can withdraw if adherence to the contract can no longer be expected of him.

§ 325. The right to demand compensation for damage in case of a synallagmatic contract is not excluded by withdrawal.

§ 326. (1) If, the debtor is not required to perform under § 275 paragraphs (1) to (3), the claim counter-performance is inapplicable; in the case of partial performance, § 441 paragraph (3) applies mutatis mutandis. sentence 1 does not apply if the debtor, in the case of failure to perform in conformity with the contract, does not have to effect subsequent fulfilment under § 275 paragraphs (1) to (3).

(2) If the creditor is solely or predominantly responsible for the circumstance due to which the debtor does not have to effect subsequent fulfilment under § 275 paragraphs (1) to (3), or if this circumstance for which the debtor is not responsible occurs at a time when the creditor is in default of acceptance, the debtor retains the right to counter-performance. He must, however, allow to be credited against him what he saves as a result of the release from performance or through other use of his labour acquires or wilfully refrains from acquiring.
(3) If the creditor demands under § 285 the return of the replacement obtained for the object owed or assignment of the claim to replacement under § 285, he remains obliged to render counter-performance. The latter is reduced, however, under the requirement of § 441 paragraph (3) in so far as the value of the replacement or of the claim to replacement falls short of the value of the performance owed.
(4) In so far as the counter-performance that is not owed under this provision is effected, what has been performed can be demanded back under §§ 346 to 348.
(5) If the debtor does not have to perform under § 275 paragraphs (1) to (3), the creditor may withdraw; § 323 applies mutatis mutandis to the withdrawal, with the proviso that setting of a period of time is unnecessary.

[Titles 3 and 4 are omitted.]

Title 5. Right of Withdrawal; the right of withdrawal and right to return in consumer contracts

Subtitle 1. Withdrawal [Rücktritt]

§ 346. (1) Where a contracting party has contractually reserved the right to withdraw or the party has a statutory right to withdraw, in case of withdrawal, the performances received are to be returned and the benefits derived are to be restored.
(2) Instead of the return or restoration, the creditor is to provide compensation for value, in so far as
1. the return or the restoration of that which was obtained is precluded by its nature,
2. he used up, disposed of, burdened, processed or transformed the received object,
3. the received object has deteriorated or is lost; however, the deterioration that occurred through the designated use of the object is not to be taken into account.
If the contract determines a counter-performance, the calculation of compensation for value is to be based on it; if the compensation for value for the benefit of use of a loan is to be made, it can be shown that the value of the benefit of use was lower.
(3) The obligation to compensate for value does not apply,
1. if the defect entitling the withdrawal only become apparent during the processing or transformation of the object,
2. in so far as the creditor is responsible for the deterioration or loss or the damage would also have occurred to him,
3. if in the case of a statutory right to withdrawal the deterioration or loss has occurred to the person entitled, even though he used the care that he tends to apply to his own affairs.
A remaining enrichment is to be restored.
(4) The creditor can demand compensation for damage according to the standards of §§280 to 283 for a violation of a duty under paragraph 1.

[§ 347 is omitted.]

§ 348. The duties of the parties deriving from the withdrawal are to be performed concurrently. The provisions of §§ 320, 322 apply mutatis mutandis.

§ 349. The withdrawal occurs by declaration to the other party.

§ 350. If no time limit is fixed for the exercise of a contractual right of withdrawal, the other party can fix for the person entitled an appropriate period of time for the exercise. The right to withdraw extinguishes when the withdrawal is not declared before the expiry of the period of time.

[The remainder of Division 3 and Division 4 are omitted.]

Division 5. Assignment of a claim

§ 398. The creditor of a claim [Forderung] can, by contract with another, transfer that claim to this other (assignment) [Abtretung]. The new creditor takes the place of the old creditor with the conclusion of the contract.

§ 399. A claim cannot be assigned if the performance to another person than the original creditor cannot take place without alteration of its content or if the assignment has been excluded by agreement with the debtor.

[§§ 400 – 406 are omitted.]

§ 407. (1) The new creditor must, after the assignment, allow a performance that the debtor makes to the previous creditor, as well as any legal transaction undertaken after the assignment between the debtor and the previous creditor in respect to the claim, allow it to be asserted against him, unless the debtor is aware of the assignment at the moment of performance or the undertaking of the legal transaction.
(2) If, in a legal dispute between the debtor and the previous creditor that has become pending at a court after the assignment, a final and non-appealable judgment in respect to the claim has been made, the new creditor must allow the judgment to be asserted against him, unless the debtor was aware of the assignment on commencement of the legal proceedings started.

[§ 408 is omitted.]

§ 409. (1) If the creditor notifies the debtor that he has assigned the claim, the debtor must allow the notified assignment to be asserted against him, also if it does not take place or has no effect. It is equivalent to a notice that the creditor creates a deed [Urkunde] relating to the assignment to the new creditor identified in the deed and the latter presents it to the debtor.
(2) The notice can only be revoked with the permission of the person who is identified as the new creditor.

[The remainder of Division 5 and Divisions 6 – 7 are omitted.]

Division 8. Particular types of obligation relationships

Title 1. Sale, exchange

Subtitle 1. General provisions

§ 433. (1) By a contract of sale [Kaufvertrag], the seller of an object is obliged to deliver the object to the buyer and to provide ownership of the object. The seller must provide the object to the buyer free from physical and legal defects [Sach- und Rechtsmängeln].
(2) The buyer is obliged to pay the seller the agreed purchase price and to take delivery of the purchased object.

§ 434. (1) The object is free from physical defects [Sachmangel] if it possesses the agreed upon properties [Beschaffenheit] when the risk passes [Gefahrübergang]. In so far as that the properties are not agreed, the object is free of physical defects
1. if it is suitable for the intended use under the contract, or otherwise
2. if it is suitable for the customary use and possesses the properties that are usual in objects of the same kind and which the buyer may expect given the nature of the object.
Properties under sentence 2 no. 2 includes characteristics which the buyer can expect from the public statements by the seller, the producer (§ 4 paragraphs (1) and (2) of the Product Liability Act [Produkthaftungsgesetz]) or his assistant, in particular in advertising or labeling about the specific characteristics of the object, unless the seller was not aware and did not have to be aware of the statement, or at the point in time of the conclusion of the contract it had been corrected in an equivalent manner, or it could not have influenced the decision to purchase.
(2) It is also a physical defect if the agreed installation by the seller or his assistants has been carried out improperly. A physical defect further exists in an object that is to be installed if the installation instructions are defective, unless the object has been installed correctly.
(3) It is equivalent to a physical defect if the seller supplies a different object or too small a quantity.

Part V. Private Law

§ 435. The object is free of legal defects [Rechtsmängeln] if third parties cannot enforce any rights against the buyer in relation to the object, or only those that have been taken over in the contract of sale. It is equivalent to a legal defect if a right that does not exist is registered in the Land Register.

[§ 436 is omitted.]

§ 437. If the object is defective, the buyer may, provided the pre-requisites of the following provisions are met and unless otherwise specified,
1. under § 439, demand subsequent fulfilment [Nacherfüllung],
2. under §§ 440, 323 and 326 paragraph (5) withdraw from the agreement or under § 441 reduce the purchase price, and
3. under §§ 440, 280, 281, 283 and 311a, demand compensation for damage, or under § 284, compensation for futile expenditure.

§ 438. (1) The claims cited in § 437 nos. 1 and 3 become prescribed
1. in thirty years, if the defect consists of
a) a property right [dinglich recht] a third party on the basis of which return of the purchased object may be demanded, or
b) some other right which is registered in the Land Register,
2. in five years
a) in relation to a construction, and
b) in relation to an object that has been used for a construction in accordance with its usual manner it is used and has caused the defectiveness of the building, and
3. otherwise in two years.
(2) In the case of a piece of land the prescription period commences upon the delivery of possession, in other cases upon delivery of the object.
(3) Contrary to paragraph (1) nos. 2 and 3 and paragraph (2), claims become prescribed after the regular prescription period, if the seller wilfully kept silent about the defect. In the case of paragraph (1) no. 2, however, the prescription period does not take effect before the expiry of the period determined there.
(4) §218 applies to the right of withdrawal referred to in § 437. Notwithstanding the ineffectiveness of a withdrawal under § 218 paragraph (1), the buyer may refuse payment of the purchase price in so far as he would be entitled to do so on the basis of withdrawal. If he makes use of this right, the seller may withdraw from the contract.
(5) § 218 and paragraph § (4) sentence 2 above apply correspondingly to the right to reduction referred to in § 437.

§ 439. (1) The buyer may, as subsequent fulfilment, at his option, demand the removal of the defect or delivery of an object free of defects.
(2) The seller must bear all the necessary expenditure for the purpose of subsequent fulfilment, in particular transport, road tolls, labour and materials costs.
(3) Without prejudice to § 275 paragraphs (2) and (3), the seller may refuse to provide the kind of subsequent fulfilment chosen by the buyer, if it is only possible with disproportionate cost. In this connection, account must be taken in particular of the value of the object when free of defects, the significance of the defect and the question whether recourse could be had to the other kind of subsequent fulfilment without substantial detriment to the buyer. The claim of the buyer is restricted in that case to the other kind of subsequent fulfilment; the right of the seller to refuse this as well remains unaffected subject to the pre-requisites of sentence 1.
(4) If the seller delivers an object free from defects for the purpose of subsequent fulfilment, he may demand from the buyer the retransfer [Rückgewähr] of the defective object in accordance with §§ 346 to 348.

§ 440. Except in the cases of § 281 paragraph 2 and § 323 paragraph 2, the setting of a period of time is also not necessary when the seller refuses both kinds of subsequent fulfillment pursuant to § 439 paragraph 3 or when the kind of subsequent fulfillment due to the buyer has failed or cannot be expected of him. A subsequent improvement [Nachbesserung] is regarded as failed after the second unsuccessful attempt, unless something else results in particular from the nature of the object or the defect or other circumstances.

§ 441. (1) Instead of withdrawing the buyer can reduce the purchase price by a declaration to the seller. The ground for exclusion in § 323 paragraph 5 sentence 2 does not apply.
(2) Where on the side of the buyer or on the side of seller several take part, the reduction can only be declared by all or to all.

(3) In the case of reduction, the purchase price is to be reduced in the proportion in which the value of the object in a defect free state at the time of the conclusion of the contract would have stood to the actual value. The reduction is, to the extent necessary, to be determined by appraisal.
(4) Where the buyer paid more than the reduced purchase price, the surplus amount is to be reimbursed by the seller. § 346 paragraph 1 and § 347 paragraph 1 apply mutatis mutandis.

§ 442. (1) The rights of the buyer concerning a defect are excluded if he knew of the defect at the conclusion of the contract. Where the defect remains unknown to the buyer due to gross negligence, the buyer can only assert his rights arising out of the defect if the seller fraudulently concealed the defect or gave a guarantee concerning the properties of the object.
(2) A right that is registered in the land register is to be rectified by the seller, also if the buyer is aware of it.

§ 443. (1) Where the seller or a third party gives a guarantee concerning the properties of the object or therefor, that the object will retain a certain property for a certain period (guarantee of durability) [Haltbarkeitsgarantie], the buyer is entitled, in case of a guarantee claim, without prejudice to statutory claims, to the rights arising from the guarantee, on the terms provided by the declaration of guarantee and the relevant advertising against the person who granted the guarantee.
(2) In so far as a guarantee of durability has been give, it is presumed that a physical defect occurring during its validity period gives rise to the rights under the guarantee.

§ 444. The seller cannot invoke an agreement by which the rights of the buyer arising from a defect are excluded or limited, in so far as he fraudulently concealed the defect or gave a guarantee concerning the properties of the object.

[§ 445 is omitted.]

§ 446. With the delivery of the object sold, the risk of accidental loss or accidental deterioration passes to the buyer. From the delivery, the buyer is entitled to the benefits and he bears the burdens of the object. It is equivalent to delivery, when the buyer is in default of acceptance.

§ 447. (1) Where the seller, at request of the buyer, ships the object sold to another place than the place of performance, the risk passes to the buyer as soon as the seller hands the object over to the freight forwarder, carrier or any other person or body, responsible for the performance of shipment.
(2) Where the buyer gave a particular instruction concerning the manner of shipment, and the seller without good reason derogates from the instruction, the seller is responsible to the buyer for the resulting damage.

§ 448. (1) The seller bears the costs of delivery of the object, the buyer the costs of acceptance and the shipment of the object to another place than the place of performance.
(2) The buyer of a piece of land bears the costs of authentication of the sales contract and the deed, the registration in the land register and the declarations required for the registration.

§ 449. (1) If the seller of a movable object has reserved his right of ownership until payment of the purchase price, in case of doubt, it is presumed that the right of ownership is transferred under the suspensive condition [afschießenden Bedingung] of full payment of the purchase price.
(2) On the basis of the reservation of ownership [Eigentumsvorbehalt], the seller of the object can only claim back the object if he has withdrawn from the contract.
(3) The agreement on a reservation of ownership is void in so far as the transfer of ownership is made dependent on the payment of claims to a third person, in particular one to a business connected to the seller.

[The remainder of Title 2 and Title 3 are omitted.]

Title 4. Gift

§ 516. (1) A donation [Zuwendung] by means of which someone enriches another person from his own patrimony [Vermögen] is a gift [Schenkung] if both parties are in agreement that the donation occurs gratuitously.
(2) If the donation occurs without the intention of the other party, the donor may request him to make a declaration as to acceptance specifying an appropriate period of time. After expiry of the period of time, the gift is deemed to

be accepted if the other party has not previously rejected it. In the case of rejection, return of what has been donated may be demanded according to the provisions on the return of unjust enrichment.

[§ 517 is omitted.]

§ 518. (1) For the validity of a contract by which a performance is promised as a gift, the notarial authentication of the promise is required. The same applies to a promise or a declaration of acknowledgement when a promise to fulfil an obligation or the acknowledgement of an obligation in the manner referred to in §§ 780 and 781 is made as a gift.
(2) A defect of form is cured by the effectuation of the performance promised.

[The remainder of Title 4 is omitted.]

Title 5. Lease contract [Mietvertrag], agricultural lease contract [Pachtvertrag]

[Subtitle 1 is omitted.]

Subtitle 2. Lease for living space

Chapter 4. Change of contracting parties

[§§ 563 – 565 are omitted.]

§ 566. (1) If the leased living space, after the lessee has taken up the lease, is transferred to a third party, the acquirer will take the place of the lessor in respect to the rights and obligations that follow from the lease for the duration of his ownership.
(2) If the acquirer does not fulfill his obligations, the lessor is liable in the same was as a surety who has waived the defence of unexhausted remedies [Einrede der Vorausklage] for the damage to be compensated for by the acquirer. If the lessee obtains knowledge of the transfer of ownership through a notification by the lessor, the lessor is released from liability, unless the lessee cancels the lease at the earliest date at which cancellation is permitted.

[The remainder of Title 5 and Titles 6 – 11 are omitted.]

Title 12. Mandate and contract for the management of the affairs of another [Auftrag und Geschäftsbesorgungsvertrag]

[§§ 662 – 666 are omitted.]

§ 667. The mandatary [Beauftragte] is obliged to return to the mandator [Auftraggeber] everything he receives to perform the mandate [Auftrag] and that which he obtains from carrying out the transaction.

[§§ 668 – 672 are omitted.]

§ 673. In case of doubt, the mandate is extinguished on the death of the mandatary. If the mandate is extinguished, the heir of the mandatary must notify the mandator of the death without undue delay and, if postponement entails risk, must continue carrying out the transaction entrusted to him until the mandator can make other arrangements; the mandate is to this extent deemed to continue.

[The remainder of Title 12 and Titles 13 – 26 are omitted.]

Title 27. Wrongful acts [Unerlaubte Handlungen]

§ 823. (1) A person who intentionally [vorsätzlich] or negligently [fahrlässig], unlawfully injures the life, body, health, freedom, property or another right of another person is obliged to compensate the other party for the damage arising there from.

(2) The same duty arises for a person who infringes a law intended to protect another. If, according to the contents of the law, an infringement is possible even without fault [Verschulden], the duty to compensate only arises in the case of fault.

§ 824. (1) A person who contrary to the truth asserts or disseminates a fact that is capable of endangering the credit of another or to lead to other disadvantages for his income or advancement shall compensate the other for the damage arising there from even if he does not know that the fact is untrue, but should have known of it.
(2) A communication, the untruth of which is unknown to the person making it, will not oblige a person to compensate for damage if he or the recipient of the communication has a justified interest in it.

§ 825. A person who by deceitfulness, threat or abuse of a relationship of dependence, induces another person to undertake or tolerate sexual acts, is obliged to compensate him for the damage caused.

§ 826. A person who, in a manner that infringes good morals [guten Sitten], intentionally inflicts damage on another person, is obliged to compensate the other for damage.

§ 827. A person who, in a state of unconsciousness or in a state of pathological mental disturbance that excludes the free determination of will, inflicts damage on another is not responsible for that damage. Where he has temporarily brought himself in such a state through spirituous beverages or similar means, he is responsible for any damage that he unlawfully causes in this condition in the same manner as if negligence [Fahrlässigkeit] were imputable to him; the responsibility does not arise if he came into this state without fault.

§ 828. (1) A person who has not completed his seventh year of age is not responsible for the damage that he inflicts on another.
(2) A person who has completed his seventh, but not his tenth, year of age is not responsible for the damage that he inflicts on another in an accident involving a motor vehicle, railway or a cable railway. This does not apply if he intentionally caused the injury.
(3) A person who has not yet completed his eighteenth year is, in so far as his responsibility is not excluded according to paragraph (1) or (2) not responsible for damage that he inflicts on another if, when committing the damaging act, he did not possess the insight necessary to understand his responsibility.

§ 829. A person who, in one of the cases specified in §§ 823 to 826, is not responsible for damage caused by him on the basis of §§ 827 and 828, must nevertheless, in so far as compensation cannot be claimed from a third party with a duty of supervision, compensate for the damage to the extent that fairness requires according to the circumstances, and in particular the position of the parties, and he is not deprived of the means which he needs for his own reasonable subsistence as well as for the fulfilment of his statutory maintenance duties.

§ 830. (1) Where several persons, through a jointly committed wrongful act, have caused damage, each is responsible for the damage. The same applies if it is not possible to establish who of the several persons involved caused the damage through his action.
(2) Instigators and assistants are equivalent to joint actors.

§ 831. A person who appoints another to perform a task is obliged to compensate for damage which the other in the performance of his tasks unlawfully causes to a third party. The duty to compensate does not arise if the principal [Geschäftsherr], in selecting the person appointed and, in so far as he has to procure devices or equipment or to supervise the execution of the performance, observed due and necessary care [im Verkehr erforderliche Sorgfalt] in the procurement or supervision, or if the damage would have arisen notwithstanding the exercise of such care.
(2) The same responsibility arises for any person who undertakes the performance of one of the transactions specified in paragraph (1) sentence 2 for the principal by contract.

§ 832. (1) A person who is obliged by law to exercise supervision over a person who requires supervision by reason of minority or his mental or physical condition is obliged to compensate for the damage that this person unlawfully inflicts on a third party. The duty to compensate does not arise if he fulfils his duty to supervise or if the damage would even have arisen in the case of proper exercise of supervision.
(2) The same responsibility arises for a person who assumes the exercise of supervision by contract.

§ 833. If a human being is killed by an animal, or the body or health of a human being is injured, or a thing is damaged, the person who keeps the animal is obliged to compensate the injured person for the damage arising there from. The duty to compensate does not arise if the damage is caused by a domestic animal intended to serve the profession, economic activity or subsistence of the keeper of the animal and either the keeper of the animal in supervising the animal has exercised due and necessary care or the damage would also have arisen even if this care had been exercised.

§ 834. A person who undertakes under contract to exercise supervision of an animal for a person who keeps the animal is responsible for the damage inflicted by the animal on a third party in the manner specified in § 833. The responsibility does not arise if he exercises due and necessary care or if the damage would also have arisen even if such care had been exercised.

§ 835. (Repealed.)

§ 836. (1) If, by the collapse of a building or any other structure attached to a piece of land or by the dislocation of parts of the building or structure, a human being is killed, the body or health of a human being is injured or a thing is damaged, the possessor of the piece of land is, to the extent that the collapse or dislocation is a consequence of defective construction or inadequate maintenance, obliged to compensate the injured person for damage arising there from. The duty to compensate does not arise if the possessor has observed due and necessary care for the purpose of averting the danger.
(2) A previous possessor of the piece of land is responsible for the damage if the collapse or dislocation arises within one year after the termination of his possession, unless during his period of possession he exercised due and necessary care or a later possessor would have been able to avert the danger by the exercise of such care.
(3) The possessor within the meaning of these provisions is the possessor for his own benefit [Eigenbesitzer].

§ 837. If a person possesses, in the exercise of a right, on the piece of land of another, a building or another structure, the responsibility specified in § 836 applies to him instead of the possessor of the piece of land.

§ 838. A person who undertakes for the possessor the maintenance of a building or of a structure attached to a piece of land, or has to maintain the building or the other structure by virtue of a right of use to which he is entitled, is responsible for the damage caused by the collapse or the dislocation of parts in the same way as the possessor.

§ 839. (1) If an official intentionally or negligently violates the official duty incumbent upon him as against a third party, he shall compensate the third party for damage arising there from. Where only negligence is imputable to the official, he may only be held liable if the injured person is unable to obtain compensation in another way.
(2) If an official violates his official duties in a judgment in a legal matter, he is only responsible for any damage arising there from if the violation of duty consists in a criminal offence. This provision is not applicable to a breach of duty that consists of refusal or delay in the exercise of the public function.
(3) The duty to compensate does not arise if the injured person has intentionally or negligently failed to avert the damage by making use of a legal remedy.

§ 839a. (1) If an expert appointed by the court intentionally or by gross negligence provides a false expert opinion, he is liable to compensate for the damage incurred by a party to the proceedings as a result of a court decision based on this expert opinion.
(2) § 839 paragraph (3) applies mutatis mutandis.

[§§ 840 – 843 are omitted.]

§ 844. (1) In cases where death is caused, the person under the duty to compensate shall reimburse the costs of a funeral to the person under a duty to bear such costs.
(2) If the person killed, at the time of the injury, stood in a relationship to a third party on the basis of which he was obliged or might become obliged by law to provide maintenance for that person and if the third party has as a result of the death been deprived of his right to maintenance, the person under the duty to compensate shall compensate the third party for damages by payment of an annuity to the extent that the person killed would have been obliged to provide maintenance for the presumed duration of his life; the provisions of § 843 paragraphs (2) to (4) apply mutatis mutandis. The duty to compensate also arises where the third party at the time of injury had been conceived but not yet born.

[The remainder of Book 2 is omitted.]

Book 3. Property law [Sachenrecht]

Division 1. Possession [Besitz]

§ 854. (1) Possession of an object is acquired by obtaining actual control of the object.
(2) Agreement between the previous possessor and the acquirer is sufficient for acquisition if the acquirer is in a position to exercise control over the object.

§ 855. If a person exercises actual control over an object for another in the other's household or business or in a similar relationship, by virtue of which he has to follow the other's instructions relating to the object, so only the other is possessor.

§ 856. (1) Possession is terminated as a result of the possessor giving up, or losing in another way, actual control of the object.
(2) Possession is not terminated as a result of a, by its nature, temporary prevention to exercise control.

§ 857. Possession devolves on the heir.

§ 858. (1) A person who deprives the possessor against his will of the possession or interferes with the possession acts, except where the deprivation or interference is permitted by law, unlawfully (unlawful interference) [verbotene Eigenmacht].
(2) The possession obtained as a result of unlawful interference is defective. The successor in possession must allow the defectiveness to be asserted against him if he is the heir of the possessor or if he knows when he acquires possession of the defectiveness of his predecessor's possession.

§ 859. (1) The possessor may ward off unlawful interference by use of force.
(2) If a moveable object is taken away from the possessor by means of unlawful interference, the possessor may use force to remove the object from the perpetrator caught in the act or pursued.
(3) If the possessor of a piece of land is deprived of possession by unlawful interference, he may recover possession immediately after the deprivation by dispossession of the perpetrator.
(4) The possessor has the same rights against a person who under § 858 paragraph (2) must allow the defectiveness of the possession to be asserted against him.

§ 860. The rights to which the possessor is entitled under § 859 may also be exercised by the person who exercises actual control for the possessor under § 855.

§ 861. (1) If the possessor is deprived of possession by unlawful interference, he may request the person who in relation to him possesses defectively to restore possession.
(2) The claim is excluded if the removed possession was defective as against the current possessor or his predecessor and if the possession was obtained in the last year before the deprivation of possession.

§ 862. (1) If the possessor is disturbed in his possession by unlawful interference, he may request the disturber [Störer] to remove the disturbance. If further disturbances are to be feared, the possessor may apply for an injunction.
(2) The claim is excluded if the possessor possesses defectively as against the interferer or his predecessor and if the possession was obtained in the last year before the disturbance.

§ 863. Against the claims set out in §§ 861 and 862, a right to possession or to undertake the interfering act may be put forward only to establish the assertion that the deprivation or disturbance of the possession is not unlawful interference.

§ 864. (1) A claim founded on §§ 861, 862 extinguishes upon the expiry of one year after the perpetration of the unlawful interference, except where the claim is asserted by way of legal action before this date.
(2) Extinction also occurs if it is established after the perpetration of the unlawful act by a final and non-appealable judgment that the interferer holds a right to the object by virtue of which he may claim the establishment of a possessory status that corresponds to his course of action.

PART V. PRIVATE LAW

§ 865. The provisions of §§ 858 to 864 apply also in favour of a person who possesses only part of an object, in particular separate living spaces or other rooms.

§ 866. If several persons possess an object collectively, in their relationship to each other no protection of possession takes place insofar as it concerns the limits of the use to which each of them is entitled.

§ 867. If an object in the control of the possessor gets on a piece of land in the possession of another, the possessor of the piece of land must permit the possessor of the object to locate and remove the object, except where the object has meanwhile been taken into possession. The possessor of the piece of land may claim compensation for the damage caused by the locating and removal. He may refuse permission, if causation of damage is to be feared, until he is given security; the refusal is not permitted if delay entails danger.

§ 868. If a person possesses an object as a usufructuary [Nießgebraucher], pledgee [Pfandgläubiger], lessee [Pächter], tenant [Mieter], depositary [Verwahrer] or in a similar relationship, by virtue of which he is as against another entitled or obliged, to have possession for a period of time, the other person is also a possessor (indirect possession) [mittelbarer Besitz].

§ 869. If unlawful interference is perpetrated against a possessor, the claims set out under § 861, 862 also apply to the indirect possessor. In case of deprivation of possession, the indirect possessor is entitled to claim that restoration of possession to the previous possessor; if the latter cannot or does not wish to retake possession, the indirect possessor may require that possession is restored to him. Under the same pre-requisites he may, in the case of § 867, require that he is permitted to locate and remove the object.

§ 870. Indirect possession may be transferred to another by assigning the claim for restoration of property.

§ 871. If the indirect possessor is in a relationship with a third party as set out in § 868, the third party is also indirect possessor.

§ 872. A person who possesses an object as belonging to him is a possessor for his own benefit [Eigenbesitzer].

Division 2. General Provisions on rights in respect to pieces of land

§ 873. (1) The transfer of the ownership of a piece of land [Grundstück], the burdening of a piece of land with a right, as well as the transfer or burdening of such a right requires, in so far as the law does not otherwise provide, the agreement of the person entitled and the other party on the occurrence of the change of title and the registration of the change of title in the Land Register [Grundbuch].
(2) Before the registration, the parties are bound by the agreement only if the declarations are notarially authenticated or made before the land registration office [Grundbuchamt] or filed with the same, or if the person entitled has handed over to the other party an authorization for registration [Eintragungsbewilligung] that is in accordance with the provisions of the Land Register Code [Grundbuchordnung].

[§ 874 is omitted.]

§ 875. (1) The abandonment of a right in respect of a piece of land requires, in so far as the law does not provide otherwise, the declaration of the person holding the right that he abandons his right and the cancellation [Löschung] of the right in the land register. The declaration must be made to the land registration office or to the person for whose benefit it is made.
(2) Before the cancellation the person holding the right is only bound to his declaration if it has been made to the land registry office or the person, for whose benefit it is made, has handed over an authorization of cancellation in accordance with the provisions of the Land Register Code.

§ 876. If a right in respect to a piece of land is burdened with the right of a third party, the abandonment of the right that burdens the land requires the permission of that third party. If the right that is to be abandoned belongs to the owner of another piece of land and that piece of land is burdened with a right of a third party, the permission of that third party is needed, unless the right is not affected by the abandonment. The permission must be declared to the land registration office or to the person for whose benefit the declaration is made; it cannot be withdrawn.

[§§ 877 – 878 are omitted.]

§ 879. (1) The ranking of several rights that burden a piece of land are determined according to the sequence of the entries, if the rights are entered in the same section of the land register. If the rights are registered in different sections, the right entered by indicating an earlier day has priority; rights that are entered by indicating the same date have the same priority.
(2) The entry is also decisive for the order of priority, if the agreement, which is according to § 873 necessary for the acquisition of the right, was concluded only after the entry.
(3) A deviating determination of the ranking must be registered in the land register.

[§§ 880 – 882 are omitted.]

§ 883. (1) To secure a claim to the granting or abolition [Aufhebung] of a right in a piece of land or in a right burdening a piece of land or the alteration of the content or the priority of such a right, a priority notice [Vormerkung] may be entered in the land register. The registration of a priority notice is also admissible to secure a future or a conditional claim.
(2) A disposition that is made after the registration of the priority notice on the piece of land or the right is ineffective to the extent that it would defeat or adversely affect the claim. This also applies, if the disposition is made by way of compulsory execution or enforcement of an attachment or by the insolvency administrator.
(3) The priority of the right to the granting of which the claim relates is determined according to the registration of the priority notice.

[§§ 884 – 888 are omitted.]

§ 889. A right on another piece of land does not cease to exist when the owner of the land acquires the right or the holder of the right acquires ownership.

[§ 890 is omitted.]

§ 891. (1) If a right has been registered in the land register for a person, it is presumed that he is entitled to the right.
(2) If a registered right is cancelled in the land register, it is presumed that the right does not exist.

§ 892. (1) In favour of the person who acquires a right in a piece of land or a right in such a right by legal transaction, the contents of the land register are presumed to be accurate, unless an objection to the accuracy is registered or the inaccuracy is known to the acquirer. If the person entitled is restricted in favour of a particular person in his disposition of a right entered in the land register, the restriction is effective as against the acquirer only if it is apparent from the land register or known to the acquirer.
(2) If registration is necessary for the acquisition of the right, the knowledge of the acquirer at the date when the application for registration is made or, if the agreement required under § 873 is reached only later, the date of agreement, is conclusive.

§ 893. The provisions of § 892 apply mutatis mutandis if, on the basis of this right, performance is made to the person for whom a right is registered in the land register, or if, on the basis of this right, between this person and another person a legal transaction that does not fall under the provision of § 892 is made which contains a disposition of the right.

[§§ 894 – 899 are omitted.]

§ 900. (1) A person who has been registered in the land registry as owner of a piece of land, without having obtained the right of ownership, acquires the right of ownership when the registration has existed for 30 years and he has been in possession of the land for his own benefit for that time. The thirty year period is calculated in the same way as the period for prescription of a movable object. The running of the prescription period is interrupted as long as an objection to the accuracy of the registration in the land register is registered.
(2) These provisions apply mutatis mutandis when a right has been registered in the land register for a person who is not entitled to it, that gives a right to possession or the exercise of which is protected by the provisions on possession. The order of registration is decisive for the priority of the right.

Part V. Private Law

§ 901. If a right to another piece of land has been unlawfully cancelled in the land register, the right ceases to exist when the claim of the holder of the right against the owner has prescribed. The same applies, when a right that was created by operation of law on another piece of land was not registered in the land register.

§ 902. (1) The claims arising out of the registered rights are not subject to prescription. This does not apply to claims for recurrent performances in arrears or for compensation for damage.
(2) A right, against which an objection to accuracy has been registered in the land register, is equal to the right that is registered.

Division 3. Ownership [Eigentum]

Title 1. Content of ownership

§ 903. The owner of an object can, when this is not contrary to the law or the rights of third parties, do with the object what he wishes and exclude others from exercising influence The owner of an animal must, in the exercise of his powers, observe the special provisions for the protection of animals.

[The remainder of Title 1 is omitted.]

Title 2. Acquisition and loss of ownership in respect to a piece of land

§ 925. (1) The agreement between the disposer and the acquirer required for the transfer of ownership of a piece of land under § 873 (conveyance agreement) [Auflassung] must be declared in the simultaneous presence of both parties before a competent authority. Any notary is, without prejudice to the competence of other authorities, competent to receive the conveyance agreement. A conveyance agreement may also be stipulated in a judicial settlement or in a finally confirmed insolvency plan.
(2) A conveyance agreement subjected to a condition or time stipulation is ineffective.

§ 925a. The conveyance agreement shall be accepted only if the document relating to the contract required under § 311b first sentence is submitted or simultaneously drawn up.

[§§ 926 – 927 are omitted.]

§ 928. (1) The ownership of a piece of land can be abandoned by the owner declaring his abandonment [Verzicht] to the land registration office and by registering the abandonment in the land register.
[Paragraph 2 is omitted.]

Title 3. Acquisition and loss of ownership in respect to movable objects

Subtitle 1. Transfer [Übertragung]

§ 929. For the transfer of ownership of a movable object it is necessary that the owner of the object hands it over to the acquirer and that both agree that the ownership is to be transferred. If the acquirer is in possession of the object, agreement about the transfer of ownership is sufficient.

§ 930. If the owner is in possession of the object, the handing over of the object can be replaced by a legal relationship agreed upon between him and the acquirer by virtue of which the acquirer demands indirect possession.

§ 931. If a third party is in possession of the object, the handing over of the object can be replaced by the owner assigning the acquirer the claim to restoration [Anspruch auf Herausgabe].

§ 932. (1) As a result of a transfer under § 929 the acquirer becomes owner even when the object did not belong to the transferor, unless he was not in good faith [in gutem Glauben] at the time he would acquire ownership under these provisions. In the case of § 929 second sentence, this applies only if the acquirer has acquired possession from the transferor.
(2) The acquirer is not in good faith if he knew or due to gross negligence did not know that the object did not belong to the transferor.

§ 933. If an object that is transferred under § 930 does not belong to the transferor, the acquirer will become owner when the object is handed over to him by the transferor, unless he is not in good faith at that moment.

§ 934. If an object that is transferred under § 931 does not belong to the transferor, the acquirer will become owner with the assignment of the claim, if the transferor is indirect possessor of the object, or else if he demands possession of the object from a third party, unless he is not in good faith at the time of the assignment of the claim or at the time of the acquisition of possession.

§ 935. (1) The acquisition of ownership on the basis of §§ 932 to 934 does not have effect, when the object was stolen from the owner, was lost or otherwise went astray. The same applies, if the owner was only indirect possessor, when the possessor lost the object.
(2) These provisions do not apply to money or bearer documents [Inhaberpapiere] or to objects that are transferred by way of a public auction.

[§ 936 is omitted.]

Subtitle 2. Acquisitive possession [Ersitzung]

§ 937. (1) A person who possesses a movable object for ten years for himself acquires the ownership of that object (acquisitive possession) [Ersitzung].
(2) Acquisitive possession is excluded, if the acquirer is not in good faith or if he later discovers the right of ownership does not belong to him.

[The remainder of Subtitle 2 and Subtitles 3 – 4 are omitted.]

Subtitle 5. Occupatio/Taking of objects [Aneignung]

[§ 958 is omitted.]

§ 959. A movable object becomes without a master, when the owner gives up possession of the object with the intention to lose the right of ownership.

[Remainder of Subtitle 5 and Subtitle 6 are omitted.]

Title 4. Claims arising from ownership

§ 985. The owner may claim from the possessor restoration of the object [Herausgabeanspruch].

§ 986. (1) The possessor may refuse the return of the object, if he or the indirect possessor from whom he derives a right to possession is entitled to possession as against the owner. If the indirect possessor is not authorized as against the owner to grant possession to the possessor, the owner may require the possessor to return the object to the indirect possessor or, if he cannot or does not wish to resume possession, to himself.
(2) The possessor of an object that has been transferred under § 931 by assignment of the claim may raise against the new owner any defense available to him against the assigned claim.

[§§ 987 – 1003 are omitted.]

§ 1004 . (1) If the ownership is interfered with in another way than by removal or retention of possession, the owner may require the removal of the interference from the interferer. If further interferences are to be feared, the owner may ask for injunction.
(2) The claim is excluded if the owner is obliged to tolerate the interference.

[§1005 is omitted.]

§ 1006. (1) In favour of the possessor of a movable object, it is presumed that he is the owner of the object. This does not apply, however, as against a former possessor from whom the object was stolen, or lost otherwise went astray, unless it concerns money or bearer documents.

(2) In favour of a former possessor, it is presumed that during the period of his possession he was the owner of the object.
(3) In the case of indirect possession, the presumption applies to the indirect possessor.

§ 1007. (1) A person who has had a movable object in his possession may require the return of the object from possessor if he was not in good faith in the acquisition of possession.
(2) If the object was stolen from the former possessor, or was lost or otherwise went astray, he may require return even from a possessor in good faith, unless the latter is the owner of the object or has lost possession before the former owner acquired possession. This provision does not apply to money and bearer documents.
(3) The claim is excluded if the former possessor was not in good faith on the acquisition of possession or if he has given up possession. Apart from this, the provisions of §§ 986 to 1003 apply mutatis mutandis.

[Title 5 is omitted.]

Division 4. Servitudes [Dienstbarkeiten]

Title 1. Real servitudes [Grunddienstbarkeiten]

§ 1018. A piece of land can, for the benefit of an owner of another piece of land, be burdened in such a way, that the owner may use this piece of land for specific purposes or that on the piece of land certain actions cannot be undertaken or that the exercise of a certain right which follows from the ownership of the burdened piece of land as against the other piece of land is excluded.

[The remainder of Title 1 is omitted.]

Title 2. Usufruct [Nießbrauch]

Subtitle 1. Usufruct of objects

§ 1030. (1) An object can be burdened in such a way, that the person for whose benefit this burdening occurs is entitled to the use of the object and to take the fruits (Usufruct) [Nießbrauch].
(2) The usufruct can be restricted by the exclusion of certain powers of use.

[§§ 1031 – 1035 are omitted.]

§ 1036. (1) The usufructuary [Nießbraucher] is entitled to possession of the object.
(2) In the exercise of his right of usufruct he must maintain the economic purpose of the object and must act according to the ordinary rules of business.

§ 1037 (1). (1) The usufructuary is not entitled to transform [umzugestalten] the object or to change its nature.

[The remainder of § 1037 and §§ 1038 – 1060 are omitted.]

§ 1061. The right of usufruct ceases to exist with the death of the usufructuary. When the right of usufruct is created for a legal person or a partnership with legal personality, it ceases to exist with these.

[§ 1062 is omitted.]

§ 1063. (1) The right of usufruct on a movable object ceases to exist, when it falls together with the right of ownership in the same person.
(2) The right of usufruct does not cease to exist in so far as the owner has a legal interest in the continuation of the usufruct.

§ 1064. In order to end a right of usufruct on a movable object by legal transaction, a declaration of the usufructuary to the owner or the person creating the right that he ends suffices.

[§§ 1065 – 1066 are omitted.]

§ 1067. (1) If the right of usufruct is created on consumable objects, the usufructuary becomes the owner of those objects; after the termination of the right of usufruct, he must pay the creator of the right [Besteller] the value that the objects had at the time of creation of the right. Both the person creating the right and the holder of the right of usufruct can, at their own costs, ask an expert to determine the value of the object,
(2) The person creating the right can demand security when the claim for compensation of the value is endangered.

Subtitle 2. Usufruct of rights

§ 1068. (1) The object on which the right of usufruct is created can also be a right.
(2) In so far as §§ 1069 to 1084 do not provide otherwise, the provisions on the right of usufruct on objects are applicable mutatis mutandis to the right of usufruct on rights.

§ 1069. (1) The creation of a right of usufruct on rights occurs in accordance with the provisions applicable to the transfer of rights.
(2). A right of usufruct cannot be created on a right that cannot be transferred.

[§§ 1070 – 1073 are omitted.]

§ 1074. The usufructuary on a claim is entitled to seize the claim and to cancellation, if the due date of a cancellation [Kündigung] depends on the creditor. He has to secure the orderly seizure. He is not entitled to dispose over the claim in any other way.

§ 1075. (1) With the performance by the debtor to the usufructuary, the creditor receives the provided object and the usufructuary receives the usufruct on the object.
(2) If consumable objects are provided, the usufructuary acquires the right of ownership; the provision of § 1067 applies mutatis mutandis.

§ 1076. If an outstanding debt receiving interest is the subject of the right of usufruct, the provisions of §§ 1077 to 1079 apply.

§ 1077. (1) The debtor can only pay the capital to the usufructuary [Niessbraucher] and the creditor together. Each of them may request, that they will be paid together; each may demand instead of the payment a deposit for both.
2. The usufructuary and the creditor can only cancel together. The cancellation of the debtor is only effective if it is declared to the usufructuary and the creditor.

§ 1078. When the claim has become due, the usufructuary and the creditor are obliged to each other to cooperate with the payment of the claim. If the due date of the claim is dependent on a cancellation, each of them may require the cooperation of the other to the cancellation, if the payment of the claim is needed because, following the rules of normal management of assets [ordnungsmäßigen Vermögensverwaltung], their security is endangered.

§ 1079. The usufructuary and the creditor are obligated to each other to cooperate to ensure that the seized capital is invested to receive interest in accordance with the provisions applicable to the investment of ward money [Mündelgeld] and at the same time that the usufructuary receives his usufruct. The nature of the investment is determined by the usufructuary.

[§§ 1080 – 1089 are omitted.]

Title 3. Limited personal servitudes

§ 1090. A piece of land can be burdened in such a way, that the person, for whose benefit the right is created, is entitled to a specific use of the land or which grants him a power which can constitute the subject matter of a real servitude (limited personal servitude) [beschränkte persönliche Dienstbarkeit].
[The remainder of Title 3 is omitted.]

Division 5. Option to purchase [Vorkaufsrecht]

Part V. Private Law

§ 1094. (1) A piece of land can be burdened in such a way that the person, for whose benefit the right is created, is entitled as against the owner to an option to purchase.
(2) The right of preemption may also be created in favour of the respective owner of another piece of land.

[The remainder of Division 5 is omitted.]

Division 6. Real burdens [Reallasten]

§ 1105. A piece of land can be burdened in such a way that the person, for whose benefit the right is created, is entitled to receive recurrent performances from the piece of land (Real Burden) [Reallast]. As a part of the real burden, it can also be agreed that the performances that must be conducted on the land will, when on the basis of the contents of the agreement the nature and size of the burden on the land can be established, adapt itself, without further agreement, to changing circumstances.

[The remainder of Division 6 is omitted.]

Division 7. Hypothec, *Grundschuld* and *Rentenschuld*

Title 1. Hypothec

§ 1113. (1) A piece of land can be burdened in such a way that the person, for whose benefit the right is created, is entitled to be paid a specific sum of money out of the land for satisfaction of a claim to which he is entitled (Hypothec) [Hypothek].
(2) The right of hypothec can also be created for a future or conditional claim [künftige oder bedingte Forderung].

§ 1114. A share in a piece of land can, with the exception of the cases mentioned in § 3 paragraph (6) of the Land Register Code, only be burdened with a right of hypothec, if it concerns a share in a co-ownership.

[§§ 1115 – 1146 are omitted.]

§ 1147. The satisfaction of the creditor out of the land and its belongings [Gegenständen] to which the right of hypothec applies, occurs by way of compulsory execution.

[§§ 1148 – 1152 are omitted.]

§ 1153. (1) With the assignment of the claim, the right of hypothec is transferred to the new creditor.
(2). The claim cannot be assigned without the right of hypothec, the right of hypothec cannot be assigned without the claim.

[§§ 1154 – 1161 are omitted.]

§ 1162. If the hypothec-document [Hypothekenbrief] is lost or destroyed, it can be, under the cancellation proceedings [Aufgebotverfahrens], be declared to be without effect.

[§§ 1163 – 1180 are omitted.]

§ 1181. (1) If the creditor is satisfied from the piece of land, the right of hypothec ceases to exist.
(2) If the satisfaction of the creditor is made from one of the pieces of land that are burdened with a co-entitled hypothec [Gesamthypothec], the other pieces of land are also freed.
(3) The satisfaction out of the piece of land is equal to the satisfaction out of the belongings to which the right of hypothec applies.

[§ 1182 is omitted.]

§ 1183. The permission of the owner is needed for the ending [Aufhebung] by a legal transaction of a right of hypothec. The permission must be declared to the land registration office or to the creditor; it cannot be withdrawn.

[The remainder of Title 1 is omitted.]

Title 2. *Grundschuld, Rentenschuld*

Subtitle 1. *Grundschuld*

§ 1191. (1) A piece of land can be burdened in such a way, that the person for whose benefit the right is created is entitled to receive a specific sum of money out of the piece of land [Grundschuld].
(2) The right can also be created in such a way that interest from the sum of money or other secondary performances are to be paid arising from the piece of land.

§ 1192. (1) The provisions on the right of hypothec are applicable mutatis mutandis tot the *Grundschuld*, unless it does not follow from these that the right of *Grundschuld* requires a claim.
(1a) If the Grundschuld has been procured as to security of a claim [Sicherungsgrundschuld], defences, which are granted to the owner on grounds of the security agreement with the hitherto creditor or which arise from the security agreement, may be opposed to any transferor of the Grundschuld; § 1157 sentence 2 does not apply in this respect. For the remainder, § 1157 remains unaffected.
(2) The provisions on interest on the claim arising from the right of hypothec are applicable to the interest on the *Grundschuld*.

[§§ 1193 – 1198 are omitted.]

Subtitle 2. *Rentenschuld*

§ 1199. (1) A land charge can be created in such a way, that on regular and recurrent dates a certain sum of money arising from the piece of land must be paid [Rentenschuld].
(2) When the *Rentenschuld* is created the amount of money by which the *Rentenschuld* can be repaid shall be determined. This repayment amount shall be registered in the land registry.

[The remainder of Subtitle 2 is omitted.]

Division 8. Right of pledge on movable objects and on rights

Title. 1. Right of pledge on movable objects

§ 1204. (1) In order to secure a claim, a movable object can be burdened in such a way that the creditor is entitled to satisfaction of his claim from the object (Right of pledge) [Pfandrecht].
(2) The right of pledge can also be created for a future claim or conditional claim.

§ 1205. (1) To create a right of pledge it is necessary that the owner hands over the object to the creditor and both must agree, that the creditor will have a right of pledge. If the creditor is in possession of the object, it suffices that the parties agree on the creation of a right of pledge.
(2) The transfer of an object in the indirect possession of the owner can be replaced in such a way that the owner transfers indirect possession to the creditor of the pledge and notifies the possessor of taking away the existence of the pledge.

[§§ 1206 – 1227 are omitted.]

§ 1228. (1) The satisfaction of the creditor of the pledge is effected through a sale.
(2) The creditor of the pledge is entitled to sell, as soon as the claim has become completely or partially due. If the secured object is not money, the sale is only allowed once the claim is transformed into a monetary claim.

§ 1229. An agreement reached before the occurrence of the right to sell, according to which ownership of the object devolves on or will be transferred to the creditor of the pledge, if he is not satisfied or not satisfied on time, is void.

[§§ 1230 – 1249 are omitted.]

§ 1250. (1) With the assignment of the claim, the right of pledge is transferred to the new creditor. The right of pledge cannot be transferred without the claim.
(2) If the assignment of the claim excludes the transfer of the right pledge, the right pledge ceases to exist.

[§ 1251 is omitted.]

§ 1252. The right of pledge ceases to exist with the claim for which it was created.

§ 1253. (1) The right of pledge ceases to exist if the creditor of the pledge returns the object to the pledgor or to the owner. A stipulation that the right of pledge will continue to exist is ineffective.
(2) If the object under pledge is in possession of the pledgor or of the owner, it is presumed that the object was returned to him by the creditor of the pledge. The presumption also applies, if the object under pledge is in possession of a third party who demanded possession of the object from the pledgor or the owner after the creation of the right of pledge.

[§ 1254 is omitted.]

§ 1255. (1) For the ending [Aufhebung] by legal transaction of a right of pledge, a declaration by the creditor of the pledge to the pledgor or to the owner that he abandons his right, suffices.
(2) If the right of pledge is burdened with a right of a third party, the permission of that third party is required. The permission is to be declared to the person, for whose benefit it is made; it cannot be withdrawn.

§ 1256. (1) The right of pledge ceases to exist when it falls together with the right of ownership into the same hands. The right does not cease to exist as long as the claim, for which the right of pledge exists, is burdened with a right of a third party.
(2) The right of pledge is considered not to have ceased to exist, in so far as the owner has a legal interest in the continuation of the right.

[The remainder of Title 1 is omitted.]

Title 2. Right of Pledge on rights

[§1273 is omitted.]

§ 1274. (1) The creation of a right of pledge on a right is effected according to the provisions applicable to the transfer of rights. If the handing over of the object is necessary for the transfer of the right, the provisions of §§ 1205, 1206 apply.
(2) To the extent a right cannot be transferred, a right of pledge cannot be created on that right.

[The remainder of the BGB is omitted.]

Miscellaneous Private Law Statutes and Codes[20]

Code of Civil Procedure [ZivilProzeßOrdnung (ZPO)] of 12 September 1950, as last amended on 26 March 2008 (*BGBl. I* p. 441). Selected provisions: §§ 851, 869, 883(1), 887 and 888.

§ 851. (1) A claim is, in the absence of special provisions, only subject to a right of pledge if it can be assigned.
(2) An claim that cannot be assigned according to §399 of the Civil Code can in so far be subject to a right of pledge and to forced payment [Einziehung] if the subject matter of the claim [geschuldete Gegenstand] is subject of the pledge.

§ 869. The compulsory auction [Zwangsversteigerung] and the forced administration [Zwangverwaltung] are regulated by special laws.

§ 887. (1) If the debtor does not fulfill the duty to perform an act, the performance of which can be effected by a third party, the creditor can, on authority of the court of first instance [Prozessgericht des ersten Rechtszuges], granted on request, have the act performed at the expense of the debtor.
(2) The creditor can request at the same time that the debtor be ordered to pay in advance the costs that will accrue from the performance of the act, without prejudice to the right to claim extra payment, if the performance of the act leads to greater expenditure.
(3) These provisions do not apply to the compulsory enforcement [Zwangvollstreckung] for the return or provision of objects.

§ 888. (1) If an act cannot be carried out by a third party, where it exclusively depends on the will of the debtor, on application to be recognized by the court of first instance [Prozessgericht des ersten Rechtszuges], the debtor can be exhorted to perform the act through a fine and, in the situation that this cannot be collected, by imprisonment or by imprisonment. A single fine may not exceed 25.000 Euros. The provisions of the fourth section on detention apply mutatis mutandis to the imprisonment.
(2) A threat of the sanctions does not take place.
(3) These provisions do not apply in the case of an order to perform services under an employment contract.

Emphyteusis Act [Gesetz über das Erbbaurecht (ErbbauRG)] of 15 January 1919, last amended on 23 November 2007 (*BGBl. I* p. 2614). Selected provision: § 1.

§ 1. A piece of land can be burdened in such a way that the person, for whose benefit the land is burdened, reserves the right to have a building on or under the surface of a piece of land, which can be transferred and passed on by succession (Emphyteusis) [Erbbaurecht].

Ownership of an Apartment and Long Term Tenancy Act [Gesetz über das Wohnungseigentum und das Dauerwohnrecht (Wohnungseigentumsgesetz) (WoEigG)] of 15 March 1951, as last amended on 26 March 2007 (*BGBl. I* p. 370), selected provision: § 1.

§ 1. (1) Under this law apartments can be burdened with a right of ownership of apartment, parts of a building that are not suitable for habitation, can be burdened with a right of co-ownership of a part.
(2) The ownership of an apartment is the exclusive ownership of an apartment in combination with a co-ownership share in the common ownership, to which it belongs.

---

[20] Translation by B. Akkermans, H. Hauröder and N. Kornet.

Part V. Private Law

Commercial Code [Handelsgesetzbuch HGB] of 10 May 1897 as last amended on 21 December 2007 (*BGBl. I* p. 3089). Selected provision: §354a.

§ 354a. If the transfer of a monetary claim has been excluded by agreement with the debtor under § 399 of the German Civil Code and the legal transaction that created this claim is a commercial transaction for both parties, or the debtor is a public legal person [juristische Person des öffentlichen Rechts] or a public separated set of assets and debt [öffentlich-rechtliches Sondervermögen], the transfer is nevertheless valid. The debtor may however satisfy the claim to the previous creditor. Agreements to the contrary are ineffective.

Compulsory Auction and Compulsory Administration Act [Gesetz über die Zwangsversteigerung und die Zwangsverwaltung (ZVG)] of 24 March 1897, as last amended on 23 November 2007 (*BGBl. I* p. 2614 mWv 30.11.2007). Selected provision: § 15.

§ 15. The compulsory auction [Zwangsversteigerung] of a piece of land is effected by a request to the insolvency court

Insolvency Code [Insolvenzordnung (InsO)] of 5 October 1994, as last amended on 12 December 2007 (*BGBl. I* p. 2840). Selected provisions: §§ 47, 51, 115 and 116.

§ 47. A person who on the basis of a right in rem or in personam is entitled to claim that an object does not belong to the assets involved in the insolvency proceedings [Insolvenzmasse], is not a creditor of the insolvency proceedings. His claim to separation of the object is governed by the laws that apply outside the insolvency proceedings.

§ 51. The creditors mentioned in § 50 are equal to:
1. creditors, to whom a debtor, to secure the performance of a claim, transferred a movable object or a assigned a right;
2. creditors, who are entitled to a right of retention to an object, because they have used something for the benefit of the object, in so far as their claim for that use does not supersede the benefit.
3. creditors, who are entitled to a right of retention under the commercial code [Handelsgesetz]
4. The Federation [Bund], States [Länder], municipalities and associations thereof [Gemeinde Verbände], in so far as objects subject to custom duties and taxation serve them as security for public dues in accordance with statutory provisions.

§ 115. (1) Any mandate ordered by the debtor referring to the property forming part of the assets involved in the insolvency proceedings shall expire upon the opening of the insolvency proceedings.
(2) If suspension of such mandate would cause a risk, the mandatory shall continue to perform the mandated transaction until the insolvency administrator is able to otherwise take care of any such transaction himself. For this purpose the mandate shall be deemed to continue. The mandatory may claim reimbursement of his expenses incurred for such continuation as a creditor of the assets involved in the insolvency proceedings.
(3) As long as the mandatory is not at fault in being unaware of the opening of insolvency proceedings he shall benefit from the presumption that the mandate continues. The mandatory shall rank among the creditors of the insolvency proceedings with his reimbursement claims arising from such continuation.

§ 116. If anyone is obligated under a service or work contract with the debtor to manage a business transaction for the latter, § 115 shall apply mutatis mutandis. The provision governing reimbursement claims arising from a continuation of such management contract shall also apply to claims to remuneration. Sentence 1 is not applicable to contracts for the debit of money or contracts for the payment or transfer of money; these continue to have effect on the estate [Masse].

Limited Liability Company Act [Gesetz betreffend die Gesellschaften mit beschränkter Haftung (GmbHG)] of 20 April 1892 as last amended on 31 July 2009 *(BGBl.* I p. 2509)

§ 6. (1)The company must have one or more managing directors [Geschäftsführer].
(2) The managing director can only be a natural person being of unrestricted legal capacity. Managing director cannot be, he who
1. as the person in charge of the provision of his financial matters is entirely or partially subject to a reservation of consent [Einwilligungsvorbehalt] (§1903 Civil Code),
2. on the basis of a court order or an executable decision of an administrative authority, is not permitted to exercise a profession, a professional sector, a trade or a branch of trade, in so far as the object of the business coincides entirely or partially with the object of the prohibition.
3. due to one or more intentionally committed criminal offences
a. the omission of filing an application for the opening of insolvency proceedings [Insolvenzverschleppung],
b. according to §§283 to 283d of the Criminal Code [Insolvenzstraftaten],
c. false statements according to §82 of this law or §399 of the Stock Corporation Law.
d. the incorrect representation according to §400 of the Stock Corporation Law, §331 of the Commercial Code, §313 of the Law Regulating Transformation of Companies or §17 of the Disclosure Law, or
e. according to §§263 to 264a or §265b of §266a of the Criminal Code sentenced to a custodial sentence of at least one year;
has been convicted; this exclusion applies for a period of five years from the judgment becoming legally effective, not including the time during which the offender was in custody in an institution by official order.
Sentence 2, under 3 applies mutatis mutandis to a conviction abroad regarding an offence which is comparable to offences stated in sentence 2 under 3.
(3) Shareholders [Gesellschafter] or other persons can be appointed as managing directors. The appointment occurs either in the articles of association [Gesellschaftsvertrag] or in compliance with the provisions of the third section.
(4) If the articles of association [Gesellschaftsvertrag] determine that all shareholders should be entitled to the management board, then only those individuals who belong to the company at the time of the determination of this provision count as appointed directors.
(5) Shareholders who intentionally or grossly negligent leave the management to a person, who cannot be a director, are jointly [solidarisch] liable for the damage that occurs thereby, because this person violates their duties towards the company.

§ 35. (1) The company is represented judicially and extra-judicially by the managing directors. If a company does not have a managing director [Führungslosigkeit], the company will be represented by the shareholders in the event that declarations of intention are to be made to the company or documents are to be served.
(2) If several managing directors have been appointed, they are all merely jointly competent to represent the company, unless the articles of association determines otherwise. If a declaration of intention is made to the company, the delivery to one of the representatives of the company according to subparagraph 1 is sufficient. Declarations of intention can be made and documents can be served to the representatives of the company according to subparagraph 1 to the business address which is registered with the Commercial Register [Handelsregister]. Irrespective thereof, the making and the serving can also take place at the registered address of the person authorized to receive, according to §10 subparagraph 2 sentence 2.
(3) If all shares of the company are in the hands of one shareholder or besides in the hands of the company and if at the same time he is the sole managing director, §181 of the Civil Code applies to his legal transactions with the company. Legal transactions between him and the company which he represents are to be included without delay after their performance in a record.

§ 37. (1) The managing directors are obliged towards the company to comply with the restrictions on the scope of their competence to represent the company, which are laid down, by the articles of association or in so far as these do not provide otherwise by the decisions of the shareholders.
(2) A restriction of the competence of the managing director to represent the company does not have legal effect against third persons. This applies in particular in the case that the representation only concerns certain transactions or types of transactions or should only take place under certain circumstances or for a certain time or at particular places, or that the consent of the shareholders or of an organ of the company is necessary for particular transactions.

§ 43. (1) The managing directors are to exercise the due care of a prudent business manager [Geschäftsleiter] in matters concerning the company.

Part V. Private Law

(2) Managing directors who violate their obligations are held severally liable to the company for the damage caused.
[*paragraphs 3 and 4 are omitted.*]

§ 64. The managing directors are obliged to compensate the company for payments, which have been made after the occurrence of the inability to pay [Zahlungsunfähigkeit] of the company or after the declaration of its insolvency [Überschuldung]. This does not apply to payments that after this point in time would also be compatible with the care of a prudent business manager. The same obligation applies to the managing directors regarding payments being made to shareholders, in so far as these had to lead to the inability to pay of the company, unless, this also would not have been recognizable, with observance of the care referred to in sentence 2. The provisions of §43 subparagraph 3 and 4 apply mutatis mutandis to the claim for compensation.

§84. (1) With imprisonment of up to three years or a fine will be punished, he who omits as a managing director to notify the shareholders about a loss in the amount of half of the share capital.
(2) If the offender acts negligently, the punishment will be imprisonment up to one year or a fine.

Public Company Act [Aktiengesetz (AktG)] of 6 September 1965 (*BGBl.* I p. 1089), as last amended on 31 July 2009 (*BGBl.* I p. 2509).

§ 76. (1) The management board [Vorstand] is under its own responsibility to manage the company [Geschäftsführung].
(2) The management board may be composed of one or more persons. If corporations have an initial capital of more than three million Euros, it is to be composed of at least two persons, unless the articles of association [Satzung] provide that it has to be composed of one person. The provisions about the appointment of an industrial resources director [Arbeitsdirektor] remain unaffected.
(3) Member of the management board can only be a natural person being of unrestricted legal capacity. Member of the management board cannot be, he who,
1. as the person in charge of the provision of his financial matters is entirely or partially subject to a reservation of consent [Einwillingungsvorbehalt] (§1903 Civil Code),
2. on the basis of a court order or an executable decision of an administrative authority, is not permitted to exercise a profession, a professional sector, a trade or a branch of trade, in so far as the object of the business coincides entirely or partially with the object of the prohibition.
3. due to one or more intentionally committed criminal offences
a. the omission of filing an application for the opening of insolvency proceedings [Insolvenzverschleppung],
b. according to §§283 to 283d of the Criminal Code [Insolvenzstraftaten],
c. false statements according to §399 of this law or §82 of the Limited Liability Company Law.
d. the incorrect representation according to §400 of this law, §331 of the Commercial Code, §313 of the Law Regulating Transformation of Companies or §17 of the Disclosure Law, or
e. according to §§263 to 264a or §265b to §266a of the Criminal Code sentenced to a custodial sentence of at least one year;
has been convicted; this exclusion applies for a period of five years from the judgment becoming legally effective, not including the time during which the offender was in custody in an institution by official order.
Sentence 2, under 3 applies mutatis mutandis to a conviction abroad regarding an offence which is comparable to offences stated in sentence 2 under 3.

§ 77. (1) If the management board is composed of several persons, all members of the management board are merely competent to jointly manage the corporation. The articles of association or the rules of procedure of the management board may provide otherwise; it may not be determined, however, that one or more members of the management board settle disagreements in the management board against the majority of its members.
(2) The management board may adopt rules of procedure, provided the articles of association did not refer the issue of the rules of procedure to the supervisory board [Aufsichtsrat] or the supervisory board issued rules of procedure for the management board. The articles of association may govern individual questions regarding the rules of procedure in a binding way. Decisions of the management board about the rules of procedure have to be made unanimously.

§ 78. (1) The management board represents the corporation judicially and extra judicially. If a corporation does not have a management board [Führungslosigkeit], the corporation will be represented by the supervisory board in case declarations of intention are made to it or documents are served.
(2) If the management board is composed of several persons, all members of the management board are only entitled to represent the corporation jointly, unless the articles of association provide otherwise. If a declaration of intention is to be made to the corporation, the delivery to a member of the management board or in the case of subparagraph 1 sentence 2 to a member of the supervisory board is sufficient. Declarations of intention can be made and documents can be served to the representatives of the corporation according to subparagraph 1 to the business address which is registered with the Commercial Register [Handelsregister]. Irrespective thereof, the making and the serving can also take place at the registered address of the person authorized to receive, according to §10 subparagraph 2 sentence 2.
(3) The articles of association may also determine that single members of the board, alone or together with a registered officer [Prokurist] have the power to represent the company. The same may be determined by the supervisory board, if the articles of association authorized it to do so. Subparagraph 2 sentence 2 applies in these cases mutatis mutandis.
(4) Members of the management board competent to joint representation can entitle individual members to conduct certain transactions or certain types of transaction. This applies mutatis mutandis if an individual member of the management board in conjunction with a registered officer is competent to represent the corporation.

§ 82. (1) The power to represent of the board of management cannot be restricted.
(2) In the relationship of the members of the management board to the corporation, they are obliged to observe the restrictions for the power of management that have been laid down within the framework of the provisions about the stock corporation, the articles of association, the supervisory board, the general meeting and the rules of procedure of the management board and the supervisory board.

§ 93. (1) The members of the management board must apply the duty of care of a conscientious and prudent business manager. A violation of the duty of care is not at hand if the member of the management board, regarding an entrepreneurial decision, could reasonably assume, on the basis of appropriate information, to be acting in the interest of the corporation. Concerning confidential information and secrets of the corporation, namely industrial or business secrets, which the members of the management board became acquainted with through their activity in the management board, they are to maintain secrecy. The duty of sentence 3 does not apply towards a recognized examining office according to §342b of the Commercial Code within the context of an examination conducted by thereby.
(2) Members of the management board who violate their duties are liable as joint debtor [Gesamtschuldner] to the corporation to compensate for the damage caused. If it is disputable whether they exercised the care of a conscientious and prudent business manager, the burden of proof lies upon them. If the corporation effects an insurance to safeguard a member of the management board against risks arising from his professional activity for the corporation, a franchise of at least ten per cent of the damage until at least to the amount of one and a half times the fixed yearly remuneration of the member of the management board is to be provided for.
(3) The members of the management board are obliged to compensate in particular, if, contrary to this law,
1. contributed capital is refunded to the shareholders,
2. the shareholders are paid interests or shares of profit,
3. own shares of the corporation or of another corporation are subscribed, acquired, or taken as pledge or are redeemed,
4. shares are issued prior to the full performance of the face value,
5. corporation's assets are distributed,
6. payments are rendered contrary to §92 subparagraph 2,
7. remunerations are granted to members of the supervisory board,
8. credit is granted,
9. preemptive shares are issued through the contingent increase of the share capital outside of the determined purpose or prior to the full performance of the equivalent value.
(4) The duty of the corporation to compensate does not arise if the act is based on a lawful decision of the general meeting. The duty to compensate is not excluded thereby, that the supervisory board consented to the act. Not until three years after the claim arises can the corporation waive claims, and then only claims to compensation, or settle them, if the general meeting consents and a minority, whose shares together attain the tenth part of the share capital, does not lodge an objection in writing. The temporal limit does not apply if the one who is obliged to compensate is unable to pay and settles with his creditors in order to avert insolvency proceedings or if the duty to compensate is regulated by an insolvency plan.

Part V. Private Law

(5) The claim for compensation of the corporation can also be asserted by the creditors of the corporation, in so far as they cannot obtain satisfaction therefrom. This however only applies in other cases then the ones stated in subparagraph 3, if the members of the management board grossly violated the care of a conscientious and prudent business manager; subparagraph 2 sentence 2 applies mutatis mutandis. Towards the creditors, the duty to compensate will neither by a waiver or settlement by the corporation nor thereby nullified that the act is based on a decision of the general meeting. If insolvency proceedings have been opened regarding the assets [Vermögen] of the corporation, for the duration, the insolvency administrator [Insolvenzverwalter] or the private attorney [Sachverwalter] exercises the right of the creditors against the members of the management board.

§ 148 (1) Shareholders [Aktionäre], whose shares equal together the 100th part of the share capital or a proportionate amount of 100,000 Euro at the time of filing the application, may apply for admission to assert in their own name the claims for compensation of the corporation specified in §147 subparagraph 1 sentence 1. The court will allow the proceedings, if
1. the shareholders prove that they acquired the shares prior to the point in time, in which they or in the case of universal succession [Gesamtsrechtsnachfolge] their predecessors had to obtain knowledge of the alleged violations of duty or the alleged damage of the basis of a public announcement.
2. the shareholders prove, that they requested the corporation in vain, by setting a reasonable time, to start proceedings itself.
3. there are facts which justify the suspicion that the corporation by way of impropriety or gross violation of the law or the articles of association damage occurred, and
4. no reasons of interests of corporation oppose the enforcement of the claim for compensation.
[paragraphs 2 – 5 are omitted.]
6. The costs of the derivative action [Zulassungsverfahrens] are to be borne by the applicant, in so far as his application is dismissed. If the dismissal rests on opposing grounds of the interest of the corporation, which the corporation could have made known prior to the application, but did not make known, it has to reimburse the applicant for the costs. For the rest, costs is to be decided in the final judgment. If the corporation starts proceedings itself or if it takes over pending proceedings from the shareholders, it bears any costs of the applicants which accrued up until the point in time of its initiation of proceedings or take over of the proceedings and the action can only be withdrawn under the prerequisites of §93 subparagraph 4 sentence 3 with the exception of the blocking period. If the action is entirely or partially dismissed, the corporation is to reimburse the costs borne by the claimants, provided the claimant did not obtain the admittance by an intentional or grossly negligent false submission. Shareholders who act jointly as applicant or as joined party obtain in total only reimbursement of the costs of an authorized representative, in so far as another authorized representative was not indispensable for the bringing the action.

Civil Code of the Netherlands [Burgerlijk Wetboek]. Selected provisions from Books 2, 3, 5, 6 and 7.[21]

Book 2. Legal Persons [Rechtspersonen]

Title 1. General provisions

[Article 2:1 – 2:8 are omitted.]

Article 2:9 Each director [bestuurder] is responsible to the legal person [rechtspersoon] for a proper performance of the duty assigned to him. If it concerns a matter which belongs to the position of two or more directors, each of them is wholly liable for a shortcoming, unless he cannot blamed for it and he was not negligent in taking measures to avert the consequences thereof.

[The remainder of Title 1 and Titles 2 – 3 are omitted.]

Title 4. Public companies [naamloze vennootschappen]

[Divisions 1 – 4 are omitted.]

Division 5. The management of a public company and the supervision of the management board

Article 2:129. (1) Except for limitations according to the articles of association [statuten], the management board [bestuur] is responsible for managing the company.
(2) The articles of association may determine that a director, referred to by name or function, is granted more than one vote. A director cannot cast more votes than the other directors together.
(3) Decisions of the management board by or pursuant to the articles of association can only be subject to the consent of an organ of the company.
(4) The articles of association can determine that the management board is required to conduct itself according to the instructions of an organ of the company which relate to the general lines of the policy to be pursued in fields further specified in the articles of association.

Article 2:130. (1) The management board represents the company, in so far as something else does not stem from the law.
(2) The competence of representation is granted to each director. The articles of association may nevertheless determine that, it is granted to only one or more directors in addition to the management board. They can further determine that a director is only allowed to represent the company with the cooperation of one or more others.
(3) Competence of representation granted to the management board or to a director is unrestricted and unconditional, in so far as something else does not stem from the law. A restriction or condition allowed or prescribed by law for the competence of representation can only be invoked by the company.
(4) The articles of association can also grant the competence of representation to individuals other than directors.

Article 2:138. (1) In the event of bankruptcy of the public company, every director is jointly and severally liable to the estate [boedel] for the amount of the debts, in so far as these cannot be satisfied through settlement of the other benefits, if the management board performed its duty in an obviously improper way and it can be assumed that this is an important cause of the bankruptcy.
(2) Where the management board has not fulfilled its duties under Articles 10 or 394, it has not performed its duty properly and it is presumed that improper performance of the duty is an important cause for the bankruptcy. The same applies if the company is a wholly liable partner of a general partnership [vennootschap onder firma] or a limited partnership [commanditaire vennootschap] and the duties under Article 15i of book 3 are not fulfilled. An insignificant default will not be taken into account.
(3) Not liable is the director who proves that the improper performance of the duty by the management board cannot be attributed to him and that he was not negligent in taking measures to avert the consequences thereof.
[Paragraphs (4) and (5) are omitted.]

---

[21] Translation by B. Akkermans, H. Hauröder, N. Kornet and E. Ramaekers.

PART V. PRIVATE LAW

(6) The claim can only be set up on the basis of improper performance of the duty in the period of three years preceding the bankruptcy. A discharge [kwijting] granted to the director does not stand in the way of setting up the claim.
(7) For the application of this article, any person who determined or contributed to determining the policy of the company will be treated equal to a director, as if he were a director. The claim may not be set up against the administrator [bewindvoerder] appointed by the judge.
(8) This article does not impede the competence of the (official) receiver [curator] to set up a claim by virtue of the contract with the director or by virtue of Article 9.

[Paragraphs (9) and (10) of Article 2:138 and Articles 2:139 – 2: 145 are omitted.]

Article 2:146. Unless the Articles of Association determine otherwise, the public company is represented by supervisory directors [commissarissen] in all cases in which it has a conflict of interest with one or more directors. The general meeting [algemene vergadering] is competent at any time to appoint one or more other persons thereto.

[The remainder of Title 4 is omitted.]

Title 5. Private limited liability companies [besloten vennootschappen met beperkte aansprakelijkheid]

[Divisions 1 – 4 are omitted.]

Division 5. The management of the company and the supervision of the management board

Article 2:239. (1) Except for limitations according to the articles of association [statuten], the management board [bestuur] is responsible for managing the company.
(2) The articles of association may determine that a director, referred to by name or function, is granted more than one vote. A director cannot cast more votes than the other directors together.
(3) Decisions of the management board by or pursuant to the articles of association can only be subject to the consent of an organ of the company.
(4) The articles of association can determine that the management board is required to conduct itself according to the instructions of an organ of the company which relate to the general lines of the policy to be pursued in fields further specified in the articles of association.

Article 2:240. (1) The management board represents the company, in so far as something else does not stem from the law.
(2) The competence of representation is granted to each director. The articles of association may nevertheless determine that, it is granted to only one or more directors in addition to the management board. They can further determine that a director is only allowed to represent the company with the cooperation of one or more others.
(3) Competence of representation granted to the management board or to a director is unrestricted and unconditional, in so far as something else does not stem from the law. A restriction or condition allowed or prescribed by law for the competence of representation can only be invoked by the company.
(4) The articles of association can also grant the competence of representation to individuals other than directors.

[Articles 2:241 – 2:247 are omitted.]

Article 2: 248. (1) In the event of bankruptcy of the company, every director is jointly and severally liable to the estate [boedel] for the amount of the debts, in so far as these cannot be satisfied through settlement of the other benefits, if the management board performed its duty in an obviously improper way and it can be assumed that this is an important cause of the bankruptcy.
(2) Where the management board has not fulfilled its duties under Articles 10 or 394, it has not performed its duty properly and it is presumed that improper performance of the duty is an important cause for the bankruptcy. The same applies if the company is a wholly liable partner of a general partnership [vennootschap onder firma] or a limited partnership [commanditaire vennootschap] and the duties under Article 15i of book 3 are not fulfilled. An insignificant default will not be taken into account.
(3) Not liable is the director who proves that the improper performance of the duty by the management board cannot be attributed to him and that he was not negligent in taking measures to avert the consequences thereof.

[Paragraphs (4) and (5) are omitted.]
(6) The claim can only be set up on the basis of improper performance of the duty in the period of three years preceding the bankruptcy. A discharge [kwijting] granted to the director does not stand in the way of setting up the claim.
(7) For the application of this article, any person who determined or contributed to determining the policy of the company will be treated equal to a director, as if he were a director. The claim may not be set up against the administrator [bewindvoerder] appointed by the judge.
(8) This article does not impede the competence of the (official) receiver [curator] to set up a claim by virtue of the contract with the director or by virtue of Article 9.

[Paragraphs (9) and (10) of Article 2:248 and Articles 2:249 – 2:255 are omitted.]

Article 2:256. Unless the Articles of Association determine otherwise, the company is represented by supervisory directors [commissarissen] in all cases in which it has a conflict of interest with one or more directors. The general meeting [algemene vergadering] is competent at any time to appoint one or more other persons thereto.

[The remainder of Book 2 is omitted.]

Book 3. Patrimonial law in general [Vermogensrecht in het algemeen]

Title 1. General provisions

Division 1. Definitions

Article 3:1. Things [goederen] are all objects [zaken] and all patrimonial rights [vermogensrechten].

Article 3:2. Objects [zaken] are corporeal objects susceptible to human control.

Article 3:3. (1) Immovable [onroerend] are the land, not yet extracted minerals, plantings connected to the land, as well as buildings and constructions permanently connected to the land, either directly, or through combination with other buildings or constructions .
(2) Movable [roerend] are all objects that are not immovable.

Article 3:4. (1) Everything that, according to common opinion, constitutes part of an object, is a component [bestanddeel] of that object.
(2) An object that is connected with the principal object [hoofdzaak] in such a way that it cannot be separated without significant damage being done to one of the objects, becomes a component of the principal object.

[Article 3:5 is omitted.]

Article 3:6. Rights that, either separately or together with another right, are transferrable, or that provide their holder with material advantage [stoffelijk voordeel], or which are acquired in exchange for or in anticipation of material advantage, are patrimonial rights [vermogensrechten].

Article 3:7. A dependent right [afhankelijk recht] is a right that is connected to another right in such a way that it cannot exist without that other right.

Article 3:8. A limited right [beperkt recht] is a right that is derived from a more comprehensive right, which is burdened [bezwaard] by the limited right.

[Article 3:9 is omitted.]

Article 3:10. Registered objects [registergoederen] are things for the transfer or creation of which registration in the relevant public registers is necessary.

Article 3:11. Good faith [goede trouw] of a person, required for any legal effect, is not only lacking if he knew the facts or the right to which his good faith shall relate, but also if he, in the given circumstances should have known of them. Impossibility of investigation does not prevent that the person who had good reasons to doubt is regarded as someone who should have known the facts or the right.

[The remainder of Division 1, Divisions 1A and 1B are omitted]

Division 2. Registration of registered things

[Articles 16 – 20 are omitted.]

Article 3:21. (1) The rank of registrations in respect to the same registered thing [registergoed] is determined by the order of registration, unless another ranking follows by law.
(2) If two registrations are made at the same time and could lead to two incompatible rights being held by two different persons on the same object, the ranking is determined:
(a) in case the deeds that are offered for registration are passed on a different date, by the order of those dates.
(b) in case both deeds have been passed on the same day and the deeds are notarial deeds, including notarial statements, by the order of the time at which the deeds or statements have been passed.

[The remainder of Division 2 is omitted.]

Title 2. Legal acts [Rechtshandelingen]

Article 3:32. (1) Every natural person is capable of performing legal acts, unless otherwise provided by law.
(2) A legal act of an incapable person may be avoided. A unilateral legal act of an incapable person, which was not directed to one or more specific persons, is however void.

Article 3:33. A legal act requires a will which is directed towards a legal consequence and which has been manifested by a declaration.

Article 3:34. (1) If someone whose mental capabilities have been permanently or temporarily disrupted, has declared something, then a will which corresponds to the declaration is deemed to be lacking, if the disruption prevented a reasonable evaluation of the interests involved with the act, or if the declaration has been made under the influence of that disruption. A declaration is assumed to have been made under the influence of the disruption, if the legal act was disadvantageous for the mentally disturbed person, unless the disadvantage could not reasonably be foreseen at the time of the legal act.
(2) Such lack of will renders the legal act avoidable. A unilateral legal act which was not directed to one or more specific persons becomes void by lack of a will.

Article 3:35. Against him who has interpreted another's declaration or behaviour, in accordance with the sense that he could reasonably have attributed to it under the given circumstances, as a declaration of a particular scope directed towards him by that other, one cannot invoke the lack of a will which corresponds to this declaration.

Article 3:36. Against he who, as a third party on the basis of a declaration or behaviour, in accordance with the sense that he could reasonably have attributed to it under the given circumstances, has assumed the creation, existence or extinction of a particular legal relationship and has in reasonable confidence relied on the correctness of that assumption and acted accordingly, the incorrectness of that assumption with regard to this act cannot be invoked by he whose declaration or behaviour is concerned.

Article 3:37. (1) Unless otherwise provided, declarations, including notices, can be made in any form, and can be contained in one or more acts.
(2) If it is provided that a declaration must be made in writing, it can also be made by bailiff's notification, to the extent that the purpose of that provision does not suggest otherwise.
(3) A declaration which is directed to a particular person must have reached that person, in order to have effect. Nevertheless, a declaration which has not reached the person to whom it was directed in time or not at all, also has effect, if the fact that the untimely arrival or lack of arrival is the consequence of his own actions, of the actions of persons for whom he is liable, or of other circumstances concerning his person which justify that he bears the disadvantage.

(4) Where a declaration which is directed to another person has been improperly conveyed by the person or means that was chosen thereto by the sender, the information received by the recipient counts as the sender's declaration, unless the means of conveyance that was used, was determined by the recipient.
(5) Withdrawal of a declaration that is directed to a particular person must, in order to have effect, reach that person before or at the same time as the declaration that is withdrawn.

Article 3:38. (1) Unless something else stems from the law or from the nature of the legal act, a legal act can be performed under a time-limit or a condition.
(2) The fulfilment of a condition does not have retroactive effect.

Article 3:39. Unless otherwise provided by law, legal acts which have not been performed in the prescribed form, are void.

Article 3:40. (1) A legal act which, because of its content or purpose, is contrary to good morals or public order, is void.
(2) Infringement of a mandatory statutory provision renders the legal act void, however, if the provision only serves to protect one of the parties to a multilateral legal act, it is only voidable, all this to the extent that nothing else results from the purpose of the provision.
(3) The previous paragraph does not apply to provisions that are not intended to affect the validity of legal acts which are in conflict therewith.

Article 3:41. If a ground for nullity only relates to part of a legal act, then the remaining part will stay intact, to the extent that this part, given the content and purpose of the act, is not inextricably linked to the part that is void.

Article 3:42. Where the purpose of a void legal act is to such an extent in conformity with another valid legal act, that one must assume that the latter would have been performed, had the former been abandoned for reason of its invalidity, then the effect of the latter is granted to the former, unless this would be unreasonable towards an interested third party who has not participated in the legal act as a party.

Article 3:43. (1) Legal acts which, either directly, or through persons who intervene, have as their purpose the acquisition by:
(a) judges, members of the public prosecution service, assistant judges, clerks, advocates, members of the local Bar, bailiffs and notaries, of things which are the subject of a dispute before the court, in whose jurisdiction they exercise their profession;
(b) civil servants, of things which are sold by them or before them, or
(c) persons holding a public office, of things that belong to the State, provinces, municipalities or other public institutions and that have been left in their care,
are void and oblige the recipients to pay damages.
(2) Paragraph (1) subparagraph (a) does not relate to testamentary provisions, made by a testator for the benefit of his legal heirs, nor to legal acts by which these heirs acquire goods of the estate.
(3) In the situation provided under paragraph (1) subparagraph (c) the legal act is valid, if it has been performed with Our consent or if it concerns a public sale. If the legal act has its purpose the acquisition by the member of a municipal council or an alderman [wethouder], or by the burgomaster [burgemeester], the competence to give consent mentioned in the previous sentence falls to Provincial Executive [Gedeputeerde Staten] or the Queen's Commissioner respectively.

Article 3:44. (1) A legal act is voidable, where it has been brought about by threat [bedreiging], by deceit [bedrog] or by abuse of circumstances.
(2) A threat consists of a person inducing another to perform a certain legal act by wrongfully threatening this or a third party with any disadvantage to person or property. The threat must be such, that a reasonable human being could be influenced thereby.
(3) Deceit consists of a person inducing another to perform a certain legal act by an intentionally incorrect statement made for that purpose, or by intentionally withholding any fact for that purpose, which he who withheld it was obligated to disclose, or by another ruse. Recommendations generally phrased, even if they are untrue, do not in themselves constitute deceit.
(4) Abuse of circumstances consists of a person, who knows or ought to understand that another is induced to perform a legal act because of special circumstances, such as an emergency situation, dependence, thoughtlessness

[lichtzinnigheid], abnormal mental condition or inexperience, having facilitated that legal act, although what he knows or ought to understand should prevent him from doing so.
(5) If a declaration is brought about by threat, deceit or abuse of circumstances on the part of someone who is not a party to the legal act, one cannot rely on this defect as against the other party who had no reason to assume its existence.

Article 3:45. (1) If a debtor, while performing a voluntary legal act, knew or ought to know that a consequence thereof would be to prejudice one or more creditors' possibilities for redress, the legal act is voidable and the ground for annulment may be relied upon by each creditor whose possibilities for redress have been prejudiced because of the legal act, regardless of whether his claim arose before or after the legal act.
(2) A legal act other than a gratuitous one, which is either multilateral or unilateral and directed to one or several specified persons, can only be avoided because of a prejudicial act, if those with whom or towards whom the debtor performed the legal act also knew or ought to have known that a consequence thereof would be to prejudice one or more creditors.
(3) Where a gratuitous legal act is avoided because of a prejudicial act, the avoidance has no effect with regard to he who benefited and neither knew nor ought to have known that the legal act would prejudice one or more creditors, to the extent that he can show that he did not benefit from the legal act at the time of the declaration or the commencement of the action for avoidance.
(4) A creditor who opposes a legal act because he has been prejudiced, shall only avoid it in his own interest and no more than is necessary in order to remove the prejudice experienced by him.
(5) Rights to things, acquired by third parties in good faith and not gratuitously, which were the subject of an avoided legal act, shall be respected. As regards the third party who acquired gratuitously in good faith, the avoidance has no effect to the extent that he can show that he did not benefit from the legal act at the moment that the good is demanded from him.

[Articles 3:46 – 3:48 are omitted.]

Article 3:49. A voidable legal act may be avoided, either by an extrajudicial declaration, or by a judicial decision.

Article 3:50. (1) An extrajudicial declaration which avoids a legal act is directed to those who are party to the legal act, by him in whose interest the ground for avoidance exists.
(2) An extrajudicial declaration can only avoid a legal act with regard to a registered thing, which has led to a registration in the public registers or to an instrument meant for transfer of a registered thing, if all parties accept the avoidance.

Article 3:51. (1) A judicial decision avoids a legal act by upholding a ground for avoidance which has been invoked at law.
(2) A legal action for avoidance of a legal act is instituted as against those who are party to the legal act.
(3) A legal appeal based on a ground for avoidance can be made at all times to repeal a claim based on the legal act or any other judicial measure. He who makes this appeal is obliged to notify it as soon as possible to the parties to the legal act who did not appear during the proceedings.

Article 3:52. (1) Legal actions for avoidance will become prescribed:
(a) in case of incapacity: three years after the incapacity ended, or, if the incapable person has a legal representative, three years after the legal representative became aware of the act;
(b) in case of threat or abuse of circumstances: three years after this influence ceased to exist;
(c) in case of deceit, mistake or prejudice: three years after the deceit, the mistake or the prejudice has been discovered;
(d) in case of another ground for avoidance: three years after the right to invoke this ground for avoidance has come to benefit him who has this right.
(2) After the period of prescription of the action for avoidance of the legal act, it can no longer be annulled on the same ground for avoidance by an extrajudicial declaration.

Article 3:53. (1) The avoidance has retroactive effect to the time at which the legal act was performed.
(2) If the consequences of a legal act which have already manifested can only be undone with difficulty, the court, if so requested, can wholly or partially deny the avoidance its effect. It can oblige a party who is thereby unfairly benefited to pay a monetary compensation to the party who has been disadvantaged.

Article 3:54. (1) The right to invoke abuse of circumstances for the avoidance of a multilateral legal act lapses where the other party suggests a timely amendment to the consequences of the legal act, which adequately brings an end to the disadvantage.
(2) The court can, at the request of one of the parties, moreover alter the consequences of the legal act in order to lift this disadvantage, instead of pronouncing an avoidance on grounds of abuse of circumstances.

Article 3:55. (1) The right to invoke a ground for avoidance to avoid a legal act lapses, where he who has this right has confirmed the legal act, after the period of prescription relating to the action for avoidance on that ground has commenced.
(2) The right to invoke a ground for avoidance also lapses, where a person with a direct interest has set a reasonable time at the onset of the period of prescription for him who has this competence, to choose between confirmation and avoidance and where he has not made a choice within this time.

[The remainder of Title 2 and Title 3 are omitted.]

Title 4. Acquisition and loss of things

Division 1. General provisions

Article 3:80. (1) A person can acquire things under general [algemene] and under special title [bijzondere titel]
(2) A person acquires things under general title [algemene titel] by succession [erfopvolging], mixing of estates [boedelmenging], merger as meant in Article 309 of Book 2, and by separation as meant in Article 334a of Book 2.
(3) A person acquires things under special title [bijzondere titel] by transfer, by prescription and by expropriation, and further in the other ways of acquisition specified by the law for each kind.
(4) A person loses things the ways specified by the law for each kind.

Article 3:81. (1) He who is entitled to an independent and transferable right may, within the limits of that right, create the limited rights that are prescribed by law. He may also transfer his right by making a reservation of a limited right as such, provided he takes into account the rules about rights as such as well as the creation of a right as such.
(2) Limited property right are destroyed by:
a. the destruction [tenietgaan] of the right from which the limited property right is derived;
b. the expiry of time for which, or the fulfilment of a resolutive condition [ontbindende voorwaarde] under which the limited property right was created;
c. abandonment [afstand];
d. renunciation [opzegging], if the right thereto has been granted by law or has been granted upon the creation of the right to the holder of the principal right, to the holder of the limited property right, or to both persons;
e. mixing of rights (confusio) [vermenging];
and further in any other manner of destruction as provided for by law according to each type of destruction.
(3) Abandonment and mixing of rights apply those who have in turn a limited right on the destructed limited right. Mixing of rights applies neither in favour of those who have a limited right on the burdened thing and should have respected the destructed right.

Article 3:82. Dependant rights [afhankelijke rechten] follow the right to which they are connected.

Division 2. Transfer of things and abandonment of limited property rights

Article 3:83. (1) The right of ownership [eigendom], limited property rights [beperkte rechten], and claims [vorderingsrechten] are transferrable, unless the law or the nature of the right resists the transferability.
(2) The transfer of claims can also be excluded by agreement between the creditor and the debtor.
(3) All other rights are only transferrable when the law provides this.

Article 3:84. (1) The transfer of a thing requires a delivery with a valid title, made by a person with the power to dispose over that thing.
(2) The title must describe the thing with sufficient certainty.
(3) A legal act that aims to transfer the thing for security purposes or that lacks the objective to bring the thing after the transfer into the patrimony [vermogen] of the acquirer, is no valid title for the transfer of that thing.

315

(4) If transfer takes place under a conditional obligation, only a right is acquired that is subject to that same condition as the obligation.

[Article 3:85 is omitted.]

Article 3:86. (1) Regardless of the lack of power of the transferor to dispose, a transfer made in accordance with Article 90, 91 or 93 of a movable object, that is not a registered thing, or a bearer or an order right, is valid if the transfer was made for value and the acquirer was in good faith.
(2) When a limited property right is created on a thing mentioned in the previous paragraph that is transferred for value in accordance with Article 90, 91 or 93, which the acquirer neither knew of nor ought to have been known of, this right ceases to exist, in case the transfer in accordance with Article 91 was made under the same suspensive condition [opschortende voorwaarde] as under which the delivery was made.
(3) Nevertheless, the owner of a movable object, who has lost possession thereof through theft, may, for the duration of three years, to be calculated from the day of the theft, reclaim his ownership, unless:
a) the object was acquired by a natural person who does not act in the exercise of a profession or a business from a transferor whose business it is to deal with the public in similar objects, other than as an auctioneer, on business premises that are intended for such a purpose, being an immovable object or a part thereof with the land that belongs thereto, and provided that the transferor acted in the normal course of his business; or
b) it concerns money or bearer or order documents.
(4) Articles 316, 318 and 319 regarding the interruption of the prescription period of a claim apply to the period mentioned in the last paragraph mutatis mutandis.

[Article 3:86a and 3:86b are omitted.]

Article 3:87. (1) An acquirer who, within three years after his acquisition, is asked who transferred the thing to him, must without delay provide the data that is needed to find this person or which he at the time of acquisition, could consider sufficient for that purpose. If he does not fulfil this obligation, he may not invoke the protection of Articles 86 and 86a against an acquirer in good faith.
(2) The previous paragraph does not apply to money.

[Article 3:87a is omitted.]

Article 3:88. (1) Regardless of the lack of power of the transferor to dispose, the transfer of a registered thing, a non-documentary claim [recht op naam], or of another thing to which Article 86 does not apply, is valid, if the acquirer was in good faith and the lack of power to dispose was not the result of an invalid earlier transfer, that was not the consequence of a lack of the power to dispose of the transferor at that time.
(2). Paragraph 1 cannot be raised against a claim mentioned in Articles 86a paragraphs 1 and 2 and 86b paragraph 1.

Article 3:89. (1) The delivery, required for a transfer of immovable objects, is effected by a notarial deed, made between the parties, followed by the registration of that deed in the public registry. Both the transferee as well as the transferor may ask for the registration.
(2) The transfer deed must specifically mention the title of the transfer; additional conditions, which do not concern the transfer, can be left out of the deed.
(3) When someone is acting as a mandatory [gevolmachtigde] for another in the deed, the deed must specifically mention the mandate.
(4) This article is applicable *mutatis mutandis* to the delivery, required for the transfer of other registered objects [registergoederen].

Article 3:90. (1) The delivery required for the transfer of movable objects, not registered things, that are in the power of the acquirer, is made by providing the acquirer with possession of the object.
(2) If the object remains in the hands of the transferor after the transfer, the transfer has effect against a third party with an older right to the object only from the moment that the object comes into the hands of the acquirer, unless the holder of the older right agreed to the transfer.

[Article 3:91 is omitted.]

Article 3:92. (1) Where a contract has as its object that the right of ownership of an object is brought into the power of another, but only once a performance that is due by the other party is completed, it is assumed that the right of ownership is transferred under the suspensive condition [opschortende voorwaarde] of completion of that performance.
(2) A reservation of ownership [eigendomsvoorbehoud] can only be validly made in respect to claims for counter-performance based on a contract for the object delivered, or to be delivered, by the transferor to the transferee, or based on a contract for work to be performed for the transferee, as well as for claims for deficiencies of performance of such contracts. To the extent that a condition is void on this basis, it is deemed not to have been written.
(3) A condition as meant in paragraph 1 is presumed to be fulfilled, when the transferor is satisfied in any other way than by performance, if the transferee is freed from his obligation under Article 60 of Book 6, or if the prescription period in respect to the claim for performance is expired. Except for a stipulation stating otherwise, the same applies for the abandonment of the right to a counter-performance.

Article 3:93. The delivery, required for the transfer of a bearer right [recht aan toonder] of which the bearer document is in the power of the transferor, is made by the delivery of that document in the way and with the effects as set forth in Articles 90, 91 and 92. For the transfer of a right to order [recht aan order], of which the order document is in the power of the transferor, the same applies, in so far as delivery also requires an endorsement.

Article 3:94. (1) Besides the cases dealt with in the previous article, rights that can be exercised against one or more persons are delivered by a deed to that purpose, and notice to these persons by the transferor and acquirer.
(2) The delivery of a right that can be exercised against a certain, however on the date the deed is passed unknown person, that belongs on that day to the transferor, has retroactive effect, provided notice is given as soon as reasonably possible [met bekwame spoed], after that person has become known.
(3) These rights can also be delivered by authentic deed or registered deed to that purpose, without notice to those persons against whom the right can be exercised, if these rights, at the moment of delivery already exist or will be acquired directly from an already existing legal relation. The delivery cannot be invoked against those persons against whom it can be exercised until notice of the delivery has been made to them by the transferor or acquirer. For the acquirer of a right that is delivered according to the first sentence, Article 88 paragraph (1) only applies if he was in good faith at the point in time mentioned in the second sentence.
(4) Persons, against whom the right can be exercised, may demand to receive a summary of the deed and its title [uittreksel] certified by the transferor. Stipulations that are irrelevant to these persons, do not have to be included in it. Where a deed has not been made of the title, the content of the title should, in so far as it is relevant to them, be notified in writing.

[Articles 3:95 – 3:97 are omitted.]

Article 3:98. Unless the law provides otherwise, everything that this Division provides on the transfer of things, is applicable mutatis mutandis to the creation [vestiging], the transfer [overdracht] and the abandonment [afstand] of a property right on such a thing.

Division 3. Acquisition and loss through prescription

Article 3:99. 1. Rights to movable objects that are not registered objects [niet-registergoederen], bearer rights [rechten aan toonder] or order [order], are acquired by a possessor in good faith through uninterrupted possession of three years, other things through uninterrupted possession of ten years.

[The remainder of Article 3:99 and Article 3:100 are omitted.]

Article 3:101. A prescription [verjaring] begins to run at the start of the day after the start of the possession.

[Articles 3:102 – 3:104 are omitted.]

Article 3:105. (1) He who possesses a thing at the point in time when the period of prescription of the claim aimed at ending that possession is completed, acquires that thing, even if his possession was not in good faith.

(2) Where a person has lost possession involuntarily prior to that point in time, but regains it after that point in time, provided within the year after the loss of possession or on the basis of a claim brought within that year, he is regarded to be the possessor at the point in time stated in the aforementioned paragraph.

[Article 3:106 is omitted.]

Title 5. Possession and holding [Bezit en houderschap]

Article 3:107. (1) Possession is holding a thing for oneself.
(2) Possession is direct when a person is in possession, without another holding the thing for him.
(3) Possession is indirect when a person is in possession through another person holding the thing for him.
(4) Holding is direct or indirect mutatis mutandis.

Article 3:108. Whether a person holds a thing and whether he does this for himself or for another, is assessed according to the common opinion [verkeersopvatting], taking into account the following rules and otherwise on the basis of external facts.

Article 3:109. A person who holds a thing, is presumed to hold it for himself.

[Articles 3:110 and 3:111 are omitted.]

Article 3:112. Possession is acquired by taking possession [inbezitneming], by transfer or by succession under general title [opvolging onder algemene titel].

Article 3:113. (1) A person takes possession of a thing by furnishing oneself with the actual power [feitelijke macht] over it.
(2) When a thing is in the possession of another, singular and independent acts of actual power are insufficient for taking possession.

Article 3:114. A possessor transfers his possession by putting the acquirer in a position to exercise the actual power that he himself could exercise over the thing.

Article 3:115. A bilateral declaration without any actual conduct is sufficient for the transfer of possession:
a. when the transferor possesses the object and in accordance with a stipulation made at the delivery he henceforth holds it for the acquirer;
b. when the acquirer was holder [houder] of the object for the transferor;
c. when a third party held the object for the transferor, and after the transfer of the object holds it for the acquirer. In that case, possession does not pass until that third party has recognized the transfer, or otherwise the transferor or acquirer notified him of the transfer.

Article 3:116. He who succeeds another under general title, thereby succeeds that other in his possession and holding, with all the qualities and deficiencies thereof.

Article 3:117. (1) A possessor of a thing loses possession when he apparently relinquishes the thing, or when another acquires possession of the thing.
(2) As long as the conditions for the loss of possession mentioned in the previous paragraph are not met, possession that has commenced continues.

Article 3:118. (1) A possessor is in good faith when he considers himself to be the holder of the right [rechthebbende] and could reasonably consider himself so such.
(2) Once a possessor is in good faith, he is deemed to remain so.
(3) Good faith is presumed to be present; the lack of good faith must be proven.

Article 3:119. (1) The possessor of a thing is presumed to be the holder of the right [rechthebbende].
(2) In respect to registered things this presumption yields, when it is established that the other party or his predecessor in title [rechtsvoorganger] was at any time the holder of the right and that the possessor cannot base his claim on subsequent acquisition under special title for which registration in the registers is required.

[The remainder of Title 5 and Titles 6 – 7 are omitted.]

Title 8. Right of usufruct

Article 3:201. The right of usufruct [vruchtgebruik] provides the right to use things that belong to another and to enjoy the fruits thereof.

Article 3:202. A right of usufruct is established by creation [vestiging] or by prescription [verjaring].

[Articles 3:203 – 3:206 are omitted.]

Article 3:207. (1) A usufructuary [vruchtgebruiker] can use and use up the things under usufruct in accordance with the rules made upon creation of the usufruct, or where such rules are lacking, in accordance with the nature of the things and the local practice in respect to the use and using up.
(2) A usufructuary is moreover entitled to engage in all acts that can be useful for the good management of the things that are subject to the right of usufruct. With respect to all other acts concerning the things the person with the principal entitlement [hoofdgerechtigde] and usufructuary are merely jointly competent.
(3) As against the person with the principal entitlement the usufructuary is obliged with respect to the things subject to the right of usufruct and the management thereof to exercise the care of a good usufructuary.

[Articles 3:208 – 3:209 are omitted.]

Article 3:210. (1) Unless determined otherwise at the creation, the usufructuary is entitled to demand performance, both in and outside of court, of claims and to receive monetary payments under the right of usufruct.
(2) Unless determined otherwise at the creation, he is only entitled to dissolution and cancellation of contracts when this could be useful to a good management.
(3) The person with the principal entitlement is only entitled to exercise the powers mentioned in the previous paragraphs if he has obtained permission from the usufructuary or a mandate from the local court [kantonrechter]. No appeal is permitted against the mandate given by the local court by virtue of this paragraph.

[Articles 3:211 – 3:212 are omitted.]

Article 3:213. (1) That which comes in the place of the things subject to the right of usufruct, through the exercise of the power to dispose over them, belongs to the person with the principal entitlement and is likewise subject to the right of usufruct. The same applies for that which is received through collection of claims subject to the right of usufruct, and claims for compensation that comes in the place of things subject to the right of usufruct, including claims in respect of the devaluation of those things.
(2) Also subject to the right of usufruct are those advantages that a thing yields during the existence of the right of usufruct and which are not fruits.

Article 3:214. (1) Unless otherwise determined at the creation of the right of usufruct, money that is subject to the right of usufruct must be, in consultation with the person with the principal entitlement fruitfully invested or spent for the benefit of the other things subject to the right of usufruct.
(2) In the case of a dispute concerning what is to happen to the money referred to in the first paragraph, the person who at the creation of the right of usufruct was appointed thereto decides on this matter, or in the absence of such an appointment, the local court [kantonrechter]. No appeal is permitted against the decision given by the local court by virtue of this paragraph.

Article 3:215. (1) Where upon creation of a right of usufruct, or after that, the power to partially or completely alienate or use up the things under usufruct is given to the usufructuary, the person with the principal entitlement may demand the retro-transfer of the things under usufruct or the things substituted for these, unless the usufructuary or acquirers of his right prove that the things were used up or vanished by coincidence.

[The remainder of Article 3:215 is omitted.]

Article 3:216. The usufructuary is entitled to all fruits that are separated or that can be claimed during the existence of the right of usufruct. What with respect to the right of usufruct can be regarded as a fruit can be further determined at the creation of the right of usufruct.

[Articles 3:217 – 3:223 are omitted.]

Article 3:224. If a usufructuary wishes to abandon his right at his own cost, due to the burdens and duties following from the right of usufruct, the person with the principal entitlement is obliged to cooperate herewith.

[Article 3:225 is omitted.]

Article 3:226. (1) The rules concerning the right of usufruct apply mutatis mutandis to the rights of use [recht van gebruik] and a right of habitation [recht van bewoning], except the following provisions.
(2) Where only a right of use has been granted, the holder of the right has the power to use the objects that are subject to his right and to enjoy the fruits thereof, which he needs for himself and his family.
(3) Where only a right of habitation has been granted, the holder of the right has the power to live in the dwelling that is the subject of his right with his family.
(4) He who has one of the rights mentioned in this article cannot transfer or burden his right, nor allow the use by another of the object, or allow the dwelling to be inhabited by another.

Title 9. Rights of pledge and hypothec

Division 1. General provisions

Article 3:227. (1) The right of pledge [recht van pand] and the right of hypothec [recht van hypotheek] are limited rights aiming at recovering out of the things subject thereto a claim for the payment of a monetary sum with priority over other creditors. If the right is created on a registered thing, it is a right of hypothec; if the right is created on another thing, it is a right of pledge.
(2) A right of pledge or hypothec on a thing extends to all that belongs to the ownership of that thing.

Article 3:228. A right of pledge or hypothec can be created on all things that are capable of transfer.

[Articles 3:229 – 3:230 are omitted.]

Article 3:231. (1) A right of pledge or hypothec can be created for an existing as well as for a future claim. The claim can be non-documentary [op naam], to order [aan order] or to bearer [aan toonder]. It can be a claim on the pledgor or hypothecor as well as a claim on another.
(2) The claim for which a right of pledge or hypothec is given, must be sufficiently determinable.

[Articles 3:232 – 3:234 are omitted.]

Article 3:235. Every stipulation by which the pledgee [pandhouder] or hypothecee [hypotheekhouder] is given the power to appropriate the thing subject of this right, is void.

Division 2. Right of pledge

Article 3:236. (1) A right of pledge on a movable object, a right to bearer or order, or on the right of usufruct of such an object or right, is created by bringing the object, or the bearer or order document, within the power of the pledgee or of a third party on whom the parties have agreed. The creation of a right of pledge on a right to order or on the right of usufruct thereon also requires an endorsement
2. A right of pledge on other things is created in the same way as is determined for the delivery of the thing that is to be pledged.

Article 3:237. (1) A right of pledge on a movable object, on a bearer right, or on the right of usufruct on such an object or right, can also be created by authentic or registered deed, without bringing the object or bearer document into the power of the pledgee or of a third party.

[The remainder of Article 3:237 and Articles 3:238 – 3:247 are omitted.]

Article 3:248. (1) When the debtor is in default of the performance for which the right of pledge was created as security [waarborg], the pledgee is entitled to sell the thing under pledge and to recover what is owed to him from the proceeds.
(2) The parties can stipulate that the sale can only take place after a court has determined, on the request of the pledgee, that the debtor is in default.
(3) A pledgee or seizor [beslaglegger] with a lower rank can only sell the thing under pledge while upholding the higher ranked rights of pledge.

[Articles 3:249 – 3:257 are omitted.]

Article 3:258. (1) When a thing that is subject to a right of pledge, as meant in Article 236 paragraph 1, comes into the power of the pledgor, the right of pledge is terminated, unless it was created in accordance with Article 237 paragraph (1).

[The remainder of Article 3:258 and Division 3 is omitted.]

Division 4. The right of hypothec

Article 3:260. (1) A right of hypothec is created by a notarial deed between the parties in which the hypothecor [hypotheekgever] grants a right of hypothec on a registered thing to the hypothecee [hypotheeknemer], followed by registration of the deed in the relevant public registers. The deed must contain a reference to the claim for which the right of hypothec provides security, or to the facts on the bases of which that claim can be determined. In addition, the amount of money for which the right of hypothec is created, or, when the amount of money is not yet determined, the maximum amount of money that can be claimed with the right of hypothec must be mentioned. The hypothecee must in the deed choose residence in the Netherlands.

[The remainder of Article 3:260 and Articles 3:261 – 3:267 are omitted.]

Article 3:268. (1) Where a debtor is in default in respect of the performance for which the right of hypothec is created as security, the hypothecee is entitled to have the object subject to the right of hypothec sold in public, in the presence of an authorized notary.
(2) On the request of the hypothecee or the hypothecor the judge on provisionary measures [voorzieningenrechter] of the district court [rechtbank] can decide that the sale takes place through an informal sale by a contract that is presented to him on this request for approval. Where the hypothecor, hypothecee, seizor or holder of a limited right, who has an interest in higher proceeds from the sale of the object, is presented with a better offer before the proceedings dealing with the request to the court are completed, he may decide that the sale will proceed on the basis of this offer.
(3) The request mentioned in paragraph (2) must be submitted within the period set by the Code of Civil Procedure [Wetboek van Burgerlijke Rechtsvordering]. No appeal is possible against a decision of the court mentioned in paragraph (2).
(4) An execution as mentioned in the previous subparagraphs is to be made in conformity with the formalities prescribed therefor by the Code of Civil Procedure.
(5) The hypothecee cannot exercise his recovery on the object subject to the right of hypothec in any other way. Any stipulation seeking to achieve this is void.

[The remainder of Division 4 is omitted.]

Title 10. Recourse to retrieval of things

[Divisions 1 – 3 are omitted.]

Division 4. Right of retention

Article 3:290. A right of retention [retentierecht] is the power that is granted to a creditor in those cases mentioned by law, to suspend performance of a duty of delivery of an object to his debtor until the claim is satisfied.

Article 3:291. (1). The creditor can invoke his right of retention also against third parties that have acquired a right to the object after his claim had arisen and the object came into his power.
(2) He can also invoke the right of retention against third parties with an older right, if his claim results from a contract that the debtor was entitled to enter into with respect to the object, or if he had no reason to doubt the power of the debtor.
(3) The creditor cannot invoke the right of retention against the Minister of Education, Culture and Science, who, on the basis of Article 7 of the Act on the restitution of cultural goods from occupied territory, initiates a claim.

[The remainder of Title 10 is omitted.]

Title 11. Legal claims [Rechtsvorderingen]

Article 3:296. (1) Unless otherwise provided by law, the nature of an obligation or a legal act, he who is obliged as against another to give, to do or not to do something, is held to do so by the court, at the request of he who has this right.
(2) He who is held to something under a condition or time-limit may be adjudicated under that condition or time-limit.

[Articles 3:297 – 3:305d are omitted.]

Article 3:306. Unless the law determines otherwise, a claim prescribes after the completion of a period of twenty years.

Article 3:307. (1) A claim for the performance of an obligation arising from a contract to do or to give something prescribes after the completion of a period of five years after the day, following the day on which the claim became due.
(2) In case of an obligation to perform after an undetermined period of time, the prescription period mentioned in paragraph 1 will not commence until beginning of the day, following the day on which the creditor has notified to proceed to ,enforce the claim mentioned in paragraph 1 prescribes in any case after the completion of a period of twenty years after the beginning of the day, following the day on which the enforceability, if necessary after cancellation by the creditor, was at the earliest possible.

Article 3:308. Claims for the payment of interest and sums of money, life interest, dividends, lease payments, agricultural lease payments and anything else that must be paid within a year or a shorter period, prescribe after the completion of a period of five years after the day, following the day on which the claim became due.

[Articles 3:309 – 3:312 are omitted.]

Article 3:313. Unless the law provides otherwise, the prescription period for a claim for the performance of an obligation to give or to do something commences on the day, following the day on which immediate performance may be demanded.

[Articles 3:314 – 3:318 are omitted.]

Article 3:319. (1) By interruption of the prescription period of a claim, other than by initiating a demand that is followed by an award, a new prescription period commences from the following day. If a binding advice is requested and obtained, the new prescription period commences from the day on which the binding advice was rendered.
(2) The new prescription period is equal to the original, but not longer than five years. Nevertheless, the prescription will in no case have effect earlier than the day on which the original prescription period would have expired without the interruption.

[Articles 3:320 – 3:322 are omitted.]

Article 3:323. (1) By completion of the prescription of a claim for the performance of an obligation, the rights of pledge and hypothec that secure it cease to exist.

(2) Neither does the prescription prevent that the right of pledge is exercised on the thing that is subject to the right, if this thing is a movable object, a bearer or order right or the bearer or order document was brought in the power of the pledgee or a third party.
(3) The claim for the performance of an obligation for which a right of hypothec was created, does not prescribe before twenty years have passed after the day following the day on which the right of hypothec was connected to the obligation.

[The remainder of Book 3 and Book 4 are omitted.]

Book 5. Property Rights in Respect to Objects [Zakelijke rechten]

Title 1. Ownership in general

Article 5:1. (1) Ownership [Eigendom] is the most comprehensive right that a person can have to an object.
(2) The owner is free to the exclusion of everyone else, to use the object, provided that this use is not in violation of the rights of others and the limitations based upon legislative provisions and rules of unwritten law are complied with.
(3) The owner of the object becomes, without prejudice to the rights of others, owner of the fruits the object produces once these are separated.

Article 5:2. The owner of an object is entitled to demand the object from everyone else who holds it without a right to it.

Article 5:3. In so far as the law does not prescribe otherwise, the owner of an object is the owner of all its components [bestanddelen].

Title 2. Ownership of movable objects

Article 5:4. He who takes possession of a movable object that belongs to no one, acquires ownership thereof.

[Articles 5:5 – 5:13 are omitted.]

Article 5:14. (1) Ownership of a movable object that becomes a component [bestanddeel] of another movable object that can be regarded as the principal object [hoofdzaak], passes to the owner of this principal object.
(2) Where neither of the objects can be regarded as the principal object and they belong to different owners, they become co-owners of the new object, each for a share equal to the value of the object.
(3) To be regarded as the principal object is the object of which the value substantially exceeds that of the other or which according to the common opinion [verkeersopvatting] is considered as such.

Article 5:15. If movable objects that belong to different owners are united into one object through merger [vermenging], the former article applies *mutatis mutandis*.

Article 5:16. 1. When a person creates a new object from one or more movable objects, this new object becomes the property of the owner of the original objects. If these belonged to different owners, then the previous two articles apply *mutatis mutandis*.
2. When a person creates an object for himself or has an object created from or partly from one or more movable objects that do not belong to him, he becomes owner of the new object, unless the costs of creation due to their limited amount do not justify this.
3. The paragraphs above apply mutatis mutandis to the processing of materials substances into a new material or the culture of plants.

[Article 5:17 is omitted.]

Article 5:18. Ownership of a movable object is lost, when the owner relinquishes possession with the intention to free himself of ownership.

[Article 5:19 is omitted.]

PART V. PRIVATE LAW

Title 3. Ownership of immovable objects

Article 5:20. Ownership of land includes, in as far as not otherwise determined by law:
a. the surface;
b. the layers of earth beneath it;
c. the underground water that has come to the surface through a source, a well or a pump;
d. the water that is on the land and which is not in connection with water on another's land;
e. buildings and constructions that are permanently connected to the land, either directly, or through incorporation with other buildings and constructions, in so far as they are not a component of another's immovable object;
f. plants connected to the land;
2. In derogation from paragraph 1 the ownership of a network, consisting of one or more cables or pipelines, destined for transport of solid, fluid or gaseous materials, of energy or of information, which is or will be laid in, on or above the land of others, belongs to the person entitled to construct such a network or his successor in title.

[Articles 5:21 – 5:23 are omitted.]

Article 5:24. Immovable objects that do not have another owner belong to the State.

[The remainder of Title 3 is omitted.]

Title 4. Powers and duties of owners of neighbouring pieces of land

[Articles 5:37 – 5:53 are omitted.]

Article 5:54. (1) Where part of a building or construction has been constructed on, above or under the land of another person and where removal of the protruding part would be disproportionately more prejudicial to the owner of the building or construction than its preservation would be to the owner of the land, the owner of the building or construction may at any time demand that, in return for compensation, a right of servitude [erfdienstbaarheid] be granted to him in order to preserve the existing situation or that, at the option of the owner of the land, the required part of the land is transferred to him.
(2) The preceding paragraph applies mutatis mutandis to a building or construction which over time has begun to lean over the land of another person.
(3) The preceding paragraphs do not apply if this is the result of an obligation, arising from the law or a legal act, to tolerate the existing situation or if the owner of the building or construction can be held to have been in bad faith or grossly negligent with respect to the construction or his acquisition of the building or construction.

[The remainder of Title 4 and Title 5 are omitted.]

Title 6. Right of servitude [Erfdienstbaarheid]

Article 5:70. (1) A right of servitude is a burden, whereby an immovable object, the servient land, is burdened for the benefit of another immovable object, the dominant land.

[The remainder of Article 5:70 is omitted.]

Article 5:71. (1) The burden that a right of servitude imposes on the servient land, consists of a duty to allow or refrain from doing something on, above or under one of the piece of land. It can be stipulated in the deed of creation that the burden also includes a duty to establish buildings, constructions or plantation that are required for the exercise of the right of servitude, provided these buildings, constructions or plantations are entirely or partly on the servient land.
(2) The burden that a right of servitude imposes on the servient land can also consist of a duty to maintain the servient land or the buildings, constructions or plantations that are, or will be, entirely or partly on the servient land.

Article 5:72. Rights of servitude can be created by creation [vestiging] or by prescription.

[Articles 5:73 – 5:77 are omitted.]

Article 5:78. A court may, on the request of the owner of the servient land modify or terminate a right of servitude:
(a) on the basis of unforeseen circumstances, which are of such a nature that following the requirements of reasonableness and fairness unaltered continuation of the right of servitude cannot be expected of the owner of the servient land;
(b) if at least twenty years after the creation of the right of servitude have passed and the unaltered continuation of the right of servitude is contrary to the general interest [algemeen belang].

Article 5:79. A court may, on the request of the owner of the servient land, terminate a right of servitude, if the exercise of that right has become impossible or the owner of the dominant land no longer has a reasonable interest in the exercise of the right, and it cannot be assumed that the possibility to exercise the right or the reasonable interest will return with that.

[Articles 5:80 – 5:81 are omitted.]

Article 5:82. (1) If the owner of the dominant land wishes to abandon his right at his own costs, due to the burdens and obligations arising from the right of servitude, the owner of the servient land is obliged to cooperate with this.
(2) The deed of creation may provide otherwise for the duration of the first twenty years.

[Articles 5:83 – 5:85 are omitted.]

Article 5:86. Parties may agree on the duration of the right of emphyteusis in the deed of creation.

[The remainder of Title 6 is omitted.]

Title 7. Right of emphyteusis [Erfpacht]

Article 5:85. (1) The right of emphyteusis is the property right that entitles the emphyteuticarius [erfpacher] the power to hold and use the immovable object that belongs to someone else.
(2) An obligation for the emphyteuticarius to pay, periodically or not, the owner a sum of money – the canon – can be imposed on him by the deed of creation of the right.

[Article 5:86 is omitted.]

Article 5:87. (1) A right of emphyteusis can be terminated by the emphyteuticarius, unless the deed of creation provides otherwise.
(2) A right of emphyteusis can be terminated by the owner, if the emphyteuticarius is in default of payment of the canon for two consecutive years or fails to a serious extent in the performance of his obligations. The termination shall, under the penalty of nullity, be notified to those who are registered as holder of a property right or as seizor in the public registers within eight days. After the end of the right of emphyteusis, the owner is obliged to compensate the emphyteuticarius for the value that the emphyteusis has at that time, set-off with the costs he may claim from the emphyteuticarius arising out of the right of emphyteusis.
(3) A stipulation that deviates from the previous paragraph to the disadvantage of the emphyteuticarius, is void. In the deed of creation, the owner may be granted the right to terminate, except on the basis of a deficiency in the performance of his obligations by emphyteuticarius.

[Article 5:88 is omitted.]

Article 5:89. (1) Unless provided otherwise in the deed of creation, the emphyteuticarius will have the same power to enjoy the object as the owner.

[The remainder Article 5:89 and Articles 5:90 – 5:96 are omitted.]

Article 5:97. (1) If twenty five years have passed since the creation of the right of emphyteusis, a court, on the request of the owner or the emphyteuticarius, may modify or terminate the right on the basis of changed circumstances, which are of such a nature that according to the requirements of reasonableness and fairness the unaltered continuation of the deed of creation can no longer be expected of the owner or the emphyteuticarius.
(2) A court may allow the request, subject to conditions determined by it.

Part V. Private Law

(3) If a limited property right is created on the right of emphyteusis or the object, the request can only be allowed, if the holder of the limited property right is called to the procedure and the standard of paragraph 1 is also fulfilled in respect to him.

[Articles 5:98 – 5:100 are omitted.]

Title 8. Right of superficies [Opstal]

Article 5:101. (1) The right of superficies is a property right to have or acquire a right of ownership of buildings, constructions or plantations in, on or above an immovable object, that belongs to someone else

[The remainder of Article 5:101 and Title 8 is omitted.]

Title 9. Rights of apartment [Appartementsrechten]

Article 5:106. (1) An owner, holder of a right of emphyteusis or of a right of superficies, is entitled to divide his right in respect to a building and its appurtenances and to the land that belongs to it and its appurtenances, into rights of apartment.
(2) An owner, holder of a right of emphyteusis or of a right of superficies is also entitled to divide his right in respect to a piece of land into rights of apartment.
(3) A right of apartment in its turn can be divided into rights of apartment. A holder of a right of apartment is entitled to this subdivision, in so far as the deed of creation does not provide otherwise.
(4) A right of apartment is a share in the things that are included in the division, that includes the power to exclusively use specific parts of the building that by their design are meant to be or will be used separately. The share can also include the power to exclusively use certain parts of the land that belongs to the building. In case of paragraph 2, the share includes the power to exclusively use those parts of the land that by their design or designation are meant to be or will be used as a separate part.
(5) An owner of an apartment shall be understood to be a holder of a right of apartment.
(6) As a building as referred to in this title shall also be understood a group of buildings that are part of the same division into rights of apartment.
A holder of a right of emphyteusis or right of superficies is only entitled to a division into rights of apartments after obtaining permission from the owner of the land. Where the necessary permission is not granted evidently without a reasonable foundation or the owner does not respond at all, the permission may be replaced upon a petition by the person that needs it with a mandate of the local court [kantonrechter] of the district court [arrondissementsrechtbank] in which the building or the largest part of the building is situated.

[The remainder of Book 5 is omitted.]

Book 6. General Part on the Law of Obligations

Title 1. Obligations in general

Division 1. General provisions

Article 6:1. Obligations [verbintenissen] can only arise if they follow from the law.

Article 6:2. (1) Creditor [schuldeiser] and debtor [schuldenaar] are obligated to behave as against each other in accordance with the requirements of reasonableness and fairness [redelijkheid en billijkheid].
(2) A rule which governs them on the basis of law, custom or a legal act is not applicable, as far as this would be unacceptable in the given circumstances according to the standards of reasonableness and fairness.

[The remainder of Division 1 and Divisions 2 – 4 are omitted.]

Division 5. Conditional obligations

Article 6:21. An obligation is conditional [voorwaardelijk] if, according to the legal act, its effect has been made dependent on a future event.

Article 6:22. A suspensive [opschortende] condition renders the obligation effective only after the occurrence of the event; a resolutive [ontbindende] condition renders the obligation terminated.

[Article 23 is omitted.]

Article 6:24. After a resolutive condition has been fulfilled, the creditor is obliged to restore the performance already rendered, unless something else follows from the content or purpose of the legal act.

[The remainder of Article 24 and Division 5 are omitted.]

Division 6. Performance of obligations

Article 6:27. He who has to deliver an individually determined object is obliged to exercise care for delivery of this object in the manner that a careful debtor would do in the given circumstances.

Article 6:28. If the object or objects owed are only determined according to their sort, and within the mentioned sort differences in quality exist, that which the debtor delivers may not be below the good average quality.

Article 6:29. The creditor is not entitled, without the permission of the creditor, to fulfil that which is owed in parts.

Article 6:30. (1) An obligation may be performed by a person other than debtor, unless its nature or purpose oppose this.
(2) The creditor is not in default if he refuses a realization offered by a third party with the approval of the debtor.

[Articles 31 – 37 are omitted.]

Article 6:38. If no time has been determined for the performance, the obligation may be performed immediately, and performance may be demanded immediately.

Article 6:39. (1) If a time for performance has been determined, it is presumed that this only prevents the performance from being claimed earlier.
(2) Payment before the due date is not undue.

[Article 40 is omitted.]

Article 6:41. If no place for performance is determined, delivery of the object owed shall occur:
(a) in case of an individually determined object: at the place where it was situated at the time of the creation of the obligation;
(b) in case of an object determined by sort: at the place where the debtor conducts his profession or business or, in the absence thereof, where he has his residence.

[The remainder of Division 6 is omitted.]

Division 7. Rights of suspension [Opschortingsrechten]

Article 6:52. (1) A debtor who has a claim on his creditor which is due, is entitled to suspend performance of his obligation until his claim has been met, if there is sufficient connection between the claim and the obligation to justify this suspension.
(2) Such a connection can be assumed inter alia in case both obligations follow from the same legal relationship or from transactions frequently conducted by the parties.

Article 6:53. A right of suspension can also be invoked as against the creditors of the other party.

Article 6:54. No right to suspend exists:
(a) to the extent that performance of the obligation of the other party is prevented by default of the creditor;
(b) to the extent that performance of the obligation of the other party has become permanently impossible;
(c) to the extent that seizure of the other party's claim is not permitted.

Article 6:55. As soon as security has been provided for fulfilment of the obligation of the other party, the right to suspend lapses, unless that fulfilment would thereby unreasonably be delayed.

Article 6:56. The right to suspend remains even after prescription of the legal claim on the other party.

[Article 57 and Division 8 are omitted.]

Division 9. The consequences of non-performance of an obligation

§1 General provisions

Article 6:74. (1) Every deficiency in the performance [tekortkoming in de nakoming] of an obligation obliges the debtor to compensate the creditor for the damage thereby caused to him, unless the deficiency cannot be attributed to the debtor.
(2) In as far as performance is not yet permanently impossible, paragraph 1 is only applicable having taken into account what has been provided in Paragraph §2 concerning default of the debtor.

Article 6:75. A deficiency cannot be attributed to the debtor if it cannot be ascribed to his fault, or if it is not for his account pursuant to the law, a legal act or generally accepted views in society [in het verkeer geldende opvattingen].

Article 6:76. Where the debtor makes use of the help of other persons when fulfilling an obligation, he is liable for their conduct in the same manner as for his own.

Article 6:77. If, for the fulfilment of an obligation an object is used which is unsuitable to that end, then the resulting deficiency is attributed to the debtor, unless this would be unreasonable given the content and purpose of the legal act which gives rise to the obligation, generally accepted views in society and the other circumstances of the case.

Article 6:78. (1) If a deficiency cannot be attributed to the debtor, but he enjoys an advantage in connection to that deficiency that he would not otherwise have had in case of proper performance, the creditor has a right to compensation of his damage to a maximum amount of that benefit, under application of the rules concerning unjust enrichment.
(2) Where this benefit consists of a claim on a third party, the debtor can comply with the previous paragraph by transferring that claim.

Article 6:79. If a creditor, whose debtor is prevented from performing as a result of a cause that cannot be attributed to him, is nevertheless capable of providing for himself that which is due through execution or set-off, he is authorized to do so.

Article 6:80. (1) The consequences of non-performance ensue even before the claim is due:
(a) if it is certain that performance without deficiency will be impossible;
(b) if the creditor is to deduce from a statement of the debtor that there will be a deficiency in his performance; or
(c) if the creditor on good grounds fears that there will be a deficiency in the debtor's performance and the latter does not comply with a written notice which contains those grounds by declaring himself willing to honour his commitments within a reasonable time indicated in that notice.
(2) The original time at which the obligation became due remains valid with regard to damages owed due to delay and the attribution to the debtor of the fact that performance became impossible during the time that he was in default.

§2 Default of the debtor

Article 6:81. The debtor is in default [verzuim] during the time that performance is lacking after it has become due and the requirements of Articles 82 and 83 are met, except to the extent that the delay cannot be attributed to him or performance is already permanently impossible.

Article 6:82. (1) Default commences when the debtor has been given written notice of default whereby a reasonable time for performance is set, and there is no performance within this reasonable time.
(2) If the debtor temporarily cannot perform or it appears from his conduct that a notice would be useless, the notice of default [ingebrekestelling] can be made by a written statement proclaiming that he is held liable for the failure to perform.

Article 6:83. Default commences without a notice of default:
(a) where a period of time set for fulfilment lapses without the obligation having been performed, unless it appears that the time period has a different purpose;
(b) where the obligation follows from a wrongful act or is meant as damages as provided in Article 74 paragraph (1) and the obligation is not immediately performed;
(c) where the creditor is to understand from a statement of the debtor that the latter will fail to perform the obligation.

Article 6:84. Every impossibility to perform that arises during the time that the debtor was in default and which cannot be attributed to the creditor, is attributed to the debtor; the latter shall compensate the resulting damage, unless the creditor would also have suffered the damage had performance been proper and timely.

Article 6:85. The debtor is only obliged to compensate damage resulting from delay in performance as regards the time during which he was in default.

Article 6:86. The creditor may refuse performance that is offered after commencement of the default, as long as payment of the damages that have in the meantime become due, and of the costs, is not offered as well.

Article 6:87. (1) To the extent that performance is not yet permanently impossible, the obligation is converted into one to pay substitutionary damages [vervangende schadevergoeding], when the debtor is in default and the creditor informs him in writing that he claims damages instead of performance.
(2) Conversion shall not take place if it is not justified by the deficiency, given its inferior nature.

[The remainder of Division 9 is omitted.]

Division 10. Statutory duties to compensate

Article 6:95. Damage that must be compensated on the basis of a legal obligation to pay damages consists of patrimonial damage [vermogensschade] and any other disadvantage, the latter to the extent that the law grants a right to compensation thereof.

Article 6:96. (1) Patrimonial damage comprises both losses suffered as well as lost profits.
(2) Loss that can be compensated as damage to patrimony includes:
(a) reasonable costs to prevent or limit damage that was to be expected as a consequence of the event which gave rise to the liability;
(b) reasonable costs to determine damage and liability;
(c) reasonable costs to acquire extrajudicial compensation, as regards the costs under (b) and (c), subject to the extent to which, in the given case, the rules relating to legal costs are applicable on the basis of Article 241 of the Code of Civil Procedure.

Article 6:97. The court assesses the damage in a manner which is most in accordance with its nature. If the extent of the damage cannot be established accurately, it will be estimated.

Article 6:98. Only damage which is in such a way connected to the event which gave rise to the liability of the debtor, that it can be attributed to him as a consequence of this event, taking into consideration as well the nature of the liability and of the damage, can be compensated.

Article 6:99. Where the damage could be the consequence of two or more events for each of which another person is liable, and if it is certain that the damage has been caused by at least one of these events, then each of these persons is obliged to compensate the damage, unless he proves that this damage is not the consequence of an event for which he is liable.

Article 6:100. Where one and the same event has resulted in benefit as well as damage to the aggrieved party, then this benefit must be offset against the damage to be compensated when it is established, to the extent that this is reasonable.

Article 6:101. (1) Where the damage is partly a consequence of a circumstance that can be attributed to the prejudiced person [benadeelde], the duty to compensate is reduced by dividing the damage among the prejudiced person and he who has a duty to compensate in proportion to the extent to which the circumstances attributable to each have contributed to the damage, provided that a different division shall take place or the duty to compensate lapses or remains in its entirety, where fairness [billijkheid] so demands given the discrepancy between de severity of the errors made or other circumstances of the case.
(2) Where the duty to compensate concerns damage inflicted to an object which a third party kept for the aggrieved party, circumstances that can be attributed to the third party shall be attributed to the prejudiced person when applying the previous paragraph.

Article 6:102. (1) Where each of two or more persons are obliged to compensate the same damage, they are jointly and severally responsible. In order to establish what they are to contribute to each other in their mutual relationship in accordance with Article 10, the damage is divided amongst them in accordance with Article 101, unless another division follows from law or legal act.
(2) Where the damage is partly the consequence of a circumstance that can be attributed to the prejudiced person, Article 101 is applicable to the duty to compensate of each of the persons separately as meant in the previous paragraph, provided that the prejudiced person can in total not claim more from them than he would have been entitled to if only one person had been liable for the circumstances which gave rise to the duties to compensate. Where recovery from one of the persons held to contribute appears not to be entirely possible, the judge, at the request of one of them, can decide that, when applying Article 13, the part which has not been recovered will be apportioned to the prejudiced person.

Article 6:103. Damages are paid in money. Nevertheless, the court, at the request of the prejudiced person, mat award damages in another form than payment of a monetary sum. If such a decision is not complied with within a reasonable time, the prejudiced person regains his competence to demand damages in monetary form.

Article 6:104. If someone who is liable as against someone else on the basis of a wrongful act or a deficiency in the performance of an obligation has profited from that act or defect, the court may, at the request of the other person, establish the damage to the amount of that profit or to a part of it.

[The remainder of Title 2 is omitted.]

Title 3. Wrongful act

Division 1. General provisions

Article 6:162. (1) He who commits a wrongful act [onrechtmatige daad] as against another, which can be attributed to him, is obliged to compensate the damage suffered by that other as a consequence thereof.
(2) A wrongful act is considered to be a violation of a right and an act or omission [een doen of nalaten] contrary to a legal obligation or to what is socially acceptable according to unwritten law [hetgeen volgens ongeschreven recht in het maatschappelijk verkeer betaamt], all this subject to the availability of a ground for justification.
(3) A wrongful act can be attributed to the wrongdoer [dader], if it is due to his fault or to a cause that is attributed to him pursuant to the law or to generally accepted views in society [de in het verkeer geldende opvattingen].

Article 6:163. There is no obligation to pay damages where the violated norm does not extend to protect against the damage as it was suffered by the wronged person [benadeelde].

Article 6:164. Conduct [gedraging] of a child who has not yet reached the age of fourteen cannot be attributed to him as a wrongful act.

Article 6:165. (1) The circumstance that conduct by a person of fourteen years or older must be considered as an act occurring under the influence of a mental or physical deficiency is not an obstacle to attributing it as a wrongful act to the wrongdoer.
(2) If a third party is also liable as against the wronged person due to insufficient supervision, then this third party is obliged as against the wrongdoer to contribute to the compensation to the full amount of his liability as against the wronged person.

Article 6:166. (1) Where a person belonging to a group wrongfully causes damage and the likelihood of so causing damage should have discouraged these persons from acting as a group, they are jointly and severally liable [hoofdelijk aansprakelijk] if these actions can be attributed to them.
(2) Among themselves, they each bear an equal share of the compensation, unless, given the circumstances of the case, fairness [billijkheid] requires a different division.

Article 6:167. (1) Where a person is liable as against another pursuant to this title as regards incorrect or, due to its incompleteness, misleading publication of data of a factual nature, a court may, at the request of that other person, order him to publish a rectification in a manner to be indicated by the court.
(2) The same applies where there is no liability because the publication cannot be attributed as a wrongful act to the wrongdoer since he was unfamiliar with the incorrectness or incompleteness.
(3) In the case of paragraph 2, the court granting the claim may determine that the costs of the proceedings and of the publication of the rectification must be borne wholly or partially by the person who initiated the claim. Each of the parties may recover his part in the costs of the proceedings and the publication of the rectification that he must bear as a result of the judgment from anyone who is liable for the damage resulting from the publication.

Article 6:168. (1) The court may reject a claim to prohibit a wrongful act on the basis that this act ought to be tolerated for imperative reasons of public interest. The wronged person retains his right to compensation of the damage in accordance with the present title.
(2) In the case as meant in Article 170, the subordinate is not liable for this damage.
(3) If a judgment to pay damages or to provide security is not complied with, the court may nonetheless prohibit the act.

Division 2. Liability for persons and objects

Article 6:169. (1) A person who exercises parental authority or custody over a child is liable for damage caused to a third party by conduct that is to be regarded as an act of a child who has not yet reached the age of fourteen years and to whom this conduct could be attributed as a wrongful act had his age not prevented it.
(2) A person who exercises parental authority or custody over a child is liable for damage caused to a third party by a fault of that child, who has reached the age of fourteen years but not yet that of sixteen years, unless he cannot be reproached for not preventing the conduct of the child.

Article 6:170. (1) The person in whose service a subordinate fulfils his task is liable for damage caused to a third party by a fault of that subordinate, if the likelihood of the fault is increased by the order to undertake the task and the person in whose service he was, due to the legal relationship, had control over the conduct resulting in the fault.
(2) If the subordinate was in the service of a natural person and was not employed for a profession or business of this person, then the latter is only liable if the subordinate, when making the mistake, was acting in fulfilment of the task assigned to him.
(3) If the subordinate and he in whose service he was are both liable for the damage, then the subordinate need not contribute to the compensation in their mutual relationship, unless the damage is the result of wilful misconduct or deliberate recklessness [opzet of bewuste roekeloosheid]. Something other than what is determined in the previous sentence may follow from the circumstances of the case, also taking into account the nature of their relationship.

Article 6:171. Where a non-subordinate carries out activities assigned by another in the course of that person's business is liable as against a third party for a fault committed during those activities, then that other is also liable as against the third party.

Article 6:172. Where an act by a representative in the exercise of the powers attributed to him amounts to a fault as against a third party, then the represented party is also liable as against the third party.

Article 6:173. (1) The possessor [bezitter] of a movable object of which it is known that it constitutes a serious danger to persons or objects, in case it does not meet the standards that may be set for such an object in the given circumstances,, is liable if this danger manifests itself, unless there would have been no liability on the basis of the previous division if he would have had known of this danger at the time it arose.
(2) If the object does not meet the standards as meant in the previous paragraph due to a defect as meant in Division 3 of Title 3, there is no liability on the basis of the previous paragraph for damage as meant in that division, unless
(a) taking all circumstances into account, it is likely that the defect did not exist at the time at which the product was brought into circulation or that the defect arose at a later time; or
(b) it concerns damage to the object itself [zaakschade] with regard to which, pursuant to Division 3 of Title 3, there is no right to compensation on the basis of the franchise regulated in that division.
(3) The previous paragraphs do not apply to animals, vessels and aircraft.

Article 6:174. (1) The possessor of a structure which does not meet the standards that may be set in the given circumstances and which thereby constitutes a danger for persons or objects, is liable if this danger manifests itself, unless there is no liability on the basis of the previous division if he would have known of this danger at the time it arose.
(2) As regards emphyteusis [erfpacht], liability lies with the possessor of the right of emphyteusis. As regards public roads, it lies with the public authority that must take care that the road is in good condition, as regards pipes, with the person managing them, except in as far as the pipe is in a building or construction and is meant for supply and drainage of that building or edifice.
(3) As regards underground structures, liability lies with the person who, at the moment that the damage becomes known, uses the structure in the exercise of his business. If, after the damage becomes known another person becomes the user, liability remains with the person who was user at the time this [damage] became known. If the damage has become known after the use of the underground construction ended, liability lies with the person who was the last user.
(4) In this article, a structure is considered to be a building or edifice that is permanently connected to the ground, either directly, or through a connection to other buildings or edifices.
(5) The person who is registered in the public registry as owner of the construction or of the ground is presumed to be the possessor of the construction.
(6) In applying this article, a public road is considered to be both the actual road, as well as the surrounding road fixtures.

[Articles 175 – 178 are omitted.]

Article 6:179. The possessor of an animal is liable for damage caused by the animal, unless there is no liability on the basis of the previous division if he would have had control over the conduct of the animal that caused the damage.

Article 6:180. (1) In the cases of Articles 173, 174 and 179, co-possessors are jointly and severally liable.
(2) In case of transfer of an object under the suspensive condition of fulfilment of a counter-performance, the liability that is imposed upon the possessor by Articles 173, 174 and 179 lies with the acquirer from the time of this transfer.

Article 6:181. (1) Where the objects, constructions or animals as meant in Articles 173, 174 and 179 are used in the course of business, then the liability stemming from Articles 173(1), 174 paragraphs (1) and (2), first sentence, and 179 lies with the person who carries out this business, unless it concerns a construction and the cause of the damage was not related to the carrying out of the business.
(2) Where the objects, constructions or animals are used in the course of business by making them available for use in the course of another's business, then that other is considered to be the person liable pursuant to the previous paragraph.
(3) Where a substance as meant in Article 175 is used in the course of business by making this substance available for use in the course of another's profession or business, that other is considered to be the person liable pursuant to Article 175 paragraph (1).

Article 6:182. Where in the cases of Articles 176 and 177 there are at the same time two or more operators, either acting jointly or not, then they are jointly and severally liable.

Article 6:183. (1) As regards liability on the basis of this Division, the person sued may not invoke his youthful age or a mental or physical deficiency.
(2) The person who exercises parental authority or custody over a child who has not yet reached the age of fourteen years, is liable in his place on the basis of Articles 173 and 179 for the objects and animals as meant therein, unless these are used in the course of business.

[The remainder of Title 3 and Title 4 are omitted.]

Title 5. Contracts in general

Part 1. General provisions

Article 6:213. (1) A contract [overeenkomst] in the sense of this title is a multilateral legal act [meerzijdige rechtshandeling], whereby one or more parties undertake an obligation as against one or more others.
(2) The statutory provisions with regard to contracts do not apply to contracts between more than two parties to the extent that this is contrary to the purpose of the provisions concerned in relation to the nature of the contract.

Article 6:214. (1) A contract entered into by one of the parties in the exercise of his business or profession, is, apart from the statutory provisions, also subject to a standard regulation, where such a standard regulation is applicable with regard to such a contract to the branch to which the business belongs or to the profession. The special kinds of contract for which standard regulations may be established and the branch or profession to which each of these regulations is meant to apply are designated by ordinance.
(2) A standard regulation is established, altered and repealed by a committee to be appointed by Our Minister of Justice. Further rules will be laid down by law as regards the manner of assembling the committees and their method of working.
(3) The establishment, alteration or repeal of a standard regulation does not enter into force before it has been approved by Us and has been published in the Netherlands Government Gazette [Nederlandse Staatscourant] following Our endorsement order.
(4) In a standard regulation one may deviate from statutory provisions, to the extent that deviation is also permitted by contract, whether or not in compliance with a particular form. An exception is made to the previous sentence, where a statutory provision provides otherwise.
(5) Parties may deviate in their contract from a standard regulation. A standard regulation may however prescribe a particular form for deviation.

Article 6:215. Where a contract satisfies the description of two or more particular kinds of contracts regulated by law, then the provisions provided for each of these types are applicable simultaneously, except in as far as these provisions are not entirely compatible or if their purpose opposes application in relation to the nature of the contract.

Article 6:216. That which has been stipulated in this and the next three titles, is equally applicable to other multilateral patrimonial legal acts [meerzijdige vermogensrechtelijke rechtshandeling], to the extent that the purpose of the provisions concerned is not opposed thereto in relation to the nature of the legal act.

Division 2. The formation of contracts

Article 6:217. (1) A contract is formed through an offer and the acceptance thereof.
(2) Articles 219 – 225 are applicable, unless something else follows from the offer, from another legal act or from a custom.

Article 6:218. An offer is valid, void or voidable in accordance with the rules on multilateral legal acts.

Article 6:219. (1) An offer may be revoked [herroepen], unless it contains a time period for acceptance or if its irrevocability follows from the offer in another manner.
(2) The revocation may only occur, as long as the offer has not been accepted or a statement containing the acceptance has not yet been sent. If the offer contains a statement that it is made free of obligation [vrijblijvend], then the revocation may still be made without delay after the acceptance.

(3) A stipulation by which one of the parties binds himself, should the other party wish it, to conclude a particular contract with him, constitutes an irrevocable offer.

Article 6:220. (1) An offer of a reward [uitloving] for a given time may be revoked or altered for significant reasons.
(2) In case of revocation or alteration of a reward, the court may award a fair compensation to a person who has started with the preparation of the requested performance on the basis of the reward.

Article 6:221. (1) An oral offer lapses if it is not immediately accepted, a written offer if it is not accepted within a reasonable time.
(2) An offer lapses when it is rejected.

Article 6:222. An offer does not lapse due to death or loss of legal capacity of one of the parties, nor because one of the parties loses the competence to conclude the contract as a consequence of legal administration.

Article 6:223. (1) The offeror may regard a late acceptance as having been made in time, provided that he immediately informs the other party thereof.
(2) If an acceptance occurs too late, but the offeror understands or ought to understand that this was not clear to the other party, then the acceptance counts as having been made in time, unless he immediately informs the other party that he considers the offer to have lapsed.

Article 6:224. If an acceptance does not reach the offeror at all or not in time due to a circumstance on the basis of which it nevertheless has effect following Article 37 paragraph (3), second sentence, of Book 3, then the contract is deemed to have been formed at the time at which the declaration would have been received without the hindering circumstance.

Article 6:225. (1) An acceptance which deviates from the offer constitutes a new offer and as a rejection of the original.
(2) If a reply to an offer containing an acceptance deviates from that offer only on insignificant points, then this reply counts as acceptance and the contract is formed in conformity with this acceptance, unless the offeror instantaneously objects to the differences.
(3) If offer and acceptance refer to different sets of conditions, then the second reference does not have effect where the applicability of the set of conditions as indicated in the first reference is therein not also expressly rejected.

Article 6:226. If the law provides, for the formation of a contract, a pre-requisite concerning form, this pre-requisite is equally applicable to a contract whereby a party for whose benefit it is intended commits to conclude such a contract, unless the purpose of the pre-requisite suggests otherwise.

Article 6:227. The obligations which parties undertake must be determinable.

[Articles 227a – 227c are omitted.]

Article 6:228. (1) A contract which has been concluded under the influence of mistake [dwaling] and would not have been concluded under a correct impression of the situation, is voidable:
(a) if the mistake is attributable to information from the other party, unless the latter was allowed to presume that the contract would also be concluded without this information;
(b) if the other party should have informed the mistaken person in relation to what he knew or should have known regarding the mistake;
(c) if the other party, when concluding the contract, has relied on the same wrong impression as the mistaken person, unless, even under a correct impression of the situation, he would not have had to understand that the mistaken person ought to have been deterred from concluding the contract.
(2) The avoidance may not be grounded on a mistake which only concerns an exclusively future circumstance or which, with regard to the nature of the contract, generally accepted views in society [de in het verkeer geldende opvattingen] or the circumstances of the case should remain for the account of the mistaken person.

Article 6:229. A contract that aims to build upon an existing legal relationship between the parties, is voidable, if this legal relationship does not exist, unless given the nature of the contract, generally accepted views in society or the circumstances of the case, this absence should remain for the account of the mistaken party.

Article 6:230. (1) The right to avoid on the basis of Articles 228 and 229 lapses, where the other party proposes in time an alteration of the consequences of the contract, which sufficiently eliminates the disadvantage suffered by the person entitled to avoid in case the agreement is maintained.
(2) Furthermore, the court may, at the request of one of the parties, instead of pronouncing the avoidance, alter the consequences of the agreement to eliminate this disadvantage.

Division 3. General conditions

Article 6:231. In this Division:
(a) general conditions [algemene voorwaarden] are: one or more terms drawn up in order to be included in a number of contracts, with the exception of terms that concern the essence of the performances, to the extent that the latter stipulations are clearly and understandably formulated;
(b) the user is: he who uses general conditions in a contract;
(c) the other party is: he who by signing a document or in another manner has accepted the application of general conditions.

Article 6:232. The other party is bound to the general conditions even if, at the time of conclusion of the contract, the user understood or ought to have understood that he did not know the content thereof.

Article 6:233. A term in general conditions is voidable
(a) if, given the nature and other content of the contract, the manner in which the general conditions have come about, the mutually identifiable interests of the parties and the other circumstances of the case, it is unreasonably onerous for the other party; or
(b) if the user has not offered the other party a reasonable opportunity to become acquainted with the general conditions.

Article 6:234. (1) The user has offered the other party the opportunity as meant in Article 233(b), if
(a) he has either provided the other party with the general conditions before or at the time of conclusion of the contract, or
(b) if this is not reasonably possible, he has informed the other party before conclusion of the contract that the conditions are available for inspection with him or have been deposited at a Chamber of Commerce [Kamer van Koophandel en Fabrieken] indicated by him or at the registry of a court, and that they will be sent upon request, or
(c) if the contract is concluded electronically, he has provided the other party electronically with the general conditions before or at the time of conclusion of the contract, in such a manner that they can be saved by him and are accessible to him for consultation at a later time, or, if this is not reasonably possible, has informed the other party before conclusion of the contract where he may consult the conditions electronically, and that they will be sent upon request, electronically or in another manner.
(2) If the other party has not been provided with the conditions before or at the time of conclusion of the contract, then the terms are also voidable, if the user does not immediately and at his own expense send the conditions to the other party upon his request.
(3) The provisions of paragraphs (1) under (b) and (2) concerning the obligation to send are not applicable, in as far as such forwarding cannot reasonably be demanded of the user.

Article 6:235. (1) The grounds for avoidance as meant in Articles 233 and 234 may not be invoked by
(a) a legal person as meant in Article 360 of Book 2, that has at the time of conclusion of the agreement recently published its annual account, or with regard to which at that time Article 403 paragraph (1) of Book 2 was recently applied;
(b) a party to whom subparagraph (a) does not apply, if at the aforementioned time he employs fifty or more persons or if at that time it follows from a report pursuant to the Trade Register Act 1996 [Handelsregisterwet 1996] that he employs fifty or more persons.
(2) The ground for avoidance as meant in Article 233 paragraph (a) may also be invoked by a party for whom the general conditions have been used by a representative, provided that the other party repeatedly concludes contracts to which the same or practically the same general conditions are applicable.

3) The grounds for avoidance as meant in Articles 233 and 234 may not be invoked by a party that has repeatedly used the same or practically the same general conditions in his agreements.
(4) The time period as meant in Article 52 paragraph (1) under (d) of Book 3 starts at the beginning of the day, following that on which the term has been invoked.

Article 6:236. In a contract between a user and another party, who is a natural person not acting in the exercise of a profession or business, a term in the general conditions is considered to be unreasonably onerous
(a) where it deprives the other party entirely and unconditionally of the right to demand the performance promised by the user;
(b) where it excludes or restricts the other party's right to dissolve, as regulated in Division 5 of Title 5;
(c) where it excludes or restricts the other party's right, pursuant to the law, to suspend performance or grants the user a more far-reaching right to suspend than he is entitled to according to the law;
(d) where it leaves the assessment of the question whether the user has failed to fulfil one or more of his obligations to himself, or makes the exercise of the rights that the other party has according to the law with regard to such a deficiency dependent upon the condition that the latter has first brought a legal action against a third party;
(e) where the other party grants the user permission in advance to pass his obligations stemming from the contract to a third party in one of the ways as meant in Division 3 of Title 2, unless the other party has at all times the right to dissolve the contract, or unless the user is liable as against the other party for performance by the third party, or unless the passing takes place in relation to the transfer of a company to which both these obligations as well as the rights acquired in exchange belong;
(f) where it, in case the rights of the user stemming from the contract are transferred to a third party, has as its purpose to exclude or restrict rights or defences which the other party could invoke against that third party according to the law;
(g) where it shortens a statutory period of prescription or expiry within which the other party must invoke a particular right to a period of prescription or expiry of less than a year;
(h) where it obliges the other party, in case during performance of the contract damage is caused to a third party by the user or by a person or object for which the latter is liable, to either compensate the third party for this damage, or to bear a larger part of it in his relation to the user than he would be obliged to according to the law;
(i) where it gives the user the right to raise the price stipulated by him within three months after conclusion of the contract, unless the other party has in that case the right to dissolve the contract;
(j) where it leads, in the case of a contract for the regular delivery of objects, including electricity, or for the regular provision of services, to tacit extension or renewal for more than a year;
(k) where it excludes or restricts the right of the other party to provide evidence, or where it alters the allocation of the burden of proof as follows from the law to the disadvantage of the other party, either by containing a declaration from the latter regarding the quality of the performance owed to him, or by placing upon him the burden of proving that a shortcoming of the user can be attributed to him;
(l) where it deviates from Article 37 of Book 3 to the disadvantage of the other party, unless it relates to the form of declarations to be made by the other party or determines that the user may continue to consider the address provided to him by the other party as such until he has been informed of a new address;
(m) as a result of which the other party who, at the time of conclusion of the contract has his habitual residence in a municipality in the Netherlands, chooses a residence for other reasons than in case he will at any time not have a known actual residence in that municipality, unless the contract relates to a registered object and a residence is chosen at the offices of a notary;
(n) where it provides for the adjudication of a dispute by a person other than the court that would be competent pursuant to the law, or one or more arbiters, unless it provides the other party with a time period of at least one month after the user has invoked the term in writing as against him, to choose a court that is competent pursuant to the law for adjudication of the dispute.

Article 6:237. In a contract between a user and another party, who is a natural person not acting in the exercise of a profession or business, a term in general conditions is presumed to be unreasonably onerous
(a) where, given the circumstances of the case, it gives the user an unusually long or insufficiently determined time period to react to an offer or other declaration of the other party;
(b) where it extensively restricts the content of the obligations of the user with regard to what the other party, taking into account the statutory rules that apply to the contract, could reasonably expect without this term;
(c) where it grants the user the right to provide a performance that deviates essentially from the promised performance, unless the other party has in that case the right to dissolve the contract;

(d) where it frees the user of being bound by the contract or grants him the right thereto on other grounds than those mentioned in the contract, which are of such a nature that he can no longer be required to be bound;
(e) where it gives the user an unusually long or insufficiently determined time period for performance;
(f) where it frees the user or a third party wholly or partially of a statutory obligation to pay damages;
(g) where it excludes or restricts the right to settle granted to the other party by law or grants the user a more extensive right to settle than he is entitled to pursuant to the law;
(h) where it imposes as a sanction on certain acts of the other party, including omission, the loss of rights to which he is entitled or of the right to invoke certain defences, except in as far as these acts justify the loss of these rights or defences;
(i) where, in case the contract is ended on grounds other than the fact that the other party has failed to perform his obligation, it obliges the other party to pay a sum of money, except in as far as it concerns a reasonable compensation for loss suffered by the user or profit of which he has been deprived;
(j) where it obliges the other party to conclude a contract with the user or with a third party, unless this, taking into account the connection of that contract with the contract as meant in this article, may reasonably be required of the other party;
(k) where it lays down a time period of more than one year for a contract as meant in Article 236 under (j), unless the other party has the right to cancel the contract after each year;
(l) where it binds the other party to a time period for cancellation that is longer than three months or longer than the time period for cancellation of the contract by the user;
(m) where it requires, for the validity of a declaration to be made by the other party, a stricter form than required for a private document [onderhandse akte];
(n) where it determines that a mandate granted by the other party is irrevocable or does not end at his death or his coming under legal guardianship [ondercuratelestelling], unless the mandate has as its purpose the delivery of a registered thing.

[Articles 6:238 – 6:245 are omitted.]

Article 6:246. Neither Articles 231 – 244, nor the provisions of the ordinances [algemene maatregelen van bestuur] as meant in Article 239 paragraph (1) may be deviated from. The right to avoid a term pursuant to this division by an extrajudicial declaration cannot be excluded.

Article 6:247. (1) This division applies to contracts between parties acting in the exercise of a profession or business which are both established in the Netherlands, irrespective of the law governing the contract.
(2) This division does not apply to contracts between parties acting in the exercise of a profession or business that are not both established in the Netherlands, irrespective of the law governing the contract.
(3) A party is established in the Netherlands in the sense of paragraphs (1) and (2), if its central administration, or, where the performance is to be carried out according to the contract by a place of business other than the central administration, this other place of business is located in the Netherlands.
(4) This division applies to contracts between a user and another party, natural person, not acting in the exercise of a profession or business, if the other party has his habitual residence in the Netherlands, irrespective of the law governing the contract.

Division 4. Legal Consequences of Contracts

Article 6:248. (1) A contract does not only contain the legal consequences agreed upon by the parties, but also those which, in relation to the nature of the contract, stem from the law, custom or the requirements of reasonableness and fairness [redelijkheid en billijkheid].
(2) A provision which has effect as between the parties as a consequence of the contract is not applicable, to the extent that this would be unacceptable in the given circumstances according to the standards of reasonableness and fairness.

[Articles 6:249 – 6:251 are omitted.]

Article 6:252. (1) It may be stipulated by contract that the duty of one of the parties to tolerate or not to do something in respect to a registered thing [registergoed] that belongs to that party, shall pass onto those that acquire the registered thing under specific title, and the persons who acquire a right to use the object from the holder of a right shall also be bound.

(2) To effect the stipulation mentioned in paragraph (1), the it is required that the parties draw up a notarial deed of their contract, followed by registration in the public land registers. The person who is subject to the duty must choose residence in the Netherlands in the deed of creation.
(3) Also after registration, the stipulation will have no effect:
(a) against those that have acquired a right to the thing or a right to use the thing under specific title before registration.
(b) against the seizor of the thing or of a right on that thing, when the summons [proces-verbaal] for the seizure was registered before registration of the deed.
(c) against those who have acquired their right from a person that was not bound by the agreed upon duty under (a) or (b).
(4) If a counter-performance has been agreed upon for the duty, then with the passing of the duty, the right to the counter-performance will pass in so far as this relates to the period after the passing and this duty to perform has also been entered in the register.
(5) This article does not apply to those duties that limit a holder of a right in his powers to transfer or burden his right.

[Articles 6:253 – 6:257 are omitted.]

Article 6:258. (1) The court may, at the request of one of the parties, modify the consequences of a contract or dissolve it wholly or partially on grounds of unforeseen circumstances which are of such a nature that the other party may not expect unaltered continuation of the contract according to the standards of reasonableness and fairness. The modification or dissolution may be granted retroactive effect.
(2) A modification or dissolution will not be pronounced to the extent that the circumstances are for the account of he who relies on them on the basis of the nature of the contract or public opinion.
(3) For the application of this article, he to whom a right or obligation from a contract has been transferred is equal to a party to that contract.

[Articles 6:259 – 6: 260 are omitted.]

Division 5. Synallagmatic Contracts [Wederkerige overeenkomsten]

Article 6:261. (1) A contract is synallagmatic if each of the parties assumes an obligation towards the other in order to acquire the performance to which the other party commits himself.
(2) The provisions regarding synallagmatic contracts are applicable mutatis mutandis to other legal relationships with the purpose of mutual execution of performances, in as far as the nature of those legal relationships is not opposed to it.

Article 6:262. (1) If one of the parties does not honour his commitment, then the other party is authorized to suspend his parallel obligations.
(2) In case of partial or improper performance, suspension is only allowed, to the extent that it is justified by the deficiency.

Article 6:263. (1) The party that is obliged to perform first, is nevertheless authorized to suspend performance of his obligation, if after the contract was concluded he gained knowledge of circumstances which give good grounds to fear that the other party will not perform his parallel obligations.
(2) In case there are good grounds to fear that performance will only be partial or improper, suspension is only allowed in as far as it is justified by the deficiency.

Article 6:264. In case of suspension on the basis of Articles 262 and 263, Articles 54 under (b) and (c) and 55 are not applicable.

Article 6:265. (1) Every deficiency in the performance of one of a party's obligations authorizes the other party to dissolve the contract wholly or partially, unless the deficiency, given its special nature or its insignificant meaning, does not justify this dissolution [ontbinding] and its consequences.
(2) To the extent that performance is not permanently or temporarily impossible, the right to dissolution only arises when the debtor is in default.

Article 6:266. (1) A dissolution cannot be based on a deficiency in the performance of an obligation with regard to which the creditor himself is in default.
(2) If, during the default of the creditor, however, proper performance becomes wholly or partially impossible, then the contract may be dissolved, if through fault of the debtor or his subordinate there has been a lack of care which could have been required from him in the given circumstances.

Article 6:267. (1) The dissolution takes place by way of a written declaration of the person who is so entitled. If the contract was formed electronically, it can also be dissolved by a declaration brought about electronically. Article 227a paragraph (1) is applicable mutatis mutandis.
(2) It may also be pronounced by a court upon his request.

Article 6:268. The right to extrajudicial dissolution lapses through prescription of the legal claim for dissolution. The prescription does not impede a judicial or extrajudicial dissolution to avert a legal claim or other judicial measure which is based on the contract.

Article 6:269. The dissolution does not have retroactive effect, except where an offer to perform, made after the dissolution has been claimed, does not have effect, if the dissolution is pronounced.

Article 6:270. A partial dissolution contains an equal decrease of the mutual performances in quantity or quality.

Article 6:271. A dissolution releases the parties of the obligations affected thereby. In as far as these have already been performed, the legal ground for this performance remains intact, but an obligation arises for the parties to undo the performances already received by them.

Article 6:272. (1) If the nature of the contract excludes that it be undone, then compensation comes in its place to the amount of its value at the time of receipt.
(2) If the performance was not in conformity with the contract, then this compensation is limited to the amount of the value that the performance actually had for the recipient at that time in the given circumstances.

Article 6:273. A party who has received a performance, is, from the time at which he reasonably ought to take dissolution into account, obliged to take care as a careful debtor that the restoration [ongedaanmaking] of the owed performance as a consequence of that dissolution, will be possible. Article 78 applies mutatis mutandis.

[The remainder of Book 6 is omitted.]

Book 7. Special Types of Contract

Title 1. Sale and Exchange

Division 1. Sale: General Provisions

Article 7:1. Sale [koop] is a contract by which one person binds himself to give an object and the other party to pay a price in money therefor.

Article 7:2. (1) The sale of an immovable object intended for habitation or a part thereof, where the buyer is a natural person not acting in the exercise of a profession or business, is to be concluded in writing.
(2) The deed or a copy thereof which has been drawn up between the parties is to be handed over to the buyer, in exchange for a dated receipt from the seller if required. During three days after this handing over, the buyer has the right to dissolve the sale. If after the buyer has exercised this right, a new sale is entered within six months between the same parties in respect of the same object or the same part, then the right does not arise again.
(3) Paragraphs 1 and 2 apply mutatis mutandis to the sale of participation and membership rights that grant rights to the use of an immovable object intended for habitation or a part thereof.
(4) Paragraphs 1 – 3 cannot be derogated from to the disadvantage of the buyer, except in case of a standard regulation as meant in Article 214 of Book 6.
(5) Paragraphs 1 – 4 are not applicable to a hire purchase and to a public auction in the presence of a notary. Neither are they applicable to a sale as meant in Article 48a under a.

PART V. PRIVATE LAW

[Article 7:3 is omitted.]

Article 7:4. When the sale is concluded without the price being determined, the buyer owes a reasonable one; for the determination of the price account is to be taken of the price the seller commonly demands at the time of the conclusion of the contract.

Article 7:5. (1) In this title a 'consumer sale' means: the sale of a movable object, including electricity, which is concluded by a seller acting in the exercise of a profession or business, and a buyer, natural person, not acting in the exercise of a profession or a business.
(2) If the object is sold by a representative [gevolmachtigde] who acts in the exercise of a profession or a business, the sale will be regarded as a consumer sale, unless the buyer knows, at the time the contract is concluded that the principal [volmachtgever] does not act in exercise of a profession or a business.
(3) The previous paragraphs are not applicable if the contract concerns water that is delivered by pipelines to the consumer.
(4) If the movable object still has to be produced and the contract by virtue of which the object has to be delivered satisfies the description of Article 750, the contract will be regarded as a consumer sale, if the contract is concluded by a (building) contractor [aannemer] who acts in the exercise of a profession or a business, and a customer [opdrachtgever], natural person, not acting in the exercise of a profession or a business. The provisions of this title and of Division 1 of Title 12 apply simultaneously. In the case of conflict the provisions of this title are applicable.

Article 7:6. (1) In a consumer sale, divisions 1 – 7 of this title cannot be derogated from to the disadvantage of the buyer and the rights and claims which the law accords to the buyer regarding a deficiency in the performance of the duties of the seller may not be restricted or excluded.
(2) Paragraph 1 is not applicable to Articles 11, 12, 13, 26 and 35, but stipulations in general conditions whereby these articles are derogated from to the disadvantage of the buyer, are deemed to be unreasonably burdensome.
(3) The applicability to the consumer sale of a right that does not or only partially offers the protection by way of directive 99/44/EC of the European Parliament and the Council of the European Union of 25 May1999 concerning certain aspects of consumer sales of and associated guarantees (O.J. L171), cannot result in the buyer losing the protection he is entitled to by virtue of this directive through the mandatory provisions of the law of the Member State of the European Union or another state which is party to the Agreement creating the European Economic Area, where he has his habitual residence.

Article 7:6a. (1) If in the case of a consumer sale, certain characteristics are promised by the seller or producer in a guarantee, in the absence whereof certain rights or claims are granted to the buyer, the buyer can exercise them notwithstanding all other rights or claims the law grants the buyer.
(2) In a guarantee it must be specified in a clear and understandable manner which rights and claims referred to in paragraph 1 are granted to the buyer and it is to be stated that they are accorded to the buyer notwithstanding the rights and claims which he is entitled to by law. Furthermore, in a guarantee, the name and the address either of the seller or of the producer from whom the guarantee originated are to be stated as well as the duration and the territory for which the guarantee will have effect.
(3) The information referred to in paragraph 2 is to be provided to buyer on his demand. This occurs in writing or on another permanently accessible information medium at the disposal of the buyer. .
(4) The rights and claims granted to the buyer by the seller or producer in a certificate of guarantee are also available to him if the object does not possess the characteristics which were promised by that seller or producer in an advertisement.
(5) In this article the following means:
a. Guarantee: a promise made in a certificate of guarantee or advertisement as meant in paragraph 1;
b. Producer: the manufacturer of the object, the person who imports the object into the European Economic Area, as well as anyone else who presents himself to be the producer by placing his name, his trademark or any other distinguishing feature on the object.

Article 7:7. (1) The person to whom an object has been sent and who may reasonably assume that this sending occurred in order to induce him to purchase, is irrespective of any other contrary statement by the sender to him entitled to keep the object for free, unless it can be attributed to him that the sending occurred.
(2) The sending to a natural person not acting in the exercise of a profession or a business, of an object not ordered by this person with a demand for payment of the price, , return or safe keeping, is not permitted. Where an

object is nevertheless sent in the sense of the first sentence, then that which is determined in paragraph 1 regarding the power to retain the object for free applies mutatis mutandis.
(3) If the recipient, in the situations meant in paragraphs 1 – 2, returns the object, the costs therefor are for the account of the sender.
(4) Paragraph 2 applies mutatis mutandis to the performance on behalf of a natural person, not acting in the exercise of a profession or a business, of a service that has not been ordered by that person.

[Article 7:8 is omitted.]

Division 2. Duties of the seller

Article 7:9. (1)The seller is obliged to transfer ownership of the sold object including any appurtenances and to deliver them. The appurtenances include the existing proofs of title; in so far as the seller thereby retains an interest, he is simply under a duty to provide a copy or an excerpt to the buyer on his demand and for his account.
(2) To deliver means bringing the buyer into possession of the object.
(3) In the case of a sale with a reservation of title, delivery means putting the object under the control of the buyer.

Article 7:10. (1) The object is at the risk of the buyer from the delivery, even if the ownership has not yet been transferred. Accordingly, he still owes the purchase price, notwithstanding the loss or deterioration of the object by a cause that cannot be attributed to the seller.
(2) The same applies from the moment at which the buyer is in default with the performance of an act with which he is to cooperate for the delivery. Depending on the sort of specific objects being sold, default of the buyer only causes the risk to pass to him once the seller has identified the objects destined for the performance of the contract and notified the buyer thereof.
(3) If the buyer on good grounds invokes his right to dissolution [ontbinding] of the sale or substitution of the object, these remain at the risk of the seller.
(4) When the object remained at the risk of the seller after delivery, the loss or deterioration thereof through the fault of the buyer will be likewise remains for the account of the seller. Nevertheless, the moment he must reasonably take into account the fact that he will have to return the object, the buyer has to care for the preservation thereof as a careful debtor; Article 78 of Book 6 applies mutatis mutandis.

Article 7:11. If in a consumer sale the object is delivered to the buyer by the seller or the carrier appointed by this person, the object is only at the risk of the buyer from delivery, even if it has been delivered already earlier in the sense of Article 9.

[Article 7:12 is omitted.]

Article 7:13. If in a consumer sale the object is delivered to the buyer by the seller or the carrier appointed by this person, the costs therefor can only be claimed in so far as they were specified separately by the seller at the conclusion of the contract or information was provided by the seller on what basis they are calculated by him. The same applies to costs due for activities which the seller performs for the buyer in relation to the sale.

[Article 7:14 is omitted.]

Article 7:15. (1) The seller is obliged to transfer ownership of the object sold free from all special burdens and restrictions, with the exception of those which the buyer has explicitly accepted.
(2) Notwithstanding any provisions to the contrary, the seller warrants the absence of burdens and restrictions which might stem from facts that are capable of registration in the public register, but which were not registered therein at the time of the conclusion of the contract.

[Article 7:16 is omitted.]

Article 7:17. (1) The delivered object must comply with the contract.
(2) An object does not comply with the contract if, in light of the nature of the object and the information that the seller gave about the object, it does not possess the characteristics which the buyer on the basis of the contract could have expected. The buyer may expect that the object has the characteristics which are necessary for ordinary use thereof and of which he did not need to doubt their presence, as well as the characteristics that are necessary for a particular use that is provided for in the contract.

Part V. Private Law

(3) Another object than contracted for or an object of a different kind likewise does not comply with the contract. The same applies if the delivered object differs in number, size or weight from that which was contracted for.
(4) If the purchaser has been shown or was provided with a sample or model, then the object has to be identical to it, unless it was merely provided for the purpose of identification, without requiring the object to comply with it.
(5) The buyer cannot invoke that the object does not comply with the contract when he knew or reasonably could have known this at the time of the conclusion of the contract. The buyer can also not invoke that the object does not comply with the contract when this is attributable to defects or unsuitability of raw materials originating from the buyer, unless the seller should have warned him of these defects or unsuitability.
(6) In case of the sale of an immovable object, the reference to size is presumed to merely be meant as an indication without the object having to comply therewith.

Article 7:18. (1) When evaluating the question, whether an object delivered on the basis of a consumer sale complies with the contract, announcements made by or on behalf of a previous seller of the object, acting in the exercise of a profession or a business, which were made public with regards to the object count as notifications of the seller, except in so far as this person neither knew of a certain announcement nor ought to have known of it or ultimately at the time of the conclusion of the contract revoked the announcement in a for the buyer clear way, or the sale could not be influenced by that announcement.
(2) In a consumer contract, is presumed that the object did not comply with the contract at delivery, if the deviation from the agreed upon manifests itself within a period of six months after the delivery, unless the nature of the object or the nature of the deviation oppose this.
(3) If in a consumer sale, the seller is obliged to take care of the installation of the object and such installation was performed badly, this amounts to a lack of conformity of the object to the contract. The same applies if the installation by the buyer was executed badly by the buyer and this is to be attributed to the instruction sheet, which was given to the buyer with the delivery of the object.
(4) In the case of compulsory enforcement, the buyer cannot invoke that the object is tainted with a burden or a restriction that it should not have been vested with, or that it does not comply with the contract, unless the seller knew of this.
(5) The same applies if the sale takes place by way of imminent execution, provided that the buyer knew of it or ought to have known of it. In a consumer sale the buyer however can invoke that the object does not comply with the contract.

[Article 7:19 is omitted.]

Division 3. Special consequences of non-performance of the duties of the seller

Article 7:20. If the object is tainted with a burden or restriction that should not have rested upon it, the buyer may demand the burden or restriction be removed, provided the seller can reasonably comply therewith.

Article 7:21. (1) If the delivered object does not comply with the contract, the buyer can demand:
a. delivery of that which is lacking;
b. repair of the delivered object, provided the seller can reasonably comply therewith.
c. replacement of the delivered object, unless the deviation from that which was contracted for is too trivial to justify this, or that the object after the time that the buyer could reasonably take into consideration restoration [ongedaanmaking], is lost or has deteriorated because he did not care for the preservation thereof as a careful debtor.
(2) The costs of performance of the duties meant in paragraph 1 cannot be charged to the buyer.
(3) The seller is obliged to, also in light of the nature of the object and the particular use of the object which is provided for by the contract, within a reasonable time and without serious inconvenience to the buyer, fulfil his duties mentioned in paragraph 1.
(4) In a consumer sale, in derogation from paragraph 1, the buyer is only not entitled to repair or replacement of the delivered object, if repair or replacement is impossible or it cannot be required of the seller.
(5) Repair or replacement cannot be required of the seller, in a consumer sale, if the costs thereof are not in proportion to the costs of the exercise of another right or another claim which is accorded to the buyer, in light of the value of the object if it would conform with the contract, the extent of the deviation from that which was contracted for and the question whether the exercise of another right or another claim does not cause serious inconvenience to the buyer.

(6) If the seller did not, in a consumer sale, within a reasonable period of time after he was notified in writing by the buyer to do so, fulfil his duty to repair or replace the object, the buyer is authorized to have the repair take place by a third person and to claim the costs therefor from the seller.

Article 7:22. (1) If the delivered object does not comply with the contract, then in a consumer sale, the buyer is authorized to:
a. dissolve the contract, unless the deviation from that which was contracted for, in view of its trivial significance, would not justify such dissolution and its consequences.
b. reduce the price in proportion to the degree of deviation from that which was contracted for.
(2) The competences referred to in paragraph 1 only arise where repair and replacement cannot be required of the seller, or the seller was deficient in performance of a duty meant in Article 21 paragraph 3.
(3) In so far as this division did not derogate therefrom, the provisions of Division 5 of Title 5 of Book 6 in respect of dissolution of a contract apply mutatis mutandis to the powers referred to in paragraph 1 subparagraph b.
(4) The rights and powers mentioned in paragraph 1 and Articles 20 and 21 are accorded to the buyer without prejudice to all other rights and claims.

Article 7:23. (1) The buyer can no longer invoke that that which was delivered does not comply with the contract, if he does not notify the seller thereof within adequate time [bekwame tijd] after he has discovered it or reasonably ought to have discovered it. If it appears, however, that the object lacks a characteristic that according to the seller it possessed, or if the deviation is related to facts which he knew or ought to have known, but which he did not disclose, then the notification must take place within adequate time after the discovery. In a consumer sale, the notification has to occur within adequate time after the discovery, with a notification within a period of two months after the discovery being timely.
(2) Legal claims and defences grounded on facts that could justify the proposition that the delivered object does not comply with the contract, prescribe after a period of two years after the notification made in accordance with paragraph 1. However, the buyer retains the power to counter a claim for payment of the price with his right to reduction thereof or to damages.
(3) The period does not run as long as the buyer cannot exercise his right as a consequence of the intent of the seller.

Article 7:24. (1) If on the basis of a consumer sale an object has been delivered that does not possess the characteristics which the buyer could have expected on the basis of the contract, the buyer has against the seller the right to damages in accordance with Divisions 9 and 10 of Title 1 of Book 6.
(2) If the deficiency consists of a defect as meant in Division 3 of Title 3 of Book 6, the seller is not liable for damage as meant in that division, unless
a. he knew of the defect or ought to have known of it,
b. he guaranteed the absence of the defect, or
c. it concerns damage to the object with respect to which by virtue of Division 3 of Title 3 of Book 6, no right to compensation exists on the basis of the franchise regulated in that division, notwithstanding his defences by virtue of Divisions 9 and 10 of Title 1 of Book 6.

Article 7:25. (1) If the buyer, in the case of deficiency as meant in Article 24, has exercised one or more of his rights in respect of the deficiency against the seller, the seller has the right to damages from the person from whom he bought the object, provided this person also in the contract acted in the exercise of his profession or business. The costs of defence only will be compensated in so far as they were made reasonably by the seller.
(2) Paragraph 1 cannot be derogated from to the disadvantage of the seller.
(3) The right of damages by virtue of paragraph 1 is not accorded to the seller, if the deviation concerns facts which he knew or ought to have known, or its cause lies in a circumstance that occurred after the object had been delivered to him.
(4) If an object lacks a characteristic which according to the seller it possessed, the right of the seller to damages by virtue of paragraph 1 is restricted to the amount to which he could have been entitled if he had not made the promise.
(5) The previous paragraphs apply mutatis mutandis to recovery based on earlier contracts.
(6) The previous paragraphs are not applicable in so far as it concerns damage as meant in Article 24 paragraph 2.

Division 4. Duties of the buyer

Article 7:26. (1) The buyer is obliged to pay the price.

(2) The payment has to be made at the time and the place of delivery. In a consumer sale, the buyer can be obliged to pay in advance at most half of the purchase price.

[The remainder of Article 7:26 and Article 7:27 are omitted.]

Article 7:28. In a consumer sale, the claim for payment of the purchase price prescribes after a period of two years.

Article 7:29. (1) Where the buyer has received the object, but he intends to reject it, he must take charge of its preservation as a careful debtor; he has a right of retention to the object until he has been reimbursed by the seller for the costs reasonably made by him.
(2) The buyer who intends to reject an object that was sent to him and that was put at his disposal at the place of destination must in so far as this does not require the payment of the purchase price and without serious inconvenience or unreasonable expenses, take possession of it, unless the seller is present at the place of destination or someone else there who is authorized to be charged with the care of the object on his behalf.

Article 7:30. When in the situations of Article 29, the object is susceptible to loss or deterioration or when the safekeeping results in serious inconvenience or unreasonable expense, the buyer is bound to sell the object in an appropriate manner.

[Division 5 is omitted.]

Division 6. Special cases of dissolution

Article 7:33. If the delivery of a movable good on a certain day is essential and on that day the buyer does not take possession, such conduct provides grounds to dissolve as meant in Article 265 of Book 6.

Article 7:34. The seller can dissolve the sale by way of written declaration, if the failure to take possession gives him good grounds to fear that the price will not be paid.

Article 7: 35. (1) If the seller in a consumer sale, by virtue of a stipulation made in the contract, increases the purchase price after the conclusion of the contract, the buyer is authorized to dissolve the contract by way of written declaration, unless it is stipulated that the delivery will take place more than three months after the purchase.
(2) For the application of paragraph 1, purchase price means the amount which at the conclusion of the contract subject to price changes was mentioned as the provisional purchase price.

Division 7. Damages

Article 7:36. (1) In the case of dissolution of the sale, if the object has a current price, the damages amounts to the difference between the price determined in the contract and the current price on the day of non-performance.
(2) In order to calculate these damages the current price to be taken into account is that of the market where the sale took place, or, if there is no such current price or it would be inconvenient to apply it, the price on the market which can reasonably replace it; with this differences in the costs for the carriage of the object are to be taken into consideration.

Article 7:37. Where the buyer or the seller concluded a cover purchase and in doing so he proceeded in a reasonable manner, he will be entitled to the difference between the agreed upon price and the price of the cover purchase.

Article 7:38. The provisions of the two previous articles do not exclude the right to higher damages in case more damage is suffered.

[The remainder of Title 1 and Titles 2 – 3 are omitted.]

Title 4. Lease

Division 4. The passing of lease on the transfer of the leased object and the termination of the lease

Article 7:226. (1) Transfer of ownership of an object in respect of which also a lease contract is made and creation or transfer of an independent right of usufruct, emphyteusis or superficies on the object in respect of which a lease contract is made, by the lessor, results in a passing of the rights and obligations of the lessor that pursuant to the lease contract become due after that time, to the acquirer.
(2) Transfer by a creditor of the lessor shall be equal to a transfer made by the lessor.
(3) The transferee shall only be bound by those stipulations in the lease contract that directly relate to granting the use of the object against a counter-performance to be paid by the lessee.
(4) No derogation can be made from the preceding paragraphs in case of the lease of a constructed immoveable object or of a part of that object and of a caravan referred to in Article 235 and of a caravan site referred to in Article 236.

Article 7:227. In the case of creation or assignment of a limited property right to a leased object does not fall under Article 226, paragraph (1), the holder must, as regards the lessee, refrain from exercising his right in a way that interferes with the lessee's use.

[The remainder of the Civil Code is omitted.]

Sale of Goods Act 1979 [An Act to consolidate the law relating to the sale of goods] (c. 54).

Part I: Contracts to Which Act Applies

Section 1. (1) This Act applies to contracts of sale of goods made on or after (but not to those made before) 1 January 1894.
(2) In relation to contracts made on certain dates, this Act applies subject to the modification of certain of its sections as mentioned in Schedule 1 below.
(3) Any such modification is indicated in the section concerned by a reference to Schedule 1 below.
(4) Accordingly, where a section does not contain such a reference, this Act applies in relation to the contract concerned without such modification of the section.

Part II: Formation of Contract

Contract of sale

Section 2. (1) A contract of sale of goods is a contract by which the seller transfers or agrees to transfer the property in goods to the buyer for a money consideration, called the price.
(2) There may a contract of sale between one part owner and another.
(3) A contract of sale may be absolute or conditional.
(4) Where under a contract of sale the property in the goods is transferred from the seller to the buyer the contact is called a sale.
(5) Where under a contract of sale the transfer of the property in the goods is to take place at a future time or subject to some condition later to be fulfilled the contract is called an agreement to sell.
(6) An agreement to sell becomes a sale when the time elapses or the conditions are fulfilled subject to which the property in the goods is to be transferred.

Section 3. (1) Capacity to buy and sell is regulated by the general law concerning capacity to contract and to transfer and acquire property.
(2) Where necessaries are sold and delivered to a minor or to a person who by reason of mental incapacity or drunkenness is incompetent to contract, he must pay a reasonable price for them.
(3) In subsection (2) above 'necessaries' means goods suitable to the condition in life of the minor or other person concerned and to his actual requirements at the time of the sale and delivery.

Formalities of contract

Section 4. (1) Subject to this and any other Act, a contract of sale may be made in writing (either with or without seal), or by word of mouth, or partly in writing and partly by word of mouth, or may be implied from the conduct of the parties.
(2) Nothing in this section affects the law relating to corporations.

Subject matter of contract

Section 5. (1) The goods which form the subject of a contract of sale may be either existing goods, owned or possessed by the seller, or goods to be manufactured or acquired by him after the making of the contract of sale, in this Act called future goods.
(2) There may be a contract for the sale of goods the acquisition of which by the seller depends on a contingency which may or may not happen.
(3) Where by a contract of sale the seller purports to effect a present sale of future goods, the contract operates as an agreement to sell the goods.

Section 6. Where there is a contract for the sale of specific goods, and the goods without the knowledge of the seller have perished at the time when a contract is made, the contract is void.

Section 7. Where there is an agreement to sell specific goods and subsequently the goods, without any fault on the part of the seller or buyer, perish before the risk passes to the buyer, the agreement is avoided.

Part V. Private Law

The price

Section 8. (1) The price in a contract of sale may be fixed by the contract, or may be left to be fixed in a manner agreed by the contract, or may be determined by the course of dealing between the parties.
(2) Where the price is not determined as mentioned in subsection (1) above the buyer must pay a reasonable price.
(3) What is a reasonable price is a question of fact dependent on the circumstances of each particular case.

Section 9. (1) Where there is an agreement to sell goods on the terms that the price is to be fixed by the valuation of a third party, and he cannot or does not make the valuation, the agreement is avoided; but if the goods or any part of them have been delivered to and appropriated by the buyer he must pay a reasonable price for them.
(2) Where the third party is prevented from making the valuation by the fault of the seller or buyer, the party not at fault may maintain an action for damages against the party at fault.

Implied terms etc.

Section 10. (1) Unless a different intention appears from the terms of the contract, stipulations as to time of payment are not of the essence of a contract of sale.
(2) Whether any other stipulation as to time is or is not of the essence of the contract depends on the terms of the contract.
(3) In a contract of sale 'month' prima facie means calendar month.

Section 11. (1) This section does not apply to Scotland.
(2) Where a contract of sale is subject to a condition to be fulfilled by the seller, the buyer may waive the condition, or may elect to treat the breach of the condition as a breach of warranty and not as a ground for treating the contract as repudiated.
(3) Whether a stipulation in a contract of sale is a condition, the breach of which may give rise to a right to treat the contract as repudiated, or a warranty, the breach of which may give rise to a claim for damages but not to a right to reject the goods and treat the contract as repudiated, depends in each case on the construction of the contract; and a stipulation may be a condition, though called a warranty in the contract.
(4) Subject to section 35A below where a contract of sale is not severable and the buyer has accepted the goods or part of them, the breach of a condition to be fulfilled by the seller can only be treated as a breach of warranty, and not as a ground for rejecting the goods and treating the contract as repudiated, unless there is an express or implied term of the contract to that effect.
(6) Nothing in this section affects a condition or warranty whose fulfilment is excused by law by reason of impossibility or otherwise.
[Subsection 7 is omitted.]

Section 12. (1) In a contract of sale, other than one to which subsection (3) below applies, there is an implied term on the part of the seller that in the case of a sale he has a right to sell the goods, and in the case of an agreement to sell he will have such a right at the time when the property is to pass.
(2) In a contract of sale, other than one to which subsection (3) below applies, there is also an implied term that—
(a) the goods are free, and will remain free until the time when the property is to pass, from any charge or encumbrance not disclosed or known to the buyer before the contract is made, and
(b) the buyer will enjoy quiet possession of the goods except so far as it may be disturbed by the owner or other person entitled to the benefit of any charge or encumbrance so disclosed or known.
(3) This subsection applies to a contract of sale in the case of which there appears from the contract or is to be inferred from its circumstances an intention that the seller should transfer only such title as he or a third person may have.
(4) In a contract to which subsection (3) above applies there is an implied term that all charges or encumbrances known to the seller and not known to the buyer have been disclosed to the buyer before the contract is made.
(5) In a contract to which subsection (3) above applies there is also an implied term that none of the following will disturb the buyer's quiet possession of the goods, namely—
(a) the seller;
(b) in a case where the parties to the contract intend that the seller should transfer only such title as a third person may have, that person;
(c) anyone claiming through or under the seller or that third person otherwise than under a charge or encumbrance disclosed or known to the buyer before the contract is made.

(5A) As regards England and Wales and Northern Ireland, the term implied by subsection (1) above is a condition and the terms implied by subsections (2), (4) and (5) above are warranties.
[Subsection 6 is omitted.]

Section 13. (1) Where there is a contract for the sale of goods by description, there is an implied term that the goods will correspond with the description.
(1A) As regards England and Wales and Northern Ireland, the term implied by subsection (1) above is a condition.
(2) If the sale is by sample as well as by description it is not sufficient that the bulk of the goods corresponds with the sample if the goods do not also correspond with the description.
(3) A sale of goods is not prevented from being a sale by description by reason only that, being exposed for sale or hire, they are selected by the buyer.
[Subsection 4 is omitted.]

Section 14. (1) Except as provided by this section and section 15 below and subject to any other enactment, there is no implied term about the quality or fitness for any particular purpose of goods supplied under a contract of sale.
(2) Where the seller sells goods in the course of a business, there is an implied term that the goods supplied under the contract are of satisfactory quality.
(2A) For the purposes of this Act, goods are of satisfactory quality if they meet the standard that a reasonable person would regard as satisfactory, taking account of any description of the goods, the price (if relevant) and all the other relevant circumstances.
(2B) For the purposes of this Act, the quality of goods includes their state and condition and the following (among others) are in appropriate cases aspects of the quality of goods—
(a) fitness for all the purposes for which goods of the kind in question are commonly supplied,
(b) appearance and finish,
(c) freedom from minor defects,
(d) safety, and
(e) durability.
(2C) The term implied by subsection (2) above does not extend to any matter making the quality of goods unsatisfactory—
(a) which is specifically drawn to the buyer's attention before the contract is made,
(b) where the buyer examines the goods before the contract is made, which that examination ought to reveal, or
(c) in the case of a contract for sale by sample, which would have been apparent on a reasonable examination of the sample.
(2D) If the buyer deals as consumer or, in Scotland, if a contract of sale is a consumer contract, the relevant circumstances mentioned in subsection (2A) above include any public statements on the specific characteristics of the goods made about them by the seller, the producer or his representative, particularly in advertising or on labelling.
(2E) A public statement is not by virtue of subsection (2D) above a relevant circumstance for the purposes of subsection (2A) above in the case of a contract of sale, if the seller shows that—
(a) at the time the contract was made, he was not, and could not reasonably have been, aware of the statement,
(b) before the contract was made, the statement had been withdrawn in public or, to the extent that it contained anything which was incorrect or misleading, it had been corrected in public, or
(c) the decision to buy the goods could not have been influenced by the statement.
(2F) Subsections (2D) and (2E) above do not prevent any public statement from being a relevant circumstance for the purposes of subsection (2A) above (whether or not the buyer deals as consumer or, in Scotland, whether or not the contract of sale is a consumer contract) if the statement would have been such a circumstance apart from those subsections.
(3) Where the seller sells goods in the course of a business and the buyer, expressly or by implication, makes known—
(a) to the seller, or
(b) where the purchase price of part of it is payable by instalments and the goods were previously sold by a credit-broker to the seller, to that credit-broker,
any particular purpose for which the goods are being bought, there is an implied term that the goods supplied under the contract are reasonably fit for that purpose, whether or not that is a purpose for which such goods are commonly supplied, except where the circumstances show that the buyer does not rely, or that it is unreasonable for him to rely, on the skill or judgment of the seller or credit-broker.
(4) An implied term about quality or fitness for a particular purpose may be annexed to a contract of sale by usage.

(5) The preceding provisions of this section apply to a sale by a person who in the course of a business is acting as agent for another as they apply to a sale by a principal in the course of a business, except where that other is not selling in the course of a business and either the buyer knows that fact or reasonable steps are taken to bring it to the notice of the buyer before the contract is made.
(6) As regards England and Wales and Northern Ireland, the terms implied by subsections (2) and (3) above are conditions.
[Subsections 7 and 8 are omitted.]

Sale by sample

Section 15. (1) A contract of sale is a contract for sale by sample where there is an express or implied term to that effect in the contract.
(2) In the case of a contract for sale by sample there is an implied term—
(a) that the bulk will correspond with the sample in quality;
(c) that the goods will be free from any defect, making their quality unsatisfactory, which would not be apparent on reasonable examination of the sample.
(3) As regards England and Wales and Northern Ireland, the term implied by subsection (2) above is a condition.
[Subsection 2(b) repealed and subsection 4 is omitted.]

Miscellaneous

Section 15A. (1) Where in the case of a contract of sale—
(a) the buyer would, apart from this subsection, have the right to reject goods by reason of a breach on the part of the seller of a term implied by section 13, 14 or 15 above, but
(b) the breach is so slight that it would be unreasonable for him to reject them,
then, if the buyer does not deal as consumer, the breach is not to be treated as a breach of condition but may be treated as a breach of warranty.
(2) This section applies unless a contrary intention appears in, or is to be implied from, the contract.
(3) It is for the seller to show that a breach fell within subsection (1)(b) above.
(4) This section does not apply to Scotland.

Part III: Effects of the Contract

Transfer of property as between seller and buyer

Section 16. Subject to section 20A below where there is a contract for the sale of unascertained goods no property in the goods is transferred to the buyer unless and until the goods are ascertained.

Section 17. (1) Where there is a contract for the sale of specific or ascertained goods the property in them is transferred to the buyer at such time as the parties to the contract intend it to be transferred.
(2) For the purpose of ascertaining the intention of the parties regard shall be had to the terms of the contract, the conduct of the parties and the circumstances of the case.

Section 18. Unless a different intention appears, the following are rules for ascertaining the intention of the parties as to the time at which the property in the goods is to pass to the buyer.
Rule 1.—Where there is an unconditional contract for the sale of specific goods in a deliverable state the property in the goods passes to the buyer when the contract is made, and it is immaterial whether the time of payment or the time of delivery, or both, be postponed.
Rule 2.—Where there is a contract for the sale of specific goods and the seller is bound to do something to the goods for the purpose of putting them into a deliverable state, the property does not pass until the thing is done and the buyer has notice that it has been done.
Rule 3.—Where there is a contract for the sale of specific goods in a deliverable state but the seller is bound to weigh, measure, test, or do some other act or thing with reference to the goods for the purpose of ascertaining the price, the property does not pass until the act or thing is done and the buyer has notice that it has been done.
Rule 4.—When goods are delivered to the buyer on approval or on sale or return or other similar terms the property in the goods passes to the buyer:—
(a) when he signifies his approval or acceptance to the seller or does any other act adopting the transaction;

(b) if he does not signify his approval or acceptance to the seller but retains the goods without giving notice of rejection, then, if a time has been fixed for the return of the goods, on the expiration of that time, and, if no time has been fixed, on the expiration of a reasonable time.

Rule 5.—(1) Where there is a contract for the sale of unascertained or future goods by description, and goods of that description and in a deliverable state are unconditionally appropriated to the contract, either by the seller with the assent of the buyer or by the buyer with the assent of the seller, the property in the goods then passes to the buyer; and the assent may be express or implied, and may be given either before or after the appropriation is made.
(2) Where, in pursuance of the contract, the seller delivers the goods to the buyer or to a carrier or other bailee or custodier (whether named by the buyer or not) for the purpose of transmission to the buyer, and does not reserve the right of disposal, he is to be taken to have unconditionally appropriated the goods to the contract.
(3) Where there is a contract for the sale of a specified quantity of unascertained goods in a deliverable state forming part of a bulk which is identified either in the contract or by subsequent agreement between the parties and the bulk is reduced to (or to less than) that quantity, then, if the buyer under that contract is the only buyer to whom goods are then due out of the bulk—
(a) the remaining goods are to be taken as appropriated to that contract at the time when the bulk is so reduced; and
(b) the property in those goods then passes to that buyer.
(4) Paragraph (3) above applies also (with the necessary modifications) where a bulk is reduced to (or to less than) the aggregate of the quantities due to a single buyer under separate contracts relating to that bulk and he is the only buyer to whom goods are then due out of that bulk.

Section 19. (1) Where there is a contract for the sale of specific goods or where goods are subsequently appropriated to the contract, the seller may, by the terms of the contract or appropriation, reserve the right of disposal of the goods until certain conditions are fulfilled; and in such a case, notwithstanding the delivery of the goods to the buyer, or to a carrier or other bailee or custodier for the purpose of transmission to the buyer, the property in the goods does not pass to the buyer until the conditions imposed by the seller are fulfilled.
(2) Where goods are shipped, and by the bill of lading the goods are deliverable to the order of the seller or his agent, the seller is prima facie to be taken to reserve the right of disposal.
(3) Where the seller of goods draws on the buyer for the price, and transmits the bill of exchange and bill of lading to the buyer together to secure acceptance or payment of the bill of exchange, the buyer is bound to return the bill of lading if he does not honour the bill of exchange, and if he wrongfully retains the bill of lading the property in the goods does not pass to him.

Section 20. (1) Unless otherwise agreed, the goods remain at the seller's risk until the property in them is transferred to the buyer, but when the property in them is transferred to the buyer the goods are at the buyer's risk whether delivery has been made or not.
(2) But where delivery has been delayed through the fault of either buyer or seller the goods are at the risk of the party at fault as regards any loss which might not have occurred but for such fault.
(3) Nothing in this section affects the duties or liabilities of either seller or buyer as a bailee or custodier of the goods of the other party.
(4) In a case where the buyer deals as consumer or, in Scotland, where there is a consumer contract in which the buyer is a consumer, subsections (1) to (3) above must be ignored and the goods remain at the seller's risk until they are delivered to the consumer.

Section 20A. (1) This section applies to a contract for the sale of a specified quantity of unascertained goods if the following conditions are met—
(a) the goods or some of them form part of a bulk which is identified either in the contract or by subsequent agreement between the parties; and
(b) the buyer has paid the price for some or all of the goods which are the subject of the contract and which form part of the bulk.
(2) Where this section applies, then (unless the parties agree otherwise), as soon as the conditions specified in paragraphs (a) and (b) of subsection (1) above are met or at such later time as the parties may agree—
(a) property in an undivided share in the bulk is transferred to the buyer, and
(b) the buyer becomes an owner in common of the bulk.
(3) Subject to subsection (4) below, for the purposes of this section, the undivided share of a buyer in a bulk at any time shall be such share as the quantity of goods paid for and due to the buyer out of the bulk bears to the quantity of goods in the bulk at that time.

Part V. Private Law

(4) Where the aggregate of the undivided shares of buyers in a bulk determined under subsection (3) above would at any time exceed the whole of the bulk at that time, the undivided share in the bulk of each buyer shall be reduced proportionately so that the aggregate of the undivided shares is equal to the whole bulk.
(5) Where a buyer has paid the price for only some of the goods due to him out of a bulk, any delivery to the buyer out of the bulk shall, for the purposes of this section, be ascribed in the first place to the goods in respect of which payment has been made.
(6) For the purposes of this section payment of part of the price for any goods shall be treated as payment for a corresponding part of the goods.

Section 20B. (1) A person who has become an owner in common of a bulk by virtue of section 20A above shall be deemed to have consented to—
(a) any delivery of goods out of the bulk to any other owner in common of the bulk, being goods which are due to him under
his contract;
(b) any dealing with or removal, delivery or disposal of goods in the bulk by any other person who is an owner in common of the bulk in so far as the goods fall within that co-owner's undivided share in the bulk at the time of the dealing, removal, delivery or disposal.
(2) No cause of action shall accrue to anyone against a person by reason of that person having acted in accordance with paragraph (a) or (b) of subsection (1) above in reliance on any consent deemed to have been given under that subsection.
(3) Nothing in this section or section 20A above shall—
(a) impose an obligation on a buyer of goods out of a bulk to compensate any other buyer of goods out of that bulk for any shortfall in the goods received by that other buyer;
(b) affect any contractual arrangement between buyers of goods out of a bulk for adjustments between themselves; or
(c) affect the rights of any buyer under his contract.

Transfer of title

Section 21. (1) Subject to this Act, where goods are sold by a person who is not their owner, and who does not sell them under the authority or with the consent of the owner, the buyer acquires no better title to the goods than the seller had, unless the owner of the goods is by his conduct precluded from denying the seller's authority to sell.
(2) Nothing in this Act affects—
(a) the provisions of the Factors Acts or any enactment enabling the apparent owner of goods to dispose of them as if he were their true owner;
(b) the validity of any contract of sale under any special common law or statutory power of sale or under the order of a court of competent jurisdiction.

[Section 22 is omitted.]

Section 23. When the seller of goods has a voidable title to them, but his title has not been avoided at the time of the sale, the buyer acquires a good title to the goods, provided he buys them in good faith and without notice of the seller's defect of title.

Section 24. Where a person having sold goods continues or is in possession of the goods, or of the documents of title to the goods, the delivery or transfer by that person, or by a mercantile agent acting for him, of the goods or documents of title under any sale, pledge, or other disposition thereof, to any person receiving the same in good faith and without notice of the previous sale, has the same effect as if the person making the delivery or transfer were expressly authorised by the owner of the goods to make the same.

Section 25. (1) Where a person having bought or agreed to buy goods obtains, with the consent of the seller, possession of the goods or the documents of title to the goods, the delivery or transfer by that person, or by a mercantile agent acting for him, of the goods or documents of title, under any sale, pledge, or other disposition thereof, to any person receiving the same in good faith and without notice of any lien or other right of the original seller in respect of the goods, has the same effect as if the person making the delivery or transfer were a mercantile agent in possession of the goods or documents of title with the consent of the owner.
(2) For the purposes of subsection (1) above—

(a) the buyer under a conditional sale agreement is to be taken not to be a person who has bought or agreed to buy goods, and
(b) 'conditional sale agreement' means an agreement for the sale of goods which is a consumer credit agreement within the meaning of the Consumer Credit Act 1974 under which the purchase price or part of it is payable by instalments, and the property in the goods is to remain in the seller (notwithstanding that the buyer is to be in possession of the goods) until such conditions as to the payment of instalments or otherwise as may be specified in the agreement are fulfilled.
(3) Paragraph 9 of Schedule 1 below applies in relation to a contract under which a person buys or agrees to buy goods and which is made before the appointed day.
(4) In subsection (3) above and paragraph 9 of Schedule 1 below references to the appointed day are to the day appointed for the purposes of those provisions by an order of the Secretary of State made by statutory instrument.

Section 26. In sections 24 and 25 above 'mercantile agent' means a mercantile agent having in the customary course of his business as such agent authority either—
(a) to sell goods, or
(b) to consign goods for the purpose of sale, or
(c) to buy goods, or
(d) to raise money on the security of goods.

Part IV: Performance of the Contract

Section 27. It is the duty of the seller to deliver the goods, and of the buyer to accept and pay for them, in accordance with the terms of the contract of sale.

Section 28. Unless otherwise agreed, delivery of the goods and payment of the price are concurrent conditions, that is to say, the seller must be ready and willing to give possession of the goods to the buyer in exchange for the price and the buyer must be ready and willing to pay the price in exchange for possession of the goods.

Section 29. (1) Whether it is for the buyer to take possession of the goods or for the seller to send them to the buyer is a question depending in each case on the contract, express or implied, between the parties.
(2) Apart from any such contract, express or implied, the place of delivery is the seller's place of business if he has one, and if not, his residence; except that, if the contract is for the sale of specific goods, which to the knowledge of the parties when the contract is made are in some other place, then that place is the place of delivery.
(3) Where under the contract of sale the seller is bound to send the goods to the buyer, but no time for sending them is fixed, the seller is bound to send them within a reasonable time.
(4) Where the goods at the time of sale are in the possession of a third person, there is no delivery by seller to buyer unless and until the third person acknowledges to the buyer that he holds the goods on his behalf; but nothing in this section affects the operation of the issue or transfer of any document of title to goods.
(5) Demand or tender of delivery may be treated as ineffectual unless made at a reasonable hour; and what is a reasonable hour is a question of fact.
(6) Unless otherwise agreed, the expenses of and incidental to putting the goods into a deliverable state must be borne by the seller.

Section 30. (1) Where the seller delivers to the buyer a quantity of goods less than he contracted to sell, the buyer may reject them, but if the buyer accepts the goods so delivered he must pay for them at the contract rate.
(2) Where the seller delivers to the buyer a quantity of goods larger than he contracted to sell, the buyer may accept the goods included in the contract and reject the rest, or he may reject the whole.
(2A) A buyer who does not deal as consumer may not—
(a) where the seller delivers a quantity of goods less than he contracted to sell, reject the goods under subsection (1) above, or
(b) where the seller delivers a quantity of goods larger than he contracted to sell, reject the whole under subsection (2) above, if the shortfall or, as the case may be, excess is so slight that it would be unreasonable for him to do so.
(2B) It is for the seller to show that a shortfall or excess fell within subsection (2A) above.
(2C) Subsections (2A) and (2B) above do not apply to Scotland.
(2D) Where the seller delivers a quantity of goods—
(a) less than he contracted to sell, the buyer shall not be entitled to reject the goods under subsection (1) above,
(b) larger than he contracted to sell, the buyer shall not be entitled to reject the whole under subsection (2) above, unless the shortfall or excess is material.

(2E) Subsection (2D) above applies to Scotland only.
(3) Where the seller delivers to the buyer a quantity of goods larger than he contracted to sell and the buyer accepts the whole of the goods so delivered he must pay for them at the contract rate.
(5) This section is subject to any usage of trade, special agreement, or course of dealing between the parties.

Section 31. (1) Unless otherwise agreed, the buyer of goods is not bound to accept delivery of them by instalments.
(2) Where there is a contract for the sale of goods to be delivered by stated instalments, which are to be separately paid for, and the seller makes defective deliveries in respect of one or more instalments, or the buyer neglects or refuses to take delivery of or pay for one or more instalments, it is a question in each case depending on the terms of the contract and the circumstances of the case whether the breach of contract is a repudiation of the whole contract or whether it is a severable breach giving rise to a claim for compensation but not to a right to treat the whole contract as repudiated.

Section 32. (1) Where, in pursuance of a contract of sale, the seller is authorised or required to send the goods to the buyer, delivery of the goods to a carrier (whether named by the buyer or not) for the purpose of transmission to the buyer is prima facie deemed to be delivery of the goods to the buyer.
(2) Unless otherwise authorised by the buyer, the seller must make such contact with the carrier on behalf of the buyer as may be reasonable having regard to the nature of the goods and the other circumstances of the case; and if the seller omits to do so, and the goods are lost or damaged in course of transit, the buyer may decline to treat the delivery to the carrier as a delivery to himself or may hold the seller responsible in damages.
(3) Unless otherwise agreed, where goods are sent by the seller to the buyer by a route involving sea transit, under circumstances in which it is usual to insure, the seller must give such notice to the buyer as may enable him to insure them during their sea transit, and if the seller fails to do so, the goods are at his risk during such sea transit.
(4) In a case where the buyer deals as consumer or, in Scotland, where there is a consumer contract in which the buyer is a consumer, subsections (1) to (3) above must be ignored, but if in pursuance of a contract of sale the seller is authorised or required to send the goods to the buyer, delivery of the goods to the carrier is not delivery of the goods to the buyer.

Section 33. Where the seller of goods agrees to deliver them at his own risk at a place other than that where they are when sold, the buyer must nevertheless (unless otherwise agreed) take any risk of deterioration in the goods necessarily incident to the course of transit.

Section 34. Unless otherwise agreed, when the seller tenders delivery of goods to the buyer, he is bound on request to afford the buyer a reasonable opportunity of examining the goods for the purpose of ascertaining whether they are in conformity with the contract and, in the case of a contract for sale by sample, of comparing the bulk with the sample.

Section 35. (1) The buyer is deemed to have accepted the goods subject to subsection (2) below—
(a) when he intimates to the seller that he has accepted them, or
(b) when the goods have been delivered to him and he does any act in relation to them which is inconsistent with the ownership of the seller.
(2) Where goods are delivered to the buyer, and he has not previously examined them, he is not deemed to have accepted them under subsection (1) above until he has had a reasonable opportunity of examining them for the purpose—
(a) of ascertaining whether they are in conformity with the contract, and
(b) in the case of a contract for sale by sample, of comparing the bulk with the sample.
(3) Where the buyer deals as consumer or (in Scotland) the contract of sale is a consumer contract, the buyer cannot lose his right to rely on subsection (2) above by agreement, waiver or otherwise.
(4) The buyer is also deemed to have accepted the goods when after the lapse of a reasonable time he retains the goods without intimating to the seller that he has rejected them.
(5) The questions that are material in determining for the purposes of subsection (4) above whether a reasonable time has elapsed include whether the buyer has had a reasonable opportunity of examining the goods for the purpose mentioned in subsection (2) above.
(6) The buyer is not by virtue of this section deemed to have accepted the goods merely because—
(a) he asks for, or agrees to, their repair by or under an arrangement with the seller, or
(b) the goods are delivered to another under a sub-sale or other disposition.

(7) Where the contract is for the sale of goods making one or more commercial units, a buyer accepting any goods included in a unit is deemed to have accepted all the goods making the unit; and in this subsection 'commercial unit' means a unit division of which would materially impair the value of the goods or the character of the unit.
(8) Paragraph 10 of Schedule 1 below applies in relation to a contract made before 22 April 1967 or (in the application of this Act to Northern Ireland) 28 July 1967.

Section 35A. (1)If the buyer—
(a) has the right to reject the goods by reason of a breach on the part of the seller that affects some or all of them, but
(b) accepts some of the goods, including, where there are any goods unaffected by the breach, all such goods, he does not by accepting them lose his right to reject the rest.
(2) In the case of a buyer having the right to reject an instalment of goods, subsection (1) above applies as if references to the goods were references to the goods comprised in the instalment.
(3) For the purposes of subsection (1) above, goods are affected by a breach if by reason of the breach they are not in conformity with the contract.
(4) This section applies unless a contrary intention appears in, or is to be implied from, the contract.

Section 36. Unless otherwise agreed, where goods are delivered to the buyer, and he refuses to accept them, having the right to do so, he is not bound to return them to the seller, but it is sufficient if he intimates to the seller that he refuses to accept them.

Section 37. (1) When the seller is ready and willing to deliver the goods, and requests the buyer to take delivery, and the buyer does not within a reasonable time after such request take delivery of the goods, he is liable to the seller for any loss occasioned by his neglect or refusal to take delivery, and also for a reasonable charge for the care and custody of the goods.
(2) Nothing in this section affects the rights of the seller where the neglect or refusal of the buyer to take delivery amounts to a repudiation of the contract.

Part V: Rights of Unpaid Seller Against the Goods

Preliminary

Section 38. (1) The seller of goods is an unpaid seller within the meaning of this Act—
(a) when the whole of the price has not been paid or tendered;
(b) when a bill of exchange or other negotiable instrument has been received as conditional payment, and the condition on which it was received has not been fulfilled by reason of the dishonour of the instrument or otherwise.
(2) In this Part of this Act 'seller' includes any person who is in the position of a seller, as, for instance, an agent of the seller to whom the bill of lading has been indorsed, or a consignor or agent who has himself paid (or is directly responsible for) the price.

Section 39. (1) Subject to this and any other Act, notwithstanding that the property in the goods may have passed to the buyer, the unpaid seller of goods, as such, has by implication of law—
(a) a lien on the goods or right to retain them for the price while he is in possession of them;
(b) in the case of the insolvency of the buyer, a right of stopping the goods in transit after he has parted with the possession of them;
(c) a right of re-sale as limited by this Act.
(2) Where the property in goods has not passed to the buyer, the unpaid seller has (in addition to his other remedies) a right of withholding delivery similar to and coextensive with his rights of lien or retention and stoppage in transit where the property has passed to the buyer.

Unpaid seller's lien

Section 41. (1) Subject to this Act, the unpaid seller of goods who is in possession of them is entitled to retain possession of them until payment or tender of the price in the following cases:-
(a) where the goods have been sold without any stipulation as to credit;
(b) where the goods have been sold on credit but the term of credit has expired;
(c) where the buyer becomes insolvent.

(2) The seller may exercise his lien or right of retention notwithstanding that he is in possession of the goods as agent or bailee or custodier for the buyer.

Section 42. Where an unpaid seller has made part delivery of the goods, he may exercise his lien or right of retention on the remainder, unless such part delivery has been made under such circumstances as to show an agreement to waive the lien or right of retention.

Section 43. (1) The unpaid seller of goods loses his lien or right of retention in respect of them-
(a) when he delivers the goods to a carrier or other bailee or custodier for the purpose of transmission to the buyer without reserving the right of disposal of the goods;
(b) when the buyer or his agent lawfully obtains possession of the goods;
(c) by waiver of the lien or right of retention.
(2) An unpaid seller of goods who has a lien or right of retention in respect of them does not lose his lien or right of retention by reason only that he has obtained judgment or decree for the price of the goods.

Stoppage in transit

Section 44. Subject to this Act, when the buyer of goods becomes insolvent the unpaid seller who has parted with the possession of the goods has the right of stopping them in transit, that is to say, he may resume possession of the goods as long as they are in course of transit, and may retain them until payment or tender of the price.

Section 45. (1) Goods are deemed to be in course of transit from the time when they are delivered to a carrier or other bailee or custodier for the purpose of transmission to the buyer, until the buyer or his agent in that behalf takes delivery of them from the carrier or other bailee or custodier.
(2) If the buyer or his agent in that behalf obtains delivery of the goods before their arrival at the appointed destination, the transit is at an end.
(3) If, after the arrival of the goods at the appointed destination, the carrier or other bailee or custodier acknowledges to the buyer or his agent that he holds the goods on his behalf and continues in possession of them as bailee or custodier for the buyer or his agent, the transit is at an end, and it is immaterial that a further destination for the goods may have been indicated by the buyer.
(4) If the goods are rejected by the buyer, and the carrier or other bailee or custodier continues in possession of them, the transit is not deemed to be at an end, even if the seller has refused to receive them back.
(5) When goods are delivered to a ship chartered by the buyer it is a question depending on the circumstances of the particular case whether they are in the possession of the master as a carrier or as agent to the buyer.
(6) Where the carrier or other bailee or custodier wrongfully refuses to deliver the goods to the buyer or his agent in that behalf, the transit is deemed to be at an end.
(7) Where part delivery of the goods has been made to the buyer or his agent in that behalf, the remainder of the goods may be stopped in transit, unless such part delivery has been made under such circumstances as to show an agreement to give up possession of the whole of the goods.

Section 46. (1) The unpaid seller may exercise his right of stoppage in transit either by taking actual possession of the goods or by giving notice of his claim to the carrier or other bailee or custodier in whose possession the goods are.
(2) The notice may be given either to the person in actual possession of the goods or to his principal.
(3) If given to the principal, the notice is ineffective unless given at such time and under such circumstances that the principal, by the exercise of reasonable diligence, may communicate it to his servant or agent in time to prevent a delivery to the buyer.
(4) When notice of stoppage in transit is given by the seller to the carrier or other bailee or custodier in possession of the goods, he must re-deliver the goods to, or according to the directions of, the seller; and the expenses of the re-delivery must be borne by the seller.

Re-sale etc by buyer

Section 47. (1) Subject to this Act, the unpaid seller's right of lien or retention or stoppage in transit is not affected by any sale or other disposition of the goods which the buyer may have made, unless the seller has assented to it.
(2) Where a document of title to goods has been lawfully transferred to any person as buyer or owner of the goods, and that person transfers the document to a person who takes it in good faith and for valuable consideration, then-

(a) if the last-mentioned transfer was by way of sale the unpaid seller's right of lien or retention or stoppage in transit is defeated; and
(b) if the last-mentioned transfer was made by way of pledge or other disposition for value, the unpaid seller's right of lien or retention or stoppage in transit can only be exercised subject to the rights of the transferee.

Rescission and re-sale by seller

Section 48. (1) Subject to this section, a contract of sale is not rescinded by the mere exercise by an unpaid seller of his right of lien or retention or stoppage in transit.
(2) Where an unpaid seller who has exercised his right of lien or retention or stoppage in transit re-sells the goods, the buyer acquires a good title to them as against the original buyer.
(3) Where the goods are of a perishable nature, or where the unpaid seller gives notice to the buyer of his intention to re-sell, and the buyer does not within a reasonable time pay or tender the price, the unpaid seller may re-sell the goods and recover from the original buyer damages for any loss occasioned by his breach of contract.
(4) Where the seller expressly reserves the right of re-sale in case the buyer should make default, and on the buyer making default re-sells the goods, the original contract of sale is rescinded but without prejudice to any claim the seller may have for damages.

Part 5A: Additional Rights of Buyer in Consumer Cases

Introductory

Section 48A. (1) This section applies if—
(a) the buyer deals as consumer or, in Scotland, there is a consumer contract in which the buyer is a consumer, and
(b) the goods do not conform to the contract of sale at the time of delivery.
(2) If this section applies, the buyer has the right—
(a) under and in accordance with section 48B below, to require the seller to repair or replace the goods, or
(b) under and in accordance with section 48C below—
(i) to require the seller to reduce the purchase price of the goods to the buyer by an appropriate amount, or
(ii) to rescind the contract with regard to the goods in question.
(3) For the purposes of subsection (1)(b) above goods which do not conform to the contract of sale at any time within the period of six months starting with the date on which the goods were delivered to the buyer must be taken not to have so conformed at that date.
(4) Subsection (3) above does not apply if—
(a) it is established that the goods did so conform at that date;
(b) its application is incompatible with the nature of the goods or the nature of the lack of conformity.

Section 48B. (1) If section 48A above applies, the buyer may require the seller—
(a) to repair the goods, or
(b) to replace the goods.
(2) If the buyer requires the seller to repair or replace the goods, the seller must—
(a) repair or, as the case may be, replace the goods within a reasonable time but without causing significant inconvenience to the buyer;
(b) bear any necessary costs incurred in doing so (including in particular the cost of any labour, materials or postage).
(3) The buyer must not require the seller to repair or, as the case may be, replace the goods if that remedy is—
(a) impossible, or
(b) disproportionate in comparison to the other of those remedies, or
(c) disproportionate in comparison to an appropriate reduction in the purchase price under paragraph (a), or rescission under paragraph (b), of section 48C(1) below.
(4) One remedy is disproportionate in comparison to the other if the one imposes costs on the seller which, in comparison to those imposed on him by the other, are unreasonable, taking into account—
(a) the value which the goods would have if they conformed to the contract of sale,
(b) the significance of the lack of conformity, and
(c) whether the other remedy could be effected without significant inconvenience to the buyer.
(5) Any question as to what is a reasonable time or significant inconvenience is to be determined by reference to—
(a) the nature of the goods, and
(b) the purpose for which the goods were acquired.

Part V. Private Law

Section 48C. (1) If section 48A above applies, the buyer may—
(a) require the seller to reduce the purchase price of the goods in question to the buyer by an appropriate amount, or
(b) rescind the contract with regard to those goods,
if the condition in subsection (2) below is satisfied.
(2) The condition is that—
(a) by virtue of section 48B(3) above the buyer may require neither repair nor replacement of the goods; or
(b) the buyer has required the seller to repair or replace the goods, but the seller is in breach of the requirement of section 48B(2)(a) above to do so within a reasonable time and without significant inconvenience to the buyer.
(3) For the purposes of this Part, if the buyer rescinds the contract, any reimbursement to the buyer may be reduced to take account of the use he has had of the goods since they were delivered to him.

Section 48D. (1) If the buyer requires the seller to repair or replace the goods the buyer must not act under subsection (2) until he has given the seller a reasonable time in which to repair or replace (as the case may be) the goods.
(2) The buyer acts under this subsection if—
(a) in England and Wales or Northern Ireland he rejects the goods and terminates the contract for breach of condition;
(b) in Scotland he rejects any goods delivered under the contract and treats it as repudiated;
(c) he requires the goods to be replaced or repaired (as the case may be).

Section 48E. (1) In any proceedings in which a remedy is sought by virtue of this Part the court, in addition to any other power it has, may act under this section.
(2) On the application of the buyer the court may make an order requiring specific performance or, in Scotland, specific implement by the seller of any obligation imposed on him by virtue of section 48B above.
(3) Subsection (4) applies if—
(a) the buyer requires the seller to give effect to a remedy under section 48B or 48C above or has claims to rescind under section 48C, but
(b) the court decides that another remedy under section 48B or 48C is appropriate.
(4) The court may proceed—
(a) as if the buyer had required the seller to give effect to the other remedy, or if the other remedy is rescission under section 48C
(b) as if the buyer had claimed to rescind the contract under that section.
(5) If the buyer has claimed to rescind the contract the court may order that any reimbursement to the buyer is reduced to take account of the use he has had of the goods since they were delivered to him.
(6) The court may make an order under this section unconditionally or on such terms and conditions as to damages, payment of the price and otherwise as it thinks just.

Section 48F. For the purposes of this Part, goods do not conform to a contract of sale if there is, in relation to the goods, a breach of an express term of the contract or a term implied by section 13, 14 or 15 above.

Part VI: Actions for Breach of Contract

Seller's remedies

Section 49. (1) Where, under a contract of sale, the property in the goods has passed to the buyer and he wrongfully neglects or refuses to pay for the goods according to the terms of the contract, the seller may maintain an action against him for the price of the goods.
(2) Where, under a contract of sale, the price is payable on a day certain irrespective of delivery and the buyer wrongfully neglects or refuses to pay such price, the seller may maintain an action for the price, although the property in goods has not passed and the goods have not been appropriated to the contract.
(3) Nothing in this section prejudices the right of the seller in Scotland to recover interest on the price from the date of tender of the goods, or from the date on which the price was payable, as the case may be.

Section 50. (1) Where the buyer wrongfully neglects or refuses to accept and pay for the goods, the seller may maintain an action against him for damages for non-acceptance.
(2) The measure of damages is the estimated loss directly and naturally resulting in the ordinary course of events, from the buyer's breach of contract.

(3) Where there is an available market for the goods in question the measure of damages is prima facie to be ascertained by the difference between the contract price and the market or current price at the time or times when the goods ought to have been accepted or (if no time was fixed for acceptance) at the time of the refusal to accept.

Buyer's remedies

Section 51. (1) Where the seller wrongfully neglects or refuses to deliver the goods to the buyer, the buyer may maintain an action against the seller for damages for non-delivery.
(2) The measure of damages is the estimated loss directly and naturally resulting, in the ordinary course of events, from the seller's breach of contract.
(3) Where there is an available market for the goods in question the measure of damages is prima facie to be ascertained by the difference between the contract price and the market or current price of the goods at the time or times when they ought to have been delivered or (if no time was fixed) at the time of the refusal to deliver.

Section 52. (1) If any action for breach of contract to deliver specific or ascertained goods the court may, if it thinks fit, on the plaintiff's application, by its judgment or decree direct that the contract shall be performed specifically, without giving the defendant the option of retaining the goods on payment of damages.
(2) The plaintiff's application may be made at any time before judgment or decree.
(3) The judgment or decree may be unconditional, or on such terms and conditions as to damages, payment of the price and otherwise as seem just to the court.
(4) The provisions of this section shall be deemed to be supplementary to, and not in derogation of, the right of specific implement in Scotland.

Section 53. (1) Where there is a breach of warranty by the seller, or where the buyer elects (or is compelled) to treat any breach of a condition on the part of the seller as a breach of warranty, the buyer is not by reason only of such breach of warranty entitled to reject the goods; but he may—
(a) set up against the seller the breach of warranty in diminution of extinction of the price, or
(b) maintain an action against the seller for damages for the breach of warranty.
(2) The measure of damages for breach of warranty is the estimated loss directly and naturally resulting, in the ordinary course of events, from the breach of warranty.
(3) In the case of breach of warranty of quality such loss is prima facie the difference between the value of the goods at the time of delivery to the buyer and the value they would have had if they had fulfilled the warranty.
(4) The fact that the buyer has set up the breach of warranty in diminution or extinction of the price does not prevent him from maintaining an action for the same breach of warranty if he has suffered further damage.
(5) This section does not apply to Scotland.

Interest, etc.

Section 54. Nothing in this Act affects the right of the buyer or the seller to recover interest or special damages in any case where by law interest or special damages may be recoverable, or to recover money paid where the consideration for the payment of it has failed.

Part VII Supplementary

Section 55. (1) Where a right duty or liability would arise under a contract of sale of goods by implication of law, it may (subject to the Unfair Contract Terms Act 1977) be negatived or varied by express agreement, or by the course of dealing between the parties, or by such usage as binds both parties to the contract.
(2) An express term does not negative a term implied by this Act unless inconsistent with it.
[Subsection 3 omitted.]

Section 57. (1) Where goods are put up for sale by auction in lots, each lot is prima facie deemed to be the subject of a separate contract of sale.
(2) A sale by auction is complete when the auctioneer announces its completion by the fall of the hammer, or in other customary manner; and until the announcement is made any bidder may retract his bid.
(3) A sale by auction may be notified to be subject to a reserve or upset price, and a right to bid may also be reserved expressly by or on behalf of the seller.

Part V. Private Law

(4) Where a sale by auction is not notified to be subject to a right to bid by or on behalf of the seller, it is not lawful for the seller to bid himself or to employ any person to bid at the sale, or for the auctioneer knowingly to take any bid from the seller or any such person.
(5) A sale contravening subsection (4) above may be treated as fraudulent by the buyer.
(6) Where, in respect of a sale by auction, a right to bid is expressly reserved (but not otherwise) the seller or any one person on his behalf may bid at the auction.

Section 59. Where a reference is made in this Act to a reasonable time the question what is a reasonable time is a question of fact.

Section 60. Where a right, duty or liability is declared by this Act, it may (unless otherwise provided by this Act) be enforced by action.

Section 61. (1) In this Act, unless the context or subject matter otherwise requires,—
'action' includes counterclaim and set-off, and in Scotland condescendence and claim and compensation;
'bulk' means a mass or collection of goods of the same kind which—
(a) is contained in a defined space or area; and
(b) is such that any goods in the bulk are interchangeable with any other goods therein of the same number or quantity;
'business' includes a profession and the activities of any government department (including a Northern Ireland department) or local or public authority;
'buyer' means a person who buys or agrees to buy goods;
'consumer contract' has the same meaning as in section 25(1) of the Unfair Contract Terms Act 1977; and for the purposes of this Act the onus of proving that a contract is not to be regarded as a consumer contract shall lie on the seller
'contract of sale' includes an agreement to sell as well as a sale,
'credit-broker' means a person acting in the course of a business of credit brokerage carried on by him, that is a business of effecting introductions of individuals desiring to obtain credit—
(a) to persons carrying on any business so far as it relates to the provision of credit, or
(b) to other persons engaged in credit brokerage;
'defendant' includes in Scotland defender, respondent, and claimant in a multiplepoinding;
'delivery' means voluntary transfer of possession from one person to another; except that in relation to sections 20A and 20B above it includes such appropriation of goods to the contract as results in property in the goods being transferred to the buyer;
'document of title to goods' has the same meaning as it has in the Factors Acts;
'Factors Acts' means the Factors Act 1889, the Factors (Scotland) Act 1890, and any enactment amending or substituted for the same;
'fault' means wrongful act or default;
'future goods' means goods to be manufactured or acquired by the seller after the making of the contract of sale;
'goods' includes all personal chattels other than things in action and money, and in Scotland all corporeal moveables except money; and in particular 'goods' includes emblements, industrial growing crops, and things attached to or forming part of the land which are agreed to be severed before sale or under the contract of sale; and includes an undivided share in goods;
'plaintiff' includes pursuer, complainer, claimant in a multiplepoinding and defendant or defender counter-claiming;
'producer' means the manufacturer of goods, the importer of goods into the European Economic Area or any person purporting to be a producer by placing his name, trade mark or other distinctive sign on the goods;
'property' means the general property in goods, and not merely a special property;
'repair' means, in cases where there is a lack of conformity in goods for the purposes of section 48F of this Act, to bring the goods into conformity with the contract;
'sale' includes a bargain and sale as well as a sale and delivery;
'seller' means a person who sells or agrees to sell goods;
'specific goods' means goods identified and agreed on at the time a contract of sale is made; and includes an undivided share, specified as a fraction or percentage, of goods identified and agreed on as aforesaid;
'warranty' (as regards England and Wales and Northern Ireland) means an agreement with reference to goods which are the subject of a contract of sale, but collateral to the main purpose of such contract, the breach of which gives rise to a claim for damages, but not to a right to reject the goods and treat the contract as repudiated.

(3) A thing is deemed to be done in good faith within the meaning of this Act when it is in fact done honestly, whether it is done negligently or not.
(4) A person is deemed to be insolvent within the meaning of this Act if he has either ceased to pay his debts in the ordinary course of business or he cannot pay his debts as they become due.
(5) Goods are in a deliverable state within the meaning of this Act when they are in such a state that the buyer would under the contract be bound to take delivery of them.
(5A) References in this Act to dealing as consumer are to be construed in accordance with Part I of the Unfair Contract Terms Act 1977; and, for the purposes of this Act, it is for a seller claiming that the buyer does not deal as consumer to show that he does not.
[Subsection 6 is omitted.]

Section 62. (1) The rules in bankruptcy relating to contracts of sale apply to those contracts, notwithstanding anything in this Act.
(2) The rules of the common law, including the law merchant, except in so far as they are inconsistent with the provisions of this Act, and in particular the rules relating to the law of principal and agent and the effect of fraud, misrepresentation, duress or coercion, mistake, or other invalidating cause, apply to contracts for the sale of goods.
(3) Nothing in this Act or the Sale of Goods Act 1893 affects the enactments relating to bills of sale, or any enactment relating to the sale of goods which is not expressly repealed or amended by this Act or that.
(4) The provisions of this Act about contracts of sale do not apply to a transaction in the form of a contract of sale which is intended to operate by way of mortgage, pledge, charge, or other security.
(5) Nothing in this Act prejudices or affects the landlord's right of hypothec or sequestration for rent in Scotland.

Miscellaneous Private Law Statutes

Law of Property Act 1925 [An Act to consolidate the enactments relating to conveyancing and the law of property in England and Wales] (c.20). Selected provisions: Sections 1, 52, 101, 136 and 198.

Section 1. (1) The only estates in land which are capable of subsisting or of being conveyed or created at law are—
a) An estate in fee simple absolute in possession;
b) A term of years absolute.
(2) The only interests or charges in or over land which are capable of subsisting or of being conveyed or created at law are—
(a) An easement, right, or privilege in or over land for an interest equivalent to an estate in fee simple absolute in possession or a term of years absolute;
(b) A rentcharge in possession issuing out of or charged on land being either perpetual or for a term of years absolute;
(c) A charge by way of legal mortgage;
(d) . . . and any other similar charge on land which is not created by an instrument;
(e) Rights of entry exercisable over or in respect of a legal term of years absolute, or annexed, for any purpose, to a legal rentcharge.
(3) All other estates, interests, and charges in or over land take effect as equitable interests

Section 52. (1) All conveyances of land or of any interest therein are void for the purpose of conveying or creating a legal estate unless made by deed.
[Subsection 2 is omitted.]

Section 101. (1) A mortgagee, where the mortgage is made by deed, shall, by virtue of this Act, have the following powers, to the like extent as if they had been in terms conferred by the mortgage deed, but not further (namely):
(i) A power, when the mortgage money has become due, to sell, or to concur with any other person in selling, the mortgaged property, or any part thereof, either subject to prior charges or not, and either together or in lots, by public auction or by private contract, subject to such conditions respecting title, or evidence of title, or other matter, as the mortgagee thinks fit, with power to vary any contract for sale, and to buy in at an auction, or to rescind any contract for sale, and to re-sell, without being answerable for any loss occasioned thereby; and
(ii) A power, at any time after the date of the mortgage deed, to insure and keep insured against loss or damage by fire any building, or any effects or property of an insurable nature, whether affixed to the freehold or not, being or forming part of the property which or an estate or interest wherein is mortgaged, and the premiums paid for any such insurance shall be a charge on the mortgaged property or estate or interest, in addition to the mortgage money, and with the same priority, and with interest at the same rate, as the mortgage money; and
(iii) A power, when the mortgage money has become due, to appoint a receiver of the income of the mortgaged property, or any part thereof; or, if the mortgaged property consists of an interest in income, or of a rentcharge or an annual or other periodical sum, a receiver of that property or any part thereof; and
(iv) A power, while the mortgagee is in possession, to cut and sell timber and other trees ripe for cutting, and not planted or left standing for shelter or ornament, or to contract for any such cutting and sale, to be completed within any time not exceeding twelve months from the making of the contract.
[Subsections 2 – 6 are omitted.]

Section 136. (1) Any absolute assignment by writing under the hand of the assignor (not purporting to be by way of charge only) of any debt or other legal thing in action, of which express notice in writing has been given to the debtor, trustee or other person from whom the assignor would have been entitled to claim such debt or thing in action, is effectual in law (subject to equities having priority over the right of the assignee) to pass and transfer from the date of such notice-
(a) the legal right to such debt or thing in action;
(b) all legal and other remedies for the same; and
(c) the power to give a good discharge for the same without the concurrence of the assignor:
Provided that, if the debtor, trustee or other person liable in respect of such debt or thing in action has notice-
(a) that the assignment is disputed by the assignor or any person claiming under him; or

Part V. Private Law

(b) of any other opposing or conflicting claims to such debt or thing in action; he may, if he thinks fit, either call upon the persons making claim thereto to interplead concerning the same, or pay the debt or other thing in action into court under the provisions of the Trustee Act, 1925.
[Subsection 2 is omitted.]

Section 198. (1) The registration of any instrument or matter in any register kept under the Land Charges Act 1972 […] shall be deemed to constitute actual notice of such instrument or matter, and of the fact of such registration, to all persons and for all purposes connected with the land affected, as from the date of registration or other prescribed dates and so long as the registration continues in force.
[Subsection 2 is omitted.]

Misrepresentation Act 1967 [An Act to amend the law relating to innocent misrepresentations and to amend sections 11 and 35 of the Sale of Goods Act 1893] (c. 7). Selected provisions: Sections 1 – 3.

Section 1. Where a person has entered into a contract after a misrepresentation has been made to him, and –
(a) the misrepresentation has become a term of the contract; or
(b) the contract has been performed;
or both, then, if otherwise he would be entitled to rescind the contract without alleging fraud, he shall be so entitled, subject to the provisions of this Act, notwithstanding the matters mentioned in paragraphs (a) and (b) of this section.

Section 2. (1) Where a person has entered into a contract after a misrepresentation has been made to him by another party thereto and as a result thereof he has suffered loss, then, if the person making the misrepresentation would be liable to damages in respect thereof had the misrepresentation been made fraudulently, that person shall be so liable notwithstanding that the misrepresentation was not made fraudulently, unless he proves that he had reasonable ground to believe and did believe up to the time the contract was made that the facts represented were true.
(2) Where a person has entered into a contract after a misrepresentation has been made to him otherwise than fraudulently, and he would be entitled, by reason of the misrepresentation, to rescind the contract, then, if it is claimed, in any proceedings arising out of the contract, that the contract ought to be or has been rescinded the court or arbitrator may declare the contract subsisting and award damages in lieu of rescission, if of opinion that it would be equitable to do so, having regard to the nature of the misrepresentation and the loss that would be caused by it if the contract were upheld, as well as to the loss that rescission would cause to the other party.
(3) Damages may be awarded against a person under subsection (2) of this section whether or not he is liable to damages under subsection (1) thereof, but where he is so liable any award under the said subsection (2) shall be taken into account in assessing his liability under the said subsection (1).

Section 3. If a contract contains a term which would exclude or restrict—
(a) any liability to which a party to a contract may be subject by reason of any misrepresentation made by him before the contract was made; or
(b) any remedy available to another party to the contract by reason of such a misrepresentation,
that term shall be of no effect except in so far as it satisfies the requirement of reasonableness as stated in section 11(1) of the Unfair Contract Terms Act 1977; and it is for those claiming that the term satisfies that requirement to show that it does.

Torts (Interference with Goods) Act 1977 [An Act to amden the law concerning conversion and other torts affecting goods] (c. 32). Selected provisions: Sections 1 – 11 and 14.

Section 1. In this Act "wrongful interference", or "wrongful interference with goods", means—
(a) conversion of goods (also called trover),
(b) trespass to goods,
(c) negligence so far at it results in damage to goods or to an interest in goods.
(d) subject to section 2, any other tort so far as it results in damage to goods or to an interest in goods.

Section 2. (1) Detinue is abolished.
(2) An action lies in conversion for loss or destruction of goods which a bailee has allowed to happen in breach of his duty to his bailor (that is to say it lies in a case which is not otherwise conversion, but would have been detinue before detinue was abolished).

Section 3. (1) In proceedings for wrongful interference against a person who is in possession or in control of the goods relief may be given in accordance with this section, so far as appropriate.
(2) The relief is—
(a) an order for delivery of the goods, and for payment of any consequential damages, or
(b) an order for delivery of the goods, but giving the defendant the alternative of paying damages by reference to the value of the goods, together in either alternative with payment of any consequential damages, or
(c) damages.
(3) Subject to rules of court—
(a) relief shall be given under only one of paragraphs (a), (b) and (c) of subsection (2),
(b) relief under paragraph (a) of subsection (2) is at the discretion of the court, and the claimant may choose between the others.
(4) If it is shown to the satisfaction of the court that an order under subsection (2)(a) has not been complied with, the court may—
(a) revoke the order, or the relevant part of it, and
(b) make an order for payment of damages by reference to the value of the goods.
(5) Where an order is made under subsection (2)(b) the defendant may satisfy the order by returning the goods at any time before execution of judgment, but without prejudice to liability to pay any consequential damages.
(6) An order for delivery of the goods under subsection (2)(a) or (b) may impose such conditions as may be determined by the court, or pursuant to rules of court, and in particular, where damages by reference to the value of the goods would not be the whole of the value of the goods, may require an allowance to be made by the claimant to reflect the difference. For example, a bailor's action against the bailee may be one in which the measure of damages is not the full value of the goods, and then the court may order delivery of the goods, but require the bailor to pay the bailee a sum reflecting the difference.
(7) Where under subsection (1) or subsection (2) of section 6 an allowance is to be made in respect of an improvement of the goods, and an order is made under subsection (2)(a) or (b), the court may assess the allowance to be made in respect of the improvement, and by the order require, as a condition for delivery of the goods, that allowance to be made by the claimant.
(8) This section is without prejudice—
(a) to the remedies afforded by section 133 of the Consumer Credit Act 1974, or
(b) to the remedies afforded by sections 35, 42 and 44 of the Hire-Purchase Act 1965, or to those sections of the Hire-Purchase Act (Northern Ireland) 1966 (so long as those sections respectively remain in force), or
(c) to any jurisdiction to afford ancillary or incidental relief.

Section 4. (1) In this section "proceedings" means proceedings for wrongful interference.
(2) On the application of any person in accordance with rules of court, the High Court shall, in such circumstances as may be specified in the rules, have power to make an order providing for the delivery up of any goods which are or may become the subject matter of subsequent proceedings in the court, or as to which any question may arise in proceedings.
(3) Delivery shall be, as the order may provide, to the claimant or to a person appointed by the court for the purpose, and shall be on such terms and conditions as may be specified in the order.
[Subsections 4 and 5 are omitted.]

Part V. Private Law

Section 5. (1) Where damages for wrongful interference are, or would fall to be, assessed on the footing that the claimant is being compensated—
(a) for the whole of his interest in the goods, or
(b) for the whole of his interest in the goods subject to a reduction for contributory negligence, payment of the assessed damages (under all heads), or as the case may be settlement of a claim for damages for the wrong (under all heads), extinguishes the claimant's title to that interest.
[Subsection 2 is omitted.]
(3) It is hereby declared that subsection (1) does not apply where damages are assessed on the footing that the claimant is being compensated for the whole of his interest in the goods, but the damages paid are limited to some lesser amount by virtue of any enactment or rule of law.
(4) Where under section 7(3) the claimant accounts over to another person (the "third party") so as to compensate (under all heads) the third party for the whole of his interest in the goods, the third party's title to that interest is extinguished.
(5) This section has effect subject to any agreement varying the respective rights of the parties to the agreement, and where the claim is made in court proceedings has effect subject to any order of the court.

Section 6. (1) If in proceedings for wrongful interference against a person (the "improver") who has improved the goods, it is shown that the improver acted in the mistaken but honest belief that he had a good title to them, an allowance shall be made for the extent to which, at the time as at which the goods fall to be valued in assessing damages, the value of the goods is attributable to the improvement.
(2) If, in proceedings for wrongful interference against a person ("the purchaser") who has purported to purchase the goods—
(a) from the improver, or
(b) where after such a purported sale the goods passed by a further purported sale on one or more occasions, on any such occasion,
it is shown that the purchaser acted in good faith, an allowance shall be made on the principle set out in subsection (1).
For example, where a person in good faith buys a stolen car from the improver and is sued in conversion by the true owner the damages may be reduced to reflect the improvement, but if the person who bought the stolen car from the improver sues the improver for failure of consideration, and the improver acted in good faith, subsection (3) below will ordinarily make a comparable reduction in the damages he recovers from the improver.
(3) If in a case within subsection (2) the person purporting to sell the goods acted in good faith, then in proceedings by the purchaser for recovery of the purchase price because of failure of consideration, or in any other proceedings founded on that failure of consideration, an allowance shall, where appropriate, be made on the principle set out in subsection (1).
(4) This section applies, with the necessary modifications, to a purported bailment or other disposition of goods as it applies to a purported sale of goods.

Section 7. (1) In this section "double liability" means the double liability of the wrongdoer which can arise—
(a) where one of two or more rights of action for wrongful interference is founded on a possessory title, or
(b) where the measure of damages in an action for wrongful interference founded on a proprietary title is or includes the entire value of the goods, although the interest is one of two or more interests in the goods.
(2) In proceedings to which any two or more claimants are parties, the relief shall be such as to avoid double liability of the wrongdoer as between those claimants.
(3) On satisfaction, in whole or in part, of any claim for an amount exceeding that recoverable if subsection (2) applied, the claimant is liable to account over to the other person having a right to claim to such extent as will avoid double liability.
(4) Where, as the result of enforcement of a double liability, any claimant is unjustly enriched to any extent, he shall be liable to reimburse the wrongdoer to that extent.
For example, if a converter of goods pays damages first to a finder of the goods, and then to the true owner, the finder is unjustly enriched unless he accounts over to the true owner under subsection (3); and then the true owner is unjustly enriched and becomes liable to reimburse the converter of the goods.

Section 8. (1) The defendant in an action for wrongful interference shall be entitled to show, in accordance with rules of court, that a third party has a better right than the plaintiff as respects all or any part of the interest claimed by the plaintiff, or in right of which he sues, and any rule of law (sometimes called jus tertii) to the contrary is abolished.
(2) Rules of court relating to proceedings for wrongful interference may—

(a) require the plaintiff to give particulars of his title,
(b) require the plaintiff to identify any person who, to his knowledge, has or claims any interest in the goods,
(c) authorise the defendant to apply for directions as to whether any person should be joined with a view to establishing whether he has a better right than the plaintiff, or has a claim as a result of which the defendant might be doubly liable,
(d) where a party fails to appear on an application within paragraph (c), or to comply with any direction given by the court on such an application, authorise the court to deprive him of any right of action against the defendant for the wrong either unconditionally, or subject to such terms or conditions as may be specified.
(3) Subsection (2) is without prejudice to any other power of making rules of court.

Section 9. (1) This section applies where goods are the subject of two or more claims for wrongful interference (whether or not the claims are founded on the same wrongful act, and whether or not any of the claims relates also to other goods).
(2) Where goods are the subject of two or more claims under section 6 this section shall apply as if any claim under section 6(3) were a claim for wrongful interference.
(3) If proceedings have been brought in a county court on one of those claims, county court rules may waive, or allow a court to waive, any limit (financial or territorial) on the jurisdiction of county courts or the County Courts so as to allow another of those claims to be brought in the same county court.
(4) If proceedings are brought on one of the claims in the High Court, and proceedings on any other are brought in a county court, whether prior to the High Court proceedings or not, the High Court may, on the application of the defendant, after notice has been given to the claimant in the county court proceedings—
(a) order that the county court proceedings be transferred to the High Court, and
(b) order security for costs or impose such other terms as the court thinks fit.

Section 10. (1) Co-ownership is no defence to an action founded on conversion or trespass to goods where the defendant without the authority of the other co-owner—
(a) destroys the goods, or disposes of the goods in a way giving a good title to the entire property in the goods, or otherwise does anything equivalent to the destruction of the other's interest in the goods, or
(b) purports to dispose of the goods in a way which would give a good title to the entire property in the goods if he was acting with the authority of all co-owners of the goods.
(2) Subsection (1) shall not affect the law concerning execution or enforcement of judgments, or concerning any form of distress.
(3) Subsection (1)(a) is by way of restatement of existing law so far as it relates to conversion.

Section 11. (1) Contributory negligence is no defence in proceedings founded on conversion, or on intentional trespass to goods.
(2) Receipt of goods by way of pledge is conversion if the delivery of the goods is conversion.
(3) Denial of title is not of itself conversion.

[Sections 12 and 13 are omitted.]

Section 14. Interpretation
(1) In this Act, unless the context otherwise requires –
[…]
"goods" includes all chattels personal other than things in action and money ...
[The remainder of the section is omitted.]

PART V. PRIVATE LAW

Unfair Contract Terms Act 1977 [An Act to impose further limits on the extent to which under the law of England and Wales and Northern Ireland civil liability for breach of contract, of for negligence or other breach of duty, can be avoided by means of contract terms and otherwise, and under the law of Scotland civil liability can be avoided by means of contract terms] (c. 50). Selected provisions: Sections 1 – 14 and Schedule 2.

Part I

Section 1. (1) For the purposes of this Part of this Act, "negligence" means the breach—
(a) of any obligation, arising from the express or implied terms of a contract, to take reasonable care or exercise reasonable skill in the performance of the contract;
(b) of any common law duty to take reasonable care or exercise reasonable skill (but not any stricter duty);
(c) of the common duty of care imposed by the Occupiers' Liability Act 1957 or the Occupiers' Liability Act (Northern Ireland) 1957.
(2) This Part of this Act is subject to Part III; and in relation to contracts, the operation of sections 2 to 4 and 7 is subject to the exceptions made by Schedule 1.
(3) In the case of both contract and tort, sections 2 to 7 apply (except where the contrary is stated in section 6(4)) only to business liability, that is liability for breach of obligations or duties arising—
(a) from things done or to be done by a person in the course of a business (whether his own business or another's); or
(b) from the occupation of premises used for business purposes of the occupier;
and references to liability are to be read accordingly but liability of an occupier of premises for breach of an obligation or duty towards a person obtaining access to the premises for recreational or educational purposes, being liability for loss or damage suffered by reason of the dangerous state of the premises, is not a business liability of the occupier unless granting that person such access for the purposes concerned falls within the business purposes of the occupier.
(4) In relation to any breach of duty or obligation, it is immaterial for any purpose of this Part of this Act whether the breach was inadvertent or intentional, or whether liability for it arises directly or vicariously.

Section 2. (1) A person cannot by reference to any contract term or to a notice given to persons generally or to particular persons exclude or restrict his liability for death or personal injury resulting from negligence.
(2) In the case of other loss or damage, a person cannot so exclude or restrict his liability for negligence except in so far as the term or notice satisfies the requirement of reasonableness.
(3) Where a contract term or notice purports to exclude or restrict liability for negligence a person's agreement to or awareness of it is not of itself to be taken as indicating his voluntary acceptance of any risk.

Section 3. (1) This section applies as between contracting parties where one of them deals as consumer or on the other's written standard terms of business.
(2) As against that party, the other cannot by reference to any contract term—
(a) when himself in breach of contract, exclude or restrict any liability of his in respect of the breach; or
(b) claim to be entitled—
(i) to render a contractual performance substantially different from that which was reasonably expected of him, or
(ii) in respect of the whole or any part of his contractual obligation, to render no performance at all,
except in so far as (in any of the cases mentioned above in this subsection) the contract term satisfies the requirement of reasonableness.

Section 4. (1) A person dealing as consumer cannot by reference to any contract term be made to indemnify another person (whether a party to the contract or not) in respect of liability that may be incurred by the other for negligence or breach of contract, except in so far as the contract term satisfies the requirement of reasonableness.
(2) This section applies whether the liability in question—
(a) is directly that of the person to be indemnified or is incurred by him vicariously;
(b) is to the person dealing as consumer or to someone else.

Section 5. (1) In the case of goods of a type ordinarily supplied for private use or consumption, where loss or damage—
(a) arises from the goods proving defective while in consumer use; and
(b) results from the negligence of a person concerned in the manufacture or distribution of the goods,

liability for the loss or damage cannot be excluded or restricted by reference to any contract term or notice contained in or operating by reference to a guarantee of the goods.
(2) For these purposes—
(a) goods are to be regarded as "in consumer use" when a person is using them, or has them in his possession for use, otherwise than exclusively for the purposes of a business; and
(b) anything in writing is a guarantee if it contains or purports to contain some promise or assurance (however worded or presented) that defects will be made good by complete or partial replacement, or by repair, monetary compensation or otherwise.
(3) This section does not apply as between the parties to a contract under or in pursuance of which possession or ownership of the goods passed.

Section 6. (1) Liability for breach of the obligations arising from—
(a) section 12 of the Sale of Goods Act 1979 (seller's implied undertakings as to title, etc);
(b) section 8 of the Supply of Goods (Implied Terms) Act 1973 (the corresponding thing in relation to hire-purchase),
cannot be excluded or restricted by reference to any contract term.
(2) As against a person dealing as consumer, liability for breach of the obligations arising from—
(a) section 13, 14 or 15 of the 1979 Act (seller's implied undertakings as to conformity of goods with description or sample, or as to their quality or fitness for a particular purpose);
(b) section 9, 10 or 11 of the 1973 Act (the corresponding things in relation to hire-purchase),
cannot be excluded or restricted by reference to any contract term.
(3) As against a person dealing otherwise than as consumer, the liability specified in subsection (2) above can be excluded or restricted by reference to a contract term, but only in so far as the term satisfies the requirement of reasonableness.
(4) The liabilities referred to in this section are not only the business liabilities defined by section 1(3), but include those arising under any contract of sale of goods or hire-purchase agreement.

Section 7. (1) Where the possession or ownership of goods passes under or in pursuance of a contract not governed by the law of sale of goods or hire-purchase, subsections (2) to (4) below apply as regards the effect (if any) to be given to contract terms excluding or restricting liability for breach of obligation arising by implication of law from the nature of the contract.
(2) As against a person dealing as consumer, liability in respect of the goods' correspondence with description or sample, or their quality or fitness for any particular purpose, cannot be excluded or restricted by reference to any such term.
(3) As against a person dealing otherwise than as consumer, that liability can be excluded or restricted by reference to such a term, but only in so far as the term satisfies the requirement of reasonableness.
(3A) Liability for breach of the obligations arising under section 2 of the Supply of Goods and Services Act 1982 (implied terms about title etc in certain contracts for the transfer of the property in goods) cannot be excluded or restricted by references to any such term.
(4) Liability in respect of—
(a) the right to transfer ownership of the goods, or give possession; or
(b) the assurance of quiet possession to a person taking goods in pursuance of the contract,
cannot (in a case to which subsection (3A) above does not apply) be excluded or restricted by reference to any such term except in so far as the term satisfies the requirement of reasonableness.
(5) This section does not apply in the case of goods passing on a redemption of trading stamps within the Trading Stamps Act 1964 or the Trading Stamps Act (Northern Ireland) 1965.

Section 8. (This section substitutes the Misrepresentation Act 1967, s 3 and the Misrepresentation Act (Northern Ireland) 1967, s 3).

Section 9. (1) Where for reliance upon it a contract term has to satisfy the requirement of reasonableness, it may be found to do so and be given effect accordingly notwithstanding that the contract has been terminated either by breach or by a party electing to treat it as repudiated.
(2) Where on a breach the contract is nevertheless affirmed by a party entitled to treat it as repudiated, this does not of itself exclude the requirement of reasonableness in relation to any contract term.

Part V. Private Law

Section 10. A person is not bound by any contract term prejudicing or taking away rights of his which arise under, or in connection with the performance of, another contract, so far as those rights extend to the enforcement of another's liability which this Part of this Act prevents that other from excluding or restricting.

Section 11. (1) In relation to a contract term, the requirement of reasonableness for the purposes of this Part of this Act, section 3 of the Misrepresentation Act 1967 and section 3 of the Misrepresentation Act (Northern Ireland) 1967 is that the term shall have been a fair and reasonable one to be included having regard to the circumstances which were, or ought reasonably to have been, known to or in the contemplation of the parties when the contract was made.
(2) In determining for the purposes of section 6 or 7 above whether a contract term satisfies the requirement of reasonableness, regard shall be had in particular to the matters specified in Schedule 2 to this Act; but this subsection does not prevent the court or arbitrator from holding, in accordance with any rule of law, that a term which purports to exclude or restrict any relevant liability is not a term of the contract.
(3) In relation to a notice (not being a notice having contractual effect), the requirement of reasonableness under this Act is that it should be fair and reasonable to allow reliance on it, having regard to all the circumstances obtaining when the liability arose or (but for the notice) would have arisen.
(4) Where by reference to a contract term or notice a person seeks to restrict liability to a specified sum of money, and the question arises (under this or any other Act) whether the term or notice satisfies the requirement of reasonableness, regard shall be had in particular (but without prejudice to subsection (2) above in the case of contract terms) to—
(a) the resources which he could expect to be available to him for the purpose of meeting the liability should it arise; and
(b) how far it was open to him to cover himself by insurance.
(5) It is for those claiming that a contract term or notice satisfies the requirement of reasonableness to show that it does.

Section 12. (1) A party to a contract "deals as consumer" in relation to another party if—
(a) he neither makes the contract in the course of a business nor holds himself out as doing so; and
(b) the other party does make the contract in the course of a business; and
(c) in the case of a contract governed by the law of sale of goods or hire purchase, or by section 7 of this Act, the goods passing under or in pursuance of the contract are of a type ordinarily supplied for private use or consumption.
(1A) But if the first party mentioned in subsection (1) is an individual paragraph (c) of that subsection must be ignored.
(2) But the buyer is not in any circumstances to be regarded as dealing as consumer—
(a) if he is an individual and the goods are second hand goods sold at public auction at which individuals have the opportunity of attending the sale in person;
(b) if he is not an individual and the goods are sold by auction or by competitive tender.
(3) Subject to this, it is for those claiming that a party does not deal as consumer to show that he does not.

Section 13. (1) To the extent that this Part of this Act prevents the exclusion or restriction of any liability it also prevents—
(a) making the liability or its enforcement subject to restrictive or onerous conditions;
(b) excluding or restricting any right or remedy in respect of the liability, or subjecting a person to any prejudice in consequence of his pursuing any such right or remedy;
(c) excluding or restricting rules of evidence or procedure;
and (to that extent) sections 2 and 5 to 7 also prevent excluding or restricting liability by reference to terms and notices which exclude or restrict the relevant obligation or duty.
(2) But an agreement in writing to submit present or future differences to arbitration is not to be treated under this Part of this Act as excluding or restricting any liability.

Section 14. In this Part of this Act—
"business" includes a profession and the activities of any government department or local or public authority;
"goods" has the same meaning as in the Sale of Goods Act 1979;
"hire-purchase agreement" has the same meaning as in the Consumer Credit Act 1974;
"negligence" has the meaning given by section 1(1);
"notice" includes an announcement, whether or not in writing, and any other communication or pretended communication; and

"personal injury" includes any disease and any impairment of physical or mental condition.

[The remainder of the Act and Schedule 1 are omitted.]

Schedule 2: "Guidelines" for Application of Reasonableness Test

The matters to which regard is to be had in particular for the purposes of sections 6(3), 7(3) and (4), 20 and 21 are any of the following which appear to be relevant—
(a) the strength of the bargaining positions of the parties relative to each other, taking into account (among other things) alternative means by which the customer's requirements could have been met;
(b) whether the customer received an inducement to agree to the term, or in accepting it had an opportunity of entering into a similar contract with other persons, but without having to accept a similar term;
(c) whether the customer knew or ought reasonably to have known of the existence and extent of the term (having regard, among other things, to any custom of the trade and any previous course of dealing between the parties);
(d) where the term excludes or restricts any relevant liability if some condition is not complied with, whether it was reasonable at the time of the contract to expect that compliance with that condition would be practicable;
(e) whether the goods were manufactured, processed or adapted to the special order of the customer.

Limitation Act 1980 [An Act to consolidate the Limitation Acts 1939 to 1980] (c. 58). Selected provisions: Sections 3, 5 and 17.

Section 3. (2) Where any such cause of action has accrued to any person and the period prescribed for bringing that action has expired and he [the claimant] has not during that period recovered possession of the chattel, the title of that person to the chattel shall be extinguished.

Section 5. An action founded on simple contract shall not be brought after the expiration of six years from the date on which the cause of action accrued.

Section 17. Subject to –
(a) section 18 of this Act; […]
at the expiration of the period prescribed by this Act for any person to bring an action to recover land (including a redemption action) he title of that person to the land shall be extinguished

Insolvency Act 1986 [An Act to consolidate the enactments relating to company insolvency and winding up (including the winding up of companies that are not insolvent, and of unregistered companies); enactments relating to the insolvency and bankruptcy of individuals; and other enactments bearing on those two subject matters, including the functions and qualification of insolvency practitioners, the public administration of insolvency, the penalisation and redress of malpractice and wrongdoing, and the avoidance of certain transactions at an undervalue] (c. 45). Selected provision: Section 283.

Section 283. (1) Subject as follows, a bankrupt's estate for the purposes of any of this Group of Parts comprises –
(a) all property belonging to or vested in the bankrupt at the commencement of the bankruptcy, and
(b) any property which by virtue of any of the following provisions of this Part is comprised in that estate or is treated as falling within the preceding paragraph.
(2) Subsection (1) does not apply to –
(a) such tools, books, vehicles and other items of equipment as are necessary to the bankrupt for use personally by him in his employment, business or vocation;
(b) such clothing, bedding, furniture, household equipment and provisions as are necessary for satisfying the basic domestic needs of the bankrupt and his family. …
(3) Subsection (1) does not apply to –
(a) property held by the bankrupt on trust for any other person, or
(b) the right of nomination to a vacant ecclesiastical benefice.

Part V. Private Law

Minors' Contracts Act 1987 [An Act to amend the law relating to minors' contracts] (c. 13). Selected provisions: Sections 2 and 3.

Section 2. Where—
(a) a guarantee is given in respect of an obligation of a party to a contract made after the commencement of this Act, and
(b) the obligation is unenforceable against him (or he repudiates the contract) because he was a minor when the contract was made,
the guarantee shall not for that reason alone be unenforceable against the guarantor.

Section 3. (1) Where—
(a) a person ("the plaintiff") has after the commencement of this Act entered into a contract with another ("the defendant"), and
(b) the contract is unenforceable against the defendant (or he repudiates it) because he was a minor when the contract was made,
the court may, if it is just and equitable to do so, require the defendant to transfer to the plaintiff any property acquired by the defendant under the contract, or any property representing it.
(2) Nothing in this section shall be taken to prejudice any other remedy available to the plaintiff.

Law of Property (Miscellaneous Provisions) Act 1989 [An Act to make new provision with respect to deeds and their execution and contracts for the sale or other disposition of interests in land; and to abolish the rule of law known as the rule in Bain v. Fothergill] (c. 34). Selected Provisions: Sections 1 and 2.

Section 1. (1) Any rule of law which—
(a) restricts the substances on which a deed may be written;
(b) requires a seal for the valid execution of an instrument as a deed by an individual; or
(c) requires authority by one person to another to deliver an instrument as a deed on his behalf to be given by deed, is abolished.
(2) An instrument shall not be a deed unless—
(a) it makes it clear on its face that it is intended to be a deed by the person making it or, as the case may be, by the parties to it (whether by describing itself as a deed or expressing itself to be executed or signed as a deed or otherwise); and
(b) it is validly executed as a deed by that person or, as the case may be, one or more of those parties.
(3) An instrument is validly executed as a deed by an individual if, and only if—
(a) it is signed—
(i) by him in the presence of a witness who attests the signature; or
(ii) at his direction and in his presence and the presence of two witnesses who each attest the signature; and
(b) it is delivered as a deed by him or a person authorised to do so on his behalf.
(4) In subsections (2) and (3) above "sign", in relation to an instrument, includes making one's mark on the instrument and "signature" is to be construed accordingly.
(5) Where a solicitor or licensed conveyancer, or an agent or employee of a solicitor or licensed conveyancer, in the course of or in connection with a transaction involving the disposition or creation of an interest in land, purports to deliver an instrument as a deed on behalf of a party to the instrument, it shall be conclusively presumed in favour of a purchaser that he is authorised so to deliver the instrument.
(6) In subsection (5) above—
"disposition" and "purchaser" have the same meanings as in the [1925 c. 20.] Law of Property Act 1925; and "interest in land" means any estate, interest or charge in or over land or in or over the proceeds of sale of land.
(7) Where an instrument under seal that constitutes a deed is required for the purposes of an Act passed before this section comes into force, this section shall have effect as to signing, sealing or delivery of an instrument by an individual in place of any provision of that Act as to signing, sealing or delivery.
[Subsections 8 – 11 are omitted.]

Section 2. (1) A contract for the sale or other disposition of an interest in land can only be made in writing and only by incorporating all the terms which the parties have expressly agreed in one document or, where contracts are exchanged, in each.

(2) The terms may be incorporated in a document either by being set out in it or by reference to some other document.
(3) The document incorporating the terms or, where contracts are exchanged, one of the documents incorporating them (but not necessarily the same one) must be signed by or on behalf of each party to the contract.
(4) Where a contract for the sale or other disposition of an interest in land satisfies the conditions of this section by reason only of the rectification of one or more documents in pursuance of an order of a court, the contract shall come into being, or be deemed to have come into being, at such time as may be specified in the order.
(5) This section does not apply in relation to—
(a) a contract to grant such a lease as is mentioned in section 54(2) of the [1925 c. 20.] Law of Property Act 1925 (short leases);
(b) a contract made in the course of a public auction; or
(c) a contract regulated under the [1986 c. 60.] Financial Services Act 1986;
and nothing in this section affects the creation or operation of resulting, implied or constructive trusts.
(6) In this section—
"disposition" has the same meaning as in the Law of Property Act 1925;
"interest in land" means any estate, interest or charge in or over land or in or over the proceeds of sale of land.
[Subsections 7 – 8 are omitted.]

Land Registration Act 2002 [An Act to make provision about land registration; and for connected purposes] (c. 9). Selected provisions: Schedule 1.

Schedule 1 Unregistered interests which override first registration
1 A leasehold estate in land granted for a term not exceeding seven years from the date of the grant, except for a lease the grant of which falls within section 4(1) (d), (e) or (f).
2 An interest belonging to a person in actual occupation, so far as relating to land of which he is in actual occupation, except for an interest under a settlement und the Settled Land Act 1925.
3 A legal easement or profit a prendre.
4 A customary right.
5 A public right.
6 A local land charge
[Paragraphs 7 – 9 are omitted.]
10 A franchise.
11 A manorial right.
12 A right to rent which was reserved to the Crown on the granting of any freehold estate (whether or not the right is still vested in the Crown).
13 A non-statutory right in respect of an embankment or sea or river wall.
14 A right to payment in lieu of tithe.

Mental Capacity Act 2005 [An Act to make new provision relating to persons who lack capacity; to establish a superior court of record called the Court of Protection in place of the office of the Supreme Court called by that name; to make provision in connection with the Convention on the International Protection of Adults signed at the Hague on 13th January 2000; and for connected purposes] (c. 9). Selected provisions: Sections 1 – 4 and 7.

Part I Persons Who Lack Capacity

Preliminary

Section 1. (1) The following principles apply for the purposes of this Act.
(2) A person must be assumed to have capacity unless it is established that he lacks capacity.
(3) A person is not to be treated as unable to make a decision unless all practicable steps to help him to do so have been taken without success.
(4) A person is not to be treated as unable to make a decision merely because he makes an unwise decision.
(5) An act done, or decision made, under this Act for or on behalf of a person who lacks capacity must be done, or made, in his best interests.
(6) Before the act is done, or the decision is made, regard must be had to whether the purpose for which it is needed can be as effectively achieved in a way that is less restrictive of the person's rights and freedom of action.

Section 2. (1) For the purposes of this Act, a person lacks capacity in relation to a matter if at the material time he is unable to make a decision for himself in relation to the matter because of an impairment of, or a disturbance in the functioning of, the mind or brain.
(2) It does not matter whether the impairment or disturbance is permanent or temporary.
(3) A lack of capacity cannot be established merely by reference to—
(a) a person's age or appearance, or
(b) a condition of his, or an aspect of his behaviour, which might lead others to make unjustified assumptions about his capacity.
(4) In proceedings under this Act or any other enactment, any question whether a person lacks capacity within the meaning of this Act must be decided on the balance of probabilities.
(5) No power which a person ("D") may exercise under this Act—
(a) in relation to a person who lacks capacity, or
(b) where D reasonably thinks that a person lacks capacity,
is exercisable in relation to a person under 16.
(6) Subsection (5) is subject to section 18(3).

Section 3. (1) For the purposes of section 2, a person is unable to make a decision for himself if he is unable—
(a) to understand the information relevant to the decision,
(b) to retain that information,
(c) to use or weigh that information as part of the process of making the decision, or
(d) to communicate his decision (whether by talking, using sign language or any other means).
(2) A person is not to be regarded as unable to understand the information relevant to a decision if he is able to understand an explanation of it given to him in a way that is appropriate to his circumstances (using simple language, visual aids or any other means).
(3) The fact that a person is able to retain the information relevant to a decision for a short period only does not prevent him from being regarded as able to make the decision.
(4) The information relevant to a decision includes information about the reasonably foreseeable consequences of—
(a) deciding one way or another, or
(b) failing to make the decision.

Section 4. (1) In determining for the purposes of this Act what is in a person's best interests, the person making the determination must not make it merely on the basis of—
(a) the person's age or appearance, or
(b) a condition of his, or an aspect of his behaviour, which might lead others to make unjustified assumptions about what might be in his best interests.

(2) The person making the determination must consider all the relevant circumstances and, in particular, take the following steps.
(3) He must consider—
(a) whether it is likely that the person will at some time have capacity in relation to the matter in question, and
(b) if it appears likely that he will, when that is likely to be.
(4) He must, so far as reasonably practicable, permit and encourage the person to participate, or to improve his ability to participate, as fully as possible in any act done for him and any decision affecting him.
(5) Where the determination relates to life-sustaining treatment he must not, in considering whether the treatment is in the best interests of the person concerned, be motivated by a desire to bring about his death.
(6) He must consider, so far as is reasonably ascertainable—
(a) the person's past and present wishes and feelings (and, in particular, any relevant written statement made by him when he had capacity),
(b) the beliefs and values that would be likely to influence his decision if he had capacity, and
(c) the other factors that he would be likely to consider if he were able to do so.
(7) He must take into account, if it is practicable and appropriate to consult them, the views of—
(a) anyone named by the person as someone to be consulted on the matter in question or on matters of that kind,
(b) anyone engaged in caring for the person or interested in his welfare,
(c) any donee of a lasting power of attorney granted by the person, and
(d) any deputy appointed for the person by the court,
as to what would be in the person's best interests and, in particular, as to the matters mentioned in subsection (6).
(8) The duties imposed by subsections (1) to (7) also apply in relation to the exercise of any powers which—
(a) are exercisable under a lasting power of attorney, or
(b) are exercisable by a person under this Act where he reasonably believes that another person lacks capacity.
(9) In the case of an act done, or a decision made, by a person other than the court, there is sufficient compliance with this section if (having complied with the requirements of subsections (1) to (7)) he reasonably believes that what he does or decides is in the best interests of the person concerned.
(10) "Life-sustaining treatment" means treatment which in the view of a person providing health care for the person concerned is necessary to sustain life.
(11) "Relevant circumstances" are those—
(a) of which the person making the determination is aware, and
(b) which it would be reasonable to regard as relevant.

Section 7. (1) If necessary goods or services are supplied to a person who lacks capacity to contract for the supply, he must pay a reasonable price for them.
(2) "Necessary" means suitable to a person's condition in life and to his actual requirements at the time when the goods or services are supplied.

PART VI

Civil Procedure

Code of Civil Procedure [Code de procédure civile] as consolidated on 3 May 2010. Selected provisions: Book I, Title I, Chapter I.[22]

Book I. Provisions common to all courts

Title I. Preliminary provisions

Chapter I. Guiding principles of the procedure

Section I. Proceedings

Article 1. Only the parties institute proceedings, except for cases where statute provides otherwise. They are free to bring them to an end before they are concluded by means of a judgment or by operation of law.

Article 2. The parties conduct proceedings under the duties that are incumbent upon them. It is for them to carry out procedural acts within the required forms and time limits.

Article 3. The judge oversees the proper conduct of proceedings; he has the power to set time limits and to order the necessary measures.

Section II. The object of the litigation

Article 4. The object of the litigation is determined by the respective claims of the parties.
These claims are set by the initiating action and by the arguments of the defence. However, the object of the litigation may be modified by incidental demands where they are connected to the original claims by a sufficient link.

Article 5. The judge must pronounce himself on all that is claimed and only on what is claimed.

Section III. The facts

Article 6. To support their claims, the parties have the duty to allege facts to base them on.

Article 7. The judge cannot base his decision on fact which were not under discussion.
Among the elements of the discussion, the judge may even take into consideration facts which the parties have not explicitly invoked to support their claims.

Article 8. The judge may invite the parties to provide explanations on facts which he deems necessary for a resolution of the litigation.

Section IV. Evidence

Article 9. It is incumbent upon each party to prove, in accordance with statute, the facts necessary for the success of its claim.

Article 10. The judge has the power to order ex officio any legally admissible investigative measure.

Article 11. The parties are held to provide their cooperation to investigative measures, under the reservation for the judge to draw all consequences of an abstention or refusal.
If a party holds an element of evidence, the judge may, upon request of the other party, compel it to provide it, if necessary under a periodic penalty. He may, upon request of one of the parties, demand or order, if necessary under the same penalty, the provision of any documents held by third parties where there is no legitimate impediment.

---

[22] Translation by Ph. Kiiver.

Section V. The law

Article 12. The judge resolves the litigation in accordance with the legal rules that apply thereto.
He must give or restore to facts and disputed acts their exact qualification without taking into account the definition that the parties have proposed.
However, he may not change the definition or legal ground where the parties, by virtue of an express agreement and for rights of which they can freely dispose, have bound him by qualifications and points of law to which they agree to restrict the discussion.
Where a litigation has arisen, the parties may also, in the same matters and under the same conditions, confer upon the judge the task of an amicable arbiter, subject to appeal if they have not explicitly renounced it.

Article 13. The judge may invite the parties to provide explanations on points of law which he deems necessary for the resolution of the litigation.

Section VI. The adversarial procedure

Article 14. No party may be judged without having been heard or addressed.

Article 15. The parties must inform one another in due time of the points of fact on which they base their claims, the elements of evidence which they provide and the points of law that they invoke, so that each may organize its defence.

Article 16. The judge must, in all circumstances, see to the respect of, and respect himself, the principle of adversarial procedure.
He may rely, in his decision, only on points, explanations and documents invoked or provided by the parties if they could discuss them in an adversarial manner.
He may not base his decision on points of law which he has raised ex officio without first having invited the parties to present their opinions.

Article 17. Where statute allows or necessity requires that a measure be ordered without a party knowing, it has the right of appropriate remedy against the decision to which it objects.

Section VII. The defence

Article 18. The parties may mount their defence themselves, except for cases where representation is obligatory.

Article 19. The parties choose freely their counsel either to be represented or to be assisted in accordance with what statute allows or prescribes.

Article 20. The judge may always hear the parties themselves.

Section VIII. Conciliation

Article 21. It belongs to the tasks of the judge to conciliate between the parties.

Section IX. The oral hearing

Article 22. Oral hearings are public, except for cases where statute demands or allows that they be held in chambers.

Article 23. The judge is not held to resort to an interpreter where he commands the language in which the parties express themselves.

Article 23-1. If one of the parties suffers from deafness, the judge appoints for its assistance, by order not subject to appeal, an interpreter of sign language or of completed spoken language, or any qualified person commanding a language or method allowing to communicate with the deaf. The judge may equally resort to any technical facility allowing to communicate with that party.

However, the preceding paragraph does not apply if the party that suffers from deafness appears with the assistance of a person of its choice in order to ensure communication with it.

Section X. The duty of restraint

Article 24. The parties are held to always respect that is due to justice.
The judge may, depending on the gravity of the infringements, pronounce, even ex officio, injunctions, suppress writings, declare them defamatory, order the printing and publication of his judgments.

[The remainder of the Code is omitted.]

Code of Civil Procedure [Zivilprozessordnung] in the version promulgated on 5 December 2005 (*BGBl.* I p. 3202; 2006 I p. 431; 2007 I p. 1781), last amended by the statute of 24 September 2009 (*BGBl.* I p. 3145). Selected provisions from Book I.[23]

Book 1. General Provisions

Chapter 1. Courts

Title 1. Subject-matter competence of the courts and value provisions

§ 1. Subject-matter jurisdiction of the courts is determined by the Judicial Organization Act [Gerichtsverfassung].

[§§ 2-11 are omitted.]

Title 2. Competence

§ 12. The court where a person has its general forum [Gerichtsstand] is competent for all claims brought against it, unless an exclusive forum has been established for a claim.

§ 13. The general forum of a person is determined by its residence.

[§§ 14-16 are omitted.]

§ 17. (1) The general forum of municipalities, corporations as well as those companies, cooperative societies or other associations and of those foundations, institutions and estates which may be sued as such is determined by their seat. The seat is considered to be, unless anything else is concluded, the place where the management is carried out.
[The remaining subparagraphs are omitted.]

[§§ 18-34 are omitted.]

§ 35. From among several competent courts the plaintiff may choose.

[§§ 35a-37 are omitted.]

Title 3. Agreement about the competence of the courts

§ 38. (1) A court of first instance not competent in principle becomes competent by express or tacit agreement of the parties, if the contracting parties are merchants, legal persons of public law or special assets of public law.
(2) The competence of a court of first instance may furthermore be agreed upon if at least one of the parties does not have its general forum inside the country. The agreement must be concluded in writing or, if it is concluded orally, must be confirmed in writing. If one of the parties has its general forum inside the country, then for within the country only one court may be chosen, at which that party has its general forum or where a special forum applies.
(3) In all other cases, a forum agreement is only permitted if has been concluded expressly and in writing
1. after the dispute arose, or
2. for the case that the party to be sued in court, after the conclusion of the contract, transfers its residence or habitual sojourn outside the area of application of this Act or its residence or habitual sojourn is unknown when the claim is brought.

[§§ 39-40 are omitted.]

---

[23] Translation by G. Rotering.

Title 4. Exclusion and rejection of the court by the parties

[§§ 41-49 are omitted.]

Chapter 2. Parties

Title 1. Capacity to be a party; capacity to conduct proceedings

§ 50. (1) He who has legal capacity [rechtsfähig] has capacity to be a party.
(2) An association without legal capacity may sue and be sued; in such a dispute, the association has the status of an association with legal capacity.

§ 51. (1) The capacity of a party to appear in court, the representation of parties that do not have capacity to conduct proceedings by other persons (legal representatives) and the necessity of a special authorization to conduct proceedings is determined pursuant to the provisions of private law to the extent that the following paragraphs do not contain deviating provisions.
[The remaining subparagraphs are omitted.]

[§§ 52-58 are omitted.]

Title 2. Joinder of parties

§ 59. Several persons may jointly sue or be sued as joint parties if they are a legal community with respect to the object of the dispute or if their rights or obligations arise from the same factual and legal ground.

§ 60. Several persons may also jointly sue or be sued as joint parties if claims or obligations of the same kind and arising from a substantially similar factual and legal ground form the object of the dispute.

[§§ 61-63 are omitted.]

Title 3. Participation of third parties in the dispute

[§§ 64-77 are omitted.]

Title 4. Agents in proceedings and advisors

§ 78. (1) Before the district courts [Landgerichte] and courts of appeal [Oberlandesgerichte] the parties must be represented by an attorney [Rechtsanwalt]. Where a supreme State court has been established in a State pursuant to § 8 of the Introductory Act to the Judicial Organization Act [Einführungsgesetz zum Gerichtsverfassungsgesetz], parties must be represented by an attorney before that court as well. Before the Federal Supreme Court [Bundesgerichtshof] parties must be represented by an attorney accredited with the Federal Supreme Court.
[The remaining subparagraphs are omitted.]

[§§ 78a-78c are omitted.]

§ 79. (1) Insofar as representation by attorneys is not prescribed, the parties may conduct the dispute themselves. Parties which bring another's pecuniary claim or a pecuniary claim assigned to them in order to collect it on another's behalf must be represented by an attorney as an agent to the extent that they would not be entitled to represent the creditor pursuant to subparagraph 2 or do not collect a claim whose original creditor they are.
[The remaining subparagraphs are omitted.]

[§§ 80-90 are omitted.]

Title 5. Costs of the dispute

§ 91. (1) The losing party is to bear the costs of the dispute, in particular to compensate the opponent for their expenses to the extent that they were necessary for an adequate prosecution or defence of rights. The

compensation of costs also includes compensation of the opponent for the loss of time caused by necessary travelling or the necessary meeting of appointments; the provisions applicable to the compensation of witnesses apply mutatis mutandis.
(2) The legal fees and expenses of the attorney of the winning party are to be reimbursed in all proceedings, the travel expenses of an attorney not established in the district of the court where proceedings take place and not resident at the seat of the court where proceedings take place, however only to the extent that his engagement was necessary for an adequate prosecution or defence of rights. The costs of several attorneys are to be reimbursed only to such extent that they do not exceed the costs of a single attorney or where a substitution of the attorney needed to take place. In self-representation, the attorney is to be compensated for the fees and costs which he would be entitled to demand as fees and costs of an attorney acting as an agent.
(3) The costs of a dispute within the meaning of subparagraphs 1 and 2 also include the fees arising from a conciliation procedure before a conciliation authority established or recognized by the State judicial administration; this does not apply if more than one year has passed between the completion of the conciliation procedure and the bringing of the claim.
(4) The costs of a dispute within the meaning of subparagraph 1 also include costs that the winning party had paid to the losing party in the course of the dispute.

[§§ 92-97 are omitted.]

§ 98. The costs of an agreed settlement [Vergleich] are to be regarded as mutually compensatory unless the parties have agreed otherwise. The same applies concerning the costs of the dispute cleared by settlement unless they have already been finally decided upon in court.

[§§ 99-107 are omitted.]

Title 6. Provision of securities

[§§ 108-113 are omitted.]

Title 7. Legal aid and advance on legal costs

[§§ 114-127a are omitted.]

Chapter 3. Procedure

Title 1. Oral hearing

§ 128. (1) The parties debate the legal dispute orally before the deciding court.
(2) With the consent of the parties, which is revocable only in case of a substantial change of the state of the proceedings, the court may hand down a decision without an oral hearing. It determines forthwith the deadline until which written memorials may be submitted and the date of the pronunciation of the judgment. A decision without oral hearing is prohibited if more than three months have passed since the giving of consent by the parties.
(3) Where only a decision about the costs is outstanding, it may be made without an oral hearing.
(4) Decisions of the court that are not judgments may be made without oral hearing, unless otherwise specified.

[§ 128a is omitted.]

§ 129. (1) In proceedings with attorneys [Anwaltsprozesse] the oral hearing is prepared by written memorials.
(2) In other proceedings, the parties may be obliged by court order to prepare the oral hearing by written memorials or declarations to be submitted to the registry for the record.

[§ 129a is omitted.]

§ 130. The preparatory written memorials shall contain:
1. the designation of the parties and their legal representatives by name, occupation or trade, place of residence and status as a party; the designation of the court and the object of the dispute; the number of attachments;
2. the applications the party intends to bring forward during the session of the court;

3. the declaration of the factual circumstances supporting the reasons for the applications;
4. the declaration about the factual statements of the opponent;
5. the designation of the evidence the party intends to use for the support or refutation of factual statements, as well as the declaration about the evidence designated by the opponent;
6. the signature of the person responsible for the written memorial, in cases of submission by telefax service the reproduction of the signature on the copy.

[§§ 130a-130b are omitted.]

§ 131. (1) The preparatory written memorial is to have the documents that are in possession of the parties and referenced in the written memorial attached in the original or as copies.
(2) Where only specific parts of a document come under consideration, the attachment of an excerpt suffices that contains the introduction, the place pertaining to the matter, the conclusion, the date and the signature.
(3) If the documents are already known to the opponent or are of significant volume, their accurate description, with the offer to allow access, suffices.

§ 132. (1) The preparatory written memorial that contains new facts or submissions is to be filed so timely that it can be served at least one week before the oral hearing. The same applies to a written memorial which concerns interim proceedings.
(2) The preparatory written memorial that contains a counterstatement to a new submission is to be filed so timely that it can be served at least three days before the oral hearing. This does not apply if it concerns a written counterstatement in interim proceedings.

§ 133. (1) The parties shall attach to the written memorial which they file with the court, the number of copies required for service of the written memorials and their attachments. This does not apply to electronically communicated documents as well as attachments that are available to the opponent in the original or as copies.
(2) In case of service from attorney to attorney (§ 195), the parties are to submit with the court, immediately after service, a copy of their preparatory written memorials and the attachments intended for the court where proceedings take place.

[§§ 134-135 are omitted.]

§ 136. (1) The presiding judge opens and directs the hearing [Verhandlung].
(2) He gives permission to speak and he may withdraw it from him who fails to follow his orders. He is to allow any member of the court to ask questions upon request.
(3) He is to see to it that the matter is exhaustively argued and the hearing is completed without interruption; where necessary, he is to determine the session for the continuation of the hearing immediately.
(4) He closes the hearing if, in the view of the court, the matter has been completely argued, and pronounces the judgments and decisions of the court.

§ 137. (1) The oral hearings are commenced with the parties submitting their applications.
(2) The pleadings of the parties are to be pronounced in free speech; they are to comprise the substance of the dispute's factual and legal aspects.
(3) Reference to documents is permissible, to the extent that no party objects and the court deems it appropriate. Readings of documents only takes place to the extent that the literal content is relevant.
(4) In proceedings with attorneys, apart from the attorney, also the party itself is to be granted permission to speak upon request.

§ 138. (1) The parties are to submit their declarations concerning factual circumstances exhaustively and truthfully.
(2) Each party is to make declarations concerning the facts asserted by the opponent.
(3) Facts which are not explicitly denied are to be deemed as admitted, unless the intention to deny them emanates from the other declarations of the party.
(4) A declaration of lack of knowledge is permissible only concerning facts which have been neither personal acts of the party nor objects of its own perception.

§ 139. (1) The court is to evaluate the facts and the dispute together with the parties with respect to the factual and legal aspects, to the extent that is necessary, and to ask questions. It is to effect that the parties declare themselves timely and completely concerning all relevant facts, and especially supplement incomplete statements concerning the asserted facts, designate evidence and submit the pertinent applications.

(2) The point may base its decision on a point that a party has evidently overlooked or considered insignificant, where not only an ancillary claim is concerned, only when it has pointed it out and has given an opportunity to comment. The same applies to a point that the court assesses differently than both parties.

(3) The court is to call attention to concerns that exist with regard to points that have to be taken into account ex officio.

(4) Notice pursuant to this provision is to be given as soon as possible and to be noted in the record. Its issuance can only be proven by the content of the record. Against the content of the record, only evidence of forgery is admissible.

(5) Where a party cannot immediately comment on a court notice, the court shall, upon its request, determine a time limit during which it may subsequently file a comment in a written memorial.

§ 140. Where an order of the presiding judge concerning the direction of the case or a question put by the presiding judge or a member of the court is contested as being inadmissible by one of the persons involved in the hearing, the court decides.

§ 141. (1) The court shall order personal appearance of both parties when it appears necessary for the clarification of the factual circumstances. If a party cannot be expected to personally attend the hearing due to great distance or for other important reasons, the court abstains from ordering its appearance.

(2) If appearance is ordered, the party is to be summoned ex officio. The party itself is to be notified, even if it has appointed an agent for the case; delivery of the summons is not required.

(3) If the party is absent from the hearing, it may be fined in the same manner as a witness who fails to appear at a hearing. This does not apply if the party sends a representative to the hearing who is authorized to clarify the facts of the situation and to make the required declarations, especially to conclude a settlement. The party is to be warned of the consequences of its absence in the summons.

§ 142. (1) The court may order that a party or a third party submit the certificates and other documents in its possession to which it made reference. The court may set a time period for this and order that the submitted documents remain in the court registry for a time period to be determined by it.

(2) Third parties are not obliged to submit, to the extent that submission cannot be expected of them or they have the right to refuse to give evidence pursuant to §§ 383 to 385. §§ 386 to 390 apply mutatis mutandis.

[Subparagraph (3) is omitted.]

§ 143. The court may order parties to submit dossiers in their possession, to the extent that they consist of documents that concern the hearing and the decision on the matter.

§ 144. (1) The court may order visual inspection as well as assessment by an expert. It may, to this end, order a party or a third party to submit an object in their possession and determine a term for this. It may also order toleration of the measure pursuant to the first sentence, provided it does not pertain to a dwelling.

(2) Third parties are not obliged to submit or tolerate, to the extent that this cannot be expected of them or they have the right to refuse to give evidence pursuant to §§ 383 to 385. §§ 386 to 390 apply mutatis mutandis.

(3) The procedure is regulated by the provisions that have as their object visual inspection or assessment by an exert upon request.

§ 145. (1) The court may order that several claims raised in one action be heard in separate proceedings.

[The remaining subparagraphs are omitted.]

§ 146. The court may order that, in the case of several independent means of attack or defence (causes of action, objections, replies, etc.) referring to the same claim, the proceedings are initially to be limited to one or several of these means of attack or defence.

§ 147. The court may order the joining of several proceedings pending before it involving the same or different parties for the purpose of simultaneous hearing and decision, if the claims which form the object of these proceeding are legally connected or could have been asserted in one action.

§ 148. The court may, if the decision of the dispute wholly or in part depends on the existence or inexistence of a legal relationship which is the object of another pending dispute or is to be established by an administrative authority, order that the proceedings be suspended until the conclusion of the other dispute or the decision by the administrative authority.

[§§ 149-158 are omitted.]

§ 159. (1) Minutes are to be made with regard to the hearing and any taking of evidence. A recording clerk of the court registry may be called in, if this is required owing to the expected volume of the minutes, the particular difficulty of the matter or for another important reason.
[Subparagraph (2) is omitted.]

[§§ 160-165 are omitted.]

Title 2. Service procedure

Subtitle 1. Service ex officio

§ 166. (1) Service [Zustellung] is the notification of a document to a person in the manner provided for in this title. (2) Documents whose service is mandatory or ordered by the court, are to be served ex officio, unless otherwise provided.

[§ 167 is omitted.]

§ 168 (1) The court registry carries out services pursuant to §§ 173 to 175. It may assign service to a contractor engaged pursuant to § 33 (1) of the Post Act [Postgesetz] (post) or to a judicial clerk. The assignment to the post is issued by the court registry on the designated pre-printed form.
(2) The presiding judge of the court where proceedings take place or a member assigned by him may assign service to a bailiff or another authority where service pursuant to the first paragraph is not expected to succeed.

[§§ 169-176 are omitted.]

§ 177. The document can be delivered to the person that is to be served at any place where it is encountered.

[§§ 178-190 are omitted.]

Subtitle 2. Service upon request by the parties

§ 191. Where service upon request by the parties is permissible or required, the provisions on service ex officio apply mutatis mutandis, provided that no deviations arise from the following provisions.

[§§ 192-195 are omitted.]

§§ 195a-213a. (Repealed).

Title 3. Summons, dates and time limits

[§§ 214-229 are omitted.]

Title 4. Consequences of default; Restitutio in integrum

§ 230. Default [Versäumung] of a step in the proceedings has as its general consequence that the party will be excluded with the step in the proceeding to be undertaken.

[§§ 231 is omitted.]

§ 232. (Repealed).

§ 233. Where a party was prevented, through no fault of its own, from complying with a statutory term [Notfrist] or a time limit for founding an appeal [Berufung], an appeal on points of law [Revision], appeal against rejection of appeal on points of law [Nichtzulassungsbeschwerde] or complaint [Rechtsbeschwerde] or with the period of § 234 (1), restitutio in integrum is to be allowed upon request.

[§§ 234-238 are omitted.]

Title 5. Interruption and suspension of proceedings

[The remainder of Book I – §§ 239-252 – is omitted.]

Code of Civil Procedure [Wetboek van Burgerlijke Rechtsvordering]. Selected provisions from Title I of Book I.[24]

Book 1. The method of procedure before district courts [rechtbanken], courts of appeal [hoven] and the Supreme Court [Hoge Raad]

Title 1. General provisions

Division 1. Jurisdiction of the Dutch judge

Article 1. Without prejudice to what is determined in treaties and EC regulations, the jurisdiction of the Dutch judge is governed by the following provisions.

[*The remainder of Division 1 is omitted.*]

Division 2. Single-judge and multi-member chambers

Article 15. (1) In the district court [rechtbank] cases, save for exceptions stipulated in statute, are considered and decided by a single-judge chamber.
(2) If the single-judge chamber considers the case ill-suited to be considered and decided by a single judge, it refers the case to a multi-member chamber, consisting of three members. The single-judge chamber may also refer a case to a multi-member chamber in other cases.
[*The remainder of Article 15 is omitted.*]

Article 16. (1) In the court of appeal [gerechtshof] cases, save for exceptions stipulated in statute, are considered and decided by a multi-member chamber consisting of three justices [raadsheren].
[*The remainder of Article 16 is omitted.*]

Article 17. (1) In the Supreme Court [Hoge Raad] cases, save for exceptions stipulated in statute, are considered and decided by five members of the multi-member chamber.
[*The remainder of Article 17 and Division 2 are omitted.*]

Division 3. General rules for proceedings

Article 19. The judge provides the parties, to and fro, with the opportunity to bring forward and explain their positions and comment on each other's positions and on all documents and other facts that have been brought to the knowledge of the judge in the proceedings, all of which unless something else flows from statute. In his decision [beslissing] the judge does not base his judgment, to the detriment of one of the parties, on documents or other facts on which that party has not been able to comment sufficiently.

Article 20. (1) The judge guards against unreasonable delay of proceedings and takes, where necessary, upon request of a party or ex officio, measures.
(2) Parties are obliged with respect to one another to prevent unreasonable delay of proceedings.

Article 21. Parties are obliged to bring forward completely and truthfully the facts that are of importance for the decision. If this obligation is not observed, the judge may draw the conclusions he considers appropriate.

Article 22. The judge may, in all cases and in each state of proceedings, order the parties or one of them to explain certain arguments or to submit certain documents which relate to the case. Parties may refuse this where there are serious reasons to do so. The judge decides whether the refusal is justified, failing which he may draw the conclusions he considers appropriate.

Article 23. The judge decides on everything the parties have claimed or requested.

---

[24] Translation by M. Dekker.

Article 24. The judge investigates and decides the case on the basis of that on which parties have founded their claim, request or defence, unless something else flows from statute.

Article 25. The judge complements the legal grounds ex officio.

Article 26. The judge may not refuse to decide.

Article 27. (1) The court session is public. The judge may however order either full or partial consideration behind closed doors or with admission of certain persons only:
a. in the interest of the public order or good morals,
b. in the interest of the security of the state,
c. if the interests of minors or the respect for the private life of the parties so require, or
d. if publicity would seriously compromise the interest of good administration of justice.
(2) If someone disrupts the order during the court session, the judge may have him removed.

Article 28. (1) The decision is handed down in public.
(2) Without prejudice to Articles 231 (1) and 290 (3), the registrar provides everyone who so desires with a copy of judgments [vonnissen], superior rulings [arresten] and orders [beschikkingen], unless such provision, in the opinion of the registrar, must be refused fully or partially for the protection of important interests of others, including those of the parties. In the latter case the registrar may limit himself to providing an anonymized copy of or excerpt from the judgment, superior ruling or order.
(3) Judgments, superior rulings and orders are understood to include the documents that are attached to the ruling [uitspraak]. No copy of or excerpt from other documents that belong to the case file is provided to third parties.
(4) Of judgments, superior rulings and orders in cases that have been considered behind closed doors, only an anonymized copy or excerpt is provided.
[*The remainder of Article 28 is omitted.*]

[*The remainder of the Code is omitted.*]

Civil Procedure Rules 1998 as amended. Selected provisions: Parts 1, 7, 15, 26 and 31.

Part 1. Overriding objective

1.1. (1) These Rules are a new procedural code with the overriding objective of enabling the court to deal with cases justly.
(2) Dealing with a case justly includes, so far as is practicable –
(a) ensuring that the parties are on an equal footing;
(b) saving expense;
(c) dealing with the case in ways which are proportionate –
(i) to the amount of money involved;
(ii) to the importance of the case;
(iii) to the complexity of the issues; and
(iv) to the financial position of each party;
(d) ensuring that it is dealt with expeditiously and fairly; and
(e) allotting to it an appropriate share of the court's resources, while taking into account the need to allot resources to other cases.

1.2. The court must seek to give effect to the overriding objective when it –
(a) exercises any power given to it by the Rules; or
(b) interprets any rule subject to rules 76.2 and 79.2.

1.3. The parties are required to help the court to further the overriding objective.

1.4. (1) The court must further the overriding objective by actively managing cases.
(2) Active case management includes –
(a) encouraging the parties to co-operate with each other in the conduct of the proceedings;
(b) identifying the issues at an early stage;
(c) deciding promptly which issues need full investigation and trial and accordingly disposing summarily of the others;
(d) deciding the order in which issues are to be resolved;
(e) encouraging the parties to use an alternative dispute resolution procedure if the court considers that appropriate and facilitating the use of such procedure;
(f) helping the parties to settle the whole or part of the case;
(g) fixing timetables or otherwise controlling the progress of the case;
(h) considering whether the likely benefits of taking a particular step justify the cost of taking it;
(i) dealing with as many aspects of the case as it can on the same occasion;
(j) dealing with the case without the parties needing to attend at court;
(k) making use of technology; and
(l) giving directions to ensure that the trial of a case proceeds quickly and efficiently.

[Parts 2 – 6 are omitted.]

Part 7. How to start proceedings – The claim form

7.1. Restrictions on where proceedings may be started are set out in the relevant practice directions supplementing this Part.

7.2. (1) Proceedings are started when the court issues a claim form at the request of the claimant.
(2) A claim form is issued on the date entered on the form by the court.

7.3. A claimant may use a single claim form to start all claims which can be conveniently disposed of in the same proceedings.

7.4. (1) Particulars of claim must –
(a) be contained in or served with the claim form; or

(b) subject to paragraph (2) be served on the defendant by the claimant within 14 days after service of the claim form.
(2) Particulars of claim must be served on the defendant no later than the latest time for serving a claim form.
(3) Where the claimant serves particulars of claim separately from the claim form in accordance with paragraph (1)(b), the claimant must, within 7 days of service on the defendant, file a copy of the particulars except where –
(a) paragraph 5.2(4) of Practice Direction 7C applies; or
(b) paragraph 6.4 of Practice Direction 7E applies.

7.5. (1) Where the claim form is served within the jurisdiction, the claimant must complete the step required by the following table in relation to the particular method of service chosen, before 12.00 midnight on the calendar day four months after the date of issue of the claim form.

Method of service	Step required
First class post, document exchange or other service which provides for delivery on the next business day	Posting, leaving with, delivering to or collection by the relevant service provider
Delivery of the document to or leaving it at the relevant place	Delivering to or leaving the document at the relevant place
Personal service under rule 6.5	Completing the relevant step required by rule 6.5(3)
Fax	Completing the transmission of the fax
Other electronic method	Sending the e-mail or other electronic transmission

(2) Where the claim form is to be served out of the jurisdiction, the claim form must be served in accordance with Section IV of Part 6 within 6 months of the date of issue.

7.6. (1) The claimant may apply for an order extending the period for compliance with rule 7.5.
(2) The general rule is that an application to extend the time for compliance with rule 7.5 must be made –
(a) within the period specified by rule 7.5; or
(b) where an order has been made under this rule, within the period for service specified by that order.
(3) If the claimant applies for an order to extend the time for compliance after the end of the period specified by rule 7.5 or by an order made under this rule, the court may make such an order only if –
(a) the court has failed to serve the claim form; or
(b) the claimant has taken all reasonable steps to comply with rule 7.5 but has been unable to do so; and
(c) in either case, the claimant has acted promptly in making the application.
(4) An application for an order extending the time for compliance with rule 7.5 –
(a) must be supported by evidence; and
(b) may be made without notice.

7.7. (1) Where a claim form has been issued against a defendant, but has not yet been served on him, the defendant may serve a notice on the claimant requiring him to serve the claim form or discontinue the claim within a period specified in the notice.
(2) The period specified in a notice served under paragraph (1) must be at least 14 days after service of the notice.
(3) If the claimant fails to comply with the notice, the court may, on the application of the defendant –
(a) dismiss the claim; or
(b) make any other order it thinks just.

7.8. (1) When particulars of claim are served on a defendant, whether they are contained in the claim form, served with it or served subsequently, they must be accompanied by –
(a) a form for defending the claim;
(b) a form for admitting the claim; and
(c) a form for acknowledging service.
(2) Where the claimant is using the procedure set out in Part 8 –
(a) paragraph (1) does not apply; and

(b) a form for acknowledging service must accompany the claim form.

7.9. A practice direction –
(a) may set out the circumstances in which the court may give a fixed date for a hearing when it issues a claim;
(b) may list claims in respect of which there is a specific claim form for use and set out the claim form in question; and
(c) may disapply or modify these Rules as appropriate in relation to the claims referred to in paragraphs (a) and (b).

7.10. (1) There shall be a Production Centre for the issue of claim forms and other related matters.
(2) Practice Direction 7C makes provision for –
(a) which claimants may use the Production Centre;
(b) the type of claims which the Production Centre may issue;
(c) the functions which are to be discharged by the Production Centre;
(d) the place where the Production Centre is to be located; and
(e) other related matters.
(3) Practice Direction 7C may disapply or modify these Rules as appropriate in relation to claims issued by the Production Centre.

7.11. (1) A claim under section 7(1)(a) of the Human Rights Act 1998 in respect of a judicial act may be brought only in the High Court.
(2) Any other claim under section 7(1)(a) of that Act may be brought in any court.

7.12. (1) A practice direction may make provision for a claimant to start a claim by requesting the issue of a claim form electronically.
(2) The practice direction may, in particular –
(a) specify –
(i) the types of claim which may be issued electronically; and
(ii) the conditions which a claim must meet before it may be issued electronically;
(b) specify –
(i) the court where the claim will be issued; and
(ii) the circumstances in which the claim will be transferred to another court;
(c) provide for the filing of other documents electronically where a claim has been started electronically;
(d) specify the requirements that must be fulfilled for any document filed electronically; and
(e) provide how a fee payable on the filing of any document is to be paid where that document is filed electronically.
(3) The practice direction may disapply or modify these Rules as appropriate in relation to claims started electronically.

[Parts 8 – 14 are omitted.]

Part 15. Defence and reply

15.1. This Part does not apply where the claimant uses the procedure set out in Part 8.

15.2. A defendant who wishes to defend all or part of a claim must file a defence.

15.3. If a defendant fails to file a defence, the claimant may obtain default judgment if Part 12 allows it.

15.4. (1) The general rule is that the period for filing a defence is –
(a) 14 days after service of the particulars of claim; or
(b) if the defendant files an acknowledgment of service under Part 10, 28 days after service of the particulars of claim.
(2) The general rule is subject to the following rules –
(a) rule 6.35;
(b) rule 11;
(c) rule 24.4(2); and

(d) rule 6.12(3).

15.5. (1) The defendant and the claimant may agree that the period for filing a defence specified in rule 15.4 shall be extended by up to 28 days.
(2) Where the defendant and the claimant agree to extend the period for filing a defence, the defendant must notify the court in writing.

15.6. A copy of the defence must be served on every other party.

15.7. Part 20 applies to a defendant who wishes to make a counterclaim.

15.8. If a claimant files a reply to the defence, he must –
(a) file his reply when he files his allocation questionnaire; and
(b) serve his reply on the other parties at the same time as he files it.

15.9. A party may not file or serve any statement of case after a reply without the permission of the court.

15.10. (1) Where –
(a) the only claim is for a specified amount of money; and
(b) the defendant states in his defence that he has paid to the claimant the amount claimed,
the court will send notice to the claimant requiring him to state in writing whether he wishes the proceedings to continue.
(2) When the claimant responds, he must serve a copy of his response on the defendant.
(3) If the claimant fails to respond under this rule within 28 days after service of the court's notice on him the claim shall be stayed.
(4) Where a claim is stayed under this rule any party may apply for the stay to be lifted.

15.11. (1) Where –
(a) at least 6 months have expired since the end of the period for filing a defence specified in rule 15.4;
(b) no defendant has served or filed an admission or filed a defence or counterclaim; and
(c) the claimant has not entered or applied for judgment under Part 12, or Part 24,
the claim shall be stayed.
(2) Where a claim is stayed under this rule any party may apply for the stay to be lifted.

[Parts 16 – 25 are omitted.]

Part 26. Case management – preliminary stage

26.1. (1) This Part provides for –
(a) the automatic transfer of some defended cases between courts; and
(b) the allocation of defended cases to case management tracks.
(2) There are three tracks –
(a) the small claims track;
(b) the fast track; and
(c) the multi-track.

26.2. (1) This rule applies to proceedings where –
(a) the claim is for a specified amount of money;
(b) the claim was commenced in a court which is not the defendant's home court;
(c) the claim has not been transferred to another defendant's home court under rule 13.4 or rule 14.12; and
(d) the defendant is an individual.
(2) This rule does not apply where the claim was commenced in a specialist list.
(3) Where this rule applies, the court will transfer the proceedings to the defendant's home court when a defence is filed, unless paragraph (4) applies.
(4) Where the claimant notifies the court under rule 15.10 or rule 14.5 that he wishes the proceedings to continue, the court will transfer the proceedings to the defendant's home court when it receives that notification from the claimant.

(5) Where –
(a) the claim is against two or more defendants with different home courts; and
(b) the defendant whose defence is filed first is an individual,
proceedings are to be transferred under this rule to the home court of that defendant.
(6) The time when a claim is automatically transferred under this rule may be varied by a practice direction in respect of claims issued by the Production Centre.

26.3. (1) When a defendant files a defence the court will serve an allocation questionnaire on each party unless –
(a) rule 15.10 or rule 14.5 applies; or
(b) the court dispenses with the need for a questionnaire.
(2) Where there are two or more defendants and at least one of them files a defence, the court will serve the allocation questionnaire under paragraph (1) –
(a) when all the defendants have filed a defence; or
(b) when the period for the filing of the last defence has expired,
whichever is the sooner.
(3) Where proceedings are automatically transferred to the defendant's home court under rule 26.2, the court in which the proceedings have been commenced will serve an allocation questionnaire before the proceedings are transferred.
(4) Where –
(a) rule 15.10 or rule 14.5 applies; and
(b) the proceedings are not automatically transferred to the defendant's home court under rule 26.2,
the court will serve an allocation questionnaire on each party when the claimant files a notice indicating that he wishes the proceedings to continue.
(5) The court may, on the application of the claimant, serve an allocation questionnaire earlier than it would otherwise serve it under this rule.
(6) Each party must file the completed allocation questionnaire no later than the date specified in it, which shall be at least 14 days after the date when it is deemed to be served on the party in question.
(6A) The date for filing the completed allocation questionnaire may not be varied by agreement between the parties.
(7) The time when the court serves an allocation questionnaire under this rule may be varied by a practice direction in respect of claims issued by the Production Centre.

26.4. (1) A party may, when filing the completed allocation questionnaire, make a written request for the proceedings to be stayed while the parties try to settle the case by alternative dispute resolution or other means.
(2) Where –
(a) all parties request a stay under paragraph (1); or
(b) the court, of its own initiative, considers that such a stay would be appropriate,
the court will direct that the proceedings, either in whole or in part, be stayed for one month, or for such specified period as it considers appropriate.
(3) The court may extend the stay until such date or for such specified period as it considers appropriate.
(4) Where the court stays the proceedings under this rule, the claimant must tell the court if a settlement is reached.
(5) If the claimant does not tell the court by the end of the period of the stay that a settlement has been reached, the court will give such directions as to the management of the case as it considers appropriate.

26.5. (1) The court will allocate the claim to a track –
(a) when every defendant has filed an allocation questionnaire, or
(b) when the period for filing the allocation questionnaires has expired,
whichever is the sooner, unless it has –
(i) stayed the proceedings under rule 26.4; or
(ii) dispensed with the need for allocation questionnaires.
(2) If the court has stayed the proceedings under rule 26.4, it will allocate the claim to a track at the end of the period of the stay.
(3) Before deciding the track to which to allocate proceedings or deciding whether to give directions for an allocation hearing to be fixed, the court may order a party to provide further information about his case.
(4) The court may hold an allocation hearing if it thinks it is necessary.
(5) If a party fails to file an allocation questionnaire, the court may give any direction it considers appropriate.

26.6. (1) The small claims track is the normal track for –
(a) any claim for personal injuries where –
(i) the value of the claim is not more than £5,000; and
(ii) the value of any claim for damages for personal injuries is not more than £1,000;
(b) any claim which includes a claim by a tenant of residential premises against a landlord where –
(i) the tenant is seeking an order requiring the landlord to carry out repairs or other work to the premises;
(ii) the cost of the repairs or other work to the premises is estimated to be not more than £1,000; and
(iii) the value of any other claim for damages is not more than £1,000.
(2) For the purposes of paragraph (1) 'damages for personal injuries' means damages claimed as compensation for pain, suffering and loss of amenity and does not include any other damages which are claimed.
(3) Subject to paragraph (1), the small claims track is the normal track for any claim which has a value of not more than £5,000.
(4) Subject to paragraph (5), the fast track is the normal track for any claim –
(a) for which the small claims track is not the normal track; and
(b) which has a value –
(i) for proceedings issued on or after 6th April 2009, of not more than £25,000; or
(ii) for proceedings issued before 6th April 2009, of not more than £15,000.
(5) The fast track is the normal track for the claims referred to in paragraph (4) only if the court considers that –
(a) the trial is likely to last for no longer than one day; and
(b) oral expert evidence at trial will be limited to –
(i) one expert per party in relation to any expert field; and
(ii) expert evidence in two expert fields.
(6) The multi-track is the normal track for any claim for which the small claims track or the fast track is not the normal track.

26.7. (1) In considering whether to allocate a claim to the normal track for that claim under rule 26.6, the court will have regard to the matters mentioned in rule 26.8(1).
(2) The court will allocate a claim which has no financial value to the track which it considers most suitable having regard to the matters mentioned in rule 26.8(1).
(3) The court will not allocate proceedings to a track if the financial value of the claim, assessed by the court under rule 26.8, exceeds the limit for that track unless all the parties consent to the allocation of the claim to that track.
(4) The court will not allocate a claim to the small claims track, if it includes a claim by a tenant of residential premises against his landlord for a remedy in respect of harassment or unlawful eviction.

26.8. (1) When deciding the track for a claim, the matters to which the court shall have regard include –
(a) the financial value, if any, of the claim;
(b) the nature of the remedy sought;
(c) the likely complexity of the facts, law or evidence;
(d) the number of parties or likely parties;
(e) the value of any counterclaim or other Part 20 claim and the complexity of any matters relating to it;
(f) the amount of oral evidence which may be required;
(g) the importance of the claim to persons who are not parties to the proceedings;
(h) the views expressed by the parties; and
(i) the circumstances of the parties.
(2) It is for the court to assess the financial value of a claim and in doing so it will disregard –
(a) any amount not in dispute;
(b) any claim for interest;
(c) costs; and
(d) any contributory negligence.
(3) Where –
(a) two or more claimants have started a claim against the same defendant using the same claim form; and
(b) each claimant has a claim against the defendant separate from the other claimants,
the court will consider the claim of each claimant separately when it assesses financial value under paragraph (1).

26.9. (1) When it has allocated a claim to a track, the court will serve notice of allocation on every party.
(2) When the court serves notice of allocation on a party, it will also serve –
(a) a copy of the allocation questionnaires filed by the other parties; and
(b) a copy of any further information provided by another party about his case.

26.10. The court may subsequently re-allocate a claim to a different track.

26.11. An application for a claim to be tried with a jury must be made within 28 days of service of the defence.

[Parts 27 – 30 are omitted.]

Part 31. Disclosure and inspection of documents

31.1. (1) This Part sets out rules about the disclosure and inspection of documents.
(2) This Part applies to all claims except a claim on the small claims track.

31.2. A party discloses a document by stating that the document exists or has existed.

31.3. (1) A party to whom a document has been disclosed has a right to inspect that document except where –
(a) the document is no longer in the control of the party who disclosed it;
(b) the party disclosing the document has a right or a duty to withhold inspection of it; or
(c) paragraph (2) applies.
(2) Where a party considers that it would be disproportionate to the issues in the case to permit inspection of documents within a category or class of document disclosed under rule 31.6(b) –
(a) he is not required to permit inspection of documents within that category or class; but
(b) he must state in his disclosure statement that inspection of those documents will not be permitted on the grounds that to do so would be disproportionate.

31.4. In this Part –
'document' means anything in which information of any description is recorded; and
'copy', in relation to a document, means anything onto which information recorded in the document has been copied, by whatever means and whether directly or indirectly.

31.5. (1) An order to give disclosure is an order to give standard disclosure unless the court directs otherwise.
(2) The court may dispense with or limit standard disclosure.
(3) The parties may agree in writing to dispense with or to limit standard disclosure.

31.6. Standard disclosure requires a party to disclose only –
(a) the documents on which he relies; and
(b) the documents which –
(i) adversely affect his own case;
(ii) adversely affect another party's case; or
(iii) support another party's case; and
(c) the documents which he is required to disclose by a relevant practice direction.

31.7. (1) When giving standard disclosure, a party is required to make a reasonable search for documents falling within rule 31.6(b) or (c).
(2) The factors relevant in deciding the reasonableness of a search include the following –
(a) the number of documents involved;
(b) the nature and complexity of the proceedings;
(c) the ease and expense of retrieval of any particular document; and
(d) the significance of any document which is likely to be located during the search.
(3) Where a party has not searched for a category or class of document on the grounds that to do so would be unreasonable, he must state this in his disclosure statement and identify the category or class of document.

31.8. (1) A party's duty to disclose documents is limited to documents which are or have been in his control.
(2) For this purpose a party has or has had a document in his control if –
(a) it is or was in his physical possession;
(b) he has or has had a right to possession of it; or
(c) he has or has had a right to inspect or take copies of it.

PART VI. CIVIL PROCEDURE

31.9. (1) A party need not disclose more than one copy of a document.
(2) A copy of a document that contains a modification, obliteration or other marking or feature –
(a) on which a party intends to rely; or
(b) which adversely affects his own case or another party's case or supports another party's case;
shall be treated as a separate document.

31.10. (1) The procedure for standard disclosure is as follows.
(2) Each party must make and serve on every other party, a list of documents in the relevant practice form.
(3) The list must identify the documents in a convenient order and manner and as concisely as possible.
(4) The list must indicate –
(a) those documents in respect of which the party claims a right or duty to withhold inspection; and
(b)
(i) those documents which are no longer in the party's control; and
(ii) what has happened to those documents.
(5) The list must include a disclosure statement.
(6) A disclosure statement is a statement made by the party disclosing the documents –
(a) setting out the extent of the search that has been made to locate documents which he is required to disclose;
(b) certifying that he understands the duty to disclose documents; and
(c) certifying that to the best of his knowledge he has carried out that duty.
(7) Where the party making the disclosure statement is a company, firm, association or other organisation, the statement must also –
(a) identify the person making the statement; and
(b) explain why he is considered an appropriate person to make the statement.
(8) The parties may agree in writing –
(a) to disclose documents without making a list; and
(b) to disclose documents without the disclosing party making a disclosure statement.
(9) A disclosure statement may be made by a person who is not a party where this is permitted by a relevant practice direction.

31.11. (1) Any duty of disclosure continues until the proceedings are concluded.
(2) If documents to which that duty extends come to a party's notice at any time during the proceedings, he must immediately notify every other party.

31.12. (1) The court may make an order for specific disclosure or specific inspection.
(2) An order for specific disclosure is an order that a party must do one or more of the following things –
(a) disclose documents or classes of documents specified in the order;
(b) carry out a search to the extent stated in the order;
(c) disclose any documents located as a result of that search.
(3) An order for specific inspection is an order that a party permit inspection of a document referred to in rule 31.3(2).

31.13. The parties may agree in writing, or the court may direct, that disclosure or inspection or both shall take place in stages.

31.14. (1) A party may inspect a document mentioned in –
(a) a statement of case;
(b) a witness statement;
(c) a witness summary; or
(d) an affidavit.
(e) (Revoked).
(2) Subject to rule 35.10(4), a party may apply for an order for inspection of any document mentioned in an expert's report which has not already been disclosed in the proceedings.

31.15. Where a party has a right to inspect a document –
(a) that party must give the party who disclosed the document written notice of his wish to inspect it;
(b) the party who disclosed the document must permit inspection not more than 7 days after the date on which he received the notice; and

(c) that party may request a copy of the document and, if he also undertakes to pay reasonable copying costs, the party who disclosed the document must supply him with a copy not more than 7 days after the date on which he received the request.

31.16. (1) This rule applies where an application is made to the court under any Act for disclosure before proceedings have started.
(2) The application must be supported by evidence.
(3) The court may make an order under this rule only where –
(a) the respondent is likely to be a party to subsequent proceedings;
(b) the applicant is also likely to be a party to those proceedings;
(c) if proceedings had started, the respondent's duty by way of standard disclosure, set out in rule 31.6, would extend to the documents or classes of documents of which the applicant seeks disclosure; and
(d) disclosure before proceedings have started is desirable in order to –
(i) dispose fairly of the anticipated proceedings;
(ii) assist the dispute to be resolved without proceedings; or
(iii) save costs.
(4) An order under this rule must –
(a) specify the documents or the classes of documents which the respondent must disclose; and
(b) require him, when making disclosure, to specify any of those documents –
(i) which are no longer in his control; or
(ii) in respect of which he claims a right or duty to withhold inspection.
(5) Such an order may –
(a) require the respondent to indicate what has happened to any documents which are no longer in his control; and
(b) specify the time and place for disclosure and inspection.

31.17. (1) This rule applies where an application is made to the court under any Act for disclosure by a person who is not a party to the proceedings.
(2) The application must be supported by evidence.
(3) The court may make an order under this rule only where –
(a) the documents of which disclosure is sought are likely to support the case of the applicant or adversely affect the case of one of the other parties to the proceedings; and
(b) disclosure is necessary in order to dispose fairly of the claim or to save costs.
(4) An order under this rule must –
(a) specify the documents or the classes of documents which the respondent must disclose; and
(b) require the respondent, when making disclosure, to specify any of those documents –
(i) which are no longer in his control; or
(ii) in respect of which he claims a right or duty to withhold inspection.
(5) Such an order may –
(a) require the respondent to indicate what has happened to any documents which are no longer in his control; and
(b) specify the time and place for disclosure and inspection.

31.18. Rules 31.16 and 31.17 do not limit any other power which the court may have to order –
(a) disclosure before proceedings have started; and
(b) disclosure against a person who is not a party to proceedings.

31.19. (1) A person may apply, without notice, for an order permitting him to withhold disclosure of a document on the ground that disclosure would damage the public interest.
(2) Unless the court orders otherwise, an order of the court under paragraph (1) –
(a) must not be served on any other person; and
(b) must not be open to inspection by any person.
(3) A person who wishes to claim that he has a right or a duty to withhold inspection of a document, or part of a document, must state in writing –
(a) that he has such a right or duty; and
(b) the grounds on which he claims that right or duty.
(4) The statement referred to in paragraph (3) must be made –
(a) in the list in which the document is disclosed; or
(b) if there is no list, to the person wishing to inspect the document.
(5) A party may apply to the court to decide whether a claim made under paragraph (3) should be upheld.

(6) For the purpose of deciding an application under paragraph (1) or paragraph (3) the court may –
(a) require the person seeking to withhold disclosure or inspection of a document to produce that document to the court; and
(b) invite any person, whether or not a party, to make representations.
(7) An application under paragraph (1) or paragraph (5) must be supported by evidence.
(8) This Part does not affect any rule of law which permits or requires a document to be withheld from disclosure or inspection on the ground that its disclosure or inspection would damage the public interest.

31.20. Where a party inadvertently allows a privileged document to be inspected, the party who has inspected the document may use it or its contents only with the permission of the court.

31.21. A party may not rely on any document which he fails to disclose or in respect of which he fails to permit inspection unless the court gives permission.

31.22. (1) A party to whom a document has been disclosed may use the document only for the purpose of the proceedings in which it is disclosed, except where –
(a) the document has been read to or by the court, or referred to, at a hearing which has been held in public;
(b) the court gives permission; or
(c) the party who disclosed the document and the person to whom the document belongs agree.
(2) The court may make an order restricting or prohibiting the use of a document which has been disclosed, even where the document has been read to or by the court, or referred to, at a hearing which has been held in public.
(3) An application for such an order may be made –
(a) by a party; or
(b) by any person to whom the document belongs.

31.23. (1) Proceedings for contempt of court may be brought against a person if he makes, or causes to be made, a false disclosure statement, without an honest belief in its truth.
(2) Proceedings under this rule may be brought only –
(a) by the Attorney General; or
(b) with the permission of the court.

[The remaining Parts are omitted.]

Council Regulation (EC) No 1206/2001 of 28 May 2001 on cooperation between the courts of the Member States in the taking of evidence in civil or commercial matters.

[The Preamble is omitted.]

CHAPTER I. GENERAL PROVISIONS

Article 1. 1. This Regulation shall apply in civil or commercial matters where the court of a Member State, in accordance with the provisions of the law of that State, requests:
(a) the competent court of another Member State to take evidence; or
(b) to take evidence directly in another Member State.
2. A request shall not be made to obtain evidence which is not intended for use in judicial proceedings, commenced or contemplated.
3. In this Regulation, the term 'Member State' shall mean Member States with the exception of Denmark.

Article 2. 1. Requests pursuant to Article 1(1)(a), hereinafter referred to as 'requests', shall be transmitted by the court before which the proceedings are commenced or contemplated, hereinafter referred to as the 'requesting court', directly to the competent court of another Member State, hereinafter referred to as the 'requested court', for the performance of the taking of evidence.
2. Each Member State shall draw up a list of the courts competent for the performance of taking of evidence according to this Regulation. The list shall also indicate the territorial and, where appropriate, the special jurisdiction of those courts.

Article 3. 1. Each Member State shall designate a central body responsible for:
(a) supplying information to the courts;
(b) seeking solutions to any difficulties which may arise in respect of a request;
(c) forwarding, in exceptional cases, at the request of a requesting court, a request to the competent court.
2. A federal State, a State in which several legal systems apply or a State with autonomous territorial entities shall be free to designate more than one central body.
3. Each Member State shall also designate the central body referred to in paragraph 1 or one or several competent authority(ies) to be responsible for taking decisions on requests pursuant to Article 17.

CHAPTER II. TRANSMISSION AND EXECUTION OF REQUESTS

Section 1. Transmission of the request

Article 4. 1. The request shall be made using form A or, where appropriate, form I in the Annex. It shall contain the following details:
(a) the requesting and, where appropriate, the requested court;
(b) the names and addresses of the parties to the proceedings and their representatives, if any;
(c) the nature and subject matter of the case and a brief statement of the facts;
(d) a description of the taking of evidence to be performed;
(e) where the request is for the examination of a person:
— the name(s) and address(es) of the person(s) to be examined,
— the questions to be put to the person(s) to be examined or a statement of the facts about which he is (they are) to be examined,
— where appropriate, a reference to a right to refuse to testify under the law of the Member State of the requesting court,
— any requirement that the examination is to be carried out under oath or affirmation in lieu thereof, and any special form to be used,
— where appropriate, any other information that the requesting court deems necessary;
(f) where the request is for any other form of taking of evidence, the documents or other objects to be inspected;
(g) where appropriate, any request pursuant to Article 10(3) and (4), and Articles 11 and 12 and any information necessary for the application thereof.
2. The request and all documents accompanying the request shall be exempted from authentication or any equivalent formality.

Part VI. Civil Procedure

3. Documents which the requesting court deems it necessary to enclose for the execution of the request shall be accompanied by a translation into the language in which the request was written.

Article 5. The request and communications pursuant to this Regulation shall be drawn up in the official language of the requested Member State or, if there are several official languages in that Member State, in the official language or one of the official languages of the place where the requested taking of evidence is to be performed, or in another language which the requested Member State has indicated it can accept. Each Member State shall indicate the official language or languages of the institutions of the European Community other than its own which is or are acceptable to it for completion of the forms.

Article 6. Requests and communications pursuant to this Regulation shall be transmitted by the swiftest possible means, which the requested Member State has indicated it can accept. The transmission may be carried out by any appropriate means, provided that the document received accurately reflects the content of the document forwarded and that all information in it is legible.

Section 2. Receipt of request

Article 7. 1. Within seven days of receipt of the request, the requested competent court shall send an acknowledgement of receipt to the requesting court using form B in the Annex. Where the request does not comply with the conditions laid down in Articles 5 and 6, the requested court shall enter a note to that effect in the acknowledgement of receipt.
2. Where the execution of a request made using form A in the Annex, which complies with the conditions laid down in Article 5, does not fall within the jurisdiction of the court to which it was transmitted, the latter shall forward the request to the competent court of its Member State and shall inform the requesting court thereof using form A in the Annex.

Article 8. 1. If a request cannot be executed because it does not contain all of the necessary information pursuant to Article 4, the requested court shall inform the requesting court thereof without delay and, at the latest, within 30 days of receipt of the request using form C in the Annex, and shall request it to send the missing information, which should be indicated as precisely as possible.
2. If a request cannot be executed because a deposit or advance is necessary in accordance with Article 18(3), the requested court shall inform the requesting court thereof without delay and, at the latest, within 30 days of receipt of the request using form C in the Annex and inform the requesting court how the deposit or advance should be made. The requested Court shall acknowledge receipt of the deposit or advance without delay, at the latest within 10 days of receipt of the deposit or the advance using form D.

Article 9. 1. If the requested court has noted on the acknowledgement of receipt pursuant to Article 7(1) that the request does not comply with the conditions laid down in Articles 5 and 6 or has informed the requesting court pursuant to Article 8 that the request cannot be executed because it does not contain all of the necessary information pursuant to Article 4, the time limit pursuant to Article 10 shall begin to run when the requested court received the request duly completed.
2. Where the requested court has asked for a deposit or advance in accordance with Article 18(3), this time limit shall begin to run when the deposit or the advance is made.

Section 3. Taking of evidence by the requested court

Article 10. 1. The requested court shall execute the request without delay and, at the latest, within 90 days of receipt of the request.
2. The requested court shall execute the request in accordance with the law of its Member State.
3. The requesting court may call for the request to be executed in accordance with a special procedure provided for by the law of its Member State, using form A in the Annex. The requested court shall comply with such a requirement unless this procedure is incompatible with the law of the Member State of the requested court or by reason of major practical difficulties. If the requested court does not comply with the requirement for one of these reasons it shall inform the requesting court using form E in the Annex.
4. The requesting court may ask the requested court to use communications technology at the performance of the taking of evidence, in particular by using videoconference and teleconference.
The requested court shall comply with such a requirement unless this is incompatible with the law of the Member State of the requested court or by reason of major practical difficulties.

If the requested court does not comply with the requirement for one of these reasons, it shall inform the requesting court, using form E in the Annex.

If there is no access to the technical means referred to above in the requesting or in the requested court, such means may be made available by the courts by mutual agreement.

Article 11. 1. If it is provided for by the law of the Member State of the requesting court, the parties and, if any, their representatives, have the right to be present at the performance of the taking of evidence by the requested court.

2. The requesting court shall, in its request, inform the requested court that the parties and, if any, their representatives, will be present and, where appropriate, that their participation is requested, using form A in the Annex. This information may also be given at any other appropriate time.

3. If the participation of the parties and, if any, their representatives, is requested at the performance of the taking of evidence, the requested court shall determine, in accordance with Article 10, the conditions under which they may participate.

4. The requested court shall notify the parties and, if any, their representatives, of the time when, the place where, the proceedings will take place, and, where appropriate, the conditions under which they may participate, using form F in the Annex.

5. Paragraphs 1 to 4 shall not affect the possibility for the requested court of asking the parties and, if any their representatives, to be present at or to participate in the performance of the taking of evidence if that possibility is provided for by the law of its Member State.

Article 12. 1. If it is compatible with the law of the Member State of the requesting court, representatives of the requesting court have the right to be present in the performance of the taking of evidence by the requested court.

2. For the purpose of this Article, the term 'representative' shall include members of the judicial personnel designated by the requesting court, in accordance with the law of its Member State. The requesting court may also designate, in accordance with the law of its Member State, any other person, such as an expert.

3. The requesting court shall, in its request, inform the requested court that its representatives will be present and, where appropriate, that their participation is requested, using form A in the Annex. This information may also be given at any other appropriate time.

4. If the participation of the representatives of the requesting court is requested in the performance of the taking of evidence, the requested court shall determine, in accordance with Article 10, the conditions under which they may participate.

5. The requested court shall notify the requesting court, of the time when, and the place where, the proceedings will take place, and, where appropriate, the conditions under which the representatives may participate, using form F in the Annex.

Article 13. Where necessary, in executing a request the requested court shall apply the appropriate coercive measures in the instances and to the extent as are provided for by the law of the Member State of the requested court for the execution of a request made for the same purpose by its national authorities or one of the parties concerned.

Article 14. 1. A request for the hearing of a person shall not be executed when the person concerned claims the right to refuse to give evidence or to be prohibited from giving evidence,

(a) under the law of the Member State of the requested court; or

(b) under the law of the Member State of the requesting court, and such right has been specified in the request, or, if need be, at the instance of the requested court, has been confirmed by the requesting court.

2. In addition to the grounds referred to in paragraph 1, the execution of a request may be refused only if:

(a) the request does not fall within the scope of this Regulation as set out in Article 1; or

(b) the execution of the request under the law of the Member State of the requested court does not fall within the functions of the judiciary; or

(c) the requesting court does not comply with the request of the requested court to complete the request pursuant to Article 8 within 30 days after the requested court asked it to do so; or

(d) a deposit or advance asked for in accordance with Article 18(3) is not made within 60 days after the requested court asked for such a deposit or advance.

3. Execution may not be refused by the requested court solely on the ground that under the law of its Member State a court of that Member State has exclusive jurisdiction over the subject matter of the action or that the law of that Member State would not admit the right of action on it.

4. If execution of the request is refused on one of the grounds referred to in paragraph 2, the requested court shall notify the requesting court thereof within 60 days of receipt of the request by the requested court using form H in the Annex.

Article 15. If the requested court is not in a position to execute the request within 90 days of receipt, it shall inform the requesting court thereof, using form G in the Annex. When it does so, the grounds for the delay shall be given as well as the estimated time that the requested court expects it will need to execute the request.

Article 16. The requested court shall send without delay to the requesting court the documents establishing the execution of the request and, where appropriate, return the documents received from the requesting court. The documents shall be accompanied by a confirmation of execution using form H in the Annex.

Section 4. Direct taking of evidence by the requesting court

Article 17. 1. Where a court requests to take evidence directly in another Member State, it shall submit a request to the central body or the competent authority referred to in Article 3(3) in that State, using form I in the Annex.
2. Direct taking of evidence may only take place if it can be performed on a voluntary basis without the need for coercive measures.
Where the direct taking of evidence implies that a person shall be heard, the requesting court shall inform that person that the performance shall take place on a voluntary basis.
3. The taking of evidence shall be performed by a member of the judicial personnel or by any other person such as an expert, who will be designated, in accordance with the law of the Member State of the requesting court.
4. Within 30 days of receiving the request, the central body or the competent authority of the requested Member State shall inform the requesting court if the request is accepted and, if necessary, under what conditions according to the law of its Member State such performance is to be carried out, using form J.
In particular, the central body or the competent authority may assign a court of its Member State to take part in the performance of the taking of evidence in order to ensure the proper application of this Article and the conditions that have been set out.
The central body or the competent authority shall encourage the use of communications technology, such as videoconferences and teleconferences.
5. The central body or the competent authority may refuse direct taking of evidence only if:
(a) the request does not fall within the scope of this Regulation as set out in Article 1;
(b) the request does not contain all of the necessary information pursuant to Article 4; or
(c) the direct taking of evidence requested is contrary to fundamental principles of law in its Member State.
6. Without prejudice to the conditions laid down in accordance with paragraph 4, the requesting court shall execute the request in accordance with the law of its Member State.

Section 5. Costs

Article 18. 1. The execution of the request, in accordance with Article 10, shall not give rise to a claim for any reimbursement of taxes or costs.
2. Nevertheless, if the requested court so requires, the requesting court shall ensure the reimbursement, without delay, of:
— the fees paid to experts and interpreters, and
— the costs occasioned by the application of Article 10(3) and(4).
The duty for the parties to bear these fees or costs shall be governed by the law of the Member State of the requesting court.
3. Where the opinion of an expert is required, the requested court may, before executing the request, ask the requesting court for an adequate deposit or advance towards the requested costs. In all other cases, a deposit or advance shall not be a condition for the execution of a request.
The deposit or advance shall be made by the parties if that is provided for by the law of the Member State of the requesting court.

CHAPTER III. FINAL PROVISIONS

Article 19. 1. The Commission shall draw up and regularly update a manual, which shall also be available electronically, containing the information provided by the Member States in accordance with Article 22 and the agreements or arrangements in force, according to Article 21.

2. The updating or making of technical amendments to the standard forms set out in the Annex shall be carried out by the Commission. Those measures, designed to amend non-essential elements of this Regulation, shall be adopted in accordance with the regulatory procedure with scrutiny referred to in Article 20(2).

Article 20. 1. The Commission shall be assisted by a committee.
2. Where reference is made to this paragraph, Article 5a(1) to (4) and Article 7 of Decision 1999/468/EC shall apply, having regard to the provisions of Article 8 thereof.

Article 21. 1. This Regulation shall, in relation to matters to which it applies, prevail over other provisions contained in bilateral or multilateral agreements or arrangements concluded by the Member States and in particular the Hague Convention of 1 March 1954 on Civil Procedure and the Hague Convention of 18 March 1970 on the Taking of Evidence Abroad in Civil or Commercial Matters, in relations between the Member States party thereto.
2. This Regulation shall not preclude Member States from maintaining or concluding agreements or arrangements between two or more of them to further facilitate the taking of evidence, provided that they are compatible with this Regulation.
3. Member States shall send to the Commission:
(a) by 1 July 2003, a copy of the agreements or arrangements maintained between the Member States referred to in paragraph 2;
(b) a copy of the agreements or arrangements concluded between the Member States referred to in paragraph 2 as well as drafts of such agreements or arrangements which they intend to adopt; and
(c) any denunciation of, or amendments to, these agreements or arrangements.

Article 22. By 1 July 2003 each Member State shall communicate to the Commission the following:
(a) the list pursuant to Article 2(2) indicating the territorial and, where appropriate, the special jurisdiction of the courts;
(b) the names and addresses of the central bodies and competent authorities pursuant to Article 3, indicating their territorial jurisdiction;
(c) the technical means for the receipt of requests available to the courts on the list pursuant to Article 2(2);
(d) the languages accepted for the requests as referred to in Article 5.
Member States shall inform the Commission of any subsequent changes to this information.

Article 23. No later than 1 January 2007, and every five years thereafter, the Commission shall present to the European Parliament, the Council and the Economic and Social Committee a report on the application of this Regulation, paying special attention to the practical application of Article 3(1)(c) and 3, and Articles 17 and 18.

Article 24. 1. This Regulation shall enter into force on 1 July 2001.
2. This Regulation shall apply from 1 January 2004, except for Articles 19, 21 and 22, which shall apply from 1 July 2001.
This Regulation shall be binding in its entirety and directly applicable in the Member States in accordance with the Treaty establishing the European Community.

[The Annex is omitted.]

Regulation (EC) No 805/2004 of the European Parliament and of the Council of 21 April 2004 creating a European Enforcement Order for uncontested claims.

[The Preamble is omitted.]

CHAPTER I. SUBJECT MATTER, SCOPE AND DEFINITIONS

Article 1. The purpose of this Regulation is to create a European Enforcement Order for uncontested claims to permit, by laying down minimum standards, the free circulation of judgments, court settlements and authentic instruments throughout all Member States without any intermediate proceedings needing to be brought in the Member State of enforcement prior to recognition and enforcement.

Article 2. 1. This Regulation shall apply in civil and commercial matters, whatever the nature of the court or tribunal. It shall not extend, in particular, to revenue, customs or administrative matters or the liability of the State for acts and omissions in the exercise of State authority ('acta iure imperii').
2. This Regulation shall not apply to:
(a) the status or legal capacity of natural persons, rights in property arising out of a matrimonial relationship, wills and succession;
(b) bankruptcy, proceedings relating to the winding-up of insolvent companies or other legal persons, judicial arrangements, compositions and analogous proceedings;
(c) social security;
(d) arbitration.
3. In this Regulation, the term 'Member State' shall mean Member States with the exception of Denmark.

Article 3. 1. This Regulation shall apply to judgments, court settlements and authentic instruments on uncontested claims.
A claim shall be regarded as uncontested if:
(a) the debtor has expressly agreed to it by admission or by means of a settlement which has been approved by a court or concluded before a court in the course of proceedings; or
(b) the debtor has never objected to it, in compliance with the relevant procedural requirements under the law of the Member State of origin, in the course of the court proceedings; or
(c) the debtor has not appeared or been represented at a court hearing regarding that claim after having initially objected to the claim in the course of the court proceedings, provided that such conduct amounts to a tacit admission of the claim or of the facts alleged by the creditor under the law of the Member State of origin; or
(d) the debtor has expressly agreed to it in an authentic instrument.
2. This Regulation shall also apply to decisions delivered following challenges to judgments, court settlements or authentic instruments certified as European Enforcement Orders.

Article 4. For the purposes of this Regulation, the following definitions shall apply:
1. 'judgment': any judgment given by a court or tribunal of a Member State, whatever the judgment may be called, including a decree, order, decision or writ of execution, as well as the determination of costs or expenses by an officer of the court;
2. 'claim': a claim for payment of a specific sum of money that has fallen due or for which the due date is indicated in the judgment, court settlement or authentic instrument;
3. 'authentic instrument':
(a) a document which has been formally drawn up or registered as an authentic instrument, and the authenticity of which:
(i) relates to the signature and the content of the instrument; and
(ii) has been established by a public authority or other authority empowered for that purpose by the Member State in which it originates;
or
b) an arrangement relating to maintenance obligations concluded with administrative authorities or authenticated by them;
4. 'Member State of origin': the Member State in which the judgment has been given, the court settlement has been approved or concluded or the authentic instrument has been drawn up or registered, and is to be certified as a European Enforcement Order;

5. 'Member State of enforcement': the Member State in which enforcement of the judgment, court settlement or authentic instrument certified as a European Enforcement Order is sought;
6. 'court of origin': the court or tribunal seised of the proceedings at the time of fulfilment of the conditions set out in Article 3(1)(a), (b) or (c);
7. in Sweden, in summary proceedings concerning orders to pay (betalningsföreläggande), the expression 'court' includes the Swedish enforcement service (kronofogdemyndighet).

CHAPTER II. EUROPEAN ENFORCEMENT ORDER

Article 5. A judgment which has been certified as a European Enforcement Order in the Member State of origin shall be recognised and enforced in the other Member States without the need for a declaration of enforceability and without any possibility of opposing its recognition.

Article 6. 1. A judgment on an uncontested claim delivered in a Member State shall, upon application at any time to the court of origin, be certified as a European Enforcement Order if:
(a) the judgment is enforceable in the Member State of origin; and
(b) the judgment does not conflict with the rules on jurisdiction as laid down in sections 3 and 6 of Chapter II of Regulation (EC) No 44/2001; and
(c) the court proceedings in the Member State of origin met the requirements as set out in Chapter III where a claim is uncontested within the meaning of Article 3(1)(b) or (c); and
(d) the judgment was given in the Member State of the debtor's domicile within the meaning of Article 59 of Regulation (EC) No 44/2001, in cases where
— a claim is uncontested within the meaning of Article 3(1)(b) or (c); and
— it relates to a contract concluded by a person, the consumer, for a purpose which can be regarded as being outside his trade or profession; and
— the debtor is the consumer.
2. Where a judgment certified as a European Enforcement Order has ceased to be enforceable or its enforceability has been suspended or limited, a certificate indicating the lack or limitation of enforceability shall, upon application at any time to the court of origin, be issued, using the standard form in Annex IV.
3. Without prejudice to Article 12(2), where a decision has been delivered following a challenge to a judgment certified as a European Enforcement Order in accordance with paragraph 1 of this Article, a replacement certificate shall, upon application at any time, be issued, using the standard form in Annex V, if that decision on the challenge is enforceable in the Member State of origin.

Article 7. Where a judgment includes an enforceable decision on the amount of costs related to the court proceedings, including the interest rates, it shall be certified as a European Enforcement Order also with regard to the costs unless the debtor has specifically objected to his obligation to bear such costs in the course of the court proceedings, in accordance with the law of the Member State of origin.

Article 8. If only parts of the judgment meet the requirements of this Regulation, a partial European Enforcement Order certificate shall be issued for those parts.

Article 9. 1. The European Enforcement Order certificate shall be issued using the standard form in Annex I.
2. The European Enforcement Order certificate shall be issued in the language of the judgment.

Article 10. 1. The European Enforcement Order certificate shall, upon application to the court of origin, be
(a) rectified where, due to a material error, there is a discrepancy between the judgment and the certificate;
(b) withdrawn where it was clearly wrongly granted, having regard to the requirements laid down in this Regulation.
2. The law of the Member State of origin shall apply to the rectification or withdrawal of the European Enforcement Order certificate.
3. An application for the rectification or withdrawal of a European Enforcement Order certificate may be made using the standard form in Annex VI.
4. No appeal shall lie against the issuing of a European Enforcement Order certificate.

Article 11. The European Enforcement Order certificate shall take effect only within the limits of the enforceability of the judgment.

CHAPTER III. MINIMUM STANDARDS FOR UNCONTESTED CLAIMS PROCEDURES

Article 12. 1. A judgment on a claim that is uncontested within the meaning of Article 3(1)(b) or (c) can be certified as a European Enforcement Order only if the court proceedings in the Member State of origin met the procedural requirements as set out in this Chapter.

2. The same requirements shall apply to the issuing of a European Enforcement Order certificate or a replacement certificate within the meaning of Article 6(3) for a decision following a challenge to a judgment where, at the time of that decision, the conditions of Article 3(1)(b) or (c) are fulfilled.

Article 13. 1. The document instituting the proceedings or an equivalent document may have been served on the debtor by one of the following methods:
(a) personal service attested by an acknowledgement of receipt, including the date of receipt, which is signed by the debtor;
(b) personal service attested by a document signed by the competent person who effected the service stating that the debtor has received the document or refused to receive it without any legal justification, and the date of the service;
(c) postal service attested by an acknowledgement of receipt including the date of receipt, which is signed and returned by the debtor;
(d) service by electronic means such as fax or e-mail, attested by an acknowledgement of receipt including the date of receipt, which is signed and returned by the debtor.

2. Any summons to a court hearing may have been served on the debtor in compliance with paragraph 1 or orally in a previous court hearing on the same claim and stated in the minutes of that previous court hearing.

Article 14. 1. Service of the document instituting the proceedings or an equivalent document and any summons to a court hearing on the debtor may also have been effected by one of the following methods:
(a) personal service at the debtor's personal address on persons who are living in the same household as the debtor or are employed there;
(b) in the case of a self-employed debtor or a legal person, personal service at the debtor's business premises on persons who are employed by the debtor;
(c) deposit of the document in the debtor's mailbox;
(d) deposit of the document at a post office or with competent public authorities and the placing in the debtor's mailbox of written notification of that deposit, provided that the written notification clearly states the character of the document as a court document or the legal effect of the notification as effecting service and setting in motion the running of time for the purposes of time limits;
(e) postal service without proof pursuant to paragraph 3 where the debtor has his address in the Member State of origin;
(f) electronic means attested by an automatic confirmation of delivery, provided that the debtor has expressly accepted this method of service in advance.

2. For the purposes of this Regulation, service under paragraph 1 is not admissible if the debtor's address is not known with certainty.

3. Service pursuant to paragraph 1, (a) to (d), shall be attested by:
(a) a document signed by the competent person who effected the service, indicating:
(i) the method of service used; and
(ii) the date of service; and
(iii) where the document has been served on a person other than the debtor, the name of that person and his relation to the debtor,
or
(b) an acknowledgement of receipt by the person served, for the purposes of paragraphs 1(a) and (b).

Article 15. Service pursuant to Articles 13 or 14 may also have been effected on a debtor's representative.

Article 16. In order to ensure that the debtor was provided with due information about the claim, the document instituting the proceedings or the equivalent document must have contained the following:
(a) the names and the addresses of the parties;
(b) the amount of the claim;
(c) if interest on the claim is sought, the interest rate and the period for which interest is sought unless statutory interest is automatically added to the principal under the law of the Member State of origin;
(d) a statement of the reason for the claim.

Article 17. The following must have been clearly stated in or together with the document instituting the proceedings, the equivalent document or any summons to a court hearing:
(a) the procedural requirements for contesting the claim, including the time limit for contesting the claim in writing or the time for the court hearing, as applicable, the name and the address of the institution to which to respond or before which to appear, as applicable, and whether it is mandatory to be represented by a lawyer;
(b) the consequences of an absence of objection or default of appearance, in particular, where applicable, the possibility that a judgment may be given or enforced against the debtor and the liability for costs related to the court proceedings.

Article 18. 1. If the proceedings in the Member State of origin did not meet the procedural requirements as set out in Articles 13 to 17, such non-compliance shall be cured and a judgment may be certified as a European Enforcement Order if:
(a) the judgment has been served on the debtor in compliance with the requirements pursuant to Article 13 or Article 14; and
(b) it was possible for the debtor to challenge the judgment by means of a full review and the debtor has been duly informed in or together with the judgment about the procedural requirements for such a challenge, including the name and address of the institution with which it must be lodged and, where applicable, the time limit for so doing; and
(c) the debtor has failed to challenge the judgment in compliance with the relevant procedural requirements.
2. If the proceedings in the Member State of origin did not comply with the procedural requirements as set out in Article 13 or Article 14, such non-compliance shall be cured if it is proved by the conduct of the debtor in the court proceedings that he has personally received the document to be served in sufficient time to arrange for his defence.

Article 19. 1. Further to Articles 13 to 18, a judgment can only be certified as a European Enforcement Order if the debtor is entitled, under the law of the Member State of origin, to apply for a review of the judgment where:
(a) (i) the document instituting the proceedings or an equivalent document or, where applicable, the summons to a court hearing, was served by one of the methods provided for in Article 14; and
(ii) service was not effected in sufficient time to enable him to arrange for his defence, without any fault on his part; or
(b) the debtor was prevented from objecting to the claim by reason of force majeure, or due to extraordinary circumstances without any fault on his part,
provided in either case that he acts promptly.
2. This Article is without prejudice to the possibility for Member States to grant access to a review of the judgment under more generous conditions than those mentioned in paragraph 1.

CHAPTER IV. ENFORCEMENT

Article 20. 1. Without prejudice to the provisions of this Chapter, the enforcement procedures shall be governed by the law of the Member State of enforcement.
A judgment certified as a European Enforcement Order shall be enforced under the same conditions as a judgment handed down in the Member State of enforcement.
2. The creditor shall be required to provide the competent enforcement authorities of the Member State of enforcement with:
(a) a copy of the judgment which satisfies the conditions necessary to establish its authenticity; and
(b) a copy of the European Enforcement Order certificate which satisfies the conditions necessary to establish its authenticity; and
(c) where necessary, a transcription of the European Enforcement Order certificate or a translation thereof into the official language of the Member State of enforcement or, if there are several official languages in that Member State, the official language or one of the official languages of court proceedings of the place where enforcement is sought, in conformity with the law of that Member State, or into another language that the Member State of enforcement has indicated it can accept. Each Member State may indicate the official language or languages of the institutions of the European Community other than its own which it can accept for the completion of the certificate. The translation shall be certified by a person qualified to do so in one of the Member States.
3. No security, bond or deposit, however described, shall be required of a party who in one Member State applies for enforcement of a judgment certified as a European Enforcement Order in another Member State on the ground that he is a foreign national or that he is not domiciled or resident in the Member State of enforcement.

Article 21. 1. Enforcement shall, upon application by the debtor, be refused by the competent court in the Member State of enforcement if the judgment certified as a European Enforcement Order is irreconcilable with an earlier judgment given in any Member State or in a third country, provided that:
(a) the earlier judgment involved the same cause of action and was between the same parties; and
(b) the earlier judgment was given in the Member State of enforcement or fulfils the conditions necessary for its recognition in the Member State of enforcement; and
(c) the irreconcilability was not and could not have been raised as an objection in the court proceedings in the Member State of origin.
2. Under no circumstances may the judgment or its certification as a European Enforcement Order be reviewed as to their substance in the Member State of enforcement.

Article 22. This Regulation shall not affect agreements by which Member States undertook, prior to the entry into force of Regulation (EC) No 44/2001, pursuant to Article 59 of the Brussels Convention on jurisdiction and the enforcement of judgments in civil and commercial matters, not to recognise judgments given, in particular in other Contracting States to that Convention, against defendants domiciled or habitually resident in a third country where, in cases provided for in Article 4 of that Convention, the judgment could only be founded on a ground of jurisdiction specified in the second paragraph of Article 3 of that Convention.

Article 23. Where the debtor has
— challenged a judgment certified as a European Enforcement Order, including an application for review within the meaning of Article 19, or
— applied for the rectification or withdrawal of a European Enforcement Order certificate in accordance with Article 10,
the competent court or authority in the Member State of enforcement may, upon application by the debtor:
(a) limit the enforcement proceedings to protective measures; or
(b) make enforcement conditional on the provision of such security as it shall determine; or
(c) under exceptional circumstances, stay the enforcement proceedings.

CHAPTER V. COURT SETTLEMENTS AND AUTHENTIC INSTRUMENTS

Article 24. 1. A settlement concerning a claim within the meaning of Article 4(2) which has been approved by a court or concluded before a court in the course of proceedings and is enforceable in the Member State in which it was approved or concluded shall, upon application to the court that approved it or before which it was concluded, be certified as a European Enforcement Order using the standard form in Annex II.
2. A settlement which has been certified as a European Enforcement Order in the Member State of origin shall be enforced in the other Member States without the need for a declaration of enforceability and without any possibility of opposing its enforceability.
3. The provisions of Chapter II, with the exception of Articles 5, 6(1) and 9(1), and of Chapter IV, with the exception of Articles 21(1) and 22, shall apply as appropriate.

Article 25. 1. An authentic instrument concerning a claim within the meaning of Article 4(2) which is enforceable in one Member State shall, upon application to the authority designated by the Member State of origin, be certified as a European Enforcement Order, using the standard form in Annex III.
2. An authentic instrument which has been certified as a European Enforcement Order in the Member State of origin shall be enforced in the other Member States without the need for a declaration of enforceability and without any possibility of opposing its enforceability.
3. The provisions of Chapter II, with the exception of Articles 5, 6(1) and 9(1), and of Chapter IV, with the exception of Articles 21(1) and 22, shall apply as appropriate.

CHAPTER VI. TRANSITIONAL PROVISION

Article 26. This Regulation shall apply only to judgments given, to court settlements approved or concluded and to documents formally drawn up or registered as authentic instruments after the entry into force of this Regulation.

CHAPTER VII. RELATIONSHIP WITH OTHER COMMUNITY INSTRUMENTS

Article 27. This Regulation shall not affect the possibility of seeking recognition and enforcement, in accordance with Regulation (EC) No 44/2001, of a judgment, a court settlement or an authentic instrument on an uncontested claim.

Article 28. This Regulation shall not affect the application of Regulation (EC) No 1348/2000.

CHAPTER VIII. GENERAL AND FINAL PROVISIONS

Article 29. The Member States shall cooperate to provide the general public and professional circles with information on:
(a) the methods and procedures of enforcement in the Member States; and
(b) the competent authorities for enforcement in the Member States,
in particular via the European Judicial Network in civil and commercial matters established in accordance with Decision 2001/470/EC (9).

Article 30. 1. The Member States shall notify the Commission of:
(a) the procedures for rectification and withdrawal referred to in Article 10(2) and for review referred to in Article 19(1);
(b) the languages accepted pursuant to Article 20(2)(c);
(c) the lists of the authorities referred to in Article 25;
and any subsequent changes thereof.
2. The Commission shall make the information notified in accordance with paragraph 1 publicly available through publication in the Official Journal of the European Union and through any other appropriate means.

Article 31. The Commission shall amend the standard forms set out in the Annexes. Those measures, designed to amend non-essential elements of this Regulation, shall be adopted in accordance with the regulatory procedure with scrutiny referred to in Article 32(2).

Article 32. 1. The Commission shall be assisted by the committee referred to in Article 75 of Regulation (EC) No 44/2001.
2. Where reference is made to this paragraph, Article 5a(1) to (4) and Article 7 of Decision 1999/468/EC shall apply, having regard to the provisions of Article 8 thereof.

Article 33. This Regulation shall enter into force on 21 January 2005.
It shall apply from 21 October 2005, with the exception of Articles 30, 31 and 32, which shall apply from 21 January 2005.
This Regulation shall be binding in its entirety and directly applicable in the Member States in accordance with the Treaty establishing the European Community.

[The Annex is omitted.]

Regulation (EC) No 1896/2006 of the European Parliament and of the Council of 12 December 2006 creating a European order for payment procedure.

[The Preamble is omitted.]

Article 1. 1. The purpose of this Regulation is:
(a) to simplify, speed up and reduce the costs of litigation in cross-border cases concerning uncontested pecuniary claims by creating a European order for payment procedure; and
(b) to permit the free circulation of European orders for payment throughout the Member States by laying down minimum standards, compliance with which renders unnecessary any intermediate proceedings in the Member State of enforcement prior to recognition and enforcement.
2. This Regulation shall not prevent a claimant from pursuing a claim within the meaning of Article 4 by making use of another procedure available under the law of a Member State or under Community law.

Article 2. 1. This Regulation shall apply to civil and commercial matters in cross-border cases, whatever the nature of the court or tribunal. It shall not extend, in particular, to revenue, customs or administrative matters or the liability of the State for acts and omissions in the exercise of State authority ('acta iure imperii').
2. This Regulation shall not apply to:
(a) rights in property arising out of a matrimonial relationship, wills and succession;
(b) bankruptcy, proceedings relating to the winding-up of insolvent companies or other legal persons, judicial arrangements, compositions and analogous proceedings;
(c) social security;
(d) claims arising from non-contractual obligations, unless:
(i) they have been the subject of an agreement between the parties or there has been an admission of debt, or
(ii) they relate to liquidated debts arising from joint ownership of property.
3. In this Regulation, the term 'Member State' shall mean Member States with the exception of Denmark.

Article 3. 1. For the purposes of this Regulation, a cross-border case is one in which at least one of the parties is domiciled or habitually resident in a Member State other than the Member State of the court seised.
2. Domicile shall be determined in accordance with Articles 59 and 60 of Council Regulation (EC) No 44/2001 of 22 December 2000 on jurisdiction and the recognition and enforcement of judgments in civil and commercial matters.
3. The relevant moment for determining whether there is a cross-border case shall be the time when the application for a European order for payment is submitted in accordance with this Regulation.

Article 4. The European order for payment procedure shall be established for the collection of pecuniary claims for a specific amount that have fallen due at the time when the application for a European order for payment is submitted.

Article 5. For the purposes of this Regulation, the following definitions shall apply:
1) 'Member State of origin' means the Member State in which a European order for payment is issued;
2) 'Member State of enforcement' means the Member State in which enforcement of a European order for payment is sought;
3) 'court' means any authority in a Member State with competence regarding European orders for payment or any other related matters;
4) 'court of origin' means the court which issues a European order for payment.

Article 6. 1. For the purposes of applying this Regulation, jurisdiction shall be determined in accordance with the relevant rules of Community law, in particular Regulation (EC) No 44/2001.
2. However, if the claim relates to a contract concluded by a person, the consumer, for a purpose which can be regarded as being outside his trade or profession, and if the defendant is the consumer, only the courts in the Member State in which the defendant is domiciled, within the meaning of Article 59 of Regulation (EC) No 44/2001, shall have jurisdiction.

Article 7. 1. An application for a European order for payment shall be made using standard form A as set out in Annex I.
2. The application shall state:

PART VI. CIVIL PROCEDURE

(a) the names and addresses of the parties, and, where applicable, their representatives, and of the court to which the application is made;
(b) the amount of the claim, including the principal and, where applicable, interest, contractual penalties and costs;
(c) if interest on the claim is demanded, the interest rate and the period of time for which that interest is demanded unless statutory interest is automatically added to the principal under the law of the Member State of origin;
(d) the cause of the action, including a description of the circumstances invoked as the basis of the claim and, where applicable, of the interest demanded;
(e) a description of evidence supporting the claim;
(f) the grounds for jurisdiction; and
(g) the cross-border nature of the case within the meaning of Article 3.
3. In the application, the claimant shall declare that the information provided is true to the best of his knowledge and belief and shall acknowledge that any deliberate false statement could lead to appropriate penalties under the law of the Member State of origin.
4. In an Appendix to the application the claimant may indicate to the court that he opposes a transfer to ordinary civil proceedings within the meaning of Article 17 in the event of opposition by the defendant. This does not prevent the claimant from informing the court thereof subsequently, but in any event before the order is issued.
5. The application shall be submitted in paper form or by any other means of communication, including electronic, accepted by the Member State of origin and available to the court of origin.
6. The application shall be signed by the claimant or, where applicable, by his representative. Where the application is submitted in electronic form in accordance with paragraph 5, it shall be signed in accordance with Article 2(2) of Directive 1999/93/EC of the European Parliament and of the Council of 13 December 1999 on a Community framework for electronic signatures. The signature shall be recognised in the Member State of origin and may not be made subject to additional requirements.
6. However, such electronic signature shall not be required if and to the extent that an alternative electronic communications system exists in the courts of the Member State of origin which is available to a certain group of pre-registered authenticated users and which permits the identification of those users in a secure manner. Member States shall inform the Commission of such communications systems.

Article 8. The court seised of an application for a European order for payment shall examine, as soon as possible and on the basis of the application form, whether the requirements set out in Articles 2, 3, 4, 6 and 7 are met and whether the claim appears to be founded. This examination may take the form of an automated procedure.

Article 9. 1. If the requirements set out in Article 7 are not met and unless the claim is clearly unfounded or the application is inadmissible, the court shall give the claimant the opportunity to complete or rectify the application. The court shall use standard form B as set out in Annex II.
2. Where the court requests the claimant to complete or rectify the application, it shall specify a time limit it deems appropriate in the circumstances. The court may at its discretion extend that time limit.

Article 10. 1. If the requirements referred to in Article 8 are met for only part of the claim, the court shall inform the claimant to that effect, using standard form C as set out in Annex III. The claimant shall be invited to accept or refuse a proposal for a European order for payment for the amount specified by the court and shall be informed of the consequences of his decision. The claimant shall reply by returning standard form C sent by the court within a time limit specified by the court in accordance with Article 9(2).
2. If the claimant accepts the court's proposal, the court shall issue a European order for payment, in accordance with Article 12, for that part of the claim accepted by the claimant. The consequences with respect to the remaining part of the initial claim shall be governed by national law.
3. If the claimant fails to send his reply within the time limit specified by the court or refuses the court's proposal, the court shall reject the application for a European order for payment in its entirety.

Article 11. 1. The court shall reject the application if:
(a) the requirements set out in Articles 2, 3, 4, 6 and 7 are not met; or
(b) the claim is clearly unfounded; or
(c) the claimant fails to send his reply within the time limit specified by the court under Article 9(2); or
(d) the claimant fails to send his reply within the time limit specified by the court or refuses the court's proposal, in accordance with Article 10.
The claimant shall be informed of the grounds for the rejection by means of standard form D as set out in Annex IV.
2. There shall be no right of appeal against the rejection of the application.

3. The rejection of the application shall not prevent the claimant from pursuing the claim by means of a new application for a European order for payment or of any other procedure available under the law of a Member State.

Article 12. 1. If the requirements referred to in Article 8 are met, the court shall issue, as soon as possible and normally within 30 days of the lodging of the application, a European order for payment using standard form E as set out in Annex V.
1. The 30-day period shall not include the time taken by the claimant to complete, rectify or modify the application.
2. The European order for payment shall be issued together with a copy of the application form. It shall not comprise the information provided by the claimant in Appendices 1 and 2 to form A.
3. In the European order for payment, the defendant shall be advised of his options to:
(a) pay the amount indicated in the order to the claimant; or
(b) oppose the order by lodging with the court of origin a statement of opposition, to be sent within 30 days of service of the order on him.
4. In the European order for payment, the defendant shall be informed that:
(a) the order was issued solely on the basis of the information which was provided by the claimant and was not verified by the court;
(b) the order will become enforceable unless a statement of opposition has been lodged with the court in accordance with Article 16;
(c) where a statement of opposition is lodged, the proceedings shall continue before the competent courts of the Member State of origin in accordance with the rules of ordinary civil procedure unless the claimant has explicitly requested that the proceedings be terminated in that event.
5. The court shall ensure that the order is served on the defendant in accordance with national law by a method that shall meet the minimum standards laid down in Articles 13, 14 and 15.

Article 13. The European order for payment may be served on the defendant in accordance with the national law of the State in which the service is to be effected, by one of the following methods:
(a) personal service attested by an acknowledgement of receipt, including the date of receipt, which is signed by the defendant;
(b) personal service attested by a document signed by the competent person who effected the service stating that the defendant has received the document or refused to receive it without any legal justification, and the date of service;
(c) postal service attested by an acknowledgement of receipt, including the date of receipt, which is signed and returned by the defendant;
(d) service by electronic means such as fax or e-mail, attested by an acknowledgement of receipt, including the date of receipt, which is signed and returned by the defendant.

Article 14. 1. The European order for payment may also be served on the defendant in accordance with the national law of the State in which service is to be effected, by one of the following methods:
(a) personal service at the defendant's personal address on persons who are living in the same household as the defendant or are employed there;
(b) in the case of a self-employed defendant or a legal person, personal service at the defendant's business premises on persons who are employed by the defendant;
(c) deposit of the order in the defendant's mailbox;
(d) deposit of the order at a post office or with competent public authorities and the placing in the defendant's mailbox of written notification of that deposit, provided that the written notification clearly states the character of the document as a court document or the legal effect of the notification as effecting service and setting in motion the running of time for the purposes of time limits;
(e) postal service without proof pursuant to paragraph 3 where the defendant has his address in the Member State of origin;
(f) electronic means attested by an automatic confirmation of delivery, provided that the defendant has expressly accepted this method of service in advance.
2. For the purposes of this Regulation, service under paragraph 1 is not admissible if the defendant's address is not known with certainty.
3. Service pursuant to paragraph 1(a), (b), (c) and (d) shall be attested by:
(a) a document signed by the competent person who effected the service, indicating:
(i) the method of service used; and
(ii) the date of service; and

(iii) where the order has been served on a person other than the defendant, the name of that person and his relation to the defendant; or
(b) an acknowledgement of receipt by the person served, for the purposes of paragraphs (1)(a) and (b).

Article 15. Service pursuant to Articles 13 or 14 may also be effected on a defendant's representative.

Article 16. 1. The defendant may lodge a statement of opposition to the European order for payment with the court of origin using standard form F as set out in Annex VI, which shall be supplied to him together with the European order for payment.
2. The statement of opposition shall be sent within 30 days of service of the order on the defendant.
3. The defendant shall indicate in the statement of opposition that he contests the claim, without having to specify the reasons for this.
4. The statement of opposition shall be submitted in paper form or by any other means of communication, including electronic, accepted by the Member State of origin and available to the court of origin.
5. The statement of opposition shall be signed by the defendant or, where applicable, by his representative. Where the statement of opposition is submitted in electronic form in accordance with paragraph 4, it shall be signed in accordance with Article 2(2) of Directive 1999/93/EC. The signature shall be recognised in the Member State of origin and may not be made subject to additional requirements.
5. However, such electronic signature shall not be required if and to the extent that an alternative electronic communications system exists in the courts of the Member State of origin which is available to a certain group of pre-registered authenticated users and which permits the identification of those users in a secure manner. Member States shall inform the Commission of such communications systems.

Article 17. 1. If a statement of opposition is entered within the time limit laid down in Article 16(2), the proceedings shall continue before the competent courts of the Member State of origin in accordance with the rules of ordinary civil procedure unless the claimant has explicitly requested that the proceedings be terminated in that event.
Where the claimant has pursued his claim through the European order for payment procedure, nothing under national law shall prejudice his position in subsequent ordinary civil proceedings.
2. The transfer to ordinary civil proceedings within the meaning of paragraph 1 shall be governed by the law of the Member State of origin.
3. The claimant shall be informed whether the defendant has lodged a statement of opposition and of any transfer to ordinary civil proceedings.

Article 18. 1. If within the time limit laid down in Article 16(2), taking into account an appropriate period of time to allow a statement to arrive, no statement of opposition has been lodged with the court of origin, the court of origin shall without delay declare the European order for payment enforceable using standard form G as set out in Annex VII. The court shall verify the date of service.
2. Without prejudice to paragraph 1, the formal requirements for enforceability shall be governed by the law of the Member State of origin.
3. The court shall send the enforceable European order for payment to the claimant.

Article 19. A European order for payment which has become enforceable in the Member State of origin shall be recognised and enforced in the other Member States without the need for a declaration of enforceability and without any possibility of opposing its recognition.

Article 20. 1. After the expiry of the time limit laid down in Article 16(2) the defendant shall be entitled to apply for a review of the European order for payment before the competent court in the Member State of origin where:
(a) (i) the order for payment was served by one of the methods provided for in Article 14, and
(ii) service was not effected in sufficient time to enable him to arrange for his defence, without any fault on his part, or
(b) the defendant was prevented from objecting to the claim by reason of force majeure or due to extraordinary circumstances without any fault on his part,
provided in either case that he acts promptly.
2. After expiry of the time limit laid down in Article 16(2) the defendant shall also be entitled to apply for a review of the European order for payment before the competent court in the Member State of origin where the order for payment was clearly wrongly issued, having regard to the requirements laid down in this Regulation, or due to other exceptional circumstances.

3. If the court rejects the defendant's application on the basis that none of the grounds for review referred to in paragraphs 1 and 2 apply, the European order for payment shall remain in force.
3. If the court decides that the review is justified for one of the reasons laid down in paragraphs 1 and 2, the European order for payment shall be null and void.

Article 21. 1. Without prejudice to the provisions of this Regulation, enforcement procedures shall be governed by the law of the Member State of enforcement.
A European order for payment which has become enforceable shall be enforced under the same conditions as an enforceable decision issued in the Member State of enforcement.
2. For enforcement in another Member State, the claimant shall provide the competent enforcement authorities of that Member State with:
(a) a copy of the European order for payment, as declared enforceable by the court of origin, which satisfies the conditions necessary to establish its authenticity; and
(b) where necessary, a translation of the European order for payment into the official language of the Member State of enforcement or, if there are several official languages in that Member State, the official language or one of the official languages of court proceedings of the place where enforcement is sought, in conformity with the law of that Member State, or into another language that the Member State of enforcement has indicated it can accept. Each Member State may indicate the official language or languages of the institutions of the European Union other than its own which it can accept for the European order for payment. The translation shall be certified by a person qualified to do so in one of the Member States.
3. No security, bond or deposit, however described, shall be required of a claimant who in one Member State applies for enforcement of a European order for payment issued in another Member State on the ground that he is a foreign national or that he is not domiciled or resident in the Member State of enforcement.

Article 22. 1. Enforcement shall, upon application by the defendant, be refused by the competent court in the Member State of enforcement if the European order for payment is irreconcilable with an earlier decision or order previously given in any Member State or in a third country, provided that:
(a) the earlier decision or order involved the same cause of action between the same parties; and
(b) the earlier decision or order fulfils the conditions necessary for its recognition in the Member State of enforcement; and
(c) the irreconcilability could not have been raised as an objection in the court proceedings in the Member State of origin.
2. Enforcement shall, upon application, also be refused if and to the extent that the defendant has paid the claimant the amount awarded in the European order for payment.
3. Under no circumstances may the European order for payment be reviewed as to its substance in the Member State of enforcement.

Article 23. Where the defendant has applied for a review in accordance with Article 20, the competent court in the Member State of enforcement may, upon application by the defendant:
(a) limit the enforcement proceedings to protective measures; or
(b) make enforcement conditional on the provision of such security as it shall determine; or
(c) under exceptional circumstances, stay the enforcement proceedings.

Article 24. Representation by a lawyer or another legal professional shall not be mandatory:
(a) for the claimant in respect of the application for a European order for payment;
(b) for the defendant in respect of the statement of opposition to a European order for payment.

Article 25. 1. The combined court fees of a European order for payment procedure and of the ordinary civil proceedings that ensue in the event of a statement of opposition to a European order for payment in a Member State shall not exceed the court fees of ordinary civil proceedings without a preceding European order for payment procedure in that Member State.
2. For the purposes of this Regulation, court fees shall comprise fees and charges to be paid to the court, the amount of which is fixed in accordance with national law.

Article 26. All procedural issues not specifically dealt with in this Regulation shall be governed by national law.

Article 27. This Regulation shall not affect the application of Council Regulation (EC) No 1348/2000 of 29 May 2000 on the service in the Member States of judicial and extrajudicial documents in civil and commercial matters.

Article 28. Member States shall cooperate to provide the general public and professional circles with information on:
(a) costs of service of documents; and
(b) which authorities have competence with respect to enforcement for the purposes of applying Articles 21, 22 and 23,
in particular via the European Judicial Network in civil and commercial matters established in accordance with Council Decision 2001/470/EC.

Article 29. 1. By 12 June 2008, Member States shall communicate to the Commission:
(a) which courts have jurisdiction to issue a European order for payment;
(b) the review procedure and the competent courts for the purposes of the application of Article 20;
(c) the means of communication accepted for the purposes of the European order for payment procedure and available to the courts;
(d) languages accepted pursuant to Article 21(2)(b).
Member States shall apprise the Commission of any subsequent changes to this information.
2. The Commission shall make the information notified in accordance with paragraph 1 publicly available through publication in the Official Journal of the European Union and through any other appropriate means.

Article 30. The standard forms set out in the Annexes shall be updated or technically adjusted, ensuring full conformity with the provisions of this Regulation, in accordance with the procedure referred to in Article 31(2).

Article 31. 1. The Commission shall be assisted by the committee established by Article 75 of Regulation (EC) No 44/2001.
2. Where reference is made to this paragraph, Article 5a(1)-(4) and Article 7 of Decision 1999/468/EC shall apply, having regard to the provisions of Article 8 thereof.
3. The Committee shall adopt its Rules of Procedure.

Article 32. By 12 December 2013, the Commission shall present to the European Parliament, the Council and the European Economic and Social Committee a detailed report reviewing the operation of the European order for payment procedure. That report shall contain an assessment of the procedure as it has operated and an extended impact assessment for each Member State.
To that end, and in order to ensure that best practice in the European Union is duly taken into account and reflects the principles of better legislation, Member States shall provide the Commission with information relating to the cross-border operation of the European order for payment. This information shall cover court fees, speed of the procedure, efficiency, ease of use and the internal payment order procedures of the Member States.
The Commission's report shall be accompanied, if appropriate, by proposals for adaptation.

Article 33. This Regulation shall enter into force on the day following the date of its publication in the Official Journal of the European Union.
It shall apply from 12 December 2008, with the exception of Articles 28, 29, 30 and 31 which shall apply from 12 June 2008.
This Regulation shall be binding in its entirety and directly applicable in the Member States in accordance with the Treaty establishing the European Community.

[The Annex is omitted.]

Regulation (EC) No 861/2007 of the European Parliament and of the Council of 11 July 2007 establishing a European Small Claims Procedure.

[The Preamble is omitted.]

CHAPTER I. SUBJECT MATTER AND SCOPE

Article 1. This Regulation establishes a European procedure for small claims (hereinafter referred to as the "European Small Claims Procedure"), intended to simplify and speed up litigation concerning small claims in cross-border cases, and to reduce costs. The European Small Claims Procedure shall be available to litigants as an alternative to the procedures existing under the laws of the Member States.
This Regulation also eliminates the intermediate proceedings necessary to enable recognition and enforcement, in other Member States, of judgments given in one Member State in the European Small Claims Procedure.

Article 2. 1. This Regulation shall apply, in cross-border cases, to civil and commercial matters, whatever the nature of the court or tribunal, where the value of a claim does not exceed EUR 2000 at the time when the claim form is received by the court or tribunal with jurisdiction, excluding all interest, expenses and disbursements. It shall not extend, in particular, to revenue, customs or administrative matters or to the liability of the State for acts and omissions in the exercise of State authority (acta jure imperii).
2. This Regulation shall not apply to matters concerning:
(a) the status or legal capacity of natural persons;
(b) rights in property arising out of a matrimonial relationship, maintenance obligations, wills and succession;
(c) bankruptcy, proceedings relating to the winding-up of insolvent companies or other legal persons, judicial arrangements, compositions and analogous proceedings;
(d) social security;
(e) arbitration;
(f) employment law;
(g) tenancies of immovable property, with the exception of actions on monetary claims; or
(h) violations of privacy and of rights relating to personality, including defamation.
3. In this Regulation, the term "Member State" shall mean Member States with the exception of Denmark.

Article 3. 1. For the purposes of this Regulation, a cross-border case is one in which at least one of the parties is domiciled or habitually resident in a Member State other than the Member State of the court or tribunal seised.
2. Domicile shall be determined in accordance with Articles 59 and 60 of Regulation (EC) No 44/2001.
3. The relevant moment for determining whether there is a cross-border case is the date on which the claim form is received by the court or tribunal with jurisdiction.

CHAPTER II. THE EUROPEAN SMALL CLAIMS PROCEDURE

Article 4. 1. The claimant shall commence the European Small Claims Procedure by filling in standard claim Form A, as set out in Annex I, and lodging it with the court or tribunal with jurisdiction directly, by post or by any other means of communication, such as fax or e-mail, acceptable to the Member State in which the procedure is commenced. The claim form shall include a description of evidence supporting the claim and be accompanied, where appropriate, by any relevant supporting documents.
2. Member States shall inform the Commission which means of communication are acceptable to them. The Commission shall make such information publicly available.
3. Where a claim is outside the scope of this Regulation, the court or tribunal shall inform the claimant to that effect. Unless the claimant withdraws the claim, the court or tribunal shall proceed with it in accordance with the relevant procedural law applicable in the Member State in which the procedure is conducted.
4. Where the court or tribunal considers the information provided by the claimant to be inadequate or insufficiently clear or if the claim form is not filled in properly, it shall, unless the claim appears to be clearly unfounded or the application inadmissible, give the claimant the opportunity to complete or rectify the claim form or to supply supplementary information or documents or to withdraw the claim, within such period as it specifies. The court or tribunal shall use standard Form B, as set out in Annex II, for this purpose.
Where the claim appears to be clearly unfounded or the application inadmissible or where the claimant fails to complete or rectify the claim form within the time specified, the application shall be dismissed.

5. Member States shall ensure that the claim form is available at all courts and tribunals at which the European Small Claims Procedure can be commenced.

Article 5. 1. The European Small Claims Procedure shall be a written procedure. The court or tribunal shall hold an oral hearing if it considers this to be necessary or if a party so requests. The court or tribunal may refuse such a request if it considers that with regard to the circumstances of the case, an oral hearing is obviously not necessary for the fair conduct of the proceedings. The reasons for refusal shall be given in writing. The refusal may not be contested separately.
2. After receiving the properly filled in claim form, the court or tribunal shall fill in Part I of the standard answer Form C, as set out in Annex III.
A copy of the claim form, and, where applicable, of the supporting documents, together with the answer form thus filled in, shall be served on the defendant in accordance with Article 13. These documents shall be dispatched within 14 days of receiving the properly filled in claim form.
3. The defendant shall submit his response within 30 days of service of the claim form and answer form, by filling in Part II of standard answer Form C, accompanied, where appropriate, by any relevant supporting documents, and returning it to the court or tribunal, or in any other appropriate way not using the answer form.
4. Within 14 days of receipt of the response from the defendant, the court or tribunal shall dispatch a copy thereof, together with any relevant supporting documents to the claimant.
5. If, in his response, the defendant claims that the value of a non-monetary claim exceeds the limit set out in Article 2(1), the court or tribunal shall decide within 30 days of dispatching the response to the claimant, whether the claim is within the scope of this Regulation. Such decision may not be contested separately.
6. Any counterclaim, to be submitted using standard Form A, and any relevant supporting documents shall be served on the claimant in accordance with Article 13. Those documents shall be dispatched within 14 days of receipt.
The claimant shall have 30 days from service to respond to any counterclaim.
7. If the counterclaim exceeds the limit set out in Article 2(1), the claim and counterclaim shall not proceed in the European Small Claims Procedure but shall be dealt with in accordance with the relevant procedural law applicable in the Member State in which the procedure is conducted.
Articles 2 and 4 as well as paragraphs 3, 4 and 5 of this Article shall apply, mutatis mutandis, to counterclaims.

Article 6. 1. The claim form, the response, any counterclaim, any response to a counterclaim and any description of relevant supporting documents shall be submitted in the language or one of the languages of the court or tribunal.
2. If any other document received by the court or tribunal is not in the language in which the proceedings are conducted, the court or tribunal may require a translation of that document only if the translation appears to be necessary for giving the judgment.
3. Where a party has refused to accept a document because it is not in either of the following languages:
(a) the official language of the Member State addressed, or, if there are several official languages in that Member State, the official language or one of the official languages of the place where service is to be effected or to where the document is to be dispatched; or
(b) a language which the addressee understands,
the court or tribunal shall so inform the other party with a view to that party providing a translation of the document.

Article 7. 1. Within 30 days of receipt of the response from the defendant or the claimant within the time limits laid down in Article 5(3) or (6), the court or tribunal shall give a judgment, or:
(a) demand further details concerning the claim from the parties within a specified period of time, not exceeding 30 days;
(b) take evidence in accordance with Article 9; or
(c) summon the parties to an oral hearing to be held within 30 days of the summons.
2. The court or tribunal shall give the judgment either within 30 days of any oral hearing or after having received all information necessary for giving the judgment. The judgment shall be served on the parties in accordance with Article 13.
3. If the court or tribunal has not received an answer from the relevant party within the time limits laid down in Article 5(3) or (6), it shall give a judgment on the claim or counterclaim.

Article 8. The court or tribunal may hold an oral hearing through video conference or other communication technology if the technical means are available.

Article 9. 1. The court or tribunal shall determine the means of taking evidence and the extent of the evidence necessary for its judgment under the rules applicable to the admissibility of evidence. The court or tribunal may admit the taking of evidence through written statements of witnesses, experts or parties. It may also admit the taking of evidence through video conference or other communication technology if the technical means are available.
2. The court or tribunal may take expert evidence or oral testimony only if it is necessary for giving the judgment. In making its decision, the court or tribunal shall take costs into account.
3. The court or tribunal shall use the simplest and least burdensome method of taking evidence.

Article 10. Representation by a lawyer or another legal professional shall not be mandatory.

Article 11. The Member States shall ensure that the parties can receive practical assistance in filling in the forms.

Article 12. 1. The court or tribunal shall not require the parties to make any legal assessment of the claim.
2. If necessary, the court or tribunal shall inform the parties about procedural questions.
3. Whenever appropriate, the court or tribunal shall seek to reach a settlement between the parties.

Article 13. 1. Documents shall be served by postal service attested by an acknowledgement of receipt including the date of receipt.
2. If service in accordance with paragraph 1 is not possible, service may be effected by any of the methods provided for in Articles 13 or 14 of Regulation (EC) No 805/2004.

Article 14. 1. Where the court or tribunal sets a time limit, the party concerned shall be informed of the consequences of not complying with it.
2. The court or tribunal may extend the time limits provided for in Article 4(4), Article 5(3) and (6) and Article 7(1), in exceptional circumstances, if necessary in order to safeguard the rights of the parties.
3. If, in exceptional circumstances, it is not possible for the court or tribunal to respect the time limits provided for in Article 5(2) to (6) and Article 7, it shall take the steps required by those provisions as soon as possible.

Article 15. 1. The judgment shall be enforceable notwithstanding any possible appeal. The provision of a security shall not be required.
2. Article 23 shall also apply in the event that the judgment is to be enforced in the Member State where the judgment was given.

Article 16. The unsuccessful party shall bear the costs of the proceedings. However, the court or tribunal shall not award costs to the successful party to the extent that they were unnecessarily incurred or are disproportionate to the claim.

Article 17. 1. Member States shall inform the Commission whether an appeal is available under their procedural law against a judgment given in the European Small Claims Procedure and within what time limit such appeal shall be lodged. The Commission shall make that information publicly available.
2. Article 16 shall apply to any appeal.

Article 18. 1. The defendant shall be entitled to apply for a review of the judgment given in the European Small Claims Procedure before the court or tribunal with jurisdiction of the Member State where the judgment was given where:
(a) (i) the claim form or the summons to an oral hearing were served by a method without proof of receipt by him personally, as provided for in Article 14 of Regulation (EC) No 805/2004; and
(ii) service was not effected in sufficient time to enable him to arrange for his defence without any fault on his part, or
(b) the defendant was prevented from objecting to the claim by reason of force majeure, or due to extraordinary circumstances without any fault on his part,
provided in either case that he acts promptly.
2. If the court or tribunal rejects the review on the basis that none of the grounds referred to in paragraph 1 apply, the judgment shall remain in force.
If the court or tribunal decides that the review is justified for one of the reasons laid down in paragraph 1, the judgment given in the European Small Claims Procedure shall be null and void.

Article 19. Subject to the provisions of this Regulation, the European Small Claims Procedure shall be governed by the procedural law of the Member State in which the procedure is conducted.

CHAPTER III. RECOGNITION AND ENFORCEMENT IN ANOTHER MEMBER STATE

Article 20. 1. A judgment given in a Member State in the European Small Claims Procedure shall be recognised and enforced in another Member State without the need for a declaration of enforceability and without any possibility of opposing its recognition.
2. At the request of one of the parties, the court or tribunal shall issue a certificate concerning a judgment in the European Small Claims Procedure using standard Form D, as set out in Annex IV, at no extra cost.

Article 21. 1. Without prejudice to the provisions of this Chapter, the enforcement procedures shall be governed by the law of the Member State of enforcement.
Any judgment given in the European Small Claims Procedure shall be enforced under the same conditions as a judgment given in the Member State of enforcement.
2. The party seeking enforcement shall produce:
(a) a copy of the judgment which satisfies the conditions necessary to establish its authenticity; and
(b) a copy of the certificate referred to in Article 20(2) and, where necessary, the translation thereof into the official language of the Member State of enforcement or, if there are several official languages in that Member State, the official language or one of the official languages of court or tribunal proceedings of the place where enforcement is sought in conformity with the law of that Member State, or into another language that the Member State of enforcement has indicated it can accept. Each Member State may indicate the official language or languages of the institutions of the European Union other than its own which it can accept for the European Small Claims Procedure. The content of Form D shall be translated by a person qualified to make translations in one of the Member States.
3. The party seeking the enforcement of a judgment given in the European Small Claims Procedure in another Member State shall not be required to have:
(a) an authorised representative; or
(b) a postal address
in the Member State of enforcement, other than with agents having competence for the enforcement procedure.
4. No security, bond or deposit, however described, shall be required of a party who in one Member State applies for enforcement of a judgment given in the European Small Claims Procedure in another Member State on the ground that he is a foreign national or that he is not domiciled or resident in the Member State of enforcement.

Article 22. 1. Enforcement shall, upon application by the person against whom enforcement is sought, be refused by the court or tribunal with jurisdiction in the Member State of enforcement if the judgment given in the European Small Claims Procedure is irreconcilable with an earlier judgment given in any Member State or in a third country, provided that:
(a) the earlier judgment involved the same cause of action and was between the same parties;
(b) the earlier judgment was given in the Member State of enforcement or fulfils the conditions necessary for its recognition in the Member State of enforcement; and
(c) the irreconcilability was not and could not have been raised as an objection in the court or tribunal proceedings in the Member State where the judgment in the European Small Claims Procedure was given.
2. Under no circumstances may a judgment given in the European Small Claims Procedure be reviewed as to its substance in the Member State of enforcement.

Article 23. Where a party has challenged a judgment given in the European Small Claims Procedure or where such a challenge is still possible, or where a party has made an application for review within the meaning of Article 18, the court or tribunal with jurisdiction or the competent authority in the Member State of enforcement may, upon application by the party against whom enforcement is sought:
(a) limit the enforcement proceedings to protective measures;
(b) make enforcement conditional on the provision of such security as it shall determine; or
(c) under exceptional circumstances, stay the enforcement proceedings.

CHAPTER IV. FINAL PROVISIONS

Article 24. The Member States shall cooperate to provide the general public and professional circles with information on the European Small Claims Procedure, including costs, in particular by way of the European Judicial Network in Civil and Commercial Matters established in accordance with Decision 2001/470/EC.

Article 25. 1. By 1 January 2008 the Member States shall communicate to the Commission:
(a) which courts or tribunals have jurisdiction to give a judgment in the European Small Claims Procedure;
(b) which means of communication are accepted for the purposes of the European Small Claims Procedure and available to the courts or tribunals in accordance with Article 4(1);
(c) whether an appeal is available under their procedural law in accordance with Article 17 and with which court or tribunal this may be lodged;
(d) which languages are accepted pursuant to Article 21(2)(b); and
(e) which authorities have competence with respect to enforcement and which authorities have competence for the purposes of the application of Article 23.
Member States shall apprise the Commission of any subsequent changes to this information.
2. The Commission shall make the information notified in accordance with paragraph 1 publicly available through publication in the Official Journal of the European Union and through any other appropriate means.

Article 26. The measures designed to amend non-essential elements of this Regulation, including by supplementing it, relating to updates or technical amendments to the forms in the Annexes shall be adopted in accordance with the regulatory procedure with scrutiny referred to in Article 27(2).

Article 27. 1. The Commission shall be assisted by a Committee.
2. Where reference is made to this paragraph, Article 5a(1) to (4), and Article 7 of Decision 1999/468/EC shall apply, having regard to the provisions of Article 8 thereof.

Article 28. By 1 January 2014, the Commission shall present to the European Parliament, the Council and the European Economic and Social Committee a detailed report reviewing the operation of the European Small Claims Procedure, including the limit of the value of the claim referred to in Article 2(1). That report shall contain an assessment of the procedure as it has operated and an extended impact assessment for each Member State.
To that end and in order to ensure that best practice in the European Union is duly taken into account and reflects the principles of better legislation, Member States shall provide the Commission with information relating to the cross-border operation of the European Small Claims Procedure. This information shall cover court fees, speed of the procedure, efficiency, ease of use and the internal small claims procedures of the Member States.
The Commission's report shall be accompanied, if appropriate, by proposals for adaptation.

Article 29. This Regulation shall enter into force on the day following its publication in the Official Journal of the European Union.
It shall apply from 1 January 2009, with the exception of Article 25, which shall apply from 1 January 2008.
This Regulation shall be binding in its entirety and directly applicable in the Member States in accordance with the Treaty establishing the European Community.

[The Annex is omitted.]

Regulation (EC) No 1393/2007 of the European Parliament and of the Council of 13 November 2007 on the service in the Member States of judicial and extrajudicial documents in civil or commercial matters (service of documents), and repealing Council Regulation (EC) No 1348/2000.

[The Preamble is omitted.]

CHAPTER I. GENERAL PROVISIONS

Article 1. 1. This Regulation shall apply in civil and commercial matters where a judicial or extrajudicial document has to be transmitted from one Member State to another for service there. It shall not extend in particular to revenue, customs or administrative matters or to liability of the State for actions or omissions in the exercise of state authority (acta iure imperii).
2. This Regulation shall not apply where the address of the person to be served with the document is not known.
3. In this Regulation, the term "Member State" shall mean the Member States with the exception of Denmark.

Article 2. 1. Each Member State shall designate the public officers, authorities or other persons, hereinafter referred to as "transmitting agencies", competent for the transmission of judicial or extrajudicial documents to be served in another Member State.
2. Each Member State shall designate the public officers, authorities or other persons, hereinafter referred to as "receiving agencies", competent for the receipt of judicial or extrajudicial documents from another Member State.
3. A Member State may designate one transmitting agency and one receiving agency, or one agency to perform both functions. A federal State, a State in which several legal systems apply or a State with autonomous territorial units shall be free to designate more than one such agency. The designation shall have effect for a period of five years and may be renewed at five-year intervals.
4. Each Member State shall provide the Commission with the following information:
(a) the names and addresses of the receiving agencies referred to in paragraphs 2 and 3;
(b) the geographical areas in which they have jurisdiction;
(c) the means of receipt of documents available to them; and
(d) the languages that may be used for the completion of the standard form set out in Annex I.
Member States shall notify the Commission of any subsequent modification of such information.

Article 3. Each Member State shall designate a central body responsible for:
(a) supplying information to the transmitting agencies;
(b) seeking solutions to any difficulties which may arise during transmission of documents for service;
(c) forwarding, in exceptional cases, at the request of a transmitting agency, a request for service to the competent receiving agency.
A federal State, a State in which several legal systems apply or a State with autonomous territorial units shall be free to designate more than one central body.

CHAPTER II. JUDICIAL DOCUMENTS

Section 1. Transmission and service of judicial documents

Article 4. 1. Judicial documents shall be transmitted directly and as soon as possible between the agencies designated pursuant to Article 2.
2. The transmission of documents, requests, confirmations, receipts, certificates and any other papers between transmitting agencies and receiving agencies may be carried out by any appropriate means, provided that the content of the document received is true and faithful to that of the document forwarded and that all information in it is easily legible.
3. The document to be transmitted shall be accompanied by a request drawn up using the standard form set out in Annex I. The form shall be completed in the official language of the Member State addressed or, if there are several official languages in that Member State, the official language or one of the official languages of the place where service is to be effected, or in another language which that Member State has indicated it can accept. Each Member State shall indicate the official language or languages of the institutions of the European Union other than its own which is or are acceptable to it for completion of the form.
4. The documents and all papers that are transmitted shall be exempted from legalisation or any equivalent formality.

5. When the transmitting agency wishes a copy of the document to be returned together with the certificate referred to in Article 10, it shall send the document in duplicate.

Article 5. 1. The applicant shall be advised by the transmitting agency to which he forwards the document for transmission that the addressee may refuse to accept it if it is not in one of the languages provided for in Article 8.
2. The applicant shall bear any costs of translation prior to the transmission of the document, without prejudice to any possible subsequent decision by the court or competent authority on liability for such costs.

Article 6. 1. On receipt of a document, a receiving agency shall, as soon as possible and in any event within seven days of receipt, send a receipt to the transmitting agency by the swiftest possible means of transmission using the standard form set out in Annex I.
2. Where the request for service cannot be fulfilled on the basis of the information or documents transmitted, the receiving agency shall contact the transmitting agency by the swiftest possible means in order to secure the missing information or documents.
3. If the request for service is manifestly outside the scope of this Regulation or if non-compliance with the formal conditions required makes service impossible, the request and the documents transmitted shall be returned, on receipt, to the transmitting agency, together with the notice of return using the standard form set out in Annex I.
4. A receiving agency receiving a document for service but not having territorial jurisdiction to serve it shall forward it, as well as the request, to the receiving agency having territorial jurisdiction in the same Member State if the request complies with the conditions laid down in Article 4(3) and shall inform the transmitting agency accordingly using the standard form set out in Annex I. That receiving agency shall inform the transmitting agency when it receives the document, in the manner provided for in paragraph 1.

Article 7. 1. The receiving agency shall itself serve the document or have it served, either in accordance with the law of the Member State addressed or by a particular method requested by the transmitting agency, unless that method is incompatible with the law of that Member State.
2. The receiving agency shall take all necessary steps to effect the service of the document as soon as possible, and in any event within one month of receipt. If it has not been possible to effect service within one month of receipt, the receiving agency shall:
(a) immediately inform the transmitting agency by means of the certificate in the standard form set out in Annex I, which shall be drawn up under the conditions referred to in Article 10(2); and
(b) continue to take all necessary steps to effect the service of the document, unless indicated otherwise by the transmitting agency, where service seems to be possible within a reasonable period of time.

Article 8. 1. The receiving agency shall inform the addressee, using the standard form set out in Annex II, that he may refuse to accept the document to be served at the time of service or by returning the document to the receiving agency within one week if it is not written in, or accompanied by a translation into, either of the following languages:
(a) a language which the addressee understands; or
(b) the official language of the Member State addressed or, if there are several official languages in that Member State, the official language or one of the official languages of the place where service is to be effected.
2. Where the receiving agency is informed that the addressee refuses to accept the document in accordance with paragraph 1, it shall immediately inform the transmitting agency by means of the certificate provided for in Article 10 and return the request and the documents of which a translation is requested.
3. If the addressee has refused to accept the document pursuant to paragraph 1, the service of the document can be remedied through the service on the addressee in accordance with the provisions of this Regulation of the document accompanied by a translation into a language provided for in paragraph 1. In that case, the date of service of the document shall be the date on which the document accompanied by the translation is served in accordance with the law of the Member State addressed. However, where according to the law of a Member State, a document has to be served within a particular period, the date to be taken into account with respect to the applicant shall be the date of the service of the initial document determined pursuant to Article 9(2).
4. Paragraphs 1, 2 and 3 shall also apply to the means of transmission and service of judicial documents provided for in Section 2.
5. For the purposes of paragraph 1, the diplomatic or consular agents, where service is effected in accordance with Article 13, or the authority or person, where service is effected in accordance with Article 14, shall inform the addressee that he may refuse to accept the document and that any document refused must be sent to those agents or to that authority or person respectively.

Article 9. 1. Without prejudice to Article 8, the date of service of a document pursuant to Article 7 shall be the date on which it is served in accordance with the law of the Member State addressed.
2. However, where according to the law of a Member State a document has to be served within a particular period, the date to be taken into account with respect to the applicant shall be that determined by the law of that Member State.
3. Paragraphs 1 and 2 shall also apply to the means of transmission and service of judicial documents provided for in Section 2.

Article 10. 1. When the formalities concerning the service of the document have been completed, a certificate of completion of those formalities shall be drawn up in the standard form set out in Annex I and addressed to the transmitting agency, together with, where Article 4(5) applies, a copy of the document served.
2. The certificate shall be completed in the official language or one of the official languages of the Member State of origin or in another language which the Member State of origin has indicated that it can accept. Each Member State shall indicate the official language or languages of the institutions of the European Union other than its own which is or are acceptable to it for completion of the form.

Article 11. 1. The service of judicial documents coming from a Member State shall not give rise to any payment or reimbursement of taxes or costs for services rendered by the Member State addressed.
2. However, the applicant shall pay or reimburse the costs occasioned by:
(a) recourse to a judicial officer or to a person competent under the law of the Member State addressed;
(b) the use of a particular method of service.
Costs occasioned by recourse to a judicial officer or to a person competent under the law of the Member State addressed shall correspond to a single fixed fee laid down by that Member State in advance which respects the principles of proportionality and non-discrimination. Member States shall communicate such fixed fees to the Commission.

Section 2. Other means of transmission and service of judicial documents

Article 12. Each Member State shall be free, in exceptional circumstances, to use consular or diplomatic channels to forward judicial documents, for the purpose of service, to those agencies of another Member State which are designated pursuant to Articles 2 or 3.

Article 13. 1. Each Member State shall be free to effect service of judicial documents on persons residing in another Member State, without application of any compulsion, directly through its diplomatic or consular agents.
2. Any Member State may make it known, in accordance with Article 23(1), that it is opposed to such service within its territory, unless the documents are to be served on nationals of the Member State in which the documents originate.

Article 14. Each Member State shall be free to effect service of judicial documents directly by postal services on persons residing in another Member State by registered letter with acknowledgement of receipt or equivalent.

Article 15. Any person interested in a judicial proceeding may effect service of judicial documents directly through the judicial officers, officials or other competent persons of the Member State addressed, where such direct service is permitted under the law of that Member State.

CHAPTER III. EXTRAJUDICIAL DOCUMENTS

Article 16. Extrajudicial documents may be transmitted for service in another Member State in accordance with the provisions of this Regulation.

CHAPTER IV. FINAL PROVISIONS

Article 17. Measures designed to amend non-essential elements of this Regulation relating to the updating or to the making of technical amendments to the standard forms set out in Annexes I and II shall be adopted in accordance with the regulatory procedure with scrutiny referred to in Article 18(2).

Article 18. 1. The Commission shall be assisted by a committee.

2. Where reference is made to this paragraph, Article 5a(1) to (4), and Article 7 of Decision 1999/468/EC shall apply, having regard to the provisions of Article 8 thereof.

Article 19. 1. Where a writ of summons or an equivalent document has had to be transmitted to another Member State for the purpose of service under the provisions of this Regulation and the defendant has not appeared, judgment shall not be given until it is established that:
(a) the document was served by a method prescribed by the internal law of the Member State addressed for the service of documents in domestic actions upon persons who are within its territory; or
(b) the document was actually delivered to the defendant or to his residence by another method provided for by this Regulation;
and that in either of these cases the service or the delivery was effected in sufficient time to enable the defendant to defend.
2. Each Member State may make it known, in accordance with Article 23(1), that the judge, notwithstanding the provisions of paragraph 1, may give judgment even if no certificate of service or delivery has been received, if all the following conditions are fulfilled:
(a) the document was transmitted by one of the methods provided for in this Regulation;
(b) a period of time of not less than six months, considered adequate by the judge in the particular case, has elapsed since the date of the transmission of the document;
(c) no certificate of any kind has been received, even though every reasonable effort has been made to obtain it through the competent authorities or bodies of the Member State addressed.
3. Notwithstanding paragraphs 1 and 2, the judge may order, in case of urgency, any provisional or protective measures.
4. When a writ of summons or an equivalent document has had to be transmitted to another Member State for the purpose of service under the provisions of this Regulation and a judgment has been entered against a defendant who has not appeared, the judge shall have the power to relieve the defendant from the effects of the expiry of the time for appeal from the judgment if the following conditions are fulfilled:
(a) the defendant, without any fault on his part, did not have knowledge of the document in sufficient time to defend, or knowledge of the judgment in sufficient time to appeal; and
(b) the defendant has disclosed a prima facie defence to the action on the merits.
An application for relief may be filed only within a reasonable time after the defendant has knowledge of the judgment.
Each Member State may make it known, in accordance with Article 23(1), that such application will not be entertained if it is filed after the expiry of a time to be stated by it in that communication, but which shall in no case be less than one year following the date of the judgment.
5. Paragraph 4 shall not apply to judgments concerning the status or capacity of persons.

Article 20. 1. This Regulation shall, in relation to matters to which it applies, prevail over other provisions contained in bilateral or multilateral agreements or arrangements concluded by the Member States, and in particular Article IV of the Protocol to the Brussels Convention of 1968 and the Hague Convention of 15 November 1965.
2. This Regulation shall not preclude individual Member States from maintaining or concluding agreements or arrangements to expedite further or simplify the transmission of documents, provided that they are compatible with this Regulation.
3. Member States shall send to the Commission:
(a) a copy of the agreements or arrangements referred to in paragraph 2 concluded between the Member States as well as drafts of such agreements or arrangements which they intend to adopt; and
(b) any denunciation of, or amendments to, these agreements or arrangements.

Article 21. This Regulation shall not affect the application of Article 23 of the Convention on civil procedure of 17 July 1905, Article 24 of the Convention on civil procedure of 1 March 1954 or Article 13 of the Convention on international access to justice of 25 October 1980 between the Member States party to those Conventions.

Article 22. 1. Information, including in particular personal data, transmitted under this Regulation shall be used by the receiving agency only for the purpose for which it was transmitted.
2. Receiving agencies shall ensure the confidentiality of such information, in accordance with their national law.
3. Paragraphs 1 and 2 shall not affect national laws enabling data subjects to be informed of the use made of information transmitted under this Regulation.
4. This Regulation shall be without prejudice to Directives 95/46/EC and 2002/58/EC.

Article 23. 1. Member States shall communicate to the Commission the information referred to in Articles 2, 3, 4, 10, 11, 13, 15 and 19. Member States shall communicate to the Commission if, according to their law, a document has to be served within a particular period as referred to in Articles 8(3) and 9(2).
2. The Commission shall publish the information communicated in accordance with paragraph 1 in the Official Journal of the European Union with the exception of the addresses and other contact details of the agencies and of the central bodies and the geographical areas in which they have jurisdiction.
3. The Commission shall draw up and update regularly a manual containing the information referred to in paragraph 1, which shall be available electronically, in particular through the European Judicial Network in Civil and Commercial Matters.

Article 24. No later than 1 June 2011, and every five years thereafter, the Commission shall present to the European Parliament, the Council and the European Economic and Social Committee a report on the application of this Regulation, paying special attention to the effectiveness of the agencies designated pursuant to Article 2 and to the practical application of Article 3(c) and Article 9. The report shall be accompanied if need be by proposals for adaptations of this Regulation in line with the evolution of notification systems.

Article 25. 1. Regulation (EC) No 1348/2000 shall be repealed as from the date of application of this Regulation.
2. References made to the repealed Regulation shall be construed as being made to this Regulation and should be read in accordance with the correlation table in Annex III.

Article 26. This Regulation shall enter into force on the 20th day following its publication in the Official Journal of the European Union.
It shall apply from 13 November 2008 with the exception of Article 23 which shall apply from 13 August 2008.
This Regulation shall be binding in its entirety and directly applicable in the Member States in accordance with the Treaty establishing the European Community.

[The Annex is omitted.]

Directive 2008/52/EC of the European Parliament and of the Council of 21 May 2008 on certain aspects of mediation in civil and commercial matters.

[The Preamble is omitted.]

Article 1. 1. The objective of this Directive is to facilitate access to alternative dispute resolution and to promote the amicable settlement of disputes by encouraging the use of mediation and by ensuring a balanced relationship between mediation and judicial proceedings.
2. This Directive shall apply, in cross-border disputes, to civil and commercial matters except as regards rights and obligations which are not at the parties' disposal under the relevant applicable law. It shall not extend, in particular, to revenue, customs or administrative matters or to the liability of the State for acts and omissions in the exercise of State authority (acta iure imperii).
3. In this Directive, the term "Member State" shall mean Member States with the exception of Denmark.

Article 2. 1. For the purposes of this Directive a cross-border dispute shall be one in which at least one of the parties is domiciled or habitually resident in a Member State other than that of any other party on the date on which:
(a) the parties agree to use mediation after the dispute has arisen;
(b) mediation is ordered by a court;
(c) an obligation to use mediation arises under national law; or
(d) for the purposes of Article 5 an invitation is made to the parties.
2. Notwithstanding paragraph 1, for the purposes of Articles 7 and 8 a cross-border dispute shall also be one in which judicial proceedings or arbitration following mediation between the parties are initiated in a Member State other than that in which the parties were domiciled or habitually resident on the date referred to in paragraph 1(a), (b) or (c).
3. For the purposes of paragraphs 1 and 2, domicile shall be determined in accordance with Articles 59 and 60 of Regulation (EC) No 44/2001.

Article 3. For the purposes of this Directive the following definitions shall apply:
(a) "Mediation" means a structured process, however named or referred to, whereby two or more parties to a dispute attempt by themselves, on a voluntary basis, to reach an agreement on the settlement of their dispute with the assistance of a mediator. This process may be initiated by the parties or suggested or ordered by a court or prescribed by the law of a Member State.
It includes mediation conducted by a judge who is not responsible for any judicial proceedings concerning the dispute in question. It excludes attempts made by the court or the judge seised to settle a dispute in the course of judicial proceedings concerning the dispute in question.
(b) "Mediator" means any third person who is asked to conduct a mediation in an effective, impartial and competent way, regardless of the denomination or profession of that third person in the Member State concerned and of the way in which the third person has been appointed or requested to conduct the mediation.

Article 4. 1. Member States shall encourage, by any means which they consider appropriate, the development of, and adherence to, voluntary codes of conduct by mediators and organisations providing mediation services, as well as other effective quality control mechanisms concerning the provision of mediation services.
2. Member States shall encourage the initial and further training of mediators in order to ensure that the mediation is conducted in an effective, impartial and competent way in relation to the parties.

Article 5. 1. A court before which an action is brought may, when appropriate and having regard to all the circumstances of the case, invite the parties to use mediation in order to settle the dispute. The court may also invite the parties to attend an information session on the use of mediation if such sessions are held and are easily available.
2. This Directive is without prejudice to national legislation making the use of mediation compulsory or subject to incentives or sanctions, whether before or after judicial proceedings have started, provided that such legislation does not prevent the parties from exercising their right of access to the judicial system.

Article 6. 1. Member States shall ensure that it is possible for the parties, or for one of them with the explicit consent of the others, to request that the content of a written agreement resulting from mediation be made enforceable. The content of such an agreement shall be made enforceable unless, in the case in question, either the

content of that agreement is contrary to the law of the Member State where the request is made or the law of that Member State does not provide for its enforceability.
2. The content of the agreement may be made enforceable by a court or other competent authority in a judgment or decision or in an authentic instrument in accordance with the law of the Member State where the request is made.
3. Member States shall inform the Commission of the courts or other authorities competent to receive requests in accordance with paragraphs 1 and 2.
4. Nothing in this Article shall affect the rules applicable to the recognition and enforcement in another Member State of an agreement made enforceable in accordance with paragraph 1.

Article 7. 1. Given that mediation is intended to take place in a manner which respects confidentiality, Member States shall ensure that, unless the parties agree otherwise, neither mediators nor those involved in the administration of the mediation process shall be compelled to give evidence in civil and commercial judicial proceedings or arbitration regarding information arising out of or in connection with a mediation process, except:
(a) where this is necessary for overriding considerations of public policy of the Member State concerned, in particular when required to ensure the protection of the best interests of children or to prevent harm to the physical or psychological integrity of a person; or
(b) where disclosure of the content of the agreement resulting from mediation is necessary in order to implement or enforce that agreement.
2. Nothing in paragraph 1 shall preclude Member States from enacting stricter measures to protect the confidentiality of mediation.

Article 8. 1. Member States shall ensure that parties who choose mediation in an attempt to settle a dispute are not subsequently prevented from initiating judicial proceedings or arbitration in relation to that dispute by the expiry of limitation or prescription periods during the mediation process.
2. Paragraph 1 shall be without prejudice to provisions on limitation or prescription periods in international agreements to which Member States are party.

Article 9. Member States shall encourage, by any means which they consider appropriate, the availability to the general public, in particular on the Internet, of information on how to contact mediators and organisations providing mediation services.

Article 10. The Commission shall make publicly available, by any appropriate means, information on the competent courts or authorities communicated by the Member States pursuant to Article 6(3).

Article 11. Not later than 21 May 2016, the Commission shall submit to the European Parliament, the Council and the European Economic and Social Committee a report on the application of this Directive. The report shall consider the development of mediation throughout the European Union and the impact of this Directive in the Member States. If necessary, the report shall be accompanied by proposals to adapt this Directive.

Article 12. 1. Member States shall bring into force the laws, regulations, and administrative provisions necessary to comply with this Directive before 21 May 2011, with the exception of Article 10, for which the date of compliance shall be 21 November 2010 at the latest. They shall forthwith inform the Commission thereof. When they are adopted by Member States, these measures shall contain a reference to this Directive or shall be accompanied by such reference on the occasion of their official publication. The methods of making such reference shall be laid down by Member States.
2. Member States shall communicate to the Commission the text of the main provisions of national law which they adopt in the field covered by this Directive.

Article 13. This Directive shall enter into force on the 20th day following its publication in the Official Journal of the European Union.

Article 14. This Directive is addressed to the Member States.

PART VII

Private International Law

Implementation Act of the Civil Code [Einführungsgesetz zum Bürgerlichen Gesetzbuch (EGBGB)] of 21 September 1994 (*BGBl. I* p. 2494; 1997 I p. 1061), last amended by Article 5 of the Law of 26 March 2008 (*BGBl.* I p. 441).[25] Selected provisions: 3 – 6, 10, 14, 17, 19 – 20, 23, 43 – 46.

Part I. General provisions

[Chapter 1 is omitted.]

Chapter 2. Private international law

Division 1. Referral

Article 3. (1) In cases with a connection to the law of a foreign state, the following provisions determine which legal systems shall be applied (private international law). References to substantive regulations [Sachvorschriften] see to the legal norms of the applicable legal system with the exception of those of private international law.
(2) Regulations in international agreements take precedence over the provisions of this Act, in as far as they have become directly applicable domestic law. Regulations in legal instruments of the European Communities remain unaffected.
(3) In as far as references in the third and fourth chapter place the patrimony of a person under the law of a state, they do not relate to objects that are not located in this state and, pursuant to the law of the state in which they are located, are subject to specific regulations.

Article 4. (1) If the law of another state is referred to, then its private international law is to be applied as well, in as far as it does not contradict the purpose of the referral. If the law of the other state refers back to German law, then the German substantive regulations shall be applied.
(2) To the extent that parties may choose the law of a state, they may only refer to the substantive regulations.
(3) If the law of a state with several legal subsystems is referred to, without indicating the applicable one, then the law of that state determines which legal subsystem is to be applied. If no such regulation exists, then the legal subsystem is to be applied with which the case is most closely connected.

Article 5. (1) If the law of the state is referred to, of which a person is a national, and if that person is a national of several states, then the law of the state must be applied with which the person has the closest connection, especially because of his habitual residence or because of the course of his life. If the person is also German, then this legal status takes precedence.
(2) If a person is stateless or if his nationality cannot be established, then the law of the state must be applied in which he has his habitual residence or, for lack thereof, has his residence.
(3) If the law of a state in which a person has his residence or his habitual residence is referred to and if a person not having the full capacity to conduct legal acts changes the residence without the consent of the legal representative, then this change alone does not lead to the application of another law.

Article 6. A legal rule of another state is not to be applied, if its application leads to a result which is manifestly incompatible with essential principles of German law. It is especially not to be applied if the application is incompatible with fundamental rights.

Division 2. Rights of natural persons and legal transactions

[Articles 7 – 9 are omitted.]

Article 10. (1) A person's name is governed by the law of the state of which the person is a national.
(2) Spouses may at the time of or after entering into the marriage [Eheschliessung] choose in the presence of the civil status registrar [Standesbeamter] the name that they will use in the future
1. in accordance with the law of a state, of which one of the spouses is a national, notwithstanding Article 5 paragraph (1), or
2. in accordance with German law, if one of them has his habitual residence in the country.

---

[25] Translation by E. Ramaekers.

Declarations made after the entry into the marriage must be authenticated. For the consequences of a choice for the name of a child, § 1617c of the Civil Code is to be applied mutatis mutandis.
(3) The custodian may in the presence of the registrar determine, that a child shall acquire the family name
1. in accordance with the law of a state, of which one of the parents is a national, notwithstanding article 5 paragraph 1,
2. in accordance with German law, if one parent has his habitual residence in the country, or
3. in accordance with the law of the state, of which the person bestowing the name is a national.
Declarations made after the registration of the birth must be authenticated.
(4) Repealed.

[Articles 11 – 13 are omitted.]

Article 14. (1) The general effects of marriage are governed by
1. the law of the state of which both spouses are a national or of which both were last nationals during their marriage, if one of them is still a national of this state, otherwise
2. the law of the State in which both spouses have, or last had during the marriage, their habitual residence, if one of them still has his habitual residence there, or instead
3. the law of the state with which the spouses together are in another way most closely connected.
(2) If one of the spouses has more than one nationality, then the spouses may, notwithstanding Article 5 paragraph (1), choose the law of one of these states in case the other spouse also has that nationality.
(3) Spouses may choose the law of the state of which one of the spouses is a national, if the provisions of paragraph (1) section (1) do not apply and
1. neither spouse is a national of the state in which both spouses have their habitual residence, or
2. the spouses do not have their habitual residence in the same state.
The effects of the choice of law end if the spouses acquire a common nationality.
(4) The choice of law must be authenticated by a notary. If it is not chosen in the country, it suffices if it is in conformity with the formal requirements for a marriage agreement [Ehevertrag] according to the chosen law or the place of the choice of law.

[Articles 15 – 16 are omitted.]

Article 17. (1) Divorce [Scheidung] is governed by the law, which at the time the request for divorce is filed applies to the general effects of marriage. If the marriage cannot be dissolved in accordance herewith, the divorce is governed by German law, if the spouse who seeks the divorce is German at this time or was German at the time of the marriage.
(2) A marriage may within the country only be dissolved by a court.
(3) The alimonial regime [Versorgungsausgleich] is governed by the applicable law in accordance with paragraph 1 sentence 1; it may only be executed if it is known under the law of one of the states of which the spouses are a national at the time when the request for divorce is filed. If an alimonial regime cannot take place in accordance therewith, then it is to be executed in accordance with German law at the request of one of the spouses,
1. if the other spouse during the marriage has acquired an allowance claim within the country [Versorgungsanwartschaft] or
2. if the general effects of the marriage during part of the time of the marriage were governed by a legal system which recognizes the alimonial regime,
in as far as its execution is not incompatible with fairness [Billigkeit], with a view to the financial situations of both spouses also during the time not spent in the country.

[Articles 17a – 18 are omitted.]

Article 19. (1) The parentage of a child is governed by the law of the state, in which the child has its habitual residence. It may also be established in relation to each parent in accordance with the law of the state, of which this parent is a national. If the mother is married, then the parentage may further be established in accordance with the law which, in accordance with Article 14 paragraph (1), governs the general effects of her marriage at the moment of birth; if the marriage has previously been dissolved by way of death, then the moment of dissolution is decisive.
(2) If the parents are not married to each other, the obligations of the father to the mother by virtue of her pregnancy are governed by the law of the state, in which the mother has her habitual residence.

Article 20. The parentage may be contested in accordance with any law which determine the conditions for its exisence. The child may contest the parentage in any case in accordance with the law of the state, in which he has his habitual residence.

[Articles 21 – 22 are omitted.]

Article 23. The requirement and the granting of consent by the child and by a person, with whom the child has a relation under family law, to a declaration of parentage, a granting of a name or an acceptance as child are in addition governed by the law of the state, of which the child is a national. To the extent necessary for the well-being of the child, German law is to be applied instead.

[Article 24 and Divisions 4 – 5 are omitted.]

Division 6. Property law

Article 43. (1) Rights to an object are governed by the law of the state where the object is located.
(2) If an object in respect to which rights are created enters another state, then these rights may not be exercised in contravention of the legal system of this state.
(3) If a right with respect to an object, which enters the country, has not been previously acquired, then events in another state as well as within the country are to be taken into account as regards such acquisition within the country.

[Articles 44 – 45 are omitted.]

Article 46. If a substantially closer connection exists with the law of a state than with the law, which would be decisive pursuant to Articles 43 to 45, then the former law is to be applied.

[The remainder of the Act is omitted.]

Private International Law Act relating to the Dissolution of Marriage and Judicial Separation [Wet conflictenrecht inzake ontbinding huwelijk en scheiding van tafel en bed (Wet conflictenrecht echtscheiding)] of 25 March 1981, *Stb*. 166.[26]

Article 1. (1) Whether dissolution of marriage or judicial separation may be demanded or requested and on what grounds is determined
(a) where the parties have a common national law: by that law;
(b) where a common national law is absent: by the law of the country in which the parties have their habitual residence;
(c) where the parties do not have a common national law and do not have their habitual residence in the same country: by Netherlands law.
(2) In application of the preceding paragraph, lack of a common national law is considered to be equal to the case in which one of the parties lacks a genuine connection with the country of common nationality. In that case the common national law is nevertheless applied, if the parties have jointly chosen this law or if such a choice by one of the parties remains uncontested.
(3) Where one party possesses the nationality of more than one country, then his national law is considered to be the law of that country of which he possesses the nationality and with which he, taking into account all circumstances, has the strongest connection.
(4) Without prejudice to the preceding paragraphs, Netherlands law is applied, if the parties have jointly chosen this law or if such a choice by one of the parties remains uncontested.

Article 2. (1) A dissolution of marriage or judicial separation, acquired outside the Kingdom after a proper judicial procedure, is recognized in the Netherlands, if it has been brought about by the decision of a judge or other authority that had jurisdiction in the matter.
(2) A dissolution of marriage or judicial separation acquired outside the Kingdom, which does not meet one or more of the requirements laid down in the previous paragraph, is nevertheless recognized in the Netherlands, if it is apparent that the other party to the foreign proceedings has, explicitly or implicitly, either during those proceedings agreed with, or after those proceedings acquiesced to the dissolution of the marriage or the judicial separation.

Article 3. A dissolution of marriage outside the Kingdom brought about exclusively by a unilateral declaration of the man, is not recognized, unless
(a) the dissolution of the marriage in this form is in accordance with the personal law [personele wet] of the man;
(b) the dissolution has legal effect at the place where it occurred; and
(c) it is apparent that the woman, explicitly or implicitly, has agreed with the dissolution of the marriage or has acquiesced thereto.

[Article 4 is omitted.]

---

[26] Translation by E. Ramaekers.

Private International Law Act relating to Legal Familial Relations based on Parentage [Wet houdende regeling van het conflictenrecht inzake de familierechtelijke betrekkingen uit hoofde van afstamming (Wet conflictenrecht afstamming)] of 14 March 2002. *Stb.* 153.[27] Selected provisions: 1 – 10.

Chapter 1. Legal familial relations by birth

Article 1. (1) Whether legal familial relations [familierechtelijke betrekkingen] are created by birth between a child and the woman who gave birth to it and the man with whom she is or has been married, shall be determined according to the law of the state of the common nationality of the woman and the man or, where such does not exist, according to the law of the state where both the woman and the man each have their habitual residence, or where such also does not exist, according to the law of the state of the habitual residence of the child.
(2) For the application of paragraph (1), the time of birth of the child or, if the marriage of the parents was dissolved prior to that time, the time of the dissolution, shall be determinative.
(3) If the woman and the man possess more than one common nationality, they will be deemed, for the application of paragraph (1), not to have a common nationality.

Article 2. (1) Whether the legal familial relations referred to in Article 1may be annulled in legal proceedings for a declaration that the denial [of paternity] [ontkenning] is valid, shall be determined according to the law which, pursuant to that Article, that is applicable in respect of the existence of such relations.
(2) If, according to the law referred to in paragraph (1), denial is not or no longer possible, the court may, where this is in the best interests of the child and the parents and the child make a joint application for that purpose, apply another law mentioned in Article 1 or apply the law of the state of the habitual residence of the child at the time of the denial or Netherlands law.
(3) Notwithstanding the applicable law pursuant to paragraph (1) or (2), Article 212 of Book 1of the Civil Code is applicable to the legal procedure referred to in those paragraphs.
(4) Whether legal familial relations between a child and the man who is or has been married to his mother may be annulled by a declaration of denial by the mother before the Registrar of Births, Deaths, Marriages and Registered Partnerships [ambtenaar van de burgerlijke stand], shall be determined according to the law that is applicable pursuant to Article 1 to the existence of such relations. Without prejudice to paragraphs (1) and (2), such a declaration may be made only if the man who is or has been married to the mother and is still living consents thereto and if legal familial relations between the child and another man are or will be established at the same time.

Article 3. (1) Whether legal familial relations are created by birth between a woman and a child to whom she gave birth outside of marriage, shall be determined according to the law of the state of the nationality of the woman. In any event, such relations shall be established if the woman has her habitual residence in the Netherlands.
(2) For the application of paragraph (1) the time of birth shall be determinative.
(3) Paragraphs (1) and (2) shall not affect the application of the Convention on the establishment of maternal descent of natural children concluded in Brussels on 12th September 1962 (Trb. 1963, No. 93).

Chapter 2. Legal familial relations by recognition of or judicial establishment of paternity

Article 4. (1) Whether the recognition [of paternity] [erkenning] by a man establishes legal familial relations between him and a child shall be determined, where the right of the man and the conditions for recognition are concerned, according to the law of the state whose nationality the man possesses. If, according to that law, recognition is not or no longer possible, the law of the state of the habitual residence of the child shall be determinative. If, according to that law, this is also not or no longer possible, then the law of the state whose nationality the child possesses shall be determinative. If, according to that law, this will also not or no longer be possible, then the law of the state of the habitual residence of the man shall be determinative.
(2) Notwithstanding the applicable law pursuant to paragraph (1), Netherlands law shall determine whether a Netherlands married man has the right to recognise a child of a woman other than his spouse.
(3) The instrument of recognition and the subsequent entry of the recognition shall record the law that was applied pursuant to paragraph (1) or (2).
(4) Notwithstanding the applicable law pursuant to paragraph (1), the law of the state whose nationality the mother, respectively the child, possesses, is applicable to the consent of the mother respectively the child, for the

---

[27] Translation by N. Kornet and K. Saarloos.

purposes of the recognition. If the mother respectively the child possesses Netherlands nationality, Netherlands law is applicable. If the applicable law does not provide for recognition, the law of the state of the habitual residence of the mother respectively the child is applicable. The law that is applicable to the consent also determines whether, in the absence of consent, it may be replaced by a judicial decision.
(5) For the application of the preceding paragraphs the time of recognition and of the consent shall be determinative.

Article 5. Whether and in which manner a recognition may be annulled shall be determined, where the right of the man and the conditions for recognition are concerned, according to the law applied pursuant to Article 4 (1) and (2) and, where the consent of the mother respectively of the child is concerned, according to the law that is applicable pursuant to Article 4 paragraph (4).

Article 6. (1). Whether and under which conditions the paternity of a man may be judicially established, shall be decided according to the law of the state of the common nationality of the man and the mother or, where such does not exist, according to the law of the state of their common habitual residence or, where such also does not exist, according to the law of the state of the habitual residence of the child.
(2) For the application of paragraph (1), the time of the lodging of the application shall be determinative. If the man or the mother has already died at that time, then, in the absence of common nationality at the time of his death, the law of the state of the common habitual residence of the man and the mother at that time is applicable or, where such does not exist, the law of the state of the habitual residence of the child at the time of the lodging of the application.
(3) If both the man and the woman have more than one common nationality, they will be deemed, for the application of the preceding paragraphs, not to have a common nationality.

Chapter 3. Legal familial relations by legitimation

Article 7. (1). Whether a child is legitimised by the marriage of one of its parents or by a later decision of a judicial or other competent authority shall be determined according to the Convention on the legitimation resulting from marriage concluded in Rome on 10 December 1970 (Trb. 1972, No. 61).
(2) If application of paragraph (1) does not result in legitimation, legal familial relations may be established by legitimation according to the law of the state of the habitual residence of the child.
(3) Paragraphs (1) and (2) do not apply if one of the parents possesses the Netherlands nationality and the marriage was not validly performed in accordance with the provisions of Articles 4 and 5 of the Private International Law (Marriages) Act [Wet conflictenrecht huwelijk].
(4) For the application of the preceding paragraphs, the time of the marriage of the parents or, for the establishment of legal familial relations by a decision of a judicial or other competent authority, the time of the lodging of the application or claim shall be determinative.

Chapter 4. The Contents of the Legal Familial Relations on Account of Parentage

Article 8. (1). Without prejudice to what has been provided for special subject matters, the content of the legal familial relations between the parents and the child shall be determined according to the law of the state of the common nationality of the parents or, where such does not exist, according to the law of the state of their common habitual residence or, where such also does not exist, according to the law of the state of the habitual residence of the child.
(2) If legal familial relations only exist between the mother and the child, the content of such legal familial relations shall be determined according to the law of the state of the common nationality of the mother and the child. In the absence of a common nationality it shall be determined according to the law of the habitual residence of the child.
(3) If the woman and the man have more than one common nationality, they will be deemed, for the application of the preceding paragraphs, not to have a common nationality.

Chapter 5. Recognition of Judicial Decisions, Legal Facts and Legal Acts Established Abroad whereby Legal Familial Relations on Account of Parentage were Established or Altered

Article 9. (1) An irrevocable foreign judicial decision whereby legal familial relations by reason of parentage are established or altered, shall be recognised in the Netherlands, unless

(a) there has been a manifestly insufficient connection with the legal environment [rechtssfeer] of this country to found the jurisdiction of that court;
(b) there was a lack of a proper investigation or proper legal process undertaken prior to the decision, or
(c) the recognition of the decision would be manifestly contrary to public policy.
(2) The recognition of the decision may not be refused because of a violation of public policy, even if a Netherlands national is involved, on the sole ground that another law had been applied thereto than would have resulted under the provisions of this Act.
(3) The decision is not capable of recognition if it is irreconcilable with a decision of a Netherlands court that has become irrevocable as regards the establishment or alteration of the same legal familial relations.
(4) The preceding paragraphs shall not affect the application of the Convention referred to in Article 7 paragraph (1).

Article 10. (1). The provisions of Article 9 paragraph (1) (b) and (c), (2) and (3) apply mutatis mutandis to legal facts or legal acts established abroad whereby legal familial relations were established or altered and which have been recorded in an instrument drawn up by a competent authority in accordance with local provisions..
(2) There is, in any event, a ground for refusal as referred to in Article 9 paragraph (l) (c) with respect to a recognition,
(a) if the recognition is made by a Netherlands national who, according to Netherlands law, would not have been entitled to recognise the child;
(b) if, where the consent of the mother or the child is concerned, the legal requirements of the law that is applicable pursuant to Article 4 paragraph (4) were not complied with, or
(c) if the instrument manifestly relates to a sham transaction.
(3) The preceding paragraphs shall not affect the application of the Convention mentioned in Article 7 paragraph (1).

[Articles 11 – 13 are omitted.]

The Netherlands: Private International Law Act Relating to Corporations

Private International Law Act relating to Corporations [Wet houdende regels van international privaatrecht met betrekking to corporaties (Wet conflictenrecht corporaties)] of 17 December 1997, as last amended by the Statute of 20 November 2006, *Stb.* 2006, 600.[28] Selected provisions: Articles 1 – 6.

Article 1. In this Act, the following shall mean:
(a) corporations are: partnerships and companies [vennootschappen], associations [verenigingen], co-operatives [coöperaties], mutual insurance societies [onderlinge waarborgmaatschappijen], foundations [stichtingen] and other bodies operating externally as an independent unit or organization and interest groupings [samenwerkingsverbanden].
(b) an officer is: a person who is, without being an organ, pursuant to the law applicable to it and its articles of association or the agreement establishing the interest grouping competent to represent the corporation.

Article 2. A corporation which, pursuant to its agreement or deed of incorporation [akte van oprichting], has at the time of its incorporation its seat or, or in the absence thereof, its centre of external operations on the territory of the state under the law of which it has been incorporated, shall be governed by the law of that state.

Article 3. The law applicable to the corporation governs, besides its incorporation, in particular the following matters:
(a) the possession of legal personality, or its capacity to bear rights and obligations, to perform legal acts and to act at law;
(b) the internal structure of the corporation and all matters related thereto;
(c) the competence of bodies and officers of the corporation to represent it;
(d) the liability of directors [bestuurders], supervisory board members [commissarissen] and other officers as such as against the corporation;
(e) the question who is, besides the corporation, liable for acts through which the corporation is bound by virtue of a particular function such as founder, partner [vennoot], shareholder, member, director, supervisory board member or other officer of the corporation;
(f) the termination of the existence of the corporation.

Article 4. If a corporation which has legal personality transfers its statutory seat to another country and the law of the state of the original seat and that of the state of the new seat recognize the continued existence of the corporation as a legal person at the time the seat is transferred, then its continued existence as a legal person is also recognized according to Netherlands law. From the time the seat is transferred, the law of the state of the new seat governs the matters referred to in Article 3, unless if, pursuant to that law, the law of the state of the original seat remains applicable thereto.

Article 5. Notwithstanding what is laid down in Articles 2 and 3, Articles 138 and 149 of Book 2 of the Civil Code are applicable or applicable mutatis mutandis to the liability of directors and supervisory board members of a corporation governed by foreign law pursuant to Article 2 or Article 4, which is subject in the Netherlands to a levying of corporate income taxes, if the corporation is declared bankrupt in the Netherlands. Those persons who are charged with the management of the business conducted in the Netherlands are also liable as directors.

Article 5a. (1) The Public Prosecution Service [Openbare Ministerie] may request the court at Utrecht to issue a declaration of law that the purpose or the activities of a corporation are in violation of public order as meant in Article 20 of Book 2 of the Civil Code.
(2) The declaration has effect for and against everyone starting on the first day after the day of the ruling. The declaration is published under the care of the registrar in the Government Gazette [Staatscourant]. If the corporation is registered in the Trade Register [Handelsregister], then the declaration shall also be registered therein.
(3) The court may place the assets of the corporation that are located in the Netherlands under a legal regime [bewind] if so requested. Article 22 of Book 2 of the Civil Code applies mutatis mutandis.
(4) The assets of a corporation that are located in the Netherlands and with regard to which the court has issued a declaration of law as meant in the first paragraph, are wound up by one or more liquidators to be appointed by [the court]. Articles 23 to 24 of Book 2 of the Civil Code apply mutatis mutandis.

---

[28] Translation by E. Ramaekers and N. Kornet.

Article 5b. A corporation which is not a Dutch legal person and is mentioned in the list, as meant in Article 2, third paragraph, of Council Regulation (EC) n° 2580/2001 of 27 December 2001 (OJ L 344) or in Annex I of Council Regulation (EC) n° 881/2002 of 27 May 2002 (OJ L 139) or is mentioned and indicated with a star in the Annex to Common Position n° 2001/931 of the Council of 27 December 2001 (OJ L 344) is prohibited by operation of law and not competent to perform legal acts.

Article 6. This Act does not derogate from what is laid down in the Act on Pro Forma Foreign Companies.

[Articles 7 – 10 are omitted.]

Pro Forma Foreign Companies Act [Wet houdende regels met betrekking tot naar buitenlands recht opgerichte, rechtspersoonlijkheid bezittende kapitaalvennootschappen die hun werkzaamheden geheel of nagenoeg geheel in Nederland verrichten en geen werkelijke band hebben met de staat naar welks recht zij zijn opgericht (Wet formeel buitenlandse vennootschappen)] of 17 December 1997, as last amended by the Statute of 28 January 1999, *Stb.* **2005, 230.**[29] **Selected provisions: Articles 1 – 7.**

Article 1. (1) In this Act, a pro forma foreign company means a capital company [kapitaalvennootschap] with legal personality incorporated according to another law than Netherlands law, which conducts its business entirely or almost entirely in the Netherlands and without any actual connection with the state where the law applies in accordance with which it was incorporation. In this Article, the countries of the Kingdom of the Netherlands are considered as states.
(2) The following Articles of this Act do not apply, with the exception of Article 6, to companies to which the law of one of the Member States of the European Union or of a state that is a party to the Agreement on the European Economic Area of 2 May 1992 is applicable.

Article 2. (1) The directors of a pro forma foreign company are obliged to disclose for registration in the Trade Register [handelsregister] that the company meets the description of Article 1, and to deposit at the office of the trade register an authentic copy or a copy authenticated by a director, drafted in Dutch, French, German or English, of the deed of incorporation [akte van oprichting] and of the articles of association [statuten], if these have been laid down in a separate document. They are moreover obliged to disclose for registration the register in which and the number under which that company is registered and the date of the first registration. Furthermore, they are obliged to disclose for registration the name, personal data, where it concerns a natural person, and the residence of the holder of all shares in the capital of the company or of a partner in matrimonial property [huwelijksgemeenschap] or registered partnership property [gemeenschap van een geregistreerd partnerschap] to which all shares in the capital of the company belong, not taking into account the shares held by the company or its subsidiary companies. The directors of a pro forma foreign company are obliged to disclose every change to what has been registered in the Trade Register pursuant to the law, with mention of the date on which it takes effect. Actions on the basis of this Act cannot be performed by proxy.
(2) The trade register, as meant in the first paragraph, is the Trade Register which is held by the Chamber of Commerce [Kamer van Koophandel en Fabrieken] that is competent in accordance with Articles 6 and 7 of the Trade Register Act 1996 [Handelsregisterwet 1996].

Article 3. (1) All writings, printed documents and announcements in which a pro forma foreign company is a party or which are issued by it, with the exception of telegrams and advertisements, must mention the full name of the company, its legal form, its statutory seat and the place of establishment of its enterprise, as well as, if it must be registered in a register pursuant to the applicable law, the register in which and the number under which the company is registered and the date of the first registration. It must furthermore mention under which number the company is registered in the Trade Register and that the company is a pro forma foreign company. It is prohibited to use in the writings, documents or announcements an indication which, contrary to the truth, entails that the enterprise belongs to a Netherlands legal person.
(2) If the capital of the company is mentioned, then in any case it must be mentioned what amount has been issued and how much of the issued amount has been paid up.
(3) If the company continues to exist after its dissolution, 'in liquidation' ['in liquidatie'] must be added to its name.

Article 4. (1) The issued capital of a pro forma foreign company and the paid-up part thereof must at least amount to the amount of the minimum capital as meant in Article 178, second paragraph, of Book 2 of the Civil Code [Burgerlijk Wetboek], such as this amount is at the time when the company first meets the description of Article 1.
(2) At the time when the company first meets the description of Article 1, its own net worth [eigen vermogen] must at least amount to the amount of the minimum capital as meant in the first paragraph.
(3) The directors are obliged to deposit, together with the filing as meant in Article 2, first paragraph, in the Trade Register as meant in that article, a copy of a declaration of a registered accountant [registeraccountant] or an accountant-administrative consultant [accountant-administratieconsulent], stating that the company fulfils the first and second paragraph. The second and third sentence of Article 204a, second paragraph, of Book 2 of the Civil

---

[29] Translation by E. Ramaekers and N. Kornet.

Code apply mutatis mutandis. The declaration shall relate to a date that is not earlier than five months from the time when the company first meets the description of Article 1.

(4) The directors are, in addition to the company, jointly and severally liable [hoofdelijk aansprakelijk] for every legal act performed during their management, through which the company is bound during the period of time before Article 2, first sentence, and the first until the third sentence of this article, are complied with, or during any other period of time during which the first paragraph is not complied with or the own net worth falls below the amount as meant in the first paragraph due to payments to shareholders or repurchase of shares.

Article 5. (1) Without prejudice to the second paragraph, Article 10 of Book 2 of the Civil Code applies mutatis mutandis to a pro forma foreign company. The obligations laid down therein apply to the directors of the company.

(2) The directors are obliged to draw up an annual account and an annual report each year within five months after the end of the fiscal year, subject to an extension of this term with a maximum of six months pursuant to a competent decision taken on the basis of special circumstances. Title 9 of Book 2 of the Civil Code applies mutatis mutandis to the annual account, the annual report and the other data, taking into account that the publication pursuant to Article 394 of that book takes place by deposit at the office of the trade register as meant in Article 2, second paragraph.

(3) The directors are obliged every calendar year before 1 April of that year to deposit at the office of the trade register proof of the registration in the register where the company must be registered pursuant to the applicable law. Such proof may not be filed more than four weeks prior to the date of deposit.

Article 6. As regards a pro forma foreign company, Articles 249, 260 and 261 of Book 2 of the Civil Code apply mutatis mutandis.

Article 7. For the application of Articles 2 to 6, directors of the company are considered equal to those who are charged with the day-to-day management of the company's enterprise.

[Articles 8 – 11 are omitted.]

Private International Law Act relating to Property Law [Wet houdende regeling van het conflictenrecht betreffende het goederenrechtelijke regime met betrekking tot zaken, vorderingsrechten, aandelen en giraal overdraagbare effecten (Wet Goederenrecht goederenrecht)] of 25 February 2008, Stb. 70.[30]

Title 1. General provisions

Article 1. (1) This statute does not derogate from the Convention on the Law Applicable to Trusts and on their Recognition concluded on 1 July 1985 in The Hague (Trb. 1985, 141), nor from the Statute on the conflict of laws on trusts. Without prejudice to what follows from that Convention and that Statute, a legal act pertaining to a transfer governed by Netherlands law to the trustee of a trust as meant in article 1 of that statute which is governed by foreign law, does not constitute an invalid title on the sole ground that that legal act has as its purpose to transfer that thing [goed] for security purposes or lacks the purpose to bring the thing within the patrimony [vermogen] of the receiver after the transfer.
(2) This statute does not derogate from Directive 93/7/EEC of the Council of the European Communities of 15 March 1993 on the return of cultural objects unlawfully removed from the territory of a Member State (OJ L74) nor from the Implementation statute on the protection of cultural objects against illegal export.
(3) In this statute, application of the law of a state is considered to mean the application of the legal rules that apply in that state with the exception of private international law.

Title 2. The property law rules relating to objects

Article 2. (1) Unless otherwise provided in the second and third paragraph, the property law rules [goederenrechtelijk regime] relating to an object [zaak] are governed by the law of the state on whose territory the object is located.
(2) Without prejudice to article 3 of the Statute of 18 March 1993, Stb. 168, containing several provisions of private international law with regard to maritime law, inland navigation law and aviation law, the property law rules with regard to registered ships are governed by the law of the state where the ship is registered.
(3) The property law rules with regard to registered aircraft and aircraft that are exclusively registered in a nationality registry as meant in article 17 of the Convention on International Civil Aviation concluded on 7 December 1944 at Chicago, Stb. 1947, H 165, is governed by the law of the state where the aircraft is registered or entered into the nationality registry.(4) The law as meant in the previous paragraphs particularly determines:
(a) whether an object is movable or immovable;
(b) what a component [bestanddeel] of an object is;
(c) whether an object is susceptible to transfer of ownership thereof or creation of a right in respect thereto;
(d) which requirements are laid down for transfer or creation;
(e) what rights may exist in respect to an object and what the nature and content of these rights are;
(f) in what way these rights arise, alter, pass and perish and what their mutual relationship is.
(5) For the application of the previous paragraph, as far as the acquisition, the creation, the passing, the alteration or the perishing of rights to an object are concerned, the time at which the required legal facts occur is decisive.
(6) The preceding paragraphs are applicable mutatis mutandis in case of transfer and creation of rights to real rights.

Article 3. (1) The property-effects [goederenrechtelijke gevolgen] of a retention of ownership are governed by the law of the state on whose territory the object is located at the moment of the delivery. This is without prejudice to the obligations which may follow from the law that is applicable to the retention of title clause.
(2) Contrary to the first sentence of the first paragraph parties may agree that the property-effects of a retention of title of an object intended for export are governed by the law of the state of destination where on the basis of that law the retention of title does not loose its effect until the price has been fully paid. The choice of law thereby agreed upon only has effect if the object is actually imported in the indicated state of destination.
(3) The preceding paragraphs are applicable mutatis mutandis to the property-effects of the leasing of objects that are intended for use abroad.

---

[30] Translation by E. Ramaekers.

Article 4. Without prejudice to Article 6, introduction and sub a, of the Statute of 18 March 1993, Stb. 168, containing several provisions of private international law relating to maritime law, inland navigation law and aviation law, the coming into existence and the content of a right of retention are determined by the law that governs the underlying legal relationship. A right of retention may only be enforced to the extent that the law of the state on whose territory the object is located permits it.

Article 5. Rights with respect to an object, which have been acquired or created in accordance with the applicable law pursuant to this statute, shall remain, even where that object is moved to another state. These rights may not be exercised in a manner which is incompatible with the law of the state on whose territory the object is located at the time of such exercise.

Article 6. The legal effects of the acquisition of an object of a person without the power to dispose are governed by the law of the state on whose territory the object is located at the time of that acquisition.

Article 7. (1) If the possession of an object has been involuntarily lost and after this loss it is unknown in which state the object is, the legal effects of legal acts in the area of property law [goederenrechtelijke rechtshandelingen], performed by the owner or his successor in title, are governed by the law of the state on whose territory the object was located before the loss of possession.
(2) If in the case as meant in the previous paragraph the loss is covered by insurance, then the law which governs the insurance agreement determines whether and in which way the ownership passes to the insurer.

Article 8. (1) The property law rules with regard to an object which is being transported pursuant to a contract of international transport, are governed by the law of the state of destination.
(2) If the transport as meant in the first paragraph takes place in execution of a sales contract or another contract which obliges to transfer the transported object, or in execution of a contract which obliges to create rights with respect to that object, then a choice of the law applicable for the said contract which is included in that contract is, contrary to the first paragraph, considered to relate also to the property law rules as regards the transported object.

Title 3. The property law rules with regard to claims

Article 9. If a claim is laid down in a document, the law of the state on whose territory the document is located determines whether the claim is a non-documentary claim [vordering op naam] or a bearer claim [vordering aan toonder].

Article 10. (1) The susceptibility of a non-documentary claim to transfer or to the creation of rights with respect thereto is governed by the law that is applicable to the claim.
(2) Otherwise the property law rules with regard to a non-documentary claim are governed by the law that is applicable to the agreement obliging the transfer or creation of rights. That law particularly determines:
(a) what requirements are laid down for a transfer or creation;
(b) who is authorized to exercise the rights contained in the claim;
(c) what rights may be created with respect to the claim and what the nature and content of these rights are;
(d) in what manner those rights alter, pass or perish and what their mutual relationship is.
(3) The relations between the assignee [cessionaris], the authorized person and the debtor, the conditions under which the transfer of a non-documentary claim or the creation with respect thereto of a right may be invoked as against the debtor, as well as the question whether the debtor is released through payment, are governed by the law which is applicable to the claim.

Article 11. (1) The property law rules with regard to a bearer claim are governed by the law of the state on whose territory the bearer document is located. Article 10, first and second paragraph, is applicable mutatis mutandis to the question which subject matters are governed by that law.
(2) The relations between the acquirer and the debtor, the conditions under which the transfer of the claim or the creation of a right with respect thereto may be invoked against the debtor, as well as the question whether the debtor is released through payment, are governed by the law which is applicable to the claim.
(3) Articles 5 and 6 are applicable mutatis mutandis to bearer claims.

Council Regulation (EC) No. 44/2001 on jurisdiction and the recognition and enforcement of judgments in civil and commercial matters [Brussels I] (*OJ* L012, 16.1.2001 pp. 1 – 23) [footnotes omitted].

THE COUNCIL OF THE EUROPEAN UNION,
Having regard to the Treaty establishing the European Community, and in particular Article 61(c) and Article 67(1) thereof,
Having regard to the proposal from the Commission,
Having regard to the opinion of the European Parliament,
Having regard to the opinion of the Economic and Social Committee,
Whereas:
(1) The Community has set itself the objective of maintaining and developing an area of freedom, security and justice, in which the free movement of persons is ensured. In order to establish progressively such an area, the Community should adopt, amongst other things, the measures relating to judicial cooperation in civil matters which are necessary for the sound operation of the internal market.
(2) Certain differences between national rules governing jurisdiction and recognition of judgments hamper the sound operation of the internal market. Provisions to unify the rules of conflict of jurisdiction in civil and commercial matters and to simplify the formalities with a view to rapid and simple recognition and enforcement of judgments from Member States bound by this Regulation are essential.
(3) This area is within the field of judicial cooperation in civil matters within the meaning of Article 65 of the Treaty.
(4) In accordance with the principles of subsidiarity and proportionality as set out in Article 5 of the Treaty, the objectives of this Regulation cannot be sufficiently achieved by the Member States and can therefore be better achieved by the Community. This Regulation confines itself to the minimum required in order to achieve those objectives and does not go beyond what is necessary for that purpose.
(5) On 27 September 1968 the Member States, acting under Article 293, fourth indent, of the Treaty, concluded the Brussels Convention on Jurisdiction and the Enforcement of Judgments in Civil and Commercial Matters, as amended by Conventions on the Accession of the New Member States to that Convention (hereinafter referred to as the "Brussels Convention"). On 16 September 1988 Member States and EFTA States concluded the Lugano Convention on Jurisdiction and the Enforcement of Judgments in Civil and Commercial Matters, which is a parallel Convention to the 1968 Brussels Convention. Work has been undertaken for the revision of those Conventions, and the Council has approved the content of the revised texts. Continuity in the results achieved in that revision should be ensured.
(6) In order to attain the objective of free movement of judgments in civil and commercial matters, it is necessary and appropriate that the rules governing jurisdiction and the recognition and enforcement of judgments be governed by a Community legal instrument which is binding and directly applicable.
(7) The scope of this Regulation must cover all the main civil and commercial matters apart from certain well-defined matters.
(8) There must be a link between proceedings to which this Regulation applies and the territory of the Member States bound by this Regulation. Accordingly common rules on jurisdiction should, in principle, apply when the defendant is domiciled in one of those Member States.
(9) A defendant not domiciled in a Member State is in general subject to national rules of jurisdiction applicable in the territory of the Member State of the court seised, and a defendant domiciled in a Member State not bound by this Regulation must remain subject to the Brussels Convention.
(10) For the purposes of the free movement of judgments, judgments given in a Member State bound by this Regulation should be recognised and enforced in another Member State bound by this Regulation, even if the judgment debtor is domiciled in a third State.
(11) The rules of jurisdiction must be highly predictable and founded on the principle that jurisdiction is generally based on the defendant's domicile and jurisdiction must always be available on this ground save in a few well-defined situations in which the subject-matter of the litigation or the autonomy of the parties warrants a different linking factor. The domicile of a legal person must be defined autonomously so as to make the common rules more transparent and avoid conflicts of jurisdiction.
(12) In addition to the defendant's domicile, there should be alternative grounds of jurisdiction based on a close link between the court and the action or in order to facilitate the sound administration of justice.
(13) In relation to insurance, consumer contracts and employment, the weaker party should be protected by rules of jurisdiction more favourable to his interests than the general rules provide for.
(14) The autonomy of the parties to a contract, other than an insurance, consumer or employment contract, where only limited autonomy to determine the courts having jurisdiction is allowed, must be respected subject to the exclusive grounds of jurisdiction laid down in this Regulation.

(15) In the interests of the harmonious administration of justice it is necessary to minimise the possibility of concurrent proceedings and to ensure that irreconcilable judgments will not be given in two Member States. There must be a clear and effective mechanism for resolving cases of lis pendens and related actions and for obviating problems flowing from national differences as to the determination of the time when a case is regarded as pending. For the purposes of this Regulation that time should be defined autonomously.

(16) Mutual trust in the administration of justice in the Community justifies judgments given in a Member State being recognised automatically without the need for any procedure except in cases of dispute.

(17) By virtue of the same principle of mutual trust, the procedure for making enforceable in one Member State a judgment given in another must be efficient and rapid. To that end, the declaration that a judgment is enforceable should be issued virtually automatically after purely formal checks of the documents supplied, without there being any possibility for the court to raise of its own motion any of the grounds for non-enforcement provided for by this Regulation.

(18) However, respect for the rights of the defence means that the defendant should be able to appeal in an adversarial procedure, against the declaration of enforceability, if he considers one of the grounds for non-enforcement to be present. Redress procedures should also be available to the claimant where his application for a declaration of enforceability has been rejected.

(19) Continuity between the Brussels Convention and this Regulation should be ensured, and transitional provisions should be laid down to that end. The same need for continuity applies as regards the interpretation of the Brussels Convention by the Court of Justice of the European Communities and the 1971 Protocol should remain applicable also to cases already pending when this Regulation enters into force.

(20) The United Kingdom and Ireland, in accordance with Article 3 of the Protocol on the position of the United Kingdom and Ireland annexed to the Treaty on European Union and to the Treaty establishing the European Community, have given notice of their wish to take part in the adoption and application of this Regulation.

(21) Denmark, in accordance with Articles 1 and 2 of the Protocol on the position of Denmark annexed to the Treaty on European Union and to the Treaty establishing the European Community, is not participating in the adoption of this Regulation, and is therefore not bound by it nor subject to its application.

(22) Since the Brussels Convention remains in force in relations between Denmark and the Member States that are bound by this Regulation, both the Convention and the 1971 Protocol continue to apply between Denmark and the Member States bound by this Regulation.

(23) The Brussels Convention also continues to apply to the territories of the Member States which fall within the territorial scope of that Convention and which are excluded from this Regulation pursuant to Article 299 of the Treaty.

(24) Likewise for the sake of consistency, this Regulation should not affect rules governing jurisdiction and the recognition of judgments contained in specific Community instruments.

(25) Respect for international commitments entered into by the Member States means that this Regulation should not affect conventions relating to specific matters to which the Member States are parties.

(26) The necessary flexibility should be provided for in the basic rules of this Regulation in order to take account of the specific procedural rules of certain Member States. Certain provisions of the Protocol annexed to the Brussels Convention should accordingly be incorporated in this Regulation.

(27) In order to allow a harmonious transition in certain areas which were the subject of special provisions in the Protocol annexed to the Brussels Convention, this Regulation lays down, for a transitional period, provisions taking into consideration the specific situation in certain Member States.

(28) No later than five years after entry into force of this Regulation the Commission will present a report on its application and, if need be, submit proposals for adaptations.

(29) The Commission will have to adjust Annexes I to IV on the rules of national jurisdiction, the courts or competent authorities and redress procedures available on the basis of the amendments forwarded by the Member State concerned; amendments made to Annexes V and VI should be adopted in accordance with Council Decision 1999/468/EC of 28 June 1999 laying down the procedures for the exercise of implementing powers conferred on the Commission,

HAS ADOPTED THIS REGULATION:

Chapter I. Scope

Article 1. 1. This Regulation shall apply in civil and commercial matters whatever the nature of the court or tribunal. It shall not extend, in particular, to revenue, customs or administrative matters.

2. The Regulation shall not apply to:

(a) the status or legal capacity of natural persons, rights in property arising out of a matrimonial relationship, wills and succession;
(b) bankruptcy, proceedings relating to the winding-up of insolvent companies or other legal persons, judicial arrangements, compositions and analogous proceedings;
(c) social security;
(d) arbitration.
3. In this Regulation, the term 'Member State' shall mean Member States with the exception of Denmark.

Chapter II. Jurisdiction

Section 1. General provisions

Article 2. 1. Subject to this Regulation, persons domiciled in a Member State shall, whatever their nationality, be sued in the courts of that Member State.
2. Persons who are not nationals of the Member State in which they are domiciled shall be governed by the rules of jurisdiction applicable to nationals of that State.

Article 3. 1. Persons domiciled in a Member State may be sued in the courts of another Member State only by virtue of the rules set out in Sections 2 to 7 of this Chapter.
2. In particular the rules of national jurisdiction set out in Annex I shall not be applicable as against them.

Article 4. 1. If the defendant is not domiciled in a Member State, the jurisdiction of the courts of each Member State shall, subject to Articles 22 and 23, be determined by the law of that Member State.
2. As against such a defendant, any person domiciled in a Member State may, whatever his nationality, avail himself in that State of the rules of jurisdiction there in force, and in particular those specified in Annex I, in the same way as the nationals of that State.

Section 2. Special jurisdiction

Article 5 A person domiciled in a Member State may, in another Member State, be sued:
1. (a) in matters relating to a contract, in the courts for the place of performance of the obligation in question;
(b) for the purpose of this provision and unless otherwise agreed, the place of performance of the obligation in question shall be:
- in the case of the sale of goods, the place in a Member State where, under the contract, the goods were delivered or should have been delivered,
- in the case of the provision of services, the place in a Member State where, under the contract, the services were provided or should have been provided,
(c) if subparagraph (b) does not apply then subparagraph (a) applies;
2. in matters relating to maintenance, in the courts for the place where the maintenance creditor is domiciled or habitually resident or, if the matter is ancillary to proceedings concerning the status of a person, in the court which, according to its own law, has jurisdiction to entertain those proceedings, unless that jurisdiction is based solely on the nationality of one of the parties;
3. in matters relating to tort, delict or quasi-delict, in the courts for the place where the harmful event occurred or may occur;
4. as regards a civil claim for damages or restitution which is based on an act giving rise to criminal proceedings, in the court seised of those proceedings, to the extent that that court has jurisdiction under its own law to entertain civil proceedings;
5. as regards a dispute arising out of the operations of a branch, agency or other establishment, in the courts for the place in which the branch, agency or other establishment is situated;
6. as settlor, trustee or beneficiary of a trust created by the operation of a statute, or by a written instrument, or created orally and evidenced in writing, in the courts of the Member State in which the trust is domiciled;
7. as regards a dispute concerning the payment of remuneration claimed in respect of the salvage of a cargo or freight, in the court under the authority of which the cargo or freight in question:
(a) has been arrested to secure such payment, or
(b) could have been so arrested, but bail or other security has been given;
provided that this provision shall apply only if it is claimed that the defendant has an interest in the cargo or freight or had such an interest at the time of salvage.

Article 6. A person domiciled in a Member State may also be sued:
1. where he is one of a number of defendants, in the courts for the place where any one of them is domiciled, provided the claims are so closely connected that it is expedient to hear and determine them together to avoid the risk of irreconcilable judgments resulting from separate proceedings;
2. as a third party in an action on a warranty or guarantee or in any other third party proceedings, in the court seised of the original proceedings, unless these were instituted solely with the object of removing him from the jurisdiction of the court which would be competent in his case;
3. on a counter-claim arising from the same contract or facts on which the original claim was based, in the court in which the original claim is pending;
4. in matters relating to a contract, if the action may be combined with an action against the same defendant in matters relating to rights in rem in immovable property, in the court of the Member State in which the property is situated.

Article 7. Where by virtue of this Regulation a court of a Member State has jurisdiction in actions relating to liability from the use or operation of a ship, that court, or any other court substituted for this purpose by the internal law of that Member State, shall also have jurisdiction over claims for limitation of such liability.

Section 3. Jurisdiction in matters relating to insurance

Article 8. In matters relating to insurance, jurisdiction shall be determined by this Section, without prejudice to Article 4 and point 5 of Article 5.

Article 9. 1. An insurer domiciled in a Member State may be sued:
(a) in the courts of the Member State where he is domiciled, or
(b) in another Member State, in the case of actions brought by the policyholder, the insured or a beneficiary, in the courts for the place where the plaintiff is domiciled,
(c) if he is a co-insurer, in the courts of a Member State in which proceedings are brought against the leading insurer.
2. An insurer who is not domiciled in a Member State but has a branch, agency or other establishment in one of the Member States shall, in disputes arising out of the operations of the branch, agency or establishment, be deemed to be domiciled in that Member State.

Article 10. In respect of liability insurance or insurance of immovable property, the insurer may in addition be sued in the courts for the place where the harmful event occurred. The same applies if movable and immovable property are covered by the same insurance policy and both are adversely affected by the same contingency.

Article 11. 1. In respect of liability insurance, the insurer may also, if the law of the court permits it, be joined in proceedings which the injured party has brought against the insured.
2. Articles 8, 9 and 10 shall apply to actions brought by the injured party directly against the insurer, where such direct actions are permitted.
3. If the law governing such direct actions provides that the policyholder or the insured may be joined as a party to the action, the same court shall have jurisdiction over them.

Article 12. 1. Without prejudice to Article 11(3), an insurer may bring proceedings only in the courts of the Member State in which the defendant is domiciled, irrespective of whether he is the policyholder, the insured or a beneficiary.
2. The provisions of this Section shall not affect the right to bring a counter-claim in the court in which, in accordance with this Section, the original claim is pending.

Article 13. The provisions of this Section may be departed from only by an agreement:
1. which is entered into after the dispute has arisen, or
2. which allows the policyholder, the insured or a beneficiary to bring proceedings in courts other than those indicated in this Section, or
3. which is concluded between a policyholder and an insurer, both of whom are at the time of conclusion of the contract domiciled or habitually resident in the same Member State, and which has the effect of conferring jurisdiction on the courts of that State even if the harmful event were to occur abroad, provided that such an agreement is not contrary to the law of that State, or

4. which is concluded with a policyholder who is not domiciled in a Member State, except in so far as the insurance is compulsory or relates to immovable property in a Member State, or
5. which relates to a contract of insurance in so far as it covers one or more of the risks set out in Article 14.

Article 14. The following are the risks referred to in Article 13(5):
1. any loss of or damage to:
(a) seagoing ships, installations situated offshore or on the
high seas, or aircraft, arising from perils which relate to their use for commercial purposes;
(b) goods in transit other than passengers' baggage where the transit consists of or includes carriage by such ships or aircraft;
2. any liability, other than for bodily injury to passengers or loss of or damage to their baggage:
(a) arising out of the use or operation of ships, installations or aircraft as referred to in point 1(a) in so far as, in respect of the latter, the law of the Member State in which such aircraft are registered does not prohibit agreements on jurisdiction regarding insurance of such risks;
(b) for loss or damage caused by goods in transit as described in point 1(b);
3. any financial loss connected with the use or operation of ships, installations or aircraft as referred to in point 1(a), in particular loss of freight or charter-hire;
4. any risk or interest connected with any of those referred to in points 1 to 3;
5. notwithstanding points 1 to 4, all large risks as defined in Council Directive 73/239/EEC (1), as amended by Council Directives 88/357/EEC (2) and 90/618/EEC (3), as they may be amended.

Section 5. Jurisdiction over consumer contracts

Article 15. 1. In matters relating to a contract concluded by a person, the consumer, for a purpose which can be regarded as being outside his trade or profession, jurisdiction shall be determined by this Section, without prejudice to Article 4 and point 5 of Article 5, if:
(a) it is a contract for the sale of goods on instalment credit terms; or
(b) it is a contract for a loan repayable by instalments, or for any other form of credit, made to finance the sale of goods; or
(c) in all other cases, the contract has been concluded with a person who pursues commercial or professional activities in the Member State of the consumer's domicile or, by any means, directs such activities to that Member State or to several States including that Member State, and the contract falls within the scope of such activities.
2. Where a consumer enters into a contract with a party who is not domiciled in the Member State but has a branch, agency or other establishment in one of the Member States, that party shall, in disputes arising out of the operations of the branch, agency or establishment, be deemed to be domiciled in that State.
3. This Section shall not apply to a contract of transport other than a contract which, for an inclusive price, provides for a combination of travel and accommodation.

Article 16. 1. A consumer may bring proceedings against the other party to a contract either in the courts of the Member State in which that party is domiciled or in the courts for the place where the consumer is domiciled.
2. Proceedings may be brought against a consumer by the other party to the contract only in the courts of the Member State in which the consumer is domiciled.
3. This Article shall not affect the right to bring a counter-claim in the court in which, in accordance with this Section, the original claim is pending.

Article 17. The provisions of this Section may be departed from only by an agreement:
1. which is entered into after the dispute has arisen; or
2. which allows the consumer to bring proceedings in courts other than those indicated in this Section; or
3. which is entered into by the consumer and the other party to the contract, both of whom are at the time of conclusion of the contract domiciled or habitually resident in the same Member State, and which confers jurisdiction on the courts of that Member State, provided that such an agreement is not contrary to the law of that Member State.

Section 5. Jurisdiction over individual contracts of employment

Article 18. 1. In matters relating to individual contracts of employment, jurisdiction shall be determined by this Section, without prejudice to Article 4 and point 5 of Article 5.

2. Where an employee enters into an individual contract of employment with an employer who is not domiciled in a Member State but has a branch, agency or other establishment in one of the Member States, the employer shall, in disputes arising out of the operations of the branch, agency or establishment, be deemed to be domiciled in that Member State.

Article 19. An employer domiciled in a Member State may be sued:
1. in the courts of the Member State where he is domiciled; or
2. in another Member State:
(a) in the courts for the place where the employee habitually carries out his work or in the courts for the last place where he did so, or
(b) if the employee does not or did not habitually carry out his work in any one country, in the courts for the place where the business which engaged the employee is or was situated.

Article 20. 1. An employer may bring proceedings only in the courts of the Member State in which the employee is domiciled.
2. The provisions of this Section shall not affect the right to bring a counter-claim in the court in which, in accordance with this Section, the original claim is pending.

Article 21. The provisions of this Section may be departed from only by an agreement on jurisdiction:
1. which is entered into after the dispute has arisen; or
2. which allows the employee to bring proceedings in courts other than those indicated in this Section.

Section 6. Exclusive jurisdiction

Article 22. The following courts shall have exclusive jurisdiction, regardless of domicile:
1. in proceedings which have as their object rights in rem in immovable property or tenancies of immovable property, the courts of the Member State in which the property is situated. However, in proceedings which have as their object tenancies of immovable property concluded for temporary private use for a maximum period of six consecutive months, the courts of the Member State in which the defendant is domiciled shall also have jurisdiction, provided that the tenant is a natural person and that the landlord and the tenant are domiciled in the same Member State;
2. in proceedings which have as their object the validity of the constitution, the nullity or the dissolution of companies or other legal persons or associations of natural or legal persons, or of the validity of the decisions of their organs, the courts of the Member State in which the company, legal person or association has its seat. In order to determine that seat, the court shall apply its rules of private international law;
3. in proceedings which have as their object the validity of entries in public registers, the courts of the Member State in which the register is kept;
4. in proceedings concerned with the registration or validity of patents, trade marks, designs, or other similar rights required to be deposited or registered, the courts of the Member State in which the deposit or registration has been applied for, has taken place or is under the terms of a Community instrument or an international convention deemed to have taken place. Without prejudice to the jurisdiction of the European Patent Office under the Convention on the Grant of European Patents, signed at Munich on 5 October 1973, the courts of each Member State shall have exclusive jurisdiction, regardless of domicile, in proceedings concerned with the registration or validity of any European patent granted for that State;
5. in proceedings concerned with the enforcement of judgments, the courts of the Member State in which the judgment has been or is to be enforced.

Section 7. Prorogation of jurisdiction

Article 23. 1. If the parties, one or more of whom is domiciled in a Member State, have agreed that a court or the courts of a Member State are to have jurisdiction to settle any disputes which have arisen or which may arise in connection with a particular legal relationship, that court or those courts shall have jurisdiction. Such jurisdiction shall be exclusive unless the parties have agreed otherwise. Such an agreement conferring jurisdiction shall be either:
(a) in writing or evidenced in writing; or
(b) in a form which accords with practices which the parties have established between themselves; or

(c) in international trade or commerce, in a form which accords with a usage of which the parties are or ought to have been aware and which in such trade or commerce is widely known to, and regularly observed by, parties to contracts of the type involved in the particular trade or commerce concerned.
2. Any communication by electronic means which provides a durable record of the agreement shall be equivalent to 'writing'.
3. Where such an agreement is concluded by parties, none of whom is domiciled in a Member State, the courts of other Member States shall have no jurisdiction over their disputes unless the court or courts chosen have declined jurisdiction.
4. The court or courts of a Member State on which a trust instrument has conferred jurisdiction shall have exclusive jurisdiction in any proceedings brought against a settlor, trustee or beneficiary, if relations between these persons or their rights or obligations under the trust are involved.
5. Agreements or provisions of a trust instrument conferring jurisdiction shall have no legal force if they are contrary to Articles 13, 17 or 21, or if the courts whose jurisdiction they purport to exclude have exclusive jurisdiction by virtue of Article 22.

Article 24. Apart from jurisdiction derived from other provisions of this Regulation, a court of a Member State before which a defendant enters an appearance shall have jurisdiction. This rule shall not apply where appearance was entered to contest the jurisdiction, or where another court has exclusive jurisdiction by virtue of Article 22.

Section 8. Examination as to jurisdiction and admissibility

Article 25. Where a court of a Member State is seised of a claim which is principally concerned with a matter over which the courts of another Member State have exclusive jurisdiction by virtue of Article 22, it shall declare of its own motion that it has no jurisdiction.

Article 26. 1. Where a defendant domiciled in one Member State is sued in a court of another Member State and does not enter an appearance, the court shall declare of its own motion that it
has no jurisdiction unless its jurisdiction is derived from the provisions of this Regulation.
2. The court shall stay the proceedings so long as it is not shown that the defendant has been able to receive the document instituting the proceedings or an equivalent document in sufficient time to enable him to arrange for his defence, or that all necessary steps have been taken to this end.
3. Article 19 of Council Regulation (EC) No 1348/2000 of 29 May 2000 on the service in the Member States of judicial and extrajudicial documents in civil or commercial matters (1) shall apply instead of the provisions of paragraph 2 if the document instituting the proceedings or an equivalent document had to be transmitted from one Member State to another pursuant to this Regulation.
4. Where the provisions of Regulation (EC) No 1348/2000 are not applicable, Article 15 of the Hague Convention of 15 November 1965 on the Service Abroad of Judicial and Extrajudicial Documents in Civil or Commercial Matters shall apply if the document instituting the proceedings or an equivalent document had to be transmitted pursuant to that Convention.

Section 9. Lis pendens – related actions

Article 27. 1. Where proceedings involving the same cause of action and between the same parties are brought in the courts of different Member States, any court other than the court first seised shall of its own motion stay its proceedings until such time as the jurisdiction of the court first seised is established.
2. Where the jurisdiction of the court first seised is established, any court other than the court first seised shall decline jurisdiction in favour of that court.

Article 28. 1. Where related actions are pending in the courts of different Member States, any court other than the court first seised may stay its proceedings.
2. Where these actions are pending at first instance, any court other than the court first seised may also, on the application of one of the parties, decline jurisdiction if the court first seised has jurisdiction over the actions in question and its law permits the consolidation thereof.
3. For the purposes of this Article, actions are deemed to be related where they are so closely connected that it is expedient to hear and determine them together to avoid the risk of irreconcilable judgments resulting from separate proceedings.

Article 29. Where actions come within the exclusive jurisdiction of several courts, any court other than the court first seised shall decline jurisdiction in favour of that court.

Article 30. For the purposes of this Section, a court shall be deemed to be seised:
1. at the time when the document instituting the proceedings or an equivalent document is lodged with the court, provided that the plaintiff has not subsequently failed to take the steps he was required to take to have service effected on the defendant, or
2. if the document has to be served before being lodged with the court, at the time when it is received by the authority responsible for service, provided that the plaintiff has not subsequently failed to take the steps he was required to take to have the document lodged with the court.

Section 10. Provisional, including protective, measures

Article 31. Application may be made to the courts of a Member State for such provisional, including protective, measures as may be available under the law of that State, even if, under this
Regulation, the courts of another Member State have jurisdiction as to the substance of the matter.

Chapter III. Recognition and Enforcement

Article 32. For the purposes of this Regulation, .judgment. means any judgment given by a court or tribunal of a Member State, whatever the judgment may be called, including a decree, order, decision or writ of execution, as well as the determination of costs or expenses by an officer of the court.

Section 1. Recognition

Article 33. 1. A judgment given in a Member State shall be recognised in the other Member States without any special procedure being required.
2. Any interested party who raises the recognition of a judgment as the principal issue in a dispute may, in accordance with the procedures provided for in Sections 2 and 3 of this Chapter, apply for a decision that the judgment be recognised.
3. If the outcome of proceedings in a court of a Member State depends on the determination of an incidental question of recognition that court shall have jurisdiction over that question.

Article 34. A judgment shall not be recognised:
1. if such recognition is manifestly contrary to public policy in the Member State in which recognition is sought;
2. where it was given in default of appearance, if the defendant was not served with the document which instituted the proceedings or with an equivalent document in sufficient time and in such a way as to enable him to arrange for his defence, unless the defendant failed to commence proceedings to challenge the judgment when it was possible for him to do so;
3. if it is irreconcilable with a judgment given in a dispute between the same parties in the Member State in which recognition is sought;
4. if it is irreconcilable with an earlier judgment given in another Member State or in a third State involving the same cause of action and between the same parties, provided that the earlier judgment fulfils the conditions necessary for its recognition in the Member State addressed.

Article 35. 1. Moreover, a judgment shall not be recognised if it conflicts with Sections 3, 4 or 6 of Chapter II, or in a case provided for in Article 72.
2. In its examination of the grounds of jurisdiction referred to in the foregoing paragraph, the court or authority applied to shall be bound by the findings of fact on which the court of the Member State of origin based its jurisdiction.
3. Subject to the paragraph 1, the jurisdiction of the court of the Member State of origin may not be reviewed. The test of public policy referred to in point 1 of Article 34 may not be applied to the rules relating to jurisdiction.

Article 36. Under no circumstances may a foreign judgment be reviewed as to its substance.

Article 37. 1. A court of a Member State in which recognition is sought of a judgment given in another Member State may stay the proceedings if an ordinary appeal against the judgment has been lodged.

2. A court of a Member State in which recognition is sought of a judgment given in Ireland or the United Kingdom may stay the proceedings if enforcement is suspended in the State of origin, by reason of an appeal.

Section 2. Enforcement

Article 38. 1. A judgment given in a Member State and enforceable in that State shall be enforced in another Member State when, on the application of any interested party, it has been declared enforceable there.
2. However, in the United Kingdom, such a judgment shall be enforced in England and Wales, in Scotland, or in Northern Ireland when, on the application of any interested party, it has been registered for enforcement in that part of the United Kingdom.

Article 39. 1. The application shall be submitted to the court or competent authority indicated in the list in Annex II.
2. The local jurisdiction shall be determined by reference to the place of domicile of the party against whom enforcement is sought, or to the place of enforcement.

Article 40. 1. The procedure for making the application shall be governed by the law of the Member State in which enforcement is sought.
2. The applicant must give an address for service of process within the area of jurisdiction of the court applied to. However, if the law of the Member State in which enforcement is sought does not provide for the furnishing of such an address, the applicant shall appoint a representative ad litem.
3. The documents referred to in Article 53 shall be attached to the application.

Article 41. The judgment shall be declared enforceable immediately on completion of the formalities in Article 53 without any review under Articles 34 and 35. The party against whom enforcement is sought shall not at this stage of the proceedings be entitled to make any submissions on the application.

Article 42. 1. The decision on the application for a declaration of enforceability shall forthwith be brought to the notice of the applicant in accordance with the procedure laid down by the law of the Member State in which enforcement is sought.
2. The declaration of enforceability shall be served on the party against whom enforcement is sought, accompanied by the judgment, if not already served on that party.

Article 43. 1. The decision on the application for a declaration of enforceability may be appealed against by either party.
2. The appeal is to be lodged with the court indicated in the list in Annex III.
3. The appeal shall be dealt with in accordance with the rules governing procedure in contradictory matters.
4. If the party against whom enforcement is sought fails to appear before the appellate court in proceedings concerning an appeal brought by the applicant, Article 26(2) to (4) shall apply even where the party against whom enforcement is sought is not domiciled in any of the Member States.
5. An appeal against the declaration of enforceability is to be lodged within one month of service thereof. If the party against whom enforcement is sought is domiciled in a Member State other than that in which the declaration of enforceability was given, the time for appealing shall be two months and shall run from the date of service, either on him in person or at his residence. No extension of time may be granted on account of distance.

Article 44. The judgment given on the appeal may be contested only by the appeal referred to in Annex IV.

Article 45. 1. The court with which an appeal is lodged under Article 43 or Article 44 shall refuse or revoke a declaration of enforceability only on one of the grounds specified in Articles 34 and 35. It shall give its decision without delay.
2. Under no circumstances may the foreign judgment be reviewed as to its substance.

Article 46. 1. The court with which an appeal is lodged under Article 43 or Article 44 may, on the application of the party against whom enforcement is sought, stay the proceedings if an ordinary appeal has been lodged against the judgment in the Member State of origin or if the time for such an appeal has not yet expired; in the latter case, the court may specify the time within which such an appeal is to be lodged.
2. Where the judgment was given in Ireland or the United Kingdom, any form of appeal available in the Member State of origin shall be treated as an ordinary appeal for the purposes of paragraph 1.

3. The court may also make enforcement conditional on the provision of such security as it shall determine.

Article 47. 1. When a judgment must be recognised in accordance with this Regulation, nothing shall prevent the applicant from availing himself of provisional, including protective, measures in accordance with the law of the Member State requested without a declaration of enforceability under Article 41 being required.
2. The declaration of enforceability shall carry with it the power to proceed to any protective measures.
3. During the time specified for an appeal pursuant to Article 43(5) against the declaration of enforceability and until any such appeal has been determined, no measures of enforcement may be taken other than protective measures against the property of the party against whom enforcement is sought.

Article 48. 1. Where a foreign judgment has been given in respect of several matters and the declaration of enforceability cannot be given for all of them, the court or competent authority shall give it for one or more of them.
2. An applicant may request a declaration of enforceability limited to parts of a judgment.

Article 49. A foreign judgment which orders a periodic payment by way of a penalty shall be enforceable in the Member State in which enforcement is sought only if the amount of the payment has been finally determined by the courts of the Member State of origin.

Article 50. An applicant who, in the Member State of origin has benefited from complete or partial legal aid or exemption from costs or expenses, shall be entitled, in the procedure provided for in this Section, to benefit from the most favourable legal aid or the most extensive exemption from costs or expenses provided for by the law of the Member State addressed.

Article 51. No security, bond or deposit, however described, shall be required of a party who in one Member State applies for enforcement of a judgment given in another Member State on the ground that he is a foreign national or that he is not domiciled or resident in the State in which enforcement is sought.

Article 52. In proceedings for the issue of a declaration of enforceability, no charge, duty or fee calculated by reference to the value of the matter at issue may be levied in the Member State in which enforcement is sought.

Section 3. Common provisions

Article 53. 1. A party seeking recognition or applying for a declaration of enforceability shall produce a copy of the judgment which satisfies the conditions necessary to establish its authenticity.
2. A party applying for a declaration of enforceability shall also produce the certificate referred to in Article 54, without prejudice to Article 55.

Article 54. The court or competent authority of a Member State where a judgment was given shall issue, at the request of any interested party, a certificate using the standard form in Annex V to this Regulation.

Article 55. 1. If the certificate referred to in Article 54 is not produced, the court or competent authority may specify a time for its production or accept an equivalent document or, if it considers that it has sufficient information before it, dispense with its production.
2. If the court or competent authority so requires, a translation of the documents shall be produced. The translation shall be certified by a person qualified to do so in one of the Member States.

Article 56. No legalisation or other similar formality shall be required in respect of the documents referred to in Article 53 or Article 55(2), or in respect of a document appointing a representative ad litem.

Chapter IV. Authentic Instruments and Court Settlements

Article 57. 1. A document which has been formally drawn up or registered as an authentic instrument and is enforceable in one Member State shall, in another Member State, be declared enforceable there, on application made in accordance with the procedures provided for in Articles 38, et seq. The court with which an appeal is lodged under Article 43 or Article 44 shall refuse or revoke a declaration of enforceability only if enforcement of the instrument is manifestly contrary to public policy in the Member State addressed.

2. Arrangements relating to maintenance obligations concluded with administrative authorities or authenticated by them shall also be regarded as authentic instruments within the meaning of paragraph 1.
3. The instrument produced must satisfy the conditions necessary to establish its authenticity in the Member State of origin.
4. Section 3 of Chapter III shall apply as appropriate. The competent authority of a Member State where an authentic instrument was drawn up or registered shall issue, at the request of any interested party, a certificate using the standard form in Annex VI to this Regulation.

Article 58. A settlement which has been approved by a court in the course of proceedings and is enforceable in the Member State in which it was concluded shall be enforceable in the State addressed under the same conditions as authentic instruments. The court or competent authority of a Member State where a court settlement was approved shall issue, at the request of any interested party, a certificate using the standard form in Annex V to this Regulation.

Chapter V. General Provisions

Article 59. 1. In order to determine whether a party is domiciled in the Member State whose courts are seised of a matter, the court shall apply its internal law.
2. If a party is not domiciled in the Member State whose courts are seised of the matter, then, in order to determine whether the party is domiciled in another Member State, the court shall apply the law of that Member State.

Article 60. 1. For the purposes of this Regulation, a company or other legal person or association of natural or legal persons is domiciled at the place where it has its:
(a) statutory seat, or
(b) central administration, or
(c) principal place of business.
2. For the purposes of the United Kingdom and Ireland .statutory seat. means the registered office or, where there is no such office anywhere, the place of incorporation or, where there is no such place anywhere, the place under the law of which the formation took place.
3. In order to determine whether a trust is domiciled in the Member State whose courts are seised of the matter, the court shall apply its rules of private international law.

Article 61. Without prejudice to any more favourable provisions of national laws, persons domiciled in a Member State who are being prosecuted in the criminal courts of another Member
State of which they are not nationals for an offence which was not intentionally committed may be defended by persons qualified to do so, even if they do not appear in person. However, the court seised of the matter may order appearance in person; in the case of failure to appear, a judgment given in the civil action without the person concerned having had the opportunity to arrange for his defence need not be recognised or enforced in the other Member States.

Article 62. In Sweden, in summary proceedings concerning orders to pay (betalningsföreläggande) and assistance (handräckning), the expression 'court' includes the 'Swedish enforcement service' (kronofogdemyndighet).

Article 63. 1. A person domiciled in the territory of the Grand Duchy of Luxembourg and sued in the court of another Member State pursuant to Article 5(1) may refuse to submit to the jurisdiction of that court if the final place of delivery of the goods or provision of the services is in Luxembourg.
2. Where, under paragraph 1, the final place of delivery of the goods or provision of the services is in Luxembourg, any agreement conferring jurisdiction must, in order to be valid, be accepted in writing or evidenced in writing within the meaning of Article 23(1)(a).
3. The provisions of this Article shall not apply to contracts for the provision of financial services.
4. The provisions of this Article shall apply for a period of six years from entry into force of this Regulation.

Article 64. 1. In proceedings involving a dispute between the master and a member of the crew of a seagoing ship registered in Greece or in Portugal, concerning remuneration or other conditions of service, a court in a Member State shall establish whether the diplomatic or consular officer responsible for the ship has been notified of the dispute. It may act as soon as
that officer has been notified.
2. The provisions of this Article shall apply for a period of six years from entry into force of this Regulation.

Article 65. 1. The jurisdiction specified in Article 6(2), and Article 11 in actions on a warranty of guarantee or in any other third party proceedings may not be resorted to in Germany and Austria. Any person domiciled in another Member State may be sued in the courts:
(a) of Germany, pursuant to Articles 68 and 72 to 74 of the Code of Civil Procedure (Zivilprozessordnung) concerning third-party notices,
(b) of Austria, pursuant to Article 21 of the Code of Civil Procedure (Zivilprozessordnung) concerning third-party notices.
2. Judgments given in other Member States by virtue of Article 6(2), or Article 11 shall be recognised and enforced in Germany and Austria in accordance with Chapter III. Any effects which judgments given in these States may have on third parties by application of the provisions in paragraph 1 shall also be recognised in the other Member States.

Chapter VI. Transitional Provisions

Article 66. 1. This Regulation shall apply only to legal proceedings instituted and to documents formally drawn up or registered as authentic instruments after the entry into force thereof.
2. However, if the proceedings in the Member State of origin were instituted before the entry into force of this Regulation, judgments given after that date shall be recognised and enforced in accordance with Chapter III,
(a) if the proceedings in the Member State of origin were instituted after the entry into force of the Brussels or the Lugano Convention both in the Member State or origin and in the Member State addressed;
(b) in all other cases, if jurisdiction was founded upon rules which accorded with those provided for either in Chapter II or in a convention concluded between the Member State of origin and the Member State addressed which was in force when the proceedings were instituted.

Chapter VII. Relations with other Instruments

Article 67. This Regulation shall not prejudice the application of provisions governing jurisdiction and the recognition and enforcement of judgments in specific matters which are contained in Community instruments or in national legislation harmonised pursuant to such instruments.

Article 68. 1. This Regulation shall, as between the Member States, supersede the Brussels Convention, except as regards the territories of the Member States which fall within the territorial scope of that Convention and which are excluded from this Regulation pursuant to Article 299 of the Treaty.
2. In so far as this Regulation replaces the provisions of the Brussels Convention between Member States, any reference to the Convention shall be understood as a reference to this Regulation.

Article 69. Subject to Article 66(2) and Article 70, this Regulation shall, as between Member States, supersede the following conventions and treaty concluded between two or more of them: *Omitted*

Article 70. 1. The Treaty and the Conventions referred to in Article 69 shall continue to have effect in relation to matters to which this Regulation does not apply.
2. They shall continue to have effect in respect of judgments given and documents formally drawn up or registered as authentic instruments before the entry into force of this Regulation.

Article 71. 1. This Regulation shall not affect any conventions to which the Member States are parties and which in relation to particular matters, govern jurisdiction or the recognition or
enforcement of judgments.
2. With a view to its uniform interpretation, paragraph 1 shall be applied in the following manner:
(a) this Regulation shall not prevent a court of a Member State, which is a party to a convention on a particular matter, from assuming jurisdiction in accordance with that convention, even where the defendant is domiciled in another Member State which is not a party to that convention. The court hearing the action shall, in any event, apply Article 26 of this Regulation;
(b) judgments given in a Member State by a court in the exercise of jurisdiction provided for in a convention on a particular matter shall be recognised and enforced in the other Member States in accordance with this Regulation. Where a convention on a particular matter to which both the Member State of origin and the Member State addressed are parties lays down conditions for the recognition or enforcement of judgments, those conditions shall apply. In any event, the provisions of this Regulation which concern the procedure for recognition and enforcement of judgments may be applied.

Article 72. This Regulation shall not affect agreements by which Member States undertook, prior to the entry into force of this Regulation pursuant to Article 59 of the Brussels Convention, not to recognise judgments given, in particular in other Contracting States to that Convention, against defendants domiciled or habitually resident in a third country where, in cases provided for in Article 4 of that Convention, the judgment could only be founded on a ground of jurisdiction specified in the second paragraph of Article 3 of that Convention.

Chapter VIII. Final Provisions

Article 73. No later than five years after the entry into force of this Regulation, the Commission shall present to the European Parliament, the Council and the Economic and Social Committee a report on the application of this Regulation. The report shall be accompanied, if need be, by proposals for adaptations to this Regulation.

Article 74. 1. The Member States shall notify the Commission of the texts amending the lists set out in Annexes I to IV. The Commission shall adapt the Annexes concerned accordingly.
2. The updating or technical adjustment of the forms, specimens of which appear in Annexes V and VI, shall be adopted in accordance with the advisory procedure referred to in Article 75(2).

Article 75. 1. The Commission shall be assisted by a committee.
2. Where reference is made to this paragraph, Articles 3 and 7 of Decision 1999/468/EC shall apply.
3. The Committee shall adopt its rules of procedure.

Article 76. This Regulation shall enter into force on 1 March 2002.
This Regulation is binding in its entirety and directly applicable in the Member States in accordance with the Treaty establishing the European Community.

Council Regulation (EC) No 2201/2003 of 27 November 2003 concerning jurisdiction and the recognition and enforcement of judgments in matrimonial matters and the matters of parental responsibility, repealing Regulation (EC) No 1347/2000 [Brussels II] (*OJ* L 338, 23.12.2003, p. 1–29) [footnotes omitted].

THE COUNCIL OF THE EUROPEAN UNION,
Having regard to the Treaty establishing the European Community, and in particular Article 61(c) and Article 67(1) thereof,
Having regard to the proposal from the Commission,
Having regard to the opinion of the European Parliament,
Having regard to the opinion of the European Economic and Social Committee,
Whereas:
(1) The European Community has set the objective of creating an area of freedom, security and justice, in which the free movement of persons is ensured. To this end, the Community is to adopt, among others, measures in the field of judicial cooperation in civil matters that are necessary for the proper functioning of the internal market.
(2) The Tampere European Council endorsed the principle of mutual recognition of judicial decisions as the cornerstone for the creation of a genuine judicial area, and identified visiting rights as a priority.
(3) Council Regulation (EC) No 1347/2000 sets out rules on jurisdiction, recognition and enforcement of judgments in matrimonial matters and matters of parental responsibility for the children of both spouses rendered on the occasion of the matrimonial proceedings. The content of this Regulation was substantially taken over from the Convention of 28 May 1998 on the same subject matter.
(4) On 3 July 2000 France presented an initiative for a Council Regulation on the mutual enforcement of judgments on rights of access to children.
(5) In order to ensure equality for all children, this Regulation covers all decisions on parental responsibility, including measures for the protection of the child, independently of any link with a matrimonial proceeding.
(6) Since the application of the rules on parental responsibility often arises in the context of matrimonial proceedings, it is more appropriate to have a single instrument for matters of divorce and parental responsibility.
(7) The scope of this Regulation covers civil matters, whatever the nature of the court or tribunal.
(8) As regards judgments on divorce, legal separation or marriage annulment, this Regulation should apply only to the dissolution of matrimonial ties and should not deal with issues such as the grounds for divorce, property consequences of the marriage or any other ancillary measures.
(9) As regards the property of the child, this Regulation should apply only to measures for the protection of the child, i.e. (i) the designation and functions of a person or body having charge of the child's property, representing or assisting the child, and (ii) the administration, conservation or disposal of the child's property. In this context, this Regulation should, for instance, apply in cases where the parents are in dispute as regards the administration of the child's property. Measures relating to the child's property which do not concern the protection of the child should continue to be governed by Council Regulation (EC) No 44/2001 of 22 December 2000 on jurisdiction and the recognition and enforcement of judgments in civil and commercial matters.
(10) This Regulation is not intended to apply to matters relating to social security, public measures of a general nature in matters of education or health or to decisions on the right of asylum and on immigration. In addition it does not apply to the establishment of parenthood, since this is a different matter from the attribution of parental responsibility, nor to other questions linked to the status of persons. Moreover, it does not apply to measures taken as a result of criminal offences committed by children.
(11) Maintenance obligations are excluded from the scope of this Regulation as these are already covered by Council Regulation No 44/2001. The courts having jurisdiction under this Regulation will generally have jurisdiction to rule on maintenance obligations by application of Article 5(2) of Council Regulation No 44/2001.
(12) The grounds of jurisdiction in matters of parental responsibility established in the present Regulation are shaped in the light of the best interests of the child, in particular on the criterion of proximity. This means that jurisdiction should lie in the first place with the Member State of the child's habitual residence, except for certain cases of a change in the child's residence or pursuant to an agreement between the holders of parental responsibility.
(13) In the interest of the child, this Regulation allows, by way of exception and under certain conditions, that the court having jurisdiction may transfer a case to a court of another Member State if this court is better placed to hear the case. However, in this case the second court should not be allowed to transfer the case to a third court.
(14) This Regulation should have effect without prejudice to the application of public international law concerning diplomatic immunities. Where jurisdiction under this Regulation cannot be exercised by reason of the existence of diplomatic immunity in accordance with international law, jurisdiction should be exercised in accordance with national law in a Member State in which the person concerned does not enjoy such immunity.

Part VII. Private International Law

(15) Council Regulation (EC) No 1348/2000 of 29 May 2000 on the service in the Member States of judicial and extrajudicial documents in civil or commercial matters should apply to the service of documents in proceedings instituted pursuant to this Regulation.

(16) This Regulation should not prevent the courts of a Member State from taking provisional, including protective measures, in urgent cases, with regard to persons or property situated in that State.

(17) In cases of wrongful removal or retention of a child, the return of the child should be obtained without delay, and to this end the Hague Convention of 25 October 1980 would continue to apply as complemented by the provisions of this Regulation, in particular Article 11. The courts of the Member State to or in which the child has been wrongfully removed or retained should be able to oppose his or her return in specific, duly justified cases. However, such a decision could be replaced by a subsequent decision by the court of the Member State of habitual residence of the child prior to the wrongful removal or retention. Should that judgment entail the return of the child, the return should take place without any special procedure being required for recognition and enforcement of that judgment in the Member State to or in which the child has been removed or retained.

(18) Where a court has decided not to return a child on the basis of Article 13 of the 1980 Hague Convention, it should inform the court having jurisdiction or central authority in the Member State where the child was habitually resident prior to the wrongful removal or retention. Unless the court in the latter Member State has been seised, this court or the central authority should notify the parties. This obligation should not prevent the central authority from also notifying the relevant public authorities in accordance with national law.

(19) The hearing of the child plays an important role in the application of this Regulation, although this instrument is not intended to modify national procedures applicable.

(20) The hearing of a child in another Member State may take place under the arrangements laid down in Council Regulation (EC) No 1206/2001 of 28 May 2001 on cooperation between the courts of the Member States in the taking of evidence in civil or commercial matters.

(21) The recognition and enforcement of judgments given in a Member State should be based on the principle of mutual trust and the grounds for non-recognition should be kept to the minimum required.

(22) Authentic instruments and agreements between parties that are enforceable in one Member State should be treated as equivalent to "judgments" for the purpose of the application of the rules on recognition and enforcement.

(23) The Tampere European Council considered in its conclusions (point 34) that judgments in the field of family litigation should be "automatically recognised throughout the Union without any intermediate proceedings or grounds for refusal of enforcement". This is why judgments on rights of access and judgments on return that have been certified in the Member State of origin in accordance with the provisions of this Regulation should be recognised and enforceable in all other Member States without any further procedure being required. Arrangements for the enforcement of such judgments continue to be governed by national law.

(24) The certificate issued to facilitate enforcement of the judgment should not be subject to appeal. It should be rectified only where there is a material error, i.e. where it does not correctly reflect the judgment.

(25) Central authorities should cooperate both in general matter and in specific cases, including for purposes of promoting the amicable resolution of family disputes, in matters of parental responsibility. To this end central authorities shall participate in the European Judicial Network in civil and commercial matters created by Council Decision 2001/470/EC of 28 May 2001 establishing a European Judicial Network in civil and commercial matters.

(26) The Commission should make publicly available and update the lists of courts and redress procedures communicated by the Member States.

(27) The measures necessary for the implementation of this Regulation should be adopted in accordance with Council Decision 1999/468/EC of 28 June 1999 laying down the procedures for the exercise of implementing powers conferred on the Commission.

(28) This Regulation replaces Regulation (EC) No 1347/2000 which is consequently repealed.

(29) For the proper functioning of this Regulation, the Commission should review its application and propose such amendments as may appear necessary.

(30) The United Kingdom and Ireland, in accordance with Article 3 of the Protocol on the position of the United Kingdom and Ireland annexed to the Treaty on European Union and the Treaty establishing the European Community, have given notice of their wish to take part in the adoption and application of this Regulation.

(31) Denmark, in accordance with Articles 1 and 2 of the Protocol on the position of Denmark annexed to the Treaty on European Union and the Treaty establishing the European Community, is not participating in the adoption of this Regulation and is therefore not bound by it nor subject to its application.

(32) Since the objectives of this Regulation cannot be sufficiently achieved by the Member States and can therefore be better achieved at Community level, the Community may adopt measures, in accordance with the principle of subsidiarity as set out in Article 5 of the Treaty. In accordance with the principle of proportionality, as set out in that Article, this Regulation does not go beyond what is necessary in order to achieve those objectives.

(33) This Regulation recognises the fundamental rights and observes the principles of the Charter of Fundamental Rights of the European Union. In particular, it seeks to ensure respect for the fundamental rights of the child as set out in Article 24 of the Charter of Fundamental Rights of the European Union,

HAS ADOPTED THE PRESENT REGULATION:

Chapter 1. Scope and Definitions

Article 1. 1. This Regulation shall apply, whatever the nature of the court or tribunal, in civil matters relating to:
(a) divorce, legal separation or marriage annulment;
(b) the attribution, exercise, delegation, restriction or termination of parental responsibility.
2. The matters referred to in paragraph 1(b) may, in particular, deal with:
(a) rights of custody and rights of access;
(b) guardianship, curatorship and similar institutions;
(c) the designation and functions of any person or body having charge of the child's person or property, representing or assisting the child;
(d) the placement of the child in a foster family or in institutional care;
(e) measures for the protection of the child relating to the administration, conservation or disposal of the child's property.
3. This Regulation shall not apply to:
(a) the establishment or contesting of a parent-child relationship;
(b) decisions on adoption, measures preparatory to adoption, or the annulment or revocation of adoption;
(c) the name and forenames of the child;
(d) emancipation;
(e) maintenance obligations;
(f) trusts or succession;
(g) measures taken as a result of criminal offences committed by children.

Article 2. For the purposes of this Regulation:
1. the term "court" shall cover all the authorities in the Member States with jurisdiction in the matters falling within the scope of this Regulation pursuant to Article 1;
2. the term "judge" shall mean the judge or an official having powers equivalent to those of a judge in the matters falling within the scope of the Regulation;
3. the term "Member State" shall mean all Member States with the exception of Denmark;
4. the term "judgment" shall mean a divorce, legal separation or marriage annulment, as well as a judgment relating to parental responsibility, pronounced by a court of a Member State, whatever the judgment may be called, including a decree, order or decision;
5. the term "Member State of origin" shall mean the Member State where the judgment to be enforced was issued;
6. the term "Member State of enforcement" shall mean the Member State where enforcement of the judgment is sought;
7. the term "parental responsibility" shall mean all rights and duties relating to the person or the property of a child which are given to a natural or legal person by judgment, by operation of law or by an agreement having legal effect. The term shall include rights of custody and rights of access;
8. the term "holder of parental responsibility" shall mean any person having parental responsibility over a child;
9. the term "rights of custody" shall include rights and duties relating to the care of the person of a child, and in particular the right to determine the child's place of residence;
10. the term "rights of access" shall include in particular the right to take a child to a place other than his or her habitual residence for a limited period of time;
11. the term "wrongful removal or retention" shall mean a child's removal or retention where:
(a) it is in breach of rights of custody acquired by judgment or by operation of law or by an agreement having legal effect under the law of the Member State where the child was habitually resident immediately before the removal or retention;
and
(b) provided that, at the time of removal or retention, the rights of custody were actually exercised, either jointly or alone, or would have been so exercised but for the removal or retention. Custody shall be considered to be exercised jointly when, pursuant to a judgment or by operation of law, one holder of parental responsibility cannot decide on the child's place of residence without the consent of another holder of parental responsibility.

Part VII. Private International Law

Chapter II. Jurisdiction

Section 1. Divorce, legal separation and marriage annulment

Article 3. 1. In matters relating to divorce, legal separation or marriage annulment, jurisdiction shall lie with the courts of the Member State
(a) in whose territory:
- the spouses are habitually resident, or
- the spouses were last habitually resident, insofar as one of them still resides there, or
- the respondent is habitually resident, or
- in the event of a joint application, either of the spouses is habitually resident, or
- the applicant is habitually resident if he or she resided there for at least a year immediately before the application was made, or
- the applicant is habitually resident if he or she resided there for at least six months immediately before the application was made and is either a national of the Member State in question or, in the case of the United Kingdom and Ireland, has his or her "domicile" there;
(b) of the nationality of both spouses or, in the case of the United Kingdom and Ireland, of the "domicile" of both spouses.
2. For the purpose of this Regulation, "domicile" shall have the same meaning as it has under the legal systems of the United Kingdom and Ireland.

Article 4. The court in which proceedings are pending on the basis of Article 3 shall also have jurisdiction to examine a counterclaim, insofar as the latter comes within the scope of this Regulation.

Article 5. Without prejudice to Article 3, a court of a Member State that has given a judgment on a legal separation shall also have jurisdiction for converting that judgment into a divorce, if the law of that Member State so provides.

Article 6. A spouse who:
(a) is habitually resident in the territory of a Member State; or
(b) is a national of a Member State, or, in the case of the United Kingdom and Ireland, has his or her "domicile" in the territory of one of the latter Member States,
may be sued in another Member State only in accordance with Articles 3, 4 and 5.

Article 7. 1. Where no court of a Member State has jurisdiction pursuant to Articles 3, 4 and 5, jurisdiction shall be determined, in each Member State, by the laws of that State.
2. As against a respondent who is not habitually resident and is not either a national of a Member State or, in the case of the United Kingdom and Ireland, does not have his "domicile" within the territory of one of the latter Member States, any national of a Member State who is habitually resident within the territory of another Member State may, like the nationals of that State, avail himself of the rules of jurisdiction applicable in that State.

Section 2. Parental responsibililty

Article 8. 1. The courts of a Member State shall have jurisdiction in matters of parental responsibility over a child who is habitually resident in that Member State at the time the court is seised.
2. Paragraph 1 shall be subject to the provisions of Articles 9, 10 and 12.

Article 9. Continuing jurisdiction of the child's former habitual residence
1. Where a child moves lawfully from one Member State to another and acquires a new habitual residence there, the courts of the Member State of the child's former habitual residence shall, by way of exception to Article 8, retain jurisdiction during a three-month period following the move for the purpose of modifying a judgment on access rights issued in that Member State before the child moved, where the holder of access rights pursuant to the judgment on access rights continues to have his or her habitual residence in the Member State of the child's former habitual residence.
2. Paragraph 1 shall not apply if the holder of access rights referred to in paragraph 1 has accepted the jurisdiction of the courts of the Member State of the child's new habitual residence by participating in proceedings before those courts without contesting their jurisdiction.

Article 10. In case of wrongful removal or retention of the child, the courts of the Member State where the child was habitually resident immediately before the wrongful removal or retention shall retain their jurisdiction until the child has acquired a habitual residence in another Member State and:
(a) each person, institution or other body having rights of custody has acquiesced in the removal or retention; or
(b) the child has resided in that other Member State for a period of at least one year after the person, institution or other body having rights of custody has had or should have had knowledge of the whereabouts of the child and the child is settled in his or her new environment and at least one of the following conditions is met:
(i) within one year after the holder of rights of custody has had or should have had knowledge of the whereabouts of the child, no request for return has been lodged before the competent authorities of the Member State where the child has been removed or is being retained;
(ii) a request for return lodged by the holder of rights of custody has been withdrawn and no new request has been lodged within the time limit set in paragraph (i);
(iii) a case before the court in the Member State where the child was habitually resident immediately before the wrongful removal or retention has been closed pursuant to Article 11(7);
(iv) a judgment on custody that does not entail the return of the child has been issued by the courts of the Member State where the child was habitually resident immediately before the wrongful removal or retention.

Article 11. 1. Where a person, institution or other body having rights of custody applies to the competent authorities in a Member State to deliver a judgment on the basis of the Hague Convention of 25 October 1980 on the Civil Aspects of International Child Abduction (hereinafter "the 1980 Hague Convention"), in order to obtain the return of a child that has been wrongfully removed or retained in a Member State other than the Member State where the child was habitually resident immediately before the wrongful removal or retention, paragraphs 2 to 8 shall apply.
2. When applying Articles 12 and 13 of the 1980 Hague Convention, it shall be ensured that the child is given the opportunity to be heard during the proceedings unless this appears inappropriate having regard to his or her age or degree of maturity.
3. A court to which an application for return of a child is made as mentioned in paragraph 1 shall act expeditiously in proceedings on the application, using the most expeditious procedures available in national law.
Without prejudice to the first subparagraph, the court shall, except where exceptional circumstances make this impossible, issue its judgment no later than six weeks after the application is lodged.
4. A court cannot refuse to return a child on the basis of Article 13b of the 1980 Hague Convention if it is established that adequate arrangements have been made to secure the protection of the child after his or her return.
5. A court cannot refuse to return a child unless the person who requested the return of the child has been given an opportunity to be heard.
6. If a court has issued an order on non-return pursuant to Article 13 of the 1980 Hague Convention, the court must immediately either directly or through its central authority, transmit a copy of the court order on non-return and of the relevant documents, in particular a transcript of the hearings before the court, to the court with jurisdiction or central authority in the Member State where the child was habitually resident immediately before the wrongful removal or retention, as determined by national law. The court shall receive all the mentioned documents within one month of the date of the non-return order.
7. Unless the courts in the Member State where the child was habitually resident immediately before the wrongful removal or retention have already been seised by one of the parties, the court or central authority that receives the information mentioned in paragraph 6 must notify it to the parties and invite them to make submissions to the court, in accordance with national law, within three months of the date of notification so that the court can examine the question of custody of the child.
Without prejudice to the rules on jurisdiction contained in this Regulation, the court shall close the case if no submissions have been received by the court within the time limit.
8. Notwithstanding a judgment of non-return pursuant to Article 13 of the 1980 Hague Convention, any subsequent judgment which requires the return of the child issued by a court having jurisdiction under this Regulation shall be enforceable in accordance with Section 4 of Chapter III below in order to secure the return of the child.

Article 12. 1. The courts of a Member State exercising jurisdiction by virtue of Article 3 on an application for divorce, legal separation or marriage annulment shall have jurisdiction in any matter relating to parental responsibility connected with that application where:
(a) at least one of the spouses has parental responsibility in relation to the child; and

(b) the jurisdiction of the courts has been accepted expressly or otherwise in an unequivocal manner by the spouses and by the holders of parental responsibility, at the time the court is seised, and is in the superior interests of the child.
2. The jurisdiction conferred in paragraph 1 shall cease as soon as:
(a) the judgment allowing or refusing the application for divorce, legal separation or marriage annulment has become final;
(b) in those cases where proceedings in relation to parental responsibility are still pending on the date referred to in (a), a judgment in these proceedings has become final;
(c) the proceedings referred to in (a) and (b) have come to an end for another reason.
3. The courts of a Member State shall also have jurisdiction in relation to parental responsibility in proceedings other than those referred to in paragraph 1 where:
(a) the child has a substantial connection with that Member State, in particular by virtue of the fact that one of the holders of parental responsibility is habitually resident in that Member State or that the child is a national of that Member State; and
(b) the jurisdiction of the courts has been accepted expressly or otherwise in an unequivocal manner by all the parties to the proceedings at the time the court is seised and is in the best interests of the child.
4. Where the child has his or her habitual residence in the territory of a third State which is not a contracting party to the Hague Convention of 19 October 1996 on jurisdiction, applicable law, recognition, enforcement and cooperation in respect of parental responsibility and measures for the protection of children, jurisdiction under this Article shall be deemed to be in the child's interest, in particular if it is found impossible to hold proceedings in the third State in question.

Article 13. 1. Where a child's habitual residence cannot be established and jurisdiction cannot be determined on the basis of Article 12, the courts of the Member State where the child is present shall have jurisdiction.
2. Paragraph 1 shall also apply to refugee children or children internationally displaced because of disturbances occurring in their country.

Article 14. Where no court of a Member State has jurisdiction pursuant to Articles 8 to 13, jurisdiction shall be determined, in each Member State, by the laws of that State.

Article 15. 1. By way of exception, the courts of a Member State having jurisdiction as to the substance of the matter may, if they consider that a court of another Member State, with which the child has a particular connection, would be better placed to hear the case, or a specific part thereof, and where this is in the best interests of the child:
(a) stay the case or the part thereof in question and invite the parties to introduce a request before the court of that other Member State in accordance with paragraph 4; or
(b) request a court of another Member State to assume jurisdiction in accordance with paragraph 5.
2. Paragraph 1 shall apply:
(a) upon application from a party; or
(b) of the court's own motion; or
(c) upon application from a court of another Member State with which the child has a particular connection, in accordance with paragraph 3.
A transfer made of the court's own motion or by application of a court of another Member State must be accepted by at least one of the parties.
3. The child shall be considered to have a particular connection to a Member State as mentioned in paragraph 1, if that Member State:
(a) has become the habitual residence of the child after the court referred to in paragraph 1 was seised; or
(b) is the former habitual residence of the child; or
(c) is the place of the child's nationality; or
(d) is the habitual residence of a holder of parental responsibility; or
(e) is the place where property of the child is located and the case concerns measures for the protection of the child relating to the administration, conservation or disposal of this property.
4. The court of the Member State having jurisdiction as to the substance of the matter shall set a time limit by which the courts of that other Member State shall be seised in accordance with paragraph 1.
If the courts are not seised by that time, the court which has been seised shall continue to exercise jurisdiction in accordance with Articles 8 to 14.
5. The courts of that other Member State may, where due to the specific circumstances of the case, this is in the best interests of the child, accept jurisdiction within six weeks of their seisure in accordance with paragraph 1(a) or

1(b). In this case, the court first seised shall decline jurisdiction. Otherwise, the court first seised shall continue to exercise jurisdiction in accordance with Articles 8 to 14.
6. The courts shall cooperate for the purposes of this Article, either directly or through the central authorities designated pursuant to Article 53.

Section 3. Common provisions

Article 16. 1. A court shall be deemed to be seised:
(a) at the time when the document instituting the proceedings or an equivalent document is lodged with the court, provided that the applicant has not subsequently failed to take the steps he was required to take to have service effected on the respondent; or
(b) if the document has to be served before being lodged with the court, at the time when it is received by the authority responsible for service, provided that the applicant has not subsequently failed to take the steps he was required to take to have the document lodged with the court.

Article 17. Where a court of a Member State is seised of a case over which it has no jurisdiction under this Regulation and over which a court of another Member State has jurisdiction by virtue of this Regulation, it shall declare of its own motion that it has no jurisdiction.

Article 18. 1. Where a respondent habitually resident in a State other than the Member State where the action was brought does not enter an appearance, the court with jurisdiction shall stay the proceedings so long as it is not shown that the respondent has been able to receive the document instituting the proceedings or an equivalent document in sufficient time to enable him to arrange for his defence, or that all necessary steps have been taken to this end.
2. Article 19 of Regulation (EC) No 1348/2000 shall apply instead of the provisions of paragraph 1 of this Article if the document instituting the proceedings or an equivalent document had to be transmitted from one Member State to another pursuant to that Regulation.
3. Where the provisions of Regulation (EC) No 1348/2000 are not applicable, Article 15 of the Hague Convention of 15 November 1965 on the service abroad of judicial and extrajudicial documents in civil or commercial matters shall apply if the document instituting the proceedings or an equivalent document had to be transmitted abroad pursuant to that Convention.

Article 19. 1. Where proceedings relating to divorce, legal separation or marriage annulment between the same parties are brought before courts of different Member States, the court second seised shall of its own motion stay its proceedings until such time as the jurisdiction of the court first seised is established.
2. Where proceedings relating to parental responsibility relating to the same child and involving the same cause of action are brought before courts of different Member States, the court second seised shall of its own motion stay its proceedings until such time as the jurisdiction of the court first seised is established.
3. Where the jurisdiction of the court first seised is established, the court second seised shall decline jurisdiction in favour of that court.
In that case, the party who brought the relevant action before the court second seised may bring that action before the court first seised.

Article 20. 1. In urgent cases, the provisions of this Regulation shall not prevent the courts of a Member State from taking such provisional, including protective, measures in respect of persons or assets in that State as may be available under the law of that Member State, even if, under this Regulation, the court of another Member State has jurisdiction as to the substance of the matter.
2. The measures referred to in paragraph 1 shall cease to apply when the court of the Member State having jurisdiction under this Regulation as to the substance of the matter has taken the measures it considers appropriate.

Chapter III. Recognition and Enforcement

Section 1. Recognition

Article 21. 1. A judgment given in a Member State shall be recognised in the other Member States without any special procedure being required.
2. In particular, and without prejudice to paragraph 3, no special procedure shall be required for updating the civil-status records of a Member State on the basis of a judgment relating to divorce, legal separation or marriage

annulment given in another Member State, and against which no further appeal lies under the law of that Member State.
3. Without prejudice to Section 4 of this Chapter, any interested party may, in accordance with the procedures provided for in Section 2 of this Chapter, apply for a decision that the judgment be or not be recognised.
The local jurisdiction of the court appearing in the list notified by each Member State to the Commission pursuant to Article 68 shall be determined by the internal law of the Member State in which proceedings for recognition or non-recognition are brought.
4. Where the recognition of a judgment is raised as an incidental question in a court of a Member State, that court may determine that issue.

Article 22. A judgment relating to a divorce, legal separation or marriage annulment shall not be recognised:
(a) if such recognition is manifestly contrary to the public policy of the Member State in which recognition is sought;
(b) where it was given in default of appearance, if the respondent was not served with the document which instituted the proceedings or with an equivalent document in sufficient time and in such a way as to enable the respondent to arrange for his or her defence unless it is determined that the respondent has accepted the judgment unequivocally;
(c) if it is irreconcilable with a judgment given in proceedings between the same parties in the Member State in which recognition is sought; or
(d) if it is irreconcilable with an earlier judgment given in another Member State or in a non-Member State between the same parties, provided that the earlier judgment fulfils the conditions necessary for its recognition in the Member State in which recognition is sought.

Article 23. A judgment relating to parental responsibility shall not be recognised:
(a) if such recognition is manifestly contrary to the public policy of the Member State in which recognition is sought taking into account the best interests of the child;
(b) if it was given, except in case of urgency, without the child having been given an opportunity to be heard, in violation of fundamental principles of procedure of the Member State in which recognition is sought;
(c) where it was given in default of appearance if the person in default was not served with the document which instituted the proceedings or with an equivalent document in sufficient time and in such a way as to enable that person to arrange for his or her defence unless it is determined that such person has accepted the judgment unequivocally;
(d) on the request of any person claiming that the judgment infringes his or her parental responsibility, if it was given without such person having been given an opportunity to be heard;
(e) if it is irreconcilable with a later judgment relating to parental responsibility given in the Member State in which recognition is sought;
(f) if it is irreconcilable with a later judgment relating to parental responsibility given in another Member State or in the non-Member State of the habitual residence of the child provided that the later judgment fulfils the conditions necessary for its recognition in the Member State in which recognition is sought. or
(g) if the procedure laid down in Article 56 has not been complied with.

Article 24. The jurisdiction of the court of the Member State of origin may not be reviewed. The test of public policy referred to in Articles 22(a) and 23(a) may not be applied to the rules relating to jurisdiction set out in Articles 3 to 14.

Article 25. The recognition of a judgment may not be refused because the law of the Member State in which such recognition is sought would not allow divorce, legal separation or marriage annulment on the same facts.

Article 26. Under no circumstances may a judgment be reviewed as to its substance.

Article 27. 1. A court of a Member State in which recognition is sought of a judgment given in another Member State may stay the proceedings if an ordinary appeal against the judgment has been lodged.
2. A court of a Member State in which recognition is sought of a judgment given in Ireland or the United Kingdom may stay the proceedings if enforcement is suspended in the Member State of origin by reason of an appeal.

Section 2. Application for a declaration of enforceability

Article 28. 1. A judgment on the exercise of parental responsibility in respect of a child given in a Member State which is enforceable in that Member State and has been served shall be enforced in another Member State when, on the application of any interested party, it has been declared enforceable there.
2. However, in the United Kingdom, such a judgment shall be enforced in England and Wales, in Scotland or in Northern Ireland only when, on the application of any interested party, it has been registered for enforcement in that part of the United Kingdom.

Article 29. 1. An application for a declaration of enforceability shall be submitted to the court appearing in the list notified by each Member State to the Commission pursuant to Article 68.
2. The local jurisdiction shall be determined by reference to the place of habitual residence of the person against whom enforcement is sought or by reference to the habitual residence of any child to whom the application relates. Where neither of the places referred to in the first subparagraph can be found in the Member State of enforcement, the local jurisdiction shall be determined by reference to the place of enforcement.

Article 30. 1. The procedure for making the application shall be governed by the law of the Member State of enforcement.
2. The applicant must give an address for service within the area of jurisdiction of the court applied to. However, if the law of the Member State of enforcement does not provide for the furnishing of such an address, the applicant shall appoint a representative ad litem.
3. The documents referred to in Articles 37 and 39 shall be attached to the application.

Article 31. 1. The court applied to shall give its decision without delay. Neither the person against whom enforcement is sought, nor the child shall, at this stage of the proceedings, be entitled to make any submissions on the application.
2. The application may be refused only for one of the reasons specified in Articles 22, 23 and 24.
3. Under no circumstances may a judgment be reviewed as to its substance.

Article 32. The appropriate officer of the court shall without delay bring to the notice of the applicant the decision given on the application in accordance with the procedure laid down by the law of the Member State of enforcement.

Article 33. Appeal against the decision
1. The decision on the application for a declaration of enforceability may be appealed against by either party.
2. The appeal shall be lodged with the court appearing in the list notified by each Member State to the Commission pursuant to Article 68.
3. The appeal shall be dealt with in accordance with the rules governing procedure in contradictory matters.
4. If the appeal is brought by the applicant for a declaration of enforceability, the party against whom enforcement is sought shall be summoned to appear before the appellate court. If such person fails to appear, the provisions of Article 18 shall apply.
5. An appeal against a declaration of enforceability must be lodged within one month of service thereof. If the party against whom enforcement is sought is habitually resident in a Member State other than that in which the declaration of enforceability was given, the time for appealing shall be two months and shall run from the date of service, either on him or at his residence. No extension of time may be granted on account of distance.

Article 34. The judgment given on appeal may be contested only by the proceedings referred to in the list notified by each Member State to the Commission pursuant to Article 68.

Article 35. 1. The court with which the appeal is lodged under Articles 33 or 34 may, on the application of the party against whom enforcement is sought, stay the proceedings if an ordinary appeal has been lodged in the Member State of origin, or if the time for such appeal has not yet expired. In the latter case, the court may specify the time within which an appeal is to be lodged.
2. Where the judgment was given in Ireland or the United Kingdom, any form of appeal available in the Member State of origin shall be treated as an ordinary appeal for the purposes of paragraph 1.

Article 36. 1. Where a judgment has been given in respect of several matters and enforcement cannot be authorised for all of them, the court shall authorise enforcement for one or more of them.

2. An applicant may request partial enforcement of a judgment.

Section 3. Provisions common to Sections 1 and 2

Article 37. 1. A party seeking or contesting recognition or applying for a declaration of enforceability shall produce:
(a) a copy of the judgment which satisfies the conditions necessary to establish its authenticity; and
(b) the certificate referred to in Article 39.
2. In addition, in the case of a judgment given in default, the party seeking recognition or applying for a declaration of enforceability shall produce:
(a) the original or certified true copy of the document which establishes that the defaulting party was served with the document instituting the proceedings or with an equivalent document; or
(b) any document indicating that the defendant has accepted the judgment unequivocally.

Article 38. 1. If the documents specified in Article 37(1)(b) or (2) are not produced, the court may specify a time for their production, accept equivalent documents or, if it considers that it has sufficient information before it, dispense with their production.
2. If the court so requires, a translation of such documents shall be furnished. The translation shall be certified by a person qualified to do so in one of the Member States.

Article 39. The competent court or authority of a Member State of origin shall, at the request of any interested party, issue a certificate using the standard form set out in Annex I (judgments in matrimonial matters) or in Annex II (judgments on parental responsibility).

Section 4. Enforceability of certain judgments concerning rights of access and of certain judgments which require the return of the child

Article 40. 1. This Section shall apply to:
(a) rights of access; and
(b) the return of a child entailed by a judgment given pursuant to Article 11(8).
2. The provisions of this Section shall not prevent a holder of parental responsibility from seeking recognition and enforcement of a judgment in accordance with the provisions in Sections 1 and 2 of this Chapter.

Article 41. 1. The rights of access referred to in Article 40(1)(a) granted in an enforceable judgment given in a Member State shall be recognised and enforceable in another Member State without the need for a declaration of enforceability and without any possibility of opposing its recognition if the judgment has been certified in the Member State of origin in accordance with paragraph 2.
Even if national law does not provide for enforceability by operation of law of a judgment granting access rights, the court of origin may declare that the judgment shall be enforceable, notwithstanding any appeal.
2. The judge of origin shall issue the certificate referred to in paragraph 1 using the standard form in Annex III (certificate concerning rights of access) only if:
(a) where the judgment was given in default, the person defaulting was served with the document which instituted the proceedings or with an equivalent document in sufficient time and in such a way as to enable that person to arrange for his or her defense, or, the person has been served with the document but not in compliance with these conditions, it is nevertheless established that he or she accepted the decision unequivocally;
(b) all parties concerned were given an opportunity to be heard; and
(c) the child was given an opportunity to be heard, unless a hearing was considered inappropriate having regard to his or her age or degree of maturity.
The certificate shall be completed in the language of the judgment.
3. Where the rights of access involve a cross-border situation at the time of the delivery of the judgment, the certificate shall be issued ex officio when the judgment becomes enforceable, even if only provisionally. If the situation subsequently acquires a cross-border character, the certificate shall be issued at the request of one of the parties.

Article 42. 1. The return of a child referred to in Article 40(1)(b) entailed by an enforceable judgment given in a Member State shall be recognised and enforceable in another Member State without the need for a declaration of enforceability and without any possibility of opposing its recognition if the judgment has been certified in the Member State of origin in accordance with paragraph 2.

Even if national law does not provide for enforceability by operation of law, notwithstanding any appeal, of a judgment requiring the return of the child mentioned in Article 11(b)(8), the court of origin may declare the judgment enforceable.

2. The judge of origin who delivered the judgment referred to in Article 40(1)(b) shall issue the certificate referred to in paragraph 1 only if:

(a) the child was given an opportunity to be heard, unless a hearing was considered inappropriate having regard to his or her age or degree of maturity;

(b) the parties were given an opportunity to be heard; and

(c) the court has taken into account in issuing its judgment the reasons for and evidence underlying the order issued pursuant to Article 13 of the 1980 Hague Convention.

In the event that the court or any other authority takes measures to ensure the protection of the child after its return to the State of habitual residence, the certificate shall contain details of such measures.

The judge of origin shall of his or her own motion issue that certificate using the standard form in Annex IV (certificate concerning return of the child(ren)).

The certificate shall be completed in the language of the judgment.

Article 43. 1. The law of the Member State of origin shall be applicable to any rectification of the certificate.

2. No appeal shall lie against the issuing of a certificate pursuant to Articles 41(1) or 42(1).

Article 44. The certificate shall take effect only within the limits of the enforceability of the judgment.

Article 45. 1. A party seeking enforcement of a judgment shall produce:

(a) a copy of the judgment which satisfies the conditions necessary to establish its authenticity; and

(b) the certificate referred to in Article 41(1) or Article 42(1).

2. For the purposes of this Article,

- the certificate referred to in Article 41(1) shall be accompanied by a translation of point 12 relating to the arrangements for exercising right of access,

- the certificate referred to in Article 42(1) shall be accompanied by a translation of its point 14 relating to the arrangements for implementing the measures taken to ensure the child's return.

The translation shall be into the official language or one of the official languages of the Member State of enforcement or any other language that the Member State of enforcement expressly accepts. The translation shall be certified by a person qualified to do so in one of the Member States.

Section 5. Authentic instruments and agreements

Article 46. Documents which have been formally drawn up or registered as authentic instruments and are enforceable in one Member State and also agreements between the parties that are enforceable in the Member State in which they were concluded shall be recognised and declared enforceable under the same conditions as judgments.

Section 6. Other Provisions

Article 47. 1. The enforcement procedure is governed by the law of the Member State of enforcement.

2. Any judgment delivered by a court of another Member State and declared to be enforceable in accordance with Section 2 or certified in accordance with Article 41(1) or Article 42(1) shall be enforced in the Member State of enforcement in the same conditions as if it had been delivered in that Member State.

In particular, a judgment which has been certified according to Article 41(1) or Article 42(1) cannot be enforced if it is irreconcilable with a subsequent enforceable judgment.

Article 48. 1. The courts of the Member State of enforcement may make practical arrangements for organising the exercise of rights of access, if the necessary arrangements have not or have not sufficiently been made in the judgment delivered by the courts of the Member State having jurisdiction as to the substance of the matter and provided the essential elements of this judgment are respected.

2. The practical arrangements made pursuant to paragraph 1 shall cease to apply pursuant to a later judgment by the courts of the Member State having jurisdiction as to the substance of the matter.

Part VII. Private International Law

Article 49. The provisions of this Chapter, with the exception of Section 4, shall also apply to the determination of the amount of costs and expenses of proceedings under this Regulation and to the enforcement of any order concerning such costs and expenses.

Article 50. An applicant who, in the Member State of origin, has benefited from complete or partial legal aid or exemption from costs or expenses shall be entitled, in the procedures provided for in Articles 21, 28, 41, 42 and 48 to benefit from the most favourable legal aid or the most extensive exemption from costs and expenses provided for by the law of the Member State of enforcement.

Article 51. No security, bond or deposit, however described, shall be required of a party who in one Member State applies for enforcement of a judgment given in another Member State on the following grounds:
(a) that he or she is not habitually resident in the Member State in which enforcement is sought; or
(b) that he or she is either a foreign national or, where enforcement is sought in either the United Kingdom or Ireland, does not have his or her "domicile" in either of those Member States.

Article 52. No legalisation or other similar formality shall be required in respect of the documents referred to in Articles 37, 38 and 45 or in respect of a document appointing a representative ad litem.

Chapter IV. Cooperation between Central Authorities in Matters of Parental Responsibility

Article 53. Each Member State shall designate one or more central authorities to assist with the application of this Regulation and shall specify the geographical or functional jurisdiction of each. Where a Member State has designated more than one central authority, communications shall normally be sent direct to the relevant central authority with jurisdiction. Where a communication is sent to a central authority without jurisdiction, the latter shall be responsible for forwarding it to the central authority with jurisdiction and informing the sender accordingly.

Article 54. The central authorities shall communicate information on national laws and procedures and take measures to improve the application of this Regulation and strengthening their cooperation. For this purpose the European Judicial Network in civil and commercial matters created by Decision No 2001/470/EC shall be used.

Article 55. The central authorities shall, upon request from a central authority of another Member State or from a holder of parental responsibility, cooperate on specific cases to achieve the purposes of this Regulation. To this end, they shall, acting directly or through public authorities or other bodies, take all appropriate steps in accordance with the law of that Member State in matters of personal data protection to:
(a) collect and exchange information:
(i) on the situation of the child;
(ii) on any procedures under way; or
(iii) on decisions taken concerning the child;
(b) provide information and assistance to holders of parental responsibility seeking the recognition and enforcement of decisions on their territory, in particular concerning rights of access and the return of the child;
(c) facilitate communications between courts, in particular for the application of Article 11(6) and (7) and Article 15;
(d) provide such information and assistance as is needed by courts to apply Article 56; and
(e) facilitate agreement between holders of parental responsibility through mediation or other means, and facilitate cross-border cooperation to this end.

Article 56. 1. Where a court having jurisdiction under Articles 8 to 15 contemplates the placement of a child in institutional care or with a foster family and where such placement is to take place in another Member State, it shall first consult the central authority or other authority having jurisdiction in the latter State where public authority intervention in that Member State is required for domestic cases of child placement.
2. The judgment on placement referred to in paragraph 1 may be made in the requesting State only if the competent authority of the requested State has consented to the placement.
3. The procedures for consultation or consent referred to in paragraphs 1 and 2 shall be governed by the national law of the requested State.
4. Where the authority having jurisdiction under Articles 8 to 15 decides to place the child in a foster family, and where such placement is to take place in another Member State and where no public authority intervention is

required in the latter Member State for domestic cases of child placement, it shall so inform the central authority or other authority having jurisdiction in the latter State.

Article 57. 1. Any holder of parental responsibility may submit, to the central authority of the Member State of his or her habitual residence or to the central authority of the Member State where the child is habitually resident or present, a request for assistance as mentioned in Article 55. In general, the request shall include all available information of relevance to its enforcement. Where the request for assistance concerns the recognition or enforcement of a judgment on parental responsibility that falls within the scope of this Regulation, the holder of parental responsibility shall attach the relevant certificates provided for in Articles 39, 41(1) or 42(1).
2. Member States shall communicate to the Commission the official language or languages of the Community institutions other than their own in which communications to the central authorities can be accepted.
3. The assistance provided by the central authorities pursuant to Article 55 shall be free of charge.
4. Each central authority shall bear its own costs.

Article 58. 1. In order to facilitate the application of this Regulation, central authorities shall meet regularly.
2. These meetings shall be convened in compliance with Decision No 2001/470/EC establishing a European Judicial Network in civil and commercial matters.

Chapter V. Relations with other Instruments

Article 59. 1. Subject to the provisions of Articles 60, 63, 64 and paragraph 2 of this Article, this Regulation shall, for the Member States, supersede conventions existing at the time of entry into force of this Regulation which have been concluded between two or more Member States and relate to matters governed by this Regulation.
2. (a) Finland and Sweden shall have the option of declaring that the Convention of 6 February 1931 between Denmark, Finland, Iceland, Norway and Sweden comprising international private law provisions on marriage, adoption and guardianship, together with the Final Protocol thereto, will apply, in whole or in part, in their mutual relations, in place of the rules of this Regulation. Such declarations shall be annexed to this Regulation and published in the Official Journal of the European Union. They may be withdrawn, in whole or in part, at any moment by the said Member States.
(b) The principle of non-discrimination on the grounds of nationality between citizens of the Union shall be respected.
(c) The rules of jurisdiction in any future agreement to be concluded between the Member States referred to in subparagraph (a) which relate to matters governed by this Regulation shall be in line with those laid down in this Regulation.
(d) Judgments handed down in any of the Nordic States which have made the declaration provided for in subparagraph (a) under a forum of jurisdiction corresponding to one of those laid down in Chapter II of this Regulation, shall be recognised and enforced in the other Member States under the rules laid down in Chapter III of this Regulation.
3. Member States shall send to the Commission:
(a) a copy of the agreements and uniform laws implementing these agreements referred to in paragraph 2(a) and (c);
(b) any denunciations of, or amendments to, those agreements or uniform laws.

Article 60. In relations between Member States, this Regulation shall take precedence over the following Conventions in so far as they concern matters governed by this Regulation:
(a) the Hague Convention of 5 October 1961 concerning the Powers of Authorities and the Law Applicable in respect of the Protection of Minors;
(b) the Luxembourg Convention of 8 September 1967 on the Recognition of Decisions Relating to the Validity of Marriages;
(c) the Hague Convention of 1 June 1970 on the Recognition of Divorces and Legal Separations;
(d) the European Convention of 20 May 1980 on Recognition and Enforcement of Decisions concerning Custody of Children and on Restoration of Custody of Children; and
(e) the Hague Convention of 25 October 1980 on the Civil Aspects of International Child Abduction.

Article 61. Relation with the Hague Convention of 19 October 1996 on Jurisdiction, Applicable law, Recognition, Enforcement and Cooperation in Respect of Parental Responsibility and Measures for the Protection of Children

PART VII. PRIVATE INTERNATIONAL LAW

As concerns the relation with the Hague Convention of 19 October 1996 on Jurisdiction, Applicable law, Recognition, Enforcement and Cooperation in Respect of Parental Responsibility and Measures for the Protection of Children, this Regulation shall apply:
(a) where the child concerned has his or her habitual residence on the territory of a Member State;
(b) as concerns the recognition and enforcement of a judgment given in a court of a Member State on the territory of another Member State, even if the child concerned has his or her habitual residence on the territory of a third State which is a contracting Party to the said Convention.

Article 62. 1. The agreements and conventions referred to in Articles 59(1), 60 and 61 shall continue to have effect in relation to matters not governed by this Regulation.
2. The conventions mentioned in Article 60, in particular the 1980 Hague Convention, continue to produce effects between the Member States which are party thereto, in compliance with Article 60.

Article 63. 1. This Regulation shall apply without prejudice to the International Treaty (Concordat) between the Holy See and Portugal, signed at the Vatican City on 7 May 1940.
2. Any decision as to the invalidity of a marriage taken under the Treaty referred to in paragraph 1 shall be recognised in the Member States on the conditions laid down in Chapter III, Section 1.
3. The provisions laid down in paragraphs 1 and 2 shall also apply to the following international treaties (Concordats) with the Holy See:
(a) "Concordato lateranense" of 11 February 1929 between Italy and the Holy See, modified by the agreement, with additional Protocol signed in Rome on 18 February 1984;
(b) Agreement between the Holy See and Spain on legal affairs of 3 January 1979.
4. Recognition of the decisions provided for in paragraph 2 may, in Italy or in Spain, be subject to the same procedures and the same checks as are applicable to decisions of the ecclesiastical courts handed down in accordance with the international treaties concluded with the Holy See referred to in paragraph 3.
5. Member States shall send to the Commission:
(a) a copy of the Treaties referred to in paragraphs 1 and 3;
(b) any denunciations of or amendments to those Treaties.

Chapter VI. Transitional Provisions

Article 64. 1. The provisions of this Regulation shall apply only to legal proceedings instituted, to documents formally drawn up or registered as authentic instruments and to agreements concluded between the parties after its date of application in accordance with Article 72.
2. Judgments given after the date of application of this Regulation in proceedings instituted before that date but after the date of entry into force of Regulation (EC) No 1347/2000 shall be recognised and enforced in accordance with the provisions of Chapter III of this Regulation if jurisdiction was founded on rules which accorded with those provided for either in Chapter II or in Regulation (EC) No 1347/2000 or in a convention concluded between the Member State of origin and the Member State addressed which was in force when the proceedings were instituted.
3. Judgments given before the date of application of this Regulation in proceedings instituted after the entry into force of Regulation (EC) No 1347/2000 shall be recognised and enforced in accordance with the provisions of Chapter III of this Regulation provided they relate to divorce, legal separation or marriage annulment or parental responsibility for the children of both spouses on the occasion of these matrimonial proceedings.
4. Judgments given before the date of application of this Regulation but after the date of entry into force of Regulation (EC) No 1347/2000 in proceedings instituted before the date of entry into force of Regulation (EC) No 1347/2000 shall be recognised and enforced in accordance with the provisions of Chapter III of this Regulation provided they relate to divorce, legal separation or marriage annulment or parental responsibility for the children of both spouses on the occasion of these matrimonial proceedings and that jurisdiction was founded on rules which accorded with those provided for either in Chapter II of this Regulation or in Regulation (EC) No 1347/2000 or in a convention concluded between the Member State of origin and the Member State addressed which was in force when the proceedings were instituted.

Chapter VII. Final Provisions

Article 65. No later than 1 January 2012, and every five years thereafter, the Commission shall present to the European Parliament, to the Council and to the European Economic and Social Committee a report on the application of this Regulation on the basis of information supplied by the Member States. The report shall be accompanied if need be by proposals for adaptations.

Article 66. With regard to a Member State in which two or more systems of law or sets of rules concerning matters governed by this Regulation apply in different territorial units:
(a) any reference to habitual residence in that Member State shall refer to habitual residence in a territorial unit;
(b) any reference to nationality, or in the case of the United Kingdom "domicile", shall refer to the territorial unit designated by the law of that State;
(c) any reference to the authority of a Member State shall refer to the authority of a territorial unit within that State which is concerned;
(d) any reference to the rules of the requested Member State shall refer to the rules of the territorial unit in which jurisdiction, recognition or enforcement is invoked.

Article 67. The Member States shall communicate to the Commission within three months following the entry into force of this Regulation:
(a) the names, addresses and means of communication for the central authorities designated pursuant to Article 53;
(b) the languages accepted for communications to central authorities pursuant to Article 57(2); and
(c) the languages accepted for the certificate concerning rights of access pursuant to Article 45(2).
The Member States shall communicate to the Commission any changes to this information.
The Commission shall make this information publicly available.

Article 68. The Member States shall notify to the Commission the lists of courts and redress procedures referred to in Articles 21, 29, 33 and 34 and any amendments thereto.
The Commission shall update this information and make it publicly available through the publication in the Official Journal of the European Union and any other appropriate means.

Article 69. Any amendments to the standard forms in Annexes I to IV shall be adopted in accordance with the consultative procedure set out in Article 70(2).

Article 70. 1. The Commission shall be assisted by a committee (committee).
2. Where reference is made to this paragraph, Articles 3 and 7 of Decision 1999/468/EC shall apply.
3. The committee shall adopt its rules of procedure.

Article 71. 1. Regulation (EC) No 1347/2000 shall be repealed as from the date of application of this Regulation.
2. Any reference to Regulation (EC) No 1347/2000 shall be construed as a reference to this Regulation according to the comparative table in Annex V.

Article 72. This Regulation shall enter into force on 1 August 2004.
The Regulation shall apply from 1 March 2005, with the exception of Articles 67, 68, 69 and 70, which shall apply from 1 August 2004.
This Regulation shall be binding in its entirety and directly applicable in the Member States in accordance with the Treaty establishing the European Community.

[The annexes are omitted.]

Regulation (EC) 864/2007 of the European Parliament and of the Council of 11 July 2007 on the law applicable to non-contractual obligations [Rome II] (*OJ* L199, 31.7.2007, pp. 40 – 49) [footnotes omitted].

THE EUROPEAN PARLIAMENT AND THE COUNCIL OF THE EUROPEAN UNION,
Having regard to the Treaty establishing the European Community, and in particular Articles 61(c) and 67 thereof,
Having regard to the proposal from the Commission,
Having regard to the opinion of the European Economic and Social Committee,
Acting in accordance with the procedure laid down in Article 251 of the Treaty in the light of the joint text approved by the Conciliation Committee on 25 June 2007,
Whereas:
(1) The Community has set itself the objective of maintaining and developing an area of freedom, security and justice. For the progressive establishment of such an area, the Community is to adopt measures relating to judicial cooperation in civil matters with a cross-border impact to the extent necessary for the proper functioning of the internal market.
(2) According to Article 65(b) of the Treaty, these measures are to include those promoting the compatibility of the rules applicable in the Member States concerning the conflict of laws and of jurisdiction.
(3) The European Council meeting in Tampere on 15 and 16 October 1999 endorsed the principle of mutual recognition of judgments and other decisions of judicial authorities as the cornerstone of judicial cooperation in civil matters and invited the Council and the Commission to adopt a programme of measures to implement the principle of mutual recognition.
(4) On 30 November 2000, the Council adopted a joint Commission and Council programme of measures for implementation of the principle of mutual recognition of decisions in civil and commercial matters. The programme identifies measures relating to the harmonisation of conflict-of-law rules as those facilitating the mutual recognition of judgments.
(5) The Hague Programme, adopted by the European Council on 5 November 2004, called for work to be pursued actively on the rules of conflict of laws regarding non-contractual obligations (Rome II).
(6) The proper functioning of the internal market creates a need, in order to improve the predictability of the outcome of litigation, certainty as to the law applicable and the free movement of judgments, for the conflict-of-law rules in the Member States to designate the same national law irrespective of the country of the court in which an action is brought.
(7) The substantive scope and the provisions of this Regulation should be consistent with Council Regulation (EC) No 44/2001 of 22 December 2000 on jurisdiction and the recognition and enforcement of judgments in civil and commercial matters (Brussels I) and the instruments dealing with the law applicable to contractual obligations.
(8) This Regulation should apply irrespective of the nature of the court or tribunal seised.
(9) Claims arising out of acta iure imperii should include claims against officials who act on behalf of the State and liability for acts of public authorities, including liability of publicly appointed office-holders. Therefore, these matters should be excluded from the scope of this Regulation.
(10) Family relationships should cover parentage, marriage, affinity and collateral relatives. The reference in Article 1(2) to relationships having comparable effects to marriage and other family relationships should be interpreted in accordance with the law of the Member State in which the court is seised.
(11) The concept of a non-contractual obligation varies from one Member State to another. Therefore for the purposes of this Regulation non-contractual obligation should be understood as an autonomous concept. The conflict-of-law rules set out in this Regulation should also cover non-contractual obligations arising out of strict liability.
(12) The law applicable should also govern the question of the capacity to incur liability in tort/delict.
(13) Uniform rules applied irrespective of the law they designate may avert the risk of distortions of competition between Community litigants.
(14) The requirement of legal certainty and the need to do justice in individual cases are essential elements of an area of justice. This Regulation provides for the connecting factors which are the most appropriate to achieve these objectives. Therefore, this Regulation provides for a general rule but also for specific rules and, in certain provisions, for an "escape clause" which allows a departure from these rules where it is clear from all the circumstances of the case that the tort/delict is manifestly more closely connected with another country. This set of rules thus creates a flexible framework of conflict-of-law rules. Equally, it enables the court seised to treat individual cases in an appropriate manner.
(15) The principle of the lex loci delicti commissi is the basic solution for non-contractual obligations in virtually all the Member States, but the practical application of the principle where the component factors of the case are spread over several countries varies. This situation engenders uncertainty as to the law applicable.

(16) Uniform rules should enhance the foreseeability of court decisions and ensure a reasonable balance between the interests of the person claimed to be liable and the person who has sustained damage. A connection with the country where the direct damage occurred (lex loci damni) strikes a fair balance between the interests of the person claimed to be liable and the person sustaining the damage, and also reflects the modern approach to civil liability and the development of systems of strict liability.

(17) The law applicable should be determined on the basis of where the damage occurs, regardless of the country or countries in which the indirect consequences could occur. Accordingly, in cases of personal injury or damage to property, the country in which the damage occurs should be the country where the injury was sustained or the property was damaged respectively.

(18) The general rule in this Regulation should be the lex loci damni provided for in Article 4(1). Article 4(2) should be seen as an exception to this general principle, creating a special connection where the parties have their habitual residence in the same country. Article 4(3) should be understood as an 'escape clause' from Article 4(1) and (2), where it is clear from all the circumstances of the case that the tort/delict is manifestly more closely connected with another country.

(19) Specific rules should be laid down for special torts/delicts where the general rule does not allow a reasonable balance to be struck between the interests at stake.

(20) The conflict-of-law rule in matters of product liability should meet the objectives of fairly spreading the risks inherent in a modern high-technology society, protecting consumers' health, stimulating innovation, securing undistorted competition and facilitating trade. Creation of a cascade system of connecting factors, together with a foreseeability clause, is a balanced solution in regard to these objectives. The first element to be taken into account is the law of the country in which the person sustaining the damage had his or her habitual residence when the damage occurred, if the product was marketed in that country. The other elements of the cascade are triggered if the product was not marketed in that country, without prejudice to Article 4(2) and to the possibility of a manifestly closer connection to another country.

(21) The special rule in Article 6 is not an exception to the general rule in Article 4(1) but rather a clarification of it. In matters of unfair competition, the conflict-of-law rule should protect competitors, consumers and the general public and ensure that the market economy functions properly. The connection to the law of the country where competitive relations or the collective interests of consumers are, or are likely to be, affected generally satisfies these objectives.

(22) The non-contractual obligations arising out of restrictions of competition in Article 6(3) should cover infringements of both national and Community competition law. The law applicable to such non-contractual obligations should be the law of the country where the market is, or is likely to be, affected. In cases where the market is, or is likely to be, affected in more than one country, the claimant should be able in certain circumstances to choose to base his or her claim on the law of the court seised.

(23) For the purposes of this Regulation, the concept of restriction of competition should cover prohibitions on agreements between undertakings, decisions by associations of undertakings and concerted practices which have as their object or effect the prevention, restriction or distortion of competition within a Member State or within the internal market, as well as prohibitions on the abuse of a dominant position within a Member State or within the internal market, where such agreements, decisions, concerted practices or abuses are prohibited by Articles 81 and 82 of the Treaty or by the law of a Member State.

(24) "Environmental damage" should be understood as meaning adverse change in a natural resource, such as water, land or air, impairment of a function performed by that resource for the benefit of another natural resource or the public, or impairment of the variability among living organisms.

(25) Regarding environmental damage, Article 174 of the Treaty, which provides that there should be a high level of protection based on the precautionary principle and the principle that preventive action should be taken, the principle of priority for corrective action at source and the principle that the polluter pays, fully justifies the use of the principle of discriminating in favour of the person sustaining the damage. The question of when the person seeking compensation can make the choice of the law applicable should be determined in accordance with the law of the Member State in which the court is seised.

(26) Regarding infringements of intellectual property rights, the universally acknowledged principle of the lex loci protectionis should be preserved. For the purposes of this Regulation, the term 'intellectual property rights' should be interpreted as meaning, for instance, copyright, related rights, the sui generis right for the protection of databases and industrial property rights.

(27) The exact concept of industrial action, such as strike action or lock-out, varies from one Member State to another and is governed by each Member State's internal rules. Therefore, this Regulation assumes as a general principle that the law of the country where the industrial action was taken should apply, with the aim of protecting the rights and obligations of workers and employers.

(28) The special rule on industrial action in Article 9 is without prejudice to the conditions relating to the exercise of such action in accordance with national law and without prejudice to the legal status of trade unions or of the representative organisations of workers as provided for in the law of the Member States.

(29) Provision should be made for special rules where damage is caused by an act other than a tort/delict, such as unjust enrichment, negotiorum gestio and culpa in contrahendo.

(30) Culpa in contrahendo for the purposes of this Regulation is an autonomous concept and should not necessarily be interpreted within the meaning of national law. It should include the violation of the duty of disclosure and the breakdown of contractual negotiations. Article 12 covers only non-contractual obligations presenting a direct link with the dealings prior to the conclusion of a contract. This means that if, while a contract is being negotiated, a person suffers personal injury, Article 4 or other relevant provisions of this Regulation should apply.

(31) To respect the principle of party autonomy and to enhance legal certainty, the parties should be allowed to make a choice as to the law applicable to a non-contractual obligation. This choice should be expressed or demonstrated with reasonable certainty by the circumstances of the case. Where establishing the existence of the agreement, the court has to respect the intentions of the parties. Protection should be given to weaker parties by imposing certain conditions on the choice.

(32) Considerations of public interest justify giving the courts of the Member States the possibility, in exceptional circumstances, of applying exceptions based on public policy and overriding mandatory provisions. In particular, the application of a provision of the law designated by this Regulation which would have the effect of causing non-compensatory exemplary or punitive damages of an excessive nature to be awarded may, depending on the circumstances of the case and the legal order of the Member State of the court seised, be regarded as being contrary to the public policy (ordre public) of the forum.

(33) According to the current national rules on compensation awarded to victims of road traffic accidents, when quantifying damages for personal injury in cases in which the accident takes place in a State other than that of the habitual residence of the victim, the court seised should take into account all the relevant actual circumstances of the specific victim, including in particular the actual losses and costs of after-care and medical attention.

(34) In order to strike a reasonable balance between the parties, account must be taken, in so far as appropriate, of the rules of safety and conduct in operation in the country in which the harmful act was committed, even where the non-contractual obligation is governed by the law of another country. The term "rules of safety and conduct" should be interpreted as referring to all regulations having any relation to safety and conduct, including, for example, road safety rules in the case of an accident.

(35) A situation where conflict-of-law rules are dispersed among several instruments and where there are differences between those rules should be avoided. This Regulation, however, does not exclude the possibility of inclusion of conflict-of-law rules relating to non-contractual obligations in provisions of Community law with regard to particular matters.

This Regulation should not prejudice the application of other instruments laying down provisions designed to contribute to the proper functioning of the internal market in so far as they cannot be applied in conjunction with the law designated by the rules of this Regulation. The application of provisions of the applicable law designated by the rules of this Regulation should not restrict the free movement of goods and services as regulated by Community instruments, such as Directive 2000/31/EC of the European Parliament and of the Council of 8 June 2000 on certain legal aspects of information society services, in particular electronic commerce, in the Internal Market (Directive on electronic commerce).

(36) Respect for international commitments entered into by the Member States means that this Regulation should not affect international conventions to which one or more Member States are parties at the time this Regulation is adopted. To make the rules more accessible, the Commission should publish the list of the relevant conventions in the Official Journal of the European Union on the basis of information supplied by the Member States.

(37) The Commission will make a proposal to the European Parliament and the Council concerning the procedures and conditions according to which Member States would be entitled to negotiate and conclude on their own behalf agreements with third countries in individual and exceptional cases, concerning sectoral matters, containing provisions on the law applicable to non-contractual obligations.

(38) Since the objective of this Regulation cannot be sufficiently achieved by the Member States, and can therefore, by reason of the scale and effects of this Regulation, be better achieved at Community level, the Community may adopt measures, in accordance with the principle of subsidiarity set out in Article 5 of the Treaty. In accordance with the principle of proportionality set out in that Article, this Regulation does not go beyond what is necessary to attain that objective.

(39) In accordance with Article 3 of the Protocol on the position of the United Kingdom and Ireland annexed to the Treaty on European Union and to the Treaty establishing the European Community, the United Kingdom and Ireland are taking part in the adoption and application of this Regulation.

(40) In accordance with Articles 1 and 2 of the Protocol on the position of Denmark, annexed to the Treaty on European Union and to the Treaty establishing the European Community, Denmark does not take part in the adoption of this Regulation, and is not bound by it or subject to its application,

HAVE ADOPTED THIS REGULATION:

Chapter 1. Scope

Article 1. 1. This Regulation shall apply, in situations involving a conflict of laws, to non-contractual obligations in civil and commercial matters. It shall not apply, in particular, to revenue, customs or administrative matters or to the liability of the State for acts and omissions in the exercise of State authority (acta iure imperii).
2. The following shall be excluded from the scope of this Regulation:
(a) non-contractual obligations arising out of family relationships and relationships deemed by the law applicable to such relationships to have comparable effects including maintenance obligations;
(b) non-contractual obligations arising out of matrimonial property regimes, property regimes of relationships deemed by the law applicable to such relationships to have comparable effects to marriage, and wills and succession;
(c) non-contractual obligations arising under bills of exchange, cheques and promissory notes and other negotiable instruments to the extent that the obligations under such other negotiable instruments arise out of their negotiable character;
(d) non-contractual obligations arising out of the law of companies and other bodies corporate or unincorporated regarding matters such as the creation, by registration or otherwise, legal capacity, internal organisation or winding-up of companies and other bodies corporate or unincorporated, the personal liability of officers and members as such for the obligations of the company or body and the personal liability of auditors to a company or to its members in the statutory audits of accounting documents;
(e) non-contractual obligations arising out of the relations between the settlors, trustees and beneficiaries of a trust created voluntarily;
(f) non-contractual obligations arising out of nuclear damage;
(g) non-contractual obligations arising out of violations of privacy and rights relating to personality, including defamation.
3. This Regulation shall not apply to evidence and procedure, without prejudice to Articles 21 and 22.
4. For the purposes of this Regulation, "Member State" shall mean any Member State other than Denmark.

Article 2. 1. For the purposes of this Regulation, damage shall cover any consequence arising out of tort/delict, unjust enrichment, negotiorum gestio or culpa in contrahendo.
2. This Regulation shall apply also to non-contractual obligations that are likely to arise.
3. Any reference in this Regulation to:
(a) an event giving rise to damage shall include events giving rise to damage that are likely to occur; and
(b) damage shall include damage that is likely to occur.

Article 3. Any law specified by this Regulation shall be applied whether or not it is the law of a Member State.

Chapter II. Torts/Delicts

Article 4. 1. Unless otherwise provided for in this Regulation, the law applicable to a non-contractual obligation arising out of a tort/delict shall be the law of the country in which the damage occurs irrespective of the country in which the event giving rise to the damage occurred and irrespective of the country or countries in which the indirect consequences of that event occur.
2. However, where the person claimed to be liable and the person sustaining damage both have their habitual residence in the same country at the time when the damage occurs, the law of that country shall apply.
3. Where it is clear from all the circumstances of the case that the tort/delict is manifestly more closely connected with a country other than that indicated in paragraphs 1 or 2, the law of that other country shall apply. A manifestly closer connection with another country might be based in particular on a pre-existing relationship between the parties, such as a contract, that is closely connected with the tort/delict in question.

Article 5. 1. Without prejudice to Article 4(2), the law applicable to a non-contractual obligation arising out of damage caused by a product shall be:

(a) the law of the country in which the person sustaining the damage had his or her habitual residence when the damage occurred, if the product was marketed in that country; or, failing that,
(b) the law of the country in which the product was acquired, if the product was marketed in that country; or, failing that,
(c) the law of the country in which the damage occurred, if the product was marketed in that country.
However, the law applicable shall be the law of the country in which the person claimed to be liable is habitually resident if he or she could not reasonably foresee the marketing of the product, or a product of the same type, in the country the law of which is applicable under (a), (b) or (c).
2. Where it is clear from all the circumstances of the case that the tort/delict is manifestly more closely connected with a country other than that indicated in paragraph 1, the law of that other country shall apply. A manifestly closer connection with another country might be based in particular on a pre-existing relationship between the parties, such as a contract, that is closely connected with the tort/delict in question.

Article 6. 1. The law applicable to a non-contractual obligation arising out of an act of unfair competition shall be the law of the country where competitive relations or the collective interests of consumers are, or are likely to be, affected.
2. Where an act of unfair competition affects exclusively the interests of a specific competitor, Article 4 shall apply.
3. (a) The law applicable to a non-contractual obligation arising out of a restriction of competition shall be the law of the country where the market is, or is likely to be, affected.
(b) When the market is, or is likely to be, affected in more than one country, the person seeking compensation for damage who sues in the court of the domicile of the defendant, may instead choose to base his or her claim on the law of the court seised, provided that the market in that Member State is amongst those directly and substantially affected by the restriction of competition out of which the non-contractual obligation on which the claim is based arises; where the claimant sues, in accordance with the applicable rules on jurisdiction, more than one defendant in that court, he or she can only choose to base his or her claim on the law of that court if the restriction of competition on which the claim against each of these defendants relies directly and substantially affects also the market in the Member State of that court.
4. The law applicable under this Article may not be derogated from by an agreement pursuant to Article 14.

Article 7. The law applicable to a non-contractual obligation arising out of environmental damage or damage sustained by persons or property as a result of such damage shall be the law determined pursuant to Article 4(1), unless the person seeking compensation for damage chooses to base his or her claim on the law of the country in which the event giving rise to the damage occurred.

Article 8. 1. The law applicable to a non-contractual obligation arising from an infringement of an intellectual property right shall be the law of the country for which protection is claimed.
2. In the case of a non-contractual obligation arising from an infringement of a unitary Community intellectual property right, the law applicable shall, for any question that is not governed by the relevant Community instrument, be the law of the country in which the act of infringement was committed.
3. The law applicable under this Article may not be derogated from by an agreement pursuant to Article 14.

Article 9. Without prejudice to Article 4(2), the law applicable to a non-contractual obligation in respect of the liability of a person in the capacity of a worker or an employer or the organisations representing their professional interests for damages caused by an industrial action, pending or carried out, shall be the law of the country where the action is to be, or has been, taken.

Chapter III. Unjust Enrichment, Negotiorum Gestio and Culpa in Contrahendo

Article 10. 1. If a non-contractual obligation arising out of unjust enrichment, including payment of amounts wrongly received, concerns a relationship existing between the parties, such as one arising out of a contract or a tort/delict, that is closely connected with that unjust enrichment, it shall be governed by the law that governs that relationship.
2. Where the law applicable cannot be determined on the basis of paragraph 1 and the parties have their habitual residence in the same country when the event giving rise to unjust enrichment occurs, the law of that country shall apply.
3. Where the law applicable cannot be determined on the basis of paragraphs 1 or 2, it shall be the law of the country in which the unjust enrichment took place.

4. Where it is clear from all the circumstances of the case that the non-contractual obligation arising out of unjust enrichment is manifestly more closely connected with a country other than that indicated in paragraphs 1, 2 and 3, the law of that other country shall apply.

Article 11. 1. If a non-contractual obligation arising out of an act performed without due authority in connection with the affairs of another person concerns a relationship existing between the parties, such as one arising out of a contract or a tort/delict, that is closely connected with that non-contractual obligation, it shall be governed by the law that governs that relationship.
2. Where the law applicable cannot be determined on the basis of paragraph 1, and the parties have their habitual residence in the same country when the event giving rise to the damage occurs, the law of that country shall apply.
3. Where the law applicable cannot be determined on the basis of paragraphs 1 or 2, it shall be the law of the country in which the act was performed.
4. Where it is clear from all the circumstances of the case that the non-contractual obligation arising out of an act performed without due authority in connection with the affairs of another person is manifestly more closely connected with a country other than that indicated in paragraphs 1, 2 and 3, the law of that other country shall apply.

Article 12. 1. The law applicable to a non-contractual obligation arising out of dealings prior to the conclusion of a contract, regardless of whether the contract was actually concluded or not, shall be the law that applies to the contract or that would have been applicable to it had it been entered into.
2. Where the law applicable cannot be determined on the basis of paragraph 1, it shall be:
(a) the law of the country in which the damage occurs, irrespective of the country in which the event giving rise to the damage occurred and irrespective of the country or countries in which the indirect consequences of that event occurred; or
(b) where the parties have their habitual residence in the same country at the time when the event giving rise to the damage occurs, the law of that country; or
(c) where it is clear from all the circumstances of the case that the non-contractual obligation arising out of dealings prior to the conclusion of a contract is manifestly more closely connected with a country other than that indicated in points (a) and (b), the law of that other country.

Article 13. For the purposes of this Chapter, Article 8 shall apply to non-contractual obligations arising from an infringement of an intellectual property right.

Chapter IV. Freedom of Choice

Article 14. 1. The parties may agree to submit non-contractual obligations to the law of their choice:
(a) by an agreement entered into after the event giving rise to the damage occurred; or
(b) where all the parties are pursuing a commercial activity, also by an agreement freely negotiated before the event giving rise to the damage occurred.
The choice shall be expressed or demonstrated with reasonable certainty by the circumstances of the case and shall not prejudice the rights of third parties.
2. Where all the elements relevant to the situation at the time when the event giving rise to the damage occurs are located in a country other than the country whose law has been chosen, the choice of the parties shall not prejudice the application of provisions of the law of that other country which cannot be derogated from by agreement.
3. Where all the elements relevant to the situation at the time when the event giving rise to the damage occurs are located in one or more of the Member States, the parties' choice of the law applicable other than that of a Member State shall not prejudice the application of provisions of Community law, where appropriate as implemented in the Member State of the forum, which cannot be derogated from by agreement.

Chapter V. Common Rules

Article 15. The law applicable to non-contractual obligations under this Regulation shall govern in particular:
(a) the basis and extent of liability, including the determination of persons who may be held liable for acts performed by them;
(b) the grounds for exemption from liability, any limitation of liability and any division of liability;
(c) the existence, the nature and the assessment of damage or the remedy claimed;
(d) within the limits of powers conferred on the court by its procedural law, the measures which a court may take to prevent or terminate injury or damage or to ensure the provision of compensation;

(e) the question whether a right to claim damages or a remedy may be transferred, including by inheritance;
(f) persons entitled to compensation for damage sustained personally;
(g) liability for the acts of another person;
(h) the manner in which an obligation may be extinguished and rules of prescription and limitation, including rules relating to the commencement, interruption and suspension of a period of prescription or limitation.

Article 16. Nothing in this Regulation shall restrict the application of the provisions of the law of the forum in a situation where they are mandatory irrespective of the law otherwise applicable to the non-contractual obligation.

Article 17. In assessing the conduct of the person claimed to be liable, account shall be taken, as a matter of fact and in so far as is appropriate, of the rules of safety and conduct which were in force at the place and time of the event giving rise to the liability.

Article 18. The person having suffered damage may bring his or her claim directly against the insurer of the person liable to provide compensation if the law applicable to the non-contractual obligation or the law applicable to the insurance contract so provides.

Article 19. Where a person (the creditor) has a non-contractual claim upon another (the debtor), and a third person has a duty to satisfy the creditor, or has in fact satisfied the creditor in discharge of that duty, the law which governs the third person's duty to satisfy the creditor shall determine whether, and the extent to which, the third person is entitled to exercise against the debtor the rights which the creditor had against the debtor under the law governing their relationship.

Article 20. If a creditor has a claim against several debtors who are liable for the same claim, and one of the debtors has already satisfied the claim in whole or in part, the question of that debtor's right to demand compensation from the other debtors shall be governed by the law applicable to that debtor's non-contractual obligation towards the creditor.

Article 21. A unilateral act intended to have legal effect and relating to a non-contractual obligation shall be formally valid if it satisfies the formal requirements of the law governing the non-contractual obligation in question or the law of the country in which the act is performed.

Article 22. 1. The law governing a non-contractual obligation under this Regulation shall apply to the extent that, in matters of non-contractual obligations, it contains rules which raise presumptions of law or determine the burden of proof.
2. Acts intended to have legal effect may be proved by any mode of proof recognised by the law of the forum or by any of the laws referred to in Article 21 under which that act is formally valid, provided that such mode of proof can be administered by the forum.

Chapter VI. Other Provisions

Article 23. 1. For the purposes of this Regulation, the habitual residence of companies and other bodies, corporate or unincorporated, shall be the place of central administration.
Where the event giving rise to the damage occurs, or the damage arises, in the course of operation of a branch, agency or any other establishment, the place where the branch, agency or any other establishment is located shall be treated as the place of habitual residence.
2. For the purposes of this Regulation, the habitual residence of a natural person acting in the course of his or her business activity shall be his or her principal place of business.

Article 24. The application of the law of any country specified by this Regulation means the application of the rules of law in force in that country other than its rules of private international law.

Article 25. 1. Where a State comprises several territorial units, each of which has its own rules of law in respect of non-contractual obligations, each territorial unit shall be considered as a country for the purposes of identifying the law applicable under this Regulation.
2. A Member State within which different territorial units have their own rules of law in respect of non-contractual obligations shall not be required to apply this Regulation to conflicts solely between the laws of such units.

Article 26. The application of a provision of the law of any country specified by this Regulation may be refused only if such application is manifestly incompatible with the public policy (ordre public) of the forum.

Article 27. This Regulation shall not prejudice the application of provisions of Community law which, in relation to particular matters, lay down conflict-of-law rules relating to non-contractual obligations.

Article 28. 1. This Regulation shall not prejudice the application of international conventions to which one or more Member States are parties at the time when this Regulation is adopted and which lay down conflict-of-law rules relating to non-contractual obligations.
2. However, this Regulation shall, as between Member States, take precedence over conventions concluded exclusively between two or more of them in so far as such conventions concern matters governed by this Regulation.

Chapter VII. Final Provisions

Article 29. 1. By 11 July 2008, Member States shall notify the Commission of the conventions referred to in Article 28(1). After that date, Member States shall notify the Commission of all denunciations of such conventions.
2. The Commission shall publish in the Official Journal of the European Union within six months of receipt:
(i) a list of the conventions referred to in paragraph 1;
(ii) the denunciations referred to in paragraph 1.

Article 30. 1. Not later than 20 August 2011, the Commission shall submit to the European Parliament, the Council and the European Economic and Social Committee a report on the application of this Regulation. If necessary, the report shall be accompanied by proposals to adapt this Regulation. The report shall include:
(i) a study on the effects of the way in which foreign law is treated in the different jurisdictions and on the extent to which courts in the Member States apply foreign law in practice pursuant to this Regulation;
(ii) a study on the effects of Article 28 of this Regulation with respect to the Hague Convention of 4 May 1971 on the law applicable to traffic accidents.
2. Not later than 31 December 2008, the Commission shall submit to the European Parliament, the Council and the European Economic and Social Committee a study on the situation in the field of the law applicable to non-contractual obligations arising out of violations of privacy and rights relating to personality, taking into account rules relating to freedom of the press and freedom of expression in the media, and conflict-of-law issues related to Directive 95/46/EC of the European Parliament and of the Council of 24 October 1995 on the protection of individuals with regard to the processing of personal data and on the free movement of such data [7].

Article 31. This Regulation shall apply to events giving rise to damage which occur after its entry into force.

Article 32. This Regulation shall apply from 11 January 2009, except for Article 29, which shall apply from 11 July 2008.
This Regulation shall be binding in its entirety and directly applicable in the Member States in accordance with the Treaty establishing the European Community.

EU: ROME I REGULATION

Regulation (EC) 593/2008 of 17 June 2008 of the European Parliament and the Council on the law applicable to contractual obligations [Rome I] (*OJ* L177, 4.7.2008, pp. 6 – 16) [footnotes omitted].

THE EUROPEAN PARLIAMENT AND THE COUNCIL OF THE EUROPEAN UNION,
Having regard to the Treaty establishing the European Community, and in particular Article 61(c) and the second indent of Article 67(5) thereof,
Having regard to the proposal from the Commission,
Having regard to the opinion of the European Economic and Social Committee,
Acting in accordance with the procedure laid down in Article 251 of the Treaty,
Whereas:
(1) The Community has set itself the objective of maintaining and developing an area of freedom, security and justice. For the progressive establishment of such an area, the Community is to adopt measures relating to judicial cooperation in civil matters with a cross-border impact to the extent necessary for the proper functioning of the internal market.
(2) According to Article 65, point (b) of the Treaty, these measures are to include those promoting the compatibility of the rules applicable in the Member States concerning the conflict of laws and of jurisdiction.
(3) The European Council meeting in Tampere on 15 and 16 October 1999 endorsed the principle of mutual recognition of judgments and other decisions of judicial authorities as the cornerstone of judicial cooperation in civil matters and invited the Council and the Commission to adopt a programme of measures to implement that principle.
(4) On 30 November 2000 the Council adopted a joint Commission and Council programme of measures for implementation of the principle of mutual recognition of decisions in civil and commercial matters. The programme identifies measures relating to the harmonisation of conflict-of-law rules as those facilitating the mutual recognition of judgments.
(5) The Hague Programme, adopted by the European Council on 5 November 2004, called for work to be pursued actively on the conflict-of-law rules regarding contractual obligations (Rome I).
(6) The proper functioning of the internal market creates a need, in order to improve the predictability of the outcome of litigation, certainty as to the law applicable and the free movement of judgments, for the conflict-of-law rules in the Member States to designate the same national law irrespective of the country of the court in which an action is brought.
(7) The substantive scope and the provisions of this Regulation should be consistent with Council Regulation (EC) No 44/2001 of 22 December 2000 on jurisdiction and the recognition and enforcement of judgments in civil and commercial matters (Brussels I) and Regulation (EC) No 864/2007 of the European Parliament and of the Council of 11 July 2007 on the law applicable to non-contractual obligations (Rome II).
(8) Family relationships should cover parentage, marriage, affinity and collateral relatives. The reference in Article 1(2) to relationships having comparable effects to marriage and other family relationships should be interpreted in accordance with the law of the Member State in which the court is seised.
(9) Obligations under bills of exchange, cheques and promissory notes and other negotiable instruments should also cover bills of lading to the extent that the obligations under the bill of lading arise out of its negotiable character.
(10) Obligations arising out of dealings prior to the conclusion of the contract are covered by Article 12 of Regulation (EC) No 864/2007. Such obligations should therefore be excluded from the scope of this Regulation.
(11) The parties' freedom to choose the applicable law should be one of the cornerstones of the system of conflict-of-law rules in matters of contractual obligations.
(12) An agreement between the parties to confer on one or more courts or tribunals of a Member State exclusive jurisdiction to determine disputes under the contract should be one of the factors to be taken into account in determining whether a choice of law has been clearly demonstrated.
(13) This Regulation does not preclude parties from incorporating by reference into their contract a non-State body of law or an international convention.
(14) Should the Community adopt, in an appropriate legal instrument, rules of substantive contract law, including standard terms and conditions, such instrument may provide that the parties may choose to apply those rules.
(15) Where a choice of law is made and all other elements relevant to the situation are located in a country other than the country whose law has been chosen, the choice of law should not prejudice the application of provisions of the law of that country which cannot be derogated from by agreement. This rule should apply whether or not the choice of law was accompanied by a choice of court or tribunal. Whereas no substantial change is intended as compared with Article 3(3) of the 1980 Convention on the Law Applicable to Contractual Obligations (the Rome

Convention), the wording of this Regulation is aligned as far as possible with Article 14 of Regulation (EC) No 864/2007.

(16) To contribute to the general objective of this Regulation, legal certainty in the European judicial area, the conflict-of-law rules should be highly foreseeable. The courts should, however, retain a degree of discretion to determine the law that is most closely connected to the situation.

(17) As far as the applicable law in the absence of choice is concerned, the concept of "provision of services" and "sale of goods" should be interpreted in the same way as when applying Article 5 of Regulation (EC) No 44/2001 in so far as sale of goods and provision of services are covered by that Regulation. Although franchise and distribution contracts are contracts for services, they are the subject of specific rules.

(18) As far as the applicable law in the absence of choice is concerned, multilateral systems should be those in which trading is conducted, such as regulated markets and multilateral trading facilities as referred to in Article 4 of Directive 2004/39/EC of the European Parliament and of the Council of 21 April 2004 on markets in financial instruments, regardless of whether or not they rely on a central counterparty.

(19) Where there has been no choice of law, the applicable law should be determined in accordance with the rule specified for the particular type of contract. Where the contract cannot be categorised as being one of the specified types or where its elements fall within more than one of the specified types, it should be governed by the law of the country where the party required to effect the characteristic performance of the contract has his habitual residence. In the case of a contract consisting of a bundle of rights and obligations capable of being categorised as falling within more than one of the specified types of contract, the characteristic performance of the contract should be determined having regard to its centre of gravity.

(20) Where the contract is manifestly more closely connected with a country other than that indicated in Article 4(1) or (2), an escape clause should provide that the law of that other country is to apply. In order to determine that country, account should be taken, inter alia, of whether the contract in question has a very close relationship with another contract or contracts.

(21) In the absence of choice, where the applicable law cannot be determined either on the basis of the fact that the contract can be categorised as one of the specified types or as being the law of the country of habitual residence of the party required to effect the characteristic performance of the contract, the contract should be governed by the law of the country with which it is most closely connected. In order to determine that country, account should be taken, inter alia, of whether the contract in question has a very close relationship with another contract or contracts.

(22) As regards the interpretation of contracts for the carriage of goods, no change in substance is intended with respect to Article 4(4), third sentence, of the Rome Convention. Consequently, single-voyage charter parties and other contracts the main purpose of which is the carriage of goods should be treated as contracts for the carriage of goods. For the purposes of this Regulation, the term "consignor" should refer to any person who enters into a contract of carriage with the carrier and the term "the carrier" should refer to the party to the contract who undertakes to carry the goods, whether or not he performs the carriage himself.

(23) As regards contracts concluded with parties regarded as being weaker, those parties should be protected by conflict-of-law rules that are more favourable to their interests than the general rules.

(24) With more specific reference to consumer contracts, the conflict-of-law rule should make it possible to cut the cost of settling disputes concerning what are commonly relatively small claims and to take account of the development of distance-selling techniques. Consistency with Regulation (EC) No 44/2001 requires both that there be a reference to the concept of directed activity as a condition for applying the consumer protection rule and that the concept be interpreted harmoniously in Regulation (EC) No 44/2001 and this Regulation, bearing in mind that a joint declaration by the Council and the Commission on Article 15 of Regulation (EC) No 44/2001 states that "for Article 15(1)(c) to be applicable it is not sufficient for an undertaking to target its activities at the Member State of the consumer's residence, or at a number of Member States including that Member State; a contract must also be concluded within the framework of its activities". The declaration also states that "the mere fact that an Internet site is accessible is not sufficient for Article 15 to be applicable, although a factor will be that this Internet site solicits the conclusion of distance contracts and that a contract has actually been concluded at a distance, by whatever means. In this respect, the language or currency which a website uses does not constitute a relevant factor.".

(25) Consumers should be protected by such rules of the country of their habitual residence that cannot be derogated from by agreement, provided that the consumer contract has been concluded as a result of the professional pursuing his commercial or professional activities in that particular country. The same protection should be guaranteed if the professional, while not pursuing his commercial or professional activities in the country where the consumer has his habitual residence, directs his activities by any means to that country or to several countries, including that country, and the contract is concluded as a result of such activities.

(26) For the purposes of this Regulation, financial services such as investment services and activities and ancillary services provided by a professional to a consumer, as referred to in sections A and B of Annex I to Directive 2004/39/EC, and contracts for the sale of units in collective investment undertakings, whether or not covered by Council Directive 85/611/EEC of 20 December 1985 on the coordination of laws, regulations and administrative provisions relating to undertakings for collective investment in transferable securities (UCITS), should be subject to Article 6 of this Regulation. Consequently, when a reference is made to terms and conditions governing the issuance or offer to the public of transferable securities or to the subscription and redemption of units in collective investment undertakings, that reference should include all aspects binding the issuer or the offeror to the consumer, but should not include those aspects involving the provision of financial services.

(27) Various exceptions should be made to the general conflict-of-law rule for consumer contracts. Under one such exception the general rule should not apply to contracts relating to rights in rem in immovable property or tenancies of such property unless the contract relates to the right to use immovable property on a timeshare basis within the meaning of Directive 94/47/EC of the European Parliament and of the Council of 26 October 1994 on the protection of purchasers in respect of certain aspects of contracts relating to the purchase of the right to use immovable properties on a timeshare basis.

(28) It is important to ensure that rights and obligations which constitute a financial instrument are not covered by the general rule applicable to consumer contracts, as that could lead to different laws being applicable to each of the instruments issued, therefore changing their nature and preventing their fungible trading and offering. Likewise, whenever such instruments are issued or offered, the contractual relationship established between the issuer or the offeror and the consumer should not necessarily be subject to the mandatory application of the law of the country of habitual residence of the consumer, as there is a need to ensure uniformity in the terms and conditions of an issuance or an offer. The same rationale should apply with regard to the multilateral systems covered by Article 4(1)(h), in respect of which it should be ensured that the law of the country of habitual residence of the consumer will not interfere with the rules applicable to contracts concluded within those systems or with the operator of such systems.

(29) For the purposes of this Regulation, references to rights and obligations constituting the terms and conditions governing the issuance, offers to the public or public take-over bids of transferable securities and references to the subscription and redemption of units in collective investment undertakings should include the terms governing, inter alia, the allocation of securities or units, rights in the event of over-subscription, withdrawal rights and similar matters in the context of the offer as well as those matters referred to in Articles 10, 11, 12 and 13, thus ensuring that all relevant contractual aspects of an offer binding the issuer or the offeror to the consumer are governed by a single law.

(30) For the purposes of this Regulation, financial instruments and transferable securities are those instruments referred to in Article 4 of Directive 2004/39/EC.

(31) Nothing in this Regulation should prejudice the operation of a formal arrangement designated as a system under Article 2(a) of Directive 98/26/EC of the European Parliament and of the Council of 19 May 1998 on settlement finality in payment and securities settlement systems.

(32) Owing to the particular nature of contracts of carriage and insurance contracts, specific provisions should ensure an adequate level of protection of passengers and policy holders. Therefore, Article 6 should not apply in the context of those particular contracts.

(33) Where an insurance contract not covering a large risk covers more than one risk, at least one of which is situated in a Member State and at least one of which is situated in a third country, the special rules on insurance contracts in this Regulation should apply only to the risk or risks situated in the relevant Member State or Member States.

(34) The rule on individual employment contracts should not prejudice the application of the overriding mandatory provisions of the country to which a worker is posted in accordance with Directive 96/71/EC of the European Parliament and of the Council of 16 December 1996 concerning the posting of workers in the framework of the provision of services.

(35) Employees should not be deprived of the protection afforded to them by provisions which cannot be derogated from by agreement or which can only be derogated from to their benefit.

(36) As regards individual employment contracts, work carried out in another country should be regarded as temporary if the employee is expected to resume working in the country of origin after carrying out his tasks abroad. The conclusion of a new contract of employment with the original employer or an employer belonging to the same group of companies as the original employer should not preclude the employee from being regarded as carrying out his work in another country temporarily.

(37) Considerations of public interest justify giving the courts of the Member States the possibility, in exceptional circumstances, of applying exceptions based on public policy and overriding mandatory provisions. The concept

of "overriding mandatory provisions" should be distinguished from the expression "provisions which cannot be derogated from by agreement" and should be construed more restrictively.

(38) In the context of voluntary assignment, the term "relationship" should make it clear that Article 14(1) also applies to the property aspects of an assignment, as between assignor and assignee, in legal orders where such aspects are treated separately from the aspects under the law of obligations. However, the term "relationship" should not be understood as relating to any relationship that may exist between assignor and assignee. In particular, it should not cover preliminary questions as regards a voluntary assignment or a contractual subrogation. The term should be strictly limited to the aspects which are directly relevant to the voluntary assignment or contractual subrogation in question.

(39) For the sake of legal certainty there should be a clear definition of habitual residence, in particular for companies and other bodies, corporate or unincorporated. Unlike Article 60(1) of Regulation (EC) No 44/2001, which establishes three criteria, the conflict-of-law rule should proceed on the basis of a single criterion; otherwise, the parties would be unable to foresee the law applicable to their situation.

(40) A situation where conflict-of-law rules are dispersed among several instruments and where there are differences between those rules should be avoided. This Regulation, however, should not exclude the possibility of inclusion of conflict-of-law rules relating to contractual obligations in provisions of Community law with regard to particular matters.

This Regulation should not prejudice the application of other instruments laying down provisions designed to contribute to the proper functioning of the internal market in so far as they cannot be applied in conjunction with the law designated by the rules of this Regulation. The application of provisions of the applicable law designated by the rules of this Regulation should not restrict the free movement of goods and services as regulated by Community instruments, such as Directive 2000/31/EC of the European Parliament and of the Council of 8 June 2000 on certain legal aspects of information society services, in particular electronic commerce, in the Internal Market (Directive on electronic commerce).

(41) Respect for international commitments entered into by the Member States means that this Regulation should not affect international conventions to which one or more Member States are parties at the time when this Regulation is adopted. To make the rules more accessible, the Commission should publish the list of the relevant conventions in the Official Journal of the European Union on the basis of information supplied by the Member States.

(42) The Commission will make a proposal to the European Parliament and to the Council concerning the procedures and conditions according to which Member States would be entitled to negotiate and conclude, on their own behalf, agreements with third countries in individual and exceptional cases, concerning sectoral matters and containing provisions on the law applicable to contractual obligations.

(43) Since the objective of this Regulation cannot be sufficiently achieved by the Member States and can therefore, by reason of the scale and effects of this Regulation, be better achieved at Community level, the Community may adopt measures, in accordance with the principle of subsidiarity as set out in Article 5 of the Treaty. In accordance with the principle of proportionality, as set out in that Article, this Regulation does not go beyond what is necessary to attain its objective.

(44) In accordance with Article 3 of the Protocol on the position of the United Kingdom and Ireland, annexed to the Treaty on European Union and to the Treaty establishing the European Community, Ireland has notified its wish to take part in the adoption and application of the present Regulation.

(45) In accordance with Articles 1 and 2 of the Protocol on the position of the United Kingdom and Ireland, annexed to the Treaty on European Union and to the Treaty establishing the European Community, and without prejudice to Article 4 of the said Protocol, the United Kingdom is not taking part in the adoption of this Regulation and is not bound by it or subject to its application.

(46) In accordance with Articles 1 and 2 of the Protocol on the position of Denmark, annexed to the Treaty on European Union and to the Treaty establishing the European Community, Denmark is not taking part in the adoption of this Regulation and is not bound by it or subject to its application,

HAVE ADOPTED THIS REGULATION:

Chapter I. Scope

Article 1. 1. This Regulation shall apply, in situations involving a conflict of laws, to contractual obligations in civil and commercial matters.
It shall not apply, in particular, to revenue, customs or administrative matters.
2. The following shall be excluded from the scope of this Regulation:
(a) questions involving the status or legal capacity of natural persons, without prejudice to Article 13;

(b) obligations arising out of family relationships and relationships deemed by the law applicable to such relationships to have comparable effects, including maintenance obligations;
(c) obligations arising out of matrimonial property regimes, property regimes of relationships deemed by the law applicable to such relationships to have comparable effects to marriage, and wills and succession;
(d) obligations arising under bills of exchange, cheques and promissory notes and other negotiable instruments to the extent that the obligations under such other negotiable instruments arise out of their negotiable character;
(e) arbitration agreements and agreements on the choice of court;
(f) questions governed by the law of companies and other bodies, corporate or unincorporated, such as the creation, by registration or otherwise, legal capacity, internal organisation or winding-up of companies and other bodies, corporate or unincorporated, and the personal liability of officers and members as such for the obligations of the company or body;
(g) the question whether an agent is able to bind a principal, or an organ to bind a company or other body corporate or unincorporated, in relation to a third party;
(h) the constitution of trusts and the relationship between settlors, trustees and beneficiaries;
(i) obligations arising out of dealings prior to the conclusion of a contract;
(j) insurance contracts arising out of operations carried out by organisations other than undertakings referred to in Article 2 of Directive 2002/83/EC of the European Parliament and of the Council of 5 November 2002 concerning life assurance the object of which is to provide benefits for employed or self-employed persons belonging to an undertaking or group of undertakings, or to a trade or group of trades, in the event of death or survival or of discontinuance or curtailment of activity, or of sickness related to work or accidents at work.
3. This Regulation shall not apply to evidence and procedure, without prejudice to Article 18.
4. In this Regulation, the term "Member State" shall mean Member States to which this Regulation applies. However, in Article 3(4) and Article 7 the term shall mean all the Member States.

Article 2. Any law specified by this Regulation shall be applied whether or not it is the law of a Member State.

Chapter II. Uniform rules

Article 3. 1. A contract shall be governed by the law chosen by the parties. The choice shall be made expressly or clearly demonstrated by the terms of the contract or the circumstances of the case. By their choice the parties can select the law applicable to the whole or to part only of the contract.
2. The parties may at any time agree to subject the contract to a law other than that which previously governed it, whether as a result of an earlier choice made under this Article or of other provisions of this Regulation. Any change in the law to be applied that is made after the conclusion of the contract shall not prejudice its formal validity under Article 11 or adversely affect the rights of third parties.
3. Where all other elements relevant to the situation at the time of the choice are located in a country other than the country whose law has been chosen, the choice of the parties shall not prejudice the application of provisions of the law of that other country which cannot be derogated from by agreement.
4. Where all other elements relevant to the situation at the time of the choice are located in one or more Member States, the parties' choice of applicable law other than that of a
Member State shall not prejudice the application of provisions of Community law, where appropriate as implemented in the Member State of the forum, which cannot be derogated from by agreement.
5. The existence and validity of the consent of the parties as to the choice of the applicable law shall be determined in accordance with the provisions of Articles 10, 11 and 13.

Article 4. 1. To the extent that the law applicable to the contract has not been chosen in accordance with Article 3 and without prejudice to Articles 5 to 8, the law governing the contract shall be determined as follows:
(a) a contract for the sale of goods shall be governed by the law of the country where the seller has his habitual residence;
(b) a contract for the provision of services shall be governed by the law of the country where the service provider has his habitual residence;
(c) a contract relating to a right in rem in immovable property or to a tenancy of immovable property shall be governed by the law of the country where the property is situated;
(d) notwithstanding point (c), a tenancy of immovable property concluded for temporary private use for a period of no more than six consecutive months shall be governed by the law of the country where the landlord has his habitual residence, provided that the tenant is a natural person and has his habitual residence in the same country;

(e) a franchise contract shall be governed by the law of the country where the franchisee has his habitual residence;
(f) a distribution contract shall be governed by the law of the country where the distributor has his habitual residence;
(g) a contract for the sale of goods by auction shall be governed by the law of the country where the auction takes place, if such a place can be determined;
(h) a contract concluded within a multilateral system which brings together or facilitates the bringing together of multiple third-party buying and selling interests in financial instruments, as defined by Article 4(1), point (17) of Directive 2004/39/EC, in accordance with non-discretionary rules and governed by a single law, shall be governed by that law.
2. Where the contract is not covered by paragraph 1 or where the elements of the contract would be covered by more than one of points (a) to (h) of paragraph 1, the contract shall be governed by the law of the country where the party required to effect the characteristic performance of the contract has his habitual residence.
3. Where it is clear from all the circumstances of the case that the contract is manifestly more closely connected with a country other than that indicated in paragraphs 1 or 2, the law of that other country shall apply.
4. Where the law applicable cannot be determined pursuant to paragraphs 1 or 2, the contract shall be governed by the law of the country with which it is most closely connected.

Article 5. 1. To the extent that the law applicable to a contract for the carriage of goods has not been chosen in accordance with Article 3, the law applicable shall be the law of the country of habitual residence of the carrier, provided that the place of receipt or the place of delivery or the habitual residence of the consignor is also situated in that country. If those requirements are not met, the law of the country where the place of delivery as agreed by the parties is situated shall apply.
2. To the extent that the law applicable to a contract for the carriage of passengers has not
been chosen by the parties in accordance with the second subparagraph, the law applicable shall be the law of the country where the passenger has his habitual residence, provided that either the place of departure or the place of destination is situated in that country. If these requirements are not met, the law of the country where the carrier has his habitual residence shall apply.
The parties may choose as the law applicable to a contract for the carriage of passengers in accordance with Article 3 only the law of the country where:
(a) the passenger has his habitual residence; or
(b) the carrier has his habitual residence; or
(c) the carrier has his place of central administration; or
(d) the place of departure is situated; or
(e) the place of destination is situated.
3. Where it is clear from all the circumstances of the case that the contract, in the absence of a choice of law, is manifestly more closely connected with a country other than that indicated in paragraphs 1 or 2, the law of that other country shall apply.

Article 6. 1. Without prejudice to Articles 5 and 7, a contract concluded by a natural person for a purpose which can be regarded as being outside his trade or profession ("the consumer") with another person acting in the exercise of his trade or profession ("the professional") shall be governed by the law of the country where the consumer has his habitual residence, provided that the professional:
(a) pursues his commercial or professional activities in the country where the consumer has his habitual residence, or
(b) by any means, directs such activities to that country or to several countries including that country,
and the contract falls within the scope of such activities.
2. Notwithstanding paragraph 1, the parties may choose the law applicable to a contract which fulfils the requirements of paragraph 1, in accordance with Article 3. Such a choice
may not, however, have the result of depriving the consumer of the protection afforded to him by provisions that cannot be derogated from by agreement by virtue of the law which, in the absence of choice, would have been applicable on the basis of paragraph 1.
3. If the requirements in points (a) or (b) of paragraph 1 are not fulfilled, the law applicable to a contract between a consumer and a professional shall be determined pursuant to Articles 3 and 4.
4. Paragraphs 1 and 2 shall not apply to:
(a) a contract for the supply of services where the services are to be supplied to the consumer exclusively in a country other than that in which he has his habitual
residence;

(b) a contract of carriage other than a contract relating to package travel within the meaning of Council Directive 90/314/EEC of 13 June 1990 on package travel,
package holidays and package tours;
(c) a contract relating to a right in rem in immovable property or a tenancy of immovable property other than a contract relating to the right to use immovable properties on a timeshare basis within the meaning of Directive 94/47/EC;
(d) rights and obligations which constitute a financial instrument and rights and obligations constituting the terms and conditions governing the issuance or offer to the public and public take-over bids of transferable securities, and the subscription and redemption of units in collective investment undertakings in so far as these activities do not constitute provision of a financial service;
(e) a contract concluded within the type of system falling within the scope of Article 4(1), point (h).

Article 7. 1. This Article shall apply to contracts referred to in paragraph 2, whether or not the risk covered is situated in a Member State, and to all other insurance contracts covering risks situated inside the territory of the Member States. It shall not apply to reinsurance contracts.
2. An insurance contract covering a large risk as defined in Article 5(d) of the First Council Directive 73/239/EEC of 24 July 1973 on the coordination of laws, regulations and administrative provisions relating to the taking-up and pursuit of the business of direct insurance other than life assurance1 shall be governed by the law chosen by the parties in accordance with Article 3 of this Regulation.
To the extent that the applicable law has not been chosen by the parties, the insurance contract shall be governed by the law of the country where the insurer has his habitual residence. Where it is clear from all the circumstances of the case that the contract is manifestly more closely connected with another country, the law of that other country shall apply.
3. In the case of an insurance contract other than a contract falling within paragraph 2, only the following laws may be chosen by the parties in accordance with Article 3:
(a) the law of any Member State where the risk is situated at the time of conclusion of
the contract;
(b) the law of the country where the policy holder has his habitual residence;
(c) in the case of life assurance, the law of the Member State of which the policy holder
is a national;
(d) for insurance contracts covering risks limited to events occurring in one
Member State other than the Member State where the risk is situated, the law of that
Member State;
(e) where the policy holder of a contract falling under this paragraph pursues a commercial or industrial activity or a liberal profession and the insurance contract covers two or more risks which relate to those activities and are situated in different Member States, the law of any of the Member States concerned or the law of the country of habitual residence of the policy holder.
Where, in the cases set out in points (a), (b) or (e), the Member States referred to grant greater freedom of choice of the law applicable to the insurance contract, the parties may take advantage of that freedom.
To the extent that the law applicable has not been chosen by the parties in accordance with this paragraph, such a contract shall be governed by the law of the Member State in which the risk is situated at the time of conclusion of the contract.
4. The following additional rules shall apply to insurance contracts covering risks for which a Member State imposes an obligation to take out insurance:
(a) the insurance contract shall not satisfy the obligation to take out insurance unless it complies with the specific provisions relating to that insurance laid down by the Member State that imposes the obligation. Where the law of the Member State in which the risk is situated and the law of the Member State imposing the obligation to take out insurance contradict each other, the latter shall prevail;
(b) by way of derogation from paragraphs 2 and 3, a Member State may lay down that the insurance contract shall be governed by the law of the Member State that imposes the obligation to take out insurance.
5. For the purposes of paragraph 3, third subparagraph, and paragraph 4, where the contract covers risks situated in more than one Member State, the contract shall be considered as constituting several contracts each relating to only one Member State.
6. For the purposes of this Article, the country in which the risk is situated shall be determined in accordance with Article 2(d) of the Second Council Directive 88/357/EEC of 22 June 1988 on the coordination of laws, regulations and administrative provisions relating to direct insurance other than life assurance and laying down provisions to facilitate the effective exercise of freedom to provide services1 and, in the case of life assurance, the country in

which the risk is situated shall be the country of the commitment within the meaning of Article 1(1)(g) of Directive 2002/83/EC.

Article 8. 1. An individual employment contract shall be governed by the law chosen by the parties in accordance with Article 3. Such a choice of law may not, however, have the result of depriving the employee of the protection afforded to him by provisions that cannot be derogated from by agreement under the law that, in the absence of choice, would have been applicable pursuant to paragraphs 2, 3 and 4 of this Article.
2. To the extent that the law applicable to the individual employment contract has not been chosen by the parties, the contract shall be governed by the law of the country in which or, failing that, from which the employee habitually carries out his work in performance of the contract. The country where the work is habitually carried out shall not be deemed to have changed if he is temporarily employed in another country.
3. Where the law applicable cannot be determined pursuant to paragraph 2, the contract shall be governed by the law of the country where the place of business through which the employee was engaged is situated.
4. Where it appears from the circumstances as a whole that the contract is more closely connected with a country other than that indicated in paragraphs 2 or 3, the law of that other country shall apply.

Article 9. 1. Overriding mandatory provisions are provisions the respect for which is regarded as crucial by a country for safeguarding its public interests, such as its political, social or economic organisation, to such an extent that they are applicable to any situation falling within their scope, irrespective of the law otherwise applicable to the contract under this Regulation.
2. Nothing in this Regulation shall restrict the application of the overriding mandatory provisions of the law of the forum.
3. Effect may be given to the overriding mandatory provisions of the law of the country where the obligations arising out of the contract have to be or have been performed, in so far as those overriding mandatory provisions render the performance of the contract unlawful. In considering whether to give effect to those provisions, regard shall be had to their nature and purpose and to the consequences of their application or non-application.

Article 10. 1. The existence and validity of a contract, or of any term of a contract, shall be determined by the law which would govern it under this Regulation if the contract or term were valid.
2. Nevertheless, a party, in order to establish that he did not consent, may rely upon the law of the country in which he has his habitual residence if it appears from the circumstances that it would not be reasonable to determine the effect of his conduct in accordance with the law specified in paragraph 1.

Article 11. 1. A contract concluded between persons who, or whose agents, are in the same country at the time of its conclusion is formally valid if it satisfies the formal requirements of the law which governs it in substance under this Regulation or of the law of the country where it is concluded.
2. A contract concluded between persons who, or whose agents, are in different countries at the time of its conclusion is formally valid if it satisfies the formal requirements of the law which governs it in substance under this Regulation, or of the law of either of the countries where either of the parties or their agent is present at the time of conclusion, or of the law of the country where either of the parties had his habitual residence at that time.
3. A unilateral act intended to have legal effect relating to an existing or contemplated contract is formally valid if it satisfies the formal requirements of the law which governs or would govern the contract in substance under this Regulation, or of the law of the country where the act was done, or of the law of the country where the person by whom it was done had his habitual residence at that time.
4. Paragraphs 1, 2 and 3 of this Article shall not apply to contracts that fall within the scope of Article 6. The form of such contracts shall be governed by the law of the country where the consumer has his habitual residence.
5. Notwithstanding paragraphs 1 to 4, a contract the subject matter of which is a right in rem in immovable property or a tenancy of immovable property shall be subject to the requirements of form of the law of the country where the property is situated if by that law:
(a) those requirements are imposed irrespective of the country where the contract is concluded and irrespective of the law governing the contract, and
(b) those requirements cannot be derogated from by agreement.

Article 12. 1. The law applicable to a contract by virtue of this Regulation shall govern in particular:
(a) interpretation;
(b) performance;
(c) within the limits of the powers conferred on the court by its procedural law, the consequences of a total or partial breach of obligations, including the assessment of damages in so far as it is governed by rules of law;

(d) the various ways of extinguishing obligations, and prescription and limitation of actions;
(e) the consequences of nullity of the contract.
2. In relation to the manner of performance and the steps to be taken in the event of defective performance, regard shall be had to the law of the country in which performance takes place.

Article 13. In a contract concluded between persons who are in the same country, a natural person who would have capacity under the law of that country may invoke his incapacity resulting from the law of another country, only if the other party to the contract was aware of that incapacity at the time of the conclusion of the contract or was not aware thereof as a result of negligence.

Article 14. 1. The relationship between assignor and assignee under a voluntary assignment or contractual subrogation of a claim against another person ("the debtor") shall be governed by the law that applies to the contract between the assignor and assignee under this Regulation.
2. The law governing the assigned or subrogated claim shall determine its assignability, the relationship between the assignee and the debtor, the conditions under which the assignment or subrogation can be invoked against the debtor and whether the debtor's obligations have been discharged.
3. The concept of assignment in this Article includes outright transfers of claims, transfers of claims by way of security and pledges or other security rights over claims.

Article 15. Where a person ("the creditor") has a contractual claim against another ("the debtor") and a third person has a duty to satisfy the creditor, or has in fact satisfied the creditor in discharge of that duty, the law which governs the third person's duty to satisfy the creditor shall determine whether and to what extent the third person is entitled to exercise against the debtor the rights which the creditor had against the debtor under the law governing their relationship.

Article 16. If a creditor has a claim against several debtors who are liable for the same claim, and one of the debtors has already satisfied the claim in whole or in part, the law governing the debtor's obligation towards the creditor also governs the debtor's right to claim recourse from the other debtors. The other debtors may rely on the defences they had against the creditor to the extent allowed by the law governing their obligations towards the creditor.

Article 17. Where the right to set-off is not agreed by the parties, set-off shall be governed by the law applicable to the claim against which the right to set-off is asserted.

Article 18. 1. The law governing a contractual obligation under this Regulation shall apply to the extent that, in matters of contractual obligations, it contains rules which raise presumptions of law or determine the burden of proof.
2. A contract or an act intended to have legal effect may be proved by any mode of proof recognised by the law of the forum or by any of the laws referred to in Article 11 under which that contract or act is formally valid, provided that such mode of proof can be administered by the forum.

Chapter III. Other provisions

Article 19. 1. For the purposes of this Regulation, the habitual residence of companies and other bodies, corporate or unincorporated, shall be the place of central administration.
The habitual residence of a natural person acting in the course of his business activity shall be his principal place of business.
2. Where the contract is concluded in the course of the operations of a branch, agency or any other establishment, or if, under the contract, performance is the responsibility of such a branch, agency or establishment, the place where the branch, agency or any other establishment is located shall be treated as the place of habitual residence.
3. For the purposes of determining the habitual residence, the relevant point in time shall be the time of the conclusion of the contract.

Article 20. The application of the law of any country specified by this Regulation means the application of the rules of law in force in that country other than its rules of private international law, unless provided otherwise in this Regulation.

Article 21. The application of a provision of the law of any country specified by this Regulation may be refused only if such application is manifestly incompatible with the public policy ("ordre public") of the forum.

Article 22. 1. Where a State comprises several territorial units, each of which has its own rules of law in respect of contractual obligations, each territorial unit shall be considered as a country for the purposes of identifying the law applicable under this Regulation.
2. A Member State where different territorial units have their own rules of law in respect of contractual obligations shall not be required to apply this Regulation to conflicts solely between the laws of such units.

Article 23. With the exception of Article 7, this Regulation shall not prejudice the application of provisions of Community law which, in relation to particular matters, lay down conflict-of-law rules relating to contractual obligations.

Article 24. 1. This Regulation shall replace the Rome Convention in the Member States, except as regards the territories of the Member States which fall within the territorial scope of that Convention and to which this Regulation does not apply pursuant to Article 299 of the Treaty.
2. In so far as this Regulation replaces the provisions of the Rome Convention, any reference to that Convention shall be understood as a reference to this Regulation.

Article 25. 1. This Regulation shall not prejudice the application of international conventions to which one or more Member States are parties at the time when this Regulation is adopted and which lay down conflict-of-law rules relating to contractual obligations.
2. However, this Regulation shall, as between Member States, take precedence over conventions concluded exclusively between two or more of them in so far as such conventions concern matters governed by this Regulation.

Article 26. 1. By 17 June 2009, Member States shall notify the Commission of the conventions referred to in Article 25(1). After that date, Member States shall notify the Commission of all denunciations of such conventions.
2. Within six months of receipt of the notifications referred to in paragraph 1, the Commission shall publish in the Official Journal of the European Union:
(a) a list of the conventions referred to in paragraph 1;
(b) the denunciations referred to in paragraph 1.

Article 27. 1. By 17 June 2013, the Commission shall submit to the European Parliament, the Council and the European Economic and Social Committee a report on the application of this Regulation. If appropriate, the report shall be accompanied by proposals to amend this Regulation. The report shall include:
(a) a study on the law applicable to insurance contracts and an assessment of the impact
of the provisions to be introduced, if any; and
(b) an evaluation on the application of Article 6, in particular as regards the coherence of
Community law in the field of consumer protection.
2. By 17 June 2010, the Commission shall submit to the European Parliament, the Council and the European Economic and Social Committee a report on the question of the effectiveness of an assignment or subrogation of a claim against third parties and the priority of the assigned or subrogated claim over a right of another person. The report shall be accompanied, if appropriate, by a proposal to amend this Regulation and an assessment of the impact of the provisions to be introduced.

Article 28. This Regulation shall apply to contracts concluded after 17 December 2009.

Chapter IV. Final provisions

Article 29. This Regulation shall enter into force on the twentieth day following its publication in the Official Journal of the European Union.
It shall apply from 17 December 2009 except for Article 26 which shall apply from 17 June 2009.
This Regulation shall be binding in its entirety and directly applicable in the Member States in accordance with the Treaty establishing the European Community.

Convention on the Law Applicable to Contractual Obligations, concluded at Rome on 19 June 1980 [Rome Convention] (*OJ* L 266 , 9.10.1980, pp. 1 – 19). Selected provisions: 1 – 22.

[The Preamble is omitted.]

Title I. Scope of the Convention

Article 1. 1. The rules of this Convention shall apply to contractual obligations in any situation involving a choice between the laws of different countries.
2. They shall not apply to:
(a) questions involving the status or legal capacity of natural persons, without prejudice to Article 11;
(b) contractual obligations relating to:
- wills and succession,
- rights in property arising out of a matrimonial relationship,
- rights and duties arising out of a family relationship, parentage, marriage or affinity, including maintenance obligations in respect of children who are not legitimate;
(c) obligations arising under bills of exchange, cheques and promissory notes and other negotiable instruments to the extent that the obligations under such other negotiable instruments arise out of their negotiable character;
(d) arbitration agreements and agreements on the choice of court;
(e) questions governed by the law of companies and other bodies corporate or unincorporate such as the creation, by registration or otherwise, legal capacity, internal organization or winding up of companies and other bodies corporate or unincorporate and the personal liability of officers and members as such for the obligations of the company or body;
(f) the question whether an agent is able to bind a principal, or an organ to bind a company or body corporate or unincorporate, to a third party;
(g) the constitution of trusts and the relationship between settlors, trustees and beneficiaries;
(h) evidence and procedure, without prejudice to Article 14.
(3) The rules of this Convention do not apply to contracts of insurance which cover risks situated in the territories of the Member States of the European Economic Community. In order to determine whether a risk is situated in these territories the court shall apply its internal law.
(4) The preceding paragraph does not apply to contracts of re-insurance.

Article 2. Any law specified by this Convention shall be applied whether or not it is the law of a Contracting State.

Title II. Uniform Rules

Article 3. (1) A contract shall be governed by the law chosen by the parties. The choice must be expressed or demonstrated with reasonable certainty by the terms of the contract or the circumstances of the case. By their choice the parties can select the law applicable to the whole or a part only of the contract.
(2) The parties may at any time agree to subject the contract to a law other than that which previously governed it, whether as a result of an earlier choice under this Article or of other provisions of this Convention. Any variation by the parties of the law to be applied made after the conclusion of the contract shall not prejudice its formal validity under Article 9 or adversely affect the rights of third parties.
(3) The fact that the parties have chosen a foreign law, whether or not accompanied by the choice of a foreign tribunal, shall not, where all the other elements relevant to the situation at the time of the choice are connected with one country only, prejudice the application of rules of the law of that country which cannot be derogated from by contract, hereinafter called "mandatory rules".
(4) The existence and validity of the consent of the parties as to the choice of the applicable law shall be determined in accordance with the provisions of Articles 8, 9 and 11.

Article 4. (1) To the extent that the law applicable to the contract has not been chosen in accordance with Article 3, the contract shall be governed by the law of the country with which it is most closely connected. Nevertheless, a severable part of the contract which has a closer connection with another country may by way of exception be governed by the law of that other country.
(2) Subject to the provisions of paragraph 5 of this Article, it shall be presumed that the contract is most closely connected with the country where the party who is to effect the performance which is characteristic of the contract

has, at the time of conclusion of the contract, his habitual residence, or, in the case of a body corporate or unincorporate, its central administration. However, if the contract is entered into in the course of that party's trade or profession, that country shall be the country in which the principal place of business is situated or, where under the terms of the contract the performance is to be effected through a place of business other than the principal place of business, the country in which that other place of business is situated.
(3) Notwithstanding the provisions of paragraph 2 of this Article, to the extent that the subject matter of the contract is a right in immovable property or a right to use immovable property it shall be presumed that the contract is most closely connected with the country where the immovable property is situated.
(4) A contract for the carriage of goods shall not be subject to the presumption in paragraph 2. In such a contract if the country in which, at the time the contract is concluded, the carrier has his principal place of business is also the country in which the place of loading or the place of discharge or the principal place of business of the consignor is situated, it shall be presumed that the contract is most closely connected with that country. In applying this paragraph single voyage charter-parties and other contracts the main purpose of which is the carriage of goods shall be treated as contracts for the carriage of goods.
(5) Paragraph 2 shall not apply if the characteristic performance cannot be determined, and the presumptions in paragraphs 2, 3 and 4 shall be disregarded if it appears from the circumstances as a whole that the contract is more closely connected with another country.

Article 5. (1) This Article applies to a contract the object of which is the supply of goods or services to a person ("the consumer") for a purpose which can be regarded as being outside his trade or profession, or a contract for the provision of credit for that object.
(2) Notwithstanding the provisions of Article 3, a choice of law made by the parties shall not have the result of depriving the consumer of the protection afforded to him by the mandatory rules of the law of the country in which he has his habitual residence:
- if in that country the conclusion of the contract was preceded by a specific invitation addressed to him or by advertising, and he had taken in that country all the steps necessary on his part for the conclusion of the contract, or
- if the other party or his agent received the consumer's order in that country, or
- if the contract is for the sale of goods and the consumer travelled from that country to another country and there gave his order, provided that the consumer's journey was arranged by the seller for the purpose of inducing the consumer to buy.
(3) Notwithstanding the provisions of Article 4, a contract to which this Article applies shall, in the absence of choice in accordance with Article 3, be governed by the law of the country in which the consumer has his habitual residence if it is entered into in the circumstances described in paragraph 2 of this Article.
(4) This Article shall not apply to: (a) a contract of carriage;
(b) a contract for the supply of services where the services are to be supplied to the consumer exclusively in a country other than that in which he has his habitual residence.
(5) Notwithstanding the provisions of paragraph 4, this Article shall apply to a contract which, for an inclusive price, provides for a combination of travel and accommodation.

Article 6. (1) Notwithstanding the provisions of Article 3, in a contract of employment a choice of law made by the parties shall not have the result of depriving the employee of the protection afforded to him by the mandatory rules of the law which would be applicable under paragraph 2 in the absence of choice.
(2) Notwithstanding the provisions of Article 4, a contract of employment shall, in the absence of choice in accordance with Article 3, be governed:
(a) by the law of the country in which the employee habitually carries out his work in performance of the contract, even if he is temporarily employed in another country ; or
(b) if the employee does not habitually carry out his work in any one country, by the law of the country in which the place of business through which he was engaged is situated; unless it appears from the circumstances as a whole that the contract is more closely connected with another country, in which case the contract shall be governed by the law of that country.

Article 7. (1) When applying under this Convention the law of a country, effect may be given to the mandatory rules of the law of another country with which the situation has a close connection, if and in so far as, under the law of the latter country, those rules must be applied whatever the law applicable to the contract. In considering whether to give effect to these mandatory rules, regard shall be had to their nature and purpose and to the consequences of their application or non-application.

2. Nothing in this Convention shall restrict the application of the rules of the law of the forum in a situation where they are mandatory irrespective of the law otherwise applicable to the contract.

Article 8. 1. The existence and validity of a contract, or of any term of a contract, shall be determined by the law which would govern it under this Convention if the contract or term were valid.
2. Nevertheless a party may rely upon the law of the country in which he has his habitual residence to establish that he did not consent if it appears from the circumstances that it would not be reasonable to determine the effect of his conduct in accordance with the law specified in the preceding paragraph.

Article 9. 1 A contract concluded between persons who are in the same country is formally valid if it satisfies the formal requirements of the law which governs it under this Convention or of the law of the country where it is concluded.
2. A contract concluded between persons who are in different countries is formally valid if it satisfies the formal requirements of the law which governs it under this Convention or of the law of one of those countries.
3. Where a contract is concluded by an agent, the country in which the agent acts is the relevant country for the purposes of paragraphs 1 and 2.
4. An act intended to have legal effect relating to an existing or contemplated contract is formally valid if it satisfies the formal requirements of the law which under this Convention governs or would govern the contract or of the law of the country where the act was done.
5. The provisions of the preceding paragraphs shall not apply to a contract to which Article 5 applies, concluded in the circumstances described in paragraph 2 of Article 5. The formal validity of such a contract is governed by the law of the country in which the consumer has his habitual residence.
6. Notwithstanding paragraphs 1 to 4 of this Article, a contract the subject matter of which is a right in immovable property or a right to use immovable property shall be subject to the mandatory requirements of form of the law of the country where the property is situated if by that law those requirements are imposed irrespective of the country where the contract is concluded and irrespective of the law governing the contract.

Article 10. 1. The law applicable to a contract by virtue of Articles 3 to 6 and 12 of this Convention shall govern in particular:
(a) interpretation;
(b) performance;
(c) within the limits of the powers conferred on the court by its procedural law, the consequences of breach, including the assessment of damages in so far as it is governed by rules of law;
(d) the various ways of extinguishing obligations, and prescription and limitation of actions;
(e) the consequences of nullity of the contract.
2. In relation to the manner of performance and the steps to be taken in the event of defective performance regard shall be had to the law of the country in which performance takes place.

Article 11. In a contract concluded between persons who are in the same country, a natural person who would have capacity under the law of that country may invoke his incapacity resulting from another law only if the other party to the contract was aware of this incapacity at the time of the conclusion of the contract or was not aware thereof as a result of negligence.

Article 12. 1. The mutual obligations of assignor and assignee under a voluntary assignment of a right against another person ("the debtor") shall be governed by the law which under this Convention applies to the contract between the assignor and assignee.
2. The law governing the right to which the assignment relates shall determine its assignability, the relationship between the assignee and the debtor, the conditions under which the assignment can be invoked against the debtor and any question whether the debtor's obligations have been discharged.

Article 13. 1. Where a person ("the creditor") has a contractual claim upon another ("the debtor"), and a third person has a duty to satisfy the creditor, or has in fact satisfied the creditor in discharge of that duty, the law which governs the third person's duty to satisfy the creditor shall determine whether the third person is entitled to exercise against the debtor the rights which the creditor had against the debtor under the law governing their relationship and, if so, whether he may do so in full or only to a limited extent.
2. The same rule applies where several persons are subject to the same contractual claim and one of them has satisfied the creditor.

Part VII. Private International Law

Article 14. 1. The law governing the contract under this Convention applies to the extent that it contains, in the law of contract, rules which raise presumptions of law or determine the burden of proof.
2. A contract or an act intended to have legal effect may be proved by any mode of proof recognized by the law of the forum or by any of the laws referred to in Article 9 under which that contract or act is formally valid, provided that such mode of proof can be administered by the forum.

Article 15. The application of the law of any country specified by this Convention means the application of the rules of law in force in that country other than its rules of private international law.

Article 16. The application of a rule of the law of any country specified by this Convention may be refused only if such application is manifestly incompatible with the public policy ("ordre public") of the forum.

Article 17. This Convention shall apply in a Contracting State to contracts made after the date on which this Convention has entered into force with respect to that State.

Article 18. In the interpretation and application of the preceding uniform rules, regard shall be had to their international character and to the desirability of achieving uniformity in their interpretation and application.

Article 19. 1. Where a State comprises several territorial units each of which has its own rules of law in respect of contractual obligations, each territorial unit shall be considered as a country for the purposes of identifying the law applicable under this Convention.
2. A State within which different territorial units have their own rules of law in respect of contractual obligations shall not be bound to apply this Convention to conflicts solely between the laws of such units.

Article 20. This Convention shall not affect the application of provisions which, in relation to particular matters, lay down choice of law rules relating to contractual obligations and which are or will be contained in acts of the institutions of the European Communities or in national laws harmonized in implementation of such acts.

Article 21. This Convention shall not prejudice the application of international conventions to which a Contracting State is, or becomes, a party.

Article 22. 1. Any Contracting State may, at the time of signature, ratification, acceptance or approval, reserve the right not to apply:
(a) the provisions of Article 7 (1);
(b) the provisions of Article 10 (1) (e).
2. Any Contracting State may also, when notifying an extension of the Convention in accordance with Article 27 (2), make one or more of these reservations, with its effect limited to all or some of the territories mentioned in the extension.
3. Any Contracting State may at any time withdraw a reservation which it has made; the reservation shall cease to have effect on the first day of the third calendar month after notification of the withdrawal.

[The final provisions are omitted.]

Convention on the law applicable to surnames and given names, concluded at Munich on 5 September 1980 (*UNTS* 1990, Vol. 1553, 1-26995, pp. 8 – 11. Authentic text: French).

[The Preamble is omitted]

Article 1. 1. An individual's surnames and given names shall be determined according to the law of the State of which he is a national. To this end alone, the circumstances governing surnames and given names shall be defined according to the law of that State.
2. In cases involving a change of nationality, the law of the State of the new nationality shall apply.

Article 2. The law designated by this Convention shall apply even in the case of a non-contracting State.

Article 3. All birth certificates must indicate the child's surnames and given names.

Article 4. The implementation of the law designated by this Convention may not be disallowed unless it is manifestly incompatible with public policy.

Article 5. 1. If the registrar drawing up a certificate is unable to ascertain the applicable law to determine the surnames and given names of the person concerned, he shall apply the internal law of his country and shall so inform the authority to which he is responsible.
2. Certificates thus drawn up may be corrected by means of a procedure which each State undertakes to institute free of charge.

Article 6. 1. Any State may, at the time of signature, ratification, acceptance, approval or accession reserve the right to apply its internal law when the person concerned is normally resident in its territory.
2. The determination of surnames and given names under that law shall apply only for the contracting State which reserved that right.
3. No other reservations shall be permitted.
4. Any State party to this Convention may, at any time, withdraw its reservation in whole or in part. Such withdrawal shall be notified to the Swiss Federal Council and shall take effect on the first day of the third month following that in which the notification is received.

Article 7. This Convention shall be ratified, accepted or approved and the instruments of ratification, acceptance or approval shall be deposited with the Swiss Federal Council.

Article 8. 1. This Convention shall enter into force on the first day of the third month following that in which the third instrument of ratification, acceptance, approval or accession is deposited.
2. For any State which ratifies, accepts, approves or accedes to this Convention after its entry into force, the Convention shall take effect on the first day of the third month following that in which the State deposits the instrument of ratification, acceptance, approval or accession.

Article 9. Any State may accede to this Convention. The instrument of accession shall be deposited with the Swiss Federal Council.

Article 10. 1. Any State may, at the time of signature, ratification, acceptance, approval or accession, or at any time subsequent thereto, declare that this Convention shall apply to all the territories for whose international relations it is responsible, or to one or more of them.
2. This declaration shall be notified to the Swiss Federal Council, and the extension of applicability shall take effect at the time the Convention enters into force for the State concerned or, subsequently, on the first day of the third month following that in which the notification is received.
3. Any such extension of applicability may be withdrawn by notification to the Swiss Federal Council, and the Convention shall cease to apply to the designated territory on the first day of the third month following that in which the notification is received.

Article 11. 1. This Convention shall remain in force indefinitely.
2. However, any State party to this Convention shall have the power to denounce it at any time after one year has elapsed from the date on which the Convention entered into force *vis-à-vis* that State. The denunciation shall be notified to the Swiss Federal Council, and shall take effect on the first day of the sixth month following that in which the notification is received. The Convention shall remain in force *vis-à-vis* the other States.

Article 12. 1. The Swiss Federal Council shall notify the States members of the International Commission on Civil Status and any other State having acceded to this Convention:
(a) Of the deposit of any instrument of ratification, acceptance, approval or accession;
(b) Of any date of entry into force of the Convention;
(c) Of any declaration concerning reservations or withdrawal thereof;
(d) Of any declaration concerning the territorial applicability of the Convention or withdrawal thereof, with the date on which it takes effect;
(e) Of any denunciation of the Convention and the date on which it takes effect.
2. The Swiss Federal Council shall inform the Secretary-General of the International Commission on Civil Status of any notification made in application of paragraph 1.
3. Upon the entry into force of this Convention, a certified copy thereof shall be transmitted by the Swiss Federal Council to the Secretary-General of the United Nations for purposes of registration and publication, pursuant to Article 102 of the Charter of the United Nations.

Convention on the recognition of decisions concerning the marriage bond, concluded at Luxembourg on 8 September 1967 (*UNTS* 1978, Vol. 1081,1-16547, pp. 239 – 245. Authentic text: French).

[The Preamble is omitted.]

Article 1. Any decision concerning the dissolution, relaxation, existence or non-existence, validity or nullity of the marriage bond rendered in one of the Contracting States shall, without prejudice to respect for the provisions of articles 2, 3 and 4, be recognized in the other Contracting States with the same authority as in the one in which it was rendered, where the following conditions are met:
1) The decision is not incompatible, in the State in which it is invoked, with a decision which has become a res judicata, rendered or recognized in that State;
2) The parties have been in a position to state their grounds;
3) The decision is not manifestly contrary to the public order of the State in which it is invoked.

Article 2. Recognition of a foreign decision may not be refused on the sole grounds that the authority which rendered it was not competent under the private international law of the State in which that decision is invoked, except where the two spouses are nationals of that State.

Article 3. Recognition of a foreign decision which has applied a law other than that indicated by the private international law of the State in which that decision is invoked may not be refused on those sole grounds except the twofold condition:
1) That the two spouses were nationals of that State, or only one of them if it is a question of a decision rejecting his or her application;
2) That the decision led to a result contrary to that which would have resulted from the application of the law indicated by the private international law of the State in which that decision is invoked.

Article 4. When two incompatible foreign decisions are invoked, the decision which became a res judicata first shall be the only one recognized.

Article 5. Decisions rendered in the matters referred to in article 1 by the authorities of one of the Contracting States and invoked in another Contracting State shall not be subjected to any investigation except insofar as concerns the conditions stated above.

Article 6. The legislation of each Contracting State shall determine the competent authority with respect to recognition and the procedure to be followed. That authority, for each Contracting State, shall be specified in an annex to this Convention.

Article 7. The recognition provided for in this Convention shall apply only to the provisions of the foreign decision concerning the dissolution, relaxation, existence or non-existence, validity or nullity of the marriage bond, and to its provisions ruling on the offences of the parties or of one of them or, in the case of annulment, on their good faith. That recognition may not be called into question even on the occasion of the examination of a provision regulating questions relating to patrimony or child care, or any other accessory or temporary provision.

Article 8. The decisions recognized in a Contracting State in application of this Convention shall, without formalities, be entered on the records of civil status and on the other public records of that State, where the law of that State provides for public announcement of decisions of the same nature rendered in its territory.

Article 9. Where a decision to dissolve or annul a marriage has been recognized in a Contracting State in application of this Convention, the celebration of a new marriage may not be refused in that State on the sole grounds that the law of another State does not allow or does not recognize that dissolution or that annulment.

Article 10. If an application has previously been brought before an authority of one of the Contracting States concerning the dissolution, relaxation, existence or non-existence, validity or nullity of the marriage bond, the authorities of the other Contracting States shall abstain from ruling, even ex officio, on the merits of any application brought before them for the same purpose and involving the same parties acting in the same capacity. However, the authority last seized shall have the option of establishing a waiting period of at least one year, upon the expiry of which it may render a decision if the application made previously has not yet been judged on its merits.

Article 11. For the purposes of this Convention, the terms "nationals of a State" include persons possessing the nationality of that State, as well as those whose personal status is governed by the laws of that State.

Article 12. This Convention shall apply, between the State in which the decision was rendered and that in which it is invoked, only to decisions subsequent to its entry into force between those two States.

Article 13. This Convention shall not preclude the application of international conventions or rules of municipal law more favourable to the recognition of foreign decisions.

Article 14. The Contracting States shall notify the Swiss Federal Council of the completion of the procedures required by their Constitution to render this Convention applicable in their territory. The Swiss Federal Council shall advise the Contracting States and the Secretary- General of the International Commission on Civil Status of any notification under the preceding paragraph.

Article 15. This Convention shall enter into force on the thirtieth day following the date of deposit of the second notification and shall take effect thereafter between the two States having completed this formality. In the case of each signatory State, subsequently completing the formality provided for in the preceding article, this Convention shall take effect on the thirtieth day following the date of deposit of its notification.

Article 16. Each Contracting State may declare, at the time of signature, the notification provided for in Article 14 or accession that it extends to the exequatur of the accessory or temporary provisions referred to in article 7, second paragraph, the regime provided for by this Convention. This declaration may also be made at a later date and at any time by notification addressed to the Swiss Federal Council. The Swiss Federal Council shall advise each of the Contracting States and the Secretary-General of the International Commission on Civil Status of this notification. The declaration provided for in paragraph 2 of this article shall take effect on the
thirtieth day following the date upon which the Swiss Federal Council receives such notification.

Article 17. Any Contracting State may declare, at the time of signature, the notification provided for in article 14 or accession, that as far as it is concerned this Convention shall apply to only one or several of the subjects mentioned in article 1. Any State which has made a declaration in accordance with the provisions of the first paragraph of this article may subsequently declare at any time, by notification addressed to the Swiss Federal Council, that it extends the application of the Convention to other matters mentioned in article 1. The Swiss Federal Council shall advise each of the Contracting States and the Secretary-General of the International Commission on Civil Status of such notification. The declaration referred to in the second paragraph of this article shall take effect on the thirtieth day following the date on which the Swiss Federal Council receives such notification.

Article 18. Each Contracting State may declare, at the time of signature, the notification provided for in article 14 or accession, that it reserves the right:
1) Not to recognize decisions concerning the dissolution of marriage rendered in a Contracting State between two spouses who are nationals only of States whose law does not allow such dissolution;
2) To apply article 9 only to the annulment of marriage.

Article 19. This Convention shall apply ipso jure throughout the metropolitan territory of each Contracting State. Any Contracting State may declare, at the time of signature, the notification provided for in article 14 or accession, or subsequently by notification addressed to the Swiss Federal Council, that the provisions of this Convention shall be applicable to one or more of its extra-metropolitan territories, States or territories for which it assumes international responsibility. The Swiss Federal Council shall advise each of the Contracting States and the Secretary-General of the International Commission on Civil Status of this last-mentioned notification. The provisions of this Convention shall become applicable in the one or more territories designated in the notification on the sixtieth day following the date on which the Swiss Federal Council receives such notification. Any State which has made a declaration, under the provisions of the second paragraph of this article, may subsequently declare at any time, by notification addressed to the Swiss Federal Council, that this Convention will cease to be applicable to one or more of the States or territories designated in the declaration. The Swiss Federal Council shall advise each of the Contracting States and the Secretary-General of the International Commission on Civil Status of the new notification. The Convention shall cease to be applicable in the designated territory on the sixtieth day following the date on which the Swiss Federal Council receives such notification.

Article 20. Any State member of the Council of Europe or the International Commission on Civil Status may accede to this Convention. A State desiring to accede shall give notice of its intention by an instrument which shall be deposited with the Swiss Federal Council. The latter shall advise each of the Contracting States and the Secretary-General of the International Commission on Civil Status of any deposit of an instrument of accession. The Convention shall enter into force, in respect of the acceding State, on the thirtieth day following the date of deposit of the instrument of accession. The deposit of the instrument of accession may take place only after the entry into force of this Convention.

Article 21. This Convention shall remain in force indefinitely. Each of the Contracting States shall, however, have the right to denounce it at any time by means of a notification in writing addressed to the Swiss Federal Council, which shall in form the other Contracting States and the Secretary-General of the International Commission on Civil Status thereof. This right of denunciation may not be exercised before the expiry of a period of one year from the notification provided for in article 14 or from accession. The denunciation shall take effect six months after the date on which the Swiss Federal Council receives the notification provided for in the first paragraph of this article.

Convention on the Recognition of Divorces and Legal Separations, concluded at The Hague on 1 June 1970 (*UNTS* 1975 Vol. 978, 1-14236 pp. 400 -411, Authentic texts: French and English).

[The Preamble is omitted.]

Article 1. The present Convention shall apply to the recognition in one Contracting State of divorces and legal separations obtained in another Contracting State which follow judicial or other proceedings officially recognized in that State and which are legally effective there.
The Convention does not apply to findings of fault or to ancillary orders pronounced on the making of a decree of divorce or legal separation; in particular, it does not apply to orders relating to pecuniary obligations or to the custody of children.

Article 2. Such divorces and legal separations shall be recognized in all other Contracting States, subject to the remaining terms of this Convention, if, at the date of the institution of the proceedings in the State of the divorce or legal separation (hereinafter called "the State of origin") –
(1) the respondent had his habitual residence there; or
(2) the petitioner had his habitual residence there and one of the following further conditions was fulfilled –
a) such habitual residence had continued for not less than one year immediately prior to the institution of proceedings;
b) the spouses last habitually resided there together; or
(3) both spouses were nationals of that State; or
(4) the petitioner was a national of that State and one of the following further conditions was fulfilled –
a) the petitioner had his habitual residence there; or
b) he had habitually resided there for a continuous period of one year falling, at least in part, within the two years preceding the institution of the proceedings; or
(5) the petitioner for divorce was a national of that State and both the following further conditions were fulfilled –
a) the petitioner was present in that State at the date of institution of the proceedings and
b) the spouses last habitually resided together in a State whose law, at the date of institution of the proceedings, did not provide for divorce.

Article 3. Where the State of origin uses the concept of domicile as a test of jurisdiction in matters of divorce or legal separation, the expression "habitual residence" in Article 2 shall be deemed to include domicile as the term is used in that State. Nevertheless, the preceding paragraph shall not apply to the domicile of dependence of a wife.

Article 4. Where there has been a cross-petition, a divorce or legal separation following upon the petition or cross-petition shall be recognized if either falls within the terms of Articles 2 or 3.

Article 5. Where a legal separation complying with the terms of this Convention has been converted into a divorce in the State of origin, the recognition of the divorce shall not be refused for the reason that the conditions stated in Articles 2 or 3 were no longer fulfilled at the time of the institution of the divorce proceedings.

Article 6. Where the respondent has appeared in the proceedings, the authorities of the State in which recognition of a divorce or legal separation is sought shall be bound by the findings of fact on which jurisdiction was assumed.
The recognition of a divorce or legal separation shall not be refused –
a) because the internal law of the State in which such recognition is sought would not allow divorce or, as the case may be, legal separation upon the same facts, or,
b) because a law was applied other than that applicable under the rules of private international law of that State.
Without prejudice to such review as may be necessary for the application of other provisions of this Convention, the authorities of the State in which recognition of a divorce or legal separation is sought shall not examine the merits of the decision.

Article 7. Contracting States may refuse to recognize a divorce when, at the time it was obtained, both the parties were nationals of States which did not provide for divorce and of no other State.

Article 8. If, in the light of all the circumstances, adequate steps were not taken to give notice of the proceedings for a divorce or legal separation to the respondent, or if he was not afforded a sufficient opportunity to present his case, the divorce or legal separation may be refused recognition.

Article 9. Contracting States may refuse to recognize a divorce or legal separation if it is incompatible with a previous decision determining the matrimonial status of the spouses and that decision either was rendered in the State in which recognition is sought, or is recognized, or fulfils the conditions required for recognition, in that State.

Article 10. Contracting States may refuse to recognize a divorce or legal separation if such recognition is manifestly incompatible with their public policy ("ordre public").

Article 11. A State which is obliged to recognize a divorce under this Convention may not preclude either spouse from remarrying on the ground that the law of another State does not recognize that divorce.

Article 12. Proceedings for divorce or legal separation in any Contracting State may be suspended when proceedings relating to the matrimonial status of either party to the marriage are pending in another Contracting State.

Article 13. In the application of this Convention to divorces or legal separations obtained or sought to be recognized in Contracting States having, in matters of divorce or legal separation, two or more legal systems applying in different territorial units –
(1) any reference to the law of the State of origin shall be construed as referring to the law of the territory in which the divorce or separation was obtained;
(2) any reference to the law of the State in which recognition is sought shall be construed as referring to the law of the forum; and
(3) any reference to domicile or residence in the State of origin shall be construed as referring to domicile or residence in the territory in which the divorce or separation was obtained.

Article 14. For the purposes of Articles 2 and 3, where the State of origin has in matters of divorce or legal separation two or more legal systems applying in different territorial units –
(1) Article 2, sub-paragraph (3), shall apply where both spouses were nationals of the State of which the territorial unit where the divorce or legal separation was obtained forms a part, and that regardless of the habitual residence of the spouses;
(2) Article 2, sub-paragraphs (4) and (5), shall apply where the petitioner was a national of the State of which the territorial unit where the divorce or legal separation was obtained forms a part.

Article 15. In relation to a Contracting State having, in matters of divorce or legal separation, two or more legal systems applicable to different categories of persons, any reference to the law of that State shall be construed as referring to the legal system specified by the law of that State.

Article 16. When, for the purposes of this Convention, it is necessary to refer to the law of a State, whether or not it is a Contracting State, other than the State of origin or the State in which recognition is sought, and having in matters of divorce or legal separation two or more legal systems of territorial or personal application, reference shall be made to the system specified by the law of that State.

Article 17. This Convention shall not prevent the application in a Contracting State of rules of law more favourable to the recognition of foreign divorces and legal separations.

Article 18. This Convention shall not affect the operation of other conventions to which one or several Contracting States are or may in the future become Parties and which contain provisions relating to the subject-matter of this Convention. Contracting States, however, should refrain from concluding other conventions on the same matter incompatible with the terms of this Convention, unless for special reasons based on regional or other ties; and, notwithstanding the terms of such conventions, they undertake to recognize in accordance with this Convention divorces and legal separations granted in Contracting States which are not Parties to such other conventions.

Article 19. Contracting States may, not later than the time of ratification or accession, reserve the right –
(1) to refuse to recognize a divorce or legal separation between two spouses who, at the time of the divorce or legal separation, were nationals of the State in which recognition is sought, and of no other State, and a law other than that indicated by the rules of private international law of the State of recognition was applied, unless the result reached is the same as that which would have been reached by applying the law indicated by those rules;

(2) to refuse to recognize a divorce when, at the time it was obtained, both parties habitually resided in States which did not provide for divorce. A State which utilizes the reservation stated in this paragraph may not refuse recognition by the application of Article 7.

Article 20. Contracting States whose law does not provide for divorce may, not later than the time of ratification or accession, reserve the right not to recognize a divorce if, at the date it was obtained, one of the spouses was a national of a State whose law did not provide for divorce. This reservation shall have effect only so long as the law of the State utilizing it does not provide for divorce.

Article 21. Contracting States whose law does not provide for legal separation may, not later than the time of ratification or accession, reserve the right to refuse to recognize a legal separation when, at the time it was obtained, one of the spouses was a national of a Contracting State whose law did not provide for legal separation.

Article 22. Contracting States may, from time to time, declare that certain categories of persons having their nationality need not be considered their nationals for the purposes of this Convention.

Article 23. If a Contracting State has more than one legal system in matters of divorce or legal separation, it may, at the time of signature, ratification or accession, declare that this Convention shall extend to all its legal systems or only to one or more of them, and may modify its declaration by submitting another declaration at anytime thereafter. These declarations shall be notified to the Ministry of Foreign Affairs of the Netherlands, and shall state expressly the legal systems to which the Convention applies. Contracting States may decline to recognize a divorce or legal separation if, at the date on which recognition is sought, the Convention is not applicable to the legal system under which the divorce or legal separation was obtained.

Article 24. This Convention applies regardless of the date on which the divorce or legal separation was obtained. Nevertheless a Contracting State may, not later than the time of ratification or accession, reserve the right not to apply this Convention to a divorce or to a legal separation obtained before the date on which, in relation to that State, the Convention comes into force.

Article 25. Any State may, not later than the moment of its ratification or accession, make one or more of the reservations mentioned in Articles 19, 20, 21 and 24 of the present Convention. No other reservation shall be permitted. Each Contracting State may also, when notifying an extension of the Convention in accordance with Article 29, make one or more of the said reservations, with its effect limited to all or some of the territories mentioned in the extension. Each Contracting State may at any time withdraw a reservation it has made. Such a withdrawal shall be notified to the Ministry of Foreign Affairs of the Netherlands. Such a reservation shall cease to have effect on the sixtieth day after the notification referred to in the preceding paragraph.

Article 26. The present Convention shall be open for signature by the States represented at the Eleventh Session of the Hague Conference on Private International Law. It shall be ratified, and the instruments of ratification shall be deposited with the Ministry of Foreign Affairs of the Netherlands.

Article 27. The present Convention shall enter into force on the sixtieth day after the deposit of the third instrument of ratification referred to in the second paragraph of Article 26. The Convention shall enter into force for each signatory State which ratifies subsequently on the sixtieth day after the deposit of its instrument of ratification.

Article 28. Any State not represented at the Eleventh Session of the Hague Conference on Private International Law which is a Member of this Conference or of the United Nations or of a specialized agency of that Organization, or a Party to the Statute of the International Court of Justice may accede to the present Convention after it has entered into force in accordance with the first paragraph of Article 27. The instrument of accession shall be deposited with the Ministry of Foreign Affairs of the Netherlands. The Convention shall enter into force for a State acceding to it on the sixtieth day after the deposit of its instrument of accession. The accession will have effect only as regards the relations between the acceding State and such Contracting States as will have declared their acceptance of the accession. Such a declaration shall be deposited at the Ministry of Foreign Affairs of the Netherlands; this Ministry shall forward, through diplomatic channels, a certified copy to each of the Contracting States. The Convention will enter into force as between the acceding State and the State that has declared its acceptance of the accession on the sixtieth day after the deposit of the declaration of acceptance.

Part VII. Private International Law

Article 29. Any State may, at the time of signature, ratification or accession, declare that the present Convention shall extend to all the territories for the international relations of which it is responsible, or to one or more of them. Such a declaration shall take effect on the date of entry into force of the Convention for the State concerned. At any time thereafter, such extensions shall be notified to the Ministry of Foreign Affairs of the Netherlands. The extension will have effect only as regards the relations with such Contracting States as will have declared their acceptance of the extensions. Such a declaration shall be deposited at the Ministry of Foreign Affairs of the Netherlands; this Ministry shall forward, through diplomatic channels, a certified copy to each of the Contracting States. The extension will take effect in each case sixty days after the deposit of the declaration of acceptance.

Article 30. The present Convention shall remain in force for five years from the date of its entry into force in accordance with the first paragraph of Article 27, even for States which have ratified it or acceded to it subsequently. If there has been no denunciation, it shall be renewed tacitly every five years. Any denunciation shall be notified to the Ministry of Foreign Affairs of the Netherlands, at least six months before the end of the five year period. It may be limited to certain of the territories to which the Convention applies. The denunciation shall have effect only as regards the State which has notified it. The Convention shall remain in force for the other Contracting States.

Article 31. The Ministry of Foreign Affairs of the Netherlands shall give notice to the States referred to in Article 26, and to the States which have acceded in accordance with Article 28, of the following –
a) the signatures and ratifications referred to in Article 26;
b) the date on which the present Convention enters into force in accordance with the first paragraph of Article 27;
c) the accessions referred to in Article 28 and the dates on which they take effect;
d) the extensions referred to in Article 29 and the dates on which they take effect;
e) the denunciations referred to in Article 30;
f) the reservations and withdrawals referred to in Articles 19, 20, 21, 24 and 25;
g) the declarations referred to in Articles 22, 23, 28 and 29.

PART VIII

Company Law

Directive 2009/101/EC of the European Parliament and of the Council of 16 September 2009 on coordination of safeguards which, for the protection of the interests of members and third parties, are required by Member States of companies within the meaning of the second paragraph of Article 48 of the Treaty, with a view to making such safeguards equivalent (amended "First Company Law Directive")(*OJ* L 258, 01.10.009 pp. 11 -19) [footnotes omitted].

THE EUROPEAN PARLIAMENT AND THE COUNCIL OF THE EUROPEAN UNION,
Having regard to the Treaty establishing the European Community, and in particular Article 44(2)(g) thereof,
Having regard to the General Programme for the abolition of restrictions on freedom of establishment, and in particular Title VI thereof,
Having regard to the proposal from the Commission,
Having regard to the opinion of the European Economic and Social Committee, Acting in accordance with the procedure laid down in Article 251 of the Treaty,
Whereas:
(1) First Council Directive 68/151/EEC of 9 March 1968 on coordination of safeguards which, for the protection of the interests of members and others, are required by Member States of companies within the meaning of the second paragraph of Article 58 of the Treaty, with a view to making such safeguards equivalent throughout the Community has been substantially amended several times. In the interests of clarity and rationality that Directive should be codified.
(2) The coordination of national provisions concerning disclosure, the validity of obligations entered into by, and the nullity of, companies limited by shares or otherwise having limited liability is of special importance, particularly for the purpose of protecting the interests of third parties.
(3) The basic documents of the company should be disclosed in order that third parties may be able to ascertain their contents and other information concerning the company, especially particulars of the persons who are authorised to bind the company.
(4) Without prejudice to substantive requirements and formalities established by the national law of the Member States, companies should be able to choose to file their compulsory documents and particulars by paper means or by electronic means.
(5) Interested parties should be able to obtain from the register a copy of such documents and particulars by paper means as well as by electronic means.
(6) Member States should be allowed to decide to keep the national gazette, designated for publication of compulsory documents and particulars, in paper form or electronic form, or to provide for disclosure by equally effective means.
(7) Cross-border access to company information should be facilitated by allowing, in addition to the mandatory disclosure made in one of the languages permitted in the company's Member State, voluntary registration in additional languages of the required documents and particulars. Third parties acting in good faith should be able to rely on the translations thereof.
(8) It is appropriate to clarify that the statement of the compulsory particulars set out in this Directive should be included in all company letters and order forms, whether they are in paper form or use any other medium. In the light of technological developments, it is also appropriate to provide that these statements be placed on any company website.
(9) The protection of third parties should be ensured by provisions which restrict to the greatest possible extent the grounds on which obligations entered into in the name of the company are not valid.
(10) It is necessary, in order to ensure certainty in the law as regards relations between the company and third parties, and also between members, to limit the cases in which nullity can arise and the retroactive effect of a declaration of nullity, and to fix a short time limit within which third parties may enter objection to any such declaration.
(11) This Directive should be without prejudice to the obligations of the Member States relating to the time limits for transposition into national law of the Directives set out in Annex I, Part B,
HAVE ADOPTED THIS DIRECTIVE:

Chapter I. Scope

Article 1. The coordination measures prescribed by this Directive shall apply to the laws, regulations and administrative provisions of the Member States relating to the following types of company:

Part VIII. European Company Law

Belgium: naamloze vennootschap, | société anonyme, | commanditaire vennootschap op aandelen, | société en commandite par actions, | personenvennootschap met beperkte aansprakelijkheid; | société de personnes à responsabilité limitée; |
Bulgaria: акционерно дружество, дружество с ограничена отговорност, командитно дружество с акции;
Czech Republic: společnost s ručením omezeným, akciová společnost;
Denmark: aktieselskab, kommanditaktieselskab, anpartsselskab;
Germany: die Aktiengesellschaft, die Kommanditgesellschaft auf Aktien, die Gesellschaft mit beschränkter Haftung;
Estonia: aktsiaselts, osaühing;
Ireland: Companies incorporated with limited liability;
Greece: ανώνυμη εταιρία, εταιρία περιωρισμένης ευθύνης, ετερόρρυθμη κατά μετοχές εταιρία;
Spain: la sociedad anónima, la sociedad comanditaria por acciones, la sociedad de responsabilidad limitada;
France: société anonyme, société en commandite par actions, société à responsabilité limitée, société par actions simplifiée;
Italy: società per azioni, società in accomandita per azioni, società a responsabilità limitata;
Cyprus: δημόσιες εταιρείες περιορισμένης ευθύνης με μετοχές ή με εγγύηση, ιδιωτικές εταιρείες περιορισμένης ευθύνης με μετοχές ή με εγγύηση;
Latvia: akciju sabiedrība, sabiedrība ar ierobežotu atbildību, komanditsabiedrība;
Lithuania: akcinė bendrovė, uždaroji akcinė bendrovė;
Luxembourg: société anonyme, société en commandite par actions, société à responsabilité limitée;
Hungary: részvénytársaság, korlátolt felelősségű társaság;
Malta: kumpannija pubblika/public limited liability company, kumpannija privata/private limited liability company;
The Netherlands: naamloze vennootschap, besloten vennootschap met beperkte aansprakelijkheid;
Austria: die Aktiengesellschaft, die Gesellschaft mit beschränkter Haftung;
Poland: spółka z ograniczoną odpowiedzialnością, spółka komandytowo-akcyjna, spółka akcyjna;
Portugal: a sociedade anónima de responsabilidade limitada, a sociedade em comandita por acções, a sociedade por quotas de responsabilidade limitada;
Romania: societate pe acțiuni, societate cu răspundere limitată, societate în comandită pe acțiuni;
Slovenia: delniška družba, družba z omejeno odgovornostjo, komaditna delniška družba;
Slovakia: akciová spoločnosť, spoločnosť s ručením obmedzeným;
Finland: yksityinen osakeyhtiö/privat aktiebolag, julkinen osakeyhtiö/publikt aktiebolag;
Sweden: aktiebolag;
United Kingdom: Companies incorporated with limited liability.

Chapter II. Disclosure

Article 2. Member States shall take the measures required to ensure compulsory disclosure by companies as referred to in Article 1 of at least the following documents and particulars:
(a) the instrument of constitution, and the statutes if they are contained in a separate instrument;
(b) any amendments to the instruments mentioned in point (a), including any extension of the duration of the company;
(c) after every amendment of the instrument of constitution or of the statutes, the complete text of the instrument or statutes as amended to date;
(d) the appointment, termination of office and particulars of the persons who either as a body constituted pursuant to law or as members of any such body:
(i) are authorised to represent the company in dealings with third parties and in legal proceedings; it must be apparent from the disclosure whether the persons authorised to represent the company may do so alone or must act jointly;
(ii) take part in the administration, supervision or control of the company;
(e) at least once a year, the amount of the capital subscribed, where the instrument of constitution or the statutes mention an authorised capital, unless any increase in the capital subscribed necessitates an amendment of the statutes;
(f) the accounting documents for each financial year which are required to be published in accordance with Council Directives 78/660/EEC [6], 83/349/EEC [7], 86/635/EEC [8] and 91/674/EEC [9];
(g) any change of the registered office of the company;
(h) the winding-up of the company;

(i) any declaration of nullity of the company by the courts;
(j) the appointment of liquidators, particulars concerning them, and their respective powers, unless such powers are expressly and exclusively derived from law or from the statutes of the company;
(k) the termination of the liquidation and, in Member States where striking off the register entails legal consequences, the fact of any such striking off.

Article 3. 1. In each Member State, a file shall be opened in a central register, commercial register or companies register, for each of the companies registered therein.
2. For the purposes of this Article, "by electronic means" shall mean that the information is sent initially and received at its destination by means of electronic equipment for the processing (including digital compression) and storage of data, and entirely transmitted, conveyed and received in a manner to be determined by Member States by wire, by radio, by optical means or by other electromagnetic means.
3. All documents and particulars which must be disclosed pursuant to Article 2 shall be kept in the file, or entered in the register; the subject matter of the entries in the register must in every case appear in the file. Member States shall ensure that the filing by companies, as well as by other persons and bodies required to make or assist in making notifications, of all documents and particulars which must be disclosed pursuant to Article 2 is possible by electronic means. In addition, Member States may require all, or certain categories of, companies to file all, or certain types of, such documents and particulars by electronic means.
All documents and particulars referred to in Article 2 which are filed, whether by paper means or by electronic means, shall be kept in the file, or entered in the register, in electronic form. To this end, Member States shall ensure that all such documents and particulars which are filed by paper means are converted by the register to electronic form.
The documents and particulars referred to in Article 2 that have been filed by paper means up to 31 December 2006 shall not be required to be converted automatically into electronic form by the register. Member States shall nevertheless ensure that they are converted into electronic form by the register upon receipt of an application for disclosure by electronic means submitted in accordance with the measures adopted to give effect to paragraph 4.
4. A copy of the whole or any part of the documents or particulars referred to in Article 2 must be obtainable on application. Applications may be submitted to the register by paper means or by electronic means as the applicant chooses.
Copies as referred to in the first subparagraph must be obtainable from the register by paper means or by electronic means as the applicant chooses. This shall apply in the case of all documents and particulars already filed. However, Member States may decide that all, or certain types of, documents and particulars filed by paper means on or before a date which may not be later than 31 December 2006 shall not be obtainable from the register by electronic means if a specified period has elapsed between the date of filing and the date of the application submitted to the register. Such specified period may not be less than 10 years.
The price of obtaining a copy of the whole or any part of the documents or particulars referred to in Article 2, whether by paper means or by electronic means, shall not exceed the administrative cost thereof.
Paper copies supplied shall be certified as "true copies", unless the applicant dispenses with such certification. Electronic copies supplied shall not be certified as "true copies", unless the applicant explicitly requests such a certification.
Member States shall take the necessary measures to ensure that certification of electronic copies guarantees both the authenticity of their origin and the integrity of their contents, by means at least of an advanced electronic signature within the meaning of Article 2(2) of Directive 1999/93/EC [10].
5. Disclosure of the documents and particulars referred to in paragraph 3 shall be effected by publication in the national gazette designated for that purpose by the Member State, either of the full text or of a partial text, or by means of a reference to the document which has been deposited in the file or entered in the register. The national gazette designated for that purpose may be kept in electronic form.
Member States may decide to replace publication in the national gazette with equally effective means, which shall entail at least the use of a system whereby the information disclosed can be accessed in chronological order through a central electronic platform.
6. The documents and particulars may be relied on by the company as against third parties only after they have been disclosed in accordance with paragraph 5, unless the company proves that the third parties had knowledge thereof.
However, with regard to transactions taking place before the sixteenth day following the disclosure, the documents and particulars shall not be relied on as against third parties who prove that it was impossible for them to have had knowledge thereof.

7. Member States shall take the necessary measures to avoid any discrepancy between what is disclosed in accordance with paragraph 5 and what appears in the register or file.
However, in cases of discrepancy, the text disclosed in accordance with paragraph 5 may not be relied on as against third parties; such third parties may nevertheless rely thereon, unless the company proves that they had knowledge of the texts deposited in the file or entered in the register.
Third parties may, moreover, always rely on any documents and particulars in respect of which the disclosure formalities have not yet been completed, save where non-disclosure causes them not to have effect.

Article 4. 1. Documents and particulars which must be disclosed pursuant to Article 2 shall be drawn up and filed in one of the languages permitted by the language rules applicable in the Member State in which the file referred to in Article 3(1) is opened.
2. In addition to the mandatory disclosure referred to in Article 3, Member States shall allow documents and particulars referred to in Article 2 to be disclosed voluntarily in accordance with Article 3 in any official language(s) of the Community.
Member States may prescribe that the translation of such documents and particulars be certified.
Member States shall take the necessary measures to facilitate access by third parties to the translations voluntarily disclosed.
3. In addition to the mandatory disclosure referred to in Article 3, and to the voluntary disclosure provided for under paragraph 2 of this Article, Member States may allow the documents and particulars concerned to be disclosed, in accordance with Article 3, in any other language(s).
Member States may prescribe that the translation of such documents and particulars be certified.
4. In cases of discrepancy between the documents and particulars disclosed in the official languages of the register and the translation voluntarily disclosed, the latter may not be relied upon as against third parties. Third parties may nevertheless rely on the translations voluntarily disclosed, unless the company proves that the third parties had knowledge of the version which was the subject of the mandatory disclosure.

Article 5. Member States shall prescribe that letters and order forms, whether they are in paper form or use any other medium, are to state the following particulars:
(a) the information necessary in order to identify the register in which the file mentioned in Article 3 is kept, together with the number of the company in that register;
(b) the legal form of the company, the location of its registered office and, where appropriate, the fact that the company is being wound up.
Where, in those documents, mention is made of the capital of the company, the reference shall be to the capital subscribed and paid up.
Member States shall prescribe that company websites are to contain at least the particulars mentioned in the first paragraph and, if applicable, a reference to the capital subscribed and paid up.

Article 6. Each Member State shall determine by which persons the disclosure formalities are to be carried out.

Article 7. Member States shall provide for appropriate penalties at least in the case of:
(a) failure to disclose accounting documents as required by Article 2(f);
(b) omission from commercial documents or from any company website of the compulsory particulars provided for in Article 5.

Chapter III. Validity of obligations entered into by the company

Article 8. If, before a company being formed has acquired legal personality, action has been carried out in its name and the company does not assume the obligations arising from such action, the persons who acted shall, without limit, be jointly and severally liable therefor, unless otherwise agreed.

Article 9. Completion of the formalities of disclosure of the particulars concerning the persons who, as an organ of the company, are authorised to represent it shall constitute a bar to any irregularity in their appointment being relied upon as against third parties unless the company proves that such third parties had knowledge thereof.

Article 10. 1. Acts done by the organs of the company shall be binding upon it even if those acts are not within the objects of the company, unless such acts exceed the powers that the law confers or allows to be conferred on those organs.
However, Member States may provide that the company shall not be bound where such acts are outside the objects of the company, if it proves that the third party knew that the act was outside those objects or could not in view of the circumstances have been unaware of it; disclosure of the statutes shall not of itself be sufficient proof thereof.
2. The limits on the powers of the organs of the company, arising under the statutes or from a decision of the competent organs, may not be relied on as against third parties, even if they have been disclosed.
3. If the national law provides that authority to represent a company may, in derogation from the legal rules governing the subject, be conferred by the statutes on a single person or on several persons acting jointly, that law may provide that such a provision in the statutes may be relied on as against third parties on condition that it relates to the general power of representation; the question whether such a provision in the statutes can be relied on as against third parties shall be governed by Article 3.

Chapter IV. Nullity of the company

Article 11. In all Member States whose laws do not provide for preventive, administrative or judicial control, at the time of formation of a company, the instrument of constitution, the company statutes and any amendments to those documents shall be drawn up and certified in due legal form.

Article 12. The laws of the Member States may not provide for the nullity of companies otherwise than in accordance with the following provisions:
(a) nullity must be ordered by decision of a court of law;
(b) nullity may be ordered only on the grounds:
(i) that no instrument of constitution was executed or that the rules of preventive control or the requisite legal formalities were not complied with;
(ii) that the objects of the company are unlawful or contrary to public policy;
(iii) that the instrument of constitution or the statutes do not state the name of the company, the amount of the individual subscriptions of capital, the total amount of the capital subscribed or the objects of the company;
(iv) of failure to comply with the provisions of the national law concerning the minimum amount of capital to be paid up;
(v) of the incapacity of all the founder members;
(vi) that, contrary to the national law governing the company, the number of founder members is less than two.
Apart from the foregoing grounds of nullity, a company shall not be subject to any cause of non-existence, absolute nullity, relative nullity or declaration of nullity.

Article 13. 1. The question whether a decision of nullity pronounced by a court of law may be relied on as against third parties shall be governed by Article 3. Where the national law entitles a third party to challenge the decision, he may do so only within six months of public notice of the decision of the court being given.
2. Nullity shall entail the winding-up of the company, as may dissolution.
3. Nullity shall not of itself affect the validity of any commitments entered into by or with the company, without prejudice to the consequences of the company's being wound up.
4. The laws of each Member State may make provision for the consequences of nullity as between members of the company.
5. Holders of shares in the capital shall remain obliged to pay up the capital agreed to be subscribed by them but which has not been paid up, to the extent that commitments entered into with creditors so require.

Chapter V. General provisions

Article 14. Member States shall communicate to the Commission the text of the main provisions of national law which they adopt in the field covered by this Directive.

Article 15. The Commission shall present to the European Parliament and to the Council, by no later than 1 January 2012, a report, together with a proposal, if appropriate, for amendment of the provisions of Article 2(f) and Articles 3, 4, 5 and 7 in the light of the experience acquired in applying those provisions, of their aims and of the technological developments observed at the time.

Article 16. Directive 68/151/EEC, as amended by the acts listed in Annex I, Part A, is hereby repealed, without prejudice to the obligations of the Member States relating to the time limits for transposition into national law of the Directives set out in Annex I, Part B. References to the repealed Directive shall be construed as references to this Directive and shall be read in accordance with the correlation table in Annex II.

Article 17. This Directive shall enter into force on the 20th day following its publication in the Official Journal of the European Union.

Article 18. This Directive is addressed to the Member States.

Council Directive 77/91/EEC of 13 December 1976 on coordination of safeguards which, for the protection of the interests of members and others, are required by Member States of companies within the meaning of the second paragraph of Article 58 of the Treaty, in respect of the formation of public limited liability companies and the maintenance and alteration of their capital, with a view to making such safeguards equivalent ("Second Company Law Directive") (*O J* L 026, 31.01.1977 pp. 1 –13). Consolidated version as last amended by Directive 2009/109/EC of the European Parliament and of the Council of 16 September 2009 amending Council Directives 77/91/EEC, 78/855/EEC and 82/891/EEC, and Directive 2005/56/EC as regards reporting and documentation requirements in the case of mergers and divisions. [footnotes omitted].

THE COUNCIL OF THE EUROPEAN COMMUNITIES,
Having regard to the Treaty establishing the European Economic Community, and in particular Article 54 (3) (g) thereof,
Having regard to the proposal from the Commission,
Having regard to the opinion of the European Parliament, Having regard to the opinion of the Economic and Social Committee,
Whereas the coordination provided for in Article 54 (3) (g) and in the General Programme for the abolition of restrictions on freedom of establishment, which was begun by Directive 68/151/EEC, is especially important in relation to public limited liability companies, because their activities predominate in the economy of the Member States and frequently extend beyond their national boundaries;
Whereas in order to ensure minimum equivalent protection for both shareholders and creditors of public limited liability companies, the coordination of national provisions relating to their formation and to the maintenance, increase or reduction of their capital is particularly important;
Whereas in the territory of the Community, the statutes or instrument of incorporation of a public limited liability company must make it possible for any interested person to acquaint himself with the basic particulars of the company, including the exact composition of its capital;
Whereas Community provisions should be adopted for maintaining the capital, which constitutes the creditors' security, in particular by prohibiting any reduction thereof by distribution to shareholders where the latter are not entitled to it and by imposing limits on the company's right to acquire its own shares;
Whereas it is necessary, having regard to the objectives of Article 54 (3) (g), that the Member States' laws relating to the increase or reduction of capital ensure that the principles of equal treatment of shareholders in the same position and of protection of creditors whose claims exist prior to the decision on reduction are observed and harmonized,

HAS ADOPTED THIS DIRECTIVE:

Article 1. 1. The coordination measures prescribed by this Directive shall apply to the provisions laid down by law, regulation or administrative action in Member States relating to the following types of company:
in Belgium:la société anonymede naamloze vennootschap;
in Denmark:aktieselskabet;
in France:la société anonyme;
in Germany:die Aktiengesellschaft;
in Ireland:the public company limited by shares, the public company limited by guarantee and having a share capital;
in Italy:la società per azioni;
in Luxembourg:la société anonyme;
in the Netherlands:de naamloze vennootschap;
in the United Kingdom:the public company limited by shares, the public company limited by guarantee and having a share capital;
in Greece: η ανώνυμη εταιρία;
in Spain:la sociedad anónima;
in Portugal: a sociedade anonima de responsabilidade limitada;
in Austria: die Aktiengesellschaft;
in Finland: julkinen osakeyhtiö/publikt aktiebolag;
in Sverige:aktiebolag;
in the Czech Republic:akciová společnost;
in Estonia: aktsiaselts;

in Cyprus:Δημόσιες εταιρείες περιορισμένης ευθύνης με μετοχές, δημόσιες εταιρείες περιορισμένης ευθύνης με εγγύηση που διαθέτουν με- τοχικό κεφάλαιο; in Latvia: akciju sabiedrība; in Lithuania:akcinė bendrovė;
in Hungary:nyilvánosan működő részvénytársaság;
in Malta:kumpanija pubblika/public limited liability company;
in Poland:spółka akcyjna;
in Slovenia:delniška družba;
in Slovakia:akciová spoločnosť;
in Bulgaria:акционерно дружество;
in Romania:societate pe acţiuni.
The name for any company of the above types shall comprise or be accompanied by a description which is distinct from the description required of other types of companies.
2. The Member States may decide not to apply this Directive to investment companies with variable capital and to cooperatives incorporated as one of the types of company listed in paragraph 1. In so far as the laws of the Member States make use of this option, they shall require such companies to include the words 'investment company with variable capital' or 'cooperative' in all documents indicated in Article 4 of Directive 68/151/EEC. The expression 'investment company with variable capital', within the meaning of this Directive, means only those companies:
— the exclusive object of which is to invest their funds in various stocks and shares, land or other assets with the sole aim of spreading investment risks and giving their shareholders the benefit of the results of the management of their assets,
— which offer their own shares for subscription by the public, and
— the statutes of which provide that, within the limits of a minimum and maximum capital, they may at any time issue, redeem or resell their shares.

Article 2. The statutes or the instrument of incorporation of the company shall always give at least the following information:
(a) the type and name of the company;
(b) the objects of the company;
(c) — when the company has no authorized capital, the amount of the subscribed capital,
— when the company has an authorized capital, the amount thereof and also the amount of the capital subscribed at the time the company is incorporated or is authorized to commence business, and at the time of any change in the authorized capital, without prejudice to Article 2 (1) (e) of Directive 68/151/EEC;
(d) in so far as they are not legally determined, the rules governing the number of and the procedure for appointing members of the bodies responsible for representing the company with regard to third parties, administration, management, supervision or control of the company and the allocation of powers among those bodies;
(e) the duration of the company, except where this is indefinite.

Article 3. The following information at least must appear in either the statutes or the instrument of incorporation or a separate document published in accordance with the procedure laid down in the laws of each Member State in accordance with Article 3 of Directive 68/151/EEC:
(a) the registered office;
(b) the nominal value of the shares subscribed and, at least once a year, the number thereof;
(c) the number of shares subscribed without stating the nominal value, where such shares may be issued under national law;
(d) the special conditions if any limiting the transfer of shares;
(e) where there are several classes of shares, the information under (b),
(c) and (d) for each class and the rights attaching to the shares of each class;
(f) whether the shares are registered or bearer, where national law provides for both types, and any provisions relating to the conversion of such shares unless the procedure is laid down by law;
(g) the amount of the subscribed capital paid up at the time the company is incorporated or is authorized to commence business;
(h) the nominal value of the shares or, where there is not nominal value, the number of shares issued for a consideration other than in cash, together with the nature of the consideration and the name of the person providing this consideration;
(i) the identity of the natural or legal persons or companies or firms by whom or in whose name the statutes or the instrument of incorporation, or where the company was not formed at the same time, the drafts of these documents, have been signed;

(j) the total amount, or at least an estimate, of all the costs payable by the company or chargeable to it by reason of its formation and, where appropriate, before the company is authorized to commence business;
(k) any special advantage granted, at the time the company is formed or up to the time it receives authorization to commence business, to anyone who has taken part in the formation of the company or in transactions leading to the grant of such authorization.

Article 4. 1. Where the laws of a Member State prescribe that a company may not commence business without authorization, they shall also make provision for responsibility for liabilities incurred by or on behalf of the company during the period before such authorization is granted or refused.
2. Paragraph 1 shall not apply to liabilities under contracts concluded by the company conditionally upon its being granted authorization to commence business.

Article 5. 1. Where the laws of a Member State require a company to be formed by more than one member, the fact that all the shares are held by one person or that the number of members has fallen below the legal minimum after incorporation of the company shall not lead to the automatic dissolution of the company.
2. If in the cases referred to in paragraph 1, the laws of a Member State permit the company to be wound up by order of the court, the judge having jurisdiction must be able to give the company sufficient time to regularize its position.
3. Where such a winding up order is made the company shall enter into liquidation.

Article 6. 1. The laws of the Member States shall require that, in order that a company may be incorporated or obtain authorization to commence business, a minimum capital shall be subscribed the amount of which shall be not less than 25 000 ecus.
The ecus shall be that defined by Commission Decision No 3289/75/ECSC (1). The equivalent in national currency shall be calculated initially at the rate applicable on the date of adoption of this Directive.
2. If the equivalent of the ecus in national currency is altered so that the value of the minimum capital in national currency remains less than 22 500 ecus for a period of one year, the Commission shall inform the Member State concerned that it must amend its legislation to comply with paragraph 1 within 12 months following the expiry of that period. However, the Member State may provide that the amended legislation shall not apply to companies already in existence until 18 months after its entry into force.
3. Every five years the Council, acting on a proposal from the Commission, shall examine and, if need be, revise the amounts expressed in this Article in ecus in the light of economic and monetary trends in the Community and of the tendency towards allowing only large and medium-sized undertakings to opt for the types of company listed in Article 1 (1).

Article 7. The subscribed capital may be formed only of assets capable of economic assessment. However, an undertaking to perform work or supply services may not form part of these assets.

Article 8. 1. Shares may not be issued at a price lower than their nominal value, or, where there is no nominal value, their accountable par. 2. However, Member States may allow those who undertake to place shares in the exercise of their profession to pay less than the total price of the shares for which they subscribe in the course of this transaction.

Article 9. 1. Shares issued for a consideration must be paid up at the time the company is incorporated or is authorized to commence business at not less than 25 % of their nominal value or, in the absence of a nominal value, their accountable par.
2. However, where shares are issued for a consideration other than in cash at the time the company is incorporated or is authorized to commence business, the consideration must be transferred in full within five years of that time.

Article 10. 1. A report on any consideration other than in cash shall be drawn up before the company is incorporated or is authorized to commence business, by one or more independent experts appointed or approved by an administrative or judicial authority. Such experts may be natural persons as well as legal persons and companies or firms under the laws of each Member State.
2. The experts' report shall contain at least a description of each of the assets comprising the consideration as well as of the methods of valuation used and shall state whether the values arrived at by the application of these methods correspond at least to the number and nominal value or, where there is no nominal value, to the accountable par and, where appropriate, to the premium on the shares to be issued for them.

PART VIII. EUROPEAN COMPANY LAW

3. The expert's (SIC! experts') report shall be published in the manner laid down by the laws of each Member State, in accordance with Article 3 of Directive 68/151/EEC.
4. Member States may decide not to apply this Article where 90 % of the nominal value, or where there is no nominal value, of the accountable par, of all the shares is issued to one or more companies for a consideration other than in cash, and where the following requirements are met:
(a) with regard to the company in receipt of such consideration, the persons referred to in Article 3 (i) have agreed to dispense with the expert's (SIC! experts') report;
(b) such agreement has been published as provided for in paragraph 3;
(c) the companies furnishing such consideration have reserves which may not be distributed under the law or the statutes and which are at least equal to the nominal value or, where there is no nominal value, the accountable par of the shares issued for consideration other than in cash;
(d) the companies furnishing such consideration guarantee, up to an amount equal to that indicated in paragraph (c), the debts of the recipient company arising between the time the shares are issued for a consideration other than in cash and one year after the publication of that company's annual accounts for the financial year during which such consideration was furnished. Any transfer of these shares is prohibited within this period;
(e) the guarantee referred to in (d) has been published as provided for in paragraph 3;
(f) the companies furnishing such consideration shall place a sum equal to that indicated in (c) into a reserve which may not be distributed until three years after publication of the annual accounts of the recipient company for the financial year during which such consideration was furnished or, if necessary, until such later date as all claims relating to the guarantee referred to in (d) which are submitted during this period have been settled.
5. Member States may decide not to apply this Article to the formation of a new company by way of merger or division where an independent expert's report on the draft terms of merger or division is drawn up. Where Member States decide to apply this Article in the cases referred to in the first subparagraph, they may provide that the report under this Article and the independent expert's report on the draft terms of merger or division may be drawn up by the same expert or experts.

Article 10a. 1. Member States may decide not to apply Article 10(1), (2) and (3) where, upon a decision of the administrative or management body, transferable securities as defined in point 18 of Article 4(1) of Directive 2004/39/EC of the European Parliament and of the Council of 21 April 2004 on markets in financial instruments (1) or moneymarket instruments as defined in point 19 of Article 4(1) of that Directive are contributed as consideration other than in cash, and those securities or money-market instruments are valued at the weighted average price at which they have been traded on one or more regulated market(s) as defined in point 14 of Article 4(1) of that Directive during a sufficient period, to be determined by national law, preceding the effective date of the contribution of the respective consideration other than in cash. However, where that price has been affected by exceptional circumstances that would significantly change the value of the asset at the effective date of its contribution, including situations where the market for such transferable securities or money-market instruments has become illiquid, a revaluation shall be carried out on the initiative and under the responsibility of the administrative or management body. For the purposes of the aforementioned revaluation, Article 10(1), (2) and (3) shall apply.
2. Member States may decide not to apply Article 10(1), (2) and (3) where, upon a decision of the administrative or management body, assets, other than the transferable securities and money-market instruments referred to in paragraph 1, are contributed as consideration other than in cash which have already been subject to a fair value opinion by a recognised independent expert and where the following conditions are fulfilled:
(a) the fair value is determined for a date not more than six months before the effective date of the asset contribution; Directive as last amended by Directive 2006/31/EC (OJ L 114, 27.4.2006, p. 60).
(b) the valuation has been performed in accordance with generally accepted valuation standards and principles in the Member State, which are applicable to the kind of assets to be contributed. In the case of new qualifying circumstances that would significantly change the fair value of the asset at the effective date of its contribution, a revaluation shall be carried out on the initiative and under the responsibility of the administrative or management body. For the purposes of the aforementioned revaluation, Article 10(1), (2) and (3) shall apply. In the absence of such a revaluation, one or more shareholders holding an aggregate percentage of at least 5 % of the company's subscribed capital on the day the decision on the increase in the capital is taken may demand a valuation by an independent expert, in which case Article 10(1), (2) and (3) shall apply. Such shareholder(s) may submit a demand up until the effective date of the asset contribution, provided that, at the date of the demand, the shareholder(s) in question still hold(s) an aggregate percentage of at least 5 % of the company's subscribed capital, as it was on the day the decision on the increase in the capital was taken.
3. Member States may decide not to apply Article 10(1), (2) and (3) where, upon a decision of the administrative or management body, assets, other than the transferable securities and money-market instruments referred to in

paragraph 1, are contributed as consideration other than in cash whose fair value is derived by individual asset from the statutory accounts of the previous financial year provided that the statutory accounts have been subject to an audit in accordance with Directive 2006/43/EC of the European Parliament and of the Council of 17 May 2006 on statutory audits of annual accounts and consolidated accounts. The second and third subparagraphs of paragraph 2 shall apply mutatis mutandis.

Article 10b. 1. Where consideration other than in cash as referred to in Article 10a occurs without an expert's report as referred to in Article 10(1), (2) and (3), in addition to the requirements set out in point (h) of Article 3 and within one month after the effective date of the asset contribution, a declaration containing the following shall be published:
(a) a description of the consideration other than in cash at issue;
(b) its value, the source of this valuation and, where appropriate, the method of valuation;
(c) a statement whether the value arrived at corresponds at least to the number, to the nominal value or, where there is no nominal value, the accountable par and, where appropriate, to the premium on the shares to be issued for such consideration;
(d) a statement that no new qualifying circumstances with regard to the original valuation have occurred. That publication shall be effected in the manner laid down by the laws of each Member State in accordance with Article 3 of Directive 68/151/EEC.
2. Where consideration other than in cash is proposed to be made without an expert's report as referred to in Article 10(1), (2) and (3) in relation to an increase in the capital proposed to be made under Article 25(2), an announcement containing the date when the decision on the increase was taken and the information listed in paragraph 1 shall be published, in the manner laid down by the laws of each Member State in accordance with Article 3 of Directive 68/151/EEC, before the contribution of the asset as consideration other than in cash is to become effective. In that event, the declaration pursuant to paragraph 1 shall be limited to the statement that no new qualifying circumstances have occurred since the aforementioned announcement was published.
3. Each Member State shall provide for adequate safeguards ensuring compliance with the procedure set out in Article 10a and in this Article where a contribution for a consideration other than in cash is made without an expert's report as referred to in Article 10(1), (2) and (3).

Article 11. 1. If, before the expiry of a time limit laid down by national law of at least two years from the time the company is incorporated or is authorized to commence business, the company acquires any asset belonging to a person or company or firm referred to in Article 3 (i) for a consideration of not less than one-tenth of the subscribed capital, the acquisition shall be examined and details of it published in the manner provided for in Article 10(1), (2) and (3) and it shall be submitted for the approval of the general meeting. Articles 10a and 10b shall apply mutatis mutandis. Member States may also require these provisions to be applied when the assets belong to a shareholder or to any other person.
2. Paragraph 1 shall not apply to acquisitions effected in the normal course of the company's business, to acquisitions effected at the instance or under the supervision of an administrative or judicial authority, or to stock exchange acquisitions.

Article 12. Subject to the provisions relating to the reduction of subscribed capital, the shareholders may not be released from the obligation to pay up their contributions.

Article 13. Pending coordination of national laws at a subsequent date, Member States shall adopt the measures necessary to require provision of at least the same safeguards as are laid down in Articles 2 to 12 in the event of the conversion of another type of company into a public limited liability company.

Article 14. Articles 2 to 13 shall not prejudice the provisions of Member States on competence and procedure relating to the modification of the statutes or of the instrument of incorporation.

Article 15. 1. (a) Except for cases of reductions of subscribed capital, no distribution to shareholders may be made when on the closing date of the last financial year the net assets as set out in the company's annual accounts are, or following such a distribution would become, lower than the amount of the subscribed capital plus those reserves which may not be distributed under the law or the statutes.
(b) Where the uncalled part of the subscribed capital is not included in the assets shown in the balance sheet, this amount shall be deducted from the amount of subscribed capital referred to in paragraph (a).

(c) The amount of a distribution to shareholders may not exceed the amount of the profits at the end of the last financial year plus any profits brought forward and sums drawn from reserves available for this purpose, less any losses brought forward and sums placed to reserve in accordance with the law or the statutes.
(d) The expression 'distribution' used in subparagraphs (a) and (c) includes in particular the payment of dividends and of interest relating to shares.
2. When the laws of a Member State allow the payment of interim dividends, the following conditions at least shall apply:
(a) interim accounts shall be drawn up showing that the funds available for distribution are sufficient,
(b) the amount to be distributed may not exceed the total profits made since the end of the last financial year for which the annual accounts have been drawn up, plus any profits brought forward and sums drawn from reserves available for this purpose, less losses brought forward and sums to be placed to reserve pursuant to the requirements of the law or the statutes.
3. Paragraphs 1 and 2 shall not affect the provisions of the Member States as regards increases in subscribed capital by capitalization of reserves.
4. The laws of a Member State may provide for derogations from paragraph 1 (a) in the case of investment companies with fixed capital. The expression 'investment company with fixed capital', within the meaning of this paragraph (SIC! paragraph,) means only those companies:
— the exclusive object of which is to invest their funds in various stocks and shares, land or other assets with the sole aim of spreading investment risks and giving their shareholders the benefit of the results of the management of their assets, and
— which offer their own shares for subscription by the public. In so far as the laws of Member States make use of this option they shall:
(a) require such companies to include the expression 'investment company' in all documents indicated in Article 4 of Directive 68/151/EEC;
(b) not permit any such company whose net assets fall below the amount specified in paragraph 1 (a) to make a distribution to shareholders when on the closing date of the last financial year the company's total assets as set out in the annual accounts are, or following such distribution would become, less than one-and-ahalf times the amount of the company's total liabilities to creditors as set out in the annual accounts;
(c) require any such company which makes a distribution when its net assets fall below the amount specified in paragraph 1 (a) to include in its annual accounts a note to that effect.

Article 16. Any distribution made contrary to Article 15 must be returned by shareholders who have received it if the company proves that these shareholders knew of the irregularity of the distributions made to them, or could not in view of the circumstances have been unaware of it.

Article 17. 1. In the case of a serious loss of the subscribed capital, a general meeting of shareholders must be called within the period laid down by the laws of the Member States, to consider whether the company should be wound up or any other measures taken.
2. The amount of a loss deemed to be serious within the meaning of paragraph 1 may not be set by the laws of Member States at a figure higher than half the subscribed capital.

Article 18. 1. The shares of a company may not be subscribed for by the company itself.
2. If the shares of a company have been subscribed for by a person acting in his own name, but on behalf of the company, the subscriber shall be deemed to have subscribed for them for his own account.
3. The persons or companies or firms referred to in Article 3 (i) or, in cases of an increase in subscribed capital, the members of the administrative or management body shall be liable to pay for shares subscribed in contravention of this Article. However, the laws of a Member State may provide that any such person may be released from his obligation if he proves that no fault is attributable to him personally.

Article 19. 1. Without prejudice to the principle of equal treatment of all shareholders who are in the same position, and to Directive 2003/6/EC of the European Parliament and of the Council of 28 January 2003 on insider dealing and market manipulation (market abuse), Member States may permit a company to acquire its own shares, either itself or through a person acting in his own name but on the company's behalf. To the extent that the acquisitions are permitted, Member States shall make such acquisitions subject to the following conditions:
(a) authorisation shall be given by the general meeting, which shall determine the terms and conditions of such acquisitions, and, in particular, the maximum number of shares to be acquired, the duration of the period for which the authorisation is given, the maximum length of which shall be determined by national law without, however, exceeding five years, and, in the case of acquisition for value, the maximum and minimum consideration.

Members of the administrative or management body shall satisfy themselves that, at the time when each authorised acquisition is effected, the conditions referred to in points (b) and (c) are respected;
(b) the acquisitions, including shares previously acquired by the company and held by it, and shares acquired by a person acting in his own name but on the company's behalf, may not have the effect of reducing the net assets below the amount mentioned in points (a) and (b) of Article 15(1);
(c) only fully paid-up shares may be included in the transaction. Furthermore, Member States may subject acquisitions within the meaning of the first subparagraph to any of the following conditions:
(i) that the nominal value or, in the absence thereof, the accountable par of the acquired shares, including shares previously acquired by the company and held by it, and shares acquired by a person acting in his own name but on the company's behalf, may not exceed a limit to be determined by Member States. This limit may not be lower than 10 % of the subscribed capital;
(ii) that the power of the company to acquire its own shares within the meaning of the first subparagraph, the maximum number of shares to be acquired, the duration of the period for which the power is given and the maximum or minimum consideration are laid down in the statutes or in the instrument of incorporation of the company;
(iii) that the company complies with appropriate reporting and notification requirements;
(iv) that certain companies, as determined by Member States, may be required to cancel the acquired shares provided that an amount equal to the nominal value of the shares cancelled must be included in a reserve which cannot be distributed to the shareholders, except in the event of a reduction in the subscribed capital. This reserve may be used only for the purposes of increasing the subscribed capital by the capitalisation of reserves;
(v) that the acquisition shall not prejudice the satisfaction of creditors' claims.
2. The laws of a Member State may provide for derogations from the first sentence of paragraph 1 (a) where the acquisition of a company's own shares is necessary to prevent serious and imminent harm to the company. In such a case, the next general meeting must be informed by the administrative or management body of the reasons for and nature of the acquisitions effected, of the number and nominal value or, in the absence of a nominal value, the accountable par, of the shares acquired, of the proportion of the subscribed capital which they represent, and of the consideration for these shares.
3. Member States may decide not to apply the first sentence of paragraph 1 (a) to shares acquired by either the company itself or by a person acting in his own name but on the company's behalf, for distribution to that company's employees or to the employees of an associate company. Such shares must be distributed within 12 months of their acquisition.

Article 20. 1. Member States may decide not to apply Article 19 to: (a) shares acquired in carrying out a decision to reduce capital, or in the circumstances referred to in Article 39;
(b) shares acquired as a result of a universal transfer of assets;
(c) fully paid-up shares acquired free of charge or by banks and other financial institutions as purchasing commission;
(d) shares acquired by virtue of a legal obligation or resulting from a court ruling for the protection of minority shareholders in the event, particularly, of a merger, a change in the company's object or form, transfer abroad of the registered office, or the introduction of restrictions on the transfer of shares;
(e) shares acquired from a shareholder in the event of failure to pay them up;
(f) shares acquired in order to indemnify minority shareholders in associated companies;
(g) fully paid-up shares acquired under a sale enforced by a court order for the payment of a debt owed to the company by the owner of the shares;
(h) fully paid-up shares issued by an investment company with fixed capital, as defined in the second subparagraph of Article 15 (4), and acquired at the investor's request by that company or by an associate company. Article 15 (4) (a) shall apply. These acquisitions may not have the effect of reducing the net assets below the amount of the subscribed capital plus any reserves the distribution of which is forbidden by law.
2. Shares acquired in the cases listed in paragraph 1 (b) to (g) above must, however, be disposed of within not more than three years of their acquisition unless the nominal value or, in the absence of a nominal value, the accountable par of the shares acquired, including shares which the company may have acquired through a person acting in his own name but on the company's behalf, does not exceed 10 % of the subscribed capital. 3. If the shares are not disposed of within the period laid down in paragraph 2, they must be cancelled. The laws of a Member State may make this cancellation subject to a corresponding reduction in the subscribed capital. Such a reduction must be prescribed where the acquisition of shares to be cancelled results in the net assets having fallen below the amount specified in points (a) and (b) of Article 15(1).

Article 21. Shares acquired in contravention of Articles 19 and 20 shall be disposed of within one year of their acquisition. Should they not be disposed of within that period, Article 20 (3) shall apply.

Article 22. 1. Where the laws of a Member State permit a company to acquire its own shares, either itself or through a person acting in his own name but on the company's behalf, they shall make the holding of these shares at all times subject to at least the following conditions:
(a) among the rights attaching to the shares, the right to vote attaching to the company's own shares shall in any event be suspended;
(b) if the shares are included among the assets shown in the balance sheet, a reserve of the same amount, unavailable for distribution, shall be included among the liabilities.
2. Where the laws of a Member State permit a company to acquire its own shares, either itself or through a person acting in his own name but on the company's behalf, they shall require the annual report to state at least:
(a) the reasons for acquisitions made during the financial year;
(b) the number and nominal value or, in the absence of a nominal value, the accountable par of the shares acquired and disposed of during the financial year and the proportion of the subscribed capital which they represent;
(c) in the case of acquisition or disposal for a value, the consideration for the shares;
(d) the number and nominal value or, in the absence of a nominal value, the accountable par of all the shares acquired and held by the company and the proportion of the subscribed capital which they represent.

Article 23. 1. Where Member States permit a company to, either directly or indirectly, advance funds or make loans or provide security, with a view to the acquisition of its shares by a third party, they shall make such transactions subject to the conditions set out in the second, third, fourth and fifth subparagraphs. The transactions shall take place under the responsibility of the administrative or management body at fair market conditions, especially with regard to interest received by the company and with regard to security provided to the company for the loans and advances referred to in the first subparagraph. The credit standing of the third party or, in the case of multiparty transactions, of each counterparty thereto shall have been duly investigated. The transactions shall be submitted by the administrative or management body to the general meeting for prior approval, whereby the general meeting shall act in accordance with the rules for a quorum and a majority laid down in Article 40. The administrative or management body shall present a written report to the general meeting, indicating the reasons for the transaction, the interest of the company in entering into such a transaction, the conditions on which the transaction is entered into, the risks involved in the transaction for the liquidity and solvency of the company and the price at which the third party is to acquire the shares. This report shall be submitted to the register for publication in accordance with Article 3 of Directive 68/151/EEC. The aggregate financial assistance granted to third parties shall at no time result in the reduction of the net assets below the amount specified in points (a) and (b) of Article 15(1), taking into account also any reduction of the net assets that may have occurred through the acquisition, by the company or on behalf of the company, of its own shares in accordance with Article 19(1). The company shall include, among the liabilities in the balance sheet, a reserve, unavailable for distribution, of the amount of the aggregate financial assistance. Where a third party by means of financial assistance from a company acquires that company's own shares within the meaning of Article 19(1) or subscribes for shares issued in the course of an increase in the subscribed capital, such acquisition or subscription shall be made at a fair price.
2. Paragraph 1 shall not apply to transactions concluded by banks and other financial institutions in the normal course of business, nor to transactions effected with a view to the acquisition of shares by or for the company's employees or the employees of an associate company. However, these transactions may not have the effect of reducing the net assets below the amount specified in Article 15 (1) (a).
3. Paragraph 1 shall not apply to transactions effected with a view to acquisition of shares as described in Article 20 (1) (h).

Article 23a. In cases where individual members of the administrative or management body of the company being party to a transaction referred to in Article 23(1), or of the administrative or management body of a parent undertaking within the meaning of Article 1 of Council Directive 83/349/EEC of 13 June 1983 on consolidated accounts or such parent undertaking itself, or individuals acting in their own name, but on behalf of the members of such bodies or on behalf of such undertaking, are counterparties to such a transaction, Member States shall ensure through adequate safeguards that such transaction does not conflict with the company's best interests.

Article 24. 1. The acceptance of the company's own shares as security, either by the company itself or through a person acting in his own name but on the company's behalf, shall be treated as an acquisition for the purposes of Articles 19, 20 (1), 22 and 23.

2. The Member States may decide not to apply paragraph 1 to transactions concluded by banks and other financial institutions in the normal course of business.

Article 24a. 1. (a) The subscription, acquisition or holding of shares in a public limited-liability company by another company within the meaning of Article 1 of Directive 68/151/EEC in which the public limited-liability company directly or indirectly holds a majority of the voting rights or on which it can directly or indirectly exercise a dominant influence shall be regarded as having been effected by the public limited-liability company itself;
(b) subparagraph (a) shall also apply where the other company is governed by the law of a third country and has a legal form comparable to those listed in Article 1 of Directive 68/151/EEC.
2. However, where the public limited-liability company holds a majority of the voting rights indirectly or can exercise a dominant influence indirectly, Member States need not apply paragraph 1 if they provide for the suspension of the voting rights attached to the shares in the public limited-liability company held by the other company.
3. In the absence of coordination of national legislation on groups of companies, Member States may:
(a) define the cases in which a public limited-liability company shall be regarded as being able to exercise a dominant influence on another company; if a Member State exercises this option, its national law must in any event provide that a dominant influence can be exercised if a public limited-liability company:
— has the right to appoint or dismiss a majority of the members of the administrative organ, of the management organ or of the supervisory organ, and is at the same time a shareholder or member of the other company or
— is a shareholder or member of the other company and has sole control of a majority of the voting rights of its shareholders or members under an agreement concluded with other shareholders or members of that company. Member States shall not be obliged to make provision for any cases other than those referred to in the first and second indents;
(b) define the cases in which a public limited-liability company shall be regarded as indirectly holding voting rights or as able indirectly to exercise a dominant influence;
(c) specify the circumstances in which a public limited-liability company shall be regarded as holding voting rights.
4. (a) Member States need not apply paragraph 1 where the subscription, acquisition or holding is effected on behalf of a person other than the person subscribing, acquiring or holding the shares, who is neither the public limited liability company referred to in paragraph 1 nor another company in which the public limited-liability company directly or indirectly holds a majority of the voting rights or on which it can directly or indirectly exercise a dominant influence.
(b) Member States need not apply paragraph 1 where the subscription, acquisition or holding is effected by the other company in its capacity and in the context of its activities as a professional dealer in securities, provided that it is a member of a stock exchange situated or operating within a Member State, or is approved or supervised by an authority of a Member State competent to supervise professional dealers in securities which, within the meaning of this Directive, may include credit institutions.
5. Member States need not apply paragraph 1 where shares in a public limited-liability company held by another company were acquired before the relationship between the two companies corresponded to the criteria laid down in paragraph 1. However, the voting rights attached to those shares shall be suspended and the shares shall be taken into account when it is determined whether the condition laid down in Article 19 (1) (b) is fulfilled.
6. Member States need not apply Article 20 (2) or (3) or Article 21 where shares in a public limited-liability company are acquired by another company on condition that they provide for:
(a) the suspension of the voting rights attached to the shares in the public limited-liability company held by the other company, and
(b) the members of the administrative or the management organ of the public limited-liability company to be obliged to buy back from the other company the shares referred to in Article 20 (2) and (3) and Article 21 at the price at which the other company acquired them; this sanction shall be inapplicable only where the members of the administrative or the management organ of the public limitedliability company prove that that company played no part whatsoever in the subscription for or acquisition of the shares in question.

Article 25. 1. Any increase in capital must be decided upon by the general meeting. Both this decision and the increase in the subscribed capital shall be published in the manner laid down by the laws of each Member State, in accordance with Article 3 of Directive 68/151/EEC.
2. Nevertheless, the statutes or instrument of incorporation or the general meeting, the decision of which must be published in accordance with the rules referred to in paragraph 1, may authorize an increase in the subscribed capital up to a maximum amount which they shall fix with due regard for any maximum amount provided for by

Part VIII. European Company Law

law. Where ppropriate, the increase in the subscribed capital shall be decided on within the limits of the amount fixed, (SIC! fixed) by the company body empowered to do so. The power of such body in this respect shall be for a maximum period of five years and may be renewed one or more times by the general meeting, each time for a period not exceeding five years.

3. Where there are several classes of shares, the decision by the general meeting concerning the increase in capital referred to in paragraph 1 or the authorization to increase the capital referred to in paragraph 2, shall be subject to a separate vote at least for each class of shareholder whose rights are affected by the transaction.

4. This Article shall apply to the issue of all securities which are convertible into shares or which carry the right to subscribe for shares, but not to the conversion of such securities, nor to the exercise of the right to subscribe.

Article 26. Shares issued for a consideration, in the course of an increase in subscribed capital, must be paid up to at least 25 % of their nominal value or, in the absence of a nominal value, of their accountable par. Where provision is made for an issue premium, it must be paid in full.

Article 27. 1. Where shares are issued for a consideration other than in cash in the course of an increase in the subscribed capital the consideration must be transferred in full within a period of five years from the decision to increase the subscribed capital.

2. The consideration referred to in paragraph 1 shall be the subject of a report drawn up before the increase in capital is made by one or more experts who are independent of the company and appointed or approved by an administrative or judicial authority. Such experts may be natural persons as well as legal persons and companies and firms under the laws of each Member State. Article 10(2) and (3) and Articles 10a and 10b shall apply.

3. Member States may decide not to apply paragraph 2 in the event of an increase in subscribed capital made in order to give effect to a merger, a division or a public offer for the purchase or exchange of shares and to pay the shareholders of the company which is being absorbed or divided or which is the object of the public offer for the purchase or exchange of shares.
In the case of a merger or a division, however, Member States shall apply the first subparagraph only where an independent expert's report on the draft terms of merger or division is drawn up. Where Member States decide to apply paragraph 2 in the case of a merger or a division, they may provide that the report under this Article and the independent expert's report on the draft terms of merger or division may be drawn up by the same expert or experts.

4. Member States may decide not to apply paragraph 2 if all the shares issued in the course of an increase in subscribed capital are issued for a consideration other than in cash to one or more companies, on condition that all the shareholders in the company which receive the consideration have agreed not to have an experts' report drawn up and that the requirements of Article 10 (4) (b) to (f) are met.

Article 28. Where an increase in capital is not fully subscribed, the capital will be increased by the amount of the subscriptions received only if the conditions of the issue so provide.

Article 29. 1. Whenever the capital is increased by consideration in cash, the shares must be offered on a pre-emptive basis to shareholders in proportion to the capital represented by their shares.

2. The laws of a Member State:
(a) need not apply paragraph 1 above to shares which carry a limited right to participate in distributions within the meaning of Article 15 and/or in the company's assets in the event of liquidation; or
(b) may permit, where the subscribed capital of a company having several classes of shares carrying different rights with regard to voting, or participation in distributions within the meaning of Article 15 or in assets in the event of liquidation, is increased by issuing new shares in only one of these classes, the right of preemption of shareholders of the other classes to be exercised only after the exercise of this right by the shareholders of the class in which the new shares are being issued.

3. Any offer of subscription on a pre-emptive basis and the period within which this right must be exercised shall be published in the national gazette appointed in accordance with Directive 68/151/EEC. However, the laws of a Member State need not provide for such publication where all a company's shares are registered. In such case, all the company's shareholders must be informed in writing. The right of preemption must be exercised within a period which shall not be less than 14 days from the date of publication of the offer or from the date of dispatch of the letters to the shareholders. The right of pre-emption may not be restricted or withdrawn by the statutes or instrument of incorporation. This may, however, be done by decision of the general meeting. The administrative or management body shall be required to present to such a meeting a written report indicating the reasons for restriction or withdrawal of the right of preemption, and justifying the proposed issue price. The general meeting

shall act in accordance with the rules for a quorum and a majority laid down in Article 40. Its decision shall be published in the manner laid down by the laws of each Member State, in accordance with Article 3 of Directive 68/151/EEC.

5. The laws of a Member State may provide that the statutes, the instrument of incorporation or the general meeting, acting in accordance with the rules for a quorum, a majority and publication set out in paragraph 4, may give the power to restrict or withdraw the right of pre-emption to the company body which is empowered to decide on an increase in subscribed capital within the limit of the authorized capital. This power may not be granted for a longer period than the power for which provision is made in Article 25 (2).

6. Paragraphs 1 to 5 shall apply to the issue of all securities which are convertible into shares or which carry the right to subscribe for shares, but not to the conversion of such securities, nor to the exercise of the right to subscribe.

7. The right of pre-emption is not excluded for the purposes of paragraphs 4 and 5 where, in accordance with the decision to increase the subscribed capital, shares are issued to banks or other financial institutions with a view to their being offered to shareholders of the company in accordance with paragraphs 1 and 3.

Article 30. Any reduction in the subscribed capital, except under a court order, must be subject at least to a decision of the general meeting acting in accordance with the rules for a quorum and a majority laid down in Article 40 without prejudice to Articles 36 and 37. Such decision shall be published in the manner laid down by the laws of each Member State in accordance with Article 3 of Directive 68/151/EEC. The notice convening the meeting must specify at least the purpose of the reduction and the way in which it is to be carried out.

Article 31. Where there are several classes of shares, the decision by the general meeting concerning a reduction in the subscribed capital shall be subject to a separate vote, at least for each class of shareholders whose rights are affected by the transaction.

Article 32. 1. In the event of a reduction in the subscribed capital, at least the creditors whose claims antedate the publication of the decision on the reduction shall at least have the right to obtain security for claims which have not fallen due by the date of that publication. Member States may not set aside such a right unless the creditor has adequate safeguards, or unless such safeguards are not necessary having regard to the assets of the company. Member States shall lay down the conditions for the exercise of the right provided for in the first subparagraph. In any event, Member States shall ensure that the creditors are authorised to apply to the appropriate administrative or judicial authority for adequate safeguards provided that they can credibly demonstrate that due to the reduction in the subscribed capital the satisfaction of their claims is at stake, and that no adequate safeguards have been obtained from the company.

2. The laws of the Member States shall also stipulate at least that the reduction shall be void or that no payment may be made for the benefit of the shareholders, until the creditors have obtained satisfaction or a court has decided that their application should not be acceded to.

3. This Article shall apply where the reduction in the subscribed capital is brought about by the total or partial waiving of the payment of the balance of the shareholders' contributions.

Article 33. 1. Member States need not apply Article 32 to a reduction in the subscribed capital whose purpose is to offset losses incurred or to include sums of money in a reserve provided that, following this operation, the amount of such reserve is not more than 10 % of the reduced subscribed capital. Except in the event of a reduction in the subscribed capital, this reserve may not be distributed to shareholders; it may be used only for offsetting losses incurred or for increasing the subscribed capital by the capitalization of such reserve, in so far as the Member States permit such an operation.

2. In the cases referred to in paragraph 1 the laws of the Member States must at least provide for the measures necessary to ensure that the amounts deriving from the reduction of subscribed capital may not be used for making payments or distributions to shareholders or discharging shareholders from the obligation to make their contributions.

Article 34. The subscribed capital may not be reduced to an amount less than the minimum capital laid down in accordance with Article 6. However, Member States may permit such a reduction if they also provide that the decision to reduce the subscribed capital may take effect only when the subscribed capital is increased to an amount at least equal to the prescribed minimum.

Article 35. Where the laws of a Member State authorize total or partial redemption of the subscribed capital without reduction of the latter, they shall at least require that the following conditions are observed:

(a) where the statutes or instrument of incorporation provide for redemption, the latter shall be decided on by the general meeting voting at least under the usual conditions of quorum and majority. Where the statutes or instrument of incorporation do not provide for redemption, the latter shall be decided upon by the general meeting acting at least under the conditions of quorum and majority laid down in Article 40. The decision must be published in the manner prescribed by the laws of each Member State, in accordance with Article 3 of Directive 68/151/EEC;
(b) only sums which are available for distribution within the meaning of Article 15 (1) may be used for redemption purposes;
(c) shareholders whose shares are redeemed shall retain their rights in the company, with the exception of their rights to the repayment of their investment and participation in the distribution of an initial dividend on unredeemed shares.

Article 36. 1. Where the laws of a Member State may allow companies to reduce their subscribed capital by compulsory withdrawal of shares, they shall require that at least the following conditions are observed:
(a) compulsory withdrawal must be prescribed or authorized by the statutes or instrument of incorporation before subscription of the shares which are to be withdrawn are subscribed for;
(b) where the compulsory withdrawal is merely authorized by the statutes or instrument of incorporation, it shall be decided upon by the general meeting unless it has been unanimously approved by the shareholders concerned;
(c) the company body deciding on the compulsory withdrawal shall fix the terms and manner thereof, where they have not already been fixed by the statutes or instrument of incorporation;
(d) Article 32 shall apply except in the case of fully paid-up shares which are made available to the company free of charge or are withdrawn using sums available for distribution in accordance with Article 15 (1); in these cases, an amount equal to the nominal value or, in the absence thereof, to the accountable par of all the withdrawn shares must be included in a reserve. Except in the event of a reduction in the subscribed capital this reserve may not be distributed to shareholders. It can be used only for offsetting losses incurred or for increasing the subscribed capital by the capitalization of such reserve, in so far as Member States permit such an operation;
(e) the decision on compulsory withdrawal shall be published in the manner laid down by the laws of each Member State in accordance with Article 3 of Directive 68/151/EEC.
2. Articles 30 (1), 31, 33 and 40 shall not apply to the cases to which paragraph 1 refers.

Article 37. 1. In the case of a reduction in the subscribed capital by the withdrawal of shares acquired by the company itself or by a person acting in his own name but on behalf of the company, the withdrawal must always be decided on by the general meeting.
2. Article 32 shall apply unless the shares are fully paid up and are acquired free of charge or using sums available for distribution in accordance with Article 15 (1); in these cases an amount equal to the nominal value or, in the absence thereof, to the accountable par of all the shares withdrawn must be included in a reserve. Except in the event of a reduction in the subscribed capital, this reserve may not be distributed to shareholders. It may be used only for offsetting losses incurred or for increasing the subscribed capital by the capitalization of such reserve, in so far as the Member States permit such an operation.
3. Articles 31, 33 and 40 shall not apply to the cases to which paragraph 1 refers.

Article 38. In the cases covered by Articles 35, 36 (1) (b) and 37 (1), when there are several classes of shares, the decision by the general meeting concerning redemption of the subscribed capital or its reduction by withdrawal of shares shall be subject to a separate vote, at least for each class of shareholders whose rights are affected by the transaction.

Article 39. Where the laws of a Member State authorize companies to issue redeemable shares, they shall require that the following conditions, at least, are complied with for the redemption of such shares:
(a) redemption must be authorized by the company's statutes or instrument of incorporation before the redeemable shares are subscribed for;
(b) the shares must be fully paid up;
(c) the terms and the manner of redemption must be laid down in the company's statutes or instrument of incorporation;
(d) redemption can be only effected by using sums available for distribution in accordance with Article 15 (1) or the proceeds of a new issue made with a view to effecting such redemption;
(e) an amount equal to the nominal value or, in the absence thereof, to the accountable par of all the redeemed shares must be included in a reserve which cannot be distributed to the shareholders, except in the event of a

reduction in the subscribed capital; it may be used only for the purpose of increasing the subscribed capital by the capitalization of reserves;

(f) subparagraph (e) shall not apply to redemption using the proceeds of a new issue made with a view to effecting such redemption;

(g) where provision is made for the payment of a premium to shareholders in consequence of a redemption, the premium may be paid only from sums available for distribution in accordance with Article 15 (1), or from a reserve other than that referred to in (e) which may not be distributed to shareholders except in the event of a reduction in the subscribed capital; this reserve may be used only for the purposes of increasing the subscribed capital by the capitalization of reserves or for covering the costs referred to in Article 3 (j) or the cost of issuing shares or debentures or for the payment of a premium to holders of redeemable shares or debentures;

(h) notification of redemption shall be published in the manner laid down by the laws of each Member State in accordance with Article 3 of Directive 68/151/EEC.

Article 40. 1. The laws of the Member States shall provide that the decisions referred to in Articles 29 (4) and (5), 30, 31, 35 and 38 must be taken at least by a majority of not less than two-thirds of the votes attaching to the securities or the subscribed capital represented.

2. The laws of the Member States may, however, lay down that a simple majority of the votes specified in paragraph 1 is sufficient when at least half the subscribed capital is represented.

Article 41. 1. Member States may derogate from Article 9(1), the first sentence of point (a) of Article 19(1), and Articles 25, 26 and 29 to the extent that such derogations are necessary for the adoption or application of provisions designed to encourage the participation of employees, or other groups of persons defined by national law, in the capital of undertakings.

2. Member States may decide not to apply Article 19 (1) (a), first sentence, and Articles 30, 31, 36, 37, 38 and 39 to companies incorporated under a special law which issue both capital shares and workers' shares, the latter being issued to the company's employees as a body, who are represented at general meetings of shareholders by delegates having the right to vote.

Article 42. For the purposes of the implementation of this Directive, the laws of the Member States shall ensure equal treatment to all shareholders who are in the same position.

Article 43. 1. Member States shall bring into force the laws, regulations and administrative provisions needed in order to comply with this Directive within two years of its notification. They shall forthwith inform the Commission thereof.

2. Member States may decide not to apply Article 3 (g), (i), (j) and (k) to companies already in existence at the date of entry into force of the provisions referred to in paragraph 1. They may provide that the other provisions of this Directive shall not apply to such companies until 18 months after that date. However, this time limit may be three years in the case of Articles 6 and 9 and five years in the case of unregistered companies in the United Kingdom and Ireland.

3. Member States shall ensure that they communicate to the Commission the text of the main provisions of national law which they adopt in the field covered by this Directive.

Article 44. This Directive is addressed to the Member States.

Council Directive 78/855/EEC of 9 October 1978 based on Article 54 (3) (g) of the Treaty concerning mergers of public limited liability companies ("Third Company Law Directive") (*OJ* L 295, 20.10.1978, pp. 36–43). Consolidated version as last amended by Directive 2009/109/EC of the European Parliament and of the Council of 16 September 2009 amending Council Directives 77/91/EEC, 78/855/EEC and 82/891/EEC, and Directive 2005/56/EC as regards reporting and documentation requirements in the case of mergers and divisions [footnotes omitted].

THE COUNCIL OF THE EUROPEAN COMMUNITIES,
Having regard to the Treaty establishing the European Economic Community, and in particular Article 54 (3) (g) thereof,
Having regard to the proposal from the Commission ,
Having regard to the opinion of the European Parliament,
Having regard to the opinion of the Economic and Social Committee,
Whereas the coordination provided for in Article 54 (3) (g) and in the general programme for the abolition of restrictions on freedom of establishment was begun with Directive 68/151/EEC ;
Whereas this coordination was continued as regards the formation of public limited liability companies and the maintenance and alteration of their capital with Directive 77/91/EEC, and as regards the annual accounts of certain types of companies with Directive 78/660/EEC;
Whereas the protection of the interests of members and third parties requires that the laws of the Member States relating to mergers of public limited liability companies be coordinated and that provision for mergers should be made in the laws of all the Member States;
Whereas in the context of such coordination it is particularly important that the shareholders of merging companies be kept adequately informed in as objective a manner as possible and that their rights be suitably protected;
Whereas the protection of employees' rights in the event of transfers of undertakings, businesses or parts of businesses is at present regulated by Directive 77/187/EEC;
Whereas creditors, including debenture holders, and persons having other claims on the merging companies must be protected so that the merger does not adversely affect their interests;
Whereas the disclosure requirements of Directive 68/151/EEC must be extended to include mergers so that third parties are kept adequately informed;
Whereas the safeguards afforded to members and third parties in connection with mergers must be extended to cover certain legal practices which in important respects are similar to merger, so that the obligation to provide such protection cannot be evaded;
Whereas to ensure certainty in the law as regards relations between the companies concerned, between them and third parties, and between the members, the cases in which nullity can arise must be limited by providing that defects be remedied wherever that is possible and by restricting the period within which nullification proceedings may be commenced,

HAS ADOPTED THIS DIRECTIVE:

Article 1. 1. The coordination measures laid down by this Directive shall apply to the laws, regulations and administrative provisions of the Member States relating to the following types of company:
Germany: die Aktiengesellschaft,
Belgium: la société anonyme/de naamloze vennootschap,
Denmark: aktieselskaber,
France: la société anonyme,
Ireland: public companies limited by shares, and public companies limited by guarantee having a share capital,
Italy: la società per azioni,
Luxembourg: la société anonyme,
the Netherlands: de naamloze vennootschap,
the United Kingdom: public companies limited by shares, and public companies limited by guarantee having a share capital,
Greece: η ανώνυμη εταιρία,
Spain: la sociedad anónima,
Portugal: a sociedade anónima de responsabilidade limitada,
Austria: die Aktiengesellschaft,
Finland: julkinen osakeyhtiö / publikt aktiebolag,
Sweden: aktiebolag,

the Czech Republic: akciová společnost,
Estonia: aktsiaselts,
Cyprus: Δημόσιες εταιρείες περιορισμένης ευθύνης με μετοχές, δημόσιες ετα- ιρείες περιορισμένης ευθύνης με εγγύηση που διαθέτουν μετοχικό κεφάλαιο,
Latvia: akciju sabiedrība,
Lithuania: akcinė bendrovė,
Hungary: részvénytársaság,
Malta: kumpanija pubblika/public limited liability company, kumpanija privata/private limited liability company,
Poland: spółka akcyjna,
Slovenia: delniška družba,
Slovakia: akciová spoločnosť,
Bulgaria: акционерно дружество,
Romania: societate pe acţiuni.
2. The Member States need not apply this Directive to cooperatives incorporated as one of the types of company listed in paragraph 1. In so far as the laws of the Member States make use of this option, they shall require such companies to include the word cooperative' in all the documents referred to in Article 4 of Directive 68/151/EEC.
3. The Member States need not apply this Directive in cases where the company or companies which are being acquired or will cease to exist are the subject of bankruptcy proceedings, proceedings relating to the winding-up of insolvent companies, judicial arangements, compositions and analogous proceedings.

Chapter I. Regulation of merger by the acquisition of one or more companies by another and of merger by the formation of a new company

Article 2. The Member States shall, as regards companies governed by their national laws, make provision for rules governing merger by the acquisition of one or more companies by another and merger by the formation of a new company.

Article 3. 1. For the purposes of this Directive, 'merger by acquisition' shall mean the operation whereby one or more companies are wound up without going into liquidation and transfer to another all their assets and liabilities in exchange for the issue to the shareholders of the company or companies being acquired of shares in the acquiring company and a cash payment, if any, not exceeding 10 % of the nominal value of the shares so issued or, where they have no nominal value, of their accounting par value.
2. A Member State's laws may provide that merger by acquisition may also be effected where one or more of the companies being acquired is in liquidation, provided that this option is restricted to companies which have not yet begun to distribute their assets to their shareholders.

Article 4. 1. For the purposes of this Directive, 'merger by the formation of a new company' shall mean the operation whereby several companies are wound up without going into liquidation and transfer to a company that they set up all their assets and liabilities in exchange for the issue to their shareholders of shares in the new company and a cash payment, if any, not exceeding 10 % of the nominal value of the shares so issued or, where they have no nominal value, of their accounting par value.
2. A Member State's laws may provide that merger by the formation of a new company may also be effected where one or more of the companies which are ceasing to exist is in liquidation, provided that this option is restricted to companies which have not yet begun to distribute their assets to their shareholders.

Chapter II. Merger by acquisition

Article 5. 1. The administrative or management bodies of the merging companies shall draw up draft terms of merger in writing.
2. Draft terms of merger shall specify at least:
(a) the type, name and registered office of each of the merging companies;
(b) the share exchange ratio and the amount of any cash payment;
(c) the terms relating to the allotment of shares in the acquiring company;
(d) the date from which the holding of such shares entitles the holders to participate in profits and any special conditions affecting that entitlement;
(e) the date from which the transactions of the company being acquired shall be treated for accounting purposes as being those of the acquiring company;

(f) the rights conferred by the acquiring company on the holders of shares to which special rights are attached and the holders of securities other than shares, or the measures proposed concerning them;
(g) any special advantage granted to the experts referred to in Article 10 (1) and members of the merging companies' administrative, management, supervisory or controlling bodies.

Article 6. Draft terms of merger must be published in the manner prescribed by the laws of each Member State in accordance with Article 3 of Directive 68/151/EEC, for each of the merging companies, at least one month before the date fixed for the general meeting which is to decide thereon. Any of the merging companies shall be exempt from the publication requirement laid down in Article 3 of Directive 68/151/EEC if, for a continuous period beginning at least one month before the day fixed for the general meeting which is to decide on the draft terms of merger and ending not earlier than the conclusion of that meeting, it makes the draft terms of such merger available on its website free of charge for the public. Member States shall not subject that exemption to any requirements or constraints other than those which are necessary in order to ensure the security of the website and the authenticity of the documents, and may impose such requirements or constraints only to the extent that they are proportionate in order to achieve those objectives. By way of derogation from the second paragraph, Member States may require that publication be effected via the central electronic platform referred to in Article 3(4) of Directive 68/151/EEC. Member States may alternatively require that such publication be made on any other website designated by them for that purpose. Where Member States avail themselves of one of those possibilities, they shall ensure that companies are not charged a specific fee for such publication. Where a website other than the central electronic platform is used, a reference giving access to that website shall be published on the central electronic platform at least one month before the day fixed for the general meeting. That reference shall include the date of publication of the draft terms of merger on the website and shall be accessible to the public free of charge. Companies shall not be charged a specific fee for such publication. The prohibition precluding the charging to companies of a specific fee for publication, laid down in the third and fourth paragraphs, shall not affect the ability of Member States to pass on to companies the costs in respect of the central electronic platform. Member States may require companies to maintain the information for a specific period after the general meeting on their website or, where applicable, on the central electronic platform or the other website designated by the Member State concerned. Member States may determine the consequences of temporary disruption of access to the website or to the central electronic platform, caused by technical or other factors.

Article 7. 1. A merger shall require at least the approval of the general meeting of each of the merging companies. The laws of the Member States shall provide that this decision shall require a majority of not less than two thirds of the votes attaching either to the shares or to the subscribed capital represented. The laws of a Member State may, however, provide that a simple majority of the votes specified in the first subparagraph shall be sufficient when at least half of the subscribed capital is represented. Moreover, where appropriate, the rules governing alterations to the memorandum and articles of association shall apply.
2. Where there is more than one class of shares, the decision concerning a merger shall be subject to a separate vote by at least each class of shareholders whose rights are affected by the transaction.
3. The decision shall cover both the approval of the draft terms of merger and any alterations to the memorandum and articles of association necessitated by the merger.

Article 8. The laws of a Member State need not require approval of the merger by the general meeting of the acquiring company if the following conditions are fulfilled:
(a) the publication provided for in Article 6 must be effected, for the acquiring company, at least one month before the date fixed for the general meeting of the company or companies being acquired which are to decide on the draft terms of merger;
(b) at least one month before the date specified in (a), all shareholders of the acquiring company must be entitled to inspect the documents specified in Article 11 (1) at the registered office of the acquiring company;
(c) one or more shareholders of the acquiring company holding a minimum percentage of the subscribed capital must be entitled to require that a general meeting of the acquiring company be called to decide whether to approve the merger. This minimum percentage may not be fixed at more than 5 %. The Member States may, however, provide for the exclusion of non-voting shares from this calculation. For the purposes of point (b) of the first paragraph, Article 11(2), (3) and (4) shall apply.

Article 9. 1. The administrative or management bodies of each of the merging companies shall draw up a detailed written report explaining the draft terms of merger and setting out the legal and economic grounds for them, in particular the share exchange ratio. That report shall also describe any special valuation difficulties which have arisen.

2. The administrative or management bodies of each of the companies involved shall inform the general meeting of their company and the administrative or management bodies of the other companies involved so that the latter may inform their respective general meetings of any material change in the assets and liabilities between the date of preparation of the draft terms of merger and the date of the general meetings which are to decide on the draft terms of merger.
3. Member States may provide that the report referred to in paragraph 1 and/or the information referred to in paragraph 2 shall not be required if all the shareholders and the holders of other securities conferring the right to vote of each of the companies involved in the merger have so agreed.

Article 10. 1. One or more experts, acting on behalf of each of the merging companies but independent of them, appointed or approved by a judicial or administrative authority, shall examine the draft terms of merger and draw up a written report to the shareholders. However, the laws of a Member State may provide for the appointment of one or more independent experts for all the merging companies, if such appointment is made by a judicial or administrative authority at the joint request of those companies. Such experts may, depending on the laws of each Member State, be natural or legal persons or companies or firms.
2. In the report mentioned in paragraph 1 the experts must in any case state whether in their opinion the share exchange ratio is fair and reasonable. Their statement must at least:
(a) indicate the method or methods used to arrive at the share exchange ratio proposed;
(b) state whether such method or methods are adequate in the case in question, indicate the values arrived at using each such method and give an opinion on the relative importance attributed to such methods in arriving at the value decided on. The report shall also describe any special valuation difficulties which have arisen.
3. Each expert shall be entitled to obtain from the merging companies all relevant information and documents and to carry out all necessary investigations.
4. Neither an examination of the draft terms of merger nor an expert report shall be required if all the shareholders and the holders of other securities conferring the right to vote of each of the companies involved in the merger have so agreed.

Article 11. 1. All shareholders shall be entitled to inspect at least the following documents at the registered office at least one month before the date fixed for the general meeting which is to decide on the draft terms of merger:
(a) the draft terms of merger;
(b) the annual accounts and annual reports of the merging companies for the preceding three financial years;
(c) where applicable, an accounting statement drawn up as at a date which must not be earlier than the first day of the third month preceding the date of the draft terms of merger, if the latest annual accounts relate to a financial year which ended more than six months before that date;
(d) where applicable, the reports of the administrative or management bodies of the merging companies provided for in Article 9;
(e) where applicable, the reports provided for in Article 10.
For the purposes of point (c) of the first subparagraph, an accounting statement shall not be required if the company publishes a half-yearly financial report in accordance with Article 5 of Directive 2004/109/EC and makes it available to shareholders in accordance with this paragraph. Furthermore, Member States may provide that an accounting statement shall not be required if all the shareholders and the holders of other securities conferring the right to vote of each of the companies involved in the merger have so agreed.
2. The accounting statement provided for in paragraph 1 (c) shall be drawn up using the same methods and the same layout as the last annual balance sheet. However, the laws of a Member State may provide that:
(a) it shall not be necessary to take a fresh physical inventory;
(b) the valuations shown in the last balance sheet shall be altered only to reflect entries in the books of account; the following shall nevertheless be taken into account:
— interim depreciation and provisions,
— material changes in actual value not shown in the books.
3. Every shareholder shall be entitled to obtain, on request and free of charge, full or, if so desired, partial copies of the documents referred to in paragraph 1.
Where a shareholder has consented to the use by the company of electronic means for conveying information, such copies may be provided by electronic mail.
4. A company shall be exempt from the requirement to make the documents referred to in paragraph 1 available at its registered office if, for a continuous period beginning at least one month before the day fixed for the general meeting which is to decide on the draft terms of merger and ending not earlier than the conclusion of that meeting, it makes them available on its website. Member States shall not subject that exemption to any requirements or constraints other than those which are necessary in order to ensure the security of the website and the authenticity

of the documents and may impose such requirements or constraints only to the extent that they are proportionate in order to achieve those objectives. Paragraph 3 shall not apply if the website gives shareholders the possibility, throughout the period referred to in the first subparagraph of this paragraph, of downloading and printing the documents referred to in paragraph 1. However, in that case Member States may provide that the company is to make those documents available at its registered office for consultation by the shareholders. Member States may require companies to maintain the information on their website for a specific period after the general meeting. Member States may determine the consequences of temporary disruption of access to the website caused by technical or other factors.

Article 12. Protection of the rights of the employees of each of the merging companies shall be regulated in accordance with Directive 77/187/EEC.

Article 13. 1. The laws of the Member States must provide for an adequate system of protection of the interests of creditors of the merging companies whose claims antedate the publication of the draft terms of merger and have not fallen due at the time of such publication.
2. To that end, the laws of the Member States shall at least provide that such creditors shall be entitled to obtain adequate safeguards where the financial situation of the merging companies makes such protection necessary and where those creditors do not already have such safeguards. Member States shall lay down the conditions for the protection provided for in paragraph 1 and in the first subparagraph of this paragraph. In any event, Member States shall ensure that the creditors are authorised to apply to the appropriate administrative or judicial authority for adequate safeguards provided that they can credibly demonstrate that due to the merger the satisfaction of their claims is at stake and that no adequate safeguards have been obtained from the company.
3. Such protection may be different for the creditors of the acquiring company and for those of the company being acquired.

Article 14. Without prejudice to the rules governing the collective exercise of their rights, Article 13 shall apply to the debenture holders of the merging companies, except where the merger has been approved by a meeting of the debenture holders, if such a meeting is provided for under national laws, or by the debenture holders individually.

Article 15. Holders of securities, other than shares, to which special rights are attached, must be given rights in the acquiring company at least equivalent to those they possessed in the company being acquired, unless the alteration of those rights has been approved by a meeting of the holders of such securities, if such a meeting is provided for under national laws, or by the holders of those securities individually, or unless the holders are entitled to have their securities repurchased by the acquiring company.

Article 16. 1. Where the laws of a Member State do not provide for judicial or administrative preventive supervision of the legality of mergers, or where such supervision does not extend to all the legal acts required for a merger, the minutes of the general meetings which decide on the merger and, where appropriate, the merger contract subsequent to such general meetings shall be drawn up and certified in due legal form. In cases where the merger need not be approved by the general meetings of all the merging companies, the draft terms of merger must be drawn up and certified in due legal form.
2. The notary or the authority competent to draw up and certify the document in due legal form must check and certify the existence and validity of the legal acts and formalities required of the company for which he or it is acting and of the draft terms of merger.

Article 17. The laws of the Member States shall determine the date on which a merger takes effect.

Article 18. 1. A merger must be publicized in the manner prescribed by the laws of each Member State, in accordance with Article 3 of Directive 68/151/EEC, in respect of each of the merging companies.
2. The acquiring company may itself carry out the publication formalities relating to the company or companies being acquired.

Article 19. 1. A merger shall have the following consequences ipso jure and simultaneously:
(a) the transfer, both as between the company being acquired and the acquiring company and as regards third parties, to the acquiring company of all the assets and liabilities of the company being acquired;
(b) the shareholders of the company being acquired become shareholders of the acquiring company;
(c) the company being acquired ceases to exist.
2. No shares in the acquiring company shall be exchanged for shares in the company being acquired held either:

(a) by the acquiring company itself or through a person acting in his own name but on its behalf;or
(b) by the company being acquired itself or through a person acting in his own name but on its behalf.
3. The foregoing shall not affect the laws of Member States which require the completion of special formalities for the transfer of certain assets, rights and obligations by the acquired company to be effective as against third parties. The acquiring company may carry out these formalities itself; however, the laws of the Member States may permit the company being acquired to continue to carry out these formalities for a limited period which cannot, save in exceptional cases, be fixed at more than six months from the date on which the merger takes effect.

Article 20. The laws of the Member States shall at least lay down rules governing the civil liability towards the shareholders of the company being acquired of the members of the administrative or management bodies of that company in respect of misconduct on the part of members of those bodies in preparing and implementing the merger.

Article 21. The laws of the Member States shall at least lay down rules governing the civil liability towards the shareholders of the company being acquired of the experts responsible for drawing up on behalf of that company the report referred to in Article 10 (1) in respect of misconduct on the part of those experts in the performance of their duties.

Article 22. 1. The laws of the Member States may lay down nullity rules for mergers in accordance with the following conditions only:
(a) nullity must be ordered in a court judgment;
(b) mergers which have taken effect pursuant to Article 17 may be declared void only if there has been no judicial or administrative preventive supervision of their legality, or if they have not been drawn up and certified in due legal form, or if it is shown that the decision of the general meeting is void or voidable under national law;
(c) nullification proceedings may not be initiated more than six months after the date on which the merger becomes effective as against the person alleging nullity or if the situation has been rectified;
(d) where it is possible to remedy a defect liable to render a merger void, the competent court shall grant the companies involved a period of time within which to rectify the situation;
(e) a judgment declaring a merger void shall be published in the manner prescribed by the laws of each Member State in accordance with Article 3 of Directive 68/151/EEC;
(f) where the laws of a Member State permit a third party to challenge such a judgment, he may do so only within six months of publication of the judgment in the manner prescribed by Directive 68/151/EEC;
(g) a judgment declaring a merger void shall not of itself affect the validity of obligations owed by or in relation to the acquiring company which arose before the judgment was published and after the date referred to in Article 17;
(h) companies which have been parties to a merger shall be jointly and severally liable in respect of the obligations of the acquiring company referred to in (g).
2. By way of derogation from paragraph 1 (a), the laws of a Member State may also provide for the nullity of a merger to be ordered by an administrative authority if an appeal against such a decision lies to a court. Subparagraphs (b), (d), (e), (f), (g) and (h) shall apply by analogy to the administrative authority. Such nullification, proceedings may not be initiated more than six months after the date referred to in Article 17.
3. The foregoing shall not affect the laws of the Member States on the nullity of a merger pronounced following any supervision other than judicial or administrative preventive supervision of legality.

Chapter III. Merger by formation of a new company

Article 23. 1. Articles 5, 6, 7 and 9 to 22 shall apply, without prejudice to Articles 11 and 12 of Directive 68/151/EEC, to merger by formation of a new company. For this purpose, 'merging companies' and 'company being acquired' shall mean the companies which will cease to exist, and 'acquiring company' shall mean the new company.
2. Article 5 (2) (a) shall also apply to the new company.
3. The draft terms of merger and, if they are contained in a separate document, the memorandum or draft memorandum of association and the articles or draft articles of association of the new company shall be approved at a general meeting of each of the companies that will cease to exist.

Chapter IV. Acquisition of one company by another which holds 90 % or more of its shares

Article 24. The Member States shall make provision, in respect of companies governed by their laws, for the operation whereby one or more companies are wound up without going into liquidation and transfer all their assets and liabilities to another company which is the holder of all their shares and other securities conferring the right to vote at general meetings.

Such operations shall be regulated by the provisions of Chapter II. However, Member States shall not impose the requirements set out in points (b), (c) and (d) of Article 5(2), Articles 9 and 10, Article 11(1)(d) and (e), Article 19(1)(b) and Articles 20 and 21.

Article 25. Member States shall not apply Article 7 to the operations referred to in Article 24 if the following conditions are fulfilled:
(a) the publication provided for in Article 6 must be effected, as regards each company involved in the operation, at least one month before the operation takes effect;
(b) at least one month before the operation takes effect, all shareholders of the acquiring company must be entitled to inspect the documents specified in Article 11 (1) (a), (b) and (c) at the company's registered office
(c) Article 8 (c) must apply. For the purposes of point (b) of the first paragraph, Article 11(2), (3) and (4) shall apply.

Article 26. The Member States may apply Articles 24 and 25 to operations whereby one or more companies are wound up without going into liquidation and transfer all their assets and liabilities to another company, if all the shares and other securities specified in Article 24 of the company or companies being acquired are held by the acquiring company and/or by persons holding those shares and securities in their own names but on behalf of that company.

Article 27. Where a merger by acquisition is carried out by a company which holds 90 % or more, but not all, of the shares and other securities conferring the right to vote at general meetings of the company or companies being acquired, Member States shall not require approval of the merger by the general meeting of the acquiring company if the following conditions are fulfilled:
(a) the publication provided for in Article 6 must be effected, as regards the acquiring company, at least one month before the date fixed for the general meeting of the company or companies being acquired which is to decide on the draft terms of merger;
(b) at least one month before the date specified in point (a), all shareholders of the acquiring company must be entitled to inspect the documents specified in points (a), (b) and, where applicable, (c), (d) and (e) of Article 11(1) at the company's registered office;
(c) Article 8 (c) must apply.
For the purposes of point (b) of the first paragraph, Article 11(2), (3) and (4) shall apply.

Article 28. Member States shall not impose the requirements set out in Articles 9, 10 and 11 in the case of a merger within the meaning of Article 27 if the following conditions are fulfilled:
(a) the minority shareholders of the company being acquired must be entitled to have their shares acquired by the acquiring company;
(b) if they exercise that right, they must be entitled to receive consideration corresponding to the value of their shares;
(c) in the event of disagreement regarding such consideration, it must be possible for the value of the consideration to be determined by a court or by an administrative authority designated by the Member State for that purpose.
A Member State need not apply the first paragraph if the laws of that Member State entitle the acquiring company, without a previous public takeover offer, to require all the holders of the remaining securities of the company or companies to be acquired to sell those securities to it prior to the merger at a fair price.

Article 29. The Member States may apply Articles 27 and 28 to operations whereby one or more companies are wound up without going into liquidation and transfer all their assets and liabilities to another company if 90 % or more, but not all, of the shares and other securities referred to in Article 27 of the company or companies being acquired are held by that acquiring company and/or by persons holding those shares and securities in their own names but on behalf of that company.

Chapter V. Other operations treated as mergers

Article 30. Where in the case of one of the operations referred to in Article 2 the laws of a Member State permit a cash payment to exceed 10 %, Chapters II and III and Articles 27, 28 and 29 shall apply.

Article 31. Where the laws of a Member State permit one of the operations referred to in Articles 2, 24 and 30, without all of the transferring companies thereby ceasing to exist, Chapter II, except for Article 19 (1) (c), Chapter III or Chapter IV shall apply as appropriate.

Chapter VI. Final provisions

Article 32. 1. The Member States shall bring into force the laws, regulations and administrative provisions necessary for them to comply with this Directive within three years of its notification. They shall forthwith inform the Commission thereof.
2. However, provision may be made for a delay of five years from the entry into force of the provisions referred to in paragraph 1 for the application of those provisions to unregistered companies in the United Kingdom and Ireland.
3. The Member States need not apply Articles 13, 14 and 15 as regards the holders of convertible debentures and other convertible securities if, at the time when the laws, regulations and administrative provisions referred to in paragraph 1 come into force, the position of these holders in the event of a merger has previously been determined by the conditions of issue.
4. The Member States need not apply this Directive to mergers or to operations treated as mergers for the preparation or execution of which an act or formality required by national law has already been completed when the provisions referred to in paragraph 1 enter into force.

Article 33. This Directive is addressed to the Member States.

Council Directive 78/660/EEC of 25 July 1978 based on Article 54 (3) (g) of the Treaty on the annual accounts of certain types of companies ("Fourth Company Law Directive") *(OJ* L 222 , 14.08.1978 pp. 11 - 31). Consolidated version as last amended by Directive 2009/49/EC of the European Parliament and of the Council of 18 June 2009 amending Council Directives 78/660/EEC and 83/349/EEC as regards certain disclosure requirements for medium-sized companies and the obligation to draw up consolidated accounts [footnotes omitted].

THE COUNCIL OF THE EUROPEAN COMMUNITIES,
Having regard to the Treaty establishing the European Economic Community, and in particular Article 54 (3) (g) thereof,
Having regard to the proposal from the Commission, Having regard to the opinion of the European Parliament,
Having regard to the opinion of the Economic and Social Committee,
Whereas the coordination of national provisions concerning the presentation and content of annual accounts and annual reports, the valuation methods, used therein and their publication in respect of certain companies with limited liability is of special importance for the protection of members and third parties;
Whereas simultaneous coordination is necessary in these fields for these forms of company because, on the one hand, these companies' activities frequently extend beyond the frontiers of their national territories and, on the other, they offer no safeguards to third parties beyond the amounts of their net assets; whereas, moreover, the necessity for and the urgency of such coordination have been recognized and confirmed by Article 2 (1) (f) of Directive 68/151/EEC;
Whereas it is necessary, moreover, to establish in the Community minimum equivalent legal requirements as regards the extent of the financial information that should be made available to the public by companies that are in competition with one another;
Whereas annual accounts must give a true and fair view of a company's assets and liabilities, financial position and profit or loss; whereas to this end a mandatory layout must be prescribed for the balance sheet and the profit and loss account and whereas the minimum content of the notes on the accounts and the annual report must be laid down; whereas, however, derogations may be granted for certain companies of minor economic or social importance;
Whereas the different methods for the valuation of assets and liabilities must be coordinated to the extent necessary to ensure that annual accounts disclose comparable and equivalent information;
Whereas the annual accounts of all companies to which this Directive applies must be published in accordance with Directive 68/151/EEC; whereas, however, certain derogations may likewise be granted in this area for small and medium-sized companies;
Whereas annual accounts must be audited by authorized persons whose minimum qualifications will be the subject of subsequent coordination; whereas only small companies may be relieved of this audit obligation;
Whereas, when a company belongs to a group, it is desirable that group accounts giving a true and fair view of the activities of the group as a whole be published; whereas, however, pending the entry into force of a Council Directive on consolidated accounts, derogations from certain provisions of this Directive are necessary;
Whereas, in order to meet the difficulties arising from the present position regarding legislation in certain Member States, the period allowed for the implementation of certain provisions of this Directive must be longer than the period generally laid down in such cases,

HAS ADOPTED THIS DIRECTIVE:

Article 1.1. The coordination measures prescribed by this Directive shall apply to the laws, regulations and administrative provisions of the Member States relating to the following types of companies:
in Germany: die Aktiengesellschaft, die Kommanditgesellschaft auf Aktien, die Gesellschaft mit beschränkter Haftung;
in Belgium: la société anonyme/de naamloze vennootschap, la société en commandite par actions / de commanditaire vennootschap op aandelen, la société de personnes à responsabilité limitée/de personenvennootschap met beperkte aansprakelijkheid;
in Denmark: aktieselskaber, kommanditaktieselskaber, anpartsselskaber;
in France: la société anonyme, la société en commandite par actions, la société à responsabilité limitée;
in Ireland: public companies limited by shares or by guarantee, private companies limited by shares or by guarantee;
in Italy: la società per azioni, la società in accomandita per azioni, la società a responsabilità limitata;
in Luxembourg: la société anonyme, la société en commandite par actions, la société à responsabilité limitée;
in the Netherlands: de naamloze vennootschap, de besloten vennootschap met beperkte aansprakelijkheid;

Part VIII. European Company Law

in the United Kingdom: public companies limited by shares or by guarantee, private companies limited by shares or by guarantee;
in Greece: η ανώνυμη εταιρία, η εταιρία περιωρισμένης ευθύνης, η ετερόρρυθμη κατά μετοχές εταιρία;
in Spain: la sociedad anónima, la sociedad comanditiara por acciones, la sociedad de responsabilidad limitada;
in Portugal: a sociedade anónima, de responsabilidade limitada, a sociedade em comandita por acções, a sociedadepor quotas de responsabilidade limitada;
in Austria: die Aktiengesellschaft, die Gesellschaft mit beschränkter Haftung;
in Finland: osakeyhtiö/aktiebolag;
in Sweden: aktiebolag;
in the Czech Republic: společnost s ručením omezeným, akciová společnost;
in Estonia: aktsiaselts, osaühing;
in Cyprus: Δημόσιες εταιρείες περιορισμένης ευθύνης με μετοχές ή με εγγύηση, ιδιωτικές εταιρείες περιορισμένης ευθύνης με μετοχές ή με εγγύηση;
in Latvia: akciju sabiedrība, sabiedrība ar ierobežotu atbildību;
in Lithuania: akcinės bendrovės, uždarosios akcinės bendrovės;
in Hungary: részvénytársaság, korlátolt felelősségű társaság;
in Malta: kumpanija pubblika —public limited liability company,kumpannija privata —private limited liability company, soċjeta in akkomandita bil-kapital maqsum f'azzjonijiet —partnership en commandite with the capital divided into shares;
in Poland: spółka akcyjna, spółka z ograniczoną odpowiedzialnością, spółka komandytowo-akcyjna;
in Slovenia: delniška družba, družba z omejeno odgovornostjo, komanditna delniška družba;
in Slovakia: akciová spoločnosť, spoločnosť s ručením obmedzeným;
in Bulgaria: акционерно дружество, дружество с ограничена отговорност, командитно дружество с акции;
in Romania: societate pe acțiuni, societate cu răspundere limitată, societate în comandită pe acțiuni.
The coordination measures prescribed by this Directive shall also apply to the Member States' laws, regulations and administrative provisions relating to the following types of company:
(a) in Germany: die offene Handelsgesellschaft, die Kommanditgesellschaft;
(b) in Belgium: la société en nom collectif/de vennootschap onder firma, la société en commandité (SIC! commandite) simple/de gewone commanditaire vennootschap;
(c) in Denmark: interessentskaber, kommanditselskaber;
(d) in France: la société en nom collectif, la société en commandite simple;
(e) in Greece: η ομόρρυθμος εταιρία, η ετερόρρυθμος εταιρία;
(f) in Spain: sociedad colectiva, sociedad en comandita simple;
(g) in Ireland: partnerships, limited partnerships, unlimited companies;
(h) in Italy: la società in nome collettivo, la società in accomandita semplice;
(i) in Luxembourg: la société en nom collectif, la société en commandite simple;
(j) in the Netherlands: de vennootschap onder firma, de commanditaire vennootschap;
(k) in Portugal: sociedade em nome colectivo, sociedade em comandita simples;
(l) in the United Kingdom: partnerships, limited partnerships, unlimited companies;
(m) in Austria: die offene Handelsgesellschaft, die Kommanditgesellschaft;
(n) in Finland: avoin yhtiö/ öppet bolag, kommandiittiyhtiö/kommanditbolag;
(o) in Sweden: handelsbolag, kommanditbolag;
(p) in the Czech Republic: veřejná obchodní společnost, komanditní společnost, družstvo;
(q) in Estonia: täisühing, usaldusühing;
(r) in Cyprus: Ομόρρυθμες και ετερόρρυθμες εταιρείες (συνεταιρισμοί);
(s) in Latvia: pilnsabiedrība, komanditsabiedrība;
(t) in Lithuania: tikrosios ūkinės bendrijos, komanditinės ūkinės bendrijos;
(u) in Hungary: közkereseti társaság, betéti társaság, közös vállalat, egyesülés;
(v) in Malta: Soċjeta f'isem kollettiv jew soċjeta in akkomandita, bil-kapital li mhux maqsum f'azzjonijiet meta s-soċji kollha li għandhom responsabbilita' llimitata huma soċjetajiet tat-tip deskritt f'sub paragrafu 1 —Partnership en nom collectif or partnership en
commandite with capital that is not divided into shares, when all the partners with unlimited liability are partnerships as described in
sub-paragraph 1;
(w) in Poland: spółka jawna, spółka komandytowa;
(x) in Slovenia: družba z neomejeno odgovornostjo, komanditna družba;
(y) in Slovakia: verejná obchodná spoločnosť, komanditná spoločnosť;
(z) in Bulgaria: събирателно дружество, командитно дружество.

(aa) in Romania: asocietate în nume colectiv, societate în comandită simplă
where all members having unlimited liability are companies of the types set out in the first subparagraph or companies which are not governed by the laws of a Member State but which have a legal form comparable to those referred to in Directive 68/151/EEC.
This Directive shall also apply to the types of companies or firms referred to in the second subparagraph where all members having unlimited liability are themselves companies of the types set out in that or the first subparagraph.
2. Pending subsequent coordination, the Member States need not apply the provisions of this Directive to banks and other financial institutions or to insurance companies.

Section I. General provisions

Article 2. 1. The annual accounts shall comprise the balance sheet, the profit and loss account and the notes on the accounts. These documents shall constitute a composite whole. Member States may permit or require the inclusion of other statements in the annual accounts in addition to the documents referred to in the first subparagraph.
2. They shall be drawn up clearly and in accordance with the provisions of this Directive.
3. The annual accounts shall give a true and fair view of the company's assets, liabilities, financial position and profit or loss.
4. Where the application of the provision of this Directive would not be sufficient to give a true and fair view within the meaning of paragraph 3, additional information must be given.
5. Where in exceptional cases the application of a provision of this Directive is incompatible with the obligation laid down in paragraph 3, that provision must be departed from in order to give a true and fair view within the meaning of paragraph 3. Any such departure must be disclosed in the notes on the accounts together with an explanation of the reasons for it and a statement of its effect on the assets, liabilities, financial position and profit or loss. The Member States may define the exceptional cases in question and lay down the relevant special rules.
6. The Member States may authorize or require the disclosure in the annual accounts of other information as well as that which must be disclosed in accordance with this Directive.

Section II. General provisions concerning the balance sheet and the profit and loss account

Article 3. The layout of the balance sheet and of the profit and loss account, particularly as regards the form adopted for their presentation, may not be changed from one financial year to the next. Departures from this principle shall be permitted in exceptional cases. Any such departure must be disclosed in the notes on the accounts together with an explanation of the reasons therefor.

Article 4. 1. In the balance sheet and in the profit and loss account the items prescribed in Articles 9, 10 and 23 to 26 must be shown separately in the order indicated. A more detailed subdivision of the items shall be authorized provided that the layouts are complied with. New items may be added provided that their contents are not covered by any of the items prescribed by the layouts. Such subdivision or new items may be required by the Member States.
2. The layout, nomenclature and terminology of items in the balance sheet and profit and loss account that are preceded by Arabic numerals must be adapted where the special nature of an undertaking so requires. Such adaptations may be required by the Member States of undertakings forming part of a particular economic sector.
3. The balance sheet and profit and loss account items that are preceded by Arabic numerals may be, combined where:
(a) they are immaterial in amount for the purposes of Article 2 (3); or
(b) such combination makes for greater clarity, provided that the items so combined are dealt with separately in the notes on the accounts. Such combination may be required by the Member States.
4. In respect of each balance sheet and profit and loss account item the figure relating to the corresponding item for the preceding financial year must be shown. The Member States may provide that, where these figures are not comparable, the figure for the preceding financial year must be adjusted. In any case, non-comparability and any adjustment of the figures must be disclosed in the notes on the accounts, with relevant comments.
5. Save where there is a corresponding item for the preceding financial year within the meaning of paragraph 4, a balance sheet or profit and loss account item for which there is no amount shall not be shown.
6. Member States may permit or require the presentation of amounts within items in the profit and loss account and balance sheet to have regard to the substance of the reported transaction or arrangement. Such permission or requirement may be restricted to certain classes of company and/or to consolidated accounts as defined in the Seventh Council Directive 83/349/EEC of 13 June 1983 on consolidated accounts.

Article 5. 1. By way of derogation from Article 4 (1) and (2), the Member States may prescribe special layouts for the annual accounts of investment companies and of financial holding companies provided that these layouts give a view of these companies equivalent to that provided for in Article 2 (3).
2. For the purposes of this Directive, 'investment companies' shall mean only:
(a) those companies the sole object of which is to invest their funds in various securities, real property and other assets with the sole aim of spreading investment risks and giving their shareholders the benefit of the results of the management of their assets;
(b) those companies associated with investment companies with fixed capital if the sole object of the companies so associated is to acquire fully paid shares issued by those investment companies without prejudice to the provisions of Article 20 (1) (h) of Directive 77/91/EEC (2).
3. For the purposes of this Directive, 'financial holding companies' shall mean only those companies the sole object of which is to acquire holdings in other undertakings, and to manage such holdings and turn them to profit, without involving themselves directly or indirectly in the management of those undertakings, the aforegoing without prejudice to their rights as shareholders. The limitations imposed on the activities of these companies must be such that compliance with them can be supervised by an administrative or judicial authority.

Article 6. The Member States may authorize or require adaptation of the layout of the balance sheet and profit and loss account in order to include the appropriation of profit or the treatment of loss.

Article 7. Any set-off between asset and liability items, or between income and expenditure items, shall be prohibited.

Section III. Layout of the balance sheet

Article 8. For the presentation of the balance sheet, the Member States shall prescribe one or both of the layouts prescribed by Articles 9 and 10. If a Member State prescribes both, it may allow companies to choose between them. Member States may permit or require companies to adopt the presentation of the balance sheet set out in Article 10a as an alternative to the layouts otherwise prescribed or permitted.

Article 9. A. Subscribed capital unpaid of which there has been called (unless national law provides that called-up capital be shown under 'Liabilities'. In that case, the part of the capital called but not yet paid must appear as an asset either under A or under D (II) (5)).
B. Formation expenses as defined by national law, and in so far as national law permits their being shown as an asset. National law may also provide for formation expenses to be shown as the first item under 'Intangible assets'.
C. Fixed assets
I. Intangible assets
1. Costs of research and development, in so far as national law permits their being shown as assets.
2. Concessions, patents, licences, trade marks and similar rights and assets, if they were:
(a) acquired for valuable consideration and need not be shown under C (I) (3); or
(b) created by the undertaking itself, in so far as national law permits their being shown as assets.
3. Goodwill, to the extent that it was acquired for valuable consideration.
4. Payments on account.
II. Tangible assets
1. Land and buildings.
2. Plant and machinery.
3. Other fixtures and fittings, tools and equipment.
4. Payments on account and tangible assets in course of construction.
III. Financial assets
1. Shares in affiliated undertakings.
2. Loans to affiliated undertakings.
3. Participating interests.
4. Loans to undertakings with which the company is linked by virtue of participating interests.
5. Investments held as fixed assets.
6. Other loans.
7. Own shares (with an indication of their nominal value or, in the absence of a nominal value, their accounting par value) to the extent that national law permits their being shown in the balance sheet.
D. Current assets

I. Stocks
1. Raw materials and consumables.
2. Work in progress.
3. Finished goods and goods for resale.
4. Payments on account.
II. Debtors
(Amounts becoming due and payable after more than one year must be shown separately for each item.)
1. Trade debtors.
2. Amounts owed by affiliated undertakings.
3. Amounts owed by undertakings with which the company is linked by virtue of participating interests.
4. Other debtors.
5. Subscribed capital called but not paid (unless national law provides that called-up capital be shown as an asset under A).
6. Prepayments and accrued income (unless national law provides for such items to be shown as an asset under E).
III. Investments
1. Shares in affiliated undertakings.
2. Own shares (with an indication of their nominal value or, in the absence of a nominal value, their accounting par value) to the extent that national law permits their being shown in the balance sheet.
3. Other investments.
IV. Cash at bank and in hand
E. Prepayments and accrued income
(unless national law provides for such items to be shown as an asset under D (II) (6)).
F. Loss for the financial year
(unless national law provides for it to be shown under A (VI) under 'Liabilities').
Liabilities
A. Capital and reserves
I. Subscribed capital (unless national law provides for called-up capital to be shown under this item. In that case, the amounts of subscribed capital and paid-up capital must be shown separately).
II. Share premium account
III. Revaluation reserve
IV. Reserves
1. Legal reserve, in so far as national law requires such a reserve.
2. Reserve for own shares, in so far as national law requires such a reserve, without prejudice to Article 22 (1) (b) of Directive 77/91/EEC.
3. Reserves provided for by the articles of association.
4. Other reserves.
V. Profit or loss brought forward
VI. Profit or loss for the financial year
(unless national law requires that this item be shown under F under 'Assets' or under E under 'Liabilities').
B. Provisions
1. Provisions for pensions and similar obligations.
2. Provisions for taxation.
3. Other provisions.
C. Creditors
(Amounts becoming due and payable within one year and amounts becoming due and payable after more than one year must be shown
separately for each item and for the aggregate of these items.)
1. Debenture loans, showing convertible loans separately.
2. Amounts owed to credit institutions.
3. Payments received on account of orders in so far as they are not shown separately as deductions from stocks.
4. Trade creditors.
5. Bills of exchange payable.
6. Amounts owed to affiliated undertakings.
7. Amounts owed to undertakings with which the company is linked by virtue of participating interests.
8. Other creditors including tax and social security.
9. Accruals and deferred income (unless national law provides for such items to be shown under D under 'Liabilities').
D. Accruals and deferred income

Part VIII. European Company Law

(unless national law provides for such items to be shown under C (9) under 'Liabilities').
E. Profit for the financial year
(unless national law provides for it to be shown under A (VI) under 'Liabilities').

Article 10. A. Subscribed capital unpaid of which there has been called (unless national law provides that called-up capital be shown under
L. In that case, the part of the capital called but not yet paid must appear either under A or under D (11) (5)).
B. Formation expenses
as defined by national law, and in so far as national law permits their being shown as an asset. National law may also provide for formation expenses to be shown as the first item under 'Intangible assets'.
C. Fixed assets
I. Intangible assets
1. Costs of research and development, in so far as national law permits their being shown as assets.
2. Concessions, patents, licences, trade marks and similar rights and assets, if they were:
(a) acquired for valuable consideration and need not be shown under C (I) (3); or
(b) created by the undertaking itself, in so far as national law permits their being shown as assets.
3. Goodwill, to the extent that it was acquired for valuable consideration.
4. Payments on account.
II. Tangible assets
1. Land and buildings.
2. Plant and machinery.
3. Other fixtures and fittings, tools and equipment.
4. Payments on account and tangible assets in course of construction.
III. Financial assets
1. Shares in affiliated undertakings.
2. Loans to affiliated undertakings.
3. Participating interests.
4. Loans to undertakings with which the company is linked by virtue of participating interests.
5. Investments held as fixed assets.
6. Other loans.
7. Own shares (with an indication of their nominal value or, in the absence of a nominal value, their accounting par value)
to the extent that national law permits their being shown in the balance sheet.
D. Current assets
I. Stocks
1. Raw materials and consumables.
2. Work in progress.
3. Finished goods and goods for resale.
4. Payments on account.
II. Debtors
(Amounts becoming due and payable after more than one year must be shown separately for each item.)
1. Trade debtors.
2. Amounts owed by affiliated undertakings.
3. Amounts owed by undertakings with which the company is linked by virtue of participating interests.
4. Other debtors.
5. Subscribed capital called but not paid (unless national law provides that called-up capital be shown under A).
6. Prepayments and accrued income (unless national law provides that such items be shown under E).
III. Investments
1. Shares in affiliated undertakings.
2. Own shares (with an indication of their nominal value or, in the absence of a nominal value, their accounting par value)
to the extent that national law permits their being shown in the balance sheet.
3. Other investments.
IV. Cash at bank and in hand.
E. Prepayments and accrued income
(unless national law provides for such items to be shown under D (II) (6)).
F. Creditors: amounts be coming due and payable within one year
1. Debenture loans, showing convertible loans separately.

2. Amounts owed to credit institutions.
3. Payments received on account of orders in so far as they are not shown separately as deductions from stocks.
4. Trade creditors.
5. Bills of exchange payable.
6. Amounts owed to affiliated undertakings.
7. Amounts owed to undertakings with which the company is linked by virtue of participating interests.
8. Other creditors including tax and social security.
9. Accruals and deferred income (unless national law provides for such items to be shown under K).
G. Net current assets/liabilities (taking into account prepayments and accrued income when shown under E and accruals and deferred income when shown under K).
H. Total assets less current liabilities
I. Creditors: amounts becoming due and payable after more than one year
1. Debenture loans, showing convertible loans separately.
2. Amounts owed to credit institutions.
3. Payments received on account of orders in so far as they are not shown separately as deductions from stocks.
4. Trade creditors.
5. Bills of exchange payable.
6. Amounts owed to affiliated undertakings.
7. Amounts owed to undertakings with which the company is linked by virtue of participating interests.
8. Other creditors including tax and social security.
9. Accruals and deferred income (unless national law provides for such items to be shown under K).
J. Provisions
1. Provisions for pensions and similar obligations.
2. Provisions for taxation.
3. Other provisions.
K. Accruals and deferred income
(unless national law provides for such items to be shown under F (9) or I (9) or both).
L. Capital and reserves
I. Subscribed capital (unless national law provides for called-up capital to be shown under this item. In that case, the amounts of subscribed capital and paid-up capital must be shown separately).
II. Share premium account
III. Revaluation reserve
IV. Reserves
1. Legal reserve, in so far as national law requires such a reserve.
2. Reserve for own shares, in so far as national law requires such a reserve, without prejudice to Article 22 (1) (b) of Directive 77/91/EEC.
3. Reserves provided for by the articles of association.
4. Other reserves.
V. Profit or loss brought forward
VI. Profit or loss for the financial year

Article 10a. Instead of the presentation of balance sheet items in accordance with Articles 9 and 10, Member States may permit or require companies, or certain classes of company, to present those items on the basis of a distinction between current and non-current items provided that the information given is at least equivalent to that otherwise required by Articles 9 and 10.

Article 11. The Member States may permit companies which on their balance sheet dates do not exceed the limits of two of the three following criteria:
— balance sheet total: EUR 4 400 000,
— net turnover: EUR 8 800 000,
— average number of employees during the financial year: 50
to draw up abridged balance sheets showing only those items preceded by letters and roman numerals in Articles 9 and 10, disclosing separately the information required in brackets in D (II) under 'Assets' and C under 'Liabilities' in Article 9 and in D (II) in Article 10, but in total for each.
Member States may waive the application of Article 15 (3) (a) and (4) to the abridged balance sheet. In the case of those Member States which have not adopted the euro, the amount in national currency equivalent to the amounts specified in the first paragraph shall be that obtained by applying the exchange rate published in the Official Journal of the European Union on the date of the entry into force of any Directive setting those amounts.

Article 12. 1. Where on its balance sheet date, a company exceeds or ceases to exceed the limits of two of the three criteria indicated in Article 11, that fact shall affect the application of the derogation provided for in that Article only if it occurs in two consecutive financial years.
2. For the purposes of translation into national currencies, the amounts in European units of account specified in Article 11 may be increased by not more than 10 %.
3. The balance sheet total referred to in Article 11 shall consist of the assets in A to E under 'Assets' in the layout prescribed in Article 9 or those in A to E in the layout prescribed in Article 10.

Article 13. 1. Where an asset or liability relates to more than one layout item, its relationship to other items must be disclosed either under the item where it appears or in the notes on the accounts, if such disclosure is essential to the comprehension of the annual accounts.
2. Own shares and shares in affiliated undertakings may be shown only under the items prescribed for that purpose.

Article 14. All commitments by way of guarantee of any kind must, if there is no obligation to show them as liabilities, be clearly set out at the foot of the balance sheet or in the notes on the accounts, and a distinction made between the various types of guarantee which national law recognizes; specific disclosure must be made of any valuable security which has been provided. Commitments of this kind existing in respect of affiliated undertakings must be shown separately.

Section IV. Special provisions relating to certain balance sheet items

Article 15. 1. Whether particular assets are to be shown as fixed assets or current assets shall depend upon the purpose for which they are intended.
2. Fixed assets shall comprise those assets which are intended for use on a continuing basis for the purposes of the undertaking's activities.
3. (a) Movements in the various fixed asset items shall be shown in the balance sheet or in the notes on the accounts. To this end there shall be shown separately, starting with the purchase price or production cost, for each fixed asset item, on the one hand, the additions, disposals and transfers during the financial year and, on the other, the cumulative value adjustments at the balance sheet date and the rectifications made during the financial year to the value adjustments of previous financial years. Value adjustments shall be shown either in the balance sheet, as clear deductions from the relevant items, or in the notes on the accounts.
(b)If, when annual accounts are drawn up in accordance with this Directive for the first time, the purchase price or production cost of a fixed asset cannot be determined without undue expense or delay, the residual value at the beginning of the financial year may be treated as the purchase price or production cost. Any application of this provision must be disclosed in the notes on the accounts.
(c)Where Article 33 is applied, the movements in the various fixed asset items referred to in subparagraph (a) of this paragraph shall be shown starting with the purchase price or production cost resulting from revaluation.
4. Paragraph 3 (a) and (b) shall apply to the presentation of 'Formation expenses'.

Article 16. Rights to immovables and other similar rights as defined by national law must be shown under 'Land and buildings'.

Article 17. For the purposes of this Directive, participating interest shall mean rights in the capital of other undertakings, whether or not represented by certificates, which, by creating a durable link with those undertakings, are intended to contribute to the company's activities. The holding of part of the capital of another company shall be presumed to constitute a participating interest where it exceeds a percentage fixed by the Member States which may not exceed 20 %.

Article 18. Expenditure incurred during the financial year but relating to a subsequent financial year, together with any income which, though relating to the financial year in question, is not due until after its expiry must be shown under 'Prepayments and accrued income'. The Member States may, however, provide that such income shall be included in 'Debtors'. Where such income is material, it must be disclosed in the notes on the accounts.

Article 19. Value adjustments shall comprise all adjustments intended to take account of reductions in the values of individual assets established at the balance sheet date whether that reduction is final or not.

Article 20. 1. Provisions are intended to cover liabilities the nature of which is clearly defined and which at the date of the balance sheet are either likely to be incurred, or certain to be incurred but uncertain as to amount or as to the date on which they will arise.
2. The Member States may also authorize the creation of provisions intended to cover charges which have their origin in the financial year under review or in a previous financial year, the nature of which is clearly defined and which at the date of the balance sheet are either likely to be incurred, or certain to be incurred but uncertain as to amount or as to the date on which they will arise.
3. Provisions may not be used to adjust the values of assets.

Article 21. Income receivable before the balance sheet date but relating to a subsequent financial year, together with any charges which, though relating to the financial year in question, will be paid only in the course of a subsequent financial year, must be shown under 'Accruals and deferred income'. The Member States may, however, provide that such charges shall be included in 'Creditors'. Where such charges are material, they must be disclosed in the notes on the accounts.

Section V. Layout of the profit and loss account

Article 22. For the presentation of the profit and loss account, the Member States shall prescribe one or more of the layouts provided for in Articles 23 to 26. If a Member State prescribes more than one layout, it may allow companies to choose from among them.
By way of derogation from Article 2(1), Member States may permit or require all companies, or any classes of company, to present a statement of their performance instead of the presentation of profit and loss items in accordance with Articles 23 to 26, provided that the information given is at least equivalent to that otherwise required by those Articles.

Article 23. 1. Net turnover.
2. Variation in stocks of finished goods and in work in progress.
3. Work performed by the undertaking for its own purposes and capitalized.
4. Other operating income.
5. (a) Raw materials and consumables.
(b) Other external charges.
6. Staff costs:
(a) wages and salaries;
(b) social security costs, with a separate indication of those relating to pensions.
7. (a) Value adjustments in respect of formation expenses and of tangible and intangible fixed assets.
(b) Value adjustments in respect of current assets, to the extent that they exceed the amount of value adjustments which are normal
in the undertaking concerned.
8. Other operating charges.
9. Income from participating interests, with a separate indication of that derived from affiliated undertakings.
10. Income from other investments and loans forming part of the fixed assets, with a separate indication of that derived from affiliated
undertakings.
11. Other interest receivable and similar income, with a separate indication of that derived from affiliated undertakings.
12. Value adjustments in respect of financial assets and of investments held as current assets.
13. Interest payable and similar charges, with a separate indication of those concerning affiliated undertakings.
14. Tax on profit or loss on ordinary activities.
15. Profit or loss on ordinary activities after taxation.
16. Extraordinary income.
17. Extraordinary charges.
18. Extraordinary profit or loss.
19. Tax on extraordinary profit or loss.
20. Other taxes not shown under the above items.
21. Profit or loss for the financial year.

Article 24. A. Charges.
1. Reduction in stocks of finished goods and in work in progress:

2. (a) raw materials and consumables;
(b) other external charges.
3. Staff costs:
(a) wages and salaries;
(b) social security costs, with a separate indication of those relating to pensions.
4. (a) Value adjustments in respect of formation expenses and of tangible and intangible fixed assets.
(b) Value adjustments in respect of current assets, to the extent that they exceed the amount of value adjustments which are normal in the undertaking concerned.
5. Other operating charges.
6. Value adjustments in respect of financial assets and of investments held as current assets.
7. Interest payable and similar charges, with a separate indication of those concerning affiliated undertakings.
8. Tax on profit or loss on ordinary activities.
9. Profit or loss on ordinary activities after taxation.
10. Extraordinary charges.
11. Tax on extraordinary profit or loss.
12. Other taxes not shown under the above items.
13. Profit or loss for the financial year.
B. Income
1. Net turnover.
2. Increase in stocks of finished goods and in work in progress.
3. Work performed by the undertaking for its own purposes and capitalized.
4. Other operating income.
5. Income from participating interests, with a sepa-rate indication of that derived from affiliated undertakings.
6. Income from other investments and loans forming part of the fixed assets, with a separate indication of that derived from affiliated undertakings.
7. Other interest receivable and similar income, with a separate indication of that derived from affiliated undertakings.
8. Profit or loss on ordinary activities after taxation.
9. Extraordinary income.
10. Profit or loss for the financial year.

Article 25. 1. Net turnover.
2. Cost of sales (including value adjustments).
3. Gross profit or loss.
4. Distribution costs (including value adjustments).
5. Administrative expenses (including value adjustments).
6. Other operating income.
7. Income from participating interests, with a separate indication of that derived from affiliated undertakings.
8. Income from other investments and loans forming part of the fixed assets, with a separate indication of that derived from affiliated
undertakings.
9. Other interest receivable and similar income with a separate indication of that derived from affiliated undertakings.
10. Value adjustments in respect of financial assets and of investments held as current assets.
11. Interest payable and similar charges, with a separate indication of those concerning affiliated undertakings.
12. Tax on profit or loss on ordinary activities.
13. Profit or loss on ordinary activities after taxation.
14. Extraordinary income.
15. Extraordinary charges.
16. Extraordinary profit or loss.
17. Tax on extraordinary profit or loss.
18. Other taxes not shown under the above items.
19. Profit or loss for the financial year.

Article 26. A. Charges
1. Cost of sales (including value adjustments).
2. Distribution costs (including value adjustments).
3. Administrative expenses (including value adjustments).

4. Value adjustments in respect of financial assets and of investments held as current assets.
5. Interest payable and similar charges, with a separate indication of those concerning affiliated undertakings.
6. Tax on profit or loss on ordinary activities.
7. Profit or loss on ordinary activities after taxation.
8. Extraordinary charges.
9. Tax on extraordinary profit or loss.
10. Other taxes not shown under the above items.
11. Profit or loss for the financial year.
B. Income
1. Net turnover.
2. Other operating income.
3. Income from participating interests, with a separate indication of that derived from affiliated undertakings.
4. Income from other investments and loans forming part of the fixed assets, with a separate indication of that derived from affiliated undertakings.
5. Other interest receivable and similar income with a separate indication of that derived from affiliated undertakings.
6. Profit or loss on ordinary activities after taxation.
7. Extraordinary income.
8. Profit or loss for the financial year.

Article 27. The Member States may permit companies which on their balance sheet dates do not exceed the limits of two of the three following criteria:
— balance sheet total: EUR 17 500 000,
— net turnover: EUR 35 000 000,
— average number of employees during the financial year: 250 to adopt layouts different from those prescribed in Articles 23 to 26
within the following limits:
(a) in Article 23: 1 to 5 inclusive may be combined under one item called 'Gross profit or loss';
(b) in Article 24: A (1), A (2) and B (1) to B (4) inclu-sive may be combined under one item called 'Gross profit or loss';
(c) in Article 25: (1), (2), (3) and (6) may be combined under one item called 'Gross profit or loss';
(d) in Article 26, A (1), B (1) and B (2) may be combined under one item called 'Gross profit or loss'. Article 12 shall apply.
In the case of those Member States which have not adopted the euro, the amount in national currency equivalent to the amounts specified in the first paragraph shall be that obtained by applying the exchange rate published in the Official Journal of the European Union on the date of the entry into force of any Directive setting those amounts.

Section VI. Special provisions relating to certain items in the profit and loss account

Article 28. The net turnover shall comprise the amounts derived from the sale of products and the provision of services falling within the company's ordinary activities, after deduction of sales rebates and of value added tax and other taxes directly linked to the turnover.

Article 29. 1. Income and charges that arise otherwise than in the course of the company's ordinary activities must be shown under 'Extraordinary income and extraordinary charges'.
2. Unless the income and charges referred to in paragraph 1 are immaterial for the assessment of the results, explanations of their amount and nature must be given in the notes on the accounts. The same shall apply to income and charges relating to another financial year.

Article 30. The Member States may permit taxes on the profit or loss on ordinary activities and taxes on the extraordinary profit or loss to be shown in total as one item in the profit and loss account before 'Other taxes not shown under the above items'. In that case, 'Profit or loss on ordinary activities after taxation' shall be omitted from the layouts prescribed in Articles 23 to 26.
Where this derogation is applied, companies must disclose in the notes on the accounts the extent to which the taxes on the profit or loss affect the profit or loss on ordinary activities and the 'Extraordinary profit or loss'.

Section VII. Valuation rules

Article 31. 1. The Member States shall ensure that the items shown in the annual accounts are valued in accordance with the following general principles:
(a) the company must be presumed to be carrying on its business as a going concern;
(b) the methods of valuation must be applied consistently from one financial year to another;
(c) valuation must be made on a prudent basis, and in particular:
(aa) only profits made at the balance sheet date may be included,
 (bb) account must be taken of all liabilities arising in the course of the financial year concerned or of a previous one, even if such
liabilities become apparent only between the date of the balance sheet and the date on which it is drawn up,
(cc) account must be taken of all depreciation, whether the result of the financial year is a loss or a profit;
(d) account must be taken of income and charges relating to the financial year, irrespective of the date of receipt or payment of
such income or charges;
(e) the components of asset and liability items must be valued separately;
(f) the opening balance sheet for each financial year must correspond to the closing balance sheet for the preceding financial year.
1a. In addition to those amounts recorded pursuant to paragraph
(1)(c)(bb), Member States may permit or require account to be taken of all foreseeable liabilities and potential losses arising in the course of the financial year concerned or of a previous one, even if such liabilities or losses become apparent only between the date of the balance sheet and the date on which it is drawn up.
2. Departures from these general principles shall be permitted in exceptional cases. Any such departures must be disclosed in the notes
on the accounts and the reasons for them given together with an assessment of their effect on the assets, liabilities, financial position
and profit or loss.

Article 32. The items shown in the annual accounts shall be valued in accordance with Articles 34 to 42, which are based on the principle of purchase price or production cost.

Article 33. 1. The Member States may declare to the Commission that they reserve the power, by way of derogation from Article 32 and pending subsequent coordination, to permit or require in respect of all companies or any classes of companies:
(a) valuation by the replacement value method for tangible fixed assets with limited useful economic lives and for stocks;
(b) valuation by methods other than that provided for in (a) which are designed to take account of inflation for the items shown in annual accounts, including capital and reserves;
(c) revaluation of fixed assets.
Where national law provides for valuation methods as indicated in (a), (b) and (c), it must define their content and limits and the rules for their application. The application of any such method, the balance sheet and profit and loss account items concerned and the method by which the values shown are calculated shall be disclosed in the notes on the accounts.
2. (a) Where paragraph 1 is applied, the amount of the difference between valuation by the method used and valuation in accordance with the general rule laid down in Article 32 must be entered in the revaluation reserve under 'Liabilities'. The treatment of this item for taxation purposes must be explained either in the balance sheet or in the notes on the accounts. For purposes of the application of the last subparagraph of paragraph 1, companies shall, whenever the amount of the reserve has been changed in the course of the financial year, publish in the notes on the accounts inter alia a table showing:
— the amount of the revaluation reserve at the beginning of the financial year,
— the revaluation differences transferred to the revaluation reserve during the financial year,
— the amounts capitalized or otherwise transferred from the revaluation reserve during the financial year, the nature of any such transfer being diclosed,
— the amount of the revaluation reserve at the end of the financial year.
(b) The revaluation reserve may be capitalized in whole or in part at any time.
(c) The revaluation reserve must be reduced to the extent that the amounts transferred thereto are no longer necessary for the implementation of the valuation method used and the achievement of its purpose. The Member States may lay down rules governing the application of the revaluation reserve, provided that transfers to the profit

and loss account from the revaluation reserve may be made only to the extent that the amounts transferred have been entered as charges in the profit and loss account or reflect increases in value which have been actually realized. These amounts must be disclosed separately in the profit and loss account. No part of the revaluation reserve may be distributed, either directly or indirectly, unless it represents gains actually realized.
(d) Save as provided under (b) and (c) the revaluation reserve may not be reduced.
3. Value adjustments shall be calculated each year on the basis of the value adopted for the financial year in question, save that by way of derogation from Articles 4 and 22, the Member States may permit or require that only the amount of the value adjustments arising as a result of the application of the general rule laid down in Article 32 be shown under the relevant items in the layouts prescribed in Articles 23 to 26 and that the difference arising as a result of the valuation method adopted under this Article be shown separately in the layouts. Furthermore, Articles 34 to 42 shall apply mutatis mutandis.
4. Where paragraph 1 is applied, the following must be disclosed, either in the balance sheet or in the notes on the accounts, separately for each balance sheet item as provided for in the layouts prescribed in Articles 9 and 10, except for stocks, either:
(a) the amount at the balance sheet date of the valuation made in accordance with the general rule laid down in Article 32 and the amount of the cumulative value adjustments; or
(b) the amount at the balance sheet date of the difference between the valuation made in accordance with this Article and that resulting from the application of Article 32 and, where appropriate, the cumulative amount of the additional value adjustments.
5. Without prejudice to Article 52 the Council shall, on a proposal from the Commission and within seven years of the notification of this Directive, examine and, where necessary, amend this Article in the light of economic and monetary trends in the Community.

Article 34. 1. (a) Where national law authorizes the inclusion of formation expenses under 'Assets', they must be written off within a maximum period of five years.
(b) In so far as formation expenses have not been completely written off, no distribution of profits shall take place unless the amount of the reserves available for distribution and profits brought forward is at least equal to that of the expenses not written off.
2. The amounts entered under 'Formation expenses' must be explained in the notes on the accounts.

Article 35. 1. (a) Fixed assets must be valued at purchase price or production cost, without prejudice to (b) and (c) below.
(b) The purchase price or production cost of fixed assets with limited useful economic lives must be reduced by value adjustments calculated to write off the value of such assets systematically over their useful economic lives.
(c) (aa) Value adjustments may be made in respect of financial fixed assets, so that they are valued at the lower figure to be attributed to them at the balance sheet date.
(bb) Value adjustments must be made in respect of fixed assets, whether their useful economic lives are limited or not, so that they are valued at the lower figure to be attributed to them at the balance sheet date if it is expected that the reduction in their value will be permanent.
(cc) The value adjustments referred to in (aa) and (bb) must be charget to the profit and loss account and disclosed separately in the notes on the accounts if they have not been shown separately in the profit and loss account.
(dd) Valuation at the lower of the values provided for in (aa) and (bb) may not be continued if the reasons for which the value adjustments were made have ceased to apply.
(d) If fixed assets are the subject of exceptional value adjustments for taxation purposes alone, the amount of the adjustments and the reasons for making them shall be indicated in the notes on the accounts.
2. The purchase price shall be calculated by adding to the price paid the expenses incidental thereto.
3. (a) The production cost shall be calculated by adding to the purchasing price of the raw materials and consumables the costs directly attributable to the product in question.
(b) A reasonable proportion of the costs which are only indirectly attributable to the product in question may be added into the production costs to the extent that they relate to the period of production.
4. Interest on capital borrowed to finance the production of fixed assets may be included in the production costs to the extent that it relates to the period of production. In that event, the inclusion of such interest under 'Assets' must be disclosed in the notes on the accounts.

Article 36. By way of derogation from Article 35 (1) (c) (cc), the Member States may allow investment companies within the meaning of Article 5 (2) to set off value adjustments to investments directly against 'Capital and reserves'. The amounts in question must be shown separately under 'Liabilities' in the balance sheet.

Article 37. 1. Article 34 shall apply to costs of research and development. In exceptional cases, however, the Member States may permit derogations from Article 34 (1) (a). In that case, they may also provide for derogations from Article 34 (1) (b). Such derogations and the reasons for them must be disclosed in the notes on the accounts.
2. Article 34 (1) (a) shall apply to goodwill. The Member States may, however, permit companies to write goodwill off systematically over a limited period exceeding five years provided that this period does not exceed the useful economic life of the asset and is disclosed in the notes on the accounts together with the supporting reasons therefore.

Article 38. Tangible fixed assets, raw materials and consumables which are constantly being replaced and the overall value of which is of secondary importance to the undertaking may be shown under 'Assets' at a fixed quantity and value, if the quantity, value and composition thereof do not vary materially.

Article 39. 1. (a) Current assets must be valued at purchase price or production cost, without prejudice to (b) and (c) below.
(b) Value adjustments shall be made in respect of current assets with a view to showing them at the lower market value or, in particular circumstances, another lower value to be attributed to them at the balance sheet date.
(c) The Member States may permit exceptional value adjustments where, on the basis of a reasonable commercial assessment, these are necessary if the valuation of these items is not to be modified in the near future because of fluctuations in value. The amount of these value adjustments must be disclosed separately in the profit and loss account or in the notes on the accounts.
(d) Valuation at the lower value provided for in (b) and (c) may not be continued if the reasons for which the value adjustments were made have ceased to apply.
(e) If current assets are the subject of exceptional value adjustments for taxation purposes alone, the amount of the adjustments and the reasons for making them must be disclosed in the notes on the accounts.
2. The definitions of purchase price and of production cost given in Article 35 (2) and (3) shall apply. The Member States may also apply Article 35 (4). Distribution costs may not be included in production costs.

Article 40. 1. The Member States may permit the purchase price or production cost of stocks of goods of the same category and all fungible items including investments to be calculated either on the basis of weighted average prices or by the 'first in, first out' (FIFO) method, the 'last in, first out' (LIFO) method, or some similar method.
2. Where the value shown in the balance sheet, following application of the methods of calculation specified in paragraph 1, differs materially, at the balance sheet date, from the value on the basis of the last known market value prior to the balance sheet date, the amount of that difference must be disclosed in total by category in the notes on the accounts.

Article 41. 1. Where the amount repayable on account of any debt is greater than the amount received, the difference may be shown as an asset. It must be shown separately in the ba-lance sheet or in the notes on the accounts.
2. The amount of this difference must be written off by a reasonable amount each year and completely written off no later than the time of repayment of the debt.

Article 42. Provisions may not exceed in amount the sums which are necessary. The provisions shown in the balance sheet under 'Other provisions' must be disclosed in the notes on the accounts if they are material.

Section VIIa. Valuation at fair value

Article 42a. 1. By way of derogation from Article 32 and subject to the conditions set out in paragraphs 2 to 4 of this Article, Member States shall permit or require in respect of all companies or any classes of companies valuation at fair value of financial instruments, including derivatives. Such permission or requirement may be restricted to consolidated accounts as defined in Directive 83/349/EEC.
2. For the purpose of this Directive commodity-based contracts that give either contracting party the right to settle in cash or some other financial instrument shall be considered to be derivative financial instruments, except when:
(a) they were entered into and continue to meet the company's expected purchase, sale or usage requirements;
(b) they were designated for such purpose at their inception; and
(c) they are expected to be settled by delivery of the commodity.
3. Paragraph 1 shall apply only to liabilities that are:
(a) held as part of a trading portfolio; or
(b) derivative financial instruments.

4. Valuation according to paragraph 1 shall not apply to:
(a) to non-derivative financial instruments held to maturity;
(b) to loans and receivables originated by the company and not held for trading purposes; and
(c) to interests in subsidiaries, associated undertakings and joint ventures, equity instruments issued by the company, contracts for contingent consideration in a business combination as well as other financial instruments with such special characteristics that the instruments, according to what is generally accepted, should be accounted for differently from other financial instruments.
5. By way of derogation from Article 32, Member States may in respect of any assets and liabilities which qualify as hedged items under a fair value hedge accounting system, or identified portions of such assets or liabilities, permit valuation at the specific amount required under that system.
5a. By way of derogation from the provisions of paragraphs 3 and 4, Member States may, in accordance with international accounting standards as adopted by Commission Regulation (EC) No 1725/2003 of 29 September 2003 adopting certain international accounting standards in accordance with Regulation (EC) No 1606/2002 of the European Parliament and of the Council, as amended until 5 September 2006, permit or require valuation of financial instruments, together with the associated disclosure requirements which are provided for in international accounting standards adopted in accordance with Regulation (EC) No 1606/2002 of the European Parliament and of the Council of 19 July 2002 on the application of international accounting standards.

Article 42b. 1. The fair value referred to in Article 42a shall be determined by reference to:
(a) a market value, for those financial instruments for which a reliable market can readily be identified. Where a market value is not readily identifiable for an instrument but can be identified for its components of for a similar instrument, the market value may be derived from that of its components or of the similar instrument; or
(b) a value resulting from generally accepted valuation models and techniques, for those instruments for which a reliable market cannot be readily identified. Such valuation models and techniques shall ensure a reasonable approximation of the market value.
2. Those financial instruments that cannot be measured reliably by any of the methods described in paragraph 1, shall be measured in accordance with Articles 34 to 42.

Article 42c. 1. Notwithstanding Article 31(1)(c), where a financial instrument is valued in accordance with Article 42b, a change in the value shall be included in the profit and loss account. However, such a change shall be included directly in equity, in a fair value reserve, where:
(a) the instrument accounted for is a hedging instrument under a system of hedge accounting that allows some or all of the change in value not to be shown in the profit and loss account; or
(b) the change in value relates to an exchange difference arising on a monetary item that forms part of a company's net investment in a foreign entity.
2. Member States may permit or require a change in the value on an available for sale financial asset, other than a derivative financial instrument, to be included directly in equity, in the fair value reserve.
3. The fair value reserve shall be adjusted when amounts shown therein are no longer necessary for the implementation of paragraphs 1 and 2.

Article 42d. Where valuation at fair value of financial instruments has been applied, the notes on the accounts shall disclose:
(a) the significant assumptions underlying the valuation models and techniques where fair values have been determined in accordance with Article 42b(1)(b);
(b) per category of financial instruments, the fair value, the changes in value included directly in the profit and loss account as well as changes included in the fair value reserve;
(c) for each class of derivative financial instruments, information about the extent and the nature of the instruments, including significant terms and conditions that may affect the amount, timing and certainty of future cash flows; and
(d) a table showing movements in the fair value reserve during the financial year.

Article 42e. By way of derogation from Article 32, Member States may permit or require in respect of all companies or any classes of company the valuation of specified categories of assets other than financial instruments at amounts determined by reference to fair value.
Such permission or requirement may be restricted to consolidated accounts as defined in Directive 83/349/EEC.

PART VIII. EUROPEAN COMPANY LAW

Article 42f. Notwithstanding Article 31(1)(c), Member States may permit or require in respect of all companies or any classes of company that, where an asset is valued in accordance with Article 42e, a change in the value is included in the profit and loss account.

Section VIII. Contents of the notes on the accounts

Article 43. 1. In addition to the information required under other provisions of this Directive, the notes on the accounts must set out information in respect of the following matters at least:
(1) the valuation methods applied to the various items in the annual accounts, and the methods employed in calculating the value adjustments. For items included in the annual accounts which are or were originally expressed in foreign currency, the bases of conversion used to express them in local currency must be disclosed;
(2) the name and registered office of each of the undertakings in which the company, either itself or through a person acting in his own name but on the company's behalf, holds at least a percentage of the capital which the Member States cannot fix at more than 20 %, showing the proportion of the capital held, the amount of capital and reserves, and the profit or loss for the latest financial year of the undertaking concerned for which accounts have been adopted. This information may be omitted where for the purposes of Article 2 (3) it is of negligible importance only. The information concerning capital and reserves and the profit or loss may also be omitted where the undertaking concerned does not publish its balance sheet and less than 50 % of its capital is held (directly or irdirectly) by the company; the name, the head or registered office and the legal form of each of the undertakings of which the company or firm is a member having unlimited liability. This information may be omitted where for the purposes of Article 2 (3) it is of negligible importance only;
(3) the number and the nominal value or, in the absence of a nominal value, the accounting par value of the shares subscribed during the financial year within the limits of an authorized capital, without prejudice as far as the amount of this capital is concerned to Article 2 (1) (e) of Directive 68/151/EEC or to Article 2 (c) of Directive 77/91/EEC;
(4) where there is more than one class of shares, the number and the nominal value or, in the absence of a nominal value, the accounting par value for each class;
(5) the existence of any participation certificates, convertible debentures or similar securities or rights, with an indication of their number and the rights they confer;
(6) amounts owed by the company becoming due and payable after more than five years as well as the company's entire debts covered by valuable security furnished by the company with an indication of the nature and form of the security. This information must be disclosed separately for each creditors item, as provided for in the layouts prescribed in Articles 9, 10 and 10a ;
(7) the total amount of any financial commitments that are not included in the balance sheet, in so far as this information is of assistance in assessing the financial position. Any commitments concerning pensions and affiliated undertakings must be disclosed separately;
(7a) the nature and business purpose of the company's arrangements that are not included in the balance sheet and the financial impact on the company of those arrangements, provided that the risks or benefits arising from such arrangements are material and in so far as the disclosure of such risks or benefits is necessary for assessing the financial position of the company. Member States may permit the companies referred to in Article 27 to limit the information required to be disclosed by this point to the nature and business purpose of such arrangements;
(7b) transactions which have been entered into with related parties by the company, including the amount of such transactions, the nature of the related party relationship and other information about the transactions necessary for an understanding of the financial position of the company, if such transactions are material and have not been concluded under normal market conditions. Information about individual transactions may be aggregated according to their nature except where separate information is necessary for an understanding of the effects of related party transactions on the financial position of the company. Member States may permit the companies referred to in Article 27 to omit the disclosures prescribed in this point unless those companies are of a type referred to in Article 1(1) of Directive 77/91/EEC, in which case Member States may limit disclosure to, as a minimum, transactions entered into directly or indirectly between:
(i) the company and its major shareholders, and
(ii) the company and the members of the administrative, management and supervisory bodies. Member States may exempt transactions entered into between two or more members of a group provided that subsidiaries which are party to the transaction are wholly owned by such a member. 'Related party' has the same meaning as in international accounting standards adopted in accordance with Regulation (EC) No 1606/2002;
(8) the net turnover within the meaning of Article 28, broken down by categories of activity and into geographical markets in so far as, taking account of the manner in which the sale of products and the provision of services

falling within the company's ordinary activities are organized, these categories and markets differ substantially from one another;
(9) the average number of persons employed during the financial year, broken down by categories and, if they are not disclosed separately in the profit and loss account, the staff costs relating to the financial year, broken down as provided for in Article 23 (6);
(10) the extent to which the calculation of the profit or loss for the financial year has been affected by a valuation of the items which, by way of derogation from the principles enunciated in Articles 31 and 34 to 42c , was made in the financial year in question or in an earlier financial year with a view to obtaining tax relief. Where the influence of such a valuation on future tax charges is material, details must be disclosed;
(11) the difference between the tax charged for the financial year and for earlier financial years and the amount of tax payable in respect of those years, provided that this difference is material for purposes of future taxation. This amount may also be disclosed in the balance sheet as a cumulative amount under a separate item with an appropriate heading;
(12) the amount of the emoluments granted in respect of the financial year to the members of the administrative, managerial and supervisory bodies by reason of their responsibilities, and any commitments arising or entered into in respect of retirement pensions for former members of those bodies, with an indication of the total for each category;
(13) the amount of advances and credits granted to the members of the administrative, managerial and supervisory bodies, with indications of the interest rates, main conditions and any amounts repaid, as well as commitments entered into on their behalf by way of guarantees of any kind, with an indication of the total for each category;
14. where valuation at fair value of financial instruments has not been applied in accordance with Section 7a:
(a) for each class of derivative financial instruments:
(i) the fair value of the instruments, if such a value can be determined by any of the methods prescribed in Article 42b(1);
(ii) information about the extent and the nature of the instruments; and
(b) for financial fixed assets covered by Article 42a, carried at an amount in excess of their fair value and without use being made of the option to make a value adjustment in accordance with Article 35(1)(c)(aa):
(i) the book value and the fair value of either the individual assets or appropriate groupings of those individual assets;
(ii) the reasons for not reducing the book value, including the nature of the evidence that provides the basis for the belief that the book value will be recovered;
(15) separately, the total fees for the financial year charged by the statutory auditor or audit firm for the statutory audit of annual accounts, the total fees charged for other assurance services, the total fees charged for tax advisory services and the total fees charged for other non-audit services. Member States may provide that this requirement shall not apply where the company is included within the consolidated accounts required to be drawn up under Article 1 of Directive 83/349/EEC, provided that such information is given in the notes to the consolidated accounts.
2. Pending subsequent coordination, the Member States need not apply paragraph 1 (2) to financial holding companies within the meaning of Article 5 (3).
3. Member States may waive the requirement to provide the information referred to in paragraph 1 point 12 where such information makes it possible to identify the position of a specific member of such a body.

Article 44. 1. Member States may permit the companies referred to in Article 11 to draw up abridged notes on their accounts without the information required in Article 43(1)(5) to (12), (14)(a) and (15). However, the notes must disclose the information specified in rticle 43(1)(6) in total for all the items concerned.
2. Member States may also permit the companies ref erred to in paragraph 1 to be exempted from the obligation to disclose in the notes on their accounts the information prescribed in Article 15 (3) (a) and (4), Articles 18, 21 and 29 (2), the second subparagraph of Article 30, Article 34 (2), Article 40 (2) and the second subparagraph of Article 42.
3. Article 12 shall apply.

Article 45. 1. The Member States may allow the disclosures prescribed in Article 43 (1) (2):
(a) to take the form of a statement deposited in accordance with Article 3 (1) and (2) of Directive 68/151/EEC; this must be disclosed in the notes on the accounts;
(b) to be omitted when their nature is such that they would be seriously prejudicial to any of the undertakings to which Article 43 (1) (2) relates. The Member States may make such omissions subject to prior administrative or judicial authorization. Any such omission must be disclosed in the notes on the accounts.

2. Paragraph 1(b) shall also apply to the information specified in Article 43(1)(8). The Member States may permit the companies referred to in Article 27 to omit disclosure of the information specified in Articles 34(2) and 43(1)(8). The Member States may also permit the companies referred to in Article 27 to omit disclosure of the information specified in Article 43(1)(15), provided that such information is delivered to the public oversight system referred to in Article 32 of Directive 2006/43/EC of the European Parliament and of the Council of 17 May 2006 on statutory audit of annual accounts and consolidated accounts when requested by such a public oversight system.

Section IX. Contents of the annual report

Article 46. 1. (a) The annual report shall include at least a fair review of the development and performance of the company's business and of its position, together with a description of the principal risks and uncertainties that it faces. The review shall be a balanced and comprehensive analysis of the development and performance of the company's business and of its position, consistent with the size and complexity of the business;
(b) To the extent necessary for an understanding of the company's development, performance or position, the analysis shall include both financial and, where appropriate, non-financial key performance indicators relevant to the particular business, including information relating to environmental and employee matters;
(c) In providing its analysis, the annual report shall, where appropriate, include references to and additional explanations of amounts reported in the annual accounts.
2. The report shall also give an indication of:
(a) any important events that have occurred since the end of the financial year;
(b) the company's likely future development;
(c) activities in the field of research and development;
(d) the information concerning acquisitions of own shares prescribed by Article 22 (2) of Directive 77/91/EEC.
(e) the existence of branches of the company;
(f) in relation to the company's use of financial instruments and where material for the assessment of its assets, liabilities, financial position and profit or loss,
— the company's financial risk management objectives and policies, including its policy for hedging each major type of forecasted transaction for which hedge accounting is used, and
— the company's exposure to price risk, credit risk, liquidity risk and cash flow risk.
3. Member States may waive the obligation on companies covered by Article 11 to prepare annual reports, provided that the information referred to in Article 22 (2) of Directive 77/91/EEC concerning the acquisition by a company of its own shares is given in the notes to their accounts.
4. Member States may choose to exempt companies covered by Article 27 from the obligation in paragraph 1(b) above in so far as it relates to non-financial information.

Article 46a. 1. A company whose securities are admitted to trading on a regulated market within the meaning of Article 4(1), point (14) of Directive 2004/39/EC of the European Parliament and of the Council of 21 April 2004 on markets in financial instruments shall include a corporate governance statement in its annual report. That statement shall be included as a specific section of the annual report and shall contain at least the following information:
(a) a reference to:
(i) the corporate governance code to which the company is subject, and/or
(ii) the corporate governance code which the company may have voluntarily decided to apply, and/or
(iii) all relevant information about the corporate governance practices applied beyond the requirements under national law.
Where points (i) and (ii) apply, the company shall also indicate where the relevant texts are publicly available; where point (iii) applies, the company shall make its corporate governance practices publicly available;
(b) to the extent to which a company, in accordance with national law, departs from a corporate governance code referred to under points (a)(i) or (ii), an explanation by the company as to which parts of the corporate governance code it departs from and the reasons for doing so.
Where the company has decided not to apply any provisions of a corporate governance code referred to under points (a)(i) or (ii), it shall explain its reasons for doing so;
(c) a description of the main features of the company's internal control and risk management systems in relation to the financial reporting process;
(d) the information required by Article 10(1), points (c), (d), (f), (h) and (i) of Directive 2004/25/EC of the European Parliament and of the Council of 21 April 2004 on takeover bids, where the company is subject to that Directive;

(e) unless the information is already fully provided for in national laws or regulations, the operation of the shareholder meeting and its key powers, and a description of shareholders' rights and how they can be exercised;
(f) the composition and operation of the administrative, management and supervisory bodies and their committees.
2. Member States may permit the information required by this Article to be set out in a separate report published together with the annual report in the manner set out in Article 47 or by means of a reference in the annual report where such document is publicly available on the company's website. In the event of a separate report, the corporate governance statement may contain a reference to the annual report where the information required in paragraph 1, point (d) is made available. Article 51(1), second subparagraph shall apply to the provisions of paragraph 1, points (c) and (d) of this Article. For the remaining information, the statutory auditor shall check that the corporate governance statement has been produced.
3. Member States may exempt companies which have only issued securities other than shares admitted to trading on a regulated market, within the meaning of Article 4(1), point (14) of Directive 2004/39/EC, from the application of the provisions of paragraph 1, points (a), (b), (e) and (f), unless such companies have issued shares which are traded in a multilateral trading facility, within the meaning of Article 4(1), point (15) of Directive 2004/39/EC.

Section X. Publication

Article 47 1. The annual accounts, duly approved, and the annual report, together with the opinion submitted by the person responsible for auditing the accounts, shall be published as laid down by the laws of each Member State in accordance with Article 3 of Directive 68/151/EEC. The laws of a Member State may, however, permit the annual report not to be published as stipulated above. It must be possible to obtain a copy of all or part of any such report upon request. The price of such a copy must not exceed its administrative cost.
1a. The Member State of a company or firm referred to in Article 1 (1), second and third subparagraphs (entity concerned) may exempt that entity from publishing its accounts in accordance with Article 3 of Directive 68/151/EEC, provided that those accounts are available to the public at its head office, where:
(a) all the members having unlimited liability of the entity concerned are the companies referred to in the first subparagraph of Article 1 (1) governed by the laws of Member States other than the Member State whose law governs that entity and none of those companies publishes the accounts of the entity concerned with its own accounts; or
(b) all the members having unlimited liability are companies which are not governed by the laws of a Member State but which have a legal form comparable to those referred to in Directive 68/151/EEC. Copies of the accounts must be obtainable upon request. The price of such a copy may not exceed its administrative cost. Appropriate sanctions must be provided for failure to comply with the publication obligation imposed in this paragraph.
2. By way of derogation from paragraph 1, the Member States may permit the companies referred to in Article 11 to publish:
(a) abridged balance sheets showing only those items preceded by letters and roman numerals in Articles 9 and 10, disclosing separately the information required in brackets in D (II) under 'Assets' and C under 'Liabilities' in Article 9 and in D (11) in Article 10, but in total for all the items concerned; and
(b) abridged notes on their accounts in accordance with Article 44. Article 12 shall apply. In addition, the Member States may relieve such companies from the obligation to publish their profit and loss accounts and annual reports and the opinions of the persons responsible for auditing the accounts.
3. The Member States may permit the companies mentioned in Article 27 to publish:
(a) abridged balance sheets showing only those items preceded by letters and roman numerals in Articles 9 and 10 disclosing separately, either in the balance sheet or in the notes on the accounts:
— C (I) (3), C (II) (1), (2), (3) and (4), C (III) (1), (2), (3), (4) and (7), D (II) (2), (3) and (6) and D (III) (1) and (2) under 'Assets' and C, (1), (2), (6), (7) and (9) under 'Liabilities in Article 9,
— C (I) (3), C (II) (1), (2), (3) and (4), C (III) (1), (2), (3), (4) and (7), D (II) (2), (3) and (6), D (III) (1) and (2), F (1), (2), (6), (7) and (9) and (I) (1), (2), (6), (7) and (9) in Article 10,
— the information required in brackets in D (II) under 'Assets' and C under 'Liabilities' in Article 9, in total for all the items concerned and separately for D (II) (2) and (3) under 'Assets' and C (1), (2), (6), (7) and (9) under 'Liabilities',
— the information required in brackets in D (11) in Article 10, in total for all the items concerned, and separately for D (II) (2) and (3); (b) abridged notes on their accounts without the information required in Article 43 (1) (5), (6), (8), (10) and (11). However, the notes on the accounts must give the information specified in Article 43 (1) (6) in total for all the items concerned.
This paragraph shall be without prejudice to paragraph 1 in so far as it relates to the profit and loss account, the annual report and the opinion of the person responsible for auditing the accounts.

Article 12 shall apply.

Article 48 .Whenever the annual accounts and the annual report are published in full, they must be reproduced in the form and text on the basis of which the person responsible for auditing the accounts has drawn up his opinion. They must be accompanied by the full text of his report.

Article 49. If the annual accounts are not published in full, it must be indicated that the version published is abridged and reference must be made to the register in which the accounts have been filed in accordance with Article 47 (1). Where such filing has not yet been effected, the fact must be disclosed. The report of the person or persons responsible for auditing the annual accounts (hereinafter: the statutory auditors) shall not accompany this publication, but it shall be disclosed whether an unqualified, qualified or adverse audit opinion was expressed, or whether the statutory auditors were unable to express an audit opinion. It shall also be disclosed whether the report of the statutory auditors included a reference to any matters to which the statutory auditors drew attention by way of emphasis without qualifying the audit opinion.

Article 50. The following must be published together with the annual accounts, and in like manner:
— the proposed appropriation of the profit or treatment of the loss,
— the appropriation of the profit or treatment of the loss, where these items do not appear in the annual accounts.

Article 50a. Annual accounts may be published in the currency in which they were drawn up and in ecus, translated at the exchange rate prevailing on the balance sheet date. That rate shall be disclosed in the notes on the accounts.

Section XA. Duty and liability for drawing up and publishing the annual accounts and the annual report

Article 50b. Member States shall ensure that the members of the administrative, management and supervisory bodies of the company have collectively the duty to ensure that the annual accounts, the annual report and, when provided separately, the corporate governance statement to be provided pursuant to Article 46a are drawn up and published in accordance with the requirements of this Directive and, where applicable, in accordance with the international accounting standards adopted in accordance with Regulation (EC) No 1606/2002. Such bodies shall act within the competences assigned to them by national law.

Article 50c. Member States shall ensure that their laws, regulations and administrative provisions on liability apply to the members of the administrative, management and supervisory bodies referred to in Article 50b, at least towards the company, for breach of the duty referred to in Article 50b.

Section XI. Auditing

Article 51. 1. The annual accounts of companies shall be audited by one or more persons approved by Member States to carry out statutory audits on the basis of the Eighth Council Directive 84/253/EEC of 10 April 1984 on the approval of persons responsible for carrying out the statutory audits of accounting documents. The statutory auditors shall also express an opinion concerning the consistency or otherwise of the annual report with the annual accounts for the same financial year.
2. The Member States may relieve the companies referred to in Article 11 from the obligation imposed by paragraph 1.
Article 12 shall apply.
3. Where the exemption provided for in paragraph 2 is granted the Member States shall introduce appropriate sanctions into their laws for cases in which the annual accounts or the annual reports of such companies are not drawn up in accordance with the requirements of this Directive.

Article 51a. 1. The report of the statutory auditors shall include:
(a) an introduction which shall at least identify the annual accounts that are the subject of the statutory audit, together with the financial reporting framework that has been applied in their preparation;
(b) a description of the scope of the statutory audit which shall at least identify the auditing standards in accordance with which the statutory audit was conducted;
(c) an audit opinion which shall state clearly the opinion of the statutory auditors as to whether the annual accounts give a true and fair view in accordance with the relevant financial reporting framework and, where appropriate, whether the annual accounts comply with statutory requirements; the audit opinion shall be either unqualified,

qualified, an adverse opinion or, if the statutory auditors are unable to express an audit opinion, a disclaimer of opinion;
(d) a reference to any matters to which the statutory auditors draw attention by way of emphasis without qualifying the audit opinion;
(e) an opinion concerning the consistency or otherwise of the annual report with the annual accounts for the same financial year.
2. The report shall be signed and dated by the statutory auditors.

Section XII. Final provisions

Article 52. 1. A Contact Committee shall be set up under the auspices of the Commission. Its function shall be:
(a) to facilitate, without prejudice to the provisions of Articles 169 and 170 of the Treaty, harmonized application of this Directive through regular meetings dealing in particular with practical problems arising in connection with its application;
(b) to advise the Commission, if necessary, on additions or amendments to this Directive.
2. The Contact Committee shall be composed of representatives of the Member States and representatives of the Commission. The chairman shall be a representative of the Commission. The Commission shall provide the secretariat.
3. The Committee shall be convened by the chairman either on his own initiative or at the request of one of its members.

Article 53. 2. Every five years the Council, acting on a proposal from the Commission, shall examine and, if need be, revise the amounts expressed in European units of account in this Directive, in the light of economic and monetary trends in the Community.

Article 53a. Member States shall not make available the exemptions set out in Articles 11, 27, 43(1), points (7a) and (7b), 46, 47 and 51 in the case of companies whose securities are admitted to trading on a regulated market within the meaning of Article 4(1), point (14) of Directive 2004/39/EC.

Article 55. 1. The Member States shall bring into force the laws, regulations and administrative provisions necessary for them to comply with this Directive within two years of its notification. They shall forthwith inform the Commission thereof.
2. The Member States may stipulate that the provisions referred to in paragraph 1 shall not apply until 18 months after the end of the period provided for in that paragraph. That period of 18 months may, however, be five years:
(a) in the case of unregistered companies in the United Kingdom and Ireland;
(b) for purposes of the application of Articles 9 and 10 and Articles 23 to 26 concerning the layouts for the balance sheet and the profit and loss account, where a Member State has brought other layouts for these documents into force not more than three years before the notification of this Directive;
(c) for purposes of the application of this Directive as regards the calculation and disclosure in balance sheets of depreciation relating to assets covered by the asset items mentioned in Article 9, C (II) (2) and (3), and Article 10, C (II) (2) and (3);
(d) for purposes of the application of Article 47 (1) of this Directive except as regards companies already under an obligation of publication under Article 2 (1) (f) of Directive 68/151/EEC. In this case the second subparagraph of Article 47 (1) of this Directive shall apply to the annual account and to the opinion drawn up by the person responsible for auditing the accounts;
(e) for purposes of the application of Article 51 (1) of this Directive. Furthermore, this period of 18 months may be extended to eight years for companies the principal object of which is shipping and which are already in existence on the entry into force of the provisions referred to in paragraph 1.
3. The Member States shall ensure that they communicate to the Commission the texts of the main provisions of national law which they adopt in the field covered by this Directive.

Article 56. 1. The obligation to show in annual accounts the items prescribed by Articles 9, 10, 10a and 23 to 26 which relate to affiliated undertakings, as defined by Article 41 of Directive 83/349/EEC, and the obligation to provide information concerning these undertakings in accordance with Articles 13 (2), and 14 and point 7 of Article 43 (1) shall enter into force on the date fixed in Article 49 (2) of that Directive.
2. The notes on the accounts must also disclose:
(a) the name and registered office of the undertaking which draws up the consolidated accounts of the largest body of undertakings of which the company forms part as a subsidiary undertaking;

(b) the name and registered office of the undertaking which draws up the consolidated accounts of the smallest body of undertakings of which the company forms part as a subsidiary undertaking and which is also included in the body of undertakings referred to in (a) above;
(c) the place where copies of the consolidated accounts referred to in (a) and (b) above may be obtained provided that they are available.

Article 57 Notwithstanding the provisions of Directives 68/151/EEC and 77/91/EEC, a Member State need not apply the provisions of this Directive concerning the content, auditing and publication of annual accounts to companies governed by their national laws which are subsidiary undertakings, as defined in Directive 83/349/EEC, where the following conditions are fulfilled:
(a) the parent undertaking must be subject to the laws of a Member State;
(b) all shareholders or members of the subsidiary undertaking must have declared their agreement to the exemption from such obligation; this declaration must be made in respect of every financial year;
(c) the parent undertaking must have declared that it guarantees the commitments entered into by the subsidiary undertaking;
(d) the declarations referred to in (b) and (c) must be published by the subsidiary undertaking as laid down by the laws of the Member State in accordance with Article 3 of Directive 68/151/EEC;
(e) the subsidiary undertaking must be included in the consolidated accounts drawn up by the parent undertaking in accordance with Directive 83/349/EEC;
(f) the above exemption must be disclosed in the notes on the consolidated accounts drawn up by the parent undertaking;
(g) the consolidated accounts referred to in (e), the consolidated annual report, and the report by the person responsible for auditing those accounts must be published for the subsidiary undertaking as laid down by the laws of the Member State in accordance with Article 3 of Directive 68/151/EEC.

Article 57a. 1. Member States may require the companies referred to in the first subparagraph of Article 1 (1) governed by their law, which are members having unlimited liability of any of the companies and firms listed in Article 1 (1), second and third subparagraphs (entity concerned), to draw up, have audited and publish, with their own accounts, the accounts of the entity concerned in conformity with the provisions of this Directive. In this case, the requirements of this Directive do not apply to the entity concerned.
2. Member States need not apply the requirements of this Directive to the entity concerned where:
(a) the accounts of this entity are drawn up, audited and published in conformity with the provisions of this Directive by a company which is a member having unlimited liability of the entity and is governed by the law of another Member State;
(b) the entity concerned is included in consolidated accounts drawn up, audited and published in accordance with Directive 83/349/EEC by a member having unlimited liability or where the entity concerned is included in the consolidated accounts of a larger body of undertakings drawn up, audited and published in conformity with Council Directive 83/349/EEC by a parent undertaking governed by the law of a Member State. The exemption must be disclosed in the notes on the consolidated accounts.
3. In these cases, the entity concerned must reveal to whomsoever so requests the name of the entity publishing the accounts.

Article 58. A Member State need not apply the provisions of this Directive concerning the auditing and publication of the profit-and-loss account to companies governed by their national laws which are parent undertakings for the purposes of Directive 83/349/EEC where the following conditions are fulfilled:
(a) the parent undertaking must draw up consolidated accounts in accordance with Directive 83/349/EEC and be included in the consolidated accounts;
(b) the above exemption must be disclosed in the notes on the annual accounts of the parent undertaking;
(c) the above exemption must be disclosed in the notes on the consolidated accounts drawn up by the parent undertaking;
(d) the profit or loss of the parent company, determined in accordance with this Directive, must be shown in the balance sheet of the parent company.

Article 59. 1. A Member State may require or permit that participating interests, as defined in Article 17, in the capital of undertakings over the operating and financial policies of which significant influence is exercised, be shown in the balance sheet in accordance with paragraphs 2 to 9 below, as sub-items of the items 'shares in affiliated undertakings' or 'participating interests', as the case may be. An undertaking shall be presumed to exercise a significant influence over another undertaking where it has 20 % or more of the 'shareholders' or 'members' voting rights in that undertaking. Article 2 of Directive 83/349/EEC shall apply.

2. When this Article is first applied to a participating interest covered by paragraph 1, it shall be shown in the balance sheet either :

(a) at its book value calculated in accordance with Section 7 or 7a . The difference between that value and the amount corresponding to the proportion of capital and reserves represented by the participating interest shall be disclosed separately in the balance sheet or in the notes on the accounts. That difference shall be calculated as at the date as at which the method is applied for the first time; or

(b) at the amount corresponding to the proportion of the capital and reserves represented by the participating interest. The difference between that amount and the book value calculated in accordance with Section 7 or 7a shall be disclosed separately in the balance sheet or in the notes on the accounts. That difference shall be calculated as at the date as at which the method is applied for the first time.

(c) A Member State may prescribe the application of one or other of the above paragraphs. The balance sheet or the notes on the account must indicate whether (a) or (b) above has been used.

(d) In addition, when applying (a) and (b) above, a Member State may require or permit calculation of the difference as at the date of acquisition of the participating interest referred to in paragraph 1 or, where the acquisition took place in two or more stages, as at the date as at which the holding became a participating interest within the meaning of paragraph 1 above.

3. Where the assets or liabilities of an undertaking in which a participating interest within the meaning of paragraph 1 above is held have been valued by methods other than those used by the company drawing up the annual accounts, they may, for the purpose of calculating the difference referred to in paragraph 2 (a) or (b) above, be revalued by the methods used by the company drawing up the annual accounts. Disclosure must be made in he notes on the accounts where such revaluation has not been carried out. A Member State may require such revaluation.

4. The book value referred to in paragraph 2 (a) above, or the amount corresponding to the proportion of capital and reserves referred to in paragraph 2 (b) above, shall be increased or reduced by the amount of the variation which has taken place during the financial year in the proportion of capital and reserves represented by that participating interest; it shall be reduced by the amount of the dividends relating to the participating interest.

5. In so far as a positive difference covered by paragraph 2 (a) or (b) above cannot be related to any category of asset or liability, it shall be dealt with in accordance with the rules applicable to the item 'goodwill'.

6. (a) The proportion of the profit or loss attributable to participating interests within the meaning of paragraph 1 above shall be shown in the profit-and-loss account as a separate item with an appropriate heading.

(b) Where that amount exceeds the amount of dividends already received or the payment of which can be claimed, the amount of the difference must be placed in a reserve which cannot be distributed to shareholders.

(c) A Member State may require or permit that the proportion of the profit or loss attributable to the participating interests referred to in paragraph 1 above be shown in the profit-andloss account only to the extent of the amount corresponding to dividends already received or the payment of which can be claimed.

7. The eliminations referred to in Article 26 (1) (c) of Directive 83/349/EEC shall be effected in so far as the facts are known or can be ascertained. Article 26 (2) and (3) of that Directive shall apply.

8. Where an undertaking in which a participating interest within the meaning of paragraph 1 above is held draws up consolidated accounts, the foregoing paragraphs shall apply to the capital and reserves shown in such consolidated accounts.

9. This Article need not be applied where a participating interest as defined in paragraph 1 is not material for the purposes of Article 2 (3).

Article 60. Pending subsequent coordination, the Member States may prescribe that investments in which investment companies within the meaning of Article 5 (2) have invested their funds shall be valued on the basis of their fair value. In that case, the Member States may also waive the obligation on investment companies with variable capital to show separately the value adjustments referred to in Article 36.

Article 60a. Member States shall lay down the rules on penalties applicableto infringements of the national provisions adopted pursuant to this Directive and shall take all the measures necessary to ensure that theyare implemented. The penalties provided for must be effective, proportionate and dissuasive.

Article 61. A Member State need not apply the provisions of point 2 of Article 43(1) of this Directive concerning the amount of capital and reserves and profits and losses of the undertakings concerned to companies governed by their national laws which are parent undertakings for the purposes of Directive 83/349/EEC:

(a) where the undertakings concerned are included in consolidated accounts drawn up by that parent undertaking, or in the consolidated accounts of a larger body of undertakings as referred to in Article 7 (2) of Directive 83/349/EEC; or

(b) where the holdings in the undertakings concerned have been dealt with by the parent undertaking in its annual accounts in accordance with Article 59, or in the consolidated accounts drawn up by that parent undertaking in accordance with Article 33 of Directive 83/349/EEC.

Article 61a. Not later than 1 July 2007, the Commission shall review the provisions in Articles 42a to 42f, Article 43(1)(10) and (14), Article 44(1), Article 46(2)(f) and Article 59(2)(a) and (b) in the light of the experience acquired in applying provisions on fair value accounting, with particular regard to IAS 39 as endorsed in accordance with Regulation (EC) No 1606/2002, and taking account of international developments in the field of accounting and, if appropriate, submit a proposal to the European Parliament and the Council with a view to amending the abovementioned Articles.

Article 62. This Directive is addressed to the Member States.

Directive 83/349 on Consolidated Accounts

Council Directive 83/349/EEC of 13 June 1983 based on the Article 54 (3) (g) of the Treaty on consolidated accounts ("Seventh Company Law Directive") (*OJ* L 193, 18.7.1983, pp. 1–17). Consolidated version as last amended by Directive 2009/49/EC of the European Parliament and of the Council of 18 June 2009 amending Council Directives 78/660/EEC and 83/349/EEC as regards certain disclosure requirements for medium-sized companies and the obligation to draw up consolidated accounts [footnotes omitted].

THE COUNCIL OF THE EUROPEAN COMMUNITIES,

Having regard to the Treaty establishing the European Economic Community, and in particular Article 54 (3) (g) thereof,

Having regard to the proposal from the Commission,

Having regard to the opinion of the European Parliament,

Having regard to the opinion of the Economic and Social Committee,

Whereas on 25 July 1978 the Council adopted Directive 78/660/EEC on the coordination of national legislation governing the annual accounts of certain types of companies; whereas many companies are members of bodies of undertakings; whereas consolidated accounts must be drawn up so that financial information concerning such bodies of undertakings may be conveyed to members and third parties; whereas national legislation governing consolidated accounts must therefore be coordinated in order to achieve the objectives of comparability and equivalence in the information which companies must publish within the Community;

Whereas, in the determination of the conditions for consolidation, account must be taken not only of cases in which the power of control is based on a majority of voting rights but also of those in which it is based on agreements, where these are permitted; whereas, furthermore, Member States in which the possibility occurs must be permitted to cover cases in which in certain circumstances control has been effectively exercised on the basis of a minority holding; whereas the Member States must be permitted to cover the case of bodies of undertakings in which the undertakings exist on an equal footing with each other;

Whereas the aim of coordinating the legislation governing consolidated accounts is to protect the interests subsisting in companies with share capital; whereas such protection implies the principle of the preparation of consolidated accounts where such a company is a member of a body of undertakings, and that such accounts must be drawn up at least where such a subsidiary is a parent undertaking; whereas, furthermore, the cause of full information also requires that a subsidiary undertaking which is itself a parent undertaking draw up consolidated accounts; whereas, nevertheless, such a parent undertaking may, and, in certain circumstances, must be exempted from the obligation to draw up such consolidated accounts provided that its members and third parties are sufficiently protected;

Whereas, for bodies of undertakings not exceeding a certain size, exemption from the obligation to prepare consolidated accounts may be justified; whereas, accordingly, maximum limits must be set for such exemptions; whereas it follows therefrom that the Member States may either provide that it is sufficient to exceed the limit of one only of the three criteria for the exemption not to apply or adopt limits lower than those prescribed in the Directive;

Whereas consolidated accounts must give a true and fair view of the assets and liabilities, the financial position and the profit and loss of all the undertakings consolidated taken as a whole; whereas, therefore consolidation should in principle include all of those undertakings; whereas such consolidation requires the full incorporation of the assets and liabilities and of the income and expenditure of those undertakings and the separate disclosure of the interests of persons outwith such bodies; whereas, however, the necessary corrections must be made to eliminate the effects of the financial relations between the undertakings consolidated;

Whereas a number of principles relating to the preparation of consolidated accounts and valuation in the context of such accounts must be laid down in order to ensure that items are disclosed consistently, and may readily be compared not only as regards the methods used in their valuation but also as regards the periods covered by the accounts;

Whereas participating interests in he capital of undertakings over which undertakings included in a consolidation exercise significant influence must be included in consolidated accounts by means of the equity method;

Whereas the notes on consolidated accounts must give details of the undertakings to be consolidated;

Whereas certain derogations originally provided for on a transitional basis in Directive 78/660/EEC may be continued subject to review at a later date,

HAS ADOPTED THIS DIRECTIVE:

Section I. Conditions for the preparation of consolidated accounts

Article 1. 1. A Member State shall require any undertaking governed by its national law to draw up consolidated accounts and a consolidated annual report if that undertaking (a parent undertaking):
(a) has a majority of the shareholders' or members' voting rights in another undertaking (a subsidiary undertaking); or
(b) has the right to appoint or remove a majority of the members of the administrative, management or supervisory body of another undertaking (a subsidiary undertaking) and is at the same time a shareholder in or member of that undertaking; or
(c) has the right to exercise a dominant influence over an undertaking (a subsidiary undertaking) of which it is a shareholder or member, pursuant to a contract entered into with that undertaking or to a provision in its memorandum or articles of association, where the law governing that subsidiary undertaking permits its being subject to such contracts or provisions. A Member State need not prescribe that a parent undertaking must be a shareholder in or member of its subsidiary undertaking. Those Member States the laws of which do not provide for each contracts or clauses shall not be required to apply this provision; or
(d) is a shareholder in or member of an undertaking, and:
(aa) a majority of the members of the administrative, management or supervisory bodies of that undertaking (a subsidiary undertaking) who have held office during the financial year, during the preceding financial year and up to the time when the consolidated accounts are drawn up, have been appointed solely as a result of the exercise of its voting rights; or
(bb) controls alone, pursuant to an agreement with other shareholders in or members of that undertaking (a subsidiary undertaking), a majority of shareholders' or members' voting rights in that undertaking. The Member States may introduce more detailed provisions concerning the form and contents of such agreements. The Member States shall prescribe at least the arrangements referred to in (bb) above. They may make the application of (aa) above dependent upon the holding's representing 20 % or more of the shareholders' or members' voting rights. However, (aa) above shall not apply where another undertaking has the rights referred to in subparagraphs (a), (b) or (c) above with regard to that subsidiary undertaking.
2. Apart from the cases mentioned in paragraph 1 the Member States may require any undertaking governed by their national law to draw up consolidated accounts and a consolidated annual report if:
(a) that undertaking (a parent undertaking) has the power to exercise, or actually exercises, dominant influence or control over another undertaking (the subsidiary undertaking); or
(b) that undertaking (a parent undertaking) and another undertaking (the subsidiary undertaking) are managed on a unified basis by the parent undertaking.

Article 2. 1. For the purposes of Article 1 (1) (a), (b) and (d), the voting rights and the rights of appointment and removal of any other subsidiary undertaking as well as those of any person acting in his own name but on behalf of the parent undertaking or of another subsidiary undertaking must be added to those of the parent undertaking.
2. For the purposes of Article 1 (1) (a), (b) and (d), the rights mentioned in paragraph 1 above must be reduced by the rights:
(a) attaching to shares held on behalf of a person who is neither the parent undertaking nor a subsidiary thereof; or
(b) attaching to shares held by way of security, provided that the rights in question are exercised in accordance with the instructions received, or held in connection with the granting of loans as part of normal business activities, provided that the voting rights are exercised in the interests of the person providing the security.
3. For the purposes of Article 1 (1) (a) and (d), the total of the shareholders' or members' voting rights in the subsidiary undertaking must be reduced by the voting rights attaching to the shares held by that undertaking itself by a subsidiary undertaking of that undertaking or by a person acting in his own name but on behalf of those undertakings.

Article 3. 1. Without prejudice to Articles 13 and 15, a parent undertaking and all of its subsidiary undertakings shall be undertakings to be consolidated regardless of where the registered offices of such subsidiary undertakings are situated.
2. For the purposes of paragraph 1 above any subsidiary undertaking of a subsidiary undertaking shall be considered a subsidiary undertaking of the parent undertaking which is the parent of the undertaking to be consolidated.

Article 4. 1. For the purposes of this Directive, a parent undertaking and all of its subsidiary undertakings shall be undertakings to be consolidated where either the parent undertaking or one or more subsidiary undertakings is established as one of the following types of company:

(a) in Germany:die Aktiengesellschaft, die Kommanditgesellschaft auf Aktien, die Gesellschaft mit beschränkter Haftung;
(b) in Belgium :la société anonyme / de naamloze vennootschap — la société en commandite par actions / de commanditaire vennootschap op aandelen — la société de personnes à responsabilité limitée / de personenvennootschap met beperkte aansprakelijkheid;
(c) in Denmark: aktieselskaber, kommanditaktieselskaber, anpartsselskaber;
(d) in France: la société anonyme, la société en commandite par actions, la société à responsabilité limitée;
(e) in Greece: η ανώνυμη εταιρία, η εταιρία περιορισμένης ευθύνης, η ετερ- όρρυθμη κατά μετοχές εταιρία;
(f) in Ireland: public companies limited by shares or by guarantee, private companies limited by shares or by guarantee;
(g) in Italy: la società per azioni, la società in accomandita per azioni, la società a responsabilità limitata;
(h) in Luxembourg: la société anonyme, la société en commandite par actions, la société à responsabilité limitée;
(i) in the Netherlands: de naamloze vennootschap, de besloten vennootschap met beperkte aansprakelijkheid;
(j) in the United Kingdom: public companies limited by shares or by guarantee, private companies limited by shares or by guarantee;
(k) in Spain: la sociedad anónima, la sociedad comanditaria por acciones, la sociedad de responsabilidad limitada;
(l) in Portugal: a sociedade anónima de responsabilidade limitada, a sociedade em comandita por acções, a sociedade por quotas de responsabilidade limitada;
(m) in Austria: die Aktiengesellschaft, die Gesellschaft mit beschränkter Haftung;
(n) in Finland: osakeyhtiö / aktiebolag;
(o) in Sweden: aktiebolag;
(p) in the Czech Republic: společnost s ručením omezeným, akciová společnost;
(q) in Estonia: aktsiaselts, osaühing;
(r) in Cyprus: Δημόσιες εταιρείες περιορισμένης ευθύνης με μετοχές ή με εγγύηση, ιδιωτικές εταιρείες περιορισμένης ευθύνης με μετοχές ή με εγγύηση;
(s) in Latvia: akciju sabiedrība, sabiedrība ar ierobežotu atbildību;
(t) in Lithuania: akcinės bendrovės, uždarosios akcinės bendrovės;
(u) in Hungary: részvénytársaság, korlátolt felelősségű társaság;
(v) in Malta: kumpanija pubblika—public limited liability company,kumpannija privata—private limited liability company,
soċjeta in akkomandita bil-kapital maqsum f'azzjonijiet—partnership en commandite with the capital divided into shares;
(w) in Poland: spółka akcyjna, spółka z ograniczoną odpowiedzialnością, spółka komandytowo-akcyjna;
(x) in Slovenia: delniška družba, družba z omejeno odgovornostjo, komanditna delniška družba;
(y) in Slovakia: akciová spoločnosť, spoločnosť s ručením obmedzeným;
(z) in Bulgaria: акционерно дружество, дружество с ограничена отговорност, командитно дружество с акции;
(aa) in Romania: societate pe acțiuni, societate cu răspundere limitată, societate în comandită pe acțiuni.
The first subparagraph shall also apply where either the parent undertaking or one or more subsidiary undertakings is constituted as one of the types of company mentioned in Article 1 (1), second or third subparagraph of Directive 78/660/EEC.
2. The Member States may, however, grant exemption from the obligation imposed in Article 1 (1) where the parent undertaking is not constituted as one of the types of company mentioned in Article 4 (1) of this Directive or in Article 1 (1), second or third subparagraph of Directive 78/660/EEC.

Article 5. 1. A Member State may grant exemption from the obligation imposed in Article 1 (1) where the parent undertaking is a financial holding company as defined in Article 5 (3) of Directive 78/660/EEC, and:
(a) it has not intervened during the financial year, directly or indirectly, in the management of a subsidiary undertaking;
(b) it has not exercised the voting rights attaching to its participating interest in respect of the appointment of a member of a subsidiary undertaking's administrative, management or supervisory bodies during the financial year or the five preceding financial years or, where the exercise of voting rights was necessary for the operation of the administrative, management or supervisory bodies of the subsidiary undertaking, no shareholder in or member of the parent undertaking with majority voting rights or member of the administrative, management or supervisory bodies of that undertaking or of a member thereof with majority voting rights is a member of the administrative, management or supervisory bodies of the subsidiary undertaking and the members of those bodies so appointed have fulfilled their functions without any interference or influence on the part of the parent undertaking or of any of its subsidiary undertakings;

(c) it has made loans only to undertakings in which it holds participating interests. Where such loans have been made to other parties, they must have been repaid by the end of the previous financial year; and
(d) the exemption is granted by an administrative authority after fulfilment of the above conditions has been checked.
2. (a) Where a financial holding company has been exempted, Article 43 (2) of Directive 78/660/EEC shall not apply to its annual accounts with respect to any majority holdings in subsidiary undertakings as from the date provided for in Article 49 (2).
(b) The disclosures in respect of such majority holdings provided for in point 2 of Article 43 (1) of Directive 78/660/EEC may be omitted when their nature is such that they would be seriously prejudicial to the company, to its shareholders or members or to one of its subsidiaries. A Member State may make such omissions subject to prior administrative or judicial authorization. Any such omission must be disclosed in the notes on the accounts.

Article 6. 1. Without prejudice to Articles 4 (2) and 5, a Member State may provide for an exemption from the obligation imposed in Article 1 (1) if as at the balance sheet date of a parent undertaking the undertakings to be consolidated do not together, on the basis of their latest annual accounts, exceed the limits of two of the three criteria laid down in Article 27 of Directive 78/660/EEC.
2. A Member State may require or permit that the set-off referred to in Article 19 (1) an the elimination referred to in Article 26 (1) (a) and (b) be not effected when the aforementioned limits are calculated. In that case, the limits for the balance sheet total and net turnover criteria shall be increased by 20 %.
3. Article 12 of Directive 78/660/EEC shall apply to the above criteria.
4. This Article shall not apply where one of the undertakings to be consolidated is a company whose securities are admitted to trading on a regulated market of any Member State within the meaning of Article 1(13) of Council Directive 93/22/EEC of 10 May 1993 on investment services in the securities field.

Article 7. 1. Notwithstanding Articles 4 (2), 5 and 6, a Member State shall exempt from the obligation imposed in Article 1 (1) any parent undertaking governed by its national law which is also a subsidiary undertaking if its own parent undertaking is governed by the law of a Member State in the following two cases:
(a) where that parent undertaking holds all of the shares in the exempted undertaking. The shares in that undertaking held by members of its administrative, management or supervisory bodies. pursuant to an obligation in law or in the memorandum or articles of association shall be ignored for this purpose; or
(b) where that parent undertaking holds 90 % or more of the shares in the exempted undertaking and the remaining shareholders in or members of that undertaking have approved the exemption.
2. Exemption shall be conditional upon compliance with all of the following conditions:
(a) the exempted undertaking and, without prejudice to Articles 13 and 15, all of its subsidiary undertakings must be consolidated in the accounts of a larger body of undertakings, the parent undertaking of which is governed by the law of a Member State;
(b) (aa) the consolidated accounts referred to in (a) above and the consolidated annual report of the larger body of undertakings must be drawn up by the parent undertaking of that body and audited, according to the law of the Member State by which the parent undertaking of that larger body of undertakings is governed, in accordance with this Directive;
(bb) the consolidated accounts referred to in (a) above and the consolidated annual report referred to in (aa) above, the report by the person responsible for auditing those accounts and, where appropriate, the appendix referred to in Article 9 must be published for the exempted undertaking in the manner prescribed by the law of the Member State governing that undertaking in accordance with Article 38. That Member State may require that those documents be published in its official language and that the translation be certified;
(c) the notes on the annual accounts of the exempted undertaking must disclose:
(aa) the name and registered office of the parent undertaking that draws up the consolidated accounts referred to in (a) above; and
(bb) the exemption from the obligation to draw up consolidated accounts and a consolidated annual report.
3. This Article shall not apply to companies whose securities are admitted to trading on a regulated market of any Member State within the meaning of Article 1(13) of Directive 93/22/EEC.

Article 8. 1. In cases not covered by Article 7 (1), a Member State may, without prejudice to Articles 4 (2), 5 and 6, exempt from the obligation imposed in Article 1 (1) any parent undertaking governed by its national law which is also a subsidiary undertaking, the parent undertaking of which is governed by the law of a Member State, provided that all the conditions set out in Article 7 (2) are fulfilled and that the shareholders in or members of the exempted undertaking who own a minimum proportion of the subscribed capital of that undertaking have not requested the preparation of consolidated accounts at least six months before the end of the financial year. The

Member States may fix that proportion at not more than 10 % for public limited liability companies and for limited partnerships with share capital, and at not more than 20 % for undertakings of other types.
2. A Member State may not make it a condition for this exemption that the parent undertaking which prepared the consolidated accounts described in Article 7 (2) (a) must also be governed by its national law.
3. A Member State may not make exemption subject to conditions concerning the preparation and auditing of the consolidated accounts referred to in Article 7 (2) (a).

Article 9. 1. A Member State may make the exemptions provided for in Articles 7 and 8 dependent upon the disclosure of additional information, in accordance with this Directive, in the consolidated accounts referred to in Article 7 (2) (a), or in an appendix thereto, if that information is required of undertakings governed by the national law of that Member State which are obliged to prepare consolidated accounts and are in the same circumstances.
2. A Member State may also make exemption dependent upon the disclosure, in the notes on the consolidated accounts referred to in Article 7 (2) (a), or in the annual accounts of the exempted undertaking, of all or some of the following information regarding the body of undertakings, the parent undertaking of which it is exempting from the obligation to draw up consolidated accounts:
— the amount of the fixed assets,
— the net turnover,
— the profit or loss for the financial year and the amount of the capital and reserves,
— the average number of persons employed during the financial year.

Article 10. Articles 7 to 9 shall not affect any Member State's legislation on the drawing up of consolidated accounts or consolidated annual reports in so far as those documents are required:
— for the information of employees of their representatives, or
— by an administrative or judicial authority for its own purposes.

Article 11. 1. Without prejudice to Articles 4 (2), 5 and 6, a Member State may exempt from the obligation imposed in Article 1 (1) any parent undertaking governed by its national law which is also a subsidiary undertaking of a parent undertaking not governed by the law of a Member State, if all of the following conditions are fulfilled:
(a) the exempted undertaking and, without prejudice to Articles 13 and 15, all of its subsidiary undertakings must be consolidated in the accounts of a larger body of undertakings;
(b) the consolidated accounts referred to in (a) above and, where appropriate, the consolidated annual report must be drawn up in accordance with this Directive or in a manner equivalent to consolidated accounts and consolidated annual reports drawn up in accordance with this Directive;
(c) the consolidated accounts referred to in (a) above must have been audited by one or more persons authorized to audit accounts under the national law governing the undertaking which drew them up.
2. Articles 7 (2) (b) (bb) and (c) an 8 to 10 shall apply.
3. A Member State may provide for exemptions under this Article only if it provides for the same exemptions under Articles 7 to 10.

Article 12. 1. Without prejudice to Articles 1 to 10, a Member State may require any undertaking governed by its national law to draw up consolidated accounts and a consolidated annual report if:
(a) that undertaking and one or more other undertakings with which it is not connected, as described in Article 1 (1) or (2), are managed on a unified basis pursuant to a contract concluded with that undertaking or provisions in the memorandum or articles of association of those undertakings; or
(b) the administrative, management or supervisory bodies of that undertaking and of one or more other undertakings with which it is not connected, as described in Article 1 (1) or (2), consist for the major part of the same persons in office during the financial year and until the consolidated accounts are drawn up.
2. Where paragraph 1 above is applied, undertakings related as defined in that paragraph together with all of their subsidiary undertakings shall be undertakings to be consolidated, as defined in this Directive, where one or more of those undertakings is established as one of the types of company listed in Article 4.
3. Articles 3, 4 (2), 5, 6, 13 to 28, 29 (1), (3), (4) and (5), 30 to 38 and 39 (2) shall apply to the consolidated accounts and the consolidated annual report covered by this Article, references to parent undertakings being understood to refer to all the undertakings specified in paragraph 1 above. Without prejudice to Article 19 (2), however, the items 'capital', 'share premium account', 'revaluation reserve', 'reserves', 'profit or loss brought forward', and 'profit or loss for the financial year' to be included in the consolidated accounts shall be the aggregate amounts attributable to each of the undertakings specified in paragraph 1.

Article 13. 1. An undertaking need not be included in consolidated accounts where it is not material for the purposes of Article 16 (3).
2. Where two or more undertakings satisfy the requirements of paragraph 1 above, they must nevertheless be included in consolidated accounts if, as a whole, they are material for the purposes of Article 16 (3).
2a. Without prejudice to Article 4(2) and Articles 5 and 6, any parent undertaking governed by the national law of a Member State which only has subsidiary undertakings which are not material for the purposes of Article 16(3), both individually and as a whole, shall be exempted from the obligation imposed in Article 1(1).
3. In addition, an undertaking need not be included in consolidated accounts where:
(a) severe long-term restrictions substantially hinder:
(aa) the parent undertaking in the exercise of its rights over the assets or management of that undertaking; or
(bb) the exercise of unified management of that undertaking where it is in one of the relationships defined in Article 12 (1); or
(b) the information necessary for the preparation of consolidated accounts in accordance with this Directive cannot be obtained without disproportionate expense or undue delay; or
(c) the shares of that undertaking are held exclusively with a view to their subsequent resale.

Article 14. 1. Where the activities of one or more undertakings to be consolidated are so different that their inclusion in the consolidated accounts would be incompatible with the obligation imposed in Article 16 (3), such undertakings must, without prejudice to Article 33 of this Directive, be excluded from the consolidation.
2. Paragraph 1 above shall not be applicable merely by virtue of the fact that the undertakings to be consolidated are partly industrial, partly commercial, and partly provide services, or because such undertakings carry on industrial or commercial activities involving different products or provide different services.
3. Any application of paragraph 1 above and the reasons therefor must be disclosed in the notes on the accounts. Where the annual or consolidated accounts of the undertakings thus excluded from the consolidation are not published in the same Member State in accordance with Directive 68/151/EEC [6], they must be attached to the consolidated accounts or made available to the public. In the latter case it must be possible to obtain a copy of such documents upon request. The price of such a copy must not exceed its administrative cost.

Article 15. 1. A Member State may, for the purposes of Article 16 (3), permit the omission from consolidated accounts of any parent undertaking not carrying on any industrial or commercial activity which holds shares in a subsidiary undertaking on the basis of a joint arrangement with one or more undertakings not included in the consolidated accounts.
2. The annual accounts of the parent undertaking shall be attached to the consolidated accounts.
3. Where use is made of this derogation either Article 59 of Directive 78/660/EEC shall apply to the parent undertaking's annual accounts or the information which would have resulted from its application must be given in the notes on those accounts.

Section II. The preparation of consolidated accounts

Article 16. 1. Consolidated accounts shall comprise the consolidated balance sheet, the consolidated profit-and-loss account and the notes on the accounts. These documents shall constitute a composite whole. Member States may permit or require the inclusion of other statements in the consolidated accounts in addition to the documents referred to in the first subparagraph.
2. Consolidated accounts shall be drawn up clearly and in accordance with this Directive.
3. Consolidated accounts shall give a true and fair view of the assets, liabilities, financial position and profit or loss of the undertakings included therein taken as a whole.
4. Where the application of the provisions of this Directive would not be sufficient to give a true and fair view within the meaning of paragraph 3 above, additional information must be given.
5. Where, in exceptional cases, the application of a provision of Articles 17 to 35 and 39 is incompatible with the obligation imposed in paragraph 3 above, that provision must be departed from in order to give a true and fair view within the meaning of paragraph 3. Any such departure must be disclosed in the notes on the accounts together with an explanation of the reasons for it and a statement of its effect on the assets, liabilities, financial position and profit or loss. The Member States may define the exceptional cases in question and lay down the relevant special rules.
6. A Member State may require or permit the disclosure in the consolidated accounts of other information as well as that which must be disclosed in accordance with this Directive.

Article 17. 1. Articles 3 to 10a, 13 to 26 and 28 to 30 of Directive 78/660/EEC shall apply in respect of the layout of consolidated accounts, without prejudice to the provisions of this Directive and taking account of the essential adjustments resulting from the particular characteristics of consolidated accounts as compared with annual accounts.
2. Where there are special circumstances which would entail undue expense a Member State may permit stocks to be combined in the consolidated accounts.

Article 18. The assets and liabilities of undertakings included in a consolidation shall be incorporated in full in the consolidated balance sheet.

Article 19. 1. The book values of shares in the capital of undertakings included in a consolidation shall be set off against the proportion which they represent of the capital and reserves of those undertakings:
(a) That set-off shall be effected on the basis of book values as at the date as at which such undertakings are included in the consolidations for the first time. Differences arising from such set-offs shall as far as possible be entered directly against those items in the consolidated balance sheet which have values above or below their book values.
(b) A Member State may require or permit set-offs on the basis of the values of identifiable assets and liabilities as at the date of acquisition of the shares or, in the event of acquisition in two or more stages, as at the date on which the undertaking became a subsidiary.
(c) Any difference remaining after the application of (a) or resulting from the application of (b) shall be shown as a separate item in the consolidated balance sheet with an appropriate heading. That item, the methods used and any significant changes in relation to the preceding financial year must be explained in the notes on the accounts. Where the offsetting of positive and negative differences is authorized by a Member State, a breakdown of such differences must also be given in the notes on the accounts.
2. However, paragraph 1 above shall not apply to shares in the capital of the parent undertaking held either by that undertaking itself or by another undertaking included in the consolidation. In the consolidated accounts such shares shall be treated as own shares in accordance with Directive 78/660/EEC.

Article 20. 1. A Member State may require or permit the book values of shares held in the capital of an undertaking included in the consolidation to be set off against the corresponding percentage of capital only, provided that:
(a) the shares held represent at least 90 % of the nominal value or, in the absence of a nominal value, of the accounting par value of the shares of that undertaking other than shares of the kind described in Article 29 (2) (a) of Directive 77/91 EEC (1);
(b) the proportion referred to in (a) above has been attained pursuant to an arrangement providing for the issue of shares by an undertaking included in the consolidation; and
(c) the arrangement referred to in (b) above did not include a cash payment exceeding 10 % of the nominal value or, in the absence of nominal value, of the accounting par value of the shares issued.
2. Any difference arising under paragraph 1 above shall be added to or deducted from consolidated reserves as appropriate.
3. The application of the method described in paragraph 1 above, the resulting movement in reserves and the names and registered offices of the undertakings concerned shall be disclosed in the notes on the accounts.

Article 21. The amount attributable to shares in subsidiary undertakings included in the consolidation held by persons other than the undertakings included in the consolidation shall be shown in the consolidated balance sheet as a separate item with an appropriate heading.

Article 22. The income and expenditure of undertakings included in a consolidation shall be incorporated in full in the consolidated profit-and-loss account.

Article 23. The amount of any profit or loss attributable to shares in subsidiary undertakings included in the consolidation held by persons other than the undertakings included in the consolidation shall be shown in the consolidated profit-and-loss account as a separate item with an appropriate heading.

Article 24. Consolidated accounts shall be drawn up in accordance with the principles enunciated in Articles 25 to 28.

Article 25. 1. The methods of consolidation must be applied consistently from one financial year to another.

2. Derogations from the provisions of paragraph 1 above shall be permitted in exceptional cases. Any such derogations must be disclosed in the notes on the accounts and the reasons for them given together with an assessment of their effect on the assets, liabilities, financial position and profit or loss of the undertakings included in the consolidation taken as a whole.

Article 26. 1. Consolidated accounts shall show the assets, liabilities, financial positions and profits or losses of the undertakings included in a consolidation as if the latter were a single undertaking. In particular:
(a) debts and claims between the undertakings included in a consolidation shall be eliminated from the consolidated accounts;
(b) income and expenditure relating to transactions between the undertakings included in a consolidation shall be eliminated from the consolidated accounts;
(c) where profits and losses resulting from transactions between the undertakings included in a consolidation are included in the book values of assets, they shall be eliminated from the consolidated accounts. Pending subsequent coordination, however, a Member State may allow the eliminations mentioned above to be effected in proportion to the percentage of the capital held by the parent undertaking in each of the subsidiary undertakings included in the consolidation.
2. A Member State may permit derogations from the provisions of paragraph 1 (c) above where a transaction has been concluded according to normal market conditions and where the elimination of the profit or loss would entail undue expense. Any such derogations must be disclosed and where the effect on the assets, liabilities, financial position and profit or loss of the undertakings, included in the consolidation, taken as a whole, is material, that fact must be disclosed in the notes on the consolidated accounts.
3. Derogations from the provisions of paragraph 1 (a), (b) or (c) above shall be permitted where the amounts concerned are not material for the purposes of Article 16 (3).

Article 27. 1. Consolidated accounts must be drawn up as at the same date as the annual accounts of the parent undertaking.
2. A Member State may, however, require or permit consolidated accounts to be drawn up as at another date in order to take account of the balance sheet dates of the largest number or the most important of the undertakings included in the consolidation. Where use is made of this derogation that fact shall be disclosed in the note on the consolidated accounts together with the reasons therefor. In addition, account must be taken or disclosure made of important events concerning the assets and liabilities, the financial position or the profit or loss of an undertaking included in a consolidation which have occurred between that undertaking's balance sheet date and the consolidated balance sheet date.
3. Where an undertaking's balance sheet date precedes the consolidated balance sheet date by more than three months, that undertaking shall be consolidated on the basis of interim accounts drawn up as at the consolidated balance sheet date.

Article 28. If the composition of the undertakings included in a consolidation has changed significantly in the course of a financial year, the consolidated accounts must include information which makes the comparison of successive sets of consolidated accounts meaningful. Where such a change is a major one, a Member State may require or permit this obligation to be fulfilled by the preparation of an adjusted opening balance sheet and an adjusted profit-and-loss account.

Article 29. 1. Assets and liabilities to be included in consolidated accounts shall be valued according to uniform methods and in accordance with Sections 7 and 7a and Article 60 of Directive 78/660/EEC.
2. (a) An undertaking which draws up consolidated accounts must apply the same methods of valuation as in its annual accounts.
However, a Member State may require or permit the use in consolidated accounts of other methods of valuation in accordance with the abovementioned Articles of Directive 78/660/EEC.
(b) Where use is made of this derogation that fact shall be disclosed in the notes on the consolidated accounts and the reasons therefor given.
3. Where assets and liabilities to be included in consolidated accounts have been valued by undertakings included in the consolidation by methods differing from those used for the consolidation, they must be revalued in accordance with the methods used for the consolidation, unless the results of such revaluation are not material for the purposes of Article 16 (3). Departures from this principle shall be permitted in exceptional cases. Any such departures shall be disclosed in the notes on the consolidated accounts and the reasons for them given.
4. Account shall be taken in the consolidated balance sheet and in the consolidated profit-and-loss account of any difference arising on consolidation between the tax chargeable for the financial year and for preceding financial

years and the amount of tax paid or payable in respect of those years, provided that it is probable that an actual charge to tax will arise within the foreseeable future for one of the undertakings included in the consolidation.
5. Where assets to be included in consolidated accounts have been the subject of exceptional value adjustments solely for tax purposes, they shall be incorporated in the consolidated accounts only after those adjustments have been eliminated. A Member State may, however, require or permit that such assets be incorporated in the consolidated accounts without the elimination of the adjustments, provided that their amounts, together with the reasons for them, are disclosed in the notes on the consolidated accounts.

Article 30. 1. A separate item as defined in Article 19 (1) (c) which corresponds to a positive consolidation difference shall be dealt with in accordance with the rules laid down in Directive 78/660/EEC for the item 'goodwill'.
2. A Member State may permit a positive consolidation difference to be immediately and clearly deducted from reserves.

Article 31. An amount shown as a separate item, as defined in Article 19 (1) (c), which corresponds to a negative consolidation difference may be transferred to the consolidated profit-and-loss account only:
(a) where that difference corresponds to the expectation at the date of acquisition of unfavourable future results in that undertaking, or to the expectation of costs which that undertaking would incur, in so far as such an expectation materializes; or
(b) in so far as such a difference corresponds to a realized gain.

Article 32. 1. Where an undertaking included in a consolidation manages another undertaking jointly with one or more undertakings not included in that consolidation, a Member State may require or permit the inclusion of that other undertaking in the consolidated accounts in proportion to the rights in its capital held by the undertaking included in the consolidation.
2. Articles 13 to 31 shall apply mutatis mutandis to the proportional consolidation referred to in paragraph 1 above.
3. Where this Article is applied, Article 33 shall not apply if the undertaking proportionally consolidated is an associated undertaking as defined in Article 33.

Article 33. 1. Where an undertaking included in a consolidation exercises a significant influence over the operating and financial policy of an undertaking not included in the consolidation (an associated undertaking) in which it holds a participating interest, as defined in Article 17 of Directive 78/660/EEC, that participating interest shall be shown in the consolidated balance sheet as a separate item with an appropriate heading. An undertaking shall be presumed to exercise a significant influence over another undertaking where it has 20 % or more of the shareholders' or members' voting rights in that undertaking. Article 2 shall apply.
2. When this Article is applied for the first time to a participating interest covered by paragraph 1 above, that participating interest shall be shown in the consolidated balance sheet either:
(a) at its book value calculated in accordance with the valuation rules laid down in Directive 78/660/EEC. The difference between that value and the amount corresponding to the proportion of capital and reserves represented by that participating interest shall be disclosed separately in the consolidated balance sheet or in the notes on the accounts. That difference shall be calculated as at the date as at which that method is used for the first time; or
(b) at an amount corresponding to the proportion of the associated undertaking's capital and reserves represented by that participating interest. The difference between that amount and the book value calculated in accordance with the valuation rules laid down in Directive 78/660/EEC shall be disclosed separately in the consolidated balance sheet or in the notes on the accounts. That difference shall be calculated as at the date as at which that method is used for the first time.
(c) A Member State may prescribe the application of one or other of (a) and (b) above. The consolidated balance sheet or the notes on the accounts must indicate whether (a) or (b) has been used.
(d) In addition, for the purposes of (a) and (b) above, a Member State may require or permit the calculation of the difference as at the date of acquisition of the shares or, where they were acquired in two or more stages, as at the date on which the undertaking became an associated undertaking.
3. Where an associated undertaking's assets or liabilities have been valued by methods other than those used for consolidation in accordance with Article 29 (2), they may, for the purpose of calculating the difference referred to in paragraph 2 (a) or (b) above, be revalued by the methods used for consolidation. Where such revaluation has not been carried out that fact must be disclosed in the notes on the accounts. A Member State may require such revaluation.

4. The book value referred to in paragraph 2 (a) above, or the amount corresponding to the proportion of the associated undertaking's capital and reserves referred to in paragraph 2 (b) above, shall be increased or reduced by the amount of any variation which has taken place during the financial year in the proportion of the associated undertaking's capital and reserves represented by that participating interest; it shall be reduced by the amount of the dividends relating to that participating interest.

5. In so far as the positive difference referred to in paragraph 2 (a) or
(b) above cannot be related to any category of assets or liabilities it shall be dealt with in accordance with Articles 30 and 39 (3).

6. The proportion of the profit or loss of the associated undertakings attributable to such participating interests shall be shown in the consolidated profit-and-loss account as a separate item under an appropriate heading.

7. The eliminations referred to in Article 26 (1) (c) shall be effected in so far as the facts are known or can be ascertained. Article 26 (2) and (3) shall apply.

8. Where an associated undertaking draws up consolidated accounts the foregoing provisions shall apply to the capital and reserves shown in such consolidated accounts.

9. This Article need not be applied where the participating interest in the capital of the associated undertaking is not material for the purposes of Article 16 (3).

Article 34. In addition to the information required under other provisions of this Directive, the notes on the accounts must set out information in respect of the following matters at least:

1. The valuation methods applied to the various items in the consolidated accounts, and the methods employed in calculating the value adjustments. For items included in the consolidated accounts which are or were originally expressed in foreign currency the bases of conversion used to express them in the currency in which the consolidated accounts are drawn up must be disclosed.

2. (a) The names and registered offices of the undertakings included in the consolidation; the proportion of the capital held in undertakings included in the consolidation, other than the parent undertaking, by the undertakings included in the consolidation or by persons acting in their own names but on behalf of those undertakings; which of the conditions referred to in Articles 1 and 12 (1) following application of Article 2 has formed the basis on which the consolidation has been carried out. The latter disclosure may, however, be omitted where consolidation has been carried out on the basis of Article 1 (1) (a) and where the proportion of the capital and the proportion of the voting rights held are the same.

(b) The same information must be given in respect of undertakings excluded from a consolidation pursuant to Article 13 and an explanation must be given for the exclusion of the undertakings referred to in Article 13.

3 (a) The names and registered offices of undertakings associated with an undertaking included in the consolidation as described in Article 33 (1) and the proportion of their capital held by undertakings included in the consolidation or by persons acting in their own names but on behalf of those undertakings.

(b) The same information must be given in respect of the associated undertakings referred to in Article 33 (9), together with the reasons for applying that provision.

4. The names and registered offices of undertakings proportionally consolidated pursuant to Article 32, the factors on which joint management is based, and the proportion of their capital held by the undertakings included in the consolidation or by persons acting in their own names but on behalf of those undertakings.

5. The name and registered office of each of the undertakings, other than those referred to in paragraphs 2, 3 and 4 above, in which undertakings included in the consolidation, either themselves or through persons acting in their own names but on behalf of those undertakings, hold at least a percentage of the capital which the Member States cannot fix at more than 20 %, showing the proportion of the capital held, the amount of the capital and reserves, and the profit or loss for the latest financial year of the undertaking concerned for which accounts have been adopted. This information may be omitted where, for the purposes of Article 16 (3), it is of negligible importance only. The information concerning capital and reserves and the profit or loss may also be omitted where the undertaking concerned does not publish its balance sheet and where less than 50 % of its capital is held (directly or indirectly) by the abovementioned undertakings.

6. The total amount shown as owed in the consolidated balance sheet and becoming due and payable after more than five years, as well as the total amount shown as owed in the consolidated balance sheet and covered by valuable security furnished by undertakings included in the consolidation, with an indication of the nature and form of the security.

7. The total amount of any financial commitments that are not included in the consolidated balance sheet, in so far as this information is of assistance in assessing the financial position of the undertakings included in the consolidation taken as a whole. Any ommitments concerning pensions and affiliated undertakings which are not included in the consolidation must be disclosed separately.

7a. The nature and business purpose of any arrangements that are not included in the consolidated balance sheet, and the financial impact of those arrangements, provided that the risks or benefits arising from such arrangements are material and in so far as the disclosure of such risks or benefits is necessary for assessing the financial position of the undertakings included in the consolidation taken as a whole.

7b. The transactions, save for intra-group transactions, entered into by the parent undertaking, or by other undertakings included in the consolidation, with related parties, including the amounts of such transactions, the nature of the related party relationship as well as other information about the transactions necessary for an understanding of the financial position of the undertakings included in the consolidation taken as a whole, if such transactions are material and have not been concluded under normal market conditions. Information about individual transactions may be aggregated according to their nature except where separate information is necessary for an understanding of the effects of the related party transactions on the financial position of the undertakings included in the consolidation taken as a whole.

8. The consolidated net turnover as defined in Article 28 of Directive 78/660/EEC broken down by categories of activity and into geographical markets in so far as, taking account of the manner in which the sale of products and the provision of services falling within the ordinary activities of the undertakings included in the consolidation taken as a whole are organized, these categories and markets differ substantially from one another.

9.(a) The average number of persons employed during the financial year by undertakings included in the consolidation broken down by categories and, if they are not disclosed separately in the consolidated profit-and-loss account, the staff costs relating to the financial year.

(b) The average number of persons employed during the financial year by undertakings to which Article 32 has been applied shall be disclosed separately.

10. The extent to which the calculation of the consolidated profit or loss for the financial year has been affected by a valuation of the items which, by way of derogation from the principles enunciated in Articles 31 and 34 to Article 42c of Directive 78/660/EEC and in Article 29 (5) of this Directive, was made in the financial year in question or in an earlier financial year with a view to obtaining tax relief. Where the influence of such a valuation on the future tax charges of the undertakings included in the consolidation taken as a whole is material, details must be disclosed.

11. The difference between the tax charged to the consolidated profitand- loss account for the financial year and to those for earlier financial years and the amount of tax payable in respect of those years, provided that this difference is material for the purposes of future taxation. This amount may also be disclosed in the balance sheet as a cumulative amount under a separate item with an appropriate heading.

12. The amount of the emoluments granted in respect of the financial year to the members of the administrative, managerial and supervisory bodies of the parent undertaking by reason of their responsibilities in the parent undertaking and its subsidiary undertakings, and any commitments arising or entered into under the same conditions in respect of retirement pensions for former members of those bodies, with an indication of the total for each category. A Member State may require that emoluments granted by reason of responsibilities assumed in undertakings linked as described in Article 32 or 33 shall also be included with the information specified in the first sentence.

13. The amount of advances and credits granted to the members of the administrative, managerial and supervisory bodies of the parent undertaking by that undertaking or by one of its subsidiary undertakings, with indications of the interest rates, main conditions and any amounts repaid, as well as commitments entered into on their behalf by way of guarantee of any kind with an indication of the total for each category. A Member State may require that advances and credits granted by undertakings linked as described in Article 32 or 33 shall also be included with the information specified in the first sentence.

14. Where valuation at fair value of financial instruments has been applied in accordance with Section 7a of Directive 78/660/EEC:
(a) the significant assumptions underlying the valuation models and techniques where fair values have been determined in accordance with Article 42b(1)(b) of that Directive;
(b) per category of financial instruments, the fair value, the changes in value included directly in the profit and loss account as well as, in accordance with Article 42c of that Directive, changes included in the fair value reserve;
(c) for each class of derivative financial instruments, information about the extent and the nature of the instruments, including significant terms and conditions that may affect the amount, timing and certainty of future cash flows; and
(d) a table showing movements in the fair value reserve during the financial year.

15. Where valuation at fair value of financial instruments has not been applied in accordance with Section 7a of Directive 78/660/EEC:
(a) for each class of derivative instruments:
(i) the fair value of the instruments, if such a value can be determined by any of the methods prescribed in

Article 42b(1) of that Directive;
(ii) information about the extent and the nature of the instruments; and
(b) for financial fixed assets covered by Article 42a of that Directive, carried at an amount in excess of their fair value and without use being made of the option to make a value adjustment in accordance with Article 35(1)(c)(aa) of that Directive:
(i) the book value and the fair value of either the individual assets or appropriate groupings of those individual assets;
(ii) the reasons for not reducing the book value, including the nature of the evidence that provides the basis for the belief that the book value will be recovered.
16. Separately, the total fees for the financial year charged by the statutory auditor or audit firm for the statutory audit of the consolidated accounts, the total fees charged for other assurance services, the total fees charged for tax advisory services and the total fees charged for other non-audit services.

Article 35. 1. A Member State may allow the disclosures prescribed in Article 34 (2), (3), (4) and (5):
(a) to take the form of a statement deposited in accordance with Article 3 (1) and (2) of Directive 68/151/EEC; this must be disclosed in the notes on the accounts;
(b) to be omitted when their nature is such that they would be seriously prejudicial to any of the undertakings affected by these provisions. A Member State may make such omissions subject to prior administrative or judicial authorization. Any such omission must be disclosed in the notes on the accounts.
2. Paragraph 1 (b) shall also apply to the information prescribed in Article 34 (8).

Section III. The consolidated annual report

Article 36. 1. The consolidated annual report shall include at least a fair review of the development and performance of the business and of the position of the undertakings included in the consolidation taken as a whole, together with a description of the principal risks and uncertainties that they face. The review shall be a balanced and comprehensive analysis of the development and performance of the business and of the position of the undertakings included in the consolidation taken as a whole, consistent with the size and complexity of the business. To the extent necessary for an understanding of such development, performance or position, the analysis shall include both financial and, where appropriate, non-financial key performance indicators relevant to the particular business, including information relating to environmental and employee matters. In providing its analysis, the consolidated annual report shall, where appropriate, provide references to and additional explanations of amounts reported in the consolidated accounts.
2. In respect of those undertakings, the report shall also give an indication of:
(a) any important events that have occurred since the end of the financial year;
(b) the likely future development of those undertakings taken as a whole;
(c) the activities of those undertakings taken as whole in the field of research and development;
(d) the number and nominal value or, in the absence of a nominal value, the accounting par value of all of the parent undertaking's shares held by that undertaking itself, by subsidiary undertakings of that undertaking or by a person acting in his own name but on behalf of those undertakings. A Member State may require or permit the disclosure of these particulars in the notes on the accounts;
(e) in relation to the use by the undertakings of financial instruments and, where material for the assessment of assets, liabilities, financial position and profit or loss,
— the financial risk management objectives and policies of the undertakings, including their policies for hedging each major type of forecasted transaction for which hedge accounting is used, and
— the exposure to price risk, credit risk, liquidity risk and cash flow risk;
(f) a description of the main features of the group's internal control and risk management systems in relation to the process for preparing consolidated accounts, where an undertaking has its securities admitted to trading on a regulated market within the meaning of Article 4(1), point (14) of Directive 2004/39/EC of the European Parliament and of the Council of 21 April 2004 on markets in financial instruments (1). In the event that the consolidated annual report and the annual report are presented as a single report, this information must be included in the section of the report containing the corporate governance statement as provided for by Article 46a of Directive 78/660/EEC.
If a Member State permits the information required by paragraph 1 of Article 46a of Directive 78/660/EEC to be set out in a separate report published together with the annual report in the manner prescribed by Article 47 of that Directive, the information provided under the first subparagraph shall also form part of that separate report. Article 37(1), second subparagraph of this Directive shall apply.

3. Where a consolidated annual report is required in addition to an annual report, the two reports may be presented as a single report. In preparing such a single report, it may be appropriate to give greater emphasis to those matters which are significant to the undertakings included in the consolidation taken as a whole.

Section IIIA. Duty and liability for drawing up and publishing the consolidated accounts and the consolidated annual report

Article 36a. Member States shall ensure that the members of the administrative, management and supervisory bodies of undertakings drawing up the consolidated accounts and the consolidated annual report have collectively the duty to ensure that the consolidated accounts, the consolidated annual report and, when provided separately, the corporate governance statement to be provided pursuant to Article 46a of Directive 78/660/EEC are drawn up and published in accordance with the requirements of this Directive and, where applicable, in accordance with the international accounting standards adopted in accordance with Regulation (EC) No 1606/2002 of the European Parliament and of the Council of 19 July 2002 on the application of international accounting standards. Such bodies shall act within the competences assigned to them by national law.

Article 36b. Member States shall ensure that their laws, regulations and administrative provisions on liability apply to the members of the administrative, management and supervisory bodies referred to in Article 36a, at least towards the undertaking drawing up the consolidated accounts, for breach of the duty referred to in Article 36a.

Section IV. The auditing of consolidated accounts

Article 37. 1. The consolidated accounts of companies shall be audited by one or more persons approved by the Member State whose laws govern the parent undertaking to carry out statutory audits on the basis of the Eighth Council Directive 84/253/EEC of 10 April 1984 on the approval of persons responsible for carrying out the statutory audits of accounting documents.
The person or persons responsible for auditing the consolidated accounts (hereinafter: the statutory auditors) shall also express an opinion concerning the consistency or otherwise of the consolidated annual report with the consolidated accounts for the same financial year.
2. The report of the statutory auditors shall include:
(a) an introduction which shall at least identify the consolidated accounts which are the subject of the statutory audit, together with the financial reporting framework that has been applied in their preparation;
(b) a description of the scope of the statutory audit which shall at least identify the auditing standards in accordance with which the statutory audit was conducted;
(c) an audit opinion which shall state clearly the opinion of the statutory auditors as to whether the consolidated accounts give a true and fair view in accordance with the relevant financial reporting framework and, where appropriate, whether the consolidated accounts comply with statutory requirements; the audit opinion shall be either unqualified, qualified, an adverse opinion or, if the statutory auditors are unable to express an audit opinion, a disclaimer of opinion;
(d) a reference to any matters to which the statutory auditors draw attention by way of emphasis without qualifying the audit opinion;
(e) an opinion concerning the consistency or otherwise of the consolidated annual report with the consolidated accounts for the same financial year.
3. The report shall be signed and dated by the statutory auditors.
4. Where the annual accounts of the parent undertaking are attached to the consolidated accounts, the report of the statutory auditors required by this Article may be combined with any report of the statutory auditors on the annual accounts of the parent undertaking required by Article 51 of Directive 78/660/EEC.

Section V. The publication of consolidated accounts

Article 38. 1. Consolidated accounts, duly approved, and the consolidated annual report, together with the opinion submitted by the person responsible for auditing the consolidated accounts, shall be published for the undertaking which drew up the consolidated accounts as laid down by the laws of the Member State which govern it in accordance with Article 3 of Directive 68/151/EEC.
2. The second subparagraph of Article 47 (1) of Directive 78/660/EEC shall apply with respect to the consolidated annual report.

PART VIII. EUROPEAN COMPANY LAW

3. The following shall be substituted for the second subparagraph of Article 47 (1) of Directive 78/660/EEC: 'It must be possible to obtain a copy of all or part of any such report upon request. The price of such a copy must not exceed its administrative cost.'
4. However, where the undertaking which drew up the consolidated accounts is not established as one of the types of company listed in Article 4 and is not required by its national law to publish the documents referred to in paragraph 1 in the same manner as prescribed in Article 3 of Directive 68/151/EEC, it must at least make them available to the public at its head office. It must be possible to obtain a copy of such documents upon request. The price of such a copy must not exceed its administrative cost.
5. Articles 48 and 49 of Directive 78/660/EEC shall apply.
6. The Member States shall provide for appropriate sanctions for failure to comply with the publication obligations imposed in this Article.
7. Paragraphs 2 and 3 shall not be applied in respect of companies whose securities are admitted to trading on a regulated market of any Member State within the meaning of Article 1(13) of Directive 93/22/EEC.

Article 38a. Consolidated accounts may be published in the currency in which they were drawn up and in ecus, translated at the exchange rate prevailing on the consolidated balance sheet date.
That rate shall be disclosed in the notes on the accounts.

Section VI. Transitional and final provisions

Article 39. 1. When, for the first time, consolidated accounts are drawn up in accordance with this Directive for a body of undertakings which was already connected, as described in Article 1 (1), before application of the provisions referred to in Article 49 (1), a Member State may require or permit that, for the purposes of Article 19 (1) account be taken of the book value of a holding and the proportion of the capital and reserves that it represents as at a date before or the same as that of the first consolidation.
2. Paragraph 1 above shall apply mutatis mutandis to the valuation for the purposes of Article 33 (2) of a holding, or of the proportion of capital and reserves that it represents, in the capital of an undertaking associated with an undertaking included in the consolidation, and to the proportional consolidation referred to in Article 32.
3. Where the separate item defined in Article 19 (1) corresponds to a positive consolidation difference which arose before the date of the first consolidated accounts drawn up in accordance with this Directive, a Member State may:
(a) for the purposes of Article 30 (1), permit the calculation of the limited period of more than five years provided for in Article 37 (2) of Directive 78/660/EEC as from the date of the first consolidated accounts drawn up in accordance with this Directive; and
(b) for the purposes of Article 30 (2), permit the deduction to be made from reserves as at the date of the first consolidated accounts drawn up in accordance with this Directive.

Article 40. 1. Until expiry of the deadline imposed for the application in national law of the Directives supplementing Directive 78/660/EEC as regards the harmonization of the rules governing the annual accounts of banks and other financial institutions and insurance undertakings, a Member State may derogate from the provisions of this Directive concerning the layout of consolidated accounts, the methods of valuing the items included in those accounts and the information to be given in the notes on the accounts:
(a) with regard to any undertaking to be consolidated which is a bank, another financial institution or an insurance undertaking;
(b) where the undertakings to be consolidated comprise principally banks, financial institutions or insurance undertakings.
They may also derogate from Article 6, but only in so far as the limits and criteria to be applied to the above undertakings are concerned.
2. In so far as a Member State has not required all undertakings which are banks, other financial institutions or insurance undertakings to draw up consolidated accounts before implementation of the provisions referred to in Article 49 (1), it may, until its national law implements one of the Directives mentioned in paragraph 1 above, but not in respect of financial years ending after 1993:
(a) suspend the application of the obligation imposed in Article 1 (1) with respect to any of the above undertakings which is a parent undertaking. That fact must be disclosed in the annual accounts of the parent undertaking and the information prescribed in point 2 of Article 43 (1) of Directive 78/660/EEC must be given for all subsidiary undertakings;
(b) where consolidated accounts are drawn up and without prejudice to Article 33, permit the omission from the consolidation of any of the above undertakings which is a subsidiary undertaking. The information prescribed in Article 34 (2) must be given in the notes on the accounts in respect of any such subsidiary undertaking.

3. In the cases referred to in paragraph 2 (b) above, the annual or consolidated accounts of the subsidiary undertaking must, in so far as their publication is compulsory, be attached to the consolidated accounts or, in the absence of consolidated accounts, to the annual accounts of the parent undertaking or be made available to the public. In the latter case it must be possible to obtain a copy of such documents upon request. The price of such a copy must not exceed its administrative cost.

Article 41. 1. Undertakings which are connected as described in Article 1 (1) (a), (b) and (d) (bb), and those other undertakings which are similarly connected with one of the aforementioned undertakings, shall be affiliated undertakings for the purposes of this Directive and of Directive 78/660/EEC. 'Related party' has the same meaning as in international accounting standards adopted in accordance with Regulation (EC) No 1606/2002.
2. Where a Member State prescribes the preparation of consolidated accounts pursuant to Article 1 (1) (c), (d) (aa) or (2) or Article 12 (1), the undertakings which are connected as described in those Articles and those other undertakings which are connected similarly, or are connected as described in paragraph 1 above to one of the aforementioned undertakings, shall be affiliated undertakings as defined in paragraph 1.
3. Even where a Member State does not prescribe the preparation of consolidated accounts pursuant to Article 1 (1) (c), (d) (aa) or (2) or Article 12 (1), it may apply paragraph 2 of this Article.
4. Articles 2 and 3 (2) shall apply.
5. When a Member State applies Article 4 (2), it may exclude from the application of paragraph 1 above affiliated undertakings which are parent undertakings and which by virtue of their legal form are not required by that Member State to draw up consolidated accounts in accordance with the provisions of this Directive as well as parent undertakings with a similar legal form.

Article 42. The following shall be substituted for Article 56 of Directive 78/660/EEC: 'Article 56
1. The obligation to show in annual accounts the items prescribed by Articles 9, 10 and 23 to 26 which relate to affiliated undertakings, as defined by Article 41 of Directive 83/349/EEC, and the obligation to provide information concerning these undertakings in accordance with Articles 13 (2), and 14 and point 7 of Article 43 (1) shall enter into force on the date fixed in Article 49 (2) of that Directive.
2. The notes on the accounts must also disclose:
(a) the name and registered office of the undertaking which draws up the consolidated accounts of the largest body of undertakings of which the company forms part as a subsidiary undertaking;
(b) the name and registered office of the undertaking which draws up the consolidated accounts of the smallest body of undertakings of which the company forms part as a subsidiary undertaking and which is also included in the body of undertakings referred to in (a) above;
(c) the place where copies of the consolidated accounts referred to in (a) and (b) above may be obtained provided that they are available.

Article 43. The following shall be substituted for Article 57 of Directive 78/660/EEC: 'Article 57
Notwithstanding the provisions of Directives 68/151/EEC and 77/91/EEC, a Member State need not apply the provisions of this Directive concerning the content, auditing and publication of annual accounts to companies governed by their national laws which are subsidiary undertakings, as defined in Directive 83/349/EEC, where the following conditions are fulfilled:
(a) the parent undertaking must be subject to the laws of a Member State;
(b) all shareholders or members of the subsidiary undertaking must have declared their agreement to the exemption from such obligation; this declaration must be made in respect of every financial year;
(c) the parent undertaking must have declared that it guarantees the commitments entered into by the subsidiary undertaking;
(d) the declarations referred to in (b) and (c) must be published by the subsidiary undertaking as laid down by the laws of the Member State in accordance with Article 3 of Directive 68/151/EEC;
(e) the subsidiary undertaking must be included in the consolidated accounts drawn up by the parent undertaking in accordance with Directive 83/349/EEC;
(f) the above exemption must be disclosed in the notes on the consolidated accounts drawn up by the parent undertaking;
(g) the consolidated accounts referred to in (e), the consolidated annual report, and the report by the person responsible for auditing those accounts must be published for the subsidiary undertaking as laid down by the laws of the Member State in accordance with Article 3 of Directive 68/151/EEC.'

Article 44. The following shall be substituted for Article 58 of Directive 78/660/EEC: 'Article 58
A Member State need not apply the provisions of this Directive concerning the auditing and publication of the profit-and-loss account to companies governed by their national laws which are parent undertakings for the purposes of Directive 83/349/EEC where the following conditions are fulfilled:
(a) the parent undertaking must draw up consolidated accounts in accordance with Directive 83/349/EEC and be included in the consolidated accounts;
(b) the above exemption must be disclosed in the notes on the annual accounts of the parent undertaking;
(c) the above exemption must be disclosed in the notes on the consolidated accounts drawn up by the parent undertaking;
(d) the profit or loss of the parent company, determined in accordance with this Directive, must be shown in the balance sheet of the parent company.'

Article 45. The following shall be substituted for Article 59 of Directive 78/660/EEC: 'Article 59
1. A Member State may require or permit that participating interests, as defined in Article 17, in the capital of undertakings over the operating and financial policies of which significant influence is exercised, be shown in the balance sheet in accordance with paragraphs 2 to 9 below, as sub-items of the items "shares in affiliated undertakings" or "participating interests", as the case may be. An undertaking shall be presumed to exercise a significant influence over another undertaking where it has 20 % or more of the shareholders' or members' voting rights in that undertaking. Article 2 of Directive 83/349/EEC shall apply.
2. When this Article is first applied to a participating interest covered by paragraph 1, it shall be shown in the balance sheet either:
(a) at its book value calculated in accordance with Articles 31 to 42. The difference between that value and the amount corresponding to the proportion of capital and reserves represented by the participating interest shall be disclosed separately in the balance sheet or in the notes on the accounts. That difference shall be calculated as at the date as at which the method is applied for the first time; or
(b) at the amount corresponding to the proportion of the capital and reserves represented by the participating interest. The difference between that amount and the book value calculated in accordance with Articles 31 to 42 shall be disclosed separately in the balance sheet or in the notes on the accounts. That difference shall be calculated as at the date as at which the method is applied for the first time.
(c) A Member State may prescribe the application of one or other of the above paragraphs. The balance sheet or the notes on the account must indicate whether (a) or (b) above has been used.
(d) In addition, when applying (a) and (b) above, a Member State may require or permit calculation of the difference as at the date of acquisition of the participating interest referred to in paragraph 1 or, where the acquisition took place in two or more stages, as at the date as at which the holding became a participating interest within the meaning of paragraph 1 above.
3. Where the assets or liabilities of an undertaking in which a participating interest within the meaning of paragraph 1 above is held have been valued by methods other than those used by the company drawing up the annual accounts, they may, for the purpose of calculating the difference referred to in paragraph 2 (a) or (b) above, be revalued by the methods used by the company drawing up the annual accounts. Disclosure must be made in the notes on the accounts where such revaluation has not been carried out. A Member State may require such revaluation.
4. The book value referred to in paragraph 2 (a) above, or the amount corresponding to the proportion of capital and reserves referred to in paragraph 2 (b) above, shall be increased or reduced by the amount of the variation which has taken place during the financial year in the proportion of capital and reserves represented by that participating interest; it shall be reduced by the amount of the dividends relating to the participating interest.
5. In so far as a positive difference covered by paragraph 2 (a) or (b) above cannot be related to any category of asset or liability, it shall be dealt with in accordance with the rules applicable to the item "goodwill".
6. (a) The proportion of the profit or loss attributable to participating interests within the meaning of paragraph 1 above shall be shown in the profit-and-loss account as a separate item with an appropriate heading.
(b) Where that amount exceeds the amount of dividends already received or the payment of which can be claimed, the amount of the difference must be placed in a reserve which cannot be distributed to shareholders.
(c) A Member State may require or permit that the proportion of the profit or loss attributable to the participating interests referred to in paragraph 1 above be shown in the profit-and-loss account only to the extent of the amount corresponding to dividends already received or the payment of which can be claimed.
7. The eliminations referred to in Article 26 (1) (c) of Directive 83/349/EEC shall be effected in so far as the facts are known or can be ascertained. Article 26 (2) and (3) of that Directive shall apply.

8. Where an undertaking in which a participating interest within the meaning of paragraph 1 above is held draws up consolidated accounts, the foregoing paragraphs shall apply to the capital and reserves shown in such consolidated accounts.
9. This Article need not be applied where a participating interest as defined in paragraph 1 is not material for the purposes of Article 2 (3).'

Article 46. The following shall be substituted for Article 61 of Directive 78/660/EEC: 'Article 61
A Member State need not apply the provisions of point 2 of Article 43 (1) of this Directive concerning the amount of capital and reserves and profits and losses of the undertakings concerned to companies governed by their national laws which are parent undertakings for the purposes of Directive 83/349/EEC:
(a) where the undertakings concerned are included in consolidated accounts drawn up by that parent undertaking, or in the consolidated accounts of a larger body of undertakings as referred to in Article 7 (2) of Directive 83/349/EEC; or
(b) where the holdings in the undertakings concerned have been dealt with by the parent undertaking in its annual accounts in accordance with Article 59, or in the consolidated accounts drawn up by that parent undertaking in accordance with Article 33 of Directive 83/349/EEC.'

Article 47. The Contact Committee set up pursuant to Article 52 of Directive 78/660/EEC shall also:
(a) facilitate, without prejudice to Articles 169 and 170 of the Treaty, harmonized application of this Directive through regular meetings dealing, in particular, with practical problems arising in connection with its application;
(b) advise the Commission, if necessary, on additions or amendments to this Directive.

Article 48. Member States shall lay down the rules on penalties applicable to infringements of the national provisions adopted pursuant to this Directive and shall take all the measures necessary to ensure that they are implemented. The penalties provided for must be effective, proportionate and dissuasive.

Article 49. 1. The Member States shall bring into force the laws, regulations and administrative provisions necessary for them to comply with this Directive before 1 January 1988. They shall forthwith inform the Commission thereof.
2. A Member State may provide that the provisions referred to in paragraph 1 above shall first apply to consolidated accounts for financial years beginning on 1 January 1990 or during the calendar year 1990.
3. The Member States shall ensure that they communicate to the Commission the texts of the main provisions of national law which they adopt in the field covered by this Directive.

Article 50. 1. Five years after the date referred to in Article 49 (2), the Council, acting on a proposal from the Commission, shall examine and if need be revise Articles 1 (1) (d) (second subparagraph), 4 (2), 5, 6, 7 (1), 12, 43 and 44 in the light of the experience acquired in applying this Directive, the aims of this Directive and the economic and monetary situation at the time.
2. Paragraph 1 above shall not affect Article 53 (2) of Directive 78/660/EEC.

Article 50a. Not later than 1 January 2007, the Commission shall review the provisions in Article 29(1), Article 34(10), (14) and (15) and Article 36(2)(e) in the light of the experience acquired in applying provisions on fair value accounting and taking account of international developments in the field of accounting and, if appropriate, submit a proposal to the European Parliament and the Council with a view to amending the abovementioned Articles.

Article 51. This Directive is addressed to the Member States.

Directive 2005/56/EC of the European Parliament and of the Council of 26 October 2005 on cross-border mergers of limited liability companies ("Tenth Company Law Directive") (*O J* L 310, 25.11.2005, pp. 1). Consolidated version as last amended by Directive 2009/109/EC of the European Parliament and of the Council of 16 September 2009 amending Council Directives 77/91/EEC, 78/855/EEC and 82/891/EEC, and Directive 2005/56/EC as regards reporting and documentation requirements in the case of mergers and divisions [footnotes omitted].

THE EUROPEAN PARLIAMENT AND THE COUNCIL OF THE EUROPEAN UNION,
Having regard to the Treaty establishing the European Community, and in particular Article 44 thereof,
Having regard to the proposal from the Commission,
Having regard to the opinion of the European Economic and Social Committee, Acting in accordance with the procedure laid down in Article 251 of the Treaty,
Whereas:
(1) There is a need for cooperation and consolidation between limited liability companies from different Member States. However, as regards cross-border mergers of limited liability companies, they encounter many legislative and administrative difficulties in the Community. It is therefore necessary, with a view to the completion and functioning of the single market, to lay down Community provisions to facilitate the carrying-out of crossborder mergers between various types of limited liability company governed by the laws of different Member States.
(2) This Directive facilitates the cross-border merger of limited liability companies as defined herein. The laws of the Member States are to allow the cross-border merger of a national limited liability company with a limited liability company from another Member State if the national law of the relevant Member States permits mergers between such types of company.
(3) In order to facilitate cross-border merger operations, it should be laid down that, unless this Directive provides otherwise, each company taking part in a cross-border merger, and each third party concerned, remains subject to the provisions and formalities of the national law which would be applicable in the case of a national merger. None of the provisions and formalities of national law, to which reference is made in this Directive, should introduce restrictions on freedom of establishment or on the free movement of capital save where these can be justified in accordance with the case-law of the Court of Justice and in particular by requirements of the general interest and are both necessary for, and proportionate to, the attainment of such overriding requirements.
(4) The common draft terms of the cross-border merger are to be drawn up in the same terms for each of the companies concerned in the various Member States. The minimum content of such common draft terms should therefore be specified, while leaving the companies free to agree on other items.
(5) In order to protect the interests of members and others, both the common draft terms of cross-border mergers and the completion of the cross-border merger are to be publicised for each merging company via an entry in the appropriate public register.
(6) The laws of all the Member States should provide for the drawing-up at national level of a report on the common draft terms of the cross-border merger by one or more experts on behalf of each of the companies that are merging. In order to limit experts' costs connected with cross-border mergers, provision should be made for the possibility of drawing up a single report intended for all members of companies taking part in a cross-border merger operation. The common draft terms of the cross-border merger are to be approved by the general meeting of each of those companies.
(7) In order to facilitate cross-border merger operations, it should be provided that monitoring of the completion and legality of the decision-making process in each merging company should be carried out by the national authority having jurisdiction over each of those companies, whereas monitoring of the completion and legality of the cross-border merger should be carried out by the national authority having jurisdiction over the company resulting from the cross-border merger. The national authority in question may be a court, a notary or any other competent authority appointed by the Member State concerned. The national law determining the date on which the cross-border merger takes effect, this being the law to which the company resulting from the cross-border merger is subject, should also be specified.
(8) In order to protect the interests of members and others, the legal effects of the cross-border merger, distinguishing as to whether the company resulting from the cross-border merger is an acquiring company or a new company, should be specified. In the interests of legal certainty, it should no longer be possible, after the date on which a cross-border merger takes effect, to declare the merger null and void.
(9) This Directive is without prejudice to the application of the legislation on the control of concentrations between undertakings, both at Community level, by Regulation (EC) No 139/2004 (1), and at the level of Member States.
(10) This Directive does not affect Community legislation regulating credit intermediaries and other financial undertakings and national rules made or introduced pursuant to such Community legislation.

Part VIII. European Company Law

(11) This Directive is without prejudice to a Member State's legislation demanding information on the place of central administration or the principal place of business proposed for the company resulting from the cross-border merger.

(12) Employees' rights other than rights of participation should remain subject to the national provisions referred to in Council Directive 98/59/EC of 20 July 1998 on collective redundancies, Council Directive 2001/23/EC of 12 March 2001 on the safeguarding of employees' rights in the event of transfers of undertakings, businesses or parts of undertakings or businesses, Directive 2002/14/EC of the European Parliament and of the Council establishing a general framework for informing and consulting employees in the European Community and Council Directive 94/45/EC of 22 September 1994 on the establishment of a European Works Council or a procedure in Community-scale undertakings and Community-scale groups of undertakings for the purposes of informing and consulting employees.

(13) If employees have participation rights in one of the merging companies under the circumstances set out in this Directive and, if the national law of the Member State in which the company resulting from the cross-border merger has its registered office does not provide for the same level of participation as operated in the relevant merging companies, including in committees of the supervisory board that have decision-making powers, or does not provide for the same entitlement to exercise rights for employees of establishments resulting from the crossborder merger, the participation of employees in the company resulting from the cross-border merger and their involvement in the definition of such rights are to be regulated. To that end, the principles and procedures provided for in Council Regulation (EC) No 2157/2001 of 8 October 2001 on the Statute for a European company (SE) (3) and in Council Directive 2001/86/EC of 8 October 2001 supplementing the Statute for a European company with regard to the involvement of employees, are to be taken as a basis, subject, however, to modifications that are deemed necessary because the resulting company will be subject to the national laws of the Member State where it has its registered office. A prompt start to negotiations under Article 16 of this Directive, with a view to not unnecessarily delaying mergers, may be ensured by Member States in accordance with Article 3(2)(b) of Directive 2001/86/EC.

(14) For the purpose of determining the level of employee participation operated in the relevant merging companies, account
should also be taken of the proportion of employee representatives amongst the members of the management group, which covers the profit units of the companies, subject to employee participation.

(15) Since the objective of the proposed action, namely laying down rules with common features applicable at transnational level, cannot be sufficiently achieved by the Member States and can therefore, by reason of the scale and impact of the proposed action, be better achieved at Community level, the Community may adopt measures in accordance with the principle of subsidiarity as set out in Article 5 of the Treaty. In accordance with the principle of proportionality as set out in that Article, this Directive does not go beyond what is necessary to achieve that objective.

(16) In accordance with paragraph 34 of the Interinstitutional Agreement on better law-making , Member States should be encouraged to draw up, for themselves and in the interest of the Community, their own tables which will, as far as possible, illustrate the correlation between this Directive and the transposition measures and to make them public,

HAVE ADOPTED THIS DIRECTIVE:

Article 1. Scope. This Directive shall apply to mergers of limited liability companies formed in accordance with the law of a Member State and having their registered office, central administration or principal place of business within the Community, provided at least two of them are governed by the laws of different Member States (hereinafter referred to as cross-border mergers).

Article 2. Definitions. For the purposes of this Directive:
1) 'limited liability company', hereinafter referred to as 'company', means:
(a) a company as referred to in Article 1 of Directive 68/151/EEC (1), or
(b) a company with share capital and having legal personality, possessing separate assets which alone serve to cover its debts and subject under the national law governing it to conditions concerning guarantees such as are provided for by Directive 68/151/EEC for the protection of the interests of members and others;
2. 'merger' means an operation whereby:
(a) one or more companies, on being dissolved without going into liquidation, transfer all their assets and liabilities to another existing company, the acquiring company, in exchange for the issue to their members of securities or shares representing the capital of that other company and, if applicable, a cash payment not exceeding

10 % of the nominal value, or, in the absence of a nominal value, of the accounting par value of those securities or shares; or

(b) two or more companies, on being dissolved without going into liquidation, transfer all their assets and liabilities to a company that they form, the new company, in exchange for the issue to their members of securities or shares representing the capital of that new company and, if applicable, a cash payment not exceeding 10 % of the nominal value, or in the absence of a nominal value, of the accounting par value of those securities or shares; or

(c) a company, on being dissolved without going into liquidation, transfers all its assets and liabilities to the company holding all the securities or shares representing its capital.

Article 3. Further provisions concerning the scope. 1. Notwithstanding Article 2(2), this Directive shall also apply to cross-border mergers where the law of at least one of the Member States concerned allows the cash payment referred to in points (a) and (b) of Article 2(2) to exceed 10 % of the nominal value, or, in the absence of a nominal value, of the accounting par value of the securities or shares representing the capital of the company resulting from the cross-border merger.

2. Member States may decide not to apply this Directive to crossborder mergers involving a cooperative society even in the cases where the latter would fall within the definition of 'limited liability company' as laid down in Article 2(1).

3. This Directive shall not apply to cross-border mergers involving a company the object of which is the collective investment of capital provided by the public, which operates on the principle of riskspreading and the units of which are, at the holders' request, repurchased or redeemed, directly or indirectly, out of the assets of that company. Action taken by such a company to ensure that the stock exchange value of its units does not vary significantly from its net asset value shall be regarded as equivalent to such repurchase or redemption.

Article 4. Conditions relating to cross-border mergers. 1. Save as otherwise provided in this Directive,
(a) cross-border mergers shall only be possible between types of companies which may merge under the national law of the relevant Member States, and
(b) a company taking part in a cross-border merger shall comply with the provisions and formalities of the national law to which it is subject. The laws of a Member State enabling its national authorities to oppose a given internal merger on grounds of public interest shall also be applicable to a cross-border merger where at least one of the merging companies is subject to the law of that Member State. This provision shall not apply to the extent that Article 21 of Regulation (EC) No 139/2004 is applicable.

2. The provisions and formalities referred to in paragraph 1(b) shall, in particular, include those concerning the decision-making process relating to the merger and, taking into account the cross-border nature of the merger, the protection of creditors of the merging companies, debenture holders and the holders of securities or shares, as well as of employees as regards rights other than those governed by Article 16. A Member State may, in the case of companies participating in a crossborder merger and governed by its law, adopt provisions designed to ensure appropriate protection for minority members who have opposed the cross-border merger.

Article 5. Common draft terms of cross-border mergers. The management or administrative organ of each of the merging companies shall draw up the common draft terms of cross-border merger. The common draft terms of cross-border merger shall include at least the following particulars:

(a) the form, name and registered office of the merging companies and those proposed for the company resulting from the cross-border merger;
(b) the ratio applicable to the exchange of securities or shares representing the company capital and the amount of any cash payment;
(c) the terms for the allotment of securities or shares representing the capital of the company resulting from the cross-border merger;
(d) the likely repercussions of the cross-border merger on employment;
(e) the date from which the holding of such securities or shares representing the company capital will entitle the holders to share in profits and any special conditions affecting that entitlement;
(f) the date from which the transactions of the merging companies will be treated for accounting purposes as being those of the company resulting from the cross-border merger;
(g) the rights conferred by the company resulting from the cross-border merger on members enjoying special rights or on holders of securities other than shares representing the company capital, or the measures proposed concerning them;
(h) any special advantages granted to the experts who examine the draft terms of the cross-border merger or to members of the administrative, management, supervisory or controlling organs of the merging companies;

PART VIII. EUROPEAN COMPANY LAW

(i) the statutes of the company resulting from the cross-border merger;
(j) where appropriate, information on the procedures by which arrangements for the involvement of employees in the definition of their rights to participation in the company resulting from the cross-border merger are determined pursuant to Article 16;
(k) information on the evaluation of the assets and liabilities which are transferred to the company resulting from the cross-border merger;
(l) dates of the merging companies' accounts used to establish the conditions of the cross-border merger.

Article 6. 1. The common draft terms of the cross-border merger shall be published in the manner prescribed by the laws of each Member State in accordance with Article 3 of Directive 68/151/EEC for each of the merging companies at least one month before the date of the general meeting which is to decide thereon.
Any of the merging companies shall be exempt from the publication requirement laid down in Article 3 of Directive 68/151/EEC if, for a continuous period beginning at least one month before the day fixed for the general meeting which is to decide on the common draft terms of cross-border merger and ending not earlier than the conclusion of that meeting, it makes the common draft terms of such merger available on its website free of charge for the public. Member States shall not subject that exemption to any requirements or constraints other than those which are necessary in order to ensure the security of the website and the authenticity of the documents and may impose such requirements or constraints only to the extent that they are proportionate in order to achieve those objectives. By way of derogation from the second subparagraph, Member States may require that publication be effected via the central electronic platform referred to in Article 3(4) of Directive 68/151/EEC. Member States may alternatively require that such publication be made on any other website designated by them for that purpose. Where Member States avail themselves of one of those possibilities, they shall ensure that companies are not charged a specific fee for such publication. Where a website other than the central electronic platform is used, a reference giving access to that website shall be published on the central electronic platform at least one month before the day fixed for the general meeting. That reference shall include the date of publication of the common draft terms of cross-border merger on the website and shall be accessible to the public free of charge. Companies shall not be charged a specific fee for such publication. The prohibition precluding the charging to companies of a specific fee for publication, laid down in the third and fourth subparagraphs, shall not affect the ability of Member States to pass on to companies the costs in respect of the central electronic platform. Member States may require companies to maintain the information for a specific period after the general meeting on their website or, where applicable, on the central electronic platform or the other website designated by the Member State concerned.
Member States may determine the consequences of temporary disruption of access to the website or to the central electronic platform, caused by technical or other factors.
2. For each of the merging companies and subject to the additional requirements imposed by the Member State to which the company concerned is subject, the following particulars shall be published in the national gazette of that Member State:
(a) the type, name and registered office of every merging company;
(b) the register in which the documents referred to in Article 3(2) of Directive 68/151/EEC are filed in respect of each merging company, and the number of the entry in that register;
(c) an indication, for each of the merging companies, of the arrangements made for the exercise of the rights of creditors and of any minority members of the merging companies and the address at which complete information on those arrangements may be obtained free of charge.

Article 7. Report of the management or administrative organ. The management or administrative organ of each of the merging companies shall draw up a report intended for the members explaining and justifying the legal and economic aspects of the cross-border merger and explaining the implications of the cross-border merger for members, creditors and employees.
The report shall be made available to the members and to the representatives of the employees or, where there are no such representatives, to the employees themselves, not less than one month before the date of the general meeting referred to in Article 9.
Where the management or administrative organ of any of the merging companies receives, in good time, an opinion from the representatives of their employees, as provided for under national law, that opinion shall be appended to the report.

Article 8. 1. An independent expert report intended for members and made available not less than one month before the date of the general meeting referred to in Article 9 shall be drawn up for each merging company. Depending on the law of each Member State, such experts may be natural persons or legal persons.

2. As an alternative to experts operating on behalf of each of the merging companies, one or more independent experts, appointed for that purpose at the joint request of the companies by a judicial or administrative authority in the Member State of one of the merging companies or of the company resulting from the cross-border merger or approved by such an authority, may examine the common draft terms of crossborder merger and draw up a single written report to all the members.

3. The expert report shall include at least the particulars provided for by Article 10(2) of Council Directive 78/855/EEC of 9 October 1978 concerning mergers of public limited liability companies (1). The experts shall be entitled to secure from each of the merging companies all information they consider necessary for the discharge of their duties.

4. Neither an examination of the common draft terms of cross-border merger by independent experts nor an expert report shall be required if all the members of each of the companies involved in the cross-border merger have so agreed.

Article 9. 1. After taking note of the reports referred to in Articles 7 and 8, the general meeting of each of the merging companies shall decide on the approval of the common draft terms of cross-border merger.

2. The general meeting of each of the merging companies may reserve the right to make implementation of the cross-border merger conditional on express ratification by it of the arrangements decided on with respect to the participation of employees in the company resulting from the cross-border merger.

3. The laws of a Member State need not require approval of the merger by the general meeting of the acquiring company if the conditions laid down in Article 8 of Directive 78/855/EEC are fulfilled.

Article 10. 1. Each Member State shall designate the court, notary or other authority competent to scrutinise the legality of the cross-border merger as regards that part of the procedure which concerns each merging company subject to its national law.

2. In each Member State concerned the authority referred to in paragraph 1 shall issue, without delay to each merging company subject to that State's national law, a certificate conclusively attesting to the proper completion of the pre-merger acts and formalities.

3. If the law of a Member State to which a merging company is subject provides for a procedure to scrutinise and amend the ratio applicable to the exchange of securities or shares, or a procedure to compensate minority members, without preventing the registration of the cross-border merger, such procedure shall only apply if the other merging companies situated in Member States which do not provide for such procedure explicitly accept, when approving the draft terms of the cross-border merger in accordance with Article 9(1), the possibility for the members of that merging company to have recourse to such procedure, to be initiated before the court having jurisdiction over that merging company. In such cases, the authority referred to in paragraph 1 may issue the certificate referred to in paragraph 2 even if such procedure has commenced. The certificate must, however, indicate that the procedure is pending. The decision in the procedure shall be binding on the company resulting from the cross-border merger and all its members.

Article 11. 1. Each Member State shall designate the court, notary or other authority competent to scrutinise the legality of the cross-border merger as regards that part of the procedure which concerns the completion of the cross-border merger and, where appropriate, the formation of a new company resulting from the cross-border merger where the company created by the cross-border merger is subject to its national law. The said authority shall in particular ensure that the merging companies have approved the common draft terms of crossborder merger in the same terms and, where appropriate, that arrangements for employee participation have been determined in accordance with Article 16.

2. To that end each merging company shall submit to the authority referred to in paragraph 1 the certificate referred to in Article 10(2) within six months of its issue together with the common draft terms of cross-border merger approved by the general meeting referred to in Article 9.

Article 12. The law of the Member State to whose jurisdiction the company resulting from the cross-border merger is subject shall determine the date on which the cross-border merger takes effect. That date must be after the scrutiny referred to in Article 11 has been carried out.

Article 13. The law of each of the Member States to whose jurisdiction the merging companies were subject shall determine, with respect to the territory of that State, the arrangements, in accordance with Article 3 of Directive 68/151/EEC, for publicising completion of the cross-border merger in the public register in which each of the companies is required to file documents.

PART VIII. EUROPEAN COMPANY LAW

The registry for the registration of the company resulting from the crossborder merger shall notify, without delay, the registry in which each of the companies was required to file documents that the cross-border merger has taken effect. Deletion of the old registration, if applicable, shall be effected on receipt of that notification, but not before.

Article 14. 1. A cross-border merger carried out as laid down in points (a) and (c) of Article 2(2) shall, from the date referred to in Article 12, have the following consequences:
(a) all the assets and liabilities of the company being acquired shall be transferred to the acquiring company;
(b) the members of the company being acquired shall become members of the acquiring company;
(c) the company being acquired shall cease to exist.
2. A cross-border merger carried out as laid down in point (b) of Article 2(2) shall, from the date referred to in Article 12, have the following consequences:
(a) all the assets and liabilities of the merging companies shall be transferred to the new company;
(b) the members of the merging companies shall become members of the new company;
(c) the merging companies shall cease to exist.
3. Where, in the case of a cross-border merger of companies covered by this Directive, the laws of the Member States require the completion of special formalities before the transfer of certain assets, rights and obligations by the merging companies becomes effective against third parties, those formalities shall be carried out by the company resulting from the cross-border merger.
4. The rights and obligations of the merging companies arising from contracts of employment or from employment relationships and existing at the date on which the cross-border merger takes effect shall, by reason of that cross-border merger taking effect, be transferred to the company resulting from the cross-border merger on the date on which the cross-border merger takes effect.
5. No shares in the acquiring company shall be exchanged for shares in the company being acquired held either:
(a) by the acquiring company itself or through a person acting in his or her own name but on its behalf;
(b) by the company being acquired itself or through a person acting in his or her own name but on its behalf.

Article 15. 1. Where a cross-border merger by acquisition is carried out by a company which holds all the shares and other securities conferring the right to vote at general meetings of the company or companies being acquired:
— Articles 5, points (b), (c) and (e), 8 and 14(1), point (b) shall not apply,
— Article 9(1) shall not apply to the company or companies being acquired.
2. Where a cross-border merger by acquisition is carried out by a company which holds 90 % or more, but not all, of the shares and other securities conferring the right to vote at general meetings of the company or companies being acquired, reports by an independent expert or experts and the documents necessary for scrutiny shall be required only to the extent that the national law governing either the acquiring company or the company or companies being acquired so requires, in accordance with Directive 78/855/EEC.

Article 16. 1. Without prejudice to paragraph 2, the company resulting from the cross-border merger shall be subject to the rules in force concerning registered office.
2. However, the rules in force concerning employee participation, if any, in the Member State where the company resulting from the crossborder merger has its registered office shall not apply, where at least one of the merging companies has, in the six months before the publication of the draft terms of the cross-border merger as referred to in Article 6, an average number of employees that exceeds 500 and is operating under an employee participation system within the meaning of Article 2(k) of Directive 2001/86/EC, or where the national law applicable to the company resulting from the cross-border merger does not
(a) provide for at least the same level of employee participation as operated in the relevant merging companies, measured by reference to the proportion of employee representatives amongst the members of the administrative or supervisory organ or their committees or of the management group which covers the profit units of the company, subject to employee representation, or
(b) provide for employees of establishments of the company resulting from the cross-border merger that are situated in other Member States the same entitlement to exercise participation rights as is enjoyed by those employees employed in the Member State where the company resulting from the cross-border merger has its registered office.
3. In the cases referred to in paragraph 2, the participation of employees in the company resulting from the cross-border merger and their involvement in the definition of such rights shall be regulated by the Member States, mutatis mutandis and subject to paragraphs 4 to 7 below, in accordance with the principles and procedures laid down in Article 12(2), (3) and (4) of Regulation (EC) No 2157/2001 and the following provisions of Directive 2001/86/EC:
(a) Article 3(1), (2) and (3), (4) first subparagraph, first indent, and second subparagraph, (5) and (7);

(b) Article 4(1), (2), points (a), (g) and (h), and (3);
(c) Article 5;
(d) Article 6;
(e) Article 7(1), (2) first subparagraph, point (b), and second subparagraph, and (3). However, for the purposes of this Directive, the percentages required by Article 7(2), first subparagraph, point (b) of Directive 2001/86/EC for the application of the standard rules contained in part 3 of the Annex to that Directive shall be raised from 25 to 33 1/3 %;
(f) Articles 8, 10 and 12;
(g) Article 13(4);
(h) part 3 of the Annex, point (b).
4. When regulating the principles and procedures referred to in paragraph 3, Member States:
(a) shall confer on the relevant organs of the merging companies the right to choose without any prior negotiation to be directly subject to the standard rules for participation referred to in paragraph 3(h), as laid down by the legislation of the Member State in which the company resulting from the cross-border merger is to have its registered office, and to abide by those rules from the date of registration;
(b) shall confer on the special negotiating body the right to decide, by a majority of two thirds of its members representing at least two thirds of the employees, including the votes of members representing employees in at least two different Member States, not to open negotiations or to terminate negotiations already opened and to rely on the rules on participation in force in the Member State where the registered office of the company resulting from the cross-border merger will be situated;
(c) may, in the case where, following prior negotiations, standard rules for participation apply and notwithstanding these rules, determine to limit the proportion of employee representatives in the administrative organ of the company resulting from the cross-border merger. However, if in one of the merging companies employee representatives constituted at least one third of the administrative or supervisory board, the limitation may never result in a lower proportion of employee representatives in the administrative organ than one third.
5. The extension of participation rights to employees of the company resulting from the cross-border merger employed in other Member States, referred to in paragraph 2(b), shall not entail any obligation for Member States which choose to do so to take those employees into account when calculating the size of workforce thresholds giving rise to participation rights under national law.
6. When at least one of the merging companies is operating under an employee participation system and the company resulting from the cross-border merger is to be governed by such a system in accordance with the rules referred to in paragraph 2, that company shall be obliged to take a legal form allowing for the exercise of participation rights.
7. When the company resulting from the cross-border merger is operating under an employee participation system, that company shall be obliged to take measures to ensure that employees' participation rights are protected in the event of subsequent domestic mergers for a period of three years after the cross-border merger has taken effect, by applying mutatis mutandis the rules laid down in this Article.

Article 17. A cross-border merger which has taken effect as provided for in Article 12 may not be declared null and void.

Article 18. Five years after the date laid down in the first paragraph of Article 19, the Commission shall review this Directive in the light of the experience acquired in applying it and, if necessary, propose its amendment.

Article 19. Member States shall bring into force the laws, regulations and administrative provisions necessary to comply with this Directive by 15 December 2007. When Member States adopt these measures, they shall contain a reference to this Directive or shall be accompanied by such reference on the occasion of their official publication. The methods of making such reference shall be laid down by Member States.

Article 20. This Directive shall enter into force on the 20th day following its publication in the Official Journal of the European Union.

Article 21. This Directive is addressed to the Member States.

Council Directive 89/666/EEC of 21 December 1989 concerning disclosure requirements in respect of branches opened in a Member State by certain types of company governed by the law of another State ("Eleventh Company Law Directive") (*OJ* L 395 , 30.12.1989 pp. 36 -39) [footnotes omitted].

THE COUNCIL OF THE EUROPEAN COMMUNITIES,
Having regard to the Treaty establishing the European Economic Community, and in particular Article 54 thereof,
Having regard to the proposal from the Commission, In cooperation with the European Parliament,
Having regard to the opinion of the Economic and Social Committee,
Whereas in order to facilitate the exercise of the freedom of establishment in respect of companies covered by Article 58 of the Treaty, Article 54 (3) (g) and the general programme on the elimination of restrictions on the freedom of establishment require coordination of the safeguards required of companies and firms in the Member States for the protection of the interests of members and others;
Whereas hitherto this coordination has been effected in respect of disclosure by the adoption of the First Directive 68/151/EEC covering companies with share capital, as last amended by the 1985 Act of Accession; whereas it was continued in the field of accounting by the Fourth Directive 78/660/EEC on the annual accounts of certain types of companies, as last amended by the 1985 Act of Accession, the Seventh Directive 83/349/EEC on consolidated accounts, as amended by the 1985 Act of Accession, and the Eighth Directive 84/253/EEC on the persons responsible for carrying out the statutory audits of accounting documents;
Whereas these Directives apply to companies as such but do not cover their branches; whereas the opening of a branch, like the creation of a subsidiary, is one of the possibilities currently open to companies in the exercise of their right of establishment in another Member State;
Whereas in respect of branches the lack of coordination, in particular concerning disclosure, gives rise to some disparities, in the protection of shareholders and third parties, between companies which operate in other Member States by opening branches and those which operate there by creating subsidiaries;
Whereas in this field the differences in the laws of the Member States may interfere with the exercise of the right of establishment; whereas it is therefore necessary to eliminate such differences in order to safeguard, inter alia, the exercise of that right;
Whereas to ensure the protection of persons who deal with companies through the intermediary of branches, measures in respect of disclosure are required in the Member State in which a branch is situated; whereas, in certain respects, the economic and social influence of a branch may be comparable to that of a subsidiary company, so that there is public interest in disclosure of the company at the branch; whereas to effect such disclosure it is necessary to make use of the procedure already instituted for companies with share capital within the Community;
Whereas such disclosure relates to a range of important documents and particulars and amendments thereto;
Whereas such disclosure, with the exception of the powers of representation, the name and legal form and the winding-up of the company and the insolvency proceedings to which it is subject, may be confined to information concerning a branch itself together with a reference to the register of the company of which that branch is part, since under existing Community rules all information covering the company as such is available in that register;
Whereas national provisions in respect of the disclosure of accounting documents relating to a branch can no longer be justified following the coordination of national law in respect of the drawing up, audit and disclosure of companies' accounting documents; whereas it is accordingly sufficient to disclose, in the register of the branch, the accounting documents as audited and disclosed by the company;
Whereas letters and order forms used by a branch must give at least the same information as letters and order forms used by the company, and state the register in which the branch is entered;
Whereas to ensure that the purposes of this Directive are fully realized and to avoid any discrimination on the basis of a company's country of origin, this Directive must also cover branches opened by companies governed by the law of non-member countries and set up in legal forms comparable to companies to which Directive 68/151/EEC applies; whereas for these branches it is necessary to apply certain provisions different from those that apply to the branches of companies governed by the law of other Member States since the Directives referred to above do not apply to companies from non-member countries;
Whereas this Directive in no way affects the disclosure requirements for branches under other provisions of, for example, employment law on workers' rights to information and tax law, or for statistical purposes;

HAS ADOPTED THIS DIRECTIVE:

PART VIII. EUROPEAN COMPANY LAW

Section I. Branches of companies from other Member States

Article 1. 1. Documents and particulars relating to a branch opened in a Member State by a company which is governed by the law of another Member State and to which Directive 68/151/EEC applies shall be disclosed pursuant to the law of the Member State of the branch, in accordance with Article 3 of that Directive.

2. Where disclosure requirements in respect of the branch differ from those in respect of the company, the branch's disclosure requirements shall take precedence with regard to transactions carried out with the branch.

Article 2. 1. The compulsory disclosure provided for in Article 1 shall cover the following documents and particulars only:
(a) the address of the branch;
(b) the activities of the branch;
(c) the register in which the company file mentioned in Article 3 of Council Directive 68/151/EEC is kept, together with the registration number in that register;
(d) the name and legal form of the company and the name of the branch if that is different from the name of the company;
(e) the appointment, termination of office and particulars of the persons who are authorized to represent the company in dealings with third parties and in legal proceedings;
- as a company organ constituted pursuant to law or as members of any such organ, in accordance with the disclosure by the company as provided for in Article 2 (1) (d) of Directive 68/151/EEC,
- as permanent representatives of the company for the activities of the branch, with an indication of the extent of their powers;
(f) the winding-up of the company, the appointment of liquidators, particulars concerning them and their powers and the termination of the liquidation in accordance with disclosure by the company as provided for in Article 2 (1) (h), (j) and (k) of Directive 68/151/EEC,
- insolvency proceedings, arrangements, compositions, or any analogous proceedings to which the company is subject;
(g) the accounting documents in accordance with Article 3;
(h) the closure of the branch.

2. The Member State in which the branch has been opened may provide for the disclosure, as referred to in Article 1, of
(a) the signature of the persons referred to in paragraph 1 (e) and (f) of this Article;
(b) the instruments of constitution and the memorandum and articles of association if they are contained in a separate instrument in accordance with Article 2 (1) (a), (b) and (c) of Directive 68/151/EEC, together with amendments to those documents;
(c) an attestation from the register referred to in paragraph 1 (c) of this Article relating to the existence of the company;
(d) an indication of the securities on the company's property situated in that Member State, provided such disclosure relates to the validity of those securities.

Article 3. The compulsory disclosure provided for by Article 2 (1) (g) shall be limited to the accounting documents of the company as drawn up, audited and disclosed pursuant to the law of the Member State by which the company is governed in accordance with Directives 78/660/EEC, 83/349/EEC and 84/253/EEC.

Article 4. The Member State in which the branch has been opened may stipulate that the documents referred to in Article 2 (2) (b) and Article 3 must be published in another official language of the Community and that the translation of such documents must be certified.

Article 5. Where a company has opened more than one branch in a Member State, the disclosure referred to in Article 2 (2) (b) and Article 3 may be made in the register of the branch of the company's choice. In this case, compulsory disclosure by the other branches shall cover the particulars of the branch register of which disclosure was made, together with the number of that branch in that register.

Article 6. The Member States shall prescribe that letters and order forms used by a branch shall state, in addition to the information prescribed by Article 4 of Directive 68/151/EEC, the register in which the file in respect of the branch is kept together with the number of the branch in that register.

Section II. Branches of companies from third countries

Article 7. 1. Documents and particulars concerning a branch opened in a Member State by a company which is not governed by the law of a Member State but which is of a legal form comparable with the types of company to which Directive 68/151/EEC applies shall be disclosed in accordance with the law of the Member State of the branch as laid down in Article 3 of that Directive.
2. Article 1 (2) shall apply.

Article 8. The compulsory disclosure provided for in Article 7 shall cover at least the following documents and particulars:
(a) the address of the branch;
(b) the activities of the branch;
(c) the law of the State by which the company is governed;
(d) where that law so provides, the register in which the company is entered and the registration number of the company in that register;
(e) the instruments of constitution, and memorandum and articles of association if they are contained in a separate instrument, with all amendments to these documents;
(f) the legal form of the company, its principal place of business and its object and, at least annually, the amount of subscribed capital if these particulars are not given in the documents referred to in subparagraph (e);
(g) the name of the company and the name of the branch if that is different from the name of the company;
(h) the appointment, termination of office and particulars of the persons who are authorized to represent the company in dealings with third parties and in legal proceedings:
- as a company organ constituted pursuant to law or as members of any such organ,
- as permanent representatives of the company for the activities of the branch. The extent of the powers of the persons authorized to represent the company must be stated, together with whether they may do so alone or must act jointly;
(i) - the winding-up of the company and the appointment of liquidators, particulars concerning them and their powers and the termination of the liquidation;
- insolvency proceedings, arrangements, compositions or any analogous proceedings to which the company is subject;
(j) the accounting documents in accordance with Article 7;
(k) the closure of the branch.

Article 9. 1. The compulsory disclosure provided for by Article 8 (1) (j) shall apply to the accounting documents of the company as drawn up, audited and disclosed pursuant to the law of the State which governs the company. Where they are not drawn up in accordance with or in a manner equivalent to Directives 78/660/EEC and 83/349/EEC, Member States may require that accounting documents relating to the activities of the branch be drawn up and disclosed.
2. Articles 4 and 5 shall apply.

Article 10. The Member States shall prescribe that letters and order forms used by a branch state the register in which the file in respect of the branch is kept together with the number of the branch in that register. Where the law of the State by which the company is governed requires entry in a register, the register in which the company is entered, and the registration number of the company in that register must also be stated.

Section III. Indication of branches in the company's annual report

Article 11. The following subparagraph is added to Article 46 (2) of Directive 78/660/EEC: '(e) the existence of branches of the company'.

Section IV. Transitional and final provisions

Article 12. The Member States shall provide for appropriate penalties in the event of failure to disclose the matters set out in Articles 1, 2, 3, 7, 8 and 9 and of omission from letters and order forms of the compulsory particulars provided for in Articles 6 and 10.

Article 13. Each Member State shall determine who shall carry out the disclosure formalities provided for in this Directive.

Article 14. 1. Articles 3 and 9 shall not apply to branches opened by credit institutions and financial institutions covered by Directive 89/117/EEC (8).
2. Pending subsequent coordination, the Member States need not apply Articles 3 and 9 to branches opened by insurance companies.

Article 15. Article 54 of Directive 78/660/EEC and Article 48 of Directive 83/349/EEC shall be deleted.

Article 16. 1. Member States shall adopt the laws, regulations and administrative provisions necessary to comply with this Directive not later than 1 January 1992. They shall forthwith inform the Commission thereof.
2. Member States shall stipulate that the provisions referred to in paragraph 1 shall apply from 1 January 1993 and, with regard to accounting documents, shall apply for the first time to annual accounts for the financial year beginning on 1 January 1993 or during 1993.
3. Member States shall communicate to the Commission the texts of the provisions of national law which they adopt in the field covered by this Directive.

Article 17. The Contact Committee set up pursuant to Article 52 of Directive 78/660/EEC shall also:
(a) facilitate, without prejudice to Articles 169 and 170 of the Treaty, the harmonized application of this Directive, through regular meetings dealing, in particular, with practical problems arising in connection with its application;
(b) advise the Commission, if necessary, on any additions or amendments to this Directive.

Article 18. This Directive is addressed to the Member States.

Directive 2009/102/EC of the European Parliament and of the Council of 16 September 2009 in the area of company law on single-member private limited liability companies ("Twelfth Company Law Directive") (Text with EEA relevance) (*OJ* L 258 , 01.10.2009 pp. 20 –25) [footnotes omitted].

THE EUROPEAN PARLIAMENT AND THE COUNCIL OF THE EUROPEAN UNION,
Having regard to the Treaty establishing the European Community, and in particular Article 44 thereof,
Having regard to the proposal from the Commission,
Having regard to the opinion of the European Economic and Social Committee, Acting in accordance with the procedure laid down in Article 251 of the Treaty, Whereas:
(1) Twelfth Council Company Law Directive 89/667/EEC of 21 December 1989 on single-member private limited-liability companies has been substantially amended several times. In the interests of clarity and rationality the said Directive should be codified.
(2) Certain safeguards which, for the protection of the interests of members and others, are required by Member States of companies and firms within the meaning of the second paragraph of Article 48 of the Treaty should be coordinated with a view to making such safeguards equivalent throughout the Community.
(3) In this field, First Council Directive 68/151/EEC of 9 March 1968 on coordination of safeguards which, for the protection of the interests of members and others, are required by Member States of companies within the meaning of the second paragraph of Article 58 of the Treaty, with a view to making such safeguards equivalent throughout the Community, Fourth Council Directive 78/660/EEC of 25 July 1978 based on Article 54(3)(g) of the Treaty on the annual accounts of certain types of companies and Seventh Council Directive 83/349/EEC of 13 June 1983 based on Article 54(3)(g) of the Treaty on consolidated accounts, respectively concerning disclosure, the validity of commitments, nullity, annual accounts and consolidated accounts, apply to all share-capital companies. However, Second Council Directive 77/91/EEC of 13 December 1976 on coordination of safeguards which, for the protection of the interests of members and others, are required by Member States of companies within the meaning of the second paragraph of Article 58 of the Treaty, in respect of the formation of public limited liability companies and the maintenance and alteration of their capital, with a view to making such safeguards equivalent, Third Council Directive 78/855/EEC of 9 October 1978 based on Article 54(3)(g) of the Treaty concerning mergers of public limited liability companies, and Sixth Council Directive 82/891/EEC of 17 December 1982 based on Article 54(3)(g) of the Treaty, concerning the division of public limited liability companies, relating respectively to formation and capital, mergers and divisions, apply only to public limited liability companies.
(4) A legal instrument is required allowing the limitation of liability of the individual entrepreneur throughout the Community, without prejudice to the laws of the Member States, which, in exceptional circumstances, require that entrepreneur to be liable for the obligations of his undertaking.
(5) A private limited liability company may be a single-member company from the time of its formation, or may become one because its shares have come to be held by a single shareholder. Pending the coordination of national provisions on the laws relating to groups, Member States may lay down certain special provisions and penalties for cases where a natural person is the sole member of several companies or where a single-member company or any other legal person is the sole member of a company. The sole aim of this power is to take account of the differences which exist in certain national laws. For that purpose, Member States may in specific cases lay down restrictions on the use of single-member companies or remove the limits on the liabilities of sole members. Member States are free to lay down rules to cover the risks that single-member companies may present as a consequence of having single members, particularly in order to ensure that the subscribed capital is paid.
(6) The fact that all the shares have come to be held by a single shareholder and the identity of the sole member should be disclosed by an entry in a register accessible to the public.
(7) Decisions taken by the sole member exercising the powers of the general meeting should be recorded in writing.
(8) Contracts between a sole member and his company as represented by him should likewise be recorded in writing, in so far as such contracts do not relate to current operations concluded under normal conditions.
(9) This Directive should be without prejudice to the obligations of the Member States relating to the time limits for transposition into national law and application of the Directives set out in Annex II, Part B,

HAVE ADOPTED THIS DIRECTIVE:

Article 1. The coordination measures prescribed by this Directive shall apply to the laws, regulations and administrative provisions of the Member States relating to the types of company listed in Annex I.

Article 2. 1. A company may have a sole member when it is formed and also when all its shares come to be held by a single person (single-member company).

2. Member States may, pending coordination of national laws relating to groups, lay down special provisions or penalties for cases where:
(a) a natural person is the sole member of several companies; or
(b) a single-member company or any other legal person is the sole member of a company.

Article 3. Where a company becomes a single-member company because all its shares come to be held by a single person, that fact, together with the identity of the sole member, must either be recorded in the file or entered in the register as referred to in Article 3(1) and (2) of Directive 68/151/EEC or be entered in a register kept by the company and accessible to the public.

Article 4. 1. The sole member shall exercise the powers of the general meeting of the company.
2. Decisions taken by the sole member in the field referred to in paragraph 1 shall be recorded in minutes or drawn up in writing.

Article 5. 1. Contracts between the sole member and his company as represented by him shall be recorded in minutes or drawn up in writing.
2. Member States need not apply paragraph 1 to current operations concluded under normal conditions.

Article 6. Where a Member State allows single-member companies as defined by Article 2(1) in the case of public limited companies as well, this Directive shall apply.

Article 7. A Member State need not allow the formation of single-member companies where its legislation provides that an individual entrepreneur may set up an undertaking the liability of which is limited to a sum dedicated to a stated activity, on condition that safeguards are laid down for such undertakings which are equivalent to those imposed by this Directive or by any other Community provisions applicable to the companies referred to in Article 1.

Article 8. Member States shall communicate to the Commission the texts of the main provisions of national law which they adopt in the field covered by this Directive.

Article 9. Directive 89/667/EEC, as amended by the acts listed in Annex II, Part A, is repealed, without prejudice to the obligations of the Member States relating to the time limits for transposition into national law and application of the Directives set out in Annex II, Part B. References to the repealed Directive shall be construed as references to this Directive and shall be read in accordance with the correlation table in Annex III.

Article 10. This Directive shall enter into force on the 20th day following its publication in the Official Journal of the European Union.

Article 11. This Directive is addressed to the Member States.

Annex I. Types of companies referred to in Article 1
Belgium: "société privée à responsabilité limitée/besloten vennootschap met beperkte aansprakelijkheid",
Bulgaria: "дружество с ограничена отговорност, акционерно дружество",
Czech Republic: "společnost s ručením omezeným",
Denmark: "anpartsselskaber",
Germany: "Gesellschaft mit beschränkter Haftung",
Estonia: "aktsiaselts, osaühing",
Ireland: "private company limited by shares or by guarantee",
Greece: "εταιρεία περιορισμένης ευθύνης",
Spain: "sociedad de responsabilidad limitada",
France: "société à responsabilité limitée",
Italy: "società a responsabilità limitata",
Cyprus: "ιδιωτική εταιρεία περιορισμένης ευθύνης με μετοχές ή με εγγύηση",
Latvia: "sabiedrība ar ierobežotu atbildību",
Lithuania: "uždaroji akcinė bendrovė",
Luxembourg: "société à responsabilité limitée",
Hungary: "korlátolt felelősségű társaság, részvénytársaság",
Malta: "kumpannija privata/Private limited liability company",

The Netherlands: "besloten vennootschap met beperkte aansprakelijkheid",
Austria: "Aktiengesellschaft, Gesellschaft mit beschränkter Haftung",
Poland: "spółka z ograniczoną odpowiedzialnością",
Portugal: "sociedade por quotas",
Romania: "societate cu răspundere limitată",
Slovenia: "družba z omejeno odgovornostjo",
Slovakia: "spoločnosť s ručením obmedzeným",
Finland: "osakeyhtiö/aktiebolag",
Sweden: "aktiebolag",
United Kingdom: "private company limited by shares or by guarantee".

Directive 2004/25/EC of the European Parliament and the Council of 21 April 2004 on takeover bids (Text with EEA relevance) ("Thirteenth Company Law Directive") (*O J* L 142 , 30.04.2004 pp. 12 – 23) [footnotes omitted].

THE EUROPEAN PARLIAMENT AND THE COUNCIL OF THE EUROPEAN UNION,
Having regard to the Treaty establishing the European Community, and in particular Article 44(1) thereof, Having regard to the proposal from the Commission ,
Having regard to the opinion of the European Economic and Social Committee ,
Acting in accordance with the procedure laid down in Article 251 of the Treaty ,
Whereas:
(1) In accordance with Article 44(2)(g) of the Treaty, it is necessary to coordinate certain safeguards which, for the protection of the interests of members and others, Member States require of companies governed by the law of a Member State the securities of which are admitted to trading on a regulated market in a Member State, with a view to making such safeguards equivalent throughout the Community.
(2) It is necessary to protect the interests of holders of the securities of companies governed by the law of a Member State when those companies are the subject of takeover bids or of changes of control and at least some of their securities are admitted to trading on a regulated market in a Member State.
(3) It is necessary to create Community-wide clarity and transparency in respect of legal issues to be settled in the event of takeover bids and to prevent patterns of corporate restructuring within the Community from being distorted by arbitrary differences in governance and management cultures.
(4) In view of the public-interest purposes served by the central banks of the Member States, it seems inconceivable that they should be the targets of takeover bids. Since, for historical reasons, the securities of some of those central banks are listed on regulated markets in Member States, it is necessary to exclude them explicitly from the scope of this Directive.
(5) Each Member State should designate an authority or authorities to supervise those aspects of bids that are governed by this Directive and to ensure that parties to takeover bids comply with the rules made pursuant to this Directive. All those authorities should cooperate with one another.
(6) In order to be effective, takeover regulation should be flexible and capable of dealing with new circumstances as they arise and should accordingly provide for the possibility of exceptions and derogations. However, in applying any rules or exceptions laid down or in granting any derogations, supervisory authorities should respect certain general principles.
(7) Self-regulatory bodies should be able to exercise supervision.
(8) In accordance with general principles of Community law, and in particular the right to a fair hearing, decisions of a supervisory authority should in appropriate circumstances be susceptible to review by an independent court or tribunal. However, Member States should be left to determine whether rights are to be made available which may be asserted in administrative or judicial proceedings, either in proceedings against a supervisory authority or in proceedings between parties to a bid.
(9) Member States should take the necessary steps to protect the holders of securities, in particular those with minority holdings, when control of their companies has been acquired. The Member States should ensure such protection by obliging the person who has acquired control of a company to make an offer to all the holders of that company's securities for all of their holdings at an equitable price in accordance with a common definition. Member States should be free to establish further instruments for the protection of the interests of the holders of securities, such as the obligation to make a partial bid where the offeror does not acquire control of the company or the obligation to announce a bid at the same time as control of the company is acquired.
(10) The obligation to make a bid to all the holders of securities should not apply to those controlling holdings already in existence on the date on which the national legislation transposing this Directive enters into force.
(11) The obligation to launch a bid should not apply in the case of the acquisition of securities which do not carry the right to vote at ordinary general meetings of shareholders. Member States should, however, be able to provide that the obligation to make a bid to all the holders of securities relates not only to securities carrying voting rights but also to securities which carry voting rights only in specific circumstances or which do not carry voting rights.
(12) To reduce the scope for insider dealing, an offeror should be required to announce his/her decision to launch a bid as soon as possible and to inform the supervisory authority of the bid.
(13) The holders of securities should be properly informed of the terms of a bid by means of an offer document. Appropriate information should also be given to the representatives of the company's employees or, failing that, to the employees directly.
(14) The time allowed for the acceptance of a bid should be regulated.
(15) To be able to perform their functions satisfactorily, supervisory authorities should at all times be able to require the parties to a bid to provide information concerning themselves and should cooperate and supply

information in an efficient and effective manner, without delay, to other authorities supervising capital markets.
(16) In order to prevent operations which could frustrate a bid, the powers of the board of an offeree company to engage in operations of an exceptional nature should be limited, without unduly hindering the offeree company in carrying on its normal business activities.
(17) The board of an offeree company should be required to make public a document setting out its opinion of the bid and the reasons on which that opinion is based, including its views on the effects of implementation on all the company's interests, and specifically on employment.
(18) In order to reinforce the effectiveness of existing provisions concerning the freedom to deal in the securities of companies covered by this Directive and the freedom to exercise voting rights, it is essential that the defensive structures and mechanisms envisaged by such companies be transparent and that they be regularly presented in reports to general meetings of shareholders.
(19) Member States should take the necessary measures to afford any offeror the possibility of acquiring majority interests in other companies and of fully exercising control of them. To that end, restrictions on the transfer of securities, restrictions on voting rights, extraordinary appointment rights and multiple voting rights should be removed or suspended during the time allowed for the acceptance of a bid and when the general meeting of shareholders decides on defensive measures, on amendments to the articles of association or on the removal or appointment of board members at the first general meeting of shareholders following closure of the bid. Where the holders of securities have suffered losses as a result of the removal of rights, equitable compensation should be provided for in accordance with the technical arrangements laid down by Member States.
(20) All special rights held by Member States in companies should be viewed in the framework of the free movement of capital and the relevant provisions of the Treaty. Special rights held by Member States in companies which are provided for in private or public national law should be exempted from the 'breakthrough' rule if they are compatible with the Treaty.
(21) Taking into account existing differences in Member States' company law mechanisms and structures, Member States should be allowed not to require companies established within their territories to apply the provisions of this Directive limiting the powers of the board of an offeree company during the time allowed for the acceptance of a bid and those rendering ineffective barriers, provided for in the articles of association or in specific agreements. In that event Member States should at least allow companies established within their territories to make the choice, which must be reversible, to apply those provisions. Without prejudice to international agreements to which the European Community is a party, Member States should be allowed not to require companies which apply those provisions in accordance with the optional arrangements to apply them when they become the subject of offers launched by companies which do not apply the same provisions, as a consequence of the use of those optional arrangements.
(22) Member States should lay down rules to cover the possibility of a bid's lapsing, the offeror's right to revise his/her bid, the possibility of competing bids for a company's securities, the disclosure of the result of a bid, the irrevocability of a bid and the conditions permitted.
(23) The disclosure of information to and the consultation of representatives of the employees of the offeror and the offeree company should be governed by the relevant national provisions, in particular those adopted pursuant to Council Directive 94/45/EC of 22 September 1994 on the establishment of a European Works Council or a procedure in Community-scale undertakings and Community-scale groups of undertakings for the purposes of informing and consulting employees, Council Directive 98/59/EC of 20 July 1998 on the approximation of the laws of the Member States relating to collective redundancies, Council Directive 2001/86/EC of 8 October 2001 supplementing the statute for a European Company with regard to the involvement of employees and Directive 2002/14/EC of the European Parliament and of the Council of 11 March 2002 establishing a general framework for informing and consulting employees in the European Community — Joint declaration of the European Parliament, the Council and the Commission on employee representation . The employees of the companies concerned, or their representatives, should nevertheless be given an opportunity to state their views on the foreseeable effects of the bid on employment. Without prejudice to the rules of Directive 2003/6/EC of the European Parliament and of the Council of 28 January 2003 on insider dealing and market manipulation (market abuse) Member States may always apply or introduce national provisions concerning the disclosure of information to and the consultation of representatives of the employees of the offeror before an offer is launched.
(24) Member States should take the necessary measures to enable an offeror who, following a takeover bid, has acquired a certain percentage of a company's capital carrying voting rights to require the holders of the remaining securities to sell him/her their securities. Likewise, where, following a takeover bid, an offeror has acquired a certain percentage of a company's capital carrying voting rights, the holders of the remaining securities should be able to require him/her to buy their securities. These squeeze-out and sell-out procedures should apply only under specific conditions linked to takeover bids. Member States may continue to apply national rules to squeeze-out and sell-out procedures in other circumstances.

(25) Since the objectives of the action envisaged, namely to establish minimum guidelines for the conduct of takeover bids and ensure an adequate level of protection for holders of securities throughout the Community, cannot be sufficiently achieved by the Member States because of the need for transparency and legal certainty in the case of cross-border takeovers and acquisitions of control, and can therefore, by reason of the scale and effects of the action, be better achieved at Community level, the Community may adopt measures, in accordance with the principle of subsidiarity as set out in Article 5 of the Treaty. In accordance with the principle of proportionality as set out in that Article, this Directive does not go beyond what is necessary to achieve those objectives.

(26) The adoption of a Directive is the appropriate procedure for the establishment of a framework consisting of certain common principles and a limited number of general requirements which Member States are to implement through more detailed rules in accordance with their national systems and their cultural contexts.

(27) Member States should, however, provide for sanctions for any infringement of the national measures transposing this Directive.

(28) Technical guidance and implementing measures for the rules laid down in this Directive may from time to time be necessary, to take account of new developments on financial markets. For certain provisions, the Commission should accordingly be empowered to adopt implementing measures, provided that these do not modify the essential elements of this Directive and the Commission acts in accordance with the principles set out in this Directive, after consulting the European Securities Committee established by Commission Decision 2001/528/EC. The measures necessary for the implementation of this Directive should be adopted in accordance with Council Decision 1999/468/EC of 28 June 1999 laying down the procedures for the exercise of implementing powers conferred on the Commission and with due regard to the declaration made by the Commission in the European Parliament on 5 February 2002 concerning the implementation of financial services legislation. For the other provisions, it is important to entrust a contact committee with the task of assisting Member States and the supervisory authorities in the implementation of this Directive and of advising the Commission, if necessary, on additions or amendments to this Directive. In so doing, the contact committee may make use of the information which Member States are to provide on the basis of this Directive concerning takeover bids that have taken place on their regulated markets.

(29) The Commission should facilitate movement towards the fair and balanced harmonisation of rules on takeovers in the European Union. To that end, the Commission should be able to submit proposals for the timely revision of this Directive,

HAVE ADOPTED THIS DIRECTIVE:

Article 1. 1. This Directive lays down measures coordinating the laws, regulations, administrative provisions, codes of practice and other arrangements of the Member States, including arrangements established by organisations officially authorised to regulate the markets (hereinafter referred to as 'rules'), relating to takeover bids for the securities of companies governed by the laws of Member States, where all or some of those securities are admitted to trading on a regulated market within the meaning of Directive 93/22/EEC (2) in one or more Member States (hereinafter referred to as a 'regulated market').

2. This Directive shall not apply to takeover bids for securities issued by companies, the object of which is the collective investment of capital provided by the public, which operate on the principle of risk-spreading and the units of which are, at the holders' request, repurchased or redeemed, directly or indirectly, out of the assets of those companies. Action taken by such companies to ensure that the stock exchange value of their units does not vary significantly from their net asset value shall be regarded as equivalent to such repurchase or redemption.

3. This Directive shall not apply to takeover bids for securities issued by the Member States' central banks.

Article 2. 1. For the purposes of this Directive:
(a) 'takeover bid' or 'bid' shall mean a public offer (other than by the offeree company itself) made to the holders of the securities of a
company to acquire all or some of those securities, whether mandatory or voluntary, which follows or has as its objective the acquisition of control of the offeree company in accordance with national law;
(b) 'offeree company' shall mean a company, the securities of which are the subject of a bid;
(c) 'offeror' shall mean any natural or legal person governed by public or private law making a bid;
(d) 'persons acting in concert' shall mean natural or legal persons who cooperate with the offeror or the offeree company on the basis of an agreement, either express or tacit, either oral or written, aimed either at acquiring control of the offeree company or at frustrating the successful outcome of a bid;
(e) 'securities' shall mean transferable securities carrying voting rights in a company;

(f) 'parties to the bid' shall mean the offeror, the members of the offeror's board if the offeror is a company, the offeree company, holders of securities of the offeree company and the members of the board of the offeree company, and persons acting in concert with such parties;
(g) 'multiple-vote securities' shall mean securities included in a distinct and separate class and carrying more than one vote each.
2. For the purposes of paragraph 1(d), persons controlled by another person within the meaning of Article 87 of Directive 2001/34/EC shall be deemed to be persons acting in concert with that other person and with each other.

Article 3. 1. For the purpose of implementing this Directive, Member States shall ensure that the following principles are complied with:
(a) all holders of the securities of an offeree company of the same class must be afforded equivalent treatment; moreover, if a person acquires control of a company, the other holders of securities must be protected;
(b) the holders of the securities of an offeree company must have sufficient time and information to enable them to reach a properly informed decision on the bid; where it advises the holders of securities, the board of the offeree company must give its views on the effects of implementation of the bid on employment, conditions of employment and the locations of the company's places of business;
(c) the board of an offeree company must act in the interests of the company as a whole and must not deny the holders of securities the opportunity to decide on the merits of the bid;
(d) false markets must not be created in the securities of the offeree company, of the offeror company or of any other company concerned by the bid in such a way that the rise or fall of the prices of the securities becomes artificial and the normal functioning of the markets is distorted;
(e) an offeror must announce a bid only after ensuring that he/she can fulfil in full any cash consideration, if such is offered, and after taking all reasonable measures to secure the implementation of any other type of consideration;
(f) an offeree company must not be hindered in the conduct of its affairs for longer than is reasonable by a bid for its securities.
2. With a view to ensuring compliance with the principles laid down in paragraph 1, Member States:
(a) shall ensure that the minimum requirements set out in this Directive are observed;
(b) may lay down additional conditions and provisions more stringent than those of this Directive for the regulation of bids.

Article 4. 1. Member States shall designate the authority or authorities competent to supervise bids for the purposes of the rules which they make or introduce pursuant to this Directive. The authorities thus designated shall be either public authorities, associations or private bodies recognised by national law or by public authorities expressly empowered for that purpose by national law. Member States shall inform the Commission of those designations, specifying any divisions of functions that may be made. They shall ensure that those authorities exercise their functions impartially and independently of all parties to a bid.
2. (a) The authority competent to supervise a bid shall be that of the Member State in which the offeree company has its registered
office if that company's securities are admitted to trading on a regulated market in that Member State.
(b) If the offeree company's securities are not admitted to trading on a regulated market in the Member State in which the company has its registered office, the authority competent to supervise the bid shall be that of the Member State on the regulated market of which the company's securities are admitted to trading. If the offeree company's securities are admitted to trading on regulated markets in more than one Member State, the authority competent to supervise the bid shall be that of the Member State on the regulated market of which the securities were first admitted to trading.
(c) If the offeree company's securities were first admitted to trading on regulated markets in more than one Member State simultaneously, the offeree company shall determine which of the supervisory authorities of those Member States shall be the authority competent to supervise the bid by notifying those regulated markets and their supervisory authorities on the first day of trading. If the offeree company's securities have already been admitted to trading on regulated markets in more than one Member
State on the date laid down in Article 21(1) and were admitted simultaneously, the supervisory authorities of those Member States shall agree which one of them shall be the authority competent to supervise the bid within four weeks of the date laid down in Article 21(1). Otherwise, the offeree company shall determine which of those authorities shall be the competent authority on the first day of trading following that four-week period.
(d) Member States shall ensure that the decisions referred to in (c) are made public.
(e) In the cases referred to in (b) and (c), matters relating to the consideration offered in the case of a bid, in particular the price, and matters relating to the bid procedure, in particular the information on the offeror's

decision to make a bid, the contents of the offer document and the disclosure of the bid, shall be dealt with in accordance with the rules of the Member State of the competent authority. In matters relating to the information to be provided to the employees of the offeree company and in matters relating to company law, in particular the percentage of voting rights which confers control and any derogation from the obligation to launch a bid, as well as the conditions under which the board of the offeree company may undertake any action which might result in the frustration of the bid, the applicable rules and the competent authority shall be those of the Member State in which the offeree company has its registered office.

3. Member States shall ensure that all persons employed or formerly employed by their supervisory authorities are bound by professional secrecy. No information covered by professional secrecy may be divulged to any person or authority except under provisions laid down by law.

4. The supervisory authorities of the Member States for the purposes of this Directive and other authorities supervising capital markets, in particular in accordance with Directive 93/22/EEC, Directive 2001/34/EC, Directive 2003/6/EC and Directive 2003/71/EC of the European Parliament and of the Council of 4 November 2003 on the prospectus to be published when securities are offered to the public or admitted to trading shall cooperate and supply each other with information wherever necessary for the application of the rules drawn up in accordance with this Directive and in particular in cases covered by paragraph 2(b), (c) and (e). Information thus exchanged shall be covered by the obligation of professional secrecy to which persons employed or formerly employed by the supervisory authorities receiving the information are subject. Cooperation shall include the ability to serve the legal documents necessary to enforce measures taken by the competent authorities in connection with bids, as well as such other assistance as may reasonably be requested by the supervisory authorities concerned for the purpose of investigating any actual or alleged breaches of the rules made or introduced pursuant to this Directive.

5. The supervisory authorities shall be vested with all the powers necessary for the purpose of carrying out their duties, including that of ensuring that the parties to a bid comply with the rules made or introduced pursuant to this Directive. Provided that the general principles laid down in Article 3(1) are respected, Member States may provide in the rules that they make or introduce pursuant to this Directive for derogations from those rules:

(i) by including such derogations in their national rules, in order to take account of circumstances determined at national level and/or

(ii) by granting their supervisory authorities, where they are competent, powers to waive such national rules, to take account of the circumstances referred to in (i) or in other specific circumstances, in which case a reasoned decision must be required.

6. This Directive shall not affect the power of the Member States to designate judicial or other authorities responsible for dealing with disputes and for deciding on irregularities committed in the course of bids or the power of Member States to regulate whether and under which circumstances parties to a bid are entitled to bring administrative or judicial proceedings. In particular, this Directive shall not affect the power which courts may have in a Member State to decline to hear legal proceedings and to decide whether or not such proceedings affect the outcome of a bid. This Directive shall not affect the power of the Member States to determine the legal position concerning the liability of supervisory authorities or concerning litigation between the parties to a bid.

Article 5. 1. Where a natural or legal person, as a result of his/her own acquisition or the acquisition by persons acting in concert with him/her, holds securities of a company as referred to in Article 1(1) which, added to any existing holdings of those securities of his/hers and the holdings of those securities of persons acting in concert with him/her, directly or indirectly give him/her a specified percentage of voting rights in that company, giving him/her control of that company, Member States shall ensure that such a person is required to make a bid as a means of protecting the minority shareholders of that company. Such a bid shall be addressed at the earliest opportunity to all the holders of those securities for all their holdings at the equitable price as defined in paragraph 4.

2. Where control has been acquired following a voluntary bid made in accordance with this Directive to all the holders of securities for all their holdings, the obligation laid down in paragraph 1 to launch a bid shall no longer apply.

3. The percentage of voting rights which confers control for the purposes of paragraph 1 and the method of its calculation shall be determined by the rules of the Member State in which the company has its registered office.

4. The highest price paid for the same securities by the offeror, or by persons acting in concert with him/her, over a period, to be determined by Member States, of not less than six months and not more than 12 before the bid referred to in paragraph 1 shall be regarded as the equitable price. If, after the bid has been made public and before the offer closes for acceptance, the offeror or any person acting in concert with him/her purchases securities at a price higher than the offer price, the offeror shall increase his/her offer so that it is not less than the highest price paid for the securities so acquired. Provided that the general principles laid down in Article 3(1) are respected,

Member States may authorise their supervisory authorities to adjust the price referred to in the first subparagraph in circumstances and in accordance with criteria that are clearly determined. To that end, they may draw up a list of circumstances in which the highest price may be adjusted either upwards or downwards, for example where the highest price was set by agreement between the purchaser and a seller, where the market prices of the securities in question have been manipulated, where market prices in general or certain market prices in particular have been affected by exceptional occurrences, or in order to enable a firm in difficulty to be rescued. They may also determine the criteria to be applied in such cases, for example the average market value over a particular period, the break-up value of the company or other objective valuation criteria generally used in financial analysis. Any decision by a supervisory authority to adjust the equitable price shall be substantiated and made public.

5. By way of consideration the offeror may offer securities, cash or a combination of both. However, where the consideration offered by the offeror does not consist of liquid securities admitted to trading on a regulated market, it shall include a cash alternative.

In any event, the offeror shall offer a cash consideration at least as an alternative where he/she or persons acting in concert with him/her, over a period beginning at the same time as the period determined by the Member State in accordance with paragraph 4 and ending when the offer closes for acceptance, has purchased for cash securities carrying 5 % or more of the voting rights in the offeree company. Member States may provide that a cash consideration must be offered, at least as an alternative, in all cases.

6. In addition to the protection provided for in paragraph 1, Member States may provide for further instruments intended to protect the interests of the holders of securities in so far as those instruments do not hinder the normal course of a bid.

Article 6. 1. Member States shall ensure that a decision to make a bid is made public without delay and that the supervisory authority is informed of the bid. They may require that the supervisory authority must be informed before such a decision is made public. As soon as the bid has been made public, the boards of the offeree company and of the offeror shall inform the representatives of their respective employees or, where there are no such representatives, the employees themselves.

2. Member States shall ensure that an offeror is required to draw up and make public in good time an offer document containing the information necessary to enable the holders of the offeree company's securities to reach a properly informed decision on the bid. Before the offer document is made public, the offeror shall communicate it to the supervisory authority. When it is made public, the boards of the offeree company and of the offeror shall communicate it to the representatives of their respective employees or, where there are no such representatives, to the employees themselves. Where the offer document referred to in the first subparagraph is subject to the prior approval of the supervisory authority and has been approved, it shall be recognised, subject to any translation required, in any other Member State on the market of which the offeree company's securities are admitted to trading, without its being necessary to obtain the approval of the supervisory authorities of that Member State. Those authorities may require the inclusion of additional information in the offer document only if such information is specific to the market of a Member State or Member States on which the offeree company's securities are admitted to trading and relates to the formalities to be complied with to accept the bid and to receive the consideration due at the close of the bid as well as to the tax arrangements to which the consideration offered to the holders of the securities will be subject.

3. The offer document referred to in paragraph 2 shall state at least:

(a) the terms of the bid;

(b) the identity of the offeror and, where the offeror is a company, the type, name and registered office of that company;

(c) the securities or, where appropriate, the class or classes of securities for which the bid is made;

(d) the consideration offered for each security or class of securities and, in the case of a mandatory bid, the method employed in determining it, with particulars of the way in which that consideration is to be paid;

(e) the compensation offered for the rights which might be removed as a result of the breakthrough rule laid down in Article 11(4), with particulars of the way in which that compensation is to be paid and the method employed in determining it;

(f) the maximum and minimum percentages or quantities of securities which the offeror undertakes to acquire;

(g) details of any existing holdings of the offeror, and of persons acting in concert with him/her, in the offeree company;

(h) all the conditions to which the bid is subject; 2004L0025 — EN— 20.04.2009 —001.001 —11

(i) the offeror's intentions with regard to the future business of the offeree company and, in so far as it is affected by the bid, the offeror company and with regard to the safeguarding of the jobs of their employees and management, including any material change in

the conditions of employment, and in particular the offeror's strategic plans for the two companies and the likely repercussions on employment and the locations of the companies' places of business;
(j) the time allowed for acceptance of the bid;
(k) where the consideration offered by the offeror includes securities of any kind, information concerning those securities;
(l) information concerning the financing for the bid;
(m) the identity of persons acting in concert with the offeror or with the offeree company and, in the case of companies, their types, names, registered offices and relationships with the offeror and, where possible, with the offeree company;
(n) the national law which will govern contracts concluded between the offeror and the holders of the offeree company's securities as a result of the bid and the competent courts.
4. The Commission may adopt rules modifying the list in paragraph
3. Those measures, designed to amend non-essential elements of this Directive, shall be adopted in accordance with the regulatory procedure with scrutiny referred to in Article 18(2).
5. Member States shall ensure that the parties to a bid are required to provide the supervisory authorities of their Member State at any time on request with all the information in their possession concerning the bid that is necessary for the supervisory authority to discharge its functions.

Article 7. 1. Member States shall provide that the time allowed for the acceptance of a bid may not be less than two weeks nor more than 10 weeks from the date of publication of the offer document. Provided that the general principle laid down in Article 3(1)(f) is respected, Member States may provide that the period of 10 weeks may be extended on condition that the offeror gives at least two weeks' notice of his/her intention of closing the bid.
2. Member States may provide for rules changing the period referred to in paragraph 1 in specific cases. A Member State may authorise a supervisory authority to grant a derogation from the period referred to in paragraph 1 in order to allow the offeree company to call a general meeting of shareholders to consider the bid.

Article 8. 1. Member States shall ensure that a bid is made public in such a way as to ensure market transparency and integrity for the securities of the offeree company, of the offeror or of any other company affected by the bid, in particular in order to prevent the publication or dissemination of false or misleading information.
2. Member States shall provide for the disclosure of all information and documents required by Article 6 in such a manner as to ensure that they are both readily and promptly available to the holders of securities at least in those Member States on the regulated markets of which the offeree company's securities are admitted to trading and to the representatives of the employees of the offeree company and the offeror or, where there are no such representatives, to the employees themselves.

Article 9. 1. Member States shall ensure that the rules laid down in paragraphs 2 to 5 are complied with.
2. During the period referred to in the second subparagraph, the board of the offeree company shall obtain the prior authorisation of the general meeting of shareholders given for this purpose before taking any action, other than seeking alternative bids, which may result in the frustration of the bid and in particular before issuing any shares which may result in a lasting impediment to the offeror's acquiring control of the offeree company. Such authorisation shall be mandatory at least from the time the board of the offeree company receives the information referred to in the first sentence of Article 6(1) concerning the bid and until the result of the bid is made public or the bid lapses. Member States may require that such authorisation be obtained at an earlier stage, for example as soon as the board of the offeree company becomes aware that the bid is imminent.
3. As regards decisions taken before the beginning of the period referred to in the second subparagraph of paragraph 2 and not yet partly or fully implemented, the general meeting of shareholders shall approve or confirm any decision which does not form part of the normal course of the company's business and the implementation of which may result in the frustration of the bid.
4. For the purpose of obtaining the prior authorisation, approval or confirmation of the holders of securities referred to in paragraphs 2 and 3, Member States may adopt rules allowing a general meeting of shareholders to be called at short notice, provided that the meeting does not take place within two weeks of notification's being given.
5. The board of the offeree company shall draw up and make public a document setting out its opinion of the bid and the reasons on which it is based, including its views on the effects of implementation of the bid on all the company's interests and specifically employment, and on the offeror's strategic plans for the offeree company and their likely repercussions on employment and the locations of the company's places of business as set out in the offer document in accordance with Article 6(3)(i). The board of the offeree company shall at the same time communicate that opinion to the representatives of its employees or, where there are no such representatives, to the

employees themselves. Where the board of the offeree company receives in good time a separate opinion from the representatives of its employees on the effects of the bid on employment, that opinion shall be appended to the document.

6. For the purposes of paragraph 2, where a company has a two-tier board structure 'board' shall mean both the management board and the supervisory board.

Article 10. 1. Member States shall ensure that companies as referred to in Article 1(1) publish detailed information on the following:
(a) the structure of their capital, including securities which are not admitted to trading on a regulated market in a Member State, where appropriate with an indication of the different classes of shares and, for each class of shares, the rights and obligations attaching to it and the percentage of total share capital that it represents;
(b) any restrictions on the transfer of securities, such as limitations on the holding of securities or the need to obtain the approval of the company or other holders of securities, without prejudice to Article 46 of Directive 2001/34/EC;
(c) significant direct and indirect shareholdings (including indirect shareholdings through pyramid structures and cross-shareholdings) within the meaning of Article 85 of Directive 2001/34/EC;
(d) the holders of any securities with special control rights and a description of those rights;
(e) the system of control of any employee share scheme where the control rights are not exercised directly by the employees;
(f) any restrictions on voting rights, such as limitations of the voting rights of holders of a given percentage or number of votes, deadlines for exercising voting rights, or systems whereby, with the company's cooperation, the financial rights attaching to securities are separated from the holding of securities;
(g) any agreements between shareholders which are known to the company and may result in restrictions on the transfer of securities and/or voting rights within the meaning of Directive 2001/34/EC;
(h) the rules governing the appointment and replacement of board members and the amendment of the articles of association;
(i) the powers of board members, and in particular the power to issue or buy back shares;
(j) any significant agreements to which the company is a party and which take effect, alter or terminate upon a change of control of the company following a takeover bid, and the effects thereof, except where their nature is such that their disclosure would be seriously prejudicial to the company; this exception shall not apply where the company is specifically obliged to disclose such information on the basis of other legal requirements;
(k) any agreements between the company and its board members or employees providing for compensation if they resign or are made redundant without valid reason or if their employment ceases because of a takeover bid.
2. The information referred to in paragraph 1 shall be published in the company's annual report as provided for in Article 46 of Directive 78/660/EEC (1) and Article 36 of Directive 83/349/EEC.
3. Member States shall ensure, in the case of companies the securities of which are admitted to trading on a regulated market in a Member State, that the board presents an explanatory report to the annual general meeting of shareholders on the matters referred to in paragraph 1.

Article 11. 1. Without prejudice to other rights and obligations provided for in Community law for the companies referred to in Article 1(1), Member States shall ensure that the provisions laid down in paragraphs 2 to 7 apply when a bid has been made public.
2. Any restrictions on the transfer of securities provided for in the articles of association of the offeree company shall not apply vis-à-vis the offeror during the time allowed for acceptance of the bid laid down in Article 7(1). Any restrictions on the transfer of securities provided for in contractual agreements between the offeree company and holders of its securities, or in contractual agreements between holders of the offeree company's securities entered into after the adoption of this Directive, shall not apply vis-à-vis the offeror during the time allowed for acceptance of the bid laid down in Article 7(1).
3. Restrictions on voting rights provided for in the articles of association of the offeree company shall not have effect at the general meeting of shareholders which decides on any defensive measures in accordance with Article 9. Restrictions on voting rights provided for in contractual agreements between the offeree company and holders of its securities, or in contractual agreements between holders of the offeree company's securities entered into after the adoption of this Directive, shall not have effect at the general meeting of shareholders which decides on any defensive measures in accordance with Article 9. Multiple-vote securities shall carry only one vote each at the general meeting of shareholders which decides on any defensive measures in accordance with Article 9.
4. Where, following a bid, the offeror holds 75 % or more of the capital carrying voting rights, no restrictions on the transfer of securities or on voting rights referred to in paragraphs 2 and 3 nor any extraordinary rights of shareholders concerning the appointment or removal of board members provided for in the articles of association

of the offeree company shall apply; multiple-vote securities shall carry only one vote each at the first general meeting of shareholders following closure of the bid, called by the offeror in order to amend the articles of association or to remove or appoint board members. To that end, the offeror shall have the right to convene a general meeting of shareholders at short notice, provided that the meeting does not take place within two weeks of notification.
5. Where rights are removed on the basis of paragraphs 2, 3, or 4 and/or Article 12, equitable compensation shall be provided for any loss suffered by the holders of those rights. The terms for determining such compensation and the arrangements for its payment shall be set by Member States.
6. Paragraphs 3 and 4 shall not apply to securities where the restrictions on voting rights are compensated for by specific pecuniary advantages.
7. This Article shall not apply either where Member States hold securities in the offeree company which confer special rights on the Member States which are compatible with the Treaty, or to special rights provided for in national law which are compatible with the Treaty or to cooperatives.

Article 12. 1. Member States may reserve the right not to require companies as referred to in Article 1(1) which have their registered offices within their territories to apply Article 9(2) and (3) and/or Article 11.
2. Where Member States make use of the option provided for in paragraph 1, they shall nevertheless grant companies which have their registered offices within their territories the option, which shall be reversible, of applying Article 9(2) and (3) and/or Article 11, without prejudice to Article 11(7). The decision of the company shall be taken by the general meeting of shareholders, in accordance with the law of the Member State in which the company has its registered office in accordance with the rules applicable to amendment of the articles of association. The decision shall be communicated to the supervisory authority of the Member State in which the company has its registered office and to all the supervisory authorities of Member States in which its securities are admitted to trading on regulated markets or where such admission has been requested.
3. Member States may, under the conditions determined by national law, exempt companies which apply Article 9(2) and (3) and/or Article 11 from applying Article 9(2) and (3) and/or Article 11 if they become the subject of an offer launched by a company which does not apply the same Articles as they do, or by a company controlled, directly or indirectly, by the latter, pursuant to Article 1 of Directive 83/349/EEC.
4. Member States shall ensure that the provisions applicable to the respective companies are disclosed without delay.
5. Any measure applied in accordance with paragraph 3 shall be subject to the authorisation of the general meeting of shareholders of the offeree company, which must be granted no earlier than 18 months before the bid was made public in accordance with Article 6(1).

Article 13. Other rules applicable to the conduct of bids. Member States shall also lay down rules which govern the conduct of bids, at least as regards the following:
(a) the lapsing of bids;
(b) the revision of bids;
(c) competing bids;
(d) the disclosure of the results of bids;
(e) the irrevocability of bids and the conditions permitted.

Article 14. Information for and consultation of employees' representatives. This Directive shall be without prejudice to the rules relating to information and to consultation of representatives of and, if Member States so provide, co-determination with the employees of the offeror and the offeree company governed by the relevant national provisions, and in particular those adopted pursuant to Directives 94/45/EC, 98/59/EC, 2001/86/EC and 2002/14/EC.

Article 15. 1. Member States shall ensure that, following a bid made to all the holders of the offeree company's securities for all of their securities, paragraphs 2 to 5 apply.
2. Member States shall ensure that an offeror is able to require all the holders of the remaining securities to sell him/her those securities at a fair price. Member States shall introduce that right in one of the following situations:
(a) where the offeror holds securities representing not less than 90 % of the capital carrying voting rights and 90 % of the voting rights in the offeree company, or
(b) where, following acceptance of the bid, he/she has acquired or has firmly contracted to acquire securities representing not less than 90 % of the offeree company's capital carrying voting rights and 90 % of the voting rights comprised in the bid. In the case referred to in (a), Member States may set a higher threshold that may not, however, be higher than 95 % of the capital carrying voting rights and 95 % of the voting rights.

3. Member States shall ensure that rules are in force that make it possible to calculate when the threshold is reached. Where the offeree company has issued more than one class of securities, Member States may provide that the right of squeeze-out can be exercised only in the class in which the threshold laid down in paragraph 2 has been reached.
4. If the offeror wishes to exercise the right of squeeze-out he/she shall do so within three months of the end of the time allowed for acceptance of the bid referred to in Article 7.
5. Member States shall ensure that a fair price is guaranteed. That price shall take the same form as the consideration offered in the bid or shall be in cash. Member States may provide that cash shall be offered at least as an alternative. Following a voluntary bid, in both of the cases referred to in paragraph 2(a) and (b), the consideration offered in the bid shall be presumed to be fair where, through acceptance of the bid, the offeror has acquired securities representing not less than 90 % of the capital carrying voting rights comprised in the bid. Following a mandatory bid, the consideration offered in the bid shall be presumed to be fair.

Article 16. 1. Member States shall ensure that, following a bid made to all the holders of the offeree company's securities for all of their securities, paragraphs 2 and 3 apply.
2. Member States shall ensure that a holder of remaining securities is able to require the offeror to buy his/her securities from him/her at a fair price under the same circumstances as provided for in Article 15(2).
3. Article 15(3) to (5) shall apply mutatis mutandis.

Article 17. Member States shall determine the sanctions to be imposed for infringement of the national measures adopted pursuant to this Directive and shall take all necessary steps to ensure that they are put into effect. The sanctions thus provided for shall be effective, proportionate and dissuasive. Member States shall notify the Commission of those measures no later than the date laid down in Article 21(1) and of any subsequent change thereto at the earliest opportunity.

Article 18. 1. The Commission shall be assisted by the European Securities Committee established by Decision 2001/528/EC (hereinafter referred to as 'the Committee').
2. Where reference is made to this paragraph, Article 5a(1) to (4) and Article 7 of Decision 1999/468/EC shall apply, having regard to the provisions of Article 8 thereof.

Article 19. 1. A contact committee shall be set up which has as its functions:
(a) to facilitate, without prejudice to Articles 226 and 227 of the Treaty, the harmonised application of this Directive through regular meetings dealing with practical problems arising in connection with its application;
(b) to advise the Commission, if necessary, on additions or amendments to this Directive.
2. It shall not be the function of the contact committee to appraise the merits of decisions taken by the supervisory authorities in individual cases.

Article 20. Five years after the date laid down in Article 21(1), the Commission shall examine this Directive in the light of the experience acquired in applying it and, if necessary, propose its revision. That examination shall include a survey of the control structures and barriers to takeover bids that are not covered by this Directive. To that end, Member States shall provide the Commission annually with information on the takeover bids which have been launched against companies the securities of which are admitted to trading on their regulated markets. That information shall include the nationalities of the companies involved, the results of the offers and any other information relevant to the understanding of how takeover bids operate in practice.

Article 21. 1. Member States shall bring into force the laws, regulations and administrative provisions necessary to comply with this Directive no later than 20 May 2006. They shall forthwith inform the Commission thereof. When Member States adopt those provisions, they shall contain a reference to this Directive or shall be accompanied by such reference on the occasion of their official publication. The methods of making such reference shall be laid down by the Member States.
2. Member States shall communicate to the Commission the text of the main provisions of national law that they adopt in the fields covered by this Directive.

Article 22. This Directive shall enter into force on the 20th day after that of its publication in the Official Journal of the European Union.

Article 23. This Directive is addressed to the Member States.

Directive 2007/36/EC of the European Parliament and of the Council of 11 July 2007 on the exercise of certain rights of shareholders in listed companies (*OJ* L 184 , 14.07.2007 p. 17 – 24) [footnotes omitted].

THE EUROPEAN PARLIAMENT AND THE COUNCIL OF THE EUROPEAN UNION,
Having regard to the Treaty establishing the European Community, and in particular Articles 44 and 95 thereof,
Having regard to the proposal from the Commission, Having regard to the opinion of the European Economic and Social Committee ,
Acting in accordance with the procedure laid down in Article 251 of the Treaty,
Whereas:
(1) In its Communication to the Council and the European Parliament of 21 May 2003, entitled "Modernising Company Law and enhancing Corporate Governance in the European Union — A Plan to Move Forward", the Commission indicated that new tailored initiatives should be taken with a view to enhancing shareholders' rights in listed companies and that problems relating to cross-border voting should be solved as a matter of urgency.
(2) In its Resolution of 21 April 2004 , the European Parliament expressed its support for the Commission's intention to strengthen shareholders' rights, in particular through the extension of the rules on transparency, proxy voting rights, the possibility of participating in general meetings via electronic means and ensuring that cross-border voting rights are able to be exercised.
(3) Holders of shares carrying voting rights should be able to exercise those rights given that they are reflected in the price that has to be paid at the acquisition of the shares. Furthermore, effective shareholder control is a prerequisite to sound corporate governance and should, therefore, be facilitated and encouraged. It is therefore necessary to adopt measures to approximate the laws of the Member States to this end. Obstacles which deter shareholders from voting, such as making the exercise of voting rights subject to the blocking of shares during a certain period before the general meeting, should be removed. However, this Directive does not affect existing Community legislation on units issued by collective investment undertakings or on units acquired or disposed of in such undertakings.
(4) The existing Community legislation is not sufficient to achieve this objective. Directive 2001/34/EC of the European Parliament and of the Council of 28 May 2001 on the admission of securities to official stock exchange listing and on information to be published on those securities focuses on the information issuers have to disclose to the market and accordingly does not deal with the shareholder voting process itself. Moreover, Directive 2004/109/EC of the European Parliament and of the Council of 15 December 2004 on the harmonisation of transparency requirements in relation to information about issuers whose securities are admitted to trading on a regulated market imposes on issuers an obligation to make available certain information and documents relevant to general meetings, but such information and documents are to be made available in the issuer's home Member State. Therefore, certain minimum standards should be introduced with a view to protecting investors and promoting the smooth and effective exercise of shareholder rights attaching to voting shares. As regards rights other than the right to vote, Member States are free to extend the application of these minimum standards also to non-voting shares, to the extent that those shares do not enjoy such standards already.
(5) Significant proportions of shares in listed companies are held by shareholders who do not reside in the Member State in which the company has its registered office. Non-resident shareholders should be able to exercise their rights in relation to the general meeting as easily as shareholders who reside in the Member State in which the company has its registered office. This requires that existing obstacles which hinder the access of non-resident shareholders to the information relevant to the general meeting and the exercise of voting rights without physically attending the general meeting be removed. The removal of these obstacles should also benefit resident shareholders who do not or cannot attend the general meeting.
(6) Shareholders should be able to cast informed votes at, or in advance of, the general meeting, no matter where they reside. All shareholders should have sufficient time to consider the documents intended to be submitted to the general meeting and determine how they will vote their shares. To this end, timely notice should be given of the general meeting, and shareholders should be provided with the complete information intended to be submitted to the general meeting. The possibilities which modern technologies offer to make information instantly accessible should be exploited. This Directive presupposes that all listed companies already have an Internet site.
(7) Shareholders should, in principle, have the possibility to put items on the agenda of the general meeting and to table draft resolutions for items on the agenda. Without prejudice to different time-frames and modalities which are currently in use across the Community, the exercise of those rights should be made subject to two basic rules, namely that any threshold required for the exercise of those rights should not exceed 5 % of the company's share capital and that all shareholders should in every case receive the final version of the agenda in sufficient time to prepare for the discussion and voting on each item on the agenda.

(8) Every shareholder should, in principle, have the possibility to ask questions related to items on the agenda of the general meeting and to have them answered, while the rules on how and when questions are to be asked and answered should be left to be determined by Member States.

(9) Companies should face no legal obstacles in offering to their shareholders any means of electronic participation in the general meeting. Voting without attending the general meeting in person, whether by correspondence or by electronic means, should not be subject to constraints other than those necessary for the verification of identity and the security of electronic communications. However, this should not prevent Member States from adopting rules aimed at ensuring that the results of the voting reflect the intentions of the shareholders in all circumstances, including rules aimed at addressing situations where new circumstances occur or are revealed after a shareholder has cast his vote by correspondence or by electronic means.

(10) Good corporate governance requires a smooth and effective process of proxy voting. Existing limitations and constraints which make proxy voting cumbersome and costly should therefore be removed. But good corporate governance also requires adequate safeguards against a possible abuse of proxy voting. The proxy holder should therefore be bound to observe any instructions he may have received from the shareholder and Member States should be able to introduce appropriate measures ensuring that the proxy holder does not pursue any interest other than that of the shareholder, irrespective of the reason that has given rise to the conflict of interests. Measures against possible abuse may, in particular, consist of regimes which Member States may adopt in order to regulate the activity of persons who actively engage in the collection of proxies or who have in fact collected more than a certain significant number of proxies, notably to ensure an adequate degree of reliability and transparency. Shareholders have an unfettered right under this Directive to appoint such persons as proxy holders to attend and vote at general meetings in their name. This Directive does not, however, affect any rules or sanctions that Member States may impose on such persons where votes have been cast by making fraudulent use of proxies collected. Moreover, this Directive does not impose any obligation on companies to verify that proxy holders cast votes in accordance with the voting instructions of the appointing shareholders.

(11) Where financial intermediaries are involved, the effectiveness of voting upon instructions relies, to a great extent, on the efficiency of the chain of intermediaries, given that investors are frequently unable to exercise the voting rights attached to their shares without the cooperation of every intermediary in the chain, who may not have an economic stake in the shares. In order to enable the investor to exercise his voting rights in cross-border situations, it is therefore important that intermediaries facilitate the exercise of voting rights. Further consideration should be given to this issue by the Commission in the context of a Recommendation, with a view to ensuring that investors have access to effective voting services and that voting rights are exercised in accordance with the instructions given by those investors.

(12) While the timing of disclosure to the administrative, management or supervisory body as well as to the public of votes cast in advance of the general meeting electronically or by correspondence is an important matter of corporate governance, it can be determined by Member States.

(13) Voting results should be established through methods that reflect the voting intentions expressed by shareholders, and they should be made transparent after the general meeting at least through the company's Internet site.

(14) Since the objective of this Directive, namely to allow shareholders effectively to make use of their rights throughout the Community, cannot be sufficiently achieved by the Member States on the basis of the existing Community legislation and can therefore, by reason of the scale and effects of the measures, be better achieved at Community level, the Community may adopt measures, in accordance with the principle of subsidiarity as set out in Article 5 of the Treaty. In accordance with the principle of proportionality, as set out in that Article, this Directive does not go beyond what is necessary in order to achieve that objective.

(15) In accordance with paragraph 34 of the Interinstitutional Agreement on better law-making, Member States are encouraged to draw up, for themselves and in the interests of the Community, their own tables illustrating, as far as possible, the correlation between this Directive and the transposition measures, and to make them public,

HAVE ADOPTED THIS DIRECTIVE:

Chapter I. General provisions

Article 1. 1. This Directive establishes requirements in relation to the exercise of certain shareholder rights attaching to voting shares in relation to general meetings of companies which have their registered office in a Member State and whose shares are admitted to trading on a regulated market situated or operating within a Member State.

2. The Member State competent to regulate matters covered in this Directive shall be the Member State in which the company has its registered office, and references to the "applicable law" are references to the law of that Member State.
3. Member States may exempt from this Directive the following types of companies:
(a) collective investment undertakings within the meaning of Article 1(2) of Council Directive 85/611/EEC of 20 December 1985 on the coordination of laws, regulations and administrative provisions relating to undertakings for collective investment in transferable securities (UCITS);
(b) undertakings the sole object of which is the collective investment of capital provided by the public, which operate on the principle of risk spreading and which do not seek to take legal or management control over any of the issuers of their underlying investments, provided that these collective investment undertakings are authorised and subject to the supervision of competent authorities and that they have a depositary exercising functions equivalent to those under Directive 85/611/EEC;
(c) cooperative societies.

Article 2. For the purposes of this Directive the following definitions shall apply:
(a) "regulated market" means a market as defined in Article 4(1), point 14, of Directive 2004/39/EC of the European Parliament and of the Council of 21 April 2004 on markets in financial instruments;
(b) "shareholder" means the natural or legal person that is recognised as a shareholder under the applicable law;
(c) "proxy" means the empowerment of a natural or legal person by a shareholder to exercise some or all rights of that shareholder in the general meeting in his name.

Article 3. This Directive shall not prevent Member States from imposing further obligations on companies or from otherwise taking further measures to facilitate the exercise by shareholders of the rights referred to in this Directive.

Chapter II. General meetings of shareholders

Article 4. The company shall ensure equal treatment for all shareholders who are in the same position with regard to participation and the exercise of voting rights in the general meeting.

Article 5. 1. Without prejudice to Articles 9(4) and 11(4) of Directive 2004/25/EC of the European Parliament and of the Council of 21 April 2004 on takeover bids, Member States shall ensure that the company issues the convocation of the general meeting in one of the manners specified in paragraph 2 of this Article not later than on the 21st day before the day of the meeting. Member States may provide that, where the company offers the facility for shareholders to vote by electronic means accessible to all shareholders, the general meeting of shareholders may decide that it shall issue the convocation of a general meeting which is not an annual general meeting in one of the manners specified in paragraph 2 of this Article not later than on the 14th day before the day of the meeting. This decision is to be taken by a majority of not less than two thirds of the votes attaching to the shares or the subscribed capital represented and for a duration not later than the next annual general meeting. Member States need not apply the minimum periods referred to in the first and second subparagraphs for the second or subsequent convocation of a general meeting issued for lack of a quorum required for the meeting convened by the first convocation, provided that this Article has been complied with for the first convocation and no new item is put on the agenda, and that at least 10 days elapse between the final convocation and the date of the general meeting.
2. Without prejudice to further requirements for notification or publication laid down by the competent Member State as defined in Article 1(2), the company shall be required to issue the convocation referred to in paragraph 1 of this Article in a manner ensuring fast access to it on a non-discriminatory basis. The Member State shall require the company to use such media as may reasonably be relied upon for the effective dissemination of information to the public throughout the Community. The Member State may not impose an obligation to use only media whose operators are established on its territory. The Member State need not apply the first subparagraph to companies that are able to identify the names and addresses of their shareholders from a current register of shareholders, provided that the company is under an obligation to send the convocation to each of its registered shareholders. In either case the company may not charge any specific cost for issuing the convocation in the prescribed manner.
3. The convocation referred to in paragraph 1 shall at least:
(a) indicate precisely when and where the general meeting is to take place, and the proposed agenda for the general meeting;
(b) contain a clear and precise description of the procedures that shareholders must comply with in order to be able to participate and to cast their vote in the general meeting. This includes information concerning:

(i) the rights available to shareholders under Article 6, to the extent that those rights can be exercised after the issuing of the convocation, and under Article 9, and the deadlines by which those rights may be exercised; the convocation may confine itself to stating only the deadlines by which those rights may be exercised, provided it contains a reference to more detailed information concerning those rights being made available on the Internet site of the company;
(ii) the procedure for voting by proxy, notably the forms to be used to vote by proxy and the means by which the company is prepared to accept electronic notifications of the appointment of proxy holders; and
(iii) where applicable, the procedures for casting votes by correspondence or by electronic means;
(c) where applicable, state the record date as defined in Article 7(2) and explain that only those who are shareholders on that date shall have the right to participate and vote in the general meeting;
(d) indicate where and how the full, unabridged text of the documents and draft resolutions referred to in points (c) and (d) of paragraph 4 may be obtained;
(e) indicate the address of the Internet site on which the information referred to in paragraph 4 will be made available.
4. Member States shall ensure that, for a continuous period beginning not later than on the 21 day before the day of the general meeting and including the day of the meeting, the company shall make available to its shareholders on its Internet site at least the following information:
(a) the convocation referred to in paragraph 1;
(b) the total number of shares and voting rights at the date of the convocation (including separate totals for each class of shares where the company's capital is divided into two or more classes of shares);
(c) the documents to be submitted to the general meeting;
(d) a draft resolution or, where no resolution is proposed to be adopted, a comment from a competent body within the company, to be designated by the applicable law, for each item on the proposed agenda of the general meeting; moreover, draft resolutions tabled by shareholders shall be added to the Internet site as soon as practicable after the company has received them;
(e) where applicable, the forms to be used to vote by proxy and to vote by correspondence, unless those forms are sent directly to each shareholder.
Where the forms referred to in point (e) cannot be made available on the Internet for technical reasons, the company shall indicate on its Internet site how the forms can be obtained on paper. In this case the company shall be required to send the forms by postal services and free of charge to every shareholder who so requests.
Where, pursuant to Articles 9(4) or 11(4) of Directive 2004/25/EC, or to the second subparagraph of paragraph 1 of this Article, the convocation of the general meeting is issued later than on the 21st day before the meeting, the period specified in this paragraph shall be shortened accordingly.

Article 6. 1. Member States shall ensure that shareholders, acting individually or collectively:
(a) have the right to put items on the agenda of the general meeting, provided that each such item is accompanied by a justification or a draft resolution to be adopted in the general meeting; and
(b) have the right to table draft resolutions for items included or to be included on the agenda of a general meeting.
Member States may provide that the right referred to in point (a) may be exercised only in relation to the annual general meeting, provided that shareholders, acting individually or collectively, have the right to call, or to require the company to call, a general meeting which is not an annual general meeting with an agenda including at least all the items requested by those shareholders.
Member States may provide that those rights shall be exercised in writing (submitted by postal services or electronic means).
2. Where any of the rights specified in paragraph 1 is subject to the condition that the relevant shareholder or shareholders hold a minimum stake in the company, such minimum stake shall not exceed 5 % of the share capital.
3. Each Member State shall set a single deadline, with reference to a specified number of days prior to the general meeting or the convocation, by which shareholders may exercise the right referred to in paragraph 1, point (a). In the same manner each Member State may set a deadline for the exercise of the right referred to in paragraph 1, point (b).
4. Member States shall ensure that, where the exercise of the right referred to in paragraph 1, point (a) entails a modification of the agenda for the general meeting already communicated to shareholders, the company shall make available a revised agenda in the same manner as the previous agenda in advance of the applicable record date as defined in Article 7(2) or, if no record date applies, sufficiently in advance of the date of the general meeting so as to enable other shareholders to appoint a proxy or, where applicable, to vote by correspondence.

Article 7. 1. Member States shall ensure:
(a) that the rights of a shareholder to participate in a general meeting and to vote in respect of any of his shares are not subject to any requirement that his shares be deposited with, or transferred to, or registered in the name of, another natural or legal person before the general meeting; and
(b) that the rights of a shareholder to sell or otherwise transfer his shares during the period between the record date, as defined in paragraph 2, and the general meeting to which it applies are not subject to any restriction to which they are not subject at other times.
2. Member States shall provide that the rights of a shareholder to participate in a general meeting and to vote in respect of his shares shall be determined with respect to the shares held by that shareholder on a specified date prior to the general meeting (the record date).
Member States need not apply the first subparagraph to companies that are able to identify the names and addresses of their shareholders from a current register of shareholders on the day of the general meeting.
3. Each Member State shall ensure that a single record date applies to all companies. However, a Member State may set one record date for companies which have issued bearer shares and another record date for companies which have issued registered shares, provided that a single record date applies to each company which has issued both types of shares. The record date shall not lie more than 30 days before the date of the general meeting to which it applies. In implementing this provision and Article 5(1), each Member State shall ensure that at least eight days elapse between the latest permissible date for the convocation of the general meeting and the record date. In calculating that number of days those two dates shall not be included. In the circumstances described in Article 5(1), third subparagraph, however, a Member State may require that at least six days elapse between the latest permissible date for the second or subsequent convocation of the general meeting and the record date. In calculating that number of days those two dates shall not be included.
4. Proof of qualification as a shareholder may be made subject only to such requirements as are necessary to ensure the identification of shareholders and only to the extent that they are proportionate to achieving that objective.

Article 8. 1. Member States shall permit companies to offer to their shareholders any form of participation in the general meeting by electronic means, notably any or all of the following forms of participation:
(a) real-time transmission of the general meeting;
(b) real-time two-way communication enabling shareholders to address the general meeting from a remote location;
(c) a mechanism for casting votes, whether before or during the general meeting, without the need to appoint a proxy holder who is physically present at the meeting.
2. The use of electronic means for the purpose of enabling shareholders to participate in the general meeting may be made subject only to such requirements and constraints as are necessary to ensure the identification of shareholders and the security of the electronic communication, and only to the extent that they are proportionate to achieving those objectives.
This is without prejudice to any legal rules which Member States have adopted or may adopt concerning the decision-making process within the company for the introduction or implementation of any form of participation by electronic means.

Article 9. 1. Every shareholder shall have the right to ask questions related to items on the agenda of the general meeting. The company shall answer the questions put to it by shareholders.
2. The right to ask questions and the obligation to answer are subject to the measures which Member States may take, or allow companies to take, to ensure the identification of shareholders, the good order of general meetings and their preparation and the protection of confidentiality and business interests of companies. Member States may allow companies to provide one overall answer to questions having the same content.
Member States may provide that an answer shall be deemed to be given if the relevant information is available on the company's Internet site in a question and answer format.

Article 10. 1. Every shareholder shall have the right to appoint any other natural or legal person as a proxy holder to attend and vote at a general meeting in his name. The proxy holder shall enjoy the same rights to speak and ask questions in the general meeting as those to which the shareholder thus represented would be entitled.
Apart from the requirement that the proxy holder possess legal capacity, Member States shall abolish any legal rule which restricts, or allows companies to restrict, the eligibility of persons to be appointed as proxy holders.
2. Member States may limit the appointment of a proxy holder to a single meeting, or to such meetings as may be held during a specified period.

Without prejudice to Article 13(5), Member States may limit the number of persons whom a shareholder may appoint as proxy holders in relation to any one general meeting. However, if a shareholder has shares of a company held in more than one securities account, such limitation shall not prevent the shareholder from appointing a separate proxy holder as regards shares held in each securities account in relation to any one general meeting. This does not affect rules prescribed by the applicable law that prohibit the casting of votes differently in respect of shares held by one and the same shareholder.

3. Apart from the limitations expressly permitted in paragraphs 1 and 2, Member States shall not restrict or allow companies to restrict the exercise of shareholder rights through proxy holders for any purpose other than to address potential conflicts of interest between the proxy holder and the shareholder, in whose interest the proxy holder is bound to act, and in doing so Member States shall not impose any requirements other than the following:

(a) Member States may prescribe that the proxy holder disclose certain specified facts which may be relevant for the shareholders in assessing any risk that the proxy holder might pursue any interest other than the interest of the shareholder;

(b) Member States may restrict or exclude the exercise of shareholder rights through proxy holders without specific voting instructions for each resolution in respect of which the proxy holder is to vote on behalf of the shareholder;

(c) Member States may restrict or exclude the transfer of the proxy to another person, but this shall not prevent a proxy holder who is a legal person from exercising the powers conferred upon it through any member of its administrative or management body or any of its employees.

A conflict of interest within the meaning of this paragraph may in particular arise where the proxy holder:

(i) is a controlling shareholder of the company, or is another entity controlled by such shareholder;

(ii) is a member of the administrative, management or supervisory body of the company, or of a controlling shareholder or controlled entity referred to in point (i);

(iii) is an employee or an auditor of the company, or of a controlling shareholder or controlled entity referred to in (i);

(iv) has a family relationship with a natural person referred to in points (i) to (iii).

4. The proxy holder shall cast votes in accordance with the instructions issued by the appointing shareholder. Member States may require proxy holders to keep a record of the voting instructions for a defined minimum period and to confirm on request that the voting instructions have been carried out.

5. A person acting as a proxy holder may hold a proxy from more than one shareholder without limitation as to the number of shareholders so represented. Where a proxy holder holds proxies from several shareholders, the applicable law shall enable him to cast votes for a certain shareholder differently from votes cast for another shareholder.

Article 11. 1. Member States shall permit shareholders to appoint a proxy holder by electronic means. Moreover, Member States shall permit companies to accept the notification of the appointment by electronic means, and shall ensure that every company offers to its shareholders at least one effective method of notification by electronic means.

2. Member States shall ensure that proxy holders may be appointed, and that such appointment be notified to the company, only in writing. Beyond this basic formal requirement, the appointment of a proxy holder, the notification of the appointment to the company and the issuance of voting instructions, if any, to the proxy holder may be made subject only to such formal requirements as are necessary to ensure the identification of the shareholder and of the proxy holder, or to ensure the possibility of verifying the content of voting instructions, respectively, and only to the extent that they are proportionate to achieving those objectives.

3. The provisions of this Article shall apply mutatis mutandis for the revocation of the appointment of a proxy holder.

Article 12. Member States shall permit companies to offer their shareholders the possibility to vote by correspondence in advance of the general meeting. Voting by correspondence may be made subject only to such requirements and constraints as are necessary to ensure the identification of shareholders and only to the extent that they are proportionate to achieving that objective.

Article 13. 1. This Article applies where a natural or legal person who is recognised as a shareholder by the applicable law acts in the course of a business on behalf of another natural or legal person (the client).

2. Where the applicable law imposes disclosure requirements as a prerequisite for the exercise of voting rights by a shareholder referred to in paragraph 1, such requirements shall not go beyond a list disclosing to the company the identity of each client and the number of shares voted on his behalf.

3. Where the applicable law imposes formal requirements on the authorisation of a shareholder referred to in paragraph 1 to exercise voting rights, or on voting instructions, such formal requirements shall not go beyond what is necessary to ensure the identification of the client, or the possibility of verifying the content of voting instructions, respectively, and is proportionate to achieving those objectives.

4. A shareholder referred to in paragraph 1 shall be permitted to cast votes attaching to some of the shares differently from votes attaching to the other shares.

5. Where the applicable law limits the number of persons whom a shareholder may appoint as proxy holders in accordance with Article 10(2), such limitation shall not prevent a shareholder referred to in paragraph 1 of this Article from granting a proxy to each of his clients or to any third party designated by a client.

Article 14. 1. The company shall establish for each resolution at least the number of shares for which votes have been validly cast, the proportion of the share capital represented by those votes, the total number of votes validly cast as well as the number of votes cast in favour of and against each resolution and, where applicable, the number of abstentions.

However, Member States may provide or allow companies to provide that if no shareholder requests a full account of the voting, it shall be sufficient to establish the voting results only to the extent needed to ensure that the required majority is reached for each resolution.

2. Within a period of time to be determined by the applicable law, which shall not exceed 15 days after the general meeting, the company shall publish on its Internet site the voting results established in accordance with paragraph 1.

3. This Article is without prejudice to any legal rules that Member States have adopted or may adopt concerning the formalities required in order for a resolution to become valid or the possibility of a subsequent legal challenge to the voting result.

Chapter III. Final provisions

Article 15. Member States shall bring into force the laws, regulations and administrative provisions necessary to comply with this Directive by 3 August 2009 at the latest. They shall forthwith communicate to the Commission the text of those measures.

Notwithstanding the first paragraph, Member States which on 1 July 2006 had in force national measures restricting or prohibiting the appointment of a proxy holder in the case of Article 10(3), second subparagraph, point (ii), shall bring into force the laws, regulations and administrative provisions necessary in order to comply with Article 10(3) as concerns such restriction or prohibition by 3 August 2012 at the latest. Member States shall forthwith communicate the number of days specified under Articles 6(3) and 7(3), and any subsequent changes thereof, to the Commission, which shall publish this information in the Official Journal of the European Union.

When Member States adopt the measures referred to in the first paragraph, they shall contain a reference to this Directive or shall be accompanied by such reference on the occasion of their official publication. The methods of making such reference shall be laid down by the Member States.

Article 16. This Directive shall enter into force on the 20th day following its publication in the Official Journal of the European Union.

Article 17. This Directive is addressed to the Member States.

Directive 2004/109/EC of the European Parliament and the Council of 15 December 2004 on the harmonisation of transparency requirements in relation to information about issuers whose securities are admitted to trading on a regulated market and amending Directive 2001/34/EC (*O J* L 390 , 31.12.2004 pp. 38 -57) [footnotes omitted].

THE EUROPEAN PARLIAMENT AND THE COUNCIL OF THE EUROPEAN UNION,
Having regard to the Treaty establishing the European Community, and in particular Articles 44 and 95 thereof,
Having regard to the proposal from the Commission, Having regard to the opinion of the European Economic and Social Committee,
Having regard to the opinion of the European Central Bank,
Acting in accordance with the procedure laid down in Article 251 of the Treaty,
Whereas:
(1) Efficient, transparent and integrated securities markets contribute to a genuine single market in the Community and foster growth and job creation by better allocation of capital and by reducing costs. The disclosure of accurate, comprehensive and timely information about security issuers builds sustained investor confidence and allows an informed assessment of their business performance and assets. This enhances both investor protection and market efficiency.
(2) To that end, security issuers should ensure appropriate transparency for investors through a regular flow of information. To the same end, shareholders, or natural persons or legal entities holding voting rights or financial instruments that result in an entitlement to acquire existing shares with voting rights, should also inform issuers of the acquisition of or other changes in major holdings in companies so that the latter are in a position to keep the public informed.
(3) The Commission Communication of 11 May 1999, entitled 'Implementing the framework for financial markets: Action Plan', identifies a series of actions that are needed in order to complete the single market for financial services. The Lisbon European Council of March 2000 calls for the implementation of that Action Plan by 2005. The Action Plan stresses the need to draw up a Directive upgrading transparency requirements. That need was confirmed by the Barcelona European Council of March 2002.
(4) This Directive should be compatible with the tasks and duties conferred upon the European System of Central Banks (ESCB) and the Member States' central banks by the Treaty and the Statute of the European System of Central Banks and of the European Central Bank; particular attention in this regard needs to be given to the Member States' central banks whose shares are currently
admitted to trading on a regulated market, in order to guarantee the pursuit of primary Community law objectives.
(5) Greater harmonisation of provisions of national law on periodic and ongoing information requirements for security issuers should lead to a high level of investor protection throughout the Community. However, this Directive does not affect existing Community legislation on units issued by collective investment undertakings other than the closed-end type, or on units acquired or disposed of in such undertakings.
(6) Supervision of an issuer of shares, or of debt securities the denomination per unit of which is less than EUR 1 000, for the purposes of this Directive, would be best effected by the Member State in which the issuer has its registered office. In that respect, it is vital to ensure consistency with Directive 2003/71/EC of the European Parliament and of the Council of 4 November 2003 on the prospectus to be published when securities are offered to the public or admitted to trading. Along the same lines, some flexibility should be introduced allowing third country issuers and Community companies issuing only securities other than those mentioned above a choice of home Member State.
(7) A high level of investor protection throughout the Community would enable barriers to the admission of securities to regulated markets situated or operating within a Member State to be removed. Member States other than the home Member State should no longer be allowed to restrict admission of securities to their regulated markets by imposing more stringent requirements on periodic and ongoing information about issuers whose securities are admitted to trading on a regulated market.
(8) The removal of barriers on the basis of the home Member State principle under this Directive should not affect areas not covered by this Directive, such as rights of shareholders to intervene in the management of an issuer. Nor should it affect the home Member State's right to request the issuer to publish, in addition, parts of or all regulated information through newspapers.
(9) Regulation (EC) No 1606/2002 of the European Parliament and of the Council of 19 July 2002 on the application of international accounting standards has already paved the way for a convergence of financial reporting standards throughout the Community for issuers whose securities are admitted to trading on a regulated market and who are required to prepare consolidated accounts. Thus, a specific regime for security issuers beyond the general system for all companies, as laid down in the Company Law Directives, is already established. This Directive builds on this approach with regard to annual and interim financial reporting, including the principle of

providing a true and fair view of an issuer's assets, liabilities, financial position and profit or loss. A condensed set of financial statements, as part of a half-yearly financial report, also represents a sufficient basis for giving such a true and fair view of the first six months of an issuer's financial year.

(10) An annual financial report should ensure information over the years once the issuer's securities have been admitted to a regulated market. Making it easier to compare annual financial reports is only of use to investors in securities markets if they can be sure that this information will be published within a certain time after the end of the financial year. As regards debt securities admitted to trading on a regulated market prior to 1 January 2005 and issued by issuers incorporated in a third country, the home Member State may under certain conditions allow issuers not to prepare annual financial reports in accordance with the standards required under this Directive.

(11) This Directive introduces more comprehensive halfyearly financial reports for issuers of shares admitted to trading on a regulated market. This should allow investors to make a more informed assessment of the issuer's situation.

(12) A home Member State may provide for exemptions from half-yearly reporting by issuers of debt securities in the case of:
— credit institutions acting as small-size issuers of debt securities, or
— issuers already existing on the date of the entry into force of this Directive who exclusively issue debt securities unconditionally and irrevocably guaranteed by the home Member State or by one of its regional or local authorities, or
— during a transitional period of ten years, only in respect of those debt securities admitted to trading on a regulated market prior to 1 January 2005 which may be purchased by professional investors only. If such an exemption is given by the home Member State, it may not be extended in respect of any debt securities admitted to a regulated market thereafter.

(13) The European Parliament and the Council welcome the Commission's commitment rapidly to consider enhancing the transparency of the remuneration policies, total remuneration paid, including any contingent or deferred compensation, and benefits in kind granted to each member of administrative, management or supervisory bodies under its Action Plan for 'Modernising Company Law and Enhancing Corporate Governance in the European Union' of 21 May 2003 and the Commission's intention to make a Recommendation on this topic in the near future.

(14) The home Member State should encourage issuers whose shares are admitted to trading on a regulated market and whose principal activities lie in the extractive industry to disclose payments to governments in their annual financial report. The home Member State should also encourage an increase in the transparency of such payments within the framework established at various international financial fora.

(15) This Directive will also make half-yearly reporting mandatory for issuers of only debt securities on regulated markets. Exemptions should only be provided for wholesale markets on the basis of a denomination per unit starting at EUR 50 000, as under Directive 2003/71/EC. Where debt securities are issued in another currency, exemptions should only be possible where the denomination per unit in such a currency is, at the date of the issue, at least equivalent to EUR 50 000.

(16) More timely and more reliable information about the share issuer's performance over the financial year also requires a higher frequency of interim information. A requirement should therefore be introduced to publish an interim management statement during the first six months and a second interim management statement during the second six months of a financial year. Share issuers who already publish quarterly financial reports should not be required to publish interim management statements.

(17) Appropriate liability rules, as laid down by each Member State under its national law or regulations, should be applicable to the issuer, its administrative, management or supervisory bodies, or persons responsible within the issuer. Member States should remain free to determine the extent of the liability.

(18) The public should be informed of changes to major holdings in issuers whose shares are traded on a regulated market situated or operating within the Community. This information should enable investors to acquire or dispose of shares in full knowledge of changes in the voting structure; it should also enhance effective control of share issuers and overall market transparency of important capital movements. Information about shares or financial instruments as determined by Article 13, lodged as collateral, should be provided in certain circumstances.

(19) Articles 9 and 10(c) should not apply to shares provided to or by the members of the ESCB in carrying out their functions as monetary authorities provided that the voting rights attached to such shares are not exercised; the reference to a 'short period' in Article 11 should be understood with reference to credit operations carried out in accordance with the Treaty and the European Central Bank (ECB) legal acts, in particular the ECB Guidelines on monetary policy instruments and procedures and TARGET, and to credit operations for the purpose of performing equivalent functions in accordance with national provisions.

(20) In order to avoid unnecessary burdens for certain market participants and to clarify who actually exercises influence over an issuer, there is no need to require notification of major holdings of shares, or other financial

instruments as determined by Article 13 that result in an entitlement to acquire shares with regard to market makers or custodians, or of holdings of shares or such financial instruments acquired solely for clearing and settlement purposes, within limits and guarantees to be applied throughout the Community. The home Member State should be allowed to provide limited exemptions as regards holdings of shares in trading books of credit institutions and investment firms.

(21) In order to clarify who is actually a major holder of shares or other financial instruments in the same issuer throughout the Community, parent undertakings should not be required to aggregate their own holdings with those managed by undertakings for collective investment in transferable securities (UCITS) or investment firms, provided that such undertakings or firms exercise voting rights independently from their parent undertakings and fulfil certain further conditions.

(22) Ongoing information to holders of securities admitted to trading on a regulated market should continue to be based on the principle of equal treatment. Such equal treatment only relates to shareholders in the same position and does not therefore prejudice the issue of how many voting rights may be attached to a particular share. By the same token, holders of debt securities ranking *pari passu* should continue to benefit from equal treatment, even in the case of sovereign debt. Information to holders of shares and/or debt securities in general meetings should be facilitated. In particular, holders of shares and/or debt securities situated abroad should be more actively involved in that they should be able to mandate proxies to act on their behalf. For the same reasons, it should be decided in a general meeting of holders of shares and/or debt securities whether the use of modern information and communication technologies should become a reality. In that case, issuers should put in place arrangements in order effectively to inform holders of their shares and/or debt securities, insofar as it is possible for them to identify those holders.

(23) Removal of barriers and effective enforcement of new Community information requirements also require adequate control by the competent authority of the home Member State. This Directive should at least provide for a minimum guarantee for the timely availability of such information. For this reason, at least one filing and storage system should exist in each Member State.

(24) Any obligation for an issuer to translate all ongoing and periodic information into all the relevant languages in all the Member States where its securities are admitted to trading does not foster integration of securities markets, but has deterrent effects on cross-border admission of securities to trading on regulated markets. Therefore, the issuer should in certain cases be entitled to provide

information drawn up in a language that is customary in the sphere of international finance. Since a particular effort is needed to attract investors from other Member States and third countries, Member States should no longer prevent shareholders, persons exercising voting rights, or holders of financial instruments, from making the required notifications to the issuer in a language that is customary in the sphere of international finance.

(25) Access for investors to information about issuers should be more organised at a Community level in order to actively promote integration of European capital markets. Investors who are not situated in the issuer's home Member State should be put on an equal footing with investors situated in the issuer's home Member State, when seeking access to such information. This could be achieved if the home Member State ensures compliance with minimum quality standards for disseminating information throughout the community, in a fast manner on a non-discriminatory basis and depending on the type of regulated information in question. In addition, information which has been disseminated should be available in the home Member State in a centralized way allowing a European network to be built up, accessible at affordable prices for retail investors, while not leading to unnecessary duplication of filing requirements for issuers. Issuers should benefit from free competition when choosing the media or operators for disseminating information under this Directive.

(26) In order to further simplify investor access to corporate information across Member States, it should be left to the national supervisory authorities to formulate guidelines for setting up electronic networks, in close consultation with the other parties concerned, in particular security issuers, investors, market participants, operators of regulated markets and financial information providers. (27) So as to ensure the effective protection of investors and the proper operation of regulated markets, the rules relating to information to be published by issuers whose securities are admitted to trading on a regulated market should also apply to issuers which do not have a registered office in a Member State and which do not fall within the scope of Article 48 of the Treaty. It should also be ensured that any additional relevant information about Community issuers or third country issuers, disclosure of which is required in a third country but not in a Member State, is made available to the public in the Community.

(28) A single competent authority should be designated in each Member State to assume final responsibility for supervising compliance with the provisions adopted pursuant to this Directive, as well as for international cooperation. Such an authority should be of an administrative nature, and its independence from economic players should be ensured in order to avoid conflicts of interest. Member States may however designate another competent

PART VIII. EUROPEAN COMPANY LAW

authority for examining that information referred to in this Directive is drawn up in accordance with the relevant reporting framework and taking appropriate measures in case of discovered infringements; such an authority need not be of an administrative nature.

(29) Increasing cross-border activities require improved cooperation between national competent authorities, including a comprehensive set of provisions for the exchange of information and for precautionary measures. The organisation of the regulatory and supervisory tasks in each Member State should not hinder efficient cooperation between the competent national authorities.

(30) At its meeting on 17 July 2000, the Council set up the Committee of Wise Men on the Regulation of European securities markets. In its final report, that Committee proposed the introduction of new legislative techniques based on a four-level approach, namely essential principles, technical implementing measures, cooperation amongst national securities regulators, and enforcement of Community law. This Directive should confine itself to broad 'framework' principles, while implementing measures to be adopted by the Commission with the assistance of the European Securities Committee established by Commission Decision 2001/528/EC (1) should lay down the technical details.

(31) The Resolution adopted by the Stockholm European Council of March 2001 endorsed the final report of the Committee of Wise Men and the proposed four-level approach to make the regulatory process for Community securities legislation more efficient and transparent.

(32) According to that Resolution, implementing measures should be used more frequently, to ensure that technical provisions can be kept up to date with market and supervisory developments, and deadlines should be set for all stages of implementing rules.

(33) The Resolution of the European Parliament of 5 February 2002 on the implementation of financial services legislation also endorsed the Committee of Wise Men's report, on the basis of the solemn declaration made before the European Parliament the same day by the President of the Commission and the letter of 2 October 2001 addressed by the Internal Market Commissioner to the Chairman of the Parliament's Committee on Economic and Monetary Affairs with regard to safeguards for the European Parliament's role in this process.

(34) The European Parliament should be given a period of three months from the first transmission of draft implementing measures to allow it to examine them and to give its opinion. However, in urgent and duly justified cases, that period may be shortened. If, within that period, a Resolution is passed by the European Parliament, the Commission should re-examine the draft measures.

(35) Technical implementing measures for the rules laid down in this Directive may be necessary to take account of new developments on securities markets. The Commission should accordingly be empowered to adopt implementing measures, provided that they do not modify the essential elements of this Directive and provided that the Commission acts in accordance with the principles set out therein, after consulting the European Securities Committee.

(36) In exercising its implementing powers in accordance with this Directive, the Commission should respect the following principles:
— the need to ensure confidence in financial markets among investors by promoting high standards of transparency in financial markets;
— the need to provide investors with a wide range of competing investments and a level of disclosure and protection tailored to their circumstances;
— the need to ensure that independent regulatory authorities enforce the rules consistently, especially as regards the fight against economic crime;
— the need for high levels of transparency and consultation with all market participants and with the European Parliament and the Council;
— the need to encourage innovation in financial markets if they are to be dynamic and efficient;
— the need to ensure market integrity by close and reactive monitoring of financial innovation;
— the importance of reducing the cost of, and increasing access to, capital;
— the balance of costs and benefits to market participants on a long-term basis, including small and medium-sized businesses and small investors, in any implementing measures;
— the need to foster the international competitiveness of Community financial markets without prejudice to a much-needed extension of international cooperation;
— the need to achieve a level playing field for all market participants by establishing Community-wide regulations wherever appropriate;
— the need to respect differences in national markets where these do not unduly impinge on the coherence of the single market;
— the need to ensure coherence with other Community legislation in this area, as imbalances in information and a lack of transparency may jeopardise the operation of the markets and above all harm consumers and small investors.

(37) In order to ensure that the requirements set out in this Directive or the measures implementing this Directive are fulfilled, any infringement of those requirements or measures should be promptly detected and, if necessary, subject to penalties. To that end, measures and penalties should be sufficiently dissuasive, proportionate and consistently enforced. Member States should ensure that
decisions taken by the competent national authorities are subject to the right of appeal to the courts.
(38) This Directive aims to upgrade the current transparency requirements for security issuers and investors acquiring or disposing of major holdings in issuers whose shares are admitted to trading on a regulated market. This Directive replaces some of the requirements set out in Directive 2001/34/EC of the European Parliament and of the Council of 28 May 2001 on the admission of securities to official stock exchange listing and on information to be published on those securities. (1) In order to gather transparency requirements in a single act it is necessary to amend it accordingly. Such an amendment however should not affect the ability of Member States to impose additional requirements under Articles 42 to 63 of Directive 2001/34/EC, which remain valid.
(39) This Directive is in line with Directive 95/46/EC of the European Parliament and of the Council of 24 October 1995 on the protection of individuals with regard to the processing of personal data and on the free movement of such data.
(40) This Directive respects fundamental rights and observes the principles recognised in particular by the Charter of the Fundamental Rights of the European Union.
(41) Since the objectives of this Directive, namely to ensure investor confidence through equivalent transparency throughout the Community and thereby to complete the internal market, cannot be sufficiently achieved by the Member States on the basis of the existing Community legislation and can therefore be better achieved at Community level, the Community may adopt measures, in accordance with the principle of subsidiarity as set out in Article 5 of the Treaty. In accordance with the principle of proportionality, as set out in that Article, this Directive does not go beyond what is necessary in order to achieve these objectives.
(42) The measures necessary for implementing this Directive should be adopted in accordance with Council Decision 1999/468/EC of 28 June 1999 laying down the procedures for the exercise of implementing powers conferred on the Commission,

HAVE ADOPTED THIS DIRECTIVE:

Chapter I. General provisions

Article 1. 1. This Directive establishes requirements in relation to the disclosure of periodic and ongoing information about issuers whose securities are already admitted to trading on a regulated market situated or operating within a Member State.
2. This Directive shall not apply to units issued by collective investment undertakings other than the closed-end type, or to units acquired or disposed of in such collective investment undertakings.
3. Member States may decide not to apply the provisions mentioned in Article 16(3) and in paragraphs 2, 3 and 4 of Article 18 to securities which are admitted to trading on a regulated market issued by them or their regional or local authorities.
4. Member States may decide not to apply Article 17 to their national central banks in their capacity as issuers of shares admitted to trading on a regulated market if this admission took place before 20 January 2005.

Article 2. 1. For the purposes of this Directive the following definitions shall apply:
(a) 'securities' means transferable securities as defined in Article 4(1), point 18, of Directive 2004/39/EC of the European Parliament and of the Council of 21 April 2004 on markets in financial instruments with the exception of money-market instruments, as defined in Article 4(1), point 19, of that Directive having a maturity of less than 12 months, for which national legislation may be applicable;
(b) 'debt securities' means bonds or other forms of transferable securitised debts, with the exception of securities which are equivalent to shares in companies or which, if converted or if the rights conferred by them are exercised, give rise to a right to acquire shares or securities equivalent to shares;
(c) 'regulated market' means a market as defined in Article 4(1), point 14, of Directive 2004/39/EC;
(d) 'issuer' means a legal entity governed by private or public law, including a State, whose securities are admitted to trading on a regulated market, the issuer being, in the case of depository receipts representing securities, the issuer of the securities represented;
(e) 'shareholder' means any natural person or legal entity governed by private or public law, who holds, directly or indirectly:
(i) shares of the issuer in its own name and on its own account;
(ii) shares of the issuer in its own name, but on behalf of another natural person or legal entity;

(iii) depository receipts, in which case the holder of the depository receipt shall be considered as the shareholder of the underlying shares represented by the depository receipts;
(f) 'controlled undertaking' means any undertaking
(i) in which a natural person or legal entity has a majority of the voting rights; or
(ii) of which a natural person or legal entity has the right to appoint or remove a majority of the members of the administrative, management or supervisory body and is at the same time a shareholder in, or member of, the undertaking in question; or
(iii) of which a natural person or legal entity is a shareholder or member and alone controls a majority of the shareholders' or members' voting rights, respectively, pursuant to an agreement entered into with other shareholders or members of the undertaking in question; or
(iv) over which a natural person or legal entity has the power to exercise, or actually exercises, dominant influence or control;
(g) 'collective investment undertaking other than the closedend type' means unit trusts and investment companies:
(i) the object of which is the collective investment of capital provided by the public, and which operate on the principle of risk spreading; and
(ii) the units of which are, at the request of the holder of such units, repurchased or redeemed, directly or indirectly, out of the assets of those undertakings;
(h) 'units of a collective investment undertaking' means securities issued by a collective investment undertaking and representing rights of the participants in such an undertaking over its assets;
(i) 'home Member State' means
(i) in the case of an issuer of debt securities the denomination per unit of which is less than EUR 1 000 or an issuer of shares:
— where the issuer is incorporated in the Community, the Member State in which it has its registered office;
— where the issuer is incorporated in a third country, the Member State in which it is required to file the annual information with the competent authority in accordance with Article 10 of Directive 2003/71/EC. The definition of 'home' Member State shall be applicable to debt securities in a currency other than Euro, provided that the value of such denomination per unit is, at the date of the issue, less than EUR 1 000, unless it is nearly equivalent to EUR 1 000;
(ii) for any issuer not covered by (i), the Member State chosen by the issuer from among the Member State in which the issuer has its registered office and those Member States which have admitted its securities to trading on a regulated market on their territory. The issuer may choose only one Member State as its home Member State. Its choice shall remain valid for at least three years unless its securities are no longer admitted to trading on any regulated market in the Community;
(j) 'host Member State' means a Member State in which securities are admitted to trading on a regulated market, if different from the home Member State;
(k) 'regulated information' means all information which the issuer, or any other person who has applied for the admission of securities to trading on a regulated market without the issuer's consent, is required to disclose under this Directive, under Article 6 of Directive 2003/6/EC of the European Parliament and of the Council of 28 January 2003 on insider dealing and market manipulation (market abuse), or under the laws, regulations or administrative provisions of a Member State adopted under Article 3(1) of this Directive;
(l) 'electronic means' are means of electronic equipment for the processing (including digital compression), storage and transmission of data, employing wires, radio, optical technologies, or any other electromagnetic means;
(m) 'management company' means a company as defined in Article 1a(2) of Council Directive 85/611/EEC of 20 December 1985 on the coordination of laws, regulations and administrative provisions relating to undertakings for collective investment in transferable securities (UCITS);
(n) 'market maker' means a person who holds himself out on the financial markets on a continuous basis as being willing to deal on own account by buying and selling financial instruments against his proprietary capital at prices defined by him;
(o) 'credit institution' means an undertaking as defined in Article 1(1)(a) of Directive 2000/12/EC of the European Parliament and of the Council of 20 March 2000 relating to the taking up and pursuit of the business of credit institutions;
(p) 'securities issued in a continuous or repeated manner' means debt securities of the same issuer on tap or at least two separate issues of securities of a similar type and/or class.
2. For the purposes of the definition of 'controlled undertaking' in paragraph 1(f)(ii), the holder's rights in relation to voting, appointment and removal shall include the rights of any other undertaking controlled by the shareholder and those of any natural person or legal entity acting, albeit in its own name, on behalf of the shareholder or of any other undertaking controlled by the shareholder.

3. In order to take account of technical developments on financial markets and to ensure the uniform application of paragraph 1, the Commission shall, in accordance with the procedure referred to in Article 27(2), adopt implementing measures concerning the definitions set out in paragraph 1. The Commission shall, in particular:
(a) establish, for the purposes of paragraph 1(i)(ii), the procedural arrangements in accordance with which an issuer may make the choice of the home Member State;
(b) adjust, where appropriate for the purposes of the choice of the home Member State referred to in paragraph 1(i)(ii), the three-year period in relation to the issuer's track record in the light of any new requirement under Community law concerning admission to trading on a regulated market;
(c) establish, for the purposes of paragraph 1(l), an indicative list of means which are not to be considered as electronic means, thereby taking into account Annex V to Directive 98/34/EC of the European Parliament and of the Council of 22 June 1998 laying down a procedure for the provision of information in the field of technical standards and regulations.

Article 3. 1. The home Member State may make an issuer subject to requirements more stringent than those laid down in this Directive. The home Member State may also make a holder of shares, or a natural person or legal entity referred to in Articles 10 or 13, subject to requirements more stringent than those laid down in this Directive.
2. A host Member State may not:
(a) as regards the admission of securities to a regulated market in its territory, impose disclosure requirements more stringent than those laid down in this Directive or in Article 6 of Directive 2003/6/EC;
(b) as regards the notification of information, make a holder of shares, or a natural person or legal entity referred to in Articles 10 or 13, subject to requirements more stringent than those laid down in this Directive.

Chapter II. Periodic information

Article 4. 1. The issuer shall make public its annual financial report at the latest four months after the end of each financial year and shall ensure that it remains publicly available for at least five years.
2. The annual financial report shall comprise:
(a) the audited financial statements;
(b) the management report; and
(c) statements made by the persons responsible within the issuer, whose names and functions shall be clearly indicated, to the effect that, to the best of their knowledge, the financial statements prepared in accordance with the applicable set of accounting standards give a true and fair view of the assets, liabilities, financial position and profit or loss of the issuer and the undertakings included in the consolidation taken as a whole and that the management report includes a fair review of the development and performance of the business and the position of the issuer and the undertakings included in the consolidation taken as a whole, together with a description of the principal risks and uncertainties that they face.
3. Where the issuer is required to prepare consolidated accounts according to the Seventh Council Directive 83/349/EEC of 13 June 1983 on consolidated accounts, the audited financial statements shall comprise such consolidated accounts drawn up in accordance with Regulation (EC) No 1606/2002 and the annual accounts of the parent company drawn up in accordance with the national law of the Member State in which the parent company is incorporated. Where the issuer is not required to prepare consolidated accounts, the audited financial statements shall comprise the accounts prepared in accordance with the national law of the Member State in which the company is incorporated.
4. The financial statements shall be audited in accordance with Articles 51 and 51a of the Fourth Council Directive 78/660/EEC of 25 July 1978 on the annual accounts of certain types of companies (2) and, if the issuer is required to prepare consolidated accounts, in accordance with Article 37 of Directive 83/349/EEC. The audit report, signed by the person or persons responsible for auditing the financial statements, shall be disclosed in full to the public together with the annual financial report.
5. The management report shall be drawn up in accordance with Article 46 of Directive 78/660/EEC and, if the issuer is required to prepare consolidated accounts, in accordance with Article 36 of Directive 83/349/EEC.
6. The Commission shall, in accordance with the procedure referred to in Article 27(2), adopt implementing measures in order to take account of technical developments in financial markets and to ensure the uniform application of paragraph 1.
The Commission shall in particular specify the technical conditions under which a published annual financial report, including the audit report, is to remain available to the public. Where appropriate, the Commission may also adapt the fiveyear period referred to in paragraph 1.

Article 5. 1. The issuer of shares or debt securities shall make public a half-yearly financial report covering the first six months of the financial year as soon as possible after the end of the relevant period, but at the latest two months thereafter. The issuer shall ensure that the half-yearly financial report remains available to the public for at least five years.

2. The half-yearly financial report shall comprise:
(a) the condensed set of financial statements;
(b) an interim management report; and
(c) statements made by the persons responsible within the issuer, whose names and functions shall be clearly indicated, to the effect that, to the best of their knowledge, the condensed set of financial statements which has been prepared in accordance with the applicable set of accounting standards gives a true and fair view of the assets, liabilities, financial position and profit or loss of the issuer, or the undertakings included in the consolidation as a whole as required under paragraph 3, and that the interim management report includes a fair review of the information required under paragraph 4.

3. Where the issuer is required to prepare consolidated accounts, the condensed set of financial statements shall be prepared in accordance with the international accounting standard applicable to the interim financial reporting adopted pursuant to the procedure provided for under Article 6 of Regulation (EC) No 1606/2002. Where the issuer is not required to prepare consolidated accounts, the condensed set of financial statements shall at least contain a condensed balance sheet, a condensed profit and loss account and explanatory notes on these accounts. In preparing the condensed balance sheet and the condensed profit and loss account, the issuer shall follow the same principles for recognizing and measuring as when preparing annual financial reports.

4. The interim management report shall include at least an indication of important events that have occurred during the first six months of the financial year, and their impact on the condensed set of financial statements, together with a description of the principal risks and uncertainties for the remaining six months of the financial year. For issuers of shares, the interim management report shall also include major related parties transactions.

5. If the half-yearly financial report has been audited, the audit report shall be reproduced in full. The same shall apply in the case of an auditors' review. If the half-yearly financial report has not been audited or reviewed by auditors, the issuer shall make a statement to that effect in its report.

6. The Commission shall, in accordance with the procedure referred to in Article 27(2), adopt implementing measures in order to take account of technical developments on financial markets and to ensure the uniform application of paragraphs 1 to 5 of this Article. The Commission shall, in particular:
(a) specify the technical conditions under which a published half-yearly financial report, including the auditors' review, is to remain available to the public;
(b) clarify the nature of the auditors' review;
(c) specify the minimum content of the condensed balance sheet and profit and loss accounts and explanatory notes on these accounts, where they are not prepared in accordance with the international accounting standards adopted pursuant to the procedure provided for under Article 6 of Regulation (EC) No 1606/2002. Where appropriate, the Commission may also adapt the fiveyear period referred to in paragraph 1.

Article 6. 1. Without prejudice to Article 6 of Directive 2003/6/EC, an issuer whose shares are admitted to trading on a regulated market shall make public a statement by its management during the first six-month period of the financial year and another statement by its management during the second sixmonth period of the financial year. Such statement shall be made in a period between ten weeks after the beginning and six weeks before the end of the relevant six-month period.
It shall contain information covering the period between the beginning of the relevant six-month period and the date of publication of the statement. Such a statement shall provide:
— an explanation of material events and transactions that have taken place during the relevant period and their impact on the financial position of the issuer and its controlled undertakings, and
— a general description of the financial position and performance of the issuer and its controlled undertakings during the relevant period.

2. Issuers which, under either national legislation or the rules of the regulated market or of their own initiative, publish quarterly financial reports in accordance with such legislation or rules shall not be required to make public statements by the management provided for in paragraph 1.

3. The Commission shall provide a report to the European Parliament and the Council by 20 January 2010 on the transparency of quarterly financial reporting and statements by the management of issuers to examine whether the information provided meets the objective of allowing investors to make an informed assessment of the financial position of the issuer.
Such a report shall include an impact assessment on areas where the Commission considers proposing amendments to this Article.

Article 7. Member States shall ensure that responsibility for the information to be drawn up and made public in accordance with Articles 4, 5, 6 and 16 lies at least with the issuer or its administrative, management or supervisory bodies and shall ensure that their laws, regulations and administrative provisions on liability apply to the issuers, the bodies referred to in this Article or the persons responsible within the issuers.

Article 8. 1. Articles 4, 5 and 6 shall not apply to the following issuers:
(a) a State, a regional or local authority of a State, a public international body of which at least one Member State is a member, the ECB, and Member States' national central banks whether or not they issue shares or other securities; and
(b) an issuer exclusively of debt securities admitted to trading on a regulated market, the denomination per unit of which is at least EUR 50 000 or, in the case of debt securities denominated in a currency other than Euro, the value of such denomination per unit is, at the date of the issue, equivalent to at least EUR 50 000.
2. The home Member State may choose not to apply Article 5 to credit institutions whose shares are not admitted to trading on a regulated market and which have, in a continuous or repeated manner, only issued debt securities provided that the total nominal amount of all such debt securities remains below EUR 100 000 000 and that they have not published a prospectus under Directive 2003/71/EC.
3. The home Member State may choose not to apply Article 5 to issuers already existing at the date of the entry into force of Directive 2003/71/EC which exclusively issue debt securities unconditionally and irrevocably guaranteed by the home Member State or by one of its regional or local authorities, on a regulated market.

Chapter III. Ongoing information

Section I. Information about major holdings

Article 9. 1. The home Member State shall ensure that, where a shareholder acquires or disposes of shares of an issuer whose shares are admitted to trading on a regulated market and to which voting rights are attached, such shareholder notifies the issuer of the proportion of voting rights of the issuer held by the shareholder as a result of the acquisition or disposal where that proportion reaches, exceeds or falls below the thresholds of 5 %, 10 %, 15 %, 20 %, 25 %, 30 %, 50 % and 75 %.
The voting rights shall be calculated on the basis of all the shares to which voting rights are attached even if the exercise thereof is suspended. Moreover this information shall also be given in respect of all the shares which are in the same class and to which voting rights are attached.
2. The home Member States shall ensure that the shareholders notify the issuer of the proportion of voting rights, where that proportion reaches, exceeds or falls below the thresholds provided for in paragraph 1, as a result of events changing the breakdown of voting rights, and on the basis of the information disclosed pursuant to Article 15. Where the issuer is incorporated in a third country, the notification shall be made for equivalent events.
3. The home Member State need not apply:
(a) the 30 % threshold, where it applies a threshold of onethird;
(b) the 75 % threshold, where it applies a threshold of twothirds.
4. This Article shall not apply to shares acquired for the sole purpose of clearing and settling within the usual short settlement cycle, or to custodians holding shares in their custodian capacity provided such custodians can only exercise the voting rights attached to such shares under instructions given in writing or by electronic means.
5. This Article shall not apply to the acquisition or disposal of a major holding reaching or crossing the 5 % threshold by a market maker acting in its capacity of a market maker, provided that:
(a) it is authorised by its home Member State under Directive 2004/39/EC; and
(b) it neither intervenes in the management of the issuer concerned nor exerts any influence on the issuer to buy such shares or back the share price.
6. Home Member States under Article 2(1)(i) may provide that voting rights held in the trading book, as defined in Article 2(6) of Council Directive 93/6/EEC of 15 March 1993 on the capital adequacy of investment firms and credit institutions, of a credit institution or investment firm shall not be counted for the purposes of this Article provided that:
(a) the voting rights held in the trading book do not exceed 5 %, and
(b) the credit institution or investment firm ensures that the voting rights attaching to shares held in the trading book are not exercised nor otherwise used to intervene in the management of the issuer.
7. The Commission shall, in accordance with the procedure referred to in Article 27(2), adopt implementing measures in order to take account of technical developments on financial markets and to ensure the uniform application of paragraphs 2, 4 and 5 of this Article. The Commission shall in particular specify the maximum

Part VIII. European Company Law

length of the 'short settlement cycle' referred to in paragraph 4, as well as the appropriate control mechanisms by the competent authority of the home Member State. In addition, the Commission may draw up a list of the events referred to in paragraph 2.

Article 10. The notification requirements defined in paragraphs 1 and 2 of Article 9 shall also apply to a natural person or legal entity to the extent it is entitled to acquire, to dispose of, or to exercise voting rights in any of the following cases or a combination of them:
(a) voting rights held by a third party with whom that person or entity has concluded an agreement, which obliges them to adopt, by concerted exercise of the voting rights they hold, a lasting common policy towards the management of the issuer in question;
(b) voting rights held by a third party under an agreement concluded with that person or entity providing for the temporary transfer for consideration of the voting rights in question;
(c) voting rights attaching to shares which are lodged as collateral with that person or entity, provided the person or entity controls the voting rights and declares its intention of exercising them;
(d) voting rights attaching to shares in which that person or entity has the life interest;
(e) voting rights which are held, or may be exercised within the meaning of points (a) to (d), by an undertaking controlled by that person or entity;
(f) voting rights attaching to shares deposited with that person or entity which the person or entity can exercise at its discretion in the absence of specific instructions from the shareholders;
(g) voting rights held by a third party in its own name on behalf of that person or entity;
(h) voting rights which that person or entity may exercise as a proxy where the person or entity can exercise the voting rights at its discretion in the absence of specific instructions from the shareholders.

Article 11. 1. Articles 9 and 10(c) shall not apply to shares provided to or by the members of the ESCB in carrying out their functions as monetary authorities, including shares provided to or by members of the ESCB under a pledge or repurchase or similar agreement for liquidity granted for monetary policy purposes or within a payment system.
2. The exemption shall apply to the above transactions lasting for a short period and provided that the voting rights attaching to such shares are not exercised.

Article 12. 1. The notification required under Articles 9 and 10 shall include the following information:
(a) the resulting situation in terms of voting rights;
(b) the chain of controlled undertakings through which voting rights are effectively held, if applicable;
(c) the date on which the threshold was reached or crossed; and
(d) the identity of the shareholder, even if that shareholder is not entitled to exercise voting rights under the conditions laid down in Article 10, and of the natural person or legal entity entitled to exercise voting rights on behalf of that shareholder.
2. The notification to the issuer shall be effected as soon as possible, but not later than four trading days, the first of which shall be the day after the date on which the shareholder, or the natural person or legal entity referred to in Article 10,
(a) learns of the acquisition or disposal or of the possibility of exercising voting rights, or on which, having regard to the circumstances, should have learned of it, regardless of the date on which the acquisition, disposal or possibility of exercising voting rights takes effect; or
(b) is informed about the event mentioned in Article 9(2).
3. An undertaking shall be exempted from making the required notification in accordance with paragraph 1 if the notification is made by the parent undertaking or, where the parent undertaking is itself a controlled undertaking, by its own parent undertaking.
4. The parent undertaking of a management company shall not be required to aggregate its holdings under Articles 9 and 10 with the holdings managed by the management company under the conditions laid down in Directive 85/611/ EEC, provided such management company exercises its voting rights independently from the parent undertaking.
However, Articles 9 and 10 shall apply where the parent undertaking, or another controlled undertaking of the parent undertaking, has invested in holdings managed by such management company and the management company has no discretion to exercise the voting rights attached to such holdings and may only exercise such voting rights under direct or indirect instructions from the parent or another controlled undertaking of the parent undertaking.

5. The parent undertaking of an investment firm authorized under Directive 2004/39/EC shall not be required to aggregate its holdings under Articles 9 and 10 with the holdings which such investment firm manages on a client-by-client basis within the meaning of Article 4(1), point 9, of Directive 2004/39/EC, provided that:
— the investment firm is authorised to provide such portfolio management under point 4 of Section A of Annex I to Directive 2004/39/EC;
— it may only exercise the voting rights attached to such shares under instructions given in writing or by electronic means or it ensures that individual portfolio management services are conducted independently of any other services under conditions equivalent to those provided for under Directive 85/611/EEC by putting into place appropriate mechanisms; and
— the investment firm exercises its voting rights independently from the parent undertaking. However, Articles 9 and 10 shall apply where the parent undertaking, or another controlled undertaking of the parent undertaking, has invested in holdings managed by such investment firm and the investment firm has no discretion to exercise the voting rights attached to such holdings and may only exercise such voting rights under direct or indirect instructions from the parent or another controlled undertaking of the parent undertaking.
6. Upon receipt of the notification under paragraph 1, but no later than three trading days thereafter, the issuer shall make public all the information contained in the notification.
7. A home Member State may exempt issuers from the requirement in paragraph 6 if the information contained in the notification is made public by its competent authority, under the conditions laid down in Article 21, upon receipt of the notification, but no later than three trading days thereafter.
8. In order to take account of technical developments on financial markets and to ensure the uniform application of paragraphs 1, 2, 4, 5 and 6 of this Article, the Commission shall, in accordance with the procedure referred to in Article 27(2), adopt implementing measures:
(a) to establish a standard form to be used throughout the Community when notifying the required information to the issuer under paragraph 1 or when filing information under Article 19(3);
(b) to determine a calendar of 'trading days' for all Member States;
(c) to establish in which cases the shareholder, or the natural person or legal entity referred to in Article 10, or both, shall effect the necessary notification to the issuer;
(d) to clarify the circumstances under which the shareholder,
or the natural person or legal entity referred to in Article 10, should have learned of the acquisition or disposal;
(e) to clarify the conditions of independence to be complied with by management companies and their parent undertakings or by investment firms and their parent undertakings to benefit from the exemptions in paragraphs 4 and 5.

Article 13. 1. The notification requirements laid down in Article 9 shall also apply to a natural person or legal entity who holds, directly or indirectly, financial instruments that result in an entitlement to acquire, on such holder's own initiative alone, under a formal agreement, shares to which voting rights are attached, already issued, of an issuer whose shares are admitted to trading on a regulated market.
2. The Commission shall, in accordance with the procedure referred to in Article 27(2), adopt implementing measures in order to take account of technical developments in financial markets and to ensure the uniform application of paragraph 1.
It shall in particular determine:
(a) the types of financial instruments referred to in paragraph 1 and their aggregation;
(b) the nature of the formal agreement referred to in paragraph 1;
(c) the contents of the notification to be made, establishing a standard form to be used throughout the Community for that purpose;
(d) the notification period;
(e) to whom the notification is to be made.

Article 14. 1. Where an issuer of shares admitted to trading on a regulated market acquires or disposes of its own shares, either itself or through a person acting in his own name but on the issuer's behalf, the home Member State shall ensure that the issuer makes public the proportion of its own shares as soon as possible, but not later than four trading days following such acquisition or disposal where that proportion reaches, exceeds or falls below the thresholds of 5 % or 10 % of the voting rights. The proportion shall be calculated on the basis of the total number of shares to which voting rights are attached.
2. The Commission shall, in accordance with the procedure referred to in Article 27(2), adopt implementing measures in order to take account of technical developments in financial markets and to ensure the uniform application of paragraph 1.

Article 15. For the purpose of calculating the thresholds provided for in Article 9, the home Member State shall at least require the disclosure to the public by the issuer of the total number of voting rights and capital at the end of each calendar month during which an increase or decrease of such total number has occurred.

Article 16. 1. The issuer of shares admitted to trading on a regulated market shall make public without delay any change in the rights attaching to the various classes of shares, including changes in the rights attaching to derivative securities issued by the issuer itself and giving access to the shares of that issuer.
2. The issuer of securities, other than shares admitted to trading on a regulated market, shall make public without delay any changes in the rights of holders of securities other than shares, including changes in the terms and conditions of these securities which could indirectly affect those rights, resulting in particular from a change in loan terms or in interest rates.
3. The issuer of securities admitted to trading on a regulated market shall make public without delay of new loan issues and in particular of any guarantee or security in respect thereof. Without prejudice to Directive 2003/6/EC, this paragraph shall not apply to a public international body of which at least one Member State is member.

Section II. Information for holders of securities admitted to trading on a regulated market

Article 17. 1. The issuer of shares admitted to trading on a regulated market shall ensure equal treatment for all holders of shares who are in the same position.
2. The issuer shall ensure that all the facilities and information necessary to enable holders of shares to exercise their rights are available in the home Member State and that the integrity of data is preserved. Shareholders shall not be prevented from exercising their rights by proxy, subject to the law of the country in which the issuer is incorporated. In particular, the issuer shall:
(a) provide information on the place, time and agenda of meetings, the total number of shares and voting rights and the rights of holders to participate in meetings;
(b) make available a proxy form, on paper or, where applicable, by electronic means, to each person entitled to vote at a sharehlders' meeting, together with the notice concerning the meeting or, on request, after an announcement of the meeting;
(c) designate as its agent a financial institution through which shareholders may exercise their financial rights; and
(d) publish notices or distribute circulars concerning the allocation and payment of dividends and the issue of new shares, including information on any arrangements for allotment, subscription, cancellation or conversion.
3. For the purposes of conveying information to shareholders, the home Member State shall allow issuers the use of electronic means, provided such a decision is taken in a general meeting and meets at least the following conditions:
(a) the use of electronic means shall in no way depend upon the location of the seat or residence of the shareholder or, in the cases referred to in Article 10(a) to (h), of the natural persons or legal entities;
(b) identification arrangements shall be put in place so that the shareholders, or the natural persons or legal entities entitled to exercise or to direct the exercise of voting rights, are effectively informed;
(c) shareholders, or in the cases referred to in Article 10(a) to (e) the natural persons or legal entities entitled to acquire, dispose of or exercise voting rights, shall be contacted in writing to request their consent for the use of electronic means for conveying information and, if they do not object within a reasonable period of time, their consent shall be deemed to be given. They shall be able to request, at any time in the future, that information be conveyed in writing, and
(d) any apportionment of the costs entailed in the conveyance of such information by electronic means shall be determined by the issuer in compliance with the principle of equal treatment laid down in paragraph 1.
4. The Commission shall, in accordance with the procedure provided for in Article 27(2), adopt implementing measures in order to take account of technical developments in financial markets, to take account of developments in information and communication technology and to ensure the uniform application of paragraphs 1, 2 and 3. It shall, in particular, specify the types of financial institution through which a shareholder may exercise the financial rights provided for in paragraph 2(c).

Article 18. 1. The issuer of debt securities admitted to trading on a regulated market shall ensure that all holders of debt securities ranking pari passu are given equal treatment in respect of all the rights attaching to those debt securities.
2. The issuer shall ensure that all the facilities and information necessary to enable debt securities holders to exercise their rights are publicly available in the home Member State and that the integrity of data is preserved.

Debt securities holders shall not be prevented from exercising their rights by proxy, subject to the law of country in which the issuer is incorporated. In particular, the issuer shall:
(a) publish notices, or distribute circulars, concerning the place, time and agenda of meetings of debt securities holders, the payment of interest, the exercise of any conversion, exchange, subscription or cancellation rights, and repayment, as well as the right of those holders to participate therein;
(b) make available a proxy form on paper or, where applicable, by electronic means, to each person entitled to vote at a meeting of debt securities holders, together with the notice concerning the meeting or, on request, after an announcement of the meeting; and
(c) designate as its agent a financial institution through which debt securities holders may exercise their financial rights.
If only holders of debt securities whose denomination per unit amounts to at least EUR 50 000 or, in the case of debt securities denominated in a currency other than Euro whose denomination per unit is, at the date of the issue, equivalent to at least EUR 50 000, are to be invited to a meeting, the issuer may choose as venue any Member State, provided that all the facilities and information necessary to enable such holders to exercise their rights are made available in that Member State.
4. For the purposes of conveying information to debt securities holders, the home Member State, or the Member State chosen by the issuer pursuant to paragraph 3, shall allow issuers the use of electronic means, provided such a decision is taken in a general meeting and meets at least the following conditions:
(a) the use of electronic means shall in no way depend upon the location of the seat or residence of the debt security holder or of a proxy representing that holder;
(b) identification arrangements shall be put in place so that debt securities holders are effectively informed;
(c) debt securities holders shall be contacted in writing to request their consent for the use of electronic means for conveying information and if they do not object within a reasonable period of time, their consent shall be deemed to be given. They shall be able to request, at any time in the future, that information be conveyed in writing; and
(d) any apportionment of the costs entailed in the conveyance of information by electronic means shall be determined by the issuer in compliance with the principle of equal treatment laid down in paragraph 1.
5. The Commission shall, in accordance with the procedure provided for in Article 27(2), adopt implementing measures in order to take account of technical developments in financial markets, to take account of developments in information and communication technology and to ensure the uniform application of paragraphs 1 to 4. It shall, in particular, specify the types of financial institution through which a debt security holder may exercise the financial rights provided for in paragraph 2(c).

Chapter IV. General obligations

Article 19. 1. Whenever the issuer, or any person having requested, without the issuer's consent, the admission of its securities to trading on a regulated market, discloses regulated information, it shall at the same time file that information with the competent authority of its home Member State. That competent authority may decide to publish such filed information on its Internet site. Where an issuer proposes to amend its instrument of incorporation or statutes, it shall communicate the draft amendment to the competent authority of the home Member State and to the regulated market to which its securities have been admitted to trading. Such communication shall be effected without delay, but at the latest on the date of calling the general meeting which is to vote on, or be informed of, the amendment.
2. The home Member State may exempt an issuer from the requirement under paragraph 1 in respect of information disclosed in accordance with Article 6 of Directive 2003/6/EC or Article 12(6) of this Directive.
3. Information to be notified to the issuer in accordance with Articles 9, 10, 12 and 13 shall at the same time be filed with the competent authority of the home Member State.
4. In order to ensure the uniform application of paragraphs 1, 2 and 3, the Commission shall, in accordance with the procedure referred to in Article 27(2), adopt implementing measures. The Commission shall, in particular, specify the procedure in accordance with which an issuer, a holder of shares or other financial instruments, or a person or entity referred to in Article 10, is to file information with the competent authority of the home Member State under paragraphs 1 or 3, respectively, in order to:
(a) enable filing by electronic means in the home Member State;
(b) coordinate the filing of the annual financial report referred to in Article 4 of this Directive with the filing of the annual information referred to in Article 10 of Directive 2003/71/ EC.

Article 20. 1. Where securities are admitted to trading on a regulated market only in the home Member State, regulated information shall be disclosed in a language accepted by the competent authority in the home Member State.

2. Where securities are admitted to trading on a regulated market both in the home Member State and in one or more host Member States, regulated information shall be disclosed:
(a) in a language accepted by the competent authority in the home Member State; and
(b) depending on the choice of the issuer, either in a language accepted by the competent authorities of those host Member States or in a language customary in the sphere of international finance.
3. Where securities are admitted to trading on a regulated market in one or more host Member States, but not in the home Member State, regulated information shall, depending on the choice of the issuer, be disclosed either in a language accepted by the competent authorities of those host Member States or in a language customary in the sphere of international finance. In addition, the home Member State may lay down in its law, regulations or administrative provisions that the regulated information shall, depending on the choice of the issuer, be disclosed either in a language accepted by its competent authority or in a language customary in the sphere of international finance.
4. Where securities are admitted to trading on a regulated market without the issuer's consent, the obligations under paragraphs 1, 2 and 3 shall be incumbent not upon the issuer, but upon the person who, without the issuer's consent, has requested such admission.
5. Member States shall allow shareholders and the natural person or legal entity referred to in Articles 9, 10 and 13 to notify information to an issuer under this Directive only in a language customary in the sphere of international finance. If the issuer receives such a notification, Member States may not require the issuer to provide a translation into a language accepted by the competent authorities.
6. By way of derogation from paragraphs 1 to 4, where securities whose denomination per unit amounts to at least EUR 50 000 or, in the case of debt securities denominated in a currency other than Euro equivalent to at least EUR 50 000 at the date of the issue, are admitted to trading on a regulated market in one or more Member States, regulated information shall be disclosed to the public either in a language accepted by the competent authorities of the home and host Member States or in a language customary in the sphere of international finance, at the choice of the issuer or of the person who, without the issuer's consent, has requested such admission.
7. If an action concerning the content of regulated information is brought before a court or tribunal in a Member State, responsibility for the payment of costs incurred in the translation of that information for the purposes of the proceedings shall be decided in accordance with the law of that Member State.

Article 21. 1. The home Member State shall ensure that the issuer, or the person who has applied for admission to trading on a regulated market without the issuer's consent, discloses regulated information in a manner ensuring fast access to such information on a non-discriminatory basis and makes it available to the officially appointed mechanism referred to in paragraph 2.
The issuer, or the person who has applied for admission to trading on a regulated market without the issuer's consent, may not charge investors any specific cost for providing the information. The home Member State shall require the issuer to use such media as may reasonably be relied upon for the effective dissemination of information to the public throughout the Community. The home Member State may not impose an obligation to use only media whose operators are established on its territory.
2. The home Member State shall ensure that there is at least one officially appointed mechanism for the central storage of regulated information. These mechanisms should comply with minimum quality standards of security, certainty as to the information source, time recording and easy access by end users and shall be aligned with the filing procedure under Article 19(1).
3. Where securities are admitted to trading on a regulated market in only one host Member State and not in the home Member State, the host Member State shall ensure disclosure of regulated information in accordance with the requirements referred to in paragraph 1.
4. In order to take account of technical developments in financial markets, to take account of developments in information and communication technology and to ensure the uniform application of paragraphs 1, 2 and 3, the Commission shall adopt implementing measures in accordance with the procedure referred to in Article 27(2). The Commission shall in particular specify:
(a) minimum standards for the dissemination of regulated information, as referred to in paragraph 1;
(b) minimum standards for the central storage mechanism as referred to in paragraph 2.
The Commission may also specify and update a list of media for the dissemination of information to the public.

Article 22. 1. The competent authorities of the Member States shall draw up appropriate guidelines with a view to further facilitating public access to information to be disclosed under Directive 2003/6/EC, Directive 2003/71/EC and this Directive.The aim of those guidelines shall be the creation of:
(a) an electronic network to be set up at national level between national securities regulators, operators of regulated markets and national company registers covered by the First Council Directive 68/151/EEC of 9 March

1968 on coordination of safeguards which, for the protection of the interests of members and others, are required by Member States of companies within the meaning of the second paragraph of Article 48 (1) of the Treaty, with a view to making such safeguards equivalent throughout the Community; and
(b) a single electronic network, or a platform of electronic networks across Member States.
2. The Commission shall review the results achieved under paragraph 1 by 31 December 2006 and may, in accordance with the procedure referred to in Article 27(2), adopt implementing measures to facilitate compliance with Articles 19 and 21.

Article 23. 1. Where the registered office of an issuer is in a third country, the competent authority of the home Member State may exempt that issuer from requirements under Articles 4 to 7 and Articles 12(6), 14, 15 and 16 to 18, provided that the law of the third country in question lays down equivalent requirements or such an issuer complies with requirements of the law of a third country that the competent authority of the home Member State considers as equivalent. However, the information covered by the requirements laid down in the third country shall be filed in accordance with Article 19 and disclosed in accordance with Articles 20 and 21.
2. By way of derogation from paragraph 1, an issuer whose registered office is in a third country shall be exempted from preparing its financial statement in accordance with Article 4 or Article 5 prior to the financial year starting on or after 1 January 2007, provided such issuer prepares its financial statements in accordance with internationally accepted standards referred to in Article 9 of Regulation (EC) No 1606/ 2002.
3. The competent authority of the home Member State shall ensure that information disclosed in a third country which may be of importance for the public in the Community is disclosed in accordance with Articles 20 and 21, even if such information is not regulated information within the meaning of Article 2(1)(k).
4. In order to ensure the uniform application of paragraph 1, the Commission shall, in accordance with the procedure referred to in Article 27(2), adopt implementing measures (i) setting up a mechanism ensuring the establishment of equivalence of information required under this Directive, including financial statements and information, including financial statements, required under the law, regulations or administrative provisions of a third country;
(ii) stating that, by reason of its domestic law, regulations, administrative provisions, or of the practices or procedures based on the international standards set by international organisations, the third country where the issuer is registered ensures the equivalence of the information requirements provided for in this Directive. The Commission shall, in accordance with the procedure referred to in Article 27(2), take the necessary decisions on the equivalence of accounting standards which are used by third country issuers under the conditions set out in Article 30(3) at the latest five years following the date referred to in Article 31. If the Commission decides that the accounting standards of a third country are not equivalent, it may allow the issuers concerned to continue using such accounting standards during an appropriate transitional period.
5. In order to ensure uniform application of paragraph 2, the Commission may, in accordance with the procedure referred to in Article 27(2), adopt implementing measures defining the type of information disclosed in a third country that is of importance to the public in the Community.
6. Undertakings whose registered office is in a third country which would have required an authorisation in accordance with Article 5(1) of Directive 85/611/EEC or, with regard to portfolio management under point 4 of section A of Annex I to Directive 2004/39/EC if it had its registered office or, only in the case of an investment firm, its head office within the Community, shall also be exempted from aggregating holdings with the holdings of its parent undertaking under the requirements laid down in Article 12(4) and (5) provided that they comply with equivalent conditions of independence as management companies or investment firms.
7. In order to take account of technical developments in financial markets and to ensure the uniform application of paragraph 6, the Commission shall, in accordance with the procedure referred to in Article 27(2), adopt implementing measures stating that, by reason of its domestic law, regulations, or administrative provisions, a third country ensures the equivalence of the independence requirements provided for under this Directive and its implementing measures.

Chapter V. Competent authorities

Article 24. 1. Each Member State shall designate the central authority referred to in Article 21(1) of Directive 2003/71/EC as central competent administrative authority responsible for carrying out the obligations provided for in this Directive and for ensuring that the provisions adopted pursuant to this Directive are applied. Member States shall inform the Commission accordingly.
However, for the purpose of paragraph 4(h) Member States may designate a competent authority other than the central competent authority referred to in the first subparagraph.
2. Member States may allow their central competent authority to delegate tasks. Except for the tasks referred to in

paragraph 4(h), any delegation of tasks relating to the obligations provided for in this Directive and in its implementing measures shall be reviewed five years after the entry into force of this Directive and shall end eight years after the entry into force of this Directive. Any delegation of tasks shall be made in a specific manner stating the tasks to be undertaken and the conditions under which they are to be carried out. Those conditions shall include a clause requiring the entity in question to be organised in a manner such that conflicts of interest are avoided and information obtained from carrying out the delegated tasks is not used unfairly or to prevent competition. In any case, the final responsibility for supervising compliance with the provisions of this Directive and implementing measures adopted pursuant thereto shall lie with the competent authority designated in accordance with paragraph 1.

3. Member States shall inform the Commission and competent authorities of other Member States of any arrangements entered into with regard to the delegation of tasks, including the precise conditions for regulating the delegations.

4. Each competent authority shall have all the powers necessary for the performance of its functions. It shall at least be empowered to:

(a) require auditors, issuers, holders of shares or other financial instruments, or persons or entities referred to in Articles 10 or 13, and the persons that control them or are controlled by them, to provide information and documents;

(b) require the issuer to disclose the information required under point (a) to the public by the means and within the time limits the authority considers necessary. It may publish such information on its own initiative in the event that the issuer, or the persons that control it or are controlled by it, fail to do so and after having heard the issuer;

(c) require managers of the issuers and of the holders of shares or other financial instruments, or of persons or entities referred to in Articles 10 or 13, to notify the information required under this Directive, or under national law adopted in accordance with this Directive, and, if necessary, to provide further information and documents;

(d) suspend, or request the relevant regulated market to suspend, trading in securities for a maximum of ten days at a time if it has reasonable grounds for suspecting that the provisions of this Directive, or of national law adopted in accordance with this Directive, have been infringed by the issuer;

(e) prohibit trading on a regulated market if it finds that the provisions of this Directive, or of national law adopted in accordance with this Directive, have been infringed, or if it has reasonable grounds for suspecting that the provisions of this Directive have been infringed;

(f) monitor that the issuer discloses timely information with the objective of ensuring effective and equal access to the public in all Member States where the securities are traded and take appropriate action if that is not the case;

(g) make public the fact that an issuer, or a holder of shares or other financial instruments, or a person or entity referred to in Articles 10 or 13, is failing to comply with its obligations;

(h) examine that information referred to in this Directive is drawn up in accordance with the relevant reporting framework and take appropriate measures in case of discovered infringements; and

(i) carry out on-site inspections in its territory in accordance with national law, in order to verify compliance with the provisions of this Directive and its implementing measures. Where necessary under national law, the competent authority or authorities may use this power by applying to the relevant judicial authority and/or in cooperation with other authorities.

5. Paragraphs 1 to 4 shall be without prejudice to the possibility for a Member State to make separate legal and administrative arrangements for overseas European territories for whose external relations that Member State is responsible.

6. The disclosure to competent authorities by the auditors of any fact or decision related to the requests made by the competent authority under paragraph (4)(a) shall not constitute a breach of any restriction on disclosure of information imposed by contract or by any law, regulation or administrative provision and shall not involve such auditors in liability of any kind.

Article 25. 1. The obligation of professional secrecy shall apply to all persons who work or who have worked for the competent authority and for entities to which competent authorities may have delegated certain tasks. Information covered by professional secrecy may not be disclosed to any other person or authority except by virtue of the laws, regulations or administrative provisions of a Member State.

2. Competent authorities of the Member States shall cooperate with each other, whenever necessary, for the purpose of carrying out their duties and making use of their powers, whether set out in this Directive or in national law adopted pursuant to this Directive. Competent authorities shall render assistance to competent authorities of other Member States.

3. Paragraph 1 shall not prevent the competent authorities from exchanging confidential information. Information thus exchanged shall be covered by the obligation of professional secrecy to which the persons employed or formerly employed by the competent authorities receiving the information are subject.

4. Member States may conclude cooperation agreements providing for the exchange of information with the competent authorities or bodies of third countries enabled by their respective legislation to carry out any of the tasks assigned by this Directive to the competent authorities in accordance with Article 24. Such an exchange of information is subject to guarantees of professional secrecy at least equivalent to those referred to in this Article. Such exchange of information shall be intended for the performance of the supervisory task of the authorities or bodies mentioned. Where the information originates in another Member State, it may not be disclosed without the express agreement of the competent authorities which have disclosed it and, where appropriate, solely for the purposes for which those authorities gave their agreement.

Article 26. 1. Where the competent authority of a host Member State finds that the issuer or the holder of shares or other financial instruments, or the person or entity referred to in Article 10, has committed irregularities or infringed its obligations, it shall refer its findings to the competent authority of the home Member State.
2. If, despite the measures taken by the competent authority of the home Member State, or because such measures prove inadequate, the issuer or the security holder persists in infringing the relevant legal or regulatory provisions, the competent authority of the host Member State shall, after informing the competent authority of the home Member State, take, in accordance with Article 3(2), all the appropriate measures in order to protect investors. The Commission shall be informed of such measures at the earliest opportunity.

Chapter VI. Implementing measures

Article 27. 1. The Commission shall be assisted by the European Securities Committee, instituted by Article 1 of Decision 2001/528/EC.
2. Where reference is made to this paragraph, Articles 5 and 7 of Decision 1999/468/EC shall apply, having regard to the provisions of Article 8 thereof, provided that the implementing measures adopted in accordance with that procedure do not modify the essential provisions of this Directive. The period laid down in Article 5(6) of Decision 1999/468/EC shall be set at three months.
3. The Committee shall adopt its Rules of Procedure. 4. Without prejudice to the implementing measures already adopted by 20 January 2009 the application of the provisions of this Directive concerning the adoption of technical rules and decisions in accordance with the procedure referred to in paragraph 2 shall be suspended. On a proposal from the Commission, the European Parliament and the Council may renew the provisions concerned in accordance with the procedure laid down in Article 251 of the Treaty and, to that end, shall review them prior to the expiry of the four-year period.

Article 28. 1. Without prejudice to the right of Member States to impose criminal penalties, Member States shall ensure, in conformity with their national law, that at least the appropriate administrative measures may be taken or civil and/or administrative penalties imposed in respect of the persons responsible, where the provisions adopted in accordance with this Directive have not been complied with. Member States shall ensure that those measures are effective, proportionate and dissuasive.
2. Member States shall provide that the competent authority may disclose to the public every measure taken or penalty imposed for infringement of the provisions adopted in accordance with this Directive, save where such disclosure would seriously jeopardise the financial markets or cause disproportionate damage to the parties involved.

Article 29. Member States shall ensure that decisions taken under laws, regulations, and administrative provisions adopted in accordance with this Directive are subject to the right of appeal to the courts.

Chapter VII. Transitional and final provisions

Article 30. 1. By way of derogation from Article 5(3) of this Directive, the home Member State may exempt from disclosing financial statements in accordance with Regulation (EC) No 1606/2002 issuers referred to in Article 9 of that Regulation for the financial year starting on or after 1 January 2006.
2. Notwithstanding Article 12(2), a shareholder shall notify the issuer at the latest two months after the date in Article 31(1) of the proportion of voting rights and capital it holds, in accordance with Articles 9, 10 and 13, with issuers at that date, unless it has already made a notification containing equivalent information before that date. Notwithstanding Article 12(6), an issuer shall in turn disclose the information received in those notifications no later than three months after the date in Article 31(1).
3. Where an issuer is incorporated in a third country, the home Member State may exempt such issuer only in respect of those debt securities which have already been admitted to trading on a regulated market in the

Community prior to 1 January 2005 from drawing up its financial statements in accordance with Article 4(3) and its management report in accordance with Article 4(5) as long as
(a) the competent authority of the home Member State acknowledges that annual financial statements prepared by issuers from such a third country give a true and fair view of the issuer's assets and liabilities, financial position and results;
(b) the third country where the issuer is incorporated has not made mandatory the application of international accounting standards referred to in Article 2 of Regulation (EC) No 1606/2002; and
(c) the Commission has not taken any decision in accordance with Article 23(4)(ii) as to whether there is an equivalence between the abovementioned accounting standards and
— the accounting standards laid down in the law, regulations or administrative provisions of the third country where the issuer is incorporated, or
— the accounting standards of a third country such an issuer has elected to comply with.
4. The home Member State may exempt issuers only in respect of those debt securities which have already been admitted to trading on a regulated market in the Community prior to 1 January 2005 from disclosing half-yearly financial report in accordance with Article 5 for 10 years following 1 January 2005, provided that the home Member State had decided to allow such issuers to benefit from the provisions of Article 27 of Directive 2001/34/EC at the point of admission of those debt securities.

Article 31. 1. Member States shall take the necessary measures to comply with this Directive by 20 January 2007. They shall forthwith inform the Commission thereof. When Member States adopt these measures, they shall contain a reference to this Directive or shall be accompanied by such reference on the occasion of their official publication. The methods of making such reference shall be laid down by Member States.
2. Where Member States adopt measures pursuant to Articles 3(1), 8(2), 8(3), 9(6) or 30, they shall immediately communicate those measures to the Commission and to the other Member States.

Article 32. With effect from the date specified in Article 31(1), Directive 2001/34/EC shall be amended as follows:
(1) In Article 1, points (g) and (h) shall be deleted;
(2) Article 4 shall be deleted;
(3) In Article 6, paragraph 2 shall be deleted;
(4) In Article 8, paragraph 2 shall be replaced by the following:
'2. Member States may make the issuers of securities admitted to official listing subject to additional obligations, provided that those additional obligations apply generally for all issuers or for individual classes of issuers';
(5) Articles 65 to 97 shall be deleted;
(6) Articles 102 and 103 shall be deleted;
(7) In Article 107(3), the second subparagraph shall be deleted;
(8) In Article 108, paragraph 2 shall be amended as follows:
(a) in point (a), the words 'periodic information to be published by the companies of which shares are admitted' shall be deleted;
(b) point (b) shall be deleted;
(c) point (c)(iii) shall be deleted;
(d) point (d) shall be deleted. References made to the repealed provisions shall be construed as being made to the provisions of this Directive.

Article 33. The Commission shall by 30 June 2009 report on the operation of this Directive to the European Parliament and to the Council including the appropriateness of ending the exemption for existing debt securities after the 10-year period as provided for by Article 30(4) and its potential impact on the European financial markets.

Article 34. This Directive shall enter into force on the twentieth day following that of its publication in the *Official Journal of the European Union*.

Article 35. This Directive is addressed to the Member States.

Directive 2003/6/EC of the European Parliament and the Council of 28 January 2003 on insider dealing and market manipulation (market abuse) (*O J* L 096 , 12.04.003 pp. 6 – 25). Consolidated version as amended by Directive 2008/26/EC of the European Parliament and of the Council of 11 March 2008 [footnotes omitted].

THE EUROPEAN PARLIAMENT AND THE COUNCIL OF THE EUROPEAN UNION,
Having regard to the Treaty establishing the European Community, and in particular Article 95 thereof, Having regard to the proposal from the Commission,
Having regard to the opinion of the European Economic and Social Committee,
Having regard to the opinion of the European Central Bank,
Acting in accordance with the procedure laid down in Article 251,
Whereas:
(1) A genuine Single Market for financial services is crucial for economic growth and job creation in the Community.
(2) An integrated and efficient financial market requires market integrity. The smooth functioning of securities markets and public confidence in markets are prerequisites for economic growth and wealth. Market abuse harms the integrity of financial markets and public confidence in securities and derivatives.
(3) The Commission Communication of 11 May 1999 entitled 'Implementing the framework for financial markets: action plan' identifies a series of actions that are needed in order to complete the single market for financial services. The Lisbon European Council of April 2000 called for the implementation of that action plan by 2005. The action plan stresses the need to draw up a Directive against market manipulation.
(4) At its meeting on 17 July 2000, the Council set up the Committee of Wise Men on the Regulation of European Securities Markets. In its final report, the Committee of Wise Men proposed the introduction of new legislative techniques based on a four-level approach, namely framework principles, implementing measures, cooperation and enforcement. Level 1, the Directive, should confine itself to broad general 'framework' principles while Level 2 should contain technical implementing measures to be adopted by the Commission with the assistance of a committee.
(5) The Resolution adopted by the Stockholm European Council of March 2001 endorsed the final report of the Committee of Wise Men and the proposed four-level approach to make the regulatory process for Community securities legislation more efficient and transparent.
(6) The Resolution of the European Parliament of 5 February 2002 on the implementation of financial services legislation also endorsed the Committee of Wise Men's report, on the basis of the solemn declaration made before Parliament the same day by the Commission and the letter of 2 October 2001 addressed by the Internal Market Commissioner to the chairman of Parliament's Committee on Economic and Monetary Affairs with regard to the safeguards for the European Parliament's role in this process.
(7) The measures necessary for the implementation of this Directive should be adopted in accordance with Council Decision 1999/468/EC of 28 June 1999 laying down the procedures for the exercise of implementing powers conferred on the Commission .
(8) According to the Stockholm European Council, Level 2 implementing measures should be used more frequently, to ensure that technical provisions can be kept up to date with market and supervisory developments, and deadlines should be set for all stages of Level 2 work.
(9) The European Parliament should be given a period of three months from the first transmission of draft implementing measures to allow it to examine them and to give its opinion. However, in urgent and duly justified cases, this period may be shortened. If, within that period, a resolution is passed by the European Parliament, the Commission should re-examine the draft measures.
(10) New financial and technical developments enhance the incentives, means and opportunities for market abuse: through new products, new technologies, increasing cross-border activities and the Internet.
(11) The existing Community legal framework to protect market integrity is incomplete. Legal requirements vary from one Member State to another, leaving economic actors often uncertain over concepts, definitions and enforcement. In some Member States there is no legislation addressing the issues of price manipulation and the dissemination of misleading information.
(12) Market abuse consists of insider dealing and market manipulation. The objective of legislation against insider dealing is the same as that of legislation against market manipulation: to ensure the integrity of Community financial markets and to enhance investor confidence in those markets. It is therefore advisable to adopt combined rules to combat both insider dealing and market manipulation. A single Directive will ensure throughout the Community the same framework for allocation of responsibilities, enforcement and cooperation.
(13) Given the changes in financial markets and in Community legislation since the adoption of Council Directive 89/592/EEC of 13 November 1989 coordinating regulations on insider dealing, that Directive should now be replaced, to ensure consistency with legislation against market manipulation. A new Directive is also needed to

avoid loopholes in Community legislation which could be used for wrongful conduct and which would undermine public confidence and therefore prejudice the smooth functioning of the markets.
(14) This Directive meets the concerns expressed by the Member States following the terrorist attacks on 11 September 2001 as regards the fight against financing terrorist activities.
(15) Insider dealing and market manipulation prevent full and proper market transparency, which is a prerequisite for trading for all economic actors in integrated financial markets.
(16) Inside information is any information of a precise nature which has not been made public, relating, directly or indirectly, to one or more issuers of financial instruments or to one or more financial instruments. Information which could have a significant effect on the evolution and forming of the prices of a regulated market as such could be considered as information which indirectly relates to one or more issuers of financial instruments or to one or more related derivative financial instruments.
(17) As regards insider dealing, account should be taken of cases where inside information originates not from a profession or function but from criminal activities, the preparation or execution of which could have a significant effect on the prices of one or more financial instruments or on price formation in the regulated market as such.
(18) Use of inside information can consist in the acquisition or disposal of financial instruments by a person who knows, or ought to have known, that the information possessed is inside information. In this respect, the competent authorities should consider what a normal and reasonable person would know or should have known in the circumstances. Moreover, the mere fact that market-makers, bodies authorised to act as counterparties, or persons authorised to execute orders on behalf of third parties with inside information confine themselves, in the first two cases, to pursuing their legitimate business of buying or selling financial instruments or, in the last case, to carrying out an order dutifully, should not in itself be deemed to constitute use of such inside information.
(19) Member States should tackle the practice known as 'front running', including 'front running' in commodity derivatives, where it constitutes market abuse under the definitions contained in this Directive.
(20) A person who enters into transactions or issues orders to trade which are constitutive of market manipulation may be able to establish that his reasons for entering into such transactions or issuing orders to trade were legitimate and that the transactions and orders to trade were in conformity with accepted practice on the regulated market concerned. A sanction could still be imposed if the competent authority established that there was another, illegitimate, reason behind these transactions or orders to trade.
(21) The competent authority may issue guidance on matters covered by this Directive, e.g. definition of inside information in relation to derivatives on commodities or implementation of the definition of accepted market practices relating to the definition of market manipulation. This guidance should be in conformity with the provisions of the Directive and the implementing measures adopted in accordance with the comitology procedure.
(22) Member States should be able to choose the most appropriate way to regulate persons producing or disseminating research concerning financial instruments or issuers of financial instruments or persons producing or disseminating other information recommending or suggesting investment strategy, including appropriate mechanisms for self-regulation, which should be notified to the Commission.
(23) Posting of inside information by issuers on their internet sites should be in accordance with the rules on transfer of personal data to third countries as laid down in Directive 95/46/EC of the European Parliament and of the Council of 24 October 1995 on the protection of individuals with regard to the processing of personal data and on the movement of such data.
(24) Prompt and fair disclosure of information to the public enhances market integrity, whereas selective disclosure by issuers can lead to a loss of investor confidence in the integrity of financial markets. Professional economic actors should contribute to market integrity by various means. Such measures could include, for instance, the creation of 'grey lists', the application of 'window trading' to sensitive categories of personnel, the application of internal codes of conduct and the establishment of 'Chinese walls'. Such preventive measures may contribute to combating market abuse only if they are enforced with determination and are dutifully controlled. Adequate enforcement control would imply for instance the designation of compliance officers within the bodies concerned and periodic checks conducted by independent auditors.
(25) Modern communication methods make it possible for financial market professionals and private investors to have more equal access to financial information, but also increase the risk of the spread of false or misleading information.
(26) Greater transparency of transactions conducted by persons discharging managerial responsibilities within issuers and, where applicable, persons closely associated with them, constitutes a preventive measure against market abuse. The publication of those transactions on at least an individual basis can also be a highly valuable source of information to investors.
(27) Market operators should contribute to the prevention of market abuse and adopt structural provisions aimed at preventing and detecting market manipulation practices. Such provisions may include requirements concerning transparency of transactions concluded, total disclosure of price-regularisation agreements, a fair system of order

pairing, introduction of an effective atypical order detection scheme, sufficiently robust financial instrument reference price-fixing schemes and clarity of rules on the suspension of transactions.

(28) This Directive should be interpreted, and implemented by Member States, in a manner consistent with the requirements for effective regulation in order to protect the interests of holders of transferable securities carrying voting rights in a company (or which may carry such rights as a consequence of the exercise of rights or conversion) when the company is subject to a public take-over bid or other proposed change of control. In particular, this Directive does not in any way prevent a Member State from putting or having in place such measures as it sees fit for these purposes.

(29) Having access to inside information relating to another company and using it in the context of a public take-over bid for the purpose of gaining control of that company or proposing a merger with that company should not in itself be deemed to constitute insider dealing.

(30) Since the acquisition or disposal of financial instruments necessarily involves a prior decision to acquire or dispose taken by the person who undertakes one or other of these operations, the carrying out of this acquisition or disposal should not be deemed in itself to constitute the use of inside information.

(31) Research and estimates developed from publicly available data should not be regarded as inside information and, therefore, any transaction carried out on the basis of such research or estimates should not be deemed in itself to constitute insider dealing within the meaning of this Directive.

(32) Member States and the European System of Central Banks, national central banks or any other officially designated body, or any person acting on their behalf, should not be restricted in carrying out monetary, exchange-rate or public debt management policy.

(33) Stabilisation of financial instruments or trading in own shares in buy-back programmes can be legitimate, in certain circumstances, for economic reasons and should not, therefore, in themselves be regarded as market abuse. Common standards should be developed to provide practical guidance.

(34) The widening scope of financial markets, the rapid change and the range of new products and developments require a wide application of this Directive to financial instruments and techniques involved, in order to guarantee the integrity of Community financial markets.

(35) Establishing a level playing field in Community financial markets requires wide geographical application of the provisions covered by this Directive. As regards derivative instruments not admitted to trading but falling within the scope of this Directive, each Member State should be competent to sanction actions carried out on its territory or abroad which concern underlying financial instruments admitted to trading on a regulated market situated or operating within its territory or for which a request for admission to trading on such a regulated market has been made. Each Member State should also be competent to sanction actions carried out on its territory which concern underlying financial instruments admitted to trading on a regulated market in a Member State or for which a request for admission to trading on such a market has been made.

(36) A variety of competent authorities in Member States, having different responsibilities, may create confusion among economic actors. A single competent authority should be designated in each Member State to assume at least final responsibility for supervising compliance with the provisions adopted pursuant to this Directive, as well as international collaboration. Such an authority should be of an administrative nature guaranteeing its independence of economic actors and avoiding conflicts of interest. In accordance with national law, Member States should ensure appropriate financing of the competent authority. That authority should have adequate arrangements for consultation concerning possible changes in national legislation such as a consultative committee composed of representatives of issuers, financial services providers and consumers, so as to be fully informed of their views and concerns.

(37) A common minimum set of effective tools and powers for the competent authority of each Member State will guarantee supervisory effectiveness. Market undertakings and all economic actors should also contribute at their level to market integrity. In this sense, the designation of a single competent authority for market abuse does not exclude collaboration links or delegation under the responsibility of the competent authority, between that authority and market undertakings with a view to guaranteeing efficient supervision of compliance with the provisions adopted pursuant to this Directive.

(38) In order to ensure that a Community framework against market abuse is sufficient, any infringement of the prohibitions or requirements laid down pursuant to this Directive will have to be promptly detected and sanctioned. To this end, sanctions should be sufficiently dissuasive and proportionate to the gravity of the infringement and to the gains realised and should be consistently applied.

(39) Member States should remain alert, in determining the administrative measures and sanctions, to the need to ensure a degree of uniformity of regulation from one Member State to another.

(40) Increasing cross-border activities require improved cooperation and a comprehensive set of provisions for the exchange of information between national competent authorities. The organization of supervision and of

investigatory powers in each Member State should not hinder cooperation between the competent national authorities.

(41) Since the objective of the proposed action, namely to prevent market abuse in the form of insider dealing and market manipulation, cannot be sufficiently achieved by the Member States and can therefore, by reason of the scale and effects of the measures, be better achieved at Community level, the Community may adopt measures, in accordance with the principle of subsidiarity as set out in Article 5 of the Treaty. In accordance with the principle of proportionality, as set out in that Article, this Directive does not go beyond what is necessary in order to achieve that objective.

(42) Technical guidance and implementing measures for the rules laid down in this Directive may from time to time be necessary to take account of new developments on financial markets. The Commission should accordingly be empowered to adopt implementing measures, provided that these do not modify the essential elements of this Directive and the Commission acts according to the principles set out in this Directive, after consulting the European Securities Committee established by Commission Decision 2001/528/EC.

(43) In exercising its implementing powers in accordance with this Directive, the Commission should respect the following principles:

— the need to ensure confidence in financial markets among investors by promoting high standards of transparency in financial markets,

— the need to provide investors with a wide range of competing investments and a level of disclosure and protection tailored to their circumstances,

— the need to ensure that independent regulatory authorities enforce the rules consistently, especially as regards the fight against economic crime,

— the need for high levels of transparency and consultation with all market participants and with the European Parliament and the Council,

— the need to encourage innovation in financial markets if they are to be dynamic and efficient,

— the need to ensure market integrity by close and reactive monitoring of financial innovation,

— the importance of reducing the cost of, and increasing access to, capital,

— the balance of costs and benefits to market participants on a long-term basis (including small and medium-sized businesses and small investors) in any implementing measures,

— the need to foster the international competitiveness of EU financial markets without prejudice to a much-needed extension of international cooperation,

— the need to achieve a level playing field for all market participants by establishing EU-wide regulations every time it is appropriate,

— the need to respect differences in national markets where these do not unduly impinge on the coherence of the single market,

— the need to ensure coherence with other Community legislation in this area, as imbalances in information and a lack of transparency may jeopardise the operation of the markets and above all harm consumers and small investors.

(44) This Directive respects the fundamental rights and observes the principles recognised in particular by the Charter of Fundamental Rights of the European Union and in particular by Article 11 thereof and Article 10 of the European Convention on Human Rights. In this regard, this Directive does not in any way prevent Member States from applying their constitutional rules relating to freedom of the press and freedom of expression in the media,

HAVE ADOPTED THIS DIRECTIVE:

Article 1. 1. 'Inside information' shall mean information of a precise nature which has not been made public, relating, directly or indirectly, to one or more issuers of financial instruments or to one or more financial instruments and which, if it were made public, would be likely to have a significant effect on the prices of those financial instruments or on the price of related derivative financial instruments. In relation to derivatives on commodities, 'inside information' shall mean information of a precise nature which has not been made public, relating, directly or indirectly, to one or more such derivatives and which users of markets on which such derivatives are traded would expect to receive in accordance with accepted market practices on those markets. For persons charged with the execution of orders concerning financial instruments, 'inside information' shall also mean information conveyed by a client and related to the client's pending orders, which is of a precise nature, which relates directly or indirectly to one or more issuers of financial instruments or to one or more financial instruments, and which, if it were made public, would be likely to have a significant effect on the prices of those financial instruments or on the price of related derivative financial instruments.

2. 'Market manipulation' shall mean:

(a) transactions or orders to trade:

— which give, or are likely to give, false or misleading signals as to the supply of, demand for or price of financial instruments, or

— which secure, by a person, or persons acting in collaboration, the price of one or several financial instruments at an abnormal or artificial level, unless the person who entered into the transactions or issued the orders to trade establishes that his reasons for so doing are legitimate and that these transactions or orders to trade conform to accepted market practices on the regulated marketconcerned;

(b) transactions or orders to trade which employ fictitious devices or any other form of deception or contrivance;

(c) dissemination of information through the media, including the Internet, or by any other means, which gives, or is likely to give, false or misleading signals as to financial instruments, including the dissemination of rumours and false or misleading news, where the person who made the dissemination knew, or ought to have known, that the information was false or misleading. In respect of journalists when they act in their professional capacity such dissemination of information is to be assessed, without prejudice to Article 11, taking into account the rules governing their profession, unless those persons derive, directly or indirectly, an advantage or profits from the dissemination of the information in question. In particular, the following instances are derived from the core definition given in points (a), (b) and (c) above:

— conduct by a person, or persons acting in collaboration, to secure a dominant position over the supply of or demand for a financial instrument which has the effect of fixing, directly or indirectly, purchase or sale prices or creating other unfair trading conditions,

— the buying or selling of financial instruments at the close of the market with the effect of misleading investors acting on the basis of closing prices,

— taking advantage of occasional or regular access to the traditional or electronic media by voicing an opinion about a financial instrument (or indirectly about its issuer) while having previously taken positions on that financial instrument and profiting subsequently from the impact of the opinions voiced on the price of that instrument, without having simultaneously disclosed that conflict of interest to the public in a proper and effective way. The definitions of market manipulation shall be adapted so as to ensure that new patterns of activity that in practice constitute market manipulation can be included.

3. 'Financial instrument' shall mean:

— transferable securities as defined in Council Directive 93/22/EEC of 10 May 1993 on investment services in the securities field,

— units in collective investment undertakings,

— money-market instruments,

— financial-futures contracts, including equivalent cash-settled instruments,

— forward interest-rate agreements,

— interest-rate, currency and equity swaps,

— options to acquire or dispose of any instrument falling into these categories, including equivalent cash-settled instruments. This category includes in particular options on currency and on interest rates,

— derivatives on commodities,

— any other instrument admitted to trading on a regulated market in a Member State or for which a request for admission to trading
on such a market has been made.

4. 'Regulated market' shall mean a market as defined by Article 1(13) of Directive 93/22/EEC.

5. 'Accepted market practices' shall mean practices that are reasonably expected in one or more financial markets and are accepted by the competent authority in accordance with guidelines adopted by the Commission in accordance with the regulatory procedure with
scrutiny laid down in Article 17(2a).

6. 'Person' shall mean any natural or legal person.

7. 'Competent authority' shall mean the competent authority designated in accordance with Article 11. In order to take account of developments on financial markets and to ensure uniform application of this Directive in the Community, the Commission, shall adopt implementing measures concerning points 1, 2 and 3 of this Article. Those measures, designed to amend non-essential elements of this Directive by supplementing it, shall be adopted in accordance with the regulatory procedure with scrutiny referred to in Article 17(2a).

Article 2. 1. Member States shall prohibit any person referred to in the second subparagraph who possesses inside information from using that information by acquiring or disposing of, or by trying to acquire or dispose of, for his own account or for the account of a third party, either directly or indirectly, financial instruments to which that information relates. The first subparagraph shall apply to any person who possesses that information:

(a) by virtue of his membership of the administrative, management or supervisory bodies of the issuer; or

(b) by virtue of his holding in the capital of the issuer; or

(c) by virtue of his having access to the information through the exercise of his employment, profession or duties; or
(d) by virtue of his criminal activities.
2. Where the person referred to in paragraph 1 is a legal person, the prohibition laid down in that paragraph shall also apply to the natural persons who take part in the decision to carry out the transaction for the account of the legal person concerned.
3. This Article shall not apply to transactions conducted in the discharge of an obligation that has become due to acquire or dispose of financial instruments where that obligation results from an agreement concluded before the person concerned possessed inside information.

Article 3. Member States shall prohibit any person subject to the prohibition laid down in Article 2 from:
(a) disclosing inside information to any other person unless such disclosure is made in the normal course of the exercise of his employment, profession or duties;
(b) recommending or inducing another person, on the basis of inside information, to acquire or dispose of financial instruments to which that information relates.

Article 4. Member States shall ensure that Articles 2 and 3 also apply to any person, other than the persons referred to in those Articles, who possesses inside information while that person knows, or ought to have known, that it is inside information.

Article 5. Member States shall prohibit any person from engaging in market manipulation.

Article 6. 1. Member States shall ensure that issuers of financial instruments inform the public as soon as possible of inside information which directly concerns the said issuers. Without prejudice to any measures taken to comply with the provisions of the first subparagraph, Member States shall ensure that issuers, for an appropriate period, post on their Internet sites all inside information that they are required to disclose publicly.
2. An issuer may under his own responsibility delay the public disclosure of inside information, as referred to in paragraph 1, such as not to prejudice his legitimate interests provided that such omission would not be likely to mislead the public and provided that the issuer is able to ensure the confidentiality of that information. Member States may require that an issuer shall without delay inform the competent authority of the decision to delay the public disclosure of inside information.
3. Member States shall require that, whenever an issuer, or a person acting on his behalf or for his account, discloses any inside information to any third party in the normal exercise of his employment, profession or duties, as referred to in Article 3(a), he must make complete and effective public disclosure of that information, simultaneously in the case of an intentional disclosure and promptly in the case of a nonintentional disclosure. The provisions of the first subparagraph shall not apply if the person receiving the information owes a duty of confidentiality, regardless of whether such duty is based on a law, on regulations, on articles of association or on a contract. Member States shall require that issuers, or persons acting on their behalf or for their account, draw up a list of those persons working for them, under a contract of employment or otherwise, who have access to inside information. Issuers and persons acting on their behalf or for their account shall regularly update this list and transmit it to the competent authority whenever the latter requests it.
4. Persons discharging managerial responsibilities within an issuer of financial instruments and, where applicable, persons closely associated with them, shall, at least, notify to the competent authority the existence of transactions conducted on their own account relating to shares of the said issuer, or to derivatives or other financial instruments linked to them. Member States shall ensure that public access to information concerning such transactions, on at least an individual basis, is readily available as soon as possible.
5. Member States shall ensure that there is appropriate regulation in place to ensure that persons who produce or disseminate research concerning financial instruments or issuers of financial instruments and persons who produce or disseminate other information recommending or suggesting investment strategy, intended for distribution channels or for the public, take reasonable care to ensure that such information is fairly presented and disclose their interests or indicate conflicts of interest concerning the financial instruments to which that information relates. Details of such regulation shall be notified to the Commission.
6. Member States shall ensure that market operators adopt structural provisions aimed at preventing and detecting market manipulation practices.
7. With a view to ensuring compliance with paragraphs 1 to 5, the competent authority may take all necessary measures to ensure that the public is correctly informed.
8. Public institutions disseminating statistics liable to have a significant effect on financial markets shall disseminate them in a fair and transparent way.

9. Member States shall require that any person professionally arranging transactions in financial instruments who reasonably suspects that a transaction might constitute insider dealing or market manipulation shall notify the competent authority without delay.

10. In order to take account of technical developments on financial markets and to ensure uniform application of this Directive, the Commission shall adopt, implementing measures concerning:

— the technical modalities for appropriate public disclosure of inside information as referred to in paragraphs 1 and 3,

— the technical modalities for delaying the public disclosure of inside information as referred to in paragraph 2,

— the technical modalities designed to favour a common approach in the implementation of the second sentence of paragraph 2,

— the conditions under which issuers, or entities acting on their behalf, are to draw up a list of those persons working for them and having access to inside information, as referred to in paragraph 3, together with the conditions under which such lists are to be updated,

— the categories of persons who are subject to a duty of disclosure as referred to in paragraph 4 and the characteristics of a transaction, including its size, which trigger that duty, and the technical arrangements for disclosure to the competent authority,

— technical arrangements, for the various categories of person referred to in paragraph 5, for fair presentation of research and other information recommending investment strategy and for disclosure of particular interests or conflicts of interest as referred to in paragraph 5. Such arrangements shall take into account the rules, including self-regulation, governing the profession of journalist,

— technical arrangements governing notification to the competent authority by the persons referred to in paragraph 9.

Those measures, designed to amend non-essential elements of this Directive by supplementing it, shall be adopted in accordance with the regulatory procedure with scrutiny referred to in Article 17(2a).

Article 7. This Directive shall not apply to transactions carried out in pursuit of monetary, exchange-rate or public debt-management policy by a Member State, by the European System of Central Banks, by a national central bank or by any other officially designated body, or by any person acting on their behalf. Member States may extend this exemption to their federated States or similar local authorities in respect of the management of their public debt.

Article 8. The prohibitions provided for in this Directive shall not apply to trading in own shares in 'buy-back' programmes or to the stabilisation of a financial instrument provided such trading is carried out in accordance with implementing measures. Those measures, designed to amend non-essential elements of this Directive by supplementing it, shall be adopted in accordnce with the regulatory procedure with scrutiny referred to in Article 17(2a).

Article 9. This Directive shall apply to any financial instrument admitted to trading on a regulated market in at least one Member State, or for which a request for admission to trading on such a market has been made, irrespective of whether or not the transaction itself actually takes place on that market. Articles 2, 3 and 4 shall also apply to any financial instrument not admitted to trading on a regulated market in a Member State, but whose value depends on a financial instrument as referred to in paragraph 1. Article 6(1) to (3) shall not apply to issuers who have not requested or approved admission of their financial instruments to trading on a regulated market in a Member State.

Article 10. Each Member State shall apply the prohibitions and requirements provided for in this Directive to:
(a) actions carried out on its territory or abroad concerning financial instruments that are admitted to trading on a regulated market situated or operating within its territory or for which a request for admission to trading on such market has been made;
(b) actions carried out on its territory concerning financial instruments that are admitted to trading on a regulated market in a Member State or for which a request for admission to trading on such market has been made.

Article 11. Without prejudice to the competences of the judicial authorities, each Member State shall designate a single administrative authority competent to ensure that the provisions adopted pursuant to this Directive are applied. Member States shall establish effective consultative arrangements and procedures with market participants concerning possible changes in national legislation. These arrangements may include consultative committees within each competent authority, the membership of which should reflect as far as possible the diversity of market participants, be they issuers, providers of financial services or consumers.

Article 12. 1. The competent authority shall be given all supervisory and investigatory powers that are necessary for the exercise of its functions. It shall exercise such powers:
(a) directly; or
(b) in collaboration with other authorities or with the market undertakings; or
(c) under its responsibility by delegation to such authorities or to the market undertakings; or
(d) by application to the competent judicial authorities.
2. Without prejudice to Article 6(7), the powers referred to in paragraph 1 of this Article shall be exercised in conformity with national law and shall include at least the right to:
(a) have access to any document in any form whatsoever, and to receive a copy of it;
(b) demand information from any person, including those who are successively involved in the transmission of orders or conduct of the operations concerned, as well as their principals, and if necessary, to summon and hear any such person;
(c) carry out on-site inspections;
(d) require existing telephone and existing data traffic records;
(e) require the cessation of any practice that is contrary to the provisions adopted in the implementation of this Directive;
(f) suspend trading of the financial instruments concerned;
(g) request the freezing and/or sequestration of assets;
(h) request temporary prohibition of professional activity.
3. This Article shall be without prejudice to national legal provisions on professional secrecy.

Article 13. The obligation of professional secrecy shall apply to all persons who work or who have worked for the competent authority or for any authority or market undertaking to whom the competent authority has delegated its powers, including auditors and experts instructed by the competent authority. Information covered by professional secrecy may not be disclosed to any other person or authority except by virtue of provisions laid down by law.

Article 14. 1. Without prejudice to the right of Member States to impose criminal sanctions, Member States shall ensure, in conformity with their national law, that the appropriate administrative measures can be taken or administrative sanctions be imposed against the persons responsible where the provisions adopted in the implementation of this Directive have not been complied with. Member States shall ensure that these measures are effective, proportionate and dissuasive.
2. In accordance with the procedure laid down in Article 17(2), the Commission shall, for information, draw up a list of the administrative measures and sanctions referred to in paragraph 1.
3. Member States shall determine the sanctions to be applied for failure to cooperate in an investigation covered by Article 12.
4. Member States shall provide that the competent authority may disclose to the public every measure or sanction that will be imposed for infringement of the provisions adopted in the implementation of this Directive, unless such disclosure would seriously jeopardise the financial markets or cause disproportionate damage to the parties involved.

Article 15. Member States shall ensure that an appeal may be brought before a court against the decisions taken by the competent authority.

Article 16. 1. Competent authorities shall cooperate with each other whenever necessary for the purpose of carrying out their duties, making use of their powers whether set out in this Directive or in national law. Competent authorities shall render assistance to competent authorities of other Member States. In particular, they shall exchange information and cooperate in investigation activities.
2. Competent authorities shall, on request, immediately supply any information required for the purpose referred to in paragraph 1. Where necessary, the competent authorities receiving any such request shall immediately take the necessary measures in order to gather the required information. If the requested competent authority is not able to supply the required information immediately, it shall notify the requesting competent authority of the reasons. Information thus supplied shall be covered by the obligation of professional secrecy to which the persons employed or formerly employed by the competent authorities receiving the information are subject. The competent authorities may refuse to act on a request for information where:
— communication might adversely affect the sovereignty, security or public policy of the Member State addressed,
— judicial proceedings have already been initiated in respect of the same actions and against the same persons before the authorities of the Member State addressed, or

— where a final judgment has already been delivered in relation to such persons for the same actions in the Member State addressed.

In any such case, they shall notify the requesting competent authority accordingly, providing as detailed information as possible on those proceedings or the judgment. Without prejudice to Article 226 of the Treaty, a competent authority whose request for information is not acted upon within a reasonable time or whose request for information is rejected may bring that noncompliance to the attention of the Committee of European Securities Regulators, where discussion will take place in order to reach a rapid and effective solution. Without prejudice to the obligations to which they are subject in judicial proceedings under criminal law, the competent authorities which receive information pursuant to paragraph 1 may use it only for the exercise of their functions within the scope of this Directive and in the context of administrative or judicial proceedings specifically related to the exercise of those functions. However, where the competent authority communicating information consents thereto, the authority receiving the information may use it for other purposes or forward it to other States' competent authorities.

3. Where a competent authority is convinced that acts contrary to the provisions of this Directive are being, or have been, carried out on the territory of another Member State or that acts are affecting financial instruments traded on a regulated market situated in another Member State, it shall give notice of that fact in as specific a manner as possible to the competent authority of the other Member State. The competent authority of the other Member State shall take appropriate action. It shall inform the notifying competent authority of the outcome and, so far as possible, of significant interim developments. This paragraph shall not prejudice the competences of the competent authority that has forwarded the information. The competent authorities of the various Member States that are competent for the purposes of Article 10 shall consult each other on the proposed follow-up to their action.

4. A competent authority of one Member State may request that an investigation be carried out by the competent authority of another Member State, on the latter's territory. It may further request that members of its own personnel be allowed to accompany the personnel of the competent authority of that other Member State during the course of the investigation. The investigation shall, however, be subject throughout to the overall control of the Member State on whose territory it is conducted. The competent authorities may refuse to act on a request for an investigation to be conducted as provided for in the first subparagraph, or on a request for its personnel to be accompanied by personnel of the competent authority of another Member State as provided for in the second subparagraph, where such an investigation might adversely affect the sovereignty, security or public policy of the State addressed, or where judicial proceedings have already been initiated in respect of the same actions and against the same persons before the authorities of the State addressed or where a final judgment has already been delivered in relation to such persons for the same actions in the State addressed. In such case, they shall notify the requesting competent authority accordingly, providing information, as detailed as possible, on those proceedings or judgment. Without prejudice to the provisions of Article 226 of the Treaty, a competent authority whose application to open an inquiry or whose request for authorisation for its officials to accompany those of the other Member State's competent authority is not acted upon within a reasonable time or is rejected may bring that non-compliance to the attention of the Committee of European Securities Regulators, where discussion will take place in order to reach a rapid and effective solution.

5. In accordance with the regulatory procedure laid down in Article 17(2), the Commission shall adopt implementing measures on the working procedures for exchange of information and cross-border inspections as referred to in this Article.

Article 17. 1. The Commission shall be assisted by the European Securities Committee instituted by Decision 2001/528/EC (hereinafter referred to as the 'Committee').

2. Where reference is made to this paragraph, Articles 5 and 7 of Decision 1999/468/EC shall apply, having regard to the provisions of Article 8 thereof, provided that the implementing measures adopted according to this procedure do not modify the essential provisions of this Directive. The period laid down in Article 5(6) of Decision 1999/468/EC shall be set at three months.

2a. Where reference is made to this paragraph, Article 5a(1) to (4) and Article 7 of Decision 1999/468/EC shall apply, having regard to the provisions of Article 8 thereof.

3. By 31 December 2010, and, thereafter, at least every three years, the Commission shall review the provisions concerning its implementing powers and present a report to the European Parliament and to the Council on the functioning of those powers. The report shall examine, in particular, the need for the Commission to propose amendments to this Directive in order to ensure the appropriate scope of the implementing powers conferred on the Commission. The conclusion as to whether or not amendment is necessary shall be accompanied by a detailed statement of reasons. If necessary, the report shall be accompanied by a legislative proposal to amend the provisions conferring implementing powers on the Commission.

Part VIII. European Company Law

Article 18. Member States shall bring into force the laws, regulations and administrative provisions necessary to comply with this Directive not later than 12 October 2004. They shall forthwith inform the Commission thereof. When Member States adopt those measures, they shall contain a reference to this Directive or be accompanied by such a reference on the occasion of their official publication. Member States shall determine how such reference is to be made.

Article 19. Article 11 shall not prejudge the possibility for a Member State to make separate legal and administrative arrangements for overseas European territories for whose external relations that Member State is responsible.

Article 20. Directive 89/592/EEC and Article 68(1) and Article 81(1) of Directive 2001/34/EC of the European Parliament and of the Council of 28 May 2001 on the admission of securities to official stock exchange listing and on information to be published on those securities shall be repealed with effect from the date of entry into force of this Directive.

Article 21. This Directive shall enter into force on the day of its publication in the Official Journal of the European Union.

Article 22. This Directive is addressed to the Member States.

Council Regulation (EEC) No 2137/85 of 25 July 1985 on the European Economic Interest Grouping (EEIG) (*OJ* L 199, 31.07.1985 pp. 1 – 9) [footnotes omitted].

THE COUNCIL OF THE EUROPEAN COMMUNITIES,
Having regard to the Treaty establishing the European Economic Community, and in particular Article 235 thereof,
Having regard to the proposal from the Commission,
Having regard to the opinion of the European Parliament,
Having regard to the opinion of the Economic and Social Committee,
Whereas a harmonious development of economic activities and a continuous and balanced expansion throughout the Community depend on the establishmend and smooth functioning of a common market offering conditions analogous to those of a national market; whereas to bring about this single market and to increase its unity a legal framework which facilitates the adaptation of their activities to the economic conditions of the Community should be created for natural persons, companies, firms and other legal bodies in particular; whereas to that end it is necessary that those natural persons, companies, firms and other legal bodies should be able to cooperate effectively across frontiers;
Whereas cooperation of this nature can encounter legal, fiscal or psychological difficulties; whereas the creation of an appropriate Community legal instrument in the form of a European Economic Interest Grouping would contribute to the achievement of the abovementioned objectives and therefore proves necessary;
Whereas the Treaty does not provide the necessary powers for the creation of such a legal instrument;
Whereas a grouping's ability to adapt to economic conditions must be guaranteed by the considerable freedom for its members in their contractual relations and the internal organization of the grouping;
Whereas a grouping differs from a firm or company principally in its purpose, which is only to facilitate or develop the economic activities of its members to enable them to improve their own results; whereas, by reason of that ancillary nature, a grouping's activities must be related to the economic activities of its members but not replace them so that, to that extent, for example, a grouping may not itself, with regard to third parties, practise a profession, the concept of economic activities being interpreted in the widest sense;
Whereas access to grouping form must be made as widely available as possible to natural persons, companies, firms and other legal bodies, in keeping with the aims of this Regulation; whereas this Regulation shall not, however, prejudice the application at national level of legal rules and/or ethical codes concerning the conditions for the pursuit of business and professional activities;
Whereas this Regulation does not itself confer on any person the right to participate in a grouping, even where the conditions it lays down are fulfilled; Whereas the power provided by this Regulation to prohibit or restrict participation in grouping on grounds of public interest is without prejudice to the laws of Member States which govern the pursuit of activities and which may provide further prohibitions or restrictions or otherwise control or supervise participation in a grouping by any natural person, company, firm or other legal body or any class of them;
Whereas, to enable a grouping to achieve its purpose, it should be endowed with legal capacity and provision should be made for it to be represented vis-à-vis third parties by an organ legally separate from its membership;
Whereas the protection of third parties requires widespread publicity; whereas the members of a grouping have unlimited joint and several liability for the grouping's debts and other liabilities, including those relating to tax or social security, without, however, that principle's affecting the freedom to exclude or restrict the liability of one or more of its members in respect of a particular debt or other liability by means of a specific contract between the grouping and a third party;
Whereas matters relating to the status or capacity of natural persons and to the capacity of legal persons are governed by national law; Whereas the grounds for winding up which are peculiar to the grouping should be specific while referring to national law for its liquidation and the conclusion thereof;
Whereas groupings are subject to national laws relating to insolvency and cessation of payments; whereas such laws may provide other grounds for the winding up of groupings;
Whereas this Regulation provides that the profits or losses resulting from the activities of a grouping shall be taxable only in the hands of its members; whereas it is understood that otherwise national tax laws apply, particularly as regards the apportionment of profits, tax procedures and any obligations imposed by national tax law;
Whereas in matters not covered by this Regulation the laws of the Member States and Community law are applicable, for example with regard to:
- social and labour laws,
- competition law,
- intellectual property law;

PART VIII. EUROPEAN COMPANY LAW

Whereas the activities of groupings are subject to the provisions of Member States' laws on the pursuit and supervision of activities; whereas in the event of abuse or circumvention of the laws of a Member State by a grouping or its members that Member State may impose appropriate sanctions;
Whereas the Member States are free to apply or to adopt any laws, regulations or administrative measures which do not conflict with the scope or objectives of this Regulation;
Whereas this Regulation must enter into force immediately in its entirety; whereas the implementation of some provisions must nevertheless be deferred in order to allow the Member States first to set up the necessary machinery for the registration of groupings in their territories and the disclosure of certain matters relating to groupings; whereas, with effect from the date of implementation of this Regulation, groupings set up may operate without territorial restrictions,

HAS ADOPTED THIS REGULATION:

Article 1. 1. European Economic Interest Groupings shall be formed upon the terms, in the manner and with the effects laid down in this Regulation. Accordingly, parties intending to form a grouping must conclude a contract and have the registration provided for in Article 6 carried out.
2. A grouping so formed shall, from the date of its registration as provided for in Article 6, have the capacity, in its own name, to have rights and obligations of all kinds, to make contracts or accomplish other legal acts, and to sue and be sued.
3. The Member States shall determine whether or not groupings registered at their registries, pursuant to Article 6, have legal personality.

Article 2. 1. Subject to the provisions of this Regulation, the law applicable, on the one hand, to the contract for the formation of a grouping, except as regards matters relating to the status or capacity of natural persons and to the capacity of legal persons and, on the other hand, to the internal organization of a grouping shall be the internal law of the State in which the official address is situated, as laid down in the contract for the formation of the grouping.
2. Where a State comprises several territorial units, each of which has its own rules of law applicable to the matters referred to in paragraph 1, each territorial unit shall be considered as a State for the purposes of identifying the law applicable under this Article.

Article 3. 1. The purpose of a grouping shall be to facilitate or develop the economic activities of its members and to improve or increase the results of those activities; its purpose is not to make profits for itself. Its activity shall be related to the economic activities of its members and must not be more than ancillary to those activities.
2. Consequently, a grouping may not:
(a) exercise, directly or indirectly, a power of management or supervision over its members' own activities or over the activities of another undertaking, in particular in the fields of personnel, finance and investment;
(b) directly or indirectly, on any basis whatsoever, hold shares of any kind in a member undertaking; the holding of shares in another undertaking shall be possible only in so far as it is necessary for the achievement of the grouping's objects and if it is done on its members' behalf;
(c) employ more than 500 persons;
(d) be used by a company to make a loan to a director of a company, or any person connected with him, when the making of such loans is restricted or controlled under the Member States' laws governing companies. Nor must a grouping be used for the transfer of any property between a company and a director, or any person connected with him, except to the extent allowed by the Member States' laws governing companies. For the purposes of this provision the making of a loan includes entering into any transaction or arrangement of similar effect, and property includes moveable and immoveable property;
(e) be a member of another European Economic Interest Grouping.

Article 4. 1. Only the following may be members of a grouping:
(a) companies or firms within the meaning of the second paragraph of Article 58 of the Treaty and other legal bodies governed by public or private law, which have been formed in accordance with the law of a Member State and which have their registered or statutory office and central adminsitration in the Community; where, under the law of a Member State, a company, firm or other legal body is not obliged to have a registered or statutory office, it shall be sufficient for such a company, firm or other legal body to have its central administration in the Community;

(b) natural persons who carry on any industrial, commercial, craft or agricultural activity or who provide professional or other services in the Community.

2. A grouping must comprise at least:
(a) two companies, firms or other legal bodies, within the meaning of paragraph 1, which have their central administrations in different Member States, or
(b) two natural persons, within the meaning of paragraph 1, who carry on their principal activities in different Member States, or
(c) a company, firm or other legal body within the meaning of paragraph 1 and a natural person, of which the first has its central administration in one Member State and the second carries on his principal activity in another Member State.

3. A Member State may provide that groupings registered at its registries in accordance with Article 6 may have no more than 20 members. For this purpose, that Member State may provide that, in accordance with its laws, each member of a legal body formed under its laws, other than a registered company, shall be treated as a separate member of a grouping.

4. Any Member State may, on grounds of that State's public interest, prohibit or restrict participation in groupings by certain classes of natural persons, companies, firms, or other legal bodies.

Article 5. A contract for the formation of a grouping shall include at least:
(a) the name of the grouping preceded or followed either by the words 'European Economic Interest Grouping' or by the initials 'EEIG', unless those words or initials already form part of the name;
(b) the official address of the grouping;
(c) the objects for which the grouping is formed;
(d) the name, business name, legal form, permanent address or registered office, and the number and place of registration, if any, of each member of the grouping;
(e) the duration of the grouping, except where this is indefinite.

Article 6. A grouping shall be registered in the State in which it has its official address, at the registry designated pursuant to Article 39 (1).

Article 7. A contract for the formation of a grouping shall be filed at the registry referred to in Article 6. The following documents and particulars must also be filed at that registry: (a) any amendment to the contract for the formation of a grouping, including any change in the composition of a grouping;
(b) notice of the setting up or closure of any establishment of the grouping;
(c) any judicial decision establishing or declaring the nullity of a grouping, in accordance with Article 15;
(d) notice of the appointment of the manager or managers of a grouping, their names and any other identification particulars required by the law of the Member State in which the register is kept, notification that they may act alone or must act jointly, and the termination of any manager's appointment;
(e) notice of a member's assignment of his participation in a grouping or a proportion thereof, in accordance with Article 22 (1);
(f) any decision by members ordering or establishing the winding up of a grouping, in accordance with Article 31, or any judicial decision ordering such winding up, in accordance with Articles 31 or 32;
(g) notice of the appointment of the liquidator or liquidators of a grouping, as referred to in Article 35, their names and any other identification particulars required by the law of the Member State in which the register is kept, and the termination of any liquidator's appointment;
(h) notice of the conclusion of a grouping's liquidation, as referred to in Article 35 (2);
(i) any proposal to transfer the official address, as referred to in Article 14 (1);
(j) any clause exempting a new member from the payment of debts and other liabilities which originated prior to his admission, in accordance with Article 26 (2).

Article 8. The following must be published, as laid down in Article 39, in the gazette referred to in paragraph 1 of that Article:
(a) the particulars which must be included in the contract for the formation of a grouping, pursuant to Article 5, and any amendments thereto;
(b) the number, date and place of registration as well as notice of the termination of that registration;
(c) the documents and particulars referred to in Article 7 (b) to (j).

The particulars referred to in (a) and (b) must be published in full. The documents and particulars referred to in (c) may be published either in full or in extract form or by means of a reference to their filing at the registry, in accordance with the national legislation applicable.

Part VIII. European Company Law

Article 9. 1. The documents and particulars which must be published pursuant to this Regulation may be relied on by a grouping as against third parties under the conditions laid down by the national law applicable pursuant to Article 3 (5) and (7) of Council Directive 68/151/EEC of 9 March 1968 on coordination of safeguards which, for the protection of the interests of members and others, are required by Member States of companies within the meaning of the second paragraph of Article 58 of the Treaty, with a view to making such safeguards equivalent throughout the Community (1).

2. If activities have been carried on on behalf of a grouping before its registration in accordance with Article 6 and if the grouping does not, after its registration, assume the obligations arising out of such activities, the natural persons, companies, firms or other legal bodies which carried on those activities shall bear unlimited joint and several liability for them.

Article 10. Any grouping establishment situated in a Member State other than that in which the official address is situated shall be registered in that State. For the purpose of such registration, a grouping shall file, at the appropriate registry in that Member State, copies of the documents which must be filed at the registry of the Member State in which the official address is situated, together, if necessary, with a translation which conforms with the practice of the registry where the establishment is registered.

Article 11. Notice that a grouping has been formed or that the liquidation of a grouping has been concluded stating the number, date and place of registration and the date, place and title of publication, shall be given in the Official Journal of the European Communities after it has been published in the gazette referred to in Article 39 (1).

Article 12. The official address referred to in the contract for the formation of a grouping must be situated in the Community.
The official address must be fixed either:
(a) where the grouping has its central administration, or
(b) where one of the members of the grouping has its central administration or, in the case of a natural person, his principal activity, provided that the grouping carries on an activity there.

Article 13. The official address of a grouping may be transferred within the Community.
When such a transfer does not result in a change in the law applicable pursuant to Article 2, the decision to transfer shall be taken in accordance with the conditions laid down in the contract for the formation of the grouping.

Article 14. 1. When the transfer of the official address results in a change in the law applicable pursuant to Article 2, a transfer proposal must be drawn up, filed and published in accordance with the conditions laid down in Articles 7 and 8.
No decision to transfer may be taken for two months after publication of the proposal. Any such decision must be taken by the members of the grouping unanimously. The transfer shall take effect on the date on which the grouping is registered, in accordance with Article 6, at the registry for the new official address. That registration may not be effected until evidence has been produced that the proposal to transfer the official address has been published.

2. The termination of a grouping's registration at the registry for its old official address may not be effected until evidence has been produced that the grouping has been registered at the registry for its new official address.

3. Upon publication of a grouping's new registration the new official address may be relied on as against third parties in accordance with the conditions referred to in Article 9 (1); however, as long as the termination of the grouping's registration at the registry for the old official address has not been published, third parties may continue to rely on the old official address unless the grouping proves that such third parties were aware of the new official address.

4. The laws of a Member State may provide that, as regards groupings registered under Article 6 in that Member State, the transfer of an official address which would result in a change of the law applicable shall not take effect if, within the two-month period referred to in paragraph 1, a competent authority in that Member State opposes it. Such opposition may be based only on grounds of public interest. Review by a judicial authority must be possible.

Article 15. 1. Where the law applicable to a grouping by virtue of Article 2 provides for the nullity of that grouping, such nullity must be established or declared by judicial decision. However, the court to which the matter is referred must, where it is possible for the affairs of the grouping to be put in order, allow time to permit that to be done.
2. The nullity of a grouping shall entail its liquidation in accordance with the conditions laid down in Article 35.
3. A decision establishing or declaring the nullity of a grouping may be relied on as against third parties in accordance with the conditions laid down in Article 9 (1).
Such a decision shall not of itself affect the validity of liabilities, owed by or to a grouping, which originated before it could be relied on as against third parties in accordance with the conditions laid down in the previous subparagraph.

Article 16. 1. The organs of a grouping shall be the members acting collectively and the manager or managers. A contract for the formation of a grouping may provide for other organs; if it does it shall determine their powers.
2. The members of a grouping, acting as a body, may take any decision for the purpose of achieving the objects of the grouping.

Article 17. 1. Each member shall have one vote. The contract for the formation of a grouping may, however, give more than one vote to certain members, provided that no one member holds a majority of the votes.
2. A unanimous decision by the members shall be required to:
(a) alter the objects of a grouping;
(b) alter the number of votes allotted to each member;
(c) alter the conditions for the taking of decisions;
(d) extend the duration of a grouping beyond any period fixed in the contract for the formation of the grouping;
(e) alter the contribution by every member or by some members to the grouping's financing;
(f) alter any other obligation of a member, unless otherwise provided by the contract for the formation of the grouping;
(g) make any alteration to the contract for the formation of the grouping not covered by this paragraph, unless otherwise provided by that contract.
3. Except where this Regulation provides that decisions must be taken unanimously, the contract for the formation of a grouping may prescribe the conditions for a quorum and for a majority, in accordance with which the decisions, or some of them, shall be taken. Unless otherwise provided for by the contract, decisions shall be taken unanimously.
4. On the initiative of a manager or at the request of a member, the manager or managers must arrange for the members to be consulted so that the latter can take a decision.

Article 18. Each member shall be entitled to obtain information from the manager or managers concerning the grouping's business and to inspect the grouping's books and business records.

Article 19. 1. A grouping shall be managed by one or more natural persons appointed in the contract for the formation of the grouping or by decision of the members. No person may be a manager of a grouping if:
- by virtue of the law applicable to him, or
- by virtue of the internal law of the State in which the grouping has its official address, or
- following a judicial or administrative decision made or recognized in a Member State
he may not belong to the administrative or management body of a company, may not manage an undertaking or may not act as manager of a European Economic Interest Grouping.
2. A Member State may, in the case of groupings registered at their registries pursuant to Article 6, provide that legal persons may be managers on condition that such legal persons designate one or more natural persons, whose particulars shall be the subject of the filing provisions of Article 7 (d) to represent them.
If a Member State exercises this option, it must provide that the representative or representatives shall be liable as if they were themselves managers of the groupings concerned. The restrictions imposed in paragraph 1 shall also apply to those representatives.
3. The contract for the formation of a grouping or, failing that, a unanimous decision by the members shall determine the conditions for the appointment and removal of the manager or managers and shall lay down their powers.

Part VIII. European Company Law

Article 20. 1. Only the manager or, where there are two or more, each of the managers shall represent a grouping in respect of dealings with third parties. Each of the managers shall bind the grouping as regards third parties when he acts on behalf of the grouping, even where his acts do not fall within the objects of the grouping, unless the grouping proves that the third party knew or could not, under the circumstances, have been unaware that the act fell outside the objects of the grouping; publication of the particulars referred to in Article 5 (c) shall not of itself be proof thereof. No limitation on the powers of the manager or managers, whether deriving from the contract for the formation of the grouping or from a decision by the members, may be relied on as against thrid parties even if it is published.
2. The contract for the formation of the grouping may provide that the grouping shall be validly bound only by two or more managers acting jointly. Such a clause may be relied on as against third parties in accordance with the conditions referred to in Article 9 (1) only if it is published in accordance with Article 8.

Article 21. 1. The profits resulting from a grouping's activities shall be deemed to be the profits of the members and shall be apportioned among them in the proportions laid down in the contract for the formation of the grouping or, in the absence of any such provision, in equal shares.
2. The members of a grouping shall contribute to the payment of the amount by which expenditure exceeds income in the proportions laid down in the contract for the formation of the grouping or, in the absence of any such provision, in equal shares.

Article 22. 1. Any member of a grouping may assign his participation in the grouping, or a proportion thereof, either to another member or to a third party; the assignment shall not take effect without the unanimous authorization of the other members.
2. A member of a grouping may use his participation in the grouping as security only after the other members have given their unanimous authorization, unless otherwise laid down in the contract for the formation of the grouping. The holder of the security may not at any time become a member of the grouping by virtue of that security.

Article 23. No grouping may invite investment by the public.

Article 24. 1. The members of a grouping shall have unlimited joint and several liability for its debts and other liabilities of whatever nature. National law shall determine the consequences of such liablity.
2. Creditors may not proceed against a member for payment in respect of debts and other liabilities, in accordance with the conditions laid down in paragraph 1, before the liquidation of a grouping is concluded, unless they have first requested the grouping to pay and payment has not been made within an appropriate period.

Article 25. Letters, order forms and similar documents must indicate legibly:
(a) the name of the grouping preceded or followed either by the words 'European Economic Interest Grouping' or by the initials 'EEIG', unless those words or initials already occur in the name;
(b) the location of the registry referred to in Article 6, in which the grouping is registered, together with the number of the grouping's entry at the registry;
(c) the grouping's official address;
(d) where applicable, that the managers must act jointly;
(e) where applicable, that the grouping is in liquidation, pursuant to Articles 15, 31, 32 or 36.
Every establishment of a grouping, when registered in accordance with Article 10, must give the above particulars, together with those relating to its own registration, on the documents referred to in the first paragraph of this Article uttered by it.

Article 26. 1. A decision to admit new members shall be taken unanimously by the members of the grouping.
2. Every new member shall be liable, in accordance with the conditions laid down in Article 24, for the grouping's debts and other liabilities, including those arising out of the grouping's activities before his admission. He may, however, be exempted by a clause in the contract for the formation of the grouping or in the instrument of admission from the payment of debts and other liabilities which originated before his admission. Such a clause may be relied on as against third parties, under the conditions referred to in Article 9 (1), only if it is published in accordance with Article 8.

Article 27. 1. A member of a grouping may withdraw in accordance with the conditions laid down in the contract for the formation of a grouping or, in the absence of such conditions, with the unanimous agreement of the other members.
Any member of a grouping may, in addition, withdraw on just and proper grounds.
2. Any member of a grouping may be expelled for the reasons listed in the contract for the formation of the grouping and, in any case, if he seriously fails in his obligations or if he causes or threatens to cause serious disruption in the operation of the grouping. Such expulsion may occur only by the decision of a court to which joint application has been made by a majority of the other members, unless otherwise provided by the contract for the formation of a grouping.

Article 28. 1. A member of a grouping shall cease to belong to it on death or when he no longer complies with the conditions laid down in Article 4 (1). In addition, a Member State may provide, for the purposes of its liquidation, winding up, insolvency or cessation of payments laws, that a member shall cease to be a member of any grouping at the moment determined by those laws.
2. In the event of the death of a natural person who is a member of a grouping, no person may become a member in his place except under the conditions laid down in the contract for the formation of the grouping or, failing that, with the unanimous agreement of the remaining members.

Article 29. As soon as a member ceases to belong to a grouping, the manager or managers must inform the other members of that fact; they must also take the steps required as listed in Articles 7 and 8. In addition, any person concerned may take those steps.

Article 30. Except where the contract for the formation of a grouping provides otherwise and without prejudice to the rights acquired by a person under Articles 22 (1) or 28 (2), a grouping shall continue to exist for the remaining members after a member has ceased to belong to it, in accordance with the conditions laid down in the contract for the formation of the grouping or determined by unanimous decision of the members in question.

Article 31. 1. A grouping may be wound up by a decision of its members ordering its winding up. Such a decision shall be taken unanimously, unless otherwise laid down in the contract for the formation of the grouping. 2. A grouping must be wound up by a decision of its members:
(a) noting the expiry of the period fixed in the contract for the formation of the grouping or the existence of any other cause for winding up provided for in the contract, or
(b) noting the accomplishment of the grouping's purpose or the impossibility of pursuing it further.
Where, three months after one of the situation referred to in the first subparagraph has occurred, a members' decision establishing the winding up of the grouping has not been taken, any member may petition the court to order winding up.
3. A grouping must also be wound up by a decision of its members or of the remaining member when the conditions laid down in Article 4 (2) are no longer fulfilled.
4. After a grouping has been wound up by decision of its members, the manager or managers must take the steps required as listed in Articles 7 and 8. In addition, any person concerned may take those steps.

Article 32. 1. On application by any person concerned or by a competent authority, in the event of the infringement of Articles 3, 12 or 31 (3), the court must order a grouping to be wound up, unless its affairs can be and are put in order before the court has delivered a substantive ruling.
2. On applications by a member, the court may order a grouping to be wound up on just and proper grounds.
3. A Member State may provide that the court may, on application by a competent authority, order the winding up of a grouping which has its official address in the State to which that authority belongs, wherever the grouping acts in contravention of that State's public interest, if the law of that State provides for such a possibility in respect of registered companies or other legal bodies subject to it.

Article 33. When a member ceases to belong to a grouping for any reason other than the assignment of his rights in accordance with the conditions laid down in Article 22 (1), the value of his rights and obligations shall be determined taking into account the assets and liabilities of the grouping as they stand when he ceases to belong to it. The value of the rights and obligations of a departing member may not be fixed in advance.

Article 34. Without prejudice to Article 37 (1), any member who ceases to belong to a grouping shall remain answerable, in accordance with the conditions laid down in Article 24, for the debts and other liabilities arising out of the grouping's activities before he ceased to be a member.

Article 35. 1. The winding up of a grouping shall entail its liquidation.
2. The liquidation of a grouping and the conclusion of its liquidation shall be governed by national law.
3. A grouping shall retain its capacity, within the meaning of Article 1 (2), until its liquidation is concluded.
4. The liquidator or liquidators shall take the steps required as listed in Articles 7 and 8.

Article 36. Groupings shall be subject to national laws governing insolvency and cessation of payments. The commencement of proceedings against a grouping on grounds of its insolvency or cessation of payments shall not by itself cause the commencement of such proceedings against its members.

Article 37. 1. A period of limitation of five years after the publication, pursuant to Article 8, of notice of a member's ceasing to belong to a grouping shall be substituted for any longer period which may be laid down by the relevant national law for actions against that member in connection with debts and other liabilities arising out of the grouping's activities before he ceased to be a member.
2. A period of limitation of five years after the publication, pursuant to Article 8, of notice of the conclusion of the liquidation of a grouping shall be substituted for any longer period which may be laid down by the relevant national law for actions against a member of the grouping in connection with debts and other liabilities arising out of the grouping's activities.

Article 38. Where a grouping carries on any activity in a Member State in contravention of that State's public interest, a competent authority of that State may prohibit that activity. Review of that competent authority's decision by a judicial authority shall be possible. Article 39
1. The Member States shall designate the registry or registries responsible for effecting the registration referred to in Articles 6 and 10 and shall lay down the rules governing registration. They shall prescribe the conditions under which the documents referred to in Articles 7 and 10 shall be filed. They shall ensure that the documents and particulars referred to in Article 8 are published in the appropriate official gazette of the Member State in which the grouping has its official address, and may prescribe the manner of publication of the documents and particulars referred to in Article 8 (c).
The Member States shall also ensure that anyone may, at the appropriate registry pursuant to Article 6 or, where appropriate, Article 10, inspect the documents referred to in Article 7 and obtain, even by post, full or partial copies thereof.
The Member States may provide for the payment of fees in connection with the operations referred to in the preceding subparagraphs; those fees may not, however, exceed the administrative cost thereof.
2. The Member States shall ensure that the information to be published in the Official Journal of the European Communities pursuant to Article 11 is forwarded to the Office for Official Publications of the European Communities within one month of its publication in the official gazette referred to in paragraph 1.
3. The Member States shall provide for appropriate penalties in the event of failure to comply with the provisions of Articles 7, 8 and 10 on disclosure and in the event of failure to comply with Article 25.

Article 40. The profits or losses resulting from the activities of a grouping shall be taxable only in the hands of its members.

Article 41. 1. The Member States shall take the measures requried by virtue of Article 39 before 1 July 1989. They shall immediately communicate them to the Commission.
2. For information purposes, the Member States shall inform the Commission of the classes of natural persons, companies, firms and other legal bodies which they prohibit from participating in groupings pursuant to Article 4 (4). The Commission shall inform the other Member States.

Article 42. 1. Upon the adoption of this Regulation, a Contact Committee shall be set up under the auspices of the Commission. Its function shall be:
(a) to facilitate, without prejudice to Articles 169 and 170 of the Treaty, application of this Regulation through regular consultation dealing in particular with practical problems arising in connection with its application;
(b) to advise the Commission, if necessary, on additions or amendments to this Regulation.

2. The Contact Committee shall be composed of representatives of the Member States and representatives of the Commission. The chairman shall be a representative of the Commission. The Commission shall provide the secretariat.

3. The Contact Committee shall be convened by its chairman either on his own initiative or at the request of one of its members.

Article 43. This Regulation shall enter into force on the third day following its publication in the Official Journal of the European Communities. It shall apply from 1 July 1989, with the exception of Articles 39, 41 and 42 which shall apply as from the entry into force of the Regulation. This Regulation shall be binding in its entirety and directly applicable in all Member States.

REGULATION 2157/2001 ON STATUTE FOR A EUROPEAN COMPANY (SE)

Council Regulation (EC) No 2157/2001 of 8 October 2001 on the Statute for a European company (SE) (*O J* L 294 , 10.11.001 pp. 1 – 21) [footnotes omitted].

THE COUNCIL OF THE EUROPEAN UNION,
Having regard to the Treaty establishing the European Community, and in particular Article 308 thereof,
Having regard to the proposal from the Commission,
Having regard to the opinion of the European Parliament,
Having regard to the opinion of the Economic and Social Committee,
Whereas:
(1) The completion of the internal market and the improvement it brings about in the economic and social situation throughout the Community mean not only that barriers to trade must be removed, but also that the structures of production must be adapted to the Community dimension. For that purpose it is essential that companies the business of which is not limited to satisfying purely local needs should be able to plan and carry out the reorganisation of their business on a Community scale.
(2) Such reorganisation presupposes that existing companies from different Member States are given the option of combining their potential by means of mergers. Such operations can be carried out only with due regard to the rules of competition laid down in the Treaty.
(3) Restructuring and cooperation operations involving companies from different Member States give rise to legal and psychological difficulties and tax problems. The approximation of Member States' company law by means of Directives based on Article 44 of the Treaty can overcome some of those difficulties. Such approximation does not, however, release companies governed by different legal systems from the obligation to choose a form of company governed by a particular national law.
(4) The legal framework within which business must be carried on in the Community is still based largely on national laws and therefore no longer corresponds to the economic framework within which it must develop if the objectives set out in Article 18 of the Treaty are to be achieved. That situation forms a considerable obstacle to the creation of groups of companies from different Member States.
(5) Member States are obliged to ensure that the provisions applicable to European companies under this Regulation do not result either in discrimination arising out of unjustified different treatment of European companies compared with public limitedliability companies or in disproportionate restrictions on the formation of a European company or on the transfer of its registered office.
(6) It is essential to ensure as far as possible that the economic unit and the legal unit of business in the Community coincide. For that purpose, provision should be made for the creation, side by side with companies governed by a particular national law, of companies formed and carrying on business under the law created by a Community Regulation directly applicable in all Member States.
(7) The provisions of such a Regulation will permit the creation and management of companies with a European dimension, free from the obstacles arising from the disparity and the limited territorial application of national company law.
(8) The Statute for a European public limited-liability company (hereafter referred to as 'SE') is among the measures to be adopted by the Council before 1992 listed in the Commission's White Paper on completing the internal market, approved by the European Council that met in Milan in June 1985. The European Council that met in Brussels in 1987 expressed the wish to see such a Statute created swiftly.
(9) Since the Commission's submission in 1970 of a proposal for a Regulation on the Statute for a European public limited-liability company, amended in 1975, work on the approximation of national company law has made substantial progress, so that on those points where the functioning of an SE does not need uniform Community rules reference may be made to the law governing public limited-liability companies in the Member State where it has its registered office.
(10) Without prejudice to any economic needs that may arise in the future, if the essential objective of legal rules governing SEs is to be attained, it must be possible at least to create such a company as a means both of enabling companies from different Member States to merge or to create a holding company and of enabling companies and other legal persons carrying on economic activities and governed by the laws of different Member States to form joint subsidiaries.
(11) In the same context it should be possible for a public limitedliability company with a registered office and head office within the Community to transform itself into an SE without going into liquidation, provided it has a subsidiary in a Member State other than that of its registered office.
(12) National provisions applying to public limited-liability companies that offer their securities to the public and to securities transactions should also apply where an SE is formed by means of an offer of securities to the public and to SEs wishing to utilize such financial instruments.

PART VIII. EUROPEAN COMPANY LAW

(13) The SE itself must take the form of a company with share capital, that being the form most suited, in terms of both financing and management, to the needs of a company carrying on business on a European scale. In order to ensure that such companies are of reasonable size, a minimum amount of capital should be set so that they have sufficient assets without making it difficult for small and medium-sized undertakings to form SEs.

(14) An SE must be efficiently managed and properly supervised. It must be borne in mind that there are at present in the Community two different systems for the administration of public limitedliability companies. Although an SE should be allowed to choose between the two systems, the respective responsibilities of those responsible for management and those responsible for supervision should be clearly defined.

(15) Under the rules and general principles of private international law, where one undertaking controls another governed by a different legal system, its ensuing rights and obligations as regards the protection of minority shareholders and third parties are governed by the law governing the controlled undertaking, without prejudice to the obligations imposed on the controlling undertaking by its own law, for example the requirement to prepare consolidated accounts.

(16) Without prejudice to the consequences of any subsequent coordination of the laws of the Member States, specific rules for SEs are not at present required in this field. The rules and general principles of private international law should therefore be applied both where an SE exercises control and where it is the controlled company.

(17) The rule thus applicable where an SE is controlled by another undertaking should be specified, and for this purpose reference should be made to the law governing public limited-liability companies in the Member State in which the SE has its registered office.

(18) Each Member State must be required to apply the sanctions applicable to public limited-liability companies governed by its law in respect of infringements of this Regulation.

(19) The rules on the involvement of employees in the European company are laid down in Directive 2001/86/EC, and those provisions thus form an indissociable complement to this Regulation and must be applied concomitantly.

(20) This Regulation does not cover other areas of law such as taxation, competition, intellectual property or insolvency. The provisions of the Member States' law and of Community law are therefore applicable in the above areas and in other areas not covered by this Regulation.

(21) Directive 2001/86/EC is designed to ensure that employees have a right of involvement in issues and decisions affecting the life of their SE. Other social and labour legislation questions, in particular the right of employees to information and consultation as regulated in the Member States, are governed by the national provisions applicable, under the same conditions, to public limited-liability companies.

(22) The entry into force of this Regulation must be deferred so that each Member State may incorporate into its national law the provisions of Directive 2001/86/EC and set up in advance the necessary machinery for the formation and operation of SEs with registered offices within its territory, so that the Regulation and the Directive may be applied concomitantly.

(23) A company the head office of which is not in the Community should be allowed to participate in the formation of an SE provided that company is formed under the law of a Member State, has its registered office in that Member State and has a real and continuous link with a Member State's economy according to the principles established in the 1962 General Programme for the abolition of restrictions on freedom of establishment. Such a link exists in particular if a company has an establishment in that Member State and conducts operations therefrom.

(24) The SE should be enabled to transfer its registered office to another Member State. Adequate protection of the interests of minority shareholders who oppose the transfer, of creditors and of holders of other rights should be proportionate. Such transfer should not affect the rights originating before the transfer.

(25) This Regulation is without prejudice to any provision which may be inserted in the 1968 Brussels Convention or in any text adopted by Member States or by the Council to replace such Convention, relating to the rules of jurisdiction applicable in the case of transfer of the registered offices of a public limitedliability company from one Member State to another.

(26) Activities by financial institutions are regulated by specific directives and the national law implementing those directives and additional national rules regulating those activities apply in full to an SE.

(27) In view of the specific Community character of an SE, the 'real seat' arrangement adopted by this Regulation in respect of SEs is without prejudice to Member States' laws and does not pre-empt any choices to be made for other Community texts on company law.

(28) The Treaty does not provide, for the adoption of this Regulation, powers of action other than those of Article 308 thereof.

(29) Since the objectives of the intended action, as outlined above, cannot be adequately attained by the Member States in as much as a European public limited-liability company is being established at European level and can therefore, because of the scale and impact of such company, be better attained at Community level, the

Community may take measures in accordance with the principle of subsidiarity enshrined in Article 5 of the Treaty. In accordance with the principle of proportionality as set out in the said Article, this Regulation does not go beyond what is necessary to attain these objectives,

HAS ADOPTED THIS REGULATION:

Title I. General provisions

Article 1. 1. A company may be set up within the territory of the Community in the form of a European public limited-liability company (SocietasEuropaea or SE) on the conditions and in the manner laid down in this Regulation.
2. The capital of an SE shall be divided into shares. No shareholder shall be liable for more than the amount he has subscribed.
3. An SE shall have legal personality.
4. Employee involvement in an SE shall be governed by the provisions of Directive 2001/86/EC.

Article 2. 1. Public limited-liability companies such as referred to in Annex I, formed under the law of a Member State, with registered offices and head offices within the Community may form an SE by means of a merger provided that at least two of them are governed by the law of different Member States.
2. Public and private limited-liability companies such as referred to in Annex II, formed under the law of a Member State, with registered offices and head offices within the Community may promote the formation of a holding SE provided that each of at least two of them:
(a) is governed by the law of a different Member State, or
(b) has for at least two years had a subsidiary company governed by the law of another Member State or a branch situated in another Member State.
3. Companies and firms within the meaning of the second paragraph of Article 48 of the Treaty and other legal bodies governed by public or private law, formed under the law of a Member State, with registered offices and head offices within the Community may form a subsidiary SE by subscribing for its shares, provided that each of at least two of them:
(a) is governed by the law of a different Member State, or
(b) has for at least two years had a subsidiary company governed by the law of another Member State or a branch situated in another Member State.
4. A public limited-liability company, formed under the law of a Member State, which has its registered office and head office within the Community may be transformed into an SE if for at least two years it has had a subsidiary company governed by the law of another Member State.
5. A Member State may provide that a company the head office of which is not in the Community may participate in the formation of an SE provided that company is formed under the law of a Member State, has its registered office in that Member State and has a real and continuous link with a Member State's economy.

Article 3. 1. For the purposes of Article 2(1), (2) and (3), an SE shall be regarded as a public limited-liability company governed by the law of the Member State in which it has its registered office.
2. An SE may itself set up one or more subsidiaries in the form of SEs. The provisions of the law of the Member State in which a subsidiary SE has its registered office that require a public limitedliability company to have more than one shareholder shall not apply in the case of the subsidiary SE. The provisions of national law implementing the twelfth Council Company Law Directive (89/667/EEC) of 21 December 1989 on single-member private limited-liability companies shall apply to SEs mutatis mutandis.

Article 4. 1. The capital of an SE shall be expressed in euro.
2. The subscribed capital shall not be less than EUR 120 000.
3. The laws of a Member State requiring a greater subscribed capital for companies carrying on certain types of activity shall apply to SEs with registered offices in that Member State.

Article 5. Subject to Article 4(1) and (2), the capital of an SE, its maintenance and changes thereto, together with its shares, bonds and other similar securities shall be governed by the provisions which would apply to a public limited-liability company with a registered office in the Member State in which the SE is registered.

Article 6. For the purposes of this Regulation, 'the statutes of the SE' shall mean both the instrument of incorporation and, where they are the subject of a separate document, the statutes of the SE.

Part VIII. European Company Law

Article 7. The registered office of an SE shall be located within the Community, in the same Member State as its head office. A Member State may in addition impose on SEs registered in its territory the obligation of locating their head office and their registered office in the same place.

Article 8. 1. The registered office of an SE may be transferred to another Member State in accordance with paragraphs 2 to 13. Such a transfer shall not result in the winding up of the SE or in the creation of a new legal person.
2. The management or administrative organ shall draw up a transfer proposal and publicise it in accordance with Article 13, without prejudice to any additional forms of publication provided for by the Member State of the registered office. That proposal shall state the current name, registered office and number of the SE and shall cover:
(a) the proposed registered office of the SE;
(b) the proposed statutes of the SE including, where appropriate, its new name;
(c) any implication the transfer may have on employees' involvement;
(d) the proposed transfer timetable;
(e) any rights provided for the protection of shareholders and/or creditors.
3. The management or administrative organ shall draw up a report explaining and justifying the legal and economic aspects of the transfer and explaining the implications of the transfer for shareholders, creditors and employees.
4. An SE's shareholders and creditors shall be entitled, at least one month before the general meeting called upon to decide on the transfer, to examine at the SE's registered office the transfer proposal and the report drawn up pursuant to paragraph 3 and, on request, to obtain copies of those documents free of charge.
5. A Member State may, in the case of SEs registered within its territory, adopt provisions designed to ensure appropriate protection for minority shareholders who oppose a transfer.
6. No decision to transfer may be taken for two months after publication of the proposal. Such a decision shall be taken as laid down in Article 59.
7. Before the competent authority issues the certificate mentioned in paragraph 8, the SE shall satisfy it that, in respect of any liabilities arising prior to the publication of the transfer proposal, the interests of creditors and holders of other rights in respect of the SE (including those of public bodies) have been adequately protected in accordance with requirements laid down by the Member State where the SE has its registered office prior to the transfer. A Member State may extend the application of the first subparagraph to liabilities that arise (or may arise) prior to the transfer. The first and second subparagraphs shall be without prejudice to the application to SEs of the national legislation of Member States concerning the satisfaction or securing of payments to public bodies.
8. In the Member State in which an SE has its registered office the court, notary or other competent authority shall issue a certificate attesting to the completion of the acts and formalities to be accomplished before the transfer.
9. The new registration may not be effected until the certificate referred to in paragraph 8 has been submitted, and evidence produced that the formalities required for registration in the country of the new registered office have been completed.
10. The transfer of an SE's registered office and the consequent amendment of its statutes shall take effect on the date on which the SE is registered, in accordance with Article 12, in the register for its new registered office.
11. When the SE's new registration has been effected, the registry for its new registration shall notify the registry for its old registration. Deletion of the old registration shall be effected on receipt of that notification, but not before.
12. The new registration and the deletion of the old registration shall be publicised in the Member States concerned in accordance with Article 13.
13. On publication of an SE's new registration, the new registered office may be relied on as against third parties. However, as long as the deletion of the SE's registration from the register for its previous registered office has not been publicised, third parties may continue to rely on the previous registered office unless the SE proves that such third parties were aware of the new registered office.
14. The laws of a Member State may provide that, as regards SEs registered in that Member State, the transfer of a registered office which would result in a change of the law applicable shall not take effect if any of that Member State's competent authorities opposes it within the two-month period referred to in paragraph 6. Such opposition may be based only on grounds of public interest.
Where an SE is supervised by a national financial supervisory authority according to Community directives the right to oppose the change of registered office applies to this authority as well. Review by a judicial authority shall be possible.
15. An SE may not transfer its registered office if proceedings for winding up, liquidation, insolvency or suspension of payments or other similar proceedings have been brought against it.

16. An SE which has transferred its registered office to another Member State shall be considered, in respect of any cause of action arising prior to the transfer as determined in paragraph 10, as having its registered office in the Member States where the SE was registered prior to the transfer, even if the SE is sued after the transfer.

Article 9. 1. An SE shall be governed:
(a) by this Regulation,
(b) where expressly authorised by this Regulation, by the provisions of its statutes or
(c) in the case of matters not regulated by this Regulation or, where matters are partly regulated by it, of those aspects not covered by it, by:
(i) the provisions of laws adopted by Member States in implementation of Community measures relating specifically to SEs;
(ii) the provisions of Member States' laws which would apply to a public limited-liability company formed in accordance with the law of the Member State in which the SE has its registered office;
(iii) the provisions of its statutes, in the same way as for a public limited-liability company formed in accordance with the law of the Member State in which the SE has its registered office.
2. The provisions of laws adopted by Member States specifically for the SE must be in accordance with Directives applicable to public limited-liability companies referred to in Annex I.
3. If the nature of the business carried out by an SE is regulated by specific provisions of national laws, those laws shall apply in full to the SE.

Article 10. Subject to this Regulation, an SE shall be treated in every Member State as if it were a public limited-liability company formed in accordance with the law of the Member State in which it has its registered office.

Article 11. 1. The name of an SE shall be preceded or followed by the abbreviation SE.
2. Only SEs may include the abbreviation SE in their name.
3. Nevertheless, companies, firms and other legal entities registered in a Member State before the date of entry into force of this Regulation in the names of which the abbreviation SE appears shall not be required to alter their names.

Article 12. 1. Every SE shall be registered in the Member State in which it has its registered office in a register designated by the law of that Member State in accordance with Article 3 of the first Council Directive (68/151/ EEC) of 9 March 1968 on coordination of safeguards which, for the protection of the interests of members and others, are required by Member States of companies within the meaning of the second paragraph of Article 58 of the Treaty, with a view to making such safeguards equivalent throughout the Community (1).
2. An SE may not be registered unless an agreement on arrangements for employee involvement pursuant to Article 4 of Directive 2001/86/ EC has been concluded, or a decision pursuant to Article 3(6) of the Directive has been taken, or the period for negotiations pursuant to Article 5 of the Directive has expired without an agreement having been concluded.
3. In order for an SE to be registered in a Member State which has made use of the option referred to in Article 7(3) of Directive 2001/86/ EC, either an agreement pursuant to Article 4 of the Directive must have been concluded on the arrangements for employee involvement, including participation, or none of the participating companies must have been governed by participation rules prior to the registration of the SE.
4. The statutes of the SE must not conflict at any time with the arrangements for employee involvement which have been so determined. Where new such arrangements determined pursuant to the Directive conflict with the existing statutes, the statutes shall to the extent necessary be amended. In this case, a Member State may provide that the management organ or the administrative organ of the SE shall be entitled to proceed to amend the statutes without any further decision from the general shareholders meeting.

Article 13. Publication of the documents and particulars concerning an SE which must be publicised under this Regulation shall be effected in the manner laid down in the laws of the Member State in which the SE has its registered office in accordance with Directive 68/151/EEC.

Article 14. 1. Notice of an SE's registration and of the deletion of such a registration shall be published for information purposes in the Official Journal of the European Communities after publication in accordance with Article 13. That notice shall state the name, number, date and place of registration of the SE, the date and place of publication and the title of publication, the registered office of the SE and its sector of activity.
2. Where the registered office of an SE is transferred in accordance with Article 8, notice shall be published giving the information provided for in paragraph 1, together with that relating to the new registration.

3. The particulars referred to in paragraph 1 shall be forwarded to the Office for Official Publications of the European Communities within one month of the publication referred to in Article 13.

Title II. Formation

Section I. General

Article 15. 1. Subject to this Regulation, the formation of an SE shall be governed by the law applicable to public limited-liability companies in the Member State in which the SE establishes its registered office.
2. The registration of an SE shall be publicised in accordance with Article 13. Article 16
1. An SE shall acquire legal personality on the date on which it is registered in the register referred to in Article 12.
2. If acts have been performed in an SE's name before its registration in accordance with Article 12 and the SE does not assume the obligations arising out of such acts after its registration, the natural persons, companies, firms or other legal entities which performed those acts shall be jointly and severally liable therefor, without limit, in the absence of agreement to the contrary.

Section II. Formation by merger

Article 17. 1. An SE may be formed by means of a merger in accordance with Article 2(1).
2. Such a merger may be carried out in accordance with:
(a) the procedure for merger by acquisition laid down in Article 3(1) of the third Council Directive (78/855/EEC) of 9 October 1978 based on Article 54(3)(g) of the Treaty concerning mergers of public limited-liability companies or
(b) the procedure for merger by the formation of a new company laid down in Article 4(1) of the said Directive. In the case of a merger by acquisition, the acquiring company shall take the form of an SE when the merger takes place. In the case of a merger by the formation of a new company, the SE shall be the newly formed company.

Article 18. For matters not covered by this section or, where a matter is partly covered by it, for aspects not covered by it, each company involved in the formation of an SE by merger shall be governed by the provisions of the law of the Member State to which it is subject that apply to mergers of public limited-liability companies in accordance with Directive 78/855/EEC.

Article 19. The laws of a Member State may provide that a company governed by the law of that Member State may not take part in the formation of an SE by merger if any of that Member State's competent authorities opposes it before the issue of the certificate referred to in Article 25(2). Such opposition may be based only on grounds of public interest. Review by a judicial authority shall be possible.

Article 20. 1. The management or administrative organs of merging companies shall draw up draft terms of merger. The draft terms of merger shall include the following particulars:
(a) the name and registered office of each of the merging companies together with those proposed for the SE;
(b) the share-exchange ratio and the amount of any compensation;
(c) the terms for the allotment of shares in the SE;
(d) the date from which the holding of shares in the SE will entitle the holders to share in profits and any special conditions affecting that entitlement;
(e) the date from which the transactions of the merging companies will be treated for accounting purposes as being those of the SE;
(f) the rights conferred by the SE on the holders of shares to which special rights are attached and on the holders of securities other than shares, or the measures proposed concerning them;
(g) any special advantage granted to the experts who examine the draft terms of merger or to members of the administrative, management, supervisory or controlling organs of the merging companies;
(h) the statutes of the SE;
(i) information on the procedures by which arrangements for employee involvement are determined pursuant to Directive 2001/86/EC.
2. The merging companies may include further items in the draft terms of merger.

Article 21. For each of the merging companies and subject to the additional requirements imposed by the Member State to which the company concerned is subject, the following particulars shall be published in the national gazette of that Member State:
(a) the type, name and registered office of every merging company;
(b) the register in which the documents referred to in Article 3(2) of Directive 68/151/EEC are filed in respect of each merging company, and the number of the entry in that register;
(c) an indication of the arrangements made in accordance with Article 24 for the exercise of the rights of the creditors of the company in question and the address at which complete information on those arrangements may be obtained free of charge;
(d) an indication of the arrangements made in accordance with Article 24 for the exercise of the rights of minority shareholders of the company in question and the address at which complete information on those arrangements may be obtained free of charge;
(e) the name and registered office proposed for the SE.

Article 22. As an alternative to experts operating on behalf of each of the merging companies, one or more independent experts as defined in Article 10 of Directive 78/855/EEC, appointed for those purposes at the joint request of the companies by a judicial or administrative authority in the Member State of one of the merging companies or of the proposed SE, may examine the draft terms of merger and draw up a single report to all the shareholders. The experts shall have the right to request from each of the merging companies any information they consider necessary to enable them to complete their function.

Article 23. 1. The general meeting of each of the merging companies shall approve the draft terms of merger.
2. Employee involvement in the SE shall be decided pursuant to Directive 2001/86/EC. The general meetings of each of the merging companies may reserve the right to make registration of the SE conditional upon its express ratification of the arrangements so decided.

Article 24. 1. The law of the Member State governing each merging company shall apply as in the case of a merger of public limited-liability companies, taking into account the cross-border nature of the merger, with regard to the protection of the interests of:
(a) creditors of the merging companies;
(b) holders of bonds of the merging companies;
(c) holders of securities, other than shares, which carry special rights in the merging companies.
2. A Member State may, in the case of the merging companies governed by its law, adopt provisions designed to ensure appropriate protection for minority shareholders who have opposed the merger.

Article 25. 1. The legality of a merger shall be scrutinised, as regards the part of the procedure concerning each merging company, in accordance with the law on mergers of public limited-liability companies of the Member State to which the merging company is subject.
2. In each Member State concerned the court, notary or other competent authority shall issue a certificate conclusively attesting to the completion of the pre-merger acts and formalities.
3. If the law of a Member State to which a merging company is subject provides for a procedure to scrutinise and amend the share exchange ratio, or a procedure to compensate minority shareholders, without preventing the registration of the merger, such procedures shall only apply if the other merging companies situated in Member States which do not provide for such procedure explicitly accept, when approving the draft terms of the merger in accordance with Article 23 (1), the possibility for the shareholders of that merging company to have recourse to such procedure. In such cases, the court, notary or other competent authorities may issue the certificate referred to in paragraph 2 even if such a procedure has been commenced. The certificate must, however, indicate that the procedure is pending. The decision in the procedure shall be binding on the acquiring company and all its shareholders.

Article 26. 1. The legality of a merger shall be scrutinised, as regards the part of the procedure concerning the completion of the merger and the formation of the SE, by the court, notary or other authority competent in the Member State of the proposed registered office of the SE to scrutinise that aspect of the legality of mergers of public limitedliability companies.
2. To that end each merging company shall submit to the competent authority the certificate referred to in Article 25(2) within six months of its issue together with a copy of the draft terms of merger approved by that company.

3. The authority referred to in paragraph 1 shall in particular ensure that the merging companies have approved draft terms of merger in the same terms and that arrangements for employee involvement have been determined pursuant to Directive 2001/86/EC.
4. That authority shall also satisfy itself that the SE has been formed in accordance with the requirements of the law of the Member State in which it has its registered office in accordance with Article 15.

Article 27. 1. A merger and the simultaneous formation of an SE shall take effect on the date on which the SE is registered in accordance with Article 12.
2. The SE may not be registered until the formalities provided for in Articles 25 and 26 have been completed.

Article 28. For each of the merging companies the completion of the merger shall be publicised as laid down by the law of each Member State in accordance with Article 3 of Directive 68/151/EEC.

Article 29. 1. A merger carried out as laid down in Article 17(2)(a) shall have the following consequences ipso jure and simultaneously:
(a) all the assets and liabilities of each company being acquired are transferred to the acquiring company;
(b) the shareholders of the company being acquired become shareholders of the acquiring company;
(c) the company being acquired ceases to exist;
(d) the acquiring company adopts the form of an SE.
2. A merger carried out as laid down in Article 17(2)(b) shall have the following consequences ipso jure and simultaneously:
(a) all the assets and liabilities of the merging companies are transferred to the SE;
(b) the shareholders of the merging companies become shareholders of the SE;
(c) the merging companies cease to exist.
3. Where, in the case of a merger of public limited-liability companies, the law of a Member State requires the completion of any special formalities before the transfer of certain assets, rights and obligations by the merging companies becomes effective against third parties, those formalities shall apply and shall be carried out either by the merging companies or by the SE following its registration.
4. The rights and obligations of the participating companies on terms and conditions of employment arising from national law, practice and individual employment contracts or employment relationships and existing at the date of the registration shall, by reason of such registration be transferred to the SE upon its registration.

Article 30. A merger as provided for in Article 2(1) may not be declared null and void once the SE has been registered.
The absence of scrutiny of the legality of the merger pursuant to Articles 25 and 26 may be included among the grounds for the winding-up of the SE.

Article 31. 1. Where a merger within the meaning of Article 17(2)(a) is carried out by a company which holds all the shares and other securities conferring the right to vote at general meetings of another company, neither Article 20(1)(b), (c) and (d), Article 29(1)(b) nor Article 22 shall apply. National law governing each merging company and mergers of public limited-liability companies in accordance with Article 24 of Directive 78/855/EEC shall nevertheless apply.
2. Where a merger by acquisition is carried out by a company which holds 90 % or more but not all of the shares and other securities conferring the right to vote at general meetings of another company, reports by the management or administrative body, reports by an independent expert or experts and the documents necessary for scrutiny shall be required only to the extent that the national law governing either the acquiring company or the company being acquired so requires. Member States may, however, provide that this paragraph may apply where a company holds shares conferring 90 % or more but not all of the voting rights.

Section III. Formation of a holding SE

Article 32. 1. A holding SE may be formed in accordance with Article 2(2). A company promoting the formation of a holding SE in accordance with Article 2(2) shall continue to exist.
2. The management or administrative organs of the companies which promote such an operation shall draw up, in the same terms, draft terms for the formation of the holding SE. The draft terms shall include a report explaining and justifying the legal and economic aspects of the formation and indicating the implications for the shareholders

and for the employees of the adoption of the form of a holding SE. The draft terms shall also set out the particulars provided for in Article 20(1)(a), (b), (c), (f), (g), (h) and (i) and shall fix the minimum proportion of the shares in each of the companies promoting the operation which the shareholders must contribute to the formation of the holding SE. That proportion shall be shares conferring more than 50 % of the permanent voting rights.

3. For each of the companies promoting the operation, the draft terms for the formation of the holding SE shall be publicised in the manner laid down in each Member State's national law in accordance with Article 3 of Directive 68/151/EEC at least one month before the date of the general meeting called to decide thereon.

4. One or more experts independent of the companies promoting the operation, appointed or approved by a judicial or administrative authority in the Member State to which each company is subject in accordance with national provisions adopted in implementation of Directive 78/855/EEC, shall examine the draft terms of formation drawn up in accordance with paragraph 2 and draw up a written report for the shareholders of each company. By agreement between the companies promoting the operation, a single written report may be drawn up for the shareholders of all the companies by one or more independent experts, appointed or approved by a judicial or administrative authority in the Member State to which one of the companies promoting the operation or the proposed SE is subject in accordance with national provisions adopted in implementation of Directive 78/855/EEC.

5. The report shall indicate any particular difficulties of valuation and state whether the proposed share-exchange ratio is fair and reasonable, indicating the methods used to arrive at it and whether such methods are adequate in the case in question.

6. The general meeting of each company promoting the operation shall approve the draft terms of formation of the holding SE.

Employee involvement in the holding SE shall be decided pursuant to Directive 2001/86/EC. The general meetings of each company promoting the operation may reserve the right to make registration of the holding SE conditional upon its express ratification of the arrangements so decided.

7. These provisions shall apply mutatis mutandis to private limited liability companies.

Article 33. 1. The shareholders of the companies promoting such an operation shall have a period of three months in which to inform the promoting companies whether they intend to contribute their shares to the formation of the holding SE. That period shall begin on the date upon which the terms for the formation of the holding SE have been finally determined in accordance with Article 32.

2. The holding SE shall be formed only if, within the period referred to in paragraph 1, the shareholders of the companies promoting the operation have assigned the minimum proportion of shares in each company in accordance with the draft terms of formation and if all the other conditions are fulfilled.

3. If the conditions for the formation of the holding SE are all fulfilled in accordance with paragraph 2, that fact shall, in respect of each of the promoting companies, be publicised in the manner laid down in the national law governing each of those companies adopted in implementation of Article 3 of Directive 68/151/EEC. Shareholders of the companies promoting the operation who have not indicated whether they intend to make their shares available to the promoting companies for the purpose of forming the holding SE within the period referred to in paragraph 1 shall have a further month in which to do so.

4. Shareholders who have contributed their securities to the formation of the SE shall receive shares in the holding SE.

5. The holding SE may not be registered until it is shown that the formalities referred to in Article 32 have been completed and that the conditions referred to in paragraph 2 have been fulfilled.

Article 34. A Member State may, in the case of companies promoting such an operation, adopt provisions designed to ensure protection for minority shareholders who oppose the operation, creditors and employees.

Section IV. Formation of a subsidiary SE

Article 35. An SE may be formed in accordance with Article 2(3).

Article 36. Companies, firms and other legal entities participating in such an operation shall be subject to the provisions governing their participation in the formation of a subsidiary in the form of a public limited-liability company under national law.

Section V. Conversion of an existing public limited-liability company into an SE

Article 37. 1. An SE may be formed in accordance with Article 2(4).
2. Without prejudice to Article 12 the conversion of a public limitedliability company into an SE shall not result in the winding up of the company or in the creation of a new legal person.
3. The registered office may not be transferred from one Member State to another pursuant to Article 8 at the same time as the conversion is effected.
4. The management or administrative organ of the company in question shall draw up draft terms of conversion and a report explaining and justifying the legal and economic aspects of the conversion and indicating the implications for the shareholders and for the employees of the adoption of the form of an SE.
5. The draft terms of conversion shall be publicised in the manner laid down in each Member State's law in accordance with Article 3 of Directive 68/151/EEC at least one month before the general meeting called upon to decide thereon.
6. Before the general meeting referred to in paragraph 7 one or more independent experts appointed or approved, in accordance with the national provisions adopted in implementation of Article 10 of Directive 78/855/EEC, by a judicial or administrative authority in the Member State to which the company being converted into an SE is subject shall certify in compliance with Directive 77/91/EEC mutatis mutandis that the company has net assets at least equivalent to its capital plus those reserves which must not be distributed under the law or the Statutes.
7. The general meeting of the company in question shall approve the draft terms of conversion together with the statutes of the SE. The decision of the general meeting shall be passed as laid down in the provisions of national law adopted in implementation of Article 7 of Directive 78/855/EEC.
8. Member States may condition a conversion to a favourable vote of a qualified majority or unanimity in the organ of the company to be converted within which employee participation is organised.
9. The rights and obligations of the company to be converted on terms and conditions of employment arising from national law, practice and individual employment contracts or employment relationships and existing at the date of the registration shall, by reason of such registration be transferred to the SE.

Title III. Structure of the SE

Article 38. Under the conditions laid down by this Regulation an SE shall comprise:
(a) a general meeting of shareholders and
(b) either a supervisory organ and a management organ (two-tier system) or an administrative organ (one-tier system) depending on the form adopted in the statutes.

Section I. Two-tier system

Article 39. 1. The management organ shall be responsible for managing the SE. A Member State may provide that a managing director or managing directors shall be responsible for the current management under the same conditions as for public limited-liability companies that have registered offices within that Member State's territory.
2. The member or members of the management organ shall be appointed and removed by the supervisory organ. A Member State may, however, require or permit the statutes to provide that the member or members of the management organ shall be appointed and removed by the general meeting under the same conditions as for public limited-liability companies that have registered offices within its territory.
3. No person may at the same time be a member of both the management organ and the supervisory organ of the same SE. The supervisory organ may, however, nominate one of its members to act as a member of the management organ in the event of a vacancy.
During such a period the functions of the person concerned as a member of the supervisory organ shall be suspended. A Member State may impose a time limit on such a period.
4. The number of members of the management organ or the rules for determining it shall be laid down in the SE's statutes. A Member State may, however, fix a minimum and/or a maximum number.
5. Where no provision is made for a two-tier system in relation to public limited-liability companies with registered offices within its territory, a Member State may adopt the appropriate measures in relation to SEs.

Article 40. 1. The supervisory organ shall supervise the work of the management organ. It may not itself exercise the power to manage the SE.

2. The members of the supervisory organ shall be appointed by the general meeting. The members of the first supervisory organ may, however, be appointed by the statutes. This shall apply without prejudice to Article 47(4) or to any employee participation arrangements determined pursuant to Directive 2001/86/EC.
3. The number of members of the supervisory organ or the rules for determining it shall be laid down in the statutes. A Member State may, however, stipulate the number of members of the supervisory organ for SEs registered within its territory or a minimum and/or a maximum number.

Article 41. 1. The management organ shall report to the supervisory organ at least once every three months on the progress and foreseeable development of the SE's business.
2. In addition to the regular information referred to in paragraph 1, the management organ shall promptly pass the supervisory organ any information on events likely to have an appreciable effect on the SE.
3. The supervisory organ may require the management organ to provide information of any kind which it needs to exercise supervision in accordance with Article 40(1). A Member State may provide that each member of the supervisory organ also be entitled to this facility.
4. The supervisory organ may undertake or arrange for any investigations necessary for the performance of its duties.
5. Each member of the supervisory organ shall be entitled to examine all information submitted to it.

Article 42. The supervisory organ shall elect a chairman from among its members. If half of the members are appointed by employees, only a member appointed by the general meeting of shareholders may be elected chairman.

Section II. The one-tier system

Article 43. 1. The administrative organ shall manage the SE. A Member State may provide that a managing director or managing directors shall be responsible for the day-to-day management under the same conditions as for public limited-liability companies that have registered offices within that Member State's territory.
2. The number of members of the administrative organ or the rules for determining it shall be laid down in the SE's statutes. A Member State may, however, set a minimum and, where necessary, a maximum number of members. The administrative organ shall, however, consist of at least three members where employee participation is regulated in accordance with Directive 2001/86/EC.
3. The member or members of the administrative organ shall be appointed by the general meeting. The members of the first administrative organ may, however, be appointed by the statutes. This shall apply without prejudice to Article 47(4) or to any employee participation arrangements determined pursuant to Directive 2001/86/EC.
4. Where no provision is made for a one-tier system in relation to public limited-liability companies with registered offices within its territory, a Member State may adopt the appropriate measures in relation to SEs.

Article 44. 1. The administrative organ shall meet at least once every three months at intervals laid down by the statutes to discuss the progress and foreseeable development of the SE's business.
2. Each member of the administrative organ shall be entitled to examine all information submitted to it.

Article 45. The administrative organ shall elect a chairman from among its members. If half of the members are appointed by employees, only a member appointed by the general meeting of shareholders may be elected chairman.

Section III. Rules common to the one-tier and two-tier systems

Article 46. 1. Members of company organs shall be appointed for a period laid down in the statutes not exceeding six years.
2. Subject to any restrictions laid down in the statutes, members may be reappointed once or more than once for the period determined in accordance with paragraph 1.

Article 47. 1. An SE's statutes may permit a company or other legal entity to be a member of one of its organs, provided that the law applicable to public limited-liability companies in the Member State in which the SE's registered office is situated does not provide otherwise. That company or other legal entity shall designate a natural person to exercise its functions on the organ in question.
2. No person may be a member of any SE organ or a representative of a member within the meaning of paragraph 1 who:

(a) is disqualified, under the law of the Member State in which the SE's registered office is situated, from serving on the corresponding organ of a public limited-liability company governed by the law of that Member State, or
(b) is disqualified from serving on the corresponding organ of a public limited-liability company governed by the law of a Member State owing to a judicial or administrative decision delivered in a Member State.
3. An SE's statutes may, in accordance with the law applicable to public limited-liability companies in the Member State in which the SE's registered office is situated, lay down special conditions of eligibility for members representing the shareholders.
4. This Regulation shall not affect national law permitting a minority of shareholders or other persons or authorities to appoint some of the members of a company organ.

Article 48. 1. An SE's statutes shall list the categories of transactions which require authorisation of the management organ by the supervisory organ in the two-tier system or an express decision by the administrative organ in the one-tier system.
A Member State may, however, provide that in the two-tier system the supervisory organ may itself make certain categories of transactions subject to authorisation.
2. A Member State may determine the categories of transactions which must at least be indicated in the statutes of SEs registered within its territory.

Article 49. The members of an SE's organs shall be under a duty, even after they have ceased to hold office, not to divulge any information which they have concerning the SE the disclosure of which might be prejudicial to the company's interests, except where such disclosure is required or permitted under national law provisions applicable to public limitedliability companies or is in the public interest.

Article 50. 1. Unless otherwise provided by this Regulation or the statutes, the internal rules relating to quorums and decision-taking in SE organs shall be as follows:
(a) quorum: at least half of the members must be present or represented;
(b) decision-taking: a majority of the members present or represented.
2. Where there is no relevant provision in the statutes, the chairman of each organ shall have a casting vote in the event of a tie. There shall be no provision to the contrary in the statutes, however, where half of the supervisory organ consists of employees' representatives.
3. Where employee participation is provided for in accordance with Directive 2001/86/EC, a Member State may provide that the supervisory organ's quorum and decision-making shall, by way of derogation from the provisions referred to in paragraphs 1 and 2, be subject to the rules applicable, under the same conditions, to public limited-liability companies governed by the law of the Member State concerned.

Article 51. Members of an SE's management, supervisory and administrative organs shall be liable, in accordance with the provisions applicable to public limited-liability companies in the Member State in which the SE's registered office is situated, for loss or damage sustained by the SE following any breach on their part of the legal, statutory or other obligations inherent in their duties.

Section IV. General meeting

Article 52. The general meeting shall decide on matters for which it is given sole responsibility by:
(a) this Regulation or
(b) the legislation of the Member State in which the SE's registered office is situated adopted in implementation of Directive 2001/86/ EC. Furthermore, the general meeting shall decide on matters for which responsibility is given to the general meeting of a public limitedliability company governed by the law of the Member State in which the SE's registered office is situated, either by the law of that Member State or by the SE's statutes in accordance with that law.

Article 53. Without prejudice to the rules laid down in this section, the organisation and conduct of general meetings together with voting procedures shall be governed by the law applicable to public limited-liability companies in the Member State in which the SE's registered office is situated.

Article 54. 1. An SE shall hold a general meeting at least once each calendar year, within six months of the end of its financial year, unless the law of the Member State in which the SE's registered office is situated applicable to public limited-liability companies carrying on the same type of activity as the SE provides for more frequent

meetings. A Member State may, however, provide that the first general meeting may be held at any time in the 18 months following an SE's incorporation.
2. General meetings may be convened at any time by the management organ, the administrative organ, the supervisory organ or any other organ or competent authority in accordance with the national law applicable to public limited-liability companies in the Member State in which the SE's registered office is situated.

Article 55. 1. One or more shareholders who together hold at least 10 % of an SE's subscribed capital may request the SE to convene a general meeting and draw up the agenda therefor; the SE's statutes or national legislation may provide for a smaller proportion under the same conditions as those applicable to public limited-liability companies.
2. The request that a general meeting be convened shall state the items to be put on the agenda.
3. If, following a request made under paragraph 1, a general meeting is not held in due time and, in any event, within two months, the competent judicial or administrative authority within the jurisdiction of which the SE's registered office is situated may order that a general meeting be convened within a given period or authorise either the shareholders who have requested it or their representatives to convene a general meeting. This shall be without prejudice to any national provisions which allow the shareholders themselves to convene general meetings.

Article 56. One or more shareholders who together hold at least 10 % of an SE's subscribed capital may request that one or more additional items be put on the agenda of any general meeting. The procedures and time limits applicable to such requests shall be laid down by the national law of the Member State in which the SE's registered office is situated or, failing that, by the SE's statutes. The above proportion may be reduced by the statutes or by the law of the Member State in which the SE's registered office is situated under the same conditions as are applicable to public limited-liability companies.

Article 57. Save where this Regulation or, failing that, the law applicable to public limited-liability companies in the Member State in which an SE's registered office is situated requires a larger majority, the general meeting's decisions shall be taken by a majority of the votes validly cast.

Article 58. The votes cast shall not include votes attaching to shares in respect of which the shareholder has not taken part in the vote or has abstained or has returned a blank or spoilt ballot paper.

Article 59. 1. Amendment of an SE's statutes shall require a decision by the general meeting taken by a majority which may not be less than two thirds of the votes cast, unless the law applicable to public limitedliability companies in the Member State in which an SE's registered office is situated requires or permits a larger majority.
2. A Member State may, however, provide that where at least half of an SE's subscribed capital is represented, a simple majority of the votes referred to in paragraph 1 shall suffice.
3. Amendments to an SE's statutes shall be publicised in accordance with Article 13.

Article 60. 1. Where an SE has two or more classes of shares, every decision by the general meeting shall be subject to a separate vote by each class of shareholders whose class rights are affected thereby.
2. Where a decision by the general meeting requires the majority of votes specified in Article 59(1) or (2), that majority shall also be required for the separate vote by each class of shareholders whose class rights are affected by the decision.

Title IV. Annual accounts and consolidated accounts

Article 61. Subject to Article 62 an SE shall be governed by the rules applicable to public limited-liability companies under the law of the Member State in which its registered office is situated as regards the preparation of its annual and, where appropriate, consolidated accounts including the accompanying annual report and the auditing and publication of those accounts.

Article 62. 1. An SE which is a credit or financial institution shall be governed by the rules laid down in the national law of the Member State in which its registered office is situated in implementation of Directive 2000/12/EC of the European Parliament and of the Council of 20 March 2000 relating to the taking up and pursuit of the business of credit institutions as regards the preparation of its annual and, where appropriate, consolidated accounts, including the accompanying annual report and the auditing and publication of those accounts.
2. An SE which is an insurance undertaking shall be governed by the rules laid down in the national law of the Member State in which its registered office is situated in implementation of Council Directive 91/674/EEC of 19

December 1991 on the annual accounts and consolidated accounts of insurance undertakings (2) as regards the preparation of its annual and, where appropriate, consolidated accounts including the accompanying annual report and the auditing and publication of those accounts.

Title V. Winding up, liquidation, insolvency and, cessation of payments

Article 63. As regards winding up, liquidation, insolvency, cessation of payments and similar procedures, an SE shall be governed by the legal provisions which would apply to a public limited-liability company formed in accordance with the law of the Member State in which its registered office is situated, including provisions relating to decision-making by the general meeting.

Article 64. 1. When an SE no longer complies with the requirement laid down in Article 7, the Member State in which the SE's registered office is situated shall take appropriate measures to oblige the SE to regularise its position within a specified period either:
(a) by re-establishing its head office in the Member State in which its registered office is situated or
(b) by transferring the registered office by means of the procedure laid down in Article 8.
2. The Member State in which the SE's registered office is situated shall put in place the measures necessary to ensure that an SE which fails to regularise its position in accordance with paragraph 1 is liquidated.
3. The Member State in which the SE's registered office is situated shall set up a judicial remedy with regard to any established infringement of Article 7. That remedy shall have a suspensory effect on the procedures laid down in paragraphs 1 and 2.
4. Where it is established on the initiative of either the authorities or any interested party that an SE has its head office within the territory of a Member State in breach of Article 7, the authorities of that Member State shall immediately inform the Member State in which the SE's registered office is situated.

Article 65. Without prejudice to provisions of national law requiring additional publication, the initiation and termination of winding up, liquidation, insolvency or cessation of payment procedures and any decision to continue operating shall be publicised in accordance with Article 13.

Article 66. 1. An SE may be converted into a public limited-liability company governed by the law of the Member State in which its registered office is situated. No decision on conversion may be taken before two years have elapsed since its registration or before the first two sets of annual accounts have been approved.
2. The conversion of an SE into a public limited-liability company shall not result in the winding up of the company or in the creation of a new legal person.
3. The management or administrative organ of the SE shall draw up draft terms of conversion and a report explaining and justifying the legal and economic aspects of the conversion and indicating the implications of the adoption of the public limited-liability company for the shareholders and for the employees.
4. The draft terms of conversion shall be publicised in the manner laid down in each Member State's law in accordance with Article 3 of Directive 68/151/EEC at least one month before the general meeting called to decide thereon.
5. Before the general meeting referred to in paragraph 6, one or more independent experts appointed or approved, in accordance with the national provisions adopted in implementation of Article 10 of Directive 78/855/EEC, by a judicial or administrative authority in the Member State to which the SE being converted into a public limitedliability company is subject shall certify that the company has assets at least equivalent to its capital.
6. The general meeting of the SE shall approve the draft terms of conversion together with the statutes of the public limited-liability company. The decision of the general meeting shall be passed as laid down in the provisions of national law adopted in implementation of Article 7 of Directive 78/855/EEC.

Title VI. Additional and transitional provisions

Article 67. 1. If and so long as the third phase of economic and monetary union (EMU) does not apply to it each Member State may make SEs with registered offices within its territory subject to the same provisions as apply to public limited-liability companies covered by its legislation as regards the expression of their capital. An SE may, in any case, express its capital in euro as well. In that event the national currency/euro conversion rate shall be that for the last day of the month preceding that of the formation of the SE.
2. If and so long as the third phase of EMU does not apply to the Member State in which an SE has its registered office, the SE may, however, prepare and publish its annual and, where appropriate, consolidated accounts in euro. The Member State may require that the SE's annual and, where appropriate, consolidated accounts be prepared and

published in the national currency under the same conditions as those laid down for public limited-liability companies governed by the law of that Member State. This shall not prejudge the additional possibility for an SE of publishing its annual and, where appropriate, consolidated accounts in euro in accordance with Council Directive 90/604/EEC of 8 November 1990 amending Directive 78/60/EEC on annual accounts and Directive 83/349/EEC on consolidated accounts as concerns the exemptions for small and medium-sized companies and the publication of accounts in ecu.

Title VII. Final provisions

Article 68. 1. The Member States shall make such provision as is appropriate to ensure the effective application of this Regulation.
2. Each Member State shall designate the competent authorities within the meaning of Articles 8, 25, 26, 54, 55 and 64. It shall inform the Commission and the other Member States accordingly.

Article 69. Five years at the latest after the entry into force of this Regulation, the Commission shall forward to the Council and the European Parliament a report on the application of the Regulation and proposals for amendments, where appropriate. The report shall, in particular, analyse the appropriateness of:
(a) allowing the location of an SE's head office and registered office in different Member States;
(b) broadening the concept of merger in Article 17(2) in order to admit also other types of merger than those defined in Articles 3(1) and 4 (1) of Directive 78/855/EEC;
(c) revising the jurisdiction clause in Article 8(16) in the light of any provision which may have been inserted in the 1968 Brussels Convention or in any text adopted by Member States or by the Council to replace such Convention;
(d) allowing provisions in the statutes of an SE adopted by a Member State in execution of authorisations given to the Member States by this Regulation or laws adopted to ensure the effective application of this Regulation in respect to the SE which deviate from or are complementary to these laws, even when such provisions would not be authorised in the statutes of a public limited-liability company having its registered office in the Member State.

Article 70. This Regulation shall enter into force on 8 October 2004. This Regulation shall be binding in its entirety and directly applicable in all Member States.

Annex I. Public limited-liability companies referred to in article 2(1)
BELGIUM: la société anonyme/de naamloze vennootschap
BULGARIA: акционерно дружество
CZECH REPUBLIC: akciová společnost
DENMARK: aktieselskaber
GERMANY: die Aktiengesellschaft
ESTONIA: aktsiaselts
GREECE: ανώνυμη εταιρία
SPAIN: la sociedad anónima
FRANCE: la société anonyme
IRELAND: public companies limited by shares public companies limited by guarantee having a share capital
ITALY: società per azioni
CYPRUS: Δημόσια Εταιρεία περιορισμένης ευθύνης με μετοχές, Δημόσια Εταιρεία περιο- ρισμένης ευθύνης με εγγύηση
LATVIA: akciju sabiedrība
LITHUANIA: akcinės bendrovės
LUXEMBOURG: la société anonyme
HUNGARY: részvénytársaság
MALTA: kumpaniji pubblići / public limited liability companies
NETHERLANDS: de naamloze vennootschap
AUSTRIA: die Aktiengesellschaft
POLAND: spółka akcyjna
PORTUGAL: a sociedade anónima de responsabilidade limitada
ROMANIA: societate pe acțiuni
SLOVENIA: delniška družba
SLOVAKIA: akciová spoločnos
FINLAND: julkinen osakeyhtiö/publikt aktiebolag

Part VIII. European Company Law

SWEDEN: publikt aktiebolag
UNITED KINGDOM: public companies limited by shares public companies limited by guarantee having a share capital

Annex II. Public and private limited-liability companies referred to in article (2)

BELGIUM: la société anonyme/de naamloze vennootschap, la société privée à responsabilité limitée/besloten vennootschap met beperkte aansprakelijkheid
BULGARIA: акционерно дружество, дружество с ограничена отговорност
CZECH REPUBLIC: akciová společnost, společnost s ručením omezeným
DENMARK: aktieselskaber, anpartselskaber
GERMANY: die Aktiengesellschaft, die Gesellschaft mit beschränkter Haftung
ESTONIA: aktsiaselts ja osaühing
GREECE: ανώνυμη εταιρία εταιρία περιορισμένης ευθύνης
SPAIN: la sociedad anónima, la sociedad de responsabilidad limitada
FRANCE: la société anonyme, la société à responsabilité limitée
IRELAND: public companies limited by shares, public companies limited by guarantee having a share capital, private companies limited by shares, private companies limited by guarantee having a share capital
ITALY: società per azioni, società a responsabilità limitata
CYPRUS: Δημόσια εταιρεία περιορισμένης ευθύνης με μετοχές, δημόσια Εταιρεία περιορισμένης ευθύνης με εγγύηση, ιδιωτική εταιρεία
LATVIA: akciju sabiedrība, un sabiedrība ar ierobežotu atbildību
LITHUANIA: akcinės bendrovės, uždarosios akcinės bendrovės
LUXEMBOURG: la société anonyme, la société à responsabilité limitée
HUNGARY: részvénytársaság, korlátolt felelősségű társaság
MALTA: kumpaniji pubbliċi / public limited liability companies kumpaniji privati/private limited liability companies
NETHERLANDS: de naamloze vennootschap, de besloten vennootschap met beperkte aansprakelijkheid
AUSTRIA: die Aktiengesellschaft, die Gesellschaft mit beschränkter Haftung
POLAND: spółka akcyjna, spółka z ograniczoną odpowiedzialnością
PORTUGAL: a sociedade anónima de responsabilidade limitada, a sociedade por quotas de responsabilidade limitada
ROMANIA: societate pe acțiuni, societate cu răspundere limitată
SLOVENIA: delniška družba, družba z omejeno odgovornostjo
SLOVAKIA: akciová spoločnos', spoločnosť s ručením obmedzeným
FINLAND: osakeyhtiö aktiebolag
SWEDEN: aktiebolag
UNITED KINGDOM: public companies limited by shares, public companies limited by guarantee having a share capital, private companies limited by shares, private companies limited by guarantee having a share capital

Council Directive 2001/86/EC of 8 October 2001 supplementing the Statute for a European company with regard to the involvement of employees (*OJ* L 294 , 10.11.2001 p. 22 – 32) [footnotes omitted].

THE COUNCIL OF THE EUROPEAN UNION,
Having regard to the Treaty establishing the European Community, and in particular Article 308 thereof,
Having regard to the amended proposal from the Commission,
Having regard to the opinion of the European Parliament,
Having regard to the opinion of the Economic and Social Committee,
Whereas:
(1) In order to attain the objectives of the Treaty, Council Regulation (EC) No 2157/2001 establishes a Statute for a European company (SE).
(2) That Regulation aims at creating a uniform legal framework within which companies from different Member States should be able to plan and carry out the reorganisation of their business on a Community scale.
(3) In order to promote the social objectives of the Community, special provisions have to be set, notably in the field of employee involvement, aimed at ensuring that the establishment of an SE does not entail the disappearance or reduction of practices of employee involvement existing within the companies participating in the establishment of an SE. This objective should be pursued through the establishment of a set of rules in this field, supplementing the provisions of the Regulation.
(4) Since the objectives of the proposed action, as outlined above, cannot be sufficiently achieved by the Member States, in that the object is to establish a set of rules on employee involvement applicable to the SE, and can therefore, by reason of the scale and impact of the proposed action, be better achieved at Community level, the Community may adopt measures, in accordance with the principle of subsidiarity as set out in Article 5 of the Treaty. In accordance with the principle of proportionality, as set out in that Article, this Directive does not go beyond what is necessary to achieve these objectives.
(5) The great diversity of rules and practices existing in the Member States as regards the manner in which employees' representatives are involved in decision-making within companies makes it inadvisable to set up a single European model of employee involvement applicable to the SE.
(6) Information and consultation procedures at transnational level should nevertheless be ensured in all cases of creation of an SE.
(7) If and when participation rights exist within one or more companies establishing an SE, they should be preserved through their transfer to the SE, once established, unless the parties decide otherwise.
(8) The concrete procedures of employee transnational information and consultation, as well as, if applicable, participation, to apply to each SE should be defined primarily by means of an agreement between the parties concerned or, in the absence thereof, through the application of a set of subsidiary rules.
(9) Member States should still have the option of not applying the standard rules relating to participation in the case of a merger, given the diversity of national systems for employee involvement. Existing systems and practices of participation where appropriate at the level of participating companies must in that case be maintained by adapting registration rules.
(10) The voting rules within the special body representing the employees for negotiation purposes, in particular when concluding agreements providing for a level of participation lower than the one existing within one or more of the participating companies, should be proportionate to the risk of disappearance or reduction of existing systems and practices of participation. That risk is greater in the case of an SE established by way of transformation or merger than by way of creating a holding company or a common subsidiary.
(11) In the absence of an agreement subsequent to the negotiation between employees' representatives and the competent organs of the participating companies, provision should be made for certain standard requirements to apply to the SE, once it is established. These standard requirements should ensure effective practices of transnational information and consultation of employees, as well as their participation in the relevant organs of the SE if and when such participation existed before its establishment within the participating companies.
(12) Provision should be made for the employees' representatives acting within the framework of the Directive to enjoy, when exercising their functions, protection and guarantees which are similar to those provided to employees' representatives by the legislation and/or practice of the country of employment.

They should not be subject to any discrimination as a result of the lawful exercise of their activities and should enjoy adequate protection as regards dismissal and other sanctions.

(13) The confidentiality of sensitive information should be preserved even after the expiry of the employees' representatives terms of office and provision should be made to allow the competent organ of the SE to withhold information which would seriously harm, if subject to public disclosure, the functioning of the SE.

(14) Where an SE and its subsidiaries and establishments are subject to Council Directive 94/45/EC of 22 September 1994 on the establishment of a European Works Council or a procedure in Community-scale undertakings and Community-scale groups of undertakings for the purposes of informing and consulting employees, the provisions of that Directive and the provision transposing it into national legislation should not apply to it nor to its subsidiaries and establishments, unless the special negotiating body decides not to open negotiations or to terminate negotiations already opened.

(15) This Directive should not affect other existing rights regarding involvement and need not affect other existing representation structures, provided for by Community and national laws and practices.

(16) Member States should take appropriate measures in the event of failure to comply with the obligations laid down in this Directive.

(17) The Treaty has not provided the necessary powers for the Community to adopt the proposed Directive, other than those provided for in Article 308.

(18) It is a fundamental principle and stated aim of this Directive to secure employees' acquired rights as regards involvement in company decisions. Employee rights in force before the establishment of SEs should provide the basis for employee rights of involvement in the SE (the "before and after" principle). Consequently, that approach should apply not only to the initial establishment of an SE but also to structural changes in an existing SE and to the companies affected by structural change processes.

(19) Member States should be able to provide that representatives of trade unions may be members of a special negotiating body regardless of whether they are employees of a company participating in the establishment of an SE. Member States should in this context in particular be able to introduce this right in cases where trade union representatives have the right to be members of, and to vote in, supervisory or administrative company organs in accordance with national legislation.

(20) In several Member States, employee involvement and other areas of industrial relations are based on both national legislation and practice which in this context is understood also to cover collective agreements at various national, sectoral and/or company levels,

HAS ADOPTED THIS DIRECTIVE:

Section I General

Article 1. 1. This Directive governs the involvement of employees in the affairs of European public limited-liability companies (Societas Europaea, hereinafter referred to as "SE"), as referred to in Regulation (EC) No 2157/2001.

2. To this end, arrangements for the involvement of employees shall be established in every SE in accordance with the negotiating procedure referred to in Articles 3 to 6 or, under the circumstances specified in Article 7, in accordance with the Annex.

Article 2. For the purposes of this Directive:
(a) "SE" means any company established in accordance with Regulation (EC) No 2157/2001;
(b) "participating companies" means the companies directly participating in the establishing of an SE;
(c) "subsidiary" of a company means an undertaking over which that company exercises a dominant influence defined in accordance with Article 3(2) to (7) of Directive 94/45/EC;
(d) "concerned subsidiary or establishment" means a subsidiary or establishment of a participating company which is proposed to become a subsidiary or establishment of the SE upon its formation;
(e) "employees' representatives" means the employees' representatives provided for by national law and/or practice;
(f) "representative body" means the body representative of the employees set up by the agreements referred to in Article 4 or in accordance with the provisions of the Annex, with the purpose of informing and consulting the employees of an SE and its subsidiaries and establishments situated in the Community and, where applicable, of exercising participation rights in relation to the SE;

(g) "special negotiating body" means the body established in accordance with Article 3 to negotiate with the competent body of the participating companies regarding the establishment of arrangements for the involvement of employees within the SE;
(h) "involvement of employees" means any mechanism, including information, consultation and participation, through which employees' representatives may exercise an influence on decisions to be taken within the company;
(i) "information" means the informing of the body representative of the employees and/or employees' representatives by the competent organ of the SE on questions which concern the SE itself and any of its subsidiaries or establishments situated in another Member State or which exceed the powers of the decision-making organs in a single Member State at a time, in a manner and with a content which allows the employees' representatives to undertake an in-depth assessment of the possible impact and, where appropriate, prepare consultations with the competent organ of the SE;
(j) "consultation" means the establishment of dialogue and exchange of views between the body representative of the employees and/or the employees' representatives and the competent organ of the SE, at a time, in a manner and with a content which allows the employees' representatives, on the basis of information provided, to express an opinion on measures envisaged by the competent organ which may be taken into account in the decision-making process within the SE;
(k) "participation" means the influence of the body representative of the employees and/or the employees' representatives in the affairs of a company by way of:
- the right to elect or appoint some of the members of the company's supervisory or administrative organ, or
- the right to recommend and/or oppose the appointment of some or all of the members of the company's supervisory or administrative organ.

Section II Negotiating Procedure

Article 3. 1. Where the management or administrative organs of the participating companies draw up a plan for the establishment of an SE, they shall as soon as possible after publishing the draft terms of merger or creating a holding company or after agreeing a plan to form a subsidiary or to transform into an SE, take the necessary steps, including providing information about the identity of the participating companies, concerned subsidiaries or establishments, and the number of their employees, to start negotiations with the representatives of the companies' employees on arrangements for the involvement of employees in the SE.
2. For this purpose, a special negotiating body representative of the employees of the participating companies and concerned subsidiaries or establishments shall be created in accordance with the following provisions:
(a) in electing or appointing members of the special negotiating body, it must be ensured:
(i) that these members are elected or appointed in proportion to the number of employees employed in each Member State by the participating companies and concerned subsidiaries or establishments, by allocating in respect of a Member State one seat per portion of employees employed in that Member State which equals 10 %, or a fraction thereof, of the number of employees employed by the participating companies and concerned subsidiaries or establishments in all the Member States taken together;
(ii) that in the case of an SE formed by way of merger, there are such further additional members from each Member State as may be necessary in order to ensure that the special negotiating body includes at least one member representing each participating company which is registered and has employees in that Member State and which it is proposed will cease to exist as a separate legal entity following the registration of the SE, in so far as:
- the number of such additional members does not exceed 20 % of the number of members designated by virtue of point (i), and
- the composition of the special negotiating body does not entail a double representation of the employees concerned.
If the number of such companies is higher than the number of additional seats available pursuant to the first subparagraph, these additional seats shall be allocated to companies in different Member States by decreasing order of the number of employees they employ;
(b) Member States shall determine the method to be used for the election or appointment of the members of the special negotiating body who are to be elected or appointed in their territories. They shall take the necessary measures to ensure that, as far as possible, such members shall include at least

one member representing each participating company which has employees in the Member State concerned. Such measures must not increase the overall number of members.

Member States may provide that such members may include representatives of trade unions whether or not they are employees of a participating company or concerned subsidiary or establishment.

Without prejudice to national legislation and/or practice laying down thresholds for the establishing of a representative body, Member States shall provide that employees in undertakings or establishments in which there are no employees' representatives through no fault of their own have the right to elect or appoint members of the special negotiating body.

3. The special negotiating body and the competent organs of the participating companies shall determine, by written agreement, arrangements for the involvement of employees within the SE.

To this end, the competent organs of the participating companies shall inform the special negotiating body of the plan and the actual process of establishing the SE, up to its registration.

4. Subject to paragraph 6, the special negotiating body shall take decisions by an absolute majority of its members, provided that such a majority also represents an absolute majority of the employees. Each member shall have one vote. However, should the result of the negotiations lead to a reduction of participation rights, the majority required for a decision to approve such an agreement shall be the votes of two thirds of the members of the special negotiating body representing at least two thirds of the employees, including the votes of members representing employees employed in at least two Member States,

- in the case of an SE to be established by way of merger, if participation covers at least 25 % of the overall number of employees of the participating companies, or

- in the case of an SE to be established by way of creating a holding company or forming a subsidiary, if participation covers at least 50 % of the overall number of employees of the participating companies.

Reduction of participation rights means a proportion of members of the organs of the SE within the meaning of Article 2(k), which is lower than the highest proportion existing within the participating companies.

5. For the purpose of the negotiations, the special negotiating body may request experts of its choice, for example representatives of appropriate Community level trade union organisations, to assist it with its work. Such experts may be present at negotiation meetings in an advisory capacity at the request of the special negotiating body, where appropriate to promote coherence and consistency at Community level. The special negotiating body may decide to inform the representatives of appropriate external organisations, including trade unions, of the start of the negotiations.

6. The special negotiating body may decide by the majority set out below not to open negotiations or to terminate negotiations already opened, and to rely on the rules on information and consultation of employees in force in the Member States where the SE has employees. Such a decision shall stop the procedure to conclude the agreement referred to in Article 4. Where such a decision has been taken, none of the provisions of the Annex shall apply.

The majority required to decide not to open or to terminate negotiations shall be the votes of two thirds of the members representing at least two thirds of the employees, including the votes of members representing employees employed in at least two Member States.

In the case of an SE established by way of transformation, this paragraph shall not apply if there is participation in the company to be transformed.

The special negotiating body shall be reconvened on the written request of at least 10 % of the employees of the SE, its subsidiaries and establishments, or their representatives, at the earliest two years after the abovementioned decision, unless the parties agree to negotiations being reopened sooner. If the special negotiating body decides to reopen negotiations with the management but no agreement is reached as a result of those negotiations, none of the provisions of the Annex shall apply.

7. Any expenses relating to the functioning of the special negotiating body and, in general, to negotiations shall be borne by the participating companies so as to enable the special negotiating body to carry out its task in an appropriate manner.

In compliance with this principle, Member States may lay down budgetary rules regarding the operation of the special negotiating body. They may in particular limit the funding to cover one expert only.

Article 4. 1. The competent organs of the participating companies and the special negotiating body shall negotiate in a spirit of cooperation with a view to reaching an agreement on arrangements for the involvement of the employees within the SE.

2. Without prejudice to the autonomy of the parties, and subject to paragraph 4, the agreement referred to in paragraph 1 between the competent organs of the participating companies and the special negotiating body shall specify:
(a) the scope of the agreement;
(b) the composition, number of members and allocation of seats on the representative body which will be the discussion partner of the competent organ of the SE in connection with arrangements for the information and consultation of the employees of the SE and its subsidiaries and establishments;
(c) the functions and the procedure for the information and consultation of the representative body;
(d) the frequency of meetings of the representative body;
(e) the financial and material resources to be allocated to the representative body;
(f) if, during negotiations, the parties decide to establish one or more information and consultation procedures instead of a representative body, the arrangements for implementing those procedures;
(g) if, during negotiations, the parties decide to establish arrangements for participation, the substance of those arrangements including (if applicable) the number of members in the SE's administrative or supervisory body which the employees will be entitled to elect, appoint, recommend or oppose, the procedures as to how these members may be elected, appointed, recommended or opposed by the employees, and their rights;
(h) the date of entry into force of the agreement and its duration, cases where the agreement should be renegotiated and the procedure for its renegotiation.
3. The agreement shall not, unless provision is made otherwise therein, be subject to the standard rules referred to in the Annex.
4. Without prejudice to Article 13(3)(a), in the case of an SE established by means of transformation, the agreement shall provide for at least the same level of all elements of employee involvement as the ones existing within the company to be transformed into an SE.

Article 5. 1. Negotiations shall commence as soon as the special negotiating body is established and may continue for six months thereafter.
2. The parties may decide, by joint agreement, to extend negotiations beyond the period referred to in paragraph 1, up to a total of one year from the establishment of the special negotiating body.

Article 6. Except where otherwise provided in this Directive, the legislation applicable to the negotiation procedure provided for in Articles 3 to 5 shall be the legislation of the Member State in which the registered office of the SE is to be situated.

Article 7. 1. In order to achieve the objective described in Article 1, Member States shall, without prejudice to paragraph 3 below, lay down standard rules on employee involvement which must satisfy the provisions set out in the Annex.
The standard rules as laid down by the legislation of the Member State in which the registered office of the SE is to be situated shall apply from the date of the registration of the SE where either:
(a) the parties so agree; or
(b) by the deadline laid down in Article 5, no agreement has been concluded, and:
- the competent organ of each of the participating companies decides to accept the application of the standard rules in relation to the SE and so to continue with its registration of the SE, and
- the special negotiating body has not taken the decision provided in Article 3(6).
2. Moreover, the standard rules fixed by the national legislation of the Member State of registration in accordance with part 3 of the Annex shall apply only:
(a) in the case of an SE established by transformation, if the rules of a Member State relating to employee participation in the administrative or supervisory body applied to a company transformed into an SE;
(b) in the case of an SE established by merger:
- if, before registration of the SE, one or more forms of participation applied in one or more of the participating companies covering at least 25 % of the total number of employees in all the participating companies, or
- if, before registration of the SE, one or more forms of participation applied in one or more of the participating companies covering less than 25 % of the total number of employees in all the participating companies and if the special negotiating body so decides,
(c) in the case of an SE established by setting up a holding company or establishing a subsidiary:

- if, before registration of the SE, one or more forms of participation applied in one or more of the participating companies covering at least 50 % of the total number of employees in all the participating companies; or
- if, before registration of the SE, one or more forms of participation applied in one or more of the participating companies covering less than 50 % of the total number of employees in all the participating companies and if the special negotiating body so decides.

If there was more than one form of participation within the various participating companies, the special negotiating body shall decide which of those forms must be established in the SE. Member States may fix the rules which are applicable in the absence of any decision on the matter for an SE registered in their territory. The special negotiating body shall inform the competent organs of the participating companies of any decisions taken pursuant to this paragraph.

3. Member States may provide that the reference provisions in part 3 of the Annex shall not apply in the case provided for in point (b) of paragraph 2.

Section III Miscellaneous Provisions

Article 8. 1. Member States shall provide that members of the special negotiating body or the representative body, and experts who assist them, are not authorised to reveal any information which has been given to them in confidence.

The same shall apply to employees' representatives in the context of an information and consultation procedure.

This obligation shall continue to apply, wherever the persons referred to may be, even after the expiry of their terms of office.

2. Each Member State shall provide, in specific cases and under the conditions and limits laid down by national legislation, that the supervisory or administrative organ of an SE or of a participating company established in its territory is not obliged to transmit information where its nature is such that, according to objective criteria, to do so would seriously harm the functioning of the SE (or, as the case may be, the participating company) or its subsidiaries and establishments or would be prejudicial to them.

A Member State may make such dispensation subject to prior administrative or judicial authorisation.

3. Each Member State may lay down particular provisions for SEs in its territory which pursue directly and essentially the aim of ideological guidance with respect to information and the expression of opinions, on condition that, on the date of adoption of this Directive, such provisions already exist in the national legislation.

4. In applying paragraphs 1, 2 and 3, Member States shall make provision for administrative or judicial appeal procedures which the employees' representatives may initiate when the supervisory or administrative organ of an SE or participating company demands confidentiality or does not give information.

Such procedures may include arrangements designed to protect the confidentiality of the information in question.

Article 9. The competent organ of the SE and the representative body shall work together in a spirit of cooperation with due regard for their reciprocal rights and obligations.

The same shall apply to cooperation between the supervisory or administrative organ of the SE and the employees' representatives in conjunction with a procedure for the information and consultation of employees.

Article 10. The members of the special negotiating body, the members of the representative body, any employees' representatives exercising functions under the information and consultation procedure and any employees' representatives in the supervisory or administrative organ of an SE who are employees of the SE, its subsidiaries or establishments or of a participating company shall, in the exercise of their functions, enjoy the same protection and guarantees provided for employees' representatives by the national legislation and/or practice in force in their country of employment.

This shall apply in particular to attendance at meetings of the special negotiating body or representative body, any other meeting under the agreement referred to in Article 4(2)(f) or any meeting of the administrative or supervisory organ, and to the payment of wages for members employed by a participating company or the SE or its subsidiaries or establishments during a period of absence necessary for the performance of their duties.

Article 11. Member States shall take appropriate measures in conformity with Community law with a view to preventing the misuse of an SE for the purpose of depriving employees of rights to employee involvement or withholding such rights.

Article 12. 1. Each Member State shall ensure that the management of establishments of an SE and the supervisory or administrative organs of subsidiaries and of participating companies which are situated within its territory and the employees' representatives or, as the case may be, the employees themselves abide by the obligations laid down by this Directive, regardless of whether or not the SE has its registered office within its territory.
2. Member States shall provide for appropriate measures in the event of failure to comply with this Directive; in particular they shall ensure that administrative or legal procedures are available to enable the obligations deriving from this Directive to be enforced.

Article 13. 1. Where an SE is a Community-scale undertaking or a controlling undertaking of a Community-scale group of undertakings within the meaning of Directive 94/45/EC or of Directive 97/74/EC extending the said Directive to the United Kingdom, the provisions of these Directives and the provisions transposing them into national legislation shall not apply to them or to their subsidiaries. However, where the special negotiating body decides in accordance with Article 3(6) not to open negotiations or to terminate negotiations already opened, Directive 94/45/EC or Directive 97/74/EC and the provisions transposing them into national legislation shall apply.
2. Provisions on the participation of employees in company bodies provided for by national legislation and/or practice, other than those implementing this Directive, shall not apply to companies established in accordance with Regulation (EC) No 2157/2001 and covered by this Directive.
3. This Directive shall not prejudice:
(a) the existing rights to involvement of employees provided for by national legislation and/or practice in the Member States as enjoyed by employees of the SE and its subsidiaries and establishments, other than participation in the bodies of the SE;
(b) the provisions on participation in the bodies laid down by national legislation and/or practice applicable to the subsidiaries of the SE.
4. In order to preserve the rights referred to in paragraph 3, Member States may take the necessary measures to guarantee that the structures of employee representation in participating companies which will cease to exist as separate legal entities are maintained after the registration of the SE.

Article 14. 1. Member States shall adopt the laws, regulations and administrative provisions necessary to comply with this Directive no later than 8 October 2004, or shall ensure by that date at the latest that management and labour introduce the required provisions by way of agreement, the Member States being obliged to take all necessary steps enabling them at all times to guarantee the results imposed by this Directive. They shall forthwith inform the Commission thereof.
2. When Member States adopt these measures, they shall contain a reference to this Directive or shall be accompanied by such reference on the occasion of their official publication. The methods of making such reference shall be laid down by the Member States.

Article 15. No later than 8 October 2007, the Commission shall, in consultation with the Member States and with management and labour at Community level, review the procedures for applying this Directive, with a view to proposing suitable amendments to the Council where necessary.

Article 16. This Directive shall enter into force on the day of its publication in the Official Journal of the European Communities.

Article 17. This Directive is addressed to the Member States.

Proposal for a Council Regulation on the Statute for a European private company (Text with EEA relevance) Brussels, COM (2008) 396/3.

THE COUNCIL OF THE EUROPEAN UNION,
Having regard to the Treaty establishing the European Community, and in particular Article 308 thereof,
Having regard to the proposal from the Commission,
Having regard to the opinion of the European Parliament,
Having regard to the opinion of the European Economic and Social Committee,
Whereas:

(1) The legal framework in which business is carried out in the Community remains largely national. This exposes companies to a wide diversity of national laws, company forms and company regimes. The approximation of national laws by means of directives based on Article 44 of the Treaty can overcome some of these difficulties. Such approximation, however, does not release persons seeking to create companies from the obligation to adopt in each Member State a company form governed by the national law of that Member State.

(2) Existing Community forms of company, notably the European Company (SE), whose legal form was established by Council Regulation (EC) No 2157/2001 of 8 October 2001 on the Statute for a European Company18 are designed for large companies. The minimum capital requirement for an SE and the restrictions on its formation make that form of company unsuitable for many businesses, in particular of a smaller size. In view of the problems faced by such businesses as a result of the diversity of company law regimes and the unsuitability of the SE for small businesses, it is appropriate to provide for a European company form specifically designed for small businesses, which it is possible to create throughout the Community.

(3) Since a private company (hereinafter "SPE") which may be created throughout the Community is intended for small businesses, a legal form should be provided which is as uniform as possible throughout the Community and as many matters as possible should be left to the contractual freedom of shareholders, while a high level of legal certainty is ensured for shareholders, creditors, employees and third parties in general. Given that a high degree of flexibility and freedom is to be left to the shareholders to organise the internal affairs of the SPE, the private nature of the company should also be reflected by the fact that its shares may not be offered to the public or negotiated on the capital markets, including being admitted to trading or listed on regulated markets.

(4) In order to enable businesses to reap the full benefits of the internal market, the SPE should be able to have its registered office and principal place of business in different Member States and to transfer its registered office from one Member State to another, with or without also transferring its central administration or principal place of business.

(5) To enable businesses to gain efficiencies and save costs, the SPE should be available in every Member State, with as few variations as possible as regards the company form.

(6) To ensure a high degree of uniformity of the SPE, as many matters pertaining to the company form as possible should be governed by this Regulation, either through substantive rules or by reserving matters to the articles of association of the SPE. It is therefore appropriate to provide for a list of matters, to be set out in an Annex, in respect of which the shareholders of the SPE are obliged to lay down rules in the articles of association. In relation to those matters only Community law should apply, and consequently shareholders should be able to set out rules to regulate those matters, which are different from the rules prescribed by the law of the Member State where the SPE is registered, in relation to national forms of private limited-liability companies. National law should apply to matters where this is provided for by this Regulation and to all other matters that are not covered by the articles of this Regulation, such as insolvency, employment and tax, or are not reserved by it to the articles of association.

(7) In order to make the SPE an accessible company form for individuals and small businesses, it should be capable of being created ex nihilo or of resulting from the transformation, the merger or the division of existing national companies. The creation of an SPE by way of transformation, merger or division of companies should be governed by the applicable national law.

(8) In order to reduce the costs and administrative burdens associated with company registration, the formalities for the registration of the SPE should be limited to those requirements which are necessary to ensure legal certainty and the validity of the documents filed upon the creation of a SPE should be subject to a single verification, which may take place either before or after registration. For the purposes of registration, it is appropriate to use the registries designated by First Council Directive 68/151/EEC of 9 March 1968 on the co-ordination of safeguards which, for the protection of the interests of members and others, are required by Member States of companies within the meaning of the second paragraph of Article 58 of the Treaty, with a view to making such safeguards equivalent throughout the Community19. (9) Since small businesses often require long term financial and personal commitment, they should be able to adapt the structure of their share capital and the rights attached to shares to their specific circumstances. SPE shareholders should therefore be free to determine the rights attached to their shares, the procedure for the variation of those rights, the procedure to be followed if shares are

transferred and any restriction on such transfer. (10) In order to preserve both the operation of the SPE and the freedom of shareholders, the SPE should have the possibility of applying to court to expel shareholders who seriously harm its interests and shareholders of the SPE whose interest suffered serious harm as a result of specific events should have the right to withdraw from the SPE.
(11) The SPE should not be subject to a high mandatory capital requirement since this would be a barrier to the creation of SPEs. Creditors, however, should be protected from excessive distributions to shareholders which could affect the ability of the SPE to pay its debts. To this end, distributions that leave the SPE with liabilities exceeding the value of the assets of the SPE should be prohibited. Shareholders, however, should also be free to require the management body of the SPE to sign a solvency certificate.
(12) Since creditors should be granted protection in the event of a reduction of the capital of the SPE, certain rules should be laid down concerning when such reductions are to take effect.
(13) Since small businesses need legal structures that can be adapted to their needs and size and are able to evolve as activity develops, shareholders of the SPE should be free to determine in their articles of association the internal organisation which is best suited to their needs. An SPE may opt for one or more individual managing directors, a unitary or a dual board structure. However, mandatory rules ensuring the protection of minority shareholders should be introduced in order to avoid any unfair treatment of shareholders, in particular certain key resolutions should be adopted by a majority of no less than two-thirds of the total voting rights attached to the shares issued by the SPE. While a limit may be introduced on the right to request a resolution or to request an independent expert to investigate abuses, such right may not be made conditional on the ownership of more than 5% of the voting rights of the SPE, although the articles of association of the SPE may provide for a lower threshold.
(14) Competent national authorities should monitor the completion and legality of the transfer of the registered office of an SPE to another Member State. The timely access of shareholders, creditors and employees to the transfer proposal and to the report of the management body should be ensured.
(15) Employees' rights of participation should be governed by the legislation of the Member State in which the SPE has its registered office (the "home Member State"). The SPE should not be used for the purpose of circumventing such rights. Where the national legislation of the Member State to which the SPE transfers its registered office does not provide for at least the same level of employee participation as the home Member State, the participation of employees in the company following the transfer should in certain circumstances be negotiated. Should such negotiations fail, the provisions applying in the company before the transfer should continue to apply after the transfer.
(16) Employees' rights other than rights of participation should remain subject to Council Directive 94/45/EC of 22 September 1994 on the establishment of a European Works Council or a procedure in Community-scale undertakings and Community-scale groups of undertakings for the purposes of informing and consulting employees, Council Directive 98/59/EC of 20 July 1998 on the approximation of the laws of the Member States relating to collective redundancies, Council Directive 2001/23/EC of 12 March 2001 on the approximation of the law of the Member States relating to the safeguarding of employees' rights in the event of transfers of undertakings, businesses or parts of undertakings or businesses and Directive 2002/14/EC of the European Parliament and of the Council of 11 March 2002 establishing a general framework for informing and consulting employees in the European Community.
(17) The Member States should lay down rules on penalties applicable to infringements of the provisions of this Regulation, including infringements of the obligation to regulate in the articles of association of the SPE the matters prescribed by this Regulation, and should ensure that they are implemented. Those penalties must be effective, proportionate and dissuasive.
(18) The Treaty does not provide, for the adoption of this Regulation, powers other than those under Article 308.
(19) Since the objectives of the proposed action cannot be sufficiently achieved by the Member States in so far as they involve the creation of a company form with common features throughout the Community and can therefore, by reason of the scale of the action, be better achieved at Community level, the Community may adopt measures, in accordance with the principle of subsidiarity laid down in Article 5 of the Treaty. In accordance with the principle of proportionality as set out in that Article, this Regulation does not go beyond what is necessary to achieve those objectives

HAS ADOPTED THIS REGULATION:

Chapter I. General provisions

Article 1. This Regulation lays down the conditions governing the establishment and operation within the Community of companies in the form of a European private company with limited liability (Societas Privata Europaea, hereinafter "SPE").

Article 2. 1. For the purposes of this Regulation, the following definitions shall apply:
(a) 'shareholder' means the founding shareholder and any other person whose name is entered in the list of shareholders in accordance with Articles 15-16;
(b) 'distribution' means any financial benefit derived directly or indirectly from the SPE by a shareholder, in relation to the shares held by him, including any transfer of money or property, as well as the incurring of a debt;
(c) 'director' means any individual managing director, any member of the management, administrative board or supervisory body of an SPE;
(d) 'management body' means one or more individual managing directors, the management board (dual board) or the administrative board (unitary board), designated in the articles of association of the SPE as being responsible for the management of the SPE;
(e) 'supervisory body' means the supervisory board (dual board), designated in the articles of association of the SPE as being responsible for the supervision of the management body;
(f) 'home Member State' means the Member State in which the SPE has its registered office immediately before any transfer of its registered office to another Member State;
(g) 'host Member State' means the Member State to which the registered office of the SPE is transferred.
2. For the purposes of point (b) of paragraph 1, distributions may be made through a purchase of property, the redemption or other kind of acquisition of shares or by any other means.

Article 3. 1. An SPE shall comply with the following requirements:
(a) its capital shall be divided into shares,
(b) a shareholder shall not be liable for more than the amount he has subscribed or agreed to subscribe,
(c) it shall have legal personality,
(d) its shares shall not be offered to the public and shall not be publicly traded,
(e) it may be formed by one or more natural persons and/or legal entities, hereinafter "founding shareholders".
2. For the purposes of point (d) of paragraph 1, shares shall be regarded as 'offered to the public' where a communication is addressed to persons in any form and by any means, and it presents sufficient information on the terms of the offer and the shares to be offered so as to enable an investor to decide to purchase or subscribe to these shares, including when shares are placed through financial intermediaries.
3. For the purposes of point (e) of paragraph 1, 'legal entities' shall mean any company or firm within the meaning of the second paragraph of Article 48 of the Treaty, a European public limited-liability company as provided for in Regulation (EC) No 2001/2157, hereinafter "European Company", a European Co-operative Society as provided for in Council Regulation (EC) No 1435/2003, a European Economic Interest Grouping as provided for in Council Regulation (EEC) No 2137/85 and an SPE.

Article 4. 1. An SPE shall be governed by this Regulation and also, as regards the matters listed in Annex I, by its articles of association. However, where a matter is not covered by the articles of this Regulation or by Annex I, an SPE shall be governed by the law, including the provisions implementing Community law, which applies to private limited-liability companies in the Member State in which the SPE has its registered office, hereinafter "applicable national law".

Chapter II. Formation

Article 5. 1. Member States shall allow the formation of an SPE by any of the following methods:
(a) the creation of a SPE in accordance with this Regulation;
(b) the transformation of an existing company;
(c) the merger of existing companies;
(d) the division of an existing company.
2. Formation of the SPE by the transformation, merger or division of existing companies shall be governed by the national law applicable to the transforming company, to each of the merging companies or to the dividing company. Formation by transformation shall not give rise to the winding up of the company or any loss or interruption of its legal personality.
3. For the purposes of paragraphs 1 and 2, 'company' shall mean any form of company that may be set up under the law of the Member States, a European Company and, where applicable, an SPE.

Article 6. The name of an SPE shall be followed by the abbreviation "SPE". Only an SPE may add the abbreviation "SPE" to its name.

Article 7. An SPE shall have its registered office and its central administration or principal place of business in the Community. An SPE shall not be under any obligation to have its central administration or principal place of business in the Member State in which it has its registered office.

Article 8. 1. An SPE shall have articles of association that cover at least the matters set out in this Regulation, as provided for in Annex I.
2. The articles of association of a SPE shall be in writing and signed by every founding shareholder.
3. The articles of association and any amendments thereto may be relied upon as
follows:
(a) in relation to the shareholders and the management body of the SPE and its supervisory body, if any, from the date on which they are signed or, in the case
of amendments, adopted;
(b) in relation to third parties, in accordance with the provisions of the applicable national law implementing paragraphs 5, 6 and 7 of Article 3 of Directive
68/151/EEC.

Article 9. 1. Each SPE shall be registered in the Member State in which it has its registered office in a register designated by the applicable national law in accordance with Article 3 of
Directive 68/151/EEC24.
2. The SPE shall acquire legal personality on the date on which it is entered in the register.
3. In the case of a merger by acquisition, the acquiring company shall adopt the form of an SPE on the day the merger is registered.
In the case of a division by acquisition, the recipient company shall adopt the form of an SPE on the day the division is registered.

Article 10. 1. Application for registration shall be made by the founding shareholders of the SPE or by any person authorised by them. Such application may be made by electronic means.
2. Member States shall not require any particulars and documents to be supplied upon application for the registration of a SPE other than the following:
(a) the name of the SPE and the address of its registered office;
(b) the names, addresses and any other information necessary to identify the persons who are authorised to represent the SPE in dealings with third parties and in legal proceedings, or take part in the administration, supervision or control of the SPE;
(c) the share capital of the SPE;
(d) the share classes and the number of shares in each share class;
(e) the total number of shares;
(f) the nominal value or accountable par of the shares;
(g) the articles of association of the SPE;
(h) where the SPE was formed as a result of a transformation, merger or division of companies, the resolution on the transformation, merger or division that led to the creation of the SPE.
3. The documents and particulars referred to in paragraph 2 shall be provided in the language required by the applicable national law.
4. Registration of the SPE may be subject to only one of the following requirements:
(a) a control by an administrative or judicial body of the legality of the documents and particulars of the SPE;
(b) the certification of the documents and particulars of the SPE.
5. The SPE shall submit any change in the particulars or documents referred to in points
(a) to (g) of paragraph 2 to the register within 14 calendar days of the day on which the change takes place. After every amendment to the articles of association, the SPE shall submit its complete text to the register as amended to date.
6. The registration of an SPE shall be disclosed.

Article 11. 1. The disclosure of the documents and particulars concerning an SPE which must be disclosed under this Regulation shall be effected in accordance with the applicable national law implementing Article 3 of Directive 68/151/EEC.
2. The letters and order forms of an SPE, whether they are in paper or electronic form, as well as its website, if any, shall state the following particulars:
(a) the information necessary to identify the register referred to in Article 9, with the number of entry of the SPE in that register;

(b) the name of the SPE, the address of its registered office and, where appropriate, the fact that the company is being wound up.

Article 12. Where acts were performed on behalf of an SPE before its registration, the SPE may assume the obligations arising out of such acts after its registration. Where the SPE does not assume those obligations, the persons who performed those acts shall be jointly and severally liable, without limit.

Article 13. Branches of an SPE shall be governed by the law of the Member State in which the branch is located, including the relevant provisions implementing Council Directive 89/666/EEC25.

Chapter III. Shares

Article 14. 1. The shares of the SPE shall be entered in the list of shareholders.
2. Shares carrying the same rights and obligations shall constitute one class.
3. Subject to Article 27, the adoption of an amendment to the articles of association of the SPE which varies the rights attached to a class of shares (including any change to the procedure for varying the rights attached to a class of share) shall require the consent of a majority of not less than two-thirds of the voting rights attached to the shares issued in that class.
4. Where a share is owned by more than one person, those persons shall be regarded as one shareholder in relation to the SPE. They shall exercise their rights through a common representative, who in the absence of any notification to the SPE shall be the person whose name appears first in the list of shareholders for that share. They shall be jointly and severally liable for the commitments attached to the share.

Article 15. 1. The management body of the SPE shall draw up a list of shareholders. The list shall contain at least the following:
(a) the name and address of each shareholder;
(b) the number of shares held by the shareholder concerned, their nominal value or accountable par;
(c) where a share is owned by more than one person, the names and addresses of the co-owners and of the common representative;
(d) the date of acquisition of the shares;
(e) the amount of each consideration in cash, if any, paid or to be paid by the shareholder concerned;
(f) the value and nature of each consideration in kind, if any, provided or to be provided by the shareholder concerned;
(g) the date on which a shareholder ceases to be a member of the SPE.
2. The list of shareholders shall, unless proven otherwise, constitute evidence of the authenticity of the matters listed in points (a) to (g) of paragraph 1.
3. The list of shareholders and any amendments thereto shall be kept by the management body and may be inspected by the shareholders or third parties on request.

Article 16. 1. Subject to Article 27, a decision introducing or amending a restriction on or prohibition of the transfer of shares may be adopted only with the consent of all shareholders affected by the restriction or prohibition in question.
2. All agreements on the transfer of shares shall be in written form.
3. On notification of a transfer, the management body shall, without undue delay, enter the shareholder in the list referred to in Article 15, provided that the transfer has been executed in accordance with this Regulation and the articles of association of the SPE and the shareholder submits reasonable evidence as to his lawful ownership of the share.
4. Subject to paragraph 3, any transfer of shares shall become effective as follows:
(a) in relation to the SPE, on the day the shareholder notifies the SPE of the transfer;
(b) in relation to third parties, on the day the shareholder is entered in the list referred to in Article 15.
5. A transfer of shares shall be valid only if it complies with this Regulation and the articles of association. The provisions of the applicable national law concerning the protection of persons who acquire shares in good faith shall apply.

Article 17. 1. On the basis of a resolution of the shareholders and on an application by the SPE, the competent court may order the expulsion of a shareholder if he has caused serious harm to the SPE's interest or the

continuation of the shareholder as a member of the SPE is detrimental to its proper operation. An application to the court shall be made within 60 calendar days of the resolution of the shareholders.
2. The court shall decide whether, as an interim measure, the voting and other nonpecuniary rights of such shareholder should be suspended until a final decision is taken.
3. If the court orders the expulsion of a shareholder, it shall decide whether his shares are to be acquired by the other shareholders and/or by the SPE itself and on payment of the price of the shares.

Article 18. 1. A shareholder shall have the right to withdraw from the SPE if the activities of the SPE are being or have been conducted in a manner which causes serious harm to the interests of the shareholder as a result of one or more of the following events:
(a) the SPE has been deprived of a significant part of its assets;
(b) the registered office of the SPE has been transferred to another Member State;
(c) the activities of the SPE have changed substantially;
(d) no dividend has been distributed for at least 3 years even though the SPE's financial position would have permitted such distribution.
2. The shareholder shall submit his withdrawal in writing to the SPE stating his reasons for the withdrawal.
3. The management body of the SPE shall, on receipt of the notice referred to in paragraph 2, without undue delay, request a resolution of the shareholders on the purchase of the shareholder's shares by the other shareholders or by the SPE itself.
4. Where the shareholders of the SPE fail to adopt a resolution referred to in paragraph 3 or do not accept the shareholder's reasons for withdrawal within 30 calendar days of the submission of the notice referred to in paragraph 2, the management body shall notify the shareholder of that fact without undue delay.
5. In the case of a dispute regarding the price of the shares, their value shall be determined by an independent expert appointed by the parties or, failing an agreement between them, by the competent court or administrative authority.
6. On an application of the shareholder, the competent court may, if satisfied that the interests of the shareholder have suffered serious harm, order the acquisition of his shares by the other shareholders or by the SPE itself and the payment of the price of the shares.
An application to the court shall be made either within 60 calendar days of the resolution of the shareholders referred to in paragraph 3 or, where no resolution is adopted within 30 calendar days of the shareholder submitting his notice of withdrawal to the SPE, within 60 calendar days of the expiry of that period.

Chapter IV. Capital

Article 19. 1. Without prejudice to Article 42, the capital of the SPE shall be expressed in euro.
2. The capital of the SPE shall be fully subscribed.
3. The shares of the SPE do not need to be fully paid on issue.
4. The capital of the SPE shall be at least EUR 1.

Article 20. 1. Shareholders must pay the agreed consideration in cash or provide the agreed consideration in kind in accordance with the articles of association of the SPE.
2. Except in the case of a reduction of the share capital, shareholders may not be released from the obligation to pay or provide the agreed consideration.
3. Without prejudice to paragraphs 1 and 2, the liability of shareholders for the consideration paid or provided shall be governed by the applicable national law.

Article 21. 1. Without prejudice to Article 24, the SPE may, on the basis of a proposal of the management body, make a distribution to shareholders provided that, after the distribution, the assets of the SPE fully cover its liabilities. The SPE may not distribute those reserves that may not be distributed under its articles of association.
2. If the articles of association so require, the management body of the SPE, in addition to complying with paragraph 1, shall sign a statement, hereinafter a 'solvency certificate', before a distribution is made, certifying that the SPE will be able to pay its debts as they become due in the normal course of business within one year of the date of the distribution. Shareholders shall be provided with the solvency certificate before the resolution on the distribution referred to in Article 27 is taken. The solvency certificate shall be disclosed.

Article 22. Any shareholder who has received distributions made contrary to Article 21 must return those distributions to the SPE, provided that the SPE proves that the shareholder knew or in view of the circumstances should have been aware of the irregularities.

Article 23. 1. The SPE shall not, directly or indirectly, subscribe for its own shares.
2. In the case of acquisition by the SPE of its own shares, Articles 21 and 22 shall apply mutatis mutandis. Shares may not be purchased by the SPE unless they are fully paid. The SPE shall always have at least one issued share.
3. The right to vote and other non-pecuniary rights attached to the SPE's own shares shall be suspended, while the SPE is the registered owner of its own shares.
4. Where the SPE cancels its own shares, its share capital shall be reduced accordingly.
5. Shares acquired by the SPE in contravention of this Regulation or the articles of association shall be sold or cancelled within one year of their acquisition.
6. Subject to paragraph 5 and to the articles of association of the SPE, the cancellation of shares shall be governed by the applicable national law.
7. This Article shall apply mutatis mutandis to any shares acquired by a person acting in his own name but on behalf of the SPE.

Article 24. 1. In the case of a reduction of the share capital of the SPE, Articles 21 and 22 shall apply mutatis mutandis.
2. Following the disclosure of the resolution of the shareholders to reduce the capital of the SPE, those creditors whose claims antedate the disclosure of the resolution shall have the right to apply to the competent court for an order that the SPE provide them
with adequate safeguards. An application shall be made within 30 calendar days of the disclosure of the resolution.
3. The court may order the SPE to provide safeguards only if the creditor credibly demonstrates that due to the reduction in the capital the satisfaction of his claims is at stake, and that no adequate safeguards have been obtained from the SPE.
4. A capital reduction shall take effect as follows:
(a) where the SPE has no creditors at the time when the resolution is adopted, on its adoption;
(b) where the SPE has creditors at the time when the resolution is adopted and no creditor has made an application within 30 calendar days of the disclosure of the resolution of the shareholders, on the thirty-first calendar day following that disclosure;
(c) where the SPE has creditors at the time when the resolution is adopted and an application is made by a creditor within 30 calendar days of the disclosure of the resolution of shareholders, on the first date on which the SPE has complied with all orders by the competent court to provide adequate safeguards or, if earlier, the first date on which the court has determined, in relation to all applications that the SPE need not provide any safeguards.
5. If the purpose of a reduction of the capital is to offset losses incurred by the SPE, the reduced amount may be used only for this purpose and shall not be distributed to the shareholders.
6. A capital reduction shall be disclosed.
7. In the case of a capital reduction, the equal treatment of shareholders in the same position shall be ensured.

Article 25. 1. An SPE shall be subject to the requirements of the applicable national law as regards preparation, filing, auditing and publication of accounts.
2. The management body shall keep the books of the SPE. The bookkeeping of the SPE shall be governed by the applicable national law.

Chapter V. Organisation of the SPE

Article 26. 1. The SPE shall have a management body, which shall be responsible for the management of the SPE. The management body may exercise all the powers of the SPE not required by this Regulation or the articles of association to be exercised by the shareholders.
2. The shareholders shall determine the organisation of the SPE, subject to this Regulation.

Article 27. 1. Without prejudice to paragraph 2, at least the following matters shall be decided by a resolution of the shareholders by a majority as defined in the articles of association of the SPE:
(a) variation of rights attaching to shares;
(b) expulsion of a shareholder;
(c) withdrawal of a shareholder;
(d) approval of the annual accounts;
(e) distribution to the shareholders;
(f) acquisition of own shares;
(g) redemption of shares;

(h) increase of share capital;
(i) reduction of share capital;
(j) appointment and removal of directors and their terms of office;
(k) where the SPE has an auditor, appointment and removal of the auditor;
(l) transfer of the registered office of the SPE to another Member State;
(m) transformation of the SPE;
(n) mergers and divisions;
(o) winding up;
(p) amendments to the articles of association, not covering matters mentioned in points (a) to (o).
2. Resolutions on the matters indicated in points (a), (b), (c), (i), (l), (m) (n), (o) and (p) of paragraph 1 shall be taken by a qualified majority. For the purposes of the first subparagraph, the qualified majority may not be less than two-thirds of the total voting rights attached to the shares issued by the SPE.
3. The adoption of resolutions shall not require the organisation of a general meeting. The management body shall provide all shareholders with the proposals for resolutions together with sufficient information to enable them to take an informed decision. Resolutions shall be recorded in writing. Copies of the decisions taken shall be sent to every shareholder.
4. Resolutions of the shareholders shall comply with this Regulation and the articles of association of the SPE. The right of shareholders to challenge resolutions shall be governed by the applicable national law.
5. If the SPE has only one shareholder, he shall exercise the rights and fulfill the obligations of the shareholders of the SPE set out in this Regulation and the articles of association of the SPE.
6. Resolutions on matters indicated in paragraph 1 shall be disclosed.
7. Resolutions may be relied on as follows:
(a) in relation to the shareholders, the management body of the SPE and its supervisory body, if any, on the date they are adopted,
(b) in relation to third parties, in accordance with the provisions of the applicable national law implementing paragraphs 5, 6 and 7 of Article 3 of Directive 68/151/EEC.

Article 28. 1. Shareholders shall have the right to be duly informed and to ask questions to the management body about resolutions, annual accounts and all other matters relating to the activities of the SPE.
2. The management body may refuse to give access to the information only if doing so could cause serious harm to the business interests of the SPE.

Article 29. 1. Shareholders holding 5% of the voting rights attached to the shares of the SPE shall have the right to request the management body to submit a proposal for a resolution to the shareholders. The request must state the reasons and indicate the matters that should be subject to such resolution. If the request is refused or if the management body does not submit a proposal within 14 calendar days of receiving the request, the shareholders concerned may then submit a proposal for a resolution to the shareholders regarding the matters in question.
2. In the case of suspicion of serious breach of law or of the articles of association of the SPE, shareholders holding 5% of the voting rights attached to the shares of the SPE shall have the right to request the competent court or administrative authority to appoint an independent expert to investigate and report on the findings of the investigation to shareholders.
The expert shall be allowed access to the documents and records of the SPE and to require information from the management body.
3. The articles of association may grant the rights set out in paragraphs 1 and 2 to individual shareholders or to shareholders holding less than 5% of the voting rights attached to the shares of the SPE.

Article 30. 1. Only a natural person may be a director of an SPE.
2. A person who acts as a director without having been formally appointed shall be considered a director as regards all duties and liabilities to which the latter are subject.
3. A person who is disqualified under national law from serving as a director of a company by a judicial or administrative decision of a Member State may not become or serve as a director of an SPE.
4. Disqualification of a person serving as a director of the SPE shall be governed by the applicable national law.

Article 31. 1. A director shall have a duty to act in the best interests of the SPE. He shall act with the care and skill that can reasonably be required in the conduct of the business.
2. The duties of directors shall be owed to the SPE.

3. Subject to the articles of association of the SPE, a director shall avoid any situation that can be reasonably regarded as likely to give rise to an actual or potential conflict between his personal interests and those of the SPE or between his obligations towards the SPE and his duty to any other legal or natural person.
4. A director of the SPE shall be liable to the company for any act or omission in breach of his duties deriving from this Regulation, the articles of association of the SPE or a resolution of shareholders which causes loss or damage to the SPE. Where such breach has been committed by more than one director, all directors concerned shall be jointly and severally liable.
5. Without prejudice to the provisions of this Regulation, the liability of directors shall be governed by the applicable national law.

Article 32. Related party transactions shall be governed by the provisions of the applicable national law implementing Council Directives 78/660/EEC26 and 83/349/EEC27.

Article 33. 1. The SPE shall be represented in relation to third parties by one or more directors. Acts undertaken by the directors shall be binding on the SPE even if they are not within the objects of the SPE.
2. The articles of association of the SPE may provide that directors are to exercise jointly the general power of representation. Any other limitation of the powers of the directors, following from the articles of association, a resolution of shareholders or a decision of the management or supervisory body, if any, may not be relied on against third parties even if they have been disclosed.
3. Directors may delegate the right to represent the SPE in accordance with the articles of association.

Chapter VI. Employee participation

Article 34. 1. The SPE shall be subject to the rules on employee participation, if any, applicable in the Member State in which it has its registered office, subject to the provisions of this Article.
2. In the case of the transfer of the registered office of an SPE Article 38 shall apply.
3. In the case of a cross-border merger of an SPE with an SPE or other company registered in another Member State, the provisions of the laws of the Member States implementing Directive 2005/56/EC of the European Parliament and of the Council28 shall apply.

Chapter VII. Transfer of the registered office of the SPE

Article 35. 1. The registered office of an SPE may be transferred to another Member State in accordance with this Chapter. The transfer of the registered office of an SPE shall not result in the winding-up of the SPE or in any interruption or loss of the SPE's legal personality or affect any right or obligation under any contract entered into by the SPE existing before the transfer.
2. Paragraph 1 shall not apply to SPEs against which proceedings for winding-up, liquidation, insolvency or suspension of payments have been brought, or in respect of which preventive measures have been taken by the competent authorities to avoid the opening of such proceedings.
3. A transfer shall take effect on the date of registration of the SPE in the host Member State. From that date, for matters covered by the second paragraph of Article 4, the SPE shall be regulated by the law of the host Member State.
4. For the purpose of judicial or administrative proceedings commenced before the transfer of the registered office, the SPE shall be considered, following the registration referred to in paragraph 3, as having its registered office in the home Member State.

Article 36. 1. The management body of an SPE planning a transfer shall draw up a transfer proposal, which shall include at least the following particulars:
(a) the name of the SPE and the address of its registered office in the home Member State;
(b) the name of the SPE and the address of its proposed registered office in the host Member State;
(c) the proposed articles of association for the SPE in the host Member State;
(d) the proposed timetable for the transfer;
(e) the date from which it is proposed that the transactions of the SPE are to be regarded for accounting purposes as having been carried out in the host Member State;
(f) the consequences of the transfer for employees, and the proposed measures concerning them;
(g) where appropriate, detailed information on the transfer of the central administration or principal place of business of the SPE.

2. At least one month before the resolution of the shareholders referred to in paragraph 4 is taken, the management body of the SPE shall:
(a) submit the transfer proposal to the shareholders and employee representatives, or where there are no such representatives, to the employees of the SPE for examination and make it available to the creditors for inspection;
(b) disclose the transfer proposal.
3. The management body of the SPE shall draw up a report to the shareholders explaining and justifying the legal and economic aspects of the proposed transfer and setting out the implications of the transfer for shareholders, creditors and employees. The report shall be submitted to the shareholders and the employee representatives, or where there are no such representatives, to the employees themselves together with the transfer proposal. Where the management body receives in time the opinion of the employee representatives on the transfer, that opinion shall be submitted to the shareholders.
4. The transfer proposal shall be submitted to the shareholders for approval in accordance with the rules of the articles of association of the SPE relating to the amendment of the articles of association.
5. Where the SPE is subject to an employee participation regime, shareholders may reserve the right to make the implementation of the transfer conditional on their express ratification of the arrangements with respect to the participation of employees in the host Member State.
6. The protection of any minority shareholders who oppose the transfer and of the creditors of the SPE shall be governed by the law of the home Member State.

Article 37. 1. Each Member State shall designate a competent authority to scrutinise the legality of the transfer by verifying compliance with the transfer procedure laid down in Article 36.
2. The competent authority of the home Member State shall verify, without undue delay, that the requirements of Article 36 have been met and, if that is found to be the case, shall issue a certificate confirming that all the formalities required under the transfer procedure have been completed in the home Member State.
3. Within one month of the receipt of the certificate referred to in paragraph 2, the SPE shall present the following documents to the competent authority in the host Member State:
(a) the certificate provided for in paragraph 2;
(b) the proposed articles of association for the SPE in the host Member State, as approved by the shareholders;
(c) the transfer proposal, as approved by the shareholders. Those documents shall be deemed to be sufficient to enable the registration of the SPE in the host Member State.
4. The competent authority in the host Member State shall, within 14 calendar days of receipt of the documents referred to in paragraph 3, verify that the substantive and formal conditions required for the transfer of the registered office are met and if that
is found to be the case, take the measures necessary for the registration of the SPE.
5. The competent authority of the host Member State may refuse to register an SPE only on the grounds that the SPE does not meet all the substantive or formal requirements under this Chapter. The SPE shall be registered when it has fulfilled all requirements under this Chapter.
6. Using the notification form set out in Annex II, the competent authority of the host Member State shall, without undue delay, notify the competent authority responsible for removing the SPE from the register in the home Member State of the registration of the SPE in the host Member State. Removal from the register shall be effected as soon as, but not before, a notification has been received.
7. Registrations in the host Member State and removals from the register in the home Member State shall be disclosed.

Article 38. 1. The SPE shall be subject, as from the date of registration, to the rules in force in the host Member State, if any, concerning arrangements for the participation of employees.
2. Paragraph 1 shall not apply where the employees of the SPE in the home Member State account for at least one third of the total number of employees of the SPE including subsidiaries or branches of the SPE in any Member State, and where one of the following conditions is met:
(a) the legislation of the host Member State does not provide for at least the same level of participation as that operated in the SPE in the home Member State prior to its registration in the host Member State. The level of employee participation shall be measured by reference to the proportion of employee representatives amongst the members of the administrative or supervisory body or their committees or of the management group which covers the profit units
of the SPE, subject to employee representation;
(b) the legislation of the host Member State does not confer on the employees of establishments of the SPE that are situated in other Member States the same entitlement to exercise participation rights as such employees enjoyed before the transfer.

3. Where one of the conditions set out in points a) or b) of paragraph 2 is met, the management body of the SPE shall take the necessary steps, as soon as possible, after disclosure of the transfer proposal, to start negotiations with the representatives of the SPE's employees with a view to reaching an agreement on arrangements for the participation of the employees.

4. The agreement between the management body of the SPE and the representatives of the employees shall specify:

(a) the scope of the agreement;

(b) where, during the negotiations, the parties decide to establish arrangements for participation in the SPE following the transfer, the substance of those arrangements including, where applicable, the number of members in the company's administrative or supervisory body employees will be entitled to elect, appoint, recommend or oppose, the procedures as to how these members may be elected, appointed, recommended or opposed by employees, and their rights;

(c) the date of entry into force of the agreement and its duration, and any cases in which the agreement should be renegotiated and the procedure for its renegotiation.

5. Negotiations shall be limited to a period of six months. The parties may agree to extend negotiations beyond this period for an additional six-month period. The negotiations shall otherwise be governed by the law of the home Member State.

6. In the absence of an agreement, the participation arrangements existing in the home Member State shall be maintained.

Chapter VIII. Restructering, dissolution, and nullity

Article 39. The transformation, merger and division of the SPE shall be governed by the applicable national law.

Article 40. 1. The SPE shall be dissolved in the following circumstances:
(a) by expiry of the period for which it was established;
(b) by the resolution of the shareholders;
(c) in cases set out in the applicable national law.
2. Winding-up shall be governed by the applicable national law.
3. Liquidation, insolvency, suspension of payments and similar procedures shall be governed by the applicable national law and by Council Regulation (EC) No 1346/200029.
4. Dissolution of the SPE shall be disclosed.

Article 41. The nullity of the SPE shall be governed by the provisions of the applicable national law implementing Article 11(1) of Directive 68/151/EEC, points (a), (b), (c) and (e), except for the reference in point (c) to the objects of the company, of Article 11(2) and Article 12 of that Directive.

Chapter IX. Additional and transitional provisions

Article 42. 1. Member States in which the third phase of the economic and monetary union (EMU) does not apply may require SPEs having their registered office in their territory to express their capital in the national currency. An SPE may also express its capital in euro. The national currency/euro conversion rate shall be as on the last day of the month preceding the registration of the SPE.

2. An SPE may prepare and publish its annual and, where applicable, consolidated accounts in euro in Member States where the third phase of the economic and monetary union (EMU) does not apply. However such Member States may also require SPEs to prepare and publish their annual and, where applicable, consolidated accounts in the national currency in accordance with the applicable national law.

Chapter X. Final provisions

Article 43. Member States shall make such provision as is appropriate to ensure the effective application of this Regulation.

Article 44. The Member States shall lay down the rules on penalties applicable to infringements of the provisions of this Regulation and shall take all measures necessary to ensure that they are implemented. The penalties provided for must be effective, proportionate and dissuasive. The Member States shall notify those provisions to the Commission by 1 July 2010 at the latest and shall notify it without delay of any subsequent amendment affecting them.

Article 45. Member States shall notify the form of private limited-liability company referred to in the second paragraph of Article 4 to the Commission by 1 July 2010 at the latest. The Commission shall publish this information in the Official Journal of the European Union.

Article 46. Obligations of authorities responsible for registers
1. The authorities responsible for the register referred to in Article 9(1) shall notify the Commission before 31 March each year, of the name, registered office and registration number of the SPEs registered in and removed from the register in the preceding year as well as the total number of registered SPEs.
2. The authorities referred to in paragraph 1 shall cooperate with each other to ensure that the documents and particulars of the SPEs listed in Article 10(2) are also accessible through the registers of all other Member States.

Article 47. The Commission shall, no later than 30 June 2015, review the application of this Regulation.

Article 48. This Regulation shall enter into force on the twentieth day following that of its publication in the Official Journal of the European Union. It shall apply from 1 July 2010. This Regulation shall be binding in its entirety and directly applicable in all Member States.

Annex I. The articles of association of an SPE shall regulate at least the following:
Chapter II – Formation
– the name of the SPE,
– the names and addresses of the founding shareholders of the SPE and the nominal value or accountable par of the shares held by them,
– the initial capital of the SPE,

Chapter III. Shares
– whether sub-division, consolidation or redenomination of the shares is permitted and any applicable requirements,
– the pecuniary and non-pecuniary rights and the obligations attached to the shares (share classes), in particular
– (a) the participation in the assets and profits of the company, if any,
– (b) the votes attached to the shares, if any,
– the procedure for agreeing on any variation of the rights and obligations attached to the shares (share classes), and, subject to Article 14(3), the required majority of voting rights,
– any pre-emption rights either on issue or on transfer of shares, if any, and any applicable requirements,
– where the transfer of shares is restricted or prohibited, the details of the restriction or prohibition, in particular the form, time limit, the applicable procedure, and the rules applicable in the event of the death or dissolution of a shareholder, – where the approval of the share transfer by the SPE or by the shareholders is required or other rights are provided for shareholders or for the SPE on the transfer of shares (for example, right of first refusal), a deadline by which the transferor is to be notified of the decision,
– whether, in addition to Article 17, shareholders have any rights to require other shareholders to sell their shares, and any applicable requirements,
– whether, in addition to Article 18, shareholders have the right to sell their shares to other shareholders or to the SPE, who are obliged to buy those shares, and the applicable requirements,

Chapter IV. Capital
– the financial year of the SPE and how it may be changed,
– whether the SPE is required to establish reserves and if so, the type of reserve, the circumstances in which it is to be established and whether it is distributable,
– whether consideration in kind are to be evaluated by an independent expert and any formalities that must be complied with,
– the time when the payment or provision of the consideration is to be made and any conditions relating to such payment or provision,
– whether or not the SPE can provide financial assistance, in particular advance funds, make loans or provide security, with a view to the acquisition of its shares by a third party,
– whether interim dividends can be paid and any applicable requirements,
– whether the management body is required to sign a solvency certificate before a distribution is made, and the applicable requirements,
– the procedure the SPE must follow to recover any unlawful distribution,

– whether the acquisition of own shares is permitted and, if permitted, the procedure to be followed, including the conditions under which the shares may be held, transferred or cancelled,
– the procedure for increasing, reducing or otherwise changing the share capital, and any applicable requirements,
Chapter V – Organisation of the SPE
– the method of adopting shareholder resolutions,
– subject to the provisions of this Regulation, the majority required to adopt shareholder resolutions,
– the resolutions to be adopted by the shareholders, in addition to those listed in Article 27(1), the quorum and the required majority of voting rights,
– subject to Articles 21, 27 and 29, the rules on proposing resolutions,
– the period of time and the manner in which the shareholders are to be informed of proposals for shareholder resolutions and, if the articles of association provide for general meetings, general meetings,
– the way in which the shareholders obtain the text of any proposed shareholder resolution and any other preparatory documents in relation to the adoption of a resolution,
– the manner in which copies of an adopted resolution are made available to the shareholders,
– where the articles of association provide for the adoption of some or all resolutions at a general meeting, the manner of convening the general meeting, the working methods and the rules on voting by proxy,
– the procedure and time limits for the SPE to respond to requests from shareholders for information, to grant access to the documents of the SPE, and to notify resolutions that have been adopted by shareholders,
– whether the SPE's management body is composed of one or more managing directors, a management board (dual board) or an administrative board (unitary board),
– where there is an administrative board (unitary board), its composition and organisation,
– where there is a management board (dual board), its composition and organisation,
– where there is a management board (dual board) or one or more managing directors, whether the SPE has a supervisory body, and if so, its composition and organisation and its relationship with the management body,
– any eligibility criterion of directors,
– the procedure for appointing and removing directors,
– whether the SPE has an auditor and where the articles of association provide that the SPE should have an auditor, the procedure for his appointment, removal and resignation,
– any specific duties of directors other than those mentioned in this Regulation,
– whether situations involving an actual or potential conflict of interest by a director may be authorised and, if so, an indication of who may authorise such a conflict and the applicable requirements and procedures for the authorisation of such a conflict,
– whether related party transactions as referred to in Article 32 need to be authorised and the applicable requirements,
– the rules on representation of the SPE by the management body, in particular if the directors have the right to represent the SPE jointly or separately and any delegation of this right,
– the rules on delegation of any management power to another person.

Annex II. Notification form concerning the registration of the transfer of the registered office of an SPE notification concerning the registration of the transfer of the registered office of a European private company (SPE)

Directive 2009/38/EC of the European Parliament and of the Council of 6 May 2009 on the establishment of a European Works Council or a procedure in Community-scale undertakings and Community-scale groups of undertakings for the purposes of informing and consulting employees (Recast) Text with EEA relevance (*OJ* L 122 , 16.05.2009 pp. 28 – 44) [footnotes omitted].

THE EUROPEAN PARLIAMENT AND THE COUNCIL OF THE EUROPEAN UNION,
Having regard to the Treaty establishing the European Community, and in particular Article 137 thereof,
Having regard to the proposal from the Commission,
Having regard to the opinion of the European Economic and Social Committee ,
Having consulted the Committee of the Regions,
Acting in accordance with the procedure referred to in Article 251 of the Treaty,
Whereas:
(1) A number of substantive changes are to be made to Council Directive 94/45/EC of 22 September 1994 on the establishment of a European Works Council or a procedure in Community-scale undertakings and Community-scale groups of undertakings for the purposes of informing and consulting employees. In the interests of clarity, that Directive should be recast.
(2) Pursuant to Article 15 of Directive 94/45/EC, the Commission has, in consultation with the Member States and with management and labour at European level, reviewed the operation of that Directive and, in particular, examined whether the workforce size thresholds are appropriate, with a view to proposing suitable amendments where necessary.
(3) Having consulted the Member States and management and labour at European level, the Commission submitted, on 4 April 2000, a report on the application of Directive 94/45/EC to the European Parliament and to the Council.
(4) Pursuant to Article 138(2) of the Treaty, the Commission consulted management and labour at Community level on the possible direction of Community action in this area.
(5) Following this consultation, the Commission considered that Community action was advisable and again consulted management and labour at Community level on the content of the planned proposal, pursuant to Article 138(3) of the Treaty.
(6) Following this second phase of consultation, management and labour have not informed the Commission of their shared wish to initiate the process which might lead to the conclusion of an agreement, as provided for in Article 138(4) of the Treaty.
(7) It is necessary to modernise Community legislation on transnational information and consultation of employees with a view to ensuring the effectiveness of employees' transnational information and consultation rights, increasing the proportion of European Works Councils established while enabling the continuous functioning of existing agreements, resolving the problems encountered in the practical application of Directive 94/45/EC and remedying the lack of legal certainty resulting from some of its provisions or the absence of certain provisions, and ensuring that Community legislative instruments on information and consultation of employees are better linked.
(8) Pursuant to Article 136 of the Treaty, one particular objective of the Community and the Member States is to promote dialogue between management and labour.
(9) This Directive is part of the Community framework intended to support and complement the action taken by Member States in the field of information and consultation of employees. This framework should keep to a minimum the burden on undertakings or establishments while ensuring the effective exercise of the rights granted.
(10) The functioning of the internal market involves a process of concentrations of undertakings, cross-border mergers, take-overs, joint ventures and, consequently, a transnationalisation of undertakings and groups of undertakings. If economic activities are to develop in a harmonious fashion, undertakings and groups of undertakings operating in two or more Member States must inform and consult the representatives of those of their employees who are affected by their decisions.
(11) Procedures for informing and consulting employees as embodied in legislation or practice in the Member States are often not geared to the transnational structure of the entity which takes the decisions affecting those employees. This may lead to the unequal treatment of employees affected by decisions within one and the same undertaking or group of undertakings.
(12) Appropriate provisions must be adopted to ensure that the employees of Community-scale undertakings or Community-scale groups of undertakings are properly informed and consulted when decisions which affect them are taken in a Member State other than that in which they are employed.
(13) In order to guarantee that the employees of undertakings or groups of undertakings operating in two or more Member States are properly informed and consulted, it is necessary to set up European Works Councils or to create other suitable procedures for the transnational information and consultation of employees.

PART VIII. EUROPEAN COMPANY LAW

(14) The arrangements for informing and consulting employees need to be defined and implemented in such a way as to ensure their effectiveness with regard to the provisions of this Directive. To that end, informing and consulting the European Works Council should make it possible for it to give an opinion to the undertaking in a timely fashion, without calling into question the ability of undertakings to adapt. Only dialogue at the level where directions are prepared and effective involvement of employees' representatives make it possible to anticipate and manage change.
(15) Workers and their representatives must be guaranteed information and consultation at the relevant level of management and representation, according to the subject under discussion. To achieve this, the competence and scope of action of a European Works Council must be distinct from that of national representative bodies and must be limited to transnational matters.
(16) The transnational character of a matter should be determined by taking account of both the scope of its potential effects, and the level of management and representation that it involves. For this purpose, matters which concern the entire undertaking or group or at least two Member States are considered to be transnational. These include matters which, regardless of the number of Member States involved, are of importance for the European workforce in terms of the scope of their potential effects or which involve transfers of activities between Member States.
(17) It is necessary to have a definition of "controlling undertaking" relating solely to this Directive, without prejudice to the definitions of "group" or "control" in other acts.
(18) The mechanisms for informing and consulting employees in undertakings or groups of undertakings operating in two or more Member States must encompass all of the establishments or, as the case may be, the group's undertakings located within the Member States, regardless of whether the undertaking or the group's controlling undertaking has its central management inside or outside the territory of the Member States.
(19) In accordance with the principle of autonomy of the parties, it is for the representatives of employees and the management of the undertaking or the group's controlling undertaking to determine by agreement the nature, composition, the function, mode of operation, procedures and financial resources of European Works Councils or other information and consultation procedures so as to suit their own particular circumstances.
(20) In accordance with the principle of subsidiarity, it is for the Member States to determine who the employees' representatives are and in particular to provide, if they consider appropriate, for a balanced representation of different categories of employees.
(21) It is necessary to clarify the concepts of information and consultation of employees, in accordance with the definitions in the most recent Directives on this subject and those which apply within a national framework, with the objectives of reinforcing the effectiveness of dialogue at transnational level, permitting suitable linkage between the national and transnational levels of dialogue and ensuring the legal certainty required for the application of this Directive.
(22) The definition of "information" needs to take account of the goal of allowing employees representatives to carry out an appropriate examination, which implies that the information be provided at such time, in such fashion and with such content as are appropriate without slowing down the decision-making process in undertakings.
(23) The definition of "consultation" needs to take account of the goal of allowing for the expression of an opinion which will be useful to the decision-making process, which implies that the consultation must take place at such time, in such fashion and with such content as are appropriate.
(24) The information and consultation provisions laid down in this Directive must be implemented in the case of an undertaking or a group's controlling undertaking which has its central management outside the territory of the Member States by its representative agent, to be designated if necessary, in one of the Member States or, in the absence of such an agent, by the establishment or controlled undertaking employing the greatest number of employees in the Member States.
(25) The responsibility of undertakings or groups of undertakings in the transmission of the information required to commence negotiations must be specified in a way that enables employees to determine whether the undertaking or group of undertakings where they work is a Community-scale undertaking or group of undertakings and to make the necessary contacts to draw up a request to commence negotiations.
(26) The special negotiating body must represent employees from the various Member States in a balanced fashion. Employees' representatives must be able to cooperate to define their positions in relation to negotiations with the central management.
(27) Recognition must be given to the role that recognised trade union organisations can play in negotiating and renegotiating the constituent agreements of European Works Councils, providing support to employees' representatives who express a need for such support. In order to enable them to monitor the establishment of new European Works Councils and promote best practice, competent trade union and employers' organisations recognised as European social partners shall be informed of the commencement of negotiations. Recognised competent European trade union and employers' organisations are those social partner organisations that are

consulted by the Commission under Article 138 of the Treaty. The list of those organisations is updated and published by the Commission.

(28) The agreements governing the establishment and operation of European Works Councils must include the methods for modifying, terminating, or renegotiating them when necessary, particularly where the make-up or structure of the undertaking or group of undertakings is modified.

(29) Such agreements must lay down the arrangements for linking the national and transnational levels of information and consultation of employees appropriate for the particular conditions of the undertaking or group of undertakings. The arrangements must be defined in such a way that they respect the competences and areas of action of the employee representation bodies, in particular with regard to anticipating and managing change.

(30) Those agreements must provide, where necessary, for the establishment and operation of a select committee in order to permit coordination and greater effectiveness of the regular activities of the European Works Council, together with information and consultation at the earliest opportunity where exceptional circumstances arise.

(31) Employees' representatives may decide not to seek the setting-up of a European Works Council or the parties concerned may decide on other procedures for the transnational information and consultation of employees.

(32) Provision should be made for certain subsidiary requirements to apply should the parties so decide or in the event of the central management refusing to initiate negotiations or in the absence of agreement subsequent to such negotiations.

(33) In order to perform their representative role fully and to ensure that the European Works Council is useful, employees' representatives must report to the employees whom they represent and must be able to receive the training they require.

(34) Provision should be made for the employees' representatives acting within the framework of this Directive to enjoy, when exercising their functions, the same protection and guarantees as those provided to employees' representatives by the legislation and/or practice of the country of employment. They must not be subject to any discrimination as a result of the lawful exercise of their activities and must enjoy adequate protection as regards dismissal and other sanctions.

(35) The Member States must take appropriate measures in the event of failure to comply with the obligations laid down in this Directive.

(36) In accordance with the general principles of Community law, administrative or judicial procedures, as well as sanctions that are effective, dissuasive and proportionate in relation to the seriousness of the offence, should be applicable in cases of infringement of the obligations arising from this Directive.

(37) For reasons of effectiveness, consistency and legal certainty, there is a need for linkage between the Directives and the levels of informing and consulting employees established by Community and national law and/or practice. Priority must be given to negotiations on these procedures for linking information within each undertaking or group of undertakings. If there are no agreements on this subject and where decisions likely to lead to substantial changes in work organisation or contractual relations are envisaged, the process must be conducted at both national and European level in such a way that it respects the competences and areas of action of the employee representation bodies. Opinions expressed by the European Works Council should be without prejudice to the competence of the central management to carry out the necessary consultations in accordance with the schedules provided for in national legislation and/or practice. National legislation and/or practice may have to be adapted to ensure that the European Works Council can, where applicable, receive information earlier or at the same time as the national employee representation bodies, but must not reduce the general level of protection of employees.

(38) This Directive should be without prejudice to the information and consultation procedures referred to in Directive 2002/14/EC of the European Parliament and of the Council of 11 March 2002 establishing a general framework for informing and consulting employees in the European Community and to the specific procedures referred to in Article 2 of Council Directive 98/59/EC of 20 July 1998 on the approximation of the laws of the Member States relating to collective redundancies and Article 7 of Council Directive 2001/23/EC of 12 March 2001 on the approximation of the laws of the Member States relating to the safeguarding of employees' rights in the event of transfers of undertakings, businesses or parts of undertakings or businesses.

(39) Special treatment should be accorded to Community-scale undertakings and groups of undertakings in which there existed, on 22 September 1996, an agreement, covering the entire workforce, providing for the transnational information and consultation of employees.

(40) Where the structure of the undertaking or group of undertakings changes significantly, for example, due to a merger, acquisition or division, the existing European Works Council(s) must be adapted. This adaptation must be carried out as a priority pursuant to the clauses of the applicable agreement, if such clauses permit the required adaptation to be carried out. If this is not the case and a request establishing the need is made, negotiations, in which the members of the existing European Works Council(s) must be involved, will commence on a new agreement. In order to permit the information and consultation of employees during the often decisive period when

the structure is changed, the existing European Works Council(s) must be able to continue to operate, possibly with adaptations, until a new agreement is concluded. Once a new agreement is signed, the previously established councils must be dissolved, and the agreements instituting them must be terminated, regardless of their provisions on validity or termination.

(41) Unless this adaptation clause is applied, the agreements in force should be allowed to continue in order to avoid their obligatory renegotiation when this would be unnecessary. Provision should be made so that, as long as agreements concluded prior to 22 September 1996 under Article 13(1) of Directive 94/45/EC or under Article 3(1) of Directive 97/74/EC remain in force, the obligations arising from this Directive should not apply to them. Furthermore, this Directive does not establish a general obligation to renegotiate agreements concluded pursuant to Article 6 of Directive 94/45/EC between 22 September 1996 and 5 June 2011.

(42) Without prejudice to the possibility of the parties to decide otherwise, a European Works Council set up in the absence of agreement between the parties must, in order to fulfil the objective of this Directive, be kept informed and consulted on the activities of the undertaking or group of undertakings so that it may assess the possible impact on employees' interests in at least two different Member States. To that end, the undertaking or controlling undertaking must be required to communicate to the employees' appointed representatives general information concerning the interests of employees and information relating more specifically to those aspects of the activities of the undertaking or group of undertakings which affect employees' interests. The European Works Council must be able to deliver an opinion at the end of the meeting.

(43) Certain decisions having a significant effect on the interests of employees must be the subject of information and consultation of the employees' appointed representatives as soon as possible.

(44) The content of the subsidiary requirements which apply in the absence of an agreement and serve as a reference in the negotiations must be clarified and adapted to developments in the needs and practices relating to transnational information and consultation. A distinction should be made between fields where information must be provided and fields where the European Works Council must also be consulted, which involves the possibility of obtaining a reasoned response to any opinions expressed. To enable the select committee to play the necessary coordinating role and to deal effectively with exceptional circumstances, that committee must be able to have up to five members and be able to consult regularly.

(45) Since the objective of this Directive, namely the improvement of the right to information and to consultation of employees in Community-scale undertakings and Community-scale groups of undertakings, cannot be sufficiently achieved by the Member States and can therefore be better achieved at Community level, the Community may adopt measures, in accordance with the principle of subsidiarity as set out in Article 5 of the Treaty. In accordance with the principle of proportionality as set out in that Article, this Directive does not go beyond what is necessary in order to achieve that objective.

(46) This Directive respects fundamental rights and observes in particular the principles recognised by the Charter of Fundamental Rights of the European Union. In particular, this Directive seeks to ensure full respect for the right of workers or their representatives to be guaranteed information and consultation in good time at the appropriate levels in the cases and under the conditions provided for by Community law and national laws and practices (Article 27 of the Charter of Fundamental Rights of the European Union).

(47) The obligation to transpose this Directive into national law should be confined to those provisions which represent a substantive change as compared with the earlier Directives. The obligation to transpose the provisions which are unchanged arises under the earlier Directives.

(48) In accordance with point 34 of the Interinstitutional Agreement on better law-making, Member States are encouraged to draw up, for themselves and in the interests of the Community, tables illustrating, as far as possible, the correlation between this Directive and the transposition measures, and to make them public.

(49) This Directive should be without prejudice to the obligations of the Member States relating to the time limits set out in Annex II, Part B for transposition into national law and application of the Directives,

HAVE ADOPTED THIS DIRECTIVE:

Section I General

Article 1. 1. The purpose of this Directive is to improve the right to information and to consultation of employees in Community-scale undertakings and Community-scale groups of undertakings.

2. To that end, a European Works Council or a procedure for informing and consulting employees shall be established in every Community-scale undertaking and every Community-scale group of undertakings, where requested in the manner laid down in Article 5(1), with the purpose of informing and consulting employees. The arrangements for informing and consulting employees shall be defined and implemented in such a way as to ensure their effectiveness and to enable the undertaking or group of undertakings to take decisions effectively.

3. Information and consultation of employees must occur at the relevant level of management and representation, according to the subject under discussion. To achieve that, the competence of the European Works Council and the scope of the information and consultation procedure for employees governed by this Directive shall be limited to transnational issues.

4. Matters shall be considered to be transnational where they concern the Community-scale undertaking or Community-scale group of undertakings as a whole, or at least two undertakings or establishments of the undertaking or group situated in two different Member States.

5. Notwithstanding paragraph 2, where a Community-scale group of undertakings within the meaning of Article 2(1)(c) comprises one or more undertakings or groups of undertakings which are Community-scale undertakings or Community-scale groups of undertakings within the meaning of Article 2(1)(a) or (c), a European Works Council shall be established at the level of the group unless the agreements referred to in Article 6 provide otherwise.

6. Unless a wider scope is provided for in the agreements referred to in Article 6, the powers and competence of European Works Councils and the scope of information and consultation procedures established to achieve the purpose specified in paragraph 1 shall, in the case of a Community-scale undertaking, cover all the establishments located within the Member States and, in the case of a Community-scale group of undertakings, all group undertakings located within the Member States.

7. Member States may provide that this Directive shall not apply to merchant navy crews.

Article 2. 1. For the purposes of this Directive:
(a) "Community-scale undertaking" means any undertaking with at least 1000 employees within the Member States and at least 150 employees in each of at least two Member States;
(b) "group of undertakings" means a controlling undertaking and its controlled undertakings;
(c) "Community-scale group of undertakings" means a group of undertakings with the following characteristics:
- at least 1000 employees within the Member States,
- at least two group undertakings in different Member States, and
- at least one group undertaking with at least 150 employees in one Member State and at least one other group undertaking with at least 150 employees in another Member State;
(d) "employees' representatives" means the employees' representatives provided for by national law and/or practice;
(e) "central management" means the central management of the Community-scale undertaking or, in the case of a Community-scale group of undertakings, of the controlling undertaking;
(f) "information" means transmission of data by the employer to the employees' representatives in order to enable them to acquaint themselves with the subject matter and to examine it; information shall be given at such time, in such fashion and with such content as are appropriate to enable employees' representatives to undertake an in-depth assessment of the possible impact and, where appropriate, prepare for consultations with the competent organ of the Community-scale undertaking or Community-scale group of undertakings;
(g) "consultation" means the establishment of dialogue and exchange of views between employees' representatives and central management or any more appropriate level of management, at such time, in such fashion and with such content as enables employees' representatives to express an opinion on the basis of the information provided about the proposed measures to which the consultation is related, without prejudice to the responsibilities of the management, and within a reasonable time, which may be taken into account within the Community-scale undertaking or Community-scale group of undertakings;
(h) "European Works Council" means a council established in accordance with Article 1(2) or the provisions of Annex I, with the purpose of informing and consulting employees;
(i) "special negotiating body" means the body established in accordance with Article 5(2) to negotiate with the central management regarding the establishment of a European Works Council or a procedure for informing and consulting employees in accordance with Article 1(2).

2. For the purposes of this Directive, the prescribed thresholds for the size of the workforce shall be based on the average number of employees, including part-time employees, employed during the previous two years calculated according to national legislation and/or practice.

Article 3. 1. For the purposes of this Directive, "controlling undertaking" means an undertaking which can exercise a dominant influence over another undertaking (the controlled undertaking) by virtue, for example, of ownership, financial participation or the rules which govern it.

2. The ability to exercise a dominant influence shall be presumed, without prejudice to proof to the contrary, when an undertaking, in relation to another undertaking directly or indirectly:
(a) holds a majority of that undertaking's subscribed capital;

(b) controls a majority of the votes attached to that undertaking's issued share capital; or
(c) can appoint more than half of the members of that undertaking's administrative, management or supervisory body.
3. For the purposes of paragraph 2, a controlling undertaking's rights as regards voting and appointment shall include the rights of any other controlled undertaking and those of any person or body acting in his or its own name but on behalf of the controlling undertaking or of any other controlled undertaking.
4. Notwithstanding paragraphs 1 and 2, an undertaking shall not be deemed to be a "controlling undertaking" with respect to another undertaking in which it has holdings where the former undertaking is a company referred to in Article 3(5)(a) or (c) of Council Regulation (EC) No 139/2004 of 20 January 2004 on the control of concentrations between undertakings.
5. A dominant influence shall not be presumed to be exercised solely by virtue of the fact that an office holder is exercising his functions, according to the law of a Member State relating to liquidation, winding up, insolvency, cessation of payments, compositions or analogous proceedings.
6. The law applicable in order to determine whether an undertaking is a controlling undertaking shall be the law of the Member State which governs that undertaking.
Where the law governing that undertaking is not that of a Member State, the law applicable shall be the law of the Member State within whose territory the representative of the undertaking or, in the absence of such a representative, the central management of the group undertaking which employs the greatest number of employees is situated.
7. Where, in the case of a conflict of laws in the application of paragraph 2, two or more undertakings from a group satisfy one or more of the criteria laid down in that paragraph, the undertaking which satisfies the criterion laid down in point (c) thereof shall be regarded as the controlling undertaking, without prejudice to proof that another undertaking is able to exercise a dominant influence.

Section II Establishment of a European Works Council or an Employee Information and Consultation Procedure

Article 4. 1. The central management shall be responsible for creating the conditions and means necessary for the setting-up of a European Works Council or an information and consultation procedure, as provided for in Article 1(2), in a Community-scale undertaking and a Community-scale group of undertakings.
2. Where the central management is not situated in a Member State, the central management's representative agent in a Member State, to be designated if necessary, shall take on the responsibility referred to in paragraph 1.
In the absence of such a representative, the management of the establishment or group undertaking employing the greatest number of employees in any one Member State shall take on the responsibility referred to in paragraph 1.
3. For the purposes of this Directive, the representative or representatives or, in the absence of any such representatives, the management referred to in the second subparagraph of paragraph 2, shall be regarded as the central management.
4. The management of every undertaking belonging to the Community-scale group of undertakings and the central management or the deemed central management within the meaning of the second subparagraph of paragraph 2 of the Community-scale undertaking or group of undertakings shall be responsible for obtaining and transmitting to the parties concerned by the application of this Directive the information required for commencing the negotiations referred to in Article 5, and in particular the information concerning the structure of the undertaking or the group and its workforce. This obligation shall relate in particular to the information on the number of employees referred to in Article 2(1)(a) and (c).

Article 5. 1. In order to achieve the objective set out in Article 1(1), the central management shall initiate negotiations for the establishment of a European Works Council or an information and consultation procedure on its own initiative or at the written request of at least 100 employees or their representatives in at least two undertakings or establishments in at least two different Member States.
2. For this purpose, a special negotiating body shall be established in accordance with the following guidelines:
(a) The Member States shall determine the method to be used for the election or appointment of the members of the special negotiating body who are to be elected or appointed in their territories.
Member States shall provide that employees in undertakings and/or establishments in which there are no employees' representatives through no fault of their own, have the right to elect or appoint members of the special negotiating body.
The second subparagraph shall be without prejudice to national legislation and/or practice laying down thresholds for the establishment of employee representation bodies.

(b) The members of the special negotiating body shall be elected or appointed in proportion to the number of employees employed in each Member State by the Community-scale undertaking or Community-scale group of undertakings, by allocating in respect of each Member State one seat per portion of employees employed in that Member State amounting to 10 %, or a fraction thereof, of the number of employees employed in all the Member States taken together;
(c) The central management and local management and the competent European workers' and employers' organisations shall be informed of the composition of the special negotiating body and of the start of the negotiations.
3. The special negotiating body shall have the task of determining, with the central management, by written agreement, the scope, composition, functions, and term of office of the European Works Council(s) or the arrangements for implementing a procedure for the information and consultation of employees.
4. With a view to the conclusion of an agreement in accordance with Article 6, the central management shall convene a meeting with the special negotiating body. It shall inform the local managements accordingly.
Before and after any meeting with the central management, the special negotiating body shall be entitled to meet without representatives of the central management being present, using any necessary means for communication.
For the purpose of the negotiations, the special negotiating body may request assistance from experts of its choice which can include representatives of competent recognised Community-level trade union organisations. Such experts and such trade union representatives may be present at negotiation meetings in an advisory capacity at the request of the special negotiating body.
5. The special negotiating body may decide, by at least two-thirds of the votes, not to open negotiations in accordance with paragraph 4, or to terminate the negotiations already opened.
Such a decision shall stop the procedure to conclude the agreement referred to in Article 6. Where such a decision has been taken, the provisions in Annex I shall not apply.
A new request to convene the special negotiating body may be made at the earliest two years after the abovementioned decision unless the parties concerned lay down a shorter period.
6. Any expenses relating to the negotiations referred to in paragraphs 3 and 4 shall be borne by the central management so as to enable the special negotiating body to carry out its task in an appropriate manner.
In compliance with this principle, Member States may lay down budgetary rules regarding the operation of the special negotiating body. They may in particular limit the funding to cover one expert only.

Article 6. 1. The central management and the special negotiating body must negotiate in a spirit of cooperation with a view to reaching an agreement on the detailed arrangements for implementing the information and consultation of employees provided for in Article 1(1).
2. Without prejudice to the autonomy of the parties, the agreement referred to in paragraph 1 and effected in writing between the central management and the special negotiating body shall determine:
(a) the undertakings of the Community-scale group of undertakings or the establishments of the Community-scale undertaking which are covered by the agreement;
(b) the composition of the European Works Council, the number of members, the allocation of seats, taking into account where possible the need for balanced representation of employees with regard to their activities, category and gender, and the term of office;
(c) the functions and the procedure for information and consultation of the European Works Council and the arrangements for linking information and consultation of the European Works Council and national employee representation bodies, in accordance with the principles set out in Article 1(3);
(d) the venue, frequency and duration of meetings of the European Works Council;
(e) where necessary, the composition, the appointment procedure, the functions and the procedural rules of the select committee set up within the European Works Council;
(f) the financial and material resources to be allocated to the European Works Council;
(g) the date of entry into force of the agreement and its duration, the arrangements for amending or terminating the agreement and the cases in which the agreement shall be renegotiated and the procedure for its renegotiation, including, where necessary, where the structure of the Community-scale undertaking or Community-scale group of undertakings changes.
3. The central management and the special negotiating body may decide, in writing, to establish one or more information and consultation procedures instead of a European Works Council.
The agreement must stipulate by what method the employees' representatives shall have the right to meet to discuss the information conveyed to them.
This information shall relate in particular to transnational questions which significantly affect workers' interests.
4. The agreements referred to in paragraphs 2 and 3 shall not, unless provision is made otherwise therein, be subject to the subsidiary requirements of Annex I.

5. For the purposes of concluding the agreements referred to in paragraphs 2 and 3, the special negotiating body shall act by a majority of its members.

Article 7. 1. In order to achieve the objective set out in Article 1(1), the subsidiary requirements laid down by the legislation of the Member State in which the central management is situated shall apply:
- where the central management and the special negotiating body so decide,
- where the central management refuses to commence negotiations within six months of the request referred to in Article 5(1), or
- where, after three years from the date of this request, they are unable to conclude an agreement as laid down in Article 6 and the special negotiating body has not taken the decision provided for in Article 5(5).
2. The subsidiary requirements referred to in paragraph 1 as adopted in the legislation of the Member States must satisfy the provisions set out in Annex I.

Section III Miscellaneous Provisions

Article 8. 1. Member States shall provide that members of special negotiating bodies or of European Works Councils and any experts who assist them are not authorised to reveal any information which has expressly been provided to them in confidence.
The same shall apply to employees' representatives in the framework of an information and consultation procedure.
That obligation shall continue to apply, wherever the persons referred to in the first and second subparagraphs are, even after the expiry of their terms of office.
2. Each Member State shall provide, in specific cases and under the conditions and limits laid down by national legislation, that the central management situated in its territory is not obliged to transmit information when its nature is such that, according to objective criteria, it would seriously harm the functioning of the undertakings concerned or would be prejudicial to them.
A Member State may make such dispensation subject to prior administrative or judicial authorisation.
3. Each Member State may lay down particular provisions for the central management of undertakings in its territory which pursue directly and essentially the aim of ideological guidance with respect to information and the expression of opinions, on condition that, at the date of adoption of this Directive such particular provisions already exist in the national legislation.

Article 9. The central management and the European Works Council shall work in a spirit of cooperation with due regard to their reciprocal rights and obligations.
The same shall apply to cooperation between the central management and employees' representatives in the framework of an information and consultation procedure for workers.

Article 10. 1. Without prejudice to the competence of other bodies or organisations in this respect, the members of the European Works Council shall have the means required to apply the rights arising from this Directive, to represent collectively the interests of the employees of the Community-scale undertaking or Community-scale group of undertakings.
2. Without prejudice to Article 8, the members of the European Works Council shall inform the representatives of the employees of the establishments or of the undertakings of a Community-scale group of undertakings or, in the absence of representatives, the workforce as a whole, of the content and outcome of the information and consultation procedure carried out in accordance with this Directive.
3. Members of special negotiating bodies, members of European Works Councils and employees' representatives exercising their functions under the procedure referred to in Article 6(3) shall, in the exercise of their functions, enjoy protection and guarantees similar to those provided for employees' representatives by the national legislation and/or practice in force in their country of employment.
This shall apply in particular to attendance at meetings of special negotiating bodies or European Works Councils or any other meetings within the framework of the agreement referred to in Article 6(3), and the payment of wages for members who are on the staff of the Community-scale undertaking or the Community-scale group of undertakings for the period of absence necessary for the performance of their duties.
4. In so far as this is necessary for the exercise of their representative duties in an international environment, the members of the special negotiating body and of the European Works Council shall be provided with training without loss of wages.

Article 11. 1. Each Member State shall ensure that the management of establishments of a Community-scale undertaking and the management of undertakings which form part of a Community-scale group of undertakings which are situated within its territory and their employees' representatives or, as the case may be, employees abide by the obligations laid down by this Directive, regardless of whether or not the central management is situated within its territory.
2. Member States shall provide for appropriate measures in the event of failure to comply with this Directive; in particular, they shall ensure that adequate administrative or judicial procedures are available to enable the obligations deriving from this Directive to be enforced.
3. Where Member States apply Article 8, they shall make provision for administrative or judicial appeal procedures which the employees' representatives may initiate when the central management requires confidentiality or does not give information in accordance with that Article.
Such procedures may include procedures designed to protect the confidentiality of the information in question.

Article 12. 1. Information and consultation of the European Works Council shall be linked to those of the national employee representation bodies, with due regard to the competences and areas of action of each and to the principles set out in Article 1(3).
2. The arrangements for the links between the information and consultation of the European Works Council and national employee representation bodies shall be established by the agreement referred to in Article 6. That agreement shall be without prejudice to the provisions of national law and/or practice on the information and consultation of employees.
3. Where no such arrangements have been defined by agreement, the Member States shall ensure that the processes of informing and consulting are conducted in the European Works Council as well as in the national employee representation bodies in cases where decisions likely to lead to substantial changes in work organisation or contractual relations are envisaged.
4. This Directive shall be without prejudice to the information and consultation procedures referred to in Directive 2002/14/EC and to the specific procedures referred to in Article 2 of Directive 98/59/EC and Article 7 of Directive 2001/23/EC.
5. Implementation of this Directive shall not be sufficient grounds for any regression in relation to the situation which already prevails in each Member State and in relation to the general level of protection of workers in the areas to which it applies.

Article 13. Where the structure of the Community-scale undertaking or Community-scale group of undertakings changes significantly, and either in the absence of provisions established by the agreements in force or in the event of conflicts between the relevant provisions of two or more applicable agreements, the central management shall initiate the negotiations referred to in Article 5 on its own initiative or at the written request of at least 100 employees or their representatives in at least two undertakings or establishments in at least two different Member States.
At least three members of the existing European Works Council or of each of the existing European Works Councils shall be members of the special negotiating body, in addition to the members elected or appointed pursuant to Article 5(2).
During the negotiations, the existing European Works Council(s) shall continue to operate in accordance with any arrangements adapted by agreement between the members of the European Works Council(s) and the central management.

Article 14. 1. Without prejudice to Article 13, the obligations arising from this Directive shall not apply to Community-scale undertakings or Community-scale groups of undertakings in which, either
(a) an agreement or agreements covering the entire workforce, providing for the transnational information and consultation of employees have been concluded pursuant to Article 13(1) of Directive 94/45/EC or Article 3(1) of Directive 97/74/EC, or where such agreements are adjusted because of changes in the structure of the undertakings or groups of undertakings; or
(b) an agreement concluded pursuant to Article 6 of Directive 94/45/EC is signed or revised between 5 June 2009 and 5 June 2011.
The national law applicable when the agreement is signed or revised shall continue to apply to the undertakings or groups of undertakings referred to in point (b) of the first subparagraph.
2. Upon expiry of the agreements referred to in paragraph 1, the parties to those agreements may decide jointly to renew or revise them. Where this is not the case, the provisions of this Directive shall apply.

Article 15. No later than 5 June 2016, the Commission shall report to the European Parliament, the Council and the European Economic and Social Committee on the implementation of this Directive, making appropriate proposals where necessary.

Article 16. 1. Member States shall bring into force the laws, regulations and administrative provisions necessary to comply with Article 1(2), (3) and (4), Article 2(1), points (f) and (g), Articles 3(4), Article 4(4), Article 5(2), points (b) and (c), Article 5(4), Article 6(2), points (b), (c), (e) and (g), and Articles 10, 12, 13 and 14, as well as Annex I, point 1(a), (c) and (d) and points 2 and 3, no later than 5 June 2011 or shall ensure that management and labour introduce on that date the required provisions by way of agreement, the Member States being obliged to take all necessary steps enabling them at all times to guarantee the results imposed by this Directive.
When Member States adopt those provisions, they shall contain a reference to this Directive or be accompanied by such a reference on the occasion of their official publication. They shall also include a statement that references in existing laws, regulations and administrative provisions to the directive repealed by this Directive shall be construed as references to this Directive. Member States shall determine how such reference is to be made and how that statement is to be formulated.
2. Member States shall communicate to the Commission the text of the main provisions of national law which they adopt in the field covered by this Directive.

Article 17. Directive 94/45/EC, as amended by the Directives listed in Annex II, Part A, is repealed with effect from 6 June 2011 without prejudice to the obligations of the Member States relating to the time limit for transposition into national law of the Directives set out in Annex II, Part B.
References to the repealed Directive shall be construed as references to this Directive and shall be read in accordance with the correlation table in Annex III.

Article 18. This Directive shall enter into force on the 20th day following its publication in the Official Journal of the European Union.
Article 1(1), (5), (6) and (7), Article 2(1), points (a) to (e), (h) and (i), Article 2(2), Articles 3(1), (2), (3), (5), (6) and (7), Article 4(1), (2) and (3), Article 5(1), (3), (5) and (6), Article 5(2), point (a), Article 6(1), Article 6(2), points (a), (d) and (f), and Article 6(3), (4) and (5), and Articles 7, 8, 9 and 11, as well as Annex I, point 1(b), (e) and (f), and points 4, 5 and 6, shall apply from 6 June 2011.

Article 19. This Directive is addressed to the Member States.

Annex I Subsidiary Requirements (referred to in Article 7)
1. In order to achieve the objective set out in Article 1(1) and in the cases provided for in Article 7(1), the establishment, composition and competence of a European Works Council shall be governed by the following rules:
(a) The competence of the European Works Council shall be determined in accordance with Article 1(3).
The information of the European Works Council shall relate in particular to the structure, economic and financial situation, probable development and production and sales of the Community-scale undertaking or group of undertakings. The information and consultation of the European Works Council shall relate in particular to the situation and probable trend of employment, investments, and substantial changes concerning organisation, introduction of new working methods or production processes, transfers of production, mergers, cut-backs or closures of undertakings, establishments or important parts thereof, and collective redundancies.
The consultation shall be conducted in such a way that the employees' representatives can meet with the central management and obtain a response, and the reasons for that response, to any opinion they might express;
(b) The European Works Council shall be composed of employees of the Community-scale undertaking or Community-scale group of undertakings elected or appointed from their number by the employees' representatives or, in the absence thereof, by the entire body of employees.
The election or appointment of members of the European Works Council shall be carried out in accordance with national legislation and/or practice;
(c) The members of the European Works Council shall be elected or appointed in proportion to the number of employees employed in each Member State by the Community-scale undertaking or Community-scale group of undertakings, by allocating in respect of each Member State one seat per portion of employees employed in that Member State amounting to 10 %, or a fraction thereof, of the number of employees employed in all the Member States taken together;

(d) To ensure that it can coordinate its activities, the European Works Council shall elect a select committee from among its members, comprising at most five members, which must benefit from conditions enabling it to exercise its activities on a regular basis.
It shall adopt its own rules of procedure;
(e) The central management and any other more appropriate level of management shall be informed of the composition of the European Works Council;
(f) Four years after the European Works Council is established it shall examine whether to open negotiations for the conclusion of the agreement referred to in Article 6 or to continue to apply the subsidiary requirements adopted in accordance with this Annex.
Articles 6 and 7 shall apply, mutatis mutandis, if a decision has been taken to negotiate an agreement according to Article 6, in which case "special negotiating body" shall be replaced by "European Works Council".
2. The European Works Council shall have the right to meet with the central management once a year, to be informed and consulted, on the basis of a report drawn up by the central management, on the progress of the business of the Community-scale undertaking or Community-scale group of undertakings and its prospects. The local managements shall be informed accordingly.
3. Where there are exceptional circumstances or decisions affecting the employees' interests to a considerable extent, particularly in the event of relocations, the closure of establishments or undertakings or collective redundancies, the select committee or, where no such committee exists, the European Works Council shall have the right to be informed. It shall have the right to meet, at its request, the central management, or any other more appropriate level of management within the Community-scale undertaking or group of undertakings having its own powers of decision, so as to be informed and consulted.
Those members of the European Works Council who have been elected or appointed by the establishments and/or undertakings which are directly concerned by the circumstances or decisions in question shall also have the right to participate where a meeting is organised with the select committee.
This information and consultation meeting shall take place as soon as possible on the basis of a report drawn up by the central management or any other appropriate level of management of the Community-scale undertaking or group of undertakings, on which an opinion may be delivered at the end of the meeting or within a reasonable time.
This meeting shall not affect the prerogatives of the central management.
The information and consultation procedures provided for in the above circumstances shall be carried out without prejudice to Article 1(2) and Article 8.
4. The Member States may lay down rules on the chairing of information and consultation meetings.
Before any meeting with the central management, the European Works Council or the select committee, where necessary enlarged in accordance with the second paragraph of point 3, shall be entitled to meet without the management concerned being present.
5. The European Works Council or the select committee may be assisted by experts of its choice, in so far as this is necessary for it to carry out its tasks.
6. The operating expenses of the European Works Council shall be borne by the central management.
The central management concerned shall provide the members of the European Works Council with such financial and material resources as enable them to perform their duties in an appropriate manner.
In particular, the cost of organising meetings and arranging for interpretation facilities and the accommodation and travelling expenses of members of the European Works Council and its select committee shall be met by the central management unless otherwise agreed.
In compliance with these principles, the Member States may lay down budgetary rules regarding the operation of the European Works Council. They may in particular limit funding to cover one expert only.

Council Directive 98/59/EC of 20 July 1998 on the approximation of the laws of the Member States relating to collective redundancies (*OJ* L 225, 12.08.1998 p. 16 – 21) [footnotes omitted]

THE COUNCIL OF THE EUROPEAN UNION,
Having regard to the Treaty establishing the European Community, and in particular Article 100 thereof,
Having regard to the proposal from the Commission,
Having regard to the opinion of the European Parliament,
Having regard to the opinion of the Economic and Social Committee,
(1) Whereas for reasons of clarity and rationality Council Directive 75/129/EEC of 17 February 1975 on the approximation of the laws of the Member States relating to collective redundancies should be consolidated;
(2) Whereas it is important that greater protection should be afforded to workers in the event of collective redundancies while taking into account the need for balanced economic and social development within the Community;
(3) Whereas, despite increasing convergence, differences still remain between the provisions in force in the Member States concerning the practical arrangements and procedures for such redundancies and the measures designed to alleviate the consequences of redundancy for workers;
(4) Whereas these differences can have a direct effect on the functioning of the internal market;
(5) Whereas the Council resolution of 21 January 1974 concerning a social action programme made provision for a directive on the approximation of Member States' legislation on collective redundancies;
(6) Whereas the Community Charter of the fundamental social rights of workers, adopted at the European Council meeting held in Strasbourg on 9 December 1989 by the Heads of State or Government of 11 Member States, states, inter alia, in point 7, first paragraph, first sentence, and second paragraph; in point 17, first paragraph; and in point 18, third indent:
'7. The completion of the internal market must lead to an improvement in the living and working conditions of workers in the European Community (. . .).
The improvement must cover, where necessary, the development of certain aspects of employment regulations such as procedures for collective redundancies and those regarding bankruptcies.
(. . .)
17. Information, consultation and participation for workers must be developed along appropriate lines, taking account of the practices in force in the various Member States.
(. . .)
18. Such information, consultation and participation must be implemented in due time, particularly in the following cases:
(- . . .)
(- . . .)
- in cases of collective redundancy procedures;(- . . .)`;
(7) Whereas this approximation must therefore be promoted while the improvement is being maintained within the meaning of Article 117 of the Treaty;
(8) Whereas, in order to calculate the number of redundancies provided for in the definition of collective redundancies within the meaning of this Directive, other forms of termination of employment contracts on the initiative of the employer should be equated to redundancies, provided that there are at least five redundancies;
(9) Whereas it should be stipulated that this Directive applies in principle also to collective redundancies resulting where the establishment's activities are terminated as a result of a judicial decision;
(10) Whereas the Member States should be given the option of stipulating that workers' representatives may call on experts on grounds of the technical complexity of the matters which are likely to be the subject of the informing and consulting;
(11) Whereas it is necessary to ensure that employers' obligations as regards information, consultation and notification apply independently of whether the decision on collective redundancies emanates from the employer or from an undertaking which controls that employer;
(12) Whereas Member States should ensure that workers' representatives and/or workers have at their disposal administrative and/or judicial procedures in order to ensure that the obligations laid down in this Directive are fulfilled;
(13) Whereas this Directive must not affect the obligations of the Member States concerning the deadlines for transposition of the Directives set out in Annex I, Part B,

HAS ADOPTED THIS DIRECTIVE:

Section I Definitions and Scope

Article 1. 1. For the purposes of this Directive:
(a) 'collective redundancies' means dismissals effected by an employer for one or more reasons not related to the individual workers concerned where, according to the choice of the Member States, the number of redundancies is:
(i) either, over a period of 30 days:
- at least 10 in establishments normally employing more than 20 and less than 100 workers,
- at least 10 % of the number of workers in establishments normally employing at least 100 but less than 300 workers,
- at least 30 in establishments normally employing 300 workers or more,
(ii) or, over a period of 90 days, at least 20, whatever the number of workers normally employed in the establishments in question;
(b) 'workers' representatives' means the workers' representatives provided for by the laws or practices of the Member States.
For the purpose of calculating the number of redundancies provided for in the first subparagraph of point (a), terminations of an employment contract which occur on the employer's initiative for one or more reasons not related to the individual workers concerned shall be assimilated to redundancies, provided that there are at least five redundancies.
2. This Directive shall not apply to:
(a) collective redundancies effected under contracts of employment concluded for limited periods of time or for specific tasks except where such redundancies take place prior to the date of expiry or the completion of such contracts;
(b) workers employed by public administrative bodies or by establishments governed by public law (or, in Member States where this concept is unknown, by equivalent bodies);
(c) the crews of seagoing vessels.

Section II Information and consultation

Article 2. 1. Where an employer is contemplating collective redundancies, he shall begin consultations with the workers' representatives in good time with a view to reaching an agreement.
2. These consultations shall, at least, cover ways and means of avoiding collective redundancies or reducing the number of workers affected, and of mitigating the consequences by recourse to accompanying social measures aimed, inter alia, at aid for redeploying or retraining workers made redundant.
Member States may provide that the workers' representatives may call on the services of experts in accordance with national legislation and/or practice.
3. To enable workers' representatives to make constructive proposals, the employers shall in good time during the course of the consultations:
(a) supply them with all relevant information and
(b) in any event notify them in writing of:
(i) the reasons for the projected redundancies;
(ii) the number of categories of workers to be made redundant;
(iii) the number and categories of workers normally employed;
(iv) the period over which the projected redundancies are to be effected;
(v) the criteria proposed for the selection of the workers to be made redundant in so far as national legislation and/or practice confers the power therefor upon the employer;
(vi) the method for calculating any redundancy payments other than those arising out of national legislation and/or practice.
The employer shall forward to the competent public authority a copy of, at least, the elements of the written communication which are provided for in the first subparagraph, point (b), subpoints (i) to (v).
4. The obligations laid down in paragraphs 1, 2 and 3 shall apply irrespective of whether the decision regarding collective redundancies is being taken by the employer or by an undertaking controlling the employer.
In considering alleged breaches of the information, consultation and notification requirements laid down by this Directive, account shall not be taken of any defence on the part of the employer on the ground that the necessary information has not been provided to the employer by the undertaking which took the decision leading to collective redundancies.

Section III Procedure for collective redundances

Article 3. 1. Employers shall notify the competent public authority in writing of any projected collective redundancies.
However, Member States may provide that in the case of planned collective redundancies arising from termination of the establishment's activities as a result of a judicial decision, the employer shall be obliged to notify the competent public authority in writing only if the latter so requests.
This notification shall contain all relevant information concerning the projected collective redundancies and the consultations with workers' representatives provided for in Article 2, and particularly the reasons for the redundancies, the number of workers to be made redundant, the number of workers normally employed and the period over which the redundancies are to be effected.
2. Employers shall forward to the workers' representatives a copy of the notification provided for in paragraph 1. The workers' representatives may send any comments they may have to the competent public authority.

Article 4. 1. Projected collective redundancies notified to the competent public authority shall take effect not earlier than 30 days after the notification referred to in Article 3(1) without prejudice to any provisions governing individual rights with regard to notice of dismissal.
Member States may grant the competent public authority the power to reduce the period provided for in the preceding subparagraph.
2. The period provided for in paragraph 1 shall be used by the competent public authority to seek solutions to the problems raised by the projected collective redundancies.
3. Where the initial period provided for in paragraph 1 is shorter than 60 days, Member States may grant the competent public authority the power to extend the initial period to 60 days following notification where the problems raised by the projected collective redundancies are not likely to be solved within the initial period. Member States may grant the competent public authority wider powers of extension.
The employer must be informed of the extension and the grounds for it before expiry of the initial period provided for in paragraph 1.
4. Member States need not apply this Article to collective redundancies arising from termination of the establishment's activities where this is the result of a judicial decision.

Section IV Final Provisions

Article 5. This Directive shall not affect the right of Member States to apply or to introduce laws, regulations or administrative provisions which are more favourable to workers or to promote or to allow the application of collective agreements more favourable to workers.

Article 6. Member States shall ensure that judicial and/or administrative procedures for the enforcement of obligations under this Directive are available to the workers' representatives and/or workers.

Article 7. Member States shall forward to the Commission the text of any fundamental provisions of national law already adopted or being adopted in the area governed by this Directive.

Article 8. 1. The Directives listed in Annex I, Part A, are hereby repealed without prejudice to the obligations of the Member States concerning the deadlines for transposition of the said Directive set out in Annex I, Part B.
2. References to the repealed Directives shall be construed as references to this Directive and shall be read in accordance with the correlation table in Annex II.

Article 9. This Directive shall enter into force on the 20th day following its publication in the Official Journal of the European Communities.

Article 10. This Directive is addressed to the Member States.

PART IX

European Private Law

Council Directive 85/374/EEC of 25 July 1985 on the approximation of the laws, regulations and administrative provisions of the Member States concerning liability for defective products (*OJ* L 210, 07.08.1985, pp. 29 – 33) as amended by Directive 99/34/EC [footnotes omitted].

THE COUNCIL OF THE EUROPEAN COMMUNITIES, Having regard to the Treaty establishing the European Economic Community, and in particular Article 100 thereof,Having regard to the proposal from the Commission, Having regard to the opinion of the European Parliament, Having regard to the opinion of the Economic and Social Committee,

Whereas approximation of the laws of the Member States concerning the liability of the producer for damage caused by the defectiveness of his products is necessary because the existing divergences may distort competition and affect the movement of goods within the common market and entail a differing degree of protection of the consumer against damage caused by a defective product to his health or property;

Whereas liability without fault on the part of the producer is the sole means of adequately solving the problem, peculiar to our age of increasing technicality, of a fair apportionment of the risks inherent in modern technological production;

Whereas liability without fault should apply only to movables which have been industrially produced; whereas, as a result, it is appropriate to exclude liability for agricultural products and game, except where they have undergone a processing of an industrial nature which could cause a defect in these products; whereas the liability provided for in this Directive should also apply to movables which are used in the construction of immovables or are installed in immovables;

Whereas protection of the consumer requires that all producers involved in the production process should be made liable, in so far as their finished product, component part or any raw material supplied by them was defective;

Whereas, for the same reason, liability should extend to importers of products into the Community and to persons who present themselves as producers by affixing their name, trade mark or other distinguishing feature or who supply a product the producer of which cannot be identified;

Whereas, in situations where several persons are liable for the same damage, the protection of the consumer requires that the injured person should be able to claim full compensation for the damage from any one of them; whereas, to protect the physical well-being and property of the consumer, the defectiveness of the product should be determined by reference not to its fitness for use but to the lack of the safety which the public at large is entitled to expect; whereas the safety is assessed by excluding any misuse of the product not reasonable under the circumstances;

Whereas a fair apportionment of risk between the injured person and the producer implies that the producer should be able to free himself from liability if he furnishes proof as to the existence of certain exonerating circumstances;

Whereas the protection of the consumer requires that the liability of the producer remains unaffected by acts or omissions of other persons having contributed to cause the damage; whereas, however, the contributory negligence of the injured person may be taken into account to reduce or disallow such liability;

Whereas the protection of the consumer requires compensation for death and personal injury as well as compensation for damage to property; whereas the latter should nevertheless be limited to goods for private use or consumption and be subject to a deduction of a lower threshold of a fixed amount in order to avoid litigation in an excessive number of cases; Whereas this Directive should not prejudice compensation for pain and suffering and other non-material damages payable, where appropriate, under the law applicable to the case;

Whereas a uniform period of limitation for the bringing of action for compensation is in the interests both of the injured person and of the producer;

Whereas products age in the course of time, higher safety standards are developed and the state of science and technology progresses; whereas, therefore, it would not be reasonable to make the producer liable for an unlimited period for the defectiveness of his product; whereas, therefore, liability should expire after a reasonable length of time, without prejudice to claims pending at law;

Whereas, to achieve effective protection of consumers, no contractual derogation should be permitted as regards the liability of the producer in relation to the injured person;

Whereas under the legal systems of the Member States an injured party may have a claim for damages based on grounds of contractual liability or on grounds of non-contractual liability other than that provided for in this Directive; in so far as these provisions also serve to attain the objective of effective protection of consumers, they should remain unaffected by this Directive; whereas, in so far as effective protection of consumers in the sector of pharmaceutical products is already also attained in a Member State under a special liability system, claims based on this system should similarly remain possible;

Whereas, to the extent that liability for nuclear injury or damage is already covered in all Member States by adequate special rules, it has been possible to exclude damage of this type from the scope of this Directive;

Whereas, since the exclusion of primary agricultural products and game from the scope of this Directive may be felt, in certain Member States, in view of what is expected for the protection of consumers, to restrict unduly such protection, it should be possible for a Member State to extend liability to such products;

Whereas, for similar reasons, the possibility offered to a producer to free himself from liability if he proves that the state of scientific and technical knowledge at the time when he put the product into circulation was not such as to enable the existence of a defect to be discovered may be felt in certain Member States to restrict unduly the protection of the consumer; whereas it should therefore be possible for a Member State to maintain in its legislation or to provide by new legislation that this exonerating circumstance is not admitted; whereas, in the case of new legislation, making use of this derogation should, however, be subject to a Community stand-still procedure, in order to raise, if possible, the level of protection in a uniform manner throughout the Community;

Whereas, taking into account the legal traditions in most of the Member States, it is inappropriate to set any financial ceiling on the producer's liability without fault; whereas, in so far as there are, however, differing traditions, it seems possible to admit that a Member State may derogate from the principle of unlimited liability by providing a limit for the total liability of the producer for damage resulting from a death or personal injury and caused by identical items with the same defect, provided that this limit is established at a level sufficiently high to guarantee adequate protection of the consumer and the correct functioning of the common market;

Whereas the harmonization resulting from this cannot be total at the present stage, but opens the way towards greater harmonization; whereas it is therefore necessary that the Council receive at regular intervals, reports from the Commission on the application of this Directive, accompanied, as the case may be, by appropriate proposals;

Whereas it is particularly important in this respect that a re-examination be carried out of those parts of the Directive relating to the derogations open to the Member States, at the expiry of a period of sufficient length to gather practical experience on the effects of these derogations on the protection of consumers and on the functioning of the common market,

HAS ADOPTED THIS DIRECTIVE:

Article 1. The producer shall be liable for damage caused by a defect in his product.

Article 2. For the purpose of this Directive 'product' means all movables even if incorporated into another movable or into an immovable. 'Product' includes ellectricity.

Article 3. (1) 'Producer' means the manufacturer of a finished product, the producer of any raw material or the manufacturer of a component part and any person who, by putting his name, trade mark or other distinguishing feature on the product presents himself as its producer.
(2) Without prejudice to the liability of the producer, any person who imports into the Community a product for sale, hire, leasing or any form of distribution in the course of his business shall be deemed to be a producer within the meaning of this Directive and shall be responsible as a producer.
(3) Where the producer of the product cannot be identified, each supplier of the product shall be treated as its producer unless he informs the injured person, within a reasonable time, of the identity of the producer or of the person who supplied him with the product. The same shall apply, in the case of an imported product, if this product does not indicate the identity of the importer referred to in paragraph 2, even if the name of the producer is indicated.

Article 4. The injured person shall be required to prove the damage, the defect and the causal relationship between defect and damage.

Article 5. Where, as a result of the provisions of this Directive, two or more persons are liable for the same damage, they shall be liable jointly and severally, without prejudice to the provisions of national law concerning the rights of contribution or recourse.

Article 6. (1) A product is defective when it does not provide the safety which a person is entitled to expect, taking all circumstances into account, including:
(a) the presentation of the product;
(b) the use to which it could reasonably be expected that the product would be put;
(c) the time when the product was put into circulation.
(2) A product shall not be considered defective for the sole reason that a better product is subsequently put into circulation.

Article 7. The producer shall not be liable as a result of this Directive if he proves:

(a) that he did not put the product into circulation; or
(b) that, having regard to the circumstances, it is probable that the defect which caused the damage did not exist at the time when the product was put into circulation by him or that this defect came into being afterwards; or
(c) that the product was neither manufactured by him for sale or any form of distribution for economic purpose nor manufactured or distributed by him in the course of his business; or
(d) that the defect is due to compliance of the product with mandatory regulations issued by the public authorities; or
(e) that the state of scientific and technical knowledge at the time when he put the product into circulation was not such as to enable the existence of the defect to be discovered; or
(f) in the case of a manufacturer of a component, that the defect is attributable to the design of the product in which the component has been fitted or to the instructions given by the manufacturer of the product.

Article 8. (1) Without prejudice to the provisions of national law concerning the right of contribution or recourse, the liability of the producer shall not be reduced when the damage is caused both by a defect in product and by the act or omission of a third party.
(2) The liability of the producer may be reduced or disallowed when, having regard to all the circumstances, the damage is caused both by a defect in the product and by the fault of the injured person or any person for whom the injured person is responsible.

Article 9. For the purpose of Article 1, 'damage' means:
(a) damage caused by death or by personal injuries;
(b) damage to, or destruction of, any item of property other than the defective product itself, with a lower threshold of 500 ECU, provided that the item of property:
(i) is of a type ordinarily intended for private use or consumption, and
(ii) was used by the injured person mainly for his own private use or consumption.
This Article shall be without prejudice to national provisions relating to non-material damage.

Article 10. (1) Member States shall provide in their legislation that a limitation period of three years shall apply to proceedings for the recovery of damages as provided for in this Directive. The limitation period shall begin to run from the day on which the plaintiff became aware, or should reasonably have become aware, of the damage, the defect and the identity of the producer.
(2) The laws of Member States regulating suspension or interruption of the limitation period shall not be affected by this Directive. Article 11
Member States shall provide in their legislation that the rights conferred upon the injured person pursuant to this Directive shall be extinguished upon the expiry of a period of 10 years from the date on which the producer put into circulation the actual product which caused the damage, unless the injured person has in the meantime instituted proceedings against the producer.

Article 12. The liability of the producer arising from this Directive may not, in relation to the injured person, be limited or excluded by a provision limiting his liability or exempting him from liability.

Article 13. This Directive shall not affect any rights which an injured person may have according to the rules of the law of contractual or non-contractual liability or a special liability system existing at the moment when this Directive is notified.

Article 14. This Directive shall not apply to injury or damage arising from nuclear accidents and covered by international conventions ratified by the Member States.

Article 15. (1) Each Member State may:
by way of derogation from Article 7 (e), maintain or, subject to the procedure set out in paragraph 2 of this Article, provide in this legislation that the producer shall be liable even if he proves that the state of scientific and technical knowledge at the time when he put the product into circulation was not such as to enable the existence of a defect to be discovered.
(2) A Member State wishing to introduce the measure specified in paragraph 1 (b) shall communicate the text of the proposed measure to the Commission. The Commission shall inform the other Member States thereof.
The Member State concerned shall hold the proposed measure in abeyance for nine months after the Commission is informed and provided that in the meantime the Commission has not submitted to the Council a proposal amending this Directive on the relevant matter. However, if within three months of receiving the said information,

the Commission does not advise the Member State concerned that it intends submitting such a proposal to the Council, the Member State may take the proposed measure immediately.

If the Commission does submit to the Council such a proposal amending this Directive within the aforementioned nine months, the Member State concerned shall hold the proposed measure in abeyance for a further period of 18 months from the date on which the proposal is submitted.

(3) Ten years after the date of notification of this Directive, the Commission shall submit to the Council a report on the effect that rulings by the courts as to the application of Article 7 (e) and of paragraph 1 (b) of this Article have on consumer protection and the functioning of the common market. In the light of this report the Council, acting on a proposal from the Commission and pursuant to the terms of Article 100 of the Treaty, shall decide whether to repeal Article 7 (e).

Article 16. (1) Any Member State may provide that a producer's total liability for damage resulting from a death or personal injury and caused by identical items with the same defect shall be limited to an amount which may not be less than 70 million ECU.

(2) Ten years after the date of notification of this Directive, the Commission shall submit to the Council a report on the effect on consumer protection and the functioning of the common market of the implementation of the financial limit on liability by those Member States which have used the option provided for in paragraph 1. In the light of this report the Council, acting on a proposal from the Commission and pursuant to the terms of Article 100 of the Treaty, shall decide whether to repeal paragraph 1.

Article 17. This Directive shall not apply to products put into circulation before the date on which the provisions referred to in Article 19 enter into force.

Article 18. (1) For the purposes of this Directive, the ECU shall be that defined by Regulation (EEC) No 3180/78 (1), as amended by Regulation (EEC) No 2626/84 (2). The equivalent in national currency shall initially be calculated at the rate obtaining on the date of adoption of this Directive.

(2) Every five years the Council, acting on a proposal from the Commission, shall examine and, if need be, revise the amounts in this Directive, in the light of economic and monetary trends in the Community.

Article 19. (1) Member States shall bring into force, not later than three years from the date of notification of this Directive, the laws, regulations and administrative provisions necessary to comply with this Directive. They shall forthwith inform the Commission thereof (1).

(2) The procedure set out in Article 15 (2) shall apply from the date of notification of this Directive.

Article 20. Member States shall communicate to the Commission the texts of the main provisions of national law which they subsequently adopt in the field governed by this Directive.

Article 21. Every five years the Commission shall present a report to the Council on the application of this Directive and, if necessary, shall submit appropriate proposals to it.

Article 22. This Directive is addressed to the Member States.

Council Directive 85/577/EEC of 20 December 1985 to protect the consumer in respect of contracts negotiated away from business premises (*OJ*L 372, 31.12.1985, pp. 31-33) [footnotes omitted].

THE COUNCIL OF THE EUROPEAN COMMUNITIES,
Having regard to the Treaty establishing the European Economic Community, and in particular Article 100 thereof, Having regard to the proposal from the Commission,
Having regard to the opinion of the European Parliament,
Having regard to the opinion of the Economic and Social Committee,
Whereas it is a common form of commercial practice in the Member States for the conclusion of a contract or a unilateral engagement between a trader and consumer to be made away from the business premises of the trader, and whereas such contracts and engagements are the subject of legislation which differs from one Member State to another;
Whereas any disparity between such legislation may directly affect the functioning of the common market; whereas it is therefore necessary to approximate laws in this field;
Whereas the preliminary programme of the European Economic Community for a consumer protection and information policy provides inter alia, under paragraphs 24 and 25, that appropriate measures be taken to protect consumers against unfair commercial practices in respect of doorstep selling;
Whereas the second programme of the European Economic Community for a consumer protection and information policy confirmed that the action and priorities defined in the preliminary programme would be pursued;
Whereas the special feature of contracts concluded away from the business premises of the trader is that as a rule it is the trader who initiates the contract negotiations, for which the consumer is unprepared or which he does not except;
Whereas the consumer is often unable to compare the quality and price of the offer with other offers;
Whereas this surprise element generally exists not only in contracts made at the doorstep but also in other forms of contract concluded by the trader away from his business premises;
Whereas the consumer should be given a right of cancellation over a period of at least seven days in order to enable him to assess the obligations arising under the contract;
Whereas appropriate measures should be taken to ensure that the consumer is informed in writing of this period for reflection;
Whereas the freedom of Member States to maintain or introduce a total or partial prohibition on the conclusion of contracts away from business premises, inasmuch as they consider this to be in the interest of consumers, must not be affected;

HAS ADOPTED THIS DIRECTIVE:

Article 1. (1) This Directive shall apply to contracts under which a trader supplies goods or services to a consumer and which are concluded:- during an excursion organized by the trader away from his business premises, or-during a visit by a trader
(i) to the consumer's home or to that of another consumer;
(ii) to the consumer's place of work; where the visit does not take place at the express request of the consumer.
(2) This Directive shall also apply to contracts for the supply of goods or services other than those concerning which the consumer requested the visit of the trader, provided that when he requested the visit the consumer did not know, or could not reasonably have known, that the supply of those other goods or services formed part of the trader's commercial or professional activities.
(3) This Directive shall also apply to contracts in respect of which an offer was made by the consumer under conditions similar to those described in paragraph 1 or paragraph 2 although the consumer was not bound by that offer before its acceptance by the trader.
(4) This Directive shall also apply to offers made contractually by the consumer under conditions similar to those described in paragraph 1 or paragraph 2 where the consumer is bound by his offer.

Article 2. For the purposes of this Directive: 'consumer' means a natural person who, in transactions covered by this Directive, is acting for purposes which can be regarded as outside his trade or profession; 'trader' means a natural or legal person who, for the transaction in question, acts in his commercial or professional capacity, and anyone acting in the name or on behalf of a trader.

Article 3. (1) The Member States may decide that this Directive shall apply only to contracts for which the payment to be made by the consumer exceeds a specified amount. This amount may not exceed 60 ECU.The Council, acting on a proposal from the Commission, shall examine and, if necessary, revise this amount for the first time no later than four years after notification of the Directive and thereafter every two years, taking into account economic and monetary developments in the Community.

(2) This Directive shall not apply to:

(a) contracts for the construction, sale and rental of immovable property or contracts concerning other rights relating to immovable property.Contracts for the supply of goods and for their incorporation in immovable property or contracts for repairing immovable property shall fall within the scope of this Directive;

(b) contracts for the supply of foodstuffs or beverages or other goods intended for current consumption in the household and supplied by regular roundsmen;

(c) contracts for the supply of goods or services, provided that all three of the following conditions are met:

(i) the contract is concluded on the basis of a trader's catalogue which the consumer has a proper opportunity of reading in the absence of the trader's representative,

(ii) there is intended to be continuity of contact between the trader's representative and the consumer in relation to that or any subsequent transaction,

(iii) both the catalogue and the contract clearly inform the consumer of his right to return goods to the supplier within a period of not less than seven days of receipt or otherwise to cancel the contract within that period without obligation of any kind other than to take reasonable care of the goods;

(d) insurance contracts;

(e) contracts for securities.

(3) By way of derogation from Article 1 (2), Member States may refrain from applying this Directive to contracts for the supply of goods or services having a direct connection with the goods or services concerning which the consumer requested the visit of the trader.

Article 4. In the case of transactions within the scope of Article 1, traders shall be required to give consumers written notice of their right of cancellation within the period laid down in Article 5, together with the name and address of a person against whom that right may be exercised. Such notice shall be dated and shall state particulars enabling the contract to be identified. It shall be given to the consumer:(a) in the case of Article 1 (1), at the time of conclusion of the contract;(b)in the case of Article 1 (2), not later than the time of conclusion of the contract;(c)in the case of Article 1 (3) and 1 (4), when the offer is made by the consumer. Member States shall ensure that their national legislation lays down appropriate consumer protection measures in cases where the information referred to in this Article is not supplied.

Article 5. (1) The consumer shall have the right to renounce the effects of his undertaking by sending notice within a period of not less than seven days from receipt by the consumer of the notice referred to in Article 4, in accordance with the procedure laid down by national law. It shall be sufficient if the notice is dispatched before the end of such period.

(2) The giving of the notice shall have the effect of releasing the consumer from any obligations under the cancelled contract.

Article 6. The consumer may not waive the rights conferred on him by this Directive.

Article 7. If the consumer exercises his right of renunciation, the legal effects of such renunciation shall be governed by national laws, particularly regarding the reimbursement of payments for goods or services provided and the return of goods received.

Article 8. This Directive shall not prevent Member States from adopting or maintaining more favourable provisions to protect consumers in the field which it covers.

Article 9. (1) Member States shall take the measures necessary to comply with this Directive within 24 months of its notification (1). They shall forthwith inform the Commission thereof.

(2) Member States shall ensure that the texts of the main provisions of national law which they adopt in the field covered by this Directive are communicated to the Commission.

Article 10. This Directive is addressed to the Member States.

Council Directive 86/653/EEC of 18 December 1986 on the coordination of the laws of the Member States relating to self-employed commercial agents (*OJ* L 382 , 31/12/1986 P. 0017 – 0021) [footnotes omitted].

THE COUNCIL OF THE EUROPEAN COMMUNITIES,
Having regard to the Treaty establishing the European Economic Community, and in particular Articles 57(2) and 100 thereof,
Having regard to the proposal from the Commission,
Having regard to the opinion of the European Parliament,
Having regard to the opinion of the Economic and Social Committee,
Whereas the restrictions on the freedom of establishment and the freedom to provide services in respect of activities of intermediaries in commerce, industry and small craft industries were abolished by Directive 64/224/EEC;
Whereas the differences in national laws concerning commercial representation substantially affect the conditions of competition and the carrying-on of that activity within the Community and are detrimental both to the protection available to commercial agents vis-à-vis their principals and to the security of commercial transactions; whereas moreover those differences are such as to inhibit substantially the conclusion and operation of commerical representation contracts where principal and commercial agents are established in different Member States;
Whereas trade in goods between Member States should be carried on under conditions which are similar to those of a single market, and this necessitates approximation of the legal systems of the Member States to the extent required for the proper functioning of the common market; whereas in this regard the rules concerning conflict of laws do not, in the matter of commercial representation, remove the inconsistencies referred to above, nor would they even if they were made uniform, and accordingly the proposed harmonization is necessary notwithstanding the existence of those rules;
Whereas in this regard the legal relationship between commercial agent and principal must be given priority;
Whereas it is appropriate to be guided by the principles of Article 117 of the Treaty and to maintain improvementsalready made, when harmonizing the laws of the Member States relating to commercial agents;
Whereas additional transitional periods should be allowed for certain Member States which have to make a particular effort to adapt their regulations, especially those concerning indemnity for termination of contract between the principal and the commercial agent, to the requirements of this Directive,

HAS ADOPTED THIS DIRECTIVE:

Chapter I Scope

Article 1. (1) The harmonization measures prescribed by this Directive shall apply to the laws, regulations and administrative provisions of the Member States governing the relations between commercial agents and their principals.
(2) For the purposes of this Directive, 'commercial agent' shall mean a self-employed intermediary who has continuing authority to negotiate the sale or the purchase of goods on behalf of another person, hereinafter called the 'principal', or to negotiate and conclude such transactions on behalf of and in the name of that principal.
(3) A commercial agent shall be understood within the meaning of this Directive as not including in particular:
- a person who, in his capacity as an officer, is empowered to enter into commitments binding on a company or association,
- a partner who is lawfully authorized to enter into commitments binding on his partners,
- a receiver, a receiver and manager, a liquidator or a trustee in bankruptcy.

Article 2. (1) This Directive shall not apply to:
- commercial agents whose activities are unpaid,
- commercial agents when they operate on commodity exchanges or in the commodity market, or
- the body known is the Crown Agents for Overseas Governments and Administrations, as set up under the Crown Agents Act 1979 in the United Kingdom, or its subsidiaries.
(2) Each of the Member States shall have the right to provide that the Directive shall not apply to those persons whose activities as commercial agents are considered secondary by the law of that Member State.

Chapter II Rights and obligations

Article 3. (1) In performing has activities a commercial agent must look after his principai's interests and act dutifully and in good faith.

(2) In particular, a commercial agent must:
(a) make proper efforts to negotiate and, where appropriate, conclude the transactions he is instructed to take care of;
(b) communicate to his principal all the necessary information available to him;
(c) comply with reasonable instructions given by his principal.

Article 4. (1) In his relations with his commercial agent a principal must act dutifully and in good faith.
(2) A principal must in particular:
(a) provide his commercial agent with the necessary documentation relating to the goods concerned;
(b) obtain for his commercial agent the information necessary for the performance of the agency contract, and in particular notify the commercial agent within a reasonable period once he anticipates that the volume of commercial transactions will be significantly lower than that which the commercial agent could normally have expected.
(3) A principal must, in addition, inform the commercial agent within a reasonable period of his acceptance, refusal, and of any non-execution of a commercial transaction which the commercial agent has procured for the principal.

Article 5. The parties may not derogate from the provisions of Articles 3 and 4.

Chapter III Remuneration

Article 6. (1) In the absence of any agreement on this matter between the parties, and without prejudice to the application of the compulsory provisions of the Member States concerning the level of remuneration, a commercial agent shall be entitled to the remuneration that commercial agents appointed for the goods forming the subject of his agency contract are customarily allowed in the place where he carries on his activities. If there is no such customary practice a commercial agent shall be entitled to reasonable remuneration taking into account all the aspects of the transaction.
(2) Any part of the remuneration which varies with the number or value of business transactions shall be deemed to be commission within the meaning of this Directive.
(3) Articles 7 to 12 shall not apply if the commercial agent is not remunerated wholly or in part by commission.

Article 7. (1) A commercial agent shall be entitled to commission on commercial transactions concluded during the period covered by the agency contract:
(a) where the transaction has been concluded as a result of his action; or
(b) where the transaction is concluded with a third party whom he has previously acquired as a customer for transactions of the same kind.
(2) A commercial agent shall also be entitled to commission on transactions concluded during the period covered by the agency contract:
- either where he is entrusted with a specific geographical area or group of customers,
- or where he has an exclusive right to a specific geographical area or group of customers,
and where the transaction has been entered into with a customer belonging to that area or group.
Member State shall include in their legislation one of the possibilities referred to in the above two indents.

Article 8. A commercial agent shall be entitled to commission on commercial transactions concluded after the agency contract has terminated:
(a) if the transaction is mainly attributable to the commercial agent's efforts during the period covered by the agency contract and if the transaction was entered into within a reasonable period after that contract terminated; or
(b) if, in accordance with the conditions mentioned in Article 7, the order of the third party reached the principal or the commercial agent before the agency contract terminated.

Article 9. A commercial agent shall not be entitled to the commission referred to in Article 7, if that commission is payable, pursuant to Article 8, to the previous commercial agent, unless it is equitable because of the circumstances for the commission to be shared between the commercial agents.

Article 10. (1) The commission shall become due as soon as and to the extent that one of the following circumstances obtains:
(a) the principal has executed the transaction; or
(b) the principal should, according to his agreement with the third party, have executed the transaction; or

(c) the third party has executed the transaction.
(2) The commission shall become due at the latest when the third party has executed his part of the transaction or should have done so if the principal had executed his part of the transaction, as he should have.
(3) The commission shall be paid not later than on the last day of the month following the quarter in which it became due.
(4) Agreements to derogate from paragraphs 2 and 3 to the detriment of the commercial agent shall not be permitted.

Article 11. (1) The right to commission can be extinguished only if and to the extent that:
- it is established that the contract between the third party and the principal will not be executed, and
- that face is due to a reason for which the principal is not to blame.
(2) Any commission which the commercial agent has already received shall be refunded if the right to it is extinguished.
(3) Agreements to derogate from paragraph 1 to the detriment of the commercial agent shall not be permitted.

Article 12. (1). The principal shall supply his commercial agent with a statement of the commission due, not later than the last day of the month following the quarter in which the commission has become due. This statement shall set out the main components used in calculating the amount of commission.
(2) A commercial agent shall be entitled to demand that he be provided with all the information, and in particular an extract from the books, which is available to his principal and which he needs in order to check the amount of the commission due to him.
(3) Agreements to derogate from paragraphs 1 and 2 to the detriment of the commercial agent shall not be permitted.
(4) This Directive shall not conflict with the internal provisions of Member States which recognize the right of a commercial agent to inspect a principal's books.

Chapter IV Conclusion and termination of the agency contract

Article 13. (1) Each party shall be entitled to receive from the other on request a signed written document setting out the terms of the agency contract including any terms subsequently agreed. Waiver of this right shall not be permitted.
(2) Notwithstanding paragraph 1 a Member State may provide that an agency contract shall not be valid unless evidenced in writing.

Article 14. An agency contract for a fixed period which continues to be performed by both parties after that period has expired shall be deemed to be converted into an agency contract for an indefinite period.

Article 15. (1) Where an agency contract is concluded for an indefinite period either party may terminate it by notice.
(2) The period of notice shall be one month for the first year of the contract, two months for the second year commenced, and three months for the third year commenced and subsequent years. The parties may not agree on shorter periods of notice.
(3) Member States may fix the period of notice at four months for the fourth year of the contract, five months for the fifth year and six months for the sixth and subsequent years. They may decide that the parties may not agree to shorter periods.
(4) If the parties agree on longer periods than those laid down in paragraphs 2 and 3, the period of notice to be observed by the principal must not be shorter than that to be observed by the commercial agent.
(5) Unless otherwise agreed by the parties, the end of the period of notice must coincide with the end of a calendar month.
(6) The provision of this Article shall apply to an agency contract for a fixed period where it is converted under Article 14 into an agency contract for an indefinite period, subject to the proviso that the earlier fixed period must be taken into account in the calculation of the period of notice.

Article 16. Nothing in this Directive shall affect the application of the law of the Member States where the latter provides for the immediate termination of the agency contract:
(a) because of the failure of one party to carry out all or part of his obligations;
(b) where exceptional circumstances arise.

Article 17. (1) Member States shall take the measures necessary to ensure that the commercial agent is, after termination of the agency contract, indemnified in accordance with paragraph 2 or compensated for damage in accordance with paragraph 3.
(2) (a) The commercial agent shall be entitled to an indemnity if and to the extent that:
- he has brought the principal new customers or has significantly increased the volume of business with existing customers and the principal continues to derive substantial benefits from the business with such customers, and
- the payment of this indemnity is equitable having regard to all the circumstances and, in particular, the commission lost by the commercial agent on the business transacted with such customers. Member States may provide for such circumstances also to include the application or otherwise of a restraint of trade clause, within the meaning of Article 20;
(b) The amount of the indemnity may not exceed a figure equivalent to an indemnity for one year calculated from the commercial agent's average annual remuneration over the preceding five years and if the contract goes back less than five years the indemnity shall be calculated on the average for the period in question;
(c) The grant of such an indemnity shall not prevent the commercial agent from seeking damages.
(3) The commercial agent shall be entitled to compensation for the damage he suffers as a result of the termination of his relations with the principal.
Such damage shall be deemed to occur particularly when the termination takes place in circumstances:
- depriving the commercial agent of the commission which proper performance of the agency contract would have procured him whilst providing the principal with substantial benefits linked to the commercial agent's activities,
- and/or which have not enabled the commercial agent to amortize the costs and expenses that he had incurred for the performance of the agency contract on the principal's advice.
(4) Entitlement to the indemnity as provided for in paragraph 2 or to compensation for damage as provided for under paragraph 3, shall also arise where the agency contract is terminated as a result of the commercial agent's death.
(5) The commercial agent shall lose his entitlement to the indemnity in the instances provided for in paragraph 2 or to compensation for damage in the instances provided for in paragraph 3, if within one year following termination of the contract he has not notified the principal that he intends pursuing his entitlement.
(6) The Commission shall submit to the Council, within eight years following the date of notification of this Directive, a report on the implementation of this Article, and shall if necessary submit to it proposals for amendments.

Article 18. The indemnity or compensation referred to in Article 17 shall not be payable:
(a) where the principal has terminated the agency contract because of default attributable to the commercial agent which would justify immediate termination of the agency contract under national law;
(b) where the commercial agent has terminated the agency contract, unless such termination is justified by circumstances attributable to the principal or on grounds of age, infirmity or illness of the commercial agent in consequence of which he cannot reasonably be required to continue his activities;
(c) where, with the agreement of the principal, the commercial agent assigns his rights and duties under the agency contract to another person.

Article 19. The parties may not derogate from Articles 17 and 18 to the detriment of the commercial agent before the agency contract expires.

Article 20. (1) For the purposes of this Directive an agreement restricting the business activities of a commercial agent following termination of the agency contract is hereinafter referred to as a restraint of trade clause.
(2) A restraint of trade clause shall be valid only if and to the extent that:
(a) it is concluded in writing; and
(b) it relates to the geographical area or the group of customers and the geographical area entrusted to the commercial agent and to the kind of goods covered by his agency under the contract.
(3) A restraint of trade clause shall be valid for not more than two years after termination of the agency contract.
(4) This Article shall not affect provisions of national law which impose other restrictions on the validity or enforceability of restraint of trade clauses or which enable the courts to reduce the obligations on the parties resulting from such an agreement.

Chapter V General and final provisions

Article 21. Nothing in this Directive shall require a Member State to provide for the disclosure of information where such disclosure would be contrary to public policy.

Article 22. (1) Member States shall bring into force the provisions necessary to comply with this Directive before 1 January 1990. They shall for with inform the Commission thereof. Such provisions shall apply at least to contracts concluded after their entry into force. They shall apply to contracts in operation by 1 January 1994 at the latest.
(2) As from the notification of this Directive, Member States shall communicate to the Commission the main laws, regulations and administrative provisions which they adopt in the field governed by this Directive.
(3) However, with regard to Ireland and the United Kingdom, 1 January 1990 referred to in paragraph 1 shall be replaced by 1 January 1994.
With regard to Italy, 1 January 1990 shall be replaced by 1 January 1993 in the case of the obligations deriving from Article 17.

Article 23. This Directive is addressed to the Member States.

Council Directive 87/102/EEC of 22 December 1986 for the approximation of the laws, regulations and administrative provisions of the Member States concerning consumer credit (*OJ* L 042 , 12.02.1987 p. 0048 – 0053) as amended by Directive 90/88 and Directive 98/7 [footnotes omitted].

THE COUNCIL OF THE EUROPEAN COMMUNITIES,
Having regard to the Treaty establishing the European Economic Community, and in particular Article 100 thereof,
Having regard to the proposal from the Commission,
Having regard to the opinion of the European Parliament,
Having regard to the opinion of the Economic and Social Committee,
Whereas wide differences exist in the laws of the Member States in the field of consumer credit;
Whereas these differences of law can lead to distortions of competition between grantors of credit in the common market;
Whereas these differences limit the opportunities the consumer has to obtain credit in other Member States; whereas they affect the volume and the nature of the credit sought, and also the purchase of goods and services;
Whereas, as a result, these differences have an influence on the free movement of goods and services obtainable by consumers on credit and thus directly affect the functioning of the common market;
Whereas, given the increasing volume of credit granted in the Community to consumers, the establishment of a common market in consumer credit would benefit alike consumers, grantors of credit, manufacturers, wholesalers and retailers of goods and providers of services;
Whereas the programmes of the European Economic Community for a consumer protection and information policy provide, inter alia, that the consumer should be protected against unfair credit terms and that a harmonization of the general conditions governing consumer credit should be undertaken as a priority;
Whereas differences of law and practice result in unequal consumer protection in the field of consumer credit from one Member State to another;
Whereas there has been much change in recent years in the types of credit available to and used by consumers; whereas new forms of consumer credit have emerged and continue to develop;
Whereas the consumer should receive adequate information on the conditions and cost of credit and on his obligations; whereas this information should include, inter alia, the annual percentage rate of charge for credit, or, failing that, the total amount that the consumer must pay for credit; whereas, pending a decision on a Community method or methods of calculating the annual percentage rate of charge, Member States should be able to retain existing methods or practices for calculating this rate, or failing that, should establish provisions for indicating the total cost of the credit to the consumer;
Whereas the terms of credit may be disadvantageous to the consumer; whereas better protection of consumers can be achieved by adopting certain requirements which are to apply to all forms of credit;
Whereas, having regard to the character of certain credit agreements or types of transaction, these agreements or transactions should be partially or entirely excluded from the field of application of this Directive;
Whereas it should be possible for Member States, in consultation with the Commission, to exempt from the Directive certain forms of credit of a non-commercial character granted under particular conditions;
Whereas the practices existing in some Member States in respect of authentic acts drawn up before a notary or judge are such as to render the application of certain provisions of this Directive unnecessary in the case of such acts; whereas it should therefore be possible for Member States to exempt such acts from those provisions;
Whereas credit agreements for very large financial amounts tend to differ from the usual consumer credit agreements; whereas the application of the provisions of this Directive to agreements for very small amounts could create unnecessary administrative burdens both for consumers and grantors of credit; whereas therefore, agreements above or below specified financial limits should be excluded from the Directive;
Whereas the provision of information on the cost of credit in advertising and at the business premises of the creditor or credit broker can make it easier for the consumer to compare different offers;
Whereas consumer protection is further improved if credit agreements are made in writing and contain certain minimum particulars concerning the contractual terms;
Whereas, in the case of credit granted for the acquisition of goods, Member States should lay down the conditions in which goods may be repossessed, particularly if the consumer has not given his consent; whereas the account between the parties should upon repossession be made up in such manner as to ensure that the repossession does not entail any unjustified enrichment;

Whereas the consumer should be allowed to discharge his obligations before the due date; whereas the consumer should then be entitled to an equitable reduction in the total cost of the credit;
Whereas the assignment of the creditor's rights arising under a credit agreement should not be allowed to weaken the position of the consumer;
Whereas those Member States which permit consumers to use bills of exchange, promissory notes or cheques in connection with credit agreements should ensure that the consumer is suitably protected when so using such instruments;
Whereas, as regards goods or services which the consumer has contracted to acquire on credit, the consumer should, at least in the circumstances defined below, have rights vis-à-vis the grantor of credit which are in addition to his normal contractual rights against him and against the supplier of the goods or services; whereas the circumstances referred to above are those where the grantor of credit and the supplier of goods or services have a pre-existing agreement whereunder credit is made available exclusively by that grantor of credit to customers of that supplier for the purpose of enabling the consumer to acquire goods or services from the latter;
Whereas the ECU is as defined in Council Regulation (EEC) No 3180/78, as last amended by Regulation (EEC) No 2626/84; whereas Member States should to a limited extent be at liberty to round off the amounts in national currency resulting from the conversion of amounts of this Directive expressed in ECU; whereas the amounts in this Directive should be periodically re-examined in the light of economic and monetary trends in the Community, and, if need be, revised;
Whereas suitable measures should be adopted by Member States for authorizing persons offering credit or offering to arrange credit agreements or for inspecting or monitoring the activities of persons granting credit or arranging for credit to be granted or for enabling consumers to complain about credit agreements or credit conditions;
Whereas credit agreements should not derogate, to the detriment of the consumer, from the provisions adopted in implementation of this Directive or corresponding to its provisions; whereas those provisions should not be circumvented as a result of the way in which agreements are formulated;
Whereas, since this Directive provides for a certain degree of approximation of the laws, regulations and administrative provisions of the Member States concerning consumer credit and for a certain level of consumer protection, Member States should not be prevented from retaining or adopting more stringent measures to protect the consumer, with due regard for their obligations under the Treaty;
Whereas, not later than 1 January 1995, the Commission should present to the Council a report concerning the operation of this Directive,

HAS ADOPTED THIS DIRECTIVE:

Article 1. (1). This Directive applies to credit agreements.
(2). For the purpose of this Directive:
(a) 'consumer' means a natural person who, in transactions covered by this Directive, is acting for purposes which can be regarded as outside his trade or profession;
(b) 'creditor' means a natural or legal person who grants credit in the course of his trade, business or profession, or a group of such persons;
(c) 'credit agreement' means an agreement whereby a creditor grants or promises to grant to a consumer a credit in the form of a deferred payment, a loan or other similar financial accommodation.
Agreements for the provision on a continuing basis of a service or a utility, where the consumer has the right to pay for them, for the duration of their provision, by means of instalments, are not deemed to be credit agreements for the purpose of this Directive;
'(d) "total cost of the credit to the consumer" means all the costs, including interest and other charges, which the consumer has to pay for the credit.';
'(e) "annual percentage rate of charge" means the total cost of the credit to theconsumer, expressed as an annual percentage of the amount of the credit granted and calculated in accordance with Article 1a'.

Article 1a. (1) The annual percentage rate of charge which shall be that rate, on an annual basis which equalizes the present value of all commitments (loans, repayments and charges), future or existing, agreed by the creditor and the borrower, shall be calculated in accordance with the mathematical formula set out in Annex II.
(b) Four examples of the method of calculation are given in Annex III, by way of illustration.
(2) For the purpose of calculating the annual percentage rate of charge, the "total cost of the credit to the consumer" as defined in Article 1 (2) (d) shall be determined, with the exception of the following charges:

(i) charges payable by the borrower for non-compliance with any of his commitments laid down in the credit agreement;
(ii) charges other than the purchase price which, in purchases of goods or services, the consumer is obliged to pay whether the transaction is paid in cash or by credit;
(iii) charges for the transfer of funds and charges for keeping an account intended to receive payments towards the reimbursement of the credit the payment of interest and other charges except where the consumer doesn ot have reasonable freedom of choice in the matter and where such charges are abnormally high; this provision shall not, however, apply to charges for collection of such reimbursements or payments, whether made in cash or otherwise;
(iv) membership subscriptions to associations or groups and arising from agreements separate from the credit agreement, even though such subscriptions have an effect on the credit terms;
(v) charges for insurance or guarantees; included are, however, those designed to ensure payment to the creditor, in the event of the death, invalidity, illness or unemployment of the consumer, of a sum equal to or less than the total amount of the credit together with relevant interest and other charges which have to be imposed by the creditor as a condition for credit being granted.
(3) (repealed).
(4) (a) The annual percentage rate of charge shall be calculated at the time the credit contract is concluded, without prejudice to the provisions of Article 3 concerning advertisements and special offers.
(b) The calculation shall be made on the assumption that the credit contract is valid for the period agreed and that the creditor and the consumer fulfil their obligations under the terms and by the dates agreed.
(5) (repealed).
(6) In the case of credit contracts containing clauses allowing variations in the rate of interest and the amount or level of other charges contained in the annual percentage rate of charge but unquantifiable at the time when it is calculated, the annual percentage rate of charge shall be calculated on the assumption that interest and other charges remain fixed and will apply until the end of the credit contract. 7. Where necessary, the following assumptions may be made in calculating the annual percentage rate of charge:
- if the contract does not specify a credit limit, the amount of credit granted shall be equal to the amount fixed by the relevant Member State, without exceeding a figure equivalent to ECU 2 000;
- if there is no fixed timetable for repayment, and one cannot be deduced from the terms of the agreement and the means for repaying the credit granted, the duration of the credit shall be deemed to be one year;
- unless otherwise specified, where the contract provides for more than one repayment date, the credit will be made available and the repayments made at the earliest time provided for in the agreement.

Article 2. (1) This Directive shall not apply to:
(a) credit agreements or agreements promising to grant credit:
- intended primarily for the purpose of acquiring or retaining property rights in land or in an existing or projected building,
- intended for the purpose of renovating or improving a building as such;
(b) hiring agreements except where these provide that the title will pass ultimately to the hirer;
(c) credit granted or made available without payment of interest or any other charge;
(d) credit agreements under which no interest is charged provided the consumer agrees to repay the credit in a single payment;
(e) credit in the form of advances on a current account granted by a credit institution or financial institution other than on credit card accounts.
Nevertheless, the provisions of Article 6 shall apply to such credits;
(f) credit agreements involving amounts less than 200 ECU or more than 20 000 ECU;
(g) credit agreements under which the consumer is required to repay the credit:
- either, within a period not exceeding three months,
- or, by a maximum number of four payments within a period not exceeding 12 months.
(2) A Member State may, in consultation with the Commission, exempt from the application of this
Directive certain types of credit which fulfil the following conditions:
- they are granted at rates of charge below those prevailing in the market, and
- they are not offered to the public generally.
(3) '3. The provisions of Article 1a and of Articles 4 to 12 shall not apply to credit agreements or agreements promising to grant credit, secured by mortgage on immovable property, insofar as these are not already excluded from the Directive under paragraph 1 (a).
(4) Member States may exempt from the provisions of Articles 6 to 12 credit agreements in the form of an authentic act signed before a notary or judge.

Article 3. Without prejudice to Council Directive 84/450/EEC of 10 September 1984 relating to the approximation of the laws, regulations and administrative provisions of the Member States concerning misleading advertising, and to the rules and principles applicable to unfair advertising, any advertisement, or any offer which is displayed at business premises, in which a person offers credit or offers to arrange a credit agreement and in which a rate of interest or any figures relating to the cost of the credit are indicated, shall also include a statement of the annual percentage rate of charge, by means of a representative example if no other means is practicable.

Article 4. (1). Credit agreements shall be made in writing. The consumer shall receive a copy of the written agreement.
(2) The written agreement shall include:
(a) a statement of the annual percentage rate of charge;
(b) a statement of the conditions under which the annual percentage rate of charge may be amended
(c) a statement of the amount, number and frequency or dates of the payments which the consumer must make to repay the credit, as well as of the payments for interest and other charges; the total amount of these payments should also be indicated where possible;
(d) a statement of the cost items referred to in Article 1a (2) with the exception of expenditure related to the breach of contractual obligations which were not included in the calculation of the annual percentage rate of charge but which have to be paid by the consumer in given circumstances, together with a statement indentifying such circumstances. Where the exact amount of those items is known, that sum is to be indicated; if that is not the case, either a method of calculation or as accurate an estimate as possible is to be provided where possible.
In cases where it is not possible to state the annual percentage rate of charge, the consumer shall be provided with adequate information in the written agreement. This information shall at least include the information provided for in the second indent of Article 6 (1).
(3) The written agreement shall further include the other essential terms of the contract.
By way of illustration, the Annex to this Directive contains a list of terms which Member States may require to be included in the written agreement as being essential.

Article 5. (repealed).

Article 6. (1) Notwithstanding the exclusion provided for in Article 2 (1) (e), where there is an agreement between a credit institution or financial institution and a consumer for the granting of credit in the form of an advance on a current account, other than on credit card accounts, the consumer shall be informed at the time or before the agreement is concluded:
- of the credit limit, if any,
- of the annual rate of interest and the charges applicable from the time the agreement is concluded and the conditions under which these may be amended,
- of the procedure for terminating the agreement.
This information shall be confirmed in writing.
(2) Furthermore, during the period of the agreement, the consumer shall be informed of any change in the annual rate of interest or in the relevant charges at the time it occurs. Such information may be given in a statement of account or in any other manner acceptable to Member States.
(3). In Member States where tacitly accepted overdrafts are permissible, the Member States concerned shall ensure that the consumer is informed of the annual rate of interest and the charges applicable, and of any amendment thereof, where the overdraft extends beyond a period of three months.

Article 7. In the case of credit granted for the acquisition of goods, Member States shall lay down the conditions under which goods may be repossessed, in particular if the consumer has not given his consent. They shall further ensure that where the creditor recovers possession of the goods the account between the parties shall be made up so as to ensure that the repossession does not entail any unjustified enrichment.

Article 8. The consumer shall be entitled to discharge his obligations under a credit agreement before the time fixed by the agreement. In this event, in accordance with the rules laid down by the Member States, the consumer shall be entitled to an equitable reduction in the total cost of the credit.

Article 9. Where the creditor's rights under a credit agreement are assigned to a third person, the consumer shall be entitled to plead against that third person any defence which was available to him against the original creditor, including set-off where the latter is permitted in the Member State concerned.

Article 10. The Member States which, in connection with credit agreements, permit the consumer:
(a) to make payment by means of bills of exchange including promissory notes;
(b) to give security by means of bills of exchange including promissory notes and cheques,
shall ensure that the consumer is suitably protected when using these instruments in those ways.

Article 11. (1) Member States shall ensure that the existence of a credit agreement shall not in any way affect the rights of the consumer against the supplier of goods or services purchased by means of such an agreement in cases where the goods or services are not supplied or are otherwise not in conformity with the contract for their supply.
(2) Where:
(a) in order to buy goods or obtain services the consumer enters into a credit agreement with a person other than the supplier of them; and
(b) the grantor of the credit and the supplier of the goods or services have a pre-existing agreement whereunder credit is made available exclusively by that grantor of credit to customers of that supplier for the acquisition of goods or services from that supplier; and
(c) the consumer referred to in subparagraph (a) obtains his credit pursuant to that pre-existing agreement; and
(d) the goods or services covered by the credit agreement are not supplied, or are supplied only in part, or are not in conformity with the contract for supply of them; and
(e) the consumer has pursued his remedies against the supplier but has failed to obtain the satisfaction to which he is entitled,
the consumer shall have the right to pursue remedies against the grantor of credit. Member States shall determine to what extent and under what conditions these remedies shall be exercisable.
(3) Paragraph 2 shall not apply where the individual transaction in question is for an amount less than the equivalent of 200 ECU.

Article 12. (1) Member States shall:
(a) ensure that persons offering credit or offering to arrange credit agreements shall obtain official authorization to do so, either specifically or as suppliers of goods and services; or
(b) ensure that persons granting credit or arranging for credit to be granted shall be subject to inspection or monitoring of their activities by an institution or official body; or
(c) promote the establishment of appropriate bodies to receive complaints concerning credit agreements or credit conditions and to provide relevant information or advice to consumers regarding them.
(2) Member States may provide that the authorization referred to in paragraph 1 (a) shall not be required where persons offering to conclude or arrange credit agreements satisfy the definition in Article 1 of the first Council Directive of 12 December 1977 on the coordination of laws, regulations and administrative provisions relating to the taking up and pursuit of the business of credit institutions and are authorized in accordance with the provisions of that Directive.
Where persons granting credit or arranging for credit to be granted have been authorized both specifically, under the provisions of paragraph 1 (a) and also under the provisions of the aforementioned Directive, but the latter authorization is subsequently withdrawn, the competent authority responsible for issuing the specific authorization to grant credit under paragraph 1 (a) shall be informed and shall decide whether the persons concerned may continue to grant credit, or arrange for credit to be granted, or whether the specific authorization granted under paragraph 1 (a) should be withdrawn.

Article 13. (1) For the purposes of this Directive, the ECU shall be that defined by Regulation (EEC) No 3180/78, as amended by Regulation (EEC) No 2626/84. The equivalent in national currency shall initially be calculated at the rate obtaining on the date of adoption of this Directive.
Member States may round off the amounts in national currency resulting from the conversion of the amounts in ECU provided such rounding off does not exceed 10 ECU.
(2) Every five years, and for the first time in 1995, the Council, acting on a proposal from the Commission, shall examine and, if need be, revise the amounts in this Directive, in the light of economic and monetary trends in the Community.

Article 14. (1) Member States shall ensure that credit agreements shall not derogate, to the detriment of the consumer, from the provisions of national law implementing or corresponding to this Directive.

(2). Member States shall further ensure that the provisions which they adopt in implementation of this directive are not circumvented as a result of the way in which agreements are formulated, in particular by the device of distributing the amount of credit over several agreements.

Article 15. This Directive shall not preclude Member States from retaining or adopting more stringent provisions to protect consumers consistent with their obligations under the Treaty.

Article 16. (1) Member States shall bring into force the measures necessary to comply with this Directive not later than 1 January 1990 and shall forthwith inform the Commission thereof.
(2) Member States shall communicate to the Commission the texts of the main provisions of national law which they adopt in the field covered by this Directive.

Article 17. Not later than 1 January 1995 the Commission shall present a report to the Council concerning the operation of this Directive.

Article 18. This Directive is addressed to the Member States.

Annex I List of terms referred to in Article 4(3)
(1) Credit agreements for financing the supply of particular goods or services:
1.2 // (i) // a description of the goods or services covered by the agreement; // (ii) // the cash price and the price payable under the credit agreement; // (iii) // the amount of the deposit, if any, the number and amount of instalments and the dates on which they fall due, or the method of ascertaining any of the same if unknown at the time the agreement is concluded; // (iv) // an indication that the consumer will be entitled, as provided in Article 8, to a reduction if he repays early; // (v) // who owns the goods (if ownership does not pass immediately to the consumer) and the terms on which the consumer becomes the owner of them; // (vi) // a description of the security required, if any; // (vii) // the cooling-off period, if any; // (viii) // an indication of the insurance (s) required, if any, and, when the choice of insurer is not left to the consumer, an indication of the cost thereof //(ix) the obligation on the consumer to save a certain amount of money which must be placed in a special account'.
(2) Credit agreements operated by credit cards:
1.2 // (i) // the amount of the credit limit, if any; // (ii) // the terms of repayment or the means of determining them; // (iii) // the cooling-off period, if any.
3. Credit agreements operated by running account which are not otherwise covered by the Directive:
1.2 // (i) // the amount of the credit limit, if any, or the method of determining it; // (ii) // the terms of use and repayment; // (iii) // the cooling-off period, if any.
4. Other credit agreements covered by the Directive:
1.2 // (i) // the amount of the credit limit, if any; // (ii) // an indication of the security required, if any; // (iii) // the terms of repayment; // (iv) // the cooling-off period, if any; // (v) // an indication that the consumer will be entitled, as provided in Article 8, to a reduction if he repays early.

[Annexes II and III are omitted.]

Council Directive 93/7/EEC of 15 March 1993 on the return of cultural objects unlawfully removed from the territory of a Member State *(OJ* L 07, 27.03.1993, pp. 74 – 79) as amended by Directive 96/100 [footnotes omitted].

THE COUNCIL OF THE EUROPEAN COMMUNITIES,
Having regard to the Treaty establishing the European Economic Community, and in particular Article 100a thereof,
Having regard to the proposal from the Commission, In cooperation with the European Parliament,
Having regard to the opinion of the Economic and Social Committee,
Whereas Article 8a of the Treaty provides for the establishment, not later than 1 January 1993, of the internal market, which is to comprise an area without internal frontiers in which the free movement of goods, persons, services and capital is ensured in accordance with the provisions of the Treaty;
Whereas, under the terms and within the limits of Article 36 of the Treaty, Member States will, after 1992, retain the right to define their national treasures and to take the necessary measures to protect them in this area without internal frontiers;
Whereas arrangements should therefore be introduced enabling Member States to secure the return to their territory of cultural objects which are classified as national treasures within the meaning of the said Article 36 and have been removed from their territory in breach of the abovementioned national measures or of Council Regulation (EEC) No 3911/92 of 9 December 1992 on the export of cultural goods; whereas the implementation of these arrangements should be as simple and efficient as possible; whereas, to facilitate cooperation with regard to return, the scope of the arrangements should be confined to items belonging to common categories of cultural object; whereas the Annex to this Directive is consequently not intended to define objects which rank as 'national treasures' within the meaning of the said Article 36, but merely categories of object which may be classified as such and may accordingly be covered by the return procedure introduced by this Directive;
Whereas cultural objects classified as national treasures and forming an integral part of public collections or inventories of ecclesiastical institutions but which do not fall within these common categories should also be covered by this Directive;
Whereas administrative cooperation should be established between Member States as regards their national treasures, in close liaison with their cooperation in the field of stolen works of art and involving in particular the recording, with Interpol and other qualified bodies issuing similar lists, of lost, stolen or illegally removed cultural objects forming part of their national treasures and their public collections;
Whereas the procedure introduced by this Directive is a first step in establishing cooperation between Member States in this field in the context of the internal market; whereas the aim is mutual recognition of the relevant national laws; whereas provision should therefore be made, in particular, for the Commission to be assisted by an advisory committee;
Whereas Regulation (EEC) No 3911/92 introduces, together with this Directive, a Community system to protect Member States' cultural goods; whereas the date by which Member States have to comply with this Directive has to be as close as possible to the date of entry into force of that Regulation; whereas, having regard to the nature of their legal systems and the scope of the changes to their legislation necessary to implement this Directive, some Member States will need a longer period,

HAS ADOPTED THIS DIRECTIVE:

Article 1. For the purposes of this Directive:
(1) 'Cultural object' shall mean an object which:
- is classified, before or after its unlawful removal from the territory of a Member State, among the 'national treasures possessing artistic, historic or archaeological value' under national legislation or administrative procedures within the meaning of Article 36 of the Treaty,
and
- belongs to one of the categories listed in the Annex or does not belong to one of these categories but forms an integral part of:
- public collections listed in the inventories of museums, archives or libraries' conservation collection. For the purposes of this Directive, 'public collections' shall mean collections which are the property of a Member State, local or regional authority within a Member States or an institution situated in the territory of a Member State and defined as public in accordance with the legislation of that Member State, such institution being the property of, or significantly financed by, that Member State or a local or regional authority;
- the inventories of ecclesiastical institutions.
(2) 'Unlawfully removed from the territory of a Member State' shall mean:

- removed from the territory of a Member State in breach of its rules on the protection of national treasures or in breach of Regulation (EEC) No 3911/92, or - not returned at the end of a period of lawful temporary removal or any breach of another condition governing such temporary removal.
(3) 'Requesting Member State' shall mean the Member State from whose territory the cultural object has been unlawfully removed.
(4) 'Requested Member State' shall mean the Member State in whose territory a cultural object unlawfully removed from the territory of another Member State is located.
(5) 'Return' shall mean the physical return of the cultural object to the territory of the requesting Member State.
(6) 'Possessor' shall mean the person physically holding the cultural object on his own account.
(7) 'Holder' shall mean the person physically holding the cultural object for third parties.

Article 2. Cultural objects which have been unlawfully removed from the territory of a Member State shall be returned in accordance with the procedure and in the circumstances provided for in this Directive.

Article 3. Each Member State shall appoint one or more central authorities to carry out the tasks provided for in this Directive.
Member States shall inform the Commission of all the central authorities they appoint pursuant to this Article.
The Commission shall publish a lsit of these central authorities and any changes concerning them in the C series of the Official Journal of the European Communities.

Article 4. Member States' central authorities shall cooperate and promote consultation between the Member States' competent national authorities. The latter shall in particular:
(1) upon application by the requesting Member State, seek a specified cultural object which as been unlawfully removed from its territory, identifying the possessor and/or holder. The application must include all information needed to facilitate this search, with particular reference to the actual or presumed location of the object;
(2) notify the Member States concerned, where a cultural object is found in their own territory and there are reasonable grounds for believing that it has been unlawfully removed from the territory of another Member State;
(3) enable the competent authorities of the requesting Member State to check that the object in question is a cultural object, provided that the check is made within 2 months of the notification provided for in paragraph 2. If it is not made within the stipulated period, paragraphs 4 and 5 shall cease to apply;
(4) take any necessary measures, in cooperation with the Member State concerned, for the physical preservation of the cultural object;
(5) prevent, by the necessary interim measures, any action to evade the return procedure;
(6) act as intermediary between the prossessor and/or holder and the requesting Member State with regard to return. To this end, the competent authorities of the requested Member States may, without prejudice to Article 5, first facilitate the implementation of an arbitration procedure, in accordance with the national legislation of the requested State and provided that the requesting State and the possessor or holder give their formal approval.

Article 5. The requesting Member State may initiate, before the competent court in the requested Member State, proceedings against the possessor or, failing him, the holder, with the aim of securing the return of a cultural object which has been unlawfully removed from its territory.
Proceedings may be brought only where the document initiating them is accompanied by:
- a document describing the object covered by the request and stating that it is a cultural object,
- a declaration by the competent authorities of the requesting Member State that the cultural object has been unlawfully removed from its territory.

Article 6. The central authority of the requesting Member State shall forthwith inform the central authority of the requested Member State that proceedings have been initiated with the aim of securing the return of the object in question.
The central authority of the requested Member State shall forthwith inform the central authorities of the other Member States.

Article 7. (1) Member States shall lay down in their legislation that the return proceedings provided for in this Directive may not be brought more than one year after the requesting Member State became aware of the location of the cultural object and of the identity of its possessor or holder.
Such proceedings may, at all events, not be brought more than 30 years after the object was unlawfully removed from the territory of the requesting Member State. However, in the case of objects forming part of public collections, referred to in Article 1 (1), and ecclesiastical goods in the Member States where they are subject to

special protection arrangements under national law, return proceedings shall be subject to a time-limit of 75 years, except in Member States where proceedings are not subject to a time-limit or in the case of bilateral agreements between Member States laying down a period exceeding 75 years.
(2) Return proceedings may not be brought if removal from the national territory of the requesting Member State is no longer unlawful at the time when they are to be initiated.

Article 8. Save as otherwise provided in Articles 7 and 13, the competent court shall order the return of the cultural object in question where it is found to be a cultural object within the meaning of Article 1 (1) and to have been removed unlawfully from national teerritory.

Article 9. Where return of the object is ordered, the competent court in the requested States shall award the possessor such compensation as it deems fair according to the circumstances of the case, provided that it is satisfied that the possessor exercised due care and attention in acquiring the object. The burden of proof shall be governed by the legislation of the requested Member State.
In the case of a donation or succession, the possessor shall not be in a more favourable position than the person from whom he acquired the object by that means. The requesting Member State shall pay such compensation upon return of the object.

Article 10. Expenses incurred in implementing a decision ordering the return of a cultural object shall be borne by the requesting Member State. The same applies to the costs of the measures referred to in Article 4 (4).

Article 11. Payment of the fair compensation and of the expenses referred to in Articles 9 and 10 respectively shall be without prejudice to the requesting Member State's right to take action with a view to recovering those amounts from the persons responsible for the unlawful removal of the cultural object from its territory.

Article 12. Ownership of the cultural object after return shall be governed by that law of the requesting Member State.

Article 13. This Directive shall apply only to cultural objects unlawfully removed from the territory of a Member State on or after 1 January 1993.

Article 14. (1) Each Member State may extend its obligation to return cultural objects to cover categories of objects other than those listed in the Annex.
(2) Each Member State may apply the arrangements provided for by this Directive to requests for the return of cultural objects unlawfully removed from the territory of other Member States prior to 1 January 1993.

Article 15. This Directive shall be without prejudice to any civil or criminal proceedings that may be brought, under the national laws of the Member States, by the requesting Member State and/or the owner of a cultural object that has been stolen.

Article 16. (1) Member States shall send the Commission every three years, and for the first time in February 1996, a report on the application of this Directive.
(2) The Commission shall send the European Parliament, the Council and the Economic and Social Committee, every three years, a report reviewing the application of this Directive.
(3) The Council shall review the effectiveness of this Directive after a period of application of three years and, acting on a proposal from the Commission, make any necessary adaptations.
(4) In any event, the Council acting on a proposal from the Commission, shall examine every three years and, where appropriate, update the amounts indicated in the Annex, on the basis of economic and monetary indicators in the Community.

Article 17. The Commission shall be assisted by the Committee set up by Article 8 of Regulation (EEC) No 3911/92.
The Committee shall examine any question arising from the application of the Annex to this Directive which may be tabled by the chairman either on his own initiative or at the request of the representative of a Member State.

Article 18. Member States shall bring into force the laws, regulations and administrative provisions necessary to comply with this Directive within nine months of its adoption, except as far as the Kingdom of Belgium, the Federal Republic of Germany and the Kingdom of the Netherlands are concerned, which must conform to this

Part IX. European Private Law

Directive at the latest twelve months from the date of its adoption. They shall forthwith inform the Commission thereof. When Member States adopt these measures, they shall contain a reference to this Directive or shall be accompanied by such reference on the occasion of their official publication. The methods of making such a reference shall be laid down by the Member States.

Article 19. This Directive is addressed to the Member States.

Annex. Categories referred to in the second indent of Article 1 (1) to which objects classified as 'national treasures' within the meaning of Article 36 of the Treaty must belong in order to qualify for return under this Directive

A. (1) Archaeological objects more than 100 years old which are the products of:
- land or underwater excavations and finds,
- archaeological sites,
- archaeological collections.

(2) Elements forming an integral part of artistic, historical or religious monuments which have been dismembered, more than 100 years old.
(3) Pictures and paintings, other than those included in Category 3A or 4, executed entirely by hand on any material and in any medium.
(3A) Water-colours, gouaches and pastels executed entirely by hand on any material.
(4) Mosaics in any material executed entirely by hand, other than those falling in Categories 1 or 2, and drawings in any medium executed entirely by hand on any material.
(5) Original engravings, prints, serigraphs and lithographs with their respective plates and original posters.
(6) Original sculptures or statuary and copies produced by the same process as the original other than those in category 1.
(7) Photographs, films and negatives thereof.
(8) Incunabula and manuscripts, including maps and musical scores, singly or in collections.
(9) Books more than 100 years old, singly or in collections.
(10) Printed maps more than 200 years old.
(11) Archives and any elements thereof, of any kind, on any medium, comprising elements more than 50 years old.
(12) (a) Collections (2) and specimens from zoological, botanical, mineralogical or anatomical collections;
(b) Collections (2) of historical, palaeontological, ethnographic or numismatic interest.
(13) Means of transport more than 75 years old.
(14) Any other antique item not included in categories A 1 to A 13, more than 50 years old. The cultural objects in categories A 1 to A 14 are covered by this Directive only if their value corresponds to, or exceeds, the financial thresholds under B.

B. Financial thresholds applicable to certain categories under A (in ecus)
VALUE: 0 (Zero)
- 1 (Archaeological objects)
- 2 (Dismembered monuments)
- 8 (Incunabula and manuscripts)
- 11 (Archives)
15 000
- 4 (Mosaics and drawings)
- 5 (Engravings)
- 7 (Photographs)
- 10 (Printed maps)
30 000
- 3A. (Water colours, gouaches and pastels)`.
50 000
- 6 (Statuary)
- 9 (Books)
- 12 (Collections)
- 13 (Means of transport)
- 14 (Any other item)
150 000
- 3 (Pictures)

Council Directive 93/13/EEC of 5 April 1993 on unfair terms in consumer contracts (*OJ* L 095 , 21.04.1993, pp. 29 – 34) [footnotes omitted].

THE COUNCIL OF THE ERUOPEAN COMMUNITIES, Having regard to the Treaty establishing the European Economic Community, and in particular Article 100 A thereof, Having regard to the proposal from the Commission,
In cooperation with the European Parliament ,
Having regard to the opinion of the Economic and Social Committee,
Whereas it is necessary to adopt measures with the aim of progressively establishing the internal market before 31 December 1992; Whereas the internal market comprises an area without internal frontiers in which goods, persons, services and capital move freely;
Whereas the laws of Member States relating to the terms of contract between the seller of goods or supplier of services, on the one hand, and the consumer of them, on the other hand, show many disparities, with the result that the national markets for the sale of goods and services to consumers differ from each other and that distortions of competition may arise amongst the sellers and suppliers, notably when they sell and supply in other Member States;
Whereas, in particular, the laws of Member States relating to unfair terms in consumer contracts show marked divergences;
Whereas it is the responsibility of the Member States to ensure that contracts concluded with consumers do not contain unfair terms;
Whereas, generally speaking, consumers do not know the rules of law which, in Member States other than their own, govern contracts for the sale of goods or services; Whereas this lack of awareness may deter them from direct transactions for the purchase of goods or services in another Member State;
Whereas, in order to facilitate the establishment of the internal market and to safeguard the citizen in his role as consumer when acquiring goods and services under contracts which are governed by the laws of Member States other than his own, it is essential to remove unfair terms from those contracts;
Whereas sellers of goods and suppliers of services will thereby be helped in their task of selling goods and supplying services, both at home and throughout the internal market; whereas competition will thus be stimulated, so contributing to increased choice for Community citizens as consumers;
Whereas the two Community programmes for a consumer protection and information policy underlined the importance of safeguarding consumers in the matter of unfair terms of contract; Whereas this protection ought to be provided by laws and regulations which are either harmonized at Community level or adopted directly at that level;
Whereas in accordance with the principle laid down under the heading 'Protection of the economic interests of the consumers', as stated in those programmes: 'acquirers of goods and services should be protected against the abuse of power by the seller or supplier, in particular against one-sided standard contracts and the unfair exclusion of essential rights in contracts';
Whereas more effective protection of the consumer can be achieved by adopting uniform rules of law in the matter of unfair terms; whereas those rules should apply to all contracts concluded between sellers or suppliers and consumers; whereas as a result inter alia contracts relating to employment, contracts relating to succession rights, contracts relating to rights under family law and contracts relating to the incorporation and organization of companies or partnership agreements must be excluded from this Directive;
Whereas the consumer must receive equal protection under contracts concluded by word of mouth and written contracts regardless, in the latter case, of whether the terms of the contract are contained in one or more documents;
Whereas, however, as they now stand, national laws allow only partial harmonization to be envisaged; whereas, in particular, only contractual terms which have not been individually negotiated are covered by this Directive; whereas Member States should have the option, with due regard for the Treaty, to afford consumers a higher level of protection through national provisions that are more stringent than those of this Directive;
Whereas the statutory or regulatory provisions of the Member States which directly or indirectly determine the terms of consumer contracts are presumed not to contain unfair terms; whereas, therefore, it does not appear to be necessary to subject the terms which reflect mandatory statutory or regulatory provisions and the principles or provisions of international conventions to which the Member States or the Community are party; whereas in that respect the wording 'mandatory statutory or regulatory provisions' in Article 1 (2) also covers rules which, according to the law, shall apply between the contracting parties provided that no other arrangements have been established;
Whereas Member States must however ensure that unfair terms are not included, particularly because this Directive also applies to trades, business or professions of a public nature;

Whereas it is necessary to fix in a general way the criteria for assessing the unfair character of contract terms; Whereas the assessment, according to the general criteria chosen, of the unfair character of terms, in particular in sale or supply activities of a public nature providing collective services which take account of solidarity among users, must be supplemented by a means of making an overall evaluation of the different interests involved; whereas this constitutes the requirement of good faith; whereas, in making an assessment of good faith, particular regard shall be had to the strength of the bargaining positions of the parties, whether the consumer had an inducement to agree to the term and whether the goods or services were sold or supplied to the special order of the consumer; whereas the requirement of good faith may be satisfied by the seller or supplier where he deals fairly and equitably with the other party whose legitimate interests he has to take into account;

Whereas, for the purposes of this Directive, the annexed list of terms can be of indicative value only and, because of the cause of the minimal character of the Directive, the scope of these terms may be the subject of amplification or more restrictive editing by the Member States in their national laws;

Whereas the nature of goods or services should have an influence on assessing the unfairness of contractual terms; Whereas, for the purposes of this Directive, assessment of unfair character shall not be made of terms which describe the main subject matter of the contract nor the quality/price ratio of the goods or services supplied; whereas the main subject matter of the contract and the price/quality ratio may nevertheless be taken into account in assessing the fairness of other terms; whereas it follows, inter alia, that in insurance contracts, the terms which clearly define or circumscribe the insured risk and the insurer's liability shall not be subject to such assessment since these restrictions are taken into account in calculating the premium paid by the consumer;

Whereas contracts should be drafted in plain, intelligible language, the consumer should actually be given an opportunity to examine all the terms and, if in doubt, the interpretation most favourable to the consumer should prevail;

Whereas Member States should ensure that unfair terms are not used in contracts concluded with consumers by a seller or supplier and that if, nevertheless, such terms are so used, they will not bind the consumer, and the contract will continue to bind the parties upon those terms if it is capable of continuing in existence without the unfair provisions; whereas there is a risk that, in certain cases, the consumer may be deprived of protection under this Directive by designating the law of a non-Member country as the law applicable to the contract; whereas provisions should therefore be included in this Directive designed to avert this risk;

Whereas persons or organizations, if regarded under the law of a Member State as having a legitimate interest in the matter, must have facilities for initiating proceedings concerning terms of contract drawn up for general use in contracts concluded with consumers, and in particular unfair terms, either before a court or before an administrative authority competent to decide upon complaints or to initiate appropriate legal proceedings; whereas this possibility does not, however, entail prior verification of the general conditions obtaining in individual economic sectors;

Whereas the courts or administrative authorities of the Member States must have at their disposal adequate and effective means of preventing the continued application of unfair terms in consumer contracts,

HAS ADOPTED THIS DIRECTIVE:

Article 1. (1) The purpose of this Directive is to approximate the laws, regulations and administrative provisions of the Member States relating to unfair terms in contracts concluded between a seller or supplier and a consumer.
(2) The contractual terms which reflect mandatory statutory or regulatory provisions and the provisions or principles of international conventions to which the Member States or the Community are party, particularly in the transport area, shall not be subject to the provisions of this Directive.

Article 2. For the purposes of this Directive:
(a) 'unfair terms' means the contractual terms defined in Article 3;
(b) 'consumer' means any natural person who, in contracts covered by this Directive, is acting for purposes which are outside his trade, business or profession;
(c) 'seller or supplier' means any natural or legal person who, in contracts covered by this Directive, is acting for purposes relating to his trade, business or profession, whether publicly owned or privately owned.

Article 3. (1) A contractual term which has not been individually negotiated shall be regarded as unfair if, contrary to the requirement of good faith, it causes a significant imbalance in the parties' rights and obligations arising under the contract, to the detriment of the consumer.
(2) A term shall always be regarded as not individually negotiated where it has been drafted in advance and the consumer has therefore not been able to influence the substance of the term, particularly in the context of a pre-formulated standard contract. The fact that certain aspects of a term or one specific term have been individually

negotiated shall not exclude the application of this Article to the rest of a contract if an overall assessment of the contract indicates that it is nevertheless a pre-formulated standard contract. Where any seller or supplier claims that a standard term has been individually negotiated, the burden of proof in this respect shall be incumbent on him.
(3) The Annex shall contain an indicative and non-exhaustive list of the terms which may be regarded as unfair.

Article 4. (1) Without prejudice to Article 7, the unfairness of a contractual term shall be assessed, taking into account the nature of the goods or services for which the contract was concluded and by referring, at the time of conclusion of the contract, to all the circumstances attending the conclusion of the contract and to all the other terms of the contract or of another contract on which it is dependent.
(2) Assessment of the unfair nature of the terms shall relate neither to the definition of the main subject matter of the contract nor to the adequacy of the price and remuneration, on the one hand, as against the services or goods supplies in exchange, on the other, in so far as these terms are in plain intelligible language.

Article 5. In the case of contracts where all or certain terms offered to the consumer are in writing, these terms must always be drafted in plain, intelligible language. Where there is doubt about the meaning of a term, the interpretation most favourable to the consumer shall prevail. This rule on interpretation shall not apply in the context of the procedures laid down in Article 7 (2).

Article 6. (1) Member States shall lay down that unfair terms used in a contract concluded with a consumer by a seller or supplier shall, as provided for under their national law, not be binding on the consumer and that the contract shall continue to bind the parties upon those terms if it is capable of continuing in existence without the unfair terms.
(2) Member States shall take the necessary measures to ensure that the consumer does not lose the protection granted by this Directive by virtue of the choice of the law of a non-Member country as the law applicable to the contract if the latter has a close connection with the territory of the Member States.

Article 7. (1) Member States shall ensure that, in the interests of consumers and of competitors, adequate and effective means exist to prevent the continued use of unfair terms in contracts concluded with consumers by sellers or suppliers.
(2) The means referred to in paragraph 1 shall include provisions whereby persons or organizations, having a legitimate interest under national law in protecting consumers, may take action according to the national law concerned before the courts or before competent administrative bodies for a decision as to whether contractual terms drawn up for general use are unfair, so that they can apply appropriate and effective means to prevent the continued use of such terms.
(3) With due regard for national laws, the legal remedies referred to in paragraph 2 may be directed separately or jointly against a number of sellers or suppliers from the same economic sector or their associations which use or recommend the use of the same general contractual terms or similar terms.

Article 8. Member States may adopt or retain the most stringent provisions compatible with the Treaty in the area covered by this Directive, to ensure a maximum degree of protection for the consumer.

Article 9. The Commission shall present a report to the European Parliament and to the Council concerning the application of this Directive five years at the latest after the date in Article 10 (1).

Article 10. (1) Member States shall bring into force the laws, regulations and administrative provisions necessary to comply with this Directive no later than 31 December 1994. They shall forthwith inform the Commission thereof.
These provisions shall be applicable to all contracts concluded after 31 December 1994.
(2) When Member States adopt these measures, they shall contain a reference to this Directive or shall be accompanied by such reference on the occasion of their official publication. The methods of making such a reference shall be laid down by the Member States.
(3) Member States shall communicate the main provisions of national law which they adopt in the field covered by this Directive to the Commission.

Article 11. This Directive is addressed to the Member States.

Annex. Terms referred to in Article 3 (1)

Terms which have the object or effect of:
(a) excluding or limiting the legal liability of a seller or supplier in the event of the death of a consumer or personal injury to the latter resulting from an act or omission of that seller or supplier;
(b) inappropriately excluding or limiting the legal rights of the consumer vis-à-vis the seller or supplier or another party in the event of total or partial non-performance or inadequate performance by the seller or supplier of any of the contractual obligations, including the option of offsetting a debt owed to the seller or supplier against any claim which the consumer may have against him;
(c) making an agreement binding on the consumer whereas provision of services by the seller or supplier is subject to a condition whose realization depends on his own will alone;
(d) permitting the seller or supplier to retain sums paid by the consumer where the latter decides not to conclude or perform the contract, without providing for the consumer to receive compensation of an equivalent amount from the seller or supplier where the latter is the party cancelling the contract;
(e) requiring any consumer who fails to fulfil his obligation to pay a disproportionately high sum in compensation;
(f) authorizing the seller or supplier to dissolve the contract on a discretionary basis where the same facility is not granted to the consumer, or permitting the seller or supplier to retain the sums paid for services not yet supplied by him where it is the seller or supplier himself who dissolves the contract;
(g) enabling the seller or supplier to terminate a contract of indeterminate duration without reasonable notice except where there are serious grounds for doing so;
(h) automatically extending a contract of fixed duration where the consumer does not indicate otherwise, when the deadline fixed for the consumer to express this desire not to extend the contract is unreasonably early;
(i) irrevocably binding the consumer to terms with which he had no real opportunity of becoming acquainted before the conclusion of the contract;
(j) enabling the seller or supplier to alter the terms of the contract unilaterally without a valid reason which is specified in the contract;
(k) enabling the seller or supplier to alter unilaterally without a valid reason any characteristics of the product or service to be provided;
(l) providing for the price of goods to be determined at the time of delivery or allowing a seller of goods or supplier of services to increase their price without in both cases giving the consumer the corresponding right to cancel the contract if the final price is too high in relation to the price agreed when the contract was concluded;
(m) giving the seller or supplier the right to determine whether the goods or services supplied are in conformity with the contract, or giving him the exclusive right to interpret any term of the contract;
(n) limiting the seller's or supplier's obligation to respect commitments undertaken by his agents or making his commitments subject to compliance with a particular formality;
(o) obliging the consumer to fulfil all his obligations where the seller or supplier does not perform his;
(p) giving the seller or supplier the possibility of transferring his rights and obligations under the contract, where this may serve to reduce the guarantees for the consumer, without the latter's agreement;
(q) excluding or hindering the consumer's right to take legal action or exercise any other legal remedy, particularly by requiring the consumer to take disputes exclusively to arbitration not covered by legal provisions, unduly restricting the evidence available to him or imposing on him a burden of proof which, according to the applicable law, should lie with another party to the contract.
(2) Scope of subparagraphs (g), (j) and (l)
(a) Subparagraph (g) is without hindrance to terms by which a supplier of financial services reserves the right to terminate unilaterally a contract of indeterminate duration without notice where there is a valid reason, provided that the supplier is required to inform the other contracting party or parties thereof immediately.
(b) Subparagraph (j) is without hindrance to terms under which a supplier of financial services reserves the right to alter the rate of interest payable by the consumer or due to the latter, or the amount of other charges for financial services without notice where there is a valid reason, provided that the supplier is required to inform the other contracting party or parties thereof at the earliest opportunity and that the latter are free to dissolve the contract immediately.
Subparagraph (j) is also without hindrance to terms under which a seller or supplier reserves the right to alter unilaterally the conditions of a contract of indeterminate duration, provided that he is required to inform the consumer with reasonable notice and that the consumer is free to dissolve the contract.
(c) Subparagraphs (g), (j) and (l) do not apply to:
- transactions in transferable securities, financial instruments and other products or services where the price is linked to fluctuations in a stock exchange quotation or index or a financial market rate that the seller or supplier does not control;

- contracts for the purchase or sale of foreign currency, traveller's cheques or international money orders denominated in foreign currency;

(d) Subparagraph (l) is without hindrance to price-indexation clauses, where lawful, provided that the method by which prices vary is explicitly described.

EUPRIV

Directive 97/7/EC of the European Parliament and of the Council of 20 May 1997 on the protection of consumers in respect of distance contracts (OJ L144, 04.06.1997, pp. 19 -27) as amended by Directive 2002/65 [footnotes omitted].

THE EUROPEAN PARLIAMENT AND THE COUNCIL OF THE UNION,
Having regard to the Treaty establishing the European Community, and in particular Article 100a thereof, Having regard to the proposal from the Commission ,
Having regard to the opinion of the Economic and Social Committee,
Acting in accordance with the procedure laid down in Article 189b of the Treaty, in the light of the joint text approved by the Conciliation Committee on 27 November 1996,
(1) Whereas, in connection with the attainment of the aims of the internal market, measures must be taken for the gradual consolidation of that market;
(2) Whereas the free movement of goods and services affects not only the business sector but also private individuals; whereas it means that consumers should be able to have access to the goods and services of another Member State on the same terms as the population of that State;
(3) Whereas, for consumers, cross-border distance selling could be one of the main tangible results of the completion of the internal market, as noted, inter alia, in the communication from the Commission to the Council entitled 'Towards a single market in distribution`; whereas it is essential to the smooth operation of the internal market for consumers to be able to have dealings with a business outside their country, even if it has a subsidiary in the consumer's country of residence;
(4) Whereas the introduction of new technologies is increasing the number of ways for consumers to obtain information about offers anywhere in the Community and to place orders; whereas some Member States have already taken different or diverging measures to protect consumers in respect of distance selling, which has had a detrimental effect on competition between businesses in the internal market; whereas it is therefore necessary to introduce at Community level a minimum set of common rules in this area;
(5) Whereas paragraphs 18 and 19 of the Annex to the Council resolution of 14 April 1975 on a preliminary programme of the European Economic Community for a consumer protection and information policy point to the need to protect the purchasers of goods or services from demands for payment for unsolicited goods and from high-pressure selling methods;
(6) Whereas paragraph 33 of the communication from the Commission to the Council entitled 'A new impetus for consumer protection policy`, which was approved by the Council resolution of 23 June 1986, states that the Commission will submit proposals regarding the use of new information technologies enabling consumers to place orders with suppliers from their homes;
(7) Whereas the Council resolution of 9 November 1989 on future priorities for relaunching consumer protection policy calls upon the Commission to give priority to the areas referred to in the Annex to that resolution; whereas that Annex refers to new technologies involving teleshopping; whereas the Commission has responded to that resolution by adopting a three-year action plan for consumer protection policy in the European Economic Community (1990-1992); whereas that plan provides for the adoption of a Directive;
(8) Whereas the languages used for distance contracts are a matter for the Member States;
(9) Whereas contracts negotiated at a distance involve the use of one or more means of distance communication; whereas the various means of communication are used as part of an organized distance sales or service-provision scheme not involving the simultaneous presence of the supplier and the consumer; whereas the constant development of those means of communication does not allow an exhaustive list to be compiled but does require principles to be defined which are valid even for those which are not as yet in widespread use;
(10) Whereas the same transaction comprising successive operations or a series of separate operations over a period of time may give rise to different legal descriptions depending on the law of the Member States; whereas the provisions of this Directive cannot be applied differently according to the law of the Member States, subject to their recourse to Article 14; whereas, to that end, there is therefore reason to consider that there must at least be compliance with the provisions of this Directive at the time of the first of a series of successive operations or the first of a series of separate operations over a period of time which may be considered as forming a whole, whether that operation or series of operations are the subject of a single contract or successive, separate contracts;
(11) Whereas the use of means of distance communication must not lead to a reduction in the information provided to the consumer; whereas the information that is required to be sent to the consumer should therefore be determined, whatever the means of communication used; whereas the information supplied must also comply with the other relevant Community rules, in particular those in Council Directive 84/450/EEC of 10 September 1984 relating to the approximation of the laws, regulations and administrative provisions of the Member States concerning misleading advertising; whereas, if exceptions are made to the obligation to provide information, it is

up to the consumer, on a discretionary basis, to request certain basic information such as the identity of the supplier, the main characteristics of the goods or services and their price;

(12) Whereas in the case of communication by telephone it is appropriate that the consumer receive enough information at the beginning of the conversation to decide whether or not to continue;

(13) Whereas information disseminated by certain electronic technologies is often ephemeral in nature insofar as it is not received on a permanent medium; whereas the consumer must therefore receive written notice in good time of the information necessary for proper performance of the contract;

(14) Whereas the consumer is not able actually to see the product or ascertain the nature of the service provided before concluding the contract; whereas provision should be made, unless otherwise specified in this Directive, for a right of withdrawal from the contract; whereas, if this right is to be more than formal, the costs, if any, borne by the consumer when exercising the right of withdrawal must be limited to the direct costs for returning the goods; whereas this right of withdrawal shall be without prejudice to the consumer's rights under national laws, with particular regard to the receipt of damaged products and services or of products and services not corresponding to the description given in the offer of such products or services; whereas it is for the Member States to determine the other conditions and arrangements following exercise of the right of withdrawal;

(15) Whereas it is also necessary to prescribe a time limit for performance of the contract if this is not specified at the time of ordering;

(16) Whereas the promotional technique involving the dispatch of a product or the provision of a service to the consumer in return for payment without a prior request from, or the explicit agreement of, the consumer cannot be permitted, unless a substitute product or service is involved;

(17) Whereas the principles set out in Articles 8 and 10 of the European Convention for the Protection of Human Rights and Fundamental Freedoms of 4 November 1950 apply; whereas the consumer's right to privacy, particularly as regards freedom from certain particularly intrusive means of communication, should be recognized; whereas specific limits on the use of such means should therefore be stipulated; whereas Member States should take appropriate measures to protect effectively those consumers, who do not wish to be contacted through certain means of communication, against such contacts, without prejudice to the particular safeguards available to the consumer under Community legislation concerning the protection of personal data and privacy;

(18) Whereas it is important for the minimum binding rules contained in this Directive to be supplemented where appropriate by voluntary arrangements among the traders concerned, in line with Commission recommendation 92/295/EEC of 7 April 1992 on codes of practice for the protection of consumers in respect of contracts negotiated at a distance;

(19) Whereas in the interest of optimum consumer protection it is important for consumers to be satisfactorily informed of the provisions of this Directive and of codes of practice that may exist in this field;

(20) Whereas non-compliance with this Directive may harm not only consumers but also competitors; whereas provisions may therefore be laid down enabling public bodies or their representatives, or consumer organizations which, under national legislation, have a legitimate interest in consumer protection, or professional organizations which have a legitimate interest in taking action, to monitor the application thereof;

(21) Whereas it is important, with a view to consumer protection, to address the question of cross-border complaints as soon as this is feasible; whereas the Commission published on 14 February 1996 a plan of action on consumer access to justice and the settlement of consumer disputes in the internal market; whereas that plan of action includes specific initiatives to promote out-of-court procedures; whereas objective criteria (Annex II) are suggested to ensure the reliability of those procedures and provision is made for the use of standardized claims forms (Annex III);

(22) Whereas in the use of new technologies the consumer is not in control of the means of communication used; whereas it is therefore necessary to provide that the burden of proof may be on the supplier;

(23) Whereas there is a risk that, in certain cases, the consumer may be deprived of protection under this Directive through the designation of the law of a non-member country as the law applicable to the contract; whereas provisions should therefore be included in this Directive to avert that risk;

(24) Whereas a Member State may ban, in the general interest, the marketing on its territory of certain goods and services through distance contracts; whereas that ban must comply with Community rules; whereas there is already provision for such bans, notably with regard to medicinal products, under Council Directive 89/552/EEC of 3 October 1989 on the coordination of certain provisions laid down by law, regulation or administrative action in Member States concerning the pursuit of television broadcasting activities and Council Directive 92/28/EEC of 31 March 1992 on the advertising of medicinal products for human use,

HAVE ADOPTED THIS DIRECTIVE:

Article 1. The object of this Directive is to approximate the laws, regulations and administrative provisions of the Member States concerning distance contracts between consumers and suppliers.

Article 2. For the purposes of this Directive:
(1) 'distance contract' means any contract concerning goods or services concluded between a supplier and a consumer under an organized distance sales or service-provision scheme run by the supplier, who, for the purpose of the contract, makes exclusive use of one or more means of distance communication up to and including the moment at which the contract is concluded;
(2) 'consumer' means any natural person who, in contracts covered by this Directive, is acting for purposes which are outside his trade, business or profession;
(3) 'supplier' means any natural or legal person who, in contracts covered by this Directive, is acting in his commercial or professional capacity;
(4) 'means of distance communication' means any means which, without the simultaneous physical presence of the supplier and the consumer, may be used for the conclusion of a contract between those parties. An indicative list of the means covered by this Directive is contained in Annex I;
(5) 'operator of a means of communication' means any public or private natural or legal person whose trade, business or profession involves making one or more means of distance communication available to suppliers.

Article 3. (1) This Directive shall not apply to contracts:
- relating to any financial service to which Directive 2002/65/EC of the European Parliament and of the Council of 23 September 2002 concerning the distance marketing of consumer financial services and amending Council Directive 90/619/EEC and Directives 97/7/EC and 98/27/EC(13) applies,
- concluded by means of automatic vending machines or automated commercial premises,
- concluded with telecommunications operators through the use of public payphones,
- concluded for the construction and sale of immovable property or relating to other immovable property rights, except for rental,
- concluded at an auction.
(2) Articles 4, 5, 6 and 7 (1) shall not apply:
- to contracts for the supply of foodstuffs, beverages or other goods intended for everyday consumption supplied to the home of the consumer, to his residence or to his workplace by regular roundsmen,
- to contracts for the provision of accommodation, transport, catering or leisure services, where the supplier undertakes, when the contract is concluded, to provide these services on a specific date or within a specific period; exceptionally, in the case of outdoor leisure events, the supplier can reserve the right not to apply Article 7 (2) in specific circumstances.

Article 4. (1) In good time prior to the conclusion of any distance contract, the consumer shall be provided with the following information:
(a) the identity of the supplier and, in the case of contracts requiring payment in advance, his address;
(b) the main characteristics of the goods or services;
(c) the price of the goods or services including all taxes;
(d) delivery costs, where appropriate;
(e) the arrangements for payment, delivery or performance;
(f) the existence of a right of withdrawal, except in the cases referred to in Article 6 (3);
(g) the cost of using the means of distance communication, where it is calculated other than at the basic rate;
(h) the period for which the offer or the price remains valid;
(i) where appropriate, the minimum duration of the contract in the case of contracts for the supply of products or services to be performed permanently or recurrently.
(2) The information referred to in paragraph 1, the commercial purpose of which must be made clear, shall be provided in a clear and comprehensible manner in any way appropriate to the means of distance communication used, with due regard, in particular, to the principles of good faith in commercial transactions, and the principles governing the protection of those who are unable, pursuant to the legislation of the Member States, to give their consent, such as minors.
(3) Moreover, in the case of telephone communications, the identity of the supplier and the commercial purpose of the call shall be made explicitly clear at the beginning of any conversation with the consumer.

Article 5. (1) The consumer must receive written confirmation or confirmation in another durable medium available and accessible to him of the information referred to in Article 4 (1) (a) to (f), in good time during the performance of the contract, and at the latest at the time of delivery where goods not for delivery to third parties

are concerned, unless the information has already been given to the consumer prior to conclusion of the contract in writing or on another durable medium available and accessible to him. In any event the following must be provided:
- written information on the conditions and procedures for exercising the right of withdrawal, within the meaning of Article 6, including the cases referred to in the first indent of Article 6 (3),
- the geographical address of the place of business of the supplier to which the consumer may address any complaints,
- information on after-sales services and guarantees which exist,
- the conclusion for cancelling the contract, where it is of unspecified duration or a duration exceeding one year.
(2) Paragraph 1 shall not apply to services which are performed through the use of a means of distance communication, where they are supplied on only one occasion and are invoiced by the operator of the means of distance communication. Nevertheless, the consumer must in all cases be able to obtain the geographical address of the place of business of the supplier to which he may address any complaints.

Article 6. (1) For any distance contract the consumer shall have a period of at least seven working days in which to withdraw from the contract without penalty and without giving any reason. The only charge that may be made to the consumer because of the exercise of his right of withdrawal is the direct cost of returning the goods. The period for exercise of this right shall begin:
- in the case of goods, from the day of receipt by the consumer where the obligations laid down in Article 5 have been fulfilled,
- in the case of services, from the day of conclusion of the contract or from the day on which the obligations laid down in Article 5 were fulfilled if they are fulfilled after conclusion of the contract, provided that this period does not exceed the three-month period referred to in the following subparagraph.
If the supplier has failed to fulfil the obligations laid down in Article 5, the period shall be three months. The period shall begin:
- in the case of goods, from the day of receipt by the consumer,
- in the case of services, from the day of conclusion of the contract.
If the information referred to in Article 5 is supplied within this three-month period, the seven working day period referred to in the first subparagraph shall begin as from that moment.
(2) Where the right of withdrawal has been exercised by the consumer pursuant to this Article, the supplier shall be obliged to reimburse the sums paid by the consumer free of charge. The only charge that may be made to the consumer because of the exercise of his right of withdrawal is the direct cost of returning the goods. Such reimbursement must be carried out as soon as possible and in any case within 30 days.
(3) Unless the parties have agreed otherwise, the consumer may not exercise the right of withdrawal provided for in paragraph 1 in respect of contracts:
- for the provision of services if performance has begun, with the consumer's agreement, before the end of the seven working day period referred to in paragraph 1,
- for the supply of goods or services the price of which is dependent on fluctuations in the financial market which cannot be controlled by the supplier,
- for the supply of goods made to the consumer's specifications or clearly personalized or which, by reason of their nature, cannot be returned or are liable to deteriorate or expire rapidly,
- for the supply of audio or video recordings or computer software which were unsealed by the consumer,
- for the supply of newspapers, periodicals and magazines,
- for gaming and lottery services.
(4) The Member States shall make provision in their legislation to ensure that:
- if the price of goods or services is fully or partly covered by credit granted by the supplier, or
- if that price is fully or partly covered by credit granted to the consumer by a third party on the basis of an agreement between the third party and the supplier,
the credit agreement shall be cancelled, without any penalty, if the consumer exercises his right to withdraw from the contract in accordance with paragraph 1.
Member States shall determine the detailed rules for cancellation of the credit agreement.

Article 7. (1) Unless the parties have agreed otherwise, the supplier must execute the order within a maximum of 30 days from the day following that on which the consumer forwarded his order to the supplier.
(2) Where a supplier fails to perform his side of the contract on the grounds that the goods or services ordered are unavailable, the consumer must be informed of this situation and must be able to obtain a refund of any sums he has paid as soon as possible and in any case within 30 days.

(3) Nevertheless, Member States may lay down that the supplier may provide the consumer with goods or services of equivalent quality and price provided that this possibility was provided for prior to the conclusion of the contract or in the contract. The consumer shall be informed of this possibility in a clear and comprehensible manner. The cost of returning the goods following exercise of the right of withdrawal shall, in this case, be borne by the supplier, and the consumer must be informed of this. In such cases the supply of goods or services may not be deemed to constitute inertia selling within the meaning of Article 9.

Article 8. Member States shall ensure that appropriate measures exist to allow a consumer:
- to request cancellation of a payment where fraudulent use has been made of his payment card in connection with distance contracts covered by this Directive,
- in the event of fraudulent use, to be recredited with the sums paid or have them returned.

Article 9. Member States shall take the measures necessary to:
- prohibit the supply of goods or services to a consumer without their being ordered by the consumer beforehand, where such supply involves a demand for payment,
- exempt the consumer from the provision of any consideration in cases of unsolicited supply, the absence of a response not constituting consent.

Article 10. (1) Use by a supplier of the following means requires the prior consent of the consumer:
- automated calling system without human intervention (automatic calling machine),
- facsimile machine (fax).
(2) Member States shall ensure that means of distance communication, other than those referred to in paragraph 1, which allow individual communications may be used only where there is no clear objection from the consumer.

Article 11. (1) Member States shall ensure that adequate and effective means exist to ensure compliance with this Directive in the interests of consumers.
(2) The means referred to in paragraph 1 shall include provisions whereby one or more of the following bodies, as determined by national law, may take action under national law before the courts or before the competent administrative bodies to ensure that the national provisions for the implementation of this Directive are applied:
(a) public bodies or their representatives;
(b) consumer organizations having a legitimate interest in protecting consumers;
(c) professional organizations having a legitimate interest in acting.
(3)
(a) Member States may stipulate that the burden of proof concerning the existence of prior information, written confirmation, compliance with time-limits or consumer consent can be placed on the supplier.
(b) Member States shall take the measures needed to ensure that suppliers and operators of means of communication, where they are able to do so, cease practices which do not comply with measures adopted pursuant to this Directive.
(4) Member States may provide for voluntary supervision by self-regulatory bodies of compliance with the provisions of this Directive and recourse to such bodies for the settlement of disputes to be added to the means which Member States must provided to ensure compliance with the provisions of this Directive.

Article 12. (1) The consumer may not waive the rights conferred on him by the transposition of this Directive into national law.
(2) Member States shall take the measures needed to ensure that the consumer does not lose the protection granted by this Directive by virtue of the choice of the law of a non-member country as the law applicable to the contract if the latter has close connection with the territory of one or more Member States.

Article 13. (1) The provisions of this Directive shall apply insofar as there are no particular provisions in rules of Community law governing certain types of distance contracts in their entirety.
(2) Where specific Community rules contain provisions governing only certain aspects of the supply of goods or provision of services, those provisions, rather than the provisions of this Directive, shall apply to these specific aspects of the distance contracts.

Article 14. Member States may introduce or maintain, in the area covered by this Directive, more stringent provisions compatible with the Treaty, to ensure a higher level of consumer protection. Such provisions shall, where appropriate, include a ban, in the general interest, on the marketing of certain goods or services, particularly medicinal products, within their territory by means of distance contracts, with due regard for the Treaty.

Article 15. (1) Member States shall bring into force the laws, regulations and administrative provisions necessary to comply with this Directive no later than three years after it enters into force. They shall forthwith inform the Commission thereof.
(2) When Member States adopt the measures referred to in paragraph 1, these shall contain a reference to this Directive or shall be accompanied by such reference on the occasion of their official publication. The procedure for such reference shall be laid down by Member States.
(3) Member States shall communicate to the Commission the text of the provisions of national law which they adopt in the field governed by this Directive.
(4) No later than four years after the entry into force of this Directive the Commission shall submit a report to the European Parliament and the Council on the implementation of this Directive, accompanied if appropriate by a proposal for the revision thereof.

Article 16. Member States shall take appropriate measures to inform the consumer of the national law transposing this Directive and shall encourage, where appropriate, professional organizations to inform consumers of their codes of practice.

Article 17. The Commission shall study the feasibility of establishing effective means to deal with consumers' complaints in respect of distance selling. Within two years after the entry into force of this Directive the Commission shall submit a report to the European Parliament and the Council on the results of the studies, accompanied if appropriate by proposals.

Article 18. This Directive shall enter into force on the day of its publication in the Official Journal of the European Communities.

Article 19. This Directive is addressed to the Member States.

Annex I. Means of communication covered by Article 2 (4)
- Unaddressed printed matter
- Addressed printed matter
- Standard letter
- Press advertising with order form
- Catalogue
- Telephone with human intervention
- Telephone without human intervention (automatic calling machine, audiotext)
- Radio
- Videophone (telephone with screen)
- Videotex (microcomputer and television screen) with keyboard or touch screen
- Electronic mail
- Facsimile machine (fax)
- Television (teleshopping).

Annex II. Financial services within the meaning of Article 3 (1)
(repealed).

Directive 1999/44/EC of the European Parliament and of the Council of 25 May 1999 on certain aspects of the sale of consumer goods and associated guarantees (*OJL* 17 , 07.07.1999, pp. 12 -16) [footnotes omitted].

THE EUROPEAN PARLIAMENT AND THE COUNCIL OF THE EUROPEAN UNION,
Having regard to the Treaty establishing the European Community, and in particular Article 95 thereof,
Having regard to the proposal from the Commission,
Having regard to the opinion of the Economic and Social Committee, Acting in accordance with the procedure laid down in Article 251 of the Treaty in the light of the joint text approved by the Conciliation Committee on 18 May 1999(3),
(1) Whereas Article 153(1) and (3) of the Treaty provides that the Community should contribute to the achievement of a high level of consumer protection by the measures it adopts pursuant to Article 95 thereof;
(2) Whereas the internal market comprises an area without internal frontiers in which the free movement of goods, persons, services and capital is guaranteed; whereas free movement of goods concerns not only transactions by persons acting in the course of a business but also transactions by private individuals; whereas it implies that consumers resident in one Member State should be free to purchase goods in the territory of another Member State on the basis of a uniform minimum set of fair rules governing the sale of consumer goods;
(3) Whereas the laws of the Member States concerning the sale of consumer goods are somewhat disparate, with the result that national consumer goods markets differ from one another and that competition between sellers may be distorted;
(4) Whereas consumers who are keen to benefit from the large market by purchasing goods in Member States other than their State of residence play a fundamental role in the completion of the internal market; whereas the artificial reconstruction of frontiers and the compartmentalisation of markets should be prevented; whereas the opportunities available to consumers have been greatly broadened by new communication technologies which allow ready access to distribution systems in other Member States or in third countries; whereas, in the absence of minimum harmonisation of the rules governing the sale of consumer goods, the development of the sale of goods through the medium of new distance communication technologies risks being impeded;
(5) Whereas the creation of a common set of minimum rules of consumer law, valid no matter where goods are purchased within the Community, will strengthen consumer confidence and enable consumers to make the most of the internal market;
(6) Whereas the main difficulties encountered by consumers and the main source of disputes with sellers concern the non-conformity of goods with the contract; whereas it is therefore appropriate to approximate national legislation governing the sale of consumer goods in this respect, without however impinging on provisions and principles of national law relating to contractual and non-contractual liability;
(7) Whereas the goods must, above all, conform with the contractual specifications; whereas the principle of conformity with the contract may be considered as common to the different national legal traditions; whereas in certain national legal traditions it may not be possible to rely solely on this principle to ensure a minimum level of protection for the consumer; whereas under such legal traditions, in particular, additional national provisions may be useful to ensure that the consumer is protected in cases where the parties have agreed no specific contractual terms or where the parties have concluded contractual terms or agreements which directly or indirectly waive or restrict the rights of the consumer and which, to the extent that these rights result from this Directive, are not binding on the consumer;
(8) Whereas, in order to facilitate the application of the principle of conformity with the contract, it is useful to introduce a rebuttable presumption of conformity with the contract covering the most common situations; whereas that presumption does not restrict the principle of freedom of contract; whereas, furthermore, in the absence of specific contractual terms, as well as where the minimum protection clause is applied, the elements mentioned in this presumption may be used to determine the lack of conformity of the goods with the contract; whereas the quality and performance which consumers can reasonably expect will depend inter alia on whether the goods are new or second-hand; whereas the elements mentioned in the presumption are cumulative; whereas, if the circumstances of the case render any particular element manifestly inappropriate, the remaining elements of the presumption nevertheless still apply;
(9) Whereas the seller should be directly liable to the consumer for the conformity of the goods with the contract; whereas this is the traditional solution enshrined in the legal orders of the Member States; whereas nevertheless the seller should be free, as provided for by national law, to pursue remedies against the producer, a previous seller in the same chain of contracts or any other intermediary, unless he has renounced that entitlement; whereas this Directive does not affect the principle of freedom of contract between the seller, the producer, a previous seller or any other intermediary; whereas the rules governing against whom and how the seller may pursue such remedies are to be determined by national law;

(10) Whereas, in the case of non-conformity of the goods with the contract, consumers should be entitled to have the goods restored to conformity with the contract free of charge, choosing either repair or replacement, or, failing this, to have the price reduced or the contract rescinded;
(11) Whereas the consumer in the first place may require the seller to repair the goods or to replace them unless those remedies are impossible or disproportionate; whereas whether a remedy is disproportionate should be determined objectively; whereas a remedy would be disproportionate if it imposed, in comparison with the other remedy, unreasonable costs; whereas, in order to determine whether the costs are unreasonable, the costs of one remedy should be significantly higher than the costs of the other remedy;
(12) Whereas in cases of a lack of conformity, the seller may always offer the consumer, by way of settlement, any available remedy; whereas it is for the consumer to decide whether to accept or reject this proposal;
(13) Whereas, in order to enable consumers to take advantage of the internal market and to buy consumer goods in another Member State, it should be recommended that, in the interests of consumers, the producers of consumer goods that are marketed in several Member States attach to the product a list with at least one contact address in every Member State where the product is marketed;
(14) Whereas the references to the time of delivery do not imply that Member States have to change their rules on the passing of the risk;
(15) Whereas Member States may provide that any reimbursement to the consumer may be reduced to take account of the use the consumer has had of the goods since they were delivered to him; whereas the detailed arrangements whereby rescission of the contract is effected may be laid down in national law;
(16) Whereas the specific nature of second-hand goods makes it generally impossible to replace them; whereas therefore the consumer's right of replacement is generally not available for these goods; whereas for such goods, Member States may enable the parties to agree a shortened period of liability;
(17) Whereas it is appropriate to limit in time the period during which the seller is liable for any lack of conformity which exists at the time of delivery of the goods; whereas Member States may also provide for a limitation on the period during which consumers can exercise their rights, provided such a period does not expire within two years from the time of delivery; whereas where, under national legislation, the time when a limitation period starts is not the time of delivery of the goods, the total duration of the limitation period provided for by national law may not be shorter than two years from the time of delivery;
(18) Whereas Member States may provide for suspension or interruption of the period during which any lack of conformity must become apparent and of the limitation period, where applicable and in accordance with their national law, in the event of repair, replacement or negotiations between seller and consumer with a view to an amicable settlement;
(19) Whereas Member States should be allowed to set a period within which the consumer must inform the seller of any lack of conformity; whereas Member States may ensure a higher level of protection for the consumer by not introducing such an obligation; whereas in any case consumers throughout the Community should have at least two months in which to inform the seller that a lack of conformity exists;
(20) Whereas Member States should guard against such a period placing at a disadvantage consumers shopping across borders; whereas all Member States should inform the Commission of their use of this provision; whereas the Commission should monitor the effect of the varied application of this provision on consumers and on the internal market; whereas information on the use made of this provision by a Member State should be available to the other Member States and to consumers and consumer organisations throughout the Community; whereas a summary of the situation in all Member States should therefore be published in the Official Journal of the European Communities;
(21) Whereas, for certain categories of goods, it is current practice for sellers and producers to offer guarantees on goods against any defect which becomes apparent within a certain period; whereas this practice can stimulate competition; whereas, while such guarantees are legitimate marketing tools, they should not mislead the consumer; whereas, to ensure that consumers are not misled, guarantees should contain certain information, including a statement that the guarantee does not affect the consumer's legal rights;
(22) Whereas the parties may not, by common consent, restrict or waive the rights granted to consumers, since otherwise the legal protection afforded would be thwarted; whereas this principle should apply also to clauses which imply that the consumer was aware of any lack of conformity of the consumer goods existing at the time the contract was concluded; whereas the protection granted to consumers under this Directive should not be reduced on the grounds that the law of a non-member State has been chosen as being applicable to the contract;
(23) Whereas legislation and case-law in this area in the various Member States show that there is growing concern to ensure a high level of consumer protection; whereas, in the light of this trend and the experience acquired in implementing this Directive, it may be necessary to envisage more far-reaching harmonisation, notably by providing for the producer's direct liability for defects for which he is responsible;

(24) Whereas Member States should be allowed to adopt or maintain in force more stringent provisions in the field covered by this Directive to ensure an even higher level of consumer protection;
(25) Whereas, according to the Commission recommendation of 30 March 1998 on the principles applicable to the bodies responsible for out-of-court settlement of consumer disputes(4), Member States can create bodies that ensure impartial and efficient handling of complaints in a national and cross-border context and which consumers can use as mediators;
(26) Whereas it is appropriate, in order to protect the collective interests of consumers, to add this Directive to the list of Directives contained in the Annex to Directive 98/27/EC of the European Parliament and of the Council of 19 May 1998 on injunctions for the protection of consumers' interests,

HAVE ADOPTED THIS DIRECTIVE:

Article 1. (1) The purpose of this Directive is the approximation of the laws, regulations and administrative provisions of the Member States on certain aspects of the sale of consumer goods and associated guarantees in order to ensure a uniform minimum level of consumer protection in the context of the internal market.
(2) For the purposes of this Directive:
(a) consumer: shall mean any natural person who, in the contracts covered by this Directive, is acting for purposes which are not related to his trade, business or profession;
(b) consumer goods: shall mean any tangible movable item, with the exception of:
- goods sold by way of execution or otherwise by authority of law,
- water and gas where they are not put up for sale in a limited volume or set quantity,
- electricity;
(c) seller: shall mean any natural or legal person who, under a contract, sells consumer goods in the course of his trade, business or profession;
(d) producer: shall mean the manufacturer of consumer goods, the importer of consumer goods into the territory of the Community or any person purporting to be a producer by placing his name, trade mark or other distinctive sign on the consumer goods;
(e) guarantee: shall mean any undertaking by a seller or producer to the consumer, given without extra charge, to reimburse the price paid or to replace, repair or handle consumer goods in any way if they do not meet the specifications set out in the guarantee statement or in the relevant advertising;
(f) repair: shall mean, in the event of lack of conformity, bringing consumer goods into conformity with the contract of sale.
(3) Member States may provide that the expression "consumer goods" does not cover second-hand goods sold at public auction where consumers have the opportunity of attending the sale in person.
(4) Contracts for the supply of consumer goods to be manufactured or produced shall also be deemed contracts of sale for the purpose of this Directive.

Article 2. (1) The seller must deliver goods to the consumer which are in conformity with the contract of sale.
(2) Consumer goods are presumed to be in conformity with the contract if they:
(a) comply with the description given by the seller and possess the qualities of the goods which the seller has held out to the consumer as a sample or model;
(b) are fit for any particular purpose for which the consumer requires them and which he made known to the seller at the time of conclusion of the contract and which the seller has accepted;
(c) are fit for the purposes for which goods of the same type are normally used;
(d) show the quality and performance which are normal in goods of the same type and which the consumer can reasonably expect, given the nature of the goods and taking into account any public statements on the specific characteristics of the goods made about them by the seller, the producer or his representative, particularly in advertising or on labelling.
(3) There shall be deemed not to be a lack of conformity for the purposes of this Article if, at the time the contract was concluded, the consumer was aware, or could not reasonably be unaware of, the lack of conformity, or if the lack of conformity has its origin in materials supplied by the consumer.
(4) The seller shall not be bound by public statements, as referred to in paragraph 2(d) if he:
- shows that he was not, and could not reasonably have been, aware of the statement in question,
- shows that by the time of conclusion of the contract the statement had been corrected, or
- shows that the decision to buy the consumer goods could not have been influenced by the statement.
(5) Any lack of conformity resulting from incorrect installation of the consumer goods shall be deemed to be equivalent to lack of conformity of the goods if installation forms part of the contract of sale of the goods and the goods were installed by the seller or under his responsibility. This shall apply equally if the product, intended to be

installed by the consumer, is installed by the consumer and the incorrect installation is due to a shortcoming in the installation instructions.

Article 3. (1) The seller shall be liable to the consumer for any lack of conformity which exists at the time the goods were delivered.
(2) In the case of a lack of conformity, the consumer shall be entitled to have the goods brought into conformity free of charge by repair or replacement, in accordance with paragraph 3, or to have an appropriate reduction made in the price or the contract rescinded with regard to those goods, in accordance with paragraphs 5 and 6.
(3) In the first place, the consumer may require the seller to repair the goods or he may require the seller to replace them, in either case free of charge, unless this is impossible or disproportionate.
A remedy shall be deemed to be disproportionate if it imposes costs on the seller which, in comparison with the alternative remedy, are unreasonable, taking into account:
- the value the goods would have if there were no lack of conformity,
- the significance of the lack of conformity, and
- whether the alternative remedy could be completed without significant inconvenience to the consumer.
Any repair or replacement shall be completed within a reasonable time and without any significant inconvenience to the consumer, taking account of the nature of the goods and the purpose for which the consumer required the goods.
(4) The terms "free of charge" in paragraphs 2 and 3 refer to the necessary costs incurred to bring the goods into conformity, particularly the cost of postage, labour and materials.
(5) The consumer may require an appropriate reduction of the price or have the contract rescinded:
- if the consumer is entitled to neither repair nor replacement, or
- if the seller has not completed the remedy within a reasonable time, or
- if the seller has not completed the remedy without significant inconvenience to the consumer.
(6) The consumer is not entitled to have the contract rescinded if the lack of conformity is minor.

Article 4. Where the final seller is liable to the consumer because of a lack of conformity resulting from an act or omission by the producer, a previous seller in the same chain of contracts or any other intermediary, the final seller shall be entitled to pursue remedies against the person or persons liable in the contractual chain. the person or persons liable against whom the final seller may pursue remedies, together with the relevant actions and conditions of exercise, shall be determined by national law.

Article 5. (1) The seller shall be held liable under Article 3 where the lack of conformity becomes apparent within two years as from delivery of the goods. If, under national legislation, the rights laid down in Article 3(2) are subject to a limitation period, that period shall not expire within a period of two years from the time of delivery.
(2) Member States may provide that, in order to benefit from his rights, the consumer must inform the seller of the lack of conformity within a period of two months from the date on which he detected such lack of conformity. Member States shall inform the Commission of their use of this paragraph. The Commission shall monitor the effect of the existence of this option for the Member States on consumers and on the internal market. Not later than 7 January 2003, the Commission shall prepare a report on the use made by Member States of this paragraph. This report shall be published in the Official Journal of the European Communities.
(3) Unless proved otherwise, any lack of conformity which becomes apparent within six months of delivery of the goods shall be presumed to have existed at the time of delivery unless this presumption is incompatible with the nature of the goods or the nature of the lack of conformity.

Article 6. (1) A guarantee shall be legally binding on the offerer under the conditions laid down in the guarantee statement and the associated advertising.
(2) The guarantee shall:
- state that the consumer has legal rights under applicable national legislation governing the sale of consumer goods and make clear that those rights are not affected by the guarantee,
- set out in plain intelligible language the contents of the guarantee and the essential particulars necessary for making claims under the guarantee, notably the duration and territorial scope of the guarantee as well as the name and address of the guarantor.
(3) On request by the consumer, the guarantee shall be made available in writing or feature in another durable medium available and accessible to him.
(4) Within its own territory, the Member State in which the consumer goods are marketed may, in accordance with the rules of the Treaty, provide that the guarantee be drafted in one or more languages which it shall determine from among the official languages of the Community.

(5) Should a guarantee infringe the requirements of paragraphs 2, 3 or 4, the validity of this guarantee shall in no way be affected, and the consumer can still rely on the guarantee and require that it be honoured.

Article 7. (1) Any contractual terms or agreements concluded with the seller before the lack of conformity is brought to the seller's attention which directly or indirectly waive or restrict the rights resulting from this Directive shall, as provided for by national law, not be binding on the consumer. Member States may provide that, in the case of second-hand goods, the seller and consumer may agree contractual terms or agreements which have a shorter time period for the liability of the seller than that set down in Article 5(1). Such period may not be less than one year.
(2) Member States shall take the necessary measures to ensure that consumers are not deprived of the protection afforded by this Directive as a result of opting for the law of a non-member State as the law applicable to the contract where the contract has a close connection with the territory of the Member States.

Article 8. (1) The rights resulting from this Directive shall be exercised without prejudice to other rights which the consumer may invoke under the national rules governing contractual or non-contractual liability.
(2) Member States may adopt or maintain in force more stringent provisions, compatible with the Treaty in the field covered by this Directive, to ensure a higher level of consumer protection.

Article 9. Member States shall take appropriate measures to inform the consumer of the national law transposing this Directive and shall encourage, where appropriate, professional organisations to inform consumers of their rights.

Article 10. The Annex to Directive 98/27/EC shall be completed as follows: "10. Directive 1999/44/EC of the European Parliament and of the Council of 25 May 1999 on certain aspects of the sale of consumer goods and associated guarantees (OJ L 171, 7.7.1999, p. 12).".

Article 11. (1) Member States shall bring into force the laws, regulations and administrative provisions necessary to comply with this Directive not later than 1 January 2002. They shall forthwith inform the Commission thereof. When Member States adopt these measures, they shall contain a reference to this Directive, or shall be accompanied by such reference at the time of their official publication. The procedure for such reference shall be adopted by Member States.
(2) Member States shall communicate to the Commission the provisions of national law which they adopt in the field covered by this Directive.

Article 12. The Commission shall, not later than 7 July 2006, review the application of this Directive and submit to the European Parliament and the Council a report. The report shall examine, inter alia, the case for introducing the producer's direct liability and, if appropriate, shall be accompanied by proposals.

Article 13. This Directive shall enter into force on the day of its publication in the Official Journal of the European Communities.

Article 14. This Directive is addressed to the Member States.

Directive 2000/31/EC of the European Parliament and of the Council of 8 June 2000 on certain legal aspects of information society services, in particular electronic commerce, in the Internal Market ('Directive on electronic commerce') (*OJ* L 178, 17.07.2000, pp. 1 – 16) [footnotes omitted].

THE EUROPEAN PARLIAMENT AND THE COUNCIL OF THE EUROPEAN UNION,
Having regard to the Treaty establishing the European Community, and in particular Articles 47(2), 55 and 95 thereof,
Having regard to the proposal from the Commission,
Having regard to the opinion of the Economic and Social Committee,
Acting in accordance with the procedure laid down in Article 251 of the Treaty,
Whereas:
(1) The European Union is seeking to forge ever closer links between the States and peoples of Europe, to ensure economic and social progress; in accordance with Article 14(2) of the Treaty, the internal market comprises an area without internal frontiers in which the free movements of goods, services and the freedom of establishment are ensured; the development of information society services within the area without internal frontiers is vital to eliminating the barriers which divide the European peoples.
(2) The development of electronic commerce within the information society offers significant employment opportunities in the Community, particularly in small and medium-sized enterprises, and will stimulate economic growth and investment in innovation by European companies, and can also enhance the competitiveness of European industry, provided that everyone has access to the Internet.
(3) Community law and the characteristics of the Community legal order are a vital asset to enable European citizens and operators to take full advantage, without consideration of borders, of the opportunities afforded by electronic commerce; this Directive therefore has the purpose of ensuring a high level of Community legal integration in order to establish a real area without internal borders for information society services.
(4) It is important to ensure that electronic commerce could fully benefit from the internal market and therefore that, as with Council Directive 89/552/EEC of 3 October 1989 on the coordination of certain provisions laid down by law, regulation or administrative action in Member States concerning the pursuit of television broadcasting activities, a high level of Community integration is achieved.
(5) The development of information society services within the Community is hampered by a number of legal obstacles to the proper functioning of the internal market which make less attractive the exercise of the freedom of establishment and the freedom to provide services; these obstacles arise from divergences in legislation and from the legal uncertainty as to which national rules apply to such services; in the absence of coordination and adjustment of legislation in the relevant areas, obstacles might be justified in the light of the case-law of the Court of Justice of the European Communities; legal uncertainty exists with regard to the extent to which Member States may control services originating from another Member State.
(6) In the light of Community objectives, of Articles 43 and 49 of the Treaty and of secondary Community law, these obstacles should be eliminated by coordinating certain national laws and by clarifying certain legal concepts at Community level to the extent necessary for the proper functioning of the internal market; by dealing only with certain specific matters which give rise to problems for the internal market, this Directive is fully consistent with the need to respect the principle of subsidiarity as set out in Article 5 of the Treaty.
(7) In order to ensure legal certainty and consumer confidence, this Directive must lay down a clear and general framework to cover certain legal aspects of electronic commerce in the internal market.
(8) The objective of this Directive is to create a legal framework to ensure the free movement of information society services between Member States and not to harmonise the field of criminal law as such.
(9) The free movement of information society services can in many cases be a specific reflection in Community law of a more general principle, namely freedom of expression as enshrined in Article 10(1) of the Convention for the Protection of Human Rights and Fundamental Freedoms, which has been ratified by all the Member States; for this reason, directives covering the supply of information society services must ensure that this activity may be engaged in freely in the light of that Article, subject only to the restrictions laid down in paragraph 2 of that Article and in Article 46(1) of the Treaty; this Directive is not intended to affect national fundamental rules and principles relating to freedom of expression.
(10) In accordance with the principle of proportionality, the measures provided for in this Directive are strictly limited to the minimum needed to achieve the objective of the proper functioning of the internal market; where action at Community level is necessary, and in order to guarantee an area which is truly without internal frontiers as far as electronic commerce is concerned, the Directive must ensure a high level of protection of objectives of general interest, in particular the protection of minors and human dignity, consumer protection and the protection of public health; according to Article 152 of the Treaty, the protection of public health is an essential component of other Community policies.

Part IX. European Private Law

(11) This Directive is without prejudice to the level of protection for, in particular, public health and consumer interests, as established by Community acts; amongst others, Council Directive 93/13/EEC of 5 April 1993 on unfair terms in consumer contracts and Directive 97/7/EC of the European Parliament and of the Council of 20 May 1997 on the protection of consumers in respect of distance contracts form a vital element for protecting consumers in contractual matters; those Directives also apply in their entirety to information society services; that same Community acquis, which is fully applicable to information society services, also embraces in particular Council Directive 84/450/EEC of 10 September 1984 concerning misleading and comparative advertising, Council Directive 87/102/EEC of 22 December 1986 for the approximation of the laws, regulations and administrative provisions of the Member States concerning consumer credit, Council Directive 93/22/EEC of 10 May 1993 on investment services in the securities field, Council Directive 90/314/EEC of 13 June 1990 on package travel, package holidays and package tours, Directive 98/6/EC of the European Parliament and of the Council of 16 February 1998 on consumer production in the indication of prices of products offered to consumers, Council Directive 92/59/EEC of 29 June 1992 on general product safety, Directive 94/47/EC of the European Parliament and of the Council of 26 October 1994 on the protection of purchasers in respect of certain aspects on contracts relating to the purchase of the right to use immovable properties on a timeshare basis, Directive 98/27/EC of the European Parliament and of the Council of 19 May 1998 on injunctions for the protection of consumers' interests, Council Directive 85/374/EEC of 25 July 1985 on the approximation of the laws, regulations and administrative provisions concerning liability for defective products, Directive 1999/44/EC of the European Parliament and of the Council of 25 May 1999 on certain aspects of the sale of consumer goods and associated guarantees, the future Directive of the European Parliament and of the Council concerning the distance marketing of consumer financial services and Council Directive 92/28/EEC of 31 March 1992 on the advertising of medicinal products; this Directive should be without prejudice to Directive 98/43/EC of the European Parliament and of the Council of 6 July 1998 on the approximation of the laws, regulations and administrative provisions of the Member States relating to the advertising and sponsorship of tobacco products adopted within the framework of the internal market, or to directives on the protection of public health; this Directive complements information requirements established by the abovementioned Directives and in particular Directive 97/7/EC.

(12) It is necessary to exclude certain activities from the scope of this Directive, on the grounds that the freedom to provide services in these fields cannot, at this stage, be guaranteed under the Treaty or existing secondary legislation; excluding these activities does not preclude any instruments which might prove necessary for the proper functioning of the internal market; taxation, particularly value added tax imposed on a large number of the services covered by this Directive, must be excluded form the scope of this Directive.

(13) This Directive does not aim to establish rules on fiscal obligations nor does it pre-empt the drawing up of Community instruments concerning fiscal aspects of electronic commerce.

(14) The protection of individuals with regard to the processing of personal data is solely governed by Directive 95/46/EC of the European Parliament and of the Council of 24 October 1995 on the protection of individuals with regard to the processing of personal data and on the free movement of such data and Directive 97/66/EC of the European Parliament and of the Council of 15 December 1997 concerning the processing of personal data and the protection of privacy in the telecommunications sector which are fully applicable to information society services; these Directives already establish a Community legal framework in the field of personal data and therefore it is not necessary to cover this issue in this Directive in order to ensure the smooth functioning of the internal market, in particular the free movement of personal data between Member States; the implementation and application of this Directive should be made in full compliance with the principles relating to the protection of personal data, in particular as regards unsolicited commercial communication and the liability of intermediaries; this Directive cannot prevent the anonymous use of open networks such as the Internet.

(15) The confidentiality of communications is guaranteed by Article 5 Directive 97/66/EC; in accordance with that Directive, Member States must prohibit any kind of interception or surveillance of such communications by others than the senders and receivers, except when legally authorised.

(16) The exclusion of gambling activities from the scope of application of this Directive covers only games of chance, lotteries and betting transactions, which involve wagering a stake with monetary value; this does not cover promotional competitions or games where the purpose is to encourage the sale of goods or services and where payments, if they arise, serve only to acquire the promoted goods or services.

(17) The definition of information society services already exists in Community law in Directive 98/34/EC of the European Parliament and of the Council of 22 June 1998 laying down a procedure for the provision of information in the field of technical standards and regulations and of rules on information society services and in Directive 98/84/EC of the European Parliament and of the Council of 20 November 1998 on the legal protection of services based on, or consisting of, conditional access; this definition covers any service normally provided for remuneration, at a distance, by means of electronic equipment for the processing (including digital compression) and storage of data, and at the individual request of a recipient of a service; those services referred to in the

indicative list in Annex V to Directive 98/34/EC which do not imply data processing and storage are not covered by this definition.

(18) Information society services span a wide range of economic activities which take place on-line; these activities can, in particular, consist of selling goods on-line; activities such as the delivery of goods as such or the provision of services off-line are not covered; information society services are not solely restricted to services giving rise to on-line contracting but also, in so far as they represent an economic activity, extend to services which are not remunerated by those who receive them, such as those offering on-line information or commercial communications, or those providing tools allowing for search, access and retrieval of data; information society services also include services consisting of the transmission of information via a communication network, in providing access to a communication network or in hosting information provided by a recipient of the service; television broadcasting within the meaning of Directive EEC/89/552 and radio broadcasting are not information society services because they are not provided at individual request; by contrast, services which are transmitted point to point, such as video-on-demand or the provision of commercial communications by electronic mail are information society services; the use of electronic mail or equivalent individual communications for instance by natural persons acting outside their trade, business or profession including their use for the conclusion of contracts between such persons is not an information society service; the contractual relationship between an employee and his employer is not an information society service; activities which by their very nature cannot be carried out at a distance and by electronic means, such as the statutory auditing of company accounts or medical advice requiring the physical examination of a patient are not information society services.

(19) The place at which a service provider is established should be determined in conformity with the case-law of the Court of Justice according to which the concept of establishment involves the actual pursuit of an economic activity through a fixed establishment for an indefinite period; this requirement is also fulfilled where a company is constituted for a given period; the place of establishment of a company providing services via an Internet website is not the place at which the technology supporting its website is located or the place at which its website is accessible but the place where it pursues its economic activity; in cases where a provider has several places of establishment it is important to determine from which place of establishment the service concerned is provided; in cases where it is difficult to determine from which of several places of establishment a given service is provided, this is the place where the provider has the centre of his activities relating to this particular service.

(20) The definition of "recipient of a service" covers all types of usage of information society services, both by persons who provide information on open networks such as the Internet and by persons who seek information on the Internet for private or professional reasons.

(21) The scope of the coordinated field is without prejudice to future Community harmonisation relating to information society services and to future legislation adopted at national level in accordance with Community law; the coordinated field covers only requirements relating to on-line activities such as on-line information, on-line advertising, on-line shopping, on-line contracting and does not concern Member States' legal requirements relating to goods such as safety standards, labelling obligations, or liability for goods, or Member States' requirements relating to the delivery or the transport of goods, including the distribution of medicinal products; the coordinated field does not cover the exercise of rights of pre-emption by public authorities concerning certain goods such as works of art.

(22) Information society services should be supervised at the source of the activity, in order to ensure an effective protection of public interest objectives; to that end, it is necessary to ensure that the competent authority provides such protection not only for the citizens of its own country but for all Community citizens; in order to improve mutual trust between Member States, it is essential to state clearly this responsibility on the part of the Member State where the services originate; moreover, in order to effectively guarantee freedom to provide services and legal certainty for suppliers and recipients of services, such information society services should in principle be subject to the law of the Member State in which the service provider is established.

(23) This Directive neither aims to establish additional rules on private international law relating to conflicts of law nor does it deal with the jurisdiction of Courts; provisions of the applicable law designated by rules of private international law must not restrict the freedom to provide information society services as established in this Directive.

(24) In the context of this Directive, notwithstanding the rule on the control at source of information society services, it is legitimate under the conditions established in this Directive for Member States to take measures to restrict the free movement of information society services.

(25) National courts, including civil courts, dealing with private law disputes can take measures to derogate from the freedom to provide information society services in conformity with conditions established in this Directive.

(26) Member States, in conformity with conditions established in this Directive, may apply their national rules on criminal law and criminal proceedings with a view to taking all investigative and other measures necessary for the

detection and prosecution of criminal offences, without there being a need to notify such measures to the Commission.
(27) This Directive, together with the future Directive of the European Parliament and of the Council concerning the distance marketing of consumer financial services, contributes to the creating of a legal framework for the on-line provision of financial services; this Directive does not pre-empt future initiatives in the area of financial services in particular with regard to the harmonisation of rules of conduct in this field; the possibility for Member States, established in this Directive, under certain circumstances of restricting the freedom to provide information society services in order to protect consumers also covers measures in the area of financial services in particular measures aiming at protecting investors.
(28) The Member States' obligation not to subject access to the activity of an information society service provider to prior authorisation does not concern postal services covered by Directive 97/67/EC of the European Parliament and of the Council of 15 December 1997 on common rules for the development of the internal market of Community postal services and the improvement of quality of service consisting of the physical delivery of a printed electronic mail message and does not affect voluntary accreditation systems, in particular for providers of electronic signature certification service.
(29) Commercial communications are essential for the financing of information society services and for developing a wide variety of new, charge-free services; in the interests of consumer protection and fair trading, commercial communications, including discounts, promotional offers and promotional competitions or games, must meet a number of transparency requirements; these requirements are without prejudice to Directive 97/7/EC; this Directive should not affect existing Directives on commercial communications, in particular Directive 98/43/EC.
(30) The sending of unsolicited commercial communications by electronic mail may be undesirable for consumers and information society service providers and may disrupt the smooth functioning of interactive networks; the question of consent by recipient of certain forms of unsolicited commercial communications is not addressed by this Directive, but has already been addressed, in particular, by Directive 97/7/EC and by Directive 97/66/EC; in Member States which authorise unsolicited commercial communications by electronic mail, the setting up of appropriate industry filtering initiatives should be encouraged and facilitated; in addition it is necessary that in any event unsolicited commercial communities are clearly identifiable as such in order to improve transparency and to facilitate the functioning of such industry initiatives; unsolicited commercial communications by electronic mail should not result in additional communication costs for the recipient.
(31) Member States which allow the sending of unsolicited commercial communications by electronic mail without prior consent of the recipient by service providers established in their territory have to ensure that the service providers consult regularly and respect the opt-out registers in which natural persons not wishing to receive such commercial communications can register themselves.
(32) In order to remove barriers to the development of cross-border services within the Community which members of the regulated professions might offer on the Internet, it is necessary that compliance be guaranteed at Community level with professional rules aiming, in particular, to protect consumers or public health; codes of conduct at Community level would be the best means of determining the rules on professional ethics applicable to commercial communication; the drawing-up or, where appropriate, the adaptation of such rules should be encouraged without prejudice to the autonomy of professional bodies and associations.
(33) This Directive complements Community law and national law relating to regulated professions maintaining a coherent set of applicable rules in this field.
(34) Each Member State is to amend its legislation containing requirements, and in particular requirements as to form, which are likely to curb the use of contracts by electronic means; the examination of the legislation requiring such adjustment should be systematic and should cover all the necessary stages and acts of the contractual process, including the filing of the contract; the result of this amendment should be to make contracts concluded electronically workable; the legal effect of electronic signatures is dealt with by Directive 1999/93/EC of the European Parliament and of the Council of 13 December 1999 on a Community framework for electronic signatures; the acknowledgement of receipt by a service provider may take the form of the on-line provision of the service paid for.
(35) This Directive does not affect Member States' possibility of maintaining or establishing general or specific legal requirements for contracts which can be fulfilled by electronic means, in particular requirements concerning secure electronic signatures.
(36) Member States may maintain restrictions for the use of electronic contracts with regard to contracts requiring by law the involvement of courts, public authorities, or professions exercising public authority; this possibility also covers contracts which require the involvement of courts, public authorities, or professions exercising public authority in order to have an effect with regard to third parties as well as contracts requiring by law certification or attestation by a notary.

(37) Member States' obligation to remove obstacles to the use of electronic contracts concerns only obstacles resulting from legal requirements and not practical obstacles resulting from the impossibility of using electronic means in certain cases.
(38) Member States' obligation to remove obstacles to the use of electronic contracts is to be implemented in conformity with legal requirements for contracts enshrined in Community law.
(39) The exceptions to the provisions concerning the contracts concluded exclusively by electronic mail or by equivalent individual communications provided for by this Directive, in relation to information to be provided and the placing of orders, should not enable, as a result, the by-passing of those provisions by providers of information society services.
(40) Both existing and emerging disparities in Member States' legislation and case-law concerning liability of service providers acting as intermediaries prevent the smooth functioning of the internal market, in particular by impairing the development of cross-border services and producing distortions of competition; service providers have a duty to act, under certain circumstances, with a view to preventing or stopping illegal activities; this Directive should constitute the appropriate basis for the development of rapid and reliable procedures for removing and disabling access to illegal information; such mechanisms could be developed on the basis of voluntary agreements between all parties concerned and should be encouraged by Member States; it is in the interest of all parties involved in the provision of information society services to adopt and implement such procedures; the provisions of this Directive relating to liability should not preclude the development and effective operation, by the different interested parties, of technical systems of protection and identification and of technical surveillance instruments made possible by digital technology within the limits laid down by Directives 95/46/EC and 97/66/EC.
(41) This Directive strikes a balance between the different interests at stake and establishes principles upon which industry agreements and standards can be based.
(42) The exemptions from liability established in this Directive cover only cases where the activity of the information society service provider is limited to the technical process of operating and giving access to a communication network over which information made available by third parties is transmitted or temporarily stored, for the sole purpose of making the transmission more efficient; this activity is of a mere technical, automatic and passive nature, which implies that the information society service provider has neither knowledge of nor control over the information which is transmitted or stored.
(43) A service provider can benefit from the exemptions for "mere conduit" and for "caching" when he is in no way involved with the information transmitted; this requires among other things that he does not modify the information that he transmits; this requirement does not cover manipulations of a technical nature which take place in the course of the transmission as they do not alter the integrity of the information contained in the transmission.
(44) A service provider who deliberately collaborates with one of the recipients of his service in order to undertake illegal acts goes beyond the activities of "mere conduit" or "caching" and as a result cannot benefit from the liability exemptions established for these activities.
(45) The limitations of the liability of intermediary service providers established in this Directive do not affect the possibility of injunctions of different kinds; such injunctions can in particular consist of orders by courts or administrative authorities requiring the termination or prevention of any infringement, including the removal of illegal information or the disabling of access to it.
(46) In order to benefit from a limitation of liability, the provider of an information society service, consisting of the storage of information, upon obtaining actual knowledge or awareness of illegal activities has to act expeditiously to remove or to disable access to the information concerned; the removal or disabling of access has to be undertaken in the observance of the principle of freedom of expression and of procedures established for this purpose at national level; this Directive does not affect Member States' possibility of establishing specific requirements which must be fulfilled expeditiously prior to the removal or disabling of information.
(47) Member States are prevented from imposing a monitoring obligation on service providers only with respect to obligations of a general nature; this does not concern monitoring obligations in a specific case and, in particular, does not affect orders by national authorities in accordance with national legislation.
(48) This Directive does not affect the possibility for Member States of requiring service providers, who host information provided by recipients of their service, to apply duties of care, which can reasonably be expected from them and which are specified by national law, in order to detect and prevent certain types of illegal activities.
(49) Member States and the Commission are to encourage the drawing-up of codes of conduct; this is not to impair the voluntary nature of such codes and the possibility for interested parties of deciding freely whether to adhere to such codes.
(50) It is important that the proposed directive on the harmonisation of certain aspects of copyright and related rights in the information society and this Directive come into force within a similar time scale with a view to

establishing a clear framework of rules relevant to the issue of liability of intermediaries for copyright and relating rights infringements at Community level.
(51) Each Member State should be required, where necessary, to amend any legislation which is liable to hamper the use of schemes for the out-of-court settlement of disputes through electronic channels; the result of this amendment must be to make the functioning of such schemes genuinely and effectively possible in law and in practice, even across borders.
(52) The effective exercise of the freedoms of the internal market makes it necessary to guarantee victims effective access to means of settling disputes; damage which may arise in connection with information society services is characterised both by its rapidity and by its geographical extent; in view of this specific character and the need to ensure that national authorities do not endanger the mutual confidence which they should have in one another, this Directive requests Member States to ensure that appropriate court actions are available; Member States should examine the need to provide access to judicial procedures by appropriate electronic means.
(53) Directive 98/27/EC, which is applicable to information society services, provides a mechanism relating to actions for an injunction aimed at the protection of the collective interests of consumers; this mechanism will contribute to the free movement of information society services by ensuring a high level of consumer protection.
(54) The sanctions provided for under this Directive are without prejudice to any other sanction or remedy provided under national law; Member States are not obliged to provide criminal sanctions for infringement of national provisions adopted pursuant to this Directive.
(55) This Directive does not affect the law applicable to contractual obligations relating to consumer contracts; accordingly, this Directive cannot have the result of depriving the consumer of the protection afforded to him by the mandatory rules relating to contractual obligations of the law of the Member State in which he has his habitual residence.
(56) As regards the derogation contained in this Directive regarding contractual obligations concerning contracts concluded by consumers, those obligations should be interpreted as including information on the essential elements of the content of the contract, including consumer rights, which have a determining influence on the decision to contract.
(57) The Court of Justice has consistently held that a Member State retains the right to take measures against a service provider that is established in another Member State but directs all or most of his activity to the territory of the first Member State if the choice of establishment was made with a view to evading the legislation that would have applied to the provider had he been established on the territory of the first Member State.
(58) This Directive should not apply to services supplied by service providers established in a third country; in view of the global dimension of electronic commerce, it is, however, appropriate to ensure that the Community rules are consistent with international rules; this Directive is without prejudice to the results of discussions within international organisations (amongst others WTO, OECD, Uncitral) on legal issues.
(59) Despite the global nature of electronic communications, coordination of national regulatory measures at European Union level is necessary in order to avoid fragmentation of the internal market, and for the establishment of an appropriate European regulatory framework; such coordination should also contribute to the establishment of a common and strong negotiating position in international forums.
(60) In order to allow the unhampered development of electronic commerce, the legal framework must be clear and simple, predictable and consistent with the rules applicable at international level so that it does not adversely affect the competitiveness of European industry or impede innovation in that sector.
(61) If the market is actually to operate by electronic means in the context of globalisation, the European Union and the major non-European areas need to consult each other with a view to making laws and procedures compatible.
(62) Cooperation with third countries should be strengthened in the area of electronic commerce, in particular with applicant countries, the developing countries and the European Union's other trading partners.
(63) The adoption of this Directive will not prevent the Member States from taking into account the various social, societal and cultural implications which are inherent in the advent of the information society; in particular it should not hinder measures which Member States might adopt in conformity with Community law to achieve social, cultural and democratic goals taking into account their linguistic diversity, national and regional specificities as well as their cultural heritage, and to ensure and maintain public access to the widest possible range of information society services; in any case, the development of the information society is to ensure that Community citizens can have access to the cultural European heritage provided in the digital environment.
(64) Electronic communication offers the Member States an excellent means of providing public services in the cultural, educational and linguistic fields.
(65) The Council, in its resolution of 19 January 1999 on the consumer dimension of the information society, stressed that the protection of consumers deserved special attention in this field; the Commission will examine the degree to which existing consumer protection rules provide insufficient protection in the context of the

information society and will identify, where necessary, the deficiencies of this legislation and those issues which could require additional measures; if need be, the Commission should make specific additional proposals to resolve such deficiencies that will thereby have been identified,

HAVE ADOPTED THIS DIRECTIVE:

Chapter I. General provisions

Article 1. (1) This Directive seeks to contribute to the proper functioning of the internal market by ensuring the free movement of information society services between the Member States.
(2) This Directive approximates, to the extent necessary for the achievement of the objective set out in paragraph 1, certain national provisions on information society services relating to the internal market, the establishment of service providers, commercial communications, electronic contracts, the liability of intermediaries, codes of conduct, out-of-court dispute settlements, court actions and cooperation between Member States.
(3) This Directive complements Community law applicable to information society services without prejudice to the level of protection for, in particular, public health and consumer interests, as established by Community acts and national legislation implementing them in so far as this does not restrict the freedom to provide information society services.
(4) This Directive does not establish additional rules on private international law nor does it deal with the jurisdiction of Courts.
(5) This Directive shall not apply to:
(a) the field of taxation;
(b) questions relating to information society services covered by Directives 95/46/EC and 97/66/EC;
(c) questions relating to agreements or practices governed by cartel law;
(d) the following activities of information society services:
- the activities of notaries or equivalent professions to the extent that they involve a direct and specific connection with the exercise of public authority,
- the representation of a client and defence of his interests before the courts,
- gambling activities which involve wagering a stake with monetary value in games of chance, including lotteries and betting transactions.
(6) This Directive does not affect measures taken at Community or national level, in the respect of Community law, in order to promote cultural and linguistic diversity and to ensure the defence of pluralism.

Article 2. For the purpose of this Directive, the following terms shall bear the following meanings:
(a) "information society services": services within the meaning of Article 1(2) of Directive 98/34/EC as amended by Directive 98/48/EC;
(b) "service provider": any natural or legal person providing an information society service;
(c) "established service provider": a service provider who effectively pursues an economic activity using a fixed establishment for an indefinite period. The presence and use of the technical means and technologies required to provide the service do not, in themselves, constitute an establishment of the provider;
(d) "recipient of the service": any natural or legal person who, for professional ends or otherwise, uses an information society service, in particular for the purposes of seeking information or making it accessible;
(e) "consumer": any natural person who is acting for purposes which are outside his or her trade, business or profession;
(f) "commercial communication": any form of communication designed to promote, directly or indirectly, the goods, services or image of a company, organisation or person pursuing a commercial, industrial or craft activity or exercising a regulated profession. The following do not in themselves constitute commercial communications:
- information allowing direct access to the activity of the company, organisation or person, in particular a domain name or an electronic-mail address,
- communications relating to the goods, services or image of the company, organisation or person compiled in an independent manner, particularly when this is without financial consideration;
(g) "regulated profession": any profession within the meaning of either Article 1(d) of Council Directive 89/48/EEC of 21 December 1988 on a general system for the recognition of higher-education diplomas awarded on completion of professional education and training of at least three-years' duration(26) or of Article 1(f) of Council Directive 92/51/EEC of 18 June 1992 on a second general system for the recognition of professional education and training to supplement Directive 89/48/EEC(27);

(h) "coordinated field": requirements laid down in Member States' legal systems applicable to information society service providers or information society services, regardless of whether they are of a general nature or specifically designed for them.
(i) The coordinated field concerns requirements with which the service provider has to comply in respect of:
- the taking up of the activity of an information society service, such as requirements concerning qualifications, authorisation or notification,
- the pursuit of the activity of an information society service, such as requirements concerning the behaviour of the service provider, requirements regarding the quality or content of the service including those applicable to advertising and contracts, or requirements concerning the liability of the service provider;
(ii) The coordinated field does not cover requirements such as:
- requirements applicable to goods as such,
- requirements applicable to the delivery of goods,
- requirements applicable to services not provided by electronic means.

Article 3. (1) Each Member State shall ensure that the information society services provided by a service provider established on its territory comply with the national provisions applicable in the Member State in question which fall within the coordinated field.
(2) Member States may not, for reasons falling within the coordinated field, restrict the freedom to provide information society services from another Member State.
(3) Paragraphs 1 and 2 shall not apply to the fields referred to in the Annex.
(4) Member States may take measures to derogate from paragraph 2 in respect of a given information society service if the following conditions are fulfilled:
(a) the measures shall be:
(i) necessary for one of the following reasons:
- public policy, in particular the prevention, investigation, detection and prosecution of criminal offences, including the protection of minors and the fight against any incitement to hatred on grounds of race, sex, religion or nationality, and violations of human dignity concerning individual persons,
- the protection of public health,
- public security, including the safeguarding of national security and defence,
- the protection of consumers, including investors;
(ii) taken against a given information society service which prejudices the objectives referred to in point (i) or which presents a serious and grave risk of prejudice to those objectives;
(iii) proportionate to those objectives;
(b) before taking the measures in question and without prejudice to court proceedings, including preliminary proceedings and acts carried out in the framework of a criminal investigation, the Member State has:
- asked the Member State referred to in paragraph 1 to take measures and the latter did not take such measures, or they were inadequate,
- notified the Commission and the Member State referred to in paragraph 1 of its intention to take such measures.
(5) Member States may, in the case of urgency, derogate from the conditions stipulated in paragraph 4(b). Where this is the case, the measures shall be notified in the shortest possible time to the Commission and to the Member State referred to in paragraph 1, indicating the reasons for which the Member State considers that there is urgency.
(6) Without prejudice to the Member State's possibility of proceeding with the measures in question, the Commission shall examine the compatibility of the notified measures with Community law in the shortest possible time; where it comes to the conclusion that the measure is incompatible with Community law, the Commission shall ask the Member State in question to refrain from taking any proposed measures or urgently to put an end to the measures in question.

Chapter II. Principles

Section I. Establishment and information requirements

Article 4. (1) Member States shall ensure that the taking up and pursuit of the activity of an information society service provider may not be made subject to prior authorisation or any other requirement having equivalent effect.
(2) Paragraph 1 shall be without prejudice to authorisation schemes which are not specifically and exclusively targeted at information society services, or which are covered by Directive 97/13/EC of the European Parliament and of the Council of 10 April 1997 on a common framework for general authorisations and individual licences in the field of telecommunications services(28).

Article 5. (1) In addition to other information requirements established by Community law, Member States shall ensure that the service provider shall render easily, directly and permanently accessible to the recipients of the service and competent authorities, at least the following information:
(a) the name of the service provider;
(b) the geographic address at which the service provider is established;
(c) the details of the service provider, including his electronic mail address, which allow him to be contacted rapidly and communicated with in a direct and effective manner;
(d) where the service provider is registered in a trade or similar public register, the trade register in which the service provider is entered and his registration number, or equivalent means of identification in that register;
(e) where the activity is subject to an authorisation scheme, the particulars of the relevant supervisory authority;
(f) as concerns the regulated professions:
- any professional body or similar institution with which the service provider is registered,
- the professional title and the Member State where it has been granted,
- a reference to the applicable professional rules in the Member State of establishment and the means to access them;
(g) where the service provider undertakes an activity that is subject to VAT, the identification number referred to in Article 22(1) of the sixth Council Directive 77/388/EEC of 17 May 1977 on the harmonisation of the laws of the Member States relating to turnover taxes - Common system of value added tax: uniform basis of assessment(29).
(2) In addition to other information requirements established by Community law, Member States shall at least ensure that, where information society services refer to prices, these are to be indicated clearly and unambiguously and, in particular, must indicate whether they are inclusive of tax and delivery costs.

Section II. Commercial communications

Article 6. In addition to other information requirements established by Community law, Member States shall ensure that commercial communications which are part of, or constitute, an information society service comply at least with the following conditions:
(a) the commercial communication shall be clearly identifiable as such;
(b) the natural or legal person on whose behalf the commercial communication is made shall be clearly identifiable;
(c) promotional offers, such as discounts, premiums and gifts, where permitted in the Member State where the service provider is established, shall be clearly identifiable as such, and the conditions which are to be met to qualify for them shall be easily accessible and be presented clearly and unambiguously;
(d) promotional competitions or games, where permitted in the Member State where the service provider is established, shall be clearly identifiable as such, and the conditions for participation shall be easily accessible and be presented clearly and unambiguously.

Article 7. (1) In addition to other requirements established by Community law, Member States which permit unsolicited commercial communication by electronic mail shall ensure that such commercial communication by a service provider established in their territory shall be identifiable clearly and unambiguously as such as soon as it is received by the recipient.
(2) Without prejudice to Directive 97/7/EC and Directive 97/66/EC, Member States shall take measures to ensure that service providers undertaking unsolicited commercial communications by electronic mail consult regularly and respect the opt-out registers in which natural persons not wishing to receive such commercial communications can register themselves.

Article 8. (1) Member States shall ensure that the use of commercial communications which are part of, or constitute, an information society service provided by a member of a regulated profession is permitted subject to compliance with the professional rules regarding, in particular, the independence, dignity and honour of the profession, professional secrecy and fairness towards clients and other members of the profession.
(2) Without prejudice to the autonomy of professional bodies and associations, Member States and the Commission shall encourage professional associations and bodies to establish codes of conduct at Community level in order to determine the types of information that can be given for the purposes of commercial communication in conformity with the rules referred to in paragraph 1
(3) When drawing up proposals for Community initiatives which may become necessary to ensure the proper functioning of the Internal Market with regard to the information referred to in paragraph 2, the Commission shall

take due account of codes of conduct applicable at Community level and shall act in close cooperation with the relevant professional associations and bodies.
(4) This Directive shall apply in addition to Community Directives concerning access to, and the exercise of, activities of the regulated professions.

Section III. Contracts concluded by electronic means

Article 9. (1) Member States shall ensure that their legal system allows contracts to be concluded by electronic means. Member States shall in particular ensure that the legal requirements applicable to the contractual process neither create obstacles for the use of electronic contracts nor result in such contracts being deprived of legal effectiveness and validity on account of their having been made by electronic means.
(2) Member States may lay down that paragraph 1 shall not apply to all or certain contracts falling into one of the following categories:
(a) contracts that create or transfer rights in real estate, except for rental rights;
(b) contracts requiring by law the involvement of courts, public authorities or professions exercising public authority;
(c) contracts of suretyship granted and on collateral securities furnished by persons acting for purposes outside their trade, business or profession;
(d) contracts governed by family law or by the law of succession.
(3) Member States shall indicate to the Commission the categories referred to in paragraph 2 to which they do not apply paragraph 1. Member States shall submit to the Commission every five years a report on the application of paragraph 2 explaining the reasons why they consider it necessary to maintain the category referred to in paragraph 2(b) to which they do not apply paragraph 1.

Article 10. (1) In addition to other information requirements established by Community law, Member States shall ensure, except when otherwise agreed by parties who are not consumers, that at least the following information is given by the service provider clearly, comprehensibly and unambiguously and prior to the order being placed by the recipient of the service:
(a) the different technical steps to follow to conclude the contract;
(b) whether or not the concluded contract will be filed by the service provider and whether it will be accessible;
(c) the technical means for identifying and correcting input errors prior to the placing of the order;
(d) the languages offered for the conclusion of the contract.
(2) Member States shall ensure that, except when otherwise agreed by parties who are not consumers, the service provider indicates any relevant codes of conduct to which he subscribes and information on how those codes can be consulted electronically.
(3) Contract terms and general conditions provided to the recipient must be made available in a way that allows him to store and reproduce them.
(4) Paragraphs 1 and 2 shall not apply to contracts concluded exclusively by exchange of electronic mail or by equivalent individual communications.

Article 11. (1) Member States shall ensure, except when otherwise agreed by parties who are not consumers, that in cases where the recipient of the service places his order through technological means, the following principles apply:
- the service provider has to acknowledge the receipt of the recipient's order without undue delay and by electronic means,
- the order and the acknowledgement of receipt are deemed to be received when the parties to whom they are addressed are able to access them.
(2) Member States shall ensure that, except when otherwise agreed by parties who are not consumers, the service provider makes available to the recipient of the service appropriate, effective and accessible technical means allowing him to identify and correct input errors, prior to the placing of the order.
(3) Paragraph 1, first indent, and paragraph 2 shall not apply to contracts concluded exclusively by exchange of electronic mail or by equivalent individual communications.

Section IV. Liability of intermediary service providers

Article 12. "Mere conduit"
(1) Where an information society service is provided that consists of the transmission in a communication network of information provided by a recipient of the service, or the provision of access to a communication network,

Member States shall ensure that the service provider is not liable for the information transmitted, on condition that the provider:
(a) does not initiate the transmission;
(b) does not select the receiver of the transmission; and
(c) does not select or modify the information contained in the transmission.
(2) The acts of transmission and of provision of access referred to in paragraph 1 include the automatic, intermediate and transient storage of the information transmitted in so far as this takes place for the sole purpose of carrying out the transmission in the communication network, and provided that the information is not stored for any period longer than is reasonably necessary for the transmission.
(3) This Article shall not affect the possibility for a court or administrative authority, in accordance with Member States' legal systems, of requiring the service provider to terminate or prevent an infringement.

Article 13. "Caching"
(1) Where an information society service is provided that consists of the transmission in a communication network of information provided by a recipient of the service, Member States shall ensure that the service provider is not liable for the automatic, intermediate and temporary storage of that information, performed for the sole purpose of making more efficient the information's onward transmission to other recipients of the service upon their request, on condition that:
(a) the provider does not modify the information;
(b) the provider complies with conditions on access to the information;
(c) the provider complies with rules regarding the updating of the information, specified in a manner widely recognised and used by industry;
(d) the provider does not interfere with the lawful use of technology, widely recognised and used by industry, to obtain data on the use of the information; and
(e) the provider acts expeditiously to remove or to disable access to the information it has stored upon obtaining actual knowledge of the fact that the information at the initial source of the transmission has been removed from the network, or access to it has been disabled, or that a court or an administrative authority has ordered such removal or disablement.
(2) This Article shall not affect the possibility for a court or administrative authority, in accordance with Member States' legal systems, of requiring the service provider to terminate or prevent an infringement.

Article 14. (1) Where an information society service is provided that consists of the storage of information provided by a recipient of the service, Member States shall ensure that the service provider is not liable for the information stored at the request of a recipient of the service, on condition that:
(a) the provider does not have actual knowledge of illegal activity or information and, as regards claims for damages, is not aware of facts or circumstances from which the illegal activity or information is apparent; or
(b) the provider, upon obtaining such knowledge or awareness, acts expeditiously to remove or to disable access to the information.
(2) Paragraph 1 shall not apply when the recipient of the service is acting under the authority or the control of the provider.
(3) This Article shall not affect the possibility for a court or administrative authority, in accordance with Member States' legal systems, of requiring the service provider to terminate or prevent an infringement, nor does it affect the possibility for Member States of establishing procedures governing the removal or disabling of access to information.

Article 15. (1) Member States shall not impose a general obligation on providers, when providing the services covered by Articles 12, 13 and 14, to monitor the information which they transmit or store, nor a general obligation actively to seek facts or circumstances indicating illegal activity.
(2) Member States may establish obligations for information society service providers promptly to inform the competent public authorities of alleged illegal activities undertaken or information provided by recipients of their service or obligations to communicate to the competent authorities, at their request, information enabling the identification of recipients of their service with whom they have storage agreements.

Chapter III. Implementation

Article 16. (1) Member States and the Commission shall encourage:
(a) the drawing up of codes of conduct at Community level, by trade, professional and consumer associations or organisations, designed to contribute to the proper implementation of Articles 5 to 15;

(b) the voluntary transmission of draft codes of conduct at national or Community level to the Commission;
(c) the accessibility of these codes of conduct in the Community languages by electronic means;
(d) the communication to the Member States and the Commission, by trade, professional and consumer associations or organisations, of their assessment of the application of their codes of conduct and their impact upon practices, habits or customs relating to electronic commerce;
(e) the drawing up of codes of conduct regarding the protection of minors and human dignity.
(2) Member States and the Commission shall encourage the involvement of associations or organisations representing consumers in the drafting and implementation of codes of conduct affecting their interests and drawn up in accordance with paragraph 1(a). Where appropriate, to take account of their specific needs, associations representing the visually impaired and disabled should be consulted.

Article 17. (1) Member States shall ensure that, in the event of disagreement between an information society service provider and the recipient of the service, their legislation does not hamper the use of out-of-court schemes, available under national law, for dispute settlement, including appropriate electronic means.
(2) Member States shall encourage bodies responsible for the out-of-court settlement of, in particular, consumer disputes to operate in a way which provides adequate procedural guarantees for the parties concerned.
(3) Member States shall encourage bodies responsible for out-of-court dispute settlement to inform the Commission of the significant decisions they take regarding information society services and to transmit any other information on the practices, usages or customs relating to electronic commerce.

Article 18. (1) Member States shall ensure that court actions available under national law concerning information society services' activities allow for the rapid adoption of measures, including interim measures, designed to terminate any alleged infringement and to prevent any further impairment of the interests involved.
(2) The Annex to Directive 98/27/EC shall be supplemented as follows: "11. Directive 2000/31/EC of the European Parliament and of the Council of 8 June 2000 on certain legal aspects on information society services, in particular electronic commerce, in the internal market (Directive on electronic commerce) (OJ L 178, 17.7.2000, p. 1)."

Article 19. (1) Member States shall have adequate means of supervision and investigation necessary to implement this Directive effectively and shall ensure that service providers supply them with the requisite information.
(2) Member States shall cooperate with other Member States; they shall, to that end, appoint one or several contact points, whose details they shall communicate to the other Member States and to the Commission.
(3) Member States shall, as quickly as possible, and in conformity with national law, provide the assistance and information requested by other Member States or by the Commission, including by appropriate electronic means.
(4) Member States shall establish contact points which shall be accessible at least by electronic means and from which recipients and service providers may:
(a) obtain general information on contractual rights and obligations as well as on the complaint and redress mechanisms available in the event of disputes, including practical aspects involved in the use of such mechanisms;
(b) obtain the details of authorities, associations or organisations from which they may obtain further information or practical assistance.
(5) Member States shall encourage the communication to the Commission of any significant administrative or judicial decisions taken in their territory regarding disputes relating to information society services and practices, usages and customs relating to electronic commerce. The Commission shall communicate these decisions to the other Member States.

Article 20. Member States shall determine the sanctions applicable to infringements of national provisions adopted pursuant to this Directive and shall take all measures necessary to ensure that they are enforced. The sanctions they provide for shall be effective, proportionate and dissuasive.

Chapter IV. Final provisions

Article 21. (1) Before 17 July 2003, and thereafter every two years, the Commission shall submit to the European Parliament, the Council and the Economic and Social Committee a report on the application of this Directive, accompanied, where necessary, by proposals for adapting it to legal, technical and economic developments in the field of information society services, in particular with respect to crime prevention, the protection of minors, consumer protection and to the proper functioning of the internal market.
(2) In examining the need for an adaptation of this Directive, the report shall in particular analyse the need for proposals concerning the liability of providers of hyperlinks and location tool services, "notice and take down"

procedures and the attribution of liability following the taking down of content. The report shall also analyse the need for additional conditions for the exemption from liability, provided for in Articles 12 and 13, in the light of technical developments, and the possibility of applying the internal market principles to unsolicited commercial communications by electronic mail.

Article 22. (1) Member States shall bring into force the laws, regulations and administrative provisions necessary to comply with this Directive before 17 January 2002. They shall forthwith inform the Commission thereof.
(2) When Member States adopt the measures referred to in paragraph 1, these shall contain a reference to this Directive or shall be accompanied by such reference at the time of their official publication. The methods of making such reference shall be laid down by Member States.

Article 23. This Directive shall enter into force on the day of its publication in the Official Journal of the European Communities.

Article 24. This Directive is addressed to the Member States.

Annex. Derogations from Article 3
As provided for in Article 3(3), Article 3(1) and (2) do not apply to:
- copyright, neighbouring rights, rights referred to in Directive 87/54/EEC(1) and Directive 96/9/EC(2) as well as industrial property rights,
- the emission of electronic money by institutions in respect of which Member States have applied one of the derogations provided for in Article 8(1) of Directive 2000/46/EC(3),
- Article 44(2) of Directive 85/611/EEC(4),
- Article 30 and Title IV of Directive 92/49/EEC(5), Title IV of Directive 92/96/EEC(6), Articles 7 and 8 of Directive 88/357/EEC(7) and Article 4 of Directive 90/619/EEC(8),
- the freedom of the parties to choose the law applicable to their contract,
- contractual obligations concerning consumer contacts,
- formal validity of contracts creating or transferring rights in real estate where such contracts are subject to mandatory formal requirements of the law of the Member State where the real estate is situated,
- the permissibility of unsolicited commercial communications by electronic mail.

Directive 2000/35/EC of the European Parliament and the of the Council of 29 June 2000 on combating late payment in commercial transactions (*OJ* L 200/35, 08.08.2000, pp. 1 – 4) [footnotes omitted].

THE EUROPEAN PARLIAMENT AND THE COUNCIL OF THE EUROPEAN UNION,
Having regard to the Treaty establishing the European Community, and in particular Article 95 thereof,
Having regard to the proposal from the Commission,
Having regard to the opinion of the Economic and Social Committee,
Acting in accordance with the procedure laid down in Article 251 of the Treaty, in the light of the joint text approved by the Conciliation Committee on 4 May 2000,
Whereas:
(1) In its resolution on the integrated programme in favour of SMEs and the craft sector, the European Parliament urged the Commission to submit proposals to deal with the problem of late payment.
(2) On 12 May 1995 the Commission adopted a recommendation on payment periods in commercial transactions.
(3) In its resolution on the Commission recommendation on payment periods in commercial transactions, the European Parliament called on the Commission to consider transforming its recommendation into a proposal for a Council directive to be submitted as soon as possible.
(4) On 29 May 1997 the Economic and Social Committee adopted an opinion on the Commission's Green Paper on Public procurement in the European Union: Exploring the way forward.
(5) On 4 June 1997 the Commission published an action plan for the single market, which underlined that late payment represents an increasingly serious obstacle for the success of the single market.
(6) On 17 July 1997 the Commission published a report on late payments in commercial transactions, summarising the results of an evaluation of the effects of the Commission's recommendation of 12 May 1995.
(7) Heavy administrative and financial burdens are placed on businesses, particularly small and medium-sized ones, as a result of excessive payment periods and late payment. Moreover, these problems are a major cause of insolvencies threatening the survival of businesses and result in numerous job losses.
(8) In some Member States contractual payment periods differ significantly from the Community average.
(9) The differences between payment rules and practices in the Member States constitute an obstacle to the proper functioning of the internal market.
(10) This has the effect of considerably limiting commercial transactions between Member States. This is in contradiction with Article 14 of the Treaty as entrepreneurs should be able to trade throughout the internal market under conditions which ensure that transborder operations do not entail greater risks than domestic sales. Distortions of competition would ensue if substantially different rules applied to domestic and transborder operations.
(11) The most recent statistics indicate that there has been, at best, no improvement in late payments in many Member States since the adoption of the recommendation of 12 May 1995.
(12) The objective of combating late payments in the internal market cannot be sufficiently achieved by the Member States acting individually and can, therefore, be better achieved by the Community. This Directive does not go beyond what is necessary to achieve that objective. This Directive complies therefore, in its entirety, with the requirements of the principles of subsidiarity and proportionality as laid down in Article 5 of the Treaty.
(13) This Directive should be limited to payments made as remuneration for commercial transactions and does not regulate transactions with consumers, interest in connection with other payments, e.g. payments under the laws on cheques and bills of exchange, payments made as compensation for damages including payments from insurance companies.
(14) The fact that the liberal professions are covered by this Directive does not mean that Member States have to treat them as undertakings or merchants for purposes not covered by this Directive.
(15) This Directive only defines the term 'enforceable title' but does not regulate the various procedures of forced execution of such a title and the conditions under which forced execution of such a title can be stopped or suspended.
(16) Late payment constitutes a breach of contract which has been made financially attractive to debtors in most Member States by low interest rates on late payments and/or slow procedures for redress. A decisive shift, including compensation of creditors for the costs incurred, is necessary to reverse this trend and to ensure that the consequences of late payments are such as to discourage late payment.
(17) The reasonable compensation for the recovery costs has to be considered without prejudice to national provisions according to which a national judge can award to the creditor any additional damage caused by the debtor's late payment, taking also into account that such incurred costs may be already compensated for by the interest for late payment.

(18) This Directive takes into account the issue of long contractual payment periods and, in particular, the existence of certain categories of contracts where a longer payment period in combination with a restriction of freedom of contract or a higher interest rate can be justified.

(19) This Directive should prohibit abuse of freedom of contract to the disadvantage of the creditor. Where an agreement mainly serves the purpose of procuring the debtor additional liquidity at the expense of the creditor, or where the main contractor imposes on his suppliers and subcontractors terms of payment which are not justified on the grounds of the terms granted to himself, these may be considered to be factors constituting such an abuse. This Directive does not affect national provisions relating to the way contracts are concluded or regulating the validity of contractual terms which are unfair to the debtor.

(20) The consequences of late payment can be dissuasive only if they are accompanied by procedures for redress which are rapid and effective for the creditor. In conformity with the principle of non-discrimination contained in Article 12 of the Treaty, those procedures should be available to all creditors who are established in the Community.

(21) It is desirable to ensure that creditors are in a position to exercise a retention of title on a non-discriminatory basis throughout the Community, if the retention of title clause is valid under the applicable national provisions designated by private international law.

(22) This Directive should regulate all commercial transactions irrespective of whether they are carried out between private or public undertakings or between undertakings and public authorities, having regard to the fact that the latter handle a considerable volume of payments to business. It should therefore also regulate all commercial transactions between main contractors and their suppliers and subcontractors.

(23) Article 5 of this Directive requires that the recovery procedure for unchallenged claims be completed within a short period of time in conformity with national legislation, but does not require Member States to adopt a specific procedure or to amend their existing legal procedures in a specific way,

HAVE ADOPTED THIS DIRECTIVE:

Article 1. This Directive shall apply to all payments made as remuneration for commercial transactions.

Article 2. For the purposes of this Directive:
(1) 'commercial transactions' means transactions between undertakings or between undertakings and public authorities which lead to the delivery of goods or the provision of services for remuneration, 'public authority' means any contracting authority or entity, as defined by the Public Procurement Directives (92/ 50/EEC (1), 93/36/EEC (2), 93/37/EEC (3) and 93/ 38/EEC (4)), 'undertaking' means any organisation acting in the course of its independent economic or professional activity, even where it is carried on by a single person;
(2) 'late payment' means exceeding the contractual or statutory period of payment;
(3) 'retention of title' means the contractual agreement according to which the seller retains title to the goods in question until the price has been paid in full;
(4) 'interest rate applied by the European Central Bank to its main refinancing operations' means the interest rate applied to such operations in the case of fixed-rate tenders. In the event that a main refinancing operation was conducted according to a variable-rate tender procedure, this interest rate refers to the marginal interest rate which resulted from that tender. This applies both in the case of single-rate and variable-rate auctions;
(5) 'enforceable title' means any decision, judgment or order for payment issued by a court or other competent authority, whether for immediate payment or payment by instalments, which permits the creditor to have his claim against the debtor collected by means of forced execution; it shall include a decision, judgment or order for payment that is provisionally enforceable and remains so even if the debtor appeals against it.

Article 3. (1) Member States shall ensure that:
(a) interest in accordance with point (d) shall become payable from the day following the date or the end of the period for payment fixed in the contract;
(b) if the date or period for payment is not fixed in the contract, interest shall become payable automatically without the necessity of a reminder:
(i) 30 days following the date of receipt by the debtor of the invoice or an equivalent request for payment; or
(ii) if the date of the receipt of the invoice or the equivalent request for payment is uncertain, 30 days after the date of receipt of the goods or services; or
(iii) if the debtor receives the invoice or the equivalent request for payment earlier than the goods or the services, 30 days after the receipt of the goods or services; or
(iv) if a procedure of acceptance or verification, by which the conformity of the goods or services with the contract is to be ascertained, is provided for by statute or in the contract and if the debtor receives the invoice or the

equivalent request for payment earlier or on the date on which such acceptance or verification takes place, 30 days after this latter date;
(c) the creditor shall be entitled to interest for late payment to the extent that:
(i) he has fulfilled his contractual and legal obligations; and
(ii) he has not received the amount due on time, unless the debtor is not responsible for the delay;
(d) the level of interest for late payment ('the statutory rate'), which the debtor is obliged to pay, shall be the sum of the interest rate applied by the European Central Bank to its most recent main refinancing operation carried out before the first calendar day of the half-year in question ('the reference rate'), plus at least seven percentage points ('the margin'), unless otherwise specified in the contract. For a Member State which is not participating in the third stage of economic and monetary union, the reference rate referred to above shall be the equivalent rate set by its national central bank. In both cases, the reference rate in force on the first calendar day of the half-year in question shall apply for the following six months;
(e) unless the debtor is not responsible for the delay, the creditor shall be entitled to claim reasonable compensation from the debtor for all relevant recovery costs incurred through the latter's late payment. Such recovery costs shall respect the principles of transparency and proportionality as regards the debt in question. Member States may, while respecting the principles referred to above, fix maximum amounts as regards the recovery costs for different levels of debt.
(2) For certain categories of contracts to be defined by national law, Member States may fix the period after which interest becomes payable to a maximum of 60 days provided that they either restrain the parties to the contract from exceeding this period or fix a mandatory interest rate that substantially exceeds the statutory rate.
(3) Member States shall provide that an agreement on the date for payment or on the consequences of late payment which is not in line with the provisions of paragraphs 1(b) to (d) and 2 either shall not be enforceable or shall give rise to a claim for damages if, when all circumstances of the case, including good commercial practice and the nature of the product, are considered, it is grossly unfair to the creditor. In determining whether an agreement is grossly unfair to the creditor, it will be taken, *inter alia*, into account whether the debtor has any objective reason to deviate from the provisions of paragraphs 1(b) to (d) and 2. If such an agreement is determined to be grossly unfair, the statutory terms will apply, unless the national courts determine different conditions which are fair.
(4) Member States shall ensure that, in the interests of creditors and of competitors, adequate and effective means exist to prevent the continued use of terms which are grossly unfair within the meaning of paragraph 3.
(5) The means referred to in paragraph 4 shall include provisions whereby organisations officially recognised as, or having a legitimate interest in, representing small and medium-sized enterprises may take action according to the national law concerned before the courts or before competent administrative bodies on the grounds that contractual terms drawn up for general use are grossly unfair within the meaning of paragraph 3, so that they can apply appropriate and effective means to prevent the continued use of such terms.

Article 4. (1) Member States shall provide in conformity with the applicable national provisions designated by private international law that the seller retains title to goods until they are fully paid for if a retention of title clause has been expressly agreed between the buyer and the seller before the delivery of the goods.
(2) Member States may adopt or retain provisions dealing with down payments already made by the debtor.

Article 5. (1) Member States shall ensure that an enforceable title can be obtained, irrespective of the amount of the debt, normally within 90 calendar days of the lodging of the creditor's action or application at the court or other competent authority, provided that the debt or aspects of the procedure are not disputed. This duty shall be carried out by Member States in conformity with their respective national legislation, regulations and administrative provisions.
(2) The respective national legislation, regulations and administrative provisions shall apply the same conditions for all creditors who are established in the European Community.
(3) The 90 calendar day period referred to in paragraph 1 shall not include the following:
(a) periods for service of documents;
(b) any delays caused by the creditor, such as periods devoted to correcting applications.
(4) This Article shall be without prejudice to the provisions of the Brussels Convention on jurisdiction and enforcement of judgments in civil and commercial matters.

Article 6. (1) Member States shall bring into force the laws, regulations and administrative provisions necessary to comply with this Directive before 8 August 2002. They shall forthwith inform the Commission thereof. When Member States adopt these measures, they shall contain a reference to this Directive or shall be accompanied by such reference on the occasion of their official publication. The methods of making such reference shall be laid down by Member States.

(2) Member States may maintain or bring into force provisions which are more favourable to the creditor than the provisions necessary to comply with this Directive.
(3) In transposing this Directive, Member States may exclude:
(a) debts that are subject to insolvency proceedings instituted against the debtor;
(b) contracts that have been concluded prior to 8 August 2002; and
(c) claims for interest of less than EUR5.
(4) Member States shall communicate to the Commission the text of the main provisions of national law which they adopt in the field covered by this Directive.
(5) The Commission shall undertake two years after 8 August 2002 a review of, *inter alia*, the statutory rate, contractual payment periods and late payments, to assess the impact on commercial transactions and the operation of the legislation in practice. The results of this review and of other reviews will be made known to the European Parliament and the Council, accompanied where appropriate by proposals for improvement of this Directive.

Article 7. This Directive shall enter into force on the day of its publication in the Official Journal of the European Communities.

Article 8. This Directive is addressed to the Member States.

Directive 2002/47/EC of the European Parliament and of the Council of 6 June 2002 on financial collateral arrangements (*OJ*L 168/43, 27.06.2002) [footnotes omitted].

THE EUROPEAN PARLIAMENT AND THE COUNCIL OF THE EUROPEAN UNION,
Having regard to the Treaty establishing the European Community, and in particular Article 95 thereof,
Having regard to the proposal from the Commission,
Having regard to the opinion of the European Central Bank,
Having regard to the opinion of the Economic and Social Committee,
Acting in accordance with the procedure laid down in Article 251 of the Treaty,
Whereas: (1) Directive 98/26/EC of the European Parliament and of the Council of 19 May 1998 on settlement finality in payment and securities settlement systems constituted a milestone in establishing a sound legal framework for payment and securities settlement systems. Implementation of that Directive has demonstrated the importance of limiting systemic risk inherent in such systems stemming from the different influence of several jurisdictions, and the benefits of common rules in relation to collateral constituted to such systems.
(2) In its communication of 11 May 1999 to the European Parliament and to the Council on financial services: implementing the framework for financial markets: action plan, the Commission undertook, after consultation with market experts and national authorities, to work on further proposals for legislative action on collateral urging further progress in the field of collateral, beyond Directive 98/26/EC.
(3) A Community regime should be created for the provision of securities and cash as collateral under both security interest and title transfer structures including repurchase agreements (repos). This will contribute to the integration and cost-efficiency of the financial market as well as to the stability of the financial system in the Community, thereby supporting the freedom to provide services and the free movement of capital in the single market in financial services. This Directive focuses on bilateral financial collateral arrangements.
(4) This Directive is adopted in a European legal context which consists in particular of the said Directive 98/26/EC as well as Directive 2001/24/EC of the European Parliament and of the Council of 4 April 2001 on the reorganisation and winding up of credit institutions, Directive 2001/17/EC of the European Parliament and of the Council of 19 March 2001 on the reorganisation and winding-up of insurance undertakings and Council Regulation (EC) No 1346/2000 of 29 May 2000 on insolvency proceedings. This Directive is in line with the general pattern of these previous legal acts and is not opposed to it. Indeed, this Directive complements these existing legal acts by dealing with further issues and going beyond them in connection with particular matters already dealt with by these legal acts.
(5) In order to improve the legal certainty of financial collateral arrangements, Member States should ensure that certain provisions of insolvency law do not apply to such arrangements, in particular, those that would inhibit the effective realisation of financial collateral or cast doubt on the validity of current techniques such as bilateral close-out netting, the provision of additional collateral in the form of top-up collateral and substitution of collateral.
(6) This Directive does not address rights which any person may have in respect of assets provided as financial collateral, and which arise otherwise than under the terms of the financial collateral arrangement and otherwise than on the basis of any legal provision or rule of law arising by reason of the commencement or continuation of winding-up proceedings or reorganisation measures, such as restitution arising from mistake, error or lack of capacity.
(7) The principle in Directive 98/26/EC, whereby the law applicable to book entry securities provided as collateral is the law of the jurisdiction where the relevant register, account or centralised deposit system is located, should be extended in order to create legal certainty regarding the use of such securities held in a cross-border context and used as financial collateral under the scope of this Directive.
(8) The *lex rei sitae* rule, according to which the applicable law for determining whether a financial collateral arrangement is properly perfected and therefore good against third parties is the law of the country where the financial collateral is located, is currently recognised by all Member States. Without affecting the application of this Directive to directly-held securities, the location of book entry securities provided as financial collateral and held through one or more intermediaries should be determined. If the collateral taker has a valid and effective collateral arrangement according to the governing law of the country in which the relevant account is maintained, then the validity against any competing title or interest and the enforceability of the collateral should be governed solely by the law of that country, thus preventing legal uncertainty as a result of other unforeseen legislation.
(9) In order to limit the administrative burdens for parties using financial collateral under the scope of this Directive, the only perfection requirement which national law may impose in respect of financial collateral should be that the financial collateral is delivered, transferred, held, registered or otherwise designated so as to be in the possession or under the control of the collateral taker or of a person acting on the collateral taker's behalf while not

excluding collateral techniques where the collateral provider is allowed to substitute collateral or to withdraw excess collateral.

(10) For the same reasons, the creation, validity, perfection, enforceability or admissibility in evidence of a financial collateral arrangement, or the provision of financial collateral under a financial collateral arrangement, should not be made dependent on the performance of any formal act such as the execution of any document in a specific form or in a particular manner, the making of any filing with an official or public body or registration in a public register, advertisement in a newspaper or journal, in an official register or publication or in any other matter, notification to a public officer or the provision of evidence in a particular form as to the date of execution of a document or instrument, the amount of the relevant financial obligations or any other matter. This Directive must however provide a balance between market efficiency and the safety of the parties to the arrangement and third parties, thereby avoiding *inter alia* the risk of fraud. This balance should be achieved through the scope of this Directive covering only those financial collateral arrangements which provide for some form of dispossession, i.e. the provision of the financial collateral, and where the provision of the financial collateral can be evidenced in writing or in a durable medium, ensuring thereby the traceability of that collateral. For the purpose of this Directive, acts required under the law of a Member State as conditions for transferring or creating a security interest on financial instruments, other than book entry securities, such as endorsement in the case of instruments to order, or recording on the issuer's register in the case of registered instruments, should not be considered as formal acts.

(11) Moreover, this Directive should protect only financial collateral arrangements which can be evidenced. Such evidence can be given in writing or in any other legally enforceable manner provided by the law which is applicable to the financial collateral arrangement.

(12) The simplification of the use of financial collateral through the limitation of administrative burdens promotes the efficiency of the cross-border operations of the European Central Bank and the national central banks of Member States participating in the economic and monetary union, necessary for the implementation of the common monetary policy. Furthermore, the provision of limited protection of financial collateral arrangements from some rules of insolvency law in addition supports the wider aspect of the common monetary policy, where the participants in the money market balance the overall amount of liquidity in the market among themselves, by cross-border transactions backed by collateral.

(13) This Directive seeks to protect the validity of financial collateral arrangements which are based upon the transfer of the full ownership of the financial collateral, such as by eliminating the so-called re-characterisation of such financial collateral arrangements (including repurchase agreements) as security interests.

(14) The enforceability of bilateral close-out netting should be protected, not only as an enforcement mechanism for title transfer financial collateral arrangements including repurchase agreements but more widely, where close-out netting forms part of a financial collateral arrangement. Sound risk management practices commonly used in the financial market should be protected by enabling participants to manage and reduce their credit exposures arising from all kinds of financial transactions on a net basis, where the credit exposure is calculated by combining the estimated current exposures under all outstanding transactions with a counterparty, setting off reciprocal items to produce a single aggregated amount that is compared with the current value of the collateral.

(15) This Directive should be without prejudice to any restrictions or requirements under national law on bringing into account claims, on obligations to set-off, or on netting, for example relating to their reciprocity or the fact that they have been concluded prior to when the collateral taker knew or ought to have known of the commencement (or of any mandatory legal act leading to the commencement) of winding-up proceedings or reorganisation measures in respect of the collateral provider.

(16) The sound market practice favoured by regulators whereby participants in the financial market use top-up financial collateral arrangements to manage and limit their credit risk to each other by mark-to-market calculations of the current market value of the credit exposure and the value of the financial collateral and accordingly ask for top-up financial collateral or return the surplus of financial collateral should be protected against certain automatic avoidance rules. The same applies to the possibility of substituting for assets provided as financial collateral other assets of the same value. The intention is merely that the provision of top-up or substitution financial collateral cannot be questioned on the sole basis that the relevant financial obligations existed before that financial collateral was provided, or that the financial collateral was provided during a prescribed period. However, this does not prejudice the possibility of questioning under national law the financial collateral arrangement and the provision of financial collateral as part of the initial provision, top-up or substitution of financial collateral, for example where this has been intentionally done to the detriment of the other creditors (this covers *inter alia* actions based on fraud or similar avoidance rules which may apply in a prescribed period).

(17) This Directive provides for rapid and non-formalistic enforcement procedures in order to safeguard financial stability and limit contagion effects in case of a default of a party to a financial collateral arrangement. However, this Directive balances the latter objectives with the protection of the collateral provider and third parties by

explicitly confirming the possibility for Member States to keep or introduce in their national legislation an *a posteriori* control which the Courts can exercise in relation to the realisation or valuation of financial collateral and the calculation of the relevant financial obligations. Such control should allow for the judicial authorities to verify that the realisation or valuation has been conducted in a commercially reasonable manner.

(18) It should be possible to provide cash as collateral under both title transfer and secured structures respectively protected by the recognition of netting or by the pledge of cash collateral. Cash refers only to money which is represented by a credit to an account, or similar claims on repayment of money (such as money market deposits), thus explicitly excluding banknotes.

(19) This Directive provides for a right of use in case of security financial collateral arrangements, which increases liquidity in the financial market stemming from such reuse of 'pledged' securities. This reuse however should be without prejudice to national legislation about separation of assets and unfair treatment of creditors.

(20) This Directive does not prejudice the operation and effect of the contractual terms of financial instruments provided as financial collateral, such as rights and obligations and other conditions contained in the terms of issue and any other rights and obligations and other conditions which apply between the issuers and holders of such instruments.

(21) This Act complies with the fundamental rights and follows the principles laid down in particular in the Charter of Fundamental Rights of the European Union.

(22) Since the objective of the proposed action, namely to create a minimum regime relating to the use of financial collateral, cannot be sufficiently achieved by the Member States and can therefore, by reason of the scale and effects of the action, be better achieved at Community level, the Community may adopt measures, in accordance with the principle of subsidiarity as set out in Article 5 of the Treaty. In accordance with the principle of proportionality, as set out in that Article, this Directive does not go beyond what is necessary in order to achieve that objective,

HAVE ADOPTED THIS DIRECTIVE:

Article 1. (1) This Directive lays down a Community regime applicable to financial collateral arrangements which satisfy the requirements set out in paragraphs 2 and 5 and to financial collateral in accordance with the conditions set out in paragraphs 4 and 5.

(2) The collateral taker and the collateral provider must each belong to one of the following categories:
(a) a public authority (excluding publicly guaranteed undertakings unless they fall under points (b) to (e)) including:
(i) public sector bodies of Member States charged with or intervening in the management of public debt, and
(ii) public sector bodies of Member States authorised to hold accounts for customers;
(b) a central bank, the European Central Bank, the Bank for International Settlements, a multilateral development bank as defined in Article 1(19) of Directive 2000/12/EC of the European Parliament and of the Council of 20 March 2000 relating to the taking up and pursuit of the business of credit institutions (1), the International Monetary Fund and the European Investment Bank;
(c) a financial institution subject to prudential supervision including:
(i) a credit institution as defined in Article 1(1) of Directive 2000/12/EC, including the institutions listed in Article 2(3) of that Directive;
(ii) an investment firm as defined in Article 1(2) of Council Directive 93/22/EEC of 10 May 1993 on investment services in the securities field (1);
(iii) a financial institution as defined in Article 1(5) of Directive 2000/12/EC;
(iv) an insurance undertaking as defined in Article 1(a) of Council Directive 92/49/EEC of 18 June 1992 on the coordination of laws, regulations and administrative provisions relating to direct insurance other than life assurance (2) and a life assurance undertaking as defined in Article 1(a) of Council Directive 92/96/EEC of 10 November 1992 on the coordination of laws, regulations and administrative provisions relating to direct life assurance (3);
(v) an undertaking for collective investment in transferable securities (UCITS) as defined in Article 1(2) of Council Directive 85/611/EEC of 20 December 1985 on the coordination of laws, regulations and administrative provisions relating to undertakings for collective investment in transferable securities (UCITS) (4);
(vi) a management company as defined in Article 1a(2) of Directive 85/611/EEC;
(d) a central counterparty, settlement agent or clearing house, as defined respectively in Article 2(c), (d) and (e) of Directive 98/26/EC, including similar institutions regulated under national law acting in the futures, options and derivatives markets to the extent not covered by that Directive, and a person, other than a natural person, who acts in a trust or representative capacity on behalf of any one or more persons that includes any bondholders or holders of other forms of securitised debt or any institution as defined in points (a) to (d);

(e) a person other than a natural person, including unincorporated firms and partnerships, provided that the other party is an institution as defined in points (a) to (d).
(3) Member States may exclude from the scope of this Directive financial collateral arrangements where one of the parties is a person mentioned in paragraph 2(e). If they make use of this option Member States shall inform the Commission which shall inform the other Member States thereof.
(4) (a) The financial collateral to be provided must consist of cash or financial instruments.
(b) Member States may exclude from the scope of this Directive financial collateral consisting of the collateral provider's own shares, shares in affiliated undertakings within the meaning of seventh Council Directive 83/349/EEC of 13 June 1983 on consolidated accounts (5), and shares in undertakings whose exclusive purpose is to own means of production that are essential for the collateral provider's business or to own real property.
(5) This Directive applies to financial collateral once it has been provided and if that provision can be evidenced in writing.
The evidencing of the provision of financial collateral must allow for the identification of the financial collateral to which it applies. For this purpose, it is sufficient to prove that the book entry securities collateral has been credited to, or forms a credit in, the relevant account and that the cash collateral has been credited to, or forms a credit in, a designated account. This Directive applies to financial collateral arrangements if that arrangement can be evidenced in writing or in a legally equivalent manner.

Article 2. (1) For the purpose of this Directive:
(a) 'financial collateral arrangement' means a title transfer financial collateral arrangement or a security financial collateral arrangement whether or not these are covered by a master agreement or general terms and conditions;
(b) 'title transfer financial collateral arrangement' means an arrangement, including repurchase agreements, under which a collateral provider transfers full ownership of financial collateral to a collateral taker for the purpose of securing or otherwise covering the performance of relevant financial obligations;
(c) 'security financial collateral arrangement' means an arrangement under which a collateral provider provides financial collateral by way of security in favour of, or to, a collateral taker, and where the full ownership of the financial collateral remains with the collateral provider when the security right is established;
(d) 'cash' means money credited to an account in any currency, or similar claims for the repayment of money, such as money market deposits;
(e) 'financial instruments' means shares in companies and other securities equivalent to shares in companies and bonds and other forms of debt instruments if these are negotiable on the capital market, and any other securities which are normally dealt in and which give the right to acquire any such shares, bonds or other securities by subscription, purchase or exchange or which give rise to a cash settlement (excluding instruments of payment), including units in collective investment undertakings, money market instruments and claims relating to or rights in or in respect of any of the foregoing;
(f) 'relevant financial obligations' means the obligations which are secured by a financial collateral arrangement and which give a right to cash settlement and/or delivery of financial instruments. Relevant financial obligations may consist of or include:
(i) present or future, actual or contingent or prospective obligations (including such obligations arising under a master agreement or similar arrangement);
(ii) obligations owed to the collateral taker by a person other than the collateral provider; or
(iii) obligations of a specified class or kind arising from time to time;
(g) 'book entry securities collateral' means financial collateral provided under a financial collateral arrangement which consists of financial instruments, title to which is evidenced by entries in a register or account maintained by or on behalf of an intermediary;
(h) 'relevant account' means in relation to book entry securities collateral which is subject to a financial collateral arrangement, the register or account — which may be maintained by the collateral taker — in which the entries are made by which that book entry securities collateral is provided to the collateral taker;
(i) 'equivalent collateral':
(i) in relation to cash, means a payment of the same amount and in the same currency;
(ii) in relation to financial instruments, means financial instruments of the same issuer or debtor, forming part of the same issue or class and of the same nominal amount, currency and description or, where a financial collateral arrangement provides for the transfer of other assets following the occurrence of any event relating to or affecting any financial instruments provided as financial collateral, those other assets;
(j) 'winding-up proceedings' means collective proceedings involving realisation of the assets and distribution of the proceeds among the creditors, shareholders or members as appropriate, which involve any intervention by administrative or judicial authorities, including where the collective proceedings are terminated by a composition or other analogous measure, whether or not they are founded on insolvency or are voluntary or compulsory;

(k) 'reorganisation measures' means measures which involve any intervention by administrative or judicial authorities which are intended to preserve or restore the financial situation and which affect pre-existing rights of third parties, including but not limited to measures involving a suspension of payments, suspension of enforcement measures or reduction of claims;
(l) 'enforcement event' means an event of default or any similar event as agreed between the parties on the occurrence of which, under the terms of a financial collateral arrangement or by operation of law, the collateral taker is entitled to realise or appropriate financial collateral or a close-out netting provision comes into effect;
(m) 'right of use' means the right of the collateral taker to use and dispose of financial collateral provided under a security financial collateral arrangement as the owner of it in accordance with the terms of the security financial collateral arrangement;
(n) 'close-out netting provision' means a provision of a financial collateral arrangement, or of an arrangement of which a financial collateral arrangement forms part, or, in the absence of any such provision, any statutory rule by which, on the occurrence of an enforcement event, whether through the operation of netting or set-off or otherwise:
(i) the obligations of the parties are accelerated so as to be immediately due and expressed as an obligation to pay an amount representing their estimated current value, or are terminated and replaced by an obligation to pay such an amount; and/or
(ii) an account is taken of what is due from each party to the other in respect of such obligations, and a net sum equal to the balance of the account is payable by the party from whom the larger amount is due to the other party.
(2) References in this Directive to financial collateral being 'provided', or to the 'provision' of financial collateral, are to the financial collateral being delivered, transferred, held, registered or otherwise designated so as to be in the possession or under the control of the collateral taker or of a person acting on the collateral taker's behalf. Any right of substitution or to withdraw excess financial collateral in favour of the collateral provider shall not prejudice the financial collateral having been provided to the collateral taker as mentioned in this Directive.
(3) References in this Directive to 'writing' include recording by electronic means and any other durable medium.

Article 3. (1) Member States shall not require that the creation, validity, perfection, enforceability or admissibility in evidence of a financial collateral arrangement or the provision of financial collateral under a financial collateral arrangement be dependent on the performance of any formal act.
(2) Paragraph 1 is without prejudice to the application of this Directive to financial collateral only once it has been provided and if that provision can be evidenced in writing and where the financial collateral arrangement can be evidenced in writing or in a legally equivalent manner.

Article 4. (1) Member States shall ensure that on the occurrence of an enforcement event, the collateral taker shall be able to realise in the following manners, any financial collateral provided under, and subject to the terms agreed in, a security financial collateral arrangement:
(a) financial instruments by sale or appropriation and by setting off their value against, or applying their value in discharge of, the relevant financial obligations;
(b) cash by setting off the amount against or applying it in discharge of the relevant financial obligations.
(2) Appropriation is possible only if:
(a) this has been agreed by the parties in the security financial collateral arrangement; and
(b) the parties have agreed in the security financial collateral arrangement on the valuation of the financial instruments.
(3) Member States which do not allow appropriation on 27 June 2002 are not obliged to recognise it. If they make use of this option, Member States shall inform the Commission which in turn shall inform the other Member States thereof.
(4) The manners of realising the financial collateral referred to in paragraph 1 shall, subject to the terms agreed in the security financial collateral arrangement, be without any requirement to the effect that:
(a) prior notice of the intention to realise must have been given;
(b) the terms of the realisation be approved by any court, public officer or other person;
(c) the realisation be conducted by public auction or in any other prescribed manner; or
(d) any additional time period must have elapsed.
(5) Member States shall ensure that a financial collateral arrangement can take effect in accordance with its terms notwithstanding the commencement or continuation of winding-up proceedings or reorganisation measures in respect of the collateral provider or collateral taker.
(6) This Article and Articles 5, 6 and 7 shall be without prejudice to any requirements under national law to the effect that the realisation or valuation of financial collateral and the calculation of the relevant financial obligations must be conducted in a commercially reasonable manner.

Article 5. (1) If and to the extent that the terms of a security financial collateral arrangement so provide, Member States shall ensure that the collateral taker is entitled to exercise a right of use in relation to financial collateral provided under the security financial collateral arrangement.
(2) Where a collateral taker exercises a right of use, he thereby incurs an obligation to transfer equivalent collateral to replace the original financial collateral at the latest on the due date for the performance of the relevant financial obligations covered by the security financial collateral arrangement. Alternatively, the collateral taker shall, on the due date for the performance of the relevant financial obligations, either transfer equivalent collateral, or, if and to the extent that the terms of a security financial collateral arrangement so provide, set off the value of the equivalent collateral against or apply it in discharge of the relevant financial obligations.
(3) The equivalent collateral transferred in discharge of an obligation as described in paragraph 2, first subparagraph, shall be subject to the same security financial collateral agreement to which the original financial collateral was subject and shall be treated as having been provided under the security financial collateral arrangement at the same time as the original financial collateral was first provided.
(4) Member States shall ensure that the use of financial collateral by the collateral taker according to this Article does not render invalid or unenforceable the rights of the collateral taker under the security financial collateral arrangement in relation to the financial collateral transferred by the collateral taker in discharge of an obligation as described in paragraph 2, first subparagraph.
(5) If an enforcement event occurs while an obligation as described in paragraph 2 first subparagraph remains outstanding, the obligation may be the subject of a close-out netting provision.

Article 6. (1) Member States shall ensure that a title transfer financial collateral arrangement can take effect in accordance with its terms.
(2) If an enforcement event occurs while any obligation of the collateral taker to transfer equivalent collateral under a title transfer financial collateral arrangement remains outstanding, the obligation may be the subject of a close-out netting provision.

Article 7. (1) Member States shall ensure that a close-out netting provision can take effect in accordance with its terms:
(a) notwithstanding the commencement or continuation of winding-up proceedings or reorganisation measures in respect of the collateral provider and/or the collateral taker; and/or
(b) notwithstanding any purported assignment, judicial or other attachment or other disposition of or in respect of such rights.
(2) Member States shall ensure that the operation of a close-out netting provision may not be subject to any of the requirements that are mentioned in Article 4(4), unless otherwise agreed by the parties.

Article 8. (1) Member States shall ensure that a financial collateral arrangement, as well as the provision of financial collateral under such arrangement, may not be declared invalid or void or be reversed on the sole basis that the financial collateral arrangement has come into existence, or the financial collateral has been provided:
(a) on the day of the commencement of winding-up proceedings or reorganisation measures, but prior to the order or decree making that commencement; or
(b) in a prescribed period prior to, and defined by reference to, the commencement of such proceedings or measures or by reference to the making of any order or decree or the taking of any other action or occurrence of any other event in the course of such proceedings or measures.
(2) Member States shall ensure that where a financial collateral arrangement or a relevant financial obligation has come into existence, or financial collateral has been provided on the day of, but after the moment of the commencement of, winding-up proceedings or reorganisation measures, it shall be legally enforceable and binding on third parties if the collateral taker can prove that he was not aware, nor should have been aware, of the commencement of such proceedings or measures.
(3) Where a financial collateral arrangement contains:
(a) an obligation to provide financial collateral or additional financial collateral in order to take account of changes in the value of the financial collateral or in the amount of the relevant financial obligations, or
(b) a right to withdraw financial collateral on providing, by way of substitution or exchange, financial collateral of substantially the same value,
Member States shall ensure that the provision of financial collateral, additional financial collateral or substitute or replacement financial collateral under such an obligation or right shall not be treated as invalid or reversed or declared void on the sole basis that:

(i) such provision was made on the day of the commencement of winding-up proceedings or reorganisation measures, but prior to the order or decree making that commencement or in a prescribed period prior to, and defined by reference to, the commencement of winding-up proceedings or reorganisation measures or by reference to the making of any order or decree or the taking of any other action or occurrence of any other event in the course of such proceedings or measures; and/or
(ii) the relevant financial obligations were incurred prior to the date of the provision of the financial collateral, additional financial collateral or substitute or replacement financial collateral.
(4) Without prejudice to paragraphs 1, 2 and 3, this Directive leaves unaffected the general rules of national insolvency law in relation to the voidance of transactions entered into during the prescribed period referred to in paragraph 1(b) and in paragraph 3(i).

Article 9. (1) Any question with respect to any of the matters specified in paragraph 2 arising in relation to book entry securities collateral shall be governed by the law of the country in which the relevant account is maintained. The reference to the law of a country is a reference to its domestic law, disregarding any rule under which, in deciding the relevant question, reference should be made to the law of another country.
(2) The matters referred to in paragraph 1 are:
(a) the legal nature and proprietary effects of book entry securities collateral;
(b) the requirements for perfecting a financial collateral arrangement relating to book entry securities collateral and the provision of book entry securities collateral under such an arrangement, and more generally the completion of the steps necessary to render such an arrangement and provision effective against third parties;
(c) whether a person's title to or interest in such book entry securities collateral is overridden by or subordinated to a competing title or interest, or a good faith acquisition has occurred;
(d) the steps required for the realisation of book entry securities collateral following the occurrence of an enforcement event.

Article 10. Not later than 27 December 2006, the Commission shall present a report to the European Parliament and the Council on the application of this Directive, in particular on the application of Article 1(3), Article 4(3) and Article 5, accompanied where appropriate by proposals for its revision.

Article 11. Member States shall bring into force the laws, regulations and administrative provisions necessary to comply with this Directive by 27 December 2003 at the latest. They shall forthwith inform the Commission thereof. When Member States adopt those provisions, they shall contain a reference to this Directive or be accompanied by such reference on the occasion of their official publication. Member States shall determine how such reference is to be made.

Article 12. This Directive shall enter into force on the day of its publication in the Official Journal of the European Communities.

Article 13. This Directive is addressed to the Member States.

Directive 2005/29/EC of the European Parliament and of the Council of 11 May 2005 concerning unfair business-to-consumer commercial practices in the internal market and amending Council Directive 84/450/EEC, Directives 97/7/EC, 98/27/EC and 2002/65/EC of the European Parliament and of the Council and Regulation (EC) No 2006/2004 of the European Parliament and of the Council ('Unfair Commercial Practices Directive') (*OJL* 149 , 11.06.2000, pp. 22 -39) [footnotes omitted].

THE EUROPEAN PARLIAMENT AND THE COUNCIL OF THE EUROPEAN UNION,
Having regard to the Treaty establishing the European Community, and in particular Article 95 thereof,
Having regard to the proposal from the Commission,
Having regard to the opinion of the European Economic and Social Committee,
Acting in accordance with the procedure laid down in Article 251 of the Treaty,
Whereas:
(1) Article 153(1) and (3)(a) of the Treaty provides that the Community is to contribute to the attainment of a high level of consumer protection by the measures it adopts pursuant to Article 95 thereof.
(2) In accordance with Article 14(2) of the Treaty, the internal market comprises an area without internal frontiers in which the free movement of goods and services and freedom of establishment are ensured. The development of fair commercial practices within the area without internal frontiers is vital for the promotion of the development of cross-border activities.
(3) The laws of the Member States relating to unfair commercial practices show marked differences which can generate appreciable distortions of competition and obstacles to the smooth functioning of the internal market. In the field of advertising, Council Directive 84/450/EEC of 10 September 1984 concerning misleading and comparative advertising establishes minimum criteria for harmonising legislation on misleading advertising, but does not prevent the Member States from retaining or adopting measures which provide more extensive protection for consumers. As a result, Member States' provisions on misleading advertising diverge significantly.
(4) These disparities cause uncertainty as to which national rules apply to unfair commercial practices harming consumers' economic interests and create many barriers affecting business and consumers. These barriers increase the cost to business of exercising internal market freedoms, in particular when businesses wish to engage in cross border marketing, advertising campaigns and sales promotions. Such barriers also make consumers uncertain of their rights and undermine their confidence in the internal market.
(5) In the absence of uniform rules at Community level, obstacles to the free movement of services and goods across borders or the freedom of establishment could be justified in the light of the case-law of the Court of Justice of the European Communities as long as they seek to protect recognised public interest objectives and are proportionate to those objectives. In view of the Community's objectives, as set out in the provisions of the Treaty and in secondary Community law relating to freedom of movement, and in accordance with the Commission's policy on commercial communications as indicated in the Communication from the Commission entitled "The follow-up to the Green Paper on Commercial Communications in the Internal Market", such obstacles should be eliminated. These obstacles can only be eliminated by establishing uniform rules at Community level which establish a high level of consumer protection and by clarifying certain legal concepts at Community level to the extent necessary for the proper functioning of the internal market and to meet the requirement of legal certainty.
(6) This Directive therefore approximates the laws of the Member States on unfair commercial practices, including unfair advertising, which directly harm consumers' economic interests and thereby indirectly harm the economic interests of legitimate competitors. In line with the principle of proportionality, this Directive protects consumers from the consequences of such unfair commercial practices where they are material but recognises that in some cases the impact on consumers may be negligible. It neither covers nor affects the national laws on unfair commercial practices which harm only competitors' economic interests or which relate to a transaction between traders; taking full account of the principle of subsidiarity, Member States will continue to be able to regulate such practices, in conformity with Community law, if they choose to do so. Nor does this Directive cover or affect the provisions of Directive 84/450/EEC on advertising which misleads business but which is not misleading for consumers and on comparative advertising. Further, this Directive does not affect accepted advertising and marketing practices, such as legitimate product placement, brand differentiation or the offering of incentives which may legitimately affect consumers' perceptions of products and influence their behaviour without impairing the consumer's ability to make an informed decision.
(7) This Directive addresses commercial practices directly related to influencing consumers' transactional decisions in relation to products. It does not address commercial practices carried out primarily for other purposes, including for example commercial communication aimed at investors, such as annual reports and corporate promotional literature. It does not address legal requirements related to taste and decency which vary widely among the Member States. Commercial practices such as, for example, commercial solicitation in the streets, may be undesirable in Member States for cultural reasons. Member States should accordingly be able to continue to ban

commercial practices in their territory, in conformity with Community law, for reasons of taste and decency even where such practices do not limit consumers' freedom of choice. Full account should be taken of the context of the individual case concerned in applying this Directive, in particular the general clauses thereof.

(8) This Directive directly protects consumer economic interests from unfair business-to-consumer commercial practices. Thereby, it also indirectly protects legitimate businesses from their competitors who do not play by the rules in this Directive and thus guarantees fair competition in fields coordinated by it. It is understood that there are other commercial practices which, although not harming consumers, may hurt competitors and business customers. The Commission should carefully examine the need for Community action in the field of unfair competition beyond the remit of this Directive and, if necessary, make a legislative proposal to cover these other aspects of unfair competition.

(9) This Directive is without prejudice to individual actions brought by those who have been harmed by an unfair commercial practice. It is also without prejudice to Community and national rules on contract law, on intellectual property rights, on the health and safety aspects of products, on conditions of establishment and authorisation regimes, including those rules which, in conformity with Community law, relate to gambling activities, and to Community competition rules and the national provisions implementing them. The Member States will thus be able to retain or introduce restrictions and prohibitions of commercial practices on grounds of the protection of the health and safety of consumers in their territory wherever the trader is based, for example in relation to alcohol, tobacco or pharmaceuticals. Financial services and immovable property, by reason of their complexity and inherent serious risks, necessitate detailed requirements, including positive obligations on traders. For this reason, in the field of financial services and immovable property, this Directive is without prejudice to the right of Member States to go beyond its provisions to protect the economic interests of consumers. It is not appropriate to regulate here the certification and indication of the standard of fineness of articles of precious metal.

(10) It is necessary to ensure that the relationship between this Directive and existing Community law is coherent, particularly where detailed provisions on unfair commercial practices apply to specific sectors. This Directive therefore amends Directive 84/450/EEC, Directive 97/7/EC of the European Parliament and of the Council of 20 May 1997 on the protection of consumers in respect of distance contracts, Directive 98/27/EC of the European Parliament and of the Council of 19 May 1998 on injunctions for the protection of consumers' interests and Directive 2002/65/EC of the European Parliament and of the Council of 23 September 2002 concerning the distance marketing of consumer financial services. This Directive accordingly applies only in so far as there are no specific Community law provisions regulating specific aspects of unfair commercial practices, such as information requirements and rules on the way the information is presented to the consumer. It provides protection for consumers where there is no specific sectoral legislation at Community level and prohibits traders from creating a false impression of the nature of products. This is particularly important for complex products with high levels of risk to consumers, such as certain financial services products. This Directive consequently complements the Community acquis, which is applicable to commercial practices harming consumers' economic interests.

(11) The high level of convergence achieved by the approximation of national provisions through this Directive creates a high common level of consumer protection. This Directive establishes a single general prohibition of those unfair commercial practices distorting consumers' economic behaviour. It also sets rules on aggressive commercial practices, which are currently not regulated at Community level.

(12) Harmonisation will considerably increase legal certainty for both consumers and business. Both consumers and business will be able to rely on a single regulatory framework based on clearly defined legal concepts regulating all aspects of unfair commercial practices across the EU. The effect will be to eliminate the barriers stemming from the fragmentation of the rules on unfair commercial practices harming consumer economic interests and to enable the internal market to be achieved in this area.

(13) In order to achieve the Community's objectives through the removal of internal market barriers, it is necessary to replace Member States' existing, divergent general clauses and legal principles. The single, common general prohibition established by this Directive therefore covers unfair commercial practices distorting consumers' economic behaviour. In order to support consumer confidence the general prohibition should apply equally to unfair commercial practices which occur outside any contractual relationship between a trader and a consumer or following the conclusion of a contract and during its execution. The general prohibition is elaborated by rules on the two types of commercial practices which are by far the most common, namely misleading commercial practices and aggressive commercial practices.

(14) It is desirable that misleading commercial practices cover those practices, including misleading advertising, which by deceiving the consumer prevent him from making an informed and thus efficient choice. In conformity with the laws and practices of Member States on misleading advertising, this Directive classifies misleading practices into misleading actions and misleading omissions. In respect of omissions, this Directive sets out a limited number of key items of information which the consumer needs to make an informed transactional decision. Such information will not have to be disclosed in all advertisements, but only where the trader makes an invitation

to purchase, which is a concept clearly defined in this Directive. The full harmonisation approach adopted in this Directive does not preclude the Member States from specifying in national law the main characteristics of particular products such as, for example, collectors' items or electrical goods, the omission of which would be material when an invitation to purchase is made. It is not the intention of this Directive to reduce consumer choice by prohibiting the promotion of products which look similar to other products unless this similarity confuses consumers as to the commercial origin of the product and is therefore misleading. This Directive should be without prejudice to existing Community law which expressly affords Member States the choice between several regulatory options for the protection of consumers in the field of commercial practices. In particular, this Directive should be without prejudice to Article 13(3) of Directive 2002/58/EC of the European Parliament and of the Council of 12 July 2002 concerning the processing of personal data and the protection of privacy in the electronic communications sector.

(15) Where Community law sets out information requirements in relation to commercial communication, advertising and marketing that information is considered as material under this Directive. Member States will be able to retain or add information requirements relating to contract law and having contract law consequences where this is allowed by the minimum clauses in the existing Community law instruments. A non-exhaustive list of such information requirements in the acquis is contained in Annex II. Given the full harmonisation introduced by this Directive only the information required in Community law is considered as material for the purpose of Article 7(5) thereof. Where Member States have introduced information requirements over and above what is specified in Community law, on the basis of minimum clauses, the omission of that extra information will not constitute a misleading omission under this Directive. By contrast Member States will be able, when allowed by the minimum clauses in Community law, to maintain or introduce more stringent provisions in conformity with Community law so as to ensure a higher level of protection of consumers' individual contractual rights.

(16) The provisions on aggressive commercial practices should cover those practices which significantly impair the consumer's freedom of choice. Those are practices using harassment, coercion, including the use of physical force, and undue influence.

(17) It is desirable that those commercial practices which are in all circumstances unfair be identified to provide greater legal certainty. Annex I therefore contains the full list of all such practices. These are the only commercial practices which can be deemed to be unfair without a case-by-case assessment against the provisions of Articles 5 to 9. The list may only be modified by revision of the Directive.

(18) It is appropriate to protect all consumers from unfair commercial practices; however the Court of Justice has found it necessary in adjudicating on advertising cases since the enactment of Directive 84/450/EEC to examine the effect on a notional, typical consumer. In line with the principle of proportionality, and to permit the effective application of the protections contained in it, this Directive takes as a benchmark the average consumer, who is reasonably well-informed and reasonably observant and circumspect, taking into account social, cultural and linguistic factors, as interpreted by the Court of Justice, but also contains provisions aimed at preventing the exploitation of consumers whose characteristics make them particularly vulnerable to unfair commercial practices. Where a commercial practice is specifically aimed at a particular group of consumers, such as children, it is desirable that the impact of the commercial practice be assessed from the perspective of the average member of that group. It is therefore appropriate to include in the list of practices which are in all circumstances unfair a provision which, without imposing an outright ban on advertising directed at children, protects them from direct exhortations to purchase. The average consumer test is not a statistical test. National courts and authorities will have to exercise their own faculty of judgement, having regard to the case-law of the Court of Justice, to determine the typical reaction of the average consumer in a given case.

(19) Where certain characteristics such as age, physical or mental infirmity or credulity make consumers particularly susceptible to a commercial practice or to the underlying product and the economic behaviour only of such consumers is likely to be distorted by the practice in a way that the trader can reasonably foresee, it is appropriate to ensure that they are adequately protected by assessing the practice from the perspective of the average member of that group.

(20) It is appropriate to provide a role for codes of conduct, which enable traders to apply the principles of this Directive effectively in specific economic fields. In sectors where there are specific mandatory requirements regulating the behaviour of traders, it is appropriate that these will also provide evidence as to the requirements of professional diligence in that sector. The control exercised by code owners at national or Community level to eliminate unfair commercial practices may avoid the need for recourse to administrative or judicial action and should therefore be encouraged. With the aim of pursuing a high level of consumer protection, consumers' organisations could be informed and involved in the drafting of codes of conduct.

(21) Persons or organisations regarded under national law as having a legitimate interest in the matter must have legal remedies for initiating proceedings against unfair commercial practices, either before a court or before an administrative authority which is competent to decide upon complaints or to initiate appropriate legal proceedings.

While it is for national law to determine the burden of proof, it is appropriate to enable courts and administrative authorities to require traders to produce evidence as to the accuracy of factual claims they have made.
(22) It is necessary that Member States lay down penalties for infringements of the provisions of this Directive and they must ensure that these are enforced. The penalties must be effective, proportionate and dissuasive.
(23) Since the objectives of this Directive, namely to eliminate the barriers to the functioning of the internal market represented by national laws on unfair commercial practices and to provide a high common level of consumer protection, by approximating the laws, regulations and administrative provisions of the Member States on unfair commercial practices, cannot be sufficiently achieved by the Member States and can therefore be better achieved at Community level, the Community may adopt measures, in accordance with the principle of subsidiarity as set out in Article 5 of the Treaty. In accordance with the principle of proportionality, as set out in that Article, this Directive does not go beyond what is necessary in order to eliminate the internal market barriers and achieve a high common level of consumer protection.
(24) It is appropriate to review this Directive to ensure that barriers to the internal market have been addressed and a high level of consumer protection achieved. The review could lead to a Commission proposal to amend this Directive, which may include a limited extension to the derogation in Article 3(5), and/or amendments to other consumer protection legislation reflecting the Commission's Consumer Policy Strategy commitment to review the existing acquis in order to achieve a high, common level of consumer protection.
(25) This Directive respects the fundamental rights and observes the principles recognised in particular by the Charter of Fundamental Rights of the European Union,

HAVE ADOPTED THIS DIRECTIVE:

Chapter I. General provisions

Article 1. The purpose of this Directive is to contribute to the proper functioning of the internal market and achieve a high level of consumer protection by approximating the laws, regulations and administrative provisions of the Member States on unfair commercial practices harming consumers' economic interests.

Article 2. For the purposes of this Directive:
(a) "consumer" means any natural person who, in commercial practices covered by this Directive, is acting for purposes which are outside his trade, business, craft or profession;
(b) "trader" means any natural or legal person who, in commercial practices covered by this Directive, is acting for purposes relating to his trade, business, craft or profession and anyone acting in the name of or on behalf of a trader;
(c) "product" means any goods or service including immovable property, rights and obligations;
(d) "business-to-consumer commercial practices" (hereinafter also referred to as commercial practices) means any act, omission, course of conduct or representation, commercial communication including advertising and marketing, by a trader, directly connected with the promotion, sale or supply of a product to consumers;
(e) "to materially distort the economic behaviour of consumers" means using a commercial practice to appreciably impair the consumer's ability to make an informed decision, thereby causing the consumer to take a transactional decision that he would not have taken otherwise;
(f) "code of conduct" means an agreement or set of rules not imposed by law, regulation or administrative provision of a Member State which defines the behaviour of traders who undertake to be bound by the code in relation to one or more particular commercial practices or business sectors;
(g) "code owner" means any entity, including a trader or group of traders, which is responsible for the formulation and revision of a code of conduct and/or for monitoring compliance with the code by those who have undertaken to be bound by it;
(h) "professional diligence" means the standard of special skill and care which a trader may reasonably be expected to exercise towards consumers, commensurate with honest market practice and/or the general principle of good faith in the trader's field of activity;
(i) "invitation to purchase" means a commercial communication which indicates characteristics of the product and the price in a way appropriate to the means of the commercial communication used and thereby enables the consumer to make a purchase;
(j) "undue influence" means exploiting a position of power in relation to the consumer so as to apply pressure, even without using or threatening to use physical force, in a way which significantly limits the consumer's ability to make an informed decision;

(k) "transactional decision" means any decision taken by a consumer concerning whether, how and on what terms to purchase, make payment in whole or in part for, retain or dispose of a product or to exercise a contractual right in relation to the product, whether the consumer decides to act or to refrain from acting;
(l) "regulated profession" means a professional activity or a group of professional activities, access to which or the pursuit of which, or one of the modes of pursuing which, is conditional, directly or indirectly, upon possession of specific professional qualifications, pursuant to laws, regulations or administrative provisions.

Article 3. (1) This Directive shall apply to unfair business-to-consumer commercial practices, as laid down in Article 5, before, during and after a commercial transaction in relation to a product.
(2) This Directive is without prejudice to contract law and, in particular, to the rules on the validity, formation or effect of a contract.
(3) This Directive is without prejudice to Community or national rules relating to the health and safety aspects of products.
(4) In the case of conflict between the provisions of this Directive and other Community rules regulating specific aspects of unfair commercial practices, the latter shall prevail and apply to those specific aspects.
(5) For a period of six years from 12 June 2007, Member States shall be able to continue to apply national provisions within the field approximated by this Directive which are more restrictive or prescriptive than this Directive and which implement directives containing minimum harmonisation clauses. These measures must be essential to ensure that consumers are adequately protected against unfair commercial practices and must be proportionate to the attainment of this objective. The review referred to in Article 18 may, if considered appropriate, include a proposal to prolong this derogation for a further limited period.
(6) Member States shall notify the Commission without delay of any national provisions applied on the basis of paragraph 5.
(7) This Directive is without prejudice to the rules determining the jurisdiction of the courts.
(8) This Directive is without prejudice to any conditions of establishment or of authorisation regimes, or to the deontological codes of conduct or other specific rules governing regulated professions in order to uphold high standards of integrity on the part of the professional, which Member States may, in conformity with Community law, impose on professionals.
(9) In relation to "financial services", as defined in Directive 2002/65/EC, and immovable property, Member States may impose requirements which are more restrictive or prescriptive than this Directive in the field which it approximates.
(10) This Directive shall not apply to the application of the laws, regulations and administrative provisions of Member States relating to the certification and indication of the standard of fineness of articles of precious metal.

Article 4. Member States shall neither restrict the freedom to provide services nor restrict the free movement of goods for reasons falling within the field approximated by this Directive.

Chapter II. Unfair commercial practices

Article 5. (1) Unfair commercial practices shall be prohibited.
(2) A commercial practice shall be unfair if:
(a) it is contrary to the requirements of professional diligence, and
(b) it materially distorts or is likely to materially distort the economic behaviour with regard to the product of the average consumer whom it reaches or to whom it is addressed, or of the average member of the group when a commercial practice is directed to a particular group of consumers.
(3) Commercial practices which are likely to materially distort the economic behaviour only of a clearly identifiable group of consumers who are particularly vulnerable to the practice or the underlying product because of their mental or physical infirmity, age or credulity in a way which the trader could reasonably be expected to foresee, shall be assessed from the perspective of the average member of that group. This is without prejudice to the common and legitimate advertising practice of making exaggerated statements or statements which are not meant to be taken literally.
(4) In particular, commercial practices shall be unfair which:
(a) are misleading as set out in Articles 6 and 7, or
(b) are aggressive as set out in Articles 8 and 9.
(5) Annex I contains the list of those commercial practices which shall in all circumstances be regarded as unfair. The same single list shall apply in all Member States and may only be modified by revision of this Directive.

Section I. Misleading commercial practices

Article 6. (1) A commercial practice shall be regarded as misleading if it contains false information and is therefore untruthful or in any way, including overall presentation, deceives or is likely to deceive the average consumer, even if the information is factually correct, in relation to one or more of the following elements, and in either case causes or is likely to cause him to take a transactional decision that he would not have taken otherwise:
(a) the existence or nature of the product;
(b) the main characteristics of the product, such as its availability, benefits, risks, execution, composition, accessories, after-sale customer assistance and complaint handling, method and date of manufacture or provision, delivery, fitness for purpose, usage, quantity, specification, geographical or commercial origin or the results to be expected from its use, or the results and material features of tests or checks carried out on the product;
(c) the extent of the trader's commitments, the motives for the commercial practice and the nature of the sales process, any statement or symbol in relation to direct or indirect sponsorship or approval of the trader or the product;
(d) the price or the manner in which the price is calculated, or the existence of a specific price advantage;
(e) the need for a service, part, replacement or repair;
(f) the nature, attributes and rights of the trader or his agent, such as his identity and assets, his qualifications, status, approval, affiliation or connection and ownership of industrial, commercial or intellectual property rights or his awards and distinctions;
(g) the consumer's rights, including the right to replacement or reimbursement under Directive 1999/44/EC of the European Parliament and of the Council of 25 May 1999 on certain aspects of the sale of consumer goods and associated guarantees, or the risks he may face.
(2) A commercial practice shall also be regarded as misleading if, in its factual context, taking account of all its features and circumstances, it causes or is likely to cause the average consumer to take a transactional decision that he would not have taken otherwise, and it involves:
(a) any marketing of a product, including comparative advertising, which creates confusion with any products, trade marks, trade names or other distinguishing marks of a competitor;
(b) non-compliance by the trader with commitments contained in codes of conduct by which the trader has undertaken to be bound, where:
(i) the commitment is not aspirational but is firm and is capable of being verified, and
(ii) the trader indicates in a commercial practice that he is bound by the code.

Article 7. (1) A commercial practice shall be regarded as misleading if, in its factual context, taking account of all its features and circumstances and the limitations of the communication medium, it omits material information that the average consumer needs, according to the context, to take an informed transactional decision and thereby causes or is likely to cause the average consumer to take a transactional decision that he would not have taken otherwise.
(2) It shall also be regarded as a misleading omission when, taking account of the matters described in paragraph 1, a trader hides or provides in an unclear, unintelligible, ambiguous or untimely manner such material information as referred to in that paragraph or fails to identify the commercial intent of the commercial practice if not already apparent from the context, and where, in either case, this causes or is likely to cause the average consumer to take a transactional decision that he would not have taken otherwise.
(3) Where the medium used to communicate the commercial practice imposes limitations of space or time, these limitations and any measures taken by the trader to make the information available to consumers by other means shall be taken into account in deciding whether information has been omitted.
(4) In the case of an invitation to purchase, the following information shall be regarded as material, if not already apparent from the context:
(a) the main characteristics of the product, to an extent appropriate to the medium and the product;
(b) the geographical address and the identity of the trader, such as his trading name and, where applicable, the geographical address and the identity of the trader on whose behalf he is acting;
(c) the price inclusive of taxes, or where the nature of the product means that the price cannot reasonably be calculated in advance, the manner in which the price is calculated, as well as, where appropriate, all additional freight, delivery or postal charges or, where these charges cannot reasonably be calculated in advance, the fact that such additional charges may be payable;
(d) the arrangements for payment, delivery, performance and the complaint handling policy, if they depart from the requirements of professional diligence;

(e) for products and transactions involving a right of withdrawal or cancellation, the existence of such a right.
(5) Information requirements established by Community law in relation to commercial communication including advertising or marketing, a non-exhaustive list of which is contained in Annex II, shall be regarded as material.

Section II. Aggressive commercial practices

Article 8. A commercial practice shall be regarded as aggressive if, in its factual context, taking account of all its features and circumstances, by harassment, coercion, including the use of physical force, or undue influence, it significantly impairs or is likely to significantly impair the average consumer's freedom of choice or conduct with regard to the product and thereby causes him or is likely to cause him to take a transactional decision that he would not have taken otherwise.

Article 9. In determining whether a commercial practice uses harassment, coercion, including the use of physical force, or undue influence, account shall be taken of:
(a) its timing, location, nature or persistence;
(b) the use of threatening or abusive language or behaviour;
(c) the exploitation by the trader of any specific misfortune or circumstance of such gravity as to impair the consumer's judgement, of which the trader is aware, to influence the consumer's decision with regard to the product;
(d) any onerous or disproportionate non-contractual barriers imposed by the trader where a consumer wishes to exercise rights under the contract, including rights to terminate a contract or to switch to another product or another trader;
(e) any threat to take any action that cannot legally be taken.

Chapter III. Codes of conduct

Article 10. This Directive does not exclude the control, which Member States may encourage, of unfair commercial practices by code owners and recourse to such bodies by the persons or organisations referred to in Article 11 if proceedings before such bodies are in addition to the court or administrative proceedings referred to in that Article. Recourse to such control bodies shall never be deemed the equivalent of foregoing a means of judicial or administrative recourse as provided for in Article 11.

Chapter 4. Final provisions

Article 11. (1) Member States shall ensure that adequate and effective means exist to combat unfair commercial practices in order to enforce compliance with the provisions of this Directive in the interest of consumers. Such means shall include legal provisions under which persons or organisations regarded under national law as having a legitimate interest in combating unfair commercial practices, including competitors, may:
(a) take legal action against such unfair commercial practices; and/or
(b) bring such unfair commercial practices before an administrative authority competent either to decide on complaints or to initiate appropriate legal proceedings.
It shall be for each Member State to decide which of these facilities shall be available and whether to enable the courts or administrative authorities to require prior recourse to other established means of dealing with complaints, including those referred to in Article 10. These facilities shall be available regardless of whether the consumers affected are in the territory of the Member State where the trader is located or in another Member State.
It shall be for each Member State to decide:
(a) whether these legal facilities may be directed separately or jointly against a number of traders from the same economic sector; and
(b) whether these legal facilities may be directed against a code owner where the relevant code promotes non-compliance with legal requirements.
(2) Under the legal provisions referred to in paragraph 1, Member States shall confer upon the courts or administrative authorities powers enabling them, in cases where they deem such measures to be necessary taking into account all the interests involved and in particular the public interest:
(a) to order the cessation of, or to institute appropriate legal proceedings for an order for the cessation of, unfair commercial practices; or
(b) if the unfair commercial practice has not yet been carried out but is imminent, to order the prohibition of the practice, or to institute appropriate legal proceedings for an order for the prohibition of the practice, even without proof of actual loss or damage or of intention or negligence on the part of the trader.

Member States shall also make provision for the measures referred to in the first subparagraph to be taken under an accelerated procedure:
- either with interim effect, or
- with definitive effect, on the understanding that it is for each Member State to decide which of the two options to select.
Furthermore, Member States may confer upon the courts or administrative authorities powers enabling them, with a view to eliminating the continuing effects of unfair commercial practices the cessation of which has been ordered by a final decision:
(a) to require publication of that decision in full or in part and in such form as they deem adequate;
(b) to require in addition the publication of a corrective statement.
(3) The administrative authorities referred to in paragraph 1 must:
(a) be composed so as not to cast doubt on their impartiality;
(b) have adequate powers, where they decide on complaints, to monitor and enforce the observance of their decisions effectively;
(c) normally give reasons for their decisions.
Where the powers referred to in paragraph 2 are exercised exclusively by an administrative authority, reasons for its decisions shall always be given. Furthermore, in this case, provision must be made for procedures whereby improper or unreasonable exercise of its powers by the administrative authority or improper or unreasonable failure to exercise the said powers can be the subject of judicial review.

Article 12. Member States shall confer upon the courts or administrative authorities powers enabling them in the civil or administrative proceedings provided for in Article 11:
(a) to require the trader to furnish evidence as to the accuracy of factual claims in relation to a commercial practice if, taking into account the legitimate interest of the trader and any other party to the proceedings, such a requirement appears appropriate on the basis of the circumstances of the particular case; and
(b) to consider factual claims as inaccurate if the evidence demanded in accordance with (a) is not furnished or is deemed insufficient by the court or administrative authority.

Article 13. Member States shall lay down penalties for infringements of national provisions adopted in application of this Directive and shall take all necessary measures to ensure that these are enforced. These penalties must be effective, proportionate and dissuasive.

Article 14. Directive 84/450/EEC is hereby amended as follows:
(1) Article 1 shall be replaced by the following: "Article 1 The purpose of this Directive is to protect traders against misleading advertising and the unfair consequences thereof and to lay down the conditions under which comparative advertising is permitted."
(2) in Article 2:
- point 3 shall be replaced by the following: "3. "trader" means any natural or legal person who is acting for purposes relating to his trade, craft, business or profession and any one acting in the name of or on behalf of a trader.",
- the following point shall be added: "4. "code owner" means any entity, including a trader or group of traders, which is responsible for the formulation and revision of a code of conduct and/or for monitoring compliance with the code by those who have undertaken to be bound by it.";
(3) Article 3a shall be replaced by the following:"Article 3a. (1) Comparative advertising shall, as far as the comparison is concerned, be permitted when the following conditions are met:
(a) it is not misleading within the meaning of Articles 2(2), 3 and 7(1) of this Directive or Articles 6 and 7 of Directive 2005/29/EC of the European Parliament and of the Council of 11 May 2005 concerning unfair business-to-consumer commercial practices in the internal market;
(b) it compares goods or services meeting the same needs or intended for the same purpose;
(c) it objectively compares one or more material, relevant, verifiable and representative features of those goods and services, which may include price;
(d) it does not discredit or denigrate the trade marks, trade names, other distinguishing marks, goods, services, activities, or circumstances of a competitor;
(e) for products with designation of origin, it relates in each case to products with the same designation;
(f) it does not take unfair advantage of the reputation of a trade mark, trade name or other distinguishing marks of a competitor or of the designation of origin of competing products;
(g) it does not present goods or services as imitations or replicas of goods or services bearing a protected trade mark or trade name;

(h) it does not create confusion among traders, between the advertiser and a competitor or between the advertiser's trade marks, trade names, other distinguishing marks, goods or services and those of a competitor.
(4) Article 4 (1) shall be replaced by the following: "(1) Member States shall ensure that adequate and effective means exist to combat misleading advertising in order to enforce compliance with the provisions on comparative advertising in the interest of traders and competitors. Such means shall include legal provisions under which persons or organisations regarded under national law as having a legitimate interest in combating misleading advertising or regulating comparative advertising may:
(a) take legal action against such advertising; or
(b) bring such advertising before an administrative authority competent either to decide on complaints or to initiate appropriate legal proceedings.
It shall be for each Member State to decide which of these facilities shall be available and whether to enable the courts or administrative authorities to require prior recourse to other established means of dealing with complaints, including those referred to in Article 5.
It shall be for each Member State to decide:
(a) whether these legal facilities may be directed separately or jointly against a number of traders from the same economic sector; and
(b) whether these legal facilities may be directed against a code owner where the relevant code promotes non-compliance with legal requirements.";
(5) Article 7(1) shall be replaced by the following: "(1) This Directive shall not preclude Member States from retaining or adopting provisions with a view to ensuring more extensive protection, with regard to misleading advertising, for traders and competitors."

Article 15. (1) Article 9 of Directive 97/7/EC shall be replaced by the following: "Article 9. Given the prohibition of inertia selling practices laid down in Directive 2005/29/EC of 11 May 2005 of the European Parliament and of the Council concerning unfair business-to-consumer commercial practices in the internal market, Member States shall take the measures necessary to exempt the consumer from the provision of any consideration in cases of unsolicited supply, the absence of a response not constituting consent.
(2) Article 9 of Directive 2002/65/EC shall be replaced by the following: "Article 9. Given the prohibition of inertia selling practices laid down in Directive 2005/29/EC of 11 May 2005 of the European Parliament and of the Council concerning unfair business-to-consumer commercial practices in the internal market and without prejudice to the provisions of Member States' legislation on the tacit renewal of distance contracts, when such rules permit tacit renewal, Member States shall take measures to exempt the consumer from any obligation in the event of unsolicited supplies, the absence of a reply not constituting consent.

Article 16. (1) In the Annex to Directive 98/27/EC, point 1 shall be replaced by the following: "(1) Directive 2005/29/EC of the European Parliament and of the Council of 11 May 2005 concerning unfair business-to-consumer commercial practices in the internal market (OJ L 149, 11.6.2005, p. 22)."
(2) In the Annex to Regulation (EC) No 2006/2004 of the European Parliament and of the Council of 27 October 2004 on cooperation between national authorities responsible for the enforcement of the consumer protection law (the Regulation on consumer protection cooperation) [12] the following point shall be added: "16. Directive 2005/29/EC of the European Parliament and of the Council of 11 May 2005 concerning unfair business-to-consumer commercial practices in the internal market (OJ L 149, 11.6.2005, p. 22)."

Article 17. Member States shall take appropriate measures to inform consumers of the national law transposing this Directive and shall, where appropriate, encourage traders and code owners to inform consumers of their codes of conduct.

Article 18. (1) By 12 June 2011 the Commission shall submit to the European Parliament and the Council a comprehensive report on the application of this Directive, in particular of Articles 3(9) and 4 and Annex I, on the scope for further harmonisation and simplification of Community law relating to consumer protection, and, having regard to Article 3(5), on any measures that need to be taken at Community level to ensure that appropriate levels of consumer protection are maintained. The report shall be accompanied, if necessary, by a proposal to revise this Directive or other relevant parts of Community law.
(2) The European Parliament and the Council shall endeavour to act, in accordance with the Treaty, within two years of the presentation by the Commission of any proposal submitted under paragraph 1.

Article 19. Member States shall adopt and publish the laws, regulations and administrative provisions necessary to comply with this Directive by 12 June 2007. They shall forthwith inform the Commission thereof and inform the Commission of any subsequent amendments without delay.
They shall apply those measures by 12 December 2007. When Member States adopt those measures, they shall contain a reference to this Directive or be accompanied by such a reference on the occasion of their official publication. Member States shall determine how such reference is to be made.

Article 20. This Directive shall enter into force on the day following its publication in the Official Journal of the European Union.

Article 21. This Directive is addressed to the Member States.

Annex I. Commercial practices which are in all circumstances considered unfair
(1) Claiming to be a signatory to a code of conduct when the trader is not.
(2) Displaying a trust mark, quality mark or equivalent without having obtained the necessary authorisation.
(3) Claiming that a code of conduct has an endorsement from a public or other body which it does not have.
(4) Claiming that a trader (including his commercial practices) or a product has been approved, endorsed or authorised by a public or private body when he/it has not or making such a claim without complying with the terms of the approval, endorsement or authorisation.
(5) Making an invitation to purchase products at a specified price without disclosing the existence of any reasonable grounds the trader may have for believing that he will not be able to offer for supply or to procure another trader to supply, those products or equivalent products at that price for a period that is, and in quantities that are, reasonable having regard to the product, the scale of advertising of the product and the price offered (bait advertising).
(6) Making an invitation to purchase products at a specified price and then:
(a) refusing to show the advertised item to consumers; or
(b) refusing to take orders for it or deliver it within a reasonable time; or
(c) demonstrating a defective sample of it,
with the intention of promoting a different product (bait and switch).
(7) Falsely stating that a product will only be available for a very limited time, or that it will only be available on particular terms for a very limited time, in order to elicit an immediate decision and deprive consumers of sufficient opportunity or time to make an informed choice.
(8) Undertaking to provide after-sales service to consumers with whom the trader has communicated prior to a transaction in a language which is not an official language of the Member State where the trader is located and then making such service available only in another language without clearly disclosing this to the consumer before the consumer is committed to the transaction.
(9) Stating or otherwise creating the impression that a product can legally be sold when it cannot.
(10). Presenting rights given to consumers in law as a distinctive feature of the trader's offer.
(11). Using editorial content in the media to promote a product where a trader has paid for the promotion without making that clear in the content or by images or sounds clearly identifiable by the consumer (advertorial). This is without prejudice to Council Directive 89/552/EEC [1].
(12) Making a materially inaccurate claim concerning the nature and extent of the risk to the personal security of the consumer or his family if the consumer does not purchase the product.
(13) Promoting a product similar to a product made by a particular manufacturer in such a manner as deliberately to mislead the consumer into believing that the product is made by that same manufacturer when it is not.
(14) Establishing, operating or promoting a pyramid promotional scheme where a consumer gives consideration for the opportunity to receive compensation that is derived primarily from the introduction of other consumers into the scheme rather than from the sale or consumption of products.
(15) Claiming that the trader is about to cease trading or move premises when he is not.
(16) Claiming that products are able to facilitate winning in games of chance.
(17) Falsely claiming that a product is able to cure illnesses, dysfunction or malformations.
(18) Passing on materially inaccurate information on market conditions or on the possibility of finding the product with the intention of inducing the consumer to acquire the product at conditions less favourable than normal market conditions.
(19) Claiming in a commercial practice to offer a competition or prize promotion without awarding the prizes described or a reasonable equivalent.

(20) Describing a product as "gratis", "free", "without charge" or similar if the consumer has to pay anything other than the unavoidable cost of responding to the commercial practice and collecting or paying for delivery of the item.
(21) Including in marketing material an invoice or similar document seeking payment which gives the consumer the impression that he has already ordered the marketed product when he has not.
(22) Falsely claiming or creating the impression that the trader is not acting for purposes relating to his trade, business, craft or profession, or falsely representing oneself as a consumer.
(23) Creating the false impression that after-sales service in relation to a product is available in a Member State other than the one in which the product is sold.

Aggressive commercial practices

(24) Creating the impression that the consumer cannot leave the premises until a contract is formed.
(25) Conducting personal visits to the consumer's home ignoring the consumer's request to leave or not to return except in circumstances and to the extent justified, under national law, to enforce a contractual obligation.
(26) Making persistent and unwanted solicitations by telephone, fax, e-mail or other remote media except in circumstances and to the extent justified under national law to enforce a contractual obligation. This is without prejudice to Article 10 of Directive 97/7/EC and Directives 95/46/EC [2] and 2002/58/EC.
(27) Requiring a consumer who wishes to claim on an insurance policy to produce documents which could not reasonably be considered relevant as to whether the claim was valid, or failing systematically to respond to pertinent correspondence, in order to dissuade a consumer from exercising his contractual rights.
(28) Including in an advertisement a direct exhortation to children to buy advertised products or persuade their parents or other adults to buy advertised products for them. This provision is without prejudice to Article 16 of Directive 89/552/EEC on television broadcasting.
(29) Demanding immediate or deferred payment for or the return or safekeeping of products supplied by the trader, but not solicited by the consumer except where the product is a substitute supplied in conformity with Article 7(3) of Directive 97/7/EC (inertia selling).
(30) Explicitly informing a consumer that if he does not buy the product or service, the trader's job or livelihood will be in jeopardy.
(31) Creating the false impression that the consumer has already won, will win, or will on doing a particular act win, a prize or other equivalent benefit, when in fact either:
- there is no prize or other equivalent benefit, or
- taking any action in relation to claiming the prize or other equivalent benefit is subject to the consumer paying money or incurring a cost.

Directive 2008/122/EC of the European Parliament and of the Council of 14 January 2009 on the protection of consumers in respect of certain aspects of timeshare, long-term holiday product, resale and exchange contracts (Text with EEA relevance) (*OJ* L 33, 3.2.2009, p. 10–30) [footnotes omitted].

THE EUROPEAN PARLIAMENT AND THE COUNCIL OF THE EUROPEAN UNION,
Having regard to the Treaty establishing the European Community, and in particular Article 95 thereof,
Having regard to the proposal from the Commission,
Having regard to the opinion of the European Economic and Social Committee,
Acting in accordance with the procedure laid down in Article 251 of the Treaty,
Whereas:
(1) Since the adoption of Directive 94/47/EC of the European Parliament and of the Council of 26 October 1994 on the protection of purchasers in respect of certain aspects of contracts relating to the purchase of the right to use immovable properties on a timeshare basis, timeshare has evolved and new holiday products similar to it have appeared on the market. These new holiday products and certain transactions related to timeshare, such as resale contracts and exchange contracts, are not covered by Directive 94/47/EC. In addition, experience with the application of Directive 94/47/EC has shown that some subjects already covered need to be updated or clarified, in order to prevent the development of products aiming at circumventing this Directive.
(2) The existing regulatory gaps create appreciable distortions of competition and cause serious problems for consumers, thus hindering the smooth functioning of the internal market. Directive 94/47/EC should therefore be replaced by a new up-to-date directive. Since tourism plays an increasingly important role in the economies of the Member States, greater growth and productivity in the timeshare and long-term holiday product industries should be encouraged by adopting certain common rules.
(3) In order to enhance legal certainty and fully achieve the benefits of the internal market for consumers and businesses, the relevant laws of the Member States need to be approximated further. Therefore, certain aspects of the marketing, sale and resale of timeshares and long-term holiday products as well as the exchange of rights deriving from timeshare contracts should be fully harmonised. Member States should not be allowed to maintain or introduce in their national legislation provisions diverging from those laid down in this Directive. Where no such harmonised provisions exist, Member States should remain free to maintain or introduce national legislation in conformity with Community law. Thus, Member States should, for instance, be able to maintain or introduce provisions on the effects of exercising the right of withdrawal in legal relationships falling outside the scope of this Directive or provisions according to which no commitment may be entered into between a consumer and a trader of a timeshare or long-term holiday product, nor any payment made between those persons, as long as the consumer has not signed a credit agreement to finance the purchase of those services.
(4) This Directive should be without prejudice to the application by Member States, in accordance with Community law, of the provisions of this Directive to areas not within its scope. Member States could therefore maintain or introduce national legislation corresponding to the provisions of this Directive or certain of its provisions in relation to transactions that fall outside the scope of this Directive.
(5) The different contracts covered by this Directive should be clearly defined in such a way as to preclude circumvention of its provisions.
(6) For the purposes of this Directive, timeshare contracts should not be understood as covering multiple reservations of accommodation, including hotel rooms, in so far as multiple reservations do not imply rights and obligations beyond those arising from separate reservations. Nor should timeshare contracts be understood as covering ordinary lease contracts since the latter refer to one single continuous period of occupation and not to multiple periods.
(7) For the purposes of this Directive, long-term holiday product contracts should not be understood as covering ordinary loyalty schemes which provide discounts on future stays in the hotels of a hotel chain, since membership in the scheme is not obtained for consideration nor is the consideration paid by the consumer primarily for the purpose of obtaining discounts or other benefits in respect of accommodation.
(8) This Directive should not affect the provisions of Council Directive 90/314/EEC of 13 June 1990 on package travel, package holidays and package tours.
(9) Directive 2005/29/EC of the European Parliament and of the Council of 11 May 2005 concerning unfair business-to-consumer commercial practices in the internal market (Unfair Commercial Practices Directive) prohibits misleading, aggressive and other unfair commercial business-to-consumer practices. Given the nature of the products and the commercial practices related to timeshares, long-term holiday products, resale and exchange, it is appropriate to adopt more detailed and specific provisions regarding information requirements and sales events. The commercial purpose of invitations to sales events should be made clear to consumers. The provisions concerning pre-contractual information and the contract should be clarified and updated. In order to give

consumers the possibility to acquaint themselves with the information before the conclusion of the contract, it should be provided by means which are easily accessible to them at that time.

(10) Consumers should have the right, which should not be refused by traders, to be provided with pre-contractual information and the contract in a language, of their choice, with which they are familiar. In addition, in order to facilitate the execution and the enforcement of the contract, Member States should be allowed to determine that further language versions of the contract should be provided to consumers.

(11) In order to provide consumers with the opportunity of fully understanding their rights and obligations under the contract, they should be allowed a period during which they may withdraw from the contract without having to justify the withdrawal and without bearing any cost. Currently the length of this period varies between Member States, and experience shows that the length prescribed in Directive 94/47/EC is not sufficiently long. The period should therefore be extended in order to achieve a high level of consumer protection and more clarity for consumers and traders. The length of the period, the modalities for and the effects of exercising the right of withdrawal should be harmonised.

(12) Consumers should have effective remedies in the event that traders do not comply with the provisions regarding pre-contractual information or the contract, in particular those laying down that the contract should include all the information required and that the consumer should receive a copy of the contract at the time of its conclusion. In addition to the remedies existing under national law, consumers should benefit from an extended withdrawal period where information has not been provided by traders. The exercise of the right of withdrawal should remain free of charge during that extended period regardless of what services consumers may have enjoyed. The expiration of the withdrawal period does not preclude consumers from seeking remedies in accordance with national law for breaches of the information requirements.

(13) Council Regulation (EEC, Euratom) No 1182/71 of 3 June 1971 determining the rules applicable to periods, dates and time limits should apply to the calculation of the periods set out in this Directive.

(14) The prohibition on advance payments to traders or any third party before the end of the withdrawal period should be clarified in order to improve consumer protection. For resale contracts, the prohibition of advance payment should apply until the actual sale takes place or the resale contract is terminated, but Member States should remain free to regulate the possibility and modalities of final payments to intermediaries where resale contracts are terminated.

(15) For long-term holiday product contracts, the price to be paid in the context of a staggered payment schedule could take into consideration the possibility that subsequent amounts could be adjusted after the first year in order to ensure that the real value of those instalments is maintained, for instance to take account of inflation.

(16) In the event of a consumer withdrawing from a contract where the price is entirely or partly covered by credit granted to the consumer by the trader or by a third party on the basis of an arrangement between that third party and the trader, the credit agreement should be terminated at no cost to the consumer. The same should apply to contracts for other related services provided by the trader or by a third party on the basis of an arrangement between that third party and the trader.

(17) Consumers should not be deprived of the protection granted by this Directive where the law applicable to the contract is that of a Member State. The law applicable to a contract should be determined in accordance with the Community rules on private international law, in particular Regulation (EC) No 593/2008 of the European Parliament and of the Council of 17 June 2008 on the law applicable to contractual obligations (Rome I).Under that Regulation, the law of a third country may be applicable, in particular where consumers are targeted by traders whilst on holiday in a country other than their country of residence. Given that such commercial practices are common in the area covered by this Directive and that the contracts involve considerable amounts of money, an additional safeguard should be provided in certain specific situations, in particular where the courts of any Member State have jurisdiction over the contract, to ensure that the consumer is not deprived of the protection granted by this Directive. This concept reflects the particular needs of consumer protection arising from the typical complexity, long-term nature and financial relevance of the contracts falling within the scope of this Directive.

(18) It should be determined in accordance with Council Regulation (EC) No 44/2001 of 22 December 2000 on jurisdiction and the recognition and enforcement of judgments in civil and commercial matters which courts have jurisdiction in proceedings which have as their object matters covered by this Directive.

(19) In order to ensure that the protection afforded to consumers under this Directive is fully effective, in particular as regards compliance by traders with the information requirements both at the pre-contractual stage and in the contract, it is necessary that the Member States lay down effective, proportionate and dissuasive penalties for infringements of this Directive.

(20) It is necessary to ensure that persons or organisations having, under national law, a legitimate interest in the matter have legal remedies for initiating proceedings against infringements of this Directive.

(21) It is necessary to develop suitable and effective redress procedures in the Member States for settling disputes between consumers and traders. To this end, Member States should encourage the establishment of public or private bodies for settling disputes out of court.

(22) Member States should ensure that consumers are effectively informed of the national provisions transposing this Directive and encourage traders and code owners to inform consumers about their codes of conduct in this field. With the aim of pursuing a high level of consumer protection, consumer organisations could be informed of, and involved in, the drafting of codes of conduct.

(23) Since the objectives of this Directive cannot be sufficiently achieved by the Member States and can therefore be better achieved at Community level, the Community may adopt measures in accordance with the principle of subsidiarity as set out in Article 5 of the Treaty. In accordance with the principle of proportionality, as set out in that Article, this Directive does not go beyond what is necessary in order to eliminate the internal market barriers and achieve a high common level of consumer protection.

(24) This Directive respects the fundamental rights and observes the principles recognised in particular by the European Convention on Human Rights and Fundamental Freedoms and the Charter of Fundamental Rights of the European Union.

(25) In accordance with point 34 of the Interinstitutional agreement on better law-making [9], Member States are encouraged to draw up, for themselves and in the interests of the Community, their own tables, which will, as far as possible, illustrate the correlation between this Directive and the transposition measures, and to make them public,

HAVE ADOPTED THIS DIRECTIVE:

Article 1. (1). The purpose of this Directive is to contribute to the proper functioning of the internal market and to achieve a high level of consumer protection, by approximating the laws, regulations and administrative provisions of the Member States in respect of certain aspects of the marketing, sale and resale of timeshares and long-term holiday products as well as exchange contracts.

(2) This Directive applies to trader-to-consumer transactions.
This Directive is without prejudice to national legislation which:
(a) provides for general contract law remedies;
(b) relates to the registration of immovable or movable property and conveyance of immovable property;
(c) relates to conditions of establishment or authorisation regimes or licensing requirements; and
(d) relates to the determination of the legal nature of the rights which are the subject of the contracts covered by this Directive.

Article 2. (1) For the purposes of this Directive, the following definitions shall apply:
(a) "timeshare contract" means a contract of a duration of more than one year under which a consumer, for consideration, acquires the right to use one or more overnight accommodation for more than one period of occupation;
(b) "long-term holiday product contract" means a contract of a duration of more than one year under which a consumer, for consideration, acquires primarily the right to obtain discounts or other benefits in respect of accommodation, in isolation or together with travel or other services;
(c) "resale contract" means a contract under which a trader, for consideration, assists a consumer to sell or buy a timeshare or a long-term holiday product;
(d) "exchange contract" means a contract under which a consumer, for consideration, joins an exchange system which allows that consumer access to overnight accommodation or other services in exchange for granting to other persons temporary access to the benefits of the rights deriving from that consumer's timeshare contract;
(e) "trader" means a natural or legal person who is acting for purposes relating to that person's trade, business, craft or profession and anyone acting in the name of or on behalf of a trader;
(f) "consumer" means a natural person who is acting for purposes which are outside that person's trade, business, craft or profession;
(g) "ancillary contract" means a contract under which the consumer acquires services which are related to a timeshare contract or long-term holiday product contract and which are provided by the trader or a third party on the basis of an arrangement between that third party and the trader;
(h) "durable medium" means any instrument which enables the consumer or the trader to store information addressed personally to him in a way which is accessible for future reference for a period of time adequate for the purposes of the information and which allows the unchanged reproduction of the information stored;

(i) "code of conduct" means an agreement or set of rules not imposed by law, regulation or administrative provision of a Member State which defines the behaviour of traders who undertake to be bound by the code in relation to one or more particular commercial practices or business sectors;
(j) "code owner" means any entity, including a trader or group of traders, which is responsible for the formulation and revision of a code of conduct and/or for monitoring compliance with the code by those who have undertaken to be bound by it.
(2) In calculating the duration of a timeshare contract or a long-term holiday product contract, as defined in points (a) and (b) of paragraph 1 respectively, any provision in the contract allowing for tacit renewal or prolongation shall be taken into account.

Article 3. (1) Member States shall ensure that any advertising specifies the possibility of obtaining the information referred to in Article 4(1) and indicates where it can be obtained.
(2) Where a timeshare, long-term holiday product, resale or exchange contract is to be offered to a consumer in person at a promotion or sales event, the trader shall clearly indicate in the invitation the commercial purpose and the nature of the event.
(3) The information referred to in Article 4(1) shall be available to the consumer at any time during the event.
(4) A timeshare or a long-term holiday product shall not be marketed or sold as an investment.

Article 4. (1) In good time before the consumer is bound by any contract or offer, the trader shall provide the consumer, in a clear and comprehensible manner, with accurate and sufficient information, as follows:
(a) in the case of a timeshare contract: by means of the standard information form as set out in Annex I and information as listed in Part 3 of that form;
(b) in the case of a long-term holiday product contract: by means of the standard information form as set out in Annex II and information as listed in Part 3 of that form;
(c) in the case of a resale contract: by means of the standard information form as set out in Annex III and information as listed in Part 3 of that form;
(d) in the case of an exchange contract: by means of the standard information form as set out in Annex IV and information as listed in Part 3 of that form.
(2). The information referred to in paragraph 1 shall be provided, free of charge, by the trader on paper or on another durable medium which is easily accessible to the consumer.
(3). Member States shall ensure that the information referred to in paragraph 1 is drawn up in the language or one of the languages of the Member State in which the consumer is resident or a national, at the choice of the consumer, provided it is an official language of the Community.

Article 5 (1) Member States shall ensure that the contract is in writing, on paper or on another durable medium, and drawn up in the language or one of the languages of the Member State in which the consumer is resident or a national, at the choice of the consumer, provided it is an official language of the Community.
However, the Member State in which the consumer is resident may require that in addition:
(a) in every instance, the contract be provided to the consumer in the language or one of the languages of that Member State, provided it is an official language of the Community;
(b) in the case of a timeshare contract concerning one specific immovable property, the trader provide the consumer with a certified translation of the contract in the language or one of the languages of the Member State in which the property is situated, provided it is an official language of the Community.
The Member State on whose territory the trader carries out sale activities may require that, in every instance, the contract be provided to the consumer in the language or one of the languages of that Member State, provided it is an official language of the Community.
(2) The information referred to in Article 4(1) shall form an integral part of the contract and shall not be altered unless the parties expressly agree otherwise or the changes result from unusual and unforeseeable circumstances beyond the trader's control, the consequences of which could not have been avoided even if all due care had been exercised.
These changes shall be communicated to the consumer on paper or on another durable medium easily accessible to him, before the contract is concluded.
The contract shall expressly mention any such changes.
(3) In addition to the information referred to in Article 4(1), the contract shall include:
(a) the identity, place of residence and signature of each of the parties; and
(b) the date and place of the conclusion of the contract.

(4) Before the conclusion of the contract, the trader shall explicitly draw the consumer's attention to the existence of the right of withdrawal, the length of the withdrawal period referred to in Article 6, and the ban on advance payments during the withdrawal period referred to in Article 9.
The corresponding contractual clauses shall be signed separately by the consumer.
The contract shall include a separate standard withdrawal form, as set out in Annex V, intended to facilitate the exercise of the right of withdrawal in accordance with Article 6.
(5) The consumer shall receive a copy or copies of the contract at the time of its conclusion.

Article 6 (1) In addition to the remedies available to the consumer under national law in the event of breach of the provisions of this Directive, Member States shall ensure that the consumer is given a period of 14 calendar days to withdraw from the timeshare, long-term holiday product, resale or exchange contract, without giving any reason.
(2) The withdrawal period shall be calculated:
(a) from the day of the conclusion of the contract or of any binding preliminary contract; or
(b) from the day when the consumer receives the contract or any binding preliminary contract if it is later than the date referred to in point (a).
(3) The withdrawal period shall expire:
(a) after one year and 14 calendar days from the day referred to in paragraph 2 of this Article, where a separate standard withdrawal form as required by Article 5(4) has not been filled in by the trader and provided to the consumer in writing, on paper or on another durable medium;
(b) after three months and 14 calendar days from the day referred to in paragraph 2 of this Article, where the information referred to in Article 4(1), including the applicable standard information form set out in Annexes I to IV, has not been provided to the consumer in writing, on paper or on another durable medium.
In addition, Member States shall provide for appropriate penalties in accordance with Article 15, in particular in the event that, on expiry of the withdrawal period, the trader has failed to comply with the information requirements set out in this Directive.
(4) Where a separate standard withdrawal form as required by Article 5(4) has been filled in by the trader and provided to the consumer in writing, on paper or on another durable medium, within one year from the day referred to in paragraph 2 of this Article, the withdrawal period shall start from the day the consumer receives that form. Similarly, where the information referred to in Article 4(1), including the applicable standard information form set out in Annexes I to IV, has been provided to the consumer in writing, on paper or on another durable medium, within three months from the day referred to in paragraph 2 of this Article, the withdrawal period shall start from the day the consumer receives such information.
(5) In the event that the exchange contract is offered to the consumer together with and at the same time as the timeshare contract, only a single withdrawal period in accordance with paragraph 1 shall apply to both contracts. The withdrawal period for both contracts shall be calculated according to the provisions of paragraph 2 as they apply to the timeshare contract.

Article 7. Where the consumer intends to exercise the right of withdrawal the consumer shall, before the expiry of the withdrawal period, notify the trader on paper or on another durable medium of the decision to withdraw. The consumer may use the standard withdrawal form set out in Annex V and provided by the trader in accordance with Article 5(4). The deadline is met if the notification is sent before the withdrawal period has expired.

Article 8. (1) The exercise of the right of withdrawal by the consumer terminates the obligation of the parties to perform the contract.
(2) Where the consumer exercises the right of withdrawal, the consumer shall neither bear any cost nor be liable for any value corresponding to the service which may have been performed before withdrawal.

Article 9 (1) Member States shall ensure that in relation to timeshare, long-term holiday product and exchange contracts any advance payment, provision of guarantees, reservation of money on accounts, explicit acknowledgement of debt or any other consideration to the trader or to any third party by the consumer before the end of the withdrawal period according to Article 6, is prohibited.
(2) Member States shall ensure that in relation to resale contracts any advance payment, provision of guarantees, reservation of money on accounts, explicit acknowledgement of debt or any other consideration to the trader or to any third party by the consumer before the actual sale takes place or the resale contract is otherwise terminated, is prohibited.

Article 10 (1). For long-term holiday product contracts, payment shall be made according to a staggered payment schedule. Any payment of the price specified in the contract otherwise than in accordance with the staggered

payment schedule shall be prohibited. The payments, including any membership fee, shall be divided into yearly instalments, each of which shall be of equal value. The trader shall send a written request for payment, on paper or on another durable medium, at least fourteen calendar days in advance of each due date.
(2). From the second instalment payment onwards, the consumer may terminate the contract without incurring any penalty by giving notice to the trader within fourteen calendar days of receiving the request for payment of each instalment. This right shall not affect rights to terminate the contract under existing national legislation.

Article 11. (1) Member States shall ensure that, where the consumer exercises the right to withdraw from the timeshare or long-term holiday product contract, any exchange contract ancillary to it or any other ancillary contract is automatically terminated, at no cost to the consumer.
(2) Without prejudice to Article 15 of Directive 2008/48/EC of the European Parliament and of the Council of 23 April 2008 on credit agreements for consumers [10], where the price is fully or partly covered by a credit granted to the consumer by the trader, or by a third party on the basis of an arrangement between the third party and the trader, the credit agreement shall be terminated, at no cost to the consumer, where the consumer exercises the right to withdraw from the timeshare, long-term holiday product, resale or exchange contract.
3. The Member States shall lay down detailed rules on the termination of such contracts.

Article 12. (1). Member States shall ensure that, where the law applicable to the contract is the law of a Member State, consumers may not waive the rights conferred on them by this Directive.
(2) Where the applicable law is that of a third country, consumers shall not be deprived of the protection granted by this Directive, as implemented in the Member State of the forum if:
- any of the immovable properties concerned is situated within the territory of a Member State, or,
- in the case of a contract not directly related to immovable property, the trader pursues commercial or professional activities in a Member State or, by any means, directs such activities to a Member State and the contract falls within the scope of such activities.

Article 13. (1) Member States shall ensure that, in the interests of consumers, adequate and effective means exist to ensure compliance by traders with this Directive.
(2) The means referred to in paragraph 1 shall include provisions whereby one or more of the following bodies, as determined by national law, shall be entitled to take action in accordance with national law before the courts or competent administrative bodies to ensure that the national provisions for implementing this Directive are applied:
(a) public bodies and authorities or their representatives;
(b) consumer organisations with a legitimate interest in protecting consumers;
(c) professional organisations with a legitimate interest in taking such action.

Article 14. (1). Member States shall take appropriate measures to inform consumers of the national law transposing this Directive and shall encourage, where appropriate, traders and code owners to inform consumers of their codes of conduct.
The Commission shall encourage the drawing up at Community level, particularly by professional bodies, organisations and associations, of codes of conduct aimed at facilitating the implementation of this Directive, in conformity with Community law. It shall also encourage traders and their branch organisations to inform consumers of any such codes, including, where appropriate, by means of a specific marking.
(2) Member States shall encourage the setting up or development of adequate and effective out-of-court complaints and redress procedures for the settlement of consumer disputes under this Directive and shall, where appropriate, encourage traders and their branch organisations to inform consumers of the availability of such procedures.

Article 15. (1). Member States shall provide for appropriate penalties in the event of a trader's failure to comply with the national provisions adopted pursuant to this Directive.
(2) Those penalties shall be effective, proportionate and dissuasive.

Article 16. (1) Member States shall adopt and publish, by 23 February 2011, the laws, regulations and administrative provisions necessary to comply with this Directive. They shall forthwith communicate to the Commission the text of those provisions.
They shall apply those provisions from 23 February 2011.
When Member States adopt those provisions, they shall contain a reference to this Directive or be accompanied by such a reference on the occasion of their official publication. Member States shall determine how such reference is to be made.

(2) Member States shall communicate to the Commission the text of the main provisions of national law which they adopt in the field covered by this Directive.

Article 17. The Commission shall review this Directive and report to the European Parliament and the Council no later than 23 February 2014.
If necessary, it shall make further proposals to adapt it to developments in the area.
The Commission may request information from the Member States and the national regulatory authorities.

Article 18. Directive 94/47/EC shall be repealed.
References to the repealed Directive shall be construed as references to this Directive and shall be read in accordance with the correlation table in Annex VI.

Article 19. This Directive shall enter into force on the 20th day following its publication in the Official Journal of the European Union.

Article 20. This Directive is addressed to the Member States.

ANNEX I
STANDARD INFORMATION FORM FOR TIMESHARE CONTRACTS
Part 1:
Identity, place of residence and legal status of the trader(s) which will be party to the contract:
Short description of the product (e.g. description of the immovable property):
Exact nature and content of the right(s):
Exact period within which the right which is the subject of the contract may be exercised and, if necessary, its duration:
Date on which the consumer may start to exercise the contractual right:
If the contract concerns a specific property under construction, date when the accommodation and services/facilities will be completed/available:
Price to be paid by the consumer for acquiring the right(s):
Outline of additional obligatory costs imposed under the contract; type of costs and indication of amounts (e.g. annual fees, other recurrent fees, special levies, local taxes):
A summary of key services available to the consumer (e.g. electricity, water, maintenance, refuse collection) and an indication of the amount to be paid by the consumer for such services:
A summary of facilities available to the consumer (e.g. swimming pool or sauna):
Are these facilities included in the costs indicated above?
If not, specify what is included and what has to be paid for:
Is it possible to join an exchange scheme?
If yes, specify the name of the exchange scheme:
Indication of costs for membership/exchange:
Has the trader signed a code/codes of conduct and, if yes, where can it/they be found?
Part 2:
General information:
The consumer has the right to withdraw from this contract without giving any reason within 14 calendar days from the conclusion of the contract or any binding preliminary contract or receipt of those contracts if that takes place later.
During this withdrawal period, any advance payment by the consumer is prohibited. The prohibition concerns any consideration, including payment, provision of guarantees, reservation of money on accounts, explicit acknowledgement of debt etc. It includes not only payment to the trader, but also to third parties.
The consumer shall not bear any costs or obligations other than those specified in the contract.
In accordance with international private law, the contract may be governed by a law other than the law of the Member State in which the consumer is resident or is habitually domiciled and possible disputes may be referred to courts other than those of the Member State in which the consumer is resident or is habitually domiciled.
Signature of the consumer:
Part 3:
Additional information to which the consumer is entitled and where it can be obtained specifically (for instance, under which chapter of a general brochure) if not provided below:
1. INFORMATION ABOUT THE RIGHTS ACQUIRED

conditions governing the exercise of the right which is the subject of the contract within the territory of the Member States(s) in which the property or properties concerned are situated and information on whether those conditions have been fulfilled or, if they have not, what conditions remain to be fulfilled,

where the contract provides rights to occupy accommodation to be selected from a pool of accommodation, information on restrictions on the consumer's ability to use any accommodation in the pool at any time.

2. INFORMATION ON THE PROPERTIES

where the contract concerns a specific immovable property, an accurate and detailed description of that property and its location; where the contract concerns a number of properties (multi-resorts), an appropriate description of the properties and their location; where the contract concerns accommodation other than immovable property, an appropriate description of the accommodation and the facilities,

the services (e.g. electricity, water, maintenance, refuse collection) to which the consumer has or will have access to and under what conditions,

where applicable, the common facilities, such as swimming pool, sauna, etc., to which the consumer has or may have access and under what conditions.

3. ADDITIONAL REQUIREMENTS FOR ACCOMMODATION UNDER CONSTRUCTION (where applicable)

the state of completion of the accommodation and of the services rendering the accommodation fully operational (gas, electricity, water and telephone connections) and any facilities to which the consumer will have access,

the deadline for completion of the accommodation and of the services rendering it fully operational (gas, electricity, water and telephone connections) and a reasonable estimate of the deadline for the completion of any facilities to which the consumer will have access,

the number of the building permit and the name(s) and full address(es) of the competent authority or authorities,

a guarantee regarding completion of the accommodation or a guarantee regarding reimbursement of any payment made if the accommodation is not completed and, where appropriate, the conditions governing the operation of such guarantees.

4. INFORMATION ON THE COSTS

an accurate and appropriate description of all costs associated with the timeshare contract; how these costs will be allocated to the consumer and how and when such costs may be increased; the method for the calculation of the amount of charges relating to occupation of the property, the mandatory statutory charges (for example, taxes and fees) and the administrative overheads (for example, management, maintenance and repairs),

where applicable, information on whether there are any charges, mortgages, encumbrances or any other liens recorded against title to the accommodation.

5. INFORMATION ON TERMINATION OF THE CONTRACT

where appropriate, information on the arrangements for the termination of ancillary contracts and the consequences of such termination,

conditions for terminating the contract, the consequences of termination, and information on any liability of the consumer for any costs which might result from such termination.

6. ADDITIONAL INFORMATION

information on how maintenance and repairs of the property and its administration and management are arranged, including whether and how consumers may influence and participate in the decisions regarding these issues,

information on whether or not it is possible to join a system for the resale of the contractual rights, information about the relevant system and an indication of costs related to resale through this system,

indication of the language(s) available for communication with the trader in relation to the contract, for instance in relation to management decisions, increase of costs and the handling of queries and complaints,

where applicable, the possibility for out-of-court dispute resolution.

Acknowledgement of receipt of information:

Signature of the consumer:

ANNEX II

STANDARD INFORMATION FORM FOR LONG-TERM HOLIDAY PRODUCT CONTRACTS

Part 1:

Identity, place of residence and legal status of the trader(s) which will be party to the contract:

Short description of the product:

Exact nature and content of the right(s):

Exact period within which the right which is the subject of the contract may be exercised and, if necessary, its duration:

Date on which the consumer may start to exercise the contractual right:

Price to be paid by the consumer for acquiring the right(s), including any recurring costs the consumer can expect to incur resulting from the right to obtain access to the accommodation, travel and any related products or services as specified:

The staggered payment schedule setting out equal amounts of instalments of this price for each year of the length of the contract and the dates on which they are due to be paid:

After year 1, subsequent amounts may be adjusted to ensure that the real value of those instalments is maintained, for instance to take account of inflation.

Outline of additional obligatory costs imposed under the contract; type of costs and indication of amounts (e.g. annual membership fees):

A summary of key services available to the consumer (e.g. discounted hotel stays and flights):

Are they included in the costs indicated above?

If not, specify what is included and what has to be paid for (e.g. three-night stay included in annual membership fee, all other accommodation must be paid for separately):

Has the trader signed a code/codes of conduct and, if yes, where can it/they be found?

Part 2:

General information:

The consumer has the right to withdraw from this contract without giving any reason within 14 calendar days from the conclusion of the contract or any binding preliminary contract or receipt of those contracts if that takes place later.

During this withdrawal period, any advance payment by the consumer is prohibited. The prohibition concerns any consideration, including payment, provision of guarantees, reservation of money on accounts, explicit acknowledgement of debt etc. It includes not only payment to the trader, but also to third parties.

The consumer has the right to terminate the contract without incurring any penalty by giving notice to the trader within 14 calendar days of receiving the request for payment for each annual instalment.

The consumer shall not bear any costs or obligations other than those specified in the contract.

In accordance with international private law, the contract may be governed by a law other than the law of the Member State in which the consumer is resident or is habitually domiciled and possible disputes may be referred to courts other than those of the Member State in which the consumer is resident or is habitually domiciled.

Signature of the consumer:

Part 3:

Additional information to which the consumer is entitled and where it can be obtained specifically (for instance, under which chapter of a general brochure) if not provided below:

1. INFORMATION ABOUT THE RIGHTS ACQUIRED

an appropriate and correct description of discounts available for future bookings, illustrated by a set of examples of recent offers,

information on the restrictions on the consumer's ability to use the rights, such as limited availability or offers provided on a first-come-first-served basis, time limits on particular promotions and special discounts.

2. INFORMATION ON THE TERMINATION OF THE CONTRACT

where appropriate, information on the arrangements for the termination of ancillary contracts and the consequences of such termination,

conditions for terminating the contract, the consequences of termination, and information on any liability of the consumer for any costs which might result from such termination.

3. ADDITIONAL INFORMATION

indication of the language(s) available for communication with the trader in relation to the contract, for instance in relation to the handling of queries and complaints,

where applicable, the possibility for out-of-court dispute resolution.

Acknowledgement of receipt of information:

Signature of the consumer:

ANNEX III

STANDARD INFORMATION FORM FOR RESALE CONTRACTS

Part 1:

Identity, place of residence and legal status of the trader(s) which will be party to the contract:

Short description of the services (e.g. marketing):

Duration of the contract:

Price to be paid by the consumer for acquiring the services:

Outline of additional obligatory costs imposed under the contract; type of costs and indication of amounts (e.g. local taxes, notary fees, cost of advertising):
Has the trader signed a code/codes of conduct and, if yes, where can it/they be found?
Part 2:
General information:
The consumer has the right to withdraw from this contract without giving any reason within 14 calendar days from the conclusion of the contract or any binding preliminary contract or receipt of those contracts if that takes place later.
Any advance payment by the consumer is prohibited until the actual sale has taken place or the resale contract otherwise is terminated. The prohibition concerns any consideration, including payment, provision of guarantees, reservation of money on accounts, explicit acknowledgement of debt etc. It includes not only payment to the trader, but also to third parties.
The consumer shall not bear any costs or obligations other than those specified in the contract.
In accordance with international private law, the contract may be governed by a law other than the law of the Member State in which the consumer is resident or is habitually domiciled and possible disputes may be referred to courts other than those of the Member State in which the consumer is resident or is habitually domiciled.
Signature of the consumer:
Part 3:
Additional information to which the consumer is entitled and where it can be obtained specifically (for instance, under which chapter of a general brochure) if not provided below:
conditions for terminating the contract, the consequences of termination, and information on any liability of the consumer for any costs which might result from such termination,
indication of the language(s) available for communication with the trader in relation to the contract, for instance in relation to the handling of queries and complaints,
where applicable, the possibility for out-of-court dispute resolution.
Acknowledgement of receipt of information:
Signature of the consumer:

ANNEX IV
STANDARD INFORMATION FORM FOR EXCHANGE CONTRACTS
Part 1:
Identity, place of residence and legal status of the trader(s) which will be party to the contract:
Short description of the product:
Exact nature and content of the right(s):
Exact period within which the right which is the subject of the contract may be exercised and, if necessary, its duration:
Date on which the consumer may start to exercise the contractual right:
Price to be paid by the consumer for the exchange membership fees:
Outline of additional obligatory costs imposed under the contract; type of costs and indication of amounts (e.g. renewal fees, other recurrent fees, special levies, local taxes):
A summary of key services available to the consumer:
Are they included in the costs indicated above?
If not, specify what is included and what has to be paid for (type of costs and indication of amounts; e.g. an estimate of the price to be paid for individual exchange transactions, including any additional charges):
Has the trader signed a code/codes of conduct and, if yes, where can it/they be found?
Part 2:
General information:
The consumer has the right to withdraw from this contract without giving any reason within 14 calendar days from the conclusion of the contract or any binding preliminary contract or receipt of those contracts if that takes place later. In cases where the exchange contract is offered together with and at the same time as the timeshare contract, only a single withdrawal period shall apply to both contracts.
During this withdrawal period, any advance payment by the consumer is prohibited. The prohibition concerns any consideration, including payment, provision of guarantees, reservation of money on accounts, explicit acknowledgement of debt etc. It includes not only payment to the trader, but also to third parties.
The consumer shall not bear any costs or obligations other than those specified in the contract,
In accordance with international private law, the contract may be governed by a law other than the law of the Member State in which the consumer is resident or is habitually domiciled and possible disputes may be referred to courts other than those of the Member State in which the consumer is resident or is habitually domiciled.

Signature of the consumer:

Part 3:

Additional information to which the consumer is entitled and where it can be obtained specifically (for instance, under which chapter of a general brochure) if not provided below:

1. INFORMATION ABOUT THE RIGHTS ACQUIRED

explanation of how the exchange system works; the possibilities and modalities for exchange; an indication of the value allotted to the consumer's timeshare in the exchange system and a set of examples of concrete exchange possibilities,

an indication of the number of resorts available and the number of members in the exchange system, including any limitations on the availability of particular accommodation selected by the consumer, for example, as the result of peak periods of demand, the potential need to book a long time in advance, and indications of any restrictions on the choice resulting from the timeshare rights deposited into the exchange system by the consumer.

2. INFORMATION ON THE PROPERTIES

a brief and appropriate description of the properties and their location; where the contract concerns accommodation other than immovable property, an appropriate description of the accommodation and the facilities; description of where the consumer can obtain further information.

3. INFORMATION ON THE COSTS

information on the obligation on the trader to provide details before an exchange is arranged, in respect of each proposed exchange, of any additional charges for which the consumer is liable in respect of the exchange.

4. INFORMATION ON THE TERMINATION OF THE CONTRACT

where appropriate, information on the arrangements for the termination of ancillary contracts and the consequences of such termination,

conditions for terminating the contract, the consequences of termination, and information on any liability of the consumer for any costs which might result from such termination.

5. ADDITIONAL INFORMATION

indication of the language(s) available for communication with the trader in relation to the contract, for instance in relation to the handling of queries and complaints,

where applicable, the possibility for out-of-court dispute resolution.

Acknowledgement of receipt of information:

Signature of the consumer:

ANNEX V

SEPARATE STANDARD WITHDRAWAL FORM TO FACILITATE THE RIGHT OF WITHDRAWAL

Right of withdrawal

The consumer has the right to withdraw from this contract within 14 calendar days without giving any reason.

The right of withdrawal starts from … (to be filled in by the trader before providing the form to the consumer).

Where the consumer has not received this form, the withdrawal period starts when the consumer has received this form, but expires in any case after one year and 14 calendar days.

Where the consumer has not received all the required information, the withdrawal period starts when the consumer has received that information, but expires in any case after three months and 14 calendar days.

To exercise the right of withdrawal, the consumer shall notify the trader using the name and address indicated below by using a durable medium (e.g. written letter sent by post, e-mail). The consumer may use this form, but it is not obligatory.

Where the consumer exercises the right of withdrawal, the consumer shall not be liable for any costs.

In addition to the right of withdrawal, national contract law rules may provide for consumer rights, e.g. to terminate the contract in case of omission of information.

Ban on advance payment

During the withdrawal period any advance payment by the consumer is prohibited. The prohibition concerns any consideration, including payment, provision of guarantees, reservation of money on accounts, explicit acknowledgement of debt, etc.

It includes not only payment to the trader, but also to third parties.

Notice of withdrawal

To (Name and address of the trader) (*):

I/We (**) hereby give notice that I/We (**) withdraw from the contract,

Date of conclusion of contract (*):

Name(s) of consumer(s) (***):

Address(es) of consumer(s) (***):

Signature(s) of consumer(s) (only if this form is notified on paper) (***):

Date (***):
(*) To be filled in by the trader before providing the form to the consumer.
(**) Delete as appropriate.
(***) To be filled in by the consumer(s) where this form is used to withdraw from the contract.
Acknowledgement of receipt of information:
Signature of the consumer:

Council regulation (EC) No 1346/2000 of 29 May 2000 on insolvency proceedings (*OJ* L 16 , 30.06.2000, pp. 1 - 18) [footnotes omitted].

THE COUNCIL OF THE EUROPEAN UNION,
Having regard to the Treaty establishing the European Community, and in particular Articles 61(c) and 67(1) thereof,
Having regard to the initiative of the Federal Republic of Germany and the Republic of Finland,
Having regard to the opinion of the European Parliament,
Having regard to the opinion of the Economic and Social Committe,
Whereas:
(1) The European Union has set out the aim of establishing an area of freedom, security and justice.
(2) The proper functioning of the internal market requires that cross-border insolvency proceedings should operate efficiently and effectively and this Regulation needs to be adopted in order to achieve this objective which comes within the scope of judicial cooperation in civil matters within the meaning of Article 65 of the Treaty.
(3) The activities of undertakings have more and more cross-border effects and are therefore increasingly being regulated by Community law. While the insolvency of such undertakings also affects the proper functioning of the internal market, there is a need for a Community act requiring coordination of the measures to be taken regarding an insolvent debtor's assets.
(4) It is necessary for the proper functioning of the internal market to avoid incentives for the parties to transfer assets or judicial proceedings from one Member State to another, seeking to obtain a more favourable legal position (forum shopping).
(5) These objectives cannot be achieved to a sufficient degree at national level and action at Community level is therefore justified.
(6) In accordance with the principle of proportionality this Regulation should be confined to provisions governing jurisdiction for opening insolvency proceedings and judgments which are delivered directly on the basis of the insolvency proceedings and are closely connected with such proceedings. In addition, this Regulation should contain provisions regarding the recognition of those judgments and the applicable law which also satisfy that principle.
(7) Insolvency proceedings relating to the winding-up of insolvent companies or other legal persons, judicial arrangements, compositions and analogous proceedings are excluded from the scope of the 1968 Brussels Convention on Jurisdiction and the Enforcement of Judgments in Civil and Commercial Matters, as amended by the Conventions on Accession to this Convention.
(8) In order to achieve the aim of improving the efficiency and effectiveness of insolvency proceedings having cross-border effects, it is necessary, and appropriate, that the provisions on jurisdiction, recognition and applicable law in this area should be contained in a Community law measure which is binding and directly applicable in Member States.
(9) This Regulation should apply to insolvency proceedings, whether the debtor is a natural person or a legal person, a trader or an individual. The insolvency proceedings to which this Regulation applies are listed in the Annexes. Insolvency proceedings concerning insurance undertakings, credit institutions, investment undertakings holding funds or securities for third parties and collective investment undertakings should be excluded from the scope of this Regulation. Such undertakings should not be covered by this Regulation since they are subject to special arrangements and, to some extent, the national supervisory authorities have extremely wide-ranging powers of intervention.
(10) Insolvency proceedings do not necessarily involve the intervention of a judicial authority; the expression "court" in this Regulation should be given a broad meaning and include a person or body empowered by national law to open insolvency proceedings. In order for this Regulation to apply, proceedings (comprising acts and formalities set down in law) should not only have to comply with the provisions of this Regulation, but they should also be officially recognised and legally effective in the Member State in which the insolvency proceedings are opened and should be collective insolvency proceedings which entail the partial or total divestment of the debtor and the appointment of a liquidator.
(11) This Regulation acknowledges the fact that as a result of widely differing substantive laws it is not practical to introduce insolvency proceedings with universal scope in the entire Community. The application without exception of the law of the State of opening of proceedings would, against this background, frequently lead to difficulties. This applies, for example, to the widely differing laws on security interests to be found in the Community. Furthermore, the preferential rights enjoyed by some creditors in the insolvency proceedings are, in some cases, completely different. This Regulation should take account of this in two different ways. On the one hand, provision should be made for special rules on applicable law in the case of particularly significant rights and legal relationships (e.g. rights in rem and contracts of employment). On the other hand, national proceedings

covering only assets situated in the State of opening should also be allowed alongside main insolvency proceedings with universal scope.

(12) This Regulation enables the main insolvency proceedings to be opened in the Member State where the debtor has the centre of his main interests. These proceedings have universal scope and aim at encompassing all the debtor's assets. To protect the diversity of interests, this Regulation permits secondary proceedings to be opened to run in parallel with the main proceedings. Secondary proceedings may be opened in the Member State where the debtor has an establishment. The effects of secondary proceedings are limited to the assets located in that State. Mandatory rules of coordination with the main proceedings satisfy the need for unity in the Community.

(13) The "centre of main interests" should correspond to the place where the debtor conducts the administration of his interests on a regular basis and is therefore ascertainable by third parties.

(14) This Regulation applies only to proceedings where the centre of the debtor's main interests is located in the Community.

(15) The rules of jurisdiction set out in this Regulation establish only international jurisdiction, that is to say, they designate the Member State the courts of which may open insolvency proceedings. Territorial jurisdiction within that Member State must be established by the national law of the Member State concerned.

(16) The court having jurisdiction to open the main insolvency proceedings should be enabled to order provisional and protective measures from the time of the request to open proceedings. Preservation measures both prior to and after the commencement of the insolvency proceedings are very important to guarantee the effectiveness of the insolvency proceedings. In that connection this Regulation should afford different possibilities. On the one hand, the court competent for the main insolvency proceedings should be able also to order provisional protective measures covering assets situated in the territory of other Member States. On the other hand, a liquidator temporarily appointed prior to the opening of the main insolvency proceedings should be able, in the Member States in which an establishment belonging to the debtor is to be found, to apply for the preservation measures which are possible under the law of those States.

(17) Prior to the opening of the main insolvency proceedings, the right to request the opening of insolvency proceedings in the Member State where the debtor has an establishment should be limited to local creditors and creditors of the local establishment or to cases where main proceedings cannot be opened under the law of the Member State where the debtor has the centre of his main interest. The reason for this restriction is that cases where territorial insolvency proceedings are requested before the main insolvency proceedings are intended to be limited to what is absolutely necessary. If the main insolvency proceedings are opened, the territorial proceedings become secondary.

(18) Following the opening of the main insolvency proceedings, the right to request the opening of insolvency proceedings in a Member State where the debtor has an establishment is not restricted by this Regulation. The liquidator in the main proceedings or any other person empowered under the national law of that Member State may request the opening of secondary insolvency proceedings.

(19) Secondary insolvency proceedings may serve different purposes, besides the protection of local interests. Cases may arise where the estate of the debtor is too complex to administer as a unit or where differences in the legal systems concerned are so great that difficulties may arise from the extension of effects deriving from the law of the State of the opening to the other States where the assets are located. For this reason the liquidator in the main proceedings may request the opening of secondary proceedings when the efficient administration of the estate so requires.

(20) Main insolvency proceedings and secondary proceedings can, however, contribute to the effective realisation of the total assets only if all the concurrent proceedings pending are coordinated. The main condition here is that the various liquidators must cooperate closely, in particular by exchanging a sufficient amount of information. In order to ensure the dominant role of the main insolvency proceedings, the liquidator in such proceedings should be given several possibilities for intervening in secondary insolvency proceedings which are pending at the same time. For example, he should be able to propose a restructuring plan or composition or apply for realisation of the assets in the secondary insolvency proceedings to be suspended.

(21) Every creditor, who has his habitual residence, domicile or registered office in the Community, should have the right to lodge his claims in each of the insolvency proceedings pending in the Community relating to the debtor's assets. This should also apply to tax authorities and social insurance institutions. However, in order to ensure equal treatment of creditors, the distribution of proceeds must be coordinated. Every creditor should be able to keep what he has received in the course of insolvency proceedings but should be entitled only to participate in the distribution of total assets in other proceedings if creditors with the same standing have obtained the same proportion of their claims.

(22) This Regulation should provide for immediate recognition of judgments concerning the opening, conduct and closure of insolvency proceedings which come within its scope and of judgments handed down in direct connection with such insolvency proceedings. Automatic recognition should therefore mean that the effects

attributed to the proceedings by the law of the State in which the proceedings were opened extend to all other Member States. Recognition of judgments delivered by the courts of the Member States should be based on the principle of mutual trust. To that end, grounds for non-recognition should be reduced to the minimum necessary. This is also the basis on which any dispute should be resolved where the courts of two Member States both claim competence to open the main insolvency proceedings. The decision of the first court to open proceedings should be recognised in the other Member States without those Member States having the power to scrutinise the court's decision.

(23) This Regulation should set out, for the matters covered by it, uniform rules on conflict of laws which replace, within their scope of application, national rules of private international law. Unless otherwise stated, the law of the Member State of the opening of the proceedings should be applicable (lex concursus). This rule on conflict of laws should be valid both for the main proceedings and for local proceedings; the lex concursus determines all the effects of the insolvency proceedings, both procedural and substantive, on the persons and legal relations concerned. It governs all the conditions for the opening, conduct and closure of the insolvency proceedings.

(24) Automatic recognition of insolvency proceedings to which the law of the opening State normally applies may interfere with the rules under which transactions are carried out in other Member States. To protect legitimate expectations and the certainty of transactions in Member States other than that in which proceedings are opened, provisions should be made for a number of exceptions to the general rule.

(25) There is a particular need for a special reference diverging from the law of the opening State in the case of rights in rem, since these are of considerable importance for the granting of credit. The basis, validity and extent of such a right in rem should therefore normally be determined according to the lex situs and not be affected by the opening of insolvency proceedings. The proprietor of the right in rem should therefore be able to continue to assert his right to segregation or separate settlement of the collateral security. Where assets are subject to rights in rem under the lex situs in one Member State but the main proceedings are being carried out in another Member State, the liquidator in the main proceedings should be able to request the opening of secondary proceedings in the jurisdiction where the rights in rem arise if the debtor has an establishment there. If a secondary proceeding is not opened, the surplus on sale of the asset covered by rights in rem must be paid to the liquidator in the main proceedings.

(26) If a set-off is not permitted under the law of the opening State, a creditor should nevertheless be entitled to the set-off if it is possible under the law applicable to the claim of the insolvent debtor. In this way, set-off will acquire a kind of guarantee function based on legal provisions on which the creditor concerned can rely at the time when the claim arises.

(27) There is also a need for special protection in the case of payment systems and financial markets. This applies for example to the position-closing agreements and netting agreements to be found in such systems as well as to the sale of securities and to the guarantees provided for such transactions as governed in particular by Directive 98/26/EC of the European Parliament and of the Council of 19 May 1998 on settlement finality in payment and securities settlement systems. For such transactions, the only law which is material should thus be that applicable to the system or market concerned. This provision is intended to prevent the possibility of mechanisms for the payment and settlement of transactions provided for in the payment and set-off systems or on the regulated financial markets of the Member States being altered in the case of insolvency of a business partner. Directive 98/26/EC contains special provisions which should take precedence over the general rules in this Regulation.

(28) In order to protect employees and jobs, the effects of insolvency proceedings on the continuation or termination of employment and on the rights and obligations of all parties to such employment must be determined by the law applicable to the agreement in accordance with the general rules on conflict of law. Any other insolvency-law questions, such as whether the employees' claims are protected by preferential rights and what status such preferential rights may have, should be determined by the law of the opening State.

(29) For business considerations, the main content of the decision opening the proceedings should be published in the other Member States at the request of the liquidator. If there is an establishment in the Member State concerned, there may be a requirement that publication is compulsory. In neither case, however, should publication be a prior condition for recognition of the foreign proceedings.

(30) It may be the case that some of the persons concerned are not in fact aware that proceedings have been opened and act in good faith in a way that conflicts with the new situation. In order to protect such persons who make a payment to the debtor because they are unaware that foreign proceedings have been opened when they should in fact have made the payment to the foreign liquidator, it should be provided that such a payment is to have a debt-discharging effect.

(31) This Regulation should include Annexes relating to the organisation of insolvency proceedings. As these Annexes relate exclusively to the legislation of Member States, there are specific and substantiated reasons for the Council to reserve the right to amend these Annexes in order to take account of any amendments to the domestic law of the Member States.

(32) The United Kingdom and Ireland, in accordance with Article 3 of the Protocol on the position of the United Kingdom and Ireland annexed to the Treaty on European Union and the Treaty establishing the European Community, have given notice of their wish to take part in the adoption and application of this Regulation.
(33) Denmark, in accordance with Articles 1 and 2 of the Protocol on the position of Denmark annexed to the Treaty on European Union and the Treaty establishing the European Community, is not participating in the adoption of this Regulation, and is therefore not bound by it nor subject to its application,

HAS ADOPTED THIS REGULATION:

Chapter I. General provisions

Article 1. (1) This Regulation shall apply to collective insolvency proceedings which entail the partial or total divestment of a debtor and the appointment of a liquidator.
(2) This Regulation shall not apply to insolvency proceedings concerning insurance undertakings, credit institutions, investment undertakings which provide services involving the holding of funds or securities for third parties, or to collective investment undertakings.

Article 2. For the purposes of this Regulation:
(a) "insolvency proceedings" shall mean the collective proceedings referred to in Article 1(1). These proceedings are listed in Annex A;
(b) "liquidator" shall mean any person or body whose function is to administer or liquidate assets of which the debtor has been divested or to supervise the administration of his affairs. Those persons and bodies are listed in Annex C;
(c) "winding-up proceedings" shall mean insolvency proceedings within the meaning of point (a) involving realising the assets of the debtor, including where the proceedings have been closed by a composition or other measure terminating the insolvency, or closed by reason of the insufficiency of the assets. Those proceedings are listed in Annex B;
(d) "court" shall mean the judicial body or any other competent body of a Member State empowered to open insolvency proceedings or to take decisions in the course of such proceedings;
(e) "judgment" in relation to the opening of insolvency proceedings or the appointment of a liquidator shall include the decision of any court empowered to open such proceedings or to appoint a liquidator;
(f) "the time of the opening of proceedings" shall mean the time at which the judgment opening proceedings becomes effective, whether it is a final judgment or not;
(g) "the Member State in which assets are situated" shall mean, in the case of:
- tangible property, the Member State within the territory of which the property is situated,
- property and rights ownership of or entitlement to which must be entered in a public register, the Member State under the authority of which the register is kept,
- claims, the Member State within the territory of which the third party required to meet them has the centre of his main interests, as determined in Article 3(1);
(h) "establishment" shall mean any place of operations where the debtor carries out a non-transitory economic activity with human means and goods.

Article 3. (1) The courts of the Member State within the territory of which the centre of a debtor's main interests is situated shall have jurisdiction to open insolvency proceedings. In the case of a company or legal person, the place of the registered office shall be presumed to be the centre of its main interests in the absence of proof to the contrary.
(2) Where the centre of a debtor's main interests is situated within the territory of a Member State, the courts of another Member State shall have jurisdiction to open insolvency proceedings against that debtor only if he possesses an establishment within the territory of that other Member State. The effects of those proceedings shall be restricted to the assets of the debtor situated in the territory of the latter Member State.
(3) Where insolvency proceedings have been opened under paragraph 1, any proceedings opened subsequently under paragraph 2 shall be secondary proceedings. These latter proceedings must be winding-up proceedings.
(4) Territorial insolvency proceedings referred to in paragraph 2 may be opened prior to the opening of main insolvency proceedings in accordance with paragraph 1 only:
(a) where insolvency proceedings under paragraph 1 cannot be opened because of the conditions laid down by the law of the Member State within the territory of which the centre of the debtor's main interests is situated; or

(b) where the opening of territorial insolvency proceedings is requested by a creditor who has his domicile, habitual residence or registered office in the Member State within the territory of which the establishment is situated, or whose claim arises from the operation of that establishment.

Article 4. (1) Save as otherwise provided in this Regulation, the law applicable to insolvency proceedings and their effects shall be that of the Member State within the territory of which such proceedings are opened, hereafter referred to as the "State of the opening of proceedings".
(2) The law of the State of the opening of proceedings shall determine the conditions for the opening of those proceedings, their conduct and their closure. It shall determine in particular:
(a) against which debtors insolvency proceedings may be brought on account of their capacity;
(b) the assets which form part of the estate and the treatment of assets acquired by or devolving on the debtor after the opening of the insolvency proceedings;
(c) the respective powers of the debtor and the liquidator;
(d) the conditions under which set-offs may be invoked;
(e) the effects of insolvency proceedings on current contracts to which the debtor is party;
(f) the effects of the insolvency proceedings on proceedings brought by individual creditors, with the exception of lawsuits pending;
(g) the claims which are to be lodged against the debtor's estate and the treatment of claims arising after the opening of insolvency proceedings;
(h) the rules governing the lodging, verification and admission of claims;
(i) the rules governing the distribution of proceeds from the realisation of assets, the ranking of claims and the rights of creditors who have obtained partial satisfaction after the opening of insolvency proceedings by virtue of a right in rem or through a set-off;
(j) the conditions for and the effects of closure of insolvency proceedings, in particular by composition;
(k) creditors' rights after the closure of insolvency proceedings;
(l) who is to bear the costs and expenses incurred in the insolvency proceedings;
(m) the rules relating to the voidness, voidability or unenforceability of legal acts detrimental to all the creditors.

Article 5. Third parties' rights in rem.
(1) The opening of insolvency proceedings shall not affect the rights in rem of creditors or third parties in respect of tangible or intangible, moveable or immoveable assets - both specific assets and collections of indefinite assets as a whole which change from time to time - belonging to the debtor which are situated within the territory of another Member State at the time of the opening of proceedings.
(2) The rights referred to in paragraph 1 shall in particular mean:
(a) the right to dispose of assets or have them disposed of and to obtain satisfaction from the proceeds of or income from those assets, in particular by virtue of a lien or a mortgage;
(b) the exclusive right to have a claim met, in particular a right guaranteed by a lien in respect of the claim or by assignment of the claim by way of a guarantee;
(c) the right to demand the assets from, and/or to require restitution by, anyone having possession or use of them contrary to the wishes of the party so entitled;
(d) a right in rem to the beneficial use of assets.
(3) The right, recorded in a public register and enforceable against third parties, under which a right in rem within the meaning of paragraph 1 may be obtained, shall be considered a right in rem.
(4) Paragraph 1 shall not preclude actions for voidness, voidability or unenforceability as referred to in Article 4(2)(m).

Article 6. (1) The opening of insolvency proceedings shall not affect the right of creditors to demand the set-off of their claims against the claims of the debtor, where such a set-off is permitted by the law applicable to the insolvent debtor's claim.
(2) Paragraph 1 shall not preclude actions for voidness, voidability or unenforceability as referred to in Article 4(2)(m).

Article 7. (1) The opening of insolvency proceedings against the purchaser of an asset shall not affect the seller's rights based on a reservation of title where at the time of the opening of proceedings the asset is situated within the territory of a Member State other than the State of opening of proceedings.
(2) The opening of insolvency proceedings against the seller of an asset, after delivery of the asset, shall not constitute grounds for rescinding or terminating the sale and shall not prevent the purchaser from acquiring title

where at the time of the opening of proceedings the asset sold is situated within the territory of a Member State other than the State of the opening of proceedings.
(3) Paragraphs 1 and 2 shall not preclude actions for voidness, voidability or unenforceability as referred to in Article 4(2)(m).

Article 8. The effects of insolvency proceedings on a contract conferring the right to acquire or make use of immoveable property shall be governed solely by the law of the Member State within the territory of which the immoveable property is situated.

Article 9. (1) Without prejudice to Article 5, the effects of insolvency proceedings on the rights and obligations of the parties to a payment or settlement system or to a financial market shall be governed solely by the law of the Member State applicable to that system or market.
(2) Paragraph 1 shall not preclude any action for voidness, voidability or unenforceability which may be taken to set aside payments or transactions under the law applicable to the relevant payment system or financial market.

Article 10. The effects of insolvency proceedings on employment contracts and relationships shall be governed solely by the law of the Member State applicable to the contract of employment.

Article 11. The effects of insolvency proceedings on the rights of the debtor in immoveable property, a ship or an aircraft subject to registration in a public register shall be determined by the law of the Member State under the authority of which the register is kept.

Article 12. For the purposes of this Regulation, a Community patent, a Community trade mark or any other similar right established by Community law may be included only in the proceedings referred to in Article 3(1).

Article 13. Article 4(2)(m) shall not apply where the person who benefited from an act detrimental to all the creditors provides proof that:
- the said act is subject to the law of a Member State other than that of the State of the opening of proceedings, and
- that law does not allow any means of challenging that act in the relevant case.

Article 14. Where, by an act concluded after the opening of insolvency proceedings, the debtor disposes, for consideration, of:
- an immoveable asset, or
- a ship or an aircraft subject to registration in a public register, or
- securities whose existence presupposes registration in a register laid down by law, the validity of that act shall be governed by the law of the State within the territory of which the immoveable asset is situated or under the authority of which the register is kept.

Article 15. The effects of insolvency proceedings on a lawsuit pending concerning an asset or a right of which the debtor has been divested shall be governed solely by the law of the Member State in which that lawsuit is pending.

Chapter II. Recognition of insolvency proceedings

Article 16. (1) Any judgment opening insolvency proceedings handed down by a court of a Member State which has jurisdiction pursuant to Article 3 shall be recognised in all the other Member States from the time that it becomes effective in the State of the opening of proceedings.
This rule shall also apply where, on account of his capacity, insolvency proceedings cannot be brought against the debtor in other Member States.
(2) Recognition of the proceedings referred to in Article 3(1) shall not preclude the opening of the proceedings referred to in Article 3(2) by a court in another Member State. The latter proceedings shall be secondary insolvency proceedings within the meaning of Chapter III.

Article 17. (1) The judgment opening the proceedings referred to in Article 3(1) shall, with no further formalities, produce the same effects in any other Member State as under this law of the State of the opening of proceedings, unless this Regulation provides otherwise and as long as no proceedings referred to in Article 3(2) are opened in that other Member State.

(2) The effects of the proceedings referred to in Article 3(2) may not be challenged in other Member States. Any restriction of the creditors' rights, in particular a stay or discharge, shall produce effects vis-à-vis assets situated within the territory of another Member State only in the case of those creditors who have given their consent.

Article 18. (1) The liquidator appointed by a court which has jurisdiction pursuant to Article 3(1) may exercise all the powers conferred on him by the law of the State of the opening of proceedings in another Member State, as long as no other insolvency proceedings have been opened there nor any preservation measure to the contrary has been taken there further to a request for the opening of insolvency proceedings in that State. He may in particular remove the debtor's assets from the territory of the Member State in which they are situated, subject to Articles 5 and 7.
(2) The liquidator appointed by a court which has jurisdiction pursuant to Article 3(2) may in any other Member State claim through the courts or out of court that moveable property was removed from the territory of the State of the opening of proceedings to the territory of that other Member State after the opening of the insolvency proceedings. He may also bring any action to set aside which is in the interests of the creditors.
(3) In exercising his powers, the liquidator shall comply with the law of the Member State within the territory of which he intends to take action, in particular with regard to procedures for the realisation of assets. Those powers may not include coercive measures or the right to rule on legal proceedings or disputes.

Article 19. The liquidator's appointment shall be evidenced by a certified copy of the original decision appointing him or by any other certificate issued by the court which has jurisdiction. A translation into the official language or one of the official languages of the Member State within the territory of which he intends to act may be required. No legalisation or other similar formality shall be required.

Article 20. (1) A creditor who, after the opening of the proceedings referred to in Article 3(1) obtains by any means, in particular through enforcement, total or partial satisfaction of his claim on the assets belonging to the debtor situated within the territory of another Member State, shall return what he has obtained to the liquidator, subject to Articles 5 and 7.
(2) In order to ensure equal treatment of creditors a creditor who has, in the course of insolvency proceedings, obtained a dividend on his claim shall share in distributions made in other proceedings only where creditors of the same ranking or category have, in those other proceedings, obtained an equivalent dividend.

Article 21. (1) The liquidator may request that notice of the judgment opening insolvency proceedings and, where appropriate, the decision appointing him, be published in any other Member State in accordance with the publication procedures provided for in that State. Such publication shall also specify the liquidator appointed and whether the jurisdiction rule applied is that pursuant to Article 3(1) or Article 3(2).
(2) However, any Member State within the territory of which the debtor has an establishment may require mandatory publication. In such cases, the liquidator or any authority empowered to that effect in the Member State where the proceedings referred to in Article 3(1) are opened shall take all necessary measures to ensure such publication.

Article 22. (1) The liquidator may request that the judgment opening the proceedings referred to in Article 3(1) be registered in the land register, the trade register and any other public register kept in the other Member States.
(2) However, any Member State may require mandatory registration. In such cases, the liquidator or any authority empowered to that effect in the Member State where the proceedings referred to in Article 3(1) have been opened shall take all necessary measures to ensure such registration.

Article 23. The costs of the publication and registration provided for in Articles 21 and 22 shall be regarded as costs and expenses incurred in the proceedings.

Article 24. (1) Where an obligation has been honoured in a Member State for the benefit of a debtor who is subject to insolvency proceedings opened in another Member State, when it should have been honoured for the benefit of the liquidator in those proceedings, the person honouring the obligation shall be deemed to have discharged it if he was unaware of the opening of proceedings.
(2) Where such an obligation is honoured before the publication provided for in Article 21 has been effected, the person honouring the obligation shall be presumed, in the absence of proof to the contrary, to have been unaware of the opening of insolvency proceedings; where the obligation is honoured after such publication has been effected, the person honouring the obligation shall be presumed, in the absence of proof to the contrary, to have been aware of the opening of proceedings.

Article 25. (1) Judgments handed down by a court whose judgment concerning the opening of proceedings is recognised in accordance with Article 16 and which concern the course and closure of insolvency proceedings, and compositions approved by that court shall also be recognised with no further formalities. Such judgments shall be enforced in accordance with Articles 31 to 51, with the exception of Article 34(2), of the Brussels Convention on Jurisdiction and the Enforcement of Judgments in Civil and Commercial Matters, as amended by the Conventions of Accession to this Convention. The first subparagraph shall also apply to judgments deriving directly from the insolvency proceedings and which are closely linked with them, even if they were handed down by another court. The first subparagraph shall also apply to judgments relating to preservation measures taken after the request for the opening of insolvency proceedings.
(2) The recognition and enforcement of judgments other than those referred to in paragraph 1 shall be governed by the Convention referred to in paragraph 1, provided that that Convention is applicable.
(3) The Member States shall not be obliged to recognise or enforce a judgment referred to in paragraph 1 which might result in a limitation of personal freedom or postal secrecy.

Article 26. Any Member State may refuse to recognise insolvency proceedings opened in another Member State or to enforce a judgment handed down in the context of such proceedings where the effects of such recognition or enforcement would be manifestly contrary to that State's public policy, in particular its fundamental principles or the constitutional rights and liberties of the individual.

Chapter III. Secondary insolvency proceedings

Article 27. The opening of the proceedings referred to in Article 3(1) by a court of a Member State and which is recognised in another Member State (main proceedings) shall permit the opening in that other Member State, a court of which has jurisdiction pursuant to Article 3(2), of secondary insolvency proceedings without the debtor's insolvency being examined in that other State. These latter proceedings must be among the proceedings listed in Annex B. Their effects shall be restricted to the assets of the debtor situated within the territory of that other Member State.

Article 28. Save as otherwise provided in this Regulation, the law applicable to secondary proceedings shall be that of the Member State within the territory of which the secondary proceedings are opened.

Article 29. The opening of secondary proceedings may be requested by:
(a) the liquidator in the main proceedings;
(b) any other person or authority empowered to request the opening of insolvency proceedings under the law of the Member State within the territory of which the opening of secondary proceedings is requested.

Article 30. Where the law of the Member State in which the opening of secondary proceedings is requested requires that the debtor's assets be sufficient to cover in whole or in part the costs and expenses of the proceedings, the court may, when it receives such a request, require the applicant to make an advance payment of costs or to provide appropriate security.

Article 31. (1) Subject to the rules restricting the communication of information, the liquidator in the main proceedings and the liquidators in the secondary proceedings shall be duty bound to communicate information to each other. They shall immediately communicate any information which may be relevant to the other proceedings, in particular the progress made in lodging and verifying claims and all measures aimed at terminating the proceedings.
(2) Subject to the rules applicable to each of the proceedings, the liquidator in the main proceedings and the liquidators in the secondary proceedings shall be duty bound to cooperate with each other.
(3) The liquidator in the secondary proceedings shall give the liquidator in the main proceedings an early opportunity of submitting proposals on the liquidation or use of the assets in the secondary proceedings.

Article 32. (1) Any creditor may lodge his claim in the main proceedings and in any secondary proceedings.
(2) The liquidators in the main and any secondary proceedings shall lodge in other proceedings claims which have already been lodged in the proceedings for which they were appointed, provided that the interests of creditors in the latter proceedings are served thereby, subject to the right of creditors to oppose that or to withdraw the lodgement of their claims where the law applicable so provides.

(3) The liquidator in the main or secondary proceedings shall be empowered to participate in other proceedings on the same basis as a creditor, in particular by attending creditors' meetings.

Article 33. (1) The court, which opened the secondary proceedings, shall stay the process of liquidation in whole or in part on receipt of a request from the liquidator in the main proceedings, provided that in that event it may require the liquidator in the main proceedings to take any suitable measure to guarantee the interests of the creditors in the secondary proceedings and of individual classes of creditors. Such a request from the liquidator may be rejected only if it is manifestly of no interest to the creditors in the main proceedings. Such a stay of the process of liquidation may be ordered for up to three months. It may be continued or renewed for similar periods.
(2) The court referred to in paragraph 1 shall terminate the stay of the process of liquidation:
- at the request of the liquidator in the main proceedings,
- of its own motion, at the request of a creditor or at the request of the liquidator in the secondary proceedings if that measure no longer appears justified, in particular, by the interests of creditors in the main proceedings or in the secondary proceedings.

Article 34. (1) Where the law applicable to secondary proceedings allows for such proceedings to be closed without liquidation by a rescue plan, a composition or a comparable measure, the liquidator in the main proceedings shall be empowered to propose such a measure himself.
Closure of the secondary proceedings by a measure referred to in the first subparagraph shall not become final without the consent of the liquidator in the main proceedings; failing his agreement, however, it may become final if the financial interests of the creditors in the main proceedings are not affected by the measure proposed.
(2) Any restriction of creditors' rights arising from a measure referred to in paragraph 1 which is proposed in secondary proceedings, such as a stay of payment or discharge of debt, may not have effect in respect of the debtor's assets not covered by those proceedings without the consent of all the creditors having an interest.
(3) During a stay of the process of liquidation ordered pursuant to Article 33, only the liquidator in the main proceedings or the debtor, with the former's consent, may propose measures laid down in paragraph 1 of this Article in the secondary proceedings; no other proposal for such a measure shall be put to the vote or approved.

Article 35. If by the liquidation of assets in the secondary proceedings it is possible to meet all claims allowed under those proceedings, the liquidator appointed in those proceedings shall immediately transfer any assets remaining to the liquidator in the main proceedings.

Article 36. Where the proceedings referred to in Article 3(1) are opened following the opening of the proceedings referred to in Article 3(2) in another Member State, Articles 31 to 35 shall apply to those opened first, in so far as the progress of those proceedings so permits.

Article 37. The liquidator in the main proceedings may request that proceedings listed in Annex A previously opened in another Member State be converted into winding-up proceedings if this proves to be in the interests of the creditors in the main proceedings.
The court with jurisdiction under Article 3(2) shall order conversion into one of the proceedings listed in Annex B.

Article 38. Where the court of a Member State which has jurisdiction pursuant to Article 3(1) appoints a temporary administrator in order to ensure the preservation of the debtor's assets, that temporary administrator shall be empowered to request any measures to secure and preserve any of the debtor's assets situated in another Member State, provided for under the law of that State, for the period between the request for the opening of insolvency proceedings and the judgment opening the proceedings.

Chapter IV. Provision of information for creditors and lodgement of their claims

Article 39. Any creditor who has his habitual residence, domicile or registered office in a Member State other than the State of the opening of proceedings, including the tax authorities and social security authorities of Member States, shall have the right to lodge claims in the insolvency proceedings in writing.

Article 40. (1) As soon as insolvency proceedings are opened in a Member State, the court of that State having jurisdiction or the liquidator appointed by it shall immediately inform known creditors who have their habitual residences, domiciles or registered offices in the other Member States.
(2) That information, provided by an individual notice, shall in particular include time limits, the penalties laid down in regard to those time limits, the body or authority empowered to accept the lodgement of claims and the

other measures laid down. Such notice shall also indicate whether creditors whose claims are preferential or secured in rem need lodge their claims.

Article 41. A creditor shall send copies of supporting documents, if any, and shall indicate the nature of the claim, the date on which it arose and its amount, as well as whether he alleges preference, security in rem or a reservation of title in respect of the claim and what assets are covered by the guarantee he is invoking.

Article 42. (1) The information provided for in Article 40 shall be provided in the official language or one of the official languages of the State of the opening of proceedings. For that purpose a form shall be used bearing the heading "Invitation to lodge a claim. Time limits to be observed" in all the official languages of the institutions of the European Union.
(2) Any creditor who has his habitual residence, domicile or registered office in a Member State other than the State of the opening of proceedings may lodge his claim in the official language or one of the official languages of that other State. In that event, however, the lodgement of his claim shall bear the heading "Lodgement of claim" in the official language or one of the official languages of the State of the opening of proceedings. In addition, he may be required to provide a translation into the official language or one of the official languages of the State of the opening of proceedings.

Chapter V. Transitional and final provisions

Article 43. The provisions of this Regulation shall apply only to insolvency proceedings opened after its entry into force. Acts done by a debtor before the entry into force of this Regulation shall continue to be governed by the law which was applicable to them at the time they were done.

Article 44. (1) After its entry into force, this Regulation replaces, in respect of the matters referred to therein, in the relations between Member States, the Conventions concluded between two or more Member States, in particular:
(a) the Convention between Belgium and France on Jurisdiction and the Validity and Enforcement of Judgments, Arbitration Awards and Authentic Instruments, signed at Paris on 8 July 1899;
(b) the Convention between Belgium and Austria on Bankruptcy, Winding-up, Arrangements, Compositions and Suspension of Payments (with Additional Protocol of 13 June 1973), signed at Brussels on 16 July 1969;
(c) the Convention between Belgium and the Netherlands on Territorial Jurisdiction, Bankruptcy and the Validity and Enforcement of Judgments, Arbitration Awards and Authentic Instruments, signed at Brussels on 28 March 1925;
(d) the Treaty between Germany and Austria on Bankruptcy, Winding-up, Arrangements and Compositions, signed at Vienna on 25 May 1979;
(e) the Convention between France and Austria on Jurisdiction, Recognition and Enforcement of Judgments on Bankruptcy, signed at Vienna on 27 February 1979;
(f) the Convention between France and Italy on the Enforcement of Judgments in Civil and Commercial Matters, signed at Rome on 3 June 1930;
(g) the Convention between Italy and Austria on Bankruptcy, Winding-up, Arrangements and Compositions, signed at Rome on 12 July 1977;
(h) the Convention between the Kingdom of the Netherlands and the Federal Republic of Germany on the Mutual Recognition and Enforcement of Judgments and other Enforceable Instruments in Civil and Commercial Matters, signed at The Hague on 30 August 1962;
(i) the Convention between the United Kingdom and the Kingdom of Belgium providing for the Reciprocal Enforcement of Judgments in Civil and Commercial Matters, with Protocol, signed at Brussels on 2 May 1934;
(j) the Convention between Denmark, Finland, Norway, Sweden and Iceland on Bankruptcy, signed at Copenhagen on 7 November 1933;
(k) the European Convention on Certain International Aspects of Bankruptcy, signed at Istanbul on 5 June 1990.
(2) The Conventions referred to in paragraph 1 shall continue to have effect with regard to proceedings opened before the entry into force of this Regulation.
(3) This Regulation shall not apply:
(a) in any Member State, to the extent that it is irreconcilable with the obligations arising in relation to bankruptcy from a convention concluded by that State with one or more third countries before the entry into force of this Regulation;

(b) in the United Kingdom of Great Britain and Northern Ireland, to the extent that is irreconcilable with the obligations arising in relation to bankruptcy and the winding-up of insolvent companies from any arrangements with the Commonwealth existing at the time this Regulation enters into force.

Article 45. The Council, acting by qualified majority on the initiative of one of its members or on a proposal from the Commission, may amend the Annexes.

Article 46. No later than 1 June 2012, and every five years thereafter, the Commission shall present to the European Parliament, the Council and the Economic and Social Committee a report on the application of this Regulation. The report shall be accompanied if need be by a proposal for adaptation of this Regulation.

Article 47. This Regulation shall enter into force on 31 May 2002. This Regulation shall be binding in its entirety and directly applicable in the Member States in accordance with the Treaty establishing the European Community.

Annex A. Insolvency proceedings referred to in Article 2(a)
BELGIË-/BELGIQUE
- Het faillissement//La faillite
- Het gerechtelijk akkoord//Le concordat judiciaire
- De collectieve schuldenregeling//Le règlement collectif de dettes

DEUTSCHLAND
- Das Konkursverfahren
- Das gerichtliche Vergleichsverfahren
- Das Gesamtvollstreckungsverfahren
- Das Insolvenzverfahren

ΕΛΛΑΣ
- Πτώχευση
- Η ειδική εκκαθάριση
- Η προσωρινή διαχείριση εταιρίας. Η διοίκηση και η διαχείριση των πιστωτών
- Η υπαγωγή επιχείρησης υπό επίτροπο με σκοπό τη σύναψη συμβιβασμού με τους πιστωτές

ESPAÑA
- Concurso de acreedores
- Quiebra
- Suspensión de pagos

FRANCE
- Liquidation judiciaire
- Redressement judiciaire avec nomination d'un administrateur

IRELAND
- Compulsory winding up by the court
- Bankruptcy
- The administration in bankruptcy of the estate of persons dying insolvent
- Winding-up in bankruptcy of partnerships
- Creditors' voluntary winding up (with confirmation of a Court)
- Arrangements under the control of the court which involve the vesting of all or part of the property of the debtor in the Official Assignee for realisation and distribution
- Company examinership

ITALIA
- Fallimento
- Concordato preventivo
- Liquidazione coatta amministrativa
- Amministrazione straordinaria
- Amministrazione controllata

LUXEMBOURG
- Faillite
- Gestion contrôlée
- Concordat préventif de faillite (par abandon d'actif)
- Régime spécial de liquidation du notariat

NEDERLAND
- Het faillissement

- De surséance van betaling
- De schuldsaneringsregeling natuurlijke personen
ÖSTERREICH
- Das Konkursverfahren
- Das Ausgleichsverfahren
PORTUGAL
- O processo de falência
- Os processos especiais de recuperação de empresa, ou seja:
- A concordata
- A reconstituição empresarial
- A reestruturação financeira
- A gestão controlada
SUOMI-/FINLAND
- Konkurssi//konkurs
- Yrityssaneeraus//företagssanering
SVERIGE
- Konkurs
- Företagsrekonstruktion
UNITED KINGDOM
- Winding up by or subject to the supervision of the court
- Creditors' voluntary winding up (with confirmation by the court)
- Administration
- Voluntary arrangements under insolvency legislation
- Bankruptcy or sequestration
ANNEX B
Winding up proceedings referred to in Article 2(c)
BELGIË-/BELGIQUE
- Het faillissement//La faillite
DEUTSCHLAND
- Das Konkursverfahren
- Das Gesamtvollstreckungsverfahren
- Das Insolvenzverfahren
ΕΛΛΑΣ
- Πτώχευση
- Η ειδική εκκαθάριση
ESPAÑA
- Concurso de acreedores
- Quiebra
- Suspensión de pagos basada en la insolvencia definitiva
FRANCE
- Liquidation judiciaire
IRELAND
- Compulsory winding up
- Bankruptcy
- The administration in bankruptcy of the estate of persons dying insolvent
- Winding-up in bankruptcy of partnerships
- Creditors' voluntary winding up (with confirmation of a court)
- Arrangements under the control of the court which involve the vesting of all or part of the property of the debtor in the Official Assignee for realisation and distribution
ITALIA
- Fallimento
- Liquidazione coatta amministrativa
LUXEMBOURG
- Faillite
- Régime spécial de liquidation du notariat
NEDERLAND
- Het faillissement
- De schuldsaneringsregeling natuurlijke personen

ÖSTERREICH
- Das Konkursverfahren
PORTUGAL
- O processo de falência
SUOMI-/FINLAND
- Konkurssi//konkurs
SVERIGE
- Konkurs
UNITED KINGDOM
- Winding up by or subject to the supervision of the court
- Creditors' voluntary winding up (with confirmation by the court)
- Bankruptcy or sequestration

ANNEX C

Liquidators referred to in Article 2(b)
BELGIË-/BELGIQUE
- De curator//Le curateur
- De commissaris inzake opschorting//Le commissaire au sursis
- De schuldbemiddelaar//Le médiateur de dettes
DEUTSCHLAND
- Konkursverwalter
- Vergleichsverwalter
- Sachwalter (nach der Vergleichsordnung)
- Verwalter
- Insolvenzverwalter
- Sachwalter (nach der Insolvenzordnung)
- Treuhänder
- Vorläufiger Insolvenzverwalter
ΕΛΛΑΣ
- Ο σύνδικο
- Ο προσωρινός διαχειριστής. Η διοικούσα επιτροπή των πιστωτών
- Ο ειδικός εκκαθαριστής
- Ο επίτροπος
ESPAÑA
- Depositario-administrador
- Interventor o Interventores
- Síndicos
- Comisario
FRANCE
- Représentant des créanciers
- Mandataire liquidateur
- Administrateur judiciaire
- Commissaire à l'exécution de plan
IRELAND
- Liquidator
- Official Assignee
- Trustee in bankruptcy
- Provisional Liquidator
- Examiner
ITALIA
- Curatore
- Commissario
LUXEMBOURG
- Le curateur
- Le commissaire
- Le liquidateur
- Le conseil de gérance de la section d'assainissement du notariat
NEDERLAND
- De curator in het faillissement

- De bewindvoerder in de surséance van betaling
- De bewindvoerder in de schuldsaneringsregeling natuurlijke personen

ÖSTERREICH
- Masseverwalter
- Ausgleichsverwalter
- Sachwalter
- Treuhänder
- Besondere Verwalter
- Vorläufiger Verwalter
- Konkursgericht

PORTUGAL
- Gestor judicial
- Liquidatário judicial
- Comissão de credores

SUOMI-/FINLAND
- Pesänhoitaja//boförvaltare
- Selvittäjä//utredare

SVERIGE
- Förvaltare
- God man
- Rekonstruktör

UNITED KINGDOM
- Liquidator
- Supervisor of a voluntary arrangement
- Administrator
- Official Receiver
- Trustee
- Judicial factor

PART X

International Business Law

BUSIN

United Nations Convention on Contracts for the International Sale of Goods (Vienna, 1980)

Preamble. The States Parties to this Convention,
Bearing in Mind the broad objectives in the resolutions adopted by the sixth special session of the General Assembly of the United Nations on the establishment of a New International Economic Order,
Considering that the development of international trade on the basis of equality and mutual benefit is an important element in promoting friendly relations among States,
Beeing of the Opinion that the adoption of uniform rules which govern contracts for the international sale of goods and take into account the different social, economic and legal systems would contribute to the removal of legal barriers in international trade and promote the development of international trade,
have decreed as follows:

Chapter I : Sphere of Application

Article 1. (1) This Convention applies to contracts of sale of goods between parties whose places of business are in different States:
(a) when the States are Contracting States; or
(b) when the rules of private international law lead to the application of the law of a Contracting State.
(2) The fact that the parties have their places of business in different States is to be disregarded whenever this fact does not appear either from the contract or from any dealings between, or from information disclosed by, the parties at any time before or at the conclusion of the contract.
(3) Neither the nationality of the parties nor the civil or commercial character of the parties or of the contract is to be taken into consideration in determining the application of this Convention.

Article 2. This Convention does not apply to sales:
(a) of goods bought for personal, family or household use, unless the seller, at any time before or at the conclusion of the contract, neither knew nor ought to have known that the goods were bought for any such use;
(b) by auction;
(c) on execution or otherwise by authority of law;
(d) of stocks, shares, investment securities, negotiable instruments or money;
(e) of ships, vessels, hovercraft or aircraft;
(f) of electricity.

Article 3. (1) Contracts for the supply of goods to be manufactured or produced are to be considered sales unless the party who orders the goods undertakes to supply a substantial part of the materials necessary for such manufacture or production.
(2) This Convention does not apply to contracts in which the preponderant part of the obligations of the party who furnishes the goods consists in the supply of labour or other services.

Article 4. This Convention governs only the formation of the contract of sale and the rights and obligations of the seller and the buyer arising from such a contract. In particular, except as otherwise expressly provided in this Convention, it is not concerned with:
(a) the validity of the contract or of any of its provisions or of any usage;
(b) the effect which the contract may have on the property in the goods sold.

Article 5. This Convention does not apply to the liability of the seller for death or personal injury caused by the goods to any person.

Article 6. The parties may exclude the application of this Convention or, subject to article 12, derogate from or vary the effect of any of its provisions.

Chapter II: General Provisions

Article 7. (1) In the interpretation of this Convention, regard is to be had to its international character and to the need to promote uniformity in its application and the observance of good faith in international trade.
(2) Questions concerning matters governed by this Convention which are not expressly settled in it are to be settled in conformity with the general principles on which it is based or, in the absence of such principles, in conformity with the law applicable by virtue of the rules of private international law.

Article 8. (1) For the purposes of this Convention statements made by and other conduct of a party are to be interpreted according to his intent where the other party knew or could not have been unaware what that intent was.
(2) If the preceding paragraph is not applicable, statements made by and other conduct of a party are to be interpreted according to the understanding that a reasonable person of the same kind as the other party would have had in the same circumstances.
(3) In determining the intent of a party or the understanding a reasonable person would have had, due consideration is to be given to all relevant circumstances of the case including the negotiations, any practices which the parties have established between themselves, usages and any subsequent conduct of the parties.

Article 9. (1) The parties are bound by any usage to which they have agreed and by any practices which they have established between themselves.
(2) The parties are considered, unless otherwise agreed, to have impliedly made applicable to their contract or its formation a usage of which the parties knew or ought to have known and which in international trade is widely known to, and regularly observed by, parties to contracts of the type involved in the particular trade concerned.

Article 10. For the purposes of this Convention:
(a) if a party has more than one place of business, the place of business is that which has the closest relationship to the contract and its performance, having regard to the circumstances known to or contemplated by the parties at any time before or at the conclusion of the contract;
(b) if a party does not have a place of business, reference is to be made to his habitual residence.

Article 11. A contract of sale need not be concluded in or evidenced by writing and is not subject to any other requirement as to form. It may be proved by any means, including witnesses.

Article 12. Any provision of article 11, article 29 or Part II of this Convention that allows a contract of sale or its modification or termination by agreement or any offer, acceptance or other indication of intention to be made in any form other than in writing does not apply where any party has his place of business in a Contracting State which has made a declaration under article 96 of this Convention. The parties may not derogate from or vary the effect or this article.

Article 13. For the purposes of this Convention "writing" includes telegram and telex.

PART II: Formation of the Contract

Article 14. (1) A proposal for concluding a contract addressed to one or more specific persons constitutes an offer if it is sufficiently definite and indicates the intention of the offeror to be bound in case of acceptance. A proposal is sufficiently definite if it indicates the goods and expressly or implicitly fixes or makes provision for determining the quantity and the price.
(2) A proposal other than one addressed to one or more specific persons is to be considered merely as an invitation to make offers, unless the contrary is clearly indicated by the person making the proposal.

Article 15. (1) An offer becomes effective when it reaches the offeree.
(2) An offer, even if it is irrevocable, may be withdrawn if the withdrawal reaches the offeree before or at the same time as the offer.

Article 16. (1) Until a contract is concluded an offer may be revoked if the revocation reaches the offeree before he has dispatched an acceptance.
(2) However, an offer cannot be revoked:
(a) if it indicates, whether by stating a fixed time for acceptance or otherwise, that it is irrevocable; or
(b) if it was reasonable for the offeree to rely on the offer as being irrevocable and the offeree has acted in reliance on the offer.

Article 17. An offer, even if it is irrevocable, is terminated when a rejection reaches the offeror.

Article 18. (1) A statement made by or other conduct of the offeree indicating assent to an offer is an acceptance. Silence or inactivity does not in itself amount to acceptance.
(2) An acceptance of an offer becomes effective at the moment the indication of assent reaches the offeror. An

acceptance is not effective if the indication of assent does not reach the offeror within the time he has fixed or, if no time is fixed, within a reasonable time, due account being taken of the circumstances of the transaction, including the rapidity of the means of communication employed by the offeror. An oral offer must be accepted immediately unless the circumstances indicate otherwise.

(3) However, if, by virtue of the offer or as a result of practices which the parties have established between themselves or of usage, the offeree may indicate assent by performing an act, such as one relating to the dispatch of the goods or payment of the price, without notice to the offeror, the acceptance is effective at the moment the act is performed, provided that the act is performed within the period of time laid down in the preceding paragraph.

Article 19. (1) A reply to an offer which purports to be an acceptance but contains additions, limitations or other modifications is a rejection of the offer and constitutes a counter-offer.
(2) However, a reply to an offer which purports to be an acceptance but contains additional or different terms which do not materially alter the terms of the offer constitutes an acceptance, unless the offeror, without undue delay, objects orally to the discrepancy or dispatches a notice to that effect. If he does not so object, the terms of the contract are the terms of the offer with the modifications contained in the acceptance.
(3) Additional or different terms relating, among other things, to the price, payment, quality and quantity of the goods, place and time of delivery, extent of one party's liability to the other or the settlement of disputes are considered to alter the terms of the offer materially.

Article 20. (1) A period of time for acceptance fixed by the offeror in a telegram or a letter begins to run from the moment the telegram is handed in for dispatch or from the date shown on the letter or, if no such date is shown, from the date shown on the envelope. A period of time for acceptance fixed by the offeror by telephone, telex or other means of instantaneous communication, begins to run from the moment that the offer reaches the offeree.
(2) Official holidays or non-business days occurring during the period for acceptance are included in calculating the period. However, if a notice of acceptance cannot be delivered at the address of the offeror on the last day of the period because that day falls on an official holiday or a non-business day at the place of business of the offeror, the period is extended until the first business day which follows.

Article 21. (1) A late acceptance is nevertheless effective as an acceptance if without delay the offeror orally so informs the offeree or dispatches a notice to that effect.
(2) If a letter or other writing containing a late acceptance shows that it has been sent in such circumstances that if its transmission had been normal it would have reached the offeror in due time, the late acceptance is effective as an acceptance unless, without delay, the offeror orally informs the offeree that he considers his offer as having lapsed or dispatches a notice to that effect.

Article 22. An acceptance may be withdrawn if the withdrawal reaches the offeror before or at the same time as the acceptance would have become effective.

Article 23. A contract is concluded at the moment when an acceptance of an offer becomes effective in accordance with the provisions of this Convention.

Article 24. For the purposes of this Part of the Convention, an offer, declaration of acceptance or any other indication of intention "reaches" the addressee when it is made orally to him or delivered by any other means to him personally, to his place of business or mailing address or, if he does not have a place of business or mailing address, to his habitual residence.

Part III: Sale of Goods

Chapter I: General Provisions

Article 25. A breach of contract committed by one of the parties is fundamental if it results in such detriment to the other party as substantially to deprive him of what he is entitled to expect under the contract, unless the party in breach did not foresee and a reasonable person of the same kind in the same circumstances would not have foreseen such a result.

Article 26. A declaration of avoidance of the contract is effective only if made by notice to the other party.

Article 27. Unless otherwise expressly provided in this Part of the Convention, if any notice, request or other communication is given or made by a party in accordance with this Part and by means appropriate in the circumstances, a delay or error in the transmission of the communication or its failure to arrive does not deprive that party of the right to rely on the communication.

Article 28. If, in accordance with the provisions of this Convention, one party is entitled to require performance of any obligation by the other party, a court is not bound to enter a judgement for specific performance unless the court would do so under its own law in respect of similar contracts of sale not governed by this Convention.

Article 29. (1) A contract may be modified or terminated by the mere agreement of the parties.
(2) A contract in writing which contains a provision requiring any modification or termination by agreement to be in writing may not be otherwise modified or terminated by agreement. However, a party may be precluded by his conduct from asserting such a provision to the extent that the other party has relied on that conduct.

Chapter II: Obligations of the Seller

Article 30. The seller must deliver the goods, hand over any documents relating to them and transfer the property in the goods, as required by the contract and this Convention.

Section I. Delivery of the goods and handing over of documents

Article 31. If the seller is not bound to deliver the goods at any other particular place, his obligation to deliver consists:
(a) if the contract of sale involves carriage of the goods - in handing the goods over to the first carrier for transmission to the buyer;
(b) if, in cases not within the preceding subparagraph, the contract related to specific goods, or unidentified goods to be drawn from a specific stock or to be manufactured or produced, and at the time of the conclusion of the contract the parties knew that the goods were at, or were to be manufactured or produced at, a particular place - in placing the goods at the buyer's disposal at that place;
(c) in other cases - in placing the goods at the buyer's disposal at the place where the seller had his place of business at the time of the conclusion of the contract.

Article 32. (1) If the seller, in accordance with the contract or this Convention, hands the goods over to a carrier and if the goods are not clearly identified to the contract by markings on the goods, by shipping documents or otherwise, the seller must give the buyer notice of the consignment specifying the goods.
(2) If the seller is bound to arrange for carriage of the goods, he must make such contracts as are necessary for carriage to the place fixed by means of transportation appropriate in the circumstances and according to the usual terms for such transportation.
(3) If the seller is not bound to effect insurance in respect of the carriage of the goods, he must, at the buyer's request, provide him with all available information necessary to enable him to effect such insurance.

Article 33. The seller must deliver the goods:
(a) if a date is fixed by or determinable from the contract, on that date;
(b) if a period of time is fixed by or determinable from the contract, at any time within that period unless circumstances indicate that the buyer is to choose a date; or
(c) in any other case, within a reasonable time after the conclusion of the contract.

Article 34. If the seller is bound to hand over documents relating to the goods, he must hand them over at the time and place and in the form required by the contract. If the seller has handed over documents before that time, he may, up to that time, cure any lack of conformity in the documents, if the exercise of this right does not cause the buyer unreasonable inconvenience or unreasonable expense. However, the buyer retains any right to claim damages as provided for in this Convention.

Section II. Conformity of the goods and third party claims

Article 35. (1) The seller must deliver goods which are of the quantity, quality and description required by the contract and which are contained or packaged in the manner required by the contract.
(2) Except where the parties have agreed otherwise, the goods do not conform with the contract unless they:

(a) are fit for the purposes for which goods of the same description would ordinarily be used;
(b) are fit for any particular purpose expressly or impliedly made known to the seller at the time of the conclusion of the contract, except where the circumstances show that the buyer did not rely, or that it was unreasonable for him to rely, on the seller's skill and judgement;
(c) possess the qualities of goods which the seller has held out to the buyer as a sample or model;
(d) are contained or packaged in the manner usual for such goods or, where there is no such manner, in a manner adequate to preserve and protect the goods.
(3) The seller is not liable under subparagraphs (a) to (d) of the preceding paragraph for any lack of conformity of the goods if at the time of the conclusion of the contract the buyer knew or could not have been unaware of such lack of conformity.

Article 36. (1) The seller is liable in accordance with the contract and this Convention for any lack of conformity which exists at the time when the risk passes to the buyer, even though the lack of conformity becomes apparent only after that time.
(2) The seller is also liable for any lack of conformity which occurs after the time indicated in the preceding paragraph and which is due to a breach of any of his obligations, including a breach of any guarantee that for a period of time the goods will remain fit for their ordinary purpose or for some particular purpose or will retain specified qualities or characteristics.

Article 37. If the seller has delivered goods before the date for delivery, he may, up to that date, deliver any missing part or make up any deficiency in the quantity of the goods delivered, or deliver goods in replacement of any non-conforming goods delivered or remedy any lack of conformity in the goods delivered, provided that the exercise of this right does not cause the buyer unreasonable inconvenience or unreasonable expense. However, the buyer retains any right to claim damages as provided for in this Convention.

Article 38. (1) The buyer must examine the goods, or cause them to be examined, within as short a period as is practicable in the circumstances.
(2) If the contract involves carriage of the goods, examination may be deferred until after the goods have arrived at their destination.
(3) If the goods are redirected in transit or redispatched by the buyer without a reasonable opportunity for examination by him and at the time of the conclusion of the contract the seller knew or ought to have known of the possibility of such redirection or redispatch, examination may be deferred until after the goods have arrived at the new destination.

Article 39. (1) The buyer loses the right to rely on a lack of conformity of the goods if he does not give notice to the seller specifying the nature of the lack of conformity within a reasonable time after he has discovered it or ought to have discovered it.
(2) In any event, the buyer loses the right to rely on a lack of conformity of the goods if he does not give the seller notice thereof at the latest within a period of two years from the date on which the goods were actually handed over to the buyer, unless this time-limit is inconsistent with a contractual period of guarantee.

Article 40. The seller is not entitled to rely on the provisions of articles 38 and 39 if the lack of conformity relates to facts of which he knew or could not have been unaware and which he did not disclose to the buyer.

Article 41. The seller must deliver goods which are free from any right or claim of a third party, unless the buyer agreed to take the goods subject to that right or claim. However, if such right or claim is based on industrial property or other intellectual property, the seller's obligation is governed by article 42.

Article 42. (1) The seller must deliver goods which are free from any right or claim of a third party based on industrial property or other intellectual property, of which at the time of the conclusion of the contract the seller knew or could not have been unaware, provided that the right or claim is based on industrial property or other intellectual property:
(a) under the law of the State where the goods will be resold or otherwise used, if it was contemplated by the parties at the time of the conclusion of the contract that the goods would be resold or otherwise used in that State; or
(b) in any other case, under the law of the State where the buyer has his place of business.
(2) The obligation of the seller under the preceding paragraph does not extend to cases where:

(a) at the time of the conclusion of the contract the buyer knew or could not have been unaware of the right or claim; or
(b) the right or claim results from the seller's compliance with technical drawings, designs, formulae or other such specifications furnished by the buyer.

Article 43. (1) The buyer loses the right to rely on the provisions of article 41 or Article 42 if he does not give notice to the seller specifying the nature of the right or claim of the third party within a reasonable time after he has become aware or ought to have become aware of the right or claim.
(2) The seller is not entitled to rely on the provisions of the preceding paragraph if he knew of the right or claim of the third party and the nature of it.

Article 44. Notwithstanding the provisions of paragraph (1) of article 39 and paragraph (1) of article 43, the buyer may reduce the price in accordance with Article 50 or claim damages, except for loss of profit, if he has a reasonable excuse for his failure to give the required notice.

Section III. Remedies for breach of contract by the seller

Article 45. (1) If the seller fails to perform any of his obligations under the contract or this Convention, the buyer may:
(a) exercise the rights provided in articles 46 to 52;
(b) claim damages as provided in articles 74 to 77.
(2) The buyer is not deprived of any right he may have to claim damages by exercising his right to other remedies.
(3) No period of grace may be granted to the seller by a court or arbitral tribunal when the buyer resorts to a remedy for breach of contract.

Article 46. (1) The buyer may require performance by the seller of his obligations unless the buyer has resorted to a remedy which is inconsistent with this requirement.
(2) If the goods do not conform with the contract, the buyer may require delivery of substitute goods only if the lack of conformity constitutes a fundamental breach of contract and a request for substitute goods is made either in conjunction with notice given under article 39 or within a reasonable time thereafter.
(3) If the goods do not conform with the contract, the buyer may require the seller to remedy the lack of conformity by repair, unless this is unreasonable having regard to all the circumstances. A request for repair must be made either in conjunction with notice given under article 39 or within a reasonable time thereafter.

Article 47. (1) The buyer may fix an additional period of time of reasonable length for performance by the seller of his obligations.
(2) Unless the buyer has received notice from the seller that he will not
perform within the period so fixed, the buyer may not, during that period, resort to any remedy for breach of contract. However, the buyer is not deprived thereby of any right he may have to claim damages for delay in performance.

Article 48.(1) Subject to article 49, the seller may, even after the date for delivery, remedy at his own expense any failure to perform his obligations, if he can do so without unreasonable delay and without causing the buyer unreasonable inconvenience or uncertainty of reimbursement by the seller of expenses advanced by the buyer. However, the buyer retains any right to claim damages as provided for in this Convention.
(2) If the seller requests the buyer to make known whether he will accept performance and the buyer does not comply with the request within a reasonable time, the seller may perform within the time indicated in his request. The buyer may not, during that period of time, resort to any remedy which is inconsistent with performance by the seller.
(3) A notice by the seller that he will perform within a specified period of time is assumed to include a request, under the preceding paragraph, that the buyer make known his decision.
(4) A request or notice by the seller under paragraph (2) or (3) of this Article is not effective unless received by the buyer.

Article 49. (1) The buyer may declare the contract avoided:
(a) if the failure by the seller to perform any of his obligations under the contract or this Convention amounts to a fundamental breach of contract; or
(b) in case of non-delivery, if the seller does not deliver the goods within the additional period of time fixed by the

buyer in accordance with paragraph (1) of article 47 or declares that he will not deliver within the period so fixed.
(2) However, in cases where the seller has delivered the goods, the buyer loses the right to declare the contract avoided unless he does so:
(a) in respect of late delivery, within a reasonable time after he has become aware that delivery has been made;
(b) in respect of any breach other than late delivery, within a reasonable time:
(i) after he knew or ought to have known of the breach;
(ii) after the expiration of any additional period of time fixed by the buyer in accordance with paragraph (1) of article 47, or after the seller has declared that he will not perform his obligations within such an additional period; or
(iii) after the expiration of any additional period of time indicated by the seller in accordance with paragraph (2) of article 48, or after the buyer has declared that he will not accept performance.

Article 50. If the goods do not conform with the contract and whether or not the price has already been paid, the buyer may reduce the price in the same proportion as the value that the goods actually delivered had at the time of the delivery bears to the value that conforming goods would have had at that time. However, if the seller remedies any failure to perform his obligations in accordance with article 37 or article 48 or if the buyer refuses to accept performance by the seller in accordance with those Articles, the buyer may not reduce the price.

Article 51. (1) If the seller delivers only a part of the goods or if only a part of the goods delivered is in conformity with the contract, articles 46 to 50 apply in respect of the part which is missing or which does not conform.
(2) The buyer may declare the contract avoided in its entirety only if the failure to make delivery completely or in conformity with the contract amounts to a fundamental breach of the contract.

Article 52. (1) If the seller delivers the goods before the date fixed, the buyer may take delivery or refuse to take delivery.
(2) If the seller delivers a quantity of goods greater than that provided for in the contract, the buyer may take delivery or refuse to take delivery of the excess quantity. If the buyer takes delivery of all or part of the excess quantity, he must pay for it at the contract rate.

Chapter III : Obligations of the Buyer

Article 53. The buyer must pay the price for the goods and take delivery of them as required by the contract and this Convention.

Section I. Payment of the price

Article 54. The buyer's obligation to pay the price includes taking such steps and complying with such formalities as may be required under the contract or any laws and regulations to enable payment to be made.

Article 55. Where a contract has been validly concluded but does not expressly or implicitly fix or make provision for determining the price, the parties are considered, in the absence of any indication to the contrary, to have impliedly made reference to the price generally charged at the time of the conclusion of the contract for such goods sold under comparable circumstances in the trade concerned.

Article 56. If the price is fixed according to the weight of the goods, in case of doubt it is to be determined by the net weight.

Article 57. (1) If the buyer is not bound to pay the price at any other particular place, he must pay it to the seller:
(a) at the seller's place of business; or
(b) if the payment is to be made against the handing over of the goods or of documents, at the place where the handing over takes place.
(2) The seller must bear any increases in the expenses incidental to payment which is caused by a change in his place of business subsequent to the conclusion of the contract.

Article 58. (1) If the buyer is not bound to pay the price at any other specific time, he must pay it when the seller places either the goods or documents controlling their disposition at the buyer's disposal in accordance with the

contract and this Convention. The seller may make such payment a condition for handing over the goods or documents.
(2) If the contract involves carriage of the goods, the seller may dispatch the goods on terms whereby the goods, or documents controlling their disposition, will not be handed over to the buyer except against payment of the price.
(3) The buyer is not bound to pay the price until he has had an opportunity to examine the goods, unless the procedures for delivery or payment agreed upon by the parties are inconsistent with his having such an opportunity.

Article 59. The buyer must pay the price on the date fixed by or determinable from the contract and this Convention without the need for any request or compliance with any formality on the part of the seller.

Section II. Taking delivery

Article 60. The buyer's obligation to take delivery consists:
(a) in doing all the acts which could reasonably be expected of him in order to enable the seller to make delivery; and
(b) in taking over the goods.

Section III. Remedies for breach of contract by the buyer

Article 61. (1) If the buyer fails to perform any of his obligations under the contract or this Convention, the seller may:
(a) exercise the rights provided in articles 62 to 65;
(b) claim damages as provided in articles 74 to 77.
(2) The seller is not deprived of any right he may have to claim damages by exercising his right to other remedies.
(3) No period of grace may be granted to the buyer by a court or arbitral tribunal when the seller resorts to a remedy for breach of contract.

Article 62. The seller may require the buyer to pay the price, take delivery or perform his other obligations, unless the seller has resorted to a remedy which is inconsistent with this requirement.

Article 63. (1) The seller may fix an additional period of time of reasonable length for performance by the buyer of his obligations.
(2) Unless the seller has received notice from the buyer that he will not perform within the period so fixed, the seller may not, during that period, resort to any remedy for breach of contract. However, the seller is not deprived thereby of any right he may have to claim damages for delay in performance.

Article 64. (1) The seller may declare the contract avoided:
(a) if the failure by the buyer to perform any of his obligations under the contract or this Convention amounts to a fundamental breach of contract; or
(b) if the buyer does not, within the additional period of time fixed by the seller in accordance with paragraph (1) of article 63, perform his obligation to pay the price or take delivery of the goods, or if he declares that he will not do so within the period so fixed.
(2) However, in cases where the buyer has paid the price, the seller loses the right to declare the contract avoided unless he does so:
(a) in respect of late performance by the buyer, before the seller has become aware that performance has been rendered; or
(b) in respect of any breach other than late performance by the buyer, within a reasonable time:
(i) after the seller knew or ought to have known of the breach; or
(ii) after the expiration of any additional period of time fixed by the seller in accordance with paragraph (1) or article 63, or after the buyer has declared that he will not perform his obligations within such an additional period.

Article 65. (1) If under the contract the buyer is to specify the form, measurement or other features of the goods and he fails to make such specification either on the date agreed upon or within a reasonable time after receipt of a request from the seller, the seller may, without prejudice to any other rights he may have, make the specification himself in accordance with the requirements of the buyer that may be known to him.
(2) If the seller makes the specification himself, he must inform the buyer of the details thereof and must fix a

reasonable time within which the buyer may make a different specification. If, after receipt of such a communication, the buyer fails to do so within the time so fixed, the specification made by the seller is binding.

Chapter IV: Passing of Risk

Article 66. Loss of or damage to the goods after the risk has passed to the buyer does not discharge him from his obligation to pay the price, unless the loss or damage is due to an act or omission of the seller.

Article 67. (1) If the contract of sale involves carriage of the goods and the seller is not bound to hand them over at a particular place, the risk passes to the buyer when the goods are handed over to the first carrier for transmission to the buyer in accordance with the contract of sale. If the seller is bound to hand the goods over to a carrier at a particular place, the risk does not pass to the buyer until the goods are handed over to the carrier at that place. The fact that the seller is authorized to retain documents controlling the disposition of the goods does not affect the passage of the risk.
(2) Nevertheless, the risk does not pass to the buyer until the goods are clearly identified to the contract, whether by markings on the goods, by shipping documents, by notice given to the buyer or otherwise.

Article 68. The risk in respect of goods sold in transit passes to the buyer from the time of the conclusion of the contract. However, if the circumstances so indicate, the risk is assumed by the buyer from the time the goods were handed over to the carrier who issued the documents embodying the contract of carriage. Nevertheless, if at the time of the conclusion of the contract of sale the seller knew or ought to have known that the goods had been lost or damaged and did not disclose this to the buyer, the loss or damage is at the risk of the seller.

Article 69. (1) In cases not within articles 67 and 68, the risk passes to the buyer when he takes over the goods or, if he does not do so in due time, from the time when the goods are placed at his disposal and he commits a breach of contract by failing to take delivery.
(2) However, if the buyer is bound to take over the goods at a place other than a place of business of the seller, the risk passes when delivery is due and the buyer is aware of the fact that the goods are placed at his disposal at that place.
(3) If the contract relates to goods not then identified, the goods are considered not to be placed at the disposal of the buyer until they are clearly identified to the contract.

Article 70. If the seller has committed a fundamental breach of contract, articles 67, 68 and 69 do not impair the remedies available to the buyer on account of the breach.

Chapter V: Provisions Common to the Obligations of the Seller and of the Buyer

Section I. Anticipatory breach and instalment contracts

Article 71. (1) A party may suspend the performance of his obligations if, after the conclusion of the contract, it becomes apparent that the other party will not perform a substantial part of his obligations as a result of:
(a) a serious deficiency in his ability to perform or in his creditworthiness; or
(b) his conduct in preparing to perform or in performing the contract.
(2) If the seller has already dispatched the goods before the grounds described in the preceding paragraph become evident, he may prevent the handing over of the goods to the buyer even though the buyer holds a document which entitles him to obtain them. The present paragraph relates only to the rights in the goods as between the buyer and the seller.
(3) A party suspending performance, whether before or after dispatch of the goods, must immediately give notice of the suspension to the other party and must continue with performance if the other party provides adequate assurance of his performance.

Article 72. (1) If prior to the date for performance of the contract it is clear that one of the parties will commit a fundamental breach of contract, the other party may declare the contract avoided.
(2) If time allows, the party intending to declare the contract avoided must give reasonable notice to the other party in order to permit him to provide adequate assurance of his performance.
(3) The requirements of the preceding paragraph do not apply if the other party has declared that he will not perform his obligations.

Article 73. (1) In the case of a contract for delivery of goods by instalments, if the failure of one party to perform any of his obligations in respect of any instalment constitutes a fundamental breach of contract with respect to that instalment, the other party may declare the contract avoided with respect to that instalment.

(2) If one party's failure to perform any of his obligations in respect of any instalment gives the other party good grounds to conclude that a fundamental breach of contract will occur with respect to future instalments, he may declare the contract avoided for the future, provided that he does so within a reasonable time.

(3) A buyer who declares the contract avoided in respect of any delivery may, at the same time, declare it avoided in respect of deliveries already made or of future deliveries if, by reason of their interdependence, those deliveries could not be used for the purpose contemplated by the parties at the time of the conclusion of the contract.

Section II. Damages

Article 74. Damages for breach of contract by one party consist of a sum equal to the loss, including loss of profit, suffered by the other party as a consequence of the breach. Such damages may not exceed the loss which the party in breach foresaw or ought to have foreseen at the time of the conclusion of the contract, in the light of the facts and matters of which he then knew or ought to have known, as a possible consequence of the breach of contract.

Article 75. If the contract is avoided and if, in a reasonable manner and within a reasonable time after avoidance, the buyer has bought goods in replacement or the seller has resold the goods, the party claiming damages may recover the difference between the contract price and the price in the substitute transaction as well as any further damages recoverable under article 74.

Article 76. (1) If the contract is avoided and there is a current price for the goods, the party claiming damages may, if he has not made a purchase or resale under article 75, recover the difference between the price fixed by the contract and the current price at the time of avoidance as well as any further damages recoverable under article 74. If, however, the party claiming damages has avoided the contract after taking over the goods, the current price at the time of such taking over shall be applied instead of the current price at the time of avoidance.

(2) For the purposes of the preceding paragraph, the current price is the price prevailing at the place where delivery of the goods should have been made or, if there is no current price at that place, the price at such other place as serves as a reasonable substitute, making due allowance for differences in the cost of transporting the goods.

Article 77. A party who relies on a breach of contract must take such measures as are reasonable in the circumstances to mitigate the loss, including loss of profit, resulting from the breach. If he fails to take such measures, the party in breach may claim a reduction in the damages in the amount by which the loss should have been mitigated.

Section III. Interest

Article 78. If a party fails to pay the price or any other sum that is in arrears, the other party is entitled to interest on it, without prejudice to any claim for damages recoverable under article 74.

Section IV. Exemptions

Article 79. (1) A party is not liable for a failure to perform any of his obligations if he proves that the failure was due to an impediment beyond his control and that he could not reasonably be expected to have taken the impediment into account at the time of the conclusion of the contract or to have avoided or overcome it or its consequences.

(2) If the party's failure is due to the failure by a third person whom he has engaged to perform the whole or a part of the contract, that party is exempt from liability only if:

(a) he is exempt under the preceding paragraph; and

(b) the person whom he has so engaged would be so exempt if the provisions of that paragraph were applied to him.

(3) The exemption provided by this article has effect for the period during which the impediment exists.

(4) The party who fails to perform must give notice to the other party of the impediment and its effect on his ability to perform. If the notice is not received by the other party within a reasonable time after the party who fails to perform knew or ought to have known of the impediment, he is liable for damages resulting from such non-receipt.

(5) Nothing in this article prevents either party from exercising any right other than to claim damages under this Convention.

Article 80. A party may not rely on a failure of the other party to perform, to the extent that such failure was caused by the first party's act or omission.

Section V. Effects of avoidance

Article 81. (1) Avoidance of the contract releases both parties from their obligations under it, subject to any damages which may be due. Avoidance does not affect any provision of the contract for the settlement of disputes or any other provision of the contract governing the rights and obligations of the parties consequent upon the avoidance of the contract.
(2) A party who has performed the contract either wholly or in part may claim restitution from the other party of whatever the first party has supplied or paid under the contract. If both parties are bound to make restitution, they must do so concurrently.

Article 82. (1) The buyer loses the right to declare the contract avoided or to require the seller to deliver substitute goods if it is impossible for him to make restitution of the goods substantially in the condition in which he received them.
(2) The preceding paragraph does not apply:
(a) if the impossibility of making restitution of the goods or of making restitution of the goods substantially in the condition in which the buyer received them is not due to his act or omission;
(b) if the goods or part of the goods have perished or deteriorated as a result of the examination provided for in article 38; or
(c) if the goods or part of the goods have been sold in the normal course of business or have been consumed or transformed by the buyer in the course normal use before he discovered or ought to have discovered the lack of conformity.

Article 83. A buyer who has lost the right to declare the contract avoided or to require the seller to deliver substitute goods in accordance with article 82 retains all other remedies under the contract and this Convention.

Article 84. (1) If the seller is bound to refund the price, he must also pay interest on it, from the date on which the price was paid.
(2) The buyer must account to the seller for all benefits which he has derived from the goods or part of them:
(a) if he must make restitution of the goods or part of them; or
(b) if it is impossible for him to make restitution of all or part of the goods or to make restitution of all or part of the goods substantially in the condition in which he received them, but he has nevertheless declared the contract avoided or required the seller to deliver substitute goods.

Section VI. Preservation of the goods

Article 85. If the buyer is in delay in taking delivery of the goods or, where payment of the price and delivery of the goods are to be made concurrently, if he fails to pay the price, and the seller is either in possession of the goods or otherwise able to control their disposition, the seller must take such steps as are reasonable in the circumstances to preserve them. He is entitled to retain them until he has been reimbursed his reasonable expenses by the buyer.

Article 86. (1) If the buyer has received the goods and intends to exercise any right under the contract or this Convention to reject them, he must take such steps to preserve them as are reasonable in the circumstances. He is entitled to retain them until he has been reimbursed his reasonable expenses by the seller.
(2) If goods dispatched to the buyer have been placed at his disposal at their destination and he exercises the right to reject them, he must take possession of them on behalf of the seller, provided that this can be done without payment of the price and without unreasonable inconvenience or unreasonable expense. This provision does not apply if the seller or a person authorized to take charge of the goods on his behalf is present at the destination. If the buyer takes possession of the goods under this paragraph, his rights and obligations are governed by the preceding paragraph.

Article 87. A party who is bound to take steps to preserve the goods may deposit them in a warehouse of a third person at the expense of the other party provided that the expense incurred is not unreasonable.

Article 88. (1) A party who is bound to preserve the goods in accordance with article 85 or 86 may sell them by any appropriate means if there has been an unreasonable delay by the other party in taking possession of the goods or in taking them back or in paying the price or the cost of preservation, provided that reasonable notice of the intention to sell has been given to the other party.
(2) If the goods are subject to rapid deterioration or their preservation would involve unreasonable expense, a party who is bound to preserve the goods in accordance with article 85 or 86 must take reasonable measures to sell them. To the extent possible he must give notice to the other party of his intention to sell.
(3) A party selling the goods has the right to retain out of the proceeds of sale an amount equal to the reasonable expenses of preserving the goods and of selling them. He must account to the other party for the balance.

Part IV: Final Provisions

Article 89. The Secretary-General of the United Nations is hereby designated as the depositary for this Convention.

Article 90. This Convention does not prevail over any international agreement which has already been or may be entered into and which contains provisions concerning the matters governed by this Convention, provided that the parties have their places of business in States parties to such agreement.

Article 91. (1) This Convention is open for signature at the concluding meeting of the United Nations Conference on Contracts for the International Sale of Goods and will remain open for signature by all States at the Headquarters of the United Nations, New York until 30 September 1981.
(2) This Convention is subject to ratification, acceptance or approval by the signatory States.
(3) This Convention is open for accession by all States which are not signatory States as from the date it is open for signature.
(4) Instruments of ratification, acceptance, approval and accession are to be deposited with the Secretary-General of the United Nations.

Article 92. (1) A Contracting State may declare at the time of signature, ratification, acceptance, approval or accession that it will not be bound by Part II of this Convention or that it will not be bound by Part III of this Convention.
(2) A Contracting State which makes a declaration in accordance with the preceding paragraph in respect of Part II or Part III of this Convention is not to be considered a Contracting State within paragraph (1) of article 1 of this Convention in respect of matters governed by the Part to which the declaration applies.

Article 93. (1) If a Contracting State has two or more territorial units in which, according to its constitution, different systems of law are applicable in relation to the matters dealt with in this Convention, it may, at the time of signature, ratification, acceptance, approval or accession, declare that this Convention is to extend to all its territorial units or only to one or more of them, and may amend its declaration by submitting another declaration at any time.
(2) These declarations are to be notified to the depositary and are to state expressly the territorial units to which the Convention extends.
(3) If, by virtue of a declaration under this article, this Convention extends to one or more but not all of the territorial units of a Contracting State, and if the place of business of a party is located in that State, this place of business, for the purposes of this Convention, is considered not to be in a Contracting State, unless it is in a territorial unit to which the Convention extends.
(4) If a Contracting State makes no declaration under paragraph (1) of this Article, the Convention is to extend to all territorial units of that State.

Article 94. (1) Two or more Contracting States which have the same or closely related legal rules on matters governed by this Convention may at any time declare that the Convention is not to apply to contracts of sale or to their formation where the parties have their places of business in those States. Such declarations may be made jointly or by reciprocal unilateral declarations.
(2) A Contracting State which has the same or closely related legal rules on matters governed by this Convention as one or more non-Contracting States may at any time declare that the Convention is not to apply to contracts of sale or to their formation where the parties have their places of business in those States.
(3) If a State which is the object of a declaration under the preceding paragraph subsequently becomes a Contracting State, the declaration made will, as from the date on which the Convention enters into force in respect

of the new Contracting State, have the effect of a declaration made under paragraph (1), provided that the new Contracting State joins in such declaration or makes a reciprocal unilateral declaration.

Article 95. Any State may declare at the time of the deposit of its instrument of ratification, acceptance, approval or accession that it will not be bound by subparagraph (1)(b) of article 1 of this Convention.

Article 96. A Contracting State whose legislation requires contracts of sale to be concluded in or evidenced by writing may at any time make a declaration in accordance with article 12 that any provision of article 11, article 29, or Part II of this Convention, that allows a contract of sale or its modification or termination by agreement or any offer, acceptance, or other indication of intention to be made in any form other than in writing, does not apply where any party has his place of business in that State.

Article 97. (1) Declarations made under this Convention at the time of signature are subject to confirmation upon ratification, acceptance or approval.
(2) Declarations and confirmations of declarations are to be in writing and be formally notified to the depositary.
(3) A declaration takes effect simultaneously with the entry into force of this Convention in respect of the State concerned. However, a declaration of which the depositary receives formal notification after such entry into force takes effect on the first day of the month following the expiration of six months after the date of its receipt by the depositary. Reciprocal unilateral declarations under article 94 take effect on the first day of the month following the expiration of six months after the receipt of the latest declaration by the depositary.
(4) Any State which makes a declaration under this Convention may withdraw it at any time by a formal notification in writing addressed to the depositary. Such withdrawal is to take effect on the first day of the month following the expiration of six months after the date of the receipt of the notification by the depositary.
(5) A withdrawal of a declaration made under article 94 renders inoperative, as from the date on which the withdrawal takes effect, any reciprocal declaration made by another State under that article.

Article 98. No reservations are permitted except those expressly authorized in this Convention.

Article 99. (1) This Convention enters into force, subject to the provisions of paragraph (6) of this article, on the first day of the month following the expiration of twelve months after the date of deposit of the tenth instrument of ratification, acceptance, approval or accession, including an instrument which contains a declaration made under article 92.
(2) When a State ratifies, accepts, approves or accedes to this Convention after the deposit of the tenth instrument of ratification, acceptance, approval or accession, this Convention, with the exception of the Part excluded, enters into force in respect of that State, subject to the provisions of paragraph (6) of this article, on the first day of the month following the expiration of twelve months after the date of the deposit of its instrument of ratification, acceptance, approval or accession.
(3) A State which ratifies, accepts, approves or accedes to this Convention and is a party to either or both the Convention relating to a Uniform Law on the Formation of Contracts for the International Sale of Goods done at The Hague on 1 July 1964 (1964 Hague Formation Convention) and the Convention relating to a Uniform Law on the International Sale of Goods done at The Hague on 1 July 1964 (1964 Hague Sales Convention) shall at the same time denounce, as the case may be, either or both the 1964 Hague Sales Convention and the 1964 Hague Formation Convention by notifying the Government of the Netherlands to that effect.
(4) A State party to the 1964 Hague Sales Convention which ratifies, accepts, approves or accedes to the present Convention and declares or has declared under article 52 that it will not be bound by Part II of this Convention shall at the time of ratification, acceptance, approval or accession denounce the 1964 Hague Sales Convention by notifying the Government of the Netherlands to that effect.
(5) A State party to the 1964 Hague Formation Convention which ratifies, accepts, approves or accedes to the present Convention and declares or has declared under article 92 that it will not be bound by Part III of this Convention shall at the time of ratification, acceptance, approval or accession denounce the 1964 Hague Formation Convention by notifying the Government of the Netherlands to that effect.
(6) For the purpose of this article, ratifications, acceptances, approvals and accessions in respect of this Convention by States parties to the 1964 Hague Formation Convention or to the 1964 Hague Sales Convention shall not be effective until such denunciations as may be required on the part of those States in respect of the latter two Conventions have themselves become effective. The depositary of this Convention shall consult with the Government of the Netherlands, as the depositary of the 1964 Conventions, so as to ensure necessary co-ordination in this respect.

Article 100. (1) This Convention applies to the formation of a contract only when the proposal for concluding the contract is made on or after the date when the Convention enters into force in respect of the Contracting States referred to in subparagraph (1)(a) or the Contracting State referred to in subparagraph (1)(b) of article 1.
(2) This Convention applies only to contracts concluded on or after the date when the Convention enters into force in respect of the Contracting States referred to in subparagraph (1)(a) or the Contracting State referred to in subparagraph (1)(b) of article 1.

Article 101. (1) A Contracting State may denounce this Convention, or Part II or Part III of the Convention, by a formal notification in writing addressed to the depositary.
(2) The denunciation takes effect on the first day of the month following the expiration of twelve months after the notification is received by the depositary. Where a longer period for the denunciation to take effect is specified in the notification, the denunciation takes effect upon the expiration of such longer period after the notification is received by the depositary.

Convention on the Contract for the International Carriage of Goods by Road (CMR) (Geneva, 1956) as amended by the Protocol amending the Convention for the International Carriage of Goods by Road (Geneva, 1978)

Preamble. The Contracting Parties,
Having recognized the desirability of standardizing the conditions governing the contract for the international carriage of goods by road, particularly with respect to the documents used for such carriage and to the carrier's liability,
Have agreed as follows:

Chapter I: Scope of Application

Article 1. (1) This Convention shall apply to every contract for the carriage of goods by road in vehicles for reward, when the place of taking over of the goods and the place designated for delivery, as specified in the contract, are situated in two different countries, of which at least one is a contracting country, irrespective of the place of residence and the nationality of the parties.
(2) For the purpose of this Convention, "vehicles" means motor vehicles, articulated vehicles, trailers and semi-trailers as defined in article 4 of the Convention on Road Traffic dated 19 September 1949.
(3) This Convention shall apply also where carriage coming within its scope is carried out by States or by governmental institutions or organizations.
(4) This Convention shall not apply:
(a) To carriage performed under the terms of any international postal convention;
(b) To funeral consignments;
(c) To furniture removal.
(5) The Contracting Parties agree not to vary any of the provisions of this Convention by special agreements between two or more of them, except to make it inapplicable to their frontier traffic or to authorize the use in transport operations entirely confined to their territory of consignment notes representing a title to the goods.

Article 2. (1) Where the vehicle containing the goods is carried over part of the journey by sea, rail, inland waterways or air, and, except where the provisions of article 14 are applicable, the goods are not unloaded from the vehicle, this Convention shall nevertheless apply to the whole of the carriage. Provided that to the extent it is proved that any loss, damage or delay in delivery of the goods which occurs during the carriage by the other means of transport was not caused by act or omission of the carrier by road, but by some event which could only occurred in the course of and by reason of the carriage by that other means of transport, the liability of the carrier by road shall be determined not by this convention but in the manner in which the liability of the carrier by the other means of transport would have been determined if a contract for the carriage the goods alone had been made by the sender with the carrier by the other means of transport in accordance with the conditions prescribed by law for the carriage of goods by that means of transport. If, however, there are no such prescribed conditions, the liability of the carrier by road shall be determined by this convention.
(2) If the carrier by road is also himself the carrier by the other means of transport, his liability shall also be determined in accordance with the provisions paragraph 1 of this article, but as if, in his capacities as carrier by road and carrier by the other means of transport, he were two separate persons.

Chapter II: Persons for Whom the Carrier is Responsible

Article 3. For the purposes of this Convention the carrier shall be responsible for the acts of omissions of his agents and servants and of any other persons of whose services he makes use for the performance of the carriage, when such agents, servants or other persons are acting within the scope of their employment, as if such acts or omissions were his own.

Chapter III: Conclusion and Performance of the Contract of Carriage

Article 4. The contract of carriage shall be confirmed by the making out of a consignment note. The absence, irregularity or loss of the consignment note shall not affect the existence or the validity of the contract of carriage which shall remain subject the provisions of this Convention.

Article 5. (1) The consignment note shall be made out in three original copies signed by the sender and by the carrier. These signatures may be printed or replaced by the stamps of the sender and the carrier if the law of the country in which the consignment note has been made out so permits.
The first copy shall be handed to the sender, the second shall accompany the goods and the third
shall be retained by the carrier.
(2) When the goods which are to be carried have to be loaded in different vehicles, or are of different kinds or are divided into different lots, the sender or the carrier shall have the right to require a separate consignment note to be made out for each vehicle used, or for each kind or lot of goods.

Article 6. (1). The consignment note shall contain the following particulars:
(a) The date of the consignment note and the place at which it is made out;
(b) The name and address of the sender;
(c) The name and address of the carrier;
(d) The place and the date of taking over of the goods and the place designated for delivery;
(e) The name and address of the consignee;
(f) The description in common use of the nature of the goods and the method of packing, and, in the case of dangerous goods, their generally recognized description;
(g) The number of packages and their special marks and numbers;
(h) The gross weight of the goods or their quantity otherwise expressed;
(i) Charges relating to the carriage (carriage charges, supplementary charges, customs duties and other charges incurred from the making of the contract to the time of delivery);
(j) The requisite instructions for Customs and other formalities;
(k) A statement that the carriage is subject, notwithstanding any clause to the contrary, to the provisions of this Convention.
(2) Where applicable, the consignment note shall also contain the following particulars:
(a) A statement that trans-shipment is not allowed;
(b) Then charges which the sender undertakes to pay;
(c) The amount of "cash on delivery" charges;
(d) A declaration of the value of the goods and the amount representing special interest in delivery;
(e) The sender's instructions to the carrier regarding insurance of the goods;
(f) The agreed time limit within which the carriage is to be carried out;
(g) A list of the documents handed to the carrier.
(3) The parties may enter in the consignment note any other particulars which they may deem useful.

Article 7. (1). The sender shall be responsible for all expenses, loss and damage sustained by the carrier by reason of the inaccuracy or inadequacy of:
(a) The particulars specified in article 6, paragraph 1, (b), (d), (e), (f), (g), (h) and (j);
(b) The particular specified in article 6, paragraph 2;
(c) Any other particulars or instructions given by him to enable the consignment note to be made out or for the purpose of their being entered therein.
(2) If, at the request of the sender, the carrier enters in the consignment note the particulars referred to in paragraph 1 of this article, he shall be deemed, unless the contrary is proved, to have done so on behalf of the sender.
(3)If the consignment note does not contain the statement specified in article 6, paragraph 1 (k), the carrier shall be liable for all expenses, loss and damage sustained through such omission by
the person entitled to dispose of the goods.

Article 8 (1) On taking over the goods, the carrier shall check:
(a) The accuracy of the statements in the consignment note as to the number of packages and their marks and numbers, and
(b) The apparent condition of the goods and their packaging.
(2). Where the carrier has no reasonable means of checking the accuracy of e statements referred to in paragraph 1 (a) of this article, he shall enter his reservations in the consignment note together with the grounds on which they are based. He shall likewise specify the grounds for any reservations which he makes with regard to the apparent condition of the goods and their packaging, such reservations shall not bind the sender unless he has expressly agreed to be bound by them in the consignment note.
(3) The sender shall be entitled to require the carrier to check the gross weight the goods or their quantity otherwise expressed. He may also require the contents of the packages to be checked.The carrier shall be entitled to claim the cost of such checking. The result of the checks shall be entered in the consignment note.

Article 9. (1) The consignment note shall be prima facie evidence of the making of the contract of carriage, the conditions of the contract and the receipt of the goods by the carrier.
(2) If the consignment note contains no specific reservations by the carrier, it shall be presumed, unless the contrary is proved, that the goods and their packaging appeared to be in good condition when the carrier took them over and that the number of packages, their marks and numbers corresponded with the statements in the consignment note.

Article 10. The sender shall be liable to the carrier for damage to persons, equipment or other goods, and for any expenses due to defective packing of the goods, unless the defect was apparent or known to the carrier at the time when he took over the goods and he made no reservations concerning it.

Article 11. (1). For the purposes of the Customs or other formalities which have to be completed before delivery of the goods, the sender shall attach the necessary documents to the consignment note or place them at the disposal of the carrier and shall furnish him with all the information which he requires.
(2) The carrier shall not be under any duty to enquire into either the accuracy or the adequacy of such documents and information. The sender shall be liable to the carrier for any damage caused by the absence, inadequacy or irregularity of such documents and information, except in the case of some wrongful act or neglect on the part of the carrier.
(3) The liability of the carrier for the consequences arising from the loss or incorrect use of the documents specified in and accompanying the consignment note or deposited with the carrier shall be that of an agent, provided that the compensation payable by the carrier shall not exceed that payable in the event of loss of the goods.

Article 12. (1) The sender has the right to dispose of the goods, in particular by asking the carrier to stop the goods in transit, to change the place at which delivery is to take place or to deliver the goods to a consignee other than the consignee indicated in the consignment note.
(2) This right shall cease to exist when the second copy of the consignment note is handed to the consignee or when the consignee exercises his right under article 13, paragraph 1; from that time onwards the carrier shall obey the orders of the consignee.
(3) The consignee shall, however, have the right of disposal from the time when the consignment note is drawn up, if the sender makes an entry to that effect in the consignment note.
(4) If in exercising his right of disposal the consignee has ordered the delivery of the goods to another person, that other person shall not be entitled to name other consignees.
(5) The exercise of the right of disposal shall be subject to the following conditions:
(a) That the sender or, in the case referred to in paragraph 3 of this article, the consignee who wishes to exercise the right produces the first copy of the consignment note on which the new instructions to the carrier have been entered and indemnifies the carrier against all expenses, loss and damage involved in carrying out such instructions;
(b) That the carrying out of such instructions is possible at the time when the instructions reach the person who is to carry them out and does not either interfere with the normal working of the carriers' undertaking or prejudice the senders or consignees of other consignments;
(c) That the instructions do not result in a division of the consignment.
(6) When, by reason of the provisions of paragraph 5 (b) of this article, the carrier cannot carry out the instructions which he receives, he shall immediately notify the person who gave him such instructions.
(7) A carrier who has not carried out the instructions given under the conditions provided for in this article or who has carried them out without requiring the first copy of the consignment note to be produced, shall be liable to the person entitled to make a claim for any loss or damage caused thereby.

Article 13. (1) After arrival of the goods at the place designated for delivery, the consignee shall be entitled to require the carrier to deliver to him, against a receipt, the second copy of the consignment note and the goods. If the loss of the goods established or if the goods have not arrived after the expiry of the period provided for in article 19, the consignee shall be entitled to enforce in his own name against the carrier any rights arising from the contract of carriage.
(2) The consignee who avails himself of the rights granted to him under paragraph 1 of this article shall pay the charges shown to be due on the consignment note, but in the event of dispute on this matter the carrier shall not be required to deliver the goods unless security has been furnished by the consignee.

Article 14. (1) If for any reason it is or becomes impossible to carry out the contract in accordance with the terms laid down in the consignment note before the goods reach the place designated for delivery, the carrier shall ask for instructions from the person entitled to dispose of the goods in accordance with the provisions of article 12.
(2) Nevertheless, if circumstances are such as to allow the carriage to be carried out under conditions differing from those laid down in the consignment note and if the carrier has been unable to obtain instructions in reasonable time the person entitled to dispose of the goods in accordance with the provisions of article 12, he shall take such steps as seem to him to be in the best interests the person entitled to dispose of the goods

Article 15. (1) Where circumstances prevent delivery of the goods after their arrival at the place designated for delivery, the carrier shall ask the sender for his instructions. If the consignee refuses the goods the sender shall be entitled to dispose of them without being obliged to produce the first copy of the consignment note.
(2) Even if he has refused the goods, the consignee may nevertheless require delivery so long as the carrier has not received instructions to the contrary from the sender.
(3) When circumstances preventing delivery of the goods arise after the consignee, in exercise of his rights under article 12, paragraph 3, has given an order for the goods to be delivered to another person, paragraphs 1 and 2 of this article shall apply as if the consignee were the sender and that other person were the consignee.

Article 16. (1) The carrier shall be entitled to recover the cost of his request for instructions and any expenses entailed in carrying out such instructions, unless such expenses were caused by the
wrongful act or neglect of the carrier.
(2) In the cases referred to in article 14, paragraph 1, and in article 15, the carrier may immediately unload the goods for account of the person entitled to dispose of them and thereupon the carriage shall be deemed to be at an end. The carrier shall then hold the goods on behalf of the person so entitled. He may, however, entrust them to a third party, and in that case he shall not be under any liability except for the exercise of reasonable care in the choice of such
third party. The charges due under the consignment note and all other expenses shall remain chargeable against the goods.
(3) The carrier may sell the goods, without awaiting instructions from the person entitled to dispose of them, if the goods are perishable or their condition warrants such a course, or when the storage expenses would be out of proportion to the value of the goods. He may also proceed to the sale of the goods in other cases if after the expiry of a reasonable period he has not received from the person entitled to dispose of the goods instructions to the contrary which he may reasonably be required to carry out.
(4) If the goods have been sold pursuant to this article, the proceeds of sale, after deduction of the expenses chargeable against the goods, shall be placed at the disposal of the person entitled to dispose of the goods. If these charges exceed the proceeds of sale, the carrier shall be entitled to the difference.
(5) The procedure in the case of sale shall be determined by the law or custom of the place where the goods are situated.

Chapter IV: Liability of the Carrier

Article 17. (1) The carrier shall be liable for the total or partial loss of the goods and for damage thereto occurring between the time when he takes over the goods and the time of delivery, as well as for any delay in delivery.
(2) The carrier shall, however, be relieved of liability if the loss, damage or delay was caused by the wrongful act or neglect of the claimant, by the instructions of the claimant given otherwise than as the result of a wrongful act or neglect on the part of the carrier, by inherent vice of the goods or through circumstances which the carrier could not avoid and the consequences of which he was unable to prevent.
(3) The carrier shall not be relieved of liability by reason of the defective condition of the vehicle used by him in order to perform the carriage, or by reason of the wrongful act or neglect of the person from whom he may have hired the vehicle or of the agents or servants of the latter.
(4) Subject to article 18, paragraphs 2 to 5, the carrier shall be relieved of liability when the loss or damage arises from the special risks inherent in one more of the following circumstances:
(a) Use of open unsheeted vehicles, when their use has been expressly agreed and specified in the consignment note;
(b) The lack of, or defective condition of packing in the case of goods which, by their nature, are liable to wastage or to be damaged when not packed or when not properly packed;
(c) Handling, loading, stowage or unloading of the goods by the sender, the consignee or person acting on behalf of the sender or the consignee;

(d) The nature of certain kinds of goods which particularly exposes them to total or partial loss or to damage, especially through breakage, rust, decay, desiccation, leakage, normal wastage, or the action of moth or vermin;
(f) Insufficiency or inadequacy of marks or numbers on the packages;
(g) The carriage of livestock.
(5) Where under this article the carrier is not under any liability in respect some of the factors causing the loss, damage or delay, he shall only be liable the extent that those factors for which he is liable under this article have contributed to the loss, damage or delay.

Article 18. (1) The burden of proving that loss, damage or delay was due to one of the specified in article 17, paragraph 2, shall rest upon the carrier.
(2) When the carrier establishes that in the circumstances of the case, the loss damage could be attributed to one or more of the special risks referred to in article 17, paragraph 4, it shall be presumed that it was so caused. The claimant shall, however, be entitled to prove that the loss or damage was not, in fact, attributable either wholly or partly to one of these risks.
(3) This presumption shall not apply in the circumstances set out in article 17, paragraph 4 (a), if there has been an abnormal shortage, or a loss of any package.
(4) If the carriage is performed in vehicles specially equipped to protect the goods from the effects of heat, cold, variations in temperature or the humidity of the air, the carrier shall not be entitled to claim the benefit of article 17, paragraph 4 (d), unless he proves that all steps incumbent on him in the circumstances with respect to the choice, maintenance and use of such equipment were taken and that he complied with any special instructions issued to him.
(5) The carrier shall not be entitled to claim the benefit of article 17, paragraph 4 (f), unless he proves that all steps normally incumbent on him in the circumstances were taken and that he complied with any special instructions issued to him.

Article 19. Delay in delivery shall be said to occur when the goods have not been delivered within the agreed time-limit or when, failing an agreed time-limit, the actual duration of the carriage having regard to the circumstances of the case, and in particular, in the case of partial loads, the time required for making up a complete load in the normal way, exceeds the time it would be reasonable to allow a diligent carrier.

Article 20. (1) The fact that goods have not been delivered within thirty days following the expiry of the agreed time-limit, or, if there is no agreed time-limit, within sixty days from the time when the carrier took over the goods, shall be conclusive evidence of the loss of the goods, and the person entitled to make a claim may thereupon treat them as lost.
(2) The person so entitled may, on receipt of compensation for the missing goods, request in writing that he shall be notified immediately should the goods be recovered in the course of the year following the payment of compensation. He shall be given a written acknowledgement of such request.
(3) Within the thirty days following receipt of such notification, the person entitled as aforesaid may require the goods to be delivered to him against payment of the charges shown to be due on the consignment note and also against refund of the compensation he received less any charges included therein but without prejudice to any claims to compensation for delay in delivery under article 23 and where applicable, article 26.
(4) In the absence of the request mentioned in paragraph 2 or of any instructions given within the period of thirty days specified in paragraph 3, or if the goods are not recovered until more than one year after the payment of compensation, the carrier shall be entitled to deal with them in accordance with the law place where the goods are situated.

Article 21. Should the goods have been delivered to the consignee without collection of the "cash on delivery" charge which should have been collected by the carrier under terms of the contract of carriage, the carrier shall be liable to the sender for compensation not exceeding the amount of such charge without prejudice to his right of action against the consignee.

Article 22. (1) When the sender hands goods of a dangerous nature to the carrier, he shall inform the carrier of the exact nature of the danger and indicate if necessary, precautions to be taken. If this information has not been entered in the consignment note, the burden of proving, by some other means, that the carrier knew the exact nature of the danger constituted by the carriage of the said goods shall rest upon the sender or the consignee.
(2) Goods of a dangerous nature which, in the circumstance referred to in paragraph 1 of this article, the carrier did not know were dangerous, may, at any time or place, be unloaded, destroyed or rendered harmless by the carrier

without compensation; further, the sender shall be liable for all expenses, loss or damage arising out of their handing over for carriage or of their carriage.

Article 23. (1) When, under the provisions of this Convention, a carrier is liable for compensation in respect of total or partial loss of goods, such compensation shall be calculated by reference to the value of the goods at the place and time at which they were accepted for carriage.
(2) The value of the goods shall be fixed according to the commodity exchange price or, if there is no such price, according to the current market price or, if there is no commodity exchange price or current market price, by reference to normal value of goods of the same kind and quality.
(3) Compensation shall not, however, exceed 8.33 units of account per kilogram of gross weight short.
(4) In addition, the carriage charges, Customs duties and other charges incurred in respect of the carriage of the goods shall be refunded in full in case of total loss and in proportion to the loss sustained in case of partial loss, but no further damage shall be payable.
(5) In the case of delay if the claimant proves that damage has resulted therefrom the carrier shall pay compensation for such damage not exceeding the carriage charges.
(6) Higher compensation may only be claimed where the value of the goods or a special interest in delivery has been declared in accordance with articles 24 and 26.

Article 24. The sender may, against payment of a surcharge to be agreed upon, declare in the consignment note a value for the goods exceeding the limit laid down in article 23, paragraph 3, and in that case the amount of the declared value shall be substituted for that limit.

Article 25. (1) In case of damage, the carrier shall be liable for the amount by which the goods have diminished in value, calculated by reference to the value of the goods fixed in accordance with article 23, paragraphs 1, 2 and 4.
(2) The compensation may not, however, exceed:
(a) If the whole consignment has been damaged, the amount payable in the case of total loss;
(b) If part only of the consignment has been damaged, the amount payable in the case of loss of the part affected.

Article 26. (1) The sender may, against payment of a surcharge to be agreed upon, fix the amount of a special interest in delivery in the case of loss or damage or of the agreed time-limit being exceeded, by entering such amount in the consignment note.
(2) If a declaration of a special interest in delivery has been made, compensation for the additional loss or damage proved may be claimed, up to the total amount of the interest declared, independently of the compensation provided for in articles 23, 24 and 25.

Article 27. (1) The claimant shall be entitled to claim interest on compensation payable. Such interest, calculated at five per centum per annum, shall accrue from the date on which the claim was sent in writing to the carrier or, if no such claim has been made, from the date on which legal proceedings were instituted.
(2) When the amounts on which the calculation of the compensation is based are not expressed in the currency of the country in which payment is claimed, conversion shall be at the rate of exchange applicable on the day and at the place of payment of compensation.

Article 28. (1) In cases where, under the law applicable, loss, damage or delay arising out of carriage under this Convention gives rise to an extra-contractual claim, the carrier may avail himself of the provisions of this Convention which exclude his liability of which fix or limit the compensation due.
(2) In cases where the extra-contractual liability for loss, damage or delay of one of the persons for whom the carrier is responsible under the terms of article 3 is in issue, such person may also avail himself of the provisions of this Convention which exclude the liability of the carrier or which fix or limit the compensation due.

Article 29 (1) The carrier shall not be entitled to avail himself of the provisions of this chapter which exclude or limit his liability or which shift the burden of proof if the damage was caused by his wilful misconduct or by such default on his part as, in accordance with the law of the court or tribunal seised of the case, is considered as equivalent to wilful misconduct.
(2) The same provision shall apply if the wilful misconduct or default is committed by the agents or servants of the carrier or by any other persons of whose services he makes use for the performance of the carriage, when such agents, servants or other persons are acting within thescope of their employment. Furthermore, in such a case such agents, servants or other persons shall not be entitled to avail themselves, with regard to their personal liability, of the provisions of this chapter referred to in paragraph 1.

Chapter V: Claims and Actions

Article 30. (1) If the consignee takes delivery of the goods without duly checking their condition with the carrier or without sending him reservations giving a general indication of the loss or damage, not later than the time of delivery in the case of apparent loss or damage and within seven days of delivery, Sundays and public holidays excepted, in the case of loss or damage which is not apparent, the fact of this taking delivery shall be prima facie, evidence that he has received the goods in the condition described in the consignment note. In the case of loss or damage which is not apparent the reservations referred to shall be made in writing.
(2) When the condition of the goods has been duly checked by the consignee and the carrier, evidence contradicting the result of this checking shall only be admissible in the case of loss or damage which is not apparent and provided that the consignee has duly sent reservations in writing to the carrier within seven days, Sundays and public holidays excepted, from the date of checking.
(3) No compensation shall be payable for delay in delivery unless a reservation has been sent in writing to the carrier, within twenty-one days from the time that the goods were placed at the disposal of the consignee.
(4) In calculating the time-limits provided for in this article the date of delivery, or the date of checking, or the date when the goods were placed at the disposal of the consignee, as the case may be, shall not be included.
(5) The carrier and the consignee shall give each other every reasonable facility for making the requisite investigations and checks.

Article 31. (1) In legal proceedings arising out of carriage under this Convention, the plaintiff may bring an action in any court or tribunal of a contracting country designated by agreement between the parties and, in addition, in the courts or tribunals of a country within whose territory:
(a) The defendant is ordinarily resident, or has his principal place of business, or the branch or agency through which the contract of carriage was made, or (b) The place where the goods were taken over by the carrier or the place designated for delivery is situated.
(2) Where in respect of a claim referred to in paragraph 1 of this article an action is pending before a court or tribunal competent under that paragraph, or where in respect of such a claim a judgement has been entered by such a court or tribunal no new action shall be started between the same parties on the same grounds unless the judgement of the court or tribunal before which the first action was brought is not enforceable in the country in which the fresh proceedings are brought.
(3) When a judgement entered by a court or tribunal of a contracting country in any such action as is referred to in paragraph 1 of this article has become enforceable in that country, it shall also become enforceable in each of the other contracting States, as soon as the formalities required in the country concerned have been complied with. These formalities shall not permit the merits of the case to be re-opened.
(4) The provisions of paragraph 3 of this article shall apply to judgements after trial, judgements by default and settlements confirmed by an order of the court, but shall not apply to interim judgements or to awards of damages, in addition to costs against a plaintiff who wholly or partly fails in his action.
(5) Security for costs shall not be required in proceedings arising out of carriage under this Convention from nationals of contracting countries resident or having their place of business in one of those countries.

Article 32. (1) The period of limitation for an action arising out of carriage under this Convention shall be one year. Nevertheless, in the case of wilful misconduct, or such default as in accordance with the law of the court or tribunal seised of the case, is considered as equivalent to wilful misconduct, the period of limitation shall be three years. The period of limitation shall begin to run:
(a) In the case of partial loss, damage or delay in delivery, from the date of delivery;
(b) In the case of total loss, from the thirtieth day after the expiry of the agreed time-limit or where there is no agreed time-limit from the sixtieth day from the date on which the goods were taken over by the carrier;
(c) In all other cases, on the expiry of a period of three months after the making of the contract of carriage.
The day on which the period of limitation begins to run shall not be included in the period.
(2) A written claim shall suspend the period of limitation until such date as the carrier rejects the claim by notification in writing and returns the documents attached thereto. If a part of the claim is admitted the period of limitation shall start to run again only in respect of that part of the claim still in dispute. The burden of proof of the receipt of the claim, or of the reply and of the return of the documents, shall rest with the party relying upon these facts. The running of the period of limitation shall not be suspended by further claims having the same object.
(3) Subject to the provisions of paragraph 2 above, the extension of the period of limitation shall be governed by the law of the court or tribunal seized of the case. That law shall also govern the fresh accrual of rights of action.
(4) A right of action which has become barred by lapse of time may not be exercised by way of counterclaim or set-off.

Article 33. The contract of carriage may contain a clause conferring competence on an arbitration tribunal if the clause conferring competence on the tribunal provides that the tribunal shall apply this Convention.

Chapter VI: Provisions Relating to Carriage Performed by Successive Carrier

Article 34. If carriage governed by a single contract is performed by successive road carriers, each of them shall be responsible for the performance of the whole operation, the second carrier and each succeeding carrier becoming a party to the contract of carriage, under the terms of the consignment note, by reason of his acceptance of the goods and the consignment note.

Article 35. (1) A carrier accepting the goods from a previous carrier shall give the latter a dated and signed receipt. He shall enter his name and address on the second copy of the consignment note. Where applicable, he shall enter on the second copy of the consignment note and on the receipt reservations of the kind provided for in article 8, paragraph 2.
(2) The provisions of article 9 shall apply to the relations between successive carriers.

Article 36. Except in the case of a counterclaim or a setoff raised in an action concerning a claim based on the same contract of carriage, legal proceedings in respect of liability for loss, damage or delay may only be brought against the first carrier, the last carrier or the carrier who was performing that portion of the carriage during which the event causing the loss, damage or delay occurred, an action may be brought at the same time against several of these carriers.

Article 37. A carrier who has paid compensation in compliance with the provisions of this Convention, shall be entitled to recover such compensation, together with interest thereon and all costs and expenses incurred by reason of the claim, from the other carriers who have taken part in the carriage, subject to the following provisions:
(a) The carrier responsible for the loss or damage shall be solely liable for the compensation whether paid by himself or by another carrier;
(b) When the loss or damage has been caused by the action of two or more carriers, each of them shall pay an amount proportionate to his share of liability; should it be impossible to apportion the liability, each carrier shall be liable in proportion to the share of the payment for the carriage
which is due to him;
(c) If it cannot be ascertained to which carriers liability is attributable for the loss or damage, the amount of the compensation shall be apportioned between all the carriers as laid down in (b) above.

Article 38. If one of the carriers is insolvent, the share of the compensation due from him and unpaid by him shall be divided among the other carriers in proportion to the share of the payment for the carriage due to them.

Article 39. (1) No carrier against whom a claim is made under articles 37 and 38 shall be entitled to dispute the validity of the payment made by the carrier making the claim if the amount of the compensation was determined by judicial authority after the first mentioned carrier had been given due notice of the proceedings and afforded an opportunity of entering an appearance.
(2) A carrier wishing to take proceedings to enforce his right of recovery may make his claim before the competent court or tribunal of the country in which one of the carriers concerned is ordinarily resident, or has his principal place of business or the branch or agency through which the contract of carriage was made. All the carriers concerned may be made defendants in the same action.
(3) The provisions of article 31, paragraphs 3 and 4, shall apply to judgements entered in the proceedings referred to in articles 37 and 38.
(4) The provisions of article 32 shall apply to claims between carriers. The period of limitation shall, however, begin to run either on the date of the final judicial decision fixing the amount of compensation payable under the provisions of this Convention, or, if there is no such judicial decision, from the actual date of payment.

Article 40. Carriers shall be free to agree among themselves on provisions other than those laid down in articles 37 and 38.

Chapter VII: Nullity of Stipulation to the Convention

Article 41. (1) Subject to the provisions of article 40, any stipulation which would directly or indirectly derogate from the provisions of this Convention shall be null and void. The nullity of such a stipulation shall not involve the nullity of the other provisions of the contract.
(2) In particular, a benefit of insurance in favour of the carrier or any other similar clause, or any clause shifting the burden of proof shall be null and void.

Chapter VIII: Final Provisions

Article 42. (1) This Convention is open for signature or accession by countries members of the Economic Commission for Europe and countries admitted to the Commission in a consultative capacity under paragraph 8 of the Commission's terms of reference.
(2) Such countries as may participate in certain activities of the Economic Commission for Europe in accordance with paragraph 11 of the Commission's terms of reference may become Contracting Parties to this Convention by acceding thereto after its entry into force.
(3) The Convention shall be open for signature until 31 August 1956 inclusive. Thereafter, it shall be open for accession.
(4) This Convention shall be ratified.
(5) Ratification or accession shall be effected by the deposit of an instrument with the Secretary- General of the United Nations.

Article 43. (1) This Convention shall come into force on the ninetieth day after five of the countries referred to in article 42, paragraph 1, have deposited their instruments of ratification or accession.
(2) For any country ratifying or acceding to it after five countries have deposited their instruments of ratification or accession, this Convention shall enter into force on the ninetieth day after the said country has deposited its instrument of ratification or accession.

Article 44. (1) Any Contracting Party may denounce this Convention by so notifying the Secretary-General of the United Nations.
(2) Denunciation shall take effect twelve months after the date of receipt by the Secretary-General of the notification of denunciation.

Article 45. If, after the entry into force of this Convention, the number of Contracting Parties is reduced, as a result of denunciations, to less than five, the Convention shall cease to be in force from the date in which the last of such denunciations takes effect.

Article 46. (1) Any country may, at the time of depositing its instrument of ratification or accession or at any time thereafter, declare by notification addressed to the Secretary-General of the United Nations that this Convention shall extend to all or any of the territories for the international relations of which it is responsible. The Convention shall extend to the territory or territories named in the notification as from the ninetieth day after its receipt by the Secretary-General or, if on that day the Convention has not yet entered into force, at the time of its entry into force.
(2) Any country which has made a declaration under the preceding paragraph extending this Convention to any territory for whose international relations it is responsible may denounce the Convention separately in respect of that territory in accordance with the provisions of article 44.

Article 47. Any dispute between two or more Contracting Parties relating to the interpretation or application of this Convention, which the parties are unable to settle by negotiation or other means may, at the request of any one of the Contracting Parties concerned, be referred for settlement to the International Court of Justice.

Article 48. (1) Each Contracting Party may, at the time of signing, ratifying, or acceding to, this Convention, declare that it does not consider itself as bound by article 47 of the Convention. Other Contracting Parties shall not be bound by article 47 in respect of any Contracting Party which has entered such a reservation.
(2) Any Contracting Party having entered a reservation as provided for in paragraph 1 may at any time withdraw such reservation by notifying the Secretary-General of the United Nations.
(3) No other reservation to this Convention shall be permitted.

Article 49. (1) After this Convention has been in force for three years, any Contracting Party may, by notification to the Secretary-General of the United Nations, request that a conference be convened for the purpose of reviewing the Convention. The Secretary-General shall notify all Contracting Parties of the request and a review conference shall be convened by the Secretary-General if, within a period of four months following the date of notification by the Secretary General, not less than one-fourth of the Contracting Parties notify him of their concurrence with the request.
(2) If a conference is convened in accordance with the preceding paragraph, the Secretary-General shall notify all the Contracting Parties and invite them to submit within a period of three months such proposals as they may wish the Conference to consider. The Secretary-General shall circulate to all Contracting Parties the provisional agenda for the conference together with the texts of such proposals at least three months before the date on which the conference is to meet.
(3) The Secretary-General shall invite to any conference convened in accordance with this article all countries referred to in article 42, paragraph 1, and countries which have become Contracting Parties under article 42, paragraph 2.

Article 50. In addition to the notifications provided for in article 49, the Secretary-General of the United Nations shall notify the countries referred to in article 42, paragraph 1, and the countries which have become Contracting Parties under article 42, paragraph 2, of:
(a) Ratification and accessions under article 42;
(b) The dates of entry into force of this Convention in accordance with article 43;
(c) Denunciations under article 44;
(d) The termination of this Convention in accordance with article 45;
(e) Notifications received in accordance with article 46;
(f) Declarations and notifications received in accordance with article 48, paragraphs 1 and 2.

Article 51. After 31 August 1956, the original of this Convention shall be deposited with the Secretary-General of the United Nations, who shall transmit certified true copies to each of the countries mentioned in article 42, paragraphs 1 and 2.

International Convention for the Unification of Certain Rules of Law relating to Bills of Lading (Brussels, 1928) as modified by the Visby Amendments (Protcol to Amend the International Convention for the Unification of Certain Rules of Law relating to Bills of Lading (Brussels, 1968) and the SDR Protocol (Brussels, 1979), "The Hague-Visby Rules".

Article I. In these Rules the following words are employed, with the meanings set out below:
(a) 'Carrier' includes the owner or the charterer who enters into a contract of carriage with a shipper.
(b) 'Contract of carriage' applies only to contracts of carriage covered by a bill of lading or any similar document of title, in so far as such document relates to the carriage of goods by sea, including any bill of lading or any similar document as aforesaid issued under or pursuant to a charter party from the moment at which such bill of lading or similar document of title regulates the relations between a carrier and a holder of the same.
(c) 'Goods' includes goods, wares, merchandise, and articles of every kind whatsoever except live animals and cargo which by the contract of carriage is stated as being carried on deck and is so carried.
(d) 'Ship' means any vessel used for the carriage of goods by sea.
(e) 'Carriage of goods' covers the period from the time when the goods are loaded on to the time they are discharged from the ship.

Article II. Subject to the provisions of Article VI, under every contract of carriage of goods by sea the carrier, in relation to the loading, handling, stowage, carriage, custody, care and discharge of such goods, shall be subject to the responsibilities and liabilities and entitled to the rights and immunities hereinafter set forth.

Article III. (1) The carrier shall be bound before and at the beginning of the voyage to exercise due diligence to:
(a) Make the ship seaworthy;
(b) Properly man, equip and supply the ship;
(c) Make the holds, refrigerating and cool chambers, and all other parts of the ship in which goods are carried, fit and safe for their reception, carriage and preservation.
(2) Subject to the provisions of Article IV, the carrier shall properly and carefully load, handle, stow, carry, keep, care for, and discharge the goods carried.
(3) After receiving the goods into his charge the carrier or the master or agent of the carrier shall, on demand of the shipper, issue to the shipper a bill of lading showing among other things:
(a) The leading marks necessary for identification of the goods as the same are furnished in writing by the shipper before the loading of such goods starts, provided such marks are stamped or otherwise shown clearly upon the goods if uncovered, or on the cases or coverings in which such goods are contained, in such a manner as should ordinarily remain legible until the end of the voyage.
(b) Either the number of packages or pieces, or the quantity, or weight, as the case may be, as furnished in writing by the shipper.
(c) The apparent order and condition of the goods.
Provided that no carrier, master or agent of the carrier shall be bound to state or show in the bill of lading any marks, number, quantity or weight which he has reasonable ground for suspecting not accurately to represent the goods actually received, or which he has had no reasonable means of checking.
(4) Such a bill of lading shall be prima facie evidence of the receipt by the carrier of the goods as therein described in accordance with paragraph 3 (a), (b) and (c). However, proof to the contrary shall not be admissible when the bill of lading has been transferred to a third party acting in good faith.
(5) The shipper shall be deemed to have guaranteed to the carrier the accuracy at the time of shipment of the marks, number, quantity and weight, as furnished by him, and the shipper shall indemnify the carrier against all loss, damages and expenses arising or resulting from inaccuracies in such particulars. The right of the carrier to such indemnity shall in no way limit his responsibility and liability under the contract of carriage to any person other than the shipper.
(6) Unless notice of loss or damage and the general nature of such loss or damage be given in writing to the carrier or his agent at the port of discharge before or at the time of the removal of the goods into the custody of the person entitled to delivery thereof under the contract of carriage, or, if the loss or damage be not apparent, within three days, such removal shall be prima facie evidence of the delivery by the carrier of the goods as described in the bill of lading.
The notice in writing need not be given if the state of the goods has, at the time of their receipt, been the subject of joint survey or inspection.
Subject to paragraph 6bis the carrier and the ship shall in any event be discharged from all liability whatsoever in respect of the goods, unless suit is brought within one year of their delivery or of the date when they should have been delivered. This period, may however, be extended if the parties so agree after the cause of action has arisen.

In the case of any actual or apprehended loss or damage the carrier and the receiver shall give all reasonable facilities to each other for inspecting and tallying the goods.

(6 bis) An action for indemnity against a third person may be brought even after the expiration of the year provided for in the preceding paragraph if brought within the time allowed by the law of the Court seized of the case. However, the time allowed shall be not less than three months, commencing from the day when the person bringing such action for indemnity has settled the claim or has been served with process in the action against himself.

(7) After the goods are loaded the bill of lading to be issued by the carrier, master, or agent of the carrier, to the shipper shall, if the shipper so demands be a 'shipped' bill of lading, provided that if the shipper shall have previously taken up any document of title to such goods, he shall surrender the same as against the issue of the 'shipped' bill of lading, but at the option of the carrier such document of title may be noted at the port of shipment by the carrier, master, or agent with the name or names of the ship or ships upon which the goods have been shipped and the date or dates of shipment, and when so noted, if it shows the particulars mentioned in paragraph 3 of Article III, shall for the purpose of this article be deemed to constitute a 'shipped' bill of lading.

(8) Any clause, covenant, or agreement in a contract of carriage relieving the carrier or the ship from liability for loss or damage to, or in connection with, goods arising from negligence, fault, or failure in the duties and obligations provided in this article or lessening such liability otherwise than as provided in these Rules, shall be null and void and of no effect. A benefit of insurance in favour of the carrier or similar clause shall be deemed to be a clause relieving the carrier from liability.

Article IV. (1) Neither the carrier nor the ship shall be liable for loss or damage arising or resulting from unseaworthiness unless caused by want of due diligence on the part of the carrier to make the ship seaworthy, and to secure that the ship is properly manned, equipped and supplied, and to make the holds, refrigerating and cool chambers and all other parts of the ship in which goods are carried fit and safe for their reception, carriage and preservation in accordance with the provisions of paragraph 1 of Article III. Whenever loss or damage has resulted from unseaworthiness the burden of proving the exercise of due diligence shall be on the carrier or other person claiming exemption under this article.

(2) Neither the carrier nor the ship shall be responsible for loss or damage arising or resulting from:
(a) Act, neglect, or default of the master, mariner, pilot, or the servants of the carrier in the navigation or in the management of the ship.
(b) Fire, unless caused by the actual fault or privity of the carrier.
(c) Perils, dangers and accidents of the sea or other navigable waters.
(d) Act of God.
(e) Act of war.
(f) Act of public enemies.
(g) Arrest or restraint of princes, rulers or people, or seizure under legal process.
(h) Quarantine restrictions.
(i) Act or omission of the shipper or owner of the goods, his agent or representative.
(j) Strikes or lockouts or stoppage or restraint of labour from whatever cause, whether partial or general.
(k) Riots and civil commotions.
(l) Saving or attempting to save life or property at sea.
(m) Wastage in bulk of weight or any other loss or damage arising from inherent defect, quality or vice of the goods.
(n) Insufficiency of packing.
(o) Insufficiency or inadequacy of marks.
(p) Latent defects not discoverable by due diligence.
(q) Any other cause arising without the actual fault or privity of the carrier, or without the fault or neglect of the agents or servants of the carrier, but the burden of proof shall be on the person claiming the benefit of this exception to show that neither the actual fault or privity of the carrier nor the fault or neglect of the agents or servants of the carrier contributed to the loss or damage.

(3) The shipper shall not be responsible for loss or damage sustained by the carrier or the ship arising or resulting from any cause without the act, fault or neglect of the shipper, his agents or his servants.

(4) Any deviation in saving or attempting to save life or property at sea or any reasonable deviation shall not be deemed to be an infringement or breach of these Rules or of the contract of carriage, and the carrier shall not be liable for any loss or damage resulting therefrom.

(5) (a) Unless the nature and value of such goods have been declared by the shipper before shipment and inserted in the bill of lading, neither the carrier nor the ship shall in any event be or become liable for any loss or damage to

or in connection with the good s in an amount exceeding the equivalent of 666.67 units of account per package or unit or 2 units of account per kilo of gross weight of the goods lost or damaged, whichever is the higher.
(b) The total amount recoverable shall be calculated by reference to the value of such goods at the place and time at which the goods are discharged from the ship in accordance with the contract or should have been so discharged. The value of the goods shall be fixed according to the commodity exchange price, or, if there be no such price, according to the current market price, or, if there be no commodity exchange price or current market price, by reference to the normal value of goods of the same kind and quality.
(c) Where a container, pallet or similar article of transport is used to consolidate goods, the number of packages or units enumerated in the bill of lading as packed in such article of transport shall be deemed the number of packages or units for the purpose of this paragraph as far as these packages or units are concerned. Except as aforesaid such article of transport shall be considered the package or unit.
(d) The unit of account mentioned in this Article is the special drawing right as defined by the International Monetary Fund. The amounts mentioned in sub-paragraph (a) of this paragraph shall be converted into national currency on the basis of the value of that currency on a date to be determined by the law of the Court seized of the case.
(e) Neither the carrier nor the ship shall be entitled to the benefit of the limitation of liability provided for in this paragraph if it is proved that the damage resulted from an act or omission of the carrier done with intent to cause damage, or recklessly and with knowledge that damage would probably result.
(f) The declaration mentioned in sub-paragraph (a) of this paragraph, if embodied in the bill of lading, shall be prima facie evidence, but shall not be binding or conclusive on the carrier.
(g) By agreement between the carrier, master or agent of the carrier and the shipper other maximum amounts than those mentioned in sub-paragraph (a) of this paragraph may be fixed, provided that no maximum amount so fixed shall be less than the appropriate maximum mentioned in that sub-paragraph.
(h) Neither the carrier nor the ship shall be responsible in any event for loss or damage to, or in connection with, goods if the nature or value thereof has been knowingly mis-stated by the shipper in the bill of lading.
(6) Goods of an inflammable, explosive or dangerous nature to the shipment whereof the carrier, master or agent of the carrier has not consented with knowledge of their nature and character, may at any time before discharge be landed at any place, or destroyed or rendered innocuous by the carrier without compensation and the shipper of such goods shall be liable for all damages and expenses directly or indirectly arising out of or resulting from such shipment. If any such goods shipped with such knowledge and consent shall become a danger to the ship or cargo, they may in like manner be landed at any place, or destroyed or rendered innocuous by the carrier without liability on the part of the carrier except to general average, if any.

Article IV bis (1) The defences and limits of liability provided for in these Rules shall apply in any action against the carrier in respect of loss or damage to goods covered by a contract of carriage whether the action be founded in contract or in tort.
(2) If such an action is brought against a servant or agent of the carrier (such servant or agent not being an independent contractor), such servant or agent shall be entitled to avail himself of the defences and limits of liability which the carrier is entitled to invoke under these Rules.
(3) The aggregate of the amounts recoverable from the carrier, and such servants and agents, shall in no case exceed the limit provided for in these Rules.
(4) Nevertheless, a servant or agent of the carrier shall not be entitled to avail himself of the provisions of this article, if it is proved that the damage resulted from an act or omission of the servant or agent done with intent to cause damage or recklessly and with knowledge that damage would probably result.

Article V. A carrier shall be at liberty to surrender in whole or in part all or any of his rights and immunities or to increase any of his responsibilities and obligations under these Rules, provided such surrender or increase shall be embodied in the bill of lading issued to the shipper. The provisions of these Rules shall not be applicable to charter parties, but if bills of lading are issued in the case of a ship under a charter party they shall comply with the terms of these Rules. Nothing in these Rules shall be held to prevent the insertion in a bill of lading of any lawful provision regarding general average.

Article VI. Notwithstanding the provisions of the preceding articles, a carrier, master or agent of the carrier and a shipper shall in regard to any particular goods be at liberty to enter into any agreement in any terms as to the responsibility and liability of the carrier for such goods, and as to the rights and immunities of the carrier in respect of such goods, or his obligation as to seaworthiness, so far as this stipulation is not contrary to public policy, or the care or diligence of his servants or agents in regard to the loading, handling, stowage, carriage, custody, care and discharge of the goods carried by sea, provided that in this case no bill of lading has been or shall be issued and

that the terms agreed shall be embodied in a receipt which shall be a non-negotiable document and shall be marked as such.
An agreement so entered into shall have full legal effect.
Provided that this article shall not apply to ordinary commercial shipments made in the ordinary course of trade, but only to other shipments where the character or condition of the property to
be carried or the circumstances, terms and conditions under which the carriage is to be performed
are such as reasonably to justify a special agreement.

Article VII. Nothing herein contained shall prevent a carrier or a shipper from entering into any agreement, stipulation, condition, reservation or exemption as to the responsibility and liability of the carrier or the ship for the loss or damage to, or in connection with, the custody and care and handling of goods prior to the loading on, and subsequent to the discharge from, the ship on which the goods are carried by sea.

Article VIII. The provisions of these Rules shall not affect the rights and obligations of the carrier under any statute for the time being in force relating to the limitation of the liability of owners of sea-going vessels.

Article IX. These Rules shall not affect the provisions of any international Convention or national law governing liability for nuclear damage.

Article X. The provisions of these Rules shall apply to every bill of lading relating to the carriage of goods between ports in two different States if
(a) the bill of lading is issued in a contracting State, or
(b) the carriage is from a port in a contracting State, or
(c) the contract contained in or evidenced by the bill of lading provides that these Rules or legislation of any State giving effect to them are to govern the contract;
whatever may be the nationality of the ship, the carrier, the shipper, the consignee, or any other interested person.
(The last two paragraphs of this Article are not reproduced. They require contracting States to apply the Rules to bills of lading mentioned in the Article and authorise them to apply the Rules to other bills of lading). (Article 11 to 16 of the International Convention for the unification of certain rules of law relating to bills of lading signed at Brussels on August 25, 1974 are not reproduced. They deal with the coming into force of the Convention, procedure for ratification, accession and denunciation and the right to call for a fresh conference to consider amendments to the Rules contained in the Convention).

United Nations Convention on Contracts for the International Carriage of Goods Wholly or Partly by Sea (Rotterdam, 2009)

The States Parties to this Convention,
Reaffirming their belief that international trade on the basis of equality and mutual benefit is an important element in promoting friendly relations among States,
Convinced that the progressive harmonization and unification of international trade law, in reducing or removing legal obstacles to the flow of international trade, significantly contributes to universal economic cooperation among all States on a basis of equality, equity and common interest, and to the well-being of all peoples,
Recognizing the significant contribution of the International Convention for the Unification of Certain Rules of Law relating to Bills of Lading, signed in Brussels on 25 August 1924, and its Protocols, and of the United Nations Convention on the Carriage of Goods by Sea, signed in Hamburg on 31 March 1978, to the harmonization of the law governing the carriage of goods by sea,
Mindful of the technological and commercial developments that have taken place since the adoption of those conventions and of the need to consolidate and modernize them,
Noting that shippers and carriers do not have the benefit of a binding universal regime to support the operation of contracts of maritime carriage involving other modes of transport,
Believing that the adoption of uniform rules to govern international contracts of carriage wholly or partly by sea will promote legal certainty, improve the efficiency of international carriage of goods and facilitate new access opportunities for previously remote parties and markets, thus playing a fundamental role in promoting trade and economic development, both domestically and internationally,
Have agreed as follows:

Chapter 1 General provisions

Article 1. (Definitions) For the purposes of this Convention:
(1) "Contract of carriage" means a contract in which a carrier, against the payment of freight, undertakes to carry goods from one place to another. The contract shall provide for carriage by sea and may provide for carriage by other modes of transport in addition to the sea carriage.
(2) "Volume contract" means a contract of carriage that provides for the carriage of a specified quantity of goods in a series of shipments during an agreed period of time. The specification of the quantity may include a minimum, a maximum or a certain range.
(3) "Liner transportation" means a transportation service that is offered to the public through publication or similar means and includes transportation by ships operating on a regular schedule between specified ports in accordance with publicly available timetables of sailing dates.
(4) "Non-liner transportation" means any transportation that is not liner transportation.
(5) "Carrier" means a person that enters into a contract of carriage with a shipper.
(6) (a) "Performing party" means a person other than the carrier that performs or undertakes to perform any of the carrier's obligations under a contract of carriage with respect to the receipt, loading, handling, stowage, carriage, care, unloading or delivery of the goods, to the extent that such person acts, either directly or indirectly, at the carrier's request or under the carrier's supervision or control.
(b) "Performing party" does not include any person that is retained, directly or indirectly, by a shipper, by a documentary shipper, by the controlling party or by the consignee instead of by the carrier.
(7) "Maritime performing party" means a performing party to the extent that it performs or undertakes to perform any of the carrier's obligations during the period between the arrival of the goods at the port of loading of a ship and their departure from the port of discharge of a ship. An inland carrier is a maritime performing party only if it performs or undertakes to perform its services exclusively within a port area.
(8) "Shipper" means a person that enters into a contract of carriage with a carrier.
(9) "Documentary shipper" means a person, other than the shipper, that accepts to be named as "shipper" in the transport document or electronic transport record.
(10) "Holder" means:
(a) A person that is in possession of a negotiable transport document; and (i) if the document is an order document, is identified in it as the shipper or the consignee, or is the person to which the document is duly endorsed; or (ii) if the document is a blank endorsed order document or bearer document, is the bearer thereof; or
(b) The person to which a negotiable electronic transport record has been issued or transferred in accordance with the procedures referred to in Article 9, paragraph (1)
(11) "Consignee" means a person entitled to delivery of the goods under a contract of carriage or a transport document or electronic transport record.

(12) "Right of control" of the goods means the right under the contract of carriage to give the carrier instructions in respect of the goods in accordance with chapter 10.
(13) "Controlling party" means the person that pursuant to Article 51 is entitled to exercise the right of control.
(14) "Transport document" means a document issued under a contract of carriage by the carrier that:
(a) Evidences the carrier's or a performing party's receipt of goods under a contract of carriage; and
(b) Evidences or contains a contract of carriage.
(15) "Negotiable transport document" means a transport document that indicates, by wording such as "to order" or "negotiable" or other appropriate wording recognized as having the same effect by the law applicable to the document, that the goods have been consigned to the order of the shipper, to the order of the consignee, or to bearer, and is not explicitly stated as being "nonnegotiable" or "not negotiable".
(16) "Non-negotiable transport document" means a transport document that is not a negotiable transport document.
(17) "Electronic communication" means information generated, sent, received or stored by electronic, optical, digital or similar means with the result that the information communicated is accessible so as to be usable for subsequent reference.
(18) "Electronic transport record" means information in one or more messages issued by electronic communication under a contract of carriage by a carrier, including information logically associated with the electronic transport record by attachments or otherwise linked to the electronic transport record contemporaneously with or subsequent to its issue by the carrier, so as to become part of the electronic transport record, that:
(a) Evidences the carrier's or a performing party's receipt of goods under a contract of carriage; and
(b) Evidences or contains a contract of carriage.
(19) "Negotiable electronic transport record" means an electronic transport record:
(a) That indicates, by wording such as "to order", or "negotiable", or other appropriate wording recognized as having the same effect by the law applicable to the record, that the goods have been consigned to the order of the shipper or to the order of the consignee, and is not explicitly stated as being "non-negotiable" or "not negotiable"; and
(b) The use of which meets the requirements of Article 9, paragraph 1.
(20) "Non-negotiable electronic transport record" means an electronic transport record that is not a negotiable electronic transport record.
(21) The "issuance" of a negotiable electronic transport record means the issuance of the record in accordance with procedures that ensure that the record is subject to exclusive control from its creation until it ceases to have any effect or validity.
(22) The "transfer" of a negotiable electronic transport record means the transfer of exclusive control over the record.
(23) "Contract particulars" means any information relating to the contract of carriage or to the goods (including terms, notations, signatures and endorsements) that is in a transport document or an electronic transport record.
(24) "Goods" means the wares, merchandise, and Articles of every kind whatsoever that a carrier undertakes to carry under a contract of carriage and includes the packing and any equipment and container not supplied by or on behalf of the carrier.
(25) "Ship" means any vessel used to carry goods by sea.
(26) "Container" means any type of container, transportable tank or flat, swapbody, or any similar unit load used to consolidate goods, and any equipment ancillary to such unit load.
(27) "Vehicle" means a road or railroad cargo vehicle.
(28) "Freight" means the remuneration payable to the carrier for the carriage of goods under a contract of carriage.
(29) "Domicile" means (a) a place where a company or other legal person or association of natural or legal persons has its (i) statutory seat or place of incorporation or central registered office, whichever is applicable, (ii) central administration or (iii) principal place of business, and (b) the habitual residence of a natural person.
(30) "Competent court" means a court in a Contracting State that, according to the rules on the internal allocation of jurisdiction among the courts of that State, may exercise jurisdiction over the dispute.

Article 2. (Interpretation of this Convention) In the interpretation of this Convention, regard is to be had to its international character and to the need to promote uniformity in its application and the observance of good faith in international trade.

Article 3. (Form requirements) The notices, confirmation, consent, agreement, declaration and other communications referred to in Articles 19, paragraph 2; 23, paragraphs 1 to 4; 36, subparagraphs 1 (b), (c) and (d); 40, subparagraph 4 (b); 44; 48, paragraph 3; 51, subparagraph 1 (b); 59, paragraph 1; 63; 66; 67, paragraph 2; 75, paragraph 4; and 80, paragraphs 2 and 5, shall be in writing. Electronic communications may be used for these purposes, provided that the use of such means is with the consent of the person by which it is communicated and of the person to which it is communicated.

Article 4. (Applicability of defences and limits of liability) (1) Any provision of this Convention that may provide a defence for, or limit the liability of, the carrier applies in any judicial or arbitral proceeding, whether founded in contract, in tort, or otherwise, that is instituted in respect of loss of, damage to, or delay in delivery of goods covered by a contract of carriage or for the breach of any other obligation under this Convention against:
(a) The carrier or a maritime performing party;
(b) The master, crew or any other person that performs services on board the ship; or
(c) Employees of the carrier or a maritime performing party.
(2) Any provision of this Convention that may provide a defence for the shipper or the documentary shipper applies in any judicial or arbitral proceeding, whether founded in contract, in tort, or otherwise, that is instituted against the shipper, the documentary shipper, or their subcontractors, agents or employees.

Chapter 2 Scope of application

Article 5. (General scope of application) (1) Subject to Article 6, this Convention applies to contracts of carriage in which the place of receipt and the place of delivery are in different States, and the port of loading of a sea carriage and the port of discharge of the same sea carriage are in different States, if, according to the contract of carriage, any one of the following places is located in a Contracting State:
(a) The place of receipt;
(b) The port of loading;
(c) The place of delivery; or
(d) The port of discharge.
(2) This Convention applies without regard to the nationality of the vessel, the carrier, the performing parties, the shipper, the consignee, or any other interested parties.

Article 6. (Specific exclusions) (1) This Convention does not apply to the following contracts in liner transportation:
(a) Charter parties; and
(b) Other contracts for the use of a ship or of any space thereon.
(2) This Convention does not apply to contracts of carriage in non-liner transportation except when:
(a) There is no charter party or other contract between the parties for the use of a ship or of any space thereon; and
(b) A transport document or an electronic transport record is issued.

Article 7. (Application to certain parties) Notwithstanding Article 6, this Convention applies as between the carrier and the consignee, controlling party or holder that is not an original party to the charter party or other contract of carriage excluded from the application of this Convention. However, this Convention does not apply as between the original parties to a contract of carriage excluded pursuant to Article 6.

Chapter 3 Electronic transport records

Article 8. (Use and effect of electronic transport records) Subject to the requirements set out in this Convention:
(a) Anything that is to be in or on a transport document under this Convention may be recorded in an electronic transport record, provided the issuance and subsequent use of an electronic transport record is with the consent of the carrier and the shipper; and
(b) The issuance, exclusive control, or transfer of an electronic transport record has the same effect as the issuance, possession, or transfer of a transport document.

Article 9. (Procedures for use of negotiable electronic transport records) (1) The use of a negotiable electronic transport record shall be subject to procedures that provide for:
(a) The method for the issuance and the transfer of that record to an intended holder;
(b) An assurance that the negotiable electronic transport record retains its integrity;
(c) The manner in which the holder is able to demonstrate that it is the holder; and
(d) The manner of providing confirmation that delivery to the holder has been effected, or that, pursuant to Articles 10, paragraph 2, or 47, subparagraphs 1 (a) (ii) and (c), the electronic transport record has ceased to have any effect or validity.

(2) The procedures in paragraph 1 of this Article shall be referred to in the contract particulars and be readily ascertainable.

Article 10. (Replacement of negotiable transport document or negotiable electronic transport record) (1) If a negotiable transport document has been issued and the carrier and the holder agree to replace that document by a negotiable electronic transport record:
(a) The holder shall surrender the negotiable transport document, or all of them if more than one has been issued, to the carrier;
(b) The carrier shall issue to the holder a negotiable electronic transport record that includes a statement that it replaces the negotiable transport document; and
(c) The negotiable transport document ceases thereafter to have any effect or validity.
(2) If a negotiable electronic transport record has been issued and the carrier and the holder agree to replace that electronic transport record by a negotiable transport document:
(a) The carrier shall issue to the holder, in place of the electronic transport record, a negotiable transport document that includes a statement that it replaces the negotiable electronic transport record; and
(b) The electronic transport record ceases thereafter to have any effect or validity.

Chapter 4

Obligations of the carrier

Article 11. (Carriage and delivery of the goods) The carrier shall, subject to this Convention and in accordance with the terms of the contract of carriage, carry the goods to the place of destination and deliver them to the consignee.

Article 12. (Period of responsibility of the carrier) (1) The period of responsibility of the carrier for the goods under this Convention begins when the carrier or a performing party receives the goods for carriage and ends when the goods are delivered.
(2) (a) If the law or regulations of the place of receipt require the goods to be handed over to an authority or other third party from which the carrier may collect them, the period of responsibility of the carrier begins when the carrier collects the goods from the authority or other third party.
(b) If the law or regulations of the place of delivery require the carrier to hand over the goods to an authority or other third party from which the consignee may collect them, the period of responsibility of the carrier ends when the carrier hands the goods over to the authority or other third party.
(3) For the purpose of determining the carrier's period of responsibility, the parties may agree on the time and location of receipt and delivery of the goods, but a provision in a contract of carriage is void to the extent that it provides that:
(a) The time of receipt of the goods is subsequent to the beginning of their initial loading under the contract of carriage; or
(b) The time of delivery of the goods is prior to the completion of their final unloading under the contract of carriage.

Article 13. (Specific obligations) (1) The carrier shall during the period of its responsibility as defined in Article 12, and subject to Article 26, properly and carefully receive, load, handle, stow, carry, keep, care for, unload and deliver the goods.
(2) Notwithstanding paragraph 1 of this Article, and without prejudice to the other provisions in chapter 4 and to chapters 5 to 7, the carrier and the shipper may agree that the loading, handling, stowing or unloading of the goods is to be performed by the shipper, the documentary shipper or the consignee. Such an agreement shall be referred to in the contract particulars.

Article 14. (Specific obligations applicable to the voyage by sea) The carrier is bound before, at the beginning of, and during the voyage by sea to exercise due diligence to:
(a) Make and keep the ship seaworthy;
(b) Properly crew, equip and supply the ship and keep the ship so crewed, equipped and supplied throughout the voyage; and
(c) Make and keep the holds and all other parts of the ship in which the goods are carried, and any containers supplied by the carrier in or upon which the goods are carried, fit and safe for their reception, carriage and preservation.

Article 15. (Goods that may become a danger) Notwithstanding Articles 11 and 13, the carrier or a performing party may decline to receive or to load, and may take such other measures as are reasonable, including unloading, destroying, or rendering goods harmless, if the goods are, or reasonably appear likely to become during the carrier's period of responsibility, an actual danger to persons, property or the environment.

Article 16. (Sacrifice of the goods during the voyage by sea) Notwithstanding Articles 11, 13, and 14, the carrier or a performing party may sacrifice goods at sea when the sacrifice is reasonably made for the common safety or for the purpose of preserving from peril human life or other property involved in the common adventure.

Chapter 5 Liability of the carrier for loss, damage or delay

Article 17. (Basis of liability) (1) The carrier is liable for loss of or damage to the goods, as well as for delay in delivery, if the claimant proves that the loss, damage, or delay, or the event or circumstance that caused or contributed to it took place during the period of the carrier's responsibility as defined in chapter 4.
(2) The carrier is relieved of all or part of its liability pursuant to paragraph 1 of this Article if it proves that the cause or one of the causes of the loss, damage, or delay is not attributable to its fault or to the fault of any person referred to in Article 18.
(3) The carrier is also relieved of all or part of its liability pursuant to paragraph 1 of this Article if, alternatively to proving the absence of fault as provided in paragraph 2 of this Article, it proves that one or more of the following events or circumstances caused or contributed to the loss, damage, or delay:
(a) Act of God;
(b) Perils, dangers, and accidents of the sea or other navigable waters;
(c) War, hostilities, armed conflict, piracy, terrorism, riots, and civil commotions;
(d) Quarantine restrictions; interference by or impediments created by governments, public authorities, rulers, or people including detention, arrest, or seizure not attributable to the carrier or any person referred to in Article 18;
(e) Strikes, lockouts, stoppages, or restraints of labour;
(f) Fire on the ship;
(g) Latent defects not discoverable by due diligence;
(h) Act or omission of the shipper, the documentary shipper, the controlling party, or any other person for whose acts the shipper or the documentary shipper is liable pursuant to Article 33 or 34;
(i) Loading, handling, stowing, or unloading of the goods performed pursuant to an agreement in accordance with Article 13, paragraph 2, unless the carrier or a performing party performs such activity on behalf of the shipper, the documentary shipper or the consignee;
(j) Wastage in bulk or weight or any other loss or damage arising from inherent defect, quality, or vice of the goods;
(k) Insufficiency or defective condition of packing or marking not performed by or on behalf of the carrier;
(l) Saving or attempting to save life at sea;
(m) Reasonable measures to save or attempt to save property at sea;
(n) Reasonable measures to avoid or attempt to avoid damage to the environment; or
(o) Acts of the carrier in pursuance of the powers conferred by Articles 15 and 16.
(4) Notwithstanding paragraph 3 of this Article, the carrier is liable for all or part of the loss, damage, or delay:
(a) If the claimant proves that the fault of the carrier or of a person referred to in Article 18 caused or contributed to the event or circumstance on which the carrier relies; or
(b) If the claimant proves that an event or circumstance not listed in paragraph 3 of this Article contributed to the loss, damage, or delay, and the carrier cannot prove that this event or circumstance is not attributable to its fault or to the fault of any person referred to in Article 18.
(5) The carrier is also liable, notwithstanding paragraph 3 of this Article, for all or part of the loss, damage, or delay if:
(a) The claimant proves that the loss, damage, or delay was or was probably caused by or contributed to by (i) the unseaworthiness of the ship; (ii) the improper crewing, equipping, and supplying of the ship; or (iii) the fact that the holds or other parts of the ship in which the goods are carried, or any containers supplied by the carrier in or upon which the goods are carried, were not fit and safe for reception, carriage, and preservation of the goods; and
(b) The carrier is unable to prove either that: (i) none of the events or circumstances referred to in subparagraph 5 (a) of this Article caused the loss, damage, or delay; or (ii) it complied with its obligation to exercise due diligence pursuant to Article 14.

(6) When the carrier is relieved of part of its liability pursuant to this Article, the carrier is liable only for that part of the loss, damage or delay that is attributable to the event or circumstance for which it is liable pursuant to this Article.

Article 18. (Liability of the carrier for other persons) The carrier is liable for the breach of its obligations under this Convention caused by the acts or omissions of:
(a) Any performing party;
(b) The master or crew of the ship;
(c) Employees of the carrier or a performing party; or
(d) Any other person that performs or undertakes to perform any of the carrier's obligations under the contract of carriage, to the extent that the person acts, either directly or indirectly, at the carrier's request or under the carrier's supervision or control.

Article 19. (Liability of maritime performing parties) (1) A maritime performing party is subject to the obligations and liabilities imposed on the carrier under this Convention and is entitled to the carrier's defences and limits of liability as provided for in this Convention if:
(a) The maritime performing party received the goods for carriage in a Contracting State, or delivered them in a Contracting State, or performed its activities with respect to the goods in a port in a Contracting State; and
(b) The occurrence that caused the loss, damage or delay took place: (i) during the period between the arrival of the goods at the port of loading of the ship and their departure from the port of discharge from the ship; (ii) while the maritime performing party had custody of the goods; or (iii) at any other time to the extent that it was participating in the performance of any of the activities contemplated by the contract of carriage.
(2) If the carrier agrees to assume obligations other than those imposed on the carrier under this Convention, or agrees that the limits of its liability are higher than the limits specified under this Convention, a maritime performing party is not bound by this agreement unless it expressly agrees to accept such obligations or such higher limits.
(3) A maritime performing party is liable for the breach of its obligations under this Convention caused by the acts or omissions of any person to which it has entrusted the performance of any of the carrier's obligations under the contract of carriage under the conditions set out in paragraph 1 of this Article.
(4) Nothing in this Convention imposes liability on the master or crew of the ship or on an employee of the carrier or of a maritime performing party.

Article 20. (Joint and several liability) (1) If the carrier and one or more maritime performing parties are liable for the loss of, damage to, or delay in delivery of the goods, their liability is joint and several but only up to the limits provided for under this Convention.
(2) Without prejudice to Article 61, the aggregate liability of all such persons shall not exceed the overall limits of liability under this Convention.

Article 21. (Delay) Delay in delivery occurs when the goods are not delivered at the place of destination provided for in the contract of carriage within the time agreed.

Article 22. (Calculation of compensation) (1) Subject to Article 59, the compensation payable by the carrier for loss of or damage to the goods is calculated by reference to the value of such goods at the place and time of delivery established in accordance with Article 43.
(2) The value of the goods is fixed according to the commodity exchange price or, if there is no such price, according to their market price or, if there is no commodity exchange price or market price, by reference to the normal value of the goods of the same kind and quality at the place of delivery.
(3) In case of loss of or damage to the goods, the carrier is not liable for payment of any compensation beyond what is provided for in paragraphs 1 and 2 of this Article except when the carrier and the shipper have agreed to calculate compensation in a different manner within the limits of chapter 16.

Article 23. (Notice in case of loss, damage or delay) (1) The carrier is presumed, in absence of proof to the contrary, to have delivered the goods according to their description in the contract particulars unless notice of loss of or damage to the goods, indicating the general nature of such loss or damage, was given to the carrier or the performing party that delivered the goods before or at the time of the delivery, or, if the loss or damage is not apparent, within seven working days at the place of delivery after the delivery of the goods.

(2) Failure to provide the notice referred to in this Article to the carrier or the performing party shall not affect the right to claim compensation for loss of or damage to the goods under this Convention, nor shall it affect the allocation of the burden of proof set out in Article 17.
(3) The notice referred to in this Article is not required in respect of loss or damage that is ascertained in a joint inspection of the goods by the person to which they have been delivered and the carrier or the maritime performing party against which liability is being asserted.
(4) No compensation in respect of delay is payable unless notice of loss due to delay was given to the carrier within twenty-one consecutive days of delivery of the goods.
(5) When the notice referred to in this Article is given to the performing party that delivered the goods, it has the same effect as if that notice was given to the carrier, and notice given to the carrier has the same effect as a notice given to a maritime performing party.
(6) In the case of any actual or apprehended loss or damage, the parties to the dispute shall give all reasonable facilities to each other for inspecting and tallying the goods and shall provide access to records and documents relevant to the carriage of the goods.

Chapter 6 Additional provisions relating to particular stages of carriage

Article 24. (Deviation) When pursuant to applicable law a deviation constitutes a breach of the carrier's obligations, such deviation of itself shall not deprive the carrier or a maritime performing party of any defence or limitation of this Convention, except to the extent provided in Article 61.

Article 25. (Deck cargo on ships) (1) Goods may be carried on the deck of a ship only if:
(a) Such carriage is required by law;
(b) They are carried in or on containers or vehicles that are fit for deck carriage, and the decks are specially fitted to carry such containers or vehicles; or
(c) The carriage on deck is in accordance with the contract of carriage, or the customs, usages or practices of the trade in question.
(2) The provisions of this Convention relating to the liability of the carrier apply to the loss of, damage to or delay in the delivery of goods carried on deck pursuant to paragraph 1 of this Article, but the carrier is not liable for loss of or damage to such goods, or delay in their delivery, caused by the special risks involved in their carriage on deck when the goods are carried in accordance with subparagraphs 1 (a) or (c) of this Article.
(3) If the goods have been carried on deck in cases other than those permitted pursuant to paragraph 1 of this Article, the carrier is liable for loss of or damage to the goods or delay in their delivery that is exclusively caused by their carriage on deck, and is not entitled to the defences provided for in Article 17.
(4) The carrier is not entitled to invoke subparagraph 1 (c) of this Article against a third party that has acquired a negotiable transport document or a negotiable electronic transport record in good faith, unless the contract particulars state that the goods may be carried on deck.
(5) If the carrier and shipper expressly agreed that the goods would be carried under deck, the carrier is not entitled to the benefit of the limitation of liability for any loss of, damage to or delay in the delivery of the goods to the extent that such loss, damage, or delay resulted from their carriage on deck.

Article 26. (Carriage preceding or subsequent to sea carriage) When loss of or damage to goods, or an event or circumstance causing a delay in their delivery, occurs during the carrier's period of responsibility but solely before their loading onto the ship or solely after their discharge from the ship, the provisions of this Convention do not prevail over those provisions of another international instrument that, at the time of such loss, damage or event or circumstance causing delay:
(a) Pursuant to the provisions of such international instrument would have applied to all or any of the carrier's activities if the shipper had made a separate and direct contract with the carrier in respect of the particular stage of carriage where the loss of, or damage to goods, or an event or circumstance causing delay in their delivery occurred;
(b) Specifically provide for the carrier's liability, limitation of liability, or time for suit; and
(c) Cannot be departed from by contract either at all or to the detriment of the shipper under that instrument.

Chapter 7 Obligations of the shipper to the carrier

Article 27. (Delivery for carriage) (1) Unless otherwise agreed in the contract of carriage, the shipper shall deliver the goods ready for carriage. In any event, the shipper shall deliver the goods in such condition that they will

withstand the intended carriage, including their loading, handling, stowing, lashing and securing, and unloading, and that they will not cause harm to persons or property.
(2) The shipper shall properly and carefully perform any obligation assumed under an agreement made pursuant to Article 13, paragraph 2.
(3) When a container is packed or a vehicle is loaded by the shipper, the shipper shall properly and carefully stow, lash and secure the contents in or on the container or vehicle, and in such a way that they will not cause harm to persons or property.

Article 28. (Cooperation of the shipper and the carrier in providing information and instructions) The carrier and the shipper shall respond to requests from each other to provide information and instructions required for the proper handling and carriage of the goods if the information is in the requested party's possession or the instructions are within the requested party's reasonable ability to provide and they are not otherwise reasonably available to the requesting party.

Article 29. (Shipper's obligation to provide information, instructions and documents) (1) The shipper shall provide to the carrier in a timely manner such information, instructions and documents relating to the goods that are not otherwise reasonably available to the carrier, and that are reasonably necessary:
(a) For the proper handling and carriage of the goods, including precautions to be taken by the carrier or a performing party; and
(b) For the carrier to comply with law, regulations or other requirements of public authorities in connection with the intended carriage, provided that the carrier notifies the shipper in a timely manner of the information, instructions and documents it requires.
(2) Nothing in this Article affects any specific obligation to provide certain information, instructions and documents related to the goods pursuant to law, regulations or other requirements of public authorities in connection with the intended carriage.

Article 30. (Basis of shipper's liability to the carrier) (1) The shipper is liable for loss or damage sustained by the carrier if the carrier proves that such loss or damage was caused by a breach of the shipper's obligations under this Convention.
(2) Except in respect of loss or damage caused by a breach by the shipper of its obligations pursuant to Articles 31, paragraph 2, and 32, the shipper is relieved of all or part of its liability if the cause or one of the causes of the loss or damage is not attributable to its fault or to the fault of any person referred to in Article 34.
(3) When the shipper is relieved of part of its liability pursuant to this Article, the shipper is liable only for that part of the loss or damage that is attributable to its fault or to the fault of any person referred to in Article 34.

Article 31. (Information for compilation of contract particulars) (1) The shipper shall provide to the carrier, in a timely manner, accurate information required for the compilation of the contract particulars and the issuance of the transport documents or electronic transport records, including the particulars referred to in Article 36, paragraph 1; the name of the party to be identified as the shipper in the contract particulars; the name of the consignee, if any; and the name of the person to whose order the transport document or electronic transport record is to be issued, if any.
(2) The shipper is deemed to have guaranteed the accuracy at the time of receipt by the carrier of the information that is provided according to paragraph 1 of this Article. The shipper shall indemnify the carrier against loss or damage resulting from the inaccuracy of such information.

Article 32. (Special rules on dangerous goods) When goods by their nature or character are, or reasonably appear likely to become, a danger to persons, property or the environment:
(a) The shipper shall inform the carrier of the dangerous nature or character of the goods in a timely manner before they are delivered to the carrier or a performing party. If the shipper fails to do so and the carrier or performing party does not otherwise have knowledge of their dangerous nature or character, the shipper is liable to the carrier for loss or damage resulting from such failure to inform; and
(b) The shipper shall mark or label dangerous goods in accordance with any law, regulations or other requirements of public authorities that apply during any stage of the intended carriage of the goods. If the shipper fails to do so, it is liable to the carrier for loss or damage resulting from such failure.

Article 33. (Assumption of shipper's rights and obligations by the documentary shipper) (1) A documentary shipper is subject to the obligations and liabilities imposed on the shipper pursuant to this chapter and pursuant to Article 55, and is entitled to the shipper's rights and defences provided by this chapter and by chapter 13.

(2) Paragraph 1 of this Article does not affect the obligations, liabilities, rights or defences of the shipper.
Article 34. (Liability of the shipper for other persons) The shipper is liable for the breach of its obligations under this Convention caused by the acts or omissions of any person, including employees, agents and subcontractors, to which it has entrusted the performance of any of its obligations, but the shipper is not liable for acts or omissions of the carrier or a performing party acting on behalf of the carrier, to which the shipper has entrusted the performance of its obligations.

Chapter 8 Transport documents and electronic transport records

Article 35. (Issuance of the transport document or the electronic transport record) Unless the shipper and the carrier have agreed not to use a transport document or an electronic transport record, or it is the custom, usage or practice of the trade not to use one, upon delivery of the goods for carriage to the carrier or performing party, the shipper or, if the shipper consents, the documentary shipper, is entitled to obtain from the carrier, at the shipper's option:
(a) A non-negotiable transport document or, subject to Article 8, subparagraph (a), a non-negotiable electronic transport record; or
(b) An appropriate negotiable transport document or, subject to Article 8, subparagraph (a), a negotiable electronic transport record, unless the shipper and the carrier have agreed not to use a negotiable transport document or negotiable electronic transport record, or it is the custom, usage or practice of the trade not to use one.

Article 36. (Contract particulars) (1) The contract particulars in the transport document or electronic transport record referred to in Article 35 shall include the following information, as
furnished by the shipper:
(a) A description of the goods as appropriate for the transport;
(b) The leading marks necessary for identification of the goods;
(c) The number of packages or pieces, or the quantity of goods; and
(d) The weight of the goods, if furnished by the shipper.
(2) The contract particulars in the transport document or electronic transport record referred to in Article 35 shall also include:
(a) A statement of the apparent order and condition of the goods at the time the carrier or a performing party receives them for carriage;
(b) The name and address of the carrier;
(c) The date on which the carrier or a performing party received the goods, or on which the goods were loaded on board the ship, or on which the transport document or electronic transport record was issued; and
(d) If the transport document is negotiable, the number of originals of the negotiable transport document, when more than one original is issued.
(3) The contract particulars in the transport document or electronic transport record referred to in Article 35 shall further include:
(a) The name and address of the consignee, if named by the shipper;
(b) The name of a ship, if specified in the contract of carriage;
(c) The place of receipt and, if known to the carrier, the place of delivery; and
(d) The port of loading and the port of discharge, if specified in the contract of carriage.
(4) For the purposes of this Article, the phrase "apparent order and condition of the goods" in subparagraph 2 (a) of this Article refers to the order and condition of the goods based on:
(a) A reasonable external inspection of the goods as packaged at the time the shipper delivers them to the carrier or a performing party; and
(b) Any additional inspection that the carrier or a performing party actually performs before issuing the transport document or electronic transport record.

Article 37. (Identity of the carrier) (1) If a carrier is identified by name in the contract particulars, any other information in the transport document or electronic transport record relating to the identity of the carrier shall have no effect to the extent that it is inconsistent with
that identification.
(2) If no person is identified in the contract particulars as the carrier as required pursuant to Article 36, subparagraph 2 (b), but the contract particulars indicate that the goods have been loaded on board a named ship, the registered owner of that ship is presumed to be the carrier, unless it proves that the ship was under a bareboat charter at the time of the carriage and it identifies this bareboat charterer and indicates its address, in which case this bareboat charterer is presumed to be the carrier. Alternatively, the registered owner may rebut the presumption

of being the carrier by identifying the carrier and indicating its address. The bareboat charterer may rebut any presumption of being the carrier in the same manner.
(3) Nothing in this Article prevents the claimant from proving that any person other than a person identified in the contract particulars or pursuant to paragraph 2 of this Article is the carrier.

Article 38. (Signature) (1) A transport document shall be signed by the carrier or a person acting on its behalf.
(2) An electronic transport record shall include the electronic signature of the carrier or a person acting on its behalf. Such electronic signature shall identify the signatory in relation to the electronic transport record and indicate the carrier's authorization of the electronic transport record.

Article 39. (Deficiencies in the contract particulars) (1) The absence or inaccuracy of one or more of the contract particulars referred to in Article 36, paragraphs 1, 2 or 3, does not of itself affect the legal character or validity of the transport document or of the electronic transport record.
(2) If the contract particulars include the date but fail to indicate its significance, the date is deemed to be:
(a) The date on which all of the goods indicated in the transport document or electronic transport record were loaded on board the ship, if the contract particulars indicate that the goods have been loaded on board a ship; or
(b) The date on which the carrier or a performing party received the goods, if the contract particulars do not indicate that the goods have been loaded on board a ship.
(3) If the contract particulars fail to state the apparent order and condition of the goods at the time the carrier or a performing party receives them, the contract particulars are deemed to have stated that the goods were in apparent good order and condition at the time the carrier or a performing party received them.

Article 40. (Qualifying the information relating to the goods in the contract particulars) (1)The carrier shall qualify the information referred to in Article 36, paragraph 1, to indicate that the carrier does not assume responsibility for the accuracy of the information furnished by the shipper if:
(a) The carrier has actual knowledge that any material statement in the transport document or electronic transport record is false or misleading; or
(b) The carrier has reasonable grounds to believe that a material statement in the transport document or electronic transport record is false or misleading.
(2) Without prejudice to paragraph 1 of this Article, the carrier may qualify the information referred to in Article 36, paragraph 1, in the circumstances and in the manner set out in paragraphs 3 and 4 of this Article to indicate that the carrier does not assume responsibility for the accuracy of the information furnished by the shipper.
(3) When the goods are not delivered for carriage to the carrier or a performing party in a closed container or vehicle, or when they are delivered in a closed container or vehicle and the carrier or a performing party actually inspects them, the carrier may qualify the information referred to in Article 36, paragraph 1, if:
(a) The carrier had no physically practicable or commercially reasonable means of checking the information furnished by the shipper, in which case it may indicate which information it was unable to check; or
(b) The carrier has reasonable grounds to believe the information furnished by the shipper to be inaccurate, in which case it may include a clause providing what it reasonably considers accurate information.
(4) When the goods are delivered for carriage to the carrier or a performing party in a closed container or vehicle, the carrier may qualify the information referred to in:
(a) Article 36, subparagraphs 1 (a), (b), or (c), if:
(i) The goods inside the container or vehicle have not actually been inspected by the carrier or a performing party; and
(ii) Neither the carrier nor a performing party otherwise has actual knowledge of its contents before issuing the transport document or the electronic transport record; and
(b) Article 36, subparagraph 1 (d), if:
(i) Neither the carrier nor a performing party weighed the container or vehicle, and the shipper and the carrier had not agreed prior to the shipment that the container or vehicle would be weighed and the weight would be included in the contract particulars; or
(ii) There was no physically practicable or commercially reasonable means of checking the weight of the container or vehicle.

Article 41. (Evidentiary effect of the contract particulars) Except to the extent that the contract particulars have been qualified in the circumstances and in the manner set out in Article 40:
(a) A transport document or an electronic transport record is prima facie evidence of the carrier's receipt of the goods as stated in the contract particulars;

(b) Proof to the contrary by the carrier in respect of any contract particulars shall not be admissible, when such contract particulars are included in:
(i) A negotiable transport document or a negotiable electronic transport record that is transferred to a third party acting in good faith; or
(ii) A non-negotiable transport document that indicates that it must be surrendered in order to obtain delivery of the goods and is transferred to the consignee acting in good faith;
(c) Proof to the contrary by the carrier shall not be admissible against a consignee that in good faith has acted in reliance on any of the following contract particulars included in a non-negotiable transport document or a non negotiable electronic transport record:
(i) The contract particulars referred to in Article 36, paragraph 1, when such contract particulars are furnished by the carrier;
(ii) The number, type and identifying numbers of the containers, but not the identifying numbers of the container seals; and
(iii) The contract particulars referred to in Article 36, paragraph 2.

Article 42. ("Freight prepaid") If the contract particulars contain the statement "freight prepaid" or a statement of a similar nature, the carrier cannot assert against the holder or the consignee the fact that the freight has not been paid. This Article does not apply if the holder or the consignee is also the shipper.

Chapter 9 Delivery of the goods

Article 43. (Obligation to accept delivery) When the goods have arrived at their destination, the consignee that demands delivery of the goods under the contract of carriage shall accept delivery
of the goods at the time or within the time period and at the location agreed in the contract of carriage or, failing such agreement, at the time and location at which, having regard to the terms of the contract, the customs, usages or practices of the trade and the circumstances of the carriage, delivery could reasonably be expected.

Article 44. (Obligation to acknowledge receipt) On request of the carrier or the performing party that delivers the goods, the consignee shall acknowledge receipt of the goods from the carrier or the performing party in the manner that is customary at the place of delivery. The carrier may refuse delivery if the consignee refuses to acknowledge such receipt.

Article 45. (Delivery when no negotiable transport document or negotiable electronic transport record is issued) When neither a negotiable transport document nor a negotiable electronic transport record has been issued:
(a) The carrier shall deliver the goods to the consignee at the time and location referred to in Article 43. The carrier may refuse delivery if the person claiming to be the consignee does not properly identify itself as the consignee on the request of the carrier;
(b) If the name and address of the consignee are not referred to in the contract particulars, the controlling party shall prior to or upon the arrival of the goods at the place of destination advise the carrier of such name and address;
(c) Without prejudice to Article 48, paragraph 1, if the goods are not deliverable because (i) the consignee, after having received a notice of arrival, does not, at the time or within the time period referred to in Article 43, claim delivery of the goods from the carrier after their arrival at the place of destination, (ii) the carrier refuses delivery because the person claiming to be the consignee does not properly identify itself as the consignee, or (iii) the carrier is, after reasonable
effort, unable to locate the consignee in order to request delivery instructions, the carrier may so advise the controlling party and request instructions in respect of the delivery of the goods. If, after reasonable effort, the carrier is unable to locate the controlling party, the carrier may so advise the shipper and request instructions in respect of the delivery of the goods. If, after reasonable effort, the carrier is unable to locate the shipper, the carrier may so advise the
documentary shipper and request instructions in respect of the delivery of the goods;
(d) The carrier that delivers the goods upon instruction of the controlling party, the shipper or the documentary shipper pursuant to subparagraph (c) of this Article is discharged from its obligations to deliver the goods under the contract of carriage.

Article 46. (Delivery when a non-negotiable transport document that requires surrender is issued) When a non-negotiable transport document has been issued that indicates that it shall be surrendered in order to obtain delivery of the goods:

(a) The carrier shall deliver the goods at the time and location referred to in Article 43 to the consignee upon the consignee properly identifying itself on the request of the carrier and surrender of the non-negotiable document. The carrier may refuse delivery if the person claiming to be the consignee fails to properly identify itself on the request of the carrier, and shall refuse delivery if the non-negotiable document is not surrendered. If more than one original of the non-negotiable document has been issued, the surrender of one original will suffice and the other originals cease to have any effect or validity;
(b) Without prejudice to Article 48, paragraph 1, if the goods are not deliverable because (i) the consignee, after having received a notice of arrival, does not, at the time or within the time period referred to in Article 43, claim delivery of the goods from the carrier after their arrival at the place of destination, (ii) the carrier refuses delivery because the person claiming to be the consignee does not properly identify itself as the consignee or does not surrender the document,
or (iii) the carrier is, after reasonable effort, unable to locate the consignee in order to request delivery instructions, the carrier may so advise the shipper and request instructions in respect of the delivery of the goods. If, after reasonable effort, the carrier is unable to locate the shipper, the carrier may so advise the documentary shipper and request instructions in respect of the delivery of the goods;
(c) The carrier that delivers the goods upon instruction of the shipper or the documentary shipper pursuant to subparagraph (b) of this Article is discharged from its obligation to deliver the goods under the contract of carriage, irrespective of whether the non-negotiable transport document has been surrendered to it.

Article 47. (Delivery when a negotiable transport document or negotiable electronic transport record is issued) (1) When a negotiable transport document or a negotiable electronic transport
record has been issued:
(a) The holder of the negotiable transport document or negotiable electronic transport record is entitled to claim delivery of the goods from the carrier after they have arrived at the place of destination, in which event the carrier shall deliver the goods at the time and location referred to in Article 43 to the holder:
(i) Upon surrender of the negotiable transport document and, if the holder is one of the persons referred to in Article 1, subparagraph 10 (a) (i), upon the holder properly identifying itself; or
(ii) Upon demonstration by the holder, in accordance with the procedures referred to in Article 9, paragraph 1, that it is the holder of the negotiable electronic transport record;
(b) The carrier shall refuse delivery if the requirements of subparagraph (a) (i) or (a) (ii) of this paragraph are not met;
(c) If more than one original of the negotiable transport document has been issued, and the number of originals is stated in that document, the surrender of one original will suffice and the other originals cease to have any effect or validity. When a negotiable electronic transport record has been used, such electronic transport record ceases to have any effect or validity upon
delivery to the holder in accordance with the procedures required by Article 9, paragraph 1.
(2) Without prejudice to Article 48, paragraph 1, if the negotiable transport document or the negotiable electronic transport record expressly states that the goods may be delivered without the surrender of the transport document or the electronic transport record, the following rules apply:
(a) If the goods are not deliverable because (i) the holder, after having received a notice of arrival, does not, at the time or within the time period referred to in Article 43, claim delivery of the goods from the carrier after their arrival at the place of destination, (ii) the carrier refuses delivery because the person claiming to be a holder does not properly identify itself as one of the
persons referred to in Article 1, subparagraph 10 (a) (i), or (iii) the carrier is, after reasonable effort, unable to locate the holder in order to request delivery instructions, the carrier may so advise the shipper and request instructions in respect of the delivery of the goods. If, after reasonable effort, the carrier is unable to locate the shipper, the carrier may so advise the documentary shipper and request instructions in respect of the delivery of the goods;
(b) The carrier that delivers the goods upon instruction of the shipper or the documentary shipper in accordance with subparagraph 2 (a) of this Article is discharged from its obligation to deliver the goods under the contract of carriage to the holder, irrespective of whether the negotiable transport document has been surrendered to it, or the person claiming delivery under a negotiable
electronic transport record has demonstrated, in accordance with the procedures referred to in Article 9, paragraph 1, that it is the holder;
(c) The person giving instructions under subparagraph 2 (a) of this Article shall indemnify the carrier against loss arising from its being held liable to the holder under subparagraph 2 (e) of this Article. The carrier may refuse to follow those instructions if the person fails to provide adequate security as the carrier may reasonably request;

(d) A person that becomes a holder of the negotiable transport document or the negotiable electronic transport record after the carrier has delivered the goods pursuant to subparagraph 2 (b) of this Article, but pursuant to contractual or other arrangements made before such delivery acquires rights against the carrier under the contract of carriage, other than the right to claim delivery of the goods;
(e) Notwithstanding subparagraphs 2 (b) and 2 (d) of this Article, a holder that becomes a holder after such delivery, and that did not have and could not reasonably have had knowledge of such delivery at the time it became a holder, acquires the rights incorporated in the negotiable transport document or negotiable electronic transport record. When the contract particulars state the expected time of arrival of the goods, or indicate how to obtain information as to whether the goods have been delivered, it is presumed that the holder at the time that it became a holder had or could reasonably have had knowledge of the delivery of the goods.

Article 48. (Goods remaining undelivered) (1) For the purposes of this Article, goods shall be deemed to have remained undelivered only if, after their arrival at the place of destination:
(a) The consignee does not accept delivery of the goods pursuant to this chapter at the time and location referred to in Article 43;
(b) The controlling party, the holder, the shipper or the documentary shipper cannot be found or does not give the carrier adequate instructions pursuant to Articles 45, 46 and 47;
(c) The carrier is entitled or required to refuse delivery pursuant to Articles 44, 45, 46 and 47;
(d) The carrier is not allowed to deliver the goods to the consignee pursuant to the law or regulations of the place at which delivery is requested; or
(e) The goods are otherwise undeliverable by the carrier.
(2) Without prejudice to any other rights that the carrier may have against the shipper, controlling party or consignee, if the goods have remained undelivered, the carrier may, at the risk and expense of the person entitled to the goods, take such action in respect of the goods as circumstances may reasonably require, including:
(a) To store the goods at any suitable place;
(b) To unpack the goods if they are packed in containers or vehicles, or to act otherwise in respect of the goods, including by moving them; and
(c) To cause the goods to be sold or destroyed in accordance with the practices or pursuant to the law or regulations of the place where the goods are located at the time.
(3) The carrier may exercise the rights under paragraph 2 of this Article only after it has given reasonable notice of the intended action under paragraph 2 of this Article to the person stated in the contract particulars as the person, if any, to be notified of the arrival of the goods at the place of destination, and to one of the following persons in the order indicated, if known to the carrier: the consignee, the controlling party or the shipper.
(4) If the goods are sold pursuant to subparagraph 2 (c) of this Article, the carrier shall hold the proceeds of the sale for the benefit of the person entitled to the goods, subject to the deduction of any costs incurred by the carrier and any other amounts that are due to the carrier in connection with the carriage of those goods.
(5) The carrier shall not be liable for loss of or damage to goods that occurs during the time that they remain undelivered pursuant to this Article unless the claimant proves that such loss or damage resulted from the failure by the carrier to take steps that would have been reasonable in the circumstances to preserve the goods and that the carrier knew or ought to have known that the loss or damage to the goods would result from its failure to take such steps.

Article 49. (Retention of goods) Nothing in this Convention affects a right of the carrier or a performing party that may exist pursuant to the contract of carriage or the applicable law to
retain the goods to secure the payment of sums due.

Chapter 10 Rights of the controlling party

Article 50. (Exercise and extent of right of control) (1) The right of control may be exercised only by the controlling party and is limited to:
(a) The right to give or modify instructions in respect of the goods that do not constitute a variation of the contract of carriage;
(b) The right to obtain delivery of the goods at a scheduled port of call or, in respect of inland carriage, any place en route; and
(c) The right to replace the consignee by any other person including the controlling party.
(2) The right of control exists during the entire period of responsibility of the carrier, as provided in Article 12, and ceases when that period expires.

Article 51. (Identity of the controlling party and transfer of the right of control) (1) Except in the cases referred to in paragraphs 2, 3 and 4 of this Article:
(a) The shipper is the controlling party unless the shipper, when the contract of carriage is concluded, designates the consignee, the documentary shipper or another person as the controlling party;
(b) The controlling party is entitled to transfer the right of control to another person. The transfer becomes effective with respect to the carrier upon its notification of the transfer by the transferor, and the transferee becomes the controlling party; and
(c) The controlling party shall properly identify itself when it exercises the right of control.
(2) When a non-negotiable transport document has been issued that indicates that it shall be surrendered in order to obtain delivery of the goods:
(a) The shipper is the controlling party and may transfer the right of control to the consignee named in the transport document by transferring the document to that person without endorsement. If more than one original of the document was issued, all originals shall be transferred in order to effect a transfer of the right of control; and
(b) In order to exercise its right of control, the controlling party shall produce the document and properly identify itself. If more than one original of the document was issued, all originals shall be produced, failing which the right of control cannot be exercised.
(3) When a negotiable transport document is issued:
(a) The holder or, if more than one original of the negotiable transport document is issued, the holder of all originals is the controlling party;
(b) The holder may transfer the right of control by transferring the negotiable transport document to another person in accordance with Article 57. If more than one original of that document was issued, all originals shall be transferred to that person in order to effect a transfer of the right of control; and
(c) In order to exercise the right of control, the holder shall produce the negotiable transport document to the carrier, and if the holder is one of the persons referred to in Article 1, subparagraph 10 (a) (i), the holder shall properly identify itself. If more than one original of the document was issued, all originals shall be produced, failing which the right of control cannot be exercised.
(4) When a negotiable electronic transport record is issued:
(a) The holder is the controlling party;
(b) The holder may transfer the right of control to another person by transferring the negotiable electronic transport record in accordance with the procedures referred to in Article 9, paragraph 1; and
(c) In order to exercise the right of control, the holder shall demonstrate, in accordance with the procedures referred to in Article 9, paragraph 1, that it is the holder.

Article 52. (Carrier's execution of instructions) (1) Subject to paragraphs 2 and 3 of this Article, the carrier shall execute the instructions referred to in Article 50 if:
(a) The person giving such instructions is entitled to exercise the right of control;
(b) The instructions can reasonably be executed according to their terms at the moment that they reach the carrier; and
(c) The instructions will not interfere with the normal operations of the carrier, including its delivery practices.
(2) In any event, the controlling party shall reimburse the carrier for any reasonable additional expense that the carrier may incur and shall indemnify the carrier against loss or damage that the carrier may suffer as a result of diligently executing any instruction pursuant to this Article, including compensation that the carrier may become liable to pay for loss of or damage to other goods being carried.
(3) The carrier is entitled to obtain security from the controlling party for the amount of additional expense, loss or damage that the carrier reasonably expects will arise in connection with the execution of an instruction pursuant to this Article. The carrier may refuse to carry out the instructions if no such security is provided.
(4) The carrier's liability for loss of or damage to the goods or for delay in delivery resulting from its failure to comply with the instructions of the controlling party in breach of its obligation pursuant to paragraph 1 of this Article shall be subject to Articles 17 to 23, and the amount of the compensation payable by the carrier shall be subject to Articles 59 to 61.

Article 53. (Deemed delivery) Goods that are delivered pursuant to an instruction in accordance with Article 52, paragraph 1, are deemed to be delivered at the place of destination, and the provisions of chapter 9 relating to such delivery apply to such goods.

Article 54. (Variations to the contract of carriage) (1) The controlling party is the only person that may agree with the carrier to variations to the contract of carriage other than those referred to in Article 50, subparagraphs 1 (b) and (c).
(2) Variations to the contract of carriage, including those referred to in Article 50, subparagraphs 1 (b) and (c), shall be stated in a negotiable transport document or in a non-negotiable transport document that requires surrender, or incorporated in a negotiable electronic transport record, or, upon the request of the controlling party, shall be stated in a non-negotiable transport document
or incorporated in a non-negotiable electronic transport record. If so stated or incorporated, such variations shall be signed in accordance with Article 38.

Article 55. (Providing additional information, instructions or documents to carrier) (1) The controlling party, on request of the carrier or a performing party, shall provide in a timely manner information, instructions or documents relating to the goods not yet provided by the shipper and not otherwise reasonably available to the carrier that the carrier may reasonably need to perform its obligations under the contract of carriage.
(2) If the carrier, after reasonable effort, is unable to locate the controlling party or the controlling party is unable to provide adequate information, instructions or documents to the carrier, the shipper shall provide them. If the carrier, after reasonable effort, is unable to locate the shipper, the documentary shipper shall provide such information, instructions or documents.

Article 56. (Variation by agreement) The parties to the contract of carriage may vary the effect of Articles 50, subparagraphs 1 (b) and (c), 50, paragraph 2, and 5(2) The parties may also
restrict or exclude the transferability of the right of control referred to in Article 51, subparagraph 1 (b).

Chapter 11 Transfer of rights

Article 57. (When a negotiable transport document or negotiable electronic transport record is issued) (1)
When a negotiable transport document is issued, the holder may transfer the rights incorporated in the document by transferring it to another person:
(a) Duly endorsed either to such other person or in blank, if an order document; or
(b) Without endorsement, if: (i) a bearer document or a blank endorsed document; or (ii) a document made out to the order of a named person and the transfer is between the first holder and the named person.
(2) When a negotiable electronic transport record is issued, its holder may transfer the rights incorporated in it, whether it be made out to order or to the order of a named person, by transferring the electronic transport record in accordance with the procedures referred to in Article 9, paragraph 1.

Article 58. (Liability of holder) (1) Without prejudice to Article 55, a holder that is not the shipper and that does not exercise any right under the contract of carriage does not assume any
liability under the contract of carriage solely by reason of being a holder.
(2) A holder that is not the shipper and that exercises any right under the contract of carriage assumes any liabilities imposed on it under the contract of carriage to the extent that such liabilities are incorporated in or ascertainable from the negotiable transport document or the negotiable electronic transport record.
(3) For the purposes of paragraphs 1 and 2 of this Article, a holder that is not the shipper does not exercise any right under the contract of carriage solely because:
(a) It agrees with the carrier, pursuant to Article 10, to replace a negotiable transport document by a negotiable electronic transport record or to replace a negotiable electronic transport record by a negotiable transport document; or
(b) It transfers its rights pursuant to Article 57.

Chapter 12 Limits of liability

Article 59. (Limits of liability) (1) Subject to Articles 60 and 61, paragraph 1, the carrier's liability for breaches of its obligations under this Convention is limited to 875 units of account per package or other shipping unit, or 3 units of account per kilogram of the gross weight of the goods that are the subject of the claim or dispute, whichever amount is the higher, except when the value of the goods has been declared by the shipper and included in the contract particulars, or when a higher amount than the amount of limitation of liability set out in this Article has been agreed upon between the carrier and the shipper.
(2) When goods are carried in or on a container, pallet or similar Article of transport used to consolidate goods, or in or on a vehicle, the packages or shipping units enumerated in the contract particulars as packed in or on such

Article of transport or vehicle are deemed packages or shipping units. If not so enumerated, the goods in or on such Article of transport or vehicle are deemed one shipping unit.
(3) The unit of account referred to in this Article is the Special Drawing Right as defined by the International Monetary Fund. The amounts referred to in this Article are to be converted into the national currency of a State according to the value of such currency at the date of judgement or award or the date agreed upon by the parties. The value of a national currency, in terms of the Special Drawing Right, of a Contracting State that is a member of the International Monetary Fund is to be calculated in accordance with the method of valuation applied by the International Monetary Fund in effect at the date in question for its operations and transactions. The value of a national currency, in terms of the Special Drawing Right, of a Contracting State that is not a member of the International Monetary Fund is to be calculated in a manner to be determined by that State.

Article 60. (Limits of liability for loss caused by delay) Subject to Article 61, paragraph 2, compensation for loss of or damage to the goods due to delay shall be calculated in accordance with Article 22 and liability for economic loss due to delay is limited to an amount equivalent to two and one-half times the freight payable on the goods delayed. The total amount payable pursuant to this Article and Article 59, paragraph 1, may not exceed the limit that would be established pursuant to Article 59, paragraph 1, in respect of the total loss of the goods concerned.

Article 61. (Loss of the benefit of limitation of liability) (1) Neither the carrier nor any of the persons referred to in Article 18 is entitled to the benefit of the limitation of liability as provided in Article 59, or as provided in the contract of carriage, if the claimant proves that the loss resulting from the breach of the carrier's obligation under this Convention was attributable to a personal act or omission of the person claiming a right to limit done with the intent to cause such loss or recklessly and with knowledge that such loss would probably result.
(2) Neither the carrier nor any of the persons mentioned in Article 18 is entitled to the benefit of the limitation of liability as provided in Article 60 if the claimant proves that the delay in delivery resulted from a personal act or omission of the person claiming a right to limit done with the intent to cause the loss due to delay or recklessly and with knowledge that such loss would probably result.

Chapter 13 Time for suit

Article 62. (Period of time for suit) (1) No judicial or arbitral proceedings in respect of claims or disputes arising from a breach of an obligation under this Convention may be instituted after the
expiration of a period of two years.
(2) The period referred to in paragraph 1 of this Article commences on the day on which the carrier has delivered the goods or, in cases in which no goods have been delivered or only part of the goods have been delivered, on the last day on which the goods should have been delivered. The day on which the period commences is not included in the period.
(3) Notwithstanding the expiration of the period set out in paragraph 1 of this Article, one party may rely on its claim as a defence or for the purpose of set-off against a claim asserted by the other party.

Article 63. (Extension of time for suit) The period provided in Article 62 shall not be subject to suspension or interruption, but the person against which a claim is made may at any time during
the running of the period extend that period by a declaration to the claimant. This period may be further extended by another declaration or declarations.

Article 64. (Action for indemnity) An action for indemnity by a person held liable may be instituted after the expiration of the period provided in **Article** 62 if the indemnity action is
instituted within the later of:
(a) The time allowed by the applicable law in the jurisdiction where proceedings are instituted; or
(b) Ninety days commencing from the day when the person instituting the action for indemnity has either settled the claim or been served with process in the action against itself, whichever is earlier.

Article 65. (Actions against the person identified as the carrier) An action against the bareboat charterer or the person identified as the carrier pursuant to Article 37, paragraph 2, may be instituted after the expiration of the period provided in Article 62 if the action is instituted within the later of:
(a) The time allowed by the applicable law in the jurisdiction where proceedings are instituted; or
(b) Ninety days commencing from the day when the carrier has been identified, or the registered owner or bareboat charterer has rebutted the presumption that it is the carrier, pursuant to Article 37, paragraph 2.

Chapter 14 Jurisdiction

Article 66 (Actions against the carrier) Unless the contract of carriage contains an exclusive choice of court agreement that complies with **Article** 67 or 72, the plaintiff has the right to institute judicial proceedings under this Convention against the carrier:
(a) In a competent court within the jurisdiction of which is situated one of the following places:
(i) The domicile of the carrier;
(ii) The place of receipt agreed in the contract of carriage;
(iii) The place of delivery agreed in the contract of carriage; or
(iv) The port where the goods are initially loaded on a ship or the port where the goods are finally discharged from a ship; or
(b) In a competent court or courts designated by an agreement between the shipper and the carrier for the purpose of deciding claims against the carrier that may arise under this Convention.

Article 67. (Choice of court agreements) (1) The jurisdiction of a court chosen in accordance with Article 66, subparagraph (b), is exclusive for disputes between the parties to the contract only if the parties so agree and the agreement conferring jurisdiction:
(a) Is contained in a volume contract that clearly states the names and addresses of the parties and either (i) is individually negotiated or (ii) contains a prominent statement that there is an exclusive choice of court agreement and specifies the sections of the volume contract containing that agreement; and
(b) Clearly designates the courts of one Contracting State or one or more specific courts of one Contracting State.
(2) A person that is not a party to the volume contract is bound by an exclusive choice of court agreement concluded in accordance with paragraph 1 of this Article only if:
(a) The court is in one of the places designated in Article 66, subparagraph (a);
(b) That agreement is contained in the transport document or electronic transport record;
(c) That person is given timely and adequate notice of the court where the action shall be brought and that the jurisdiction of that court is exclusive; and
(d) The law of the court seized recognizes that that person may be bound by the exclusive choice of court agreement.

Article 68. (Actions against the maritime performing party) The plaintiff has the right to institute judicial proceedings under this Convention against the maritime performing party in a competent court within the jurisdiction of which is situated one of the following places:
(a) The domicile of the maritime performing party; or
(b) The port where the goods are received by the maritime performing party, the port where the goods are delivered by the maritime performing party or the port in which the maritime performing party performs its activities with respect to the goods.

Article 69. (No additional bases of jurisdiction) Subject to Articles 71 and 72, no judicial proceedings under this Convention against the carrier or a maritime performing party may be instituted in a court not designated pursuant to Article 66 or 68.

Article 70. (Arrest and provisional or protective measures) Nothing in this Convention affects jurisdiction with regard to provisional or protective measures, including arrest. A court in a State in which a provisional or protective measure was taken does not have jurisdiction to determine the case upon its merits unless:
(a) The requirements of this chapter are fulfilled; or
(b) An international convention that applies in that State so provides.

Article 71. (Consolidation and removal of actions) (1) Except when there is an exclusive choice of court agreement that is binding pursuant to Article 67 or 72, if a single action is brought against both the carrier and the maritime performing party arising out of a single occurrence, the action may be instituted only in a court designated pursuant to both Article 66 and Article 68. If there is no such court, such action may be instituted in a court designated pursuant to Article 68, subparagraph (b), if there is such a court.
(2) Except when there is an exclusive choice of court agreement that is binding pursuant to Article 67 or 72, a carrier or a maritime performing party that institutes an action seeking a declaration of non-liability or any other action that would deprive a person of its right to select the forum pursuant to Article 66 or 68 shall, at the request of the defendant, withdraw that action once the defendant has chosen a court designated pursuant to Article 66 or 68, whichever is applicable, where the action may be recommenced.

Article 72. (Agreement after a dispute has arisen and jurisdiction when the defendant has entered an appearance)
(1) After a dispute has arisen, the parties to the dispute may agree to resolve it in any competent court.
(2) A competent court before which a defendant appears, without contesting jurisdiction in accordance with the rules of that court, has jurisdiction.

Article 73. (Recognition and enforcement) (1) A decision made in one Contracting State by a court having jurisdiction under this Convention shall be recognized and enforced in another Contracting State in accordance with the law of such latter Contracting State when both
States have made a declaration in accordance with Article 74.
(2) A court may refuse recognition and enforcement based on the grounds for the refusal of recognition and enforcement available pursuant to its law.
(3) This chapter shall not affect the application of the rules of a regional economic integration organization that is a party to this Convention, as concerns the recognition or enforcement of judgements as between member States of the regional economic integration organization, whether adopted before or after this Convention.

Article 74. (Application of chapter 14) The provisions of this chapter shall bind only Contracting States that declare in accordance with Article 91 that they will be bound by them.

Chapter 15 Arbitration

Article 75. (Arbitration agreements) (1) Subject to this chapter, parties may agree that any dispute that may arise relating to the carriage of goods under this Convention shall be referred to
arbitration.
(2) The arbitration proceedings shall, at the option of the person asserting a claim against the carrier, take place at:
(a) Any place designated for that purpose in the arbitration agreement; or
(b) Any other place situated in a State where any of the following places is located:
(i) The domicile of the carrier;
(ii) The place of receipt agreed in the contract of carriage;
(iii) The place of delivery agreed in the contract of carriage; or
(iv) The port where the goods are initially loaded on a ship or the port where the goods are finally discharged from a ship.
(3) The designation of the place of arbitration in the agreement is binding for disputes between the parties to the agreement if the agreement is contained in a volume contract that clearly states the names and addresses of the parties and either:
(a) Is individually negotiated; or
(b) Contains a prominent statement that there is an arbitration agreement and specifies the sections of the volume contract containing the arbitration agreement.
(4) When an arbitration agreement has been concluded in accordance with paragraph 3 of this Article, a person that is not a party to the volume contract is bound by the designation of the place of arbitration in that agreement only if:
(a) The place of arbitration designated in the agreement is situated in one of the places referred to in subparagraph 2 (b) of this Article;
(b) The agreement is contained in the transport document or electronic transport record;
(c) The person to be bound is given timely and adequate notice of the place of arbitration; and
(d) Applicable law permits that person to be bound by the arbitration agreement.
(5) The provisions of paragraphs 1, 2, 3 and 4 of this Article are deemed to be part of every arbitration clause or agreement, and any term of such clause or agreement to the extent that it is inconsistent therewith is void.

Article 76. (Arbitration agreement in non-liner transportation) (1) Nothing in this Convention affects the enforceability of an arbitration agreement in a contract of carriage in non-liner transportation to which this Convention or the provisions of this Convention apply by reason of:
(a) The application of Article 7; or
(b) The parties' voluntary incorporation of this Convention in a contract of carriage that would not otherwise be subject to this Convention.
(2) Notwithstanding paragraph 1 of this Article, an arbitration agreement in a transport document or electronic transport record to which this Convention applies by reason of the application of Article 7 is subject to this chapter unless such a transport document or electronic transport record:

(a) Identifies the parties to and the date of the charter party or other contract excluded from the application of this Convention by reason of the application of Article 6; and
(b) Incorporates by specific reference the clause in the charter party or other contract that contains the terms of the arbitration agreement.

Article 77. (Agreement to arbitrate after a dispute has arisen) Notwithstanding the provisions of this chapter and chapter 14, after a dispute has arisen the parties to the dispute may agree to resolve it by arbitration in any place.

Article 78. (Application of chapter 15) The provisions of this chapter shall bind only Contracting States that declare in accordance with Article 91 that they will be bound by them.

Chapter 16 Validity of contractual terms

Article 79. (General provisions) (1) Unless otherwise provided in this Convention, any term in a contract of carriage is void to the extent that it:
(a) Directly or indirectly excludes or limits the obligations of the carrier or a maritime performing party under this Convention;
(b) Directly or indirectly excludes or limits the liability of the carrier or a maritime performing party for breach of an obligation under this Convention; or
(c) Assigns a benefit of insurance of the goods in favour of the carrier or a person referred to in Article 18.
(2) Unless otherwise provided in this Convention, any term in a contract of carriage is void to the extent that it:
(a) Directly or indirectly excludes, limits or increases the obligations under this Convention of the shipper, consignee, controlling party, holder or documentary shipper; or
(b) Directly or indirectly excludes, limits or increases the liability of the shipper, consignee, controlling party, holder or documentary shipper for breach of any of its obligations under this Convention.

Article 80. (Special rules for volume contracts) (1) Notwithstanding Article 79, as between the carrier and the shipper, a volume contract to which this Convention applies may provide for greater or lesser rights, obligations and liabilities than those imposed by this Convention.
(2) A derogation pursuant to paragraph 1 of this Article is binding only when:
(a) The volume contract contains a prominent statement that it derogates from this Convention;
(b) The volume contract is (i) individually negotiated or (ii) prominently specifies the sections of the volume contract containing the derogations;
(c) The shipper is given an opportunity and notice of the opportunity to conclude a contract of carriage on terms and conditions that comply with this Convention without any derogation under this Article; and
(d) The derogation is neither (i) incorporated by reference from another document nor (ii) included in a contract of adhesion that is not subject to negotiation.
(3) A carrier's public schedule of prices and services, transport document, electronic transport record or similar document is not a volume contract pursuant to paragraph 1 of this Article, but a volume contract may incorporate such documents by reference as terms of the contract.
(4) Paragraph 1 of this Article does not apply to rights and obligations provided in Articles 14, subparagraphs (a) and (b), 29 and 32 or to liability arising from the breach thereof, nor does it apply to any liability arising from an act or omission referred to in Article 61.
(5) The terms of the volume contract that derogate from this Convention, if the volume contract satisfies the requirements of paragraph 2 of this Article, apply between the carrier and any person other than the shipper provided that:
(a) Such person received information that prominently states that the volume contract derogates from this Convention and gave its express consent to be bound by such derogations; and
(b) Such consent is not solely set forth in a carrier's public schedule of prices and services, transport document or electronic transport record.
(6) The party claiming the benefit of the derogation bears the burden of proof that the conditions for derogation have been fulfilled.

Article 81. (Special rules for live animals and certain other goods) Notwithstanding Article 79 and without prejudice to Article 80, the contract of carriage may exclude or limit the obligations or the liability of both the carrier and a maritime performing party if:
(a) The goods are live animals, but any such exclusion or limitation will not be effective if the claimant proves that the loss of or damage to the goods, or delay in delivery, resulted from an act or omission of the carrier or of a

person referred to in Article 18, done with the intent to cause such loss of or damage to the goods or such loss due to delay or done recklessly and with knowledge that such loss or damage or such loss due to delay would probably result; or

(b) The character or condition of the goods or the circumstances and terms and conditions under which the carriage is to be performed are such as reasonably to justify a special agreement, provided that such contract of carriage is not related to ordinary commercial shipments made in the ordinary course of trade and that no negotiable transport document or negotiable electronic transport record is issued for the carriage of the goods.

Chapter 17 Matters not governed by this Convention

Article 82. (International conventions governing the carriage of goods by other modes of transport) Nothing in this Convention affects the application of any of the following international conventions in force at the time this Convention enters into force, including any future amendment to such conventions, that regulate the liability of the carrier for loss of or damage to the goods:

(a) Any convention governing the carriage of goods by air to the extent that such convention according to its provisions applies to any part of the contract of carriage;

(b) Any convention governing the carriage of goods by road to the extent that such convention according to its provisions applies to the carriage of goods that remain loaded on a road cargo vehicle carried on board a ship;

(c) Any convention governing the carriage of goods by rail to the extent that such convention according to its provisions applies to carriage of goods by sea as a supplement to the carriage by rail; or

(d) Any convention governing the carriage of goods by inland waterways to the extent that such convention according to its provisions applies to a carriage of goods without trans-shipment both by inland waterways and sea.

Article 83. (Global limitation of liability) Nothing in this Convention affects the application of any international convention or national law regulating the global limitation of liability of vessel owners.

Article 84. (General average) Nothing in this Convention affects the application of terms in the contract of carriage or provisions of national law regarding the adjustment of general average.

Article 85. (Passengers and luggage) This Convention does not apply to a contract of carriage for passengers and their luggage.

Article 86. (Damage caused by nuclear incident) No liability arises under this Convention for damage caused by a nuclear incident if the operator of a nuclear installation is liable for such damage:

(a) Under the Paris Convention on Third Party Liability in the Field of Nuclear Energy of 29 July 1960 as amended by the Additional Protocol of 28 January 1964 and by the Protocols of 16 November 1982 and 12 February 2004, the Vienna Convention on Civil Liability for Nuclear Damage of 21 May 1963 as amended by the Joint Protocol Relating to the Application of the Vienna Convention and the Paris Convention of 21 September 1988 and as amended by the
Protocol to Amend the 1963 Vienna Convention on Civil Liability for Nuclear Damage of 12 September 1997, or the Convention on Supplementary Compensation for Nuclear Damage of 12 September 1997, including any amendment to these conventions and any future convention in respect of the liability of the operator of a nuclear installation for damage caused by a nuclear incident; or

(b) Under national law applicable to the liability for such damage, provided that such law is in all respects as favourable to persons that may suffer damage as either the Paris or Vienna Conventions or the Convention on Supplementary Compensation for Nuclear Damage.

Chapter 18 Final clauses

Article 87. (Depositary) The Secretary-General of the United Nations is hereby designated as the depositary of this Convention.

Article 88. (Signature, ratification, acceptance, approval or accession) (1) This Convention is open for signature by all States at Rotterdam, the Netherlands, on 23 September 2009, and thereafter at the Headquarters of the United Nations in New York.

(2) This Convention is subject to ratification, acceptance or approval by the signatory States.

(3) This Convention is open for accession by all States that are not signatory States as from the date it is open for signature.
(4) Instruments of ratification, acceptance, approval and accession are to be deposited with the Secretary-General of the United Nations.

Article 89. (Denunciation of other conventions) (1) A State that ratifies, accepts, approves or accedes to this Convention and is a party to the International Convention for the Unification of certain Rules of Law relating to Bills of Lading signed at Brussels on 25 August 1924, to the
Protocol to amend the International Convention for the Unification of certain Rules of Law relating to Bills of Lading, signed at Brussels on 23 February 1968, or to the Protocol to amend the International Convention for the Unification of certain Rules of Law relating to Bills of Lading as Modified by the Amending Protocol of 23 February 1968, signed at Brussels on 21 December 1979, shall at the same time denounce that Convention and the protocol or protocols
thereto to which it is a party by notifying the Government of Belgium to that effect, with a declaration that the denunciation is to take effect as from the date when this Convention enters into force in respect of that State.
(2) A State that ratifies, accepts, approves or accedes to this Convention and is a party to the United Nations Convention on the Carriage of Goods by Sea concluded at Hamburg on 31 March 1978 shall at the same time denounce that Convention by notifying the Secretary-General of the United Nations to that effect, with a declaration that the denunciation is to take effect as from the date when this Convention enters into force in respect of that State.
(3) For the purposes of this Article, ratifications, acceptances, approvals and accessions in respect of this Convention by States parties to the instruments listed in paragraphs 1 and 2 of this **Article** that are notified to the depositary after this Convention has entered into force are not effective until such denunciations as may be required on the part of those States in respect of these instruments have become effective. The depositary of this Convention shall consult with the Government of Belgium, as the depositary of the instruments referred to in paragraph 1 of this Article, so as to ensure necessary coordination in this respect.

Article 90. (Reservations) No reservation is permitted to this Convention.

Article 91. (Procedure and effect of declarations) (1) The declarations permitted by Articles 74 and 78 may be made at any time. The initial declarations permitted by Article 92, paragraph 1, and Article 93, paragraph 2, shall be made at the time of signature, ratification, acceptance, approval or accession. No other declaration is permitted under this Convention.
(2) Declarations made at the time of signature are subject to confirmation upon ratification, acceptance or approval.
(3) Declarations and their confirmations are to be in writing and to be formally notified to the depositary.
(4) A declaration takes effect simultaneously with the entry into force of this Convention in respect of the State concerned. However, a declaration of which the depositary receives formal notification after such entry into force takes effect on the first day of the month following the expiration of six months after the date of its receipt by the depositary.
(5) Any State that makes a declaration under this Convention may withdraw it at any time by a formal notification in writing addressed to the depositary. The withdrawal of a declaration, or its modification where permitted by this Convention, takes effect on the first day of the month following the expiration of six months after the date of the receipt of the notification by the depositary.

Article 92. (Effect in domestic territorial units) (1) If a Contracting State has two or more territorial units in which different systems of law are applicable in relation to the matters dealt with in this Convention, it may, at the time of signature, ratification, acceptance, approval or accession, declare that this Convention is to extend to all its territorial units or only to one or more of them, and may amend its declaration by submitting another declaration at any time.
(2) These declarations are to be notified to the depositary and are to state expressly the territorial units to which the Convention extends.
(3) When a Contracting State has declared pursuant to this Article that this Convention extends to one or more but not all of its territorial units, a place located in a territorial unit to which this Convention does not extend is not considered to be in a Contracting State for the purposes of this Convention.
(4) If a Contracting State makes no declaration pursuant to paragraph 1 of this Article, the Convention is to extend to all territorial units of that State.

Article 93. (Participation by regional economic integration organizations) (1) A regional economic integration organization that is constituted by sovereign States and has competence over certain matters governed by this Convention may similarly sign, ratify, accept, approve or accede to this Convention. The regional economic integration organization shall in that case have the rights and obligations of a Contracting State, to the extent that that organization has competence over matters governed by this Convention. When the number of Contracting States is relevant in this Convention, the regional economic integration organization does not count as a Contracting State in addition to its member States which are Contracting States.
(2) The regional economic integration organization shall, at the time of signature, ratification, acceptance, approval or accession, make a declaration to the depositary specifying the matters governed by this Convention in respect of which competence has been transferred to that organization by its member States. The regional economic integration organization shall promptly notify the depositary of any changes to the distribution of competence, including new transfers of competence, specified in the declaration pursuant to this paragraph.
(3) Any reference to a "Contracting State" or "Contracting States" in this Convention applies equally to a regional economic integration organization when the context so requires.

Article 94. (Entry into force) (1) This Convention enters into force on the first day of the month following the expiration of one year after the date of deposit of the twentieth instrument of ratification, acceptance, approval or accession.
(2) For each State that becomes a Contracting State to this Convention after the date of the deposit of the twentieth instrument of ratification, acceptance, approval or accession, this Convention enters into force on the first day of the month following the expiration of one year after the deposit of the appropriate instrument on behalf of that State.
(3) Each Contracting State shall apply this Convention to contracts of carriage concluded on or after the date of the entry into force of this Convention in respect of that State.

Article 95. (Revision and amendment) (1)At the request of not less than one third of the Contracting States to this Convention, the Secretary-General of the United Nations shall convene a conference of the Contracting States for revising or amending it.
(2) Any instrument of ratification, acceptance, approval or accession deposited after the entry into force of an amendment to this Convention is deemed to apply to the Convention as amended.

Article 96. (Denunciation of this Convention) (1) A Contracting State may denounce this Convention at any time by means of a notification in writing addressed to the depositary.
(2) The denunciation takes effect on the first day of the month following the expiration of one year after the notification is received by the depositary. If a longer period is specified in the notification, the denunciation takes effect upon the expiration of such longer period after the notification is received by the depositary.

United Nations Convention on the Recognition and Enforcement of Foreign Arbitral Awards (New York, 1958)

Article I. (1) This Convention shall apply to the recognition and enforcement of arbitral awards made in the territory of a State other than the State where the recognition and enforcement of such awards are sought, and arising out of differences between persons, whether physical or legal. It shall also apply to arbitral awards not considered as domestic awards in the State where their recognition and enforcement are sought.
(2) The term "arbitral awards" shall include not only awards made by arbitrators appointed for each case but also those made by permanent arbitral bodies to which the parties have submitted.
(3) When signing, ratifying or acceding to this Convention, or notifying extension under article X hereof, any State may on the basis of reciprocity declare that it will apply the Convention to the recognition and enforcement of awards made only in the territory of another Contracting State. It may also declare that it will apply the Convention only to differences arising out of legal relationships, whether contractual or not, which are considered as commercial under the national law of the State making such declaration.

Article II. (1) Each Contracting State shall recognize an agreement in writing under which the parties undertake to submit to arbitration all or any differences which have arisen or which may arise between them in respect of a defined legal relationship, whether contractual or not, concerning a subject matter capable of settlement by arbitration.
(2) The term "agreement in writing" shall include an arbitral clause in a contract or an arbitration agreement, signed by the parties or contained in an exchange of letters or telegrams.
(3) The court of a Contracting State, when seized of an action in a matter in respect of which the parties have made an agreement within the meaning of this article, at the request of one of the parties, refer the parties to arbitration, unless it finds that the said agreement is null and void, inoperative or incapable of being performed.

Article III. Each Contracting State shall recognize arbitral awards as binding and enforce them in accordance with the rules of procedure of the territory where the award is relied upon, under the conditions laid down in the following articles. There shall not be imposed substantially more onerous conditions or higher fees or charges on the recognition or enforcement of arbitral awards to which this Convention applies than are imposed on the recognition or enforcement of domestic arbitral awards.

Article IV. (1) To obtain the recognition and enforcement mentioned in the preceding article, the party applying for recognition and enforcement shall, at the time of the application, supply:
(a) The duly authenticated original award or a duly certified copy thereof;
(b) The original agreement referred to in article II or a duly certified copy thereof.
(2) If the said award or agreement is not made in an official language of the country in which the award is relied upon, the party applying for recognition and enforcement of the award shall produce a translation of these documents into such language. The translation shall be certified by an official or sworn translator or by a diplomatic or consular agent.

Article V. (1) Recognition and enforcement of the award may be refused, at the request of the party against whom it is invoked, only if that party furnishes to the competent authority where the recognition and enforcement is sought, proof that:
(a) The parties to the agreement referred to in article II were, under the law applicable to them, under some incapacity, or the said agreement is not valid under the law to which the parties have subjected it or, failing any indication thereon, under the law of the country where the award was made; or
(b) The party against whom the award is invoked was not given proper notice of the appointment of the arbitrator or of the arbitration proceedings or was otherwise unable to present his case; or
(c) The award deals with a difference not contemplated by or not falling within the terms of the submission to arbitration, or it contains decisions on matters beyond the scope of the submission to arbitration, provided that, if the decisions on matters submitted to arbitration can be separated from those not so submitted, that part of the award which contains decisions on matters submitted to arbitration may be recognized and enforced; or
(d) The composition of the arbitral authority or the arbitral procedure was not in accordance with the agreement of the parties, or, failing such agreement, was not in accordance with the law of the country where the arbitration took place; or
(e) The award has not yet become binding on the parties, or has been set aside or suspended by a competent authority of the country in which, or under the law of which, that award was made.
(2) Recognition and enforcement of an arbitral award may also be refused if the competent authority in the country

where recognition and enforcement is sought finds that:
(a) The subject matter of the difference is not capable of settlement by arbitration under the law of that country; or
(b) The recognition or enforcement of the award would be contrary to the public policy of that country.

Article VI. If an application for the setting aside or suspension of the award has been made to a competent authority referred to in article V (1) (e), the authority before which the award is sought to be relied upon may, if it considers it proper, adjourn the decision on the enforcement of the award and may also, on the application of the party claiming enforcement of the award, order the other party to give suitable security.

Article VII. (1) The provisions of the present Convention shall not affect the validity of multilateral or bilateral agreements concerning the recognition and enforcement of arbitral awards entered into by the Contracting States nor deprive any interested party of any right he may have to avail himself of an arbitral award in the manner and to the extent allowed by the law or the treaties of the country where such award is sought to be relied upon.
(2) The Geneva Protocol on Arbitration Clauses of 1923 and the Geneva Convention on the Execution of Foreign Arbitral Awards of 1927 shall cease to have effect between Contracting States on their becoming bound and to the extent that they become bound, by this Convention.

Article VIII. (1) This Convention shall be open until 31 December 1958 for signature on behalf of any Member of the United Nations and also on behalf of any other State which is or hereafter becomes a member of any specialized agency of the United Nations, or which is or hereafter becomes a party to the Statute of the International Court of Justice, or any other State to which an invitation has been addressed by the General Assembly of the United Nations.
(2) This Convention shall be ratified and the instrument of ratification shall be deposited with the Secretary-General of the United Nations.

Article IX. (1) This Convention shall be open for accession to all States referred to in article VIII.
(2) Accession shall be effected by the deposit of an instrument of accession with the Secretary-General of the United Nations.

Article X. (1) Any State may, at the time of signature, ratification or accession, declare that this Convention shall extend to all or any of the territories for the international relations of which it is responsible. Such a declaration shall take effect when the Convention enters into force for the State concerned.
(2) At any time thereafter any such extension shall be made by notification addressed to the Secretary-General of the United Nations and shall take effect as from the ninetieth day after the day of receipt by the Secretary-General of the United Nations of this notification, or as from the date of entry into force of the Convention for the State concerned, whichever is the later.
(3) With respect to those territories to which this Convention is not extended at the time of signature, ratification or accession, each State concerned shall consider the possibility of taking the necessary steps in order to extend the application of this Convention to such territories, subject, where necessary for constitutional reasons, to the consent of the Governments of such territories.

Article XI. In the case of a federal or non-unitary State, the following provisions shall apply:
(a) With respect to those articles of this Convention that come within the legislative jurisdiction of the federal authority, the obligations of the federal Government shall to this extent be the same as those of Contracting States which are not federal States;
(b) With respect to those articles of this Convention that come within the legislative jurisdiction of constituent states or provinces which are not, under the constitutional system of the federation, bound to take legislative action, the federal Government shall bring such articles with a favourable recommendation to the notice of the appropriate authorities of constituent states or provinces at the earliest possible moment;
(c) A federal State Party to this Convention shall, at the request of any other Contracting State transmitted through the Secretary-General of the United Nations, supply a statement of the law and practice of the federation and its constituent units in regard to any particular provision of this Convention, showing the extent to which effect has been given to that provision by legislative or other action.

Article XII. (1) This Convention shall come into force on the ninetieth day following the date of deposit of the third instrument of ratification or accession.
(2) For each State ratifying or acceding to this Convention after the deposit of the third instrument of ratification or accession, this Convention shall enter into force on the ninetieth day after deposit by such State of its instrument of

ratification or accession.

Article XIII. (1) Any Contracting State may denounce this Convention by a written notification to the Secretary-General of the United Nations. Denunciation shall take effect one year after the date of receipt of the notification by the Secretary-General.
(2) Any State which has made a declaration or notification under article X may, at any time thereafter, by notification to the Secretary-General of the United Nations, declare that this Convention shall cease to extend to the territory concerned one year after the date of the receipt of the notification by the Secretary-General.
(3) This Convention shall continue to be applicable to arbitral awards in respect of which recognition and enforcement proceedings have been instituted before the denunciation takes effect.

Article XIV. A Contracting State shall not be entitled to avail itself of the present Convention against other Contracting States except to the extent that it is itself bound to apply the Convention.

Article XV. The Secretary-General of the United Nations shall notify the States contemplated in article VIII of the following:
(a) Signatures and ratifications in accordance with article VIII;
(b) Accessions in accordance with article IX;
(c) Declarations and notifications under articles I, X and XI;
(d) The date upon which this Convention enters into force in accordance with article XII;
(e) Denunciations and notifications in accordance with article XIII.

Article XVI. (1) This Convention, of which the Chinese, English, French, Russian and Spanish texts shall be equally authentic, shall be deposited in the archives of the United Nations.
(2) The Secretary-General of the United Nations shall transmit a certified copy of this Convention to the States contemplated in article VIII.

UNCITRAL Model Law on International Commercial Arbitration 1985 (as amended in 2006)[31]

Chapter I. General Provisions

Article 1. (1) This Law applies to international commercial arbitration, subject to any agreement in force between this State and any other State or States.
(2) The provisions of this Law, except articles 8, 9, 17 H, 17 I, 17 J, 35 and 36, apply only if the place of arbitration is in the territory of this State.
(3) An arbitration is international if:
(a) the parties to an arbitration agreement have, at the time of the conclusion of that agreement, their places of business in different States; or
(b) one of the following places is situated outside the State in which the parties have their places of business:
(i) the place of arbitration if determined in, or pursuant to, the arbitration agreement;
(ii) any place where a substantial part of the obligations of the commercial relationship is to be performed or the place with which the subject-matter of the dispute is most closely connected; or
(c) the parties have expressly agreed that the subject matter of the arbitration agreement relates to more than one country.
(4) For the purposes of paragraph (3) of this article:
(a) if a party has more than one place of business, the place of business is that which has the closest relationship to the arbitration agreement;
(b) if a party does not have a place of business, reference is to be made to his habitual residence.
(5) This Law shall not affect any other law of this State by virtue of which certain disputes may not be submitted to arbitration or may be submitted to arbitration only according to provisions other than those of this Law.

Article 2. For the purposes of this Law:
(a) "arbitration" means any arbitration whether or not administered by a permanent arbitral institution;
(b) "arbitral tribunal" means a sole arbitrator or a panel of arbitrator;
(c) "court" means a body or organ of the judicial system of a State;
(d) where a provision of this Law, except article 28, leaves the parties free to determine a certain issue, such freedom includes the right of the parties to authorize a third party, including an institution, to make that determination;
(e) where a provision of this Law refers to the fact that the parties have agreed or that they may agree or in any other way refers to an agreement of the parties, such agreement includes any arbitration rules referred to in that agreement;
(f) where a provision of this Law, other than in articles 25(a) and 32(2) (a), refers to a claim, it also applies to a counter-claim, and where it refers to a defence, it also applies to a defence to such counter-claim.

Article 2 A. (1) In the interpretation of this Law, regard is to be had to its international origin and to the need to promote uniformity in its application and the observance of good faith.
(2) Questions concerning matters governed by this Law which are not expressly settled in it are to be settled in conformity with the general principles on which this Law is based.

Article 3. (1) Unless otherwise agreed by the parties:
(a) any written communication is deemed to have been received if it is delivered to the addressee personally or if it is delivered at his place of business, habitual residence or mailing address; if none of these can be found after making a reasonable inquiry, a written communication is deemed to have been received if it is sent to the addressee's last-known place of business,
habitual residence or mailing address by registered letter or any other means which provides a record of the attempt to deliver it;
(b) the communication is deemed to have been received on the day it is so delivered.
(2) The provisions of this article do not apply to communications in court proceedings.

Article 4. A party who knows that any provision of this Law from which the parties may derogate or any requirement under the arbitration agreement has not been complied with and yet proceeds with the arbitration

---

[31] Reproduced with kind permission from UNCITRAL.

without stating his objection to such non-compliance without undue delay or, if a time-limit is provided therefor, within such period of time, shall be deemed to have
waived his right to object.

Article 5. In matters governed by this Law, no court shall intervene except where so provided in this Law.

Article 6. The functions referred to in articles 11(3), 11(4), 13(3), 14, 16(3) and 34(2) shall be performed by ... [Each State enacting this model law specifies the court, courts or, where referred to therein, other authority competent to perform these functions.]

Chapter II. Arbitration Agreement

Option I

Article 7. (1) "Arbitration agreement" is an agreement by the parties to submit to arbitration all or certain disputes which have arisen or which may arise between them in respect of a defined legal relationship, whether contractual or not. An arbitration agreement may be in the form of an arbitration clause in a contract or in the form of a separate agreement.
(2) The arbitration agreement shall be in writing.
(3) An arbitration agreement is in writing if its content is recorded in any form, whether or not the arbitration agreement or contract has been concluded orally, by conduct, or by other means.
(4) The requirement that an arbitration agreement be in writing is met by an electronic communication if the information contained therein is accessible so as to be useable for subsequent reference; "electronic communication" means any communication that the parties make by means of data messages; "data message" means information generated, sent, received or
stored by electronic, magnetic, optical or similar means, including, but not limited to, electronic data interchange (EDI), electronic mail, telegram, telex or telecopy.
(5) Furthermore, an arbitration agreement is in writing if it is contained in an exchange of statements of claim and defence in which the existence of an agreement is alleged by one party and not denied by the other.
(6) The reference in a contract to any document containing an arbitration clause constitutes an arbitration agreement in writing, provided that the reference is such as to make that clause part of the contract.

Option II

Article 7. "Arbitration agreement" is an agreement by the parties to submit to arbitration all or certain disputes which have arisen or which may arise between them in respect of a defined legal relationship, whether contractual or not.

Article 8. (1) A court before which an action is brought in a matter which is the subject of an arbitration agreement shall, if a party so requests not later than when submitting his first statement on the substance of the dispute, refer the parties to arbitration unless it finds that the agreement is null and void, inoperative or incapable of being performed.
(2) Where an action referred to in paragraph (1) of this article has been brought, arbitral proceedings may nevertheless be commenced or continued, and an award may be made, while the issue is pending before the court.

Article 9. It is not incompatible with an arbitration agreement for a party to request, before or during arbitral proceedings, from a court an interim measure of protection and for a court to grant such measure.

Chapter III. Composition of Arbitral Tribunal

Article 10. (1) The parties are free to determine the number of arbitrators.
(2) Failing such determination, the number of arbitrators shall be three.

Article 11. (1) No person shall be precluded by reason of his nationality from acting as an arbitrator, unless otherwise agreed by the parties.
(2) The parties are free to agree on a procedure of appointing the arbitrator or arbitrators, subject to the provisions of paragraphs (4) and (5) of this article.
(3) Failing such agreement,

(a) in an arbitration with three arbitrators, each party shall appoint one arbitrator, and the two arbitrators thus appointed shall appoint the third arbitrator; if a party fails to appoint the arbitrator within thirty days of receipt of a request to do so from the other party, or if the two arbitrators fail to agree on the third arbitrator within thirty days of their appointment, the
appointment shall be made, upon request of a party, by the court or other authority specified in article 6;
(b) in an arbitration with a sole arbitrator, if the parties are unable to agree on the arbitrator, he shall be appointed, upon request of a party, by the court or other authority specified in article 6.
(4) Where, under an appointment procedure agreed upon by the parties,
(a) a party fails to act as required under such procedure, or
(b) the parties, or two arbitrators, are unable to reach an agreement expected of them under such procedure, or
(c) a third party, including an institution, fails to perform any function entrusted to it under such procedure, any party may request the court or other authority specified in article 6 to take the necessary measure, unless the agreement on the appointment procedure provides other means for securing the appointment.
(5) A decision on a matter entrusted by paragraph (3) or (4) of this article to the court or other authority specified in article 6 shall be subject to no appeal. The court or other authority, in appointing an arbitrator, shall have due regard to any qualifications required of the arbitrator by the agreement of the parties and to such considerations as are likely to secure the appointment
of an independent and impartial arbitrator and, in the case of a sole or third arbitrator, shall take into account as well the advisability of appointing an arbitrator of a nationality other than those of the parties.

Article 12. (1) When a person is approached in connection with his possible appointment as an arbitrator, he shall disclose any circumstances likely to give rise to justifiable doubts as to his impartiality or independence. An arbitrator, from the time of his appointment and throughout the arbitral proceedings, shall without delay disclose any such circumstances to the parties unless they have already been informed of them by him.
(2) An arbitrator may be challenged only if circumstances exist that give rise to justifiable doubts as to his impartiality or independence, or if he does not possess qualifications agreed to by the parties. A party may challenge an arbitrator appointed by him, or in whose appointment he has participated, only for reasons of which he becomes aware after the appointment has been made.

Article 13. (1) The parties are free to agree on a procedure for challenging an arbitrator, subject to the provisions of paragraph (3) of this article.
(2) Failing such agreement, a party who intends to challenge an arbitrator shall, within fifteen days after becoming aware of the constitution of the arbitral tribunal or after becoming aware of any circumstance referred to in article 12(2), send a written statement of the reasons for the challenge to the arbitral tribunal. Unless the challenged arbitrator withdraws from his office or the other party agrees to the challenge, the arbitral tribunal shall decide on the challenge.
(3) If a challenge under any procedure agreed upon by the parties or under the procedure of paragraph (2) of this article is not successful, the challenging party may request, within thirty days after having received notice of the decision rejecting the challenge, the court or other authority specified in article 6 to decide on the challenge, which decision shall be subject to no
appeal; while such a request is pending, the arbitral tribunal, including the challenged arbitrator, may continue the arbitral proceedings and make an award.

Article 14. (1) If an arbitrator becomes de jure or de facto unable to perform his functions or for other reasons fails to act without undue delay, his mandate terminates if he withdraws from his office or if the parties agree on the termination. Otherwise, if a controversy remains concerning any of these grounds, any party may request the court or other authority specified in article 6 to decide on the termination of the mandate, which decision shall be subject to no appeal.
(2) If, under this article or article 13(2), an arbitrator withdraws from his office or a party agrees to the termination of the mandate of an arbitrator, this does not imply acceptance of the validity of any ground referred to in this article or article 12(2).

Article 15. Where the mandate of an arbitrator terminates under article 13 or 14 or because of his withdrawal from office for any other reason or because of the revocation of his mandate by agreement of the parties or in any other case of termination of his mandate, a substitute arbitrator shall be appointed according to the rules that were applicable to the appointment of the arbitrator
being replaced.

Chapter IV. Jurisdiction of Arbitral Tribunal

Article 16. (1) The arbitral tribunal may rule on its own jurisdiction, including any objections with respect to the existence or validity of the arbitration agreement.
For that purpose, an arbitration clause which forms part of a contract shall be treated as an agreement independent of the other terms of the contract.
A decision by the arbitral tribunal that the contract is null and void shall not entail ipso jure the invalidity of the arbitration clause.
(2) A plea that the arbitral tribunal does not have jurisdiction shall be raised not later than the submission of the statement of defence. A party is not precluded from raising such a plea by the fact that he has appointed, or participated in the appointment of, an arbitrator. A plea that the arbitral tribunal is exceeding the scope of its authority shall be raised as soon as the matter alleged to be beyond the scope of its authority is raised during the arbitral proceedings. The arbitral tribunal may, in either case, admit a later plea if it considers the delay justified.
(3) The arbitral tribunal may rule on a plea referred to in paragraph (2) of this article either as a preliminary question or in an award on the merits. If the arbitral tribunal rules as a preliminary question that it has jurisdiction, any party may request, within thirty days after having received notice of that ruling, the court specified in article 6 to decide the matter, which decision shall be subject to no appeal; while such a request is pending, the arbitral tribunal may continue the arbitral proceedings and make an award.

Chapter IV A. Interim Measures and Preliminary Orders

Section 1. Interim measures

Article 17. (1) Unless otherwise agreed by the parties, the arbitral tribunal may, at the request of a party, grant interim measures.
(2) An interim measure is any temporary measure, whether in the form of an award or in another form, by which, at any time prior to the issuance of the award by which the dispute is finally decided, the arbitral tribunal orders a party to:
(a) Maintain or restore the status quo pending determination of the dispute;
(b) Take action that would prevent, or refrain from taking action that is likely to cause, current or imminent harm or prejudice to the arbitral process itself;
(c) Provide a means of preserving assets out of which a subsequent award may be satisfied; or
(d) Preserve evidence that may be relevant and material to the resolution of the dispute.

Article 17 A. (1) The party requesting an interim measure under article 17(2)(a), (b) and (c) shall satisfy the arbitral tribunal that:
(a) Harm not adequately reparable by an award of damages is likely to result if the measure is not ordered, and such harm substantially outweighs the harm that is likely to result to the party against whom the measure is directed if the measure is granted; and
(b) There is a reasonable possibility that the requesting party will succeed on the merits of the claim. The determination on this possibility shall not affect the discretion of the arbitral tribunal in making any subsequent determination.
(2) With regard to a request for an interim measure under article 17(2)(d), the requirements in paragraphs (1)(a) and (b) of this article shall apply only to the extent the arbitral tribunal considers appropriate.

Section 2. Preliminary orders

Article 17 B. (1) Unless otherwise agreed by the parties, a party may, without notice to any other party, make a request for an interim measure together with an application for a preliminary order directing a party not to frustrate the purpose of the interim measure requested.
(2) The arbitral tribunal may grant a preliminary order provided it considers that prior disclosure of the request for the interim measure to the party against whom it is directed risks frustrating the purpose of the measure.
(3) The conditions defined under article 17A apply to any preliminary order, provided that the harm to be assessed under article 17A(1)(a), is the harm likely to result from the order being granted or not.

Article 17 C. (1) Immediately after the arbitral tribunal has made a determination in respect of an application for a preliminary order, the arbitral tribunal shall give notice to all parties of the request for the interim measure, the

application for the preliminary order, the preliminary order, if any, and all other communications, including by indicating the content of any oral communication, between any party and the arbitral tribunal in relation thereto.
(2) At the same time, the arbitral tribunal shall give an opportunity to any party against whom a preliminary order is directed to present its case at the earliest practicable time.
(3) The arbitral tribunal shall decide promptly on any objection to the preliminary order.
(4) A preliminary order shall expire after twenty days from the date on which it was issued by the arbitral tribunal. However, the arbitral tribunal may issue an interim measure adopting or modifying the preliminary order, after the party against whom the preliminary order is directed has been given notice and an opportunity to present its case.
(5) A preliminary order shall be binding on the parties but shall not be subject to enforcement by a court. Such a preliminary order does not constitute an award.

Section 3. Provisions applicable to interim measures and preliminary orders

Article 17 D. The arbitral tribunal may modify, suspend or terminate an interim measure or a preliminary order it has granted, upon application of any party or, in exceptional circumstances and upon prior notice to the parties, on the arbitral tribunal's own initiative.

Article 17 E. (1) The arbitral tribunal may require the party requesting an interim measure to provide appropriate security in connection with the measure.
(2) The arbitral tribunal shall require the party applying for a preliminary order to provide security in connection with the order unless the arbitral tribunal considers it inappropriate or unnecessary to do so.

Article 17 F. (1) The arbitral tribunal may require any party promptly to disclose any material change in the circumstances on the basis of which the measure was requested or granted.
(2) The party applying for a preliminary order shall disclose to the arbitral tribunal all circumstances that are likely to be relevant to the arbitral tribunal's determination whether to grant or maintain the order, and such obligation shall continue until the party against whom the order has been requested has had an opportunity to present its case. Thereafter, paragraph (1) of this article shall apply.

Article 17 G. The party requesting an interim measure or applying for a preliminary order shall be liable for any costs and damages caused by the measure or the order to any party if the arbitral tribunal later determines that, in the circumstances, the measure or the order should not have been granted. The arbitral tribunal may award such costs and damages at any point during the
proceedings.

Section 4. Recognition and enforcement of interim measures

Article 17 H. (1) An interim measure issued by an arbitral tribunal shall be recognized as binding and, unless otherwise provided by the arbitral tribunal, enforced upon application to the competent court, irrespective of the country in which it was issued, subject to the provisions of article 17 I.
(2) The party who is seeking or has obtained recognition or enforcement of an interim measure shall promptly inform the court of any termination, suspension or modification of that interim measure.
(3) The court of the State where recognition or enforcement is sought may, if it considers it proper, order the requesting party to provide appropriate security if the arbitral tribunal has not already made a determination with respect to security or where such a decision is necessary to protect the rights of third parties.

Article 17 I. (1) Recognition or enforcement of an interim measure may be refused only:
(a) At the request of the party against whom it is invoked if the court is satisfied that:
(i) Such refusal is warranted on the grounds set forth in article 36(1)(a)(i), (ii), (iii) or (iv); or
(ii) The arbitral tribunal's decision with respect to the provision of security in connection with the interim measure issued by the arbitral tribunal has not been complied with; or
(iii) The interim measure has been terminated or suspended by the arbitral tribunal or, where so empowered, by the court of the State in which the arbitration takes place or under the law of which that interim measure was granted; or
(b) If the court finds that:

(i) The interim measure is incompatible with the powers conferred upon the court unless the court decides to reformulate the interim measure to the extent necessary to adapt it to its own powers and procedures for the purposes of enforcing that interim measure and without modifying its substance; or
(ii) Any of the grounds set forth in article 36(1)(b)(i) or (ii), apply to the recognition and enforcement of the interim measure.
(2) Any determination made by the court on any ground in paragraph (1) of this article shall be effective only for the purposes of the application to recognize and enforce the interim measure. The court where recognition or enforcement is sought shall not, in making that determination, undertake a review of the substance of the interim measure.

Section 5. Court-ordered interim measures

Article 17 J. A court shall have the same power of issuing an interim measure in relation to arbitration proceedings, irrespective of whether their place is in the territory of this State, as it has in relation to proceedings in courts. The court shall exercise such power in accordance with its own procedures in consideration of the specific features of international arbitration.

Chapter V. Conduct of Arbitral Proceedings

Article 18. The parties shall be treated with equality and each party shall be given a full opportunity of presenting his case.

Article 19. (1) Subject to the provisions of this Law, the parties are free to agree on the procedure to be followed by the arbitral tribunal in conducting the proceedings.
(2) Failing such agreement, the arbitral tribunal may, subject to the provisions of this Law, conduct the arbitration in such manner as it considers appropriate. The power conferred upon the arbitral tribunal includes the power to determine the admissibility, relevance, materiality and weight of any evidence.

Article 20. (1) The parties are free to agree on the place of arbitration. Failing such agreement, the place of arbitration shall be determined by the arbitral tribunal having regard to the circumstances of the case, including the convenience of the parties.
(2) Notwithstanding the provisions of paragraph (1) of this article, the arbitral tribunal may, unless otherwise agreed by the parties, meet at any place it considers appropriate for consultation among its members, for hearing witnesses, experts or the parties, or for inspection of goods, other property or documents.

Article 21. Unless otherwise agreed by the parties, the arbitral proceedings in respect of a particular dispute commence on the date on which a request for that dispute to be referred to arbitration is received by the respondent.

Article 22. (1) The parties are free to agree on the language or languages to be used in the arbitral proceedings. Failing such agreement, the arbitral tribunal shall determine the language or languages to be used in the proceedings. This agreement or determination, unless otherwise specified therein, shall apply to any written statement by a party, any hearing and any award, decision or other communication by the arbitral tribunal.
(2) The arbitral tribunal may order that any documentary evidence shall be accompanied by a translation into the language or languages agreed upon by the parties or determined by the arbitral tribunal.

Article 23. (1) Within the period of time agreed by the parties or determined by the arbitral tribunal, the claimant shall state the facts supporting his claim, the points at issue and the relief or remedy sought, and the respondent shall state his defence in respect of these particulars, unless the parties have otherwise agreed as to the required elements of such statements. The parties may submit with their statements all documents they consider to be relevant or may add a reference to the documents or other evidence they will submit.
(2) Unless otherwise agreed by the parties, either party may amend or supplement his claim or defence during the course of the arbitral proceedings, unless the arbitral tribunal considers it inappropriate to allow such amendment having regard to the delay in making it.

Article 24. (1) Subject to any contrary agreement by the parties, the arbitral tribunal shall decide whether to hold oral hearings for the presentation of evidence or for oral argument, or whether the proceedings shall be conducted

on the basis of documents and other materials. However, unless the parties have agreed that no hearings shall be held, the arbitral tribunal shall hold such
hearings at an appropriate stage of the proceedings, if so requested by a party.
(2) The parties shall be given sufficient advance notice of any hearing and of any meeting of the arbitral tribunal for the purposes of inspection of goods, other property or documents.
(3) All statements, documents or other information supplied to the arbitral tribunal by one party shall be communicated to the other party. Also any expert report or evidentiary document on which the arbitral tribunal may rely in making its decision shall be communicated to the parties.

Article 25. Unless otherwise agreed by the parties, if, without showing sufficient cause,
(a) the claimant fails to communicate his statement of claim in accordance with article 23(1), the arbitral tribunal shall terminate the proceedings;
(b) the respondent fails to communicate his statement of defence in accordance with article 23(1), the arbitral tribunal shall continue the proceedings without treating such failure in itself as an admission of the claimant's allegations;
(c) any party fails to appear at a hearing or to produce documentary evidence, the arbitral tribunal may continue the proceedings and make the award on the evidence before it.

Article 26. (1) Unless otherwise agreed by the parties, the arbitral tribunal
(a) may appoint one or more experts to report to it on specific issues to be determined by the arbitral tribunal;
(b) may require a party to give the expert any relevant information or to produce, or to provide access to, any relevant documents, goods or other property for his inspection.
(2) Unless otherwise agreed by the parties, if a party so requests or if the arbitral tribunal considers it necessary, the expert shall, after delivery of his written or oral report, participate in a hearing where the parties have the opportunity to put questions to him and to present expert witnesses in order to testify on the points at issue.

Article 27. The arbitral tribunal or a party with the approval of the arbitral tribunal may request from a competent court of this State assistance in taking evidence.
The court may execute the request within its competence and according to its rules on taking evidence.

Chapter VI. Making of Award and Termination of Proceedings

Article 28. (1) The arbitral tribunal shall decide the dispute in accordance with such rules of law as are chosen by the parties as applicable to the substance of the dispute. Any designation of the law or legal system of a given State shall be construed, unless otherwise expressed, as directly referring to the substantive law of that State and not to its conflict of laws rules.
(2) Failing any designation by the parties, the arbitral tribunal shall apply the law determined by the conflict of laws rules which it considers applicable.
(3) The arbitral tribunal shall decide ex aequo et bono or as amiable compositeur only if the parties have expressly authorized it to do so.
(4) In all cases, the arbitral tribunal shall decide in accordance with the terms of the contract and shall take into account the usages of the trade applicable to the transaction.

Article 29. In arbitral proceedings with more than one arbitrator, any decision of the arbitral tribunal shall be made, unless otherwise agreed by the parties, by a majority of all its members. However, questions of procedure may be decided by a presiding arbitrator, if so authorized by the parties or all members of the arbitral tribunal.

Article 30. (1) If, during arbitral proceedings, the parties settle the dispute, the arbitral tribunal shall terminate the proceedings and, if requested by the parties and not objected to by the arbitral tribunal, record the settlement in the form of an arbitral award on agreed terms.
(2) An award on agreed terms shall be made in accordance with the provisions of article 31 and shall state that it is an award. Such an award has the same status and effect as any other award on the merits of the case.

Article 31. (1) The award shall be made in writing and shall be signed by the arbitrator or arbitrators. In arbitral proceedings with more than one arbitrator, the signatures of the majority of all members of the arbitral tribunal shall suffice, provided that the reason for any omitted signature is stated.
(2) The award shall state the reasons upon which it is based, unless the parties have agreed that no reasons are to be given or the award is an award on agreed terms under article 30.

(3) The award shall state its date and the place of arbitration as determined in accordance with article 20(1). The award shall be deemed to have been made at that place.

(4) After the award is made, a copy signed by the arbitrators in accordance with paragraph (1) of this article shall be delivered to each party.

Article 32. (1) The arbitral proceedings are terminated by the final award or by an order of the arbitral tribunal in accordance with paragraph (2) of this article.

(2) The arbitral tribunal shall issue an order for the termination of the arbitral proceedings when:

(a) the claimant withdraws his claim, unless the respondent objects thereto and the arbitral tribunal recognizes a legitimate interest on his part in obtaining a final settlement of the dispute;

(b) the parties agree on the termination of the proceedings;

(c) the arbitral tribunal finds that the continuation of the proceedings has for any other reason become unnecessary or impossible.

(3) The mandate of the arbitral tribunal terminates with the termination of the arbitral proceedings, subject to the provisions of articles 33 and 34(4).

Article 33. (1) Within thirty days of receipt of the award, unless another period of time has been agreed upon by the parties:

(a) a party, with notice to the other party, may request the arbitral tribunal to correct in the award any errors in computation, any clerical or typographical errors or any errors of similar nature;

(b) if so agreed by the parties, a party, with notice to the other party, may request the arbitral tribunal to give an interpretation of a specific point or part of the award.

If the arbitral tribunal considers the request to be justified, it shall make the correction or give the interpretation within thirty days of receipt of the request. The interpretation shall form part of the award.

(2) The arbitral tribunal may correct any error of the type referred to in paragraph (1)(a) of this article on its own initiative within thirty days of the date of the award.

(3) Unless otherwise agreed by the parties, a party, with notice to the other party, may request, within thirty days of receipt of the award, the arbitral tribunal to make an additional award as to claims presented in the arbitral proceedings but omitted from the award. If the arbitral tribunal considers the request to be justified, it shall make the additional award within sixty days.

(4) The arbitral tribunal may extend, if necessary, the period of time within which it shall make a correction, interpretation or an additional award under paragraph (1) or (3) of this article.

(5) The provisions of article 31 shall apply to a correction or interpretation of the award or to an additional award.

Chapter VII. Recourse Against Award

Article 34. (1) Recourse to a court against an arbitral award may be made only by an application for setting aside in accordance with paragraphs (2) and (3) of this article.

(2) An arbitral award may be set aside by the court specified in article 6 only if:

(a) the party making the application furnishes proof that:

(i) a party to the arbitration agreement referred to in article 7 was under some incapacity; or the said agreement is not valid under the law to which the parties have subjected it or, failing any indication thereon, under the law of this State; or

(ii) the party making the application was not given proper notice of the appointment of an arbitrator or of the arbitral proceedings or was otherwise unable to present his case; or

(iii) the award deals with a dispute not contemplated by or not falling within the terms of the submission to arbitration, or contains decisions on matters beyond the scope of the submission to

arbitration, provided that, if the decisions on matters submitted to arbitration can be separated from those not so submitted, only that part of the award which contains decisions on matters not submitted to arbitration may be set aside; or

(iv) the composition of the arbitral tribunal or the arbitral procedure was not in accordance with the agreement of the parties, unless such agreement was in conflict with a provision of this

Law from which the parties cannot derogate, or, failing such agreement, was not in accordance with this Law; or

(b) the court finds that:

(i) the subject-matter of the dispute is not capable of settlement by arbitration under the law of this State; or

(ii) the award is in conflict with the public policy of this State.

(3) An application for setting aside may not be made after three months have elapsed from the date on which the party making that application had received the award or, if a request had been made under article 33, from the date on which that request had been disposed of by the arbitral
tribunal.
(4) The court, when asked to set aside an award, may, where appropriate and so requested by a party, suspend the setting aside proceedings for a period of time determined by it in order to give the arbitral tribunal an opportunity to resume the arbitral proceedings or to take such other action
as in the arbitral tribunal's opinion will eliminate the grounds for setting aside.

Chapter VIII. Recognition and Enforcement of Awards

Article 35. (1) An arbitral award, irrespective of the country in which it was made, shall be recognized as binding and, upon application in writing to the competent court, shall be enforced subject to the provisions of this article and of article 36.
(2) The party relying on an award or applying for its enforcement shall supply the original award or a copy thereof. If the award is not made in an official language of this State, the court may request the party to supply a translation thereof into such language.

Article 36. (1) Recognition or enforcement of an arbitral award, irrespective of the country in which it was made, may be refused only:
(a) at the request of the party against whom it is invoked, if that party furnishes to the competent court where recognition or enforcement is sought proof that:
(i) a party to the arbitration agreement referred to in article 7 was under some incapacity; or the said agreement is not valid under the law to which the parties have subjected it or, failing any indication thereon, under the law of the country where the award was made; or
(ii) the party against whom the award is invoked was not given proper notice of the appointment of an arbitrator or of the arbitral proceedings or was otherwise unable to present his case; or
(iii) the award deals with a dispute not contemplated by or not falling within the terms of the submission to arbitration, or it contains decisions on matters beyond the scope of the submission to arbitration, provided that, if the decisions on matters submitted to arbitration can be separated from those not so submitted, that part of the award which contains decisions on matters submitted to arbitration may be recognized and enforced; or
(iv) the composition of the arbitral tribunal or the arbitral procedure was not in accordance with the agreement of the parties or, failing such agreement, was not in accordance with the
law of the country where the arbitration took place; or
(v) the award has not yet become binding on the parties or has been set aside or suspended by a court of the country in which, or under the law of which, that award was made; or
(b) if the court finds that:
(i) the subject-matter of the dispute is not capable of settlement by arbitration under the law of this State; or
(ii) the recognition or enforcement of the award would be contrary to the public policy of this State.
(2) If an application for setting aside or suspension of an award has been made to a court referred to in paragraph (1)(a)(v) of this article, the court where recognition or enforcement is sought may, if it considers it proper, adjourn its decision and may also, on the application of the party claiming recognition or enforcement of the award, order the other party to provide appropriate security.

Unidroit Principles of International Commercial Contracts 2004[32]

Preamble

These Principles set forth general rules for international commercial contracts.
They shall be applied when the parties have agreed that their contract be governed by them.
They may be applied when the parties have agreed that their contract be governed by general principles of law, the *lex mercatoria* or the like.
They may be applied when the parties have not chosen any law to govern their contract.
They may be used to interpret or supplement international uniform law instruments.
They may be used to interpret or supplement domestic law.
They may serve as a model for national and international legislators.

Chapter 1 – General Provisions

Article 1.1. The parties are free to enter into a contract and to determine its content.

Article 1.2. Nothing in these Principles requires a contract, statement or any other act to be made in or evidenced by a particular form. It may be proved by any means, including witnesses.

Article 1.3. A contract validly entered into is binding upon the parties. It can only be modified or terminated in accordance with its terms or by agreement or as otherwise provided in these Principles.

ARTICLE 1.4. Nothing in these Principles shall restrict the application of mandatory rules, whether of national, international or supranational origin, which are applicable in accordance with the relevant rules of private international law.

Article 1.5. The parties may exclude the application of these Principles or derogate from or vary the effect of any of their provisions, except as otherwise provided in the Principles.

Article 1.6. (1) In the interpretation of these Principles, regard is to be had to their international character and to their purposes including the need to promote uniformity in their application.
(2) Issues within the scope of these Principles but not expressly settled by them are as far as possible to be settled in accordance with their underlying general principles.

Article 1.7. (1) Each party must act in accordance with good faith and fair dealing in international trade.
(2) The parties may not exclude or limit this duty.

Article 1.8. A party cannot act inconsistently with an understanding it has caused the other party to have and upon which that other party reasonably has acted in reliance to its detriment.

Article 1.9. (1) The parties are bound by any usage to which they have agreed and by any practices which they have established between themselves.
(2) The parties are bound by a usage that is widely known to and regularly observed in international trade by parties in the particular trade concerned except where the application of such a usage would be unreasonable.

Article 1.10. (1) Where notice is required it may be given by any means appropriate to the circumstances.
(2) A notice is effective when it reaches the person to whom it is given.
(3) For the purpose of paragraph (2) a notice "reaches" a person when given to that person orally or delivered at that person's place of business or mailing address.
(4) For the purpose of this Article "notice" includes a declaration, demand, request or any other communication of intention.

Article 1.11. In these Principles

---

[32] This is a reproduction, for educational purposes, of the black letter rules, excluding commentaries, of the Principles developed by UNIDROIT; source: www.unidroit.org.

– "court" includes an arbitral tribunal;
– where a party has more than one place of business the relevant "place of business" is that which has the closest relationship to the contract and its performance, having regard to the circumstances known to or contemplated by the parties at any time before or at the conclusion of the contract;
– "obligor" refers to the party who is to perform an obligation and "obligee" refers to the party who is entitled to performance of that obligation.
– "writing" means any mode of communication that preserves a record of the information contained therein and is capable of being reproduced in tangible form.

Article 1.12. (1) Official holidays or non-business days occurring during a period set by parties for an act to be performed are included in calculating the period.
(2) However, if the last day of the period is an official holiday or a non-business day at the place of business of the party to perform the act, the period is extended until the first business day which follows, unless the circumstances indicate otherwise.
(3) The relevant time zone is that of the place of business of the party setting the time, unless the circumstances indicate otherwise.

Chapter 2 – Formation and Authority of Agents

Section 1: Formation

Article 2.1.1. A contract may be concluded either by the acceptance of an offer or by conduct of the parties that is sufficient to show agreement.

Article 2.1.2. A proposal for concluding a contract constitutes an offer if it is sufficiently definite and indicates the intention of the offeror to be bound in case of acceptance.

Article 2.1.3. (1) An offer becomes effective when it reaches the offeree.
(2) An offer, even if it is irrevocable, may be withdrawn if the withdrawal reaches the offeree before or at the same time as the offer.

Article 2.1.4. (1) Until a contract is concluded an offer may be revoked if the revocation reaches the offeree before it has dispatched an acceptance.
(2) However, an offer cannot be revoked
(a) if it indicates, whether by stating a fixed time for acceptance or otherwise, that it is irrevocable; or
(b) if it was reasonable for the offeree to rely on the offer as being irrevocable and the offeree has acted in reliance on the offer.

Article 2.1.5. An offer is terminated when a rejection reaches the offeror.

Article 2.1.6. (1) A statement made by or other conduct of the offeree indicating assent to an offer is an acceptance. Silence or inactivity does not in itself amount to acceptance.
(2) An acceptance of an offer becomes effective when the indication of assent reaches the offeror.
(3) However, if, by virtue of the offer or as a result of practices which the parties have established between themselves or of usage, the offeree may indicate assent by performing an act without notice to the offeror, the acceptance is effective when the act is performed.

Article 2.1.7. An offer must be accepted within the time the offeror has fixed or, if no time is fixed, within a reasonable time having regard to the circumstances, including the rapidity of the means of communication employed by the offeror. An oral offer must be accepted immediately unless the circumstances indicate otherwise.

Article 2.1.8. A period of acceptance fixed by the offeror begins to run from the time that the offer is dispatched. A time indicated in the offer is deemed to be the time of dispatch unless the circumstances indicate otherwise.

Article 2.1.9. (1) A late acceptance is nevertheless effective as an acceptance if without undue delay the offeror so informs the offeree or gives notice to that effect.

(2) If a communication containing a late acceptance shows that it has been sent in such circumstances that if its transmission had been normal it would have reached the offeror in due time, the late acceptance is effective as an acceptance unless, without undue delay, the offeror informs the offeree that it considers the offer as having lapsed.

Article 2.1.10. An acceptance may be withdrawn if the withdrawal reaches the offeror before or at the same time as the acceptance would have become effective.

Article 2.1.11. (1) A reply to an offer which purports to be an acceptance but contains additions, limitations or other modifications is a rejection of the offer and constitutes a counter-offer.
(2) However, a reply to an offer which purports to be an acceptance but contains additional or different terms which do not materially alter the terms of the offer constitutes an acceptance, unless the offeror, without undue delay, objects to the discrepancy. If the offeror does not object, the terms of the contract are the terms of the offer with the modifications contained in the acceptance.

Article 2.1.12. If a writing which is sent within a reasonable time after the conclusion of the contract and which purports to be a confirmation of the contract contains additional or different terms, such terms become part of the contract, unless they materially alter the contract or the recipient, without undue delay, objects to the discrepancy.

Article 2.1.13. Where in the course of negotiations one of the parties insists that the contract is not concluded until there is agreement on specific matters or in a particular form, no contract is concluded before agreement is reached on those matters or in that form.

Article 2.1.14. (1) If the parties intend to conclude a contract, the fact that they intentionally leave a term to be agreed upon in further negotiations or to be determined by a third person does not prevent a contract from coming into existence.
(2) The existence of the contract is not affected by the fact that subsequently
(a) the parties reach no agreement on the term; or (b) the third person does not determine the term, provided that there is an alternative means of rendering the term definite that is reasonable in the circumstances, having regard to the intention of the parties.

Article 2.1.15. (1) A party is free to negotiate and is not liable for failure to reach an agreement.
(2) However, a party who negotiates or breaks off negotiations in bad faith is liable for the losses caused to the other party.
(3) It is bad faith, in particular, for a party to enter into or continue negotiations when intending not to reach an agreement with the other party.

Article 2.1.16. Where information is given as confidential by one party in the course of negotiations, the other party is under a duty not to disclose that information or to use it improperly for its own purposes, whether or not a contract is subsequently concluded.
Where appropriate, the remedy for breach of that duty may include compensation based on the benefit received by the other party.

Article 2.1.17. A contract in writing which contains a clause indicating that the writing completely embodies the terms on which the parties have agreed cannot be contradicted or supplemented by evidence of prior statements or agreements. However, such statements or agreements may be used to interpret the writing.

Article 2.1.18. A contract in writing which contains a clause requiring any modification or termination by agreement to be in a particular form may not be otherwise modified or terminated. However, a party may be precluded by its conduct from asserting such a clause to the extent that the other party has reasonably acted in reliance on that conduct.

Article 2.1.19. (1) Where one party or both parties use standard terms in concluding a contract, the general rules on formation apply, subject to Articles 2.1.20 - 2.1.22.
(2) Standard terms are provisions which are prepared in advance for general and repeated use by one party and which are actually used without negotiation with the other party.

Article 2.1.20. (1) No term contained in standard terms which is of such a character that the other party could not reasonably have expected it, is effective unless it has been expressly accepted by that party.

(2) In determining whether a term is of such a character regard shall be had to its content, language and presentation.

Article 2.1.21. In case of conflict between a standard term and a term which is not a standard term the latter prevails.

Article 2.1.22. Where both parties use standard terms and reach agreement except on those terms, a contract is concluded on the basis of the agreed terms and of any standard terms which are common in substance unless one party clearly indicates in advance, or later and without undue delay informs the other party, that it does not intend to be bound by such a contract.

Section2: Authority of Agents

Article 2.2.1. (1) This Section governs the authority of a person ("the agent"), to affect the legal relations of another person ("the principal"), by or with respect to a contract with a third party, whether the agent acts in its own name or in that of the principal.
(2) It governs only the relations between the principal or the agent on the one hand, and the third party on the other.
(3) It does not govern an agent's authority conferred by law or the authority of an agent appointed by a public or judicial authority.

Article 2.2.2. (1) The principal's grant of authority to an agent may be express or implied.
(2) The agent has authority to perform all acts necessary in the circumstances to achieve the purposes for which the authority was granted.

Article 2.2.3. (1) Where an agent acts within the scope of its authority and the third party knew or ought to have known that the agent was acting as an agent, the acts of the agent shall directly affect the legal relations between the principal and the third party and no legal relation is created between the agent and the third party.
(2) However, the acts of the agent shall affect only the relations between the agent and the third party, where the agent with the consent of the principal undertakes to become the party to the contract.

Article 2.2.4. (1) Where an agent acts within the scope of its authority and the third party neither knew nor ought to have known that the agent was acting as an agent, the acts of the agent shall affect only the relations between the agent and the third party.
(2) However, where such an agent, when contracting with the third party on behalf of a business, represents itself to be the owner of that business, the third party, upon discovery of the real owner of the business, may exercise also against the latter the rights it has against the agent.

Article 2.2.5. (1) Where an agent acts without authority or exceeds its authority, its acts do not affect the legal relations between the principal and the third party.
(2) However, where the principal causes the third party reasonably to believe that the agent has authority to act on behalf of the principal and that the agent is acting within the scope of that authority, the principal may not invoke against the third party the lack of authority of the agent.

Article 2.2.6. (1) An agent that acts without authority or exceeds its authority is, failing ratification by the principal, liable for damages that will place the third party in the same position as if the agent had acted with authority and not exceeded its authority.
(2) However, the agent is not liable if the third party knew or ought to have known that the agent had no authority or was exceeding its authority.

Article 2.2.7. (1) If a contract concluded by an agent involves the agent in a conflict of interests with the principal of which the third party knew or ought to have known, the principal may avoid the contract. The right to avoid is subject to Articles 3.12 and 3.14 to 3.17.
(2) However, the principal may not avoid the contract
(a) if the principal had consented to, or knew or ought to have known of, the agent's involvement in the conflict of interests; or
(b) if the agent had disclosed the conflict of interests to the principal and the latter had not objected within a reasonable time.

Article 2.2.8. An agent has implied authority to appoint a sub-agent to perform acts which it is not reasonable to expect the agent to perform itself. The rules of this Section apply to the sub-agency.

Article 2.2.9. (1) An act by an agent that acts without authority or exceeds its authority may be ratified by the principal. On ratification the act produces the same effects as if it had initially been carried out with authority.
(2) The third party may by notice to the principal specify a reasonable period of time for ratification. If the principal does not ratify within that period of time it can no longer do so.
(3) If, at the time of the agent's act, the third party neither knew nor ought to have known of the lack of authority, it may, at any time before ratification, by notice to the principal indicate its refusal to become bound by a ratification.

Article 2.2.10. (1) Termination of authority is not effective in relation to the third party unless the third party knew or ought to have known of it.
(2) Notwithstanding the termination of its authority, an agent remains authorised to perform the acts that are necessary to prevent harm to the principal's interests.

Chapter 3 —Validity

Article 3.1. These Principles do not deal with invalidity arising from
(a) lack of capacity;
(b) immorality or illegality.

Article 3.2. A contract is concluded, modified or terminated by the mere agreement of the parties, without any further requirement.

Article 3.3. (1) The mere fact that at the time of the conclusion of the contract the performance of the obligation assumed was impossible does not affect the validity of the contract.
(2) The mere fact that at the time of the conclusion of the contract a party was not entitled to dispose of the assets to which the contract relates does not affect the validity of the contract.

Article 3.4. Mistake is an erroneous assumption relating to facts or to law existing when the contract was concluded.

Article 3.5. (1) A party may only avoid the contract for mistake if, when the contract was concluded, the mistake was of such importance that a reasonable person in the same situation as the party in error would only have concluded the contract on materially different terms or would not have concluded it at all if the true state of affairs had been known, and
(a) the other party made the same mistake, or caused the mistake, or knew or ought to have known of the mistake and it was contrary to reasonable commercial standards of fair dealing to leave the mistaken party in error; or
(b) the other party had not at the time of avoidance reasonably acted in reliance on the contract.
(2) However, a party may not avoid the contract if
(a) it was grossly negligent in committing the mistake; or
(b) the mistake relates to a matter in regard to which the risk of mistake was assumed or, having regard to the circumstances, should be borne by the mistaken party.

Article 3.6. An error occurring in the expression or transmission of a declaration is considered to be a mistake of the person from whom the declaration emanated.

Article 3.7. A party is not entitled to avoid the contract on the ground of mistake if the circumstances on which that party relies afford, or could have afforded, a remedy for non-performance.

Article 3.8. A party may avoid the contract when it has been led to conclude the contract by the other party's fraudulent representation, including language or practices, or fraudulent non-disclosure of circumstances which, according to reasonable commercial standards of fair dealing, the latter party should have disclosed.

Article 3.9. A party may avoid the contract when it has been led to conclude the contract by the other party's unjustified threat which, having regard to the circumstances, is so imminent and serious as to leave the first party no reasonable alternative. In particular, a threat is unjustified if the act or omission with which a party has been threatened is wrongful in itself, or it is wrongful to use it as a means to obtain the conclusion of the contract.

Article 3.10. (1) A party may avoid the contract or an individual term of it if, at the time of the conclusion of the contract, the contract or term unjustifiably gave the other party an excessive advantage. Regard is to be had, among other factors, to
(a) the fact that the other party has taken unfair advantage of the first party's dependence, economic distress or urgent needs, or of its improvidence, ignorance, inexperience or lack of bargaining skill, and
(b) the nature and purpose of the contract.
(2) Upon the request of the party entitled to avoidance, a court may adapt the contract or term in order to make it accord with reasonable commercial standards of fair dealing.
(3) A court may also adapt the contract or term upon the request of the party receiving notice of avoidance, provided that that party informs the other party of its request promptly after receiving such notice and before the other party has reasonably acted in reliance on it. The provisions of Article 3.13(2) apply accordingly.

Article 3.11. (1) Where fraud, threat, gross disparity or a party's mistake is imputable to, or is known or ought to be known by, a third person for whose acts the other party is responsible, the contract may be avoided under the same conditions as if the behaviour or knowledge had been that of the party itself.
(2) Where fraud, threat or gross disparity is imputable to a third person for whose acts the other party is not responsible, the contract may be avoided if that party knew or ought to have known of the fraud, threat or disparity, or has not at the time of avoidance reasonably acted in reliance on the contract.

Article 3.12. If the party entitled to avoid the contract expressly or impliedly confirms the contract after the period of time for giving notice of avoidance has begun to run, avoidance of the contract is excluded.

Article 3.13 (1) If a party is entitled to avoid the contract for mistake but the other party declares itself willing to perform or performs the contract as it was understood by the party entitled to avoidance, the contract is considered to have been concluded as the latter party understood it. The other party must make such a declaration or render such performance promptly after having been informed of the manner in which the party entitled to avoidance had understood the contract and before that party has reasonably acted in reliance on a notice of avoidance.
(2) After such a declaration or performance the right to avoidance is lost and any earlier notice of avoidance is ineffective.

Article 3.14. The right of a party to avoid the contract is exercised by notice to the other party.

Article 3.15. (1) Notice of avoidance shall be given within a reasonable time, having regard to the circumstances, after the avoiding party knew or could not have been unaware of the relevant facts or became capable of acting freely.
(2) Where an individual term of the contract may be avoided by a party under Article 3.10, the period of time for giving notice of avoidance begins to run when that term is asserted by the other party.

Article 3.16. Where a ground of avoidance affects only individual terms of the contract, the effect of avoidance is limited to those terms unless, having regard to the circumstances, it is unreasonable to uphold the remaining contract.

Article 3.17. (1) Avoidance takes effect retroactively.
(2) On avoidance either party may claim restitution of whatever it has supplied under the contract or the part of it avoided, provided that it concurrently makes restitution of whatever it has received under the contract or the part of it avoided or, if it cannot make restitution in kind, it makes an allowance for what it has received.

Article 3.18. Irrespective of whether or not the contract has been avoided, the party who knew or ought to have known of the ground for avoidance is liable for damages so as to put the other party in the same position in which it would have been if it had not concluded the contract.

Article 3.19. The provisions of this Chapter are mandatory, except insofar as they relate to the binding force of mere agreement, initial impossibility or mistake.

Article 3.20. The provisions of this Chapter apply with appropriate adaptations to any communication of intention addressed by one party to the other.

Chapter 4— Interpretation

Article 4.1. (1) A contract shall be interpreted according to the common intention of the parties.
(2) If such an intention cannot be established, the contract shall be interpreted according to the meaning that reasonable persons of the same kind as the parties would give to it in the same circumstances.

Article 4.2. (1) The statements and other conduct of a party shall be interpreted according to that party's intention if the other party knew or could not have been unaware of that intention.
(2) If the preceding paragraph is not applicable, such statements and other conduct shall be interpreted according to the meaning that a reasonable person of the same kind as the other party would give to it in the same circumstances.

Article 4.3. In applying Articles 4.1 and 4.2, regard shall be had to all the circumstances, including
(a) preliminary negotiations between the parties;
(b) practices which the parties have established between themselves;
(c) the conduct of the parties subsequent to the conclusion of the contract;
(d) the nature and purpose of the contract;
(e) the meaning commonly given to terms and expressions in the trade concerned;
(f) usages.

Article 4.4. Terms and expressions shall be interpreted in the light of the whole contract or statement in which they appear.

Article 4.5. Contract terms shall be interpreted so as to give effect to all the terms rather than to deprive some of them of effect.

Article 4.6. If contract terms supplied by one party are unclear, an interpretation against that party is preferred.

Article 4.7. Where a contract is drawn up in two or more language versions which are equally authoritative there is, in case of discrepancy between the versions, a preference for the interpretation according to a version in which the contract was originally drawn up.

Article 4.8. (1) Where the parties to a contract have not agreed with respect to a term which is important for a determination of their rights and duties, a term which is appropriate in the circumstances shall be supplied.
(2) In determining what is an appropriate term regard shall be had, among other factors, to
(a) the intention of the parties;
(b) the nature and purpose of the contract;
(c) good faith and fair dealing;
(d) reasonableness.

Chapter 5 – Content and Third Party Rights

Section 1: Content

Article 5.1.1. The contractual obligations of the parties may be express or implied.

Article 5.1.2. Implied obligations stem from
(a) the nature and purpose of the contract;
(b) practices established between the parties and usages;
(c) good faith and fair dealing;
(d) reasonableness.

Article 5.1.3. Each party shall cooperate with the other party when such co-operation may reasonably be expected for the performance of that party's obligations.

Article 5.1.4. (1) To the extent that an obligation of a party involves a duty to achieve a specific result, that party is bound to achieve that result.
(2) To the extent that an obligation of a party involves a duty of best efforts in the performance of an activity, that party is bound to make such efforts as would be made by a reasonable person of the same kind in the same circumstances.

Article 5.1.5. In determining the extent to which an obligation of a party involves a duty of best efforts in the performance of an activity or a duty to achieve a specific result, regard shall be had, among other factors, to
(a) the way in which the obligation is expressed in the contract;
(b) the contractual price and other terms of the contract;
(c) the degree of risk normally involved in achieving the expected result;
(d) the ability of the other party to influence the performance of the obligation.

Article 5.1.6. Where the quality of performance is neither fixed by, nor determinable from, the contract a party is bound to render a performance of a quality that is reasonable and not less than average in the circumstances.

Article 5.1.7. (1) Where a contract does not fix or make provision for determining the price, the parties are considered, in the absence of any indication to the contrary, to have made reference to the price generally charged at the time of the conclusion of the contract for such performance in comparable circumstances in the trade concerned or, if no such
price is available, to a reasonable price.
(2) Where the price is to be determined by one party and that determination is manifestly unreasonable, a reasonable price shall be substituted notwithstanding any contract term to the contrary.
(3) Where the price is to be fixed by a third person, and that person cannot or will not do so, the price shall be a reasonable price.
(4) Where the price is to be fixed by reference to factors which do not exist or have ceased to exist or to be accessible, the nearest equivalent factor shall be treated as a substitute.

Article 5.1.8. A contract for an indefinite period may be ended by either party by giving notice a reasonable time in advance.

Article 5.1.9. (1) An obligee may release its right by agreement with the obligor.
(2) An offer to release a right gratuitously shall be deemed accepted if the obligor does not reject the offer without delay after having become aware of it.

Section 2: Third Party Rights

Article 5.2.1. (1) The parties (the "promisor" and the "promisee") may confer by express or implied agreement a right on a third party (the "beneficiary").
(2) The existence and content of the beneficiary's right against the promisor are determined by the agreement of the parties and are subject to any conditions or other limitations under the agreement.

Article 5.2.2. The beneficiary must be identifiable with adequate certainty by the contract but need not be in existence at the time the contract is made.

Article 5.2.3. The conferment of rights in the beneficiary includes the right to invoke a clause in the contract which excludes or limits the liability of the beneficiary.

Article 5.2.4. The promisor may assert against the beneficiary all defences which the promisor could assert against the promisee.

Article 5.2.5. The parties may modify or revoke the rights conferred by the contract on the beneficiary until the beneficiary has accepted them or reasonably acted in reliance on them.

Article 5.2.6. The beneficiary may renounce a right conferred on it.

Chapter 6 —Performance

Section 1: Performance in General

Article 6.1.1. A party must perform its obligations:
(a) if a time is fixed by or determinable from the contract, at that time;
(b) if a period of time is fixed by or determinable from the contract, at any time within that period unless circumstances indicate that the other party is to choose a time;
(c) in any other case, within a reasonable time after the conclusion of the contract.

Article 6.1.2. In cases under Article 6.1.1(b) or (c), a party must perform its obligations at one time if that performance can be rendered at one time and the circumstances do not indicate otherwise.

Article 6.1.3. (1) The obligee may reject an offer to perform in part at the time performance is due, whether or not such offer is coupled with an assurance as to the balance of the performance, unless the obligee has no legitimate interest in so doing.
(2) Additional expenses caused to the obligee by partial performance are to be borne by the obligor without prejudice to any other remedy.

Article 6.1.4. (1) To the extent that the performances of the parties can be rendered simultaneously, the parties are bound to render them simultaneously unless the circumstances indicate otherwise.
(2) To the extent that the performance of only one party requires a period of time, that party is bound to render its performance first, unless the circumstances indicate otherwise.

Article 6.1.5. (1) The obligee may reject an earlier performance unless it has no legitimate interest in so doing.
(2) Acceptance by a party of an earlier performance does not affect the time for the performance of its own obligations if that time has been fixed irrespective of the performance of the other party's obligations.
(3) Additional expenses caused to the obligee by earlier performance are to be borne by the obligor, without prejudice to any other remedy.

Article 6.1.6. (1) If the place of performance is neither fixed by, nor determinable from, the contract, a party is to perform:
(a) a monetary obligation, at the obligee's place of business;
(b) any other obligation, at its own place of business.
(2) A party must bear any increase in the expenses incidental to performance which is caused by a change in its place of business subsequent to the conclusion of the contract.

Article 6.1.7. (1) Payment may be made in any form used in the ordinary course of business at the place for payment.
(2) However, an obligee who accepts, either by virtue of paragraph (1) or voluntarily, a cheque, any other order to pay or a promise to pay, is presumed to do so only on condition that it will be honoured.

Article 6.1.8. (1) Unless the obligee has indicated a particular account, payment may be made by a transfer to any of the financial institutions in which the obligee has made it known that it has an account.
(2) In case of payment by a transfer the obligation of the obligor is discharged when the transfer to the obligee's financial institution becomes effective.

Article 6.1.9. (1) If a monetary obligation is expressed in a currency other than that of the place for payment, it may be paid by the obligor in the currency of the place for payment unless
(a) that currency is not freely convertible; or
(b) the parties have agreed that payment should be made only in the currency in which the monetary obligation is expressed.
(2) If it is impossible for the obligor to make payment in the currency in which the monetary obligation is expressed, the obligee may require payment in the currency of the place for payment, even in the case referred to in paragraph (1)(b).
(3) Payment in the currency of the place for payment is to be made according to the applicable rate of exchange prevailing there when payment is due.

(4) However, if the obligor has not paid at the time when payment is due, the obligee may require payment according to the applicable rate of exchange prevailing either when payment is due or at the time of actual payment.

Article 6.1.10. Where a monetary obligation is not expressed in a particular currency, payment must be made in the currency of the place where payment is to be made.

Article 6.1.11. Each party shall bear the costs of performance of its obligations.

Article 6.1.12. (1) An obligor owing several monetary obligations to the same obligee may specify at the time of payment the debt to which it intends the payment to be applied.
However, the payment discharges first any expenses, then interest due and finally the principal.
(2) If the obligor makes no such specification, the obligee may, within a reasonable time after payment, declare to the obligor the obligation to which it imputes the payment, provided that the obligation is due and undisputed.
(3) In the absence of imputation under paragraphs (1) or (2), payment is imputed to that obligation which satisfies one of the following criteria in the order indicated:
(a) an obligation which is due or which is the first to fall due;
(b) the obligation for which the obligee has least security;
(c) the obligation which is the most burdensome for the obligor;
(d) the obligation which has arisen first.
If none of the preceding criteria applies, payment is imputed to all the obligations proportionally.

Article 6.1.13. Article 6.1.12 applies with appropriate adaptations to the imputation of performance of non-monetary obligations.

Article 6.1.14. Where the law of a State requires a public permission affecting the validity of the contract or its performance and neither that law nor the circumstances indicate otherwise (a) if only one party has its place of business in that State, that party shall take the measures necessary to obtain the permission;
(b) in any other case the party whose performance requires permission shall take the necessary measures.

Article 6.1.15. (1) The party required to take the measures necessary to obtain the permission shall do so without undue delay and shall bear any expenses incurred.
(2) That party shall whenever appropriate give the other party notice of the grant or refusal of such permission without undue delay.

Article 6.1.16. (1) If, notwithstanding the fact that the party responsible has taken all measures required, permission is neither granted nor refused within an agreed period or, where no period has been agreed, within a reasonable time from the conclusion of the contract, either party is entitled to terminate the contract.
(2) Where the permission affects some terms only, paragraph (1) does not apply if, having regard to the circumstances, it is reasonable to uphold the remaining contract even if the permission is refused.

Article 6.1.17. (1) The refusal of a permission affecting the validity of the contract renders the contract void. If the refusal affects the validity of some terms only, only such terms are void if, having regard to the circumstances, it is reasonable to uphold the remaining contract.
(2) Where the refusal of a permission renders the performance of the contract impossible in whole or in part, the rules on non-performance apply.

Section2: Hardship

Article 6.2.1. Where the performance of a contract becomes more onerous for one of the parties, that party is nevertheless bound to perform its obligations subject to the following provisions on hardship.

Article 6.2.2. There is hardship where the occurrence of events fundamentally alters the equilibrium of the contract either because the cost of a party's performance has increased or because the value of the performance a party receives has diminished, and
(a) the events occur or become known to the disadvantaged party after the conclusion of the contract;
(b) the events could not reasonably have been taken into account by the disadvantaged party at the time of the conclusion of the contract;

(c) the events are beyond the control of the disadvantaged party; and
(d) the risk of the events was not assumed by the disadvantaged party.

Article 6.2.3. (1) In case of hardship the disadvantaged party is entitled to request renegotiations. The request shall be made without undue delay and shall indicate the
grounds on which it is based.
(2) The request for renegotiation does not in itself entitle the disadvantaged party to withhold performance.
(3) Upon failure to reach agreement within a reasonable time either party may resort to the court.
(4) If the court finds hardship it may, if reasonable,
(a) terminate the contract at a date and on terms to be fixed, or
(b) adapt the contract with a view to restoring its equilibrium.

Chapter 7 —Non-Performance

Section 1: Non-Performance in General

Article 7.1.1. Non-performance is failure by a party to perform any of its obligations under the contract, including defective performance or late performance.

Article 7.1.2. A party may not rely on the non-performance of the other party to the extent that such non-performance was caused by the first party's act or omission or by another event as to which the first party bears the risk.

Article 7.1.3. (1) Where the parties are to perform simultaneously, either party may withhold performance until the other party tenders its performance.
(2) Where the parties are to perform consecutively, the party that is to perform later may withhold its performance until the first party has performed.

Article 7.1.4. (1) The non-performing party may, at its own expense, cure any nonperformance, provided that
(a) without undue delay, it gives notice indicating the proposed manner and timing of the cure;
(b) cure is appropriate in the circumstances;
(c) the aggrieved party has no legitimate interest in refusing cure; and
(d) cure is effected promptly.
(2) The right to cure is not precluded by notice of termination.
(3) Upon effective notice of cure, rights of the aggrieved party that are inconsistent with the non-performing party's performance are suspended until the time for cure has expired.
(4) The aggrieved party may withhold performance pending cure.
(5) Notwithstanding cure, the aggrieved party retains the right to claim damages for delay as well as for any harm caused or not prevented by the cure.

Article 7.1.5. (1) In a case of non-performance the aggrieved party may by notice to the other party allow an additional period of time for performance.
(2) During the additional period the aggrieved party may withhold performance of its own reciprocal obligations and may claim damages but may not resort to any other remedy. If it receives notice from the other party that the latter will not perform within that period, or if upon expiry of that period due performance has not been made, the aggrieved party may resort to any of the remedies that may be available under this Chapter.
(3) Where in a case of delay in performance which is not fundamental the aggrieved party has given notice allowing an additional period of time of reasonable length, it may terminate the contract at the end of that period. If the additional period allowed is not of reasonable length it shall be extended to a reasonable length. The aggrieved party may in its notice provide that if the other party fails to perform within the period allowed by the notice the contract shall automatically terminate.
(4) Paragraph (3) does not apply where the obligation which has not been performed is only a minor part of the contractual obligation of the non-performing party.

Article 7.1.6. A clause which limits or excludes one party's liability for non-performance or which permits one party to render performance substantially different from what the other party reasonably expected may not be invoked if it would be grossly unfair to do so, having regard to the purpose of the contract.

Article 7.1.7. (1) Non-performance by a party is excused if that party proves that the non-performance was due to an impediment beyond its control and that it could not
reasonably be expected to have taken the impediment into account at the time of the conclusion of the contract or to have avoided or overcome it or its consequences.
(2) When the impediment is only temporary, the excuse shall have effect for such period as is reasonable having regard to the effect of the impediment on the performance of the contract.
(3) The party who fails to perform must give notice to the other party of the impediment and its effect on its ability to perform. If the notice is not received by the other party within a reasonable time after the party who fails to perform knew or ought to have known of the impediment, it is liable for damages resulting from such nonreceipt.
(4) Nothing in this Article prevents a party from exercising a right to terminate the contract or to withhold performance or request interest on money due.

Section 2: Right to Performance

Article 7.2.1. Where a party who is obliged to pay money does not do so, the other party may require payment.

Article 7.2.2. Where a party who owes an obligation other than one to pay money does not perform, the other party may require performance, unless
(a) performance is impossible in law or in fact;
(b) performance or, where relevant, enforcement is unreasonably burdensome or expensive;
(c) the party entitled to performance may reasonably obtain performance from another source;
(d) performance is of an exclusively personal character; or
(e) the party entitled to performance does not require performance within a reasonable time after it has, or ought to have, become aware of the non-performance.

Article 7.2.3. The right to performance includes in appropriate cases the right to require repair, replacement, or other cure of defective performance. The provisions of Articles 7.2.1 and 7.2.2 apply accordingly.

Article 7.2.4. (1) Where the court orders a party to perform, it may also direct that this party pay a penalty if it does not comply with the order.
(2) The penalty shall be paid to the aggrieved party unless mandatory provisions of the law of the forum provide otherwise. Payment of the penalty to the aggrieved party does not exclude any claim for damages.

Article 7.2.5. (1) An aggrieved party who has required performance of a non-monetary obligation and who has not received performance within a period fixed or otherwise within a reasonable period of time may invoke any other remedy.
(2) Where the decision of a court for performance of a non-monetary obligation cannot be enforced, the aggrieved party may invoke any other remedy.

Section 3: Termination

Article 7.3.1. (1) A party may terminate the contract where the failure of the other party to perform an obligation under the contract amounts to a fundamental non-performance.
(2) In determining whether a failure to perform an obligation amounts to a fundamental non-performance regard shall be had, in particular, to whether
(a) the non-performance substantially deprives the aggrieved party of what it was entitled to expect under the contract unless the other party did not foresee and could not reasonably have foreseen such result;
(b) strict compliance with the obligation which has not been performed is of essence under the contract;
(c) the non-performance is intentional or reckless;
(d) the non-performance gives the aggrieved party reason to believe that it cannot rely on the other party's future performance;
(e) the non-performing party will suffer disproportionate loss as a result of the preparation or performance if the contract is terminated.
(3) In the case of delay the aggrieved party may also terminate the contract if the other party fails to perform before the time allowed it under Article 7.1.5 has expired.

Article 7.3.2. (1) The right of a party to terminate the contract is exercised by notice to the other party.
(2) If performance has been offered late or otherwise does not conform to the contract the aggrieved party will lose its right to terminate the contract unless it gives notice to the other party within a reasonable time after it has or ought to have become aware of the offer or of the non-conforming performance.

Article 7.3.3. Where prior to the date for performance by one of the parties it is clear that there will be a fundamental non-performance by that party, the other party may terminate the contract.

Article 7.3.4. A party who reasonably believes that there will be a fundamental non-performance by the other party may demand adequate assurance of due performance and may meanwhile withhold its own performance. Where this assurance is not provided within a reasonable time the party demanding it may terminate the contract.

Article 7.3.5. (1) Termination of the contract releases both parties from their obligation to effect and to receive future performance.
(2) Termination does not preclude a claim for damages for non-performance.
(3) Termination does not affect any provision in the contract for the settlement of disputes or any other term of the contract which is to operate even after termination.

Article 7.3.6. (1) On termination of the contract either party may claim restitution of whatever it has supplied, provided that such party concurrently makes restitution of whatever it has received. If restitution in kind is not possible or appropriate allowance should be made in money whenever reasonable.
(2) However, if performance of the contract has extended over a period of time and the contract is divisible, such restitution can only be claimed for the period after termination has taken effect.

Section 4: Damages

Article 7.4.1. Any non-performance gives the aggrieved party a right to damages either exclusively or in conjunction with any other remedies except where the non-performance is excused under these Principles.

Article 7.4.2. (1) The aggrieved party is entitled to full compensation for harm sustained as a result of the non-performance. Such harm includes both any loss which it suffered and any gain of which it was deprived, taking into account any gain to the aggrieved party resulting from its avoidance of cost or harm.
(2) Such harm may be non-pecuniary and includes, for instance, physical suffering or emotional distress.

Article 7.4.3. (1) Compensation is due only for harm, including future harm, that is established with a reasonable degree of certainty.
(2) Compensation may be due for the loss of a chance in proportion to the probability of its occurrence.
(3) Where the amount of damages cannot be established with a sufficient degree of certainty, the assessment is at the discretion of the court.

Article 7.4.4. The non-performing party is liable only for harm which it foresaw or could reasonably have foreseen at the time of the conclusion of the contract as being likely to result from its non-performance.

Article 7.4.5. Where the aggrieved party has terminated the contract and has made a replacement transaction within a reasonable time and in a reasonable manner it may recover the difference between the contract price and the price of the replacement transaction as well as damages for any further harm.

Article 7.4.6. (1) Where the aggrieved party has terminated the contract and has not made a replacement transaction but there is a current price for the performance contracted for, it may recover the difference between the contract price and the price current at the time the contract is terminated as well as damages for any further harm.
(2) Current price is the price generally charged for goods delivered or services rendered in comparable circumstances at the place where the contract should have been performed or, if there is no current price at that place, the current price at such other place that appears reasonable to take as a reference.

Article 7.4.7. Where the harm is due in part to an act or omission of the aggrieved party or to another event as to which that party bears the risk, the amount of damages shall be reduced to the extent that these factors have contributed to the harm, having regard to the conduct of each of the parties.

Article 7.4.8. (1) The non-performing party is not liable for harm suffered by the aggrieved party to the extent that the harm could have been reduced by the latter party's taking reasonable steps.
(2) The aggrieved party is entitled to recover any expenses reasonably incurred in attempting to reduce the harm.

Article 7.4.9. (1) If a party does not pay a sum of money when it falls due the aggrieved party is entitled to interest upon that sum from the time when payment is due to the time of payment whether or not the non-payment is excused.
(2) The rate of interest shall be the average bank short-term lending rate to prime borrowers prevailing for the currency of payment at the place for payment, or where no such rate exists at that place, then the same rate in the State of the currency of payment.
In the absence of such a rate at either place the rate of interest shall be the appropriate rate fixed by the law of the State of the currency of payment.
(3) The aggrieved party is entitled to additional damages if the non-payment caused it a greater harm.

Article 7.4.10. Unless otherwise agreed, interest on damages for non-performance of non-monetary obligations accrues as from the time of non-performance.

Article 7.4.11. (1) Damages are to be paid in a lump sum. However, they may be payable in instalments where the nature of the harm makes this appropriate.
(2) Damages to be paid in instalments may be indexed.

Article 7.4.12. Damages are to be assessed either in the currency in which the monetary obligation was expressed or in the currency in which the harm was suffered, whichever is more appropriate.

Article 7.4.13. (1) Where the contract provides that a party who does not perform is to pay a specified sum to the aggrieved party for such non-performance, the aggrieved party is entitled to that sum irrespective of its actual harm.
(2) However, notwithstanding any agreement to the contrary the specified sum may be reduced to a reasonable amount where it is grossly excessive in relation to the harm resulting from the non-performance and to the other circumstances.

Chapter 8 —Set-Off

Article 8.1. (1) Where two parties owe each other money or other performances of the same kind, either of them ("the first party") may set off its obligation against that of its obligee ("the other party") if at the time of set-off,
(a) the first party is entitled to perform its obligation;
(b) the other party's obligation is ascertained as to its existence and amount and performance is due.
(2) If the obligations of both parties arise from the same contract, the first party may also set off its obligation against an obligation of the other party which is not ascertained as to its existence or to its amount.

Article 8.2. Where the obligations are to pay money in different currencies, the right of set-off may be exercised, provided that both currencies are freely convertible and the parties have not agreed that the first party shall pay only in a specified currency.

Article 8.3. The right of set-off is exercised by notice to the other party.

Article 8.4.(1) The notice must specify the obligations to which it relates.
(2) If the notice does not specify the obligation against which set-off is exercised, the other party may, within a reasonable time, declare to the first party the obligation to which set-off relates. If no such declaration is made, the set-off will relate to all the obligations proportionally.

Article 8.5. (1) Set-off discharges the obligations.
(2) If obligations differ in amount, set-off discharges the obligations up to the amount of the lesser obligation.
(3) Set-off takes effect as from the time of notice.

Chapter 9 – Assignment of Rights, Transfer of Obligations, Assignment of Contracts

Section 1: Assignment of Rights

Article 9.1.1. "Assignment of a right" means the transfer by agreement from one person (the "assignor") to another person (the "assignee"), including transfer by way of security, of the assignor's right to payment of a monetary sum or other performance from a third person ("the obligor").

Article 9.1.2. This Section does not apply to transfers made under the special rules governing the transfers:
(a) of instruments such as negotiable instruments, documents of title or financial instruments, or
(b) of rights in the course of transferring a business.

Article 9.1.3. A right to non-monetary performance may be assigned only if the assignment does not render the obligation significantly more burdensome.

Article 9.1.4. (1) A right to the payment of a monetary sum may be assigned partially.
(2) A right to other performance may be assigned partially only if it is divisible, and the assignment does not render the obligation significantly more burdensome.

Article 9.1.5. A future right is deemed to be transferred at the time of the agreement, provided the right, when it comes into existence, can be identified as the right to which the assignment relates.

Article 9.1.6. A number of rights may be assigned without individual specification, provided such rights can be identified as rights to which the assignment relates at the time of the assignment or when they come into existence.

Article 9.1.7. (1) A right is assigned by mere agreement between the assignor and the assignee, without notice to the obligor.
(2) The consent of the obligor is not required unless the obligation in the circumstances is of an essentially personal character.

Article 9.1.8. The obligor has a right to be compensated by the assignor or the assignee for any additional costs caused by the assignment.

Article 9.1.9. (1) The assignment of a right to the payment of a monetary sum is effective notwithstanding an agreement between the assignor and the obligor limiting or prohibiting such an assignment. However, the assignor may be liable to the obligor for breach of contract.
(2) The assignment of a right to other performance is ineffective if it is contrary to an agreement between the assignor and the obligor limiting or prohibiting the assignment. Nevertheless, the assignment is effective if the assignee, at the time of the assignment, neither knew nor ought to have known of the agreement. The assignor may then be liable to the obligor for breach of contract.

Article 9.1.10. (1) Until the obligor receives a notice of the assignment from either the assignor or the assignee, it is discharged by paying the assignor.
(2) After the obligor receives such a notice, it is discharged only by paying the assignee.

Article 9.1.11. If the same right has been assigned by the same assignor to two or more successive assignees, the obligor is discharged by paying according to the order in which the notices were received.

Article 9.1.12. (1) If notice of the assignment is given by the assignee, the obligor may request the assignee to provide within a reasonable time adequate proof that the assignment has been made.
(2) Until adequate proof is provided, the obligor may withhold payment.
(3) Unless adequate proof is provided, notice is not effective.
(4) Adequate proof includes, but is not limited to, any writing emanating from the assignor and indicating that the assignment has taken place.

Article 9.1.13. (1) The obligor may assert against the assignee all defences that the obligor could assert against the assignor.

(2) The obligor may exercise against the assignee any right of set-off available to the obligor against the assignor up to the time notice of assignment was received.

Article 9.1.14. The assignment of a right transfers to the assignee:
(a) all the assignor's rights to payment or other performance under the contract in respect of the right assigned, and
(b) all rights securing performance of the right assigned.

Article 9.1.15. The assignor undertakes towards the assignee, except as otherwise disclosed to the assignee, that:
(a) the assigned right exists at the time of the assignment, unless the right is a future right;
(b) the assignor is entitled to assign the right;
(c) the right has not been previously assigned to another assignee, and it is free from any right or claim from a third party;
(d) the obligor does not have any defences;
(e) neither the obligor nor the assignor has given notice of set-off concerning the assigned right and will not give any such notice;
(f) the assignor will reimburse the assignee for any payment received from the obligor before notice of the assignment was given.

Section 2: Transfer of Obligations

Article 9.2.1. An obligation to pay money or render other performance may be transferred from one person (the "original obligor") to another person (the "new obligor") either
(a) by an agreement between the original obligor and the new obligor subject to Article 9.2.3, or
b) by an agreement between the obligee and the new obligor, by which the new obligor assumes the obligation.

Article 9.2.2. This Section does not apply to transfers of obligations made under the special rules governing transfers of obligations in the course of transferring a business.

Article 9.2.3. The transfer of an obligation by an agreement between the original obligor and the new obligor requires the consent of the obligee.

Article 9.2.4. (1) The obligee may give its consent in advance.
(2) If the obligee has given its consent in advance, the transfer of the obligation becomes effective when a notice of the transfer is given to the obligee or when the obligee acknowledges it.

Article 9.2.5. (1) The obligee may discharge the original obligor.
(2) The obligee may also retain the original obligor as an obligor in case the new obligor does not perform properly.
(3) Otherwise the original obligor and the new obligor are jointly and severally liable.

Article 9.2.6. (1) Without the obligee's consent, the obligor may contract with another person that this person will perform the obligation in place of the obligor, unless the obligation in the circumstances has an essentially personal character.
(2) The obligee retains its claim against the obligor.

Article 9.2.7. (1) The new obligor may assert against the obligee all defences which the original obligor could assert against the obligee.
(2) The new obligor may not exercise against the obligee any right of set-off available to the original obligor against the obligee.

Article 9.2.8. (1) The obligee may assert against the new obligor all its rights to payment or other performance under the contract in respect of the obligation transferred.
(2) If the original obligor is discharged under Article 9.2.5(1), a security granted by any person other than the new obligor for the performance of the obligation is discharged, unless that other person agrees that it should continue to be available to the obligee.
(3) Discharge of the original obligor also extends to any security of the original obligor given to the obligee for the performance of the obligation, unless the security is over an asset which is transferred as part of a transaction between the original obligor and the new obligor.

Section 3: Assignment of Contracts

Article 9.3.1. "Assignment of a contract" means the transfer by agreement from one person (the "assignor") to another person (the "assignee") of the assignor's rights and obligations arising out of a contract with another person (the "other party").

Article 9.3.2. This Section does not apply to the assignment of contracts made under the special rules governing transfers of contracts in the course of transferring a business.

Article 9.3.3. The assignment of a contract requires the consent of the other party.

Article 9.3.4. (1) The other party may give its consent in advance.
(2) If the other party has given its consent in advance, the assignment of the contract becomes effective when a notice of the assignment is given to the other party or when the other party acknowledges it.

Article 9.3.5. (1) The other party may discharge the assignor.
(2) The other party may also retain the assignor as an obligor in case the assignee does not perform properly.
(3) Otherwise the assignor and the assignee are jointly and severally liable.

Article 9.3.6. (1) To the extent that the assignment of a contract involves an assignment of rights, Article 9.1.13 applies accordingly.
(2) To the extent that the assignment of a contract involves a transfer of obligations, Article 9.2.7 applies accordingly.

Article 9.3.7. (1) To the extent that the assignment of a contract involves an assignment of rights, Article 9.1.14 applies accordingly.
(2) To the extent that the assignment of a contract involves a transfer of obligations, Article 9.2.8 applies accordingly.

Chapter 10 – Limitation Periods

Article 10.1. (1) The exercise of rights governed by these Principles is barred by the expiration of a period of time, referred to as "limitation period", according to the rules of this Chapter.
(2) This Chapter does not govern the time within which one party is required under these Principles, as a condition for the acquisition or exercise of its right, to give notice to the other party or to perform any act other than the institution of legal proceedings.

Article 10.2. (1) The general limitation period is three years beginning on the day after the day the obligee knows or ought to know the facts as a result of which the obligee's right can be exercised.
(2) In any event, the maximum limitation period is ten years beginning on the day after the day the right can be exercised.

Article 10.3. (1) The parties may modify the limitation periods.
(2) However they may not
(a) shorten the general limitation period to less than one year;
(b) shorten the maximum limitation period to less than four years;
(c) extend the maximum limitation period to more than fifteen years.

Article 10.4. (1) Where the obligor before the expiration of the general limitation period acknowledges the right of the obligee, a new general limitation period begins on the day after the day of the acknowledgement.
(2) The maximum limitation period does not begin to run again, but may be exceeded by the beginning of a new general limitation period under Art. 10.2(1).

Article 10.5. (1) The running of the limitation period is suspended
(a) when the obligee performs any act, by commencing judicial proceedings or in judicial proceedings already instituted, that is recognised by the law of the court as asserting the obligee's right against the obligor;
(b) in the case of the obligor's insolvency when the obligee has asserted its rights in the insolvency proceedings; or

(c) in the case of proceedings for dissolution of the entity which is the obligor when the obligee has asserted its rights in the dissolution proceedings.
(2) Suspension lasts until a final decision has been issued or until the proceedings have been otherwise terminated.

Article 10.6. (1) The running of the limitation period is suspended when the obligee performs any act, by commencing arbitral proceedings or in arbitral proceedings already instituted, that is recognised by the law of the arbitral tribunal as asserting the obligee's right against the obligor. In the absence of regulations for arbitral proceedings or provisions determining the exact date of the commencement of arbitral proceedings, the proceedings are deemed to commence on the date on which a request that the right in dispute should be adjudicated reaches the obligor.
(2) Suspension lasts until a binding decision has been issued or until the proceedings have been otherwise terminated.

Article 10.7. The provisions of Articles 10.5 and 10.6 apply with appropriate modifications to other proceedings whereby the parties request a third person to assist them in their attempt to reach an amicable settlement of their dispute.

Article 10.8. (1) Where the obligee has been prevented by an impediment that is beyond its control and that it could neither avoid nor overcome, from causing a limitation period to cease to run under the preceding Articles, the general limitation period is suspended so as not to expire before one year after the relevant impediment has ceased to exist.
(2) Where the impediment consists of the incapacity or death of the obligee or obligor, suspension ceases when a representative for the incapacitated or deceased party or its estate has been appointed or a successor has inherited the respective party's position. The additional one-year period under paragraph (1) applies accordingly.

Article 10.9. (1) The expiration of the limitation period does not extinguish the right.
(2) For the expiration of the limitation period to have effect, the obligor must assert it as a defence.
(3) A right may still be relied on as a defence even though the expiration of the limitation period for that right has been asserted.

Article 10.10. The obligee may exercise the right of set-off until the obligor has asserted the expiration of the limitation period.

Article 10.11. Where there has been performance in order to discharge an obligation, there is no right of restitution merely because the limitation period has expired.

PART XI

International Tax Law

TAX

OECD 2008 Model Convention with respect to Taxes on Income and on Capital.[33]

Convention between (State A) and (State B) with respect to taxes on income and on capital

Chapter I. Scope of the convention

Article 1. This Convention shall apply to persons who are residents of one or both of the Contracting States.

Article 2. (1) This Convention shall apply to taxes on income and on capital imposed on behalf of a Contracting State or of its political subdivisions or local authorities, irrespective of the manner in which they are levied.
(2) There shall be regarded as taxes on income and on capital all taxes imposed on total income, on total capital, or on elements of income or of capital, including taxes on gains from the alienation of movable or immovable property, taxes on the total amounts of wages or salaries paid by enterprises, as well as taxes on capital appreciation.
(3) The existing taxes to which the Convention shall apply are in particular:
(a) (in State A): ....
(b) (in State B): ....
(4) The Convention shall apply also to any identical or substantially similar taxes that are imposed after the date of signature of the Convention in addition to, or in place of, the existing taxes. The competent authorities of the Contracting States shall notify each other of any significant changes that have been made in their taxation laws.

Chapter II. Definitions

Article 3. (1) For the purposes of this Convention, unless the context otherwise requires:
(a) the term "person" includes an individual, a company and any other body of persons;
(b) the term "company" means any body corporate or any entity that is treated as a body corporate for tax purposes;
(c) the term "enterprise" applies to the carrying on of any business;
(d) the terms "enterprise of a Contracting State" and "enterprise of the other Contracting State" mean respectively an enterprise carried on by a resident of a Contracting State and an enterprise carried on by a resident of the other Contracting State;
(e) the term "international traffic" means any transport by a ship or aircraft operated by an enterprise that has its place of effective management in a Contracting State, except when the ship or aircraft is operated solely between places in the other Contracting State;
(f) the term "competent authority" means:
(i) (in State A): ....
(ii) (in State B): ....
(g) the term "national", in relation to a Contracting State, means:
(i) any individual possessing the nationality or citizenship of that Contracting State; and
(ii) any legal person, partnership or association deriving its status as such from the laws in force in that Contracting State;
(h) the term "business" includes the performance of professional services and of other activities of an independent character.
(2) As regards the application of the Convention at any time by a Contracting State, any term not defined therein shall, unless the context otherwise requires, have the meaning that it has at that time under the law of that State for the purposes of the taxes to which the Convention applies, any meaning under the applicable tax laws of that State prevailing over a meaning given to the term under other laws of that State.

Article 4. (1) For the purposes of this Convention, the term "resident of a Contracting State" means any person who, under the laws of that State, is liable to tax therein by reason of his domicile, residence, place of management or any other criterion of a similar nature, and also includes that State and any political subdivision or local authority thereof. This term, however, does not include any person who is liable to tax in that State in respect only of income from sources in that State or capital situated therein.

---

[33] Reproduced with kind permission from the OECD. Reference: OECD (2008), Model Tax Convention on Income and on Capital: Condensed Version 2008, p. 17-43.

(2) Where by reason of the provisions of paragraph 1 an individual is a resident of both Contracting States, then his status shall be determined as follows:
(a) he shall be deemed to be a resident only of the State in which he has a permanent home available to him; if he has a permanent home available to him in both States, he shall be deemed to be a resident only of the State with which his personal and economic relations are closer (centre of vital interests);
(b) if the State in which he has his centre of vital interests cannot be determined, or if he has not a permanent home available to him in either State, he shall be deemed to be a resident only of the State in which he has an habitual abode;
(c) if he has an habitual abode in both States or in neither of them, he shall be deemed to be a resident only of the State of which he is a national;
(d) if he is a national of both States or of neither of them, the competent authorities of the Contracting States shall settle the question by mutual agreement.
(3) Where by reason of the provisions of paragraph 1 a person other than an individual is a resident of both Contracting States, then it shall be deemed to be a resident only of the State in which its place of effective management is situated.

Article 5. (1) For the purposes of this Convention, the term "permanent establishment" means a fixed place of business through
which the business of an enterprise is wholly or partly carried on.
(2) The term "permanent establishment" includes especially:
(a) a place of management;
(b) a branch;
(c) an office;
(d) a factory;
(e) a workshop, and
(f) a mine, an oil or gas well, a quarry or any other place of extraction of natural resources.
(3) A building site or construction or installation project constitutes a permanent establishment only if it lasts more than twelve months.
(4) Notwithstanding the preceding provisions of this Article, the term "permanent establishment" shall be deemed not to include:
(a) the use of facilities solely for the purpose of storage, display or delivery of goods or merchandise belonging to the enterprise;
(b) the maintenance of a stock of goods or merchandise belonging to the enterprise solely for the purpose of storage, display or delivery;
(c) the maintenance of a stock of goods or merchandise belonging to the enterprise solely for the purpose of processing by another enterprise;
(d) the maintenance of a fixed place of business solely for the purpose of purchasing goods or merchandise or of collecting information, for the enterprise;
(e) the maintenance of a fixed place of business solely for the purpose of carrying on, for the enterprise, any other activity of a preparatory or auxiliary character;
(f) the maintenance of a fixed place of business solely for any combination of activities mentioned in subparagraphs a) to e), provided that the overall activity of the fixed place of business resulting from this combination is of a preparatory or auxiliary character.
(5) Notwithstanding the provisions of paragraphs 1 and 2, where a person — other than an agent of an independent status to whom paragraph 6 applies — is acting on behalf of an enterprise and has, and habitually exercises, in a Contracting
State an authority to conclude contracts in the name of the enterprise, that enterprise shall be deemed to have a permanent establishment in that State in respect of any activities which that person undertakes for the enterprise, unless the activities of such person are limited to those mentioned in paragraph 4 which, if exercised through a fixed place of business, would not make this fixed place of business a permanent establishment under the provisions of that paragraph.
(6) An enterprise shall not be deemed to have a permanent establishment in a Contracting State merely because it carries on business in that State through a broker, general commission agent or any other agent of an independent status, provided that such persons are acting in the ordinary course of their business.
(7) The fact that a company which is a resident of a Contracting State controls or is controlled by a company which is a resident of the other Contracting State, or which carries on business in that other State (whether through a permanent establishment or otherwise), shall not of itself constitute either company a permanent establishment of the other.

Chapter III. Taxation of income

Article 6. (1) Income derived by a resident of a Contracting State from immovable property (including income from
agriculture or forestry) situated in the other Contracting State may be taxed in that other State.
(2) The term "immovable property" shall have the meaning which it has under the law of the Contracting State in which the property in question is situated. The term shall in any case include property accessory to immovable property, livestock and equipment used in agriculture and forestry, rights to which the provisions of general law respecting landed property apply, usufruct of immovable property and rights to variable or fixed payments as consideration for the working of, or the right to work, mineral deposits, sources and other natural resources; ships, boats and aircraft shall not be regarded as immovable property.
(3) The provisions of paragraph 1 shall apply to income derived from the direct use, letting, or use in any other form of immovable property.
(4) The provisions of paragraphs 1 and 3 shall also apply to the income from immovable property of an enterprise.

Article 7. (1) The profits of an enterprise of a Contracting State shall be taxable only in that State unless the enterprise carries
on business in the other Contracting State through a permanent establishment situated therein. If the enterprise carries on
business as aforesaid, the profits of the enterprise may be taxed in the other State but only so much of them as is attributable to that permanent establishment.
(2) Subject to the provisions of paragraph 3, where an enterprise of a Contracting State carries on business in the other Contracting State through a permanent establishment situated therein, there shall in each Contracting State be attributed to that permanent establishment the profits which it might be expected to make if it were a distinct and separate enterprise engaged in the same or similar activities under the same or similar conditions and dealing wholly independently with the enterprise of which it is a permanent establishment.
(3) In determining the profits of a permanent establishment, there shall be allowed as deductions expenses which are incurred for the purposes of the permanent establishment, including executive and general administrative expenses so incurred, whether in the State in which the permanent establishment is situated or elsewhere.
(4) Insofar as it has been customary in a Contracting State to determine the profits to be attributed to a permanent establishment on the basis of an apportionment of the total profits of the enterprise to its various parts, nothing in paragraph 2 shall preclude that Contracting State from determining the profits to be taxed by such an apportionment as may be customary; the method of apportionment adopted shall, however, be such that the result shall be in accordance with the principles contained in this Article.
(5) No profits shall be attributed to a permanent establishment by reason of the mere purchase by that permanent establishment of goods or merchandise for the enterprise.
(6) For the purposes of the preceding paragraphs, the profits to be attributed to the permanent establishment shall be determined by the same method year by year unless there is good and sufficient reason to the contrary.
(7) Where profits include items of income which are dealt with separately in other Articles of this Convention, then the provisions of those Articles shall not be affected by the provisions of this Article.

Article 8. (1) Profits from the operation of ships or aircraft in international traffic shall be taxable only in the Contracting State
in which the place of effective management of the enterprise is situated.
(2) Profits from the operation of boats engaged in inland waterways transport shall be taxable only in the Contracting State in which the place of effective management of the enterprise is situated.
(3) If the place of effective management of a shipping enterprise or of an inland waterways transport enterprise is aboard a ship or boat, then it shall be deemed to be situated in the Contracting State in which the home harbour of the ship or boat is situated, or, if there is no such home harbour, in the Contracting State of which the operator of the ship or boat is a resident.
(4) The provisions of paragraph 1 shall also apply to profits from the participation in a pool, a joint business or an international operating agency.

Article 9. (1) Where
(a) an enterprise of a Contracting State participates directly or indirectly in the management, control or capital of an enterprise of the other Contracting State, or
(b) the same persons participate directly or indirectly in the management, control or capital of an enterprise of a Contracting State and an enterprise of the other Contracting State,

and in either case conditions are made or imposed between the two enterprises in their commercial or financial relations which differ from those which would be made between independent enterprises, then any profits which would, but for those conditions, have accrued to one of the enterprises, but, by reason of those conditions, have not so accrued, may be included in the profits of that enterprise and taxed accordingly.

(2) Where a Contracting State includes in the profits of an enterprise of that State and taxes accordingly profits on which an enterprise of the other Contracting State has been charged to tax in that other State and the profits so included are profits which would have accrued to the enterprise of the first-mentioned State if the conditions made between the two enterprises had been those which would have been made between independent enterprises, then that other State shall make an appropriate adjustment to the amount of the tax charged therein on those profits. In determining such adjustment, due regard shall be had to the other provisions of this Convention and the competent authorities of the Contracting States shall if necessary consult each other.

Article 10. (1) Dividends paid by a company which is a resident of a Contracting State to a resident of the other Contracting State may be taxed in that other State.

(2) However, such dividends may also be taxed in the Contracting State of which the company paying the dividends is a resident and according to the laws of that State, but if the beneficial owner of the dividends is a resident of the other Contracting State, the tax so charged shall not exceed:

(a) 5 per cent of the gross amount of the dividends if the beneficial owner is a company (other than a partnership) which holds directly at least 25 per cent of the capital of the company paying the dividends;

(b) 15 per cent of the gross amount of the dividends in all other cases. The competent authorities of the Contracting States shall by mutual agreement settle the mode of application of these limitations. This paragraph shall not affect the taxation of the company in respect of the profits out of which the dividends are paid.

(3) The term "dividends" as used in this Article means income from shares, "jouissance" shares or "jouissance" rights, mining shares, founders' shares or other rights, not being debt-claims, participating in profits, as well as income from other corporate rights which is subjected to the same taxation treatment as income from shares by the laws of the State of which the company making the distribution is a resident.

(4) The provisions of paragraphs 1 and 2 shall not apply if the beneficial owner of the dividends, being a resident of a Contracting State, carries on business in the other Contracting State of which the company paying the dividends is a resident through a permanent establishment situated therein and the holding in respect of which the dividends are paid is effectively connected with such permanent establishment. In such case the provisions of Article 7 shall apply.

(5) Where a company which is a resident of a Contracting State derives profits or income from the other Contracting State, that other State may not impose any tax on the dividends paid by the company, except insofar as such dividends are paid to a resident of that other State or insofar as the holding in respect of which the dividends are paid is effectively connected with a permanent establishment situated in that other State, nor subject the company's undistributed profits to a tax on the company's undistributed profits, even if the dividends paid or the undistributed profits consist wholly or partly of profits or income arising in such other State.

Article 11. (1) Interest arising in a Contracting State and paid to a resident of the other Contracting State may be taxed in that other State.

(2) However, such interest may also be taxed in the Contracting State in which it arises and according to the laws of that State, but if the beneficial owner of the interest is a resident of the other Contracting State, the tax so charged shall not exceed 10 per cent of the gross amount of the interest. The competent authorities of the Contracting States shall by mutual agreement settle the mode of application of this limitation.

(3) The term "interest" as used in this Article means income from debt-claims of every kind, whether or not secured by mortgage and whether or not carrying a right to participate in the debtor's profits, and in particular, income from government securities and income from bonds or debentures, including premiums and prizes attaching to such securities, bonds or debentures. Penalty charges for late payment shall not be regarded as interest for the purpose of this Article.

(4) The provisions of paragraphs 1 and 2 shall not apply if the beneficial owner of the interest, being a resident of a Contracting State, carries on business in the other Contracting State in which the interest arises through a permanent establishment situated therein and the debt-claim in respect of which the interest is paid is effectively connected with such permanent establishment. In such case the provisions of Article 7 shall apply.

(5) Interest shall be deemed to arise in a Contracting State when the payer is a resident of that State. Where, however, the person paying the interest, whether he is a resident of a Contracting State or not, has in a Contracting State a permanent establishment in connection with which the indebtedness on which the interest is paid was incurred, and such interest is borne by such permanent establishment, then such interest shall be deemed to arise in the State in which the permanent establishment is situated.

(6) Where, by reason of a special relationship between the payer and the beneficial owner or between both of them and some other person, the amount of the interest, having regard to the debt-claim for which it is paid, exceeds the amount which would have been agreed upon by the payer and the beneficial owner in the absence of such relationship, the provisions of this Article shall apply only to the last-mentioned amount. In such case, the excess part of the payments shall remain taxable according to the laws of each Contracting State, due regard being had to the other provisions of this Convention.

Article 12. (1) Royalties arising in a Contracting State and beneficially owned by a resident of the other Contracting State shall be taxable only in that other State.
(2) The term "royalties" as used in this Article means payments of any kind received as a consideration for the use of, or the right to use, any copyright of literary, artistic or scientific work including cinematograph films, any patent, trade mark, design or model, plan, secret formula or process, or for information concerning industrial, commercial or scientific experience.
(3) The provisions of paragraph 1 shall not apply if the beneficial owner of the royalties, being a resident of a Contracting State, carries on business in the other Contracting State in which the royalties arise through a permanent establishment situated therein and the right or property in respect of which the royalties are paid is effectively connected with such permanent establishment. In such case the provisions of Article 7 shall apply.
(4) Where, by reason of a special relationship between the payer and the beneficial owner or between both of them and some other person, the amount of the royalties, having regard to the use, right or information for which they are paid, exceeds the amount which would have been agreed upon by the payer and the beneficial owner in the absence of such relationship, the provisions of this Article shall apply only to the last-mentioned amount. In such case, the excess part of the payments shall remain taxable according to the laws of each Contracting State, due regard being had to the other provisions of this Convention.

Article 13. (1) Gains derived by a resident of a Contracting State from the alienation of immovable property referred to in
Article 6 and situated in the other Contracting State may be taxed in that other State.
(2) Gains from the alienation of movable property forming part of the business property of a permanent establishment which an enterprise of a Contracting State has in the other Contracting State, including such gains from the alienation of such a permanent establishment (alone or with the whole enterprise), may be taxed in that other State.
(3) Gains from the alienation of ships or aircraft operated in international traffic, boats engaged in inland waterways transport or movable property pertaining to the operation of such ships, aircraft or boats, shall be taxable only in the Contracting State in which the place of effective management of the enterprise is situated.
(4) Gains derived by a resident of a Contracting State from the alienation of shares deriving more than 50 per cent of their value directly or indirectly from immovable property situated in the other Contracting State may be taxed in that other State.
(5) Gains from the alienation of any property, other than that referred to in paragraphs 1, 2, 3 and 4, shall be taxable only in the Contracting State of which the alienator is a resident.

Article 14. (Deleted.)

Article 15. (1) Subject to the provisions of Articles 16, 18 and 19, salaries, wages and other similar remuneration derived by a resident of a Contracting State in respect of an employment shall be taxable only in that State unless the employment is exercised in the other Contracting State. If the employment is so exercised, such remuneration as is derived therefrom may be taxed in that other State.
(2) Notwithstanding the provisions of paragraph 1, remuneration derived by a resident of a Contracting State in respect of an employment exercised in the other Contracting State shall be taxable only in the first-mentioned State if:
(a) the recipient is present in the other State for a period or periods not exceeding in the aggregate 183 days in any twelve month period commencing or ending in the fiscal year concerned, and
(b) the remuneration is paid by, or on behalf of, an employer who is not a resident of the other State, and
(c) the remuneration is not borne by a permanent establishment which the employer has in the other State.
(3) Notwithstanding the preceding provisions of this Article, remuneration derived in respect of an employment exercised aboard a ship or aircraft operated in international traffic, or aboard a boat engaged in inland waterways transport, may be taxed in the Contracting State in which the place of effective management of the enterprise is situated.

Article 16. Directors' fees and other similar payments derived by a resident of a Contracting State in his capacity as a member of the board of directors of a company which is a resident of the other Contracting State may be taxed in that other State.

Article 17. (1) Notwithstanding the provisions of Articles 7 and 15, income derived by a resident of a Contracting State as an entertainer, such as a theatre, motion picture, radio or television artiste, or a musician, or as a sportsman, from his personal activities as such exercised in the other Contracting State, may be taxed in that other State.
(2) Where income in respect of personal activities exercised by an entertainer or a sportsman in his capacity as such accrues not to the entertainer or sportsman himself but to another person, that income may, notwithstanding the provisions of Articles 7 and 15, be taxed in the Contracting State in which the activities of the entertainer or sportsman are exercised.

Article 18. Subject to the provisions of paragraph 2 of Article 19, pensions and other similar remuneration paid to a resident of a Contracting State in consideration of past employment shall be taxable only in that State.

Article 19. (1) (a) Salaries, wages and other similar remuneration paid by a Contracting State or a political subdivision or a local authority thereof to an individual in respect of services rendered to that State or subdivision or authority shall be taxable only in that State.
(b) However, such salaries, wages and other similar remuneration shall be taxable only in the other Contracting State if the services are rendered in that State and the individual is a resident of that State who:
(i) is a national of that State; or
(ii) did not become a resident of that State solely for the purpose of rendering the services.
(2) (a) Notwithstanding the provisions of paragraph 1, pensions and other similar remuneration paid by, or out of funds created by, a Contracting State or a political subdivision or a local authority thereof to an individual in respect of services rendered to that State or subdivision or authority shall be taxable only in that State.
(b) However, such pensions and other similar remuneration shall be taxable only in the other Contracting State if the individual is a resident of, and a national of, that State.
(3) The provisions of Articles 15, 16, 17, and 18 shall apply to salaries, wages, pensions, and other similar remuneration in respect of services rendered in connection with a business carried on by a Contracting State or a political subdivision or a local authority thereof.

Article 20. Payments which a student or business apprentice who is or was immediately before visiting a Contracting State a resident of the other Contracting State and who is present in the first-mentioned State solely for the purpose of his education or training receives for the purpose of his maintenance, education or training shall not be taxed in that State, provided that such payments arise from sources outside that State.

Article 21. (1) Items of income of a resident of a Contracting State, wherever arising, not dealt with in the foregoing Articles of this Convention shall be taxable only in that State.
(2) The provisions of paragraph 1 shall not apply to income, other than income from immovable property as defined in paragraph 2 of Article 6, if the recipient of such income, being a resident of a Contracting State, carries on business in the other Contracting State through a permanent establishment situated therein and the right or property in respect of which the income is paid is effectively connected with such permanent establishment. In such case the provisions of Article 7 shall apply.

Chapter IV. Taxation of capital

Article 22. (1) Capital represented by immovable property referred to in Article 6, owned by a resident of a Contracting State and situated in the other Contracting State, may be taxed in that other State.
(2) Capital represented by movable property forming part of the business property of a permanent establishment which an enterprise of a Contracting State has in the other Contracting State may be taxed in that other State.
(3) Capital represented by ships and aircraft operated in international traffic and by boats engaged in inland waterways transport, and by movable property pertaining to the operation of such ships, aircraft and boats, shall be taxable only in the Contracting State in which the place of effective management of the enterprise is situated.
(4) All other elements of capital of a resident of a Contracting State shall be taxable only in that State.

Chapter V. Methods for elimination of double taxation

Article 23A. (1) Where a resident of a Contracting State derives income or owns capital which, in accordance with the provisions of this Convention, may be taxed in the other Contracting State, the first-mentioned State shall, subject to the provisions of paragraphs 2 and 3, exempt such income or capital from tax.
(2) Where a resident of a Contracting State derives items of income which, in accordance with the provisions of Articles 10 and 11, may be taxed in the other Contracting State, the first-mentioned State shall allow as a deduction from the tax on the income of that resident an amount equal to the tax paid in that other State. Such deduction shall not, however, exceed that part of the tax, as computed before the deduction is given, which is attributable to such items of income derived from that other State.
(3) Where in accordance with any provision of the Convention income derived or capital owned by a resident of a Contracting State is exempt from tax in that State, such State may nevertheless, in calculating the amount of tax on the remaining income or capital of such resident, take into account the exempted income or capital.
(4) The provisions of paragraph 1 shall not apply to income derived or capital owned by a resident of a Contracting State where the other Contracting State applies the provisions of this Convention to exempt such income or capital from tax or applies the provisions of paragraph 2 of Article 10 or 11 to such income.

Article 23B. (1) Where a resident of a Contracting State derives income or owns capital which, in accordance with the provisions of this Convention, may be taxed in the other Contracting State, the first-mentioned State shall allow:
(a) as a deduction from the tax on the income of that resident, an amount equal to the income tax paid in that other State;
(b) as a deduction from the tax on the capital of that resident, an amount equal to the capital tax paid in that other State.
Such deduction in either case shall not, however, exceed that part of the income tax or capital tax, as computed before the deduction is given, which is attributable, as the case may be, to the income or the capital which may be taxed in that other State.
(2) Where in accordance with any provision of the Convention income derived or capital owned by a resident of a Contracting State is exempt from tax in that State, such State may nevertheless, in calculating the amount of tax on the remaining income or capital of such resident, take into account the exempted income or capital.

Chapter VI. Special provisions

Article 24. (1) Nationals of a Contracting State shall not be subjected in the other Contracting State to any taxation or any requirement connected therewith, which is other or more burdensome than the taxation and connected requirements to which nationals of that other State in the same circumstances, in particular with respect to residence, are or may be subjected. This provision shall, notwithstanding the provisions of Article 1, also apply to persons who are not residents of one or both of the Contracting States.
(2) Stateless persons who are residents of a Contracting State shall not be subjected in either Contracting State to any taxation or any requirement connected therewith, which is other or more burdensome than the taxation and connected requirements to which nationals of the State concerned in the same circumstances, in particular with respect to residence, are or may be subjected.
(3) The taxation on a permanent establishment which an enterprise of a Contracting State has in the other Contracting State shall not be less favourably levied in that other State than the taxation levied on enterprises of that other State carrying on the same activities. This provision shall not be construed as obliging a Contracting State to grant to residents of the other Contracting State any personal allowances, reliefs and reductions for taxation purposes on account of civil status or family responsibilities which it grants to its own residents.
(4) Except where the provisions of paragraph 1 of Article 9, paragraph 6 of Article 11, or paragraph 4 of Article 12, apply, interest, royalties and other disbursements paid by an enterprise of a Contracting State to a resident of the other Contracting State shall, for the purpose of determining the taxable profits of such enterprise, be deductible under the same conditions as if they had been paid to a resident of the first-mentioned State. Similarly, any debts of an enterprise of a Contracting State to a resident of the other Contracting State shall, for the purpose of determining the taxable capital of such enterprise, be deductible under the same conditions as if they had been contracted to a resident of the first-mentioned State.
(5) Enterprises of a Contracting State, the capital of which is wholly or partly owned or controlled, directly or indirectly, by one or more residents of the other Contracting State, shall not be subjected in the first-mentioned State to any taxation or any requirement connected therewith which is other or more burdensome than the taxation and connected requirements to which other similar enterprises of the first-mentioned State are or may be subjected.

(6) The provisions of this Article shall, notwithstanding the provisions of Article 2, apply to taxes of every kind and description.

Article 25. (1) Where a person considers that the actions of one or both of the Contracting States result or will result for him in taxation not in accordance with the provisions of this Convention, he may, irrespective of the remedies provided by the domestic law of those States, present his case to the competent authority of the Contracting State of which he is a resident or, if his case comes under paragraph 1 of Article 24, to that of the Contracting State of which he is a national. The case must be presented within three years from the first notification of the action resulting in taxation not in accordance with the provisions of the Convention.
(2) The competent authority shall endeavour, if the objection appears to it to be justified and if it is not itself able to arrive at a satisfactory solution, to resolve the case by mutual agreement with the competent authority of the other Contracting State, with a view to the avoidance of taxation which is not in accordance with the Convention. Any agreement reached shall be implemented notwithstanding any time limits in the domestic law of the Contracting States.
(3) The competent authorities of the Contracting States shall endeavour to resolve by mutual agreement any difficulties or doubts arising as to the interpretation or application of the Convention. They may also consult together for the elimination of double taxation in cases not provided for in the Convention.
(4) The competent authorities of the Contracting States may communicate with each other directly, including through a joint commission consisting of themselves or their representatives, for the purpose of reaching an agreement in the sense of the preceding paragraphs.
(5) Where, (a) under paragraph 1, a person has presented a case to the competent authority of a Contracting State on the basis that the actions of one or both of the Contracting States have resulted for that person in taxation not in accordance with the provisions of this Convention, and
(b) the competent authorities are unable to reach an agreement to resolve that case pursuant to paragraph 2 within two years from the presentation of the case to the competent authority of the other Contracting State, any unresolved issues arising from the case shall be submitted to arbitration if the person so requests. These unresolved issues shall not, however, be submitted to arbitration if a decision on these issues has already been rendered by a court or administrative tribunal of either State. Unless a person directly affected by the case does not accept the mutual agreement that implements the arbitration decision, that decision shall be binding on both Contracting States and shall be implemented notwithstanding any time limits in the domestic laws of these States. The competent authorities of the Contracting States shall by mutual agreement settle the mode of application of this paragraph.

Article 26. (1) The competent authorities of the Contracting States shall exchange such information as is foreseeably relevant for carrying out the provisions of this Convention or to the administration or enforcement of the domestic laws concerning taxes of every kind and description imposed on behalf of the Contracting States, or of their political subdivisions or local authorities, insofar as the taxation thereunder is not contrary to the Convention. The exchange of information is not restricted by Articles 1 and 2.
(2) Any information received under paragraph 1 by a Contracting State shall be treated as secret in the same manner as information obtained under the domestic laws of that State and shall be disclosed only to persons or authorities (including courts and administrative bodies) concerned with the assessment or collection of, the enforcement or prosecution in respect of, the determination of appeals in relation to the taxes referred to in paragraph 1, or the oversight of the above. Such persons or authorities shall use the information only for such purposes. They may disclose the information in public court proceedings or in judicial decisions.
(3) In no case shall the provisions of paragraphs 1 and 2 be construed so as to impose on a Contracting State the obligation:
(a) to carry out administrative measures at variance with the laws and administrative practice of that or of the other Contracting State;
(b) to supply information which is not obtainable under the laws or in the normal course of the administration of that or of the other Contracting State;
(c) to supply information which would disclose any trade, business, industrial, commercial or professional secret or trade process, or information the disclosure of which would be contrary to public policy (ordre public).
(4) If information is requested by a Contracting State in accordance with this Article, the other Contracting State shall use its information gathering measures to obtain the requested information, even though that other State may not need such information for its own tax purposes. The obligation contained in the preceding sentence is subject to the limitations of paragraph 3 but in no case shall such limitations be construed to permit a Contracting State to decline to supply information solely because it has no domestic interest in such information.

(5) In no case shall the provisions of paragraph 3 be construed to permit a Contracting State to decline to supply information solely because the information is held by a bank, other financial institution, nominee or person acting in an agency or a fiduciary capacity or because it relates to ownership interests in a person.

Article 27. (1) The Contracting States shall lend assistance to each other in the collection of revenue claims. This assistance is not restricted by Articles 1 and 2. The competent authorities of the Contracting States may by mutual agreement settle the mode of application of this Article.
(2) The term "revenue claim" as used in this Article means an amount owed in respect of taxes of every kind and description imposed on behalf of the Contracting States, or of their political subdivisions or local authorities, insofar as the taxation thereunder is not contrary to this Convention or any other instrument to which the Contracting States are parties, as well as interest, administrative penalties and costs of collection or conservancy related to such amount.
(3) When a revenue claim of a Contracting State is enforceable under the laws of that State and is owed by a person who, at that time, cannot, under the laws of that State, prevent its collection, that revenue claim shall, at the request of the competent authority of that State, be accepted for purposes of collection by the competent authority of the other Contracting State. That revenue claim shall be collected by that other State in accordance with the provisions of its laws applicable to the enforcement and collection of its own taxes as if the revenue claim were a revenue claim of that other State.
(4) When a revenue claim of a Contracting State is a claim in respect of which that State may, under its law, take measures of conservancy with a view to ensure its collection, that revenue claim shall, at the request of the competent authority of that State, be accepted for purposes of taking measures of conservancy by the competent authority of the other Contracting State. That other State shall take measures of conservancy in respect of that revenue claim in accordance with the provisions of its laws as if the revenue claim were a revenue claim of that other State even if, at the time when such measures are applied, the revenue claim is not enforceable in the first-mentioned State or is owed by a person who has a right to prevent its collection.
(5) Notwithstanding the provisions of paragraphs 3 and 4, a revenue claim accepted by a Contracting State for purposes of paragraph 3 or 4 shall not, in that State, be subject to the time limits or accorded any priority applicable to a revenue claim under the laws of that State by reason of its nature as such. In addition, a revenue claim accepted by a Contracting State for the purposes of paragraph 3 or 4 shall not, in that State, have any priority applicable to that revenue claim under the laws of the other Contracting State.
(6) Proceedings with respect to the existence, validity or the amount of a revenue claim of a Contracting State shall not be brought before the courts or administrative bodies of the other Contracting State.
(7) Where, at any time after a request has been made by a Contracting State under paragraph 3 or 4 and before the other Contracting State has collected and remitted the relevant revenue claim to the first-mentioned State, the relevant revenue claim ceases to be
(a) in the case of a request under paragraph 3, a revenue claim of the first-mentioned State that is enforceable under the laws of that State and is owed by a person who, at that time, cannot, under the laws of that State, prevent its collection, or
(b) in the case of a request under paragraph 4, a revenue claim of the first-mentioned State in respect of which that State may, under its laws, take measures of conservancy with a view to ensure its collection
the competent authority of the first-mentioned State shall promptly notify the competent authority of the other State of that fact and, at the option of the other State, the first-mentioned State shall either suspend or withdraw its request.
(8) In no case shall the provisions of this Article be construed so as to impose on a Contracting State the obligation:
(a) to carry out administrative measures at variance with the laws and administrative practice of that or of the other Contracting State;
(b) to carry out measures which would be contrary to public policy (ordre public);
(c) to provide assistance if the other Contracting State has not pursued all reasonable measures of collection or conservancy, as the case may be, available under its laws or administrative practice;
(d) to provide assistance in those cases where the administrative burden for that State is clearly disproportionate to the benefit to be derived by the other Contracting State.

Article 28. Nothing in this Convention shall affect the fiscal privileges of members of diplomatic missions or consular posts under the general rules of international law or under the provisions of special agreements.

Article 29. (1) This Convention may be extended, either in its entirety or with any necessary modifications to any part of the territory of (State A) or of (State B) which is specifically excluded from the application of the

Convention or, to any State or territory for whose international relations (State A) or (State B) is responsible, which imposes taxes substantially similar in character to those to which the Convention applies. Any such extension shall take effect from such date and subject to such modifications and conditions, including conditions as to termination, as may be specified and agreed between the Contracting States in notes to be exchanged through diplomatic channels or in any other manner in accordance with their constitutional procedures.

(2) Unless otherwise agreed by both Contracting States, the termination of the Convention by one of them under Article 30 shall also terminate, in the manner provided for in that Article, the application of the Convention to any part of the territory of (State A) or of (State B) or to any State or territory to which it has been extended under this Article.

Chapter VII. Final provisions

Article 30. (1) This Convention shall be ratified and the instruments of ratification shall be exchanged at .... as soon as possible.
(2) The Convention shall enter into force upon the exchange of instruments of ratification and its provisions shall have effect:
(a) (in State A): ....
(b) (in State B): ....

Article 31. This Convention shall remain in force until terminated by a Contracting State. Either Contracting State may terminate the Convention, through diplomatic channels, by giving notice of termination at least six months before the end of any calendar year after the year ...... In such event, the Convention shall cease to have effect:
(a) (in State A): ....
(b) (in State B): ....

PART XII

United States Law

USA

Constitution of the United States of America of 17 September 1787, including Amendments.

Preamble
We the People of the United States, in Order to form a more perfect Union, establish Justice, insure domestic Tranquility, provide for the common defence, promote the general Welfare, and secure the Blessings of Liberty to ourselves and our Posterity, do ordain and establish this Constitution for the United States of America.

Article I.

Section 1. All legislative Powers herein granted shall be vested in a Congress of the United States, which shall consist of a Senate and House of Representatives.
Section 2. The House of Representatives shall be composed of Members chosen every second Year by the People of the several States, and the Electors in each State shall have the Qualifications requisite for Electors of the most numerous Branch of the State Legislature.
No Person shall be a Representative who shall not have attained to the Age of twenty five Years, and been seven Years a Citizen of the United States, and who shall not, when elected, be an Inhabitant of that State in which he shall be chosen.
Representatives and direct Taxes shall be apportioned among the several States which may be included within this Union, according to their respective Numbers, which shall be determined by adding to the whole Number of free Persons, including those bound to Service for a Term of Years, and excluding Indians not taxed, three fifths of all other Persons. The actual Enumeration shall be made within three Years after the first Meeting of the Congress of the United States, and within every subsequent Term of ten Years, in such Manner as they shall by Law direct.
The Number of Representatives shall not exceed one for every thirty Thousand, but each State shall have at Least one Representative; and until such enumeration shall be made, the State of New Hampshire shall be entitled to chuse three, Massachusetts eight, Rhode-Island and Providence Plantations one, Connecticut five, New-York six, New Jersey four, Pennsylvania eight, Delaware one, Maryland six, Virginia ten, North Carolina five, South Carolina five, and Georgia three.
When vacancies happen in the Representation from any State, the Executive Authority thereof shall issue Writs of Election to fill such Vacancies.
The House of Representatives shall chuse their Speaker and other Officers; and shall have the sole Power of Impeachment.
Section 3. The Senate of the United States shall be composed of two Senators from each State, chosen by the Legislature thereof for six Years; and each Senator shall have one Vote.
Immediately after they shall be assembled in Consequence of the first Election, they shall be divided as equally as may be into three Classes. The Seats of the Senators of the first Class shall be vacated at the Expiration of the second Year, of the second Class at the Expiration of the fourth Year, and of the third Class at the Expiration of the sixth Year, so that one third may be chosen every second Year; and if Vacancies happen by Resignation, or otherwise, during the Recess of the Legislature of any State, the Executive thereof may make temporary Appointments until the next Meeting of the Legislature, which shall then fill such Vacancies.
No Person shall be a Senator who shall not have attained to the Age of thirty Years, and been nine Years a Citizen of the United States, and who shall not, when elected, be an Inhabitant of that State for which he shall be chosen.
The Vice President of the United States shall be President of the Senate, but shall have no Vote, unless they be equally divided.
The Senate shall chuse their other Officers, and also a President pro tempore, in the Absence of the Vice President, or when he shall exercise the Office of President of the United States.
The Senate shall have the sole Power to try all Impeachments. When sitting for that Purpose, they shall be on Oath or Affirmation. When the President of the United States is tried, the Chief Justice shall preside: And no Person shall be convicted without the Concurrence of two thirds of the Members present.
Judgment in Cases of Impeachment shall not extend further than to removal from Office, and disqualification to hold and enjoy any Office of honor, Trust or Profit under the United States: but the Party convicted shall nevertheless be liable and subject to Indictment, Trial, Judgment and Punishment, according to Law.
Section 4. The Times, Places and Manner of holding Elections for Senators and Representatives, shall be prescribed in each State by the Legislature thereof; but the Congress may at any time by Law make or alter such Regulations, except as to the Places of chusing Senators.
The Congress shall assemble at least once in every Year, and such Meeting shall be on the first Monday in December, unless they shall by Law appoint a different Day.

Section 5. Each House shall be the Judge of the Elections, Returns and Qualifications of its own Members, and a Majority of each shall constitute a Quorum to do Business; but a smaller Number may adjourn from day to day, and may be authorized to compel the Attendance of absent Members, in such Manner, and under such Penalties as each House may provide.

Each House may determine the Rules of its Proceedings, punish its Members for disorderly Behaviour, and, with the Concurrence of two thirds, expel a Member.

Each House shall keep a Journal of its Proceedings, and from time to time publish the same, excepting such Parts as may in their Judgment require Secrecy; and the Yeas and Nays of the Members of either House on any question shall, at the Desire of one fifth of those Present, be entered on the Journal.

Neither House, during the Session of Congress, shall, without the Consent of the other, adjourn for more than three days, nor to any other Place than that in which the two Houses shall be sitting.

Section 6. The Senators and Representatives shall receive a Compensation for their Services, to be ascertained by Law, and paid out of the Treasury of the United States. They shall in all Cases, except Treason, Felony and Breach of the Peace, be privileged from Arrest during their Attendance at the Session of their respective Houses, and in going to and returning from the same; and for any Speech or Debate in either House, they shall not be questioned in any other Place.

No Senator or Representative shall, during the Time for which he was elected, be appointed to any civil Office under the Authority of the United States, which shall have been created, or the Emoluments whereof shall have been encreased during such time; and no Person holding any Office under the United States, shall be a Member of either House during his Continuance in Office.

Section 7. All Bills for raising Revenue shall originate in the House of Representatives; but the Senate may propose or concur with Amendments as on other Bills.

Every Bill which shall have passed the House of Representatives and the Senate, shall, before it become a Law, be presented to the President of the United States: If he approve he shall sign it, but if not he shall return it, with his Objections to that House in which it shall have originated, who shall enter the Objections at large on their Journal, and proceed to reconsider it. If after such Reconsideration two thirds of that House shall agree to pass the Bill, it shall be sent, together with the Objections, to the other House, by which it shall likewise be reconsidered, and if approved by two thirds of that House, it shall become a Law. But in all such Cases the Votes of both Houses shall be determined by yeas and Nays, and the Names of the Persons voting for and against the Bill shall be entered on the Journal of each House respectively. If any Bill shall not be returned by the President within ten Days (Sundays excepted) after it shall have been presented to him, the Same shall be a Law, in like Manner as if he had signed it, unless the Congress by their Adjournment prevent its Return, in which Case it shall not be a Law.

Every Order, Resolution, or Vote to which the Concurrence of the Senate and House of Representatives may be necessary (except on a question of Adjournment) shall be presented to the President of the United States; and before the Same shall take Effect, shall be approved by him, or being disapproved by him, shall be repassed by two thirds of the Senate and House of Representatives, according to the Rules and Limitations prescribed in the Case of a Bill.

Section 8. The Congress shall have Power To lay and collect Taxes, Duties, Imposts and Excises, to pay the Debts and provide for the common Defence and general Welfare of the United States; but all Duties, Imposts and Excises shall be uniform throughout the United States;

To borrow Money on the credit of the United States;

To regulate Commerce with foreign Nations, and among the several States, and with the Indian Tribes;

To establish an uniform Rule of Naturalization, and uniform Laws on the subject of Bankruptcies throughout the United States;

To coin Money, regulate the Value thereof, and of foreign Coin, and fix the Standard of Weights and Measures;

To provide for the Punishment of counterfeiting the Securities and current Coin of the United States;

To establish Post Offices and post Roads;

To promote the Progress of Science and useful Arts, by securing for limited Times to Authors and Inventors the exclusive Right to their respective Writings and Discoveries;

To constitute Tribunals inferior to the supreme Court;

To define and punish Piracies and Felonies committed on the high Seas, and Offences against the Law of Nations;

To declare War, grant Letters of Marque and Reprisal, and make Rules concerning Captures on Land and Water;

To raise and support Armies, but no Appropriation of Money to that Use shall be for a longer Term than two Years;

To provide and maintain a Navy;

To make Rules for the Government and Regulation of the land and naval Forces;

To provide for calling forth the Militia to execute the Laws of the Union, suppress Insurrections and repel Invasions;

To provide for organizing, arming, and disciplining, the Militia, and for governing such Part of them as may be employed in the Service of the United States, reserving to the States respectively, the Appointment of the Officers, and the Authority of training the Militia according to the discipline prescribed by Congress;

To exercise exclusive Legislation in all Cases whatsoever, over such District (not exceeding ten Miles square) as may, by Cession of particular States, and the Acceptance of Congress, become the Seat of the Government of the United States, and to exercise like Authority over all Places purchased by the Consent of the Legislature of the State in which the Same shall be, for the Erection of Forts, Magazines, Arsenals, dock-Yards, and other needful Buildings;--And

To make all Laws which shall be necessary and proper for carrying into Execution the foregoing Powers, and all other Powers vested by this Constitution in the Government of the United States, or in any Department or Officer thereof.

Section 9. The Migration or Importation of such Persons as any of the States now existing shall think proper to admit, shall not be prohibited by the Congress prior to the Year one thousand eight hundred and eight, but a Tax or duty may be imposed on such Importation, not exceeding ten dollars for each Person.

The Privilege of the Writ of Habeas Corpus shall not be suspended, unless when in Cases of Rebellion or Invasion the public Safety may require it.

No Bill of Attainder or ex post facto Law shall be passed.

No Capitation, or other direct, Tax shall be laid, unless in Proportion to the Census or enumeration herein before directed to be taken.

No Tax or Duty shall be laid on Articles exported from any State.

No Preference shall be given by any Regulation of Commerce or Revenue to the Ports of one State over those of another; nor shall Vessels bound to, or from, one State, be obliged to enter, clear, or pay Duties in another.

No Money shall be drawn from the Treasury, but in Consequence of Appropriations made by Law; and a regular Statement and Account of the Receipts and Expenditures of all public Money shall be published from time to time.

No Title of Nobility shall be granted by the United States: And no Person holding any Office of Profit or Trust under them, shall, without the Consent of the Congress, accept of any present, Emolument, Office, or Title, of any kind whatever, from any King, Prince, or foreign State.

Section 10. No State shall enter into any Treaty, Alliance, or Confederation; grant Letters of Marque and Reprisal; coin Money; emit Bills of Credit; make any Thing but gold and silver Coin a Tender in Payment of Debts; pass any Bill of Attainder, ex post facto Law, or Law impairing the Obligation of Contracts, or grant any Title of Nobility.

No State shall, without the Consent of the Congress, lay any Imposts or Duties on Imports or Exports, except what may be absolutely necessary for executing it's inspection Laws: and the net Produce of all Duties and Imposts, laid by any State on Imports or Exports, shall be for the Use of the Treasury of the United States; and all such Laws shall be subject to the Revision and Controul of the Congress.

No State shall, without the Consent of Congress, lay any Duty of Tonnage, keep Troops, or Ships of War in time of Peace, enter into any Agreement or Compact with another State, or with a foreign Power, or engage in War, unless actually invaded, or in such imminent Danger as will not admit of delay.

Article II.

Section 1. The executive Power shall be vested in a President of the United States of America. He shall hold his Office during the Term of four Years, and, together with the Vice President, chosen for the same Term, be elected, as follows:

Each State shall appoint, in such Manner as the Legislature thereof may direct, a Number of Electors, equal to the whole Number of Senators and Representatives to which the State may be entitled in the Congress: but no Senator or Representative, or Person holding an Office of Trust or Profit under the United States, shall be appointed an Elector.

The Electors shall meet in their respective States, and vote by Ballot for two Persons, of whom one at least shall not be an Inhabitant of the same State with themselves. And they shall make a List of all the Persons voted for, and of the Number of Votes for each; which List they shall sign and certify, and transmit sealed to the Seat of the Government of the United States, directed to the President of the Senate. The President of the Senate shall, in the Presence of the Senate and House of Representatives, open all the Certificates, and the Votes shall then be counted. The Person having the greatest Number of Votes shall be the President, if such Number be a Majority of the whole Number of Electors appointed; and if there be more than one who have such Majority, and have an equal Number of Votes, then the House of Representatives shall immediately chuse by Ballot one of them for President; and if no Person have a Majority, then from the five highest on the List the said House shall in like Manner chuse the President. But in chusing the President, the Votes shall be taken by States, the Representation from each State having one Vote; A quorum for this purpose shall consist of a Member or Members from two thirds of the States, and a Majority of all the States shall be necessary to a Choice. In every Case, after the Choice of the President, the Person having the greatest Number of Votes of the Electors shall be the Vice President. But if there should remain two or more who have equal Votes, the Senate shall chuse from them by Ballot the Vice President.

The Congress may determine the Time of chusing the Electors, and the Day on which they shall give their Votes; which Day shall be the same throughout the United States.

No Person except a natural born Citizen, or a Citizen of the United States, at the time of the Adoption of this Constitution, shall be eligible to the Office of President; neither shall any Person be eligible to that Office who shall not have attained to the Age of thirty five Years, and been fourteen Years a Resident within the United States.

In Case of the Removal of the President from Office, or of his Death, Resignation, or Inability to discharge the Powers and Duties of the said Office, the Same shall devolve on the Vice President, and the Congress may by Law provide for the Case of Removal, Death, Resignation or Inability, both of the President and Vice President, declaring what Officer shall then act as President, and such Officer shall act accordingly, until the Disability be removed, or a President shall be elected.

The President shall, at stated Times, receive for his Services, a Compensation, which shall neither be increased nor diminished during the Period for which he shall have been elected, and he shall not receive within that Period any other Emolument from the United States, or any of them.

Before he enter on the Execution of his Office, he shall take the following Oath or Affirmation:--"I do solemnly swear (or affirm) that I will faithfully execute the Office of President of the United States, and will to the best of my Ability, preserve, protect and defend the Constitution of the United States."

Section 2. The President shall be Commander in Chief of the Army and Navy of the United States, and of the Militia of the several States, when called into the actual Service of the United States; he may require the Opinion, in writing, of the principal Officer in each of the executive Departments, upon any Subject relating to the Duties of their respective Offices, and he shall have Power to grant Reprieves and Pardons for Offences against the United States, except in Cases of Impeachment.

He shall have Power, by and with the Advice and Consent of the Senate, to make Treaties, provided two thirds of the Senators present concur; and he shall nominate, and by and with the Advice and Consent of the Senate, shall appoint Ambassadors, other public Ministers and Consuls, Judges of the supreme Court, and all other Officers of the United States, whose Appointments are not herein otherwise provided for, and which shall be established by Law: but the Congress may by Law vest the Appointment of such inferior Officers, as they think proper, in the President alone, in the Courts of Law, or in the Heads of Departments.

The President shall have Power to fill up all Vacancies that may happen during the Recess of the Senate, by granting Commissions which shall expire at the End of their next Session.

Section 3. He shall from time to time give to the Congress Information of the State of the Union, and recommend to their Consideration such Measures as he shall judge necessary and expedient; he may, on extraordinary Occasions, convene both Houses, or either of them, and in Case of Disagreement between them, with Respect to the Time of Adjournment, he may adjourn them to such Time as he shall think proper; he shall receive Ambassadors and other public Ministers; he shall take Care that the Laws be faithfully executed, and shall Commission all the Officers of the United States.

Section 4. The President, Vice President and all civil Officers of the United States, shall be removed from Office on Impeachment for, and Conviction of, Treason, Bribery, or other high Crimes and Misdemeanors.

Article III.

Section 1. The judicial Power of the United States shall be vested in one supreme Court, and in such inferior Courts as the Congress may from time to time ordain and establish. The Judges, both of the supreme and inferior Courts, shall hold their Offices during good Behaviour, and shall, at stated Times, receive for their Services a Compensation, which shall not be diminished during their Continuance in Office.

Section 2. The judicial Power shall extend to all Cases, in Law and Equity, arising under this Constitution, the Laws of the United States, and Treaties made, or which shall be made, under their Authority;--to all Cases affecting Ambassadors, other public Ministers and Consuls;--to all Cases of admiralty and maritime Jurisdiction;--to Controversies to which the United States shall be a Party;--to Controversies between two or more States;--between a State and Citizens of another State;--between Citizens of different States;--between Citizens of the same State claiming Lands under Grants of different States, and between a State, or the Citizens thereof, and foreign States, Citizens or Subjects.

In all Cases affecting Ambassadors, other public Ministers and Consuls, and those in which a State shall be Party, the supreme Court shall have original Jurisdiction. In all the other Cases before mentioned, the supreme Court shall have appellate Jurisdiction, both as to Law and Fact, with such Exceptions, and under such Regulations as the Congress shall make.
The Trial of all Crimes, except in Cases of Impeachment, shall be by Jury; and such Trial shall be held in the State where the said Crimes shall have been committed; but when not committed within any State, the Trial shall be at such Place or Places as the Congress may by Law have directed.
Section 3. Treason against the United States, shall consist only in levying War against them, or in adhering to their Enemies, giving them Aid and Comfort. No Person shall be convicted of Treason unless on the Testimony of two Witnesses to the same overt Act, or on Confession in open Court.
The Congress shall have Power to declare the Punishment of Treason, but no Attainder of Treason shall work Corruption of Blood, or Forfeiture except during the Life of the Person attainted.

Article IV.

Section 1. Full Faith and Credit shall be given in each State to the public Acts, Records, and judicial Proceedings of every other State. And the Congress may by general Laws prescribe the Manner in which such Acts, Records and Proceedings shall be proved, and the Effect thereof.
Section 2. The Citizens of each State shall be entitled to all Privileges and Immunities of Citizens in the several States.
A Person charged in any State with Treason, Felony, or other Crime, who shall flee from Justice, and be found in another State, shall on Demand of the executive Authority of the State from which he fled, be delivered up, to be removed to the State having Jurisdiction of the Crime.
No Person held to Service or Labour in one State, under the Laws thereof, escaping into another, shall, in Consequence of any Law or Regulation therein, be discharged from such Service or Labour, but shall be delivered up on Claim of the Party to whom such Service or Labour may be due.
Section 3. New States may be admitted by the Congress into this Union; but no new State shall be formed or erected within the Jurisdiction of any other State; nor any State be formed by the Junction of two or more States, or Parts of States, without the Consent of the Legislatures of the States concerned as well as of the Congress.
The Congress shall have Power to dispose of and make all needful Rules and Regulations respecting the Territory or other Property belonging to the United States; and nothing in this Constitution shall be so construed as to Prejudice any Claims of the United States, or of any particular State.
Section 4. The United States shall guarantee to every State in this Union a Republican Form of Government, and shall protect each of them against Invasion; and on Application of the Legislature, or of the Executive (when the Legislature cannot be convened), against domestic Violence.

Article V.

The Congress, whenever two thirds of both Houses shall deem it necessary, shall propose Amendments to this Constitution, or, on the Application of the Legislatures of two thirds of the several States, shall call a Convention for proposing Amendments, which, in either Case, shall be valid to all Intents and Purposes, as Part of this Constitution, when ratified by the Legislatures of three fourths of the several States, or by Conventions in three fourths thereof, as the one or the other Mode of Ratification may be proposed by the Congress; Provided that no Amendment which may be made prior to the Year One thousand eight hundred and eight shall in any Manner affect the first and fourth Clauses in the Ninth Section of the first Article; and that no State, without its Consent, shall be deprived of its equal Suffrage in the Senate.

Article VI.

All Debts contracted and Engagements entered into, before the Adoption of this Constitution, shall be as valid against the United States under this Constitution, as under the Confederation.
This Constitution, and the Laws of the United States which shall be made in Pursuance thereof; and all Treaties made, or which shall be made, under the Authority of the United States, shall be the supreme Law of the Land; and the Judges in every State shall be bound thereby, any Thing in the Constitution or Laws of any State to the Contrary notwithstanding.
The Senators and Representatives before mentioned, and the Members of the several State Legislatures, and all executive and judicial Officers, both of the United States and of the several States, shall be bound by Oath or

Affirmation, to support this Constitution; but no religious Test shall ever be required as a Qualification to any Office or public Trust under the United States.

Article VII.
The Ratification of the Conventions of nine States, shall be sufficient for the Establishment of this Constitution between the States so ratifying the Same.

Done in Convention by the Unanimous Consent of the States present the Seventeenth Day of September in the Year of our Lord one thousand seven hundred and Eighty seven and of the Independence of the United States of America the Twelfth. In Witness whereof We have hereunto subscribed our Names

[The names and signatures are omitted.]

Amendments to the US Constitution

[The preamble to the Bill of Rights is omitted.]

Amendment I. Congress shall make no law respecting an establishment of religion, or prohibiting the free exercise thereof; or abridging the freedom of speech, or of the press; or the right of the people peaceably to assemble, and to petition the Government for a redress of grievances.

Amendment II. A well regulated Militia, being necessary to the security of a free State, the right of the people to keep and bear Arms, shall not be infringed.

Amendment III. No Soldier shall, in time of peace be quartered in any house, without the consent of the Owner, nor in time of war, but in a manner to be prescribed by law.

Amendment IV. The right of the people to be secure in their persons, houses, papers, and effects, against unreasonable searches and seizures, shall not be violated, and no Warrants shall issue, but upon probable cause, supported by Oath or affirmation, and particularly describing the place to be searched, and the persons or things to be seized.

Amendment V. No person shall be held to answer for a capital, or otherwise infamous crime, unless on a presentment or indictment of a Grand Jury, except in cases arising in the land or naval forces, or in the Militia, when in actual service in time of War or public danger; nor shall any person be subject for the same offence to be twice put in jeopardy of life or limb; nor shall be compelled in any criminal case to be a witness against himself, nor be deprived of life, liberty, or property, without due process of law; nor shall private property be taken for public use, without just compensation.

Amendment VI. In all criminal prosecutions, the accused shall enjoy the right to a speedy and public trial, by an impartial jury of the State and district wherein the crime shall have been committed, which district shall have been previously ascertained by law, and to be informed of the nature and cause of the accusation; to be confronted with the witnesses against him; to have compulsory process for obtaining witnesses in his favor, and to have the Assistance of Counsel for his defence.

Amendment VII. In Suits at common law, where the value in controversy shall exceed twenty dollars, the right of trial by jury shall be preserved, and no fact tried by a jury, shall be otherwise re-examined in any Court of the United States, than according to the rules of the common law.

Amendment VIII. Excessive bail shall not be required, nor excessive fines imposed, nor cruel and unusual punishments inflicted.

Amendment IX. The enumeration in the Constitution, of certain rights, shall not be construed to deny or disparage others retained by the people.

Amendment X. The powers not delegated to the United States by the Constitution, nor prohibited by it to the States, are reserved to the States respectively, or to the people.

Amendment XI. The Judicial power of the United States shall not be construed to extend to any suit in law or equity, commenced or prosecuted against one of the United States by Citizens of another State, or by Citizens or Subjects of any Foreign State.

Amendment XII. The Electors shall meet in their respective states and vote by ballot for President and Vice-President, one of whom, at least, shall not be an inhabitant of the same state with themselves; they shall name in their ballots the person voted for as President, and in distinct ballots the person voted for as Vice-President, and they shall make distinct lists of all persons voted for as President, and of all persons voted for as Vice-President, and of the number of votes for each, which lists they shall sign and certify, and transmit sealed to the seat of the government of the United States, directed to the President of the Senate; -- the President of the Senate shall, in the presence of the Senate and House of Representatives, open all the certificates and the votes shall then be counted; -- The person having the greatest number of votes for President, shall be the President, if such number be a majority of the whole number of Electors appointed; and if no person have such majority, then from the persons having the highest numbers not exceeding three on the list of those voted for as President, the House of Representatives shall choose immediately, by ballot, the President. But in choosing the President, the votes shall be taken by states, the representation from each state having one vote; a quorum for this purpose shall consist of a member or members from two-thirds of the states, and a majority of all the states shall be necessary to a choice. And if the House of Representatives shall not choose a President whenever the right of choice shall devolve upon them, before the fourth day of March next following, then the Vice-President shall act as President, as in case of the death or other constitutional disability of the President. The person having the greatest number of votes as Vice-President, shall be the Vice-President, if such number be a majority of the whole number of Electors appointed, and if no person have a majority, then from the two highest numbers on the list, the Senate shall choose the Vice-President; a quorum for the purpose shall consist of two-thirds of the whole number of Senators, and a majority of the whole number shall be necessary to a choice. But no person constitutionally ineligible to the office of President shall be eligible to that of Vice-President of the United States.

Amendment XIII. Section 1. Neither slavery nor involuntary servitude, except as a punishment for crime whereof the party shall have been duly convicted, shall exist within the United States, or any place subject to their jurisdiction.
Section 2. Congress shall have power to enforce this article by appropriate legislation.

Amendment XIV. Section 1. All persons born or naturalized in the United States, and subject to the jurisdiction thereof, are citizens of the United States and of the State wherein they reside. No State shall make or enforce any law which shall abridge the privileges or immunities of citizens of the United States; nor shall any State deprive any person of life, liberty, or property, without due process of law; nor deny to any person within its jurisdiction the equal protection of the laws.
Section 2. Representatives shall be apportioned among the several States according to their respective numbers, counting the whole number of persons in each State, excluding Indians not taxed. But when the right to vote at any election for the choice of electors for President and Vice-President of the United States, Representatives in Congress, the Executive and Judicial officers of a State, or the members of the Legislature thereof, is denied to any of the male inhabitants of such State, being twenty-one years of age, and citizens of the United States, or in any way abridged, except for participation in rebellion, or other crime, the basis of representation therein shall be reduced in the proportion which the number of such male citizens shall bear to the whole number of male citizens twenty-one years of age in such State.
Section 3. No person shall be a Senator or Representative in Congress, or elector of President and Vice-President, or hold any office, civil or military, under the United States, or under any State, who, having previously taken an oath, as a member of Congress, or as an officer of the United States, or as a member of any State legislature, or as an executive or judicial officer of any State, to support the Constitution of the United States, shall have engaged in insurrection or rebellion against the same, or given aid or comfort to the enemies thereof. But Congress may by a vote of two-thirds of each House, remove such disability.
Section 4. The validity of the public debt of the United States, authorized by law, including debts incurred for payment of pensions and bounties for services in suppressing insurrection or rebellion, shall not be questioned. But neither the United States nor any State shall assume or pay any debt or obligation incurred in aid of insurrection or rebellion against the United States, or any claim for the loss or emancipation of any slave; but all such debts, obligations and claims shall be held illegal and void.
Section 5. The Congress shall have the power to enforce, by appropriate legislation, the provisions of this article.

Amendment XV. Section 1. The right of citizens of the United States to vote shall not be denied or abridged by the United States or by any State on account of race, color, or previous condition of servitude--
Section 2. The Congress shall have the power to enforce this article by appropriate legislation.

Amendment XVI. The Congress shall have power to lay and collect taxes on incomes, from whatever source derived, without apportionment among the several States, and without regard to any census or enumeration.

Amendment XVII. The Senate of the United States shall be composed of two Senators from each State, elected by the people thereof, for six years; and each Senator shall have one vote. The electors in each State shall have the qualifications requisite for electors of the most numerous branch of the State legislatures.
When vacancies happen in the representation of any State in the Senate, the executive authority of such State shall issue writs of election to fill such vacancies: Provided, That the legislature of any State may empower the executive thereof to make temporary appointments until the people fill the vacancies by election as the legislature may direct.
This amendment shall not be so construed as to affect the election or term of any Senator chosen before it becomes valid as part of the Constitution.

Amendment XVIII. Section 1. After one year from the ratification of this article the manufacture, sale, or transportation of intoxicating liquors within, the importation thereof into, or the exportation thereof from the United States and all territory subject to the jurisdiction thereof for beverage purposes is hereby prohibited.
Section 2. The Congress and the several States shall have concurrent power to enforce this article by appropriate legislation.
Section 3. This article shall be inoperative unless it shall have been ratified as an amendment to the Constitution by the legislatures of the several States, as provided in the Constitution, within seven years from the date of the submission hereof to the States by the Congress.

Amendment XIX. The right of citizens of the United States to vote shall not be denied or abridged by the United States or by any State on account of sex.
Congress shall have power to enforce this article by appropriate legislation.

Amendment XX. Section 1. The terms of the President and the Vice President shall end at noon on the 20th day of January, and the terms of Senators and Representatives at noon on the 3d day of January, of the years in which such terms would have ended if this article had not been ratified; and the terms of their successors shall then begin.
Section 2. The Congress shall assemble at least once in every year, and such meeting shall begin at noon on the 3d day of January, unless they shall by law appoint a different day.
Section 3. If, at the time fixed for the beginning of the term of the President, the President elect shall have died, the Vice President elect shall become President. If a President shall not have been chosen before the time fixed for the beginning of his term, or if the President elect shall have failed to qualify, then the Vice President elect shall act as President until a President shall have qualified; and the Congress may by law provide for the case wherein neither a President elect nor a Vice President shall have qualified, declaring who shall then act as President, or the manner in which one who is to act shall be selected, and such person shall act accordingly until a President or Vice President shall have qualified.
Section 4. The Congress may by law provide for the case of the death of any of the persons from whom the House of Representatives may choose a President whenever the right of choice shall have devolved upon them, and for the case of the death of any of the persons from whom the Senate may choose a Vice President whenever the right of choice shall have devolved upon them.
Section 5. Sections 1 and 2 shall take effect on the 15th day of October following the ratification of this article.
Section 6. This article shall be inoperative unless it shall have been ratified as an amendment to the Constitution by the legislatures of three-fourths of the several States within seven years from the date of its submission.

Amendment XXI. Section 1. The eighteenth article of amendment to the Constitution of the United States is hereby repealed.
Section 2. The transportation or importation into any State, Territory, or Possession of the United States for delivery or use therein of intoxicating liquors, in violation of the laws thereof, is hereby prohibited.
Section 3. This article shall be inoperative unless it shall have been ratified as an amendment to the Constitution by conventions in the several States, as provided in the Constitution, within seven years from the date of the submission hereof to the States by the Congress.

Amendment XXII. Section 1. No person shall be elected to the office of the President more than twice, and no person who has held the office of President, or acted as President, for more than two years of a term to which some other person was elected President shall be elected to the office of President more than once. But this Article shall not apply to any person holding the office of President when this Article was proposed by Congress, and shall not prevent any person who may be holding the office of President, or acting as President, during the term within which this Article becomes operative from holding the office of President or acting as President during the remainder of such term.
Section 2. This article shall be inoperative unless it shall have been ratified as an amendment to the Constitution by the legislatures of three-fourths of the several States within seven years from the date of its submission to the States by the Congress.

Amendment XXIII. Section 1. The District constituting the seat of Government of the United States shall appoint in such manner as Congress may direct:
A number of electors of President and Vice President equal to the whole number of Senators and Representatives in Congress to which the District would be entitled if it were a State, but in no event more than the least populous State; they shall be in addition to those appointed by the States, but they shall be considered, for the purposes of the election of President and Vice President, to be electors appointed by a State; and they shall meet in the District and perform such duties as provided by the twelfth article of amendment.
Section 2. The Congress shall have power to enforce this article by appropriate legislation.

Amendment XXIV. Section 1. The right of citizens of the United States to vote in any primary or other election for President or Vice President, for electors for President or Vice President, or for Senator or Representative in Congress, shall not be denied or abridged by the United States or any State by reason of failure to pay poll tax or other tax.
Section 2. The Congress shall have power to enforce this article by appropriate legislation.

Amendment XXV. Section 1. In case of the removal of the President from office or of his death or resignation, the Vice President shall become President.
Section 2. Whenever there is a vacancy in the office of the Vice President, the President shall nominate a Vice President who shall take office upon confirmation by a majority vote of both Houses of Congress.
Section 3. Whenever the President transmits to the President pro tempore of the Senate and the Speaker of the House of Representatives his written declaration that he is unable to discharge the powers and duties of his office, and until he transmits to them a written declaration to the contrary, such powers and duties shall be discharged by the Vice President as Acting President.
Section 4. Whenever the Vice President and a majority of either the principal officers of the executive departments or of such other body as Congress may by law provide, transmit to the President pro tempore of the Senate and the Speaker of the House of Representatives their written declaration that the President is unable to discharge the powers and duties of his office, the Vice President shall immediately assume the powers and duties of the office as Acting President.
Thereafter, when the President transmits to the President pro tempore of the Senate and the Speaker of the House of Representatives his written declaration that no inability exists, he shall resume the powers and duties of his office unless the Vice President and a majority of either the principal officers of the executive department or of such other body as Congress may by law provide, transmit within four days to the President pro tempore of the Senate and the Speaker of the House of Representatives their written declaration that the President is unable to discharge the powers and duties of his office. Thereupon Congress shall decide the issue, assembling within forty-eight hours for that purpose if not in session. If the Congress, within twenty-one days after receipt of the latter written declaration, or, if Congress is not in session, within twenty-one days after Congress is required to assemble, determines by two-thirds vote of both Houses that the President is unable to discharge the powers and duties of his office, the Vice President shall continue to discharge the same as Acting President; otherwise, the President shall resume the powers and duties of his office.

Amendment XXVI. Section 1. The right of citizens of the United States, who are eighteen years of age or older, to vote shall not be denied or abridged by the United States or by any State on account of age.
Section 2. The Congress shall have power to enforce this article by appropriate legislation.

Amendment XXVII. No law, varying the compensation for the services of the Senators and Representatives, shall take effect, until an election of representatives shall have intervened.

Uniform Commercial Code. Selected Provisions: §§ 2-201 – 2-202, 2-204 – 2-209, 9 -109.

§ 2-201. (1) A contract for the sale of goods for the price of $5,000 or more is not enforceable by way of action or defense unless there is some record sufficient to indicate that a contract for sale has been made between the parties and signed by the party against which enforcement is sought or by the party's authorized agent or broker. A record is not insufficient because it omits or incorrectly states a term agreed upon but the contract is not enforceable under this subsection beyond the quantity of goods shown in the record.
(2) Between merchants if within a reasonable time a record in confirmation of the contract and sufficient against the sender is received and the party receiving it has reason to know its contents, it satisfies the requirements of subsection (1) against the recipient unless notice of objection to its contents is given in a record within 10 days after it is received.
(3) A contract that does not satisfy the requirements of subsection (1) but which is valid in other respects is enforceable:
(a) if the goods are to be specially manufactured for the buyer and are not suitable for sale to others in the ordinary course of the seller's business and the seller, before notice of repudiation is received and under circumstances that reasonably indicate that the goods are for the buyer, has made either a substantial beginning of their manufacture or commitments for their procurement;
(b) if the party against which enforcement is sought admits in the party's pleading, or in the party's testimony or otherwise under oath that a contract for sale was made, but the contract is not enforceable under this paragraph beyond the quantity of goods admitted; or
(c) with respect to goods for which payment has been made and accepted or which have been received and accepted (Sec. 2-606).
(4) A contract that is enforceable under this section is not unenforceable merely because it is not capable of being performed within one year or any other period after its making.

§ 2-202. (1) Terms with respect to which the confirmatory records of the parties agree or which are otherwise set forth in a record intended by the parties as a final expression of their agreement with respect to such terms as are included therein may not be contradicted by evidence of any prior agreement or of a contemporaneous oral agreement but may be supplemented by evidence of:
(a) course of performance, course of dealing, or usage of trade (Section 1-303); and
(b) consistent additional terms unless the court finds the record to have been intended also as a complete and exclusive statement of the terms of the agreement .
(2) Terms in a record may be explained by evidence of course of performance, course of dealing, or usage of trade without a preliminary determination by the court that the language used is ambiguous.

§ 2-204. (1) A contract for sale of goods may be made in any manner sufficient to show agreement, including offer and acceptance, conduct by both parties which recognizes the existence of a contract, the interaction of electronic agents, and the interaction of an electronic agent and an individual.
(2) An agreement sufficient to constitute a contract for sale may be found even if the moment of its making is undetermined.
(3) Even if one or more terms are left open, a contract for sale does not fail for indefiniteness if the parties have intended to make a contract and there is a reasonably certain basis for giving an appropriate remedy.
(4) Except as otherwise provided in Sections 2-211 through 2-213, the following rules apply:
(a) A contract may be formed by the interaction of electronic agents of the parties, even if no individual was aware of or reviewed the electronic agents' actions or the resulting terms and agreements.
(b) A contract may be formed by the interaction of an electronic agent and an individual acting on the individual's own behalf or for another person. A contract is formed if the individual takes actions that the individual is free to refuse to take or makes a statement, and the individual has reason to know that the actions or statement will:
(i) cause the electronic agent to complete the transaction or performance; or
(ii) indicate acceptance of an offer, regardless of other expressions or actions by the individual to which the electronic agent cannot react.

§ 2-205. An offer by a merchant to buy or sell goods in a signed record that by its terms gives assurance that it will be held open is not revocable, for lack of consideration, during the time stated or if no time is stated for a reasonable time, but in no event may such period of irrevocability exceed three months; but in no event may the period of irrevocability exceed three months. Any such term of assurance in a form supplied by the offeree must be separately signed by the offeror.

Part VII. United States Law

§ 2-206. (1) Unless otherwise unambiguously indicated by the language or circumstances
(a) an offer to make a contract shall be construed as inviting acceptance in any manner and by any medium reasonable in the circumstances:
(b) an order or other offer to buy goods for prompt or current shipment shall be construed as inviting acceptance either by a prompt promise to ship or by the prompt or current shipment of conforming or nonconforming goods, but the shipment of nonconforming goods is not an acceptance if the seller seasonably notifies the buyer that the shipment is offered only as an accommodation to the buyer.
(2) If the beginning of a requested performance is a reasonable mode of acceptance, an offeror that is not notified of acceptance within a reasonable time may treat the offer as having lapsed before acceptance.
(3) A definite and seasonable expression of acceptance in a record operates as an acceptance even if it contains terms additional to or different from the offer.

§ 2-207. Subject to Section 2-202, if (i) conduct by both parties recognizes the existence of a contract although their records do not otherwise establish a contract, (ii) a contract is formed by an offer and acceptance, or (iii) a contract formed in any manner is confirmed by a record that contains terms additional to or different from those in the contract being confirmed, the terms of the contract are:
(a) terms that appear in the records of both parties;
(b) terms, whether in a record or not, to which both parties agree; and
(c) terms supplied or incorporated under any provision of this Act.

§ 2-209. (1) An agreement modifying a contract within this Article needs no consideration to be binding.
(2) An agreement in a signed record which excludes modification or rescission except by a signed record may not be otherwise modified or rescinded, but except as between merchants such a requirement in a form supplied by the merchant must be separately signed by the other party.
(3) The requirements of Section 2-201 must be satisfied if the contract as modified is within its provisions.
(4) Although an attempt at modification or rescission does not satisfy the requirements of subsection (2) or (3), it may operate as a waiver.
(5) A party that has made a waiver affecting an executory portion of a contract may retract the waiver by reasonable notification received by the other party that strict performance will be required of any term waived, unless the retraction would be unjust in view of a material change of position in reliance on the waiver.

§ 9-109. (a) Except as otherwise provided in subsections (c) and (d), this article applies to:
(1) a transaction, regardless of its form, that creates a security interest in personal property or fixtures by contract;
(2) an agricultural lien;
(3) a sale of accounts, chattel paper, payment intangibles, or promissory notes;
(4) a consignment;
(5) a security interest arising under Section 2-401, 2-505, 2-711(3), or 2A-508(5), as provided in Section 9-110; and
(6) a security interest arising under Section 4-210 or 5-118.
(b) The application of this article to a security interest in a secured obligation is not affected by the fact that the obligation is itself secured by a transaction or interest to which this article does not apply.
(c) This article does not apply to the extent that:
(1) a statute, regulation, or treaty of the United States preempts this article;
(2) another statute of this State expressly governs the creation, perfection, priority, or enforcement of a security interest created by this State or a governmental unit of this State;
(3) a statute of another State, a foreign country, or a governmental unit of another State or a foreign country, other than a statute generally applicable to security interests, expressly governs creation, perfection, priority, or enforcement of a security interest created by the State, country, or governmental unit; or
(4) the rights of a transferee beneficiary or nominated person under a letter of credit are independent and superior under Section 5-114.
(d) This article does not apply to:
(1) a landlord's lien, other than an agricultural lien;
(2) a lien, other than an agricultural lien, given by statute or other rule of law for services or materials, but Section 9-333 applies with respect to priority of the lien;
(3) an assignment of a claim for wages, salary, or other compensation of an employee;
(4) a sale of accounts, chattel paper, payment intangibles, or promissory notes as part of a sale of the business out of which they arose;

(5) an assignment of accounts, chattel paper, payment intangibles, or promissory notes which is for the purpose of collection only;
(6) an assignment of a right to payment under a contract to an assignee that is also obligated to perform under the contract;
(7) an assignment of a single account, payment intangible, or promissory note to an assignee in full or partial satisfaction of a preexisting indebtedness;
(8) a transfer of an interest in or an assignment of a claim under a policy of insurance, other than an assignment by or to a health-care provider of a health-care-insurance receivable and any subsequent assignment of the right to payment, but Sections 9-315 and 9-322 apply with respect to proceeds and priorities in proceeds;
(9) an assignment of a right represented by a judgment, other than a judgment taken on a right to payment that was collateral;
(10) a right of recoupment or set-off, but:
(a) Section 9-340 applies with respect to the effectiveness of rights of recoupment or set-off against deposit accounts; and
(b) Section 9-404 applies with respect to defenses or claims of an account debtor;
(11) the creation or transfer of an interest in or lien on real property, including a lease or rents thereunder, except to the extent that provision is made for:
(a) liens on real property in Sections 9-203 and 9-308;
(b) fixtures in Section 9-334;
(c) fixture filings in Sections 9-501, 9-502, 9-512, 9-516, and 9-519; and
(d) security agreements covering personal and real property in Section 9- 604;
(12) an assignment of a claim arising in tort, other than a commercial tort claim, but Sections 9-315 and 9-322 apply with respect to proceeds and priorities in proceeds; or
(13) an assignment of a deposit account in a consumer transaction, but Sections 9-315 and 9-322 apply with respect to proceeds and priorities in proceeds.